The Transgender Studies Reader Remix

D0911903

The Transgender Studies Reader Remix assembles 50 previously published articles to orient students and scholars alike to current directions in the fast-evolving interdisciplinary field of transgender studies.

The volume is organized into ten thematic sections on trans studies' engagements with feminist theory, queer theory, Black studies, science studies, Indigeneity and coloniality, history, biopolitics, cultural production, the posthumanities, and intersectional approaches to embodied difference. It includes a selection of highly cited works from the two-volume *The Transgender Studies Reader*, more recently published essays, and some older articles in intersecting fields that are in conversation with where transgender studies is today. Editors Susan Stryker and Dylan McCarthy Blackston provide a foreword, an introduction, and a short abstract of each article that, taken together, document key texts and interdisciplinary connections foundational to the evolution of transgender studies over the past 30 years.

A handy overview for scholars, activists, and all those new to the field, this volume is also ideally suited for use as a textbook in undergraduate or graduate courses in gender studies.

Susan Stryker is Professor Emerita of Gender and Women's Studies at the University of Arizona, founding co-editor of *TSQ: Transgender Studies Quarterly*, founding co-editor of Duke University Press's ASTERISK book series, co-editor of Routledge's two previous transgender studies readers, and co-director of *Screaming Queens: The Riot at Compton's Cafeteria*.

Dylan McCarthy Blackston is Assistant Professor of Gender, Women's, and Sexuality Studies in the Department of Interdisciplinary Studies at Appalachian State University. His work examines transnational political economies of LGBTQ philanthropy, regenerative medicine, and transspecies life.

The Transgender Studies Reader Remix

Edited by
Susan Stryker and Dylan McCarthy Blackston

Routledge
Taylor & Francis Group

NEW YORK AND LONDON

First published 2023
by Routledge
605 Third Avenue, New York, NY 10158

and by Routledge
4 Park Square, Milton Park, Abingdon, Oxon, OX14 4RN

Routledge is an imprint of the Taylor & Francis Group, an informa business

Library of Congress Cataloging-in-Publication Data
Names: Stryker, Susan, editor. | Blackston, Dylan McCarthy, 1983- editor.
Title: The transgender studies reader remix / edited by Susan Stryker and Dylan McCarthy Blackston.
Description: Abindon, Oxon ; New York, NY : Routledge, 2022. | Includes bibliographical references and index.
Identifiers: LCCN 2021062412 (print) | LCCN 2021062413 (ebook) | ISBN 9781032062471 (paperback) | ISBN 9781032072722 (hardback) | ISBN 9781003206255 (ebook)
Subjects: LCSH: Gender nonconformity. | Transgender people.
Classification: LCC HQ77.9 .T72 2022 (print) | LCC HQ77.9 (ebook) | DDC 306.76/8—dc23/eng/20220111
LC record available at https://lccn.loc.gov/2021062412
LC ebook record available at https://lccn.loc.gov/2021062413

ISBN: 978-1-032-07272-2 (hbk)
ISBN: 978-1-032-06247-1 (pbk)
ISBN: 978-1-003-20625-5 (ebk)

DOI: 10.4324/9781003206255

Typeset in Bembo
by Apex CoVantage, LLC

Contents

Foreword

This is my third and final trip to the *Transgender Studies Reader* rodeo. I co-edited the first volume with my colleague Stephen Whittle in 2005 and the second with my colleague Aren Aizura in 2013. I'm pleased to now pass the torch to a next generation of scholars and scholarship in editing this remix version of the *Reader* with Dylan McCarthy Blackston.

In the nearly two decades since Stephen and I worked on that first volume, the field of transgender studies—or trans studies, or trans* studies, or even *trans study* (to mark the distinction between "trans" as an object of study versus a method of study)—has expanded exponentially and shifted focus in necessary and sometimes surprising ways. I think of this current volume as a retrospective exercise: it's a bit of a greatest hits compilation, sprinkled with some new work that documents changes in the field over the past decade as well as some older tracks in other genres that are getting sampled quite a bit these days in trans studies, all arranged into sets of interrelated conversations on topics of current interest. It's intended as a text for classroom use, a trans studies crash course between two covers, that links where the field has been to where it is now. But as to where the field is going? The crystal ball is cloudy. I hope this current volume serves not just as a backward glance that is useful in the present but as a point of departure for a next wave. Any future trans studies reader is likely to be composed of strikingly different work drawn from a new iteration of the field, a next unfolding that feels both immanent and imminent.

Looking back at my own trajectory through trans studies from the '90s to now with the benefit of hindsight, I see some things. I see, first, that it is important to historicize the point of emergence of something that called itself "transgender studies." It's important to pay attention to how the term "transgender," in particular sociocultural and linguistic contexts, articulated a break with the psychopathologizing category of "transsexual" and became an expansive identity category that some people embraced as descriptive of their lives; it opened possibilities for engaging differently with feminisms, gay/lesbian communities, and the psychomedical establishment before morphing into something else. It's equally important to ask why "studies" became a thing. The academy is part of state and capital; its pedagogical practices and production of expert knowledges are part of the reproductive process for those forms of power. The academy is also a place of critical inquiry and hence a site of sociopolitical, economic, and ideological struggle. What in the world has made *transgender* a target and a territory for the production of necessary new knowledges?

I also see how "transgender studies" was always fitfully lurching and stumbling towards what gets called "intersectionality" these days. So much of the initial conversation and so many of the earliest conversants in something that self-identified as "transgender studies" were unmarked as white while at the same time being informed by and in dialogue with feminisms of color and critical race theory. The field could reproduce able-bodied norms while at the same time recognizing that gender-non-normativity itself could limit access and mobility in ways experienced as socially disabling. It could struggle to balance the robustness of a new model for understanding gender-variance generally with the imperative not to impose a Euro-American and Anglophone frame of reference globally. States of affairs do not inevitably progress towards a better state of affairs, but I do think that trans studies has gotten better, overall, in holding itself accountable to the many forms of embodied difference transected by "transgender." I think it's become clearer how some formulations of gender transness are predicated on concepts of transformability and plasticity rooted in whiteness, as well as how practices of survival and freedom emanating from racial minority experience involve a trans-ing of bio-essentialized categories of personhood that can't be comprehended through "gender" alone. I think the field's conversation has gotten deeper and broader and drawn in a wider range of speakers who are making the space their own—and changing the conversation in the process. That's a very good thing.

I increasingly understand trans-ing as an exploratory and experimental practice for surviving within, and pointing beyond, the biocentric world order constructed in the wake of European colonization and racial chattel slavery. Trans-ing demonstrates the lie inherent in that world order's deeply naturalized ideologies, its self-serving beliefs for binding people to unjustly hierarchized categories of unevenly distributed life-chances by attributing certain meanings to their flesh. Trans-ing manifests and enacts the material truth of a potential for worlding otherwise. It shows not only that "another world is possible" but that another world is actual, and exists now. We can change what our bodies mean and what our selves become when we lovingly recognize one another in community, across difference; when we work collectively to change social structures, practices of governance, and cultural imaginaries, we thereby produce new social realities. Transness is a practice of worming one's way through the belly of the beast. It draws strength from acknowledging a commonality with non-human material existence, the different onto-epistemologies of the premodern past, the reality of Indigenous cosmologies, the survival of cultural forms that become sites of anti/colonial struggle, and the necessity of speculative visions of livable futures in which bodies and difference function within new economies of meaning. To manifest one's transness is to become semiotically unsettled within the racializing biopolitical assemblages of heteropatriarchal integrated world capitalism, in anticipation of whatever else shall come.

Whatever else shall come does not seem, from my perspective today, to be that hopeful for us *homo sapiens*, at least over the next few decades. You can't breathe the air or drink the water as forests burn and oceans rise; pathogens circulate, social pathologies intensify, contradictions deepen. We are amidst a profound transition in human affairs. If something called "transgender studies" is to have any real relevance or utility in the present, it needs to stay with this trouble, address these conditions in the late Anthropocene. It needs to be a resource for transforming *Anthropos* itself, the figure of Man that orchestrates our era, in whose name and for whose needs we now destroy the planet. Here's to the prospect of becoming something better than that. Let's live for that future, or die in pursuit of it. May the work collected in *The Transgender Studies Reader Remix* speed our journeys.

Susan Stryker

Acknowledgments

Working on this "remix" edition of the two previous Routledge transgender studies readers has been a delight for both of us, even amidst the challenges of the ongoing COVID-19 pandemic that spanned the entire project. We are both appreciative of the patience of our families, who supported us in countless ways as we completed this work. We'd both like to thank soliciting editor Kimberley Smith for approaching us with this project and for working with us as we shifted the scope away from a "transgender studies greatest hits" edition to a "remix" edition that reconceptualizes the field in light of the past decade's scholarship. We were fortunate to work as well with Routledge editorial assistant Emily Irvine, who secured permissions and diligently kept us on track throughout the publication process. Susan thanks her literary agent, Jane von Mehren of Aevitas Creative Management, for negotiating the contract with Routledge. We acknowledge our debts to Stephen Whittle, co-editor of *The Transgender Studies Reader*, and Aren Z. Aizura, co-editor of *The Transgender Studies Reader 2*, from which 22 of the 50 chapters included in *The Transgender Studies Reader Remix* have been drawn. While all of the introductory abstracts for these 22 chapters have been significantly revised and updated for republication here, we gratefully acknowledge the contributions Stephen and Aren made in co-authoring the original abstracts with *Remix* co-editor Susan Stryker. We thank Stephen for contributing to the original abstracts of Chapters 1, 2, 3, 6, 19, 21, 33, 36, and 49 and thank Aren for contributing to the original abstracts of Chapters 13, 17, 18, 26, 28, 29, 32, 34, 35, 38, 39, 41, and 42. Special thanks to AnaLouise Keating for her kind and timely assistance in gaining publication permission for the excerpt from Gloria Anzaldúa's work that we have included in this volume. Thanks as well to Paisley Currah, who granted pre-publication access to a chapter from *Sex Is as Sex Does*, which was still forthcoming at the time we went to press, and for allowing us to include an excerpt from it here. We of course thank *all* the authors of the works included in this volume, which quite literally would be nothing without them, and extend our respect and regrets to the authors whose important work remains available in the first two readers but is not included in this remixed version. We'd also like to add a special shout-out to Annie Beguhl for last-minute proofreading assistance.

Introduction

Transgender Studies Remixed

Dylan McCarthy Blackston

In 2014, a *TIME* magazine cover featured a full-length photograph of trans actor and activist Laverne Cox, with an accompanying caption that read "The Transgender Tipping Point." Their cover story, *TIME* implied, marked the moment when *transgender* crossed the threshold of cultural acceptability.[1] The cover story's subtitle, "America's next civil rights frontier," suggested that the *last* "next frontiers"—presumably gay rights or even the Black Civil Rights Movement—had been eclipsed by the need to expand the possibilities of gender. Transgender cultural acceptance was thus positioned in a progress narrative in which concerns about sexuality and race had moved on to concerns about gender-diversity.

Transgender, was not, as that story might suggest, a term only then breaking through to mainstream awareness. In their introduction to *The Transgender Studies Reader 2*, published a year before *TIME*'s "transgender tipping point," Susan Stryker and Aren Z. Aizura included a graph generated by the Google Books Ngram Viewer that charted the prevalence of *transgender* between 1900 and 2008 in Google's massive corpus of digitized and text-searchable books. The graph showed a hockey-stick-shaped line that inflected sharply in the early 1990s and shot steeply upward through 2008. A new graph (Figure 1) shows how *transgender*'s prevalence rose even more rapidly between 2008 and 2019.

Far from being a breakout phenomenon in 2014, *transgender* was already ubiquitous. As Aizura and Stryker note in that same introduction to *The Transgender Studies Reader 2*, according to a 2011 Public Religion Research Institute poll, "91 percent of people living in the U.S.A. report that they have heard the term transgender," with a strong majority (89%) agreeing that trans people should have the same rights as everybody else.[2] A 2021 Pew Research survey suggests that awareness of *transgender* has only grown in the intervening decade.[3] Nearly half of all respondents (42%) to that survey claimed to know a trans person personally (a 5% increase since 2017), while roughly a quarter knew someone who identified as non-binary or used gender-neutral pronouns. Most people overall still consider gender to be determined by assigned sex at birth (56%), while among those under 30, only 44% held that view. All the while, opinions about trans people have become increasingly polarized, to the point that we are now primary battlegrounds in the contemporary culture wars.

Heightened trans visibility and representation, in other words, did not only result in a tipping point toward greater understanding and acceptance. It has in fact gone hand in hand

DOI: 10.4324/9781003206255-1

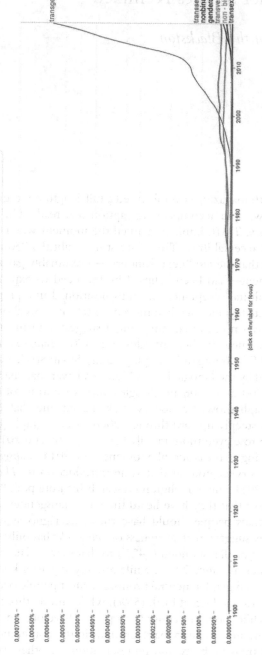

Figure 1 Screenshot of *transgender* usage on Google Ngram Viewer

with greater hostility and violence against trans people. The 2017 anthology *Trap Door: Trans Cultural Production and the Politics of Visibility*, edited by Tourmaline, Eric A. Stanley, and Joanna Burton, directly addresses this paradox. That is, visibility itself has been a trap for trans people, particular those who are already the most visible and vulnerable: trans women of color, as well as undocumented, poor, and disabled trans people.[4] One contributor to the anthology—legendary activist and Stonewall veteran Miss Major Griffin-Gracy—points out that transphobes upset to see Laverne Cox on the cover of *TIME* magazine don't aim their violent indignation at Cox; instead, it's trans women they encounter in their everyday lives who bear the brunt of their transphobic violence.

In addition to outright physical violence, trans people have been increasingly targeted by legislation that allows others to discriminate against them based on religious belief, that denies them affirming healthcare or medically assisted gender-transition, that bars them from sports or public restrooms that match their gender identity and expression, and that excludes them from gender-appropriate shelters or social services. These dangerous attempts to regulate public space and healthcare access propagate unreal fantasies that trans women are perverse men trying to infiltrate sex-segregated spaces to harm other women and girls—fantasies that have fueled the rise of transphobic "gender-critical" feminist ideology, particularly in countries where right-wing populist movements have gained strength and power. At the same time, trans men are depicted as victims of a "transgender craze" that's stealing daughters from an otherwise "natural" path to womanhood; in this depiction, transmen must be protected from themselves. In all cases, trans people are scapegoated as the signs and symptoms for all manner of social ills.

Rather than teetering on a "tipping point," *transgender* might better be imagined as a fulcrum or pivot-point around which swirl a whole host of cultural anxieties about social change, technology, and the hazy boundaries between gender, sex, race, sexuality, and species. We have plenty to feel anxious about: a fragmented social media environment that fuels the spread of misinformation; an escalating series of environmental crises driving a swell of climate refugees; an as yet insatiable demand for consumer goods and services in the global North that capacitates the extraction of resources and power from non-renewable sources to keep the wheels of racial capitalism grinding on; the precipitous rise of precarious gig-work economies in cities with unprecedented income-inequality; and a rising wave of xenophobic, racist governments and social movements that has yet to crest.

While the negative consequences of these big-picture problems affect us all, they fall especially heavily on trans people. A report from the 2015 U.S. Transgender Survey showed that trans people were at that point already four times more likely than the general population to live in poverty, twice as likely to have HIV/AIDS, and 50% more likely to have been incarcerated. Thirty percent of trans people had experienced homelessness, and nearly half—41%—had contemplated suicide.[5] The COVID-19 pandemic, layered on top of an AIDS pandemic that has never ended, has only amplified these inequities and their effects. While it's too soon to know how permanent some of the consequences of COVID-19 will be, it's already clear how the management of this pandemic, like that of others before it, created disproportionate hardships for people marginalized by race and class. In some parts of the world, gender-policing became part of public health efforts to reduce COVID-19 transmission. Panama, for example, implemented a gender-based quarantine, with women and men allowed to go out on alternating days of the week. People out on the wrong day could be fined, which created an impossible double bind for trans, nonbinary, and gender-nonconforming people who lacked government-issued identification documents confirming their genders.[6]

Remixing Transgender Studies

While COVID-19 is not the first virus to have massively reconfigured social and political life, we have certainly become newly adept in the past two years at collectively developing modes of survival through our theory and activism. Likewise, the work of trans studies as a field responds to many of the significant global changes that have taken shape in the last two years and since the publication of the two previous volumes of *The Transgender Studies Reader* in 2006 and 2013. One of the biggest changes in the field of trans studies since the second volume of the *Reader* was published was the 2014 debut of *TSQ: Transgender Studies Quarterly*, a new journal for interdisciplinary cultural studies imagined as offering a counterpoint to the more psycho-medical perspective of *International Journal of Transgenderism*, established in 1997. There's an even newer online publication, *The Journal of Applied Transgender Studies*, for more disciplinary social scientific work, as well as specialized journals such as the *International Journal of Transgender Health* and even a *Journal of Queer and Trans Religious Studies*. As a result of these new outlets for up-to-date scholarship, what a transgender studies collection needs to do has shifted. What you'll find in this book is not a survey of all scholarship on transgender topics or a selection of the most important recent works in a field. Rather, it is a set of curated conversations among scholars who imagine themselves as somehow doing interdisciplinary work in transgender cultural studies broadly defined—conversations that mix old and new work to stage intergenerational and interdisciplinary dialogues, interject historically significant work that remains relevant for understanding contemporary issues, and sample some work in adjacent fields that has been central to the development of contemporary work in trans studies. It's intended as a useful text for classroom use, as well as an introduction to and overview of the field itself and its now decades-long history.

As a field, transgender studies is no longer at a tipping point on the threshold of recognition; it has arrived. It's a vibrant area of inquiry, with a growing cadre of trans studies scholars trained and mentored by other trans studies scholars and a burgeoning presence of transgender studies material on syllabi and on the academic lecture circuit. It's worth pausing for a moment to reflect back on the field's trajectory, as documented in the previous volumes of Routledge's readers, before looking ahead to how we've remixed that work here. As Stryker and Aizura noted in the introduction to *The Transgender Studies Reader 2*, the earlier volume from 2006, edited by Stryker and Stephen Whittle, could be "taken as an account of field formation," an account that was "engaged in the kind of identity politics necessary to gain speaking positions within discourse" and which consequently "featured a good deal of auto-ethnographic and self-representational work by trans subjects."[7] Given that this was the first compilation of work in a field then already a decade-and-a-half in the making, it had a significant amount of ground to cover. Its 50 chapters included materials documenting how transgender phenomena appear in a wide range of contexts: from nineteenth-century sexological research, to early queer theory, to engagements with feminist scholarship, to visual and narrative representations of trans bodies and lives, to the importance of trans autobiography, to some field-founding essays that are still widely taught today and continue to inspire new scholarship.

The second volume of the *Reader* was a field-forming collection in its own right. Rather than seeking to trace the emergence of what has come to be known as transgender studies, the volume published only new essays to offer a time-stamped document of some of the most influential work in the field at that moment. It addressed and reframed some of the first volume's shortcomings. As the editors write, the second volume directed "its critical gaze at the inadequacies of the field's first iteration, in order to correct them, taking aim at its implicit whiteness, U.S.-centricity, Anglophone bias, and the sometimes suspect ways in which the category *transgender* has been circulated transnationally." The second volume published essays on the various ways "transgender" had migrated into international human rights discourse, philanthropy, and the work of non-governmental social service and social change organizations; how trans people were being represented in mass media and made creative work of their own; how *transgender* transects the boundaries of other body-based categories—such as species and race—that arrange biological difference in hierarchies deemed more or less worthy of life; and how the administrative regulation of gender-crossing people reflects, in part, the increased role of state surveillance in everyday life. Drawing from the vocabulary of cultural theorists Gilles Deleuze and Félix Guattari, the volume sought "to propagate *transgender* rhizomatically, in unexpected ways that trace lines of flight from the harsh realities of the present moment." It attended, in other words, to how *transgender* built on its past to develop new methodological, activist, and identitarian approaches to trans survival.

The Transgender Studies Reader Remix combines the most-cited chapters in the two previous volumes with new trans studies work and older scholarship from other fields. It asks what those potential "lines of flight" might be: what tools has transgender studies offered us to theorize and dream up new ways of living? How has the field helped us to reconceptualize histories of gender and sex in connection with other forms of embodied difference? What connections have we made or might we make across other bodies of cultural theory and activist movements to further those critical aims? How can we think and live in "trans" ways that enable us to ethically function amidst a collapsing ecology, amidst a sea of retrograde populist nationalisms threatening to engulf us all?

Much of the recent work in transgender studies seeks to develop "trans" as a mode of analysis. The *Trans-* issue of *WSQ: Women's Studies Quarterly* in 2008 was an important point of departure for this critical project, calling attention to the conceptual work performed by the prefix *trans-* itself, meaning "to cross." The introduction noted that adding the hyphen marked a distinction between the "implied nominalism" of 'trans'" (that is, "trans" as a name for an object that "trans studies" studied) and the "explicit relationality of 'trans-,' which remains open-ended and resists premature foreclosure by attachment to any single suffix."[8] In other words, the hyphen marked the difference between studying "transgender" as a thing and studying the process of how gender boundaries are crossed over, or "transed." Among other things, this shift informed a new generation of historical scholarship, helping to ask better questions about how to understand gender-variance in the past, before the term *transgender* or the concept of gender itself existed, as well as a new generation of transnational scholarship, helping to ask better questions about cross-cultural comparisons of gender-variance. The issue editors focused work they considered "doubly trans-," that is, work that put *trans-* of *transgender* into engagement with the *trans-* in other sorts of categorical crossings (such as the transnational, transgenic, transspecies, transracial).

Eva Hayward and Jami Weinstein expanded this sense of "prefixial" trans through their development of an "asteriskial" concept of transness—that is, trans with an asterisk, or trans★.[9] The asterisk as a symbol attached to the *trans-* prefix first emerged in online discussions about the relationships between various kinds of trans identities—transgender, transsexual, transvestite—and the need for a short-hand term that was not over-invested in the border wars between different kinds of transness. It referenced the fact that in database searches, the asterisk is a "wildcard operator"; an asterisk following a word in a database search multiplies the possible data retrieved or attachments generated. It can bold words when typed before the first letter and after the last, amplifying the intensity of the word among a string of others. The asterisk is used to suggest that "transing" could operate on many operands simultaneously. Unlike the hyphen, which marks a single point of attachment, the asterisk symbolically marks an undefined generative space next to trans—trans★—or even between the broken parts of words—trans★gender or trans★plantation—to signify something unnamed, perhaps ultimately unrepresentable, that serves as a placeholder for all manner of connections, both existing now or yet to come, in ever-shifting arrangements of categories, names, materialities, and processes of becoming.[10] It suggests a space of generative possibility, where ontology—the sense of being—might multiply and where new ontologies, enlivened by the possibilities of transing whatever suffix *trans-* attaches to, might emerge.

We have edited *The Transgender Studies Reader Remix* with this notion of trans★ methods in mind. The concept of a "remix" can itself be a way to think about what trans-with-an-asterisk can do. It speaks to how trans people remix the world. Remixing is a survival practice: taking existing paths, forging new ones, constantly coming up with new combinations of living to access the social, medical, and communal care needed for life. While not all trans studies scholars personally identify as trans people, this mode of survival is reflected in the intellectual work of the field. We who work in it reach across the theoretical and institutional boundaries of numerous disciplines to develop trans★ methodologies, to (re)write trans histories, to access and practice trans-focused care (medical and otherwise).

Trans★ as method is different from *transgender* as an identity label. Too often, *transgender* is merely coopted into a neoliberal vocabulary of diversity and inclusion—as the "next frontier," or even a "bridge too far"—in ways that actually eclipse both the quotidian and spectacular forms of violence many trans people face. While some trans people may be more accepted into the fold of liberal models of inclusion, the vectors of race, class, ability, sexuality, and immigration status cut across embodiments to capacitate many shifting positions in relation to gender. That is, crossing socially constructed gender boundaries is not the unique property of a "transgender person"; such crossings are characteristic of many practices of resistance, freedom, fugitivity, and disidentification from structurally oppressed positions within an ideological matrix always intent on transforming difference into social hierarchy. Focusing on the nonidentitarian features of transness as a concept or logical operator that cuts across how all the categories that rank and order life function (e.g., sex/gender, race, species, the human and the animal) enables their remixing in ways that can lead to other (potentially better?) ways of living.

A *remix* also evokes being in a club, feeling the pulse of new rhythms and unexpected twists on old beats vibrating through one's body, hearing lyrics lifted from one work transposed over the instrumental tracks of another, noticing how sounds are sampled and looped to interlace novelty with nostalgia. To experience a remix is to experience the simultaneity of the familiar and the fresh, to look back and sense previously unrecognized synergies while remaining open to the potential for the unexpected. It is to inhabit the different temporality of a nonlinear spacetime. That's what we aim for in this trans studies remix: we invite readers into a conversational spacetime spread out over decades, where some old-school tracks sound different than they did back in the day and lend resonance to contemporary sounds.

Remixing is a fraught practice. Of all the infinite ways a track can be mixed or remixed, it only comes out one particular way in any given iteration. This reader represents one particular take on how the field of trans studies could be remixed. Remixing requires cutting. Some of the source materials that could have gone into this mix simply didn't make the cut, not because they're not good or no longer relevant but simply because they don't fit the structure or rhythm we sought. Even the included essays were in many cases pared down to amplify the connections between essays in a given section, trans studies as a field, and the remix as a collection. This was exciting work to undertake but also imbued with feelings of loss. One of the hardest parts of putting the *Transgender Studies Reader Remix* together was everything we had to leave out from the first two volumes. There are brilliant and important pieces there, written not just by an earlier generation of scholars but by amazing colleagues still active in the field who are producing vital and timely work. We urge readers who want to take a deeper and more expansive dive into the field not to neglect the content of those earlier volumes. This one does not replace them.

Remixing involves not only loss but risk, particularly with regard to how it samples materials from genres with significantly different cultural and socio-political origins. It is weighted with the possibility that it may appropriate rather than respectfully recognize difference. Is it appropriative to juxtapose Black feminist work or work from the global South or Indigenous work that never imagined itself as doing "trans studies" with work originating in Anglophone trans studies in the global North that is so often unmarked as white? Or is doing so a way of changing what "transgender" means and what "transing" does by bringing trans studies into older, deeper, and broader problematics, especially those that actively shape emergent trans-of-color critique and trans scholarship as a whole? Is it offering trans methodologies for recasting *how the body means* to others who might find those methods useful?

Rhythms and Vibrations: A Remix of Trans Thinking

The Transgender Studies Reader Remix, like each of the previous volumes, contains 50 chapters. They're organized into ten sections of five chapters. Each section revolves around a central theme or topic, and we imagine the pieces chosen as all somehow talking with one another within and across sectional boundaries. As noted, this represents one particular take on how these articles can be put into conversation. We invite readers who spend time with the entire volume to notice how the works could be rearranged into other conversations and how they speak to one another across as well as within the sections as we've arranged them.

The first section, "Trans/Feminisms," pays attention to the central role that feminisms have had in transgender studies. It positions Sandy Stone's "The *Empire* Strikes Back: A Post-transexual Manifesto" as a point of departure for the field. When Stone issued her manifesto, the word "transgender" was not yet in widespread use, but it came to name the space of imaginative, critical, and theoretical possibility that Stone envisioned when she called upon like-minded gender-changing people to go beyond the limits imposed by the psychopathologizing discourse of transsexuality. Stone's title referenced Janice Raymond's book *The Transsexual Empire: The Making of the She-Male*. Raymond was one of the first TERFs—Trans Exclusionary Radical Feminists—and she had targeted Stone, a trans woman then working as a recording engineer as part of the all-lesbian Olivia Records Collective. We include "Sappho by Surgery" from Raymond's book as a representative example of the kind of transphobic feminism that has generated a robust transfeminist counter-response. One such work is "A Transvestite Answers a Feminist," by gay trans man Lou Sullivan, later an important activist and now something of a cult icon for many contemporary transmasculine people. Written before his transition when he still identified as a "heterosexual female transvestite," Sullivan offers a contemporaneous transmasculine critique of second-wave feminist frameworks hostile to transing gender. We then move beyond the United States with Karine Espineira and Sam Bourcier's chapter, "Transfeminism: Something Else, Somewhere Else," which traces the development of transfeminism in France (*transfeminismes*) and Spain (*transfeminismo*). Daniel B. Coleman, in "Transmasculine Insurgency," explores how location and feminist socio-cultural formations rooted in different racial/ethnic communities in Latinx contexts work in relation to trans life. As these authors show, transfeminism—a term coined by disability and sex-work activist Emi Koyama—emerges and is enacted differently across context.

"Trans Matters, Black Matters" remixes another foundational work in transgender studies, Susan Stryker's "My Words to Victor Frankenstein Above the Village of Chamounix: Performing Transgender Rage," with recent work in Black trans studies, trans-of-color critique, a classic work of Black feminism, and feminist science studies work on materiality. Stryker uses the figure of the monster to explore how the attribution of transness can expel one from human community while simultaneously enabling an empowering sense of connection to a primordial ontological state—the "darkness" of the chaotically generative cosmological void from which all existence spills forth. We pair this with Marquis Bey's "The Trans★-ness of Blackness, the Blackness of Trans★-ness," which develops a nuanced sense of how Black racial fugitivity and gender transness trace different roots toward the same "anoriginal lawlessness" of a groundless state of being from which difference emerges. Hortense J. Spillers's "Mama's Baby, Papa's Maybe: An American Grammar Book" is part of the genealogy of both contemporary Black feminisms and trans studies that Bey draws from and extends. Slavery and its afterlife have attenuated the possibility of Black women's inclusion in the white patrilineal ordering of gender, Spillers contends, and—in a move that preceded and informed Stryker's articulation of a (white) trans gender-monstrosity enlivened by darkness—she asks Black women to forego attempts to belong to a racialized gender ordering that will never serve them and, instead, to formulate a new "insurgent" ontological ground. Other selections in the section include "TransMaterialities: Trans★/Matter/Realities and Queer Political Imaginings," in which feminist science studies scholar Karen Barad brings a physicist's perspective to bear on the materiality of the cosmological void and puts quantum field theory into dialogue with work in queer and trans theory. A selection from Zakiyyah Iman Jackson's "Theorizing in a Void" offers a nuanced engagement with the possibilities for rupture from racial hierarchies encoded into notions of gender and the human, thus completing a circuit between Black feminisms, trans studies, and science studies.

"The Coloniality of (Trans)Gender" addresses how currently dominant ways of thinking about sex/gender are a part of an ongoing practice of European colonization. This practice not only works through the assumption that there are two kinds of bodies (sexes) and two categories of people (genders) but the even more fundamental assumption that body-difference is a naturally given way of assigning people to social categories. We open with Saylesh Wesley's "Twin-Spirited Woman: *Sts'iyóye smestíyexw slhá:li*," in which a contemporary Indigenous trans and two-spirit woman asks her grandmother—a powerful matriarch of the traditionally matrilineal, matrifocal Stó:lō people—to dream a name in their native language for the kind of person Wesley knew herself to be; doing so was a profound enactment of Indigenous survivance, asserting the power of a living culture to imagine in the present a part of itself that had been erased and suppressed through colonial violence. Postcolonial feminist philosopher María Lugones's "The Coloniality of Gender" provides a theoretical scaffolding for the rest of the work in this section and highlights how the "somato-centricity" of the Eurocentric colonial world order installed a "modern/colonial gender system" that divides people according to physical difference and expunges the multiple genders and gender roles that previously appeared in many premodern, Indigenous, and non-Western gender-systems. Deborah Miranda's "Extermination of the *Joyas*: Gendercide in Spanish California" offers a detailed account of how two-spirit people in her own ancestral culture were explicitly targeted by Spanish colonizers as part of an overarching project of cultural destruction and genocide. A short selection from Chicana feminist Gloria Anzaldúa's *Borderlands/La Frontera: The New Mestiza* traces the U.S.-México borderlands as a space of constant transition and division, where everyday survival and creative abundance take shape at once. She writes the connections between the racial and ethnic mixing that characterizes the U.S.-Mexican borderlands and the place of queer and trans people amid border space. A final piece by Aniruddha Dutta and Raina Roy, "Decolonizing Transgender in India: Some Reflections," highlights the need to bring a decolonial perspective not just to trans studies of the Americas but globally. It discusses how "transgender" as a form of identity overwrites multiple forms of gender-variance present in South Asia and in the global South more broadly and functions as a universal standard against which local variations are measured, even as the term is reworked and embodied in different ways across different transnational contexts.

"Queer Gender and Its Discontents" examines the close and sometimes contentious relationship between trans and queer studies. Queer theory tends to focus on sexuality and desire and has treated transness as the expression of a queer potential to disrupt heteronormativity. Trans studies, on the other hand, has been more attuned to questions of embodiment and identity and sees gender as a process of categorizing people that allows desire to "take shape and find its aim." We include a selection from "Subversive Bodily Acts" in Judith Butler's paradigm-shifting *Gender Trouble*, as well as one from early trans theorist Jay Prosser's critique of queer theory's skewed and partial uptake of trans phenomena in "Judith Butler: Queer Feminism, Transgender, and the Transsubstantiation of Sex." José Esteban Muñoz's "The White to Be Angry," about transfeminine drag artist Vaginal Davis, offers an excellent example of a queer-of-color disidentificatory approach to gender performativity, while Jack Halberstam's "The Transgender Look" explores queer gender representation in several important trans-developed or trans-focused films of the 1990s. Trans studies scholar Cáel M. Keegan discusses tensions in how trans studies and queer studies both have, and have not, found institutional homes in academic departments of women's studies in "Getting Disciplined: What's Trans★ About Queer Studies Now?"

"Sexology and Its Critics" historicizes and critiques the idea that trans issues are properly in the domain of scientific or medical studies of sexuality. While of course trans people want good healthcare and might need to talk with doctors and therapists, the idea that there's something inherently pathological about being trans has been a powerful way of controlling and marginalizing trans life since the nineteenth century. This section includes two case studies from late nineteenth- and early twentieth-century sexual scientists. "Case 131" in Richard von Krafft-Ebing's 1877 *Psychopathia Sexualis* documents a transmasculine life, while "Case 13" in Magnus Hirschfeld's 1910 *Transvestites* documents a transfeminine life. It's possible to read both case studies "against the grain," to recover trans perspectives from them beyond the intent of the doctors. Hirschfeld, a Jewish socialist who was himself gay, is justly remembered for trying to improve the quality of life for trans people through medical science and legal reform. But as two other contributors to this section note, the very sexological research into hormonal and surgical techniques that many trans people have found life-saving are also rooted in sexology's often explicit racism and support of eugenics. Kadji Amin's "Trans★ Plasticity and the Ontology of Race and Species" examines how late nineteenth- and early twentieth-century glandular therapies now commonly called xenotransplantations (non-human to human transfers of biomatter) functioned as a tool of eugenics and white racial and gender rejuvenation. In "The Matter of Gender," Nikki Sullivan explores how the concept of gender itself was first articulated by sexologist John Money and his colleagues at Johns Hopkins as a way of conceptualizing how trans and intersex people could have identities as men and women that did not align in normative ways with their natal genitals. Jules Gill-Peterson's "Trans of Color Critique Before Transsexuality" dives into the archive of the Johns Hopkins University Hospital, which pioneered many of the endocrinological and surgical techniques for altering the genitals of trans and intersex patients, to show how the mid-twentieth-century discourse of "transsexuality" was based on white norms that erased the ways that trans people of color both solicited and evaded the attention of medical science.

C. Riley Snorton and Jin Haritaworn's "Trans Necropolitics" opens the next section, "Regulating Embodiment." Snorton and Haritaworn, in their contribution, draw on postcolonial theorist Achille Mbembe's reworking of Michel Foucault's concept of biopolitics to point out how, for racialized and colonized subjects, the political management of their life is often solely for the purpose of orchestrating their death rather than managing their lives. They show how trans-of-color death has often been mobilized to enhance white trans life. Relatedly, much of the work in this section is characteristic of the "biopolitical turn" in trans studies in the early twenty-first century when a newly robust national security apparatus took shape amid the "War on Terror." Toby Beauchamp's "Artful Concealment and Strategic Visibility: Transgender Bodies and U.S. State Surveillance After 9/11" explores this fairly recent historic shift, while Clare Sears, in "Electric Brilliancy: Cross-Dressing Law and Freak Show Displays in Nineteenth-Century San Francisco," roots practices of surveilling gender-variance in a much deeper history of regulating public space according to white, heterosexual, and able-bodied norms. In "Incarceration, Identity Politics, and the Trans-Cis Divide," political scientist Paisley Currah examines the capitalist marketplace logics of incarceration in relation to "freeze frame" policies that work against trans peoples' access to healthcare on the inside, while legal theorist Dean Spade, in "Trans Law and Politics on a Neoliberal Landscape," explores the limitations of contemporary rights-based activism as it has taken shape amid massive prison system expansions, growing income inequality, and reductions to social safety net benefits.

"Historicizing Trans" tackles one of the liveliest topics in contemporary trans studies: using trans★ methodologies to understand gender-variance in the past, before current identity categories and gender concepts existed. The section opens with Leah DeVun and Zeb Tortorici's reflection on how we might use trans to develop cross-temporal historical analysis and, conversely, how historical analysis helps us reconsider transness in new ways. Their conceptual framing of "trans★historicities" in "Trans, Time, and History" likewise helps us to engage trans history writing from early essays such as Leslie Feinberg's "Transgender Liberation: A Movement Whose Time Has Come," to more recent work in the field. Mary Weismantel's Towards a Transgender Archeology: A Queer Rampage Through Prehistory" uses trans theory to suggest how current ideologies of a biological sex/gender binary inform a misreading of the deep human past that serves only to naturalize presentist frames of reference. Other work in this section explores much more recent history. Paul B. Preciado's "Pharmaco-Pornographic Regime: Sex, Gender, and Subjectivity in the Age of Punk Capitalism" offers a provocative riff on post-WWII techno-science that positions the pharmaceutically altered, hypersexualized trans body as the paradigmatic figure of our historical era. In "ONE, Inc. and Reed Erickson," Aaron H. Devor and Nicholas Matte offer a history of the contentious and largely unremembered support of gay activism by a wealthy trans man from the 1960s to the early 1980s, while Afsaneh Najmabadi's "Reading *Transsexuality* in Gay Tehran (Around 1979)" documents how trans and gay categories of identity rooted in a Eurocentric frame of reference shifted before and after the Iranian Revolution.

"Transing the Non/Human" begins with a classic work of feminist science studies, Donna J. Haraway's "A Cyborg Manifesto," which provided a point of departure for her student Sandy Stone's "Possttranssexual Manifesto." Haraway's cyborg offered a way to rethink many of the binaries that characterize contemporary embodiment: nature/culture, machinic/organic, human/animal, male/female, nonliving/living. Hil Malatino's "Biohacking Gender: Cyborgs, Coloniality, and the Pharmacopornographic Era" discusses both Haraway and Preciado to suggest that however liberatory it can feel to engage in DIY practices of body-transformation that point to some better posthuman cyborgian future, these very frames of reference remain embedded in capitalism and coloniality—an embeddedness that Haraway acknowledges in her work. Mel Y. Chen, in "Animals Without Genitals: Race and Transsubstantiation," reads representations of genital presence/absence in a variety of cultural texts to show how moments of "transness" make visible the way race and species operate as categories that create hierarchies between different kinds of life. In "Lessons from a Starfish," Eva Hayward similarly reads moments of transness in "The Cripple and the Starfish," a song by not-yet-out as trans artist AHNONI of Antony and the Johnsons, to put species difference and disability in conversation with trans studies in ways that open up new ways of thinking about the capacity of life to regenerate itself in new forms. In "Trans Animisms," Abram

J. Lewis links practices of magic in trans activism to the concept of animism, or ontological liveliness, in the lives and belief systems of two important mid-twentieth-century trans activists, Reed Erickson and Angela Douglas. Rather than idiosyncratic manifestations of strangeness or madness, Lewis shows how this sense of animistic magic has played a central role in trans activism.

Making creative work has long been a practice through which trans people remix and reimagine their worlds. The section of "Trans Cultural Production" includes Julian Carter's "Embracing Transition, or Dancing in the Folds of Time," which uses technical dance terminology and the metaphor of choreography to offer an expansive theorization of how "transition" can remake the relationships between bodies, time, and space. In "Performance as Intravention: Ballroom Culture and the Politics of HIV/AIDS in Detroit," Marlon M. Bailey uses performance ethnography to explore how ballroom and house culture become sites of queer and trans of color survival through creative expressions of gender and community care, while Treva Ellison offers another deeply theorized account of trans-of-color gender performance as a mode of survival within racial capitalism in "The Labor of Werqing It: The Performance and Protest Strategies of Sir Lady Java." Francisco J. Galarte, in "Transgender Chican@ Poetics," revisits the cultural production of an earlier generation of Chicana feminism and argues for an expansive *jotería* that includes trans people. A final selection from Eliza Steinbock, "Shimmering Phantasmagoria," approaches trans studies by way of film theory to suggest how transsexuality can be considered a "cinematic" mode of embodiment.

Our last set of texts is organized around the theme of "Intersectionality and Embodiment." The framework of intersectionality—a term coined by critical race theorist Kimberlé Crenshaw and a core concept of contemporary Black feminism—is rooted, by way of Pauli Murray, in a genealogy of thought that has both Black and trans/nonbinary branches. Pauli Murray, a lawyer and legal scholar whose theorization of the intersections of misogyny and racism in the experiences of Black women in the southern United States—an apartheid system Murray dubbed "Jane Crow"—informed not only the concept of intersectionality, but the anti-segregation and reproductive rights rulings of U.S. Supreme Court Justices Thurgood Marshall and Ruth Bader Ginsburg. In "Pauli Murray's Peter Panic," Simon D. Elin Fisher shows how Murray's nonbinary transness foundationally contributed to our understandings of intersectionality from a specifically trans of color perspective. We include another classic work of intersectional Black feminism, the "Black Feminist Statement" of the Combahee River Collective, for the argument it makes against the biological essentialism it saw in contemporaneous white feminism—precisely the characteristic that underpins feminist transphobia. Two other works take the concept of intersectionality in other directions. Eli Clare's "Selection from *Brilliant Imperfection: Grappling with Cure*" brings a disabilities studies framework to bear on questions of medically assisted gender-transition to critique the ways some able-bodied trans people deploy the pathologizing language of "defect" to describe their relationships with their genders. In so doing, they disavow disability stigma and imagine treatment as cure in ways that serve only to reproduce ableism. In "Hermaphrodites With Attitude," intersex activist Cheryl Chase charts connections and divergences between the intersex and transgender movements in the 1990s while placing medicalized practices of genital-cutting in a transnational feminist framework. A final essay, Christopher Joseph Lee's "Undetectibility in a Time of Trans Visibility," reminds readers of the often unacknowledged centrality of the HIV/AIDS pandemic to the historical context in which trans studies took shape. Fisher repurposes the notion of "undetectability," a term which often refers to an undetectable HIV viral load, and uses it to rethink questions of trans-of-color visibility and vulnerability to premature death through exposure to structural racism and transphobia.

We hope that you find a rhythm of your own as you read the *Remix*—whether that's by reading within sections or skipping across them, reading the chapters in order or at random. We developed the *Remix* as a specifically trans project, one that highlights the cross-disciplinary linkages already looping underneath new and old trans studies tracks.

Acknowledgments

Thank you to co-editor Susan Stryker for her sharp editorial work in this introduction, especially for her help with the final section, and for the fun of working on this project together.

Notes

1. See *TIME* cover of print edition, 9 June 2014. For the accompanying article, see Katy Steinmetz, "America's Transition," https://time.com/135480/transgender-tipping-point/.
2. See www.prri.org/research/american-attitudes-towards-transgender-people/.
3. See www.pewresearch.org/fact-tank/2021/07/27/rising-shares-of-u-s-adults-know-someone-who-is-transgender-or-goes-by-gender-neutral-pronouns/.
4. *Trap Door: Trans Cultural Production and the Politics of Visibility*, edited by Tourmaline, Eric A. Stanley, and Johanna Burton, Boston: MIT Press, 2017.
5. See "The Report of the 2015 U.S. Transgender Survey," https://transequality.org/sites/default/files/docs/usts/USTS-Full-Report-Dec17.pdf.
6. See Cristian González Cabrera, "Panama's Gender-Based Lockdown and the Resilience of Transgender Activism: An Interview with Pau González of Hombres Trans Panamá," *Human Rights Watch*, 21 July 2021, www.hrw.org/news/2021/07/21/panamas-gender-based-lockdown-and-resilience-transgender-activism#.
7. See "Introduction: Transgender Studies 2.0," *The Transgender Studies Reader 2*, edited by Susan Stryker and Aren Z. Aizura, New York: Routledge, 2013.
8. Susan Stryker, Paisley Currah, and Lisa Jean Moore, "Introduction: Trans-, Trans, or Transgender?" *WSQ: Women's Studies Quarterly* 34 (3–4) (2008): 11–22.
9. Eva Hayward and Jami Weinstein, "Introduction: Tranimalities in the Age of Trans★ Life," *TSQ: Transgender Studies Quarterly* 2 (2) (2015): 195–208.
10. Trans of color theorist and playable media designer micha cárdenas directly addresses this "asteriskial" sense of trans★ as a conceptual operator in *Poetic Operations: Trans of Color Art in Digital Media*, the first book published in the new Duke University Press book series *ASTERISK: gender, trans-, and all that comes after*.

Section I
Trans/Feminisms

1 The *Empire* Strikes Back

A Posttranssexual Manifesto

Sandy Stone

Sandy Stone had many careers before authoring this essay, which opened up the critical and conceptual space in which "transgender studies" unfolded. She worked on digital telephone technology at Bell Labs in the late 1950s, did medical research in audiology at the Menninger Clinic, and became a recording engineer for some of the biggest names in rock and roll in the '60s. In the 1970s, after her gender transition, she became a member of the lesbian music collective Olivia Records and helped popularize the Women's Music scene. This brought her to the attention of Janice Raymond, one of the first anti-trans feminists, who organized a boycott of Olivia to force Stone's expulsion. The Olivia Collective stood behind Sandy's continued involvement—most "second-wave" feminists in the '70s welcomed trans inclusion—but Stone left voluntarily, feeling her presence would become a divisive distraction. She went on earn a Ph.D. in history of consciousness at the University of California-Santa Cruz, an esteemed interdisciplinary cultural studies program, where she worked with feminist science studies scholar Donna J. Haraway. During Stone's time at UC-Santa Cruz, she had a chance to shape her thought in interaction with other feminist luminaries such as Gloria Anzaldúa, Chela Sandoval, Theresa de Lauretis, and Angela Davis. Stone wrote the first version of her manifesto as a student paper in 1987 and presented it publicly for the first time at a 1988 conference in Santa Cruz, "Other Voices, Other Worlds: Questioning Gender and Ethnicity." It was first published in the 1991 anthology *Body Guards: The Cultural Politics of Gender Ambiguity*, just as a new wave of trans activism was beginning to take shape, and was included as the opening selection of *The Transgender Studies Reader* in 2005. The title of Stone's essay referred sarcastically to Janice Raymond's transphobic 1979 book, *The Transsexual Empire*.

Stone's remarkable essay did several things at once. Along with Carol Riddell's "Divided Sisterhood," it was one of the first works to address feminist transphobia from the perspective of a feminist trans woman. It decentered the unquestioned scientific authority of transition-related medical service providers by historicizing and contextualizing their practices. It put trans issues in dialogue with post-structuralist cultural theory—including, by the time it was published, Judith Butler's influential concept of "gender performativity." Most importantly, it critiqued from within the identity category of the "transsexual," arguing that this label came from a medico-scientific discourse that required trans people to live inauthentically, trying to pass as cisgender and constructing a "plausible history" (that is, lying) to hide their pre-transition life. Her essay articulated a "counterdiscourse" that mapped the contours of a "posttranssexual" future—not yet named "transgender"—and called on trans people to speak the truth of their experience in a new way. While Stone's foundational work is inarguably in dialogue with intersectional feminisms, trans studies scholars have noted in recent years that in not explicitly calling attention to race, Stone's manifesto inadvertently contributed to the "unmarked" whiteness of trans studies in its formative period.

DOI: 10.4324/9781003206255-3

Frogs Into Princesses

The verdant hills of Casablanca look down on homes and shops jammed chockablock against narrow, twisted streets filled with the odors of spices and dung. Casablanca is a very old city, passed over by Lawrence Durrell perhaps only by a geographical accident as the winepress of love. In the more modern quarter, located on a broad, sunny boulevard, is a building otherwise unremarkable except for a small brass nameplate that identifies it as the clinic of Dr. Georges Burou. It is predominantly devoted to obstetrics and gynecology, but for many years has maintained another reputation quite unknown to the stream of Moroccan women who pass through its rooms.

Dr. Burou is being visited by journalist James Morris. Morris fidgets in an anteroom reading *Elle* and *Paris-Match* with something less than full attention, because he is on an errand of immense personal import. At last the receptionist calls for him, and he is shown to the inner sanctum. He relates:

> I was led along corridors and up staircases into the inner premises of the clinic. The atmosphere thickened as we proceeded. The rooms became more heavily curtained, more velvety, more voluptuous. Portrait busts appeared, I think, and there was a hint of heavy perfume. Presently I saw, advancing upon me through the dim alcoves of this retreat, which distinctly suggested to me the allure of a harem, a figure no less recognizably odalisque. It was Madame Burou. She was dressed in a long white robe, tasseled I think around the waist, which subtly managed to combine the luxuriance of a caftan with the hygiene of a nurse's uniform, and she was blonde herself, and carefully mysterious. . . . Powers beyond my control had brought me to Room 5 at the clinic in Casablanca, and I could not have run away then even if I had wanted to. . . . I went to say good-bye to myself in the mirror. We would never meet again, and I wanted to give that other self a long last look in the eye, and a wink for luck. As I did so a street vendor outside played a delicate arpeggio upon his flute, a very gentle merry sound which he repeated, over and over again, in sweet diminuendo down the street. Flights of angels, I said to myself, and so staggered . . . to my bed, and oblivion.[1]

Exit James Morris, enter Jan Morris, through the intervention of late twentieth-century medical practices in this wonderfully "oriental," almost religious narrative of transformation. The passage is from *Conundrum*, the story of Morris' "sex change" and the consequences for her life. Besides the wink for luck, there is another obligatory ceremony known to male-to-female transsexuals which is called "wringing the turkey's neck," although it is not recorded whether Morris performed it as well. I will return to this rite of passage later in more detail.

Making History

Imagine now a swift segue from the moiling alleyways of Casablanca to the rolling green hills of Palo Alto. The Stanford Gender Dysphoria Program occupies a small room near the campus in a quiet residential section of this affluent community. The Program, which is a counterpart to Georges Burou's clinic in Morocco, has been for many years the academic focus of Western studies of gender dysphoria syndrome, also known as transsexualism. Here are determined etiology, diagnostic criteria, and treatment.

The Program was begun in 1968, and its staff of surgeons and psychologists first set out to collect as much history on the subject of transsexualism as was available. Let me pause to provide a very brief capsule of their results. A transsexual is a person who identifies his or her gender identity with that of the "opposite" gender. Sex and gender are quite separate issues, but transsexuals commonly blur the distinction by confusing the performative character of gender with the physical "fact" of sex, referring to their perceptions of their situation as being in the "wrong body." Although the term transsexual is of recent origin, the phenomenon is not. The earliest mention of something which we can recognize *ex post facto* as transsexualism, in light of current diagnostic criteria, was of the Assyrian king Sardanapalus, who was reported to have dressed in women's clothing and spun with his wives.[2] Later instances of something very like transsexualism were reported by Philo of Judea, during the Roman Empire. In the eighteenth century the Chevalier d'Eon, who lived for thirty-nine years in the female role, was a rival of Madame Pompadour for the attention of Louis XV. The first colonial governor of New York, Lord Cornbury, came from England fully attired as a woman and remained so during his time in office.[3]

Transsexualism was not accorded the status of an "official disorder" until 1980, when it was first listed in the *American Psychiatric Association Diagnostic and Statistical Manual*. As Marie Mehl points out, this is something of a Pyrrhic victory.[4]

Prior to 1980, much work had already been done in an attempt to define criteria for differential diagnosis. An example from the 1970s is this one, from work carried out by Leslie Lothstein and reported in Walters and Ross's *Transsexualism and Sex Reassignment*:[5]

> Lothstein, in his study of ten ageing transsexuals [average age fifty-two], found that psychological testing helped to determine the extent of the patients' pathology [*sic*] [he] concluded that [transsexuals as a class] were depressed, isolated, withdrawn, schizoid individuals with profound dependency conflicts. Furthermore, they were immature, narcissistic, egocentric and potentially explosive, while their attempts to obtain [professional assistance] were demanding, manipulative, controlling, coercive, and paranoid.[6]

Here's another:

> In a study of 56 transsexuals the results on the schizophrenia and depression scales were outside the upper limit of the normal range. The authors see these profiles as reflecting the confused and bizarre life styles of the subjects.[7]

These were clinical studies, which represented a very limited class of subjects. However, the studies were considered sufficiently representative for them to be reprinted without comment in collections such as that of Walters and Ross. Further on in each paper, though, we find that each investigator invalidates his results in a brief disclaimer which is reminiscent of the fine print in a cigarette ad: In the first, by adding "It must be admitted that Lothstein's subjects could hardly be called a typical sample as nine of the ten studied had serious physical health problems" (this was a study conducted in a health clinic, not a gender clinic), and in the second, with the afterthought that "82 per cent of [the subjects] were prostitutes and atypical of transsexuals in other parts of the world."[8] Such results might have been considered marginal, hedged about as they were with markers of questionable method or excessively limited samples. Yet they came to represent transsexuals in medicolegal/psychological literature, disclaimers and all, almost to the present day.

During the same period, feminist theoreticians were developing their own analyses. The issue quickly became, and remains, volatile and divisive. Let me quote an example:

> Rape is a masculinist violation of bodily integrity. All transsexuals rape women's bodies by reducing the female form to an artifact, appropriating this body for themselves. Rape, although it is usually done by force, can also be accomplished by deception.

This quote is from Janice Raymond's 1979 book *The Transsexual Empire: The Making of The She-Male*, which occasioned the title of this paper. I read Raymond to be claiming that transsexuals are constructs of an evil phallocratic empire and were designed to invade women's spaces and appropriate women's power. Though *Empire* represented a specific moment in feminist analysis and prefigured the appropriation of liberal political language by a radical right, here in 1991, on the twelfth anniversary of its publication, it is still the definitive statement on transsexualism by a genetic female academic.[9] To clarify my stakes in this discourse let me quote another passage from *Empire*:

> Masculine behavior is notably obtrusive. It is significant that transsexually constructed lesbian-feminists have inserted themselves into the positions of importance and/or performance in the feminist community. Sandy Stone, the transsexual engineer with Olivia Records, an 'all-women' recording company, illustrates this well. Stone is not only crucial to the Olivia enterprise but plays a very dominant role there. The . . . visibility he achieved in the aftermath of the Olivia controversy . . . only serves to enhance his previously dominant role and to divide women, as men frequently do, when they make their presence necessary and vital to women. As one woman wrote: "I feel raped when Olivia passes off Sandy . . . as a real woman. After all his male privilege, is he going to cash in on lesbian feminist culture too?"

This paper, "The *Empire* Strikes Back," is about morality tales and origin myths, about telling the "truth" of gender. Its informing principle is that "technical arts are always imagined to be subordinated by the ruling artistic idea, itself rooted authoritatively in nature's own life."[10] It is about the image and the real mutually defining each other through the inscriptions and reading practices of late capitalism. It is about postmodernism, postfeminism, and (dare I say it) posttranssexualism. Throughout, the paper owes a large debt to Donna J. Haraway.

"All of Reality in Late Capitalist Culture Lusts to Become an Image for Its Own Security"[11]

Let's turn to accounts by the transsexuals themselves. During this period virtually all of the published accounts were written by male-to-females. I want to briefly consider four autobiographical accounts of male-to-female transsexuals, to see what we can learn about what they think they are doing. (I will consider female-to-male transsexuals in another paper.)

The earliest partially autobiographical account in existence is that of Lili Elbe in Niels Hoyer's book *Man Into Woman* [1933].[12] The first fully autobiographical book was the paperback *I Changed My Sex!* (not exactly a quiet, contemplative title), written by the striptease artist Hedy Jo Star in the mid-1950s.[13] Christine Jorgensen, who underwent surgery in the early 1950s and is arguably the best known of the recent transsexuals, did not publish her autobiography until 1967; instead, Star's book rode the wave of publicity surrounding Jorgensen's surgery. In 1974 *Conundrum* was published, written by the popular English journalist Jan Morris. In 1977 there was *Canary*, by musician and performer Canary Conn.[14] In addition, many transsexuals keep something they call by the argot term "O.T.F.": The Obligatory Transsexual File. This usually contains newspaper articles and bits of forbidden diary entries about "inappropriate" gender behavior. Transsexuals also collect autobiographical literature. According to the Stanford gender dysphoria program, the medical clinics do not, because they consider autobiographical accounts thoroughly unreliable. Because of this, and since a fair percentage of the literature is invisible to many library systems, these personal collections are the only source for some of this information. I am fortunate to have a few of them at my disposal.

What sort of subject is constituted in these texts? Hoyer (representing Jacobson representing Elbe, who is representing Wegener who is representing Sparre),[15] writes:

> A single glance of this man had deprived her of all her strength. She felt as if her whole personality had been crushed by him. With a single glance he had extinguished it. Something in her rebelled. She felt like a schoolgirl who had received short shrift from an idolized teacher. She was conscious of a peculiar weakness in all her members . . . it was the first time her woman's heart had trembled before her lord and master, before the man who had constituted himself her protector, and she understood why she then submitted so utterly to him and his will.[16]

We can put to this fragment all of the usual questions: Not by whom but *for* whom was Lili Elbe constructed? Under whose gaze did her text fall? And consequently what stories appear and disappear in this kind of seduction? It may come as no surprise that all of the accounts I will relate here are similar in their description of "woman" as male fetish, as replicating a socially enforced role, or as constituted by performative gender. Lili Elbe faints at the sight of blood.[17] Jan Morris, a world-class journalist who has been around the block a few times, still describes her sense of herself in relation to makeup and dress, of being on display, and is pleased when men open doors for her:

> I feel small, and neat. I am not small in fact, and not terribly neat either, but femininity conspires to make me feel so. My blouse and skirt are light, bright, crisp. My shoes make my feet look more delicate than they are, besides giving me . . . a suggestion of vulnerability that I rather like. My red and white bangles give me a racy feel, my bag matches my shoes and makes me feel well organized . . . When I walk out into the street I feel consciously ready for the world's appraisal, in a way that I never felt as a man.[18]

Hedy Jo Star, who was a professional stripper, says in *I Changed My Sex!*: "I wanted the sensual feel of lingerie against my skin, I wanted to brighten my face with cosmetics. I wanted a strong man to protect me." Here in 1991 I have also encountered a few men who are brave enough to echo this sentiment for themselves, but in 1955 it was a proprietary feminine position.

Besides the obvious complicity of these accounts in a Western white male definition of performative gender, the authors also reinforce a binary, oppositional mode of gender identification. They go from being unambiguous men, albeit unhappy men, to unambiguous women. There is no territory between.[19] Further, each constructs a specific narrative moment when their personal sexual identification changes from male to female. This moment is the moment of neocolporraphy—that is, of gender reassignment or "sex change surgery."[20] Jan Morris, on the night preceding surgery, wrote: "I went to say good-bye to myself in the mirror. We would never meet again, and I wanted to give that other self a last wink for luck."[21]

Canary Conn writes: "I'm not a *muchacho* . . . I'm a *muchacha* now . . . a girl [*sic*]."[22]

Hedy Jo Star writes: "In the instant that I awoke from the anaesthetic, I realized that I had finally become a woman."[23]

Even Lili Elbe, whose text is second-hand, used the same terms: "Suddenly it occurred to him that he, Andreas Sparre, was probably undressing for the last time." Immediately on awakening from first-stage surgery [castration in Hoyer's account], Sparre writes a note. "He gazed at the card and failed to recognize the writing. It was a woman's script." Inger carries the note to the doctor: "What do you think of this, Doctor. No man could have written it?" "No," said the astonished doctor; "no, you are quite right . . ."—an exchange which requires the reader to forget that orthography is an acquired skill. The same thing happens with Elbe's voice: "the strange thing was that your voice had completely changed . . . You have a splendid soprano voice! Simply astounding."[24] Perhaps as astounding now as then but for different reasons, since in light of present knowledge of the effects (and more to the point, the non-effects) of castration and hormones none of this could have happened. Neither has any effect on voice timbre. Hence, incidentally, the jaundiced eyes with which the clinics regard historical accounts.

If Hoyer mixes reality with fantasy and caricatures his subjects besides ("Simply astounding!"), what lessons are there in *Man Into Woman?* Partly what emerges from the book is how Hoyer deploys the strategy of building barriers within a single subject, strategies that are still in gainful employment today. Lili displaces the irruptive masculine self, still dangerously present within her, onto the Godfigure of her surgeon/therapist Werner Kreutz, whom she calls The Professor, or The Miracle Man.

The Professor is He Who molds and Lili that which is molded:

> what the Professor is now doing with Lili is nothing less than an emotional moulding, which is preceding the physical moulding into a woman. Hitherto Lili has been like clay which others had prepared and to which the Professor has given form and life . . . by a single glance the Professor awoke her heart to life, a life with all the instincts of woman.[25]

The female is immanent, the female is bone-deep, the female is instinct. With Lili's eager complicity, The Professor drives a massive wedge between the masculine and the feminine within her. In this passage, reminiscent of the "oriental" quality of Morris's narrative, the male must be annihilated or at least denied, but the female is that which exists to be *continually* annihilated:

> It seemed to her as if she no longer had any responsibility for herself, for her fate. For Werner Kreutz had relieved her of it all. Nor had she any longer a will of her own . . . there could be no past for her. Everything in the past belonged to a person who . . . was dead. Now there was only a perfectly humble woman, who was ready to obey, who was happy to submit herself to the will of another . . . her master, her creator, her Professor. Between [Andreas] and her stood Werner Kreutz. She felt secure and salvaged.[26]

Hoyer has the same problems with purity and denial of mixture that recur in many transsexual autobiographical narratives. The characters in his narrative exist in an historical period of enormous sexual repression. How is one to maintain the divide between the "male" self, whose proper object of desire is Woman, and the "female" self, whose proper object of desire is Man?

> "As a man you have always seemed to me unquestionably healthy. I have, indeed, seen with my own eyes that you attract women, and that is the clearest proof that you are a genuine fellow." He paused, and then placed his hand on Andreas' shoulder. "You won't take it amiss if I ask you a frank question? . . . Have you at any time been interested in your own kind? You know what I mean."
>
> Andreas shook his head calmly. "My word on it, Niels; never in my life. And I can add that those kind of creatures have never shown any interest in me."
>
> "Good, Andreas! That's just what I thought."[27]

Hoyer must separate the subjectivity of "Andreas," who has never felt anything for men, and "Lili," who, in the course of the narrative, wants to marry one. This salvaging procedure makes the world safe for "Lili" by erecting and maintaining an impenetrable barrier between her and "Andreas," reinforced again and again in such ways as two different handwriting styles and two different voices. The force of an imperative—a natural state toward which all things tend—to deny the potentialities of mixture, acts to preserve "pure" gender identity: at the dawn of the Nazi-led love affair with purity, no "creatures" tempt Andreas into transgressing boundaries with his "own kind."

> "I will honestly and plainly confess to you, Niels, that I have always been attracted to women. And to-day as much as ever. A most banal confession!"[28]

Banal only so long as the person inside Andreas's body who voices it is Andreas, rather than Lili. There is a lot of work being done in this passage, a microcosm of the work it takes to maintain the same polar personae in society in the large. Further, each of these writers constructs his or her account as a narrative of redemption. There is a strong element of drama, of the sense of struggle against huge odds, of over-coming perilous obstacles, and of mounting awe and mystery at the breathtaking approach and final apotheosis of the Forbidden Transformation. Oboy.

> The first operation . . . has been successful beyond all expectations. Andreas has ceased to exist, they said. His germ glands—oh, mystic words—have been removed.[29]

Oh, mystic words. The *mysterium tremendum* of deep identity hovers about a physical locus; the entire complex of male engenderment, the mysterious power of the Man-God, inhabits the "germ glands" in the way that the soul was thought to inhabit the pineal. Maleness is in the you-know-whats. For that matter, so is the ontology of the subject. Therefore Hoyer can demonstrate in the coarsest way that femaleness is lack:

> The operation which has been performed here [that is, castration] enables me to enter the clinic for women [exclusively for women].[30]

On the other hand, either Niels or Lili can be constituted by an act of *insinuation*, what the New Testament calls *endeuein*, or the putting on of the god, inserting the physical body within a shell of cultural signification:

> Andreas Sparre . . . was probably undressing for the last time. . . . For a lifetime these coverings of coat and waistcoat and trousers had enclosed him.[31]
> It is now Lili who is writing to you. I am sitting up in my bed in a silk nightdress with lace trimming, curled, powdered, with bangles, necklace, and rings . . .[32]

All these authors replicate the stereotypical male account of the constitution of woman: Dress, makeup, and delicate fainting at the sight of blood. Each of these adventurers passes directly from one pole of sexual experience to the other. If there is any intervening space in the continuum of sexuality, it is invisible. And nobody *ever* mentions wringing the turkey's neck.

No wonder feminist theorists have been suspicious. Hell, *I'm* suspicious.

How do these accounts converse with the medical/psychological texts? In a time in which more interactions occur through texts, computer conferences, and electronic media than by personal contact, and consequently when individual subjectivity can be constituted through inscription more often than through personal association, there are still moments of embodied "natural truth" that cannot be avoided. In the time period of most of these books, the most critical of these moments was the intake interview at the gender dysphoria clinic when the doctors, who were all males, decided whether the person was eligible for gender reassignment surgery. The origin of the gender dysphoria clinics is a microcosmic look at the construction of criteria for gender. The foundational idea for the gender dysphoria clinics was first, to study an interesting and potentially fundable human aberration; second, to provide help, as they understood the term, for a "correctable problem."

Some of the early nonacademic gender dysphoria clinics performed *surgery on demand*, which is to say regardless of any judgment on the part of the clinic staff regarding what came to be called appropriateness to the gender of choice. When the first academic gender dysphoria clinics were started on an experimental basis in the 1960s, the medical staff would not perform surgery on demand, because of the professional risks involved in performing experimental surgery on "sociopaths." At this time there were no official diagnostic criteria; "transsexuals" were, *ipso facto*, whoever signed up for assistance. Professionally this was a dicey situation. It was necessary to construct the category "transsexual" along customary and traditional lines, to construct plausible criteria for acceptance into a clinic. Professionally speaking, a test or a differential diagnosis was needed for transsexualism that did not depend on anything as simple and subjective as feeling that one was in the wrong body. The test needed to be objective, clinically appropriate, and repeatable. But even after considerable research, no simple and unambiguous test for gender dysphoria syndrome could be developed.[33]

The Stanford clinic was in the business of helping people, among its other agendas, as its members understood the term. Therefore the final decisions of eligibility for gender reassignment were made by the staff on the basis of an individual *sense* of the "appropriateness of the individual to their gender of choice." The clinic took on the additional role of "grooming clinic" or "charm school" because, according to the judgment of the staff, the men who presented as wanting to be women did not always "behave like" women. Stanford recognized that gender roles could be learned (to an extent). Their involvement with the grooming clinics was an effort to produce not simply anatomically legible females, but *women* . . . i.e., *gendered* females. As Norman Fisk remarked, "I now admit very candidly that . . . in the early phases we were avowedly seeking candidates who would have the best chance for success."[34] In practice this meant that the candidates for surgery were evaluated on the basis of their *performance* in the gender of choice. The criteria constituted a fully acculturated, consensual definition of gender, and *at the site of their enactment we can locate an actual instance of the apparatus of production of gender.*

This raises several sticky questions, the chief two being: Who is telling the story for whom, and how do the storytellers differentiate between the story they tell and the story they hear?

One answer is that they differentiate with great difficulty. The criteria which the researchers developed and then applied were defined recursively through a series of interactions with the candidates. The scenario worked this way: Initially, the only textbook on the subject of transsexualism was Harry Benjamin's definitive work *The Transsexual Phenomenon* [1966].[35] [Note that Benjamin's book actually postdates *I Changed My Sex!* by about ten years.] When the first clinics were constituted, Benjamin's book was the researchers' standard reference. And when the first transsexuals were evaluated for their suitability for surgery, their behavior matched up gratifyingly with Benjamin's criteria. The researchers produced papers which reported on this, and which were used as bases for funding.

It took a surprisingly long time—several years—for the researchers to realize that the reason the candidates' behavioral profiles matched Benjamin's so well was that the candidates, too, had read Benjamin's book, which was passed from hand to hand within the transsexual community, and they were only too happy to provide the behavior that led to acceptance for surgery.[36] This sort of careful repositioning created interesting problems. Among them was the determination of the permissible range of expressions of physical sexuality. This was a large gray area in the candidates' self-presentations, because Benjamin's subjects did not talk about any erotic sense of their own bodies. Consequently nobody else who came to the clinics did either. By textual authority, physical men who lived as women and who identified themselves as transsexuals, as opposed to male transvestites for whom erotic penile sensation was permissible, could not experience penile pleasure. Into the 1980s there was not a single preoperative male-to-female transsexual for whom data was available who experienced genital sexual pleasure while living in the "gender of choice."[37] The prohibition continued postoperatively in interestingly transmuted form, and remained so absolute that no postoperative transsexual would admit to experiencing sexual pleasure through masturbation either. Full membership in the assigned gender was conferred by orgasm, real or faked, accomplished through heterosexual penetration.[38] "Wringing the turkey's neck," the ritual of penile masturbation just before surgery, was the most secret of secret traditions. To acknowledge so natural a desire would be to risk "crash landing"; that is, "role inappropriateness" leading to disqualification.[39]

It was necessary to retrench. The two groups, on one hand the researchers and on the other the transsexuals, were pursuing separate ends. The researchers wanted to know what this thing they called gender dysphoria syndrome was. They wanted a taxonomy of symptoms, criteria for differential diagnosis, procedures for evaluation, reliable courses of treatment, and thorough follow-up. The transsexuals wanted surgery. They had very clear agendas regarding their relation to the researchers, and considered the doctors' evaluation criteria merely another obstacle in their path—something to be overcome. In this they unambiguously expressed Benjamin's original criterion in its simplest form: The sense of being in the "wrong" body.[40] This seems a recipe for an uneasy adversarial relationship, and it was. It continues to be, although with the passage of time there has been considerable dialogue between the two camps. Partly this has been made possible by the realization among the medical and psychological community that the expected criteria for differential diagnosis did not emerge. Consider this excerpt from a paper by Marie Mehl, written in 1986:

> There is no mental nor psychological test which successfully differentiates the transsexual from the so-called normal population. There is no more psychopathology in the transsexual population than in the population at large, although societal response to the transsexual does pose some insurmountable problems. The psychodynamic histories of transsexuals do not yield any consistent differentiation characteristics from the rest of the population.[41]

These two accounts, Mehl's statement and that of Lothstein, in which he found transsexuals to be depressed, schizoid, manipulative, controlling, and paranoid, coexist within a span of less than ten years. With the achievement of a diagnostic category in 1980—one which, after years of research, did not involve much more than the original sense of "being in the wrong body"—and consequent acceptance by the body police, i.e., the medical establishment, clinically "good" histories now exist of transsexuals in areas as widely dispersed as Australia, Sweden, Czechoslovakia, Vietnam, Singapore, China, Malaysia, India, Uganda, Sudan, Tahiti, Chile, Borneo, Madagascar, and the Aleutians.[42] (This is not a complete list.) It is a considerable stretch to fit them all into some plausible theory. Were there undiscovered or untried diagnostic techniques that would have differentiated transsexuals from the "normal" population? Were the criteria wrong, limited, or short-sighted? Did the realization that criteria were not emerging just naturally appear as a result of "scientific progress," or were there other forces at work?

Such a banquet of data creates its own problems. Concomitant with the dubious achievement of a diagnostic category is the inevitable blurring of boundaries as a vast heteroglossic account of difference, heretofore invisible to the "legitimate" professions, suddenly achieves canonization and simultaneously becomes homogenized to satisfy the constraints of the category. Suddenly the old morality tale of the truth of gender, told by a kindly white patriarch in New York in 1966, becomes pancultural in the 1980s. Emergent polyvocalities of lived experience, never represented in the discourse but present at least in potential, disappear; the *berdache* and the stripper, the tweedy housewife and the *mujerado*, the *mah'u* and the rock star, are still the same story after all, if we only try hard enough.

Whose Story Is This, Anyway?

I wish to point out the broad similarities which this peculiar juxtaposition suggests to aspects of colonial discourse with which we may be familiar: The initial fascination with the exotic, extending to professional investigators; denial of subjectivity and lack of access to the dominant discourse; followed by a species of rehabilitation.

Raising these issues has complicated life in the clinics.

"Making" history, whether autobiographic, academic, or clinical, is partly a struggle to ground an account in some natural inevitability. Bodies are screens on which we see projected the momentary settlements that emerge from ongoing struggles over beliefs and practices within the academic and medical communities. These struggles play themselves out in arenas far removed from the body. Each is an attempt to gain a high ground which is profoundly moral in character, to make an authoritative and final explanation for the way things are and consequently for the way they must continue to be. In other words, each of these accounts is culture speaking with the voice of an individual. The people who have no voice in this theorizing are the transsexuals themselves. As with males theorizing about women from the beginning of time, theorists of gender have seen transsexuals as possessing something less than agency. As with "genetic" "women," transsexuals are infantilized, considered too illogical or irresponsible to achieve true subjectivity, or clinically erased by diagnostic criteria; or else, as constructed by some radical feminist theorists, as robots of an insidious and menacing patriarchy, an alien army designed and constructed to infiltrate, pervert and destroy "true" women. In this construction as well, the transsexuals have been resolutely complicit by failing to develop an effective counterdiscourse.

Here on the gender borders at the close of the twentieth century, with the faltering of phallocratic hegemony and the bumptious appearance of heteroglossic origin accounts, we find the epistemologies of white male medical practice, the rage of radical feminist theories and the chaos of lived gendered experience meeting on the battlefield of the transsexual body: a hotly contested site of cultural inscription, a meaning machine for the production of ideal type. Representation at its most magical, the transsexual body is perfected memory, inscribed with the "true" story of Adam and Eve as the ontological account of irreducible difference, an essential biography which is part of nature. A story which culture tells itself, the transsexual body is a tactile politics of reproduction constituted through textual violence. The clinic is a technology of inscription.

Given this circumstance in which a minority discourse comes to ground in the physical, a counterdiscourse is critical. But it is difficult to generate a counterdiscourse if one is programmed to disappear. The highest purpose of the transsexual is to erase him/herself, to fade into the "normal" population as soon as possible. Part of this process is known as *constructing a plausible history*—learning to lie effectively about one's past. What is gained is acceptability in society. What is lost is the ability to authentically represent the complexities and ambiguities of lived experience, and thereby is lost that aspect of "nature" which Donna J. Haraway theorizes as Coyote—the Native American spirit animal who represents the power of continual transformation which is the heart of engaged life. Instead, authentic experience is replaced by a particular kind of story, one that supports the old constructed positions. This is expensive, and profoundly disempowering. Whether desiring to do so or not, transsexuals do not grow up in the same ways as "GGs," or genetic "naturals."[43] Transsexuals do not possess the same history as genetic "naturals," and do not share common oppression prior to gender reassignment. I am not suggesting a shared discourse. I am suggesting that in the transsexual's erased history we can find a story disruptive to the accepted discourses of gender, which originates from within the gender minority itself and which can make common cause with other oppositional discourses. But the transsexual currently occupies a position which is nowhere, which is outside the binary oppositions of gendered discourse. For a transsexual, *as a transsexual*, to generate a true, effective and representational counterdiscourse is to speak from outside the boundaries of gender, beyond the constructed oppositional nodes which have been predefined as the only positions from which discourse is possible. How, then, can the transsexual speak? If the transsexual were to speak, what would s/he say?

A Posttranssexual Manifesto

To attempt to occupy a place as speaking subject within the traditional gender frame is to become complicit in the discourse which one wishes to deconstruct. Rather, we can seize upon the textual violence inscribed in the transsexual body and turn it into a reconstructive force. Let me suggest a more familiar example. Judith Butler points out that the lesbian categories of "butch" and "femme" are not simple assimilations of lesbianism back into terms of heterosexuality. Rather, Butler introduces the concept of *cultural intelligibility*, and suggests that the contextualized and resignified "masculinity" of the butch, seen against a culturally intelligible "female" body, invokes a dissonance that both generates a sexual tension and constitutes the object of desire. She points out that this way of thinking about gendered objects of desire admits of much greater complexity than the example suggests. The lesbian butch or femme both recall the heterosexual scene but simultaneously displace it. The idea that butch and femme are "replicas" or "copies" of heterosexual exchange underestimates the erotic power of their internal dissonance.[44] In the case of the transsexual, the varieties of performative gender, seen against a culturally intelligible gendered body *which is itself a medically constituted textual violence*, generate new and unpredictable dissonances which implicate entire spectra of desire. In the transsexual as text we may find the potential to map the refigured body onto conventional gender discourse and thereby disrupt it, to take advantage of the dissonances created by such a juxtaposition to fragment and reconstitute the elements of gender in new and unexpected geometries. I suggest we start by taking Raymond's accusation that "transsexuals divide women" beyond itself, and turn it into a productive force to multiplicatively divide the old binary discourses of gender—as well as Raymond's own monistic discourse. To foreground the practices of inscription and reading which are part of this deliberate invocation of dissonance, I suggest constituting transsexuals not as a class or problematic "third gender," but rather as a *genre*—a set of embodied texts whose potential for *productive* disruption of structured sexualities and spectra of desire has yet to be explored.

In order to effect this, the genre of visible transsexuals must grow by recruiting members from the class of invisible ones, from those who have disappeared into their "plausible histories." The most critical thing a transsexual can do, the thing that *constitutes* success, is to "pass."[45] Passing means to live successfully in the gender of choice, to be accepted as a "natural" member of that gender. Passing means the denial of mixture. One and the same with passing is effacement of the prior gender role, or the construction of a plausible history. Considering that most transsexuals choose reassignment in their third or fourth decade, this means erasing a considerable portion of their personal experience. It is my contention that this process, in which both the transsexual and the medicolegal/psychological establishment are complicit, forecloses the possibility of a life grounded in the *intertextual* possibilities of the transsexual body.

To negotiate the troubling and productive multiple permeabilities of boundary and subject position that intertextuality implies, we must begin to rearticulate the foundational language by which both sexuality and transsexuality are described. For example, neither the investigators nor the transsexuals have taken the step of problematizing "wrong body" as an adequate descriptive category. In fact "wrong body" has come, virtually by default, to *define* the syndrome.[46] It is quite understandable, I think, that a phrase whose lexicality suggests the phallocentric, binary character of gender differentiation should be examined with deepest suspicion. So long as we, whether academics, clinicians, or transsexuals, ontologize both sexuality and transsexuality in this way, we have foreclosed the possibility of analyzing desire and motivational complexity in a manner which adequately describes the multiple contradictions of individual lived experience. We need a deeper analytical language for transsexual theory, one which allows for the sorts of ambiguities and polyvocalities which have already so productively informed and enriched feminist theory.

In this volume, Judith Shapiro points out that "To those who might be inclined to diagnose the transsexual's focus on the genitals as obsessive or fetishistic, the response is that they are, in fact, simply conforming to *their culture's* criteria for gender assignment" (emphasis mine). This statement points to deeper workings, to hidden discourses and experiential pluralities within the transsexual monolith. They are not yet clinically or academically visible, and with good reason. For example, in pursuit of differential diagnosis a question sometimes asked of a prospective transsexual is "Suppose that you could be a man [or woman] in every way except for your genitals; would you be content?" There are several possible answers, but only one is clinically correct.[47] Small wonder, then, that so much of these discourses revolves around the phrase "wrong body." Under the binary phallocratic founding myth by which Western bodies and subjects are authorized, only one body per gendered subject is "right." All other bodies are wrong.

As clinicians and transsexuals continue to face off across the diagnostic battlefield which this scenario suggests, the transsexuals for whom gender identity is something different from *and perhaps irrelevant to* physical genitalia are occulted by those for whom the power of the medical/psychological establishments, and their ability to act as gatekeepers for cultural norms, is the final authority for what counts as a culturally intelligible body. This is a treacherous area, and were the silenced groups to achieve voice we might well find, as feminist theorists have claimed, that the identities of individual, embodied subjects were far less implicated in physical norms, and far more diversely spread across a rich and complex structuration of identity and desire, than it is now possible to express. And yet in even the best of the current debates, the standard mode is one of relentless totalization. The most egregious example in this paper, Raymond's stunning "All transsexuals rape women's bodies" (what if she had said, e.g., "all blacks rape women's bodies"), is no less totalizing than Kates's "transsexuals . . . take on an exaggerated and stereotypical female role," or Bolin's "transsexuals try to forget their male history." There are no subjects in these discourses, only homogenized, totalized objects—fractally replicating earlier histories of minority discourses in the large. So when I speak the forgotten word, it will perhaps wake memories of other debates. The word is *some*.

Transsexuals who pass seem able to ignore the fact that by creating totalized, monistic identities, forgoing physical and subjective intertextuality, they have foreclosed the possibility of authentic relationships. Under the principle of passing, denying the destabilizing power of being "read," relationships begin as lies—and passing, of course, is not an activity restricted to transsexuals. This is familiar to the person of color whose skin is light enough to pass as white, or to the closet gay or lesbian . . . or to anyone who has chosen invisibility as an imperfect solution to personal dissonance. In essence I am rearticulating one of the arguments for solidarity which has been developed by gays, lesbians and people of color. The comparison extends further. To deconstruct the necessity for passing implies that transsexuals must take responsibility for *all* of their history, to begin to rearticulate their lives not as a series of erasures in the service of a species of feminism conceived from within a traditional frame, but as a political action begun by reappropriating difference and reclaiming the power of the refigured and reinscribed body. The disruptions of the old patterns of desire that the multiple dissonances of the transsexual body imply produce not an irreducible alterity but a myriad of alterities, whose unanticipated juxtapositions hold what Donna J. Haraway has called the promises of monsters—physicalities of constantly shifting figure and ground that exceed the frame of any possible representation.[48]

The essence of transsexualism is the act of passing. A transsexual who passes is obeying the Derridean imperative: "Genres are not to be mixed. I will not mix genres."[49] I could not ask a transsexual for anything more inconceivable than to forgo passing, to be consciously "read," to read oneself aloud—and by this troubling and productive reading, to begin to *write oneself* into the discourses by which one has been written—in effect, then, to become a (look out—dare I say it again?) posttranssexual.[50] Still, transsexuals know that silence can be an extremely high price to pay for acceptance. I want to speak directly to the brothers, sisters and others who may read/"read" this and say: I ask all of us to use the strength which brought us through the effort of restructuring identity, and which has also helped us to live in silence and denial, for a re-visioning of our lives. I know you feel that most of the work is behind you and that the price of invisibility is not great. But, although *individual* change is the foundation of all things, it is not the end of all things. Perhaps it's time to begin laying the groundwork for the next transformation.

Notes

Thanks to Gloria Anzaldúa, Laura Chernaik, Ramona Fernandez, Thyrza Goodeve, and John Hartigan for their valuable comments on earlier drafts of this paper, Judy Van Maasdam and Donald Laub of the Stanford Gender Dysphoria Program for their uneasy help, Wendy Chapkis; Nathalie Magan; the Olivia Records Collective, for whose caring in difficult times I am deeply grateful; Janice Raymond, for playing Luke Skywalker to my Darth Vader, Graham Nash and David Crosby; and to Christy Staats and Brenda Warren for their steadfastness. In particular, I thank Donna J. Haraway, whose insight and encouragement continue to inform and illuminate this work.

1. Jan Morris, *Conundrum* (New York: Harcourt Brace Jovanovich, 1974), 155.
2. In William A.W. Walters and Michael W. Ross, *Transsexualism and Sex Reassignment* (Oxford: Oxford University Press, 1986).
3. This capsule history is related in the introduction to Richard Docter's, *Transvestites and Transsexuals: Toward a Theory of Cross-Gender Behavior* (New York: Plenum Press, 1988). It is also treated by Judith Shapiro, "Transsexualism: Reflections on the Persistence of Gender and the Mutability of Sex", in this

volume, as well as by Janice Irvine in *Disorders of Desire: Sex and Gender in Modern American Sexology* (Philadelphia: Temple University Press, 1990). In chapter seven of this volume, Gary Kates argues that the Chevalier d'Eon was not a transsexual because he did not demonstrate the transsexual syndrome as Kates understands it; i.e., "intense discomfort with masculine clothes and activities, as is normal in male-to-female transsexuals." Kates's idea of the syndrome comes from standard texts. Later in this paper I discuss the mythic quality of much of this information.

4. In Mehl's introduction to Betty Steiner, ed., *Gender Dysphoria Syndrome: Development, Research, Management* (New York: Plenum Press, 1985).

5. Walters and Ross.

6. From Don Burnard and Michael W. Ross, "Psychosocial Aspects and Psychological Theory: What Can Psychological Testing Reveal?" in Walters and Ross [58, 2].

7. Walters and Ross [58, 3].

8. Walters and Ross [58, 3].

9. There is some hope to be taken that Judith Shapiro's work will supersede Raymond's as such a definitive statement. Shapiro's accounts seem excellently balanced, and she is aware that there are more accounts from transsexual scholars that have not yet entered the discourse.

10. This wonderful phrase is from Donna J. Haraway's, "Teddy Bear Patriarchy: Taxidermy in the Garden of Eden, New York City, 1908–1936," *Social Text* 11, 11:20.

11. Haraway, op.cit. The anecdotal character of this section is supported by field notes which have not yet been organized and coded. A thoroughly definitive and perhaps ethnographic version of this paper, with appropriate citations of both professionals and their subjects, awaits research time and funding.

12. The British sexologist, Norman Haine, wrote the introduction, thus making Hoyer's book a semi-medical contribution.

13. Hedy Jo Star, (Carl Rollins Hammonds), 1955. *I Changed My Sex! [From an O.T.F.]*. Star's book has disappeared from history, and I have been unable to find reference to it in any library catalog. Having held a copy in my hand, I am sorry I didn't hold tighter.

14. There was at least one other book published during this period, Renée Richards's "Second Serve," which is not treated here.

15. Niels Hoyer was a pseudonym for Ernst Ludwig Harthern Jacobson; Lili Elbe was the female name chosen by the artist Einar Wegener, whose given name was Andreas Sparre. This lexical profusion has rich implications for studies of self and its constructions, in literature and also in such emergent social settings as computer conferences, where several personalities grounded in a single body are as much the rule as the exception.

16. Hoyer [163].

17. Hoyer [147].

18. Morris [174].

19. In *Conundrum*, Morris does describe a period in her journey from masculine to feminine (from a few years before surgery to immediately afterward) during which her gender was perceived, by herself and others, as ambiguous. She is quite unambiguous, though, about the moment of transition from *male* to *female*.

20. Gender reassignment is the correct disciplinary term. In current medical discourse, sex is taken as a natural physical fact and cannot be changed.

21. Morris [115]. I was reminded of this account on the eve of my own surgery. Gee, I thought on that occasion, it would be interesting to magically become another person in that binary and final way. So I tried it myself—going to the mirror and saying goodbye to the person I saw there—and unfortunately it didn't work. A few days later, when I could next get to the mirror, the person looking back at me was still me. I still don't understand what I did wrong.

22. Canary Conn, *Canary: The Story of a Transsexual* (New York: Bantam, 1977), 271. Conn had her surgery at the clinic of Jesus Maria Barbosa in Tijuana. In this excerpt she is speaking to a Mexican nurse; hence the Spanish terms.

23. Star.

24. I admit to being every bit as astounded as the good Doctor, since except for Hoyer's account there are no other records of change in vocal pitch or timbre following administration of hormones or gender reassignment surgery. If transsexuals do succeed in altering their vocal characteristics, they do it gradually and with great difficulty. But there are more than sufficient problems with Lili Elbe's "true story," not the least of which is the scene in which Elbe finally "becomes a woman" by virtue of her physician's *implanting into her abdominal cavity a set of human ovaries*. The attention given by the media in the past decade to heart transplants and diseases of the immune system have made the lay public more aware

of the workings of the human immune response, but even in 1936 Hoyer's account would have been recognized by the medical community as questionable. Tissue rejection and the dream of mitigating it were the subjects of speculation in fiction and science fiction as late as the 1940s; e.g., the miracle drug "collodiansy" in H. Beam Piper's *One Leg Too Many* (1949).

25. Hoyer [165].

26. Hoyer [170]. For an extended discussion of texts that transmute submission into personal fulfillment cf. Sandy Stone, forthcoming, "Sweet Surrender: Gender, Spirituality, and the Ecstasy of Subjection; Pseudo-transsexual Fiction in the 1970s."

27. Hoyer [53].

28. Hoyer [53].

29. Hoyer [134].

30. Hoyer [139]. Lili Elbe's sex change took place in 1930. In the United States today, the juridical view of successful male-to-female sex change is still based upon lack; e.g., a man is a woman when "the male generative organs have been totally and irrevocably destroyed." (From a clinic letter authorizing a name change on a passport, 1980).

31. Hoyer [125].

32. Hoyer [139]. I call attention in both preceding passages to the Koine Greek verb ἐενδὲυειν, referring to the moment of baptism, when the one being baptized enters into and is entered by the Word; *endeuein* may be translated as "to enter into" but also "to put on, to insinuate oneself into, like a glove"; viz. "He [*sic*] who is baptized into Christ shall have put on Christ." In this intense homoerotic vein in which both genders are present but collapsed in the sacrifi[c]ed body cf. such examples as Fray Bernardino de Sahagun's description of rituals during which the officiating priest puts on the flayed skin of a young woman (in Frazer [589–91]).

33. The evolution and management of this problem deserves a paper in itself. It is discussed in capsule form in Donald R. Laub and Patrick Gandy, eds., *Proceedings of the Second Interdisciplinary Symposium on Gender Dysphoria Syndrome* (Stanford: Division of Reconstructive and Rehabilitation Surgery, Stanford Medical Center, 1973) and in Janice M. Irvine, *Disorders of Desire: Sex and Gender in Modern American Sexology* (Philadelphia: Temple University Press, 1990).

34. In Laub and Gandy [7]. Fisk's full remarks provide an excellent description of the aims and procedures of the Stanford group during the early years, and the tensions of conflicting agendas and various attempts at resolution are implicit in his account. For additional accounts cf. both Irvine and Shapiro, op.cit.

35. Harry Benjamin, *The Transsexual Phenomenon* (New York: Julian Press, 1966). The paper which was the foundation for the book was published as "Transsexualism and Transvestism as Psycho-somatic and Somato-Psychic Syndromes" in the *American Journal of Psychotherapy* [8:219–30 (1954)]. A much earlier paper by D.O. Cauldwell, "Psychopathia transexualis", *Sexology* 16:274–80 (1949), does not appear to have had the same effect within the field, although John Money still pays homage to it by retaining Cauldwell's single-s spelling of the term. In early documents by other workers one may sometimes trace the influence of Cauldwell or Benjamin by how the word is spelled.

36. Laub and Gandy [8, 9 *passim*].

37. The problem here is with the ontology of the term "genital," in particular with regard to its definition for such activities as preand postoperative masturbation. Engenderment ontologizes the erotic economy of body surface; as Judith Butler and others (e.g., Foucault) point out, engenderment polices which parts of the body have their erotic components switched off or on. Conflicts arise when the *same* parts become multivalent; e.g., when portions of the (physical male) urethra are used to construct portions of the (gendered female in the physical male) neoclitoris. I suggest that we use this vertiginous idea as an example of ways in which we can refigure multivalence as intervention into the constitution of binary gendered subject positions; in a binary erotic economy, "Who" experiences erotic sensation associated with these areas? (In chapter ten in this volume Judith Shapiro raises a similar point in her essay "Transsexualism: Reflections on the Persistence of Gender and the Mutability of Sex." I have chosen a site geographically quite close to the one she describes, but hopefully more ambiguous, and therefore more dissonant in these discourses in which dissonance can be a powerful and productive intervention.)

38. This act in the borderlands of subject position suggests a category missing from Marjorie Garber's excellent paper "Spare Parts: The Surgical Construction of Gender," in *differences* 1:137–59 (1990); it is an intervention into the dissymmetry between "making a man" and "making a woman" that Garber describes. To a certain extent it figures a collapse of those categories within the transsexual imaginary, although it seems reasonable to conclude that this version of the coming-of-age story

is still largely male—the male doctors and patients telling each other the stories of what Nature means for both Man and Woman. Generally female (female-to-male) patients tell the same stories from the other side.

39. The terms "wringing the turkey's neck" (male masturbation), "crash landing" (rejection by a clinical program), and "gaff" (an undergarment used to conceal male genitalia in preoperative m/f transsexuals), vary slightly in different geographical areas but are common enough to be recognized across sites.

40. Based upon Norman Fisk's remarks in Laub and Gandy [7], as well as my own notes. Part of the difficulty, as I discuss in this paper, is that the investigators (not to mention the transsexuals) have failed to problematize the phrase "wrong body" as an adequate descriptive category.

41. Walters and Ross.

42. I use the word "clinical" here and elsewhere while remaining mindful of the "Pyrrhic victory" of which Marie Mehl spoke. Now that transsexualism has the uneasy legitimacy of a diagnostic category in the DSM, how do we begin the process of getting it *out* of the book?

43. The actual meaning of "GG," a m/f transsexual slang term, is "genuine girl," (*sic*) also called "genny."

44. Judith Butler, *Gender Trouble* (New York: Routledge, 1990).

45. The opposite of passing, being *read*, provocatively invokes the inscription practices to which I have referred.

46. I am suggesting a starting point, but it is necessary to go much further. We will have to question not only how *body* is defined in these discourses, but to more critically examine who gets to say *what "body" means*.

47. In case the reader is unsure, let me supply the clinically correct answer: "No."

48. For an elaboration of this concept cf. Donna J. Haraway, "The Promises of Monsters: A Regenerative Politics for Inappropriate/d Others," in Paula Treichler, Cary Nelson, and Larry Grossberg, eds. *Cultural Studies* (New York: Routledge, 1991).

49. Jacques Derrida, "La Loi Du Genre/The Law of Genre," trans. Avital Ronell in *Glyph* 7(1980):176 (French); 202 (English).

50. I also call attention to Gloria Anzaldúa's theory of the mestiza, an illegible subject living in the borderlands between cultures, capable of partial speech in each but always only partially intelligible to each. Working against the grain of this position, Anzaldúa's "new mestiza" attempts to overcome illegibility partly by seizing control of speech and inscription and writing herself into cultural discourse. The stunning "Borderlands" is a case in point; cf. Gloria Anzaldúa, *Borderlands/La Frontera: The New Mestiza* (San Francisco: Spinsters/Aunt Lute, 1987).

2 Sappho by Surgery

The Transsexually Constructed Lesbian–Feminist

Janice G. Raymond

Feminist philosopher Janice Raymond's 1979 book *The Transsexual Empire* did not invent feminist transphobia, a discourse that first becomes visible in grassroots lesbian and feminist publications about a decade earlier, including in the work of her Ph.D. supervisor, theologian Mary Daly. Raymond's book was, however, the first to consolidate several strands of transphobic thought into a single overarching conspiracy theory that imagined trans women as a "transsexual empire" of patriarchally constructed fembots designed to infiltrate lesbian and feminist communities to destroy them from within. In the passage excerpted here from her chapter "Sappho by Surgery," Raymond goes so far as to suggest that transsexuals were invented by Nazis doing medical experiments in concentration camps. She notoriously claimed that all transsexuals, by which she actually meant only transfeminine people, perpetrate rape against cisgender women by appropriating their physical form and inserting themselves in an unwanted way in women-only spaces. In popularizing a "paranoid style" of feminist anti-trans discourse, Raymond laid the foundation for subsequent generations of so-called TERFs ("trans-exclusive radical feminists") or "gender critical" feminists while simultaneously provoking a sustained transfeminist and trans-inclusive feminist response. The article is included here not to endorse it but as a document for contemporary audiences interested in critiquing an explicitly transphobic work that unfortunately remains profoundly influential.

Transsexualism is multifaceted. From all that has been said thus far, it is clear that it raises many of the most complex questions feminism is asking about the origins and manifestations of sexism and sex-role stereotyping.* While regarded by many as an obscure issue that affects a relatively minute proportion of the population, transsexualism poses very important

---

* For a long time, I have been very hesitant about devoting a chapter of this book to what I call the "transsexually constructed lesbian-feminist." In the order this book was written, it was actually the last chapter I wrote. The recent debate and divisiveness that the transsexually constructed lesbian-feminist has produced within feminist circles has convinced me that, while transsexually constructed lesbian-feminists may be a small percentage of transsexuals, the issue needs an in-depth discussion among feminists.

    I write this chapter with the full realization that feminists look at the issue of the transsexually constructed lesbian-feminist from the vantage point of a small community in which transsexuals have been able to be very visible—not because there are that many of them, but because they immediately have center stage. Thus focusing attention on this particular aspect of the transsexual issue may only serve to inflate the issue and their presence all the more. It may also distract attention from the more central questions that transsexualism raises and the power of the medical empire that creates transsexualism to begin with.

DOI: 10.4324/9781003206255-4

feminist questions. Transsexually constructed lesbian-feminists show yet another face of patriarchy. As the male-to-constructed-female transsexual exhibits the attempt to possess women in a bodily sense while acting out the images into which men have molded women, the male-to-constructed-female who claims to be a lesbian-feminist attempts to possess women at a deeper level, this time under the guise of challenging rather than conforming to the role and behavior of stereotyped femininity. As patriarchy is neither monolithic nor one-dimensional, neither is transsexualism.

All men and male-defined realities are not blatantly macho or masculinist. Many indeed are gentle, nurturing, feeling, and sensitive, which, of course, have been the more positive qualities that are associated with stereotypical femininity. In the same way that the so-called androgynous man assumes for himself the role of *femininity*, the transsexually constructed lesbian-feminist assumes for himself the role and behavior of *feminist*. The androgynous man and the transsexually constructed lesbian-feminist deceive women in much the same way, for they lure women into believing that they are truly one of us—this time not only one in behavior but one in spirit and conviction.

Contradictions or Confirmations?

It is not accidental that most male-to-constructed-female transsexuals who claim to be feminists also claim to be lesbian-feminists. In fact, I don't know of any transsexually constructed feminists who do not also claim to be lesbians. It is this combination that is extremely important. Lesbian-feminists have spent a great deal of energy in attempting to communicate that the self-definition of lesbian, informed by feminism, is much more than just a sexual choice. It is a total perspective on life in a patriarchal society representing a primal commitment to women on all levels of existence and challenging the bulwark of a sexist society—that is, heterosexism. Thus it is not a mere sexual alternative to men, which is characterized simply by sexually relating to women instead of men, but a way of being in the world that challenges the male possession of women at perhaps its most intimate and sensitive level. In assuming the identity of lesbian-feminist, then, doesn't the transsexual renounce patriarchal definitions of selfhood and choose to fight sexism on a most fundamental level?

First of all, the transsexually constructed lesbian-feminist may have renounced femininity but not masculinity and masculinist behavior (despite deceptive appearances). If, as I have noted earlier, femininity and masculinity are different sides of the same coin, thus making it quite understandable how one could flip from one to the other, then it is important to understand that the transsexually constructed lesbian-feminist, while not exhibiting a feminine identity and role, still exhibits its obverse side—stereotypical masculinity. Thus the assumption that he has renounced patriarchal definitions of selfhood is dubious.

Masculine behavior is notably obtrusive. It is significant that transsexually constructed lesbian-feminists have inserted themselves into the positions of importance and/or performance in the feminist community. The controversy in the summer of 1977 surrounding Sandy Stone, the transsexual sound engineer for Olivia Records, an "all-women" recording

---

Because the oral and written debate concerning the transsexually constructed lesbian-feminist seems to be increasing out of proportion to their actual numbers, I think that feminists ought to consider seriously the amount of energy and space we wish to give to this discussion. However, if any space should be devoted to this issue, it is in a book that purports to be a feminist analysis of transsexualism. Furthermore, most of the commentary thus far has been limited to letters to the editor and editorial comments in feminist papers, as well as a few scattered articles in various journals. Because of limited space, these analyses are necessarily restricted. I would like, therefore, to provide an extensive and intensive analysis of the issue and to address the deeply mythic dimensions that the transsexually constructed lesbian-feminist represents.

company, illustrates this well. Stone is not only crucial to the Olivia enterprise but plays a very dominant role there.[1] The national reputation and visibility he achieved in the aftermath of the Olivia controversy is comparable, in feminist circles, to that attained by Renee Richards in the wake of the Tennis Week Open. This only serves to enhance his previously dominant role and to divide women, as men frequently do, when they make their presence necessary and vital to women. Having produced such divisiveness, one would think that if Stone's commitment to and identification with women were genuinely woman-centered, he would have removed himself from Olivia and assumed some responsibility for the divisiveness. In Boston, a transsexual named Christy Barsky has worked himself into a similar dominant position, this time coaching a women's softball team, coordinating a conference on women and violence, staffing a women's center, and performing musically at various all-women places. Thus, like Stone, he exhibits a high degree of visibility and also divides women, in the name of lesbian-feminism.

Pat Hynes has suggested that there is only an apparent similarity between a strong lesbian, woman-identified self and a transsexual who fashions himself in a lesbian-feminist image.[2] With the latter, his masculinity comes through, although it may not be recognized as such. Hynes especially points to the body language of transsexuals where she notes *subtle but perceptible* differences between, for example, the way lesbians interact with other women and the way transsexuals interact with women. One specific example of this is the way a transsexual walked into a women's restaurant with his arms around two women, one on each side, with the possessive encompassing that is characteristically masculine.

Mary Daly in explaining *why* this difference is perceptible points out that the transsexually constructed lesbian-feminist is able to deceptively act out the part of lesbian-feminist *because* he is a man with a man's history; that is, he is free of many of the residues of self-centered, self-depreciation, and self-contradiction that attend the history of women who are born with female bodies all of which is communicated both subtly and not so supply in gestures, body language, and the like.[3] Thus it is precisely *because* the transsexually constructed lesbian-feminist is a man, and *not* a woman encumbered by the scars of patriarchy that are unique to a woman's personal and social history that he can play our parts so convincingly and apparently better than we can play them ourselves. However, in the final analysis, he can only *play the part*, although the part may at times seem as, or more, plausible than the real woman (as is also the case with the male-to-constructed-female transsexual who appears more feminine than most feminine women).

What is also typically masculine in the case of the transsexually constructed lesbian-feminist is the appropriation of women's minds, convictions of feminism, and sexuality. One of the definitions of *male*, as related in Webster's, is "designed for fitting into a corresponding hollow part." This, of course, means much more than the literal signification of heterosexual intercourse. It can be taken to mean that men have been very adept at penetrating all of women's "hollow" spaces, at filling up the gaps, and of sliding into the interstices. Obviously, women who are in the process of moving out of patriarchal institutions, consciousness, and modes of living are very vulnerable and have gaps. I would imagine that it would be difficult, for example, for Olivia Records to find a female sound engineer and that such a person would be absolutely necessary to the survival of Olivia. But it would have been far more honest if Olivia had acknowledged the maleness of Sandy Stone and perhaps the necessity, at the time to employ a man in this role. As one woman wrote of Sandy Stone and the Olivia controversy: "I feel raped when Olivia passes off Sandy, a transsexual, as a real woman. After all his male privilege, is he going to cash in . . . lesbian feminist culture too?"[4]

Rape, of course, is a masculinist violation of bodily integrity. All transsexuals rape women's bodies by reducing the real female form to an artifact, appropriating this body for themselves. However, the transsexually constructed lesbian-feminist violates women's sexuality and spirit, as well. Rape, although it is usually done by force, can also be accomplished by deception. It is significant that in the case of the transsexually constructed lesbian-feminist, often he is able to gain entrance and a dominant position in women's spaces because the women involved do not know he is a transsexual and he just does not happen to mention it.

The question of deception must also be raised in the context of how transsexuals who claim to be lesbian-feminists obtained surgery in the first place. Since all transsexuals have to "pass" as feminine in order to qualify for surgery, so-called lesbian-feminist transsexuals either had to lie to the therapists and doctors, or they had a conversion experience after surgery.[5] I am highly dubious of such conversions, and the other alternative, deception, raises serious problems, of course.

Deception reaches a tragic point for all concerned if transsexuals become lesbian-feminists because they regret what they have done and cannot back off from the effects of irreversible surgery (for example, castration). Thus they revert to masculinity (but not male body appearance) by becoming the man within the woman, and more, within the women's community, getting back their maleness in a most insidious way by seducing the spirits and the sexuality of women who do not relate to men.

Because transsexuals have lost their physical "members" does not mean that they have lost their ability to penetrate women—women's mind, women's space, women's sexuality. Transsexuals merely cut off the most obvious means of invading women so that they *seem* non-invasive. However, as Mary Daly has remarked, in the case of the transsexually constructed lesbian-feminists their whole presence becomes a "member" invading women's presence and dividing us once more from each other.[6]

Furthermore, the deceptiveness of men without "members," that is, castrated men or eunuchs has historical precedent. There is a long tradition of eunuchs who were used by rulers, heads of state, and magistrates as *keepers of women*. Eunuchs were supervisors of the harem in Islam and wardens of women's apartments in many royal households. In fact, the world *eunuch*, from the Greek *eunouchos*, literally means "keeper of the bed." Eunuchs were men that other more powerful men used to keep their women in place. By fulfilling this . . . eunuchs also succeeded in winning the confidence of the ruler and securing important and influential positions.

[. . .]

Mythic Dimensions of Transsexualism

Transsexuals are living and acting out a very ancient myth, that of single parenthood by the father. This myth was prevalent in many religious traditions, including the Jewish, Greek, and Christian. Eve was born of Adam; Dionysus and Athena were born of Zeus; and Jesus was generated by God the Father in his godly birth. (Mary was a mere receptacle used to conform Jesus to earthly birth standards.) When this myth is put into the context of transsexualism, the deeper dimensions of how transsexually constructed lesbian-feminists reinforce patriarchy can be perceived.

Simone de Beauvoir has remarked that "if [woman] did not exist, men would have invented her. They did invent her. But she exists also apart from their inventiveness."[7] Men, of course, invented the feminine, and in this sense it could be said that all women who conform to this invention are transsexuals, fashioned according to man's image. Lesbian-feminists exist apart from man's inventiveness, and the political and personal ideals of lesbian-feminism have constituted a complete rebellion against the man-made invention of woman, and a context in which women begin to create ourselves in our own image. Thus the transsexual who claims to be a lesbian-feminist *seems* to be the man who creates himself in *woman's* image. This, however, is deceptive, for note that he is still created in *man's* image since he is essentially a child of the Father (in this case, the medical fathers), renouncing his mothered birth.

Mary Daly has written at length in her most recent work, *Gyn/Ecology: The Metaethics of Medical Feminism*, about the myth of Dionysus.[8] She also recites various versions of the myth along with some scholarly commentaries on it. These can shed much light on the mythic implications of the transsexually constructed lesbian-feminist. First of all, Philip Slater points out the very interesting fact that, "Instead of seeking distance from mastery over the mother, the Dionysian position incorporates her."[9] In the most popular version of the myth, Semele the mother of Dionysus while pregnant with him, is struck by Zeus with a thunderbolt and is thus consumed. Hermes saves the six-month fetal Dionysus, sews him upon Zeus's thigh, and after three more months, Zeus "births" him. Thus Zeus exterminates the woman and bears his own son, and we have single-parent fatherhood (read motherhood). Moreover, Jane Harrison has pointed out that "the word Dionysus means not 'son of Zeus' but rather Zeus Young Man, i.e., Zeus in his young form."[10] Thus Dionysus is his own father (read mother) and births himself into existence.

Whether we are talking about being born of the father, or the self (son), which in the myth are one and the same person (as in the Christian trinity), we are still talking about male mothering. At this level of analysis, it might seem that what men really envy is women's biological ability to procreate. Transsexuals illustrate the way in which men do this, by acquiring the artifacts of female biology. Even though they cannot give birth they acquire the organs that are representative of this female power. However, it is the transsexually constructed lesbian-feminist who illustrates that much more is desired than female biology—that much more is at stake than literal womb envy. He shows that female biology, whether exercised in giving birth or simply by virtue of its existence, is representative of female creativity on a profound mythic level. Thus the creative power that is associated with female biology is not envied primarily because it is able to give birth physically but because it is multidimensional, bearing culture, harmony, and true inventiveness.[11]

The transsexually constructed lesbian-feminist feeds off woman's true energy source, i.e., her woman-identified self. It is he who recognizes that if female spirit, mind, creativity, and sexuality exist anywhere in a powerful way, it is here, among lesbian-feminists. I am not saying that the lesbian-feminist is the only self and woman-identified woman. What I mean to express is that lesbianism-feminism signals a *total* giving of women's energy to women, and that it is this total woman-identified energy that the transsexual who claims to be a lesbian-feminist wants for himself. It is understandable that if men want to become women to obtain female creativity, then they will also want to assimilate those women who have withdrawn their energies from men at the most intimate and emotional levels.

This, of course, is not the usual way in which lesbian living has been harnessed. Most often, lesbian existence is simply not acknowledged, as evidenced in the laws against homosexuality, which legislate against male homosexuals, but not lesbians. It has been simply assumed that all women relate to men, and that women need men to survive. Furthermore, the mere labeling of a woman as "lesbian" has been enough to keep lesbian living harnessed or, at best, in the closet. "Lesbian is the word, the label, the condition that holds women in line. When a woman hears this word tossed her way, she knows that she . . . has crossed the terrible *boundary* of her sex role."[12] (Italics mine.)

Whereas the lesbian-feminist *crosses* the boundary of her patriarchally imposed sex role, the transsexually constructed lesbian-feminist is a *boundary violator*. This violation is also profoundly mythic, for as Norman O. Brown writes of Dionysus, he as the "mad god who breaks down boundaries."[13] Thus exhibiting qualities that are usually associated with femininity, he appeared to be the opposite of the masculine Apollo.

[. . .]

The Seduction of Lesbian-Feminists

It is not hard to understand why transsexuals want to become lesbian-feminists. They indeed have discovered where strong female energy exists and want to capture it. It is more difficult to understand why so many feminists are so ready to accept men—in this case, castrated men—into their most intimate circles. Certainly Dionysian confusion about the erasure of all boundaries is one reason that appeals to the liberal mind and masquerades as "sympathy for all oppressed groups." Women who believe this, however, fail to see that such liberalism is repressive, and that it can only favor and fortify the possession of women by men. These women also fail to recognize that accepting transsexuals into the feminist community is only another rather unique variation on the age-old theme of women nurturing men, providing them with a safe haven, and finally giving them our best energies.

The question arises: are women who accept transsexuals as lesbian-feminists expressing gratitude on some level to those men who are finally willing to join women and pay for their male privilege with their balls? Gratitude is a quality exhibited by all oppressed groups when they think that some in the class of oppressors have finally relinquished their benefits to join them. But, of course, it is doubtful that transsexuals actually give up their male privilege. As one woman put it: "A man who decides to call himself a woman is not giving up his privilege. He is simply using it in a more insidious way."[14] Furthermore, a man who decides to call himself a lesbian-feminist is getting a lot. The transsexually constructed lesbian-feminist is the man who indeed gets to be "the man" in an exclusive women's club to which he would have otherwise no access.

Women who think that these men are giving up male privilege seem to be naive about the sophisticated ways in which it is possible for men to co-opt women's energy, time, space, and sexuality. Transsexually constructed lesbian-feminists may be the first men to realize that "if you can't fight them, join them." In a short story entitled "The Women's Restaurant," by T. C. Boyle, which appeared recently in *Penthouse*, this point is well made.

The story begins by setting the scene in and around Grace & Rubie's Restaurant and is written from the point of view of the voyeuristic narrator. "It is women's restaurant. Men are not permitted What goes on there, precisely, no man knows. I am a man. I am burning to find out."[15] The narrator then proceeds to caricature Grace and Rubie as butch and femme, as well as to relate his several attempts to gain entrance. After two unsuccessful endeavors, he goes to a department store, buys a pink polyester pantsuit, a bra, pantyhose, and cosmetics with which he makes himself up to pass as a woman. He gains entrance and is able to experience what he has been missing.

> Here I was, embosomed in the very nave, the very omphalos of furtive femininity—a prize patron of the women's restaurant, a member, privy to its innermost secrets. There they were—women—chewing, drinking, digesting, chatting, giggling, crossing, and uncrossing their legs. Shoes off, feet up. Smoking cigarettes, flashing silverware, tapping time to the music. Women among women. I bathed in their soft chatter, birdsong, the laughter like falling coils of hair. I lit a cigarette and grinned. No more fairybookhero thoughts of rescuing Rubie—oh no, this was paradise.[16]

Having drunk six tequila sunrises and a carafe of dinner wine, the male intruder/narrator finds it necessary to relieve himself, but forgets to sit down when he urinates in the rest room, at which point he is discovered by Grace. The story ends with his savoring of the triumph of temporary infiltration and a plan for permanent invasion.

> I have penetrated the women's restaurant, yes, but in actuality it was little more than a rape . . . I am not satisfied. The obsession grows in me, pregnant, swelling, insatiable

with the first taste of fulfillment. Before I am through, I will drink it to satiety. I have plans. The next time I walk through those curtained doors at Grace & Rubie's there will be no dissimulation. . . . There are surgeons who can assure it.[17]

That this story appeared in *Penthouse* is no surprise. It is obvious that its editors thought it would be of interest to their readers, whether budding or closet transsexuals. In spite of the ludicrous details and caricatures, one can see that the narrator was primarily attracted to the woman-centeredness of the restaurant. "Women among women this was paradise." Such an attitude is representative of the transsexually constructed lesbian-feminist who indeed gets his "paradise," because there *were* surgeons who could "assure it." Ironically, the would-be transsexual narrator of the story says that the next time he walks through the doors, "there will be no dissimulation." Transsexualism, however, is dissimulation. As I have shown previously, to not acknowledge the fact that one is a transsexual in a women's space is indeed deception. Finally, "penetrating" the women's restaurant was "little more than a rape." Little more than a rape, indeed! What "little more" is there to such an act, unless it is the total rape of our feminist identities, minds, and convictions? The transsexually constructed lesbian-feminist, having castrated himself, turns his whole body and behavior into a phallus that can rape in many ways, all the time. In this sense, he performs *total* rape, while also functioning *totally* against women's will to lesbian-feminism.

We have seen three reasons why lesbian-feminists are seduced into accepting transsexuals: liberalism, gratitude, and naiveté. There is yet another reason—one that can be perhaps best described as the *last remnants of male identification*. This is a complex phenomenon, which has various ingredients.

On the one hand, there is fear of the label "man-hater." Are women who are so accepting of the transsexually constructed lesbian-feminist trying to prove to themselves that a lesbian-feminist (she who has been called the ultimate man-hater) is really not a man-hater after all? As Adrienne Rich has pointed out, one way of avoiding that feared label, and of allowing one's self to accept men, is to accept those men who have given up the supposed ultimate possession of manhood in a patriarchal society by self-castration.[18]

On the other hand, there is a second component to this "last remnant of male identification"—i.e., *attraction to masculine presence*. As Pat Hynes has suggested, there is an *apparent* similarity between a strong woman-identified self and a transsexual who fashions himself in a lesbian image. Because there is an *apparent* similarity, some lesbian-feminists may allow themselves to express the residues of their (buried) attraction to men or to masculine presence, while pretending to themselves that transsexually constructed lesbian-feminists are really women. This allows women to do two things: to express that attraction, yet also to decide themselves.

Self-Definition

One of the most constraining questions that transsexuals, and, in particular, transsexually constructed lesbian-feminists, pose is the question of self-definition—who is a woman, who is a lesbian-feminist? But, of course, *they* pose the question on their terms, and *we* are faced with answering it. Men have always made such questions of major concern, and this question, in true phallic fashion, is thrust upon us. How many women students writing on such a feeble feminist topic as "Should Women Be Truck Drivers, Engineers, Steam Shovel Operators?" and the like, have had their male professor scribble in the margins: "But what are the real differences between men and women?" Men, of course, have defined the supposed differences that have kept women out of such jobs and professions, and feminists have spent much energy demonstrating how these differences, if indeed they do exist, are primarily the result of socialization. Yet there are differences, and some feminists have come to realize that those differences are important whether they spring from socialization, from biology, or from the total history of existing as a woman in a patriarchal society. The point is, however, that the origin of these differences is probably not the important question, and we shall perhaps never know the total answer to it. Yet we are forced back into trying to answer it again and again.*

Transsexuals, and transsexually constructed lesbian-feminists, drag us back to answering such old questions by asking them in a new way. And thus feminists debate and divide because we keep focusing on patriarchal questions of who is a woman and who is a lesbian-feminist. It is important for us to realize that these may well be non-questions and that the only answer we can give to them is that we know who *we* are. We know that we are women who are born with female chromosomes and anatomy, and that whether or not we were socialized to be so-called normal women, patriarchy has treated and will treat us like women. Transsexuals have not had this same history. No man can have the history of being born and located in this culture as a woman. He can have the history of *wishing* to be a woman and of *acting* like a woman, but this gender experience is that of a transsexual, not of a woman. Surgery may confer the artifacts of outward and inward female organs but it cannot confer the history of being born a woman in this society.

What of persons born with ambiguous sex organs or chromosomal anomalies that place them in a biologically intersexual situation? It must be noted that practically all of them are altered shortly after birth to become anatomically male or female and are reared in accordance with the societal gender identity and role that accompanies their bodies. Persons whose sexual ambiguity is discovered later are altered in the direction of what their gender rearing has been (masculine or feminine) up to that point. Thus those who are altered shortly after birth have the history of being practically born as male or female and those who are altered later in life have their body surgically conformed to their history. When and if they do undergo surgical change, they do not become the opposite sex after a long history of functioning and being treated differently.

Although popular literature on transsexualism implies that Nature has made mistakes with transsexuals, it is really society that has made the mistake by producing conditions that create the transsexual body/mind split. While intersexed people are born with chromosomal or hormonal anomalies, which can be linked up with certain biological malfunctions, transsexualism is not of this order. The language of "Nature makes mistakes" only serves to confuse and distort the issue, taking the focus off the social system, which is actively oppressive. It succeeds in blaming an amorphous "Nature" that is made to seem oppressive and is conveniently amenable to direct control/manipulation by the instruments of hormones and surgery.

In speaking of the importance of history for self-definition, two questions must be asked. Should a person want to change his/her personal and social history and if so, *how* should one change that history in the most honest and integral way? In answer to the first question, anyone who has lived in a patriarchal society has to change personal and social history in order to be a self. History cannot be allowed to determine the boundaries, life, and location of the self. We should be change agents of our own history. Women who are feminists obviously wish to change parts of their history as women in this society; some men who are honestly dealing with feminist questions wish to change their history as men; and transsexuals wish to

---

* A parallel is the abortion issue, which can also be noted in this context. The key question, asked by men for centuries, is "when does life begin?" This question is posed in men's terms and on their turf, and is essentially unanswerable. Women torture themselves trying to answer it and thus do not assert or even develop our own questions about abortion.

change their history of *wanting* to be women. In stressing the importance of female history for female self-definition, I am not advocating a static view of such history.

What is more important, however, is *how* one changes personal history in the most honest and integral way, if one wants to break down sex-role oppression. Should nontranssexual men who wish to fight sexism take on the identity of women and/or lesbian-feminists while keeping their male anatomy intact? Why should castrated men take on these identities and self-definitions and be applauded for doing so? To what extent would concerned blacks accept whites who had undergone medicalized changes in skin color and, in the process, claimed that they had not only a black body but a black soul?

Can a transsexual assume the self-definition of lesbian-feminist just because he wants to, or does this particular self-definition proceed from certain conditions endemic to female biology and history? Women take on the self-definition of feminist and/or lesbian because that definition truly proceeds from not only the chromosomal fact of being born XX, but also from the whole history of what being born with those chromosomes means in this society. Transsexuals would be more honest if they dealt with their specific form of gender agony that inclines them to want a transsexual operation. This gender agony proceeds from the chromosomal fact of being born XY and *wishing* that one were born XX, and from the particular life history that produced such distress. The place to deal with that problem, however, is not the women's community. The place to confront and solve it is among transsexuals themselves.

One should be able to make choices about who one wants to be. But should one be able to make *any* choice? Should a white person attempt to become black, for example? The question is a moral one, which asks basically about the rightness of the choice, not the possibility of it. Should persons be able to make choices that disguise certain facets of our existence from others who have a right to know—choices that feed off others' energies, and reinforce oppression?

Jill Johnston has commented that, "many women are dedicated to working for the 'reconstructed man.'"[19] This usually means women gently or strongly prodding their significant men into androgynous behavior and action. Women who accept transsexually constructed lesbian-feminists say that these men are truly "reconstructed" in the most basic sense that women could hope for—i.e., they have paid with their balls to fight against sexism. Ultimately, however, the "reconstructed man" becomes the "reconstructed woman" who obviously considers himself equal to and a peer of genetic women in terms of his "womanhood." One transsexual openly expressed that he felt male-to-constructed-female transsexuals *surpassed* genetic women.

> Genetic women cannot possess the very special courage, brilliance, sensitivity and compassion—and overview—that derives from the transsexual experience. Free from the chains of menstruation and childbearing, transsexual women are obviously far superior to Gennys in many ways.
>
> Genetic women are becoming quite obsolete, which is obvious, and the future belongs to transsexual women. We know this, and perhaps some of you suspect it. All you have left is your "ability" to bear children, and in a world which will groan to feed 6 billion by the year 2000, that's a negative asset.[20]

Ultimately, women must ask if transsexually constructed lesbian-feminists are our peers. Are they equal to us? Questions of equality often center on proportional equality, such as "equal pay for equal work," or "equal rights to health care." I do not mean equal in this sense. Rather I use equality to mean: "like in quality, nature, or status" and "capable of meeting the requirements of a situation or a task." In these senses transsexuals are not equal to women and are not our peers. They are neither equal in "quality, nature of status" nor are they "capable of meeting the requirements of the situation" of women who have spent their whole lives as women.

Jill Johnston has written of lesbian-feminism: "The essence of the new political definition is peer grouping. Women and men are not peers and many people seriously doubt whether we ever were or if we ever could be."[21] Transsexuals are not our peers, by virtue of their history.

> It is perhaps our mistrust of the man as the biological aggressor which keeps bringing us back to the political necessity of power by peer grouping. Although we are still virtually powerless it is only by constantly adhering to this difficult principle of the power inherent in natural peers (men after all have demonstrated the success of this principle very well) that women will eventually achieve an autonomous existence.[22]

The transsexual does not display the usual phallic aggression. Instead he violates women's bodies by taking on the artifactual female organs for himself. The transsexually constructed lesbian-feminist becomes a psychological and social aggressor as well.

Transsexually constructed lesbian-feminists challenge women's preserves of autonomous existence. Their existence within the women's community basically attests to the ethic that women should not live without men—or without the "reconstructed man." How feminists assess and meet this challenge will affect the future of our genuine movement, self-definition, and power of being.

In the final analysis, transsexually constructed lesbian-feminists are in the same tradition as the man-made, made-up "lesbians" of the *Playboy* centerfolds. Every so often, *Playboy* and similar magazines feature a "Sappho Pictorial."[23] Recently, male photographers have entered the book market by portraying pseudolesbians in all sorts of positions, clothing, and contexts that could only be fantasized by a male mind.[24] In short, the manner in which women are depicted in these photographs mimics the poses of men pawing women. Men produce "lesbian" love the way they want it to be and according to their own canons of what they think it should be.

Transsexually constructed lesbian-feminists are in this tradition of pseudolesbian propaganda. Both the *Playboy* pseudolesbian and the transsexual pseudolesbian spread the "correct" (read male-defined) image of the lesbian, which in turn filters into public consciousness through the mass media as truth. By thus mutilating the true self-definition of the lesbian, men mold her image/reality according to their own. As Lisa Buck has commented, transsexualism is truly "their word made flesh!"[25]

Transsexually constructed lesbian-feminists attempt to function as image-makers of the lesbian-feminist—not only for the public-at-large, but also for the women's community. Their masquerade of the lesbian filters into women's consciousness through the feminist media as "the real thing." The ultimate tragedy of such a parody is that the reality and self-definition of lesbian-feminist becomes mutilated in women themselves. Lesbian-feminists who accept transsexually constructed lesbian-feminists as other selves are mutilating their own reality.

The various "breeds" of women that medical science can create are endless. There are the women who are hormonally hooked on continuous doses of estrogen replacement therapy. ERT supposedly will secure for them a new life of "eternal femininity."[26] There are the hysterectomized women, purified of their "potentially lethal" organs for "prophylactic" purposes.[27] Finally, there is the "she-male"—the male-to-constructed-female transsexual. And the offshoot of this "breed" is the transsexually constructed lesbian-feminist.

What all of these events point to is the particularly instrumental role that medicine has played in the control of deviant or potentially deviant women. "The Transsexual Empire" is ultimately a medical empire, based on a patriarchal medical model. This medical model has provided a "sacred canopy" of legitimations for transsexual treatment and surgery. In the name of therapy, it has medicalized moral and social questions of sex-role oppression, thereby erasing their deepest meaning.

Selection from: Raymond, Janice G., *The Transsexual Empire: The Making of the She-Male.* (New York: Teacher's College Press, 1994) pp. 99–120. Reproduced by permission of the author.

Notes

1. In June/July of 1977, twenty-two feminist musicians, sound technicians, radio women, producers, and managers sent an open letter to Olivia Records via *Sister*, a West Coast feminist newspaper. The letter focused on the employment of Sandy Stone, a male-to-constructed-female transsexual, as Olivia's recording engineer and sound technician. The signers protested Stone's presence at Olivia and the fact that Olivia did not inform women that Stone was a postoperative transsexual. They criticized Stone's participation in women-only events and accused him of taking work away from the "few competent women sound technicians in the Bay Area . . . whose opportunities are extremely limited." They noted that Stone's male privilege gave him access to his skills, and that he has never had to suffer the oppression that women face every day. The letter concluded by stating that "it is not our intention to discredit or trash Olivia," and requested that they publish a statement in response.

    In the same issue of *Sister*, Olivia replied that: 1. Surgery alone does not make a transsexual a woman. "This too-publicized step is merely the confirmation of a process that has already gone to near completion by that time." 2. Aside from a few well-publicized transsexuals, a person does not gain privilege by becoming a transsexual. Because Stone gave up his male identity and lives as a "woman" and a "lesbian," he is faced with the same kinds of oppression that "other" women and lesbians face, along with the added ostracism that results from being a transsexual. 3. A person's history is important but most significant is what that person's actions are now. 4. Day-to-day interaction with Sandy Stone has convinced the Olivia women that Sandy is a "woman we can relate to with comfort and trust." 5. Olivia did not indicate Stone's transsexual status, because they were afraid he would be "objectified." "We see transsexualism as a state of transition, and we feel that to continue to define a person primarily by that condition is to stigmatize her at the expense of her growth process as a woman." 6. Stone has trained women in technical skills and will build Olivia's recording studio where many women will apprentice. He is also writing a how-to book for women explaining the recording process. Thus Stone does not take employment away from women but provides it and may be "perhaps even the Goddess-sent engineering wizard we had so long sought."

2. Author's conversation with Pat Hynes, Cambridge, Mass., January 1978.

3. Author's conversation with Mary Daly, Boston, Mass., February 1978.

4. Rosemary Anderson, Letter entitled "Transsexual Feminism?" *Sister*, August–September 1977, p. 7.

5. Recently, questions have been raised by transsexuals who claim to be lesbian-feminists and by some professionals in gender identity clinics about clinic requirements of "passing" and about the stereotypical behavior of transsexuals. "We urge professionals *not* to assume or expect that all transsexuals will be heterosexually oriented or politically conservative and not to judge (for example) lesbianism in a male-to-female transsexual as invalid while accepting it in a genetic woman. Biological women and male-to-female transsexuals present a similarly vast range of sexual orientation and life-style choices; different choices are valid for different people Positively, we recommend a setting where the client is not forced to avow rigid self-definitions, but is permitted and even encouraged to find her/his own answers to the difficult and complex questions of sexuality and identity that confront us all." Deborah Heller Feinbloom, et al., "Lesbian/Feminist Orientation Among Male-to-Female Transsexuals," *Journal of Homosexuality* 2 (Fall 1976): 70–71.

    There are several criticisms that can be made of such a stance. First, nonstereotypical behavior is encouraged as one choice among "different choices [that] are valid for different people." Thus there is no commitment to eradicating stereotypical behavior but only to encouraging alternative behavior ("different strokes for different folks"). And thus there is no commitment to ultimately phasing out gender identity control over *various* styles of behavior. The authors' conclusions coincide with John Money's recommendations in *Sexual Signatures* for "flexible" stereotypes.

    Second, the unanswered question is why are such transsexuals and transsexual professionals still advocating surgery. Transsexual surgery would not be necessary if rigid self-definitions had not produced the phenomenon of a "female mind in a male body." This self-definition would make no sense in a society that did not accept that split. Therefore, to support behavior and orientation that is not stereotypical, yet to continue advocating transsexualism is contradictory.

Such recommendations only make the issue of "passing" and stereotypical behavior more invisible. These authors *appear* to get beyond the stereotypes, but they are actually supporting "passing" behavior on a deeper level. In effect, they are now advocating that men "pass" as lesbian-feminists, thus making a "role" out of lesbian-feminism that can be taken on by anyone. Ultimately, this brings lesbian-feminism within the confines of the gender identity clinics, where it can be observed, studied, *and controlled*—first in transsexuals, and then perhaps in lesbian-feminists. With the acceptance of transsexuals as lesbian-feminists by the gender identity clinics, the "passing" requirements only become modified. The transsexual "passes" what are the current (seemingly avant-garde) requirements of the gender identity clinics. In order to become transsexed, however, his "passing" behavior must still be "baptized" as legitimately female.

It is significant that these recommendations are coming from male-to-constructed-female transsexuals. Here is a clear admission that lesbian-feminism is perceived as important and that more is at stake in transsexual surgery than obtaining the body and the traditional role of a woman. There is a recognition here that female power/energy/creativity is at the heart of the matter. Why are there no female-to-constructed-male transsexuals, for example, who are seeking to "pass" as homosexual men?

6. Author's conversation with Mary Daly, Boston, Mass., February 1978.
7. Simone de Beauvoir, *The Second Sex* (New York: Bantam Books, 1953), p. 174.
8. See Mary Daly, *Gyn/Ecology: The Metaethics of Radical Feminism* (Boston: Beacon Press, 1978), pp. 66–67.
9. Philip Slater, *The Glory of Hera: Greek Mythology and the Greek Family* (Boston: Beacon Press, 1968), p. 211.
10. Jane Harrison, *Mythology* (New York: Harcourt, Brace and World, 1963), p. 97.
11. See comments in Chapter I about transsexual desire for female creativity as represented in female biology.
12. Radicalesbians, "The Woman Identified Woman," in Anne Koedt, Ellen Levine, and Anita Rapone, eds., *Radical Feminism* (New York: Quadrangle/New York Times Book Co., 1973), p. 241.
13. Norman O. Brown, *Love's Body* (New York: Random House, 1966), p. 116.
14. Judy Antonelli, "Open Letter to Olivia," *Sister*, August–September 1977), p. 6.
15. T. C. Boyle, "The Women's Restaurant," *Penthouse*, May 1977, p. 112.
16. *Ibid.*, p. 132.
17. *Ibid.*, p. 133.
18. Conversation with Adrienne Rich, Montague, Mass., May 1977.
19. Jill Johnston, *Lesbian Nation: The Feminist Solution* (New York: Simon & Schuster, 1973), p. 180.
20. Angela Douglas, "Letter," *Sister*, August–September 1977, p. 7.
21. Johnston, *Lesbian Nation*, p. 278.
22. *Ibid.*, p. 279.
23. See, for example, photographer J. Frederick Smith's "portfolio of stunning portraits inspired by ancient Greek poems on loving women," in *Playboy*, October 1975, pp. 126–35.
24. One photographer who is particularly obsessed with "capturing" women in pseudolesbian poses is David Hamilton. He is the creator of the following books of photography:

    Dreams of a Young Girl, text by Alain Robbe-Grillet (New York: William Morrow and Co., 1971).
    Sisters, text by Alain Robbe-Grillet (New York: William Morrow and Co., 1973). This book has an outrageous pictorial section entitled "Charms of the Harem."
    Hamilton's Movies—Bilitis (Zug, Switzerland: Swan Productions AG, 1977).

25. Lisa Buck (Unpublished notes on transsexualism, October 1977), p. 3.
26. An example of this literature is Robert Wilson's, *Feminine Forever* (New York: M. Evans, 1966). This book sold 100,000 copies in its first year, as well as being excerpted in *Look* and *Vogue*.
27. See Deborah Larned, "The Greening of the Womb," *New Times*, December 12, 1974, pp. 35–39.

3 A Transvestite Answers a Feminist*

Lou Sullivan

Lou Sullivan was a gay trans man who became a founding figure for the transmasculine community that took shape in the United States in the 1980s, before his untimely death from an AIDS-related illness in 1991. Sullivan has become an icon for a new generation of trans people in the 21st century through the publication of his remarkable journals, a biography, and frequent representation in various works of trans cultural production. In his own day, Sullivan helped recover the history of transmasculine people in Western history. He played an important role in convincing the psycho-medical gatekeepers who controlled access to medicalized gender transition that trans people could have a homosexual orientation in their self-perceived gender. Unlike many trans men, Sullivan never had a significant pre-transition history in lesbian communities. Before coming out as a gay trans man, he called himself a "heterosexual female transvestite" and identified strongly with male drag queens. In "A Transvestite Answers a Feminist," written before his social and medical transition, Sullivan provides one of the first published critiques of the new style of feminist transphobia that emerged in the early 1970s and found its canonical expression in Janice Raymond's *Transsexual Empire*. Written in response to a co-worker in the Slavic Languages Department at the University of Wisconsin-Milwaukee, where Sullivan worked as a secretary before moving to San Francisco in 1975, it was first published in *Gay Community News*.

A little over a month ago, Schlitz distributed a poster advertising their beer, featuring a "Love American Style"–type beautiful woman with a bouffant jet-black shiny hairdo and all made-up to look "sexy." Dorothy, a co-worker of mine, attached the following note to the poster and left it for me: "Sheila—would this plastic woman image be anymore excusable if this was really a man?" A bit amused, I wrote in reply: "Honey, if this was a man, she'd have to have her shit a lot more together than any of us. Believe me. (And I mean ANY of us!)" Another note from Dorothy appeared on my desk!

Dear Sheila: First of all, anyone with their shit together is constipated. Anyone who needs to keep their hair in a helmet-like style is "constipated"—Immobile, unable to move or function as a real, relaxed human. A hair style like that is a very effective way of making sure your body won't enjoy itself, and isn't sex 50 per cent body pleasure? (Other 50 per cent, of course, is mental.)

Getting your shit together means playing an act in this sense. The person who's into this scene buys a lot of funny clothing and "gets it together" on his body, not in his

DOI: 10.4324/9781003206255-5

mind, where real togetherness starts. He "gets it together" in his closet—even Alice Cooper is a "closet" queen in this respect. Now, whereas you see this superficial, bought at the department store image as implying a together personality on a man, you distain the woman who also relies on a closet full of funny, expensive clothing or make-up and lacquered hairdos as a "dumb cunt," NOT A PERSON. You very clearly stated that Joplin's trouble was her "hippy chick" image, and that often means wild clothes. Cooper dresses just as flashily, but his clothing hangup is "groovy."

The point you seem to be rather obviously trying NOT to understand is that anyone, man or woman, who must rely on a pre-packaged endorsed by *Vogue* magazine hair do or clothing is not a person, he/she is an image. This image enables the real personality to go into hiding (or conceals the fact that the person has no personality—probably more correct) because the "image" says everything about you and determines many of your actions. This is basically feminist movement thinking, so you should be aware of it. As I remember, you have put down your older makeup clad sister as being kind of a nowhere person. If people are bisexual, and the sexes are to be judged equally, what exactly makes her inferior to a transvestite? Why should I believe you? I don't believe in sex stereotyping or god, so why believe a smear of makeup is healthy on a man, but not a woman?

You're still trying to sweep mind fuck-ups under the carpet by changing the very deep and painful personality problems of the fag into some sort of ultra-cool hipness instead of realizing it's neurotic and isolating. Read Rechy's "City of Night" again. It's heartbreaking, not groovy. This scene could only appeal to someone who is absolutely terrified of communicating with other people. Yeah, they're real good at insulting each other, insulting themselves, cutting down all the institutions that oppress them . . . in short, they seem generally to react resentfully to situations, rather than mold their own lives. You say you believe in "will," but how much will do these people seem to have in this book? Can you really see this as a valid, fresh sort of life? Again, you said promiscuity without any sort of standards didn't appeal to you (it shouldn't). But when homosexuals practice this kind of non-selective fucking, bravo! After all, it's only somebody else (and a man at that) that gets emotionally hurt after every one of these one-night stands, not Sheila. And in spite of a fag's tough, oh sooooo wild'n decadent image they can hurt. If a man or woman is so tough that no pain gets through, I fear that the barriers are so high that no pleasure (probably sexual) can get through either. Remember that the mind as well as the body feels pain or pleasure, and that emotions can't be selectively repressed. A person either represses all his emotions (good and bad) or he accepts all of them. And isn't the need for a deep satisfying love an emotion?

And Sheila—I've been a Lou Reed fan, and bought all his records, for 4–5 years. He's been around for 6–7 years. Where were you and all the rest of his new supporters then? Same man making the same music, but as soon as he turned himself into a SEX-OBJECT, he gets the recognition I for one had felt he deserved as a plain MUSICIAN. Can you really think he doesn't know his music is of a secondary interest to most of his newly acquired fans? Look. No success until he decided to shove (exploit) his image (need I add up your ass?) and all of a sudden he's covered with a swarm of fruit flies. Gee, A song about shaving legs. Started shaving yours yet? If women aren't happy and satisfied as hairless sex-objects, will a man be happy as one?

I better add that I am, as always, 100 per cent against persecuting gays. I am also trying to say that they should not persecute themselves by adopting superficial roles, and going ga-ga over distorted sex-stereotype roles will only end up hurting the average gay and keep her/him from being a more "real" person.

I left the following note on Dorothy's desk in reply:

Dear Dorothy: I was startled by your heavy rap—figured either you were extremely pissed (at me?) or really wanted to understand what I was thinking. I don't know which—maybe you aren't sure yourself. It took me a while to get my thoughts and reactions together. Let's not make this a malicious encounter, but an educational one. OK?

Where does one begin to get his mind together when it is two absolute opposites? Finally I am beginning to try to reconcile a boy within me I knew was there as far back as when we kids dressed up to play cowboys and I knew it couldn't be real for me cuz I was the girl who had to be pretty and dainty and fragile and take care of the kids and cook and wait for my man to come to me. That cowboy in me could only appear as a dress-up, a pretend, but it was so real to me somehow that finally I was completely lost in it and scared someone might find out how deeply I felt it (at age 5 I had a Davy Crockett birthday party. The climax was when I appeared. I was Davy Crockett and I can still remember my thrill at the moment) and everyone else thought we were just playing, pretending, but I wasn't and it was even more frightening, cuz I knew I wasn't. (When I was 15 I stuffed a rag into my underwear for my penis and walked around like that all day, dreading exposure.)

You say flagrant queens project an "image enabling the real personality to go into hiding." What is the REAL personality in this situation—when a man wishes to appear as a woman or a woman as a man? Where do they begin to be real? Where do they begin to relax with this kind of opposition inside? To keep inside the closet, to only dress up alone in a locked room, hoping no one will ever see, afraid to open your mouth in regard to any topic coming close to your secret (What is beauty? What makes you happy? WHO DO YOU LOVE??!!!) their trying to appear straight and normal is "constipated"! That's WHY he she is an image, becuz in your own words "the image says everything about you and determines many of your actions." When he she lets himself out of the closet, dons the image of his true identity for all to see and is not scared to say "This is my lover", then he has a good start in "getting his mind together."

I challenge any person who will not admit this in themselves, such as "the woman who relies on a closet full of funny, expensive clothing or makeup and lacquered hairdos", because I could never be that . . . that which I was supposed to be and I refuse to be identified with a woman like that. I CAN'T BE! My older sister is inferior to a transvestite becuz she can't relax, she's trying so hard to deny her inner humanity and free-ness, to bottle up any susceptibility to feelings— while a transvestite at the very least, admits to himself his inner life and feelings, and, at the most, if he comes out, he's left wide open for rejection by family and friends, physical harm, denial of use of public and private facilities, easy prey for others to try and fuck his head over by saying he's sick, etc.,—all for the sake of relaxing with themselves, being free and open and alive. You ask him to come alive to the world so the world can kill him.

"Sweeping mind fuck-ups under the carpet by changing the deep and painful personality problems of the fag into ultra-cool hipness instead of realizing it's neurotic and isolating!" Dorothy. I couldn't believe you said that. The reason "**FAGS**" have deep and painful personality problems is cuz people like you "**realize** (!) they are neurotic and isolating." And then you ask them to mold their own lives! The people in Rechy have a hell of a lot more will than any straight—the will to say fuck you to all the assholes who hate them so intensely, to say fuck you to the world of people who think they're sick and say fuck you, I'm ME a lot more will than anyone else. But you say they just "seem generally to react resentfully to situations rather than mold their own lives." Where do you mold a life for yourself when all you do is battle oppressions day in and day out? Where does a black begin to mold his own life when he's alone among 200 KKKs, or a woman in a room with 50 men gawking at her tits and ass. They start at the bottom, that's where!! They band together and say fuck you everybody this is me and I'm good. Rechy's world is as valid and fresh a life as a black shouting out his SOUL or a wife splitting from her hubbie and kids and shouting her liberation.

I don't really think gays practice non-selective fucking anymore than straights. Lot and lots of gays go home from the bar alone cuz everyone there was a Gila monster, just like straights. You seem to think that's all gays do is get one-nighters. There's many more stable relationships among gays than that. Yet the rate of one-nighters is higher for gays than straights becuz of all the fear gays have of exposure, of being fucked over by straights telling them they're so sick for so long they begin to wonder themselves about their world and it's hard to have a lasting warm love with a person you've been branded from a child into thinking is sick and bad . . . someone you can never touch in public, you can never take home to mommy, you can never admit is your lover. (The two of you raise suspicion if you buy a house together, you can't take your lover to the office party or on a business trip, you can't adopt a child, and a million and five extra hassles if your couple is an older man with a 20-year-old lover.) Who can have a "deep satisfying love" under these conditions?

Six or seven years ago I was shoving rags into my underwear—that's where I was! Six or seven years ago Lou Reed was probably scared his fans would know him too well and that would be the end. "No success until he decided to exploit his image"—no success til he came out of his closet and gave others like him the courage to do the same and love and idolize him for it . . . for bringing out their lives to the public's attention as a valid, good, warm life. Yes a song about shaving legs—just like a song about natural Afros or no bras. (You'll never know if I shave my legs cuz I wear pants all the time now!)

Since you doubt men can be happy with shaved legs cuz you don't think women can be, you can come out of your closet and tell all of us how a man is to proclaim his total femininity or a woman her masculinity if not by images. You want to claim your freedom by NOT shaving your legs—so why can't a transvestite proclaim his by shaving his legs? I'm afraid you're trying to press straight standards on transvestites which just won't work . . . that's like whites judging the physical beauty of blacks by how "white" their facial features, etc., are.

Since you're adding you're 100 per cent against persecuting gays let me point out your use of chauvinist language: "fruit flies," "fags," "sex objects," "neurotic," "personality problems," "distorted sex-stereotype roles." It'd be nice if you could manage to do with that language what you did with "nigger" and "chick."

Transvestites coming out, having their own songs and idols, etc., will only "hurt" the average gay in the same sense women coming out (women's liberation) will "hurt" the average housewife.

(And double duty for all this if he's gonna pose for a Schlitz poster!)

That night Dorothy left this for me to find at work the next morning:

Just a quick note. Only wrote the way I did because you are transparently a heterosexual woman who simply cannot learn that a woman really doesn't have any lesser capabilities than a man. IF you were a lesbian as you are trying very hard to convince yourself, I certainly wouldn't have said anything to you. Also might have kept my mouth shut if you showed any interest in female homosexuals. As it is, you sit here in your "masculine" clothing (pants, masculine? nowadays?) typing and liking it. No wonder you are falling for this clothes makes the man bit. And I like you too much not to say something.

There is virtually no difference between men and women except a genital one, and anyone who limits and bases his life on his genitals is in a very bad way. That is exactly why we have a feminist movement—women were seen solely on the basis of reproductive organs, and then just couldn't take it any longer. But what are the flashy gays doing but imitating all the moronic frivolities that accrued around women in this unliberated stage? Gays are maintaining the double-standard era stereotyped woman, and as a woman who is having one hell of a time becoming fully real as a person, I cannot encourage this at all.

I would suggest you question your passivity, and so something about that. See someone if you have to. And also see if you can come up with any sort of "image" of a HUMAN—i.e., what makes a person, rather than what is a man or a woman. What happens when you discover that a man is tender, a woman aggressive; a man is spiritual, a woman is intellectual? Why get hung up on changing your sexual orientation when no difference exists in reality?

—Dorothy

But when I awoke that morning, I found this letter in my mailbox at home:

Dearest Sheila: I really feel awful about the last couple days. You were my feminist friend. We have had very similar problems in relating to other women, even feminists, so I really needed you to talk to about women's issues. Knowing I wasn't the only woman that felt isolated from others of my sex was also reassuring. You seemed to be spunkier than I was in many respects (biking up to Terre Andre; camping on the Mississippi) and I respected you for that. You were for me a direct, energetic person and good to watch in action. When my boyfriend and I stopped by, you and I could grouse about our men's super intellectualism—I needed to, because their brainy talks made me feel very left out and inferior. We were great at work—when I felt confused about some dumb office thing, you reassured me. You never put me down at work, and finally I even found out that you were as scared about phoning as I was!

So look where we are. I've got another semi-nasty note in the drawer for you; forgive me. It's nasty because you're a fine person, a fine woman, in my eyes. You're also painfully like the woman I was at your age. This little fight we're having (which I started) is mostly this age difference. I've lived through a great deal of confusion as to what a woman is and I've gone through a long period of wanting sexual "hipness." Remember the grossly insensitive (to your feelings) way I was defending your boyfriend's leaving you? Well, I was trying to defend myself and my desires for sexual hipness disguised as sexual freedom. I am so sorry, and I'm ashamed that I never apologized for my cruelty to you til now. I'm especially ashamed because I discovered a few weeks ago how wrong I was to think promiscuity and little bitty orgies made me anything special. My artwork did make me special, but I lost sight of this in my two year long resentment of my boyfriend for keeping me from my sexy'n free image. And boy oh boy, did I want an image! I just couldn't believe I was as good (smart) as he, no matter how much he told me I was. Men are smart, powerful and productive, not women, thought I, deep down inside. Well, I finally got over that. BUT—in the meantime I had lost 6 years during which I could have been developing as a strong, self-confident, self-loving person. And frankly, Sheila, I don't want to ever see another woman waste her youth on self-hatred like I wasted mine. I was so worried about you that I just exploded.

So maybe it seems like I'm patronizing you, but it's just that I've learned some truths about myself that I have a hunch apply to you. Pretty fuckin' presumptuous, ain't I? Dunno if it matters that I mean well. What I haven't learned is that people have to work thru their own problems. Maybe in my mid-30s I'll finally get that thru my thick skull.

But til then, all I can say is that masculinity and femininity, when taken as mental properties rather than physical conditions must be dumped by anyone who cares about people. "Femininity" has been used too, too long to rip off women and sensitive men, and "masculinity" has been misused to the extent of ripping off the whole world (men being the corporation heads and war-makers and women—minority ecology oppressors). I'm not talking about individuals so much as concepts (take "motherhood" as a concept and compare it to real mothers—concept has little to do with real mothers except to oppress and deceive them).

Yes, society's attitudes kill—but it's all people they kill, not just the obvious ones like blacks, freaks and gays. They killed my "Holiday Magic" sister, they killed my superficially contented mother and father, got your sister(s) and almost got me and two of my boyfriends. And it's really strange—like my parents would maintain that their images make them happy, and I know it's a lie. The only thing a person can do to get "free" is JUNK ANY KIND OF IMAGE. If "femininity" as concept is oppressive for women, it is, by its very nature, oppressive for men. If "masculinity" as concept (fear of showing emotions, social irresponsibility, hyper-competitiveness) is damaging to men, it will damage women as well. These two are socially set traps. Maybe a person hates his trap, but will he be better off in a trap someone else just jumped out of because it was a killer? How many people convince themselves to stay in a trap just because they tried to get into it so bad? What if the trap won't open when you want out? Ask a person with a prison record about that one.

I'm a wide-eyed dreamer, a utopian thru and thru. And that is why I am being such a bitch towards you right now. I so desperately want for others the peace-with-oneself that I'm having such a hard time finding. And in life any detours take years to get around. And sometimes a person can never get back on the right road. I hope that doesn't apply to us.

I felt I had to answer this letter also:

Dear Dorothy: Your letter was unexpected and surprising. I expected you to REALLY come down on me about the letter I left you. So your kind letter was more than welcome!

Dorothy, I don't feel I'm getting hung up in any "sexual hipness" (I'm not really all too sure what that means . . .) or any images. The reason I caught on so fast to what I'm doing now is cuz I always needed to do it but never had the guts to. So now I'm trying if out for size and seeing how I feel—if it's a nowhere scene, forget it. Seems I'm always going in and out of scenes . . . I guess that's how life is. For too long my boyfriend and I hid out with each other (I remember well how much I wanted to literally lock us up together in our place, board up the windows from the outside world and save us from everything). The awakening came for me when a beautiful gay came up to me on the street in the fall of '71 and I couldn't take time to even talk to him cuz I was meeting my boyfriend on the bus and it was coming a block away. And I knew when I got on that bus and left that beauty standing there that I'd never stop regretting that moment.

But now that we're untangled and I have freedom, I want to experiment in different things I've always wanted to. I'm not a lesbian. I don't want to be either. I've always thought of myself as a male homosexual (try and figure that one out—I can't). I think the reason I think that stems from my hate for the female scene. But I've always had a soft spot in my heart for transvestite and gay men becuz they seemed to me to be the most beautiful inside—the most able to abandon stereo types which, for men, I think, is a lot harder. I think they are one group that knows better than anyone that there's no difference between men and women. So I want to swim around a little—get to know some gays and transvestites, see if I can learn anything about the feelings I've had in these areas.

As long as one knows what he's doing he can't get "hung up" on it. I think I know what I'm doing and if things turn out badly, I'll know not to do it next time, right? So you're right . . . I gotta live and learn . . . don't we all?

I far from hate myself, sometimes I fear it's too much the opposite. (I love it when I find out women in the "femmy" scene hate me!) But I'm not trying to deny my "femininity," Dorothy, I'm just trying to sneak up on it thru the back door. The front door Avon lady approach didn't even work. I'd like to get the best of both worlds . . . what I'm trying to do now is find out how to get them.

—Sheila

I invited her to go to a straight bar with me that weekend to talk and drink, but she flatly turned me down, saying obviously we've "got our heads in different directions, so why bother." We never spoke about this confrontation, it had been executed entirely in writing. Ever since this exchange, over a month ago, she's been cold and offish to me. Yesterday I came to the office to visit her and she refused to even acknowledge my presence, not even to as much as look at me. I stood by the door a while and then left.

Note

* Originally published as Sullivan, Sheila. "A Transvestite Answers a Feminist" (Milwaukee: *Gay People's Union* [GPU] *News*, August 1979) pp. 9–14.

4 Transfeminism

Something Else, Somewhere Else

Karine Espineira and Sam Bourcier

The term "transfeminism" was coined by the US-based trans, intersex, disability, and sex-work advocate Emi Koyama in her 1999 essay "The Transfeminist Manifesto." The concept, translated into Spanish as *transfeminismo*, has been widely adopted in Romance-language and Latin American contexts, where it has been useful for coalition building among trans people excluded from feminist groups and for rearticulating the relationships between trans, feminist, and queer approaches to social justice activism on a range of issues such as immigration, identity documentation, anti-neoliberal protests, and sex-positivity, as well as for advancing critiques of trans-pathologization and the sex/gender binary. This article by Karine Espineira and Sam Bourcier, first published in the "Trans/Feminisms" issue of *TSQ* in 2014, examines transfeminist genealogies in France and Spain. It argues that *transfeminismo* critiques the reception of first-wave Anglophone queer theory in Europe—notably the difficulty queer theory has had in paying adequate attention to questions of embodiment and bodily difference. It notes as well that *transfeminismo* is often a better translation of the critical meaning of queerness in languages that do not have cognates for the English word *queer*.

Transfeminism started in France in the late 1990s and formally went public when the trans collective Outrans published a statement, "Transfeminismes," first in 2009 and again in revised form in 2012 (Outrans 2009, 2012, 2013). Transfeminism first entered public discourse in Spain at about the same time, in the context of a state conference on feminism in Cordoba in 2000. This article discusses the recent, interrelated development of transfeminist politics and perspectives in these two countries.

Outrans

As stated in the Outrans declaration, "transfeminism is a major opportunity to build a politics of resistance and alliance, because we consider domination to be a multilayered system that produces cross-oppressions, including transphobia. Our analysis is a feminist one, drawing from third-wave feminism, queer feminism, and postidentity feminism" (Outrans 2012). Within this coalitional politics of resistance, we see two fights that are specific to trans people: the battle against the medical and psychiatric control of trans lives, and resistance to the totalizing and compulsory system of two exclusive binary genders. Regarding the first struggle, against transpathologization, Outrans aligns itself with Stop Trans Pathologization (STP), an emancipationist group that seeks to abolish the various diagnostic classifications of

DOI: 10.4324/9781003206255-6

trans people, whether in the *Diagnostic and Statistical Manual of Mental Disorders* of the American Psychiatric Association or in the World Health Organization's (WHO) International Classification of Diseases.[1] STP is a broad coalitional movement that has managed to unite three hundred collectives on five continents, and it has contributed in a major way to thinking transfeminism in Spain. Regarding the latter struggle, in favor of gender proliferation, Outrans embraces the growing tendency to deploy such self-defining terms of identification as *FtX*, *Ft**, *FtU*, *trans'*, *trans**, *transsexual*, *trans woman*, *trans men*, *trans boy*, *trans variant*, or *gender fluid*—to name but a few of those documented by recent research (Espineira 2012; Giami et al. 2010).[2] We consider this position to emerge from a feminist critique of the sex/gender system that, on the one hand, interrogates the power relationship between men and women and, on the other hand, supports the production of new gender formations that reject and move beyond compulsory heteronormativity and its enabling gender norms (Rubin 1975, 1984). We are answering Patrick Califia's (2003: 221) call to "trash the clinic and burn down the beauty parlor" and liberate ourselves from the apparatuses that manufacture standardized femininities and masculinities.

French Transfeminism as an Offspring of Third-Wave Feminism

Third-wave feminism foregrounds "a new understanding of the power of women and girls," the "politicization of popular culture and new technologies of communication," and "the claiming of a positive sexuality open to all experience" (Mensah 2005: 15). Transfeminism's special contribution to the third wave is its insistence that a specifically transfeminist subject be included within feminism, and its demand for accountability regarding the changes that this insistence brings to feminist thinking and organizing. In her 2003 "Transfeminist Manifesto," Emi Koyama wrote that while transfeminism is certainly open to queers, intersex people, trans men, and nontrans women, it is "primarily a movement by and for trans women who view their liberation to be intrinsically linked to the liberation of all women and beyond" (Koyama 2003: 245). Four years later, Julia Serano wrote in *Whipping Girl: A Transsexual Woman on Sexism and the Scapegoating of Femininity*, "Because anti-trans discriminations is steeped in traditional sexism, it is not simply enough for trans activists to challenge binary gender norms (i.e., oppositional sexism)—we must also challenge the idea that femininity is inferior to masculinity and that femaleness is inferior to maleness. In other words, by necessity, trans activism must be at its core a feminist movement" (Serano 2007: 16).

Outrans shares this perspective and also insists on coalitional practices and intersectional analyses that expand the subject of feminism—another point of view that draws heavily from anglophone third-wave feminist traditions. Transfeminism aims to counter the homogeneity of the white, straight, and abstract subject of feminism. As did lesbian feminists, feminists of color, queer feminists, and cyber feminists before us, trans people are fighting feminism's exclusionary tendencies (Dorvil 2007). Since no definition of "oppression applies to all women any time, in any place and in any situation" (Blais et al. 2007: 143), the transfeminist paradigm relies on intersectional approaches such as Kimberlé Crenshaw's articulation of gender, race, and class (1994), and recent elaboration of intersectionality in the French context by Christine Delphy (2006), Elsa Dorlin (2008), and others.[3]

Multiplicity, variety, and hybridity remain key organizing concepts in the effort to build a feminism inclusive of ethnic, cultural, sexual, and economic minorities; women of color; lesbians; prostitutes; transsexuals; transgender people; and other marginalized groups. More recently, queer anarcho-feminist critics of capitalism have added their voices to this transfeminist call for an inclusive feminism that also encompasses antiliberals, antiracists, and anarchists.

J. Rogue notes in *Queering Anarchism* that, while "the feminist movement has a history of internal hierarchies" and that the "movement as a whole has not resolved these hierarchical tendencies," a number of groups have persistently spoken up regarding their marginalization within feminism, "in particular, transgendered women" (Rogue 2012).[4] Rogue insists that differences must be discussed rather than rejected; she explains that "one cannot address the position of women without also addressing their class, race, sexuality, ability, and all other aspects of their identity and experiences," including transgender status. All forms of oppression and exploitation are "intimately related and reinforce each other" and attempting "to address them singly (i.e., 'sexism' divorced from racism, capitalism, etc.) does not lead to a clear understanding of the patriarchal system."

Earlier French Transfeminism: Another Genealogical Thread

Transfeminism cannot be reduced to a single definition, single perspective, or single trajectory of theoretical development—even when tracing its roots in a tendency as diffuse as the feminist third wave. Excavating the history of Le Zoo—the first French queer group, founded in 1996—reveals another genealogy from which feminism entered French trans politics. Le Zoo's Q seminars (1996–2003), organized by Marie-Hélène/Sam Bourcier, helped raise feminist consciousness for many trans people doing trans politics, especially those who resisted inclusion in the *transidentités* movement they considered more normative and assimilationist, who then began to borrow concepts from feminist thought (Bourcier 1998). It was crucial for participants in Le Zoo to think through concepts of sexual difference and inequality as a basis for deconstructing gender binarity. As Maud-Yeuse Thomas noted when the *transidentités* movement was in its infancy, many assimilationist trans people did not want to be grouped together with homosexuals, prostitutes, transvestites, or the new transgender movement, and they sought instead to simply be accepted as members of a society they did not want to change (Thomas and Espineira 1998).[5] Those of us who sought to distance ourselves from this sort of trans identity politics constructed a different political and theoretical framework. We sought to disengage from the politics of binary sexual difference, which we felt could only reinscribe inequalities. We did this through trans identifications and trans practices, and by not worrying anymore about complying with the compulsory order of gender or caring whether we were either only women or only men. As two self-identified trans lesbians and their allies in Le Zoo said, "We identify as trans because we are doing politics, not because of our transsexualism" (Espineira et al. 1998: 114).

One root of French transfeminism begins in this milieu. Drawing from Monique Wittig's (1992) critique of heterosexuality as a political regime that oppresses women, as well as Judith Butler's (1990) gender performativity paradigm and her strategy of gender proliferation as resistance to the sex/gender system, Le Zoo focused on queer theory, subcultural expression, and the "epistemopolitics" of self-identified faggots, dykes, trans, bi, and queer people. The aim of Le Zoo's Q Seminar was to "widely circulate knowledge of the historical, social, political, and cultural construction of homosexuality, heterosexuality, bisexuality, transsexuality, and gender," to "highlight work that provides a hyperbolic critique of the formation and location of normative sexual and gender identities," and "to deconstruct foundational knowledges that naturalize the disciplining of bodies" (Andrieu 2008: 5). Since a new trans politics arrived on the French feminist scene via Le Zoo, a transfeminist perspective has influenced many different groups and collectives. Nowadays, all the French anarchist, antiassimilationist, and antisexist groups fight against patriarchy and see sexual difference as the origin of inequality.

Transfeminism in Spain: A Geopolitical Translation of *Queer*

The term *transfeminism* first appeared on the Spanish scene during the Jornadas Feministas Estatales (an annual national feminist conference) held in Cordoba in 2000; by the 2009 conference, it had become a familiar and persistent expression for reclaiming space for feminist trans people excluded from feminist circles and for building up a feminism based on a coalition of microgroups and identities, including "*okupas*, lesbians, anticapitalists, *maricas*, transgender people, and sex workers" (Solà 2013: 19).

More often than not, throughout the late twentieth century, both radical feminism and institutional feminism, as well as assimilationist lesbian and gay movements, have denied rights, agency, empowerment, and subcultural expression to trans people. Feminism typically reinscribes trans lives within hegemonic masculinities and femininities and, consequently, denies trans people the capacity to be feminist subjects. They may even consider trans people to be actual enemies of feminism. Transfeminism in Spain resists such feminist practices of exclusion and objectification by appropriating the term *feminism* itself, and by using the prefix *trans-* to signify a feminist trans subject or identity.[6] The *trans-* prefix is also meant to signal the process of crossing over or moving through the current impasses of feminist thought, rather than calling for "post-" feminism, as if there were no longer a need for feminist activism or analysis.

Many factors contribute to the strategy of feminism's abjected subjects' appropriating feminism for themselves, instead of subverting and transforming an insulting epithet, such as *queer* or its equivalents in Spanish. One such factor is the progress made by institutional feminism and its reformist politics of gender mainstreaming; another is the mainstreaming of the gay and lesbian movement in Europe. Queer collectives such as Smaschieramenti in Bologna have made the same move, in order to make clear that the exclusion of trans people from feminism is now over (Smaschieramenti 2011; SomMovimentonazioAnale 2012).[7] Another factor has to do with translations of *queer* in different cultural and geopolitical contexts that aim to get rid of Anglo white queer theory and English as an imperialistic language:[8] "Sin embargo, en un gesto de desplazamiento geopolitico, pero cercano a los postulados queer, el concepto 'transfeminista' està siendo reivindicado por algunos colectivos trans-bollo-marica-feministas surgidos en los últimos años en el Estado español. Un conjunto de microgrupos han reclamado esta palabra que suena mejor en castellano que el término queer" (Solà 2013: 19).[9] A similar strategy has been adopted in Brazil, where "palabra queer" is being translated as "pos-pornôs, transfeministas, loucas" (Lopes 2015).

Transfeminism might also be understood as a reaction against the theoretical excesses of first-wave white Anglo queer theory, whose poststructuralism promoted an abstract concept of political subjectivity. Transfeminism in Spain seeks to avoid this theoretical disembodiment of the political subject by consistently referencing the body and its ongoing transformations as the main means of resisting biopower through creative biopolitical production and counterproduction. A new focus on the body through trans and crip bodies, along with a new focus on sexuality through the postporn movement, takes transfeminism where queer theory failed to go (Bourcier 2012).[10]

Postporn as a Transfeminist Praxis Against Capitalism and Sex Dualism

In contrast to the Anglo queer constellation of the 1990s, transfeminism offers a new admixture of perspectives: a blend of Foucaldian biopolitics and feminist materialism rooted in the resurgence of Marxism after the recent violence of the economic crisis, and the subsequent programs of austerity and debt restructuring imposed on Spain by European and inter-national institutions after the collapse of the financial markets. Transfeminism's political horizon is not abolitionist; rather, it is counterproductive: a material proliferation of new femininities and masculinities, of "abnormal" and monstrous bodies inserted into biopolitics, which overflow the fictional but foundational dualism at the heart of capitalist modernity—so-called "sexual difference." Transfeminism is not an abstract critique of this theoretical dualism. Rather, it traffics in actually existing nonbinary lives, bodies, identities, and genders on a collective social level. Collective "artivism," especially a performance-oriented politics of representation and enspacement, plays a crucial role in transfeminism precisely because it makes visible the lie of sexual dualism. Postporn performance activism in particular has become a distinctive feature of European transfeminism—countering the neoliberal repri-vatization of the sexual sphere by publicly exposing the many ways in which the logic of binary sexual difference routinely fails.

Neoliberal politics, whether it emanates from the state or from private corporations, pro-duces neoliberal subjectivities in part by reconfiguring the relationship between private and public, sexual and social. It demands the death of embodied subjects that defy this segrega-tion of life into incommensurably separate spheres—of physical bodies that might otherwise produce new social formations and subcultures and, therefore, new bodies politic. Trans and queer urban space-making practices can counter the neoliberal spatial politics of zoning laws, social segregation, and gentrification. Many transfeminist collectives such as Quimera Rosa, Post-op, ORGIA, and Ideadestroyingmuros[11] 2005, as well as individual artists such as Diana Pornoterrorista, work against the spatial logic of neoliberalism that manifests in most cities worldwide today. In 2010, many of these artists staged a collective performance in Barcelona called "Oh-Kaña" (Post-op et al. 2010), a tribute to José Pérez Ocaña, who used to walk naked in the streets of Madrid to protest Francisco Franco's dictatorship. Through this performance they brought prosthetized, gender-fucked, and cyborg bodies; queer bodies in fetish and leather gear—that is to say, monstrous antineoliberal embodied subjectivities produced in queer sex subcultures—into such public spaces as Las Ramblas and La Boqueria.

Transfeminist bodies stand today with the freaks, the crips, and the naked queers. They share the common project of reclaiming bodies that matter precisely because they are "unpro-ductive" bodies capable of becoming bodies of pleasure dedicated to nonreproductive forms of sex, microsocial bodies that can reclaim and reconfigure space; they offer resistance to a neoliberal subjugation that aims to put bodies to work in worse conditions than ever before. Disruptive practices of embodiment have been lived by sexual minorities since at least the 1970s. Postporn practices today draw upon this resource produced by gay, lesbian, and queer BDSM cultures of the past. The passivity, anal objectification, cutting, and fist fucking that were practiced in dungeons and clubs by lesbian SM groups in the 1980s (such as Samois in San Francisco, and the Lesbian Sex Mafia in New York City) are now openly performed in the streets of Spanish cities by postporn transfeminist activists who know how to concretize and reenact their sexual and economic situations, and thereby to analyze the naturalizing and depoliticizing mechanisms at work in them.

"Queer" lately has been the target of harsh criticisms for its multiple perceived failures: internal racism, false promises of intersectionality, class privilege, the still burning issue of feminism. Chicana feminist Gloria Anzaldúa has been given a postmortem footnote in the US academy as the person who first appropriated and subverted the pejorative term *queer* (Alarcon 1990), but in Europe, queer of color feminism is routinely excluded by the queer academic jet-setters who keep asking for obscene conference fees in the middle of one of the worst economic crises we have ever faced.[12] Transfeminism in Europe, whether in Le Zoo in Paris in the 1990s or in Bologna or Barcelona today, has thus come to play the vital role of advancing a critique of queer theory and politics—a critique necessitated first by the transnationalization of "queer" along the progressivist trajectory of US modernity and, second, by the refusal within Europe to adopt the anti-identitarian stance required by first-wave US queer theory.

Is this queer corpse worth reanimating, or should we let it it die? In *Animacies*, the linguist Mel Y. Chen (2012) suggests that if such a thing as queer liveliness still exists, it is to be found in *queer*'s verbal and adjectival forms rather than its deadly nominal one. *Feminism* is a noun without a verb form, but *trans* is grammatically polymorphous. *Trans* is not about resignification; rather, it is about rematerialization. It can be a noun as well as a prefix that attaches to and dynamizes other words, providing new directions for them, bringing both feminism and queerness into new assemblages (*reagencements*). *Trans* works as well in French, Spanish, Italian, and many other languages as it does in English. What are we to make of the mobility of this little unit of grammar, its ability to animate, to cross, to "quare" (Johnson and Henderson 2005)? To quote Chen:

> Queer . . . while it continually re-animates in new formations—thanks particularly to queer of color, transnational, disability, and trans scholarship—has also achieved nominal fame as an identity; but it has simultaneously coalesced, gotten sticky, inertial, lost its animation and its drive in the context of the United States. Its nominal terminus along certain semantic paths has led it to an atemporal staticization, a lack of cognitive dynamism, an essential death, and a future imaginable only according to its modification by something else.
>
> (Chen 2012: 82–83)

Transfeminism is that "something else," and it is happening somewhere else than white Anglo feminism and queer theory in the United States.

Notes

1. Stop Trans Pathologization: "A campaign for the depathologization of trans identities. The main goals of the Campaign are the removal of the categories of 'gender dysphoria'/'gender identity disorders' from the diagnosis manuals (DSM of the American Psychiatric Association and ICD of the World Health Organization), as well as the fight for trans health rights." See Stop Trans Pathologization 2012.
2. See also the survey for the report on transphobia conducted by Arnaud Alessandrin and Karine Espineira in 2014 (Alessandrin and Espineira 2015).
3. It should be underlined that Delphy's definition of intersectionality does not include trans people and that she accuses them of ruining the feminist project to abolish gender.
4. See also Rogue 2009.
5. See also Espineira et al. 1998. At the time, we thought of many Zoo members (gays, lesbians, bis, queers, etc.) as virtual trans identities, which, later on, proved to be true.
6. The term *Spanish* is not used in a nationalistic sense here. A lot of transfeminists living in Spain are Italian.
7. Regarding Smaschieramenti, see Smaschieramenti 2010, and regarding the call for a "transfeminist block" in the demonstration against austerity in Rome on October 15, 2011, see Smaschieramenti 2011. See also the collective A/matrix based in Rome, who identified as transfeminist, write, "A/matrix é unprogetto post, trans, pop, cyber, neo, ultra, meta, iper femminista. Anche se non sembra, siamo piuttosto concrete: é la discriminante fondamentale per non imploderee/o faregomitolo" (A/matrix is a post, trans, pop, cyber, neo, ultra, meta, hyper feminist. We are more concrete than we look: being concrete is crucial for not imploding or becoming a tangle [Sconvegno 2008]). Many thanks to Alessia Acquistapace for the resources and the translation.
8. See, for instance, Lawrence La Fountain-Stoke's (2009) play on words "Queericans."
9. In Latin America, *queer* has also been translated as "*cuir*" in order to break with Anglo imperialism.
10. On the crucial part of workshops, see Bourcier 2013.
11. See "Capitalism Is a Shit" and "Pornocapitalismo" in Ideadestroyingmuros 2005.
12. See, for example, the infamous conference on sexual nationalism in Amsterdam in 2011 (Stelder 2011).

Bibliography

Alarcon, Norma. 1990. "The Theoretical Subject(s) of This Bridge Called My Back and Angloamerican Feminism." In *Making Faces, Making Souls, Haciendo Caras: Creative and Critical Perspectives by Feminists of Color*, edited by Anzaldúa Gloria, 356–369. San Francisco: Aunt Lute Books.

Alessandrin, Arnaud, and Karine Espineira. 2015. *Sociologie de la transphobie (Sociology of the Transphobia)*. Bordeaux: Maison des Sciences de l'Homme d'Aquitaine.

Andrieu, Bernard. 2008. "Entretien avec Marie-Hélène Bourcier." *Dilecta corps*, no. 4: 5–11. www.cairn.info/revue-corps-dilecta-2008-1-page-5.htm.

Blais, Mélissa, Laurence Fortin-Pellerin, Ève-Marie Lampron, and Geneviève Pagé. 2007. "Pour éviter de se noyer dans la (troisième) vague: réflexions sur l'histoire et l'actualité du féminisme radical." *Recherches féministes* 20, no. 2: 141–162.

Bourcier, Marie-Hélène/Sam, ed. 1998. *Q comme queer: Les séminaires Q du Zoo (1996–1997)*. Lille, France: Éditions GayKitschCamp.

———. 2012. "Cultural Translation, Politics of Disempowerment, and the Reinvention of Queer Politics." In *European Culture/European Queer*, edited by Lisa Downing and Robert Gillett, special issue, *Sexualities* 15, no. 1: 93–109.

———. 2013. "Bildungs-post-porn: Notes sur le post-porn, un des futurs du féminisme de la désobéissance sexuelle." *Rue Descartes: Revue du Collège international de philosophie*, no. 79: 42–60.

Butler, Judith. 1990. *Gender Trouble: Feminism and the Subversion of Identity*. New York: Routledge.

Califia, Pat. 2003. *Sex Changes: The Politics of Transgenderism*. 2nd ed. San Francisco: Cleis.

Chen, Mel Y. 2012. *Animacies, Biopolitics, Racial Mattering, and Queer Affect*. Durham, NC: Duke University Press.

Common Struggle. www.commonstruggle.org/index.php?q=node/2484.Crenshaw, Kimberlé. 1994. "Mapping the Margins: Intersectionality, Identity Politics, and Violence Against Women of Color." In *The Public Nature of Private Violence*, edited by Martha Albertson Fineman and Rixanne Mykitiuk, 93–118. New York: Routledge.

Delphy, Christine. 2006. "Antisexisme ou antiracisme? Un faux dilemme." *Nouvelles questions féministes* 25, no. 1: 59–83.

Dorlin, Elsa. 2008. *Sexe, genre, et sexualités (Sex, Gender, and Sexualities)*. Paris: Presses universitaires de France.

Dorvil, Henri, ed. 2007. *Théories et méthodologies de l'intervention sociale*. Vol. 4 of *Problèmes sociaux*. Quebec: Presses de l'Université du Québec.

Espineira, Karine. 2012. "La construction médiatique des transidentités: Une modélisation sociale et média-culturelle" ("The Media Construction of Trans Identities: A Social and Media Cultural Modelling"). PhD thesis, Université de Nice Sophia Antipolis.

Espineira, Karine, et al. 1998. "Q comme questions." *Bourcier* 1998: 112–121.

Giami, Alain, Emmanuelle Beaubatie, and Jonas Le Bail. 2010. "Caractéristiques sociodémographiques, identification de genre, parcours de transition médicopsychologiques et VIH/sida dans la population trans: Premiers résultats d'une enquête menée en France en 2010." *Bulletin épidémiologique hebdomadaire*, no. 42: 433–37.

Ideadestroyingmuros. 2005. "Who We Are." www.ideadestroyingmuros.info/bio/chi-siamo/ (accessed April 12).

Johnson, E. Patrick, and Mae G. Henderson. 2005. "Introduction: Queering Black Studies/'Quaring' Queer Studies." In *Black Queer Studies: A Critical Anthology*, edited by E. Patrick Johnson and Mae G. Henderson, 1–20. Durham, NC: Duke University Press.

Koyama, Emi. 2003. "The Transfeminist Manifesto." In *Catching a Wave: Reclaiming Feminism for the Twenty-First Century*, edited by Rory Dicker and Alison Piepmeier, 244–259. Boston: Northeastern University Press.

La Fountain-Stokes, Lawrence. 2009. *Queer Ricans: Cultures and Sexualities in the Diaspora*. Minneapolis: University of Minnesota Press.

Lopes, Denilson. 2015. "Gender and Sexuality Turn/Queer Turn." Paper presented at the seminar "Forms of Affect," King Juan Carlos Center for Latin American and Caribbean Studies (CLACS), New York University, New York, April 14.

Mensah, Maria Nengeh, ed. 2005. "Une troisième vague féministe au Québec?" In *Dialogues sur la troisième vague féministe*, 11–27. Montréal: Éditions du Remue-Ménage.

Outrans. 2009. "Trans et féministe, nos corps nous appartiennent." *News Release*, March 6.

———. 2012. "Transféminismes." www.outrans.org/infos/articles/transfeminismes/ (accessed December 2012).

———. 2013. "Le transféminisme." *L'Observatoire des transidentités*, April 2. www.observatoire-des-transidentites.com/page-8618633.html.

Post-op, et al. 2010. "Oh-Kaña." *Vimeo Video*, 11:43. June 14. vimeo.com/12566813.

Rogue, J. 2009. "Strengthening Anarchism's Gender Analysis." *Northeastern Anarchist*, no. 14.

———. 2012. "De-essentializing Anarchist Feminism: Lessons from the Trans-Feminist Movement." In *Queering Anarchism: Addressing and Undressing Power and Desire*, edited by C. B. Daring, J. Rogue, Deric Shannon, and Abbey Volcano, 39–50. Oakland, CA: AK.

Rubin, Gayle. 1975. "The Traffic in Women: Notes on the 'Political Economy' of Sex." In *Toward an Anthropology of Women*, edited by Reiter Rayna, 157–210. New York: Monthly Review Press.

———. 1984. "Thinking Sex: Notes for a Radical Theory of the Politics of Sexuality." In *Pleasure and Danger*, edited by Vance Carole, 143–178. New York: Routledge and Kegan Paul.

Serano, Julia. 2007. *Whipping Girl: A Transsexual Woman on Sexism and the Scapegoating of Femininity*. Berkeley, CA: Seal.

Sconvegno. 2008. "Le inclassificabili." In *Futuro Femminile. Passioni e ragioni nelle voci del femminismo dal dopoguerra a oggi*, edited by Reale Lorella, 19–32. Bologna: Luca Sossella Editore.

Smaschieramenti. 2010. "Manifesto per un'insurrezione PutaLesboNeraTransFemminista." *Blog*, January 1. smaschieramenti.noblogs.org/manifesto-per-uninsurrezione-putalesbonera transfemminista/.

———. 2011. "Appello per uno spezzone putatransfemministaqueer nella manifestazione del 15 ottobre." *Blog*, October 8. www.smaschieramenti.noblogs.org/post/2011/10/08/appello—per-uno-spezzone-putatransfemministaqueer-nella-manifestazione-del-15/.

Solà, Miriam. 2013. "Pre-textos, con-textos y textos." In *Transfeminismos, epistemes, fricciones y flujos (Transfeminisms, Epistemes, Frictions, and Flows)*, edited by Miriam Solà and Urko Elena, 15–30. Tafalla, Spain: Txalaparta.

Solà, Miriam, and Urko Elena, eds. 2013. *Transfeminismos, epistemes, fricciones y flujos (Transfeminisms, Epistemes, Frictions, and Flows)*. Tafalla, Spain: Txalaparta.

SomMovimentonazioAnale. 2012. "Una giornata di co-spirazione lesbica, frocia, trans e femminista nella crisi—Bologna, 15 dicembre." *Blog*, December 15. www.sommovimentonazioanale.noblogs.org/post/2012/12/15/una-giornata-di-co-spirazione-lesbica-frocia-trans-e-femminista-nella-crisi-bologna-15-dicembre/.

Stelder, Mikki. 2011. "Start with Amsterdam! An Alternative Statement on the Sexual Nationalisms Conference." *QueerIntersectional* (blog), February 16. queerintersectional.wordpress.com/2011/02/16/start-with-amsterdam-2/.

Stop Trans Pathologization. 2012. "Welcome." www.stp2012.info/old/en (accessed April 20, 2015).

Thomas, Maud-Yeuse, and Karine Espineira. 1998. "Deux lesbotrans se posent des Q." In *Q comme queer: Les séminaires Q du Zoo (1996–1997)*, edited by Marie-Hélène/Sam Bourcier, 100–104. Lille, France: Éditions GayKitschCamp.

Wittig, Monique. 1992. *The Straight Mind and Other Essays*. Boston: Beacon.

5 Transmasculine Insurgency

Masculinity and Dissidence in Feminist Movements in México

Daniel B. Coleman

This article, originally published in the "Trans/Feminisms" issue of the academic journal *TSQ: Transgender Studies Quarterly*, is framed by the questions of whether masculinity can be decolonized and if there is any such thing as feminist masculinity. Coleman, who claims Afro-Latinx, Indigenous, and white ancestry, narrates the complexities he has faced as a transmasculine two-spirit person in the United States and Chiapas, Mexico. He focuses on his experiences accessing healthcare; involvement in feminist and *transfeminismo* activist groups; and participation in the sex-positive, pro-kink *pos-porno* performance art scene. Coleman describes finding it easier and less pathologizing to access trans-focused healthcare in Mexico while at the same time feeling pushed out of feminist circles he characterizes as "inclusive of bio-women only." The article shows how trans identities are differently positioned within feminist organizing across the global North and global South; at the same time, it highlights how bio-essentialist anti-trans frameworks cross national and cultural borders. Coleman is careful to distinguish between the welcome he felt among Afro-descendant feminist communities in Chiapas, the exclusion he felt in Latina communities, and the difficulty of connecting with Indigenous feminisms as a mixed-heritage person. He suggests that the exclusions he experienced in some circles was "not innocent of, or separated from, the erasure of blackness." As a result, Coleman is committed to linking Black and trans thought, and critiques of transphobia and anti-blackness, in an overarching decolonial project that draws strongly from the Black feminist tradition exemplified by Audre Lorde's work on erotics.

I begin this brief thought experiment with the open provocation, "Can masculinity be decolonized?"

In 2014, I uprooted my life in the United States and now find myself living in San Cristóbal de las Casas, Chiapas, México. My motivations for this relocation were personal, professional, emotional, political, and existential. This place has become an important transit space for me, whether it becomes a more permanent home space or not. The doors that have opened by coming here are astounding, even though or perhaps because of what those of us residing in this country have experienced in the last year. This is particularly the case for me as a transmasculine transgender individual who has no desire to be pathologized within US medical institutions that require permission letters to authorize treatment of my "dysphoria" and to define how and what "transgender" is. With the encouragement of my former partner, far from bio-family and friends I have always known, I have finally felt for the first time the freedom to explore my transmasculinity without fear of the rejection or bullying

DOI: 10.4324/9781003206255-7

I experienced during my butch lesbian days. Here, I have been cared for by a cisgendered female doctor who works out of a home clinic, has never had a transgender patient, yet who does not flinch at ordering laboratory tests for liver function (based on information sent by a transmasculine friend in North Carolina) to determine whether my endocrine system is healthy enough to use testogel safely. She makes home visits, free of charge, to drop off *recetas* (prescriptions), no insurance required. I can order testogel here for far below US market price without a doctor's note, prescription, side-glance, or insurance coverage. Well-fitting men's clothing costs the equivalent of five to ten dollars for shirts and pants that last far longer than more flimsily made women's wear. I have a local male barber who has never questioned why I cut my hair with him, who charges about $1.50 a cut. In the United States, all these experiences of transformation would have cost thousands of dollars and required months of waiting, many doctor's visits, multiple diagnoses, interminable social hell, and isolation. In México, these experiences have become an integral part of my social, personal, and political life as a community member of Chiapas. A dear friend and colleague who is a photographer did a photo shoot with me at home for *Fotoperformance decolonial X.1: Transgresiones transfeministas desde Abya Yala con amor* (*Decolonial Photoperformance X.1: Transfeminist Transgressions from Abya Yala, with Love*) in which I explored transmasculine performativity (Chávez 2014). I also performed a piece called *(Trans)itos Transmasculinos* (*Transmasculine Transits*) as one of the invited artists for the second annual Postporn Festival in Tuxtla Gutierrez.

I begin with these anecdotes because they help narrate a complex social and political terrain. México has become a hypervigilant, militarized state dominated by the police and narco-power, where precarity and violence are quotidian realities. I, however, have the privilege of a US passport and the freedom to leave, without question, as long as I have a return ticket or my student visa—a privilege that does not extend to those traveling in the reverse direction, particularly *compañer@s* deemed "undocumented" by the state. Because of the incredibly strictly enforced gender roles prescribed for male and female appearance in México, I almost always pass as a *joven* (young man) or muchacho among all but those most intimate to me, which is key to my daily safety. Yet, within feminist movements here, there is a strong alliance to cisgendered realities as the only realities, with feminism always-already being equated with womanism, particularly in Chiapas. Within this feminist framework, my masculine physical presentation is made to represent patriarchy, violence, machismo, "wanting to be a man," succumbing to the enemy, and much more. These complex social and political realities not only determine my personal gender experience in México but also frame the larger landscape of work required of trans activism here.

I have quickly become a vocal presence for transmasculine politics in Chiapas and for bringing the "T" more meaningfully into local LGBTSTGNC identities.[1] In February of 2015, a well-known journalist in Chiapas, Patricia Chandomí, asked to interview me about transmasculinities. I eagerly accepted this invitation, given the drive I feel to debunk the prejudice around transmasculine identities, while also striving to be inclusive of the transfeminine and intersex identities that have been the source of tremendous division rather than alliance for feminists in the region.

The interview was prompted by a Facebook conversation initiated after I was tagged in an announcement for a "radical lesbian feminist" gathering. A transfeminine friend who had also been tagged had posted a response to ask if transfeminine people would be allowed to attend (given that the location was not publicly announced, and one needed to write for permission to access the space). I commented directly below this post, asking if a transmasculine presence would be honored, only to receive a retort from one of the speakers that if trans people want into these spaces so much, "they" should make their own spaces. This comment made very clear what I had always heard about feminism in Chiapas: it is inclusive of bio-women only, and anyone else will be not only rejected but also treated as outsiders and "others" who need their own spaces because feminist spaces simply cannot absorb our presence. This clarified for me two significant points: first, that feminist advances in multi-gender inclusion travel very differently between the global North and the global South; and second, that gender binaries have determined feminist practices in Chiapas up until now. What was my responsibility for, and my "response-ability" with, this information?

I have found myself deeply nourished by the writings of transfeminists from Barcelona (see especially *Transfeminismos: Epístemes, fricciones y flujos* [*Transfeminisms: Epistemes, Frictions, and Flows*], by Miriam Solá and Elena Urko [2013]), as well as by my contemporary generation of performance artists, particularly those working in México, Brazil, and Spain, who are radically transfeminist and engage in gender-exploding body practices.[2] The ways we have found to work in collaboration have been filled with so much love, along with our transgressive breaking of gender norms. The reality of feminism = womanism that I have found in Chiapas has created a significant cognitive dissonance with my transfeminist communities elsewhere in México, the rest of Latin America, and in Europe. Simultaneously, I recognize, and celebrate, that movements such as Zapatismo and the feminism within it have created tremendous pathways for indigenous bio-women to have powerful leadership positions in Chiapas, but I contend that this should not come at the expense of diverse gender and sexual positions, identities, and politics, which also exist in the region. This is the bridge that has yet to be crossed here.

Mestiza lesbian feminists have followed their own trajectory, one that parallels in many ways the advances made by indigenous women's feminism, and they, too, have an exemplary history that a rigorous feminist genealogy of Chiapanecan geopolitics simply cannot deny. But then again, these same mestizo lesbian feminists can be the biggest perpetrators of machismo and patriarchal politics when they disparage transmasculine and transfeminine identities, engage publicly and privately in transphobic hate speech, and actively exclude us from feminism by investing their energies in spaces exclusively for bio-women, without ever expressing interest in an open dialogue. While of course I understand that it is crucial for bio-women to contest violence perpetrated against them by bio-men, and while I recognize their widespread lack of access to such essential needs as contraception and safe space from domestic abuse, I also recognize that transgender individuals need not be targeted as part of those problems. I thus began to question the way feminist communities can perpetuate transphobic exclusion and violence, especially given the fierceness and radicalism of my many itinerant performance and transfeminist communities, which offered such a powerful contrast to the conservatism I was facing in my current home space in Chiapas.

I continue to explore these lived contradictions through any number of practices. After my performance in the Postporn Festival, for example, a young woman from the master's program in cultural studies at the university in Tuxtla Gutierrez approached me about writing her thesis on my *historia de vida* (a sharing of life history similar to my own oral history work), focusing on my masculinity and transition. We have since conducted many thoughtful interviews that have deepened my self-reflexivity and self-positioning in Chiapas. I have also found space and inspiration, through my quotidian body practices, to write a book chapter about sovereign erotics and the decolonization of transgender and two-spirit identities through the reclamation of First Nations' worldviews of gender, and through diasporic identity and performance (Driskill 2004; Chávez 2015).

The ultimately relatively solitary space I have had to *devenir* (to become) in the fullness of my two-spirited self has happened in a place that is politically and socially hostile to such identities and yet is so hands off regarding the medical management of this transition that the possibilities are many.[3] The coming-to-fruition of such possibilities has connected me to a global network of transfeminist performance and activist communities that, perhaps if they could be lived out on a more permanent basis, would have their own tendencies toward suffocation and intercommunity violence—but perhaps they might also allow for new ways of becoming that would in turn allow for better ways of life. Still, I have learned not to romanticize notions of "community" or "coherence" and to find deep pleasure in this becoming, when there is a personal sovereignty over the process. This allows for endless transformations.

The one axis of community that I have encountered in Chiapas that has never challenged, undermined, or been hateful toward my transmasculinity is the one of African descent, which has become part of my chosen family here. In fact, the dialogue between feminist leaders in the Afro-descendant community of Chiapas and me as a transmasculine person who claims African descent has helped to create a sense of intimacy, bonding, and friendship within the broader community of Afro-diasporic people here that all of us need. This reality has driven me to a deep, soul-sourced thinking through, primarily through Audre Lorde's erotics, of what a decolonizing masculinity might be. I have come to think about the exclusionary politics that characterizes some of my social world in Chiapas as being not innocent of, or separated from, the erasure of blackness. This is not to say that black feminism has necessarily always been trans inclusive (in fact, within the multiplicity of black feminisms, trans exclusion has often been present), but it is to say that in this space, for me in Chiapas, being black and being trans are not mutually exclusive, nor does the Afro-descendant community here practice a trans-exclusionary body politics toward me.

Drawing from the wisdom of Audre Lorde's erotics offers a starting place for considering transgender and transmasculine identities as practices of decolonization. Lorde's understanding of the erotic is not to be confused with the merely sexual, which she claims to be diametrically opposed to the erotic (Lorde 1984: 55). The erotic opens us up to the full capability of our sensing self (the five senses) in our capacity to enjoy our physical bodies and the world around us that interacts with it. Given, sexual pleasure is one small facet of the full capacities of our sensing and feeling world. Granted, Lorde speaks quite specifically about the erotic as a power held by bio-women. However, I do not interpret her words as applying exclusively to bio-women, nor do I think Lorde meant for her ideas to be an exclusionary gesture. She puts it this way: "The erotic is the measure between the beginning of our sense of self and the chaos of our strongest feelings. It is an internal sense of satisfaction to which, once we have experienced it, we know we can aspire. For having experienced the fullness of this depth of feeling and recognizing its power, in honor and self-respect we can require no less of ourselves" (Lorde 1984: 54). There is much to be recovered from Lorde's erotics that allows us to theorize the full power of our beings and the pleasures of our existence, and that can challenge medicalizing, pathologizing, and violent discourses against trans people, even (perhaps especially) within feminist circles. While sometimes this work lies in insisting that feminist and other communities expand our existing ways of seeing and being together, at other times the work insists that we decolonize the violating ways we improperly understand—or fail to see at all—the real difference of the other.

I consistently see masculinity being equated with the worst of patriarchy and colonial violence, yet in my own increasingly masculine embodiment, accomplished through the periodic use of testogel, masculinity consists of nothing more than the scent of my loins, the cut of my pants, the line of abdominal muscles, the style of my hair, and the squareness of my jaw. It is a clitoris larger than the typical female's that requires different methods of stimulation. I feel a feeling of physical strength in masculinity, but then again, I never had any problem associating physical strength with being female. I still enjoy my cycles and my swollen breasts when the natural estrogen in my body returns. These pleasures in the fullness of being will never make me less trans, less feminist, less masculine—but they are not what I currently emphasize.

Transmasculine erotics is attuned to a "yes" within ourselves. It is the choice, the risk, of fully embodying the expressions and desires our internal compass points us toward (granting, of course, that "fully embodying" for oneself traverses a spectrum from zero physical intervention to full medicalized transition). Here I understand embodiment as a way of being present, both physically and spiritually, in space. This is not about privileging masculine gender expressions over femme ones or arguing that masculine gender expressions participate in femme erasure. Rather, it is seeing others, as Lorde suggests, in accordance with the erotics present in their own embodiment, their own lives, and the embodiment of their lives.

I think of transgender and two-spirit identities as reclaiming indigenous worldviews stolen from us through hundreds of years of colonization—worldviews expressed through a language of spirituality that much of the secular West ignores or obliterates. It is important to recognize the spiritual dimension of the inalienable erotic capacity that lies within us, which is likewise always on the brink of theft by the persistence of colonial power. Asserting transmasculinity is thus an act of insurgency, a rebellion against this ongoing robbery—it is an assertion of the sense that our erotic power belongs to us alone. While it is undoubtedly important to assert that being transmasculine does not make you any less feminist, or that masculinity is not always-already a replication of patriarchy or the desire for it, there is, perhaps, a more pressing work to be done regarding the decolonization of masculinity in both *cuir* (queer) and hetero spaces through the manifestation of a sovereign transmasculine erotics.

Dissenting from feminism's normalizing practices in Chiapas has meant embodying sovereign erotic power and allowing a sense of true accountability to self and others to become our inner guide. The term "sovereign erotic" comes from Quo-Li Driskill's (2004) revolutionary work on First Nations two-spirit and decolonizing identities that also borrows from Lorde. What I intend here is to use the sovereign erotic as an important theoretical-praxical conversation about transmasculine identity in particular. After all, our gender expressions need to be guided by this erotic power, rather than by dominant social definitions of gender dysphoria. Such framings are illusions that serve only to create hatred of self, and of others. When we learn to encourage erotic fullness from our sisters and brothers in our feminist movements, then we can begin to think about true alliances. Gender expressions will then not be automatically equated with the ever-present hierarchies of colonial logic that divide us. Our energies can then shift from attack and reaction to affirmation and solidarity, from divisive exclusions to opportunities to share encounters with the fullness of our beings, across drastically different landscapes of embodiment. The erotic will force us away from judging others for the decisions (or nondecisions) they make regarding which body modification practices (if any) will fulfill their erotic needs, and it will compel us all to recognize and honor the erotic within the other. Only then, when we have known the changes that full attention to the erotic will bring to our feminist communities, can true trans/feminist alliances come into existence.

Selection from: Daniel Brittany Chávez, "Transmasculine Insurgency: Masculinity and Dissidence in Feminist Movements in México," in *TSQ: Transgender Studies Quarterly*, Volume 3, no. 1–2, pp. 58–64. Copyright 2016, Duke University Press. All rights reserved. Republished by permission of the copyright holder, Duke University Press. www.dukeupress.edu.

Notes

1. LGBTSTGNC stands for lesbian, gay, bisexual, two-spirit, trans, and gender non-conforming as used by the Audre Lorde Project (Audre Lorde Project 2015).

2. Some of the performance artists of my generation include Felipe Osorino (Lechedevirgen Trimegistro, México), La Fuliminante (Nadia Granados, México and Colombia), Sara Panamby (Brazil), Dani d'Emilia (Brazil and Spain), Anuk Guerrero (México), Joyce Jandette (México and Spain), Lia La Novia (México), La Bala Rodriguez (México), Julia Antivilio (Chile and México), and Post-Op (Spain), among numerous others.

3. While this currently quite solitary nature of my *devenir* is fine for now, it most likely will lead me to choose a different home space where I can find another trans chosen family (meaning nonblood family of trans individuals going through their own transitions), a phenomenon that at times has been called "sexilio."

Bibliography

Audre Lorde Project. 2015. alp.org (accessed May 1).

Chávez, Daniel Brittany. 2014. *Fotoperformance decolonial X.1: Transgresiones transfeministas desde Abya Yala con amor* (*Decolonial Photoperformance X.1: Transfeminist Transgressions from Abya Yala, with Love*). hysteria.mx/fotoperformance-decolonial-x-1-transgresiones—transfeministas-desde-abya-yala-con-amor/#prettyPhoto.

———. 2015. "Devenir performerx: Hacía un erótico soberano descolonial niizh manitoag" ("Becoming a Performer: Toward a Decolonial Niizh Manitoag Sovereign Erotic"). In *Andar erótico decolonial* (*Erotic Decolonial Walkings*), compiled by Raul Moarquech Ferrera-Balanquet, 83–98. Buenos Aires: Ediciones del Signo.

Driskill, Qwo-Li. 2004. "Stolen from Our Bodies: First Nations Two-Spirits/Queers and the Journey to a Sovereign Erotic." *Studies in American Indian Literatures* 16, no. 2: 50–64.

Lorde, Audre. 1984. "Uses of the Erotic: The Erotic as Power." In *Sister Outsider: Essays and Speeches*, edited by Audre Lorde, 53–59. New York: Crossing.

Solá, Miriam, and Elena Urko. 2013. *Transfeminismos: Epístemes, fricciones y flujos* (*Transfeminisms: Epistemes, Frictions, and Flows*). Barcelona: Txalaparta.

Section II

Trans Matters, Black Matters

6 My Words to Victor Frankenstein Above the Village of Chamounix

Performing Transgender Rage

Susan Stryker

Susan Stryker's retelling of the story of Frankenstein's monster from a trans perspective was first performed in 1993 and published in 1994 in the inaugural volume of *GLQ: A Journal of Lesbian and Gay Studies*. The title refers to the scene in Mary Shelley's novel in which the monster talks back to its creator, revealing itself as something other, and something more, than its maker intended. Stryker's work responded directly to Sandy Stone's call for "posttranssexual" theorizing rooted in the embodied experience of trans people. It engaged as well with longstanding feminist and leftist concerns—such as Julia Kristeva's psychoanalytic notion of abjection or Louis Althusser's Marxist concept of interpellation—as well as with the new queer theory, notably the work of Judith Butler and Eve Sedgwick. Like Stone's posttranssexual manifesto, it refuted the authority of medicine to define trans lives, and like other early transfeminist work, it addressed the explicit transphobia of Janice Raymond and Mary Daly. Rather than rejecting transphobic characterizations of trans people as inhuman monstrosities who should be cast out from human community, Stryker turned the tables and embraced monstrosity as an "egalitarian relationship with nonhuman material being" and transmuted the rage experienced over exclusion and rejection into a positive force for transforming self and society on new grounds. She drew strength from an empowering connection with the "enlivening darkness" of the generative cosmic void, an interstitial space beyond representation, from which all mattering spills forth.

Introductory Notes

The following work is a textual adaptation of a performance piece originally presented at "Rage Across the Disciplines," an arts, humanities, and social sciences conference held June 10–12, 1993, at California State University, San Marcos. The interdisciplinary nature of the conference, its theme, and the organizers' call for both performances and academic papers inspired me to be creative in my mode of presenting a topic then much on my mind. As a member of Transgender Nation—a militantly queer, direct action transsexual advocacy group—I was at the time involved in organizing a disruption and protest at the American Psychiatric Association's 1993 annual meeting in San Francisco. A good deal of the discussion at our planning meetings concerned how to harness the intense emotions emanating from transsexual experience—especially rage—and mobilize them into effective political actions. I was intrigued by the prospect of critically examining this rage in a more academic setting through an idiosyncratic application of the concept of gender performativity. My idea was to perform self-consciously a queer gender rather than simply talk about it, thus embodying

DOI: 10.4324/9781003206255-9

and enacting the concept simultaneously under discussion. I wanted the formal structure of the work to express a transgender aesthetic by replicating our abrupt, often jarring transitions between genders—challenging generic classification with the forms of my words just as my transsexuality challenges the conventions of legitimate gender and my performance in the conference room challenged the boundaries of acceptable academic discourse. During the performance, I stood at the podium wearing genderfuck drag—combat boots, threadbare Levi 501s over a black lace body suit, a shredded Transgender Nation T-shirt with the neck and sleeves cut out, a pink triangle, quartz crystal pendant, grunge metal jewelry, and a six-inch long marlin hook dangling around my neck on a length of heavy stainless steel chain. I decorated the set by draping my black leather biker jacket over my chair at the panelists' table. The jacket had handcuffs on the left shoulder, rainbow freedom rings on the right side lacings, and Queer Nation-style stickers reading SEX CHANGE, DYKE, and FUCK YOUR TRANSPHOBIA plastered on the back.

Monologue

The transsexual body is an unnatural body. It is the product of medical science. It is a technological construction. It is flesh torn apart and sewn together again in a shape other than that in which it was born. In these circumstances, I find a deep affinity between myself as a transsexual woman and the monster in Mary Shelley's Frankenstein. Like the monster, I am too often perceived as less than fully human due to the means of my embodiment; like the monster's as well, my exclusion from human community fuels a deep and abiding rage in me that I, like the monster, direct against the conditions in which I must struggle to exist.

I am not the first to link Frankenstein's monster and the transsexual body. Mary Daly makes the connection explicit by discussing transsexuality in "Boundary Violation and the Frankenstein Phenomenon," in which she characterizes transsexuals as the agents of a "necrophilic invasion" of female space (69–72). Janice Raymond, who acknowledges Daly as a formative influence, is less direct when she says that "the problem of transsexuality would best be served by morally mandating it out of existence," but in this statement she nevertheless echoes Victor Frankenstein's feelings toward the monster: "Begone, vile insect, or rather, stay, that I may trample you to dust. You reproach me with your creation" (Raymond 178; Shelley 95). It is a commonplace of literary criticism to note that Frankenstein's monster is his own dark, romantic double, the alien Other he constructs and upon which he projects all he cannot accept in himself; indeed, Frankenstein calls the monster "my own vampire, my own spirit set loose from the grave" (Shelley 74). Might I suggest that Daly, Raymond and others of their ilk similarly construct the transsexual as their own particular golem?[1]

The attribution of monstrosity remains a palpable characteristic of most lesbian and gay representations of transsexuality, displaying in unnerving detail the anxious, fearful underside of the current cultural fascination with transgenderism.[2] Because transsexuality more than any other transgender practice or identity represents the prospect of destabilizing the foundational presupposition of fixed genders upon which a politics of personal identity depends, people who have invested their aspirations for social justice in identitarian movements say things about us out of sheer panic that, if said of other minorities, would see print only in the most hate-riddled, white supremacist, Christian fascist rags. To quote extensively from one letter to the editor of a popular San Francisco gay/lesbian periodical:

> I consider transsexualism to be a fraud, and the participants in it . . . perverted. The transsexual [claims] he/she needs to change his/her body in order to be his/her "true self." Because this "true self" requires another physical form in which to manifest itself, it must therefore war with nature. One cannot change one's gender. What occurs is a

cleverly manipulated exterior: what has been done is mutation. What exists beneath the deformed surface is the same person who was there prior to the deformity. People who break or deform their bodies [act] out the sick farce of a deluded, patriarchal approach to nature, alienated from true being.

Referring by name to one particular person, self-identified as a transsexual lesbian, whom she had heard speak in a public forum at the San Francisco Women's Building, the letter-writer went on to say:

> When an estrogenated man with breasts loves a woman, that is not lesbianism, that is mutilated perversion. [This individual] is not a threat to the lesbian community, he is an outrage to us. He is not a lesbian, he is a mutant man, a self-made freak, a deformity, an insult. He deserves a slap in the face. After that, he deserves to have his body and mind made well again.[3]

When such beings as these tell me I war with nature, I find no more reason to mourn my opposition to them—or to the order they claim to represent—than Frankenstein's monster felt in its enmity to the human race. I do not fall from the grace of their company—I roar gleefully away from it like a Harley-straddling, dildo-packing leatherdyke from hell.

The stigmatization fostered by this sort of pejorative labelling is not without consequence. Such words have the power to destroy transsexual lives. On January 5, 1993, a 22-year-old pre-operative transsexual woman from Seattle, Filisa Vistima, wrote in her journal, "I wish I was anatomically 'normal' so I could go swimming. But no, I'm a mutant, Franken-stein's monster." Two months later Filisa Vistima committed suicide. What drove her to such despair was the exclusion she experienced in Seattle's queer community, some members of which opposed Filisa's participation because of her transsexuality—even though she identi-fied as and lived as a bisexual woman. The Lesbian Resource Center where she served as a volunteer conducted a survey of its constituency to determine whether it should stop offer-ing services to male-to-female transsexuals. Filisa did the data entry for tabulating the survey results; she didn't have to imagine how people felt about her kind. The Seattle Bisexual Women's Network announced that if it admitted transsexuals the SBWN would no longer be a women's organization. "I'm sure," one member said in reference to the inclusion of bisexual transsexual women, "the boys can take care of themselves." Filisa Vistima was not a boy, and she found it impossible to take care of herself. Even in death she found no support from the community in which she claimed membership. "Why didn't Filisa commit herself for psychiatric care?" asked a columnist in the Seattle Gay News. "Why didn't Filisa demand her civil rights?" In this case, not only did the angry villagers hound their monster to the edge of town, they reproached her for being vulnerable to the torches. Did Filisa Vistima commit suicide, or did the queer community of Seattle kill her?[4]

I want to lay claim to the dark power of my monstrous identity without using it as a weapon against others or being wounded by it myself. I will say this as bluntly as I know how: I am a transsexual, and therefore I am a monster. Just as the words "dyke," "fag," "queer," "slut," and "whore" have been reclaimed, respectively, by lesbians and gay men, by anti-assimilationist sexual minorities, by women who pursue erotic pleasure, and by sex industry workers, words like "creature," "monster," and "unnatural" need to be reclaimed by the transgendered. By embracing and accepting them, even piling one on top of another, we may dispel their ability to harm us. A creature, after all, in the dominant tradition of West-ern European culture, is nothing other than a created being, a made thing. The affront you humans take at being called a "creature" results from the threat the term poses to your status as "lords of creation," beings elevated above mere material existence. As in the case of being called "it," being called a "creature" suggests the lack or loss of a superior personhood. I find no shame, however, in acknowledging my egalitarian relationship with non-human material Being; everything emerges from the same matrix of possibilities. "Monster" is derived from the Latin noun monstrum, "divine portent," itself formed on the root of the verb monere, "to warn." It came to refer to living things of anomalous shape or structure, or to fabulous creatures like the sphinx who were composed of strikingly incongruous parts, because the ancients considered the appearance of such beings to be a sign of some impending supernatural event. Monsters, like angels, functioned as messengers and heralds of the extraordinary. They served to announce impending revelation, saying, in effect, "Pay attention; something of profound importance is happening."

Hearken unto me, fellow creatures. I who have dwelt in a form unmatched with my desire, I whose flesh has become an assemblage of incongruous anatomical parts, I who achieve the similitude of a natural body only through an unnatural process, I offer you this warning: the Nature you bedevil me with is a lie. Do not trust it to protect you from what I represent, for it is a fabrication that cloaks the groundlessness of the privilege you seek to maintain for yourself at my expense. You are as constructed as me; the same anarchic Womb has birthed us both. I call upon you to investigate your nature as I have been compelled to confront mine. I challenge you to risk abjection and flourish as well as have I. Heed my words, and you may well discover the seams and sutures in yourself.

Criticism

In answer to the question he poses in the title of his recent essay, "What is a Monster? (According to Frankenstein)," Peter Brooks suggests that, whatever else a monster might be, it "may also be that which eludes gender definition" (219). Brooks reads Mary Shelley's story of an overreaching scientist and his troublesome creation as an early dissent from the nineteenth-century realist literary tradition, which had not yet attained dominance as a narrative form. He understands Frankenstein to unfold textually through a narrative strategy generated by tension between a visually oriented epistemology, on the one hand, and another approach to knowing the truth of bodies that privileges verbal linguisticality, on the other (199–200). Knowing by seeing and knowing by speaking/hearing are gendered, respectively, as masculine and feminine in the critical framework within which Brooks operates. Considered in this context, Shelley's text is informed by—and critiques from a woman's point of view—the contemporary reordering of knowledge brought about by the increasingly compelling truth claims of Enlightenment science. The monster problematizes gender partly through its failure as a viable subject in the visual field; though referred to as "he," it thus offers a feminine, and potentially feminist, resistance to definition by a phallicized scopophilia. The monster accomplishes this resistance by mastering language in order to claim a position as a speaking subject and enact verbally the very subjectivity denied it in the specular realm.[5]

Transsexual monstrosity, however, along with its affect, transgender rage, can never claim quite so secure a means of resistance because of the inability of language to represent the transgendered subject's movement over time between stably gendered positions in a linguistic structure. Our situation effectively reverses the one encountered by Frankenstein's monster. Unlike the monster, we often successfully cite the culture's visual norms of gendered embodiment. This citation becomes a subversive resistance when, through a provisional use of language, we verbally declare the unnaturalness of our claim to the subject positions we nevertheless occupy.[6]

The prospect of a monster with a life and will of its own is a principal source of horror for Frankenstein. The scientist has taken up his project with a specific goal in mind—nothing less than the intent to subject nature completely to his power. He finds a means to accomplish his desires through modern science, whose devotees, it seems to him, "have acquired new and almost unlimited powers; they can command the thunders of heaven, mimic the earthquake, and even mock the invisible world with its shadows. . . . More, far more, will I achieve," thought Frankenstein. "I will pioneer a new way, explore unknown powers, and unfold to the world the deepest mysteries of creation" (Shelley 47). The fruit of his efforts is not, however, what Frankenstein anticipated. The rapture he expected to experience at the awakening of his creature turned immediately to dread. "I saw the dull yellow eyes of the creature open. His jaws opened, and he muttered some inarticulate sounds, while a grin wrinkled his cheeks. He might have spoken, but I did not hear; one hand was stretched out, seemingly to detain me, but I escaped" (Shelley 56, 57). The monster escapes, too, and parts company with its maker for a number of years. In the interim, it learns something of its situation in the world, and rather than bless its creator, the monster curses him. The very success of Mary Shelley's scientist in his self-appointed task thus paradoxically proves its futility: rather than demonstrate Frankenstein's power over materiality, the newly enlivened body of the creature attests to its maker's failure to attain the mastery he sought. Frankenstein cannot control the mind and feelings of the monster he makes. It exceeds and refutes his purposes.

My own experience as a transsexual parallels the monster's in this regard. The consciousness shaped by the transsexual body is no more the creation of the science that refigures its flesh than the monster's mind is the creation of Frankenstein. The agenda that produced hormonal and surgical sex reassignment techniques is no less pretentious, and no more noble, than Frankenstein's. Heroic doctors still endeavor to triumph over nature. The scientific discourse that produced sex reassignment techniques is inseparable from the pursuit of immortality through the perfection of the body, the fantasy of total mastery through the transcendence of an absolute limit, and the hubristic desire to create life itself.[7] Its genealogy emerges from a metaphysical quest older than modern science, and its cultural politics are aligned with a deeply conservative attempt to stabilize gendered identity in service of the naturalized heterosexual order.

None of this, however, precludes medically constructed transsexual bodies from being viable sites of subjectivity. Nor does it guarantee the compliance of subjects thus embodied with the agenda that resulted in a transsexual means of embodiment. As we rise up from the operating tables of our rebirth, we transsexuals are something more, and something other, than the creatures our makers intended us to be. Though medical techniques for sex reassignment are capable of crafting bodies that satisfy the visual and morphological criteria that generate naturalness as their effect, engaging with those very techniques produces a subjective experience that belies the naturalistic effect biomedical technology can achieve. Transsexual embodiment, like the embodiment of the monster, places its subject in an unassimilable, antagonistic, queer relationship to a Nature in which it must nevertheless exist.

Frankenstein's monster articulates its unnatural situation within the natural world with far more sophistication in Shelley's novel than might be expected by those familiar only with the version played by Boris Karloff in James Whale's classic films from the 1930s. Film critic Vito Russo suggests that Whale's interpretation of the monster was influenced by the fact that the director was a closeted gay man at the time he made his Frankenstein films. The pathos he imparted to his monster derived from the experience of his own hidden sexual identity.[8] Monstrous and unnatural in the eyes of the world, but seeking only the love of his own kind and the acceptance of human society, Whale's creature externalizes and renders visible the nightmarish loneliness and alienation that the closet can breed. But this is not the monster who speaks to me so potently of my own situation as an openly transsexual being. I emulate instead Mary Shelley's literary monster, who is quick-witted, agile, strong, and eloquent.

In the novel, the creature flees Frankenstein's laboratory and hides in the solitude of the Alps, where, by stealthy observation of the people it happens to meet, it gradually acquires a knowledge of language, literature, and the conventions of European society. At first it knows little of its own condition. "I had never yet seen a being resembling me, or who claimed any intercourse with me," the monster notes. "What did this mean? Who was I? What was I? Whence did I come? What was my destination? These questions continually recurred, but I was unable to solve them." (Shelley 116, 130). Then, in the pocket of the jacket it took as it fled the laboratory, the monster finds Victor Frankenstein's journal, and learns the particulars of its creation. "I sickened as I read," the monster says. "Increase of knowledge only discovered to me what a wretched outcast I was." (Shelley 124, 125).

Upon learning its history and experiencing the rejection of all to whom it reached out for companionship, the creature's life takes a dark turn. "My feelings were those of rage and revenge," the monster declares. "I, like the arch-fiend, bore a hell within me" (130). It would have been happy to destroy all of Nature, but it settles, finally, on a more expedient plan to murder systematically all those whom Victor Frankenstein loves. Once Frankenstein realizes that his own abandoned creation is responsible for the deaths of those most dear to him, he retreats in remorse to a mountain village above his native Geneva to ponder his complicity in the crimes the monster has committed. While hiking on the glaciers in the shadow of Mont Blanc, above the village of Chamounix, Frankenstein spies a familiar figure approaching him across the ice. Of course, it is the monster, who demands an audience with its maker. Frankenstein agrees, and the two retire together to a mountaineer's cabin. There, in a monologue that occupies nearly a quarter of the novel, the monster tells Frankenstein the tale of its creation from its own point of view, explaining to him how it became so enraged.

These are my words to Victor Frankenstein, above the village of Chamounix. Like the monster, I could speak of my earliest memories, and how I became aware of my difference from everyone around me. I can describe how I acquired a monstrous identity by taking on the label "transsexual" to name parts of myself that I could not otherwise explain. I, too, have discovered the journals of the men who made my body, and who have made the bodies of creatures like me since the 1930s. I know in intimate detail the history of this recent medical intervention into the enactment of transgendered subjectivity; science seeks to contain and colonize the radical threat posed by a particular transgender strategy of resistance to the coerciveness of gender: physical alteration of the genitals.[9] I live daily with the consequences of medicine's definition of my identity as an emotional disorder. Through the filter of this official pathologization, the sounds that come out of my mouth can be summarily dismissed as the confused ranting of a diseased mind.

Like the monster, the longer I live in these conditions, the more rage I harbor. Rage colors me as it presses in through the pores of my skin, soaking in until it becomes the blood that courses through my beating heart. It is a rage bred by the necessity of existing in external circumstances that work against my survival. But there is yet another rage within.

Journal (February 18, 1993)

Kim sat between my spread legs, her back to me, her tailbone on the edge of the table. Her left hand gripped my thigh so hard the bruises are still there a week later. Sweating and bellowing, she pushed one last time and the baby finally came. Through my lover's back, against the skin of my own belly, I felt a child move out of another woman's body and into the world. Strangers' hands snatched it away to suction the sticky green meconium from its airways. "It's a girl," somebody said. Paul, I think. Why, just then, did a jumble of dark, unsolicited feelings emerge wordlessly from some quiet back corner of my mind? This moment of miracles was not the time to deal with them. I pushed them back, knowing they were too strong to avoid for long.

After three days we were all exhausted, slightly disappointed that complications had forced us to go to Kaiser instead of having the birth at home. I wonder what the hospital staff thought of our little tribe swarming all over the delivery room: Stephanie, the midwife; Paul, the baby's father; Kim's sister Gwen; my son Wilson and me; and the two other women who make up our family, Anne and Heather. And of course Kim and the baby. She named her Denali, after the mountain in Alaska. I don't think the medical folks had a clue as to how we all considered ourselves to be related to each other. When the labor first began we all took turns shifting between various supporting roles, but as the ordeal progressed we settled into a more stable pattern. I found myself acting as birth coach. Hour after hour, through dozens of sets of contractions, I focused everything on Kim, helping her stay in control of her emotions as she gave herself over to this inexorable process, holding on to her eyes with mine to keep the pain from throwing her out of her body, breathing every breath with her, being a companion. I participated, step by increasingly intimate step, in the ritual transformation of consciousness surrounding her daughter's birth. Birth rituals work to prepare the self for a profound opening, an opening as psychic as it is corporeal. Kim's body brought this ritual process to a dramatic resolution for her, culminating in a visceral, cathartic experience. But my body left me hanging. I had gone on a journey to the point at which my companion had to go on alone, and I needed to finish my trip for myself. To conclude the birth ritual I had participated in, I needed to move something in me as profound as a whole human life.

I floated home from the hospital, filled with a vital energy that wouldn't discharge. I puttered about until I was alone: my ex had come over for Wilson; Kim and Denali were still at the hospital with Paul; Stephanie had gone, and everyone else was out for a much-needed walk. Finally, in the solitude of my home, I burst apart like a wet paper bag and spilled the emotional contents of my life through the hands I cupped like a sieve over my face. For days, as I had accompanied my partner on her journey, I had been progressively opening myself and preparing to let go of whatever was deepest within. Now everything in me flowed out, moving up from inside and out through my throat, my mouth because these things could never pass between the lips of my cunt. I knew the darkness I had glimpsed earlier would reemerge, but I had vast oceans of feeling to experience before that came up again.

Simple joy in the presence of new life came bubbling out first, wave after wave of it. I was so incredibly happy. I was so in love with Kim, had so much admiration for her strength and courage. I felt pride and excitement about the queer family we were building with Wilson, Anne, Heather, Denali, and whatever babies would follow. We've all tasted an exhilarating possibility in communal living and these nurturing, bonded kinships for which we have no adequate names. We joke about pioneering on a reverse frontier: venturing into the heart of civilization itself to reclaim biological reproduction from heterosexism and free it for our own uses. We're fierce; in a world of "traditional family values," we need to be.

Sometimes, though, I still mourn the passing of old, more familiar ways. It wasn't too long ago that my ex and I were married, woman and man. That love had been genuine, and the grief over its loss real. I had always wanted intimacy with women more than intimacy with men, and that wanting had always felt queer to me. She needed it to appear straight. The shape of my flesh was a barrier that estranged me from my desire. Like a body without a mouth, I was starving in the midst of plenty. I would not let myself starve, even if what it took to open myself for a deep connectedness cut off the deepest connections I actually had. So I abandoned one life and built this new one. The fact that she and I have begun getting along again, after so much strife between us, makes the bitterness of our separation somewhat sweet. On the day of the birth, this past loss was present even in its partial recovery; held up beside the newfound fullness in my life, it evoked a poignant, hopeful sadness that inundated me.

Frustration and anger soon welled up in abundance. In spite of all I'd accomplished, my identity still felt so tenuous. Every circumstance of life seemed to conspire against me in one vast, composite act of invalidation and erasure. In the body I was born with, I had been invisible as the person I considered myself to be; I had been invisible as a queer while the form of my body made my desires look straight. Now, as a dyke I am invisible among women; as a transsexual, I am invisible among dykes. As the partner of a new mother, I am often invisible as a transsexual, a woman, and a lesbian. I've lost track of the friends and acquaintances these past nine months who've asked me if I was the father. It shows so dramatically how much they simply don't get what I'm doing with my body. The high price of whatever visible, intelligible, self-representation I have achieved makes the continuing experience of invisibility maddeningly difficult to bear.

The collective assumptions of the naturalized order soon overwhelmed me. Nature exerts such a hegemonic oppression. Suddenly I felt lost and scared, lonely and confused. How did that little Mormon boy from Oklahoma I used to be grow up to be a transsexual leatherdyke in San Francisco with a Berkeley Ph.D.? Keeping my bearings on such a long and strange trip seemed a ludicrous proposition. Home was so far gone behind me it was gone forever, and there was no place to rest. Battered by heavy emotions, a little dazed, I felt the inner walls that protect me dissolve to leave me vulnerable to all that could harm me. I cried, and abandoned myself to abject despair over what gender had done to me.

Everything's fucked up beyond all recognition. This hurts too much to go on. I came as close today as I'll ever come to giving birth—literally. My body can't do that; I can't even bleed without a wound, and yet I claim to be a woman. How? Why have I always felt that way? I'm such a goddamned freak. I can never be a woman like other women, but I could never be a man. Maybe there really is no place for me in all creation. I'm so tired of this ceaseless movement. I do war with nature. I am alienated from Being. I'm a self-mutilated deformity, a pervert, a mutant, trapped in monstrous flesh. God, I never wanted to be trapped again. I've destroyed myself. I'm falling into darkness I am falling apart.

I enter the realm of my dreams. I am underwater, swimming upwards It is dark. I see a shimmering light above me. I break through the plane of the water's surface with my lungs bursting. I suck for air—and find only more water. My lungs are full of water. Inside and out I am surrounded by it. Why am I not dead if there is no difference between me and what I am in? There is another surface above me and I swim frantically towards it. I see a shimmering light. I break the plane of the water's surface over and over and over again. This water annihilates me. I cannot be, and yet—an excruciating impossibility—I am. I will do anything not to be here.

I will swim forever.
I will die for eternity.
I will learn to breathe water.
I will become the water.
If I cannot change my situation I will change myself.

In this act of magical transformation
I recognize myself again.

I am groundless and boundless movement. I am a furious flow.
I am one with the darkness and the wet.

And I am enraged.

Here at last is the chaos I held at bay.
Here at last is my strength.

I am not the water—
I am the wave,
and rage
is the force that moves me.

Rage
gives me back my body
as its own fluid medium.

Rage
punches a hole in water
around which I coalesce
to allow the flow to come through me.

Rage
constitutes me in my primal form.
It throws my head back
pulls my lips back over my teeth
opens my throat
and rears me up to howl: and no sound dilutes
the pure quality of my rage.

No sound
exists
in this place without language
my rage is a silent raving

Rage
throws me back at last
into this mundane reality
in this transfigured flesh
that aligns me with the power of my Being.

In birthing my rage,
my rage has rebirthed me.

Theory

A formal disjunction seems particularly appropriate at this moment because the affect I seek to examine critically, what I've termed "transgender rage," emerges from the interstices of discursive practices and at the collapse of generic categories. The rage itself is generated by the subject's situation in a field governed by the unstable but indissoluble relationship between language and materiality, a situation in which language organizes and brings into signification matter that simultaneously eludes definitive representation and demands its own perpetual rearticulation in symbolic terms. Within this dynamic field the subject must constantly police the boundary constructed by its own founding in order to maintain the fictions of "inside" and "outside" against a regime of signification/materialization whose intrinsic instability produces the rupture of subjective boundaries as one of its regular features. The affect of rage as I seek to define it is located at the margin of subjectivity and the limit of signification. It originates in recognition of the fact that the "outsideness" of a materiality that perpetually violates the foreclosure of subjective space within a symbolic order is also necessarily "inside" the subject as grounds for the materialization of its body and the formation of its bodily ego.

This primary rage becomes specifically transgender rage when the inability to foreclose the subject occurs through a failure to satisfy norms of gendered embodiment. Transgender rage is the subjective experience of being compelled to transgress what Judith Butler has referred to as the highly gendered regulatory schemata that determine the viability of bodies, of being compelled to enter a "domain of abjected bodies, a field of deformation" that in its unlivability encompasses and constitutes the realm of legitimate subjectivity (1993: 16). Transgender rage is a queer fury, an emotional response to conditions in which it becomes imperative to take up, for the sake of one's own continued survival as a subject, a set of practices that precipitates one's exclusion from a naturalized order of existence that seeks to maintain itself as the only possible basis for being a subject. However, by mobilizing gendered identities and rendering them provisional, open to strategic development and occupation, this rage enables the establishment of subjects in new modes, regulated by different codes of intelligibility. Transgender rage furnishes a means for disidentification with compulsorily assigned subject positions. It makes the transition from one gendered subject position to another possible by using the impossibility of complete subjective foreclosure to organize an outside force as an inside drive, and vice versa. Through the operation of rage, the stigma itself becomes the source of transformative power.[10]

I want to stop and theorize at this particular moment in the text because in the lived moment of being thrown back from a state of abjection in the aftermath of my lover's daughter's birth, I immediately began telling myself a story to explain my experience. I started theorizing, using all the conceptual tools my education had put at my disposal. Other true stories of those events could undoubtedly be told, but upon my return I knew for a fact what lit the fuse to my rage in the hospital delivery room. It was the non-consensuality of the baby's gendering. You see, I told myself, wiping snot off my face with a shirt sleeve, bodies are rendered meaningful only through some culturally and historically specific mode of grasping their physicality that transforms the flesh into a useful artifact. Gendering is the initial step in this transformation, inseparable from the process of forming an identity by means of which we're fitted to a system of exchange in a heterosexual economy. Authority seizes upon specific material qualities of the flesh, particularly the genitals, as outward indication of future reproductive potential, constructs this flesh as a sign, and reads it to enculturate the body. Gender attribution is compulsory; it codes and deploys our bodies in ways that materially affect us, yet we choose neither our marks nor the meanings they carry.[11] This was the act accomplished between the beginning and the end of that short sentence in the delivery room: "It's a girl." This was the act that recalled all the anguish of my own struggles with gender. But this was also the act that enjoined my complicity in the non-consensual gendering of another. A gendering violence is the founding condition of human subjectivity; having a gender is the tribal tattoo that makes one's personhood cognizable. I stood for a moment between the pains of two violations, the mark of gender and the unlivability of its absence. Could I say which one was worse? Or could I only say which one I felt could best be survived?

How can finding one's self prostrate and powerless in the presence of the Law of the Father not produce an unutterable rage? What difference does it make if the father in this instance was a pierced, tattooed, purple-haired punk fag anarchist who helped his dyke friend get pregnant? Phallogocentric language, not its particular speaker, is the scalpel that defines our flesh. I defy that Law in my refusal to abide by its original decree of my gender. Though I cannot escape its power, I can move through its medium. Perhaps if I move furiously enough, I can deform it in my passing to leave a trace of my rage. I can embrace it with a vengeance to rename myself, declare my transsexuality, and gain access to the means of my legible reinscription. Though I may not hold the stylus myself, I can move beneath it for my own deep self-sustaining pleasures.

To encounter the transsexual body, to apprehend a transgendered consciousness articulating itself, is to risk a revelation of the constructedness of the natural order. Confronting the implications of this constructedness can summon up all the violation, loss, and separation inflicted by the gendering process that sustains the illusion of naturalness. My transsexual body literalizes this abstract violence. As the bearers of this disquieting news, we transsexuals often suffer for the pain of others, but we do not willingly abide the rage of others directed against us. And we do have something else to say, if you will but listen to the monsters: the possibility of meaningful agency and action exists, even within fields of domination that bring about the universal cultural rape of all flesh. Be forewarned, however, that taking up this task will remake you in the process.

By speaking as a monster in my personal voice, by using the dark, watery images of Romanticism and lapsing occasionally into its brooding cadences and grandiose postures, I employ the same literary techniques Mary Shelley used to elicit sympathy for her scientist's creation. Like that creature, I assert my worth as a monster in spite of the conditions my monstrosity requires me to face, and redefine a life worth living. I have asked the Miltonic questions Shelley poses in the epigraph of her novel: "Did I request thee, Maker, from my clay to mould me man? Did I solicit thee from darkness to promote me?" With one voice, her monster and I answer "no" without debasing ourselves, for we have done the hard work of constituting ourselves on our own terms, against the natural order. Though we forego the privilege of naturalness, we are not deterred, for we ally ourselves instead with the chaos and blackness from which Nature itself spills forth.[12]

If this is your path, as it is mine, let me offer whatever solace you may find in this monstrous benediction: May you discover the enlivening power of darkness within yourself. May it nourish your rage. May your rage inform your actions, and your actions transform you as you struggle to transform your world.

Notes

1. While this comment is intended as a monster's disdainful dismissal, it nevertheless alludes to a substantial debate on the status of transgender practices and identities in lesbian feminism. H. S. Rubin, in a sociology dissertation in progress at Brandeis University, argues that the pronounced demographic upsurge in the female-to-male transsexual population during the 1970s and 1980s is directly related to the ascendancy within lesbianism of a "cultural feminism" that disparaged and marginalized practices smacking of an unliberated "gender inversion" model of homosexuality—especially the butch-femme roles associated with working-class lesbian bar culture. Cultural feminism thus consolidated a lesbian-feminist alliance with heterosexual feminism on a middle-class basis by capitulating to dominant ideologies of gender. The same suppression of transgender aspects of lesbian practice, I would add, simultaneously raised the spectre of male-to-female transsexual lesbians as a particular threat to the stability and purity of nontranssexual lesbian-feminist identity. See Echols for the broader context of this debate, and Raymond for the most vehement example of the anti-transgender position.

2. The current meaning of the term "transgender" is a matter of some debate. The word was originally coined as a noun in the 1970s by people who resisted categorization as either transvestites or transsexuals, and who used the term to describe their own identity. Unlike transsexuals but like transvestites, transgenders do not seek surgical alteration of their bodies but do habitually wear clothing that represents a gender other than the one to which they were assigned at birth. Unlike transvestites but like transsexuals, however, transgenders do not alter the vestimentary coding of their gender only episodically or primarily for sexual gratification; rather, they consistently and publicly express an ongoing commitment to their claimed gender identities through the same visual representational strategies used by others to signify that gender. The logic underlying this terminology reflects the widespread tendency to construe "gender" as the sociocultural manifestation of a material "sex." Thus, while transsexuals express their identities through a physical change of embodiment, transgenders do so through a non-corporeal change in public gender expression that is nevertheless more complex than a simple change of clothes.

   This essay uses "transgender" in a more recent sense, however, than its original one. That is, I use it here as an umbrella term that refers to all identities or practices that cross over, cut across, move between, or otherwise queer socially constructed sex/gender boundaries. The term includes, but is not limited to, transsexuality, heterosexual transvestism, gay drag, butch lesbianism, and such non-European identities as the Native American berdache or the Indian Hijra. Like "queer," "transgender" may also be used as a verb or an adjective. In this essay, transsexuality is considered to be a culturally and historically specific transgender practice/identity through which a transgendered subject enters into a relationship with medical, psychotherapeutic, and juridical institutions in order to gain access to certain hormonal and surgical technologies for enacting and embodying itself.

3. Mikuteit 3–4, heavily edited for brevity and clarity.

4. The preceding paragraph draws extensively on, and sometimes paraphrases, O'Hartigan and Kahler.

5. See Laqueur 1–7, for a brief discussion of the Enlightenment's effect on constructions of gender. Feminist interpretations of *Frankenstein* to which Brooks responds include Gilbert and Gubar, Jacobus, and Homans.

6. Openly transsexual speech similarly subverts the logic behind a remark by Bloom, 218, that "a beautiful 'monster,' or even a passable one, would not have been a monster."

7. Billings and Urban, 269, document especially well the medical attitude toward transsexual surgery as one of technical mastery of the body; Irvine, 259, suggests how transsexuality fits into the development of scientific sexology, though caution is advised in uncritically accepting the interpretation of transsexual experience she presents in this chapter. Meyer, in spite of some extremely transphobic concluding comments, offers a good account of the medicalization of transgender identities; for a transsexual perspective on the scientific agenda behind sex reassignment techniques, see Stone, especially the section entitled "All of reality in late capitalist culture lusts to become an image for its own security" (280–304).

8. Russo 49–50: "Homosexual parallels in *Frankenstein* (1931) and *Bride of Frankenstein* (1935) arose from a vision both films had of the monster as an antisocial figure in the same way that gay people were 'things' that should not have happened. In both films the homosexuality of director James Whale may have been a force in the vision."

9. In the absence of a reliable critical history of transsexuality, it is best to turn to the standard medical accounts themselves: see especially Benjamin, Green and Money, and Stoller. For overviews of cross-cultural variation in the institutionalization of sex/gender, see Williams, "Social Constructions/Essential Characters: A Cross-Cultural Viewpoint," 252–276; Shapiro 262–268. For accounts of particular institutionalizations of transgender practices that employ surgical alteration of the genitals, see Nanda; Roscoe. Adventurous readers curious about contemporary non-transsexual genital alteration practices may contact E.N.I.G.M.A. (Erotic Neoprimitive International Genital Modification Association), SASE to LaFarge-werks, 2329 N. Leavitt, Chicago, IL 60647.

10. See Butler, "Introduction," 4 and *passim*.

11. A substantial body of scholarship informs these observations: Gayle Rubin provides a productive starting point for developing not only a political economy of sex, but of gendered subjectivity; on gender recruitment and attribution, see Kessler and McKenna; on gender as a system of marks that naturalizes sociological groups based on supposedly shared material similarities, I have been influenced by some ideas on race in Guillaumin and by Wittig.

12. Although I mean "chaos" here in its general sense, it is interesting to speculate about the potential application of scientific chaos theory to model the emergence of stable structures of gendered identities out of the unstable matrix of material attributes, and on the production of proliferating gender identities from a relatively simple set of gendering procedures.

Works Cited

Benjamin, Harry. *The Transsexual Phenomenon*. New York: Julian, 1966.

Billings, Dwight B., and Thomas Urban. "The Socio-Medical Construction of Transsexualism: An Interpretation and Critique." *Social Problems* 29 (1981): 266–282.

Bloom, Harold. "Afterword." *Frankenstein, or The Modern Prometheus*. New York: Signet/NAL, 1965.212–223. Orig. pub. "*Frankenstein*, or The New Prometheus." *Partisan Review* 32 (1965): 611–618.

Brooks, Peter. *Body Work: Objects of Desire in Modern Narrative*. Cambridge, MA: Harvard UP, 1993.

Butler, Judith. *Bodies That Matter: On the Discursive Limits of "Sex."* New York: Routledge, 1993.

Daly, Mary. *Gyn/Ecology: The Metaethics of Radical Feminism*. Boston: Beacon, 1978.

Echols, Alice. *Daring to Be Bad: Radical Feminism in America, 1967–1975*. Minneapolis: U of Minnesota P, 1989.

Gilbert, Sandra, and Susan Gubar. "Horror's Twin: Mary Shelley's Monstrous Eve." *The Madwoman in the Attic*. New Haven: Yale UP, 1979.213–247.

Green, Richard, and John Money, eds. *Transsexualism and Sex Reassignment*. Baltimore: Johns Hopkins UP, 1969.

Guillaumin, Colette. "Race and Nature: The System of Marks." *Feminist Studies* 8 (1988): 25–44.

Homans, Margaret. "Bearing Demons: Frankenstein's Circumvention of the Maternal." *Bearing the Word*. Chicago: Chicago UP, 1986.100–119.

Irvine, Janice. *Disorders of Desire: Sex and Gender in Modern American Sexology*. Philadelphia: Temple UP, 1990.

Jacobus, Mary. "Is There a Woman in This Text?" *Reading Woman: Essays in Feminist Criticism*. New York: Columbia UP, 1986.83–109.

Kahler, Frederic. "Does Filisa Blame Seattle?" Editorial. *Bay Times* [San Francisco] 3 June 1993: 23.

Kessler, Suzanne J., and Wendy McKenna. *Gender: An Ethnomethodological Approach*. Chicago: U of Chicago P, 1985.

Laqueur, Thomas. *Making Sex: Body and Gender from the Greeks to Freud*. Cambridge, MA: Harvard UP, 1990.

Meyer, Morris. "I Dream of Jeannie: Transsexual Striptease as Scientific Display." *The Drama Review* 35.1 (1991): 25–42.

Mikuteit, Debbie. Letter. *Coming Up!* February 1986: 3–4.

Nanda, Serena. Neither Man Nor Woman: The Hijras of India. Belmont, CA: Wadsworth, 1990.

O'Hartigan, Margaret D. "I Accuse." *Bay Times* [San Francisco] 20 May 1993: 11.

Raymond, Janice G. *The Transsexual Empire: The Making of the She-Male*. Boston: Beacon, 1979.

Roscoe, Will. "Priests of the Goddess: Gender Transgression in the Ancient World." American Historical Association Meeting. 9 January 1994. San Francisco.

Rubin, Gayle. "The Traffic in Women: Notes on the 'Political Economy' of Sex." *Toward an Anthropology of Women*. Ed. Rayna R. Reiter. New York: Monthly Review Press, 1975.157–210.

Russo, Vito. *The Celluloid Closet: Homosexuality in the Movies*. New York: Harper and Row, 1981.

Shapiro, Judith. "Transsexualism: Reflections on the Persistence of Gender and the Mutability of Sex." *Body Guards: The Cultural Politics of Gender Ambiguity*. Ed. Julia Epstein and Kristina Straub. New York: Routledge, 1991.248–279.

Shelley, Mary. *Frankenstein, or The Modern Prometheus*. Orig. pub. 1817. New York: Signet/NAL, 1965.

Stoller, Robert. *Sex and Gender*. Vol. 1. New York: Science House, 1968. *The Transsexual Experiment. Vol. 2 of Sex and Gender*. London: Hogarth, 1975.

Stone, Sandy. "The Empire Strikes Back: A Posttranssexual Manifesto." *Body Guards: The Cultural Politics of Gender Ambiguity*. Ed. Julia Epstein and Kristina Straub. New York: Routledge, 1991.280–304.

Williams, Walter. *The Spirit and the Flesh: Sexual Diversity in American Indian Culture*. Boston: Beacon, 1986.

Wittig, Monique. "The Mark of Gender." *The Straight Mind and Other Essays*. Boston: Beacon, 1992.76–89.

7 The Trans*-Ness of Blackness, the Blackness of Trans*-Ness

Marquis Bey

Marquis Bey's "The Trans*-Ness of Blackness, the Blackness of Trans*-Ness" was first published in "The Issue of Blackness," a 2017 special issue of *TSQ: Transgender Studies Quarterly* that helped reorient the field toward a more substantive engagement with Black radical and feminist thought. Their work is part of the recent turn toward a Black trans studies and trans of color critique exemplified by C. Riley Snorton's influential monograph *Black on Both Sides: A Racial History of Trans Identity*. Bey is particularly concerned with the concept of "para-ontology," that is, a "besidedness" to Being that manifests in the modern world as both race and gender fugitivity. "Blackness" and "Trans*ness," Bey contends, are "nodes of one another" in that they circumvent the structures of white supremacy that seek to sink biologistic ideologies of racial hierarchy into the flesh itself. They cast Blackness and Trans*ness as "differently inflected names" that trace different roots toward an "aboriginal lawlessness" that enables an escape from ontological fixity. In doing so, Bey brings longstanding preoccupations in trans studies with a set of primordial, chaotic, interstitial, unrepresentable, and virtual conditions from which embodied being emerges (as represented in this section by Stryker and Barad) into conversation with equally longstanding preoccupations in critical Black thought (as represented in this section by Spillers and Jackson).

By black here, I don't mean a particular skin color or identity, a certain vocal affectation, musical aesthetic, or capacity for rhythm (though I *do* mean all those things, too). Instead, I mean blackness as a radical refusal of the movement of reconciliation, and thus, of whiteness. To be black and to be made black is to take seriously the work of refusal, which is an antagonism, a thorn in the side of the sovereignty of whiteness. To become black is to remain in instability, is to remain in solidarity together in instability. To become black is to be against the movement beyond sociality for the sake of becoming logical and reasonable. To become black is to refuse being made a something—to be and become nothing. Not because nothing is an absence or a lack of life, but precisely because nothing is the abundance and multiplicity out of which life is formed.

— Amaryah Shaye, "Refusing to Reconcile, Part 2"

I want to argue that "in the beginning is 'trans'": that what is original or primary is a not-yet-differentiated singularity from which distinct genders, race, species, sexes, and sexualities are generated in a form of relative stability. Fixed kinds such as the trans-gendered, trans-sexual, or trans-animal body are expressions of a more profound transitivity that is the condition for what becomes known as the human.

— Claire Colebrook, "What Is It Like to Be a Human?"

DOI: 10.4324/9781003206255-10

As I read the 341-page *Feminism Meets Queer Theory* (Weed and Schor 1997), swooning over the invigorating erudition of top-notch queer theorists, I began to wonder, quite seriously, whether this formulation of "theoretical concept 1 meets seemingly disparate, but actually not really, theoretical concept 2" would work for blackness and trans★-ness. Could a similar volume, perhaps also comprising collated essays from a special issue, be fashioned under the appellation "Blackness Meets Trans★-ness"? After fantasizing about being the one to edit this volume, perhaps alongside other, more dexterous scholars than I, I conceded that such a volume, quite simply, could not exist. Blackness cannot meet trans★-ness; trans★-ness cannot meet blackness. But why not? Black transgender people exist, a friend of mine said, as I thought out loud with her in a local café. My answer then was not as articulate as I would have liked, so I will respeak now, at this much more thoughtful and thought-fed moment: because blackness and trans★-ness, different yet intimate primordial kin, arise from the underbelly, the "undercommons" that absently saturates the conditions upon which subjectivity rests. Blackness and trans★-ness mark, as J. Kameron Carter says of blackness, "a movement of the between . . . an interstitial drama on the outskirts of the order of purity. [They mark] an improvisatory movement of doubleness, a fugitive announcement in and against the grain of the modern world's . . . investment in pure being." In short, borrowing again from Carter, I designate black and trans★ as, "to invoke [Nahum] Chandler once again, 'paraontological'" (2013: 590).

I am embarking on a cogitative journey through the para-ontological annals of the stuff of life and nonlife. Like W. E. B. Du Bois and his intellectual comrades William Shakespeare, Honoré de Balzac, and Alexandre Dumas, here in the forthcoming essay I sit with Fred Moten and Hortense J. Spillers, Alexander Weheliye, and Eva Hayward; I move arm and arm with Amaryah Shaye and Claire Colebrook—among many others, some of whom are the editors of this special issue. With these thinkers, I come to blackness and trans★-ness by way of refusal, fugitivity, anoriginality, para-ontology, and eruption. *Trans★* and *black* thus denote poetic, para-ontological forces that are only tangentially, and ultimately arbitrarily, related to bodies said to be black or transgender. They move in and through the abyss under lying ontology, rubbing up alongside it and causing it to fissure. Trans★ and black, however, as fundamentally para-ontological do not discredit the materiality of ontic subjects who are characterized by and through these identificatory markers. The relationship between my usage of these poetic forces and subjects identified with/as black or trans★ must be handled with care. But indeed, as Kai M. Green (2013: 289) writes about those who identify and are identified as black, epidermal hue and racial (and sexual and gender and class) situated-ness in history "cannot predict the politics of black people. So while race, class, gender, and sexuality will no doubt inform the way a person walks through the world, it will not provide a predetermined outcome as much as we might like it to. This is especially true when our politics or the leadership we endorse is limited by scenario." In short, racial identification will not determine one's relationship to power, thus making epidermal blackness in this case not an a priori determinant of politicality. This is what Hortense J. Spillers, quoting George Lamming, says "we definitively know now": "the nature of power [is] unrelated to pigmentation, that bad faith [is] a phenomenon which [is] independent of race" (quoted in Spillers 2012: 936).

Such is the case, too, with people who identify as transgender or gender nonconforming. Cathy Cohen writes, "People may not like this, but without an intentional politics, I don't see trans as inherently radical. I think there are many instances where marginal individuals are inserted into traditional institutions or movements and they do something to change the dynamics but they don't necessarily change these spaces and entities in a radical way that is open and more equitable." Cohen goes on to say, "I'm interested in trans feminist politics in the same way that I'm committed to a black feminist politics that is tied to a transformative liberatory agenda" (Cohen and Jackson 2015). To an extent, this is true, though I would nuance Cohen's assertion with gender-nonconforming bodies' situatedness in a gender-normative space, a hegemonic grammar that utterly disallows the very possibility of transgender; thus their very existence in a space that is constituted through the assertion of the impossibility of trans★ and nonnormative bodies is, by virtue of their inhabitation of public space, radical. This could also be said to be the case with black bodies occupying space implicitly coded in and through whiteness. No doubt, in some cases, black people or transgender folks sedulously work toward assimilation through buying into a proper black or transgender citizenship. And this entails "fading into the population . . . but also the imperative to be 'proper' in the eyes of the state: to reproduce, to find proper employment; to reorient one's 'different' body into the flow of the nationalized aspiration for possessions, property[, and] wealth" (Aizura 2006: 295). Surely, then, the two can appear at times in opposition to one another, as in those who identify as transgender and are conservative, antiblack (people), neoliberal, and so forth; and those who identify as black may be deeply transphobic. While these combinations arise, I maintain that even amid disruption one can harbor comforting compartments of hegemonic stability. Black and trans★ are both disruptive orientations indexed imperfectly by bodies said to be black or trans★ and thus can succumb to logics of white supremacy and cis sexism. The anoriginal blackness and trans★-ness that bodies cite exceed bodyness and thus can never be "captured" in perfect entirety, leaving room, as has been historically evident, for moments of clash between black people and transgender people, and their imbrications.

What I wish to delineate regarding the relationship between blackness and trans★-ness (as analytics) and black and trans★ bodies is the tangential and ultimately arbitrary connection between them, yet the metonymic nature of what can be said to be black and trans★ bodies' positionalities. That is to say, as Spillers says of black culture (though, I would assert, the logic can apply to trans★ folks as well), black and trans★ bodies speak to and as metonymic flashes of the poetic forces of blackness and trans★-ness insofar as they are imagined as "an *alternative* statement, as a *counter*statement to American culture/ civilization, or Western culture/civilization, more generally speaking, identif[ying] the cultural vocation as the space of 'contradiction, indictment, and the refusal'" (2006: 25). They are instances, not archetypes, of this fugitive, lawless force we might call "black and trans★."

As well, this is not to collapse blackness and trans★-ness, diluting their uniqueness and utility as analytics for different, though related, disciplinary fields. They are, rather, nodes of one another, inflections that, though originary and names for the nothingness upon which distinction rests, flash in different hues because of subjects' interpretive historical entrenchment. That is to say, they are differently inflected names for an anoriginal lawlessness that marks an escape from confinement and a besidedness to ontology. Manifesting in the modern world differently as race and gender fugitivity, black and trans★, though pointed at by bodies that identify as black and/or trans★, precede and provide the foundational condition for those fugitive identificatory demarcations. In short, what I seek to do is, as my title suggests, demonstrate the ways in which trans★ is black and black is trans★. Though I cannot cause the fictive "Blackness Meets Trans★ness" volume to materialize as an academic tome, I can come close by showing how they perennially speak with, through, alongside, and back to (or, alternatively, black to) one another over there on the "outskirts of the order of purity."

I. The Trans*-Ness of Blackness: A Burning Paris

To address the first clause of my title, "the Trans*-ness of Blackness," my aim is to articulate the anoriginality of that poetic, creative, fugitive force known as blackness. It bears a slight textured kinship with Michel Foucault's understanding of literature, that "third point" that is external to language and literary works and that describes an "essential blankness" (notably, I kept misreading this as "essential blackness") in which the question of "What is . . . ?" is "originally dismembered and fractured" (Foucault et al. 2015: 47). Blackness here, in another sense, riffing on Fred Moten and Stefano Harney's concept, is an undercommons, a subtending and subverting subwhere fugitives dwell, reveling in chaos. It is "not a coalition" but rather "an absolutely open secret with no professional ambition" (Moten and Harney 2014: 188)—a burning Paris, perhaps.[1] As an undercommons, blackness is a no/place that simmers alongside, or on the underside of, discernible ontology. It is a no/place, a spaceless space that renders governability ungovernable; blackness "means to render unanswerable the question of how to govern the thing that loses and finds itself to be what it is not"; blackness is the modality of constant escape, of flight, of a "held and errant pattern" that eludes (Harney and Moten 2013: 51, 49).

Additionally, blackness marks a "*break* in the passage of syntagmatic movement from one more or less stable property to another, as in the radical disjuncture between 'African' and 'American,'" says Spillers (2003: 262). As disjuncture, it rests on a modality of not only being in the interstices but also of breaking and uprooting by virtue of its escape. Or, blackness "lays in the cut," as the vernacular saying goes, and stalls the very logic of social syntax as, for example, Black Lives Matter activists—bold irruptions of corporeal, unapologetic blackness—congealed across highways to forestall traffic. Sociality as manifested in the zip and zoom of automobiles oblivious to, and thus constitutive of, the plight of blackness was socially lacerated. Blackness is "a strategy that names the new cultural situation as a *wounding*" (Spillers 2003: 262), and in this constant wounding, this constant cutting, it is the "abeyance of closure" (Carter 2013: 595). Blackness rests in the in-between, and this "between" is also a movement of flight, of escape, of fugitivity from the confines of ontological pinning down. The pinning down requires fixation and definable locations, but as in-between, blackness is that elusive interstitiality; it is that "posture of critical insurgency" about which Spillers speaks, but unlike Spillers's conceptualization, blackness cannot be achieved or arrived at (2003: 262).[2] Excessive of the logic of sovereignty—governability, logic qua logic—is blackness, and it is always smoldering, fissuring, crackling.

But why? Will blackness ever rest? No, because via its interstitial position, its undercommonality, it is perennially refusing impositions. Amaryah Shaye, whose epigraph graces the beginning of this essay, thinks of blackness, relatedly, as a "besideness," and through that besideness blackness operates "as a refusal of the unitive logic of reconciliation" (2014b). Blackness says no, then sidesteps the conversation, the imposition, and keeps it movin'.

It has also been shown, perhaps most recently, provocatively, and cogently by Michelle Wright, that thinking of blackness as "a determinable 'thing,' as a 'what' or 'who'" proves problematic (2015: 2). Blackness must move and be thought in motion. Though Wright conceives of her blackness in *Physics of Blackness* through space and time (spacetime) and through her notion of "epiphenomenal time," I am concerned more with thinking of blackness as fugitive, as volatile, as, to use her language for James Baldwin, "quantum." But although Wright is thinking differently than I am, she is, to be sure, not thinking deficiently or contrastingly. A black interlocutor she is. Her blackness, too, is a node of fugitivity.

[. . .]

Where I do wish to supplement and critique Wright is her particular handling of Spillers's work, namely, Spillers's landmark article "Mama's Baby, Papa's Maybe: An American Grammar Book." Within *Physics of Blackness*, Wright argues that Spillers's "Mama's Baby," in part, expresses that in order to resist the white supremacist "controlling images" imposed upon black women, black folks must return "to the heteronormative gender and sexuality roles that preceded enslavement" (80). This, however, is misguided on two fronts: first, black sexuality cannot be heteronormative, at least in the context of US white supremacy, because, as we learn from Roderick Ferguson in *Aberrations in Black* (2004), black people might be "heterosexual [or homosexual] but never *heteronormative* [or homonormative]" (87). Second, Spillers does not seem to be proffering a (impossible) "return" to heteronormativity; indeed, Spillers asserts something far more queer, far more, one might tentatively argue, trans★. At the end of "Mama's Baby," the penultimate paragraph reads:

> Therefore, the female, in this order of things, breaks in upon the imagination with a forcefulness that marks both a denial and an "illegitimacy." Because of this peculiar American denial, the black American male embodies the only American community of males which has had the specific occasion to learn who the female is within itself, the infant child who bears the life against the could-be fateful gamble, against the odds of pulverization and murder, including her own. It is the heritage of the mother that the African-American male must regain as an aspect of his own personhood—the power of "yes" to the "female" within.
>
> (Spillers 1987: 80)

There is a marked fugitivity in Spillers's black female as she "breaks in upon the imagination" with a force that is "both a denial and an 'illegitimacy.'" The illegitimacy that is blackness, that is lawlessness, is in full effect, historically, with black women. But if we home in on the last sentence of the above quote, we can better understand Wright's interpretive misstep. Spillers does not wish to return to heteronormative gender; on the contrary, there is something decidedly nonnormative, something even transgender, about Spillers's black heritage advancing "the power of 'yes' to the 'female' within." Heteronormative gender maintains a strict, exclusionary gender binary that Spillers, here, is undoing—transing, even. Spillers's conception of African American culture, since the mid-seventeenth century, is a tale "between the lines," which is to say, a tale that is black, that is even trans★; it is a tale in which "gender, or sex-role assignation, or the clear differentiation of sexual stuff, sustained elsewhere in the culture, does not emerge for the African-American female" (1987: 79). Quite far from advancing a return to heteronormativity, Spillers describes a black trans★ lineage within African American culture. Indeed, Spillers's claims "transly" resound in black, queer, gender-nonconforming Afrofuturist janaya (j) khan's (2015) writing when they[3] say that black trans women are integral to black liberation, the "fulcrum" of it, its "nucleus." And those who have ever taken high school biology know how consequential the nucleus is for the functioning of the entirety of the cell. Blackness, and the liberation of its corporeal bearers, is fueled by its trans★ nucleus.

[. . .]

For the remainder of this discussion of blackness, of the first clause of my title, I want to home in on Fred Moten's work, as his is the most generative and direct articulation of blackness, fugitivity, and nothingness. Fred Moten: that "black motherfucker" who, like Curtis Mayfield, will continue to remain a believer—in blackness. Moten crystallizes blackness in the most beautifully tortuous way. For him, as it is for me, when we speak of blackness we are speaking of those "irruptions of that 'thematics of flight'" (toward which Spillers moves as well) and that Kantian "nonsense" that constitutes the lawless freedom of imagination's lawlessness (see Moten 2007: 218, 220). Varying Nahum Chandler's thoughts a bit, Moten has said that "blackness is the anoriginal displacement of ontology, . . . it is ontology's anti- and ante-foundation, ontology's underground, the irreparable disturbance of ontology's time and space"—or, if I may vary Tina Campt's thinking (Campt 2014), blackness is the quotidian practice of refusal to "be"; that is, affirmation of its nothingness.

[. . .]

Always moving, always the elusive thing escaping, blackness manifests as "that desire to be free, manifest as flight, as escape, as a fugitivity that may well prove to veer away even from freedom as its telos, [and] is indexed to anoriginal lawlessness" (Moten 2007: 223). Itself a proxy for "the inadequacy of mechanistic explanation" (223), blackness stands in as a perennial refusal of lawfulness—indeed, of law—and is unable to acknowledge the law. The law can never grab blackness; blackness, in nursery rhyme fashion, is the Gingerbread Man, so run, run, run as fast as you can, but you will still not catch blackness. It is always escaping.

[. . .]

II. The Blackness of Trans*-Ness: Roots Need Not Apply

If the previous section characterized blackness's undoing of the human, and its disruption of systematicity, this section delineates similar effects of trans*-ness. So if trans*, too, is not simply a descriptor of a body, then tell me, what is it? Because we know that corporeal representation and identificatory proclamation is not enough, trans* denotes a disruptive, eruptive orientation; it denotes "unpredetermined movement," Kai M. Green writes, and is "a tool that might help readers gain a reorientation to orientation" (2015b: 191, 196). It is a mode of worldly inhabitation that fugitively engages history and space by reveling in excess, constantly refusing to limn ontological overflows—akin, perhaps, to what Matt Richardson would call the "good and messy." It is for this reason that I use *trans** instead of simply *trans* or *trans-*. Though Mel Y. Chen (2012: 137) uses the "prefixal trans-" to show that it is "not preliminarily limited to gender," and Susan Stryker, Paisley Currah, and Lisa Jean Moore note that the hyphen "marks the difference between the implied nominalism of 'trans' and the explicit relationality of 'trans-,' which remains open-ended and resists premature foreclosure by attachment to any single suffix" (2008: 11), *trans** is intended to be even more disruptive and to highlight its own dehiscence. And the asterisk is "starfishy," a regenerative cut that pulls the body back through itself, moving closer to oneself through the wound that is (on) the self—a cut that itself is that Butlerian crucial bread of possibility[4] (Hayward 2013, 2008: 72); too, it is "fingery," a "multipointed asterisk" that "both points and touches" so that it "repurposes, displaces, renames, replicates, and intensifies terms, adding yet more texture, increased vitalization" (Hayward and Weinstein 2015: 198). Additionally, however, it is celestial. Beyond our discernible stratosphere is the galactic backdrop of all that we know to be possible. Colloquially, and tellingly, known simply as "space," it is empty yet full, and it is the very condition of possibility for, essentially, that which is possible. More tellingly, it is full of stars, for which the asterisk in *trans** is a metonym. If stars stipple the pregnant celestial void, and if "almost every element on Earth was formed at the heart of a star" ("Are We Really All Made of Stardust?," 2016), then *trans** denotes the ubiquity, the transitivity, the fundamentality of the primordial force of unfixing openness. In the beginning was, in fact, trans*—because in the beginning stars floating without laws set in motion that originary trans*-ness, the fundamental openness of our world.

[. . .]

Trans* is also weighted with its etymology as all words are, and *trans** (or, *trans-*) is prefixial—across, to the side of (para-), beyond. *Trans** is elsewhere, not here, because here is known, ontologically discernible and circumscribable. By now we know that *trans** suggests, and has suggested, the unclassifiable and illegible, but I would assert that it also suggests the pervasive moving nonmovement that precedes that which is human, that which is animal, that which legibly is. Eva Hayward and Jami Weinstein (2015: 196) note the asterisk's designation of the primacy of, not the human, but the "*eventualization of life.*" That is to say, *trans** denotes its own antefoundational status, its own fugitivity insofar as it—by being prefixally *trans** and suffixally an asterisk and thus incompletely completing itself, disallowing the stabilizing force of an ontologizing root word—refuses rootedness. Syntactically and linguistically, *trans** is its own nonroot, its own para. Roots need not, indeed cannot, apply. Hence, its own nominative paradoxically marks its perpetually moving unnamability:

> If trans* is ontological, it is that insofar as it is the movement that produces beingness. In other words, trans* is not a thing or being, it is rather the processes through which thingness and beingness are constituted. In its prefixial state, trans* is prepositionally oriented—marking the *with, through, of, in,* and *across* that make life possible. Trans*life works purposefully crabwise to ontological claims; trans* can be ontological to the extent that it is the movement across precisely *vitality* itself.
>
> (Hayward and Weinstein 2015: 196–197)

"Trans* is both movement and the force of materialization that may become matter, but only prepositionally so," Hayward and Weinstein go on to write (197). Trans* is an operation, though not a mechanistic one, of locomotion and agitation, troubling and troubling ontologized states. This point, then, is an important one to make explicit: the starfishy, fingery, celestial asterisk "is the agglutinating asterisk and prefixial nature of trans that always materializes prepositional movements . . . is *moving mattering.* As such, trans* is not *not* ontological but is rather the expressive force *between, with,* and *of* that enables the asterisk to stick to particular materializations" (197). Force, a metonymic one, is what trans* is, like blackness, expressly provoking ontologization by moving beneath it and to the side of it and through it. Trans* breaks open—ever the fugitive who despises hir confinement, who, indeed, can't be confined—even the categories of transgender via engaging in a kind of "guerrilla" (em)bodying through "burrowing in and virally *disrupting* the smoothness and closure on which power depends" (Stone 2014: 92; emphasis added). Trans* is that refusal to be itself, to be sure of itself, to be sure that it is where it's at.

Trans* as transitivity, as a prefixally trans-fugitivity, enacts what C. Riley Snorton calls "transfiguration" (Snorton 2011). As an analytic of radical destabilization that "gesture[s] toward a space of transition as a site that allows us to understand the queer relationship between" feminist universality and particularities, trans*/transitivity as transfiguration operates in the space of liminality, of *transition,* which is the very site of the most radical destabilization. And this transitive/transitional space, Snorton writes, "serves as a place where particular assumptions about gender and its mapping on the body come under such scrutiny as to implode." This implosion, like blackness's volatility, is a disruptive and irruptive undercommon subversion. And this transitive, undercommon subversivity, as LaMonda H. Stallings says of hip-hop (Stallings 2013: 135), traffics in a queer above- and below-ground fluidity wherein examining the "nook and cranny spaces of transitional bodies" and subjectivities disintegrates the ontological demarcations of ontic ontology. A transfigurative transitivity unmakes ontology via its para-ontology. What Snorton is responding to in his essay "Transfiguring Masculinities in Black Women's Studies," from which the analytic concept of transfiguration is taken, is the proclivity for black male feminists to buttress a gender binary and conflate "male" with being in possession of a penis, compounding an uncritical self-reflexivity. What Snorton wishes to undo is that very assumption of penis equals male, in pursuit of a more expansive deployment of black feminism.

So if Snorton critiques the genitally normative categories of gender that black (male) feminists often unwittingly uphold, in an effort to "trans★blasphemously" concretize my theorizations, if you will, I wish here to also obviate the conflation of trans★(gender) with racial whiteness. Indeed, as Jasbir Puar explains, value is extracted from (trans★) bodies of color in order to produce transgender whiteness. Drawing on the work of Susan Stryker and Aren Aizura, Puar's project in "Bodies with New Organs: Becoming Trans, Becoming Disabled" (2015) is to always imagine an affiliation between disabilities, trans★, racial, and interspecies discourses through her concept of "becoming trans," which is to say, quite controversially, that boundaries are porous insofar as they engage the force of ontological multiplicity and, ultimately, make an end goal an always shifting impossibility: "There is no trans" (46–47, 62). Puar writes, "Trans becoming masquerades as a teleological movement, as if one could actually become trans. Trans is often mistaken as the horizon of trans and, as such, is mistaken for becoming trans as linear telos, as a prognosis that becomes the body's contemporary diagnosis and domesticates the trans body into the regulatory norms of permanence.

"*Becoming trans*, then, as opposed to trans becoming, must highlight this impossibility of linearity, permanence, and end points" (62–63). One might initially castigate Puar for erasing transgender subjects. After all, to say "there is no trans" is a rather provocative and contentious claim for a queer theorist to make. But Puar is in fact suggesting something rather profound. One cannot arrive at trans★ precisely because it is movement, excitation, and agitation. To "be" trans★ is an impossibility since trans★ is a radically unstable non/site laying the antefoundation for the possibility of Heideggerian *Dasein*. Trans★ is "force" and "intensity" rather than identity, fixed or otherwise (Puar 2014: 80). Trans★ is not linear, permanent, or an end—it is in fact the impossibility of these things.

[. . .]

III. That Alternative Groove We In

> Amiri Baraka's work is in the break, in the scene, in the music. This location, at once internal and interstitial, determines the character of Baraka's political and aesthetic intervention. Syncopation, performance, and the anarchic organization of phonic substance delineate an ontological field wherein black radicalism is set to work. . . . The black radical tradition . . . constitutes its radicalism as a cutting and abundant refusal of closure. This refusal of closure is not a rejection but an ongoing and reconstructive improvisation of ensemble; this reconstruction's motive is the sexual differentiation of sexual difference.
> — Fred Moten, *In the Break: The Aesthetics of the Black Radical Tradition*

Both the blackness of trans★-ness and the trans★-ness of blackness un/mark, in a slight recapitulation of Katherine McKittrick's phrase, "demonic non-ground." McKittrick's "demonic ground" describes "perspectives that reside in the liminal precincts of the current governing configurations of the human as man in order to abolish this figuration and create other forms of life" (Weheliye 2008: 323). A demonic ground is ground that is fugitive and unstable, "a working system that cannot have a determined, or knowable outcome," "a process that is hinged on uncertainty and non-linearity" (McKittrick 2006: xxiv). For blackness and trans★ness to un/mark a demonic nonground is a creative use of language to describe the thereness and not-thereness of the ground that is not a ground—a ground that, in not being a ground, is the condition for groundedness—which, in other words, is black and trans★. The demonic nonground resonates with Evelynn Hammonds's "black (w)hole,"[5] situating it in a black feminist genealogy, and also highlighting the accusatory, light-bearing, critical (etymologically, "demonic" or "satanic") abyss underlying the order of purity. It, too, is a space of liminality, of volatility, and in that liminality/volatility it is productive, forceful, and destructive of the human-as-man. I might alternatively call this demonic space "virtual," as virtuality is of a voidal non/space in which there is a "lively tension, a desiring orientation toward being/becoming" that is aptly described as an imaginative "scene of wild activities" (Barad 2015: 396).[6] But though demonic and virtual, there is also something sonic here in the liminality, something echoing Moten's "Black Mo'nin'" or "break," or Claudia Rankine's (2015) mournful condition of black life.[7] Or maybe this is simply to say, there is something rhythmically and interstitially poetic here.

I have been calling blackness and trans★-ness poetic forces throughout this essay, echoing Fred Moten. In this sense, they share a disciplinary affiliation with Amiri Baraka. Though one imagines Baraka would have never given much thought to his relationship to trans★-ness, Moten sees in Baraka's work the epitomization of musical interstitiality. As an archetypal black radical, Baraka dwells in the break, the undercommons, and refuses the foreclosure of his unfixing poetics. And in this refusitive posture, the fugitive posture is syncopated, uneven, differing and differential. And syncopation, like the break writ large, is a gapped chasm, which itself is, as Moten writes of black mo'nin', "the difference within invagination between what cuts and what surrounds, invagination being that principle of impurity that . . . is constantly improvised by the rupturing and augmentative power of an always already multiply and disruptively present singularity" (2003: 202). That rupturing, disruptively present singularity is what I have called "blackness," what I have called "trans★-ness."

It stands, though, that in their poetics, in Baraka's, blackness's, and trans★ness's musicality, there exists, too, a rhythmic force. We are surrounded by rhythms reverberating throughout the vibrations of worldly inhabitation, but the prevailing rhythm, the one that seeks to circumscribe our para-ontological cacophony, is what Fred Moten and Stefano Harney call a "killing rhythm." But, as they assert, "at the heart of its [the killing rhythm's] production is a certain indiscretion . . . a haptic resonance that makes possible and impossible this killing rhythm, the undercommon track that remains fugitive from the emerging logistics of this deadly rhythm and will exhaust it" (2014: 185–186). Simmering beneath the killing rhythm of hegemony is that indiscretion and fugitivity that I am calling "black" and "trans★." They reside in the undercommons, refusing the logic of logic, which is another name for the killing rhythm. "If logisticality is the resident capacity to live on the earth," Moten and Harney write, "logistics is the regulation of that capacity in the service of making the world, the zero-one, zero-one world that pursues the general antagonism of life on earth." Logic, hegemony—or as hegemonic racial and gender analogues to black and trans★, white and cisgender—attempts to create logical individuals, and this is to be firmly immersed within the symphonic trap of the killing rhythm. The killing rhythm seeks structure, fixity; it seeks "to beat out that rhythm over the undercommon track that keeps its own measure" (Moten and Harney 2014: 187–188). And the alternative rhythm facing fatal melodic extermination is, in other words, black and trans★.

The end, the demise of this logical individual who sings to the tune of the killing rhythm is, Moten and Harney assert, "flesh/blackness" (189). It is also a kind of trans★-ness, I'd add, a fatal cut, a dehiscence, a rupture to the stitches of circumscription. Characterized as a "spooky action," Moten and Harney enunciate the para-ontological sociality of blackness, and by my own extension, trans★-ness. They write:

> What one might call the social life of things is important only insofar as it allows us to imagine that social life is not a relation between things but is, rather, that field of rub and rupture that works, that is the work of, no one, nothing, in its empathic richness. The social work of social life is no work at all, but the madness remains; rub

and rupture all but emerge, but in nothing like an emergence, as something imprecision requires us to talk about as if it were some thing, not just discrete but pure. This "thing," our ~~thing~~, the alternate groove we in, the devalued and invaluable local insurgency, disobeys our most loving invocation. This gift of spirit gives itself away and zero-one is left embittered.

(188)

Blackness and trans*-ness: that "alternative groove we in," a groove that underlies grooviness and undoes it, opening it up again and again. What I have attempted here is a "grave-robbing" stratagem, as Omise'eke Natasha Tinsley and Matt Richardson (2014; 161) might say, a stratagem that insists on the necessity to "exhume tools that might help us explain what has been going on in our own backyard." I insist on this work, and my scholarly corpus in general, as a black trans* studies methodological approach to "uncovering the skeletons of racism, misogyny, and other systemic violence and piecing them together" as a way to think through the very world in which we live (161). It is an alternative song, one that moves to an alternative groove, or perhaps a groove that does not even adhere to the sonic tenets of grooviness. But that is good, because what has passed for rhythm has been structured on a necessary, constitutive "killing." In this alternatively groovy vein, blackness and trans*-ness are things, discursively marking their thereness and not-thereness, their very linguistic volatility, their elusion of syntactical nominatives, which themselves, ultimately, are a form of fixing. Ever the artfully escaping air from the enframing of life, blackness and trans*-ness embitter the binaristic zero-one formulation that is ontology. "Catch me if you can—but you can't and you never will," say blackness and trans*-ness as they skip away, holding hands, perhaps, laughing all the way (ha ha ha).

Notes

1. See the 1990 film *Paris Is Burning*, directed by Jennie Livingston. The film is a documentary about New York's underground drag scene in which genderqueer folks of color vogue, mop, perform "realness," and destabilize all that one thinks they know about gender performativity.
2. Spillers writes that "a posture of critical insurgency must be achieved. It cannot be assumed." But I might also submit that since blackness underlies possibility, it *can* be assumed, as it is the foundation of everything's foundation. In Amaryah Shaye's words, "Blackness is a thing, is a space, *that already is*" (2014a). As anoriginal, it can be assumed on the grounds that it is always, and has always been, before.
3. khan uses the singular *they* gender pronoun, so I am honoring that preference here.
4. A reference to Judith Butler's quote that "possibility is not a luxury; it is as crucial as bread" (2004: 29).
5. In reference to Evelynn Hammonds's 1994 article "Black (W)holes and the Geometry of Black Female Sexuality," in which she seeks to unearth the reasons for the silence around black women's sexuality.
6. In full, Karen Barad writes:

Virtual particles are not in the void but *of* the void. They are on the razor's edge of non/being. The void is a lively tension, a desiring orientation toward being/becoming. The void is flush with yearning, bursting with innumerable imaginings of what might yet (have) be(en). Vacuum fluctuations are virtual deviations/variations from the classical zero-energy state of the void. That is, *virtuality is the material wanderings/wonderings of nothingness; virtuality is the ongoing thought experiment the world performs with itself.* Indeed, quantum physics tells us that *the void is an endless exploration of all possible couplings of virtual particles, a "scene of wild activities."* (2015: 396)

7. These are in reference to Moten's chapter "Black Mo'nin'" and his notion of "the break" in *In the Break: The Aesthetics of the Black Radical Tradition*, and Claudia Rankine's *New York Times* article "The Condition of Black Life Is One of Mourning" (2015). Black Mo'nin' for Moten is the sonic resonances of images, the blackness, if you will, of racialized trauma. The break is that generative, black liminal space in between. As Valorie Thomas (2012: 50) writes in her chapter in *Black Cool: One Thousand Streams of Blackness*, the break "is a transformative technology that mirrors the vitality, dissonances, and underlying coherence of diasporic cultural processes." Lastly, Rankine argues that, simply, the very condition on which black life is grounded is mourning—mourning the death, essentially, of the appearance of blackness in public spaces coded as white. All these are interstitial spaces that musically and tonally resonate.

Bibliography

Aizura, Aren Z. 2006. "Of Borders and Homes: The Imaginary Community of (Trans)Sexual Citizenship." *Inter-Asia Cultural Studies* 7, no. 2: 289–309. doi:10.1080/14649370600 673953.

"Are We Really All Made of Stardust?" 2016. Physics.org. www.physics.org/article-questions.asp ?id=52 (accessed February 15, 2016).

Barad, Karen. 2015. "TransMaterialities: Trans*/Matter/Realities and Queer Political Imaginings." *GLQ* 21, nos. 2–3: 387–422. doi:10.1215/10642684-2843239.

Bey, Marquis, and Theodora Sakellarides. 2016. "When We Enter: The Blackness of Rachel Dolezal." *Black Scholar* 46, no. 3: 33–48.

Bird, Susan. 2002. "Re Kevin (Validity of Marriage of Transsexual) *[2001] FamCA 1074.*" *Southern Cross Law Review* 6: 364–371.

Brubaker, Rogers. 2016. *Trans: Gender and Race in an Age of Unsettled Identities*. Princeton, NJ: Princeton University Press.

Bussell, Sevan. 2012. "Why We Use the Asterisk." *Candiussel Corner* (blog), October 2. candius sellcorner. blogspot.com/2012/10/why-we-use-asterisk-sevan.html.

Butler, Judith. 2004. *Undoing Gender*. New York: Routledge.

Campt, Tina. 2014. "Black Feminist Futures and the Practice of Fugitivity." Helen Pond McIntyre'48 Lecture, Barnard Center for Research on Women, Barnard College, New York, October 7. bcrw.barnard. edu/blog/black-feminist-futures-and-the-practice-of-fugitivity/.

Carter, J. Kameron 2013. "Paratheological Blackness." *South Atlantic Quarterly* 112, no. 4: 589–611. doi:10.1215/00382876-2345189.

Chen, Mel Y. 2012. *Animacies: Biopolitics, Racial Mattering, and Queer Affect*. Durham, NC: Duke University Press.

Cohen, Cathy J., and Sarah J. Jackson. 2015. "Ask a Feminist: A Conversation with Cathy Cohen on Black Lives Matter, Feminism, and Contemporary Activism." *Signs: Journal of Women in Culture and Society*. signsjournal.org/ask-a-feminist-cohen-jackson/.

Colebrook, Claire. 2015. "What Is It Like to Be a Human?" *TSQ* 2, no. 2: 227–243. doi:10.1215/232 89252-2867472.

Downs, Donald Alexander. 1999. *Cornell '69: Liberalism and the Crisis of the American University*. Ithaca, NY: Cornell University Press.

Elliott, Osborn. 1969. "Universities Under the Gun—Militants at Cornell." *Newsweek*, May 5.

Ferguson, Roderick A. 2004. *Aberrations in Black: Toward a Queer of Color Critique*. Minneapolis: University of Minnesota Press.

Foucault, Michel, et al. 2015. *Language, Madness, and Desire: On Literature*. Minneapolis: University of Minnesota Press.

Gossett, Che. 2016. "Žižek's Trans/Gender Trouble." *Los Angeles Review of Books*, September 13. lareviewofbooks.org/article/zizeks-transgender-trouble/.

Green, Kai M. 2013. "'What the Eyes Did Not Wish to Behold': Lessons from Ann Allen Shockley's *Say Jesus and Come to Me*." *South Atlantic Quarterly* 112, no. 2: 285–302. doi:10.1215/00382876-2020208.

———. 2015a. "The Essential I/Eye in We: A Black TransFeminist Approach to Ethnographic Film." *Black Camera* 6, no. 2: 187–200.

———. 2015b. "'Race and Gender Are Not the Same!' Is Not a Good Response to the 'Transracial'/ Transgender Question or We Can and Must Do Better." *Feminist Wire*, June 14. www.thefeministwire.

com/2015/06/race-and-gender-are-not-the-same-is-not-a-good-response—to-the-transracial-transgen der-question-or-we-can-and-must-do-better/.

Hammonds, Evelynn. 1994. "Black (W)holes and the Geometry of Black Female Sexuality." *Differences* 6, nos. 2–3: 126–145.

Harney, Stefano, and Fred Moten. 2004. "The University and the Undercommons: Seven Theses." *Social Text*, no. 79: 101–115.

———. 2013. *The Undercommons: Fugitive Planning and Black Study*. New York: Minor Compositions.

Hayward, Eva. 2008. "More Lessons from a Starfish: Prefixial Flesh and Transspeciated Selves." *WSQ* 36, no. 3: 64–85. doi:10.1353/wsq.0.0099.

———. 2013. "Lessons from a Starfish." In *The Transgender Studies Reader 2*, edited by Susan Stryker and Aren Z. Aizura, 178–188. New York: Routledge.

Hayward, Eva, and Jami Weinstein. 2015. "Introduction: Tranimalities in the Age of Trans* Life." *TSQ* 2, no. 2: 195–208. doi:10.1215/23289252-2867446.

Jay, Martin. 1986. *Permanent Exiles: Essays on the Intellectual Migration from Germany to America*. New York: Columbia University Press.

Kelley, Robin D. G. 1994. *Race Rebels: Culture, Politics, and the Black Working Class*. New York: Maxwell Macmillan International.

Khan, Janaya. 2015. "Black Trans Women to the Front!" *Feminist Wire*, February 4. www.thefeministwire. com/2015/02/op-ed-black-trans-women-front/.

Lowery, George. 2009. "A Campus Takeover That Symbolized an Era of Change." *Cornell Chronicle*, April 16.

McKittrick, Katherine. 2006. *Demonic Grounds: Black Women and the Cartographies of Struggle*. Minneapolis: University of Minnesota Press.

Moten, Fred. 2003. *In the Break: The Aesthetics of the Black Radical Tradition*. Minneapolis: University of Minnesota Press.

———. 2007. "Preface for a Solo by Miles Davis." *Women and Performance: A Journal of Feminist Theory* 17, no. 2: 217–246. doi:10.1080/07407700701387317.

———. 2008. "Black Op." *PMLA* 123, no. 5: 1743–1747.

Moten, Fred, and Stefano Harney. 2011. "Politics Surrounded." *South Atlantic Quarterly* 110, no. 4: 985–988. doi:10.1215/00382876-1382375.

———. 2014. "Al-Khwariddim, or Savoir Faire Is Everywhere." In *Really Useful Knowledge*, edited by Brook Andrew, 185–190. Madrid: Museo Nacional Centro de Arte Reina Sofia.

Nelson, Maggie. 2015. *The Argonauts*. Minneapolis: Graywolf.

Puar, Jasbir K. 2014. "Disability." *TSQ* 1, nos. 1–2: 77–81. doi:10.1215/23289252-2399659.

———. 2015. "Bodies with New Organs: Becoming Trans, Becoming Disabled." *Social Text*, no. 124: 45–73. doi:10.1215/01642472-3125698.

Rankine, Claudia. 2015. "The Condition of Black Life Is One of Mourning." *New York Times*, June 22.

Sexton, Jared. 2010. "People-of-Color-Blindness: Notes on the Afterlife of Slavery." *Social Text*, no. 103: 31–56.

Shaye, Amaryah. 2014a. "Refusing to Reconcile, Part 2." *Women in Theology* (blog), February 16. womenintheology.org/2014/02/16/refusing-to-reconcile-part-2/.

———. 2014b. "Refusing to Reconcile, Part 3: The Best Man Holiday and the Besideness of Blackness." *Women in Theology* (blog), March 28. womenintheology.org/2014/03/28/refusing-to-reconcile-part-three-the-best-man-holiday-and-the-besideness-of-blackness/.

Snorton, C. Riley. 2011. "Transfiguring Masculinities in Black Women's Studies." *Feminist Wire*. thefeministwire.com/2011/05/transfiguring-masculinities-in-black-womens-studies/.

Spillers, Hortense J. 1987. "Mama's Baby, Papa's Maybe: An American Grammar Book." *Diacritics* 17, no. 2: 65–81. doi:10.2307/464747.

———. 2003. *Black, White, and in Color: Essays on American Literature and Culture*. Chicago: University of Chicago Press.

———. 2006. "The Idea of Black Culture." *New Centennial Review* 6, no. 3: 7–28.

———. 2012. "A Transatlantic Circuit: Baldwin at Mid-century Opening Keynote Address." *Callaloo* 35, no. 4: 929–938. doi:10.1353/cal.2013.0033.

Stallings, LaMonda Horton. 2013. "Hip Hop and the Black Ratchet Imagination." *Palimpsest* 2, no. 2: 135–139.

Stone, Sandy. 2014. "Guerrilla." *TSQ* 1, nos. 1–2: 92–96. doi:10.1215/23289252-2399704.

Stryker, Susan, Paisley Currah, and Lisa Jean Moore. 2008. "Introduction: Trans-, Trans, or Transgender?" *WSQ* 36, no. 3: 11–22. doi:10.1353/wsq.0.0112.

Thomas, Valorie. 2012. "The Break." In *Black Cool: One Thousand Streams of Blackness*, edited by Rebecca Walker, 47–58. Berkeley, CA: Soft Skull.

Tinsley, Omise'eke Natasha, and Matt Richardson. 2014. "From Black Transgender Studies to Colin Dayan: Notes on Methodology." *Small Axe* 18, no. 3: 152–161.

Tolbert, T. C. 2013. "Open, and Always, Opening—An Introduction in Three Parts." In *Troubling the Line: Trans and Genderqueer Poetry and Poetics*, edited by T. C. Tolbert and Tim Trace Peterson, 7–14. Callicoon, NY: Nightboat Books.

Tompkins, Avery. 2014. "Asterisk." *TSQ* 1, nos. 1–2: 26–27. doi:10.1215/23289252-2399497.

Weed, Elizabeth, and Naomi Schor, eds. 1997. *Feminism Meets Queer Theory*. Bloomington: Indiana University Press.

Weheliye, Alexander G. 2008. "After Man." *American Literary History* 20, no. 1: 321–336.

———. 2014. "Engendering Phonographies: Sonic Technologies of Blackness." *Small Axe* 18, no. 2: 180–190.

Wright, Michelle M. 2015. *Physics of Blackness: Beyond the Middle Passage Epistemology*. Minneapolis: University of Minnesota Press.

8 Mama's Baby, Papa's Maybe

An American Grammar Book

Hortense J. Spillers

Black feminist literary scholar Hortense J. Spillers's pathbreaking 1987 article "Mama's Baby, Papa's Maybe: An American Grammar Book" was a response to the 1965 Moynihan Report, from the U.S. Department of Labor, on "The Negro Family." The report characterized Black women through several disparaging stereotypes—the welfare queen, the neglectful mother, the matriarch who usurps the man's proper role as head of household—to cast them as deficient and improper leaders of Black family and community. Spillers calls for a radical reclamation of Black female subjectivity. She shows how chattel slavery worked to exclude Black females from the white patrilineal order and how this exclusion legally guaranteed the illegitimacy of children born to enslaved people. If Black female gendering takes place through exclusion from white patrilineal society, Black females can be considered un-gendered through slavery, their flesh reduced to a blank slate for the inscription of racial ontologies that equate Blackness with inferiority and death. Spillers suggests that Black women claim the "monstrosity" of their exclusion from a female womanhood predicated on implicitly racist criteria for gender normativity and asks them to "gain the *insurgent* ground" of new forms of personhood within new forms of sociality. Her concept of an "insurgent ground" that preexists the historical ontology of race prefigures the concept of the para-ontological deployed by Bey and the sense of a generative cosmic void in this section's selections form Barad and Jackson. Her call to imagine monstrosity as a position from which to radically intervene into the existing order of the world similarly prefigures Stryker's invocation of monstrosity in "My Words to Victor Frankenstein Above the Village of Chamounix."

Let's face it. I am a marked woman, but not everybody knows my name. "Peaches" and "Brown Sugar," "Sapphire" and "Earth Mother," "Aunty," "Granny," God's "Holy Fool," a "Miss Ebony First," or "Black Woman at the Podium": I describe a locus of confounded identities, a meeting ground of investments and privations in the national treasury of rhetorical wealth. My country needs me, and if I were not here, I would have to be invented.

W. E. B. DuBois predicted as early as 1903 that the twentieth century would be the century of the "color line." We could add to this spatiotemporal configuration another thematic of analogously terrible weight: if the "black woman" can be seen as a particular figuration of the split subject that psychoanalytic theory posits, then this century marks the site of "its" profoundest revelation. The problem before us is deceptively simple: the terms enclosed in quotation marks in the preceding paragraph isolate overdetermined nominative properties. Embedded in bizarre axiological ground, they demonstrate a sort of telegraphic coding; they

DOI: 10.4324/9781003206255-11

are markers so loaded with mythical prepossession that there is no easy way for the agents buried beneath them to come clean. In that regard, the names by which I am called in the public place render an example of signifying property *plus*. In order for me to speak a truer word concerning myself, I must strip down through layers of attenuated meanings, made an excess in time, over time, assigned by a particular historical order, and there await whatever marvels of my own inventiveness. The personal pronouns are offered in the service of a collective function.

In certain human societies, a child's identity is determined through the line of the Mother, but the United States, from at least one author's point of view, is not one of them: "In essence, the Negro community has been forced into a matriarchal structure which, because it is so far out of line with the *rest of American society*, seriously retards the progress of the group as a whole, and imposes a crushing burden on the Negro male and, in consequence, on a great many Negro women as well" (Moynihan 75; emphasis mine).

The notorious bastard, from Vico's banished Roman mothers of such sons, to Caliban, to Heathcliff, and Joe Christmas, has no official female equivalent. Because the traditional rites and laws of inheritance rarely pertain to the female child, bastard status signals to those who need to know which son of the Father's is the legitimate heir and which one the impostor. For that reason, property seems wholly the business of the male. A "she" cannot, therefore, qualify for bastard, or "natural son" status, and that she cannot provides further insight into the coils and recoils of patriarchal wealth and fortune. According to Daniel Patrick Moynihan's celebrated "Report" of the late sixties, the "Negro Family" has no Father to speak of—his Name, his Law, his Symbolic function mark the impressive missing agencies in the essential life of the black community, the "Report" maintains, and it is, surprisingly, the fault of the Daughter, or the female line. This stunning reversal of the castration thematic, displacing the Name and the Law of the Father to the territory of the Mother and Daughter, becomes an aspect of the African-American female's misnaming. We attempt to undo this misnaming in order to reclaim the relationship between Fathers and Daughters within this social matrix for a quite different structure of cultural fictions. For Daughters and Fathers are here made to manifest the very same *rhetorical* symptoms of absence and denial, to embody the double and contrastive agencies of a *prescribed* internecine degradation. "Sapphire" enacts her "Old Man" in drag, just as her "Old Man" becomes "Sapphire" in outrageous caricature.

In other words, in the historic outline of dominance, the respective subject-positions of "female" and "male" adhere to no symbolic integrity. At a time when current critical discourses appear to compel us more and more decidedly toward gender "undecidability," it would appear reactionary, if not dumb, to insist on the integrity of female/male gender. But undressing these conflations of meaning, as they appear under the rule of dominance, would restore, as figurative possibility, not only Power to the Female (for Maternity), but also Power to the Male (for Paternity). We would gain, in short, the *potential* for gender differentiation as it might express itself along a range of stress points, including human biology in its intersection with the project of culture.

Though among the most readily available "whipping boys" of fairly recent public discourse concerning African-Americans and national policy, "The Moynihan Report" is by no means unprecedented in its conclusions; it belongs, rather, to a class of symbolic paradigms that 1) inscribe "ethnicity" as a scene of negation and 2) confirm the human body as a metonymic figure for an entire repertoire of human and social arrangements. In that regard, the "Report" pursues a behavioral rule of public documentary. Under the Moynihan rule, "ethnicity" itself identifies a total objectification of human and cultural motives—the "white" family, by implication, and the "Negro Family," by outright assertion, in a constant opposition of binary meanings. Apparently spontaneous, these "actants" are *wholly* generated, with neither past nor future, as tribal currents moving out of time. Moynihan's

"Families" are pure present and always tense. "Ethnicity" in this case freezes in meaning, takes on constancy, assumes the look and the affects of the Eternal. We could say, then, that in its powerful stillness, "ethnicity," from the point of view of the "Report," embodies nothing more than a mode of memorial time, as Roland Barthes outlines the dynamics of myth [see "Myth Today" 109–59; esp. 122–23]. As a signifier that has no movement in the field of signification, the use of "ethnicity" for the living becomes purely appreciative, although one would be unwise not to concede its dangerous and fatal effects.

"Ethnicity" perceived as mythical time enables a writer to perform a variety of conceptual moves all at once. Under its hegemony, the human body becomes a defenseless target for rape and veneration, and the body, in its material and abstract phase, a resource for metaphor. For example, Moynihan's "tangle of pathology" provides the descriptive strategy for the work's fourth chapter, which suggests that "underachievement" in black males of the lower classes is primarily the fault of black females, who achieve out of all proportion, both to their numbers in the community and to the paradigmatic example before the nation: "Ours is a society which presumes male leadership in private and public affairs. . . . A subculture, such as that of the Negro American, in which this is not the pattern, is placed at a distinct disadvantage" [75]. Between charts and diagrams, we are asked to consider the impact of qualitative measure on the black male's performance on standardized examinations, matriculation in schools of higher and professional training, etc. Even though Moynihan sounds a critique on his own argument here, he quickly withdraws from its possibilities, suggesting that black males should reign because that is the way the majority culture carries things out: "It is clearly a disadvantage for a minority group to be operating under one principle, while the great majority of the population is operating on another" [75]. Those persons living according to the perceived "matriarchal" pattern are, therefore, caught in a state of social "pathology."

Even though Daughters have their own agenda with reference to this order of Fathers (imagining for the moment that Moynihan's fiction—and others like it—does not represent an adequate one and that there *is*, once we dis-cover him, a Father here), my contention that these social and cultural subjects make doubles, unstable in their respective identities, in effect transports us to a common historical ground, the socio-political order of the New World. That order, with its human sequence written in blood, *represents* for its African and indigenous peoples a scene of *actual* mutilation, dismemberment, and exile. First of all, their New-World, diasporic plight marked a *theft of the body*—a willful and violent (and unimaginable from this distance) severing of the captive body from its motive will, its active desire. Under these conditions, we lose at least *gender* difference *in the* outcome, and the female body and the male body become a territory of cultural and political maneuver, not at all gender-related, gender-specific. But this body, at least from the point of view of the captive community, focuses a private and particular space, at which point of convergence biological, sexual, social, cultural, linguistic, ritualistic, and psychological fortunes join. This profound intimacy of interlocking detail is disrupted, however, by externally imposed meanings and uses: 1) the captive body becomes the source of an irresistible, destructive sensuality; 2) at the same time—in stunning contradiction—the captive body reduces to a thing, becoming *being for* the captor; 3) in this absence *from* a subject position, the captured sexualities provide a physical and biological expression of "otherness"; 4) as a category of "otherness," the captive body translates into a potential for pornotroping and embodies sheer physical powerlessness that slides into a more general "powerlessness," resonating through various centers of human and social meaning.

But I would make a distinction in this case between "body" and "flesh" and impose that distinction as the central one between captive and liberated subject-positions. In that sense, before the "body" there is the "flesh," that zero degree of social conceptualization that does not escape concealment under the brush of discourse, or the reflexes of iconography. Even though the European hegemonies stole bodies—some of them female—out of West African communities in concert with the African "middleman," we regard this human and social irreparability as high crimes against the *flesh*, as the person of African females and African males registered the wounding. If we think of the "flesh" as a primary narrative, then we mean its seared, divided, ripped-apartness, riveted to the ship's hole, fallen, or "escaped" overboard.

One of the most poignant aspects of William Goodell's contemporaneous study of the North American slave codes gives precise expression to the tortures and instruments of captivity. Reporting an instance of Jonathan Edwards's observations on the tortures of enslavement, Goodell narrates: "The smack of the whip is all day long in the ears of those who are on the plantation, or in the vicinity; and it is used with such dexterity and severity as not only to lacerate the skin, but to tear out small portions of the flesh at almost every stake" [221]. The anatomical specifications of rupture, of altered human tissue, take on the objective description of laboratory prose—eyes beaten out, arms, backs, skulls branded, a left jaw, a right ankle, punctured; teeth missing, as the calculated work of iron, whips, chains, knives, the canine patrol, the bullet.

These undecipherable markings on the captive body render a kind of hieroglyphics of the flesh whose severe disjunctures come to be hidden to the cultural seeing by skin color. We might well ask if this phenomenon of marking and branding actually "transfers" from one generation to another, finding its various *symbolic substitutions* in an efficacy of meanings that repeat the initiating moments? As Elaine Scarry describes the mechanisms of torture [Scarry 27–59), these lacerations, woundings, fissures, tears, scars, openings, ruptures, lesions, rendings, punctures of the flesh create the distance between what I would designate a cultural *vestibularity* and the *culture*, whose state apparatus, including judges, attorneys, "owners," "soul drivers," "overseers," and "men of God," apparently colludes with a protocol of "search and destroy." This body whose flesh carries the female and the male to the frontiers of survival bears in person the marks of a cultural text whose inside has been turned outside.

The flesh is the concentration of "ethnicity" that contemporary critical discourses neither acknowledge nor discourse away. It is this "flesh and blood" entity, in the vestibule (or "pre-view") of a colonized North America, that is essentially ejected from "The Female Body in Western Culture" [see Suleiman, ed.], but it makes good theory, or commemorative "herstory" to want to "forget," or to have failed to realize, that the African female subject, under these historic conditions, is not only the target of rape—in one sense, an interiorized violation of body and mind—but also the topic of specifically *externalized* acts of torture and prostration that we imagine as the peculiar province of male brutality and torture inflicted by other males. A female body strung from a tree limb, or bleeding from the breast on any given day of field work because the "overseer," standing the length of a whip, has popped her flesh open, adds a lexical and living dimension to the narratives of women in culture and society [Davis 9]. This materialized scene of unprotected female flesh—of female flesh "ungendered"—offers a praxis and a theory, a text for living and for dying, and a method for reading both through their diverse mediations.

Among the myriad uses to which the enslaved community was put, Goodell identifies its value for medical research: "Assortments of diseased, *damaged*, and disabled Negroes, deemed incurable and otherwise worthless are *bought up*, it seems . . . by medical institutions, to be experimented and operated upon, for purposes of 'medical education' and the interest of medical science" [86–87; Goodell's emphasis]. From the *Charleston Mercury* for October 12, 1838, Goodell notes this advertisement:

'To planters and others.—Wanted, fifty Negroes, any person, having sick Negroes, considered incurable by their respective physicians, and wishing to dispose of them, Dr. 5. will pay cash for

Negroes affected with scrofula, or king's evil, confirmed hypochondriasm, apoplexy, diseases of the liver, kidneys, spleen, stomach and intestines, bladder and its appendages, diarrhea, dysentery, etc. The highest cash price will be paid, on application as above.' at No. 110 Church Street, Charleston.

[87; Goodell's emphasis]

This profitable "atomizing" of the captive body provides another angle on the divided flesh: we lose any hint or suggestion of a dimension of ethics, of relatedness between human personality and its anatomical features, between one human personality and another, between human personality and cultural institutions. To that extent, the procedures adopted for the captive flesh demarcate a total objectification, as the entire captive community becomes a living laboratory.

The captive body, then, brings into focus a gathering of social realities as well as a metaphor for *value* so thoroughly interwoven in their literal and figurative emphases that distinctions between them are virtually useless. Even though the captive flesh/body has been "liberated," and no one need pretend that even the quotation marks do not *matter*, dominant symbolic activity, the ruling episteme that releases the dynamics of naming and valuation, remains grounded in the originating metaphors of captivity and mutilation so that it is as if neither time nor history, nor historiography and its topics, shows movement, as the human subject is "murdered" over and over again by the passions of a bloodless and anonymous archaism, showing itself in endless disguise. Faulkner's young Chick Mallison in *The Mansion* calls "it" by other names—"the ancient subterrene atavistic fear . . ." [227]. And I would call it the Great Long National Shame. But people do not talk like that anymore—it is "embarrassing," just as the retrieval of mutilated female bodies will likely be "backward" for some people. Neither the shameface of the embarrassed, nor the not-looking-back of the self-assured is of much interest to us, and will not help at all if rigor is our dream. We might concede, at the very least, that sticks and bricks *might* break our bones, but words will most certainly *kill* us.

The symbolic order that I wish to trace in this writing, calling it an "American grammar," begins at the "beginning," which is really a rupture and a radically different kind of cultural continuation. The massive demographic shifts, the violent formation of a modern African consciousness, that take place on the subsaharan Continent during the initiative strikes which open the Atlantic Slave Trade in the fifteenth century of our Christ, interrupted hundreds of years of black African culture. We write and think, then, about an outcome of aspects of African-American life in the United States under the pressure of those events. I might as well add that the familiarity of this narrative does nothing to appease the hunger of recorded memory, nor does the persistence of the repeated rob these well-known, oft-told events of their power, even now, to startle. In a very real sense, every writing as revision makes the "discovery" all over again.

2

[. . .]

The conditions of "Middle Passage" are among the most incredible narratives available to the student, as it remains not easily imaginable. Late in the chronicles of the Atlantic Slave Trade, Britain's Parliament entertained discussions concerning possible "regulations" for slave vessels. A Captain Perry visited the Liverpool port, and among the ships that he inspected was "The Brookes," probably the most well-known image of the slave galley with its representative *personae* etched into the drawing like so many cartoon figures. Elizabeth Donnan's second volume carries the "Brookes Plan," along with an elaborate delineation of its dimensions from the investigative reporting of Perry himself: "Let it now be supposed . . . further, that every man slave is to be allowed six feet by one foot four inches for room, every woman five feet ten by one foot four, every boy five feet by one foot two, and every girl four feet six by one foot . . ." [2:592, n]. The owner of "The Brookes," James Jones, had recommended that "five females be reckoned as four males, and three boys or girls as equal to two grown persons" [2:592].

These scaled inequalities complement the commanding terms of the dehumanizing, ungendering, and defacing project of African persons that De Azurara's narrator might have recognized. It has been pointed out to me that these measurements do reveal the application of the gender rule to the material conditions of passage, but I would suggest that "gendering" takes place within the confines of the domestic, an essential metaphor that then spreads its tentacles for male and female subject over a wider ground of human and social purposes. Domesticity appears to gain its power by way of a common origin of cultural fictions that are grounded in the specificity of proper names, more exactly, a patronymic, which, in turn, situates those persons it "covers" in a particular place. Contrarily, the cargo of a ship might not be regarded as elements of the domestic, even though the vessel that carries it is sometimes romantically (ironically?) personified as "she." The human cargo of a slave vessel—in the fundamental effacement and remission of African family and proper names—offers a counter-narrative to notions of the domestic.

Those African persons in "Middle Passage" were literally suspended in the "oceanic," if we think of the latter in its Freudian orientation as an analogy for undifferentiated identity: removed from the indigenous land and culture, and not-yet "American" either, these captive persons, without names that their captors would recognize, were in movement across the Atlantic, but they were also *nowhere* at all. Inasmuch as, on any given day, we might imagine, the captive personality did not know where s/he was, we could say that they were the culturally "unmade," thrown in the midst of a figurative darkness that "exposed" their destinies to an unknown course. Often enough for the captains of these galleys, navigational science of the day was not sufficient to guarantee the intended destination. We might say that the slave ship, its crew, and its human-as-cargo stand for a wild and unclaimed richness of *possibility* that is not interrupted, not "counted"/"accounted," or differentiated, until its movement gains the land thousands of miles away from the point of departure. Under these conditions, one is neither female, nor male, as both subjects are taken into "account" as *quantities*. The female in "Middle Passage," as the apparently smaller physical mass, occupies "less room" in a directly translatable money economy. But she is, nevertheless, quantifiable by the same rules of accounting as her male counterpart.

It is not only difficult for the student to find "female" in "Middle Passage," but also, as Herbert S. Klein observes, "African women did not enter the Atlantic slave trade in anything like the numbers of African men. At all ages, men outnumbered women on the slave ships bound for America from Africa" [Klein 29]. Though this observation does not change the reality of African women's captivity and servitude in New World communities, it does provide a perspective from which to contemplate the *internal* African slave trade, which, according to Africanists, remained a predominantly *female* market. Klein nevertheless affirms that those females forced into the trade were segregated "from men for policing purposes" ["African Women" 35]. He claims that both "were allotted the same space between decks . . . and both were fed the same food" [35]. It is not altogether clear from Klein's observations *for whom* the "police" kept vigil. It is certainly known from evidence presented in Donnan's third volume ("New England and the Middle Colonies") that insurrection was both frequent and feared in passage, and we have not yet found a great deal of evidence to support a thesis that female captives participated in insurrectionary activity [see White 63–64]. Because it was the rule, however—not the exception—that the African female, in both indigenous African cultures and in what becomes her "home," performed tasks of hard physical labor—so much so that the quintessential "slave" is *not* a male, but a female—we wonder at the seeming docility of the subject, granting her a "feminization" that enslavement kept at bay. Indeed, across the spate of discourse that I examined for this writing, the acts of enslavement and responses to it comprise a more or less agonistic engagement of confrontational hostilities among males. The visual and historical evidence betrays the dominant discourse on the matter as incomplete, but *counter*-evidence is inadequate as well: the sexual violation of captive females and their own express rage against their oppressors did not constitute events that captains and their crews rushed to record in letters to their sponsoring companies, or sons on board in letters home to their New England mamas.

One suspects that there are several ways to snare a mockingbird, so that insurrection might have involved, from time to time, rather more subtle means than mutiny on the "Felicity," for instance. At any rate, we get very little notion in the written record of the life of women, children, and infants in "Middle Passage," and no idea of the fate of the pregnant female captive and the unborn, which startling thematic Bell Hooks addresses in the opening chapter of her pathfinding work [see Hooks 15–49]. From Hooks's lead, however, we might guess that the "reproduction of mothering" in this historic instance carries few of the benefits of a *patriarchilized* female gender, which, from one point of view, is the *only* female gender there is.

The relative silence of the record on this point constitutes a portion of the disquieting lacunae that feminist investigation seeks to fill. Such silence is the nickname of distortion, of the unknown human factor that a revised public discourse would both undo *and* reveal. This cultural subject is inscribed historically as anonymity/anomie in various public documents of European-American mal(e)venture, from Portuguese De Azurara in the middle of the fifteenth century, to South Carolina's Henry Laurens in the eighteenth.

What confuses and enriches the picture is precisely the sameness of anonymous portrayal that adheres tenaciously across the division of gender. In the vertical columns of accounts and ledgers that comprise Donnan's work, the terms "Negroes" and "Slaves" denote a common status. For instance, entries in one account, from September 1700 through September 1702, are specifically descriptive of the names of ships and the private traders in Barbados who will receive the stipulated goods, but "No. Negroes" and "Sum sold for per head" are so exactly arithmetical that it is as if these additions and multiplications belong to the other side of an equation [Donnan 2:25]. One is struck *by* the detail and precision that characterize these accounts, as a narrative, or story, is always implied by a man or woman's *name*: "Wm. Webster," "John Dunn," "Thos. Brownbill," "Robt. Knowles." But the "other" side of the page, as it were, equally precise, throws no *face* in view. It seems that nothing breaks the uniformity in this guise. If in no other way, the destruction of the African name, of kin, of linguistic, and ritual connections is so obvious in the vital stats sheet that we tend to overlook it. Quite naturally, the trader is not interested, in any *semantic* sense, in this "baggage" that he must deliver, but that he is not is all the more reason to search out the metaphorical implications of *naming* as one of the key sources of a bitter Americanizing for African persons.

The loss of the indigenous name/land provides a metaphor of displacement for other human and cultural features and relations, including the displacement of the genitalia, the female's and the male's desire that engenders future. The fact that the enslaved person's access to the issue of his/her own body is not entirely clear in this historic period throws in crisis all aspects of the blood relations, as captors apparently felt no obligation to acknowledge them. Actually trying to understand how the confusions of consanguinity worked becomes the project, because the outcome goes far to explain the rule of gender and its application to the African female in captivity.

3

Even though the essays in Claire C. Robertson's and Martin A. Klein's *Women and Slavery in Africa* have specifically to do with aspects of the internal African slave trade, some of their observations shed light on the captivities of the Diaspora. At least these observations have the benefit of altering the kind of questions we might ask of these silent chapters. For example, Robertson's essay, which opens the volume, discusses the term "slavery" in a wide variety of relationships. The enslaved person as *property* identifies the most familiar element of a most startling proposition. But to overlap *kinlessness* on the requirements of property might enlarge our view *of* the conditions *of* enslavement. Looking specifically at documents from the West African societies of Songhay and Dahomey, Claude Meillassoux elaborates several features of the property/kin less constellation that are highly suggestive for our own quite different purposes.

Meillassoux argues that "slavery creates an economic and social agent whose virtue lies in being outside the kinship system" ["Female Slavery," Robertson and Klein 50]. Because the Atlantic trade involved heterogeneous social and ethnic formations in an explicit power relationship, we certainly cannot mean "kinship system" in precisely the same way that Meillassoux observes at work within the intricate calculus of descent among West African societies. However, the idea becomes useful as a point of contemplation when we try to sharpen our own sense of the African female's reproductive uses within the diasporic enterprise of enslavement and the genetic reproduction of the enslaved. In effect, under conditions of captivity, the offspring of the female does not "belong" to the Mother, nor is s/he "related" to the "owner," though the latter "possesses" it, and in the African-American instance, often fathered it, *and*, as often, without whatever benefit of patrimony. In the social outline that Meillassoux is pursuing, the offspring *of* the enslaved, "being unrelated both to their begetters and to their owners . . . find themselves in the situation of being orphans" [50].

In the context of the United States, we could not say that the enslaved offspring was "orphaned," but the child does become, under the press of a patronymic, patrifocal, patrilineal, and patriarchal order, the man/woman on the boundary, whose human and familial status, by the very nature of the case, had yet to be defined. I would call this enforced state of breach another instance of vestibular cultural formation where "kinship" loses meaning, *since it can be invaded at any given and arbitrary moment by the property relations*. I certainly do not mean to say that African peoples in the New World did not maintain the powerful ties of sympathy that bind blood-relations in a network of feeling, of continuity. It is precisely *that* relationship—not customarily recognized by the code of slavery—that historians have long identified as the inviolable "Black Family" and further suggest that this structure remains one of the supreme social achievements *of* African-Americans under conditions of enslavement [see John Blassingame 79 ff.].

Indeed, the *revised* "Black Family" of enslavement has engendered an older tradition of historiographical and sociological writings than we usually think. Ironically enough, E. Franklin Frazier's Negro *Family in the United States* likely provides the closest *contemporary* narrative of conceptualization for the "Moynihan Report." Originally published in 1939, Frazier's work underwent two redactions in 1948 and 1966. Even though Frazier's outlook on this familial configuration remains basically sanguine, I would support Angela Davis's skeptical reading of Frazier's "Black Matriarchate" [Davis 14]. "*Except where the master's will was concerned*," Frazier contends, this matriarchal figure "developed a spirit of independence and a keen sense *of* her personal rights" [1966: 47; emphasis mine]. The "exception" in this instance tends to be overwhelming, as the African-American female's "dominance" and "strength" come to be interpreted by later generations—both black and white, oddly enough—as a "pathology," as an instrument of castration. Frazier's larger point, we might suppose, is that African-Americans developed such resourcefulness under conditions *of* captivity that "family" must be conceded as one *of* their redoubtable social attainments. This line of interpretation is pursued by Blassingame and Eugene Genovese [*Roll, Jordan, Roll* 70–75], among other U.S. historians, and indeed assumes a centrality of focus in our own thinking about the impact and outcome of captivity.

It seems clear, however, that "Family," as we practice and understand it "in the West"—the *vertical* transfer of a bloodline, of a patronymic, of titles and entitlements, *of* real estate and the prerogatives *of* "cold cash," from *fathers* to *sons* and in the supposedly free exchange *of* affectional ties between a male and a female of *his* choice—becomes the mythically revered privilege *of* a free and freed community. In that sense, African peoples in the historic Diaspora had nothing to prove, *if* the point had been that they were not capable of "family" (read "civilization"), since it is stunningly evident, in Equiano's narrative, for instance, that Africans were not only capable of the concept and the practice of "family," including "slaves," but in modes of elaboration and naming that were at least as complex as those of the "nuclear family" "in the West."

Whether or not we decide that the support systems that African-Americans derived under conditions of captivity should be called "family," or something else, strikes me as supremely impertinent. The point remains that captive persons were *forced* into patterns of *dispersal*, beginning with the Trade itself, into the *horizontal* relatedness of language groups, discourse formations, bloodlines, names, and properties by the legal arrangements of enslavement. It is true that the most "well-meaning" of "masters" (and there must have been *some) could not, did not* alter the *ideological* and hegemonic mandates of dominance. It must be conceded that African-Americans, under the press of a hostile and compulsory patriarchal order, bound and determined to destroy them, or to preserve them only in the service and at the behest of the "master" class, exercised a degree of courage and will to survive that startles the imagination even now. Although it makes good revisionist history to read this tale *liberally*, it is probably truer than we know at this distance (and truer than contemporary social practice in the community would suggest on occasion) that the captive person developed, time and again, certain ethical and sentimental features that tied her and him, *across* the landscape to others, often sold from hand to hand, of the same and different blood in a common fabric of memory and inspiration.

We might choose to call this connectedness "family," or "support structure," but that is a rather different case from the moves of a dominant symbolic order, pledged to maintain the supremacy of race. It is that order that forces "family" to modify itself when it does not mean family of the "master," or dominant enclave. It is this rhetorical and symbolic move that declares primacy over any other human and social claim, and in that political order of things, "kin," just as gender formation, has no decisive legal or social efficacy.

[. . .]

4

[. . .]

If the point is that the historic conditions of African-American women might be read as an unprecedented occasion in the national context, then gender and the arrangements of gender are both crucial and evasive. Holding, however, to a specialized reading of female gender as an *outcome* of a certain political, socio-cultural empowerment within the context of the United States, we would regard dispossession as the *loss* of gender, or one of the chief elements in an altered reading of gender: "Women are considered of no value, *unless* they continually increase their owner's stock. They were put on par with animals" [Brent 49; emphasis mine]. Linda Brent's witness appears to contradict the point I would make, but I am suggesting that even though the enslaved female reproduced other enslaved persons, we do not read "birth" in this instance as a reproduction of mothering precisely because the female, like the male, has been robbed of the parental right, the parental function. One treads dangerous ground in suggesting an equation between female gender and mothering; in fact, feminist inquiry/praxis and the actual day-to-day living of numberless American women—black and white—have gone far to break the enthrallment of a female subject-position to the theoretical and actual situation of maternity. Our task here would be lightened considerably if we could simply slide over the powerful "No," the significant *exception*. In the historic formation to which I point, however, motherhood and female gendering/ungendering appear so intimately aligned that they seem to speak the same language. At least it is plausible to say that motherhood, while it does not exhaust the problematics of female gender, offers one prominent line of approach to it. I would go farther: Because African-American women experienced uncertainty regarding their infants' lives in the historic situation, gendering, in its coeval reference to African-American women, *insinuates* an implicit and unresolved puzzle both within current feminist discourse *and* within those discursive communities that investigate the entire problematics of culture. Are we mistaken to suspect that history—at least in this instance—repeats itself yet again?

[. . .]

If we can account for an originary narrative and judicial principle that might have engendered a "Moynihan Report," many years into the twentieth century, we cannot do much better than look at Goodell's reading of the *partus sequitur ventrem*: the condition of the slave mother is "forever entailed on all her remotest posterity." This maxim of civil law, in Goodell's view, the "genuine and degrading principle of slavery, inasmuch as it places the slave upon a level with brute animals, prevails universally in the slave-holding states" [Goodell 27]. But what is the "condition" of the mother? Is it the "condition" of enslavement the writer means, or does he mean the "mark" and the "knowledge" of the *mother* upon the child that here translates into the culturally forbidden and impure? In an elision of terms, "mother" and "enslavement" are indistinct categories of the illegitimate inasmuch as each of these synonymous elements defines, in effect, a cultural situation that is *father-lacking*. Goodell, who does not only report this maxim of law as an aspect of his own factuality, but also regards it, as does Douglass, as a fundamental degradation, supposes descent and identity through the female line as comparable to a brute animality. Knowing already that there are human communities that align social reproductive procedure according to the line of the mother, and Goodell himself might have known it some years later, we can only conclude that the provisions of patriarchy, here exacerbated by the preponderant powers of an enslaving class, declare Mother Right, by definition, a negating feature of human community.

Even though we are not even talking about *any* of the matriarchal features of social production/reproduction—matrifocality, matrilinearity, matriarchy—when we speak of the enslaved person, we perceive that the dominant culture, in a fatal misunderstanding, assigns a matriarchist value where it does not belong; actually *misnames* the power of the female regarding the enslaved community. Such naming is false because the female could not, in fact, claim her child, and false, once again, because "motherhood" is not perceived in the prevailing social climate as a legitimate procedure of cultural inheritance.

The African-American male has been touched, therefore, by the *mother, handed* by her in ways that he cannot escape, and in ways that the white American male is allowed to temporize by a fatherly reprieve. This human and historic development—the text that has been inscribed on the benighted heart of the continent—takes us to the center of an inexorable difference in the depths of American women's community: the African-American woman, the mother, the daughter, becomes historically the powerful and shadowy evocation of a cultural synthesis long evaporated—the law of the Mother—only and precisely because legal enslavement removed the African-American male not so much from sight as from *mimetic* view as a partner in the prevailing social fiction of the Father's name, the Father's law.

Therefore, the female, in this order of things, breaks in upon the imagination with a forcefulness that marks both a denial and an "illegitimacy." Because of this peculiar American denial, the black American male embodies the *only* American community of males which has had the specific occasion to learn *who* the female is within itself, the infant child who bears the life against the could-be fateful gamble, against the odds of pulverization and murder, including her own. It is the heritage of the *mother* that the African-American male must regain as an aspect of his own personhood-the power of "yes" to the "female" within.

This different cultural text actually reconfigures, in historically ordained discourse, certain *representational* potentialities for African-Americans: 1) motherhood as female bloodrite is outraged, is denied, at the *very* same *time* that it becomes the founding term of a human and social enactment; 2) a dual fatherhood is set in motion, comprised of the African father's *banished* name and body and the captor father's mocking presence. In this play of paradox, only the female stands *in the flesh*, both mother and mother-dispossessed. This problematizing of gender places her, in my view, *out* of the traditional symbolics of female gender, and it is our task to make a place for this different social subject. In doing so, we are less interested in joining the ranks of gendered femaleness than gaining the *insurgent* ground as female social subject. Actually *claiming* the monstrosity (of a female with the potential to "name", which her culture imposes in blindness, "Sapphire" might rewrite after all a radically different text for a female empowerment.

From: Spillers, Hortense. "Mama's Baby, Papa's Maybe: An American Grammar Book." *dia critics* 17:2 (1987), 64–81. © 1987 Cornell University. Reprinted with permission of Johns Hopkins University Press.

Works Cited

Barthes, Roland. *Mythologies*. Trans. Annette Lavers. New York: Hill and Wang, 1972.

Blassingame, John. *The Slave Community: Plantation Life in the Antebellum South*. New York: Oxford UP, 1972.

Brent, Linda. *Incidents in the Life of a Slave Girl*. Ed. L. Maria Child. Introduced by Walter Teller. Rpt. New York: Harvest/HBJ Book, 1973.

Davis, Angela Y. *Women, Race, and Class*. New York: Random House, 1981.

De Azurara, Gomes Eannes. *The Chronicle of the Discovery and Conquest of Guinea*. Trans. C. Raymond Beazley and Edgar Prestage. London: Hakluyt Society, 1896, 1897, in Elizabeth Donnan, *Documents Illustrative of the History of the Slave Trade to America*. Washington, DC: Carnegie Institution of Washington, 1932, 1:18–41.

Donnan, Elizabeth. *Documents Illustrative of the History of the Slave Trade to America*, 4 vols. Washington, DC: The Carnegie Institution of Washington, 1932.

Douglass, Frederick. *Narrative of the Life of Frederick Douglass an American Slave, Written by Himself*. Rpt. New York: Signet Books, 1968.

El-Shabazz, Malcolm El-Hajj Malik. *Autobiography of Malcolm X*. With Alex Haley. Introduced by M. S. Handler. New York: Grove Press, 1966.

Equiano, Olaudah. "The Life of Olaudah Equiano, or Gustavus Vassa, The African, Written by Himself," in *Great Slave Narratives*. Introduced and selected by Arna Bontemps. Boston: Beacon Press, 1969.1–192.

Faulkner, William. *The Mansion*. New York: Vintage Books, 1965.

Frazier, E. Franklin. *The Negro Family in the United States*. Rev. with foreword by Nathan Glazer. Chicago: The U of Chicago P, 1966.

Genovese, Eugene. *Roll, Jordan, Roll: The World the Slaves Made*. New York: Pantheon Books, 1974.

Goodell, William. *The American Slave Code in Theory and Practice Shown by Its Statutes, Judicial Decisions, and Illustrative Facts*, 3rd ed. New York: American and Foreign Anti-Slavery Society, 1853.

Hooks, Bell. *Ain't I a Woman: Black Women and Feminism*. Boston: South End Press, 1981.

Klein, Herbert S. "African Women in the Atlantic Slave Trade." *Women and Slavery in Africa*. Ed. Claire C. Robertson and Martin A. Klein. Madison: U of Wisconsin P, 1983.29–39.

Meillassoux, Claude. "Female Slavery." *Women and Slavery in Africa*. Ed. Claire C. Robertson and Martin A. Klein. Madison: U of Wisconsin P, 1983.49–67.

Moynihan, Daniel P. "The Moynihan Report" [*The Negro Family: The Case for National Action.* Washington, DC: U.S. Department of Labor, 1965]. *The Moynihan Report and the Politics of Controversy: A Transaction Social Science and Public Policy Report.* Ed. Lee Rainwater and William L. Yancey. Cambridge: MIT Press, 1967.47–94.

Robertson, Claire C., and Martin A. Klein, eds. *Women and Slavery in Africa.* Madison: U of Wisconsin P, 1983.

Scarry, Elaine. *The Body in Pain: The Making and Unmaking of the World.* New York: Oxford UP, 1985.

Smith, Valerie. "Loopholes of Retreat: Architecture and Ideology in Harriet Jacobs's *Incidents in the Life of a Slave Girl.*" Paper presented at the 1985 American Studies Association Meeting, San Diego. Cited in Henry Louis Gates, Jr. "What's Love Got to Do with It?" *New Literary History* 18.2 (Winter 1987): 360.

Strobel, Margaret. "Slavery and Reproductive Labor in Momoasa." *Women and Slavery in Africa.* Ed. Claire C. Robertson and Martin A. Klein. Madison: U of Wisconsin P, 1983.111–130.

Suleiman, Susan Rubin, ed. *The Female Body in Western Culture.* Cambridge: Harvard UP, 1986.

Todorov, Tzvetan. *The Conquest of America: The Question of the Other.* Trans. Richard Howard. New York: Harper Colophon Books, 1984.

White, Deborah Grey. *Ar'n't I a* Woman? *Female Slaves in the Plantation South.* New York: Norton, 1985.

9 TransMaterialities

Trans★/Matter/Realities and Queer Political Imaginings

Karen Barad

Karen Barad's "TransMaterialities" is an electrifying read. Like a bolt of lightning, it zigzags thrillingly between and across many seemingly unrelated topics: quantum physics, meteorology, and Frankenstein's monster, to name but a few. Barad is theoretical particle physicist and theorist of queer/trans studies who works in cultural studies of science and technology. In this article, Barad addresses the literal materiality of desire at both cosmic and subatomic levels, to offer a jolting vision of a universe playing with itself, teeming with potential, experimenting with ever-shifting possibilities for becoming otherwise, through infinite shimmering movements across the virtual/physical boundary. Nature, in other words, is inherently queer and trans. In addition to offering a cogent introduction for non-specialists to esoteric fields of scientific study, Barad puts Stryker's "Frankenstein" article in deeper conversation with science studies while also critiquing its use of "blackness" to describe the chaotic void from which material existence emerges.

Lightning is a reaching toward, an arcing dis/juncture, a striking response to charged yearnings.[1]

A dark sky. Deep darkness, without a glimmer of light to settle the eye. Out of the blue, tenuous electrical sketches scribbled with liquid light appear/disappear faster than the human eye can detect. Flashes of potential, hints of possible lines of connection alight now and again. Desire builds, as the air crackles with anticipation. Lightning bolts are born of such charged yearnings. Branching expressions of prolonged longing, barely visible filamentary gestures, disjointed tentative luminous doodlings—each faint excitation of this desiring field is a contingent and suggestive inkling of the light show yet to come. No continuous path from sky to ground can satisfy its wild imaginings, its insistence on experimenting with different possible ways to connect, playing at all matter of errant wanderings in a virtual exploration of diverse forms of coupling and dis/connected alliance. Against a dark sky it is possible to catch glimmers of the wild energetics of indeterminacies in action.

Like lightning, this article is an exploration of charged yearnings and the sparking of new imaginaries. It is an experimental article about matter's experimental nature—its propensity to test out every un/imaginable path, every im/possibility. Matter is promiscuous and inventive in its agential wanderings: one might even dare say, imaginative. Imaginings, at least in the scientific imagination, are clearly material. Like lightning, they entail a process involving electrical potential buildup and flows of charged particles: neurons transmitting

DOI: 10.4324/9781003206255-12

electrochemical signals across synaptic gaps and through ion channels that spark awareness in our brains. This is not to suggest that imagination is merely an individual subjective experience, nor a unique capacity of the human mind. Nor is it to rely solely on a scientific imaginary of what matter is, nor a materialism that would elide questions of labor. Nor is the point to merely insist on an accounting of the material conditions of possibility for imagining, though this is surely important. Rather, what is at issue here is the nature of matter and its agential capacities for imaginative, desiring, and affectively charged forms of bodily engagements. This article explores the materiality of imagining together with the imaginative capacities of materiality—although it does so less by linear argumentation than by the zigzagged dis/continuous musings of lightning. Electrical energy runs through disparate topics in what follows: lightning, primordial ooze, frogs, Frankenstein, trans rage, queer self-birthing, the quantum vacuum, virtual particles, queer touching, bioelectricity, Franken-frogs, monstrous re/generations.

This is an experimental piece with a political investment in creating new political imaginaries and new understandings of imagining in its materiality. Not imaginaries of some future or elsewhere to arrive at or be achieved as a political goal but, rather, imaginaries with material existences in the thick now of the present—imaginaries that are attuned to the condensations of past and future condensed into each moment; imaginaries that entail superpositions of many beings and times, multiple im/possibilities that coexist and are iteratively intra-actively reconfigured; imaginaries that are material explorations of the mutual indeterminacies of being and time.[2]

Electrifying Origins/Flashes of Things to Come

> During this short voyage I saw the lightning playing on the summit of Mont Blanc in the most beautiful figures.
>
> —Mary Shelley, *Frankenstein*

Lightning is an energizing play of a desiring field. Its tortuous path is an enlivening exploration of possible connections. Not a trail from the heavens to the ground but an electrifying yearning for connection that precedes this and that, here and there, now and then.[3]

Lightning is a striking phenomenon. It jolts our memories, flashing images on the retina of our mind's eye. Lightning arouses a sense of the primordial, enlivening questions of origin and materialization. It conjures haunting cultural images of the summoning of life through its energizing effects, perhaps most memorable in the classic films *Der Golem* (1920) and *Frankenstein* (1931). And it brings to mind credible (if not uncontroversial) scientific explanations of the electrifying origins of life: nature's fury shocking primordial ooze to life, an energizing jump start. Lightning, it seems, has always danced on the razor's edge between science and imagination.

Working with his mentor, the Nobel laureate Harold Urey, in 1953, the chemist Stanley Miller began a series of experiments that would lend support to Alexander Oparin and J. S. B. Haldane's hypothesis that primitive conditions on earth would be favorable for the production of organic molecules (the basis for the evolution of life) out of inorganic ones.[4] Miller used a sparking device to mimic lightning, a crucial ingredient in this genesis story. Filling a flask with water, methane, ammonia, and hydrogen, Miller sent electrical currents through the mixture. Analyzing the resulting soup of chemicals, he found the evidence that he was looking for: "a brown broth rich in amino acids, the building blocks of proteins."[5] "It was as if they were waiting to be bidden into existence. Suddenly the origin of life looked easy."[6]

Marking the beginning of experimental research into the origins of life, the Miller–Urey experiment did not seal the deal, but it was powerfully evocative of what might (yet) have been. The theory of the electrical origins of life—inorganic matter shocked into life's organic building blocks by an electrifying energy (whose own animacy seems to belie the alleged lifelessness of so-called inanimate matter)—is a controversial piece of science that created a fair amount of heat during Miller's lifetime. But no matter how many times skeptics claim to have put it to rest, it continues to be revived.

Miller's latest experiment was completed in 2008. He was dead by then. The experiment had begun fifty-five years earlier. Miller's intellectual offspring discovered, after his death, that he had not analyzed all his data. Opening the well-marked vials that lay dormant for decades, the researchers performed the analysis. They were shocked and delighted to be able to draw a significantly more compelling result from a once-dead experiment that would breathe new life into the theory: Miller's data revealed not five but twenty-three amino acids!

Characterizing Miller's experimental apparatus as a "Frankensteinesque contraption of glass bulbs," *Scientific American* completes the electrical circuit of cultural associations.[7]

Shocking brute matter to life. What makes us think that matter is lifeless to begin with?

Lightning mucks with origins. Lightning is a lively play of in/determinacy, troubling matters of self and other, past and future, life and death. It electrifies our imaginations and our bodies. If lightning enlivens the boundary between life and death, if it exists on the razor's edge between animate and inanimate, does it not seem to dip sometimes here and sometimes there on either side of the divide?

It was in witnessing lightning's enormous power that Victor Frankenstein took upon himself the mantle of science.

> When I was about fifteen years old, . . . we witnessed a most violent and terrible thunderstorm. As I stood at the door, on a sudden I beheld a stream of fire issue from an old and beautiful oak which stood about twenty yards from our house; and so soon as the dazzling light vanished, the oak had disappeared, and nothing remained but a blasted stump. . . .
>
> Before this I was not unacquainted with the more obvious laws of electricity. On this occasion a man of great research in natural philosophy was with us, and excited by this catastrophe, he entered on the explanation of a theory which he had formed on the subject of electricity and galvanism, which was at once new and astonishing to me.[8]

And thus Victor Frankenstein was converted to galvanism.

Galvanism inspired both Mary Shelley and her famed protagonist. Shelley was fascinated by the experiments of her contemporary, Luigi Galvani, an eighteenth century physician, anatomist, and physiologist who, while preparing dinner on his balcony one stormy night—the atmosphere crackling with electrical buildup—noticed something uncanny that would change the course of his scientific studies. As he touched the frog legs—strung out on a line before him—with a pair of scissors, they twitched. Thereafter, he took it upon himself to study in a systematic fashion the application of electricity—the "spark of life," as Shelley referred to it—to frog legs and other animal parts. Galvani concluded that electricity was an innate force of life, that an "animal electricity" pervaded living organisms. As Jessica Johnson writes, "Galvani proved not only that recently-dead muscle tissue can respond to external electrical stimuli, but that muscle and nerve cells possess an intrinsic electrical force responsible for muscle contractions and nerve conduction in living organisms."[9]

It was a short leap from there to consider that if dead frog legs could be animated by electricity—the secret of life—the harnessing of nature's fury might be used to resurrect the dead or even give life to a creature made of human parts gathered from an array of different corpses. In the introduction to *Frankenstein*, Shelly writes, "Perhaps a corpse would be re-animated; galvanism had given token of such things: perhaps the component parts of a creature might be manufactured, brought together, and endured with vital warmth." Galvani's experiments sparked the interest of other scientists, and soon severed limbs and an assortment of dissected and expired animals and animal parts were animated by electrical impulses. Perhaps most (in)famously, his nephew, the physicist Giovanni Aldini, stimulated animal parts like those of cows, dogs, horses, and sheep.

Electrified by galvanism, Aldini was ready to shock nearly anything, alive or dead, that he could get his hands on. He was among the first to use electroshock treatment on those deemed mentally ill, and reported complete electrical cures. Not satisfied with his experiments on animal corpses, he performed his shock treatments on executed criminals. He recorded the findings of his 1803 experiment on the executed body of George Foster:

> The jaw began to quiver, the adjoining muscles were horribly contorted, and the left eye actually opened. . . . The action even of those muscles furthest distant from the points of contact with the arc was so much increased as almost to give an appearance of re-animation . . . vitality might, perhaps, have been restored, if many circumstances had not rendered it impossible.[10]

It is not difficult to complete the circuit of sparking disjuncture between Aldini's ghoulish experiments and those of Dr. Frankenstein.

Even while Shelley labored to write *Frankenstein*, the scientific atmosphere crackled with controversy over the nature of the relationship between life and electricity.

Bioelectricity was in the air, sparking the imagination of nineteenth-century scientists. As Cynthia Graber reports, "Many efforts, including using electricity to treat hysteria and melancholia, amounted to little more than quackery."[11] But some explorations gained scientific credibility and established the basis for current medical practices. For example, a textbook published in 1816 suggests the use of electric shock to revive a stopped heart.[12]

Monstrous Selves, Transgender Empowerment, Transgender Rage

> The monster always represents the disruption of categories, the destruction of boundaries, and the presence of impurities and so we need monsters and we need to recognize and celebrate our own monstrosities.
>
> —Judith Halberstam, *Skin Shows*

Electricity can arrest the heart. It is also capable of bringing a heart back from a state of lifelessness. It can animate its rhythmic drumbeat—the periodic pulsing of life's electrical song—in once arrested or arrhythmic hearts. Monstrosity, like electrical jolts, cuts both ways. It can serve to demonize, dehumanize, and demoralize. It can also be a source of political agency. It can empower and radicalize.

In an unforgettable, powerful, and empowering performative piece, "My Words to Victor Frankenstein above the Village of Chamounix," Susan Stryker embraces the would-be epithet of monstrosity, harnessing its energy and power to transform despair and suffering into empowering rage, self-affirmation, theoretical inventiveness, political action, and the energizing vitality of materiality in its animating possibilities.[13] Remarking on her affinity with Frankenstein's monster, she writes:

> The transsexual body is an unnatural body. It is the product of medical science. It is a technological construction. It is flesh torn apart and sewn together again in a shape other than that in which it was born. In these circumstances, I find a deep affinity between myself as a transsexual woman and the monster in Mary Shelley's *Frankenstein*. Like the monster, I am too often perceived as less than fully human due to the means of my embodiment; like the monster's as well, my exclusion from human community fuels a deep and abiding rage in me that I, like the monster, direct against the conditions in which I must struggle to exist.[14]

Making political and personal alliance with Frankenstein's monster, she intervenes in naturalizing discourses about the nature of nature, an emphasis that resonates with themes in this essay.

> Hearken unto me, fellow creatures. I who have dwelt in a form unmatched with my desire, I whose flesh has become an assemblage of incongruous anatomical parts, I who achieve the similitude of a natural body only through an unnatural process, I offer you this warning: the Nature you bedevil me with is a lie. Do not trust it to protect you from what I represent, for it is a fabrication that cloaks the groundlessness of the privilege you seek to maintain for yourself at my expense. You are as constructed as me; the same anarchic womb has birthed us both. I call upon you to investigate your nature as I have been compelled to confront mine.[15]

This passage speaks with razor-sharp directedness to those who would position their own bodies as natural against the monstrosity of trans embodiment: examine your own nature, stretch your own body out on the examining table, do the work that needs to be done on yourself (with all this charge's intended multiple meanings), and discover the seams and sutures that make up the matter of your own body. Materiality in its entangled psychic and physical manifestations is always already a patchwork, a suturing of disparate parts.[16]

Toward the end of the piece, Stryker embraces the fecundity of the "chaos and blackness"—the "anarchic womb"—as the matrix for generative nonheterosexual-reproductive birthing, "for we have done the hard work of constituting ourselves on our own terms, against the natural order. Though we forgo the privilege of naturalness, we are not deterred, for we ally ourselves instead with the chaos and blackness from which Nature itself spills forth."[17] This is a reference to the entangled birthing story that Stryker tells. She begins by sharing with the reader the joys and the pain of being in intimate connection with her partner while she was giving birth. This is a birth born of queer kinship relations: not the product of a heteronormative coupling, but a phenomenon rich with multiple entanglements, including a markedly nonnormative delivery room support team. Stryker is attuned to her partner during the birth, bodily and emotionally, yet she is also painfully aware that the physicality of birthing a being from her own womb is denied to her by the specificity of her constructed enfleshment. She describes the raw pain of being part of a process that she could not bring to fruition in the bodily way that she yearns for. This gives way to a painful birthing of transgender rage that becomes, in turn, the womb through which she rebirths herself. This radically queer configuring of spacetimemattering constitutes an uncanny topological dynamic that arrests straight tales of birthing and kinship, and gives birth to new modes of generativity, including but not limited to the generativity of a self-birthed womb. It is nearly impossible not to feel the tug of other entanglements in this queer origin story. In particular, this story reverberates with a queer reading of the Genesis moment when the earth emerges out of the chaos and the void, from a chaotic nothingness, an electrifying atmosphere silently crackling with thunderous possibilities. Nature emerges from a self-birthed womb fashioned out of a raging nothingness. A queer origin, an originary queerness, an originary birthing that is always already a rebirthing. Nature is birthed out of chaos and void, *tohu v'vohu*, an echo, a diffracted/differentiating/différancing murmuring, an originary repetition without sameness, regeneration out of a fecund nothingness.

Quantum Field Theory: Nothingness as the Scene of Wild Activities

> Physicists . . . took the vacuum as something substantial . . . the scene of wild activities.
> —Cao and Schweber

Nothingness. The void. An absence of matter. The blank page. Utter silence. No thing, no thought, no awareness. Complete ontological insensibility.[18]

From the viewpoint of classical physics, the vacuum is complete emptiness: it has no matter and no energy. But the quantum principle of ontological indeterminacy calls the existence of such a zero-energy, zero-matter state into question or, rather, makes it into a question with no decidable answer. Not a settled matter or, rather, no matter. And if the energy of the vacuum is not determinately zero, it is not determinately empty. In fact, this indeterminacy not only is responsible for the void not being nothing (while not being something) but may in fact be the source of all that is, a womb that births existence.

Birth and death, it turns out, are not the sole prerogative of the animate world; so-called inanimate beings also have finite lives. "Particles can be born and particles can die," explains one physicist. In fact, "it is a matter of birth, life, and death that requires the development of a new subject in physics, that of quantum field theory Quantum field theory is a response to the ephemeral nature of life."[19]

Quantum field theory (QFT) was invented in the 1920s, shortly after the development of (nonrelativistic single-particle) quantum mechanics. It is a theory that combines insights from the classical theory of electromagnetic fields (mid-nineteenth century), special relativity (1905), and quantum mechanics (1920s). QFT takes us to a deeper level of understanding of quantum physics.[20] It has important things to say about the nature of matter and nothingness and the indeterminateness of their alleged distinguishability and separability. QFT is a call, an alluring murmur of the insensible within the sensible to radically work the nature of being and time. According to QFT, the vacuum cannot be determinately nothing because the indeterminacy principle allows for fluctuations *of* the quantum vacuum. How can we understand "vacuum fluctuations"? First, it is necessary to know a few things about what physicists mean by the notion of a *field*.

A field in physics is something that has a physical quantity associated with every point in space-time. Or you can think of it as a pattern of energy distributed across space and time. It may be difficult to grasp this notion without specific examples. Consider a bar magnet with iron filings sprinkled around it. The filings will quickly line up in accordance with the strength and direction of the magnetic field at every point. Or consider an electric field. The electric field is a desiring field born of charged yearnings.[21] When it comes to mutual attraction the rule is opposites (i.e., opposite charges) attract. The notion of a field is a way to express the desires of each entity for the other. The attraction between a proton (a positively charged particle) and an electron (a particle with negative charge) can be expressed in terms of fields as follows: the proton emanates an electric field; the field travels outward in all directions at the speed of light. When the electric field of the proton reaches the electron, it feels the proton's desire pulling it toward it. Likewise, the electron sends out its own field, which is felt by the proton. Sitting in each other's fields, they feel a mutual tug in each other's direction.[22]

Now we add quantum physics and special relativity to classical field theory. Quantum physics enters into QFT most prominently in terms of the discretization of physical observables (quantizing or making discrete physical quantities that classical physics assumed were continuous), and the play of indeterminacy in energy and time. And special relativity speaks to matter's impermanence: matter can be converted into energy and vice versa. Putting these ideas together, we get the following. Fields are patterns of energy. When fields are quantized, the energy is quantized. But energy and matter are equivalent. And so an essential feature of QFT is that there is a correspondence between fields (energy) and particles (matter). The quantum of the electromagnetic field is a photon—a quantum of light. And electrons are understood to be the quanta of an electron field. (There are many other kinds of quanta. For example, the quantum of the gravitational field is a graviton.)

Now let us return to our question: what is a vacuum fluctuation? When it comes to the quantum vacuum, as with all quantum phenomena, ontological indeterminacy is at the heart of (the) matter . . . and no matter. Indeed, it is impossible to pin down a state of no matter or even of matter, for that matter. The crux of this strange non/state of affairs is the so-called energy-time indeterminacy principle, but because energy and matter are equivalent we will sometimes call it the "being-time" or "time-being" indeterminacy principle. The point, for our purposes, is that an indeterminacy in the energy of the vacuum translates into an indeterminacy in the number of particles associated with the vacuum, which means the vacuum is not (determinately) empty, nor is it (determinately) not empty. These particles that correspond to the quantum fluctuation of the vacuum, that are and are not there as a result of the time-being indeterminacy relation, are called "virtual particles." *Virtual particles are quantized indeterminacies-in-action.* Virtual particles are not present (and not absent), but they are material. In fact, *most of what matter is, is virtual.* Virtual particles do not traffic in a metaphysics of presence. They do not exist in space and time. They are ghostly non/existences that teeter on the edge of the infinitely fine blade between being and nonbeing. Virtuality is admittedly difficult to grasp. Indeed, this is its very nature.

Virtual particles are not in the void but *of* the void. They are on the razor's edge of non/being. The void is a lively tension, a desiring orientation toward being/becoming. The void is flush with yearning, bursting with innumerable imaginings of what might yet (have) be(en). Vacuum fluctuations are virtual deviations/variations from the classical zero-energy state of the void. That is, *virtuality is the material wanderings/wonderings of nothingness; virtuality is the ongoing thought experiment the world performs with itself.* Indeed, quantum physics tells us that *the void is an endless exploration of all possible couplings of virtual particles, a "scene of wild activities."*

The quantum vacuum is more like an ongoing questioning of the nature of emptiness than anything like a lack. The ongoing questioning of itself (and *itself* and *it* and *self*) is what generates, or rather *is*, the structure of nothingness. The vacuum is no doubt doing its own experiments with non/being. In/determinacy is not the state of a thing but an unending dynamism.

Pace Democritus, particles do not take their place in the void; rather, they are constitutively inseparable from it. And the void is not vacuous. It is a living, breathing indeterminacy of non/being. The vacuum is an extravagant inexhaustible exploration of virtuality, where virtual particles are having a field day performing experiments in being and time.[23]

[. . .]

Lightning: Responses to a Desiring Field

Lightning is an energizing response to a highly charged field. The buildup to lightning electrifies the senses; the air crackles with desire.[24]

By some mechanism that scientists have yet to fully explain, a storm cloud becomes extremely electrically polarized—electrons are stripped from the atoms that they were once attached to and gather at the lower part of the cloud closest to the earth, leaving the cloud with an overall negative charge. In response, the electrons that make up atoms of the earth's surface burrow into the ground to get farther away from the buildup of negative charges at the near edge of the cloud, leaving the earth's surface with an overall positive charge. In this way a strong electric field is set up between earth and cloud, and the yearning will not be satisfied without the buildup being discharged. The desire to find a conductive path joining the two becomes all-consuming.

[. . .]

A lightning bolt is not a straightforward resolution of the buildup of a charge difference between the earth and a storm cloud: a lightning bolt does not simply proceed from storm cloud to the earth along a unidirectional (if somewhat erratic) path; rather, flirtations alight here and there and now and again as stepped leaders and positive streamers gesture toward possible forms of connection to come. The path that lightning takes not only is not predictable but does not make its way according to some continuous unidirectional path between sky and ground. Though far from microscopic in scale, it seems that we are witnessing a quantum form of communication—a process of iterative intra-activity.[25]

[. . .]

Quantum Phenomena: Entanglements of Disparate Parts

This article is a patchwork. Made of disparate parts. Or so it may seem. But why should we understand parts as individually constructed building blocks or disconnected pieces of one or another forms of original wholeness? After all, to be a part is not to be absolutely apart but to be constituted and threaded through with the entanglements of parting. That is, if "parts," by definition, arise from divisions or cuts, it does not necessarily follow that cuts sever or break things off, either spatially or temporally, producing absolute differences of this and that, here and there, now and then. *Intra-actions* enact cuts that cut (things) together-apart (one move). So a patchwork would not be a sewing together of individual bits and pieces but a phenomenon that always already holds together, whose pattern of differentiating entangling may not be recognized but is indeed re-membered. Memory is not the recording of events held by a mind but marked historialities ingrained in the world's becoming. Memory is a field of enfolded patterns of differentiating-entangling. Remembering is not a process of recollection, of the reproduction of what was, of assembling and ordering events like puzzle pieces fit together by fixing where each has its place. Rather, it is a matter of remembering, of tracing entanglements, responding to yearnings for connection, materialized into fields of longing/belonging, of regenerating what never was but might yet have been. This article is dedicated to rememberings, to reconfiguring anew seemingly disparate parts.

The task now is to attempt to stitch together, if only imperfectly, the pieces of this monstrous article by tracing a few of the uncountable and generative entanglements in their ongoing reconfiguring. What do we have so far? Lightning, primordial ooze, electrifying origins, frogs, galvanism, Frankenstein, trans rage, queer self-birthing/regeneration, fecund void, quantum vacuum, virtual particles, indeterminate wanderings, lightning's errant pathways, queer touching, bioelectricity, Franken-frogs, monstrous re/generations, the promise of monsters, future cures, and radical im/possibilities.

Let us begin by learning just a bit more about the striking phenomena of lightning and bioelectricity. To see lightning from above the earth's atmosphere (again I encourage the reader to stop reading and have a look at this impressive phenomenon) is to see something visually akin to the flashings of the electric (pre) face of the embryonic tadpole.[26] Both the becoming of lightning and the becoming of face exhibit flashes that mark out the traces of (what might yet) be-coming. Preceding the flash of a lightning bolt, and preceding gene involvement in cell differentiation, electrons and photons play at making virtual diagrams, flashes of light painting possibilities across the sky and across an embryo, hinting at things-to-come. What I am suggesting is that as instances of the virtual play of electron-photon intra-actions that QFT tells us are the elemental happenings of electromagnetic phenomena (all such phenomena, including the ones presently under consideration), these electromagnetic phenomena in their (ongoing) be-coming illuminate an intrinsic feature of materiality: *matter's ongoing experimenting with itself—the queer dance of being-time indeterminacy, the imaginative play of presence/absence, here/there, now/then*, that holds the disparate parts together-apart.

[. . .]

Virtual Trans-Matter-Realities and Queer Political Imaginaries

> I find no shame . . . in acknowledging my egalitarian relationship with non-human material Being; everything emerges from the same matrix of possibilities.
> —Stryker, "My Words to Victor Frankenstein above the Village of Chamounix"

The promise of monsters is a regenerative politics, an invitation to explore new ways of being in touch, new forms of becoming, new possibilities for kinship, alliance, and change.[27] Regeneration understood as a quantum phenomenon brings indeterminacy's radical potential to the fore. *The indeterminacy of being-time/time-being means that matter/materiality is a matter of material wanderings/wonderings, a virtual exploration of what might yet be/have been, dispersed across spacetimebeing and condensed into each material bit-here-now, every morsel (each "dressed point") of spacetimemattering.*

The virtual is not a set of individual possibilities, one of which might yet be realized or actualized.[28] Virtual possibilities are not what is absent relative to the real's presence. They are not the roads not taken or some yet unrealized potential future, the other to actual lived reality. The virtual is a superposition of im/possibilities, energetic throbs of the nothingness, material forces of creativity and generativity. Virtual possibilities are material explorations that are integral to what matter is. Matter is not the given, the unchangeable, the bare facts of nature. It is not inanimate, lifeless, eternal. Matter is an imaginative material exploration of non/being, creatively regenerative, an ongoing trans*/formation. Matter is a condensation of dispersed and multiple beings-times, where the future and past are diffracted into now, into each moment. Matter is caught up in its own and others' desiring fields. It cannot help but touch itself in an infinite exploration of its (im/possible) be(com)ing(s). And in touching it/self, it partners promiscuously and perversely with otherness in a radical ongoing deconstruction and (re)configuring of itself. Matter is a wild exploration of trans* animacy, self-experimentations/self-re-creations, not in an autopoietic mode, but on the contrary, in a radical undoing of "self," of individualism. Ever lively, never identical with itself, it is uncountably multiple, mutable. Matter is not mere being, but its ongoing un/doing. Nature is agential trans*materiality/trans-matter-reality in its ongoing re(con)figuring, where trans is not a matter of changing *in* time, from this to that, but an undoing of "this" and "that," an ongoing reconfiguring *of* spacetimemattering in an iterative reworking of past, present, future integral to the play of the indeterminacy of being-time.[29]

The electric body—*at all scales*, atmospheric, subatomic, molecular, organismic—is a quantum phenomenon generating new imaginaries, new lines of research, new possibilities.[30] The (re)generative possibilities are endless. Fodder for potent trans★ imaginaries for reconfiguring future/past lived realities, for regenerating what never was but might yet have been. Can we cultivate bioelectrical science's radical potential, subverting Dr. Frankenstein's grab for power over life itself, aligning (neo)galvanism with trans★ desires, not in order to have control over life but to empower and galvanize the disenfranchised and breathe life into new forms of queer agency and embodiment? Can we (re)generate what was missing in fleshiness but materially present in virtuality? Can we (re)generate what our bodies sense but cannot yet touch? Can we find ways to adjust the appropriate ion potential to activate and generate new fields of re-membering? Can we learn to reconfigure our fleshliness bit by bit by slowly changing the flow of ions? Can dis-membering as well as re-membering be facilitated through such charged reconfigurings of molecular flows? Can we trans/form, regenerate, dismember, and re-member anew fleshly bodies in their materiality? And if these fleshy hopes feel cruel to us sometimes, especially perhaps when reality seems impossibly hard and fixed and our own naturalcultural bodies and desires feel immobilized, if there are times when we have to face the knife, tear ourselves open, draw blood, might a regenerative politics with all its monstrously queer possibilities still serve to recharge our imaginations and our electric body-spirits, helping us transition from momentary political and spiritual rigor mortis to living raging animacy?

Surely these imaginings of the queer potential of regenerative science (and quantum theory more generally) should not be (mis)understood as an uncritical embrace of science's utopian promise. No meditation on Frankenstein could entertain for a moment such a straight alliance with the scripted equation "science = progress," indeed, as the very incarnation of this promise. There is no illusion of queer regeneration being a bloodless affair.

The promise of regenerative medicine is surely not inherently innocent, progressive, or liberatory. It does not constitute an innocent mode of engagement with science, divorced from any heteronormative reproductive impulses. Indeed, its own quite explicit commitment to normative ideas of embodiment, able-bodiedness, and naturalness belie any such suggestion. On the contrary, its goals are to renormalize and eliminate bodily irregularities in a quest to honor Nature and her intentions, if only by doing her one better. The current bioelectric studies of regeneration are already aligning themselves with promises of curing cancer, birth defects, and disabilities because of lost body parts.[31] Levin's initial motivation was to create robots that could heal themselves. Projects in the service of the military-industrial complex, capitalism, racism, and colonialism cannot be disentangled from the practices of modern science. Nonetheless, even as "science seeks to contain and colonize the radical threat posed by a particular transgender strategy of resistance to the coerciveness of gender," and even if "its cultural politics are aligned with a deeply conservative attempt to stabilize gendered identity in service of the naturalized heterosexual order," this is not reason to believe that trans★ desires can be corralled into cooperation.[32] In alliance with this crucial point, this article engages with science in a mode that invites us to imagine not only the possibilities of subverting science's conservative agendas from the outside, as it were, but also those of opening up science from the inside and serving as midwife to its always already deconstructive nature.

Significantly, according to QFT nature is an ongoing questioning of itself—of what constitutes naturalness. Indeed, nature's indeterminacy entails its ongoing un/doing. In other words, nature itself *is* an ongoing deconstructing of naturalness. As I have shown in this brief encounter with quantum field theory, the void is "the scene of wild activities," perverse and promiscuous couplings, queer goings-on that make pre-AIDS bathhouses look tame. The void is a virtual exploration of all manner of possible trans★/formations. Nature is perverse at its core; nature is unnatural. For trans★, queer, and other marginalized people, "The collective assumptions of the naturalized order [can] overwhelm [us]. Nature exerts such a hegemonic oppression."[33] The stakes in denaturalizing nature are not insignificant. Demonstrating nature's queerness, its trans★-embodiment, exposing the monstrous face of nature itself in the undoing of naturalness holds significant political potential. The point is that the monstrously large space of agency unleashed in the indeterminate play of virtuality in all its un/doings may constitute a trans-subjective material field of im/possibilities worth exploring. And the political potential does not stop with regeneration, for there are other wild dimensions within and without that rage with possibilities. *For all its entangled history with capitalism, colonialism, and the military-industrial complex, QFT not only contains its own undoing—in a performative exploration/materialization of a subversive materialism—but in an important sense makes that very undoing its im/proper object of study.*[34]

The point is not to make trans or queer into universal features and dilute their subversive potentials. The point is to make plain the undoing of universality, the importance of the radical specificity of materiality as iterative materialization. Nor is this to set trans as an abstraction, to deny it its fleshly lived reality, sacrificing its embodiment in an appropriative embrace of the latest theory trends. What is needed is not a universalization of trans or queer experience stripped of all its specificities (as inflected through race, nationality, ethnicity, class, and other normalizing apparatuses of power), setting these terms up as concepts that float above the materiality of particular embodied experiences, but to make alliances with, to build on an already existing radical tradition (a genealogy going back at least to Marx) that troubles nature and its naturalness "all the way down." In doing so, it would be a mistake to neglect the spaces of political agency *within* science—its own deconstructive forces produce radical openings that may help us imagine not only new possibilities, new matter/realities, but also new understandings of the nature of change and its possibilities.

Queer kinship is a potent political formation, crucial to Stryker's forceful analysis. Imagine how the possibilities for alliance with nature's ongoing radical deconstruction of naturalness might enable the (re)making of queer kinship with nature. What would it mean to reclaim our trans★ natures as natural? Not to align ourselves with essence, or the history of the mobilization of "nature" on behalf of oppression, but to recognize ourselves as part of nature's doings in its very undoing of what is natural?

Stryker's queer topological musings, both in "My Words to Victor Frankenstein," where she is giving birth to her rage that births her, and also in more recent works, reverberate with the trans★ generative mode being explored here:

> From my forward-facing perspective I look back on my body as a psychically bounded space or container that becomes energetically open through the break of its surface—a rupture experienced as interior movement, a movement that becomes generative as it encloses and invests in a new space, through a perpetually reiterative process of growing new boundaries and shedding abandoned materialities: a mobile, membranous, temporally fleeting and provisional sense of enfolding and enclosure. This is the utopian space of my ongoing poesis.[35]

This topological dynamic reverberates with QFT processes, much like the one that perverse kinds of self-touching/self-re-creating electrons enact. An electron touching itself, rebirthing/regenerating itself (there is no singular birth moment, no origin, only rebirthings/regenerating), in a process of intra-active becoming, of reconfiguring and trans-forming oneself in the self's multiple and dispersive sense of it-self where the self is intrinsically a nonself.

In her "Frankenstein" piece, Stryker writes poetically of her transgender (re)birthing in a manner that echoes the literal passage of birthed body from the liquid darkness of the womb. Her voice solicits me to diffractively intercut her words there (italicized in the text below) with those (nonitalicized below) of an electron I imagine to be speaking contrapunctually of its own perpetual (re) birthing.[36]

I am an electron. I am inseparable from the darkness, the void. *It is dark. I see a shimmering light above me.* I am one with the void I was allegedly immersed in, but from which there is no possibility of extrication. There is no myself that is separable from it. *Inside and out I am surrounded by it. Why am I not dead if there is no difference between me and what I am in?* While I struggle to come into being I am virtually annihilated and re(sub)merge into the nothingness, over and over again. Time has no meaning, no directionality. My being no more than an im/possible indeterminate yearning. Bubbling up from the nothingness, I fall back into the void that fills me and surrounds me. I return to the void and reemerge once more only to fall back again. *This [void] annihilates me. I cannot be, and yet—an excruciating impossibility—I am. I will do [everything] not to be here. . . .*

I will try out every im/possibility, every virtual intra-action with all beings, all times.

I will die for eternity.
I will learn to breathe the [void].
I will become the [void].
If I cannot change my situation I will change myself.

I am transforming in intra-action with the light above me, below me, and within me, and with all manner of other beings. I am not myself. I am becoming multiple, a dispersion of disparate kinds.

In this act of magical transformation
I recognize myself again.
I am groundless and boundless movement.
I am a furious flow.
I am one with the darkness . . .
And I am enraged.

Here at last is the chaos I held at bay.
Here at last is my strength.
I am not the [void] —
I am [a] wave [a raging amplitude, a desiring field surging, being born],
and rage
is the force that moves me.
Rage
gives me back my body
as its own fluid medium.

Rage
punches a hole in [void]
around which I coalesce
to allow the flow to come through me.

Rage
constitutes me in my primal form.
It throws my head back
pulls my lips back over my
opens my throat
and rears me up to howl:
: and no sound
dilutes
the pure quality of my rage.
form.
teeth
No sound
exists
in this place without language
my rage is a silent raving.

I am one with the speaking silence of the void, the cries of im/possibility move through me, until there erupts a raging scream without sound, without language, without comprehensibility or articulation.

Rage
throws me back at last
into this mundane reality
in this transfigured flesh
that aligns me with the power of my Being.
In birthing my rage,
my rage has rebirthed me.

Let us align ourselves with the raging nothingness, the silent howling of the void, as it trans★figures fleshy possibilities. Wandering off the straight and narrow path, wonderings alight. Trans★ desires surge forth electrifying the field of dreams and transmaterialities-to-come.

From: Karen Barad, "TransMaterialities: Trans★/Matter/Realities and Queer Political Imaginings," in *GLQ: A Journal of Lesbian and Gay Studies*, Volume 21, no. 2–3, pp. 387–422. Copyright 2015, Duke University Press. All rights reserved. Republished by permission of the copyright holder, Duke University Press. www.dukeupress.edu.

Notes

I am grateful to Mel Chen and Dana Luciano for their patience and enthusiasm and for wonderful suggestions for reeling in an article that had grown to monstrous proportions. I would like to thank Susan Stryker for graciously accepting my proposal to have some of her poetics diffractively read through mine and, especially, her willingness to have her powerful poetry interrupted by the murmurings of the void (in particular, the musings of a virtual electron that is inseparable from the void). As ever, I am grateful to Fern Feldman for her feedback and ongoing support.

1. TransMaterialities is a term that arose in the planning of UCSC's 2009 "TransMaterialities: Relating across Difference" Science Studies Cluster graduate student conference, co-organized by Harlan Weaver and Martha Kenney, with faculty sponsors Donna J. Haraway and Karen Barad. The first time I saw the playful term *matterealities* was at a conference run by Monika Buscher at Lancaster University in 2007.

2. Inspired by QFT's understanding of each moment as a condensation of other beings, places, and times, this ontological-political project resonates with Marco CuevasHewitt's call for a "futurology of the present": "The futurology of the present does not prescribe a single monolithic future, but tries instead to articulate the many alternative futures continually emerging in the perpetual present. The goal of such an endeavor is to make visible the living, breathing alternatives all around us" ("Futurology of the Present: Notes on Writing, Movement, and Time," *Journal of Aesthetics and Protest* 8 [Winter 2011–12], joaap.org/issue8/futurology.htm).

3. For more on lightning's queer quantum nature, see below, and also Karen Barad, "Nature's Queer Performativity (the authorized version)," *Kvinder, Køn & Forskning/Women, Gender, and Research* 1–2 (2012): 25–53; Vicki Kirby, *Quantum Anthropologies: Life at Large* (Durham, NC: Duke University Press, 2011).

4. Charles Darwin seems to have suggested as much. See, for example, Helen Fields, "The Origins of Life," *Smithsonian Magazine*, October 2010, www.smithsonianmag.com/science-nature/The-Origins-of-Life.html.

5. Douglas Fox, "Primordial Soup's On: Scientists Repeat Evolution's Most Famous Experiment," *Scientific American*, May 28, 2007, www.scientificamerican.com/article.cfm?id=primordial-soup-urey-miller-evolution-experiment-repeated.

6. Nick Lane, quoted in Cynthia Graber, *Electric Shock: How Electricity Could Be the Key to Human Regeneration* (2012), readmatter.com.

7. Fox, "Primordial Soup's On."

8. Mary Shelley, *Frankenstein, or The Modern Prometheus* (n.p., 1818), 15.

9. Jessica P. Johnson, "Animal Electricity, circa 1781," *Scientist*, September 28, 2011, www.the-scientist.com/?articles.view/articleNo/31078/title/Animal-Electricity-circa-1781/.

10. Aldini quoted in Anne K. Mellor, "Frankenstein: A Feminist Critique of Science," in *One Culture: Essays in Science and Literature*, 287–312, eds. George Lewis Levine and Alan Rauch (Madison: University of Wisconsin Press, 1987), 304.

11. Graber, *Electric Shock*.

12. J. D. Roger, "1816 Textbook Suggests Use of Electric Shock in Treatment of Cardiac Arrest," *Canadian Journal of Cardiology* 20, no. 14 (2004): 1486.

13. Susan Stryker, "My Words to Victor Frankenstein above the Village of Chamounix," *GLQ* 1 (1994): 237–254.

14. Stryker, "My Words," 238.

15. Stryker, "My Words," 240–241.

16. For one thing, as Judith Butler points out, "Not only is the gathering of attributes under the category of sex suspect . . . indeed, the 'unity' imposed upon the body by the category of sex is a 'disunity,' a fragmentation" (quoted in *Meeting the Universe Halfway: Quantum Physics and the Entanglement of Matter and Meaning* [Durham, NC: Duke University Press, 2007], 60). But there is much more to this point. For more details on an agential realist reworking of the nature of nature, matter/ing, and the cutting together-apart of disparate parts, see Barad, *Meeting the Universe Halfway*.

17. Stryker, "My Words," 251. I am left wondering why Stryker talks about the womb as a place of "blackness" rather than say "darkness," or even, as I suggest, "nothingness" (the void). Part of my political investment in enlarging the scope of my project to include quantum field theory (QFT) is its ability to trouble the underlying metaphysics of colonialist claims such as *terrae nullius*—the alleged void that the white settler claims to encounter in "discovering undeveloped lands," that is, lands allegedly devoid of the marks of "civilization"—a logic that associates the beginning of space and time, of place and history, with the arrival of the white man. In contrast to this doctrine, according to QFT the void is full and fecund, rich and productive, actively creative and alive. Which, of course, is not the only way to contest the racist and colonialist impulses at work but is to try to further unearth and unsettle how space and time are themselves racialized.

18. Parts of this section are borrowed from Karen Barad, *What Is the Measure of Nothingness? Infinity, Virtuality, Justice/Was ist das Maß des Nichts? Unendlichkeit, Virtualität, Gerechtigkeit*, dOCUMENTA (13): 100 Notes—100 Thoughts/100 Notizen—100 Gedanken | Book N°099, English and German edition (2012).

19. A. Zee, *Quantum Field Theory in a Nutshell*, 2nd ed. (Princeton: Princeton University Press, 2010), 4.

20. Quantum field theory does not negate the findings of quantum mechanics but builds on them. Similarly, these explorations help further articulate agential realism. As I argue below: QFT entails a radical deconstruction of identity and of the equation of matter with essence in ways that transcend even the profound un/doings of (nonrelativistic) quantum mechanics.

21. The more general term *electromagnetic field*, rather than *electric field*, is sometimes used. The interchangeability is due to the fact that electricity and magnetism were unified into a single electromagnetic force in the mid-nineteenth century.
22. While the idea of a field may seem like a convenient fiction, and was in fact originally introduced as an imaginary construct to facilitate calculations, physicists in the nineteenth century began to embrace the idea that fields are real. This shift was a result of the finding that light is an electromagnetic wave made of (nothing but) changing electric and magnetic fields.
23. This is a subtle point that I develop further elsewhere (Barad, "On Touching: The Inhuman That Therefore I Am," *Differences* 22, no. 3 [2012]: 206–223): namely, the difference between the play of indeterminacy and a rapid appearance and disappearance of particles as the hallmark of virtuality. I would argue that "flashes" of potential are traces of virtuality synchronized to clock time, but this very particular manifestation is far from the only set of possibilities in the play of virtuality. I address these issues further in a forthcoming publication.
24. Parts of this section are borrowed from Barad, "Nature's Queer Performativity."
25. I have repeatedly made the point that quantum phenomena are not restricted to some alleged "micro" domain. Perhaps a(nother) large scale example like this one will help to defeat that misconception.
26. See www.discovery.com/video-topics/other/lightning-phenomena.htm.
27. This is an invocation of Donna J. Haraway, "The Promises of Monsters: A Regenerative Politics for Inappropriate/d Others," in *Cultural Studies*, eds. Lawrence Grossberg, Cary Nelson, and Paula A. Treichler (New York: Routledge, 1992), 295–337. I have in mind here also brittle stars among other creatures who display an array of nonheteronormative modes of reproduction, including asexual reproduction through regeneration. See the discussion of the brittle star in Barad, *Meeting the Universe Halfway*, chap. 8.
28. Although a common story of measurement in quantum theory is that the "wavefunction," which represents a superposition of possibilities, is collapsed on measurement and one of the possibilities is realized, I argue that there is no collapse, that measurement intra-actions reconfigure possibilities. For more details on an agential realist solution to the measurement problem, see Barad, *Meeting the Universe Halfway*, chap. 7. The notion of the *virtual* discussed here is based on my interpretation of quantum field theory. It is not the same as Gilles Deleuze's notion of the *virtual*, although there are some interesting resonances. I discuss this further in a future publication.
29. Thinking the temporalities of transitioning outside linear and external conceptions of time seems important, and this ontology gives us new understandings of being and time that may be useful. For example, what is at issue, then, is not necessarily a matter of discovering a past that was already there or remaking a past through the lens of the present but a reconfiguring, a cutting together-apart of past-present-future in the wild play of dis/identities and untimely temporalities.
30. I have tried to make the point over and over again that quantum phenomena are *not* restricted to the so-called micro scale. Scale does not precede phenomena; scale is only materialized/defined within particular phenomena.
31. This is not to suggest that curing cancer and addressing birth defects and disabilities are not worthy goals, on the contrary. But the question of what constitutes a "defect" and a "disability" needs to be thought through in conversation with disability scholars and activists, among others.
32. Stryker. "My Words," 242.
33. Stryker, "My Words," 248. The notion of a natural order is certainly important to scientific racism as well. On the historical links between scientific racism and scientific discourses on sexuality, see, for example, Siobhan Somerville, "Scientific Racism and the Emergence of the Homosexual Body," *Journal of the History of Sexuality* 5, no. 2 (1994): 243–266.
34. I take up this issue in depth in Barad, *Infinity, Nothingness, and Justice-to-Come* (book manuscript).
35. Susan Stryker, "Dungeon Intimacies: The Poetics of Transsexual Sadomasochism," *Parallax* 14, no. 1 (2008): 36–47.
36. With apologies to Susan Stryker for disrupting her powerful poem, and with gratitude to her for her generosity and willingness to be open to this experiment in entangled poetics.

10 "Theorizing in a Void"

Sublimity, Matter, and Physics in Black Feminist Poetics

Zakiyyah Iman Jackson

In this dense knot of Black feminist thought, feminist materialisms, literary studies, philosophy, and physics, Zakiyyah Iman Jackson "works through" how the black female body and black femininity might achieve representation beyond the material-discursive terrain of Western humanism. She follows Sylvia Wynter in arguing that the Enlightenment figure of Man "over-represents" the category human, thereby consigning people who are not white men to less-than-human status. She follows Hortense J. Spillers to argue that this Eurocentric paradigm is dependent upon an obfuscated Black female body that it positions as an ontological ground for racial hierarchy. "Theorizing in a void" names the process of imagining possibilities for becoming otherwise from a seeming nothingness filled with generative yet unrealized potential. She names this space the "black *mater*(nal)," a para-ontological nonform that is at once "the sublime enabling condition of the Human" and the point of potential rupture and reformation. While Jackson does not explicitly engage trans studies as a field, she points out the impossibility of comprehending the racially marked non-normativity of the black female body within the newly emergent conceptual framework of the cis/trans gender binary.

What is it like inside of a black hole?

— Evelynn Hammonds, "Black (W)holes and the Geometry
of Black Female Sexuality"

In the modern Western imagination, blackness has no value; it is nothing. As such, it marks an opposition that signals a negation, which does not refer to contradiction. For blackness refers to matter—as The Thing; it refers to that without form—it functions as a nullification of the whole signifying order that sustains value in both its economic and ethical scenes.

— Denise Ferreira da Silva, "1 (life) ÷ 0 (blackness) = ∞ − ∞ or ∞/∞:
On Matter beyond the Equation of Value"

In "The Ceremony Must Be Found: After Humanism," Sylvia Wynter (1984) argues that the "Order/Chaos" opposition has been essential to the autopoiesis, or institution and relatively stable replication, of Man as a dynamic system. Whereas Newtonian mechanics gave rise to the idea of chaos as a consternating external threat to a linear, predictable, and law-like universe, post-Newtonian chaos theory challenged this view by no longer interpreting the two tendencies—order and chaos—as purely oppositional in their origins and effects but rather as interwoven: patterns of order arise in chaos and chaos in order. For instance, structure within

DOI: 10.4324/9781003206255-13

chaos or constrained chaos is known as a strange attractor, and spontaneous chaos potentially provides pragmatic benefits to a system by allowing for the discovery of new pathways to greater efficiency. Thus chaos is not extrinsic but constitutive to the ordering processes of a system. Yet, according to Wynter, black(ened) people are *recursively* conceived as a chaotic threat encroaching from, and appropriate to, the margins of a "universalist" system of Order.

By way of introduction, I want to draw out a few key implications of Wynter's insight and engagement with chaos theory: within the logic of an antiblack imaginary, blackness functions in extended Newtonian terms as external threat, or, to use Wynter's provocative term, as a signifier of "Ultimate Chaos" against which Man has been able to vertically institute and hegemonically figure itself under the heroic sign of Order with attendant associations of Progress, Reason, and Beauty, concealing this sense of order's dependence on the abject figures constitutive to it and the systemic historical conditions of its emergence and renewal.[1] Wynter (1984: 37) writes:

> Different forms of segregating the Ultimate Chaos that was the Black—from the *apartheid* of the South to the lynchings in both North and South, to their deprivation of the vote, and confinement in an inferior secondary education sphere, to the logic of the jobless/ghetto/drugs/crime/prison archipelagoes of today—ensured that . . . the "active creation" of the type of Chaos, which the dominant model needs for the replication of its own system, would continue. It thus averted any effort to find the ceremonies which could wed the structural oppositions, liberating the Black from his Chaos function, since this function was the key to the dynamics of its own order of being.

As a signifier of blackness, the "Ultimate" in Wynter's "Ultimate Chaos" connotes both the fundamental and finality, or the end of a process, and in the context of physics, *ultimate* denotes the maximum possible strength or resistance beyond which a structure or form breaks, in other words, a threshold to rupture (37). This threshold to rupture, Wynter (1990) terms elsewhere "demonic ground." As Katherine McKittrick (2006: xxiv) has noted, while notions of the "demonic" are "unquestionably wrapped up in religious hierarchies and the supernatural, the demonic has also been understood in terms that are less ecclesiastical"; for instance, "in mathematics, physics, and computer science, the demonic connotes a working system that cannot have a determined, or knowable, outcome." It is this latter sense, nonlinearity and indeterminancy, that I would like to deepen and expand in my reading of Wynter's investigation of "the grounds" that the "absented presence" of black female iconicity provides (McKittrick 2006: xxv).

In "Beyond Miranda's Meanings: Un/Silencing the 'Demonic Ground' of Caliban's 'Woman,'" Wynter (1990: 361) argues that the "ontological absence" of black female iconicity in William Shakespeare's *The Tempest* points not simply to a silenced social subject and nullification of said subject as an object of desire in the play but more profoundly to the occlusion of modes of being/feeling/knowing, which are anxiously and persistently, even if contingently, signified by the iconicity of "the black female body" in the canonized discourses of Humanism.[2] These foreclosed modes of being/feeling/knowing, which Wynter terms "demonic ground," are discontinuous (and therefore thought to be irrational) with the racially linear teleology (read eugenic schemas) of biocentrism, which include the very hegemonic categories and ascriptions of the discourse of "gender and sexuality" itself. According to Wynter, this discourse's universalizing impetus weds an anatomical model of sexual difference to a physiognomic model of race in order to ascribe a bio-ontologizing relational and hierarchical system of value and desire to *nature*. In other words, the causality of the Human, as an imperious, linearly hierarchical, *social* system, is assigned to the order of matter itself.

Extending Wynter here, I want to suggest that the "ontological absence" she describes is not solely operative in the mode of an "absent presence," but arguably when "the black female body" is figured, figuration may paradoxically intensify a socially imposed opacity (see Browne 2015; Copeland 2013). For instance, in the development of the biocentric discourses of biology, medicine, and social science of sex/uality and reproduction, "the black female body" has functioned as a prototypical specimen and trope of disorder.[3] The development of scientific and medical images and apparatuses—take the speculum, for instance—for putative purposes of magnification and closer inspection of corporeal interiors did not progressively lead to greater clarity but was just as likely to result in the observation of a deeper opacity.[4]

As a disorderly material metaphor, "the black female body" marked the outer limits both of the "universal" order of sex-gender and of patriarchy. This order took the form not of "the gender binary," as it is often contemporarily referred to, but, instead, of a *teleological-relational hierarchy* with more than two paradigmatic positions, such that the binaristic frame of "cis" and "trans" further occludes rather than clarifies the historical logic of biocentric discourse as "the black female body" has foundationally and recursively been categorized and measured as an other gender and an other sex.[5] Such recursion conditions and is essential to the poesis and current (re)ordering of biocentric discourse.[6] In this context, what masquerades as axiomatically empirical, "the black female body," is actually an abject-conditioning material metaphor that takes on the social regulatory role of myth in a system of "universal" sex-gender. Yet our critical discourses, Wynter (1990) argues, often leave the biocentric basis of our received notions of sex, gender, and sexuality utterly unexamined despite biocentrism's mutually constitutive relation to the gendered and sexual normativities of antiblackness and empire. The term *sexual difference* evokes *racial difference*, even as it symptomatically represses the conditioning function of the "ontological absence" to which Wynter refers: in the visual epistemology of "sexual difference," the icon of "the black female body" in particular, in both its alternating and combining presences and absences, has functioned as an aporetic abject referent in making sexual difference "real," legible, and visualizable. Debates concerning (gender and racial) inscrutability and passing, the politics of the look, and those concerning the ethics of representing or refusing representation (i.e., historical violence or police terror) commonly bypass an examination of the very conditions not only of visual epistemologies of "evidence" but also of representability itself, including their foundational biocentric racializing and sexuating violence.[7] In other words, such debates further occlude the violence that is not (yet) even legible as violence.

For Wynter (1990: 355–356, 364), "demonic ground" is a "projected" "vantage point" in space or a "slot" "outside of our present governing system of meaning, or theory/ontology," yet this "silenced" ground is the condition of economies of value, affect, and desire (understood here in the broadest sense) and the "universalizing" hegemonic terms of *woman* and *patriarchal discourse.*[8] The phrase "demonic ground" "point[s] toward the epochal threshold" of a mode of being/feeling/knowing with the capacity to rupture the current order's consolidated field of meanings, affect- and behavior-regulating schemas, and order-replicating hermeneutics (356). Wynter argues that such a frame of reference or mode(l), if/when it is approached, should parallel the " 'demonic models' posited by physicists who seek to conceive of a vantage point outside the space-time orientation of the humuncular observer" (364). In referencing the displacement of the authority and hegemony of the Scholastic theological interpretative model by *studia humanitatis* and the rise of natural science, a history often metonymically recalled in the phrase "Copernican Revolution," I take Wynter to suggest that if we take seriously the constitutive absence of standpoint that she terms "demonic ground" and subject this structuring absence—which Evelynn Hammonds (1994: 137) describes as "a dense and full place in space"—to rigorous examination, such an approach would necessarily open onto a mode of thought not simply akin to physics (and scientific revolutions of the past) but one that would mutate its terms and bring about another mode of science altogether.

Man is a figuratively coded, boundary-maintaining system. When attempting to hierarchically disaggregate Order and Chaos, iconography of "the black female body" has been an essential and essentializing mechanism in the determination of Man's limits. As with the initial reception of Benoit Mandelbrot's set, "the black female body," in the discourses of Western (social) science and medicine, has been emblematized as paradigmatically dis-aesthetic or a monstrous irregularity, and, as I demonstrate below, this is a trajectory that extends into philosophical discourses as well.[9]

But in the case of Wynter's demonic ground, neither the iconography of "the black female body" nor its fleshly representationalist doubles are equivalent to it; rather, demonic ground is a sublime initiating absence that signals ontologizing racialization, sexuating domination, and violent gendered assignations, as well as the dense point of potential rupture.[10] Demonic ground alludes to the sublime because it gestures toward the superempirical, exceeding the empirical because it sets scale and the terms of scale's legibility; therefore, such a sublime capacity requires us to think the limit of representation and conceptualization beyond the representationalist terms we might associate with the iconicity of "the black female body." In this essay, I want to explore the ways that black feminist and gender theory, such as that of Wynter, has already prepared us to do this work.

In the simplest terms, I turn to questions and concerns of black *mater* because I aim to identify how blackness *even in its abstraction* is entangled with the discursive-material politics of sexual difference. My reading of the opacity and aporia structuring black femininity in the not-yet-past of Enlightenment thought, suggests that a projected black femininity functions as the ground of normativizing and hierarchical arrangement and rearrangements of sex-gender in the globalizing West.[11] I began this essay with Wynter and now proceed to read a tradition of black feminist poetics, whereby poetics implies poetry as a mode of writing and theory itself, that collectively suggests "a sort of historical a priori" where the ongoing production and nullification of black mater is the condition of possibility for relation and the dialectics of the Subject.[12] In this essay, I am thinking along the lines of Michel Foucault's historical a priori and contra Immanuel Kant, in that the seemingly self-evident ground of perception and conceptualization is not "transcendental and universal" but contingent, material, and historical. In order to bring the interventions of black feminist poetics into relief, I offer, as a first step, an analysis of Edmund Burke's and Kant's highly influential approaches to the sublime and the racialized and gendered theses undergirding their thought. Whether invisible as the absent-presence of the "unthought" or made obscurely visible via the abjection or mythification of black femininity's fleshly material metaphors, a representational strategy we might term "presenting absence" or nothingness, both are a foreclosing of the being/feeling/knowing that black femininity implies.[13] To evoke Denise Ferreira da Silva (2017), black mater here should be "taken not as a category but as a referent of another mode of existing in the world," "another horizon of existence."

What this essay does is attempt to work through the nonidentitarian terms of a black femininity, imposed and occluded, yet internal to black mater in the Western discourses of Man. This working through investigates the meeting of blackness and femininity in/as sublimity, whereby a mythical or imagined abject femininity serves as a threshold to blackness's incalculably and paradoxically dense yet voided im/materiality. Black femininity here is not a figure in the first instance but a historical a priori. When not made invisible, the black feminine sublime may become obliquely figurative in the form of material metaphors, where these representations are given mythical and/or abject representation. This essay attempts to interpret the motifs of chaos theory and physics in black gender and feminist theory and consider its implications for the increasingly central place of science (physics in particular) in recent feminist materialisms. I argue that the turn to physics metaphors in black feminism attempts to address two interrelated problems concerning representation of a black feminine sublime: scale and paradox or absurdity. Here I attempt to interpret to what effect motifs of physics perform in black feminist theory.

[. . .]

Representation and Physics in the Poetics of Black Feminism

Black feminist analysis has worked on dual registers with respect to representation(alism): thought that investigates and exposes how antiblackness generates and sustains indexicality as a mode of fraudulent referentiality and thought that more radically forgoes the mimetic imperative in order to approach, via gesture and metaphor, the nonrepresentability, or sub-limity, attributed to black femininity in the prevailing grammar of the Human (which nec-essarily requires something in excess of mimesis). In light of Hortense J. Spillers's "Mama's Baby, Papa's Maybe: An American Grammar Book" (1987), I investigate two meanings of *representation* in the discursive practices of imperial Western humanism: representative and re-presentation. The black *mater*(nal), as *mater*, as matter, is non-represent-ability because the black *mater*(nal) here gestures toward the foreclosed, enabling condition of the grammar of the Human: a dense im/material space of self-differentiation but linguistic undifferen-tiation, nonsense, or aphasia and, therefore, correspondingly *without a representative* in the "I and thou" dialectical processes of recognition, judgment, value, and decision. Regarding re-presentation, in the grammar described, when figures of the black *mater*(nal) (or repre-sentations) appear, if they appear, they function at the register of myth and, therefore, reveal that representation *performs* rather than functions *mimetically* as the notion "representation" suggests. By suggesting that representation performs, I mean to imply a doing and an imple-mentation that forestalls the vertical bifurcation of representation and matter into respective planes of transcendence and immanence and, instead, places both on the same plane in the (un)making of being.[14] Or as Wynter (2001: 38) once put it, in a gloss of the work of physi-cist David Bohm: "Transformed *meanings* have led to transformed *matter*, to a transformed mode of experiencing the *self*." Thus sensorium and its faculties are "culturally determined through the mediation of the socialized *sense of self*, as well as the 'social' situation in which the *self* is placed" (37). In what follows, I investigate both understandings of representation—representative and re-presentation—and trace how each works on the other according to and within the genealogy of black feminism in order to analyze the stakes of (in)visibility for the reigning order of the Human.[15]

In light of black femininity and black female sex/uality's predicament in discourse or, more accurately, at and as the vestibule of discourse, I ask: Why have black feminists turned to physics metaphors, in particular, to articulate a paradoxical space of visibility/invisibility in the grammar of the Human? I argue that a burden of nonrepresentability, or sublimity, has been imposed on material metaphors of the black *mater*(nal) in a manner that eschews Aristotelian norms of logic that attempt to stave off aporia and opacity, such as the law of the excluded middle, the law of noncontradiction, and the law of identity. Black feminist gesture and metaphor convey movement at the limit of thinking, where standard proto-cols of evidence are inoperable, and physics metaphors permit the bending, if not outright contradiction, of Aristotelian logic constituent to the predicament of black femininity and female sex/uality (Aristotle 1998).

[. . .]

Black feminists have often thought about the indefiniteness of black womanhood's loca-tion in ontological discourse in terms of liminality, interstitiality, or, to use Spillers's term, vestibularity, but I am going to provisionally put forward another concept—superposition—which stresses virtuality and indeterminacy rather than teleological passage or "in-between-ness." According to the Human's gendered ontologizing metrics, as in the Burke example, black femininity is figured as a superposition or the state of occupying two distinct and seemingly contradictory genders simultaneously—a predicament that underwrites the separation of both "masculine" and "feminine" in Western ontological discourse and exposes the impossibility of consistently keeping them apart. I have argued elsewhere (Jackson 2016a) that the "evacuated and overfull" appearance of the black(ened) body with respect to ontologized and ontologizing polarities, such as human-object, human-animal, for example, clears the way for a plasticization and potential fluidification of embodied minds and the fleshly matter of existence.[16]

In putting forth superposition as a way to approach black femininity's troubled and troubling ontological status vis-à-vis sex-gender and other ontologizing polarities, I want to insist on the role of measurement in parsing and ontologizing such distinctions. It is measurement (a mode of knowing that is also a means of doing/making or worlding) that parses whether figures of the black *mater*(nal) provisionally appear on one side or another of Humanism's reigning dualisms, which in fact are not dualisms at all but relational hierarchies—or, as I suggest, such appearances are undergirded by the black *mater*(nal)'s virtuality, or indeterminacy and incalculability (rather than epistemological uncertainty).[17] Barad (2012b: 6) clarifies, "Measurements are agential practices, which are not simply revelatory but performative: they help constitute and are a constitutive part of what is being measured." In other words, the means and modes of measuring are inseparable from the iterative material-discursive phenomena of the black *mater*(nal). Measurement and mattering, metric and object, are inextricable and co-constitutive or, to use Barad's term, "intra-active within phenomena," not interactions: "Measurements are world-making: matter and meaning do not pre-exist, but rather are co-constituted via measurement intra-actions" (6). Measurement is agential and constitutive with what is measured rather than disinterested; thus it matters how some *thing* is measured. Take the case of the famous wave/particle experiment: when electrons (or light) are measured using one kind of apparatus, they are waves; if they are measured in a complementary way, they are particles. As Barad explains: "What we're talking about here is not simply some object *reacting* differently to different probings but *being* differently. What is at issue is the very nature of nature" (6). In considering the black *mater*(nal), what this suggests is that there is no preexisting "black female body" with determinate boundaries and properties that precede interaction but only black *mater*(nal) phenomena or material discursive intra-actions at every scale, processual differentiation of objects within-phenomena: "cutting together-apart, entangling-differentiating (one move)" (7). Measurement, in the form of the Humanist grammar of representation, as Spillers (1987) has shown, iteratively, recursively, and perniciously marks with signifiers of abjection, lack, nullification, negation that which according to Hammonds (1994) has already and necessarily been deemed a threshold to the supersensible and immeasurable.

To put it another way, New World slavery established a field of demand that tyrannically presumed, as if by will alone, that the black(ened) via their relational proximity to black femininity in their humanity could function as infinitely malleable lexical and biological matter, at once sub/super/human. What appear as alternating, or serialized, discrete modes of (mis) recognition—sub/super/humanization or privation/superfluity—are in practice varying dimensions of a racializing demand that the black(ened) be all at once, a simultaneous actualization of seemingly discontinuous and incompatible virtualities. In examining the implications of virtual particles for questions of ontology, Barad (2012a: 210, 214) has described virtuality as a kind of thought experiment the world performs that eschews the metaphysics of presence: "They [virtual particles] do not exist in space and time. They are ghostly non/existences that teeter on the edge of the infinitely fine blade between being and nonbeing. . . . Even the smallest bits of matter are an unfathomable multitude. Each 'individual' always already includes all possible intra-actions with 'itself' through all the virtual Others, including those noncontemporaneous with 'itself.'" Barad (2012b: 16) further critiques a disavowal at the heart of representationalism; representation stills and therefore forestalls an acknowledgment of the infinite constituent to all material finities: "Representation has confessed its shortcomings throughout history: unable to convey even the palest shadow of the Infinite, it has resigned itself to incompetence in dealing with the transcendent, cursing our finitude." But what if the ever presence of ghostly potential is quantized in accordance with and at the behest of a racialized demand such that it places being in peril? And how does one represent peril when one's peril is that of representing the threshold to the infinite in all its unsettling and inarticulable power?

The ontologization of racial blackness implies the polymorphous but not seriality, in other words, the collapse of a distinction between the virtual and the actual—or an un/doing of the distinction between being and becoming as space-time matterings such that the "play of (quantum) in/determinacies" (Barad 2012a: 214) and threshold effects regulating the actual and the virtual are under erasure if not overwritten. In short, antiblackness presupposes and, indeed, demands that blackness signify neither an interstitial (in-between) nor a liminal (teleology) ontology but a virtual ontology.

In conclusion, our current moment, as Markus Gabriel (2014, 2015) has suggested, might be best characterized as a period that attempts to reduce all (im)material things to elementary particles— DNA, neurons, quarks—in an attempt to satisfy a stubborn desire that "nature," "reality," "the universe" be fully cognizable in a "theory of everything."[18] Moreover, quite often, such a pursuit is undergirded not only by a desire for nature denuded but also by a craving for a deterministic foundation for understanding "higher" order processes. For instance, once it became clear that DNA was far more recalcitrant to a deterministic understanding of biology than most ever expected, the attention was then turned to the brain as the new frontier and fundamental structure of the human being in an ever-evolving scientific foundationalism. I ask, then, how might black feminism model a "general theory" of representation and imagine a relation to science, physics in particular, that offers a challenge to the microfundamentalism of our present, particularly that of biological reductionism, our current mode of the Human, which Wynter has termed biocentrism?[19] Moreover, how might black feminist (astro)physical and quantum metaphoricity alert us to and perform a critique of *the logic* of microfundamentalism, even when the fundamentalism is the Saussurean signifier as Barad and other recent feminist materialists charge? As black feminists have shown, the "higher" scalar discourses of subjectivity, identity, and being are insufficient for making conceptual and representationalist sense of the black *mater*(nal) precisely because the foreclosing constituent to the black *mater*(nal) organizes "the discursive and material terrain" for delineating (at the very least) the ideals and failures of normative (gendered, sexual, and reproductive) subjectivity (and more, much more, incalculably more). Black feminists' physics metaphors are not proposing collapsing distinctions of scale—subatomic and macroscopic; *rather, quantum theories, not purported quantum facts* produced to speculate about the subatomic scale, are generative metaphors for approaching the contrary mechanics of the subject when that subject is black female sex/uality, femininity, and womanhood. The representational quagmire of the black *mater*(nal) and the black hole reminds us that the seduction of synthesis is a fantasy of wholeness, but wholeness is also the danger because no synthesis can be totality; rather, it is a selective bringing into order, one that presents entropy as ectropy based on a pursuit of an unassailable indexicality between representation and entities structured by incalculable processes of differentiation.

Even as the sublimity of blacken(ed) *mater*, or nonrepresentability in discourse, pulls black feminist theorizing in a nonrepresentationalist direction, black feminism, nevertheless, is minimally committed to both providing an account of antiblack representation and investigating where such representations come from. Acknowledging that discursive practices and matter are co-formative is essential, but accounting for *how* and in what mode specific speech acts or discursive traditions are co-formed with specific matterings, at specific times, and in specific contexts is something else. At and as the vestibule of the Subject, material metaphors of black femininity have not been disaggregated from *mater* in a manner that approximates a subject *in* discourse, and, therefore, black feminist critiques of representation speak to this peculiar predicament—one that can never be fully described because it exceeds the concept—the weight of which can only be approached via gesture. There is likely never going to be enough language to describe the black mater(nal)'s sublime function, and therefore, from my view, our studied critiques of it are never excessive—even if and perhaps especially when our conclusions are debatable.

From: Zakiyyah Iman Jackson, "'Theorizing in a Void': Sublimity, Matter, and Physics in Black Feminist Poetics," in *South Atlantic Quarterly*, Volume 117, no. 3, pp. 617–648. Copyright 2018, Duke University Press. All rights reserved. Republished by permission of the copyright holder, Duke University Press. www.dukeupress.edu.

Notes

1. See the discussion of antiblackness and black aesthetic movements in Taylor 1996.
2. Some critics have been troubled by Wynter's deployment of the notion of "Caliban's 'woman'" as a place marker for an absent presence she wants to analyze, but, in my reading, part of the reason Wynter uses the awkward phrase is that she is trying to question and problematize, rather than reify, "woman"; Wynter's quotation marks would appear to suggest as much. Wynter wants to trouble the nonreflexive circulation of a notion of sexual difference—hence the critical reference to Luce Irigaray at the beginning of the essay—that presumes its terms are "universal" rather than historical and local. Such a conception globalizes a biologically reductive notion of "woman," whereby "woman" follows "biological sex" or is synonymous with "female," in particular. The linearity of such an account is precisely what she wants to call into question, by naming its hegemony as Western and imperialistic, but, even more precisely, as an ideology predicated on discursive-material violence directed at a subject that we typically refer to as "black woman"—a term both inside and exceeding the logic of this system. That being said, Wynter's term "Caliban's 'woman'" runs her right into the problem of heteronormativity; her discussion of a particular "ontological absence" wants to trouble, particularly as this "ontological absence" functions in the eugenic production of gender, desire, and reproduction. Here I, too, am questioning the seemingly inescapable terms of "sexual difference," or that of the discursive-material production of sex/gender, but in a manner that presupposes neither dimorphism nor a teleological relation between sex and gender but rather is interested in tracking both the function of *black femininity* as an "absented presence" and the violence necessary to contain its ground-shifting power that can be imaged and targeted across a range of subjectivities. For another work by Wynter that attempts to think through the stakes of biocentrism as it pertains to the imperialism of "sex-gender," see Wynter's "'Genital Mutilation' or 'Symbolic Birth'? Female Circumcision, Lost Origins, and the Aculturalism of Feminist/Western Thought" (1996).
3. The literature here is long, but for work that investigates the function of "the black female body" as icon, specimen, and material metaphor in the bioscientific/medical history of sex-gender, specifically as it pertains to the mutually constitutive development of *intersex*, *trans*, and *homosexuality* as legible terms, see Doane 1999; Gilman 1985; Reis 2009; Schiebinger 1993; Somerville 1994; Stepan 1986.
4. Observation here is meant to imply both the act of empirical sense making and a statement based on sense making.
5. The popularization of the terms *cisgender* and *cissexual* has been credited to Julia Serano (2016).
6. And as I have argued elsewhere: "The violence that produces blackness necessitates that from the existential vantage point of black lived experience, gender and sexuality lose their coherence as normative

categories [T]he black body has been rendered the 'absolute index of otherness.' While particular nonblack sexual and gendered practices may be queered, blackness serves as an essential template of gendered and sexual 'deviance' that is limited to the negation not of a particular practice but of a state of being" (Jackson 2011: 359).

7. An obvious exception is Hartman 1997.

8. Greg Thomas (2001: 107) cautions against an overly narrow understanding of desire:

> While "desire" may be routinely associated with the sexual, it is *reductively* associated with it. It is reduced to the purely physical or the yearning for a particular sexual act. It is always "sexual" desire and never "social" or "cultural" desire, for lack of a better term, in which sexuality has a central place. This misunderstanding of "social" desire leads to distortion and misunderstanding of "sexual" desire, so to speak. For Wynter, it is the cultivation and control, the regulatory production or generation of "desire" and "aversion" (or "non-desire"), in the broadest sense, that is primarily at issue: the production and policing of what will be "desirable" or "undesirable" in terms of our very subjectivity, "social" subjectivity in general and perhaps "sexual" subjectivity in particular.

9. As was the case with the Mandelbrot set, establishing beauty has been imagined as necessary for the recuperation of intrinsic value. One might be tempted to simply dismiss such an aesthetic value or value in aesthetics as problematic, if aesthetic orders were not so deadly. The irony is that the invention of fractal geometry has been attributed to Mandelbrot's work in the 1970s, when ethnomathematicians like Ron Eglash (1999) have shown that fractal geometry (including algorithmic fractal practices) has been practiced in diverse design practices across continental Africa for centuries.

10. I am drawn to the metaphor of dense point offered by Rizvana Bradley's (2016: 14) reading of the work of Houston Baker because I think it resonates with that of Wynter and highlights the way Wynter's argument speaks to that of Hammonds. Additionally, one of the ways the infinite has been reimagined is via density rather than immensity.

11. This article is in conversation with, rather than teleologically follows from, my recent article "Sense of Things" (Jackson 2016b). The current article was written before, during, and after the publication of that article. This publication is another attempt to articulate and elaborate the relation between black femininity and the sublime. In "Sense of Things" (Jackson 2016b), in a reading of Nalo Hopkinson's *Brown Girl in the Ring*, I rehearse a version of this argument that is not limited to the racially ontologizing terms of sex-gender but rather places the question of sexual difference in a larger exploration of how black mater structures the terms of the empirical, more generally, or the meeting of the Kantian imagination with that of the understanding.

12. Michel Foucault ([1966] 1994: 157–158) describes the historical a priori as follows:

> It concerns a fundamental arrangement of knowledge, which orders the knowledge of beings so as to make it possible to represent them in a system of names. . . . This a priori is what, in a given period, delimits in the totality of experience a field of knowledge, defines the mode of being of the objects that appear in that field, provides man's everyday perception with theoretical powers, and defines the conditions in which he can sustain a discourse about things that is recognized to be true. Similarly, on the prompting of Rachel Jones, I am thinking with Luce Irigaray's (1993) "sensible transcendental," or the metaphorical junction of mind/body, flesh/word, immanence/transcendence, abstract/embodied, time/space, form/matter, in *An Ethics of Sexual Difference*, but, following Hortense J. Spillers (1987), I am thinking more about its psychoanalytic resonances as it pertains to matter-symbol than inquiring into its theological implications, which is how the "sensible transcendental" is usually taken up. Last, my discussion of abjection also follows and revises the theory of abjection in the work of Julia Kristeva (1982).

13. My use of the term *mythification* evokes and is informed by the work of James Snead (1994) but is primarily a response to Spillers's (1987) reading of Roland Barthes's *Mythologies* ([1957] 1972: 302–306) and the use of the term *myth* in her essay "Mama's Baby, Papa's Maybe: An American Grammar Book."

14. On the notion of performance/performativity, here I am thinking with Barad (2003: 802), who states the following: "The representationalist belief in the power of words to mirror preexisting phenomena is a metaphysical substrate that supports social constructivist, as well as traditional realist, beliefs A *performative* understanding of discursive practices challenges the representationalist belief in the power of words to represent preexisting things The move toward performative alternatives to representationalist

shifts the focus from questions of correspondence between descriptions and reality (e.g., do they mirror nature of culture?) to matters of practices/doings/actions."

15. And, in fact, in "Sense of Things" (Jackson 2016b), I suggest representationalist logics are maintained by a hegemonic mode of antiblack visuality.

16. The phrase "evacuated and overfull" is borrowed from Bradley (2016: 9).

17. Here I am thinking processes of differentiation with and along the lines of Barad, in her work on diffraction. Quoting Barad (2014: 175):

> Meaning is not ideality; meaning is material. And matter isn't what exists separately from meaning. Mattering is a matter of what comes to matter and what doesn't. Difference isn't given. It isn't fixed. Subject and object, wave and particle, position and momentum do not exist outside of specific intra-actions that enact cuts that make separations—not absolute separations, but only contingent separations *within* phenomena. Difference is understood as differencing: difference-in-the-(re)making. Differences are *within*; differences are formed through intra-activity, in the making of "this" and "that" within the phenomenon that is constituted in their inseparability (entanglement). I thank Kathrin Thiele for bringing this text to my attention.

18. For a similar argument, see also Harman 2016.

19. On "general theory," see Chandler 2013.

Bibliography

Aristotle. 1998. *The Metaphysics*. Translated by Hugh Lawson-Tancred. London: Penguin Books.

Armstrong, Meg. 1996. "'The Effects of Blackness': Gender, Race, and the Sublime in Aesthetic Theories of Burke and Kant." *Journal of Aesthetics and Art Criticism* 54, no. 3: 213–236.

Bambara, Toni Cade. 1970. "On the Issue of Roles." In *The Black Woman: An Anthology*, edited by Toni Cade Bambara, 101–110. New York: Signet.

Barad, Karen. 2003. "Posthumanist Performativity: Toward an Understanding of How Matter Comes to Matter." *Signs: Journal of Women in Culture and Society* 28, no. 3: 801–831.

———. 2012a. "On Touching—the Inhuman That Therefore I Am." *Differences* 23, no. 3: 206–223.

———. 2012b. *What Is the Measure of Nothingness? Infinity, Virtuality, Justice*. Kassel, Germany: Hatje Cantz.

———. 2014. "Diffracting Diffraction: Cutting Together-Apart." *Parallax* 20, no. 3: 168–187.

Barthes, Roland. (1957) 1972. *Mythologies*. Translated by Annette Lavers. New York: Hill and Wang.

Bennett, Jane. 2010. *Vibrant Matter: A Political Ecology of Things*. Durham, NC: Duke University Press.

Bradley, Rizvana. 2016. "Living in the Absence of a Body: The (Sus)Stain of Black Female (W)holeness." *Rhizomes: Cultural Studies of Emerging Knowledges*, no. 29. doi:10.20415/rhiz/029.e13.

Brand, Dionne. 2012. *A Map to the Door of No Return: Notes to Belonging*. Toronto: Vintage Canada.

Browne, Simone. 2015. *Dark Matters: On the Surveillance of Blackness*. Durham, NC: Duke University Press.

Burke, Edmund. (1757) 2014. *A Philosophical Inquiry into the Origin of Our Ideas of the Sublime and Beautiful*. Adelaide, South Australia: eBooks@Adelaide, University of Adelaide Library. http://ebooks.adelaide.edu.au/b/burke/edmund/sublime.

Chandler, Nahum Dimitri. 2013. *X—the Problem of the Negro as a Problem for Thought*. New York: Fordham University Press.

Coole, Diana, and Samantha Frost. 2010. "Introducing the New Materialisms." In *New Materialisms: Ontology, Agency, and Politics*, edited by Diana Coole and Samantha Frost, 1–43. Durham, NC: Duke University Press.

Copeland, Huey. 2013. *Bound to Appear: Art, Slavery, and the Site of Blackness in Multicultural America*. Chicago: University of Chicago Press.

Crenshaw, Kimberlé. 1992. "Whose Story Is It, Anyway? Feminist and Antiracist Appropriations of Anita Hill." In *Race-ing Justice, En-gendering Power: Essays on Anita Hill, Clarence Thomas, and the Construction of Social Reality*, edited by Toni Morrison, 402–440. New York: Pantheon.

Doane, Mary Ann. 1999. "Dark Continents: Epistemologies of Racial and Sexual Difference in Psychoanalysis and the Cinema." In *Visual Culture: The Reader*, edited by Jessica Evans and Stuart Hall, 448–456. London: Sage.

Eglash, Ron. 1999. *African Fractals: Modern Computing and Indigenous Design*. New Brunswick, NJ: Rutgers University Press.

Eze, Emmanuel Chukwudi. 1995. "The Color of Reason: The Idea of 'Race' in Kant's Anthropology." *Bucknell Review* 38, no. 2: 200–241.

Fanon, Frantz. 1967. *Black Skin, White Masks*. Translated by Charles Lam Markmann. New York: Grove.

Ferguson, Roderick. 2004. *Aberrations in Black: Toward a Queer of Color Critique*. Minneapolis: University of Minnesota Press.

Ferreira da Silva, Denise. 2013. "To Be Announced: Radical Praxis or Knowing (at) the Limits of Justice." *Social Text* 31, no. 1: 43–62.

———. 2017. "1 (life) ÷ 0 (blackness) = ∞ − ∞ or ∞/∞: On Matter beyond the Equation of Value." e-flux, no. 79. www.e-flux.com/journal/79/94686/1-life-0-blackness—or-on-matter-beyond-the-equation-of-value.

Foucault, Michel. (1966) 1994. *The Order of Things: An Archaeology of the Human Sciences*. New York: Vintage Books.

Freeman, Barbara Claire. 1995. *The Feminine Sublime: Gender and Excess in Women's Fiction*. Berkeley: University of California Press.

Frost, Samantha. 2011. "The Implications of the New Materialisms for Feminist Epistemology." In *Feminist Epistemology and Philosophy of Science: Power in Knowledge*, edited by Heidi E. Grasswick, 69–83. Dordrecht: Springer.

Gabriel, Markus. 2014. "Realism and Materialism." Paper presented at the "Speculations on Anonymous Materials" symposium, Kassel, Germany, January 4. YouTube video, 1:00:20. www.youtube.com/watch?v=wX1YMMKuSgs.

———. 2015. *Why the World Does Not Exist*. Cambridge, UK: Polity Press.

Gilman, Sander L. 1985. "Black Bodies, White Bodies: Toward an Iconography of Female Sexuality in Late Nineteenth-Century Art, Medicine, and Literature." *Critical Inquiry* 12, no. 1: 204–242.

Gilroy, Paul. 1993. *The Black Atlantic: Modernity and Double Consciousness*. Cambridge, MA: Harvard University Press.

Glissant, Édouard. 1997. *Poetics of Relation*. Ann Arbor: University of Michigan Press.

Hachee, Matthew. 2011. "Kant, Race, and Reason." Paper presented at the Michigan State University Philosophy Graduate Student Conference, East Lansing, March 20.

Hall, Stuart, ed. 1997. *Cultural Representations and Signifying Practices*. London: Open University Press.

Hammonds, Evelynn. 1994. "Black (W)holes and the Geometry of Black Female Sexuality." *Differences: A Journal of Feminist Cultural Studies* 6, nos. 2–3: 127–145.

Harman, Graham. 2011. "Realism Without Materialism." *SubStance* 40, no. 2: 52–72.

———. 2016. "Materialism Is Not the Solution." *Nordic Journal of Aesthetics* 24, no. 47: 94–110.

Hartman, Saidiya. 1997. *Scenes of Subjection: Terror, Slavery, and Self-Making in Nineteenth-Century America*. New York: Oxford University Press.

hooks, bell. 1992. *Representing Whiteness in the Black Imagination*. New York: Routledge.

Irigaray, Luce. 1993. *An Ethics of Sexual Difference*. Translated by Carolyn Burke and Gillian C. Gill. Ithaca, NY: Cornell University Press.

Jackson, Zakiyyah Iman. 2011. "Waking Nightmares—on David Marriott." *GLQ: A Journal of Lesbian and Gay Studies* 17, nos. 2–3: 357–363.

———. 2016a. "Losing Manhood: Animality and Plasticity in the (Neo) Slave Narrative." *Qui Parle: Critical Humanities and Social Sciences* 25, no. 1: 95–136.

———. 2016b. "Sense of Things." *Catalyst: Feminism, Theory, Technoscience* 2, no. 2. catalystjournal.org/ojs/index.php/catalyst/article/view/74.

Judy, Ronald. 1991. "Kant and the Negro." *Surfaces* 1, no. 8: 4–70.

Kant, Immanuel. (1800) 1963. *Introduction to Logic*. Translated by T. K. Abbott. Westport, CT: Greenwood.

———. 1960. *Observations on the Feeling of the Beautiful and Sublime*. Translated by John T. Goldthwait. Berkeley: University of California Press.

Keeling, Kara. 2007. *The Witch's Flight: The Cinematic, the Black Femme, and the Image of Common Sense*. Durham, NC: Duke University Press.

Kristeva, Julia. 1982. *Powers of Horror: An Essay on Abjection*. Translated by Léon S. Roudiez. New York: Columbia University Press.

McKittrick, Katherine. 2006. *Demonic Grounds: Black Women and the Cartographies of Struggle.* Minneapolis: University of Minnesota Press.

Mikkelsen, Jon M., ed. 2013. *Kant and the Concept of Race: Late Eighteenth-Century Writings.* Albany: State University of New York Press.

Morrison, Toni. 1988. "Unspeakable Things Unspoken: The Afro-American Presence in American Literature." *Michigan Quarterly Review* 28, no. 1: 1–34.

Moten, Fred. 2003. *In the Break: The Aesthetics of the Black Radical Tradition.* Minneapolis: University of Minnesota Press.

O'Grady, Lorraine. 1992. "Olympia's Maid: Reclaiming Black Female Sexuality." *Afterimage* 20, no. 1: 14–23.

Reis, Elizabeth. 2009. *Bodies in Doubt: An American History of Intersex.* Baltimore: Johns Hopkins University Press.

Schiebinger, Londa L. 1993. *Nature's Body: Gender in the Making of Modern Science.* New Brunswick, NJ: Rutgers University Press.

Scott, Darieck. 2010. *Extravagant Abjection: Blackness, Power, and Sexuality in the African American Literary Imagination.* New York: New York University Press.

Serano, Julia. 2016. *Whipping Girl: A Transsexual Woman on Sexism and the Scapegoating of Femininity.* Berkeley, CA: Seal.

Snead, James. 1994. *White Screens, Black Images: Hollywood from the Dark Side.* New York: Routledge.

Somerville, Siobhan. 1994. "Scientific Racism and the Emergence of the Homosexual Body." *Journal of the History of Sexuality* 5, no. 2: 243–266.

Spillers, Hortense. 1987. "Mama's Baby, Papa's Maybe: An American Grammar Book." *Diacritics* 17, no. 2: 65–81.

Stepan, Nancy Leys. 1986. "Race and Gender: The Role of Analogy in Science." *Isis* 77, no. 2: 261–277.

Taylor, Clyde. 1996. *The Mask of Art: Breaking the Aesthetic Contract.* Bloomington: University of Indiana Press.

Thomas, Greg. 2001. "Sex/Sexuality and Sylvia Wynter's 'Beyond . . .': Anti-colonial Ideas in 'Black Radical Tradition'." *Journal of West Indian Literature* 10, nos. 1–2: 92–118.

Tompkins, Kyla Wazana. 2016. "On the Limits and Promise of New Materialist Philosophy." *Lateral: Journal of the Cultural Studies Association* 5, no. 1. doi:10.25158/L5.1.8.

Wynter, Sylvia. 1984. "The Ceremony Must Be Found: After Humanism." *Boundary 2* 12, no. 3–13, no. 1: 19–70.

———. 1990. "Beyond Miranda's Meanings: Un/silencing the 'Demonic Ground' of Caliban's 'Woman'." Afterword in *Out of the Kumbla: Caribbean Women and Literature,* edited by Carole Boyce Davies and Elaine Savory Fido, 355–370. Trenton, NJ: Africa World Press.

———. 1996. "'Genital Mutilation' or 'Symbolic Birth'? Female Circumcision, Lost Origins, and the Aculturalism of Feminist/Western Thought." *Case Western Reserve Law Review* 47, no. 2: 501–552.

———. 2001. "Towards the Sociogenic Principle: Fanon, Identity, the Puzzle of Conscious Experience, and What It Is like to be 'Black'." In *National Identities and Sociopolitical Changes in Latin America,* edited by Mercedes Durán-Cogan and Antonio Gómez-Moriana, 30–66. New York: Routledge.

Section III

The Coloniality of (Trans) Gender

11 Twin-Spirited Woman

Sts'iyóye smestíyexw slhá:li

Saylesh Wesley

Throughout "Twin-Spirited Woman," Saylesh Wesley interweaves personal experience and cultural analysis not just to restore but to "re-story" identities lost to the history and language of her Stó:lō (Coast Salish) culture through the violence of colonization. The article was first published in the "Decolonizing Gender" issue of *TSQ: Transgender Studies Quarterly* in 2014. Wesley, a university-educated trans woman, belongs to a royal lineage in her people's traditional matriarchal society. She identifies as a two-spirit person, an identity available only to people of Indigenous heritage, which she learned about in gender studies classes. The Two-Spirit concept asserts the difference between practices of being and becoming people rooted in Indigenous cultures and cosmologies and those rooted in modern western identities or concepts of gender or sexuality. Wesley considered it necessary to reassert Stó:lō concepts for individuals such as herself if she was to assume her proper role as a woman among her people. She found no trace of this knowledge in the ethnographies, missionary accounts, and dictionaries that settler people produced about her ancestors or in the surviving traditions of Stó:lō people themselves. Rather than concluding that people such as herself did not exist in the past, she claimed the power to fill in the absences and erasures of the archival record with knowledge generated in the present as part of a continuously existing culture that makes and remakes its own sense of the world. Wesley asked her grandmother, a respected matriarch who was one of a few surviving speakers of the Stó:lō language (Halq'eméylem), to dream a new name for the kind of person Wesley considered herself. That name was "Sts'iyóye smestíyexw slhá:li," or "twin-spirited woman," based on the translation of the contemporary two-spirit concept that Wesley had taught to her grandmother. Far more than merely enabling Wesley to situate her own life within tribal language and culture, her grandmother's act of naming was a potent demonstration of the capacity of Indigenous people to assert the meaning of their own collective experience of survival.

> To decolonize our sexualities and move towards a Sovereign Erotic, we must unmask the specters of conquistadors, priests, and politicians that have invaded our spirits and psyches, insist they vacate, and begin tending the open wounds colonization leaves in our flesh A Sovereign Erotic is a return to and/or continuance of the complex realities of gender and sexuality that are ever-present in both the human and more-than-human world, but erased and hidden by colonial cultures.
> — Qwo-li Driskill, "Stolen from Our Bodies: First Nations Two-Spirits/ Queers and the Journey to a Sovereign Erotic"

The Stó:lō people of British Columbia's lower Fraser Valley have ancient stories, or *Sxōwiyám*, to turn to when seeking traditional knowledge or teachings; however, the vast majority

DOI: 10.4324/9781003206255-15

of these stories have been forgotten due to the colonial effects of assimilation. As an mtf transgendered Stó:lō citizen and PhD student in gender, sexuality, and women's studies, I have made every effort to locate any precontact stories of the Stó:lō two-spirits, but to no avail so far. In this essay, I endeavor to re-member the past differently, marshal new traditions and language together in ways that create a new vision of the future. For the Coast Salish territory, I wish to illustrate how we historically contributed to our society prior to colonization. My grandmother has overcome the colonized homophobia imposed upon her enough to coin a title for me from our Halq'eméylem language. Given it has been her acceptance I wanted most of all, I would like to propose to all living Stó:lō grandmothers, the *Sisele*, that as the traditional makers of all laws on our matriarchal lands, they support this long-overdue initiative to reclaim lost identities erased through Western gen[der]ocidal action. The restoration of lost identities back to the Stó:lō nation would further reestablish the identities deleted by Western gen[der]ocidal actions. This essay is a movement toward personal healing and internal reconciliation for the Stó:lō as a whole. I feel that what my grandmother has done for me is a perfect example for this.

As Canada currently seeks to reconcile[1] with its indigenous people against whom it practiced genocide, in my case, as an mtf person who has lost access to traditional knowledge about people like me, I feel the need for this country to atone for its gendercide. While this reconciliation is important, it is more crucial that indigenous people reconcile among themselves first.

Therefore, this essay is intended not only to regenerate the lost teachings and stories of all Stó:lō two-spirits but also to offer a new beginning toward a new realization and acceptance for all indigenous people. As a member of the Stó:lō nation, I have inquired with elders and consulted all published works for a Halq'eméylem translation, and I have found that *two-spirit* is not yet a part of the Halq'eméylem language, nor can it be found in the English-to-Halq'eméylem dictionary (First Voices 2013a). Upon my request, my grandmother has been the first to conjure a Halq'eméylem term for my transgendered identity. In the recounting of my grandmother's work, I follow the "story-work" methodology of Stó:lō scholar Jo-ann Archibald, articulated in her *Indigenous Storywork* (2008), whereby personal experience is considered in relation to stories of the elders, to craft an analysis that takes indigenous knowledge seriously. This is my story and analysis woven together.

First, I share some of my history in order to clarify how I carry both Stó:lō and Tsimshian bloodlines. Approximately three years before I was born, my maternal grandmother moved from the Fraser Valley, her traditional Stó:lō territory situated in Southwest British Columbia, Canada.[2] During this time, she was still married to my late biological maternal grandfather, who was also Coast Salish from the Musqueam nation located in Vancouver's Point Grey area. Their marriage had dwindled at this point, and they agreed to separate and divorce. She was federally contracted at the time to travel around the province to promote and help preserve all traditional fine arts that many nations were quickly losing. On one of these excursions, she landed in Terrace, a small north coast town of British Columbia. This is when she met and eventually married my late step-grandfather who was a resident of Terrace and a member of the Tsimshian nation. The Tsimshian territory spreads vastly across the Pacific Northwest Coast and geographically includes Terrace and Prince Rupert, British Columbia, as well as southern parts of Alaska. Her plan was to send for her children from her previous marriage once she was settled, and my mother, a teen at the time, was one of them. Before my grandmother had anticipated, my mother showed up on the Greyhound bus from Chilliwack, because she missed her mother too much to wait any longer. It was not long before she met my father, who was not only Tsimshian but also my step-grandfather's maternal nephew. Thus this new grandfather of mine was also my great-uncle by blood.

My parents eventually married and I was born on October 28, 1972, at the Terrace Mills Memorial Hospital. The time of my birth was 10:30 p.m. My mother almost bled to death after an extremely difficult three-hour labor, and she remained as a patient for another week to recover from a life-saving postdelivery surgery. As I was jaundiced and three weeks premature, I had to be incubated in hospital for another two weeks. This birth resulted in two quite profoundly different stories, one from my maternal (Stó:lõ) grandmother and one from my father. He tells that the night I was born, the northern lights danced across the clear night sky more brightly than he had ever witnessed, and they apparently lasted throughout the night. To him, this was a spiritual sign. What is more significant is that he was not a spiritual man. He took the northern lights as an omen that his first-born son was going to be special—which I feel I have proved true. In those days, and in a town like Terrace, a son had great expectations placed on him to become a "man of men." Terrace was, and still is, a very redneck little city; "Indians" must overcompensate for anything and everything they do. The racist attitudes toward the indigenous populations in this rural community have changed little over the years that I have visited, so I understand the double work any "Indian" has to do to fit in. I cannot imagine what my father envisioned for me as his potential "hero" of a son, but he responded to the northern lights with hope that I would do him proud and with a belief that something divine acknowledged his vision for my future. Though these hopes for me weren't necessarily achieved as he imagined they would be, I must share that he is now absolutely proud of who I have become.

My grandmother's story is different. She first told it to me when I was about thirteen years old. She shared that my mother had almost bled to death as a result of my delivery. She also explained that such a difficult birth foretells a difficult life for such a child (according to her elders). As both the Stó:lõ and Tsimshian are matrilineal, it goes without saying that I am to identify as Stó:lõ even though my blood is a blend of the two, and to this day, she maintains political jurisdiction over me. Perhaps this is why she felt she had the right to share what she did, as hurtful as it might seem. Throughout the remainder of my teenage years, it seemed that what she had foretold in regard to how tumultuous my life would become had come true. I was nearing the end of puberty. I knew that I was not the *man* that I was expected to be. Every night I prayed that a supernatural force would transform me into a "normal boy." Over the course of my lifetime and despite my family's dismay over my apparent lack of masculinity, my grandmother did love me and played a critical role in bringing me up. I spent many weekends throughout my childhood under her loving care, and there are no sad stories I can tell, except for the time she told her version of my birth. I never again felt her angst toward me until I came out as transgender. In fact, when I was a child, she would allow me to play with dolls and dress up like a bride, and she would have tea parties with me when no one else would. It hurt her to see how my family would shame me to the soul for indicating in any way that I was not supposed to be a boy. Ultimately, I loved my grandmother from the day of my memories and still do today.

I was also close to my maternal auntie, almost ten years my senior and my grandmother's youngest child. She was genderqueer like me, except the polar opposite. She, in her own crass words, "was supposed to have a pecker." By the time I was courageous enough to come out, my aunt had yet to do so. My entire family knew that she was, as everyone thought, a "lesbian," even though she later confessed to also being "trans" like me. Her story is even more painful than mine, and I will not delve into it here. When I was twenty-three, I came out to her and to the rest of my family. I started off identifying as gay, since it seemed less scary than to say I was actually a woman; however, I announced my true trans identity over the phone to my aunt. She was incarcerated at the time for dealing drugs and prostitution. She warned me: "Don't tell anyone! I don't want you to go through what I did!" She was the first in our extended family to break the ground for homophobia internally, as one might well imagine, and she faced far worse consequences for being gay than I would. Against her plea, I went ahead with revealing the truth about my identity. I was willing to be cast out from my family, but I hoped for at least some acceptance. Otherwise, I would have had to find a way to end my life for the mistake that I felt I was. Over the next little while, my aunt was released from prison, and we became even closer. My seemingly smoother journey of coming out compared to hers years earlier gave her the courage to do the same.

All this time, my grandmother had remained as diplomatically mute as possible, I think for the sake of my aunt and me. In 1997, about three years after I told our family I was gay, I phoned her: to tell her that I was transgendered and ask if she would host a "coming out" feast for us. She said she could not fathom how I came to be this deviant, and how I thought I should be blessed with such a celebration. Perhaps in her mind, I should have grown out of my feminine phase. Needless to say, the conversation ended with her hanging up the phone and me in tears. In 1999, my aunt passed away from a heroin overdose. As keen as she was to continue negotiating her queer identity, she did not survive her own demons. For my grandmother, this was a loss from which she never fully recovered. I have since prayed these words to her countless times:

> I invite you Grandmother, to shape-shift your own thought process and open your mind a bit more and see that I am still, essentially, the grandchild with whom you shared a reciprocal loving relationship. I am not asking you to change who you are in principle, but rather, that you attempt to enhance your ability to be more at peace with diversity given your late daughter's fate. Perhaps I can take this opportunity to point out metaphorically that you too are akin to being two-spirited. In your stories of your cultural immersion combined with your experience as a converted Catholic, and how you now dwell (to some degree) in both faiths, you too share your own duality. Albeit, it isn't about your gender or sexuality, but in your own words "To Thine Own Self Be True" you justify your bi-culturalism and I beg that you accept my two-spirit identity all the same. I am, after all, a descendant of your rich bloodline, so there must be some-thing worthy I can offer. The creative juices within you that produce your baskets flow through me too. I am taking what you taught me and now weave my own stories. My baskets are not literal, but they are certainly coming out to be "masterpieces" that would be finished perfectly with your loving pride.

My grandmother is a world-renowned basket weaver who not only continues to pass on her mastery of Stó:lō styles of weaving but single-handedly revived the lost Tsimshian cedar bark and spruce root weaving and taught it back to them. I have since rooted in Chilliwack because my parents also divorced after fifteen years of marriage. My mother took my sister and me back to her hometown, and here I stay. In April 2012, my grandmother's second husband tragically passed away. This event prompted her to return to Chilliwack, since it is where the bulk of her children and their families live. This was a difficult transition for her, given that she is at this point in her 80s and that she has lived in Terrace for nearly forty years. In the last two years since she returned, my relationship with her has been entirely reshaped. As well, I am now her primary caregiver. Our closeness has given me the opportunity to become her weaving apprentice. I have learned to gather and prepare strips of cedar and roots for weaving; sitting with her, I have learned basic techniques for making baskets and shawls. And as she shares with me her most cherished indigenous knowledge, I also share with her my insights about being two-spirited and how I have learned about this concept in university. Though this is uncharted territory for her, her receptiveness has clearly devel-oped. She places absolute priority on higher education for her children and grandchildren. She feels as though if she had had the opportunity to get a postsecondary education that she would have become a scientist. Instead, she only received a grade six education in an Indian residential school. Though she still wrestles with the idea that I am now a woman, she respects my academic achievements and my natural flare for weaving. Given that I have revealed the emotionally awkward aspects of our relationship here, I want to emphasize that it is the progress we have made, not the pitfalls, that I wish to spotlight. My grandmother's instinctual *trans*phobia is not her doing. This is the "good work" of the Catholic Church and the rest of the colonial project; but as mentioned, our budding friendship also works to reprogram her worldview.

While my grandmother speaks English, learned at residential school, her first language is Halq'eméylem (First Voices 2013b). And recently I asked if she could meditate and conjure a title for me as a male-to-female in our traditional language. As previously mentioned, no such thing exists in recorded history. I had already shared with her what I have learned in university about two-spirited identities and so she took some time to think about it. Eventually, she came up with a Stó:lō two-spirited identity for me in our mother tongue—an exchange that remains surreal and miraculous. She coined the term *Sts'iyóye smestíyexw slhá:li*. When she handed the piece of paper to me with this title on it, she included the English translation, "Twin-Spirited Woman," and explained that I could interpret it as "two-spirited woman," or "twin-soul woman," or "same spirit as a woman." Ultimately, she left it open for me to decide how I would like to interpret it, given that our language is much more fluid than English. As a fluent speaker of Halq'eméylem, she has taught me that our words were able to wield various contexts and concepts depending on the discussion. Therefore, she gave me permission to decipher for myself how *Sts'iyóye smestíyexw* translates. This was truly a "HALLELUJAH!" moment. I then asked her if it would have made sense to introduce my late aunt as *Sts'iyóye smestíyexw Swí:qe*, or "Twin-Spirited Man," and her response was something to the effect of "I guess if she would have wanted to."

As I state in the opening paragraphs of this essay, the Stó:lō have lost much of their Halq'eméylem language, histories, and teachings to colonization. As a result, any such focus on gender transition challenges many perspectives, particularly for gender-normative kin who must adjust their worldview once a family member discloses that she or he will change gender. I share this because I have observed how those who loved me were tremendously bewildered by my dramatic transition and how, fifteen years later, this shift is not yet finished for everyone. For the most part, my family and community members have come a long way. Many did not know how to perceive me in a literal sense; some still do not. I remain troubling and/or invisible in their presence. Most have come to a frame of mind where *I am* who *I am*. Or, "That's just the way she is," with no agenda or bias, just matter-of-fact acceptance. In other words, they have achieved true contentment with my identity and in some cases have found even more love and respect for me as a result of my transformation, given how they have witnessed my life-and-death struggle with it.

This leads to the complexities of the term *two-spirit* and how perplexing it is for everyone's psyche to negotiate. For instance, any given cisgender Stó:lō person who identifies as a contemporary two-spirit may not feel like a "twin-spirited woman" (i.e., my aforementioned late aunt might have adopted "twin-spirited man"). It only makes sense for them to choose how they wish to identify in Halq'eméylem as I have. In the introduction to the anthology *Queer Indigenous Studies* (Driskill et al. 2011), the authors suggest that the continued use of the prototype *two-spirit* is problematic: like *lesbian*, *gay*, *transgender*, and other terms, *two-spirit* "inevitably fails to represent the complexities of Indigenous constructions of sexual and gender diversity, both historically and as they are used in the present" (3). However, they also contend that two-spirit is a starting point toward the decolonization of queer indigenous identity in general. This admittedly implies that all cisgender queer people have both male and female spirits; it seems important to keep two-spirit open for such individuals to self-identify as to whether or not they understand themselves to have "two" spirits (3). Moreover, I tell my story in order to isolate my specific "queer" Stó:lō identity that makes space for other transfolk of my nation and subsequently for all queer indigenous people who remain unidentified and/or displaced from their home territory(s). In other words, I happily share the newly conceived *Sts'iyóye smestíyexw* status with any who feel it fits, though it is only an invitation. As each nonindigenous person who fits under the evolving LGBTQ spectrum has the right to self-determine where they fit and/or how they identify, it makes sense that the same goes for the Stó:lō "LGBTQ." Should any of those who do not identify as transgender wish to quest for a customized Halq'eméylem title as I have, then all the power to them.

Qwo-Li Driskill and colleagues also tell me to "talk back" to Western scholarship and compile and publish my own story: to claim first-voice authority as a contribution to the academic mainstream. Their message encourages me to bring what remains still in the proverbial closet—the lost and stolen history(s) that, until recently, remained the work of white scholars to excavate (2011: 10). However, I am grateful to some of these scholars who have engaged in this work, especially for any recent work that attempts to capture accurate and articulate accounts with clear integrity (Morgensen 2011; Rifkin 2012). However, I am fortunate to be able to bring a firsthand, lived experience to enrich this budding field. In this sense, I make every attempt to "link arms together" with other two-spirited theorists and philosophers to continue imagining what our scholarship should look like (Rifkin 2012: 18).

As previously mentioned, the term *two-spirit* is not in the English-to-Halq'eméylem dictionary. Thus it is necessary to work to reestablish the best or most appropriate "fit" to name this term and determine how it may serve as an addition to the Stó:lō gender binary.[3] Coast Salish nations traditionally hold ceremonial gatherings to "stand-up" ones who are receiving such names or honors,[4] and as our systems of passing knowledge and title down are matrilineal, only the eldest woman can legitimize this sort of work. I would thus require my grandmother to endorse this vision and support the endeavor to gift these roles back to the Stó:lō. I have truly become not only her granddaughter, but also her friend and teacher who helps to reshape her worldview, which includes my queer identity. She now understands that the "grandson" I once was remains very much alive through my female eyes. For a woman of her age and stature, this is no small feat.[5] The Catholic Church and the Canadian Indian Residential School system (which only closed in 1996[6]) have thoroughly accomplished their assimilationist goals in her. Coincidentally, it was the grandmother who raised the children prior to colonization. So, in effect, my grandmother and I have fallen back to ancestral ways of child rearing. I realize I am not a child, according to Western ideology, but I place myself in this stage given that I am "first-born" as *Sts'iyóye smestíyexw slhá:li*, and my legacy for the Stó:lō has begun.

As a philosopher and dreamer, I have come to know that fantasies of how the past could have been different are senseless, but I *do* know that there are miracles yet to unfold and that there is a possibility that my writing of this essay may very well become one. With Archibald's notion of "storywork," which gives academic freedom to scholars to cite indigenous elders and the stories they share as legitimate sources, I am secure in the fact that my grandmother has full authority to contribute to my work as she has in this essay. Storywork also has "the power to educate and heal the heart, mind, body and spirit," which is the absolute goal I have attempted to harness since the onset of my transition through the writing of this essay (Archibald 2008: back cover). Also, my work aims not only to "share back" what I have come to know but to support the change of the Coast Salish cultural landscape toward a setting that continues to honor and fulfill whatever remains necessary to please our Ancestors and to include *Sts'iyóye smestíyexw slhá:li*—while continuing to cultivate what "culture" is, how it will continue to evolve and adapt to our ever-changing world, and to "gift back" (143) fully our traditional matriarchal systems of governance and title. In order to reestablish such two-spirit roles, it is crucial that matriarchal systems replace the current Indian Act elected-chief system of governance,[7] given the grandmothers' role of making any new "laws" and/or "declarations" that hypothetically include the reclamation of *Sts'iyóye smestíyexw slhá:li.* I am certain the Ancestors have been wondering where we, as two-spirits, have been on "This Side."[8]

Current indigenous scholars such as Archibald and Driskill have contributed the use of indigenous words, names, and concepts. Many of these warriors may not have many more than my forty years, and though not all of these warriors are Stó:lō, I instinctively follow my teachings as a *xwé'lmexw te Semá:th* (Sumas Nation member) and regard them as elders, meaning that I am respectful of their knowledge and courage to speak what is in their hearts. In one of my conversations with my grandmother, she mentioned how she still notices my former "male" self peeking through my female identity. In a way, it is as though I have developed two personalities: the beloved [but vulnerable] male child who finds refuge in the arms of the protective and much more competent big sister. My grandmother explained to me in that conversation she misses her grandson but that she has come to really respect the woman I have become. It does, however, make her happy that "he" comes out and will say something funny and/or endearing in a way that only he could. As "he," I was much more emotional and extreme, with melodramatic outbursts and passion. I was not able to function well in the world, but my effect on a crowd was undoubtedly appreciated, given my alleged sweet nature. As "she," I am much more focused, serious, and even ambitious. I am well aware that it is "she" who has taken "us" this far with regard to education: I am now in a PhD program. While he remains very much a child, she has become a fully functioning adult.

I am fully committed to meeting the need to "stand-up" all roles (restorer, empowerer, healer) for future and ongoing battles toward the seemingly infinite uphill climbs toward liberation, self-determination, entitlement, title, restoration, privilege, empowerment, and decolonization. As I currently live and work on my own traditional Coast Salish territory, then perhaps the Halq'eméylem terms *xéyt* (transform it) or *meá:ylexw* (revive; come back to life) would serve more appropriately and inclusively to the aforementioned ideologies. As such, the articulation process for this essay feels intrinsically off, as if I am attempting to fight fire with fire—though this may prove to be ironically effective in other instances. Speaking in my own Halq'eméylem language would make for as close to perfect a way as possible to honor any who have been invisibilized (i.e., Stó:lō women and *Sts'iyóye smestíyexw slhá:li*). It would then seem as though I would be more effectively fighting fire with water.

[. . .]

Although the Canadian government made a very successful attempt to erase *Sts'iyóye smestíyexw*, some of us live on to tell new stories and to re-generate an entire gender and sexuality category that has been put away for so long. I invite other self-identified *Sts'iyóye smestíyexw* to pray together, laugh together, and weave our stories into a new *their* story. This invitation, of course, includes all that represent the spectrum of difference as the acronym *LGBTQ* intends, given that not all will identify as a "twin-spirit to-a-woman" as I do. There are many *Sts'iyóye smestíyexw* who have passed and who never experienced the emancipation of a true coming-out as those of us who are left behind now have the privilege to do.

My grandmother and I have come a long way since 1997. I have had to heal and spiritually strengthen myself for independence because, at that point in time, she was not able to accept my transgendered identity within her political gaze. I can now say that this has changed. *Xexa:ls* (four children of *Xa:ls*, the Creator/Transformer) have had pity on me.[9] They helped her to shape-shift her mind to one that demonstrates that transformative thinking and learning stop at no age. Now this new chapter begins, and the Coast Salish people as a whole can continue flourishing in their feasts with this new story.

Acknowledgments

Angela Pietrobon must be acknowledged for her much-appreciated edits to this paper as well as my wonderful PhD committee supervisors Deanna Reder and Dolores van der Wey.

Notes

1. See Truth and Reconciliation Commission of Canada 2014. This website details how the federal government aims to make amends and rebuild relationships with the surviving students, whose attendance in residential schools was mandatory nationwide, as well as acknowledge the travesties to which it subjected all First Nations peoples in this legislated attempt.
2. See the working map showing the First Nations peoples of British Columbia and their territories (British Columbia Ministry of Education 2014).
3. As an example, see Wesley Thomas's (2010) categorization of Navajo gender systems.
4. Coast Salish people have adopted the idea of "standing-up" individuals to receive names, honors, or blessings at traditional longhouse gatherings.
5. She is an eighty-six-year-old hereditary "Big Woman" of the *Semá:th* (Sumas) Territory, located in the Fraser Valley along the Canadian/United States border. In other words, if we went back in time five hundred years, she would be the sovereign ruler and owner of the Fraser Valley, not unlike a queen.
6. See CBC News 2008 for more information on the history of residential schools in Canada.
7. See Aboriginal Affairs and Northern Development Canada 2012 for more on elections under the Indian Act and Indian Band Election Regulations.
8. I refer to "This Side," or *third* dimension: those of us who are living in the flesh, as opposed to "The Other Side," or the Spirit world, where late Ancestors dwell, according to the Stó:lō.
9. For more information about the Stó:lō Transformer figure, sometimes referred to as "Creator," and his Divine Children (*Xa:ls* and *Xexa:ls*), see Hanson 2014.

Bibliography

Aboriginal Affairs and Northern Development Canada. 2012. "Backgrounder: Indian Act Elections." September 5. www.aadnc-aandc.gc.ca/eng/1100100016233/1100100016234.

Archibald, Jo-ann/Q'um Q'um Xiiem. 2008. *Indigenous Storywork: Educating the Heart, Mind, Body, and Spirit*. Vancouver: University of British Columbia Press.

Bergen, Rachel, and Stephanie Kelly. 2013. "Spirit Dancing: How Two UBC Students Gained Access to Report on This Secretive Aboriginal Tradition." *Canadian Journalism Project*, May 1. j-source.ca/article/spirit-dancing-how-two-ubc-students-gained-access-report-secretive-aboriginal-tradition.

British Columbia Ministry of Education. 2014. "First Nations Peoples of British Columbia." www.bced.gov.bc.ca/abed/map.htm (accessed March 6, 2014).

CBC News. 2008. "A History of Residential Schools in Canada: FAQs on Residential Schools and Compensation." May 16. www.cbc.ca/news/canada/a-history-of-residential-schools-in-canada-1.702280.

Driskill, Qwo-li. 2010. "Doubleweaving Two-Spirit Critiques: Building Alliances between Native and Queer Studies." In "Sexuality, Nationality, Indigeneity," ed. Daniel Heath Justice, Mark Rifkin, and Bethany Schneider. Special issue, *GLQ* 16, no. 1–2: 60–92.

Driskill, Qwo-Li, et al. 2011. Introduction to *Queer Indigenous Studies: Critical Interventions in Theory, Politics, and Literature*, ed. Qwo-Li Driskill et al., 1–28. Tucson: University of Arizona Press.

First Voices. 2013a. "About the People." Halq'eméylem Community Portal. www.firstvoices.com/en/Halqemeylem (accessed March 6, 2014).

———. 2013b. "Halq'eméylem Words." www.firstvoices.com/en/Halqemeylem/word/8315275ef45b39c6/Halqomelem (accessed March 6, 2014).

Hanson, Erin. 2014. "Oral Traditions." Indigenous Foundations, University of British Columbia. indigenousfoundations.arts.ubc.ca/home/culture/oral-traditions.html (accessed March 6, 2014).

Morgensen, Scott Lauria. 2011. *Spaces Between Us: Queer Settler Colonialism and Indigenous Decolonization.* Minneapolis: University of Minnesota Press.

Rifkin, Mark. 2012. *The Erotics of Sovereignty: Queer Native Writing in the Era of Self-Determination.* Minneapolis: University of Minnesota Press.

Thomas, Wesley. 2010. "Navaho Cultural Constructions of Gender and Sexuality." Trans Bodies Across the Globe, Department of Gender Studies, Indiana University Bloomington. December 17. transgenderglobe.wordpress.com/2010/12/17/navajo-cultural-constructions-of-gender-and-sexuality/.

Truth and Reconciliation Commission of Canada. 2014. "Reconciliation . . . Towards a New Relationship." www.trc.ca/websites/reconciliation/index.php?p=312 (accessed March 6, 2014).

12 The Coloniality of Gender

María Lugones

Feminist philosopher María Lugones does not directly discuss trans people or trans studies in her essay "The Coloniality of Gender," first published in *Worlds and Knowledges Otherwise* in 2008. Her framework for understanding the sex/gender binary of Eurocentric modernity as an instrument of heteropatriarchal racial capitalism nevertheless informs contemporary intersectional work in trans studies. Lugones was a leading voice in US-based third world women of color feminism who developed many useful ideas and practices for contesting misogyny and racism and for challenging the ways white feminism can reproduce colonial power relations with regard to women of color. Here, Lugones takes up Anibal Quijano's theorization of the "coloniality of power," itself drawn from the work of world-systems theorist Immanuel Wallerstein, to argue that the sex/gender concept so central to feminist analysis is itself rooted in the "somato-centricity," or body-centeredness, of the modern European world system constructed through colonization. Lugones points to scholarship on pre-colonial genders and sexualities in Latin America and Africa to show that biology has not always been a culture's most important criterion for sorting people into social categories. In doing so, her work resonates strongly with Black feminist thought that critiques biological essentialism and understands "biocentrism" to be both the legacy of the slave system and a tool of racism. It resonates with poststructuralist gender theory that denaturalizes "sex" as the proper foundation for "gender." In showing how coloniality turns biological difference into sex, class, and race hierarchies, Lugones opens the door for a deeper engagement between trans theorizing, third world and women of color feminisms, post/colonial critique, and Indigenous resistance to coloniality.

I am interested in the intersection of race, class, gender and sexuality in a way that enables me to understand the indifference that men, but, more importantly to our struggles, men who have been racialized as inferior, exhibit to the systematic violences inflicted upon women of color. I want to understand the construction of this indifference so as to make it unavoidably recognizable by those claiming to be involved in liberatory struggles. This indifference is insidious since it places tremendous barriers in the path of the struggles of women of color for our own freedom, integrity, and wellbeing and in the path of the correlative struggles towards communal integrity. The latter is crucial for communal struggles towards liberation, since it is their backbone. The indifference is found both at the level of everyday living and at the level of theorizing of both oppression and liberation. The indifference seems to me not just one of not seeing the violence because of the categorial separation of race, gender,

DOI: 10.4324/9781003206255-16

class, and sexuality. That is, it does not seem to be only a question of epistemological blinding through categorial separation.

Women of Color feminists have made clear what is revealed in terms of violent domination and exploitation once the epistemological perspective focuses on the intersection of these categories. But that has not seemed sufficient to arouse in those men who have themselves been targets of violent domination and exploitation, any recognition of their complicity or collaboration with the violent domination of women of color. In particular, theorizing global domination continues to proceed as if no betrayals or collaborations of this sort need to be acknowledged and resisted.

In this project I pursue this investigation by placing together two frameworks of analysis that I have not seen sufficiently jointly explored. I am referring, on the one hand, to the important work on gender, race and colonization done, not exclusively, but significantly by Third World and Women of Color feminists, including critical race theorists. This work has emphasized the concept of intersectionality and has exposed the historical and the theoretico-practical exclusion of non-white women from liberatory struggles in the name of "Women." The other framework is the one introduced by Anibal Quijano and which is at the center of his work, that of the coloniality of power. Placing both of these strands of analysis together permits me to arrive at what I am tentatively calling "the modern/colonial gender system." I think this understanding of gender is implied in both frameworks in large terms, but it is not explicitly articulated, or not articulated in the direction I think necessary to unveil the reach and consequences of complicity with this gender system. I think that articulating this colonial/modern gender system, both in the large strokes, and in all its detailed and lived concreteness will enable us to see what was imposed on us. It will also enable us to see its fundamental destructiveness in both a long and wide sense. The intent of this writing is to make visible the instrumentality of the colonial/modern gender system in subjecting us—both women and men of color—in all domains of existence. But it is also the project's intent to make visible the crucial disruption of bonds of practical solidarity. My intent is to provide a way of understanding, of reading, of perceiving our allegiance to this gender system. We need to place ourselves in a position to call each other to reject this gender system as we perform a transformation of communal relations. In this initial paper, I present Anibal Quijano's model that I will complicate, but one that gives us—in the logic of structural axes—a good ground from within which to understand the processes of intertwining the production of "race" and "gender."

The Coloniality of Power

Anibal Quijano thinks the intersection of race and gender in large structural terms. So, to understand that intersection in his terms, it is necessary to understand his model of global, Eurocentered capitalist power. Both "race" and gender find their meanings in this model [patrón]. Quijano understands that all power is structured in relations of domination, exploitation and conflict as social actors fight over control of "the four basic areas of human existence: sex, labor, collective authority and subjectivity/intersubjectivity, their resources and products." (Quijano, 2001–2, p. 1) What is characteristic of global, Eurocentered, capitalist power is that it is organized around two axes that Quijano terms, "the coloniality of power" and "modernity." (Quijano, 2000b, p. 342) The axes order the disputes over control of each area of existence in such a way that the meaning and forms of domination in each area are thoroughly infused by the coloniality of power and modernity. So, for Quijano, the disputes/struggles over control of "sexual access, its resources and products" define the domain of sex/gender and the disputes, in turn, can be understood as organized around the axes of coloniality and modernity.

This is too narrow an understanding of the oppressive modern/colonial constructions of the scope of gender. Quijano's lenses also assume patriarchal and heterosexual understandings of the disputes over control of sex, its resources, and products. Quijano accepts the global, Eurocentered, capitalist understanding of what gender is about. These features of the framework serve to veil the ways in which non-"white" colonized women were subjected and disempowered. The heterosexual and patriarchal character of the arrangements can themselves be appreciated as oppressive by unveiling the presuppositions of the framework. Gender does not need to organize social arrangements, including social sexual arrangements. But gender arrangements need not be either heterosexual or patriarchal. They need not be, that is, as a matter of history. Understanding these features of the organization of gender in the modern/colonial gender system—the biological dimorphism, the patriarchal and heterosexual organizations of relations—is crucial to an understanding of the differential gender arrangements along "racial" lines. Biological dimorphism, heterosexual patriarchy are all characteristic of what I call the "light" side of the colonial/modern organization of gender. Hegemonically these are written large over the meaning of gender. Quijano seems not to be aware of his accepting this hegemonic meaning of gender. In making these claims I aim to expand and complicate Quijano's approach, preserving his understanding of the coloniality of power, which is at the center of what I am calling the "modern/colonial gender system."

The coloniality of power introduces the basic and universal social classification of the population of the planet in terms of the idea of "race." (Quijano, 2001–2, p. 1) The invention of "race" is a pivotal turn as it replaces the relations of superiority and inferiority established through domination. It re-conceives humanity and human relations fictionally, in biological terms. It is important that what Quijano provides is a historical theory of social classification to replace what he terms the "Eurocentric theories of social classes." (Quijano, 2000b, p. 367) This move makes conceptual room for the coloniality of power. It makes conceptual room for the centrality of the classification of the world's population in terms of "races" in the understanding of global capitalism. It also makes conceptual room for understanding the historical disputes over control of labor, sex, collective authority and inter-subjectivity as developing in processes of long duration, rather than understanding each of the elements as pre-existing the relations of power. The elements that constitute the global, Eurocentered, capitalist model of power do not stand in separation from each other and none of them is prior to the processes that constitute the patterns. Indeed, the mythical presentation of these elements as metaphysically prior is an important aspect of the cognitive model of Eurocentered, global capitalism.

[. . .]

Europe was mythologically understood to pre-exist this pattern of power as a world capitalist center that colonized the rest of the world and as such the most advanced moment in the linear, unidirectional, continuous path of the species. A conception of humanity was consolidated according to which the world's population was differentiated in two groups: superior and inferior, rational and irrational, primitive and civilized, traditional and modern. "Primitive" referred to a prior time in the history of the species, in terms of evolutionary time. Europe came to be mythically conceived as preexisting colonial, global, capitalism and as having achieved a very advanced level in the continuous, linear, unidirectional path. Thus, from within this mythical starting point, other human inhabitants of the planet came to be mythically conceived not as dominated through conquest, nor as inferior in terms of wealth or political power, but as an anterior stage in the history of the species, in this unidirectional path. That is the meaning of the qualification "primitive." (Quijano, 2000b, pp. 343–344) We can see then the structural fit of the elements constituting Eurocentered, global capitalism in Quijano's model (pattern). Modernity and coloniality afford a complex understanding of the organization of labor. They enable us to see the fit between the thorough racialization of the division of labor and the production of knowledge. The pattern allows for heterogeneity and discontinuity. Quijano argues that the structure is not a closed totality. (Quijano, 2000b, p. 355)

We are now in a position to approach the question of the intersectionality of race and gender in Quijano's terms. I think the logic of "structural axes" does more and less than intersectionality. Intersectionality reveals what is not seen when categories such as gender and race are conceptualized as separate from each other. The move to intersect the categories has been motivated by the difficulties in making visible those who are dominated and victimized in terms of both categories. Though everyone in capitalist Eurocentered modernity is both raced and gendered, not everyone is dominated or victimized in terms of them. Crenshaw and other women of color feminists have argued that the categories have been understood as homogenous and as picking out the dominant in the group as the norm, thus "women" picks out white bourgeois women, "men" picks out white bourgeois men, "black" picks out black heterosexual men, and so on. It becomes logically clear then that the logic of categorial separation distorts what exists at the intersection, such as violence against women of color. Given the construction of the categories, the intersection misconstrues women of color. So, once intersectionality shows us what is missing, we have ahead of us the task of reconceptualizing the logic of the "intersection" so as to avoid separability. It is only when we perceive gender and race as intermeshed or fused that we actually see women of color.

The logic of structural axes shows gender as constituted by and constituting the coloniality of power. In that sense, there is no gender/race separability in Quijano's model. I think he has the logic of it right. But the axis of coloniality is not sufficient to pick out all aspects of gender. What aspects of gender are shown depends on how gender is actually conceptualized in the model. In Quijano's model (pattern,) gender seems to be contained within the organization of that "basic area of existence" that Quijano calls "sex, its resources, and products." That is, there is an account of gender within the framework that is not itself placed under scrutiny and that is too narrow and overly biologized as it presupposes sexual dimorphism, heterosexuality, patriarchal distribution of power, and so on.

Though I have not found a characterization of gender in what I have read of his work, Quijano seems to me to imply that gender difference is constituted in the disputes over control of sex, its resources, and products. Differences are shaped through the manner in which this control is organized. Sex, he understands, as biological attributes that become elaborated as social categories. He contrasts the biological quality of sex with phenotype, which does not include differential biological attributes. "The color of one's skin, the shape of one's eyes and hair "do not have any relation to the biological structure." (Quijano, 2000b, 373) Sex, on the other hand seems unproblematically biological to Quijano. [. . .]

Intersexuality

In "Definitional Dilemmas" Julie Greenberg (2002) tells us that legal institutions have the power to assign individuals to a particular racial or sexual category.

> Sex is still presumed to be binary and easily determinable by an analysis of biological factors. Despite anthropological and medical studies to the contrary, society presumes an unambiguous binary sex paradigm in which all individuals can be classified neatly as male or female (112)

She argues that throughout U.S. history the law has failed to recognize intersexuals, in spite of the fact that 1 to 4 percent of the world's population is intersexed, that is they do not fit neatly into unambiguous sex categories,

> "they have some biological indicators that are *traditionally* associated with males and some biological indicators that are *traditionally* associated with females. (my emphasis) The manner in which the law defines the terms *male*, *female*, and *sex* will have a profound impact on these individuals."
>
> (112)

The assignations reveal that what is understood to be biological sex, is socially constructed. During the late nineteenth century until WWI, reproductive function was considered a woman's essential characteristic. The presence or absence of ovaries was the ultimate criterion of sex. (113) But there are a large number of factors that can enter in "establishing someone's 'official' sex:" chromosomes, gonads, external morphology, internal morphology, hormonal patterns, phenotype, assigned sex, self-identified sex. (112) At present, chromosomes and genitalia enter into the assignment, but in a manner that reveals biology is thoroughly interpreted and itself surgically constructed.

> XY infants with "inadequate" penises must be turned into girls because society believes the essence of manhood is the ability to penetrate a vagina and urinate while standing. XX infants with "adequate" penises, however, are assigned the females sex because society and many in the medical community believe that the essence of womanhood is the ability to bear children rather than the ability to engage in satisfactory sexual intercourse.
>
> (114)

Intersexed individuals are frequently surgically and hormonally turned into males or females. These factors are taken into account in legal cases involving the right to change the sex designation on official documents, the ability to state a claim for employment discrimination based upon sex, the right to marry. (115) Greenberg reports the complexities and variety of decisions on sexual assignation in each case. The law does not recognize intersexual status. Though the law permits self-identification of one's sex in certain documents, "for the most part, legal institutions continue to base sex assignment on the traditional assumptions that sex is binary and can be easily determined by analyzing biological factors." (119)

Julie Greenberg's work enables me to point out an important assumption in the model that Quijano offers us. This is important because sexual dimorphism has been an important characteristic of what I call "the light side" of the colonial/modern gender system. Those in the "dark side" were not necessarily understood dimorphically. Sexual fears of colonizers led them to imagine the indigenous people of the Americas as hermaphrodites or intersexed, with large penises and breasts with flowing milk. But as Gunn Allen and others make clear, intersexed individuals were recognized in many tribal societies prior to colonization without assimilation to the sexual binary. It is important to consider the changes that colonization brought to understand the scope of the organization of sex and gender under colonialism and in Eurocentered global capitalism. If the latter did only recognize sexual dimorphism for white bourgeois males and females, it certainly does not follow that the sexual division is based on biology. The cosmetic and substantive corrections to biology make very clear that "gender" is antecedent to the "biological" traits and gives them meaning. The naturalizing of sexual differences is another product of the modern use of science that Quijano points out in the case of "race." It is important to see that not all different traditions correct and normalize inter-sexed people. So, as with other assumption characteristics it is important to ask how sexual dimorphism served and serves Eurocentered global capitalist domination/exploitation.

[. . .]

Non-Gendered Egalitarianism

In her *The Invention of Women*, Oyéronké Oyewùmí, raises questions about the validity of patriarchy as a valid transcultural category. (20) She does so, not by contrasting patriarchy and matriarchy, but arguing that "gender was not an organizing principle in Yoruba society prior to colonization by the West." (31) No gender system was in place.

Indeed she tells us that gender has "become important in Yoruba studies not as an artifact of Yoruba life but because Yoruba life, past and present, has been translated into English to fit the Western pattern of body-reasoning." (30) The assumption that Yoruba society included gender as an organizing principle is another case "of Western dominance in the documentation and interpretation of the world, one that is facilitated by the West's global material dominance. (32) She tells us that "researchers always find gender when they look for it." (31)

> The usual gloss of the Yoruba categories *obinrin* and *okunrin* as "female/woman" and "male/man," respectively, is a mistranslation. These categories are neither binarily opposed nor hierarchical.
>
> (32–33)

The prefixes obin and okun specify a variety of anatomy. Oyewumi translates the prefixes as referring to the anatomic male and the anatomic female, shortened as anamale and anafemale. It is important to note that she does not understand these categories as binarily opposed.

Oyewumi understands gender as introduced by the West as a tool of domination that designates two binarily opposed and hierarchical social categories. Women (the gender term) is not defined through biology, though it is assigned to anafemales. Women are defined in relation to men, the norm. Women are those who do not have a penis; those who do not have power; those who cannot participate in the public arena. (34) None of this was true of Yoruba anafemales prior to colonization.

[. . .]

We can see then that the scope of the coloniality of gender is much too narrow. Quijano assumes much of the terms of the modern/colonial gender system's hegemonic "light" side in defining the scope of gender. I have gone outside the coloniality of gender so as to think of what it hides, or disallows from consideration, about the very scope of the gender system of Eurocentered global capitalism. So, though I think that the coloniality of gender, as Quijano pointedly describes it, shows us very important aspects of the intersection of "race" and "gender," it follows rather than discloses the erasure of colonized women from most areas of social life. It accommodates rather than disrupt the narrowing of gender domination. Oyewumi's rejection of the gender lens in characterizing the inferiorization of anafemales in modern colonization makes clear the extent and scope of the inferiorization. Her understanding of gender, the colonial, Eurocentered, capitalist construction, is much more encompassing than Quijano's. She enables us to see the economic, political, cognitive inferiorization as well as the inferiorization of anafemales regarding reproductive control.

Gynecratic Egalitarianism

To assign to this great being the position of "fertility goddess" is exceedingly demeaning: it trivializes the tribes and it trivializes the power of woman. (Gunn Allen, 1986, p. 14)

As she characterizes many Native American tribes as gynecratic, Paula Gunn Allen emphasizes the centrality of the spiritual in all aspects of Indian life and thus a very different intersubjectivity from within which knowledge is produced than that of the coloniality of knowledge in modernity. Many American Indian tribes "thought that the primary potency in the universe was female, and that understanding authorizes all tribal activities." (26) Old Spider Woman, Corn Woman, Serpent Woman, Thought Woman are some of the names of powerful creators. For the gynecratic tribes, Woman is at the center and "no thing is sacred without her blessing, her thinking." (13)

Replacing this gynecratic spiritual plurality with one supreme male being as Christianity did, was crucial in subduing the tribes. [. . .]

[. . .] Among the features of the Indian society targeted for destruction were the two-sided complementary social structure; the understanding of gender; the economic distribution which often followed the system of reciprocity. The two sides of the complementary social structure included an internal female chief and an external male chief. The internal chief presided over the band, village, or tribe, maintained harmony and administered domestic affairs. The red, male, chief presided over mediations between the tribe and outsiders. (18) Gender was not understood primarily in biological terms. Most individuals fit into tribal gender roles "on the basis of proclivity, inclination, and temperament. The Yuma had a tradition of gender designation based on dreams; a female who dreamed of weapons became a male for all practical purposes." (196)

Like Oyewumi, Gunn Allen is interested in the collaboration between some Indian men and whites in undermining the power of women. It is important for us to think about these collaborations as we think of the question of indifference to the struggles of women in racialized communities against multiple forms of violence against them and the communities. The white colonizer constructed a powerful inside force as colonized men were coopted into patriarchal roles. Gunn Allen details the transformations of the Iroquois and Cherokee gynecracies and the role of Indian men in the passage to patriarchy. The British took Cherokee men to England and gave them an education in the ways of the English. These men participated during the time of the Removal Act.

> In an effort to stave off removal, the Cherokee in the early 1800s under the leadership of men such as Elias Boudinot, Major Ridge, and John Ross, and others, drafted a constitution that disenfranchised women and blacks. Modeled after the Constitution of the United States, whose favor they were attempting to curry, and in conjunction with Christian sympathizers to the Cherokee cause, the new Cherokee constitution relegated women to the position of chattel.
>
> (37)

Cherokee women had had the power to wage war, to decide the fate of captives, to speak to the men's council, they had the right to inclusion in public policy decisions, the right to choose whom and whether to marry, the right to bear arms. The Women's Council was politically and spiritually powerful. (36–37) Cherokee women lost all these powers and rights, as the Cherokee were removed and patriarchal arrangements were introduced. The Iroquois shifted from a Mother-centered, Mother-right people organized politically under the authority of the Matrons, to a patriarchal society when the Iroquois became a subject people. The feat was accomplished with the collaboration of Handsome Lake and his followers. (33)

According to Allen, many of the tribes were gynecratic, among them the Susquehanna, Hurons, Iroquois, Cherokee, Pueblo, Navajo, Narragansett, Coastal Algonkians, Montagnais. She also tells us that among the eighty-eight tribes that recognized homosexuality, those who recognized homosexuals in positive terms included the Apache, Navajo, Winnebago, Cheyenne, Pima, Crow, Shoshoni, Paiute, Osage, Acoma, Zuñi, Sioux, Pawnee, Choctaw, Creek, Seminole, Illinois, Mohave, Shasta, Aleut, Sac and Fox, Iowa, Kansas, Yuma, Aztec, Tlingit, Maya, Naskapi, Ponca, Maricopa, Lamath, Quinault, Yuki, Chilula, Kamia. Twenty of these tribes included specific references to lesbianism.

[. . .]

Allen's work not only enables us to see how narrow Quijano's conception of gender is in terms of the organization of the economy, and the organization of collective authority, she also enables us to see that the production of knowledge is gendered, the very conception of reality at every level. She also supports the questioning of biology in the construction of gender differences and introduces the important question of gender roles being chosen and dreamt. But importantly, Allen also shows us that the heterosexuality characteristic of the modern/colonial construction of gender relations, is produced, mythically constructed. But heterosexuality is not just biologized in a fictional way, it is also compulsory and it permeates the whole of the coloniality of gender, in the renewed, large sense. In this sense, global Eurocentered capitalism is heterosexualist. I think it is important to see, as we understand the depth and force of violence in the production of both the "light" and the "dark" sides of the colonial/modern gender system, that this heterosexuality has been consistently perverse, violent, demeaning, a turning of people into animals, and the turning of white women into reproducers of "the race" and "the class." Horswell's and Sigal's work complements Allen's, particularly in understanding the presence of sodomy and male homosexuality in colonial and pre-colonial America.

The Colonial/Modern Gender System

Understanding the place of gender in pre-colonial societies is pivotal to understanding the nature and scope of changes in the social structure that the processes constituting colonial/modern Eurocentered capitalism imposed. Those changes were introduced through slow, discontinuous, and heterogeneous processes that violently inferiorized colonized women. The gender system introduced was one thoroughly informed through the coloniality of power. Understanding the place of gender in pre-colonial societies is also pivotal in understanding the extent and importance of the gender system in disintegrating communal relations, egalitarian relations, ritual thinking, collective decision making, collective authority, and economies. And thus in understanding the extent to which the imposition of this gender system was as constitutive of the coloniality of power as the coloniality of power was constitutive of it. The logic of the relation between them is of mutual constitution. But it should be clear by now that the colonial, modern, gender system cannot exist without the coloniality of power, since the classification of the population in terms of race is a necessary condition of its possibility.

To think the scope of the gender system of Eurocentered global capitalism it is necessary to understand the extent to which the *very process of narrowing* of the concept of gender to the control of sex, its resources, and products constitutes gender domination. To understand this narrowing and to understand the intermeshing of racialization and gendering, it is important to think whether the social arrangements prior to colonization regarding the "sexes" gave differential meaning to them across all areas of existence. That enables us to see whether control over labor, subjectivity/intersubjectivity, collective authority, sex—Quijano's "areas of existence"—were themselves gendered. Given the coloniality of power, I think we can also say that having a "dark" and a "light side" is characteristic of the co-construction of the coloniality of power and the colonial/modern gender system. Considering critically both biological dimorphism and the position that gender socially constructs biological sex is pivotal to understand the scope, depth, and characteristics of the colonial/modern gender system. The sense is that the reduction of gender to the private, to control over sex and its resources and products is a matter of ideology, of the cognitive production of modernity that understood race as gendered and gender as raced in particularly differential ways for Europeans/"whites" and colonized/"non-white" peoples. Race is no more mythical and fictional than gender, both powerful fictions.

In the development of twentieth century feminisms, the connection between gender, class, heterosexuality as racialized was not made explicit. That feminism centered its struggle and its ways of knowing and theorizing against a characterization of women as fragile, weak in both body and mind, secluded in the private, and sexually passive. But it did not bring to consciousness that those characteristics only constructed white bourgeois womanhood. Indeed, beginning from that characterization, white bourgeois feminists theorized white womanhood as if all women were white.

It is part of their history that only white bourgeois women have consistently counted as women so described in the West. Females excluded from that description were not just their subordinates. They were also understood to be animals in a sense that went further than the identification of white women with nature, infants, and small animals. They were understood as animals in the deep sense of "without gender," sexually marked as female, but without the characteristics of femininity. Women racialized as inferior were turned from animals into various modified versions of "women" as it fit the processes of Eurocentered global capitalism. Thus heterosexual rape of Indian women, African slave women, coexisted with concubinage, as well as with the imposition of the heterosexual understanding of gender relations among the colonized—when and as it suited Euro-centered, global capitalism, and heterosexual domination of white women. But it is clear from the work of Oyewumi and Allen that there was no extension of the status of white women to colonized women even when they were turned into similes of bourgeois white women. Colonized females got the inferior status of gendering as women, without any of the privileges accompanying that status for white bourgeois women. Though, the history presented by Oyewumi and Allen should make clear to white bourgeois women that their status is much inferior to that of Native American women and Yoruba women before colonization. Oyewumi and Allen also make clear that the egalitarian understanding of the relation between anafemales, anamales, and "third" gender people has not left the imagination nor the practices of Native Americans and Yoruba. But these are matters of resistance to domination.

Erasing any history, including oral history, of the relation of white to non-white women, white feminism wrote white women large. Even though historically and contemporarily white bourgeois women knew perfectly well how to orient themselves in an organization of life that pitted them for very different treatment than non-white or working class women. White feminist struggle became one against the positions, roles, stereotypes, traits, desires imposed on white bourgeois women's subordination. No one else's gender oppression was countenanced. They understood women as inhabiting white bodies but did not bring that racial qualification to articulation or clear awareness. That is, they did not understand themselves in intersectional terms, at the intersection of race, gender, and other forceful marks of subjection or domination. Because they did not perceive these deep differences they did not see a need for creating coalitions. They presumed a sisterhood, a bond given with the subjection of gender.

Historically, the characterization of white European women as fragile and sexually passive opposed them to non-white, colonized women, including women slaves, who were characterized along a gamut of sexual aggression and perversion, and as strong enough to do any sort of labor. The following description of slave women and of slave work in the U.S. South makes clear that African slave females were not considered fragile or weak.

> First came, led by an old driver carrying a whip, forty of the largest and strongest women I ever saw together; they were all in a simple uniform dress of a bluish check stuff, the skirts reaching little below the knee; their legs and feet were bare; they carried themselves loftily, each having a hoe over the shoulder, and walking with a free, powerful swing, like *chasseurs* on the march. Behind came the cavalry, thirty strong, mostly men, but a few of them women, two of whom rode astride on the plow mules. A lean and vigilant white overseer, on a brisk pony, brought up the rear.
>
> (Takaki, 111)

> The hands are required to be in the cotton field as soon as it is light in the morning, and, with the exception of ten or fifteen minutes, which is given to them at noon to swallow their allowance of cold bacon, they are not permitted to be a moment idle until it is too dark to see, and when the moon is full, they often times labor till the middle of the night.
>
> (Takaki, 111)

Patricia Hill Collins ([1990] 2000) provides a clear sense of the dominant understanding of Black women as sexually aggressive and the genesis of that stereotype in slavery:

> The image of Jezebel originated under slavery when Black women were portrayed as being, to use Jewelle Gomez' words, "sexually aggressive wet nurses." (Clarke et al., 1983, p. 99). Jezebel's function was to relegate all Black women to the category of sexually aggressive women, thus providing a powerful rationale for the widespread sexual assaults by White men typically reported by Black slave women. (Davis, 1981; D. White, 1985) Jezebel served yet another function. If Black slave women could be portrayed as having excessive sexual appetites, then increased fertility should be the expected outcome. By suppressing the nurturing that African-American women might give their own children which would strengthen Black family networks, and by forcing Black women to work in the field, "wet nurse" White children, and emotionally nurture their White owners, slave owners effectively tied the controlling images of jezebel and mammy to the economic exploitation inherent in the institution of slavery.
>
> (Hill Collins, 82)

But it is not just black slave women who were placed outside the scope of white bourgeois femininity. In *Imperial Leather*, Anne McClintock (1995) as she tells us of Columbus' depiction of the earth as a woman's breast, evokes the "long tradition of male travel as an erotics of ravishment." (22)

> For centuries, the uncertain continents—Africa, the Americas, Asia—were figured in European lore as libidinously eroticized. Travelers' tales abounded with visions of the monstrous sexuality of far-off lands, where, as legend had it, men sported gigantic penises and women consorted with apes, feminized men's breasts flowed with milk and militarized women lopped theirs off.
>
> (22)

Within this porno tropic tradition, women figured as the epitome of sexual aberration and excess. Folklore saw them, even more than the men, as given to a lascivious venery so promiscuous as to border on the bestial.

(22)

McClintock describes the colonial scene depicted in a drawing (ca. 1575) in which Jan van der Straet "portrays the "discovery" of America as an eroticized encounter between a man and a woman." (25)

Roused from her sensual languor by the epic newcomer, the indigenous woman extends an inviting hand, insinuating sex and submission . . . Vespucci, the godlike arrival, is destined to inseminate her with his male seeds of civilization, fructify the wilderness and quell the riotous scenes of cannibalism in the background . . . The cannibals appear to be female and are spit roasting a human leg.

(26)

In the 19th century, McClintock tells us "sexual purity emerged as a controlling metaphor for racial, economic and political power." (47) With the development of evolutionary theory "anatomical criteria were sought for determining the relative position of races in the human series." (50)

The English middle-class male was placed at the pinnacle of evolutionary hierarchy. White English middle class women followed. Domestic workers, female miners and working class prostitutes were stationed on the threshold between the white and black races.

(56)

Yen Le Espiritu (1997) tells us that

representations of gender and sexuality figure strongly in the articulation of racism. Gender norms in the United States are premised upon the experiences of middle-class men and women of European origin. These Eurocentric-constructed gender norms form a backdrop of expectations for American men and women of color—expectations which racism often precludes meeting. In general, men of color are viewed not as the protector, but rather the aggressor—a threat to white women. And women of color are seen as over sexualized and thus undeserving of the social and sexual protection accorded to white middleclass women. For Asian American men and women, their exclusion from white-based cultural notions of the masculine and the feminine has taken seemingly contrasting forms: Asian men have been cast as both hypermasculine (the "Yellow Peril") and effeminate (the "model minority"); and Asian women have been rendered both superfeminine (the "China Doll") and castrating (the "Dragon Lady"). (Espiritu, 135)

This gender system congeals as Europe advances the colonial project(s). It begins to take shape during the Spanish and Portuguese colonial adventures and becomes full blown in late modernity. The gender system has a "light" and a "dark" side. The light side constructs gender and gender relations hegemonic ally. It only orders the lives of white bourgeois men and women, and it constitutes the modern/colonial meaning of "men" and "women." Sexual purity and passivity are crucial characteristics of the white bourgeois females who reproduce the class, and the colonial, and racial standing of bourgeois, white men. But equally important is the banning of white bourgeois women from the sphere of collective authority, from the production of knowledge, from most of control over the means of production. Weakness of mind and body are important in the reduction and seclusion of white bourgeois women from most domains of life, most areas of human existence. The gender system is heterosexualist, as heterosexuality permeates racialized patriarchal control over production, including knowledge production, and over collective authority. Heterosexuality is both compulsory and perverse among white bourgeois men and women since the arrangement does significant violence to the powers and rights of white bourgeois women and it serves to reproduce control over production and white bourgeois women are inducted into this reduction through bounded sexual access.

The "dark" side of the gender system was and is thoroughly violent. We have began to see the deep reductions of anamales, anafemales, and "third" genders from their ubiquitous participation in ritual, decision making, economics; their reduction to animality, to forced sex with white colonizers, to such deep labor exploitation that often people died working. Quijano tells us

> The vast Indian genocide of the first decades of colonization was not caused, in the main, by the violence of the conquest, nor by the diseases that the conquerors carried. Rather is was due to the fact that the Indians were used as throwaway labor, forced to work till death.
>
> (My translation) (Quijano, 2000a)

I want to mark the connection between the work that I am referencing here as I introduce the modern colonial gender system's "dark" side, and Quijano's coloniality of power. Unlike white feminists who have not focused on colonialism, these theorists very much see the differential construction of gender along racial lines. To some extent these theorists understand "gender" in a wider sense than Quijano, thus they think not only of control over sex, its resources and products, but also of labor as both racialized and gendered. That is, they see an articulation between labor, sex, and the coloniality of power. Oyewumi and Allen help us realize the full extent of the reach of the colonial/modern gender system into the construction of collective authority, all aspects of the relation between capital and labor, and the construction of knowledge.

There is important work done and to be done in detailing the dark and light sides of what I am calling the "modern colonial gender system." In introducing this arrangements in very large strokes, I mean to begin a conversation and a project of collaborative, participatory, research and popular education to begin to see in its details the long sense of the processes of the colonial/gender system enmeshed in the coloniality of power into the present, to uncover collaboration, and to call each other to reject it in its various guises as we recommit to communal integrity in a liberatory direction. We need to understand the organization of the social so as to make visible our collaboration with systematic racialized gender violence, so as to come to an inevitable recognition of it in our maps of reality.

Bibliography

Crenshaw, Kimberlé. 1995. "Mapping the Margins: Intersectionality, Identity Politics, and Violence Against Women of Color." In *Critical Race Theory*. Edited by Kimberlé Crenshaw, Neil Gotanda, Gary Peller, and Kendall Thomas. New York: The New Press.

Espiritu, Yen Le. 1997. "Race, Class, and Gender in Asian America." In *Making More Waves*. Edited by Elaine H. Kim, Lilia V. Villanueva and Asian Women United of California. Boston: Beacon.

Greenberg, Julie A. 2002. "Definitional Dilemmas: Male or Female? Black or White? The Law's Failure to Recognize Intersexuals and Multiracials." *In Gender Nonconformity, Race, and Sexuality. Charting the Connections*. Edited by Toni Lester. Madison: University of Wisconsin Press.

Gunn Allen, Paula. [1986] 1992. *The Sacred Hoop. Recovering the Feminine in American Indian Traditions*. Boston: Beacon Press.

Hill Collins, Patricia. [1990] 2000. *Black Feminist Thought: Knowledge, Consciousness, and the Politics of Empowerment*. New York: Routledge.

Horswell. "Toward and Andean Theory of Ritual Same-Sex Sexuality and Third-Gender Subjectivity." In *Infamous Desire. Male Homosexuality in Colonial Latin America*. Edited by Pete Sigal. Chicago and London: The University of Chicago Press.

Lugones, María. 2003. *Pilgrimages/Peregrinajes: Theorizing Coalitions Against Multiple Oppressions*. Lanham: Rowman & Littlefield.

McClintock, Anne. 1995. *Imperial Leather. Race, Gender and Sexuality in the Colonial Contest*. New York: Routledge.

Oyewumi, Oyeronke. 1997. *The Invention of Women. Making an African Sense of Western Gender Discourses*. Minneapolis: University of Minnesota Press.

Quijano, Anibal. 1991. "Colonialidad, modernidad/racionalidad." *Peru Indigena*, vol. 13, no. 29, pp. 11–29.

———. 2000a. "Colonialidad del poder, eurocentrismo y America Latina." Colonialidad del Saber, Eurocentrismo y Ciencias Sicales. CLACSO-UNESCO 2000, Buenos Aires, Argentina, pp. 201–246.

———. 2000b. "Colonialidad del Poder y Clasificacion Social." *Festschrift for Immanuel Wallerstein, part I, Journal of World Systems Research*, vol. xi, #2, summer/fall 2000.

———. 2001–2002. "Colonialidad del poder, globalización y democracia." *Revista de Ciencias Sociales de la Universidad Autónoma de Nuevo León*, Año 4, Números 7 y 8, Septiembre 2001–Abril 2002.

Sigal, Pete. 2003. "Gendered Power, the Hybrid Self, and Homosexual Desire in Late Colonial Yucatan." In *Infamous Desire. Male Homosexuality in Colonial Latin America*. Edited by Pete Sigal. Chicago and London: The University of Chicago Press.

Spelman, Elizabeth. 1988. *Inessential Woman*. Boston: Beacon.

Takaki, Ronald. 1993. *A Different Mirror*. Boston: Little, Brown, and Company.

13 Extermination of the *Joyas*

Gendercide in Spanish California

Deborah A. Miranda

Deborah A. Miranda, a literary scholar and poet of mixed Anglo, Chumash, and Ohlone heritage, uses the history of her own ancestors to discuss what Maria Lugones called the "coloniality
of gender." In "The Extermination of the *Joyas*," first published in the "Sexuality, Nationality, and
Indigeneity" special issue of *GLQ: A Journal of Lesbian and Gay Studies* in 2010, Miranda deploys
the concept of "gendercide," or the deliberate killing of an entire category of people, to examine
the mass death of two-spirit people in her native Californian lineage during Spanish colonization.
While the Spanish mockingly referred to such people as *joyas*, or "jewels," Miranda's Chumash
ancestors called them *a'qi*, which meant "undertaker." Surviving records and traditions make clear
that *a'qi* named a special ceremonial function or spiritual role and was not an identity-label like
"transgender." Many Californian cultures at the time of Spanish contact accepted that some people
with male anatomy had feminine dispositions, and those people were raised as girls and lived as
women. They also carried out the special task of guiding the spirits of the dead from this life to the
next—a treacherous journey presided over by supernatural powers of different genders that needed
the expert attention of people who understood both masculinity and femininity. The extermination of the transfeminine *joyas*, perceived through the biocentric lens of European coloniality as
"sodomites" who "sinned against nature," unraveled all of Chumash society. With no one to guide
the dead, Miranda claims, her ancestors turned to Catholicism for its burial rites—in fear, at first,
and not belief, based on an urgent and immediate need for spiritual protection.

Attempting to address the many communities from which she spoke, Paula Gunn Allen
once asserted: "I cannot do one identity. I'm simply not capable of it. And it took me
years to understand that that's one of the features of my upbringing. I was raised in a mixed
cultural group—mixed linguistic, mixed religion, mixed race—Laguna *itself* is that way.
So I get really uncomfortable in any kind of mono-cultural group."[1] Although Allen does
not speak specifically of another community—her lesbian family—in this quotation, her
legacy of activism and writing document the unspoken inclusion of sexual orientation
within her list of identities. Like Allen, my own identity is not monocultural: by blood,
I am Esselen and Chumash (California Native) as well as Jewish, French, and English.
I was born at UCLA Medical Center, raised in trailer parks and rural landscapes, possess
a PhD, and teach at a small, private southern liberal arts university. I am fluent in English,
can read Spanish, and was called to an *aliyah* at the bat mitzvah of my partner's niece. Who
am I? Where is home?

DOI: 10.4324/9781003206255-17

In my poetry and my scholarship, I have worked through issues of complex identities for much of my life, primarily those relating to my position as a mixed-blood woman with an Indian father and European American mother. But one of the most urgent questions in my life—the intersection of being Indian and being a lesbian—has always been more complicated, less easily articulated, than anything else. Here again, Allen's body of work has been most helpful. In a poem titled "Some Like Indians Endure," Allen plays with concepts of just what makes an Indian an Indian—and asks if those qualities, whatever they are, are necessarily exclusive to Indians. At the heart of this poem is this thought:

> I have it in my mind that
> dykes are indians
> they're a lot like indians . . .
> they were massacred
> lots of times
> they always came back
> like the gas
> like the clouds
> they got massacred again.[2]

This poem illustrates the multiple directions of Allen's thought: while defending the concept of Indian as something different and distinguishable from colonizing cultures around it, Allen simultaneously compares the qualities of being Indian with those of being lesbian. She comes up with lists of similarities for both identities, the lengthiness of which overwhelms her ability to keep the two apart. While Allen recognizes balance and wholeness in both her Laguna and lesbian identities, this is not necessarily something that completely expresses my own situation.

While researching material for my book "Bad Indians: A Tribal Memoir," however, I came across a page of the ethnologist J. P. Harrington's field notes that provided a doorway for me to enter into a conversation about complex identities with my ancestors.[3] Tracing my California Native ancestors from first contact with Spanish missionaries through contemporary times, my research required that I immerse myself in a rich variety of archival resources: correspondence between missionaries and their supervisors in Spain; mission records of baptism, birth, and death as well as finances and legal cases; the as-told-to testimonies of missionized Indians both before, during, and after the mission era; as well as newspapers, family oral history, photographs, and ethnological and anthropological data from earliest contact through the "salvage ethnology" era and into the present.[4] None of these archival materials came from unfiltered Indian voices; such records were impossible both because of their colonizing context and the prevalence of an oral tradition among California Indians that did not leave textual traces. The difficulties of using non-Indian archives to tell an Indian story are epic: biases, agendas, cultural pride, notions of Manifest Destiny, and the desire to "own" history mean that one can never simply read and accept even the most basic non-Native detail without multiple investigations into who collected the information, what their motivations were, who preserved the information and their motivations, the use of rhetorical devices (like the passive voice so prevalent in missionization histories: "The Missions were built using adobe bricks" rather than "Indians, often held captive and/or punished by flogging, built the Missions without compensation"). Learning how to "re-read" the archive through the eyes of a mixed-blood California Indian lesbian poet and scholar was an education in and of itself, so the fact that this essay emerges from one short, handwritten piece of information gleaned by Harrington from one of my ancestors about older ancestors should not be surprising.

To tell the story of this field note, for which I use the shorthand title "Jotos" (Spanish slang for "queer" or "faggot"), I must pull threads of several stories together. The field note is like a petroglyph; when I touch it, so much else must be known, communicated, and understood to see the power within what looks like a simple inscription, a random bit of Carmel Mission Indian trivia. Once read, this note opens out into deeper and deeper stories. Some of those stories are full of grief—like the one that follows—yet they are all essential to possessing this archival evidence and giving it a truly indigenous reading. When I say "indigenous reading," I mean a reading that enriches Native lives with meaning, survival, and love, which points to the important role of archival reconstruction in developing a robust Two-Spirit tradition today.[5] In the last two decades, the archaeology of sexuality and gender has also helped create new ways to use these biased primary sources, and I hope to pull together the many shards of information available in order to glimpse what contemporary California Indians might use in our efforts to reclaim and reinvent ourselves.[6] This essay, then, examines methods employed by the Spaniards to exterminate the *joya* (the Spanish name for third-gender people); asks what that extermination meant to California Indian cultures; explores the survival of this third gender as first *joyas*, then *jotos* (Spanish for homosexual, or faggot); and evaluates the emergence of spiritual and physical renewal of the ancestral third gender in California Indian Two-Spirit individuals.[7] It is both a personal story and a historical struggle about identity played out in many indigenous communities all over the world.

Waging Gendercide 101

Spanish colonizers—from royalty to soldier to padre—believed that American Indians were intellectually, physiologically, and spiritually immature, if not actual animals.[8] In the area eventually known as California, the genocidal policies of the Spanish Crown would lead to a severe population crash: numbering one million at first contact, California Indians plummeted to about ten thousand survivors in just over one hundred years.[9] Part of this massive loss were third-gender people, who were lost not by "passive" colonizing collateral damage such as disease or starvation, but through active, conscious, violent extermination. Speaking of the Chumash people living along the southern coast (my grandmother's tribal roots), Pedro Fages, a Spanish soldier, makes clear that the soldiers and priests colonizing Mexico and what would become California arrived with a deep abhorrence of what they viewed as homosexual relationships. In his soldier's memoir, written in 1775, Fages reports:

> I have substantial evidence that those Indian men who, both here and farther inland, are observed in the dress, clothing, and character of women—there being two or three such in each village—pass as sodomites by profession (it being confirmed that all these Indians are much addicted to this abominable vice) and permit the heathen to practice the execrable, unnatural abuse of their bodies. They are called *joyas*, and are held in great esteem. Let this mention suffice for a matter which could not be omitted,—on account of the bearing it may have on the discussion of the reduction of these natives,—with a promise to revert in another place to an excess so criminal that it seems even forbidden to speak its name . . . But we place our trust in God and expect that these accursed people will disappear with the growth of the missions. The abominable vice will be eliminated to the extent that the Catholic faith and all the other virtues are firmly implanted there, for the glory of God and the benefit of those poor ignorants.[10]

Much of what little we know about *joyas* (Spanish for "jewels," as I discuss below) is limited to observations like that of Fages, choked by Eurocentric values and mores. The majority of Spanish soldiers and priests were not interested in learning about California Indian culture and recorded only as much as was needed to dictate spiritual and corporeal discipline and/or punishment; there are no known recorded interviews with a *joya* by either priest or Spaniard, let alone the salvage ethnologists who arrived one hundred years later. In this section, I provide an overview of what first contact between *joya* and Spaniard looked like, and how that encounter leaves scars to this day in California Indian culture. The key word here is not, in fact, encounter, but *destruction*.

Weapons of Mass Destruction: The Mastiffs

As I show, while the Spanish priests' disciplinary methods might be strict and intolerant, they were at least attempting to deal with *joyas* and *joya* relationships in ways that allowed these Indians to live, albeit marginalized and shamed.

Spanish soldiers had a different, less patient method. They threw the *joyas* to their dogs. Shouting the command "Tómalos!" (take them, or sic'em), the Spanish soldiers ordered execution of *joyas* by specially bred mastiffs and greyhounds.[11] The dogs of the conquest, who had already acquired a taste for human flesh (and were frequently fed live Indians when other food was unavailable), were the colonizer's weapon of mass destruction.[12] In his history of the relationship between dogs and men, Stanley Coren explains just how efficient these weapons were: "The mastiffs of that era could weigh 250 pounds and stand nearly three feet at the shoulder. Their massive jaws could crush bones even through leather armor. The greyhounds of that period, meanwhile, could be over one hundred pounds and thirty inches at the shoulder. These lighter dogs could outrun any man, and their slashing attack could easily disembowel a person in a matter of seconds."[13] Columbus brought dogs along with him on his second journey and claimed that one dog was worth fifty soldiers in subduing the Natives.[14] On September 23, 1513, the explorer Vasco Nuñez de Balboa came on about forty indigenous men, all dressed as women, engaged in what he called "preposterous Venus." He commanded his men to give the men as "a prey to his dogges," and the men were torn apart alive.[15] Coren states matter-of-factly that "these dogs were considered to be mere weapons and sometimes instruments of torture."[16] By the time the Spaniards had expanded their territory to California, the use of dogs as weapons to kill or eat Indians, particularly *joyas*, was well established.

Was this violence against *joyas* classic homophobia (fear of people with same-sex orientation) or gendercide? I argue that gendercide is the correct term. As Maureen S. Heibert comments:

> Gendercide would then be . . . an attack on a group of victims based on the victims' gender/sex. Such an attack would only really occur if men or women are victimized because of their *primary* identity as men or women. In the case of male gendercide, male victims must be victims first and foremost because they are men, not male Bosnians, Jews, or Tutsis. Moreover, it must be the perpetrators themselves, not outside observers making ex-poste analyses, who identify a specific gender/sex as a threat and therefore a target for extermination.
>
> *As such, we must be able to explicitly show that the perpetrators target a gender victim group based on the victims' primary identity as either men or women.*[17]

Or, I must add, as a third gender? Interestingly, although Heibert doesn't consider that possibility, her argument supports my own definition of gendercide as an act of violence committed against a victim's primary gender identity.

Consider the immediate effect of Balboa's punishment of the "sodomites": when local Indians found out about the executions "upon that filthy kind of men," the Indians turned to the Spaniards "as if it had been to Hercules for refuge" and quickly rounded up all the other third-gender people in the area, "spitting in their faces and crying out to our men to take revenge of them and rid them out of the world from among men as contagious beasts."[18] This is not homophobia (widely defined as irrational fear of or aversion to homosexuals, with subsequent discrimination against homosexuals); obviously, the Indians were not suddenly surprised to find *joyas* in their midst, and dragging people to certain death went far beyond discrimination or culturally condoned chastisement. This was fear of death; more specifically, of being murdered. What the local indigenous peoples had been taught was gendercide, the killing of a particular gender *because of their gender*. As Heibert says in her description of gendercide above, "It must be the perpetrators themselves, not outside observers making ex-poste analyses, who identify a specific gender/sex as a threat and therefore a target for extermination." Now that the Spaniards had made it clear that to tolerate, harbor, or associate with the third gender meant death, and that nothing could stand against their dogs of war, the indigenous community knew that demonstrations of acquiescence to this force were essential for the survival of the remaining community—and both the community and the Spaniards knew exactly which people were marked for execution. This tragic pattern in which one segment of indigenous population was sacrificed in hopes that others would survive continues to fester in many contemporary Native communities where people with same-sex orientation are no longer part of cultural legacy but feared, discriminated against, and locked out of tribal and familial homes. We have mistakenly called this behavior "homophobia" in Indian Country; to call it gendercide would certainly require rethinking the assimilation of Euro-American cultural values and the meaning of indigenous community.

Thus the killing of the *joyas* by Spaniards was, indeed, "part of a coordinated plan of destruction"—but it was only one strategy of gendercide.

(Re-)Naming

Father Juan Crespi, part of the 1769 "Sacred Expedition" from Mexico to Alta California, traveled with an exploration party through numerous Chumash coastal villages. "We have seen heathen men wearing the dress of women," he wrote. "We have not been able to understand what it means, nor what its purpose is; time and an understanding of the language, when it is learned, will make it clear."[19] Crespi's willingness to wait for "an understanding of the language" was not, unfortunately, a common sentiment among his countrymen, and although he describes but does not attempt to name these "men wearing the dress of women," it wasn't long before someone else did.

Erasure of tribal terms, tribal group names, and personal tribal names during colonization was a strategy used by European colonizers throughout the Americas. The act of naming was, and still is, a deeply respected and important aspect of indigenous culture. Although naming ceremonies among North American Indians followed many traditions, varying according to tribe and often even by band or time period, what has never changed is an acknowledgment of the sense of power inherent in a name or in the person performing the act of naming, and the consequent right to produce self-names as utterances of empowerment. Renaming both human beings and their own names for people or objects in their world is a political act of dominance. As Stephen Greenblatt writes of Christopher Columbus's initial acts of renaming lands whose indigenous names the inhabitants had already shared with him, "The founding action of Christian imperialism is a christening. Such a christening entails the cancellation of the native name—the erasure of the alien, an exorcism, an appropriation, and a gift . . . [it is] the taking of possession, the conferral of identity."[20] To replace various tribal words for a Spanish word is indeed an appropriation of sovereignty, a "gift" that cannot be refused, and perhaps more properly called an "imposition."

Therefore, when Spaniards arrived in Alta California and encountered a class of Indians we would now identify as being "third gender," it makes sense that in exercising power over the land and inhabitants, one of the first things the Spaniards did was invent a name for the third-gender phenomenon, a name applied only to California Indians identified by Spaniards as men who dressed as women and had sex with other men. Interestingly, although Spanish morality disapproved of "sodomy" within their own culture and had a collection of words and euphemisms available to describe "el acto pecado nefando" ("the silent/unspoken sin") and its participants (*hermafrodita, sodomía, bujarrón, nefandario, maricón, amujerado*), they did not choose to apply these existing Spanish labels to California Indians.[21] Instead, overwhelmingly, primary sources use the word *joya*. As early as 1775, only six years after Crespi made his observation, the term *joya* was already in widespread use. In describing the customs of Indian women in 1775, Fages writes, "The Indian woman takes the little girls with her, that they may learn to gather seeds, and may accustom themselves to carrying the basket. In this retinue are generally included some of the worthless creatures which they call *joyas.*"[22] Although Fages states that "they" (Indians) use the word *joyas*, the slippage is obvious when we note that in 1776 or 1777, the missionaries at Mission San Antonio also reported that

> the priests were advised that two pagans had gone into one of the houses of the neophytes, one in his natural raiment, the other dressed as a woman. Such a person the Indians in their native language called a *joya*. Immediately the missionary, with the corporal and a soldier, went to the house to see what they were looking for, and there they found the two in an unspeakably sinful act. They punished them, although not so much as deserved. The priest tried to present to them the enormity of their deed. The pagan replied that that *joya* was his wife . . . along the Channel of Santa Barbara . . . many *joyas* are found.[23]

In precontact California, the linguist Leanne Hinton writes, "Over a hundred languages were spoken here, representing five or more major language families and various smaller families and linguistic isolates."[24] Adding in estimates of hundreds of different dialects, it seems clear that every California tribe would have had its own word for third-gendered people, not the generic *joya* that Spanish records give us. For example, at Mission San Diego, Father Boscana describes the biological men who dressed and lived as women or, as he put it, those who were accustomed to "marrying males with males." He writes, "Whilst yet in infancy they were selected, and instructed as they increased in years, in all the duties of the women—in their mode of dress—of walking, and dancing; so that in almost every particular, they resembled females. . . . To distinguish this detested race at this mission, they were called '*Cuit*,' in the mountains, '*Uluqui*,' and in other parts, they were known by the name of '*Coias.*'"[25] *Joya*, then, is a completely new term and must have been fashioned one way or another by the Spaniards, perhaps from an indigenous word that sounded like "joyas" or as commentary on the *joyas'* fondness for women's clothing, jewelry, and hairstyles (Spanish explorers in Mexico called hummingbirds *joyas voladoras*, or "flying jewels").[26] It seems doubtful that the Spaniards would retain a beautiful name like "jewel" to describe what they saw as the lowest, most bestial segment of the Indian community unless it was meant as a kind of sarcasm to enact a sense of power and superiority over the third-gendered people. James Sandos has some sense of this as well, writing that "the Spanish called them (jewels), a term that may have been derisive in Spanish culture but inadvertently conveyed the regard with which such men were held in Chumash culture."[27] By "derisive," Sandos perhaps means that the Spaniards were making fun of what they perceived to be a ridiculous and shameful status.

Another possibility for the origins of *joya* lies in a linguistic feat, the pun. For years, people have assumed that the California town La Jolla (the double *l* in Spanish is pronounced as a *y*) is simply a misspelling of *joya*. However, Nellie Van de Grift Sanchez writes: "*La Jolla*, a word of doubtful origin, said by some persons to mean a 'pool,' by others to be from *hoya*, a hollow surrounded by hills, and by still others to be a possible corruption of *joya*, a 'jewel.' The suggestion has been made that La Jolla was named from caves situated there which contain pools."[28] Yet another similar sounding Spanish word is *olla*, which means jar or vessel. What all these things have in common—a pool, a hollow, a vessel—is that each is a kind of container, a receptacle. Ethnologists and Spaniards alike agree that the *joya*'s role as a biological male living as a female meant, among many other things, *joyas* were sexually active with "normative" men as the recipients of anal sex. In fact, a *joya* would never consider having sex with another *joya*—this was not forbidden, simply unthinkable—so this may truly have been a case of "I'm not *joya* but my boyfriend is!"

   All in all, the renaming of the *joyas* was not likely meant to be a compliment, but strangely enough, it does reflect the respect with which precontact California Natives regarded this gender. Perhaps, as with the word *Indian*, *joya* has strong potential for reappropriation and a new signification of value. By choosing this word and not one of their established homolexemes, this act of renaming reinforces the notion that Spanish priests and soldiers sensed something else—an indefinable gender role, a "new" class of people?—going on here, something more or different than the deviant "sodomites" of their own culture.

   [. . .]

Punishment, Regendering, and Shame

The Spanish priests, viewing themselves *in loco parentis*, approached the *joya*'s behaviors through the twin disciplinary actions of physical and spiritual punishment and regendering. Both of these terms are euphemisms for violence. The consequences for being a *joya*—whether dressing as a woman, doing women's work, partnering with a normative male, or actually being caught in a sexual liaison with a man—included flogging with a leather whip (braided leather typically as thick as a fist), time in the stocks, and *corma* (a kind of hobbling device that restricted movement but allowed the Indian to work). Enforced, extended rote repetition of unfamiliar prayers on knees, verbal harassment and berating, ridicule, and shaming in front of the *joya*'s community were other forms of discipline.

   [. . .]

   [. . .] In a kind of involuntary gender reassignment, *joyas* were made to dress as men, act as men, and consort with men in contexts for which they had little if any experience. For the "normative" men, having a *joya* among them all day and night—let alone someone stripped of appropriate clothing, status, and respect—must have also been disturbing and a further disruption of cultural signification. Women, too, would have noticed and missed the presence of *joyas* within that smaller, interdependent feminine community.

   As a consequence of this regendering, renaming, and murder, one of the *joya*'s most important responsibilities, on which the well-being of the tribe depended, was completely disrupted; prohibited by the priests, the complex and deeply spiritual position of undertaker became a masterful example of colonization by appropriation.

Replacement

Most research on the indigenous third gender agrees that a person living this role had particular responsibilities to the community, especially ceremonial and religious events and tasks.[29] In California, death, burial, and mourning rituals were the exclusive province of the *joyas*; they were the undertakers of their communities. As the only members of California Indian communities who possessed the necessary training to touch the dead or handle burials without endangering themselves or the community, the absence of *joyas* in California Indian communities must have constituted a tremendously disturbing crisis.[30] As Sandra E. Hollimon states, "Perhaps most profoundly, the institution of Catholic burial programs and designated mission cemeteries would have usurped the traditional responsibilities of the *'aqi* [Ventureño Chumash word for *joya*]. The imposition of Catholic practices in combination with a tremendously high death rate among mission populations would undoubtedly have contributed to the disintegration for the guild."[31] It is hard to overstate the chaos and panic the loss of their undertakers must have produced for indigenous Californians. The journey to the afterlife was known to be a prescribed series of experiences with both male and female supernatural entities, and the *'aqi*, with their male-female liminality, were the only people who could mediate these experiences. Since the female (earth, abundance, fertility) energies were so powerful, and since the male (Sun, death-associated) energies were equally strong, the person who dealt with that moment of spiritual and bodily crossing over between life and death must have specially endowed spiritual qualities and powers, not to mention long-term training and their own quarantined tools. Baskets used to scoop up the earth of a grave, for example, were given to the *'aqi* by the deceased person's relatives as partial payment for burial services, but also because they could never again be used for the life-giving acts of cooking or gathering.[32]

The threshold of death was the realm of the *'aqi*, and no California Indian community was safe or complete without that mediator. Asserting that undertakers were exclusively *'aqi* or postmenopausal women (also called *'aqi*), Hollimon speculates that perhaps "the mediation between death and the afterlife, and between human and supernatural realms, was entrusted by the Chumash to individuals who could not be harmed by symbolic pollution of the corpse, and who were no longer (or never had been) capable of giving birth."[33] Hollimon's archaeological work allows us to understand that the "third gender" status of *joyas* may have been extended, in some fashion, to postmenopausal women as well, should they desire to pursue a career as undertaker. Another strong possibility is that elderly women stepped into the role of undertaker when persecution reduced the availability of *joyas*.

With the loss of the *'aqi*, then, came an instant and urgent need for some kind of spiritual protection and ritualization of death. This would have suited the Roman Catholic Church, which had more than enough ritual available—and priests were anxious to institute new rituals to replace what they regarded as pagan practices. While founding the San Francisco Mission, Fray Palóu wrote, "Those who die as pagans, they cremate; nor have we been able to stop this," indicating that burial—as tribes farther south practiced—was the only mortuary practice considered civilized.[34] At these same cremations, in reference to funeral rituals, Palóu noted that "there are some old women who repeatedly strike their breast with a stone they grieve much and yell quite a bit."[35] It would have been difficult to tell an elderly *joya* dressed as a woman from an elderly woman, if one did not know of the connection between *joyas* and the death ceremony; in fact, years later, when Harrington interviewed Maria Solares, a Chumash survivor of Mission Santa Ynez (and one of his major consultants), she told him that all undertakers ("aqi") were women, strong enough to carry bodies and dig deep graves, and that the role was passed from mother to daughter.[36] Harrington pointed out that the Ineseño word for *joto* was also *'aqi*, that it was strange that "women should be so strong to lift bodies," and Solares agreed, though still puzzled.[37] It seems that by the mid-1930s, the memory of *'aqi* as beloved members of the community no longer matched Solares's cultural understanding of *joto*—the long-term damage of homophobia was substantial even in linguistic terms, let alone human terms. It is not hard for me to imagine my ancestors, fearing for their spiritual well-being, their loved ones, and what remained of their communities, turning to Catholicism out of desperation. As the diseases and violence of colonization took their toll, communities were under intense pressure about the many burials or cremations to be carried out. The turn to, and dependence on, Catholic burial rituals was a form of coerced conversion that had nothing to do with Christianity, and everything to do with fear.

Through these methods, then—murder, renaming, regendering, and replacement—the *joya* gendercide was carried out. The destruction seems to cover every aspect of *joya* identity and survival. Yet, I argue, *joya* identity did not disappear entirely.

Surviving Gendercide

How could *joyas* survive such devastation? Where are they? What is their role in contemporary California Indian life?

First, it is important to note that mission records show baptisms of adult *joyas* as late as 1832, almost sixty years after Fages expressed his outrage in 1775. "Late arrivals" to the mission—adult Indians who, having lived most of their lives as "wild" Indians, were rounded up and brought in for forced baptism—actually slowed the missionization process considerably. In combination with the low life expectancy of mission-born children (two to seven years), a strong influx of adult indigenous cultural practices probably also kept the role of *joya* from fading away as quickly as might otherwise be expected (allowing younger Indians to witness or know *joyas*, as well as pass on that information orally to future generations).[38]

Second, just as the extermination of California Indians, while extensive, has been exaggerated as complete, so too is the idea that *joyas* could be gendercided out of existence. A *joya*'s conception does not depend on having a *joya* parent, unlike normative male and female sexes, who depend on both male and female for conception; as long as enough of the normative population remains alive and able to bear children, the potential for *joya* gender to emerge in some of those children also remains. To exterminate *joyas* entirely, *all* California Indian people would have had to be killed, down to the very last; thus it makes sense that during missionization and postsecularization, as in the past, *joyas* rose out of the general population spontaneously and regularly. However, those *joya* had virtually no choice but to hide their gender. Like Pueblo tribes who took their outlawed religious ceremonies underground until it was safe to practice more openly (although outsiders are understandably rarely allowed to partake or witness the ceremonies), *joyas* in California may have taken a similar tactic, removing themselves from ceremonial roles with religious connotations and hiding out in the general population. Sadly, the traditional blend of spiritual and sexual energy that was a source of *joya* empowerment suffered an abrupt division; as time passed and the few surviving elder *joyas* passed on, younger *joyas* would have been forced to function without role models, teachers, spiritual advisers, or even—eventually—oral stories of their predecessors. Walter Williams reports that he "could not find any traces of a *joya* gender in oral traditions among contemporary California Indians from missionized tribes," but adds, "that does not mean that a recognized and respected status for berdache no longer existed, or that same-sex behavior vanished. To find evidence of such continuity is extremely difficult."[39]

[. . .]

Reconstructing a Spiritual, Community-Oriented Role for Two-Spirit People

In conclusion, I suggest that contemporary California Two-Spirits are the rightful descendants of *joyas*.[40] Two-Spirit people did not cease to exist, they did not cease to be born, simply because the Spaniards killed our *joya* ancestors. This, in fact, is a crucial point: the words *gay* or *lesbian* do not fully define a Two-Spirited person, because those labels are based on an almost exclusively sexual paradigm inherited from a nonindigenous colonizing culture. The Chumash '*aqi*, or *joyas*, fulfilled important roles as spiritual community leaders, so although genocide and gendercide worked to erase their bodies, neither their spirits nor the indigenous community's spiritual needs could be murdered. This is what comes down to us as Two-Spirit people: the necessity of our roles as keepers of a dual or blended gender that holds male and female energy in various mixtures and keeps the world balanced. Although Two-Spirit people often had children in the past, and continue to do so in the present, and will into the future, we do not expect or train our children to follow in our footsteps. A Two-Spirit person is born regardless of biological genealogy. Thus we will always be with you. We *are* you. We are not outsiders, some other community that can be wiped out. We come from you, and we return to you.

Simply identifying as both Indian and gay does not make a person TwoSpirit, although it can be a courageous and important step; the danger of that assumption elides Two-Spirit responsibilities as well as the social and cultural needs of contemporary indigenous communities in relation to such issues as suicide rates, alcoholism, homelessness, and AIDS. What steps can we take to reconstruct our role in the larger indigenous community? I look back at this research on my family and find guidance, examples, strategies, and lessons that converge around six key actions:

1. reclaim a name for ourselves;
2. reclaim a place for ourselves within our tribal communities (which means serious education and presence to counteract centuries of homophobia—a literary presence, a practical presence, and a working presence);
3. resist violence against ourselves as individuals and as a community within Native America;
4. work to determine what our roles as liminal beings might be in contemporary Native and national contexts;
5. work to reclaim our histories from the colonizer's records even as we continue to know and adapt our lives to contemporary circumstances and needs; and
6. create loving, supportive, celebratory community that can work to heal the wounds inflicted by shame, internalized hatred, and fear, dealing with the legacy that, as the Chickasaw poet Linda Hogan says, "history is our illness."[41]

With the adoption of the name "Two Spirit," we have already begun the work of our lifetimes. As Sue-Ellen Jacobs, Wesley Thomas, and Sabine Lang write, "Using the word 'Two-Spirit' emphasizes the spiritual aspect of one's life and downplays the homosexual persona."[42] Significantly, this move announces and enhances the Two-Spirit need for traditionally centered lives with the community's well-being at the center. Still, we face a great problem: the lack of knowledge or spiritual training for GLBTQ Native people, particularly the mystery of blending spiritual and sexual energies to manage death/rebirth. In traditional times, there would have been older *joyas* to guide inexperienced ones; there would have been ceremony, role modeling, community support, and, most importantly, there would have been a clear role waiting to be filled.

The name Two-Spirit, then, is a way to alert others, and remind ourselves, that we have a cultural and historical responsibility to the larger community: our work is to attend to a balance of energies. We are still learning what this means; there has been no one to teach us but ourselves, our research, our stories, and our hearts. Maybe this will be the generation to figure it out. Maybe this will be the generation to reclaim our inheritance within our communities. And if it is not, I take heart from the history of the *joyas*, the impossibility of their true gendercide, and the deep, passionate, mutual need for relationship between Two Spirits and our communities.

From: Deborah A. Miranda, "Extermination of the *Joyas*: Gendercide in Spanish California," in *GLQ: A Journal of Lesbian and Gay Studies*, Volume 16, no. 1–2, pp. 253–284. Copyright 2010, Duke University Press. All rights reserved. Republished by permission of the copyright holder, Duke University Press. www.dukeupress.edu.

Notes

1. Paula Gunn Allen, "I Don't Speak the Language That Has the Sentences: An Interview with Paula Gunn Allen," *Sojourner: The Women's Forum* 24, no. 2 (1999): 26–27.
2. Paula Gunn Allen, "Some Like Indians Endure," in *Living the Spirit* (New York: St. Martin's, 1988), 9–13.
3. Elaine Mills, ed., *The Papers of John Peabody Harrington in the Smithsonian Institution, 1907–1957*, microfilm (White Plains, NY: Kraus International, 1981).
4. *Salvage ethnology* is a term coined by Jacob Gruber to refer to the paradoxical obsession of Westerners to collect artifacts, linguistic traces, and cultural knowledge of cultures that they had previously spent much effort to colonize or exterminate. Rather than basic ethnological research, the study of a culture, "salvage ethnology" was concerned with an almost fanatic search (and often the hoarding of) any remains of a colonized culture. See Jacob Gruber, "Ethnographic Salvage and the Shaping of Anthropology," *American Anthropologist*, n.s. 72 (1970): 1289–1299.
5. I use this name as it was coined during the Third International Two Spirit Gathering, to provide a positive alternative to the unacceptable term *berdache*: Two-Spirit people are "Aboriginal people who possess the sacred gifts of the female-male spirit, which exists in harmony with those of the female and the male. They have traditional respected roles within most Aboriginal cultures and societies and are contributing members of the community. Today, some Aboriginal people who are Two-Spirit also identify as being gay, lesbian, bisexual or transgender" ("Background and Recent Developments in Two-Spirit Organizing," International Two Spirit Gathering, intltwo spiritgathering.org/content/view/27/42/ [accessed July 28, 2009]).
6. The archaeology of sexuality refers to a fairly recent movement within archaeology that brings together theoretical work from gender and women's studies, science studies, philosophy, and the social sciences on sex and gender to study material remains and to approach questions often considered accessible only through texts or direct observation of behavior, such as gender or multiple genders. An excellent collection of articles on this topic is Robert Schmidt and Barbara Voss, eds., *Archaeologies of Sexuality* (London: Routledge, 2000).
7. My use of the term *third gender* relies on and refers back to work done by Will Roscoe, Sabine Lang, Wesley Thomas, Bea Medicine, and others as a way to identify a gender that is neither fully male nor fully female, nor (more importantly) simply "half and half," but a unique blend of characteristics resulting in a third or other gender. See Sue Ellen Jacobs, Wesley Thomas, and Sabine Lang, eds., *Two-Spirit People: Native American Gender Identity, Sexuality, and Spirituality* (Urbana: University of Illinois Press, 1997). As Brian Gilley summarizes, "The institution of the third gender [in Native American precontact societies] was less about an individual's sexuality and more about the ways their special qualities were incorporated into the social and religious life of their community" (*Becoming Two-Spirit: Gay Identity and Social Acceptance in Indian Country* [Lincoln: University of Nebraska Press, 2006], 11).
8. Father Gerónimo Boscana, a Franciscan priest who kept extensive notes about Native culture and customs during his stay at Mission San Juan Capistrano from 1812 until 1826, wrote that the "Indians of California may be compared to a species of monkey" ("Chinigchinich," in Alfred Robinson, *Life in California: During a Residence of Several Years in That Territory, Comprising a Description of the Country and the Missionary Establishments*, ed. Doyce B. Nunis Jr. [New York: Wiley and Putnam, 1846], 335). Postsecularization, perceptions had not changed much; in 1849 Samuel Upham commented on California Indian genealogy and eating habits: "Like his brother, the gorilla, he is a vegetarian and subsists principally on wild berries and acorns, occasionally luxuriating on snails and grasshoppers" (*Notes of a Voyage to California Via Cape Horn, Together with Scenes in El Dorado, in the Years 1849–50* [New York: Arno, 1973], 240). This attitude persisted when John Audubon wrote in his journal of a Miwok child "eating [acorns] with the judgment of a monkey, and looking very much like one." Although the journal covers the years 1840–1850, it was published in 1906, perpetuating the distorted view of California

Indians into the twentieth century (John Audubon, *Audubon's Western Journal: 1840–1850*, ed. Frank Heywood Hodder [Cleveland: Clark, 1906], 213).

9. Although most scholars still use the population estimates by Martin Baumhoff (*Ecological Determinants of Aboriginal California Populations* [Berkeley: University of California Press, 1963]); Sherburne Cook (*The Population of the California Indians, 1796–1970* [Berkeley: University of California Press, 1976]), many contemporary scholars view their numbers (150,000–350,000) as greatly outdated. In *American Indian Holocaust and Survival: A Population History since 1492* (Norman: University of Oklahoma Press, 1987), Russell Thornton, for example, writes that California Indian precontact population was "approaching 705,000" (200). In private correspondence with the author about more current population data, William Preston writes that "at this point I think Thornton's high number is totally reasonable. In fact, keeping in mind that populations no doubt fluctuated over time, I'm thinking that at times 1 million or more Native Californians were resident in that state." William Preston, e-mail message to author, July 8, 2009.

10. Pedro Fages, *A Historical, Political, and Natural Description of California by Pedro Fages, Soldier of Spain*, trans. Herbert Priestley (Berkeley: University of California Press, 1937), 33.

11. Stanley Coren, *The Pawprints of History: Dogs and the Course of Human Events* (New York: Free Press, 2003), 67–80.

12. Coren, *Pawprints of History*, 76.

13. Coren, *Pawprints of History*, 72–73.

14. Coren, *Pawprints of History*, 74.

15. Peter Martyr d'Anghera, "The Third English Book on America" [*De Orbe Novo*], trans. Richard Eden, in *The First Three English Books on America: [?1511]—1555 A.D.*, ed. Edward Arber (Birmingham, 1885), 138.

16. Coren, *Pawprints of History*, 76.

17. Maureen Heibert, " 'Too Many Cides' to Genocide Studies? Review of Jones, Adam, ed. Gendercide and Genocide," H-Genocide, H-Net Reviews, www.h-net.org/reviews/ showrev.php?id=10878 (accessed December 17, 2008); emphasis added.

18. D'Anghera, "Third English Book on America," 138.

19. Herbert E. Bolton, trans. and ed., *Fray Juan Crespi: Missionary Explorer on the Pacific Coast* (Berkeley: University of California Press, 1927), 171.

20. Stephen Greenblatt, *Marvelous Possessions: The Wonder of the New World* (Chicago: University of Chicago Press, 1991), 83.

21. Wayne Dynes, "Gay Spanish," *Homolexis*, December 25, 2006, homolexis.blogspot.com/2006_12_01_archive.html.

22. Fages, *Historical, Political, and Natural Description of California*, 59.

23. Francisco Palóu, *Palóu's Life of Fray Junipero Serra*, ed. and trans. Maynard J. Geiger (Washington, DC: American Academy of Franciscan History, 1955), 33.

24. Leanne Hinton, *Flutes of Fire: Essays on California Indian Languages* (Berkeley: Heyday, 1994), 13.

25. Boscana, "Chinigchinich," 284.

26. Connie M. Toops, *Hummingbirds: Jewels in Flight* (Stillwater, MN: Voyageur, 1992), 15.

27. James Sandos, "Christianization Among the Chumash: An Ethnohistoric Perspective," *American Indian Quarterly* 15 (1991): 71.

28. Nellie Van de Grift Sanchez, *Spanish and Indian Place Names of California: Their Meaning and Their Romance* (San Francisco: Robertson, 1914), 44.

29. For a general survey, see Jacobs, Thomas, and Lang, *Two-Spirit People*; and Will Roscoe, *Changing Ones: Third and Fourth Genders in Native North America* (New York: St. Martin's, 1998).

30. J. Alden Mason writes, "That the mention of the dead was as serious an offence among the Salinans as with other Californian Indians is well illustrated by the incident that when asked jocularly for a Salinan word of profanity, Pedro Encinales gave ca MteL and translated it 'go to the devil' (ve al diablo). [Father] Sitjar writes chavmtel 'cadaver.' " Sitjar, who compiled a useful list of Salinan words and phrases, knew enough of the Indian language to make his own translation, which apparently Pedro Encinales, the indigenous speaker, wasn't comfortable speaking (J. Alden Mason, *The Ethnology of the Salinan Indians* [Whitefish, MT: Kessinger, 2006], 167).

31. Sandra E. Hollimon, "Archaeology of the '*Aqi*: Gender and Sexuality in Prehistoric Chumash Society," in *Archaeologies of Sexuality*, ed. Robert Schmidt and Barbara Voss (New York: Routledge, 2000), 193.

32. Holliman, "Archaeology of the '*Aqi*," 192.

33. Holliman, "Archaeology of the '*Aqi*," 182.

34. Palóu, *Palóu's Life of Fray Junipero Serra*, 193.

35. Palóu, *Palóu's Life of Fray Junipero Serra*, 445.

36. Linda B. King, *The Medea Creek Cemetery (CA-LAN-243): An Investigation of Social Organization from Mortuary Practices*, UCLA Archaeological Survey Annual Report, no. 11 (Los Angeles: University of California Press, 1969), 47. I call Solares a "consultant" here rather than use the traditional ethnological term *informant* out of respect for all Native peoples who have retained and chosen to share their cultural knowledge and expertise; my purpose is to acknowledge that Indigenous knowledge puts Native consultants on an equal intellectual level with scientists and academics.

37. Hollimon suggests that "daughters" of male-bodied *'aqi* were probably fictive kinships (such as adoption) formed with other members of the same guild or role or premenopausal children of women who took up the *'aqi* role late in life, and when colonization had created a shortage in the usual mortuary profession (Holliman, "Archaeology of the *'Aqi*," 185).

38. For information about the life expectancy of mission-born children, see Robert H. Jackson and Edward Castillo, *Indians, Franciscans, and Spanish Colonization: The Impact of the Mission System on California Indians* (Albuquerque: University of New Mexico Press, 1995), 53–56.

39. Walter L. Williams, "The Abominable Sin: The Spanish Campaign Against 'Sodomy,' and the Results in Modern Latin America," in *The Spirit and the Flesh* (Boston: Beacon, 1992), 129.

40. Other indigenous peoples around the world attributed special powers and rights to Two-Spirits within their tribes; although they were not always the mediators between life and death, similar patterns may be found. Because of the limitations of this essay, I leave that to future scholars and seekers.

41. Linda Hogan, *The Woman Who Watches Over the World: A Native Memoir* (New York: Norton, 2001), 59.

42. Jacobs, Thomas, and Lang, *Two-Spirit People*, 3.

14 Selections From *Borderlands/ La Frontera: The New Mestiza*

Gloria Anzaldúa

Chicana feminist theorist Gloria Anzaldúa's 1987 book *Borderlands/La Frontera: The New Mez-tiza* is a paradigm-shifting, stylistically innovative "transgenre" work that interweaves Spanish and English poetry, creative prose, autobiography, and historical narrative. It treats the U.S.-Mexican borderlands as a real geographical place while expanding the concept of a "border-land" in more generalizable and theoretical directions. Anzaldúa develops another concept, *nepantla,* rooted in pre-Aztec Mexican culture, that describes a state of "in-betweenness"; if a border is a line that separates, *nepantla* is a realm of possible existence that abolishes that line. The brief excerpts that follow are drawn from *Borderland*'s first few pages, in a section called "The Homeland, Aztlán," and from a poem near the end, "To live in the borderlands means you." The function of the border, Anzaldúa writes, is to define who is "us" and who is "them," but the borderlands created by the "emotional residue" of this "unnatural boundary" are popu-lated by all manner of *Los atravesados,* the crossed ones, not just "Chicanos, Indians, and Blacks" but "the squint-eyed, the perverse, the queer, the troublesome, the mongrel, the mulatto, the half-breed, the half dead." To dwell in the borderlands, Anzaldúa contends, is to position one-self as the "forerunner of a new race, half and half—both man and woman, neither—a new gender." Survival there requires understanding oneself *sin fronteras,* without boundaries, stand-ing in the crossroad of one's entire experience.

The Homeland, Aztlán

El otro México
El otro México que acá hemos construido
el espacio es lo que ha sido
territorio nacional.
Esté el esfuerzo de todos nuestros hermanos
y latinoamericanos que ban sabido
progressar.

—Los Tigres del Norte[1]

"The *Aztecas del norte* . . . compose the largest single tribe or nation of Anishinabeg (Indians) found in the United States today. . . . Some call themselves Chicanos and see themselves as people whose true homeland is Aztlán [the U.S. Southwest]."[2]

DOI: 10.4324/9781003206255-18

Wind tugging at my sleeve
feet sinking into the sand
I stand at the edge where earth touches ocean
where the two overlap
a gentle coming together
at other times and places a violent clash.

Across the border in Mexico
   stark silhouette of houses gutted by waves,
      cliffs crumbling into the sea,
         silver waves marbled with spume
            gashing a hole under the border fence.
          Miro el mar atacar
       la cerca en Border Field Park
     con sus buchones de agua,
an Easter Sunday resurrection
of the brown blood in my veins.

Oigo el llorido del mar, el respiro del aire,
   my heart surges to the beat of the sea.
      In the gray haze of the sun
         the gulls' shrill cry of hunger,
            the tangy smell of the sea seeping into me.

         I walk through the hole in the fence
            to the other side.
     Under my fingers I feel the gritty wire
         rusted by 139 years
            of the salty breath of the sea.

Beneath the iron sky
Mexican children kick their soccer ball across,
run after it, entering the U.S.

        I press my hand to the steel curtain—
      chainlink fence crowned with rolled barbed wire—
rippling from the sea where Tijuana touches San Diego
      unrolling over mountains
          and plains
              and deserts,
this "Tortilla Curtain" turning into *el rio Grande*
      flowing down to the flatlands
         of the Magic Valley of South Texas
     its mouth emptying into the Gulf.

1,950 mile-long open wound
           dividing a *pueblo,* a culture,
           running down the length of my body,

staking fence rods in my flesh,
splits me splits me
    me raja me raja
This is my home
this thin edge of
    barbwire.

But the skin of the earth is seamless.
The sea cannot be fenced,
el mar does not stop at borders.
To show the white man what she thought of his
        arrogance,
Yemaya blew that wire fence down.

This land was Mexican once,
    was Indian always
        and is.
    And will be again.

Yo soy un puente tendido
    del mundo gabacho al del mojado,
lo pasado me estirá pa' 'trás
    y lo presente pa" delante.
Que la Virgen de Guadalupe me cuide
Ay, soy mexicana de este lado.

The U.S.-Mexican border *es una berida abierta* where the Third World grates against the first and bleeds. And before a scab forms it hemorrhages again, the lifeblood of two worlds merging to form a third country—a border culture. Borders are set up to define the places that are safe and unsafe, to distinguish *us them*. A border is a dividing line, a narrow strip along a steep edge. A borderland is a vague and undetermined place created by the emotional residue of an unnatural boundary. It is in a constant state of transition. The prohibited and forbidden are its inhabitants. *Los atravesados* live here: the squint-eyed, the perverse, the queer, the troublesome, the mongrel, the mulato, the half-breed, the half dead; in short, those who cross over, pass over, or go through the confines of the "normal." Gringos in the U.S. Southwest consider the inhabitants of the borderlands transgressors, aliens—whether they possess documents or not, whether they're Chicanos, Indians or Blacks. Do not enter, trespassers will be raped, maimed, strangled, gassed, shot. The only "legitimate" inhabitants are those in power, the whites and those who align themselves with whites. Tension grips the inhabitants of the borderlands like a virus. Ambivalence and unrest reside there and death is no stranger.

In the fields, *la migra*. My aunt saying, "*No corran*, don't run. They'll think you're *del otro lao*." In the confusion, Pedro ran, terrified of being caught. He couldn't speak English, couldn't tell them he was fifth generation American. *Sin papeles*—he did not carry his birth certificate to work in the fields. *La migra* took him away while we watched. *Se lo llevaron*. He tried to smile when he looked back at us, to raise his fist. But I saw the shame pushing his head down, I saw the terrible weight of shame hunch his shoulders. They deported him to Guadalajara by plane. The furthest he'd ever been to Mexico was Reynosa, a small border town opposite Hidalgo, Texas, not far from McAllen. Pedro walked all the way to the Valley. *Se lo llevaron sin un centavo al pobre. Se vino andando desde Guadalajara.*

[. . .]

To live in the Borderlands means you

are neither hispana india negra española
ni gabacha, eres mestiza, mulata, half-breed
caught in the crossfire between camps
while carrying all five races on your back
not knowing which side to turn to, run from;

To live in the Borderlands means knowing
that the *india* in you, betrayed for 500 years,
is no longer speaking to you,
that *mexicanas* call you *rajetas,*
that denying the Anglo inside you
is as bad as having denied the Indian or Black;

Cuando vives en la frontera
people walk through you, the wind steals your voice,
you're a *burra, buey,* scapegoat,
forerunner of a new race,
half and half—both woman and man, neither—
a new gender;

To live in the Borderlands means to
put *chile* in the borscht,
eat whole wheat *tortillas,*
speak Tex-Mex with a Brooklyn accent;
be stopped by *la migra* at the border checkpoints;

Living in the Borderlands means you fight hard to
resist the gold elixir beckoning from the bottle,
the pull of the gun barrel,
the rope crushing the hollow of your throat;

In the Borderlands
you are the battleground
where enemies are kin to each other;
you are at home, a stranger,

the border disputes have been settled
the volley of shots have shattered the truce
you are wounded, lost in action
dead, fighting back;

To live in the Borderlands means
    the mill with the razor white teeth wants to shred off
    your olive-red skin, crush out the kernel, your heart
    pound you pinch you roll you out
    smelling like white bread but dead;

To survive the Borderlands
    you must live *sin fronteras*
    be a crossroads.

gabacha—a Chicano term for a white woman
rajetas—literally, "split," that is, having betrayed your word
burra—donkey
buey—oxen
sin fronteras—without borders

From: Gloria Anzaldúa, *Borderlands/La Frontera: The New Mestiza*, 1987. San Francisco, CA: Aunt Lute Press.

Notes

1. Los Tigres del Norte is a *conjunto* band.
2. Jack D. Forbes, *Aztecas del Norte: The Chicanos of Aztlán* (Greenwich, CT: Fawcett Publications, Premier Books, 1973), 13, 183; Eric R. Wolf, *Sons of Shaking Earth* (Chicago, IL: University of Chicago Press, Phoenix Books, 1959), 32.

15 Decolonizing Transgender in India

Some Reflections

Aniruddha Dutta and Raina Roy

In "Decolonizing Transgender in India," first published in the "Decolonizing Gender" special issue of *TSQ: Transgender Studies Quarterly* in 2014, Aniruddha Dutta and Raina Roy discuss how the concept of *transgender* itself can function in a colonizing manner. They document how, since the 1990s, *transgender* has become a term through which international non-governmental and non-profit organizations dole out economic support for gender minorities worldwide, primarily in the context of HIV/AIDS funding. They argue that *transgender* overwrites multiple forms of gender variation long present in South Asia and in the global South more generally. At the same time, they are careful to note that transgender is not *merely* a foreign term exported and imposed on people entirely unwilling to embrace it. Many gender-variant people in the global South tactically embrace *transgender* as a conduit for resources, and some identify as both as trans and something else. The gist of their analysis is that *transgender* functions as a hegemonic master concept against which "local" sex/gender/sexuality configurations must measure and define themselves as part of resourcing their own survival. That non-consensual power imbalance is precisely what renders *transgender* part of coloniality.

How does the transnational expansion of "transgender" as a rubric of identity and activism appear when we look at the phenomenon from the vantage point of communities and social movements of gender-variant persons in the global South, specifically South Asia? This essay is a set of reflections arising out of prolonged conversations in which we compared notes on our respective experiences as activist (Raina) and ethnographer (Aniruddha, henceforth Ani) working among, and to different extents belonging to, gender/sexually marginalized communities in eastern India. If "decolonization" implies the ability to freely question, critique, and, if necessary, reject globalizing discourses or practices, this essay considers the conditions of possibility for such critical engagement with the expanding category of transgender.

We do not intend to make a prescriptive argument regarding how to make *transgender* into a more cross-culturally inclusive term—indeed, as previous critiques have pointed out, the imagination of transgender as an expansive category for all gender-variant practices and identities risks replicating colonial forms of knowledge production (Stryker and Aizura 2013: 8) or overriding other epistemologies of gender/sexual variance (Valentine 2007: 4). As we shall argue, the attempted universalization of transgender as a transnational umbrella term by the development (nongovernmental) sector, the state, and their funders tends to subsume South Asian discourses and practices of gender/sexual variance as merely "local"

DOI: 10.4324/9781003206255-19

expressions of transgender identity, often without interrogating the conceptual baggage (such as homo-trans and cis-trans binaries) associated with the transgender category. In the Indian context, this process bolsters the long-standing and continuing (post)colonial construction of hierarchies of scale between transnational, regional, and local levels of discourse and praxis, as evidenced in the relation between the hegemonic anglophone discourse of LGB-TIQ identities recognized by the state and the development sector, on one hand, and forms of gender/sexual variance that are positioned as relatively regional or local on the other. The increasing recognition of transgender identities as subjects of rights and citizenship is evident in a series of developmental, state, and legal policies, ranging from transgender-specific funding for HIV-AIDS prevention to recent directives in favor of transgender people's rights by the Supreme Court of India and the Indian Government's Ministry of Social Justice and Empowerment (UNDP 2008; SC 2014; MoSJE 2014). However, statist and developmentalist deployments of the transgender category may generalize linear narratives of transition and stable identification with the "opposite" gender as defining features of trans identities, and even when they recognize possibilities beyond the gender binary such as a "third gender," they tend to delimit and define such categories through a model of stable, consistent, and authentic identification that seeks to clearly distinguish transgender from cisgender and homosexual identities. But South Asian discourses of gender/sexual variance may blur cis-trans or homo-trans distinctions, and community formations may be based also on class/caste position rather than just the singular axis of gender identity. Emergent models of transgender identity certainly create new possibilities for social recognition and citizenship, but they may be colonizing precisely in the ways in which they may refuse or fail to comprehend many forms of gender variance relegated to the scale of the local, even though such discourses and practices may actually span multiple regions of South Asia.

However, such colonizing deployments do not necessarily exhaust or foreclose other evocations of the transgender category, particularly by people in the lower rungs of activism and the development sector. Such usages do not coalesce to a globalizing definition but may better translate or express the multifarious forms of gender/sexual variance found in India and South Asia. Thus there may be a decolonizing struggle over transgender itself, though the very emergence of transgender (rather than categories positioned as local) as a privileged site of such struggles is informed by its prior ascendance within the transnational development sector. We will not have space here to examine these hegemonic and counterhegemonic practices in all their nuances; rather, we will attempt to delineate some of the systemic conditions under which hegemonic usages of transgender emerge or counterhegemonic practices might become possible, particularly from the purview of working-class and/or *dalit* (lower or oppressed caste) communities who cannot freely access or modify statist and developmentalist usages of the transgender rubric.

Some clarifications before we begin. We realize that our collaboration and this essay itself are also implicated in the aforementioned scalar hierarchies. We are unequally positioned within transnational economies of knowledge production; Raina's location as an activist working with small community-based organizations in India restricts her access to academic and cultural capital, whereas Ani's position in US academia entails a privileged role in structuring and translating our concerns to a Northern audience. Yet we hope that our collaboration may also indicate variant circuits of dialogue and exchange that interrupt the unidirectional transmission of high-end knowledge from the "West" to the "rest," as exemplified by the dissemination of transgender itself.

Further, our analytic purview is largely limited to feminine-identified gender-variant persons assigned male at birth, particularly the *kothi* and *hijra* communities of West Bengal in eastern India, rather than masculine-identified trans or gender-variant people. *Hijra* is a well-known term connoting a structured community of feminine-identified persons who pursue distinct professions such as ritualized blessing during weddings and childbirth; *hijras* typically dress in women's clothes and may undergo penectomy and castration (orchiectomy) but also commonly designate themselves as distinct from men and women (Reddy 2005: 134; Nanda 1990). *Kothi* is one of several South Asian terms for feminine male-assigned persons who may or may not present or identify as (trans) women; while *kothis* do not form separate clans like *hijras*, some *kothis* may also join *hijra* clans or professions (Dutta 2013: 494–495). In the following sections, we consider the interface between these largely working-class, oppressed-caste communities and subcultures and transgender as an emergent category of identity and representation.

★ ★ ★

One potential risk of our critique, which we wish to guard against at the outset, is the implication of cultural dualisms between the West and the non-West. Transgender, in itself, need not be perceived as exogenous or foreign by Indians or South Asians who identify as such. Online forums such as the Facebook group Transgender India, activist groups like the Association of Transgender/Hijra in Bengal, and films on "male-to-female transgender people" like *Rupantar* (*Transformation*, dir. Amitava Sarkar, 2009) are evidence that there are already many adoptions, translations, and hybridizations of transgender as a rubric of identity. Like other seemingly foreign terms such as *lesbian* or *gay*, *transgender* has been found by many to be a suitable word for expressing who they are, and many may use the term (or its translated counterparts) in itself or in conjunction with terms like *hijra* or *kothi*. Given the hybrid postcoloniality that foundationally marks many articulations of "Indian culture" today, none of these subject positions can be seen as inauthentic vis-à-vis their sociocultural context—which would mimic right-wing religious and political viewpoints that have denounced the emergence of LGBT activism and identities as a form of corruptive Westernization.

However, while there are certainly ways in which transgender has emerged as a South Asian category of identity and community formation, the same ease of adoption, translation, and negotiation vis-à-vis the transnational circulation of "transgender" and "transsexual" categories may not be available to everyone. As Gayatri Chakravorty Spivak argues, one cannot simply endorse postcoloniality or hybridity without recognizing how agency and mobility within transnational circuits of exchange is often shaped and restricted by class/caste location and one's position within the international division of labor (Spivak 1999: 361). Only a relatively small proportion of people in India can access the Internet or have fluency in English as the hegemonic transnational medium through which categories like transgender disseminate. Moreover, as we demonstrate below, for many working-class and *dalit* gender/sexually variant communities, transgender (or TG) has arrived as a constrained rubric of representation for gaining funds and recognition, without much freedom to negotiate or alter its usages at higher levels of activism or funding. As an emergent hegemonic category, transgender may offer representation and upward mobility for people who fit official definitions, but it may elide or delegitimize working-class and *dalit* discourses and epistemologies of gender/sexual variance that are not entirely legible in terms of hegemonic usages of transgender—even as these groups, particularly *kothi-hijra* communities, must increasingly represent themselves as TG to be intelligible to high-level networks of large nongovernmental organizations (NGOs), transnational funders, and the state. Thus while "transgender" is not indubitably foreign or colonizing, its hegemonic position in discourses of activism and funding reflects inequalities within the hierarchical political economy of social movements and the nonprofit sector, even as the category may be appropriated or translated in ways that subvert these hierarchies.

An emerging body of scholarship within South Asian sexuality studies has critiqued the elitist or colonizing potentials of gay/lesbian identity politics in India, which can serve as a point of departure for critiquing the hegemonic emergence of transgender, but which we also seek to question or go beyond. In keeping with historiographical work on South Asia that has argued that colonial administration calcified ambiguous social boundaries into rigidly bound identities (Dirks 2001), this body of scholarship has claimed that the consolidation of homosexual personhood and identity during the period of globalization is largely propelled by urban activists, the law, and the state and potentially erases tropes or idioms of (particularly male) same-sex desire that are not based on personhood or interiorized identity (Khanna 2009; Katyal 2010; Boyce and Khanna 2011). Akhil Katyal argues that the interiorized conception of sexual identity, which classifies people based on their inner essence of homo or heterosexuality, may elide behavioral and habit-based idioms of desire prevalent in South Asia that do not connect same-sex practices with distinct forms of personhood (2010: 24). Paul Boyce and Akshay Khanna argue that the creation of a minoritized homosexual subject, separate from mainstream heteronormative society, by "principally urban" activists and communities is largely unsuited to the Indian context, as it erases how same-sex practices are diffusely scattered within "putatively heteronormative social formations" among actors who largely do not distinguish themselves as homosexual (2011: 90–97).

While we share concerns about the imposition of identitarian divides, we seek to go beyond this mode of critique through the gendered analytic lens offered by transgender studies. The aforementioned critique, while questioning the homo–hetero divide, takes the male-female binary for granted and assumes the unmarked gender normativity of sexually variant males/men without considering how putative participants in "same-sex" behavior may be socially marked or unmarked on the basis of gender. Often, same-sex-desiring men who do not claim a distinct identity may gain their anonymity by virtue of their masculine gendering, which permits a degree of sexual license, whereas feminized male-assigned persons (whether they desire men or not) have less access to such unmarked flexibility, being subject to stigmatizing labels like *gandu* or *chhakka* (roughly: fag, sissy), common to many South Asian languages. As Katyal notes in passing but does not analyze, *gandu* (feminized, anally-penetrated person) is a much more pejorative label than *laundebaaz*, the man who plays around with boys (2010: 24). This suggests that "same-sex" practices in South Asia are not just diffusely spread among "men" but are fundamentally constituted vis-à-vis gender normativity or variance and that gender variance, often perceived as being connected to same-sex desire, serves as a significant axis of social demarcation. Thus while sexuality may not have been a distinct axis of personhood in India prior to the emergence of the modern homosexual, the gendering of sexual behavior and the (homo)sexualization of gender variance (as in *gandu* or *chhakka*) seems to have a longer legacy, which may inform both patterns of discrimination and resistant formations of community and identity (Reddy 2005; Hall 2005). As we shall argue, people inhabiting the intersections of gender/sexual variance have not only formed communities prior to contemporary identity politics but have also been amenable to interpellation within newer rubrics such as MSM (men who have sex with men) and TG, which are thus not *only* urban or elite in origin but draw from these community formations and interact with them in potentially both liberatory and oppressive ways.

Raina's experiences as an activist and long-time participant within *kothi-hijra* communities and Ani's experiences as an ethnographer who was gradually included as a community member suggest the range and span of these communities. As a child, Raina dressed up secretly in clothes meant for (cis) women, discovered her attraction for men, and faced repeated abuse as an effeminate boy (*meyeli chhele*) in school. As an adolescent in the late 1990s, she discovered an old cruising area around Rabindra Sarovar, a chain of lakes in south Kolkata. There, she was introduced to a local community of feminine male-assigned persons, mostly poor or lower middle class, who formed a loose sisterhood among themselves and spoke a generationally inherited subcultural argot that was broadly similar to the language used by *hijra* clans (see Hall 2005). They used the terms *kothi* and *dhurani* to designate themselves, words that are unknown in standard Bengali. While they primarily cruised or undertook sex work with men outside their immediate circle, there were also less visibly articulated forms of desire (e.g., *kothis* who desired women or other *kothis*). The community included both those who wore standard male attire (*kodi kothis*) and feminine-attired *kothis* (variously called *bhelki, bheli,* or *bhorokti kothis*). *Kothis* could also switch or transition between *kodi* and *bhelki* states. Raina herself alternated between androgynous and feminine attire before mostly adopting the latter. While some of them joined *hijra* clans and professions, underwent castration-penectomy and adopted consistent feminine attire, others, like Raina, did not join *hijra* clans formally, even if they wore female-assigned clothes. Moreover, some would temporarily join *hijra* clans and professions while remaining *kodi* at other times. These varied practices do not signal an unfettered fluidity, as there were also intracommunity tensions around gender and respectability. When Raina took to feminine clothes, she was distanced by some *kodi* friends who regarded public cross-dressing and *hijras* as being disreputable. Meanwhile, some *hijras* and *bhelki kothis* regarded *kodi kothis* with suspicion for their duplicitous overlap with social masculinity and privilege. Yet friendships and sisterhood within the community also crossed these divides; some of Raina's closest friends are *kothis* who are mostly *kodi* or who cross-dress sporadically, given that they share many commonalities in terms of geographic and class location even though their precise gender identities or expressions may differ. Subsequently, as Raina moved to other cities for professional reasons, she made contacts with broadly similar communities with different names depending on cultural and linguistic context. In north Bengal and the neighboring country of Nepal, a similar spectrum of people called each other *meti*. In Delhi, *kothi* was commonly used within the community, but *hijra* clans would also call them *zenana* or *zenani* (Urdu words for effeminate/feminine persons). Through a very different trajectory as an ethnographer, Ani discovered similar communities with mutually intelligible subcultural languages in various districts of West Bengal in the late 2000s, including terms such as *kothi, dhunuri,* and *dhurani*. As zie transitioned from a relatively *kodi* youth to a more *bhelki* visibility, Ani was gradually interpellated into these communities as a friend and sister.

Taken together, our experiences indicate translocal and transregional networks that enabled us to find shelter within a range of overlapping languages and communities. As most book-length studies of gender variance in India have focused on organized *hijra gharanas* or clans (Nanda 1990; Reddy 2005), these diverse communities, and particularly their transregional connections, have been only partially and fragmentally documented in the literature (Cohen 1995; Hall 2005; Reddy 2005; Dutta 2012). Given the existence of these communities, a conceptual polarity between gender/sexual identities and more fluid practices is not adequate, since gendered differences seem to have prompted the emergence of community formations *prior* to the contemporary moment of "global queering." Rather, we may need to explore the bridges and gaps between these community formations and emergent forms of identity politics.

★ ★ ★

Transgender has emerged as a prominent category in the Indian LGBTIQ movement and development sector relatively recently, roughly around the late 2000s. While the term has been used since at least the late 1990s by upper-tier activists and within acronyms like "LGBT," its increasing adoption by relatively low-rung community-based organizations (CBOs) may be linked to shifts in the pattern of funding available to such groups. Since 2007, the Indian state and transnational funders have increasingly recognized "transgender" people, particularly male-to-female trans people, as a "high risk" group for HIV infection (NACO 2007: 13). This shift in funding has been charted elsewhere in more detail

(Dutta 2013), so we will only provide a brief contour here. The second phase of India's National AIDS Control Program (NACP-II, 1997–2007) recognized MSM as a high-risk group (NACO 2006). In this period, "transgender" was used sporadically by particular activists such as Tista Das, one of the first trans women in West Bengal to undergo modern "sex change" or gender-affirmation surgery, as distinct from *hijra* castration-penectomy (Das 2009). However, the government did not define transgender as a target group for developmental aid or HIV intervention, though it did use the colonial category "eunuch" to designate *hijras* (NACO 2006: 43). This period saw the establishment of many CBOs in eastern India that received funds under the MSM rubric, such as MANAS Bangla, a CBO network in which Raina worked for several years. These CBOs typically drew membership from *kothi-dhurani* communities rather than focus on gendernormative MSM. Raina recalls going around with other fieldworkers in various cruising sites and finding potential community members whom they would interpellate as *kothi*, which gained popularity as a more common usage relative to similar terms like *dhurani*. Lawrence Cohen has argued that the *kothi* became an "emergent reality" during the expansion of HIV-AIDS intervention projects as fieldworkers interpellated more and more people into the category (2005: 285). However, Raina's experiences suggest that the *kothi*, rather than marking a new social emergence, marked a further consolidation and expansion of the networks in which she had participated in her youth (see Dutta 2013: 501).

The third phase of the NACP (2007–12) classified *kothi* as a high-risk subgroup of feminine MSM (NACO 2007: 13). Simultaneously, "transgender" entered the NACP lexicon, but NACP guidelines took transgender to largely mean *hijra*, replacing their earlier designation as eunuchs (13). Subsequently, in 2008, the United Nations Development Programme (UNDP), a multilateral organization that assists the Indian state with its AIDS program, organized consultations to assess gaps in HIV-AIDS infrastructure, where upper-tier activists demanded greater, more specific provisions for transgender people—including and beyond *hijras*—but also conceded that it was an ambiguously defined category (UNDP 2008). This prompted UNDP to fund regional consultations organized by large metropolitan NGOs in 2009, which aimed to arrive at a common transregional definition of TG in consultation with community representatives. Transgender was defined as an umbrella term, including both *hijra* and *kothi:*

> Transgender is a gender identity. Transgender persons usually live or prefer to live in the gender role opposite to the one in which they are born. In other words, one who is biologically male but loves to feel and see herself as a female could be considered as a male to female transgender person. It is an umbrella term which includes transsexuals, cross dressers, intersexed persons, gender variant persons and many more. In eastern India there are various local names and identities, such as Kothi, Dhurani, Boudi, 50/50, Gandu, Chakka, Koena. ... Among these the most common identity is Kothi. A few transgender persons also believe in a traditional culture known as Hijra ... with with its own hierarchical social system.
>
> (SAATHII 2009: 17)

Besides obvious problems like the total exclusion of trans masculine identities, this articulation of transgender as an umbrella term resulted in the scalar subsumption of "local names" under transgender as a common (trans)national, cross-cultural signifier. As a universalizing rubric, *transgender* subsumes terms that are now posited as merely local variants, even if they actually span multiple regions of South Asia and thus belie their containment to the scale of the local. The scalar hierarchy between transnational/universal/cosmopolitan and local/particular/vernacular discourses or categories thus *emerges* during this definitional process rather than preexisting it. As transnational feminists have argued, the hierarchy between global/local cannot be taken for granted, and scale is continually in the making (Mountz and Hyndman 2006). Through such ongoing constructions of scale, the understandings of gender/sex associated with transgender become the governing rubric under which regional subordinates must be organized rather than a resource that varied idioms of gender/sexuality can negotiate in their own terms, through their own spatial or temporal scales.

Moreover, this process does not merely subsume, it also potentially elides and erases. As seen in the above document, transgender is imagined as an encompassing umbrella term that is almost infinitely extensible across various cultural contexts. Yet it is restrictively defined in biologically essentialist terms as identification with the gender "opposite" to one's "biological" sex through linear (male-to-female) transition, with only a token acknowledgment of gender variant and intersex persons who may not fit the binary. Thus while it seeks to encompass varied idioms of gender, it also carries assumptions that may contravene the discourses of gender/sexual variance that it claims to include. Following the emerging definition of transgender as a "gender identity" understood primarily through a binary transitional model, the state has tended to categorically separate funding for transgender groups from the (homo)sexual category of "men who have sex with men," belying the overlap between sexual and gender variance evidenced in the previous classification of *kothi* as MSM (WBSAPCS 2011). Thus while transgender is defined as an open-ended umbrella term, it also potentially imposes homo-trans and cis-trans borders over complex spectral communities such as Raina's friend circle in south Kolkata, with their shifting *kodi-bhelki* and *kothi-hijra* boundaries, and class/caste-based overlaps between male-attired *kothis* and those who wear feminine clothes and/or join the *hijras*. The scalar ascendance of transgender as a trans/national umbrella term tends to establish the cis/trans and homo/trans binaries (and thus the male/female, man/woman divides) as putatively cross-cultural and ontologically stable rubrics, such that local discourses or practices of gender/sexual variance are simply assumed to be intelligible and classifiable in terms of the aforementioned binaries.

Following the initial articulations of transgender as an umbrella term in the HIV-AIDS sector, recent policy directives such as a report by the Ministry of Social Justice and Empowerment (MoSJE) and a judgment by the Supreme Court of India (SC) have also defined transgender as an umbrella category, extending its use beyond HIV-AIDS prevention (MoSJE 2014: 7; SC 2014: 10). Significantly, these institutional declarations explicitly include both binary (male-to-female or female-to-male) and "third gender" identities as subjects of rights and empowerment. However, they also recommend procedures for the certification of gender either by state-appointed committees (MoSJE) or through psychological tests (SC) to legally validate someone's preferred option as male, female, or transgender/third gender, which may further entrench the state-sanctioned adjudication of the boundaries between different gender categories and between cis and trans identities (MoSJE 2014: 34; SC 2014: 84). As an umbrella term, "transgender" is therefore marked by a foundational contradiction between its supposed indefinite extensibility across different sociocultural forms of gender variance and its imposition of new categorical assumptions and identitarian boundaries. As a result, ongoing attempts to define the scope of transgender as a category for funding and representation have prompted bitter border wars and activist conflicts regarding whom to include or not. *Hijras* have been included with relatively little controversy given their old status as eunuchs or a "third gender"; indeed, in some official usages, "transgender" may primarily serve to designate *hijras* (NACO 2007: 13). However, *kothi* and similar terms become particularly controversial due to their spectral nature and previous classification as MSM. The MSM-TG border wars and attendant debates over classification have been described by one of us in detail elsewhere (Dutta 2013). For our purposes here, we will focus on the role of these conflicts in the aforementioned elision of local categories. The controversy regarding the status of *kothi* peaked during consultations in 2010 preceding the launch of Project Pehchan, a new HIV-AIDS intervention program funded by the Global Fund to Fight against AIDS, Tuberculosis and Malaria. Raina was present at one of these consultations in Kolkata, where one set of activists accused other activists, who had previously identified as *kothi* and MSM, of being men who were masquerading as TG to gain funds. This may be seen as an intensification of the existing tensions between differently gendered subject positions in *kothi-hijra* communities, as described above. On the other hand, one of Raina's *hijra* friends willfully added to the confusion by stating that she was *hijra* by profession, TG by gender identity, and MSM by sexual behavior, much to Raina's delight. Despite such attempts to confuse the boundaries, eventually, the controversy resulted in *kothi* dropping out as a term of representation within the development sector. Since 2010, most CBOs in West Bengal have officially identified their constituencies as either TG or MSM, and *kothi* has fallen out of official activist usage.

This shift has also fueled a division between public representation and intracommunity usages. Even after the ascendance of transgender, *kothi* as a term of identification has remained close to our hearts. As Raina puts it, when a *kothi* sees another community member on the streets of Kolkata, they do not usually call out to each other as "hey, you transgender!"—rather, they feel more comfortable hailing each other as *kothi*. Yet when speaking to funders or state officials, CBO leaders typically represent their constituency as transgender without referencing local terms. This disjunction between subcultural terms and official usages of transgender signals a split between the affective register of community building and the language of political representation. Even when Raina and her friends do use "transgender" among themselves, their usage is often different from official discourse and may flexibly include people who would be identified as feminine gay men or MSM by funders (e.g., Ani in hir more *kodi* days). While this suggests that intracommunity usages resist hegemonic definitions and demonstrate alternative appropriations of transgender, the split between these distinct registers also serves as a constraint that limits upward mobility in terms of linguistic facility in English and the ability to employ the politically correct discourse du jour. While both of us can negotiate between subcultural intracommunity usages and organizational discourse, most *kothis* have not had the training or privilege to be able to do so, which restricts their mobility within activism and the development sector.

★ ★ ★

Moving on from the level of official representation, the increasing circulation of transgender as a category associated with certain ideas of gender may also bolster social hierarchies and forms of stigma around gender identity and presentation. In many emergent articulations of transgender identity, "transgender" and "transsexual" are loosely conflated, and the Bengali translation, *rupantarkami* (someone who desires transformation in *roop*, or form), can signify both senses (Das 2009). In many usages, "transgender" connotes an MTF (male-to-female) or FTM (female-to-male) model of identity and the affirmation of one's womanhood or manhood through some form of transition from one sex/gender to another (Das 2009; SAATHII 2009). However, in contexts where contemporary methods of transitioning have largely not been available, people within the *kothi-hijra* spectrum have devised trajectories of sartorial, bodily, or behavioral feminization that need not imply identification with social or ontological womanhood per se but, rather, may be expressed as a separately gendered subject position. For instance, several *kothis* of our acquaintance assert than while they are *like* women or have a womanly or feminine psyche (*mone nari*), they are not women as such (also see Reddy 2005: 134). Raina herself generally presents as a (trans) woman but does not identify as either gender (Ani, having come to hir subject position via the academy and queer theory before hir introduction to these communities, is another case altogether). Further, as Gayatri Reddy argues in her ethnography of *hijras* in South India, *hijras* may elect castration-penectomy and other methods of feminization such as hormonal treatments and yet not wish to socially "pass" as women, even if they are pleased when such passing does occur (Reddy 2005: 134–136). Indeed, *hijra* livelihoods like blessing people for money *depend* on their perception as distinct from both men and women. In this context, the advent of a new discourse of trans womanhood, whether accompanied by gender affirmation surgery or not, creates new possibilities of personal and social identification, which may have life-affirming implications for some people. We do not seek to rehearse the facile critique of transsexuality as conformist and reproducing binary gender, as if nontranssexuals do not do so all the time (Valentine 2012). At the same time, both of us have encountered gendered and classed hierarchies between emergent models of trans womanhood and older forms of feminization and gender liminality. Given that *hijra* communities and *kothi* forms of public visibility (such as flamboyance, sex work, and cruising) are often socially disreputable and stigmatized, some CBO leaders actively advocate that community members fashion themselves as women rather than *hijra/kothi*—to quote one such person, "the way that you people behave in public, does any woman behave like that? No wonder you have no respect in society." Indeed, as observed by Raina, the imputation of *hijra*-like behavior may even become a form of shaming and insult within some *kothi*/trans communities, in contrast to the proud avowal of *hijra* identity by *hijra* clans. This intensification of social stigma against gender liminality by holding up (middle class, upper caste) womanhood as a more desirable and respectable ideal of self-fashioning may be paralleled by a hierarchy between castration-penectomy (called *chhibrano* in the subcultural language) and the achievement of what trans women like Tista have termed their "complete" (*sampurna*) womanhood through "sex change" surgery (Das 2013). Over the last few years, both of us have encountered *kothis* who identify as (trans) women and deride *chhibrano*, saying they would never settle for anything "less" than "full" SRS (sex reassignment surgery). Such equations between transition, womanhood, and completeness (*sampurnata*) perpetuate the stigmatization of *hijras* and nontranssexual *kothis* as less than human and heighten the challenges faced by those who cannot afford, or do not want, "complete" womanhood or "full" transition.

Further, while the aforementioned hierarchies may be seen as related to restrictive articulations of transgender identity that exclude or deride nonbinary possibilities, even inclusive definitions of the category often imply a singular or consistent model of gender identity that may elide or delegitimize various unruly and inconsistent forms of identification practiced by *kothis* and *hijras*. Even pluralistic definitions of transgender often assume a stable model of gender based on primary, consistent, and singular identities, wherein trans people may have a variety of identities, but each identity is assumed to be singular, consistent, and mutually exclusive with the others, thus reflecting the social imperative of authentic identification, as also required by modern citizenship and biopolitical power. ("Identity" in its very semantics implies singularity or, at best, the combination of singular-consistent identities). This is not to criticize people for desiring stable or officially recognized identities—many of us may need one to survive in contemporary societies—but to critique the *structural* imperative of authentic and consistent identification, which is particularly evident in defensive assertions that trans and queer people are "born this way." In our perception, this imperative is reflected in the proliferation of attempts to build stable cartographies of trans identities, such as those reflected in several popular introductory guides to gender identity and trans issues produced in the United States, which are also gaining circulation in Indian online trans spaces (Hill and Mays 2013; Kasulke 2013; Bauer 2010). Typically, these guides feature a list of trans identities led by trans men and women and followed by genderqueer people, cross-dressers, drag queens and kings, and so on (the latter categories progressively coming closer to gender instability and the cis-trans border and thus unevenly included). A trans woman, to be respected as such, has to be seen as really and only a woman: to suggest that she may potentially be *also* genderqueer, third gender—or worse, a feminine male—can only be seen as offensive misgendering. This is probably partly prompted by hostile tropes of the deceptive-pathetic transsexual in the West, wherein trans women are seen as deceptive "men" or pathetic failures at femininity (Serano 2013). To counter the forcible assignment of "real" or "birth" genders and assert the validity of trans identities, there is a systemic compulsion to exert a strong mono-gendered claim to trans womanhood (or manhood)—one fallout of which is the neat separation of binary and nonbinary identities, recreating a majority-minority dynamic wherein (trans) men and women are followed by a trail of genderqueer/bigender/agender "others." As one "Trans 101" rather despairingly states, "Just as nobody knows why there are so many cis people, nobody knows why there are so many binary identified folks" (Bauer 2010). However, this may be less an empirical constant and more the result of a system that makes it imperative to assign or claim a primary gender and confers legitimacy based on such identification, belying the shifting nonbinary positionalities occupied by many trans men and women, which must be downplayed relative to their *primary* identification. This process parallels the longstanding but never entirely successful attempt to dissociate gender variance from gay identity, wherein effeminacy/gender variance becomes downplayed within mainstream gay identities and the primary gender of gay people becomes defined in terms of masculinity (Valentine 2007). Various practices of gayness that belie stable definitions of "manhood" must be deemphasized for "gay" to retain its stable (cis) gendering and attendant privileges. Once categories such as "trans women" or "gay men" are seen as *necessarily* mono-gendered and evacuated of their historical association with gender liminality, "binary" people tend to be naturalized as majorities, leaving a trailing bunch of explicitly, exclusively nonbinary people. Such a schema would fail to understand how social or legal binary identities and nonbinary practices or subject positions may be negotiated and lived simultaneously, creating unstable assemblages rather than essentialized identities.

In contrast to the structural imperative of stable gender recognition, *hijras* and *kothis* may deploy various unruly, changeable practices of identification and citizenship arising from complex strategies of survival and self-assertion in societies that have not provided them with stable options rather than from any abstract radical politics. *Hijras* who have undergone castration-penectomy may procure and use official female identification documents and yet purposely contravene female identification in other contexts—for instance, by dramatizing physical discordance from femaleness by thickening the voice or by employing characteristic gestures such as the *thikri*, a loud clap, which immediately marks one as *hijra*. One of our *hijra* friends recently obtained a female voter card which she proudly flaunts, but she objects if otherwise perceived as a woman: in her words, "I went to a house where they mistook me for a woman: I just gave three claps!" Thus there may be *simultaneous* identifications and disidentifications with femaleness that cannot be comprehended by the aforementioned trans cartographies (or, at best, may be relegated to a "bi-gender" minority categorically separate from trans women, denying how *hijras* may be *both* women and not-women). Further, some *hijras* and *kothis* may have a combination of identity documents under "male," "female," and more recently, "other"/"transgender" categories, due to the varying circumstances in which they procured the documents. We have known *hijras* and *kothis* with multiple identity cards who have had problems accessing healthcare services due to the expectation of a stable, singular identity. Moreover, since the entry of "other" and "transgender" as official gender categories recognized by the Indian government, there have been ongoing debates about whether *hijras* and other transgender people should be classified as female or other/

transgender, often with the assumption that there could be a generalized answer to this question (see Kushala 2011). Obviously, lumping trans people into either "female" or "other" categories, each exclusive of the other, presents two problematic options. The recent MoSJE and SC directives recognize both binary-gendered trans people and a third or nonbinary category and seek to enable individual choice over identification rather than impose any one category on all trans people; however, they still operate on the assumption of a fixed and consistent identity that must be legally validated through expert committees, psychological tests, or surgery (MoSJE 2014: 34; SC 2014: 84, 108). While enabling individual access to and choice over official identification is crucial, at the same time, it may be necessary to destabilize the polarity between binary and nonbinary (or "third gender") identities—and more broadly, to question the requirement of singular, consistent identification in order to access rights and citizenship. Otherwise, emergent transgender epistemologies that attempt to classify mutually exclusive, primary gender identities over and above the binary-defying practices of many queer, trans (and even cis) lives may fail to comprehend multiple or non-coherent gendered identifications or practices enacted by a single body and may elide or erase temporally unstable or non-unidirectional trajectories of gendered transition. In such epistemologies, the subject positions and practices of *hijras* and *kothis* can only linger on as an exotic, precarious species of gender variance, as remnants of archaic forms of gender liminality, or as afterthoughts tagged on as an et cetera to trans cartographies—rather than as people who powerfully instantiate the gendered instabilities that foundationally mark many LGBTIQ subject positions and indeed, sex/gender itself.

★ ★ ★

The emergence of transgender is an ongoing and unpredictable process, and we can draw only a provisional conclusion to our reflections here. Given that transgender may serve as a useful and even life-saving rubric for service provision, politics, and funding, we do not advocate a disengagement with the category but a critique of the structural conditions and assumptions within which it functions. Rather than use transgender as an umbrella term encompassing all possible gender variant identities, it is perhaps better deployed as an analytic rubric for variant and liminal gendered *positions*, such that to access the benefits or services provided through the category (e.g., HIV prevention, gender-affirmative care, antiviolence work, crisis support), one does not have to *identify* with any pregiven understanding of transgender. This process of deontologizing transgender (dissociating it from ontological identification) has to be coupled with the critique and gradual dismantling of the scalar hierarchy between "transnational" and "local" or "regional" discourses, so as to enable more equitable conversations and engagements with other epistemologies of gender/sexual variance or marginality. Evidently, the definition of transgender as a universal(izing) term does not truly value the diverse understandings of gender/sexual variance in different regions, and even pluralistic definitions of transgender tend to recreate a majoritarian dynamic in which everyone has to have a (consistent) identity, and some identities must trail behind others. Variant imaginations of scale are crucial to challenge these colonizing implications of the transgender category, such that local or regional discourses are not compelled to be legible in terms of globalizing understandings of gender, and the latter also become accountable to the former. Beyond discursive realignments, this necessitates material transformations. The way in which each region or community may build distinctive movements and approaches, network with each other, and forge counterhegemonic translations with the transgender category is restricted through a centralized structure of activism, funding, and scholarship wherein they become just subregions within a preconstituted trans/national domain. More egalitarian exchanges necessitate a gradual dismantling of the centralized and tiered structure of social movements, with funders, NGOs, activists, and scholars based in Western or post-colonial metropolises at the top and small CBOs near the bottom. The decolonization of transgender is not likely to be achieved in isolation from the transformation of the political economy of social movements, the dismantling of scalar geographies of development, and the class/caste/racial hierarchies within which they are embedded. Therefore, in the end, we wish to stress that decolonizing transgender is not just a project to include external forms of cultural difference into existing structures and epistemologies but is internal to the deconstruction and democratization of LGBTIQ activism both inside and outside the "West."

Bibliography

Bauer, Asher. 2010. "Not Your Mom's Trans 101." *Tranarchism*, November 26. tranarchism.com/2010/11/26/not-your-moms-trans-101/.

Boyce, Paul, and Akshay Khanna. 2011. "Rights and Representations: Querying the Male-to-Male Sexual Subject in India." *Culture, Health, and Sexuality* 13, no. 1: 89–100.

Cohen, Lawrence. 1995. "The Pleasures of Castration: The Postoperative Status of Hijras, Jankhas, and Academics." In *Sexual Nature, Sexual Culture*, ed. Paul R. Abramson and Steven D. Pinkerton, 276–304. Chicago: University of Chicago Press.

———. 2005. "The Kothi Wars: AIDS Cosmopolitanism and the Morality of Classification." In *Sex in Development: Science, Sexuality, and Morality in Global Perspective*, ed. Vivienne Adams and Stacy L. Piggs, 269–303. Durham, NC: Duke University Press.

Das, Tista. 2009. "Bibhatsa-bibar" ("Monstrous"). *Swikriti Patrika*, no. 6: 9–15.

———. 2013. "Ami kichhutei tomar chhele hote chai na ma" ("I Do Not Want to Be Your Son, Ma"). *News Bangla*, June 21.

Dirks, Nicholas B. 2001. *Castes of Mind: Colonialism and the Making of Modern India*. Princeton, NJ: Princeton University Press.

Dutta, Aniruddha. 2012. "An Epistemology of Collusion: *Hijras, Kothis*, and the Historical (Dis)continuity of Gender/Sexual Identities in Eastern India." *Gender and History* 24, no. 3: 825–49.

———. 2013. "Legible Identities and Legitimate Citizens: The Globalization of Transgender and Subjects of HIV-AIDS Prevention in Eastern India." *International Feminist Journal of Politics* 15, no. 4: 494–514.

Hall, Kira. 2005. "Intertextual Sexuality: Parodies of Class, Identity, and Desire in Liminal Delhi." *Journal of Linguistic Anthropology* 15, no. 1: 125–144.

Hill, Mell Reiff, and Jay Mays. 2013. *The Gender Book*. www.thegenderbook.com/the-book/4553374748 (accessed January 14, 2014).

Kasulke, Sarah. 2013. "Everything You Always Wanted to Know About Transgender People but Were Afraid to Ask." *Buzzfeed*, July 22. www.buzzfeed.com/sbkasulke/everything-you-always-wanted-to-know-about-transgender-peopl.

Katyal, Akhil. 2010. "No 'Sexuality' for All—Some Notes from India." *Polyvocia* 2: 21–29.

Khanna, Akshay. 2009. "Taming of the Shrewd Meyeli Chhele: A Political Economy of Devel-opment's Sexual Subject." *Development* 52, no. 1: 43–51.

Kushala, S. 2011. "The Majority of Transsexuals Like to Be Women." *Bangalore Mirror*, March 21.

MoSJE (Ministry of Social Justice and Empowerment). 2014. "Report of the Expert Committee on the Issues Relating to Transgender Persons." socialjustice.nic.in/transgenderpersons.php (accessed April 16, 2014).

Mountz, Alison, and Jennifer Hyndman. 2006. "Feminist Approaches to the Global Intimate." *Women's Studies Quarterly* 34, no. 1–2: 446–463.

NACO (National AIDS Control Organization). 2006. *Annual HIV Sentinel Surveillance Report 2006*. New Delhi: Ministry of Health and Family Welfare, Government of India.

———. 2007. *Targeted Interventions under NACP III: Core High Risk Groups.* New Delhi: Ministry of Health and Family Welfare, Government of India.

Nanda, Serena. 1990. *Neither Man nor Woman: The Hijras of India.* Belmont, CA: Wadsworth.

Reddy, Gayatri. 2005. *With Respect to Sex: Negotiating Hijra Identity in South India.* Chicago: University of Chicago Press.

SAATHII (Solidarity and Action against the HIV Infection in India). 2009. *Report of the Regional TG/ Hijra Consultation in Eastern India.* www.saathii.org/orissapages/tg_hijra_issues_consultation%20.html (accessed January 14, 2014).

SC (The Supreme Court of India). 2014. *National Legal Services Authority Versus Union of India and Others.* judis.nic.in/supremecourt/imgs1.aspx?filename=41411 (accessed April 16, 2014).

Serano, Julia. 2013. "Skirt Chasers: Why the Media Depicts the Trans Revolution in Lipstick and Heels." In *The Transgender Studies Reader 2*, ed. Susan Stryker and Aren Aizura, 226–233. New York: Routledge.

Spivak, Gayatri Chakravorty. 1999. *A Critique of Postcolonial Reason: Toward a History of the Vanishing Present.* Cambridge, MA: Harvard University Press.

Stryker, Susan, and Aren Aizura, eds. 2013. *The Transgender Studies Reader 2.* New York: Routledge.

UNDP (United Nations Development Programme). 2008. *Missing Pieces: HIV Related Needs of Sexual Minorities in India.* www.ph.undp.org/content/dam/india/docs/msm_publications.pdf (accessed April 15, 2014).

Valentine, David. 2007. *Imagining Transgender: An Ethnography of a Category.* Durham, NC: Duke University Press.

———. 2012. "Sue E. Generous: Toward a Theory of Non-Transexuality." *Feminist Studies* 38, no. 1: 1–19.

WBSAPCS (West Bengal State AIDS Prevention and Control Society). 2011. *Advertisement for Inviting Applications from CBOs for Empanelment.* Kolkata: Ministry of Health and Family Welfare, Government of West Bengal.

Section IV

Queer Gender and Its Discontents

16 Selection From *Gender Trouble*

Feminism and the Subversion of Identity

Judith Butler

Feminist philosopher, activist, and public intellectual Judith Butler has played a fundamental role in shaping contemporary understandings of sex and gender, most notably for the widely misunderstood concept of "gender performativity." While some trans people understand "performative" to mean "just pretending" and therefore incompatible with asserting the authenticity of trans experience, that's not what Butler actually meant. A "performative," in speech act theory, names a class of utterances that communicate simply through the act of enunciating, like saying "I now pronounce you husband and wife." The saying of a performative is the doing of the thing it utters, unlike other sorts of speech acts—like saying "The apple is red"—that refer to objects and make statements about them. In calling gender performative, Butler suggested that the "doing" of a gender is the "being" of it. Furthermore, Butler did not consider "sex" the biological substrate of a socially constructed "gender" but rather a set of socially constructed criteria that one "cites," over and over again, to authorize a particular enactment of gender. This is not to deny the material existence of actual biological differences; rather, similar to Black and anti-colonial feminist critiques of "biocentrism," Butler shows that assigning certain meanings to biological difference is an operation of power, not a pre-given and unalterable truth. In "Bodily Inscriptions, Performative Subversions," a section of a chapter of *Gender Trouble: Feminism and the Subversion of Identity*, from 1990, Butler lays out their performative theory of gender. Despite its usefulness for trans studies, Butler has been aptly critiqued by some trans scholars, such as Jay Prosser, for imagining trans phenomena merely as sites of "gender trouble" rather than appreciating the material stakes for trans lives invested in trans identities and ways of being. In *Bodies That Matter*, the follow-up to *Gender Trouble*, Butler seems to suggest in a chapter on the murder of translatina Venus Xtravaganza in the film *Paris Is Burning* that Xtravaganza died because she "tragically misread" how power operated rather than because she was killed by transphobes. To their credit, Butler has acknowledged past deficiencies in their analysis and interpretation of trans issues, continues to refine their understanding of them through ongoing engagement with trans people, and is an outspoken advocate for trans rights.

iv. Bodily Inscriptions, Performative Subverstions

"Garbo 'got in drag' whenever she took some heavy glamour part, whenever she melted in or out of a man's arms, whenever she simply let that heavenly-flexed neck . . . bear the weight of her thrown-back head. How resplendent seems the art of acting! It is all impersonation, whether the sex underneath is true or not."

—Parker Tyler, "The Garbo Image" quoted in
Esther Newton, *Mother Camp*

DOI: 10.4324/9781003206255-21

Categories of true sex, discrete gender, and specific sexuality have constituted the stable point of reference for a great deal of feminist theory and politics. These constructs of identity serve as the points of epistemic departure from which theory emerges and politics itself is shaped. In the case of feminism, politics is ostensibly shaped to express the interests, the perspectives, of "women." But is there a political shape to "women," as it were, that precedes and prefigures the political elaboration of their interests and epistemic point of view? How is that identity shaped, and is it a political shaping that takes the very morphology and boundary of the sexed body as the ground, surface, or site of cultural inscription? What circumscribes that site as "the female body"? Is "the body" or "the sexed body" the firm foundation on which gender and systems of compulsory sexuality operate? Or is "the body" itself shaped by political forces with strategic interests in keeping that body bounded and constituted by the markers of sex?

The sex/gender distinction and the category of sex itself appear to presuppose a generalization of "the body" that preexists the acquisition of its sexed significance. This "body" often appears to be a passive medium that is signified by an inscription from a cultural source figured as "external" to that body. Any theory of the cultural constructed body, however, ought to question "the body" as a construct of suspect generality when it is figured as passive and prior to discourse. There are Christian and Cartesian precedents to such views which, prior to the emergence of vitalistic biologies in the nineteenth century, understand "the body" as so much inert matter, signifying nothing or, more specifically, signifying a profane void, the fallen state: deception, sin, the premonitional metaphorics of hell and the eternal feminine. There are many occasions in both Sartre's and Beauvoir's work where "the body" is figured as a mute facticity, anticipating some meaning that can be attributed only by a transcendent consciousness, understood in Cartesian terms as radically immaterial. But what establishes this dualism for us? What separates off "the body" as indifferent to signification, and signification itself as the act of a radically disembodied consciousness or, rather, the act that radically disembodies that consciousness? To what extent is that Cartesian dualism presupposed in phenomenology adapted to the structuralist frame in which mind/body is redescribed as culture/nature? With respect to gender discourse, to what extent do these problematic dualisms still operate within the very descriptions that are supposed to lead us out of that binarism and its implicit hierarchy? How are the contours of the body clearly marked as the taken-for-granted ground or surface upon which gender significations are inscribed, a mere facticity devoid of value, prior to significance?

Wittig suggests that a culturally specific epistemic *a priori* establishes the naturalness of "sex." But by what enigmatic means has "the body" been accepted as a *prima facie* given that admits of no genealogy? Even within Foucault's essay on the very theme of genealogy, the body is figured as a surface and the scene of a cultural inscription: "the body is the inscribed surface of events."[1] The task of genealogy, he claims, is "to expose a body totally imprinted by history." His sentence continues, however, by referring to the goal of "history"—here clearly understood on the model of Freud's "civilization"—as the "destruction of the body" (148). Forces and impulses with multiple directionalities are precisely that which history both destroys and preserves through the *Entstehung* (historical event) of inscription. As "a volume in perpetual disintegration" (148), the body is always under siege, suffering destruction by the very terms of history. And history is the creation of values and meanings by a signifying practice that requires the subjection of the body. This corporeal destruction is necessary to produce the speaking subject and its significations. This is a body, described through the language of surface and force, weakened through a "single drama" of domination, inscription, and creation (150). This is not the *modus vivendi* of one kind of history rather than another, but is, for Foucault, "history" (148) in its essential and repressive gesture.

Although Foucault writes, "Nothing in man [*sic*]—not even his body—is sufficiently stable to serve as the basis for self-recognition or for understanding other men [*sic*]" (153), he nevertheless points to the constancy of cultural inscription as a "single drama" that acts on the body. If the creation of values, that historical mode of signification, requires the destruction of the body, much as the instrument of torture in Kafka's "In the Penal Colony" destroys the body on which it writes, then there must be a body prior to that inscription, stable and self-identical, subject to that sacrificial destruction. In a sense, for Foucault, as for Nietzsche, cultural values emerge as the result of an inscription on the body, understood as a medium, indeed, a blank page; in order for this inscription to signify, however, that medium must itself be destroyed— that is, fully transvaluated into a sublimated domain of values. Within the metaphorics of this notion of cultural values is the figure of history as a relentless writing instrument, and the body as the medium which must be destroyed and transfigured in order for "culture" to emerge.

By maintaining a body prior to its cultural inscription, Foucault appears to assume a materiality prior to signification and form. Because this distinction operates as essential to the task of genealogy as he defines it, the distinction itself is precluded as an object of genealogical investigation. Occasionally in his analysis of Herculine, Foucault subscribes to a prediscursive multiplicity of bodily forces that break through the surface of the body to disrupt the regulating practices of cultural coherence imposed upon that body by a power regime, understood as a vicissitude of "history." If the presumption of some kind of precategorical source of disruption is refused, is it still possible to give a genealogical account of the demarcation of the body as such as a signifying practice? This demarcation is not initiated by a reified history or by a subject. This marking is the result of a diffuse and active structuring of the social field. This signifying practice effects a social space for and of the body within certain regulatory grids of intelligibility.

Mary Douglas's *Purity and Danger* suggests that the very contours of "the body" are established through markings that seek to establish specific codes of cultural coherence. Any discourse that establishes the boundaries of the body serves the purpose of instating and naturalizing certain taboos regarding the appropriate limits, postures, and modes of exchange that define what it is that constitutes bodies:

> ideas about separating, purifying, demarcating and punishing transgressions have as their main function to impose system on an inherently untidy experience. It is only by exaggerating the difference between within and without, above and below, male and female, with and against, that a semblance of order is created.[2]

Although Douglas clearly subscribes to a structuralist distinction between an inherently unruly nature and an order imposed by cultural means, the "untidiness" to which she refers can be redescribed as a region of *cultural* unruliness and disorder. Assuming the inevitably binary structure of the nature/culture distinction, Douglas cannot point toward an alternative configuration of culture in which such distinctions become malleable or proliferate beyond the binary frame. Her analysis, however, provides a possible point of departure for understanding the relationship by which social taboos institute and maintain the boundaries of the body as such. Her analysis suggests that what constitutes the limit of the body is never merely material, but that the surface, the skin, is systemically signified by taboos and anticipated transgressions; indeed, the boundaries of the body become, within her analysis, the limits of the social *per se*. A poststructuralist appropriation of her view might well understand the boundaries of the body as the limits of the socially *hegemonic*. In a variety of cultures, she maintains, there are

> pollution powers which inhere in the structure of ideas itself and which punish a symbolic breaking of that which should be joined or joining of that which should be

separate. It follows from this that pollution is a type of danger which is not likely to occur except where the lines of structure, cosmic or social, are clearly defined.

A polluting person is always in the wrong. He [*sic*] has developed some wrong condition or simply crossed over some line which should not have been crossed and this displacement unleashes danger for someone.[3]

In a sense, Simon Watney has identified the contemporary construction of "the polluting person" as the person with AIDS in his *Policing Desire: AIDS, Pornography, and the Media*.[4] Not only is the illness figured as the "gay disease," but throughout the media's hysterical and homophobic response to the illness there is a tactical construction of a continuity between the polluted status of the homosexual by virtue of the boundary-trespass that is homosexuality and the disease as a specific modality of homosexual pollution. That the disease is transmitted through the exchange of bodily fluids suggests within the sensationalist graphics of homophobic signifying systems the dangers that permeable bodily boundaries present to the social order as such. Douglas remarks that "the body is a model that can stand for any bounded system. Its boundaries can represent any boundaries which are threatened or precarious."[5] And she asks a question which one might have expected to read in Foucault: "Why should bodily margins be thought to be specifically invested with power and danger?"[6]

Douglas suggests that all social systems are vulnerable at their margins, and that all margins are accordingly considered dangerous. If the body is synecdochal for the social system *per se* or a site in which open systems converge, then any kind of unregulated permeability constitutes a site of pollution and endangerment. Since anal and oral sex among men clearly establishes certain kinds of bodily permeabilities unsanctioned by the hegemonic order, male homosexuality would, within such a hegemonic point of view, constitute a site of danger and pollution, prior to and regardless of the cultural presence of AIDS. Similarly, the "polluted" status of lesbians, regardless of their low-risk status with respect to AIDS, brings into relief the dangers of their bodily exchanges. Significantly, being "outside" the hegemonic order does not signify being "in" a state of filthy and untidy nature. Paradoxically, homosexuality is almost always conceived within the homophobic signifying economy as *both* uncivilized and unnatural.

The construction of stable bodily contours relies upon fixed sites of corporeal permeability and impermeability. Those sexual practices in both homosexual and heterosexual contexts that open surfaces and orifices to erotic signification or close down others effectively reinscribe the boundaries of the body along new cultural lines. Anal sex among men is an example, as is the radical remembering of the body in Wittig's *The Lesbian Body*. Douglas alludes to "a kind of sex pollution which expresses a desire to keep the body (physical and social) intact,"[7] suggesting that the naturalized notion of "the" body is itself a consequence of taboos that render that body discrete by virtue of its stable boundaries. Further, the rites of passage that govern various bodily orifices presuppose a heterosexual construction of gendered exchange, positions, and erotic possibilities. The deregulation of such exchanges accordingly disrupts the very boundaries that determine what it is to be a body at all. Indeed, the critical inquiry that traces the regulatory practices within which bodily contours are constructed constitutes precisely the genealogy of "the body" in its discreteness that might further radicalize Foucault's theory.[8]

Significantly, Kristeva's discussion of abjection in *Powers of Horror* begins to suggest the uses of this structuralist notion of a boundary-constituting taboo for the purposes of constructing a discrete subject through exclusion.[9] The "abject" designates that which has been expelled from the body, discharged as excrement, literally rendered "Other." This appears as an expulsion of alien elements, but the alien is effectively established through this expulsion.

The construction of the "not-me" as the abject establishes the boundaries of the body which are also the first contours of the subject. Kristeva writes:

> *nausea* makes me balk at that milk cream, separates me from the mother and father who proffer it. "I" want none of that element, sign of their desire; "I" do not want to listen, "I" do not assimilate it, "I" expel it. But since the food is not an "other" for "me," who am only in their desire, I expel *myself*, I spit *myself* out, I abject *myself* within the same motion through which "I" claim to establish myself.[10]

The boundary of the body as well as well as the distinction between internal and external is established through the ejection and transvaluation of something originally part of identity into a defiling otherness. As Iris Young has suggested in her use of Kristeva to understand sexism, homophobia, and racism, the repudiation of bodies for their sex, sexuality, and/or color is an "expulsion" followed by a "repulsion" that founds and consolidates culturally hegemonic identities along sex/race/sexuality axes of differentiation.[11] Young's appropriation of Kristeva shows how the operation of repulsion can consolidate "identities" founded on the instituting of the "Other" or a set of Others through exclusion and domination. What constitutes through division the "inner" and "outer" worlds of the subject is a border and boundary tenuously maintained for the purposes of social regulation and control. The boundary between the inner and outer is confounded by those excremental passages in which the inner effectively becomes outer, and this excreting function becomes, as it were, the model by which other forms of identity-differentiation are accomplished. In effect, this is the mode by which Others become shit. For inner and outer worlds to remain utterly distinct, the entire surface of the body would have to achieve an impossible impermeability. This sealing of its surfaces would constitute the seamless boundary of the subject; but this enclosure would invariably be exploded by precisely that excremental filth that it fears.

Regardless of the compelling metaphors of the spatial distinctions of inner and outer, they remain linguistic terms that facilitate and articulate a set of fantasies, feared and desired. "Inner" and "outer" make sense only with reference to a mediating boundary that strives for stability. And this stability, this coherence, is determined in large part by cultural orders that sanction the subject and compel its differentiation from the abject. Hence, "inner" and "outer" constitute a binary distinction that stabilizes and consolidates the coherent subject. When that subject is challenged, the meaning and necessity of the terms are subject to displacement. If the "inner world" no longer designates a topos, then the internal fixity of the self and, indeed, the internal locale of gender identity, become similarly suspect. The critical question is not *how* did that identity become *internalized?* as if internalization were a process or a mechanism that might be descriptively reconstructed. Rather, the question is: From what strategic position in public discourse and for what reasons has the trope of interiority and the disjunctive binary of inner/outer taken hold? In what language is "inner space" figured? What kind of figuration is it, and through what figure of the body is it signified? How does a body figure on its surface the very invisibility of its hidden depth?

From Interiority to Gender Performatives

In *Discipline and Punish* Foucault challenges the language of internalization as it operates in the service of the disciplinary regime of the subjection and subjectivation of criminals.[12] Although Foucault objected to what he understood to be the psychoanalytic belief in the "inner" truth of sex in *The History of Sexuality*, he turns to a criticism of the doctrine of internalization for separate purposes in the context of his history of criminology. In a sense, *Discipline and Punish* can be read as Foucault's effort to rewrite Nietzsche's doctrine of internalization in *On the Genealogy of Morals* on the model of *inscription*. In the context of prisoners, Foucault writes, the strategy has been not to enforce a repression of their desires, but to compel their bodies to signify the prohibitive law as their very essence, style, and necessity. That law is not literally internalized, but incorporated, with the consequence that bodies are produced which signify that law on and through the body; there the law is manifest as the essence of their selves, the meaning of their soul, their conscience, the law of their desire. In effect, the law is at once fully manifest and fully latent, for it never appears as external to the bodies it subjects and subjectivates. Foucault writes:

> It would be wrong to say that the soul is an illusion, or an ideological effect. On the contrary, it exists, it has a reality, it is produced permanently *around, on, within,* the body by the functioning of a power that is exercised on those that are punished. (my emphasis)[13]

The figure of the interior soul understood as "within" the body is signified through its inscription *on* the body, even though its primary mode of signification is through its very absence, its potent invisibility. The effect of a structuring inner space is produced through the signification of a body as a vital and sacred enclosure. The soul is precisely what the body lacks; hence, the body presents itself as a signifying lack. That lack which *is* the body signifies the soul as that which cannot show. In this sense, then, the soul is a surface signification that contests and displaces the inner/outer distinction itself, a figure of interior psychic space inscribed *on* the body as a social signification that perpetually renounces itself as such. In Foucault's terms, the soul is not imprisoned by or within the body, as some Christian imagery would suggest, but "the soul is the prison of the body."[14]

The redescription of intrapsychic processes in terms of the surface politics of the body implies a corollary redescription of gender as the disciplinary production of the figures of fantasy through the play of presence and absence on the body's surface, the construction of the gendered body through a series of exclusions and denials, signifying absences. But what determines the manifest and latent text of the body politic? What is the prohibitive law that generates the corporeal stylization of gender, the fantasied and fantastic figuration of the body? We have already considered the incest taboo and the prior taboo against homosexuality as the generative moments of gender identity, the prohibitions that produce identity along the culturally intelligible grids of an idealized and compulsory heterosexuality. The disciplinary production of gender effects a false stabilization of gender in the interests of the heterosexual construction and regulation of sexuality within the reproductive domain. The construction of coherence conceals the gender discontinuities that run rampant within heterosexual, bisexual, and gay and lesbian contexts in which gender does not necessarily follow from sex, and desire, or sexuality generally, does not seem to follow from gender—indeed, where none of these dimensions of significant corporeality express or reflect one another. When the disorganization and disaggregation of the field of bodies disrupt the regulatory fiction of heterosexual coherence, it seems that the expressive model loses its descriptive force. That regulatory ideal is then exposed as a norm and a fiction that disguises itself as a developmental law regulating the sexual field that it purports to describe.

According to the understanding of identification as an enacted fantasy or incorporation, however, it is clear that coherence is desired, wished for, idealized, and that this idealization is an effect of a corporeal signification. In other words, acts, gestures, and desire produce the effect of an internal core or substance, but produce this *on the surface* of the body, through the play of signifying absences that suggest, but never reveal, the organizing principle of identity as a cause. Such acts, gestures, enactments, generally construed, are *performative* in the sense that the essence or identity that they otherwise purport to express are *fabrications* manufactured and sustained through corporeal signs and other discursive means. That the gendered body is performative suggests that it has no ontological status apart from the various acts which constitute its reality. This also suggests that if that reality is fabricated as an interior essence, that very interiority is an effect and function of a decidedly public and social discourse, the public regulation of fantasy through the surface politics of the body, the gender border control that differentiates inner from outer, and so institutes the "integrity" of the subject. In other words, acts and gestures, articulated and enacted desires create the illusion of an interior and organizing gender core, an illusion discursively maintained for the purposes of the regulation of sexuality within the obligatory frame of reproductive heterosexuality. If the "cause" of desire, gesture, and act can be localized within the "self" of the actor, then the political regulations and disciplinary practices which produce that ostensibly coherent gender are effectively displaced from view. The displacement of a political and discursive origin of gender identity onto a psychological "core" precludes an analysis of the political constitution of the gendered subject and its fabricated notions about the ineffable interiority of its sex or of its true identity.

If the inner truth of gender is a fabrication and if a true gender is a fantasy instituted and inscribed on the surface of bodies, then it seems that genders can be neither true nor false, but are only produced as the truth effects of a discourse of primary and stable identity. In *Mother Camp: Female Impersonators in America*, anthropologist Esther Newton suggests that the structure of impersonation reveals one of the key fabricating mechanisms through which the social construction of gender takes place.[15] I would suggest as well that drag fully subverts the distinction between inner and outer psychic space and effectively mocks both the expressive model of gender and the notion of a true gender identity. Newton writes:

> At its most complex, [drag] is a double inversion that says, "appearance is an illusion." Drag says [Newton's curious personification] "my 'outside' appearance is feminine, but my essence 'inside' [the body] is masculine." At the same time it symbolizes the opposite inversion; "my appearance 'outside' [my body, my gender] is masculine but my essence 'inside' [myself] is feminine."[16]

Both claims to truth contradict one another and so displace the entire enactment of gender significations from the discourse of truth and falsity.

The notion of an original or primary gender identity is often parodied within the cultural practices of drag, cross-dressing, and the sexual stylization of butch/femme identities. Within feminist theory, such parodic identities have been understood to be either degrading to women, in the case of drag and crossdressing, or an uncritical appropriation of sex-role stereotyping from within the practice of heterosexuality, especially in the case of butch/femme lesbian identities. But the relation between the "imitation" and the "original" is, I think, more complicated than that critique generally allows. Moreover, it gives us a clue to the way in which the relationship between primary identification—that is, the original meanings accorded to gender—and subsequent gender experience might be reframed. The performance of drag plays upon the distinction between the anatomy of the performer and the gender that is being performed. But we are actually in the presence of three contingent dimensions of significant corporeality: anatomical sex, gender identity, and gender performance. If the anatomy of the performer is already distinct from the gender of the performer, and both of those are distinct from the gender of the performance, then the performance suggests a dissonance not only between sex and performance, but sex and gender, and gender and performance. As much as drag creates a unified picture of "woman" (what its critics often oppose), it also reveals the distinctness of those aspects of gendered experience which are falsely naturalized as a unity through the regulatory fiction of heterosexual coherence.

In imitating gender, drag implicitly reveals the imitative structure of gender itself—as well as its contingency. Indeed, part of the pleasure, the giddiness of the performance is in the recognition of a radical contingency in the relation between sex and gender in the face of cultural configurations of causal unities that are regularly assumed to be natural and necessary. In the place of the law of heterosexual coherence, we see sex and gender denaturalized by means of a performance which avows their distinctness and dramatizes the cultural mechanism of their fabricated unity.

The notion of gender parody defended here does not assume that there is an original which such parodic identities imitate. Indeed, the parody is *of* the very notion of an original; just as the psychoanalytic notion of gender identification is constituted by a fantasy of a fantasy, the transfiguration of an Other who is always already a "figure" in that double sense, so gender parody reveals that the original identity after which gender fashions itself is an imitation without an origin. To be more precise, it is a production which, in effect—that is, in its effect—postures as an imitation. This perpetual displacement constitutes a fluidity of identities that suggests an openness to resignification and recontextualization; parodic proliferation deprives hegemonic culture and its critics of the claim to naturalized or essentialist gender identities. Although the gender meanings taken up in these parodic styles are clearly part of hegemonic, misogynist culture, they are nevertheless denaturalized and mobilized through their parodic recontextualization. As imitations which effectively displace the meaning of the original, they imitate the myth of originality itself. In the place of an original identification which serves as a determining cause, gender identity might be reconceived as a personal/cultural history of received meanings subject to a set of imitative practices which refer laterally to other imitations and which, jointly, construct the illusion of a primary and interior gendered self or parody the mechanism of that construction.

According to Fredric Jameson's "Postmodernism and Consumer Society," the imitation that mocks the notion of an original is characteristic of pastiche rather than parody:

> Pastiche is, like parody, the imitation of a peculiar or unique style, the wearing of a stylistic mask, speech in a dead language: but it is a neutral practice of mimicry, without parody's ulterior motive, without the satirical impulse, without laughter, without that still latent feeling that there exists something *normal* compared to which what is being imitated is rather comic. Pastiche is blank parody, parody that has lost it humor.[17]

The loss of the sense of "the normal," however, can be its own occasion for laughter, especially when "the normal," "the original" is revealed to be a copy, and an inevitably failed one, an ideal that no one *can* embody. In this sense, laughter emerges in the realization that all along the original was derived.

Parody by itself is not subversive, and there must be a way to understand what makes certain kinds of parodic repetitions effectively disruptive, truly troubling, and which repetitions become domesticated and recirculated as instruments of cultural hegemony. A typology of actions would clearly not suffice, for parodic displacement, indeed, parodic laughter, depends on a context and reception in which subversive confusions can be fostered. What performance where will invert the inner/outer distinction and compel a radical rethinking of the psychological presuppositions of gender identity and sexuality? What performance where will compel a reconsideration of the *place* and stability of the masculine and the feminine? And what kind of gender performance will enact and reveal the performativity of gender itself in a way that destabilizes the naturalized categories of identity and desire?

If the body is not a "being," but a variable boundary, a surface whose permeability is politically regulated, a signifying practice within a cultural field of gender hierarchy and compulsory heterosexuality, then what language is left for understanding this corporeal enactment, gender, that constitutes its "interior" signification on its surface? Sartre would perhaps have called this act "a style of being," Foucault, "a stylistics of existence." And in my earlier reading of Beauvoir, I suggest that gendered bodies are so many "styles of the flesh." These styles all never fully self styled, for styles have a history, and those histories condition and limit the possibilities. Consider gender, for instance, as *a corporeal style*, an "act," as it were, which is both intentional and performative, where "*performative*" suggests a dramatic and contingent construction of meaning.

Wittig understands gender as the workings of "sex," where "sex" is an obligatory injunction for the body to become a cultural sign, to materialize itself in obedience to a historically delimited possibility, and to do this, not once or twice, but as a sustained and repeated corporeal project. The notion of a "project," however, suggests the originating force of a radical will, and because gender is a project which has cultural survival as its end, the term *strategy* better suggests the situation of duress under which gender performance always and variously occurs. Hence, as a strategy of survival within compulsory systems, gender is a performance with clearly punitive consequences. Discrete genders are part of what "humanizes" individuals within con temporary culture; indeed, we regularly punish those who fail to do their gender right. Because there is neither an "essence" that gender expresses or externalizes nor an objective ideal to which gender aspires, and because gender is not a fact, the various acts of gender create the idea of gender, and without those acts, there would be no gender at all. Gender is, thus, a construction that regularly conceals its genesis; the tacit collective agreement to perform, produce, and sustain discrete and polar genders as cultural fictions is obscured by the credibility of those productions—and the punishments that attend not agreeing to believe in them; the construction "compels" our belief in its necessity and naturalness. The historical possibilities materialized through various corporeal styles are nothing other than those punitively regulated cultural fictions alternately embodied and deflected under duress.

Consider that a sedimentation of gender norms produces the peculiar phenomenon of a "natural sex" or a "real woman" or any number of prevalent and compelling social fictions, and that this is a sedimentation that over time has produced a set of corporeal styles which, in reified form, appear as the natural configuration of bodies into sexes existing in a binary relation to one another. If these styles are enacted, and if they produce the coherent gendered subjects who pose as their originators, what kind of performance might reveal this ostensible "cause" to be an "effect"?

In what senses, then, is gender an act? As in other ritual social dramas, the action of gender requires a performance that is *repeated*. This repetition is at once a reenactment and reexperiencing of a set of meanings already socially established; and it is the mundane and ritualized form of their legitimation.[18] Although there are individual bodies that enact these significations by becoming stylized into gendered modes, this "action" is a public action. There are temporal and collective dimensions to these actions, and their public character is not inconsequential; indeed, the performance is effected with the strategic aim of maintaining gender within its binary frame—an aim that cannot be attributed to a subject, but, rather, must be understood to found and consolidate the subject.

Gender ought not to be construed as a stable identity or locus of agency from which various acts follow; rather, gender is an identity tenuously constituted in time, instituted in an exterior space through a *stylized repetition of acts*. The effect of gender is produced through the stylization of the body and, hence, must be understood as the mundane way in which bodily gestures, movements, and styles of various kinds constitute the illusion of an abiding gendered self. This formulation moves the conception of gender off the ground of a substantial model of identity to one that requires a conception of gender as a constituted *social temporality*. Significantly, if gender is instituted through acts which are internally discontinuous, then the *appearance of substance* is precisely that, a constructed identity, a performative accomplishment which the mundane social audience, including the actors themselves, come to believe and to perform in the mode of belief. Gender is also a norm that can never be fully internalized; "the internal" is a surface signification, and gender norms are finally phantasmatic, impossible to embody. If the ground of gender identity is the stylized repetition of acts through time and not a seemingly seamless identity, then the spatial metaphor of a "ground" will be displaced and revealed as a stylized configuration, indeed, a gendered corporealization of time. The abiding gendered self will then be shown to be structured by repeated acts that seek to approximate the ideal of a substantial ground of identity, but which, in their occasional *dis*continuity, reveal the temporal and contingent groundlessness of this "ground." The possibilities of gender transformation are to be found precisely in the arbitrary relation between such acts, in the possibility of a failure to repeat, a deformity, or a parodic repetition that exposes the phantasmatic effect of abiding identity as a politically tenuous construction.

If gender attributes, however, are not expressive but performative, then these attributes effectively constitute the identity they are said to express or reveal. The distinction between expression and performativeness is crucial. If gender attributes and acts, the various ways in which a body shows or produces its cultural signification, are performative, then there is no preexisting identity by which an act or attribute might be measured; there would be no true or false, real or distorted acts of gender, and the postulation of a true gender identity would be revealed as a regulatory fiction. That gender reality is created through sustained social performances means that the very notions of an essential sex and a true or abiding masculinity or femininity are also constituted as part of the strategy that conceals gender's performative character and the performative possibilities for proliferating gender configurations outside the restricting frames of masculinist domination and compulsory heterosexuality.

Genders can be neither true nor false, neither real nor apparent, neither original nor derived. As credible bearers of those attributes, however, genders can also be rendered thoroughly and radically *incredible*.

From: *Gender Trouble: Feminism and the Subversion of Identity*, Judith Butler, Copyright 2006 by Routledge. Reproduced by permission of Taylor & Francis Group.

Notes

1. Michel Foucault, "Nietzsche, Genealogy, History," in *Language, Counter-Memory, Practice: Selected Essays and Interviews by Michel Foucault*, trans. Donald F. Bouchard and Sherry Simon, ed. Donald F. Bouchard (Ithaca: Cornell University Press, 1977), p. 148. References in the text are to this essay.
2. Mary Douglas, *Purity and Danger* (London, Boston, and Henley: Routledge and Kegan Paul, 1969), p. 4.
3. Ibid., p. 113.
4. Simon Watney, *Policing Desire: AIDS, Pornography, and the Media* (Minneapolis: University of Minnesota Press, 1988).
5. Douglas, *Purity and Danger*, p. 115.
6. Ibid., p. 121.
7. Ibid., p. 140.
8. Foucault's essay "A Preface to Transgression" (in *Language, CounterMemory, Practice*) does provide an interesting juxtaposition with Douglas' notion of body boundaries constituted by incest taboos. Originally written in honor of Georges Bataille, this essay explores in part the metaphorical "dirt" of transgressive pleasures and the association of the forbidden orifice with the dirt-covered tomb. See pp. 46–48.
9. Kristeva discusses Mary Douglas' work in a short section of *Powers of Horror: An Essay on Abjection*, trans. Leon Roudiez (New York: Columbia University Press, 1982), originally published as *Pouvoirs de l'horreur* (Paris: Éditions de Seuil, 1980). Assimilating Douglas' insights to her own reformulation of Lacan, Kristeva writes, "Defilement is what is jettisoned from the *symbolic system*. It is what escapes that social rationality, that logical order on which a social aggregate is based, which then becomes

differentiated from a temporary agglomeration of individuals and, in short, constitutes a *classification system* or a *structure*" (p. 65).

10. Ibid., p. 3.

11. Iris Marion Young, "Abjection and Oppression: Dynamics of Unconscious Racism, Sexism, and Homophobia," paper presented at the Society of Phenomenology and Existential Philosophy Meetings, Northwestern University, 1988. In *Crises in Continental Philosophy*, eds. Arleen B. Dallery, Charles E. Scott and Holley Roberts (Albany: SUNY Press, 1990), pp. 201–214.

12. Parts of the following discussion were published in two different contexts, in my "Gender Trouble, Feminist Theory, and Psychoanalytic Discourse," in *Feminism/Postmodernism*, ed. Linda J. Nicholson (New York: Routledge, 1989); Michel Foucault, "Performative Acts and Gender Constitution: An Essay in Phenomenology and Feminist Theory," *Theatre Journal*, Vol. 20, No. 3, Winter 1988.

13. Michel Foucault, *Discipline and Punish: The Birth of the Prison*, trans. Alan Sheridan (New York: Vintage, 1979), p. 29.

14. Ibid., p. 30.

15. See the chapter "Role Models" in Esther Newton, *Mother Camp: Female Impersonators in America*, (Chicago: University of Chicago Press, 1972).

16. Ibid., p. 103.

17. Fredric Jameson, "Postmodernism and Consumer Society," in *The Anti-Aesthetic: Essays on Postmodern Culture*, ed. Hal Foster (Port Townsend, WA: Bay Press, 1983), p. 114.

18. See Victor Turner, *Dramas, Fields and Metaphors* (Ithaca: Cornell University Press, 1974). See also Clifford Geertz, "Blurred Genres: The Refiguration of Thought," in *Local Knowledge, Further Essays in Interpretive Anthropology* (New York: Basic Books, 1983).

17 "The White to Be Angry"

Vaginal Davis's Terrorist Drag

José Esteban Muñoz

This classic text by performance studies scholar José Esteban Muñoz, about drag superstar Vaginal Creme Davis, is perhaps even more relevant now, with its prescient attention to the trope of the terrorist, than when it was originally published, years before racialist constructions of terrorism became a staple of post-9/11 life. "The White to Be Angry" first appeared in the journal *Social Text* in 1997, as part of the first collection of essays within queer theory to grapple with the new problematics introduced by transgender issues. Muñoz explicates his influential concept of "disidentification" through Davis's productively off-kilter satirization of white supremacist terrorism, brilliant aesthetic reworking of Black Power militancy, postmodern glosses on gay drag performance, and unironic embrace of the aggressive urgency of urban punk subcultures. Muñoz defines disidentification as "a performative mode of tactical recognition that various minoritarian subjects employ in an effort to resist the oppressive and normalizing discourse of dominant ideology." It is a strategy whereby queer and trans people of color refuse to answer to the terms imposed on them by the dominant society while simultaneously finding ways to survive within it.

Nineteen eighty saw the debut of one of the L.A. punk scene's most critically acclaimed albums, the band X's *Los Angeles*. X was fronted by John Doe and Exene Cervenka, who were described by one writer as "poetry workshop types"[1] and who had recently migrated to Los Angeles from the East Coast. They used the occasion of their first album to describe the effect that the West Coast city had on its white denizens. The album's title track, "Los Angeles," narrates the story of a white female protagonist who had to leave Los Angeles because she started to hate "every nigger and Jew, every Mexican who gave her a lot of shit, every homosexual and the idle rich." Today, the song reads for me like a fairly standard tale of white flight from the multiethnic metropolis. Yet I can't pretend to have had access to this reading back then, since I had no contexts or reading skills for any such interpretation.

Contemplating these lyrics today leaves me with a disturbed feeling. When I was a teenager growing up in South Florida, X occupied the hallowed position of favorite band. As I attempt to situate my relation to this song and my own developmental history, I remember what X meant to me back then. Within the hermetic Cuban American community I came of age in, punk rock was not yet the almost-routine route of individuation and resistance that it is today. Back then it was the only avant-garde that I knew, the only cultural critique of normative aesthetics available to me. Yet there was a way in which I was able to escape the song's interpellating call. Though queerness was already a powerful polarity in my life, and the hissing pronunciation of "Mexican" that the song produced felt very much like

DOI: 10.4324/9781003206255-22

the epithet "spic," with which I had a great deal of experience, I somehow found a way to resist these identifications. The luxury of hindsight lets me understand that I needed X and the possibility of subculture it promised at that moment to withstand the identity-eroding effects of normativity. I was able to enact a certain misrecognition that let me imagine myself as something other than queer or racialized. But such a misrecognition demands a certain toll. The toll is one that subjects who attempt to identify with and assimilate to dominant ideologies pay every day of their lives. The price of the ticket is this: to find self within the dominant public sphere, we need to deny self. The contradictory subjectivity one is left with is not just the fragmentary subjectivity of some unspecified postmodern condition; instead, it is the story of the minoritarian subject within the majoritarian public sphere. Fortunately, this story does not end at this difficult point, this juncture of painful contradiction. Sometimes misrecognition can be *tactical*. Identification itself can also be manipulated and worked in ways that promise narratives of self that surpass the limits prescribed by dominant culture.

In this paper I will discuss the cultural work of an artist who came of age within the very same L.A. punk scene that produced X. The L.A. punk scene worked very hard to white-wash and straighten its image. While many people of color and queers were part of this cultural movement, they often remained closeted in the scene's early days. The artist whose work I will be discussing in this paper came of age in that scene and managed to resist its whitewashing and heteronormative protocols.

The work of drag superstar Vaginal Creme Davis, or, as she sometimes prefers to be called, Dr. Davis, spans several cultural production genres. It also appropriates, terroristically, both dominant culture and different subcultural movements. Davis first rose to prominence in the L.A. punk scene through her infamous zine *Fertile Latoya Jackson* and through her performances at punk shows with her Supremes-like backup singers, the Afro Sisters. *Fertile Latoya Jackson's* first incarnation was as a print zine that presented scandalous celebrity gossip. The zine was reminiscent of *Hollywood Babylon*, Kenneth Anger's two-volume tell-all history of the movie industry and the star system's degeneracy. The hand-stapled zine eventually evolved into a video magazine. At the same time as the zine became a global subcultural happening, Davis's performances in and around the L.A. punk scene, both with the Afro Sisters and solo, became semilegendary. She went on to translate her performance madness to video, starring in various productions that include *Dot* (1994), her tribute to Dorothy Parker's acerbic wit and alcoholism; *UJODoo Williamson: The Dona of Dance* (1995), her celebration of modern dance and its doyennes; and *Designy Living* (1995), a tribute to Noel Coward's *Design for Living* and Godard's *Masculine et Feminine*.

According to Davis's own self-generated legend, her existence is the result of an illicit encounter between her then forty-five-year-old African American mother and her then twenty-one-year-old Mexican American father. Davis has often reported that her parents only met once, when she was conceived under a table during a Ray Charles concert at the Hollywood Palladium in the early 1960s.

While her work with the Afro Sisters and much of her zine work deal with issues of black-ness, Davis explores her Chicana heritage with another one of her musical groups, ¡Cholita!, a band that is billed as the female Menudo. This band consists of both men and women in teenage Chicana drag who sing Latin American bubblegum pop songs with titles like "*Chicas de hoy*" ["Girls of today"]. ¡Cholita! and Davis's other bands all produce socially interrogative performances that complicate any easy understanding of race or ethnicity within the social matrix. Performance is used by these theatrical musical groups to, borrowing a phrase from George Lipsitz, "rehearse identities"[2] that have been rendered toxic within the dominant public sphere but are, through Davis's fantastic and farcical performance, restructured (yet not cleansed) so they present newly imagined notions of the self and the social. This paper focuses on the performance work done through *The White to Be Angry*, a live show and a compact disc produced by one of Davis's other subculturally acclaimed musical groups, Pedro, Muriel, and Esther. (Often referred to as PME, the band is named after a cross section of people that Davis met when waiting for a bus. Pedro was a young Latino who worked at a fast-food chain, and Muriel and Esther were two senior citizens.) This essay's first section will consider both the live performance and the CD. The issue of "passing" and its specific relation to what I am calling the cultural politics of *disidentification* will also be interrogated. I will pursue this question of "passing" in relation to both mainstream drag and a queerer modality of performance, which I will be calling Davis's *terrorist drag*. In the paper's final section I will consider Davis's relation to the discourse of "antigay."

Who's That Girl?

Disidentification is a performative mode of tactical recognition that various minoritarian subjects employ in an effort to resist the oppressive and normalizing discourse of dominant ideology. Disidentification resists the interpellating call of ideology that fixes a subject within the state power apparatus. It is a reformatting of self within the social, a third term that resists the binary of identification and counteridentification. Counteridentification often, through the very routinized workings of its denouncement of dominant discourse, reinstates that same discourse. In an interview in the magazine *aRude*, Davis offers one of the most lucid explications of a modality of performance that I call *disidentificatory*. Davis responds to the question "How did you acquire the name Vaginal Davis?" with a particularly elucidating rant:

> It came from Angela Davis—I named myself as a salute to her because I was really into the whole late '60's and early '70's militant Black era. When you come home from the inner city and you're Black you go through a stage when you try to fit the dominant culture, you kinda want to be white at first—it would be easier if you were White. Everything that's negrified or Black—you don't want to be associated with that. That's what I call the snow period—I just felt like if I had some cheap white boyfriend, my life could be perfect and I could be some treasured thing. I could feel myself projected through some White person, and have all the privileges that white people get—validation through association.[3]

The "snow period" Davis describes corresponds to the assimilationist option that minoritarian subjects often choose. Though sanctioned and encouraged by the dominant culture, the snow period is not a viable option for people of color. More often than not, snow melts in the hands of the subject who attempts to acquire privilege through associations (be they erotic, emotional, or both) with whites. Davis goes on to describe her next phase:

> Then there was a conscious shift, being that I was the first one in my family to go to college—I got militant. That's when I started reading about Angela and the Panthers, and that's when Vaginal emerged as a filtering of Angela through humor. That led to my early 1980's acapella performance entity, Vaginal Davis and the Afro Sisters (who were two white girls with afro wigs). We did a show called "we're taking over" where we portrayed the Sexualese Liberation Front which decides to kidnap all the heads of white corporate America so we could put big black dildos up their lily white buttholes and hold them for ransom. It really freaked out a lot of the middle class post-punk crowd—they didn't get the campy element of it but I didn't really care.[4]

Thus the punk rock drag diva elucidates a stage or temporal space where the person of color's consciousness turns to her or his community after an immersion in white culture and education. The ultramilitant phase that Davis describes is a powerful counteridentification with the dominant culture. At the same time, though, Davis's queer sexuality, her queerness *and* effeminacy, kept her from fully accessing Black Power militancy. Unable to pass as heterosexual black militant through simple counteridentification, Vaginal Davis instead disidentified with Black Power by selecting Angela and *not* the Panthers as a site of self-fashioning and political formation. Davis's deployment of disidentification demonstrates that it is, to employ Kimberele Crenshaw's term, an *intersectional strategy*.[5] *Intersectionality* insists on a critical hermeneutics that registers the copresence of sexuality, race, class, gender, and other identity differentials as particular components that exist simultaneously with each other. Vintage Black Power discourse contained many homophobic and masculinist elements that were toxic to queer and feminist subjects. Davis used parody and pastiche to remake Black Power, opening it up via disidentification to a self that is simultaneously black and queer. (Elsewhere, with her group ¡Cholita!, she performs a similar disidentification with Latina/o popular culture. As Graciela Grejalva, she is not an oversexed songstress, but instead a teenage Latina singing sappy bubblegum pop.)

Davis productively extends her disidentificatory strategy to her engagement with the performative practice of drag. With the advent of the mass commercialization of drag—evident in suburban multiplexes, which program such films as *To Wong Foo, Thanks for Everything, Julie Newmar* and *The Bird Cage*, or in VH1's broadcasts of RuPaul's talk show—it seems especially important at this point to distinguish different modalities of drag. Commercial drag presents a sanitized and desexualized queer subject for mass consumption, representing a certain strand of integrationist liberal pluralism. The sanitized queen is meant to be enjoyed as an entertainer who will hopefully lead to social understanding and tolerance. Unfortunately, this boom in filmic and televisual drag has had no impact on hate legislation put forth by the New Right or on homophobic violence on the nation's streets. Indeed, I want to suggest that this "boom" in drag helps one understand that a liberal-pluralist mode of political strategizing only eventuates a certain absorption, but nothing like a productive engagement, with difference. So while RuPaul, for example, hosts a talk show on VH1, one only need click the remote control to hear about the new defense-of-marriage legislation that "protects" *the* family by outlawing gay marriage. Indeed, the erosion of gay civil rights is simultaneous with the advent of higher degrees of queer visibility in the mainstream media.

But while corporate-sponsored drag has to some degree become incorporated within the dominant culture, there is also a queerer modality of drag that is performed by queer-identified drag artists in spaces of queer consumption. Félix Guattari, in a discussion of the theatrical group the Mirabelles, explains the potential political power of drag:

> The Mirabelles are experimenting with a new type of militant theater, a theater separate from an explanatory language and long tirades of good intentions, for example, on gay liberation. They resort to drag, song, mime, dance, etc., not as different ways of illustrating a theme, to "change the ideas" of spectators, but in order to trouble them, to stir up uncertain desire—zones that they always more or less refuse to explore. The question is no longer to know whether one will play feminine against masculine or the reverse, but to make bodies, all bodies, break away from the representations and restraints on the "social body."[6]

Guattari's take on the Mirabelles, specifically his appraisal of the political performance of drag, assists in the project of further evaluating the effects of queer drag. I don't simply want to assign one set of drag strategies and practices the title of "bad" drag and the other "good." But I do wish to emphasize the ways in which Davis's *terroristic drag* "stir[s] up uncertain desire[s]" and enables subjects to imagine a way of "break[ing] away from the . . . restraints on the 'social body," while sanitized corporate drag and even traditional gay drag is unable to achieve such effects. Davis's political drag is about creating an uneasiness in desire, which works to confound and subvert the social fabric. The "social body" that Guattari discusses is amazingly elastic and able to accommodate scripts on gay liberation. Drag like Davis's, however, is not easily enfolded in that social fabric because of the complexity of its intersectional nature.

There is a great diversity within drag. Julian Fleisher's *Drag Queens of New York: An Illustrated Field Guide* surveys underground drag and differentiates two dominant styles, "glamour" and "clown."[7] New York drag queens like Candis Cayne or Girlina, whose drag is relatively "real,"[8] rate high on the glamour meter. Other queens like Varla Jean Merman (who bills herself as the love child of Ethel Merman and Ernest Borgnine) and Miss Understood are representative of the over-the-top parody style of clown drag. Many famous queens, like Wigstock impresario and mad genius The "Lady" Bunny, appear squarely in the middle of Fleisher's scale.[9] On first glance Vaginal, who is in no way invoking glamour or "realness" and most certainly doesn't *pass* (in a direct sense of the word), seems to be on the side of clown drag. I want to complicate this system of evaluation and attempt a more nuanced appraisal of Vaginal Davis's style.

Vaginal Davis's drag, while comic and even hilarious, should not be dismissed as just clowning around. Her uses of humor and parody function as disidentificatory strategies whose effect on the dominant public sphere is that of a counterpublic terrorism. At the center of all of Davis's cultural productions is a radical impulse toward cultural critique. It is a critique that, according to the artist, has often escaped two groups who comprise some of drag's most avid supporters: academics and other drag queens.

> I was parodying a lot of different things. But it wasn't an intellectual-type of thing—it was innate. A lot of academics and intellectuals dismissed it because it wasn't smart enough—it was too homey, a little too country. And gay drag queens hated me. They didn't understand it. I wasn't really trying to alter myself to look like a real woman. I didn't wear false eyelashes or fake breasts. It wasn't about the realness of traditional drag—the perfect flawless make-up. I just put on a little lipstick, a little eye shadow and a wig and went out there.[10]

It is the innateness, the homeyness, and the countryness of Davis's style that draw this particular academic to the artist's work. I understand these characteristics as components of the artist's guerrilla style, a style that functions as a ground-level cultural terrorism that fiercely skewers both straight culture and reactionary components of gay culture. I would also like to link these key words—*innateness, homeyness,* and *countryness*—that Davis calls upon with a key word from the work of Antonio Gramsci that seems to be a partial cognate of these other terms: *organic.*

Gramsci attempted to both demystify the role of the intellectual and, at the same time, reassert the significance of the intellectual's role to a social movement. He explained that "Every social group, coming into existence on the original terrain of an essential function, creates together with itself, organically, one or more strata of intellectuals which give it homogeneity and an awareness of its own function not only in the economic but also in the social and political fields."[11] Davis certainly worked to bolster and cohere the L.A. punk scene, giving it a more significant "homogeneity"[12] and "awareness." At the same time, her work constituted a critique of that community's whiteness. In this way, it participated in Gramsci's project of extending the scope of Marxist analysis to look beyond class as the ultimate social division and consider *blocs*. Blocs are, in the words of John Fiske, "alliance[s] of social forces formed to promote common social interests as they can be brought together in particular historical conditions."[13] The Gramscian notion of bloc formation emphasizes the centrality of class relations in any critical analysis, while not diminishing the importance of other cultural struggles. In the lifeworld of mostly straight white punks, Davis had, as a black gay man, a strongly disidentificatory role within that community. I will suggest that her disidentifications with social blocs are productive interventions in which politics are destabilized, permitting her to come into the role of "organic intellectual." While Davis did and did not belong to the scene, she nonetheless forged a place for herself that is not *a* place, but instead the still important *position* of intellectual.

A reading of one of Davis's spin-off projects, *The White to Be Angry*, a live show and CD by her hardcore/speed metal band, Pedro, Muriel, and Esther, will ground this consideration of Vaginal Davis as organic intellectual. While I focus on this one aspect of her oeuvre, it should nonetheless be noted that my claim for her as organic intellectual has a great deal to do with the wide variety of public performances and discourses she employs. Davis disseminates her cultural critique through multiple channels of publicity: independent video, zines, public access programming, performance art, anthologized short fiction, bar drag, the L.A. punk-rock club Sucker (for which she is a weekly hostess and impresario), and three different bands (PME and !Cholita! as well as the semi-mythical Black Fag, a group that parodies famous North American punk band Black Flag). In the PME project she employs a modality of drag that is neither glamorous nor strictly comedic. Her drag is a terroristic send-up of masculinity and white supremacy. Its focus and pitch are political parody and critique, anchored in her very particular homey-organic style and humor.

"The White to Be Angry" and Passing

It is about 1:30 in the morning at Squeezebox, a modish queercore night at a bar in lower Manhattan. It is a warm June evening, and PME's show was supposed to start at midnight. I noticed the band's easily identifiable lead singer rush in at about 12:30, so I had no expectation of the show beginning before 1:00. I while away the time by watching thin and pale go-go boys and girls dancing on the bars. The boys are not the beefy, pumped-up white and Latino muscle boys of Chelsea. This, after all, is way downtown where queer style is decidedly different from the ultramasculine muscle drag of Chelsea. Still, the crowd here is extremely white, and Vaginal Davis's black six-foot-six-inch frame towers over the sea of white post-punk club goers.

Before I know it Miss Guy, a drag performer who exudes the visual style of the "white trash" Southern California punk waif,[14] stops spinning her classic eighties retro-rock, punk, and new wave discs. Then the Mistress Formika, the striking leather-clad Latina drag queen and hostess of the club, announces the band. I am positioned in the front row, to the left of the stage. I watch a figure whom I identify as Davis rush by me and mount the stage.

At this point, a clarification is necessary. Vaginal is something like the central performance persona that the artist I am discussing uses, but it is certainly not the only one. She is also the Most High Rev'rend Saint Salicia Tate, an evangelical church woman who preaches "Fornication, no! Theocracy, yes!"; Buster Butone, one of her boy drag numbers who is a bit of a gangsta and womanizer; and Kayle Hilliard, a professional pseudonym that the artist employed when she worked as an administrator at UCLA.[15] These are just a few of the artist's identities; I have yet to catalog them all.

The identity I will see tonight is a new one for me. Davis is once again in boy drag, standing on stage in military fatigues, including camouflage pants, jacket, T-shirt, and hat. The look is capped off by a long gray beard, reminiscent of the beards worn by the 1980s Texas rocker band ZZ Top. Clarence introduces himself. During the monologue we hear Vaginal's high-pitched voice explain how she finds white supremacist militiamen to be *really hot*, so hot that she herself has had a race and gender reassignment and is now Clarence. Clarence is the artist's own object of affection. Her voice drops as she inhabits the site of her object of desire and identifications. She imitates and becomes the object of her desire. The ambivalent circuits of cross-racial desire are thematized and contained in one body. This particular star-crossed coupling, black queen and white supremacist, might suggest masochism on the part of the person of color, yet such a reading would be too facile. Instead, the work done by this performance of illicit desire for the "bad" object, the toxic force, should be considered an active disidentification with strictures against cross-racial desire in communities of color and the specters of miscegenation that haunt white sexuality. The parodic performance works on Freudian distinctions between desire and identification; the "to be or to have" binary is queered and disrupted.

When the performer's voice drops and thickens, it is clear that Clarence now has the mike. He congratulates himself on his own woodsy militiaman masculinity, boasting about how great it feels to be white, male, and straight. He launches into his first number, a cut off the CD *Sawed Off Shotgun*. The song is Clarence's theme:

> I don't need a 'zooka
> Or a Ms. 38
> I feel safer in New York
> Than I do in L.A.
>
> You keep your flame thrower
> My shotgun is prettier
>
> Sawed off shot gun
> Sawed off
> Shotgun
>
> My shot gun is so warm it
> Keeps me safe in the city
> I need it at the ATM
> Or when I'm looking purdy
> In its convenient carrying case
> Graven, initialed on the face
> Sawed off shot gun
> Sawed off
> Shotgun
> Yeah . . . wow!

The singer adopts what is a typical butch, hardcore stance while performing the song. The microphone is pulled close to his face, and he bellows into it. This performance of butch masculinity complements the performance of militiaman identity. The song functions as an illustration of a particular mode of white male anxiety that feeds ultra-right-wing movements like militias and that is endemic to embattled straight white masculinity in urban multiethnic spaces like Los Angeles. The fear of an urban landscape populated by undesirable minorities is especially pronounced at privileged sites of consumerist interaction like the ATM, a public site where elites in the cityscape access capital as the lower classes stand witnesses to these mechanical transactions that punctuate class hierarchies. Through her performance of Clarence, Vaginal inhabits the image of the paranoid and embattled white male in the multiethnic city. The performer begins to subtly undermine the gender cohesion of this cultural type (a gender archetype that is always figured as heteronormative), the embattled white man in the multiethnic metropolis, by alluding to the love of "purdy" and "prettier" weapons. The eroticizing of the weapon in so overt a fashion reveals the queer specter that haunts such "impenetrable" heterosexualities. Clarence needs his gun because it "is so warm" that it keeps him "safe in the city" that he no longer feels safe in, a city where growing populations of Asians, African Americans, and Latinos pose a threat to the white majority.

Clarence is a disidentification with militiaman masculinity—not merely a counteridentification that rejects the militiaman, but a *tactical misrecognition* that consciously views the self as a militiaman. This performance is also obviously not about passing inasmuch as the whiteface makeup that the artist uses looks nothing like real white skin. Clarence has as much of a chance passing as white as Vaginal has passing as female. Rather, this disidentification works as an *interiorized passing*. The interior pass is a disidentification and tactical misrecognition of self. Aspects of the self that are toxic to the militiaman—blackness, gayness, and transvestism—are grafted on this particularly militaristic script of masculinity. The performer, through the role of Clarence, inhabits and undermines the militiaman with a fierce sense of parody.

But Davis's disidentifications are not limited to engagements with figures of white supremacy. In a similar style Clarence, during one of his other live numbers, disidentifies with the popular press image of the pathological homosexual killer. The song "Homosexual Is Criminal" tells this story:

> A homosexual
> Is a criminal
> I'm a sociopath, a pathological liar
> Bring your children near me
> I'll make them walk through the fire
>
> I have killed before and I will kill again
> You can tell my friend by my Satanic grin
> A homosexual is a criminal
>
> A homosexual is a criminal
>
> I'll eat you limb from limb
> I'll tear your heart apart
>
> Open the Frigidaire
> There'll be your body parts
> I'm gonna slit your click
> Though you don't want me to
> Bite it off real quick
> Salt'n peppa it too.

At this point in the live performance, about halfway through the number, Davis has removed the long gray beard, the jacket, and the cap. A striptease has begun. At this point Clarence starts to be undone and Davis begins to reappear. She has begun to interact lasciviously with the other members of her band. She gropes her guitarist and bass players as she cruises the audience. She is becoming queer, and as she does so she begins to perform homophobia. This public performance of homophobia indexes the specters of Jeffrey Dahmer, John Wayne Gacy, and an entire pantheon of homosexual killers. The performance magnifies images from the homophobic popular imaginary. Davis is once again inhabiting phobic images with a parodic and cutting difference. In fact, while many sectors of gay communities eschew negative images, Davis instead explodes them by inhabiting them with a difference. By becoming the serial killer, whose psychological profile is almost always white, Vaginal Davis disarticulates not only the onus of performing the positive image, which is generally borne by minoritarian subjects, but also the Dahmer paradigm where the white cannibal slaughters gay men of color. The performance of *"becoming Dahmer"* is another mode of hijacking and lampooning whiteness. Drag and minstrelsy are dramatically reconfigured; performance genres that seemed somewhat exhausted and limited are powerfully reinvigorated through Davis's "homey"-style politics.

By the last number Vaginal Davis has fully reemerged, and she is wearing a military fatigue baby-doll nightie. She is still screaming and writhing on the stage, and she is soaked in rock'n'roll sweat. The Clarence persona has disintegrated. *Long live the queen.* During an interview Davis explained to me that her actual birth name is Clarence.[16] What does it mean that the artist who negotiates various performance personas and uses Vaginal Creme Davis as a sort of base identity reserves her "birth name" for a character who represents the nation's current state of siege? Davis's drag, this reconfigured cross-sex, cross-race minstrelsy, can best be understood as *terrorist drag*—*terrorist* insofar as she is performing the nation's internal terrors around race, gender, and sexuality. It is also an aesthetic terrorism: Davis uses ground-level guerrilla representational strategies to portray some of the nation's most salient popular fantasies. The fantasies she acts out involve cultural anxieties around miscegenation, communities of color, and the queer body. Her dress does not attempt to index outmoded ideals of female glamour. She instead dresses like white supremacist militiamen and black welfare queen hookers. In other words, her drag mimesis is not concerned with the masquerade of womanliness, but instead with conjuring the nation's most dangerous citizens. She is quite literally in "terrorist drag."

While Davis's terrorist drag performance does not engage the project of passing as traditional drag at least partially does, it is useful to recognize how passing and what I am describing as disidentification resemble one another—or, to put it more accurately, how the passing entailed in traditional drag implicates elements of the disidentificatory process. Passing is often not about bald-faced opposition to a dominant paradigm or a wholesale selling out to that form. Like disidentification itself, passing can be a third modality, where a dominant structure is co-opted, worked on and against. The subject who passes can be simultaneously identifying with and rejecting a dominant form. In traditional male-to-female drag "woman" is performed, but one would be naive and deeply ensconced in heteronormative culture to consider such a performance, no matter how "real," as an actual performance of "woman." Drag performance strives to perform femininity, and femininity is not exclusively the domain of biological women. Furthermore, the drag queen is disidentifying— sometimes critically and sometimes *not*—not only with the ideal of woman but also with the a priori relationship of woman and femininity that is a tenet of gender-normative thinking. The "woman" produced in drag is not a woman but instead a public disidentification with woman. Some of the best drag that I have encountered in my research challenges the universalizing rhetorics of femininity.

Both modalities of performing the self, disidentification and passing, are often strategies of survival. (As the case of Davis and others suggests, often these modes of performance allow much more than mere survival, and subjects fully come into subjectivity in ways that are both ennobling and fierce.) Davis's work is a survival strategy on a more symbolic register than that of everyday practice. She is not passing to escape social injustice and structural racism in the way that some people of color might. Nor is she passing in the way in which "straight-acting queers" do. Her disidentification with drag plays with its prescriptive mandate to enact femininity through (often white) standards of glamour. Consider her militiaman drag. Her dark brown skin does not permit her to pass as white, the beard is obviously fake, and the fatigues look inauthentic. Realness is neither achieved nor is it the actual goal of such a project. Instead, her performance as Clarence functions as an intervention in the history of cross-race desire that saturates the phenomenon of passing. Passing is parodied, and this parody becomes a site where interracial desire is interrogated.

Davis's biting social critique phantasmatically projects the age-old threat of miscegenation, something that white supremacist groups fear the most, onto the image of a white supremacist. Cross-race desire spoils the militiaman's image.[17] It challenges the coherence of his identity, his essentialized whiteness, by invading its sense of essentialized white purity. The militiaman becomes a caricature of himself, sullied and degraded within his own logic.

Furthermore, blackface minstrelsy, the performance genre of whites performing blackness, is powerfully recycled through disidentification. The image of the fat-lipped Sambo is replaced by the image of the ludicrous white militiaman. The photographer Lyle Ashton Harris has produced a series of elegant portraits of himself in whiteface. Considered alongside Davis's work, Harris's version of whiteface is an almost *too literal* photonegative reversal. By figuring the militiaman through the vehicle of the black queen's body, Davis's whiteface interrogates white hysteria, miscegenation anxiety, and supremacy at their very core. Eric Lott, in his influential study of minstrelsy in the dominant white imagination, suggests that

> The black mask offered a way to play with collective fears of a degraded and threatening—and male—Other while at the same time maintaining some symbolic control over them.[18]

Harris's photography replicates traditional whiteface so as to challenge its tenets in a different fashion than Davis does. Harris's technique addresses the issue of "symbolic control," but does so in the form of a straightforward counteridentification. And while counteridentification is certainly not a strategy without merits, Davis's disidentification with minstrelsy offers a more polyvalent response to this history. Davis's disidentificatory take on "whiteface" both reveals the degraded character of the white supremacist and wrests "symbolic controls" from white people. The white supremacist is forced to cohabit in one body with a black queen in such a way that the image loses its symbolic force. A figure that is potentially threatening to people of color is revealed as a joke.

The dual residency in Davis's persona of both the drag queen and the white supremacist is displayed in the CD's cover art. The illustration features Clarence cleaning his gun. Occupying the background is a television set broadcasting a ranting white man reminiscent of right-wing media pundit Rush Limbaugh, a monster-truck poster titled "Pigfoot," a confederate flag, a crucifix, assorted pornography, beer bottles, and a knife stuck in the wall. Standing out in this scene is the framed photo of a black drag queen: Vaginal Davis. The flip side of the image is part of the CD's interior artwork. Vaginal sits in front of a dressing mirror wearing a showgirl outfit. She is crying on the telephone as she cooks heroin on a spoon and prepares to shoot up. A picture of Vaginal in boy drag is taped to the mirror. Among the scattered vibrators, perfume bottles, and razors is a picture of Clarence in a Marine uniform. These images represent a version of cross-racial desire (in this instance the reciprocated desire between a black hooker/showgirl and a white supremacist gun nut-militiaman) that echoes what Vaginal, in her 1995 interview, called "the snow period" when "some cheap white boyfriend" could make one's life perfect, permitting the queen of color to feel like "some treasured thing," who hopes for "the privileges that white people get—validation through association." The image of the snow queen, a gay man of color who desires white men, is exaggerated and exploded within these performances. It is important to note that this humor is not calibrated to police or moralize against crossracial desire. Instead, it renders a picture of this desire in its most fantastic and extreme form. By doing so it disturbs the coherence of the white militiaman's sexual and racial identity, an identity that locates itself as racially "pure." Concomitantly, sanitized understandings of a gay identity, which is often universalized as white, are called into question.

   [. . .]

   The cultural battle that Davis wages is fought with the darkest sense of humor and the sharpest sense of parody imaginable. Her performances represent multiple counterpublics and subjects who are liminal within those very counterpublics. She shrewdly employs performance as a modality of counterpublicity. Performance engenders, sponsors, and even *makes* worlds. The scene of speed metal and post-punk music is one which Davis ambivalently inhabits. Her blackness and queerness render her a freak among freaks. Rather than be alienated by her freakiness, she exploits its energies and its potential to enact cultural critique.

   [. . .]

   Disidentification, as a mode of analysis, registers subjects as constructed and contradictory. Davis's body, her performances, and all her myriad texts labor to create critical uneasiness and, furthermore, to create desire within uneasiness. This desire unsettles the strictures of class, race, and gender prescribed by what Guattari calls the "social body." A disidentificatory hermeneutic permits a reading and narration of the way in which Davis clears out a space, deterritorializing it and then reoccupying it with queer and black bodies. The lens of disidentification allows us to discern seams and contradictions and ultimately to understand the need for a war of positions.

From: José Esteban Muñoz, " 'The White to Be Angry': Vaginal Davis's Terrorist Drag," in *Social Text* no. 52–53, pp. 80–103. Copyright 1997, Duke University Press. All rights reserved. Republished by permission of the copyright holder, Duke University Press. www. dukeupress.edu.

Notes

This essay benefited from the thoughtful feedback of my colleagues Phillip Brian Harper, George Yudice, and Bruce Robbins. I am also grateful to audiences at Columbia University's "Passing" Conference, the University of California = Riverside's "Unnatural Acts Conference," and the Department of Ethnic Studies, University of California-Berkeley, for their comments and invitations to present this work. I am most grateful to Vaginal Davis, my muse for this project and others, who generously lent me her time, wisdom, and archives. Her work and her example kept me laughing and thinking as I prepared this paper. Dr. Davis can be contacted at editor@L.A.Weekly.com or 1-213-389-5188.

   1. Barney Hoskyns, *Waiting for the Sun: Strange Days, Weird Scenes, and the Sound of Los Angeles* (New York: St. Martin's, 1996), 307.
   2. George Lipsitz, *Dangerous Crossings: Popular Music, Postmodernism, and the Poetics of Space* (New York and London: Verso, 1994), 17.
   3. Tommy Gear and Mike Glass, "Supremely Vaginal," *aRude* 1 (Fall 1995): 42.
   4. Ibid.
   5. Kimberlé William Crenshaw, "Beyond Racism and Misogyny: Black Feminism and 2 Live Crew," in *Words That Wound: Critical Race Theory, Assaultive Speech, and the First Amendment*, eds. Mari J. Matsuda et al. (Boulder, CO: Westview, 1993), 111–132.
   6. Felix Guattari, *Soft Subversions*, ed. Sylvere Lotringer, trans. David L. Sweet and Chet Wiener (New York: Semiotext(e), 1996), 37.
   7. Julian Fleisher, *The Drag Queens of New York: An Illustrated Field Guide* (New York: Riverhead, 1996).
   8. "Realness" is mimetic of a certain high-feminine style in standard realist terms.
   9. Many of the performers I have just mentioned appear in the film documentation of New York's annual drag festival, *Wigstock: The Movie.*

10. Gear and Glass, "Supremely Vaginal," 77.

11. Antonio Gramsci, "The Formation of Intellectuals," in *The Modern Prince and Other Writings*, trans. Louis Marks (New York: International, 1959), 181.

12. Here I do not mean *homogeneity* in its more quotidian usage, the opposite of *heterogeneous*, but, instead, in a Gramscian sense that is meant to connote social cohesion.

13. John Fiske, "Opening the Hallway: Some Remarks on the Fertility of Stuart Hall's Contribution to Critical Theory," in *Stuart Hall: Critical Dialogues in Cultural Studies*, eds. David Morley and Kuan-Hsing Chen (New York: Routledge, 1996), 213–214. Also see Dick Hebdige's classic analysis of subcultures for an analysis that uses what is in part a Gramscian lens to consider group formations, *Subculture: The Meaning of Style* (London: Routledge, 1979).

14. Miss Guy's image was featured in designer Calvin Klein's CK One ad campaign. Her androgynous, nontraditional drag was seen all over the nation in print and television advertisements. This ad campaign represented a version of gender diversity that was not previously available in print advertising. Yet, once again, the campaign only led to a voyeuristic absorption with gender diversity and no real engagement with this node of difference.

15 Queercore writer Dennis Cooper, in an attempt to out the "real" Davis in *Spin* magazine, implied Hilliard was the artist's true identity. The joke was on Cooper, since Davis's professional identity as Hilliard was another "imagined identity." Davis has explained to me that her actual birth name is Clarence, which will be an important fact as my reading unfolds.

16. An alternate yet complementary reading of the name Clarence that I am offering here would link this white militiaman and the act of cross-race minstrelsy to the Bush-appointed Supreme Court Justice Clarence Thomas, an African American who has contributed to the erosion of civil rights within the nation.

17. Here I risk collapsing all antigovernment militias with more traditional domestic terrorist groups like the Ku Klux Klan or neo-Nazis. Not all militiamen are white supremacists, and the vast majority of white supremacists are not in a militia. But Davis's Clarence is definitely concerned with racist militias whose antigovernment philosophies are also overtly xenophobic and white supremacist.

18. Eric Lott, Love and Theft: Blackface Minstrelsy and the American Working Class (New York: Oxford, 1993), 25.

18 The Transgender Look

Jack Halberstam

Queer theorist Jack Halberstam has been one of the most prolific and provocative voices in post-modern cultural theory since the mid-1990s. This excerpt from "The Transgender Look," a chapter from Halberstam's 2005 book, *In a Queer Time and Place: Transgender Bodies, Subcultural Lives*, follows a lengthy discussion of the print- and visual-media archives that have accumulated around the figure of Brandon Teena, the murdered transgender teen whose story was famously fictionalized in the Academy Award-winning film *Boys Don't Cry*. It links this "Brandon archive" to a subsequent analysis of a much broader body of visual representations of gender ambiguity. The crucial conceptual pivot on which the chapter turns, highlighted here, is the "transgender gaze." In it, Halberstam reworks the concept of "the gaze," a key term in Laura Mulvey's canonical film studies essay, "Visual Pleasure and Narrative Cinema." Mulvey's essay depends on a rigid, binary economy of masculine and feminine subject positions from which a film is viewed and its characters identified with and in accordance with which a film-viewer finds his or her opportunities for "visual pleasure." Given that narrative cinema, in Mulvey's formulation, is structured by the "male gaze," women's cinematic pleasures are construed as either masochistic (identifying with the fetishized object of the male gaze) or voyeuristic (appropriating the active desire of the masculine subject presumed to be gazing). Analyzing *The Crying Game*, *Boys Don't Cry*, and *By Hook or by Crook*, Halberstam complicates Mulvey's schema by explicating the operation of the "transgender gaze," which "depends on complex relations in time and space between seeing and not seeing, appearing and disappearing, knowing and not knowing" that transgender characters invoke for mainstream film viewers. The concept presents the transgender character as a flexible figure produced through the affective responses of viewers—disgust, sympathy, and so on. On the one hand, this exploration of the "transgender gaze" offers an opportunity to find space to explore "transgender film" beyond the binary limitations of the "male gaze." On the other hand, transgender people and the materiality of trans embodiments remain secondary to Halberstam's depiction of "transgenderism" as a dynamic operation between viewer and character.

Certain social groups may be seen as having rigid and unresponsive selves and bodies, making them relatively unfit for the kind of society we now seem to desire.

—Emily Martin, *Flexible Bodies*

In the last two chapters, we have seen how an archive of print and visual materials have accumulated around the figure of Brandon Teena, a young transgender man who defied the social mandate to be and to have a singular gender identity. Here, I continue to build on that archive with a consideration of the feature film *Boys Don't Cry*, but I also try to expand the

DOI: 10.4324/9781003206255-23

archive of visual representations of gender ambiguity, placing this expanded archive within what Nick Mirzoeff calls "the postmodern globalization of the visual as everyday life" (Mirzoeff 1999, 3). I begin with a study of the transgender gaze or look as it has developed in recent queer cinema (film and video), and then in the next chapter, turn to photography and painting to examine the clash between embodiment and the visual that queer art making has documented in vivid detail. Gender ambiguity, in some sense, results from and contests the dominance of the visual within postmodernism.

The potentiality of the body to morph, shift, change, and become fluid is a powerful fantasy in transmodern cinema. [. . . T]he body in transition indelibly marks late-twentieth- and early-twenty-first-century visual fantasy. The fantasy of the shape-shifting and identity-morphing body has been nowhere more powerfully realized recently than in transgender film. In films like Neil Jordan's *The Crying Game* (1992) and *Boys Don't Cry*, the transgender character surprises audiences with his/her ability to remain attractive, appealing, and gendered while simultaneously presenting a gender at odds with sex, a sense of self not derived from the body, and an identity that operates within the heterosexual matrix without confirming the inevitability of that system of difference. But even as the transgender body becomes a symbol par excellence for flexibility, transgenderism also represents a form of Martin has called "flexible bodies." Those bodies, indeed, that fail to conform to the postmodern fantasy of flexibility that has been projected onto the transgender body may well be punished in popular representations even as they seem to be lauded. And so, Brandon in *Boys Don't Cry* and Dil in *The Crying Game* are represented as both heroic and fatally flawed.

Both *The Crying Game* and *Boys Don't Cry* rely on the successful solicitation of affect—whether it be revulsion, sympathy, or empathy—in order to give mainstream viewers access to a transgender gaze. And in both films, a relatively unknown actor pulls off the feat of credibly performing a gender at odds with the sexed body even after the body has been brutally exposed. Gender metamorphosis in these films is also used as a metaphor for other kinds of mobility or immobility. In *The Crying Game*, Dil's womanhood stands in opposition to a revolutionary subjectivity associated with the Irish Republican Army (IRA), and in *Boys Don't Cry*, Brandon's manhood represents a class-based desire to transcend small-town conflicts and a predictable life narrative of marriage, babies, domestic abuse, and alcoholism. While Brandon continues to romanticize small-town life, his girlfriend, Lana, sees him as a symbol of a much-desired elsewhere. In both films, the transgender character also seems to stand for a different form of temporality. Dil seems deliberately removed in *The Crying Game* from the time of the nation and other nationalisms, and her performance of womanhood opens up a ludic temporality. Brandon in *Boys Don't Cry* represents an alternative future for Lana by trying to be a man with no past. The dilemma for the transgender character, as we have seen in earlier chapters, is to create an alternate future while rewriting history. In *Boys Don't Cry*, director Peirce seems aware of the imperative of queer time and constructs (but fails to sustain) a transgender gaze capable of seeing through the present to a future elsewhere. In experimental moments in this otherwise brutally realistic star-crossed lovers that is located in both time and space.

The transgender film confronts powerfully the way that transgenderism is constituted as a paradox made up in equal parts of visibility and temporality: whenever the transgender character is seen to be transgendered, then he/she is both failing to pass and threatening to expose a rupture between the distinct temporal registers of past, present, and future. The exposure of a trans character whom the audience has already accepted as male or female, causes the audience to reorient themselves in relation to the film's past in order to read the film's present and prepare themselves for the film's future. When we "see" the transgender character, then, we are actually seeing cinematic time's sleight of hand. Visibility, under these circumstances, may be equated with jeopardy, danger, and exposure, and it often becomes necessary for the transgender character to disappear in order to remain viable. The transgender gaze becomes difficult to track because it depends on complex relations in time and space between seeing and not seeing, appearing and disappearing, knowing and not knowing. I will be identifying here different treatments of the transgenderism that resolve these complex problems of temporality and visibility.

In one mode that we might call the "rewind," the transgender character is presented at first as "properly" gendered, as passing in other words, and as properly located within a linear narrative; her exposure as transgender constitutes the film's narrative climax, and spells out both her own decline and the unraveling of cinematic time. The viewer literally has to rewind the film after the character's exposure in order to reorganize the narrative logic in terms of the pass. In a second mode that involves embedding several ways of looking into one, the film deploys certain formal techniques to give the viewer access to the transgender gaze in order to allow us to look *with* the transgender character instead of *at* him. Other techniques include ghosting the transgender character or allowing him to haunt the narrative after death; to remove the nodal point of normativity. [. . .]

In *By Hook or by Crook*, transgenderism is a complex dynamic between the two butch heroes, Shy and Valentine. The two collude and collaborate in their gendering, and create a closed world of queerness that is locked in place by the circuit of a gaze that never references the male or the female gaze as such. The plot of *By Hook or by Crook* involves the random meeting of two trans butches and the development of a fast friendship. Shy tries to help Valentine, who has been adopted, find his mother, while Valentine introduces the lonely Shy, whose father has just died, to an alternative form of community. The dead or missing parents imply an absence of conventional family, and afford our heroes with the opportunity to remake home, family, community, and most important, friendship. As the story evolves into a shaggy-dog tale of hide-and-seek, we leave family time far behind, entering into the shadow world of queers, loners, street people, and crazies. Transgenderism takes its place in this stability. Unlike other transgender films that remain committed to seducing the straight gaze, this one remains thoroughly committed to the transgender look, and it opens up, formally and thematically, a new mode of envisioning gender mobility. In this chapter, I pay close attention to three versions of the "transgender film"—*The Crying Game, Boys Don't Cry*, and *By Hook or by Crook*—to track the evolution of a set of strategies (each with different consequences) for representing transgender bodies, capturing transgender looks, and theorizing transgender legibility.

Crying Games

crying—verb: announce in public, utter in a loud distinct voice so as to be heard over a long distance; *noun*: the process of shedding tears (usually accompanied by sobs or other inarticulate sounds); *adj*.: conspicuously bad, offensive or reprehensible.

—*Oxford English Dictionary*

When *The Crying Game* was released, the media was instructed not to give away the "secret" at the heart of the film—but what exactly was the film's secret? Homosexuality? Transsexuality? Gender construction? Nationalist brutalities? Colonial encounters? By making the unmasking of a transvestite character into the preeminent signifier of difference and disclosure in the film, director Jordan participates, as many critics have noted, in a long tradition of transforming political conflict into erotic tension in order to offer a romantic resolution.[1] I want to discuss *The Crying Game* briefly here to illustrate the misuse or simply the avoidance of the transgender gaze in mainstream films that purport to be about gender ambiguity. By asking media and audiences to keep the film's secret, then, *The Crying Game's* producers created and deepened the illusion that the film would and could offer something new and unexpected. In fact, the secrecy constructs a mainstream viewer for the film and ignores more knowing audiences.

The Crying Game concerns a number of different erotic triangles situated within the tense political landscape of the English occupation of Northern Ireland. The film opens by animating one triangle that links two IRA operatives Fergus and Jude, to the black British soldier, Jody, whom they must kidnap. Jude lures Jody away from a fairground with a promise of sexual interaction, and then Fergus ambushes Jody and whisks him away to an IRA hideout. The whole of the opening scene plays out to the accompaniment of "When a Man Loves a Woman." The song equates femininity with trickery falsehood, and deceit, and it sets up the misogynist strands of a narrative that envision the white male as unknowing victim of feminine wiles. The first third of the film concerns the relationship between captors and captive and particularly between the warmhearted Fergus and the winning Jody. Fergus and Jody bond and connect over the picture of Jody's absent lover, Dil. After Jody dies in a foiled escape effort, Fergus leaves Ireland to escape the IRA and heads to England, where he becomes a construction worker. Fergus goes looking for Dil, and when he finds her, he romances her while seemingly unaware of her transgender identity. The last third of the film charts the course of Fergus's discovery of Dil's secret and his reentanglement with the IRA.

There are three major narrative strands in *The Crying Game*, all of which seem bound to alternative political identities, but none of which actually live up to their own potential. In the first strand, which involves the IRA we expect to hear a critique of English colonialism, English racism, and the occupation of Northern Ireland by England. Instead, the film uses Jody to critique Irish racism and Fergus to delegitimize the IRA. The second narrative strand, which concerns the romance between Fergus and Dil, seems committed to a narrative about the "naturalness" of all types of gender expression, and here we expect to see the structures of Dil's transvestism only to re-center the white male gaze, and to make the white male into the highly flexible, supremely human subject who must counter and cover for the gender rigidity of the transvestite Dil (rigidity meaning that she cannot flow back and forth between male and female; she insists on being recognized as female) and the political rigidity of the IRA "fanatic" Jude. [. . .] The third narrative strand has to do with cinematic time, and it projects an alternative ordering of time by positioning Dil as a character who seems to be able to cross back and forth between past, present, and future. When we first see Dil, she appears in a photograph representing Jody's past. When Fergus finally meets Dil, she represents his new present-tense life away from the IRA, and as the film winds down, Dil represents for Fergus a conventional future of marriage and family that awaits him when he obtains his release from jail, where he is "doing time." The seeming temporal fluidity of Dil is undercut, however, by the normative logic of the narrative's temporal drive, which seeks, through Fergus, to pin Dil down within the logic of heteronormative time.

Ultimately, the transgender character Dil never controls the gaze, and serves as a racialized fetish figure who diverts the viewer's attention from the highly charged political conflict between England and Ireland. The film characterizes Irish nationalism as a heartless and futile endeavor while depicting England ironically as a multicultural refuge, a place where formerly colonized peoples find a home. To dramatize the difference between Irish and English nationalism, the kidnapped black soldier, Jody, describes Ireland as "the only place in the world where they'll call you a nigger to your face." England, on the other hand, is marked for him by class conflicts (played out in his cricket tales), but not so much by racial disharmony. By the time Dil enters the film, about a third of the way in, England has become for Fergus a refuge and a place where he can disappear.

Disappearing is, in many ways, the name of the crying game, and the film plays with and through the fetishistic structure of cinema itself, with, in other words, the spectator's willingness to see what is not there and desire what is. In a series of scenes set in the gay bar, the Metro, where Dil performs, the viewer's gaze is sutured to Fergus's. In the first few scenes, the bar seems to be populated by so-called normal people, men and women, dancing together. But in the scene at the Metro that follows Fergus's discovery of Dil's penis, the camera again scans the bar and finds the garish and striking faces of the drag queens who populate it. Like Fergus, we formerly saw bio men and women, and like Fergus, we suddenly see the bar for what it is: a queer site. And our vision, no matter how much we recognized Dil as transgender earlier, makes this abrupt detour around the transgender gaze along with Fergus. Indeed, *The Crying Game* cannot imagine the transgender gaze any more than it can cede the gaze to an IRA perspective. Here the revelation of a queer bar community sets up new triangulations within which the relationship between Fergus/Jimmy and Dil is now coded as homosexual. The homo context erases Dil's transsexual subjectivity, and throws the male protagonist into a panic that is only resolved by the symbolic castration of Dil when Fergus cuts Dil's hair. He does this supposedly to disguise Dil and protect her from the IRA, but actually the haircut unmasks her and serves to protect Fergus from his own desires. [. . .]

Boys Don't Cry: **Beyond Tears**

Given the predominance of films that use transgender characters, but avoid the transgender gaze, Peirce's transformation of the Brandon story into the Oscar-winning *Boys Don't Cry* signaled something much more than the successful interpretation of a transgender narrative for a mainstream audience. The success of Peirce's depiction depended not simply on the impressive acting skills of Hilary Swank and her surrounding cast, nor did it rest solely on the topicality of the Brandon narrative in gay, lesbian, and transgender communities; rather, the seduction of mainstream viewers by this decidedly queer and unconventional narrative must be ascribed to the film's ability to construct and sustain a transgender gaze. [. . .] The success of *Boys Don't Cry* in cultivating an audience beyond the queer cinema circuit depends absolutely on its ability to hijack the male and female gazes, and replace them surreptitiously with transgender modes of looking and queer forms of visual pleasure.

In a gesture that has left feminist film theorists fuming for years, Laura Mulvey's classic essay "Visual Pleasure and Narrative Cinema" argued, somewhat sensibly, that the pleasure in looking was always gendered within classic cinema. Mulvey went on to claim that within those classic cinematic narrative trajectories that begin with a mystery, a murder, a checkered past, or class disadvantage, or that advance through a series of obstacles toward the desired resolution in heterosexual marriage, there exist a series of male and female points of identification (Mulvey 1990). [. . .] These gendered characters play their parts within a field of extremely limited and finite variation, and yet, because gendered spectators have already consented to limited and finite gender roles before entering the cinema, they will consent to the narrow range of narrative options within narrative cinema. Entertainment, in many ways, is the name we give to the fantasies of difference that erupt on the screen only to give way to the reproduction of sameness. [. . .]

How does conventional narrative cinema allow for variation while maintaining a high degree of conformity? [. . . S]ometimes, as we saw in *The Crying Game*, the transgender character will be evoked as a metaphor for flexible subjecthood, but will not be given a narrative in his/her own right. But every now and then, and these are the instances that I want to examine here, the gendered binary on which the stability, the pleasure, and the purchase of mainstream cinema depend will be thoroughly rescripted, allowing for another kind of gaze or look. Here, I track the potentiality of the transgender gaze or the "transverse look," as Nick Mirzoeff describes it. Mirzoeff suggests that in an age of "multiple viewpoints," we have to think beyond the gaze. He writes about a "transient, transnational, transgendered way of seeing that visual culture seeks to define, describe and deconstruct with the transverse look or glance—not a gaze, there have been enough gazes already" (Mirzoeff 2002, 18).

While Mulvey's essay created much vigorous debate in cinema studies on account of its seemingly fatalistic perspective on gender roles and relations, the messenger in many ways was being confused with the message. [. . .] Within conventional cinema, Mulvey proposed that the only way for a female viewer to access voyeuristic pleasure was to cross-identify with the male gaze; through this complicated procedure, the female spectator of a conventional visual narrative could find a position on the screen that offered a little more than the pleasure of being fetishized. Mulvey suggests that the female viewer has to suture her look to the male look. Others have talked about this as a form of transvestism—a cross- dressed look that allows the female spectator to imagine momentarily that she has the same access to power as the male viewer. The problem with the cinematic theory of masquerade, of course, is that it requires no real understanding of transvestism and of the meaning of male transvestism in particular. [. . .] But what happens [. . .] when gender constructions are overthrown and sexual difference is shaken to its very foundations?

In the classic Hollywood film text, the camera looks from one position/character and then returns the gaze from another position/character, thereby suturing the viewer to a usually male gaze and simultaneously covering over what the viewer cannot see. This dynamic of looking is called shot/reverse shot and it occupies a central position within cinematic grammar. The shot/reverse shot mode allows for the stability of narrative progression, ensures a developmental logic, and allows the viewers to insert themselves into the filmic world by imagining that their access to the characters is unmediated. The dismantling of the shot/reverse shot can be identified as the central cinematic tactic in *Boys Don't Cry*. In her stylish adaptation of the true-to-life story of Brandon, director Peirce self-consciously constructs what can only be called a transgender look. *Boys Don't Cry* establishes the legitimacy and the durability of Brandon's gender not simply by telling the tragic tale of his death by murder but by forcing spectators to adopt, if only provisionally, Brandon's gaze, a transgender look.[2] The transgender look in this film reveals the ideological content of the male and female gazes, and it disarms, temporarily, the compulsory heterosexuality of the romance genre. Brandon's gaze, obviously, dies with him in the film's brutal conclusion, but Peirce, perhaps prematurely, abandons the transgender look in the final intimate encounter between Lana and Brandon. Peirce's inability to sustain a transgender look opens up a set of questions about the inevitability and dominance of both the male/female and hetero/homo binary in narrative cinema.

One remarkable scene, about halfway through the film, clearly foregrounds the power of the transgender look, making it most visible precisely where and when it is most threatened. In a scary and nerve-racking sequence of events, Brandon finds himself cornered at Lana's house. John and Tom have forced Candace to tell them that Brandon has been charged by the police with writing bad checks and that he has been imprisoned as a woman. John and Tom now hunt Brandon, like hounds after a fox, and then they begin a long and excruciating interrogation of Brandon's gender identity. Lana protects Brandon at first by saying that she will examine him and determine whether he is a man or a woman. Lana and Brandon enter Lana's bedroom, where Lana refuses to look as Brandon unbuckles his pants, telling him, "Don't I know you're a guy." As they sit on the bed together, the camera now follows Lana's gaze out into the night sky, a utopian vision of an elsewhere into which she and Brandon long to escape. This is one of several fantasy shots in an otherwise wholly realistic film; Peirce threads these shots in which time speeds up or slows down through the film, creating an imagistic counternarrative to the story of Brandon's decline.

As Brandon and Lana sit in Lana's bedroom imagining an elsewhere that would save them from the impoverished reality they inhabit, the camera cuts back abruptly to "reality" and a still two-shot of Brandon in profile and Lana behind him. As they discuss their next move, the camera draws back slowly and makes a seamless transition to place them in the living room in front of the posse of bullies. This quiet interlude in Lana's bedroom establishes the female gaze, Lana's gaze, as a willingness to see what is not there (a condition of all fantasy), but also as a refusal to privilege the literal over the figurative (Brandon's genitalia over Brandon's gender presentation). The female gaze, in this scene, makes possible an alternative vision of time, space, and embodiment. Time slows down while the couple linger in the sanctuary of Lana's private world, her bedroom; the bedroom itself becomes an otherworldly space framed by the big night sky, and containing the perverse vision of a girl and her queer boy lover; and the body of Brandon is preserved as male, for now, by Lana's refusal to dismantle its fragile power with the scrutinizing gaze of science and "truth." That Lana's room morphs seamlessly into the living room at the end of this scene, alerts the viewer to the possibility that an alternative vision will subtend and undermine the chilling enforcement of normativity that follows.

Back in the living room—the primary domestic space of the family—events take an abrupt turn toward the tragic. Brandon is shoved now into the bathroom, a hyperreal space of sexual difference, and is violently de-pantsed by John and Tom, and then restrained by John while Tom roughly examines Brandon's crotch. The brutality of John and Tom's action here is clearly identified as a violent mode of looking, and the film identifies the male gaze with the factual, the visible, and the literal. The brutality of the male gaze, however, is more complicated than simply a castrating force; John and Tom not only want to see the site of Brandon's castration but more important, they need Lana to see it. Lana kneels in front of Brandon, confirming the scene's resemblance to a crucifixion tableau, and refuses again to raise her eyes, declining, again, to look at Brandon's unveiling.

At the point when Lana's "family" and "friends" assert their heteronormative will most forcefully on Brandon's resistant body, however, Brandon rescues himself for a moment by regaining the alternative vision of time and space that he and Lana shared moments earlier in her bedroom. A slow-motion sequence interrupts the fast and furious quasi-medical scrutiny of Brandon's body, and shots from Brandon's point of view reveal him to be in the grips of an "out-of-body" and out-of-time experience. Light shines on Brandon from above, and his anguished face peers out into the crowd of onlookers who have gathered at the bathroom door. The crowd now includes a fully clothed Brandon, a double, who returns the gaze of the tortured Brandon impassively. In this shot/reverse shot sequence between the castrated Brandon and the transgender one, the transgender gaze is constituted as a look divided within itself, a point of view that comes from two places (at least) at the same time, one clothed and one naked. The clothed Brandon is the one who was rescued by Lana's refusal to look; he is the Brandon who survives his own rape and murder; he is the Brandon to whom the audience is now sutured, a figure who combines momentarily the activity of looking with the passivity of the spectacle. And the naked Brandon is the one who will suffer, endure, and finally expire. [. . .]

Not only does *Boys Don't Cry* create a position for the transgender subject that is fortified from the traditional operations of the gaze and conventional modes of gendering but it also makes the transgender subject dependent on the recognition of a woman. In other words, Brandon can be Brandon because Lana is willing to see him as he sees himself (clothed, male, vulnerable, lacking, strong, and passionate), and she is willing to avert her gaze when his manhood is in question. With Brandon occupying the place of the male hero and the male gaze in the romance, the dynamics of looking and gendered being are permanently altered. If usually it is the female body that registers lack, insufficiency, and powerlessness, in *Boys Don't Cry*, it is Brandon who represents the general condition of incompleteness, crisis, and lack, and it is Lana who represents the fantasy of wholeness, knowledge, and pleasure.

Lana can be naked without trauma while Brandon cannot; she can access physical pleasure in a way that he cannot, but he is depicted as mobile and self-confident in a way that she is not. Exclusion and privilege cannot be assigned neatly to the couple on the basis of gender or class hierarchies; power, rather, is shared between the two subjects, and she agrees to misrecognize him as male while he sees through her social alienation and unhappiness, recognizing her as beautiful, desirable, and special.

By deploying the transgender gaze and binding it to an empowered female gaze in *Boys Don't Cry*, director Peirce, for most of the film, keeps the viewer trained on the seriousness of Brandon's masculinity and the authenticity of his presentation as opposed to its elements of masquerade. But toward the end of the film, Peirce suddenly and catastrophically divests her character of his transgender look and converts it to a lesbian and therefore female gaze. In a strange scene following the brutal rape of Brandon by John and Tom, Lana comes to Brandon as he lies sleeping in a shed outside of Candace's house. In many ways, the encounter between the two that follows seems to extend the violence enacted on Brandon's body by John and Tom since Brandon now interacts with Lana *as if he were a woman*. Lana, contrary to her previous commitment to his masculinity, seems to see him as female, and she calls him "pretty" and asks him what he was like as a girl. Brandon confesses to Lana that he has been untruthful about many things in his past, and his confession sets up the expectation that he will now appear before Lana as his "true" self. Truth here becomes sutured to nakedness as Lana disrobes Brandon, tentatively saying that she may not know "how to do this." "This" seems to refer to having sex with Brandon as a woman. They both agree that his whole journey to manhood has been pretty weird and then they move to make love. While earlier Peirce created quite graphic depictions of sex between Brandon and Lana, now the action is hidden by a Hollywood dissolve as if to suggest that the couple are now making love as opposed to having sex. The scene is disjunctive and completely breaks the flow of the cinematic text by having Lana, the one person who could see Brandon's gender separate from his sex, now see him as woman. Moreover, the scene implies that the rape has made Brandon a woman in a way that his brutal exposure earlier in the bathroom and his intimate sex scenes with Lana could not. And if the scene seems totally out of place to the viewer, it apparently felt wrong as well to Hilary Swank. There are rumors that Swank and Peirce fought over this scene, and that Peirce shot the scene without Swank by using a body double. A close reading of the end of the scene indeed shows that the Brandon figure takes off his T-shirt while the camera watches from behind. The musculature and look of Brandon's back is quite different here from the toned look of Swank's body in earlier exposure scenes.

The "love" scene raises a number of logical and practical questions about the representation of the relationship between Brandon and Lana. First, why would Brandon want to have sex within hours of a rape? Second, how does the film pull back from its previous commitment to his masculinity here by allowing his femaleness to become legible and significant to Lana's desire? Third, in what ways does this scene play against the earlier, more "plastic" sex scenes in which Brandon used a dildo and would not allow Lana to touch him? And fourth, how does this scene unravel the complexities of the transgender gaze as they have been assembled in earlier scenes between Brandon and Lana? When asked in an interview about this scene, Peirce reverts to a tired humanist narrative to explain it and says that after the rape, Brandon could not be either Brandon Teena or Teena Brandon and so he becomes truly "himself," and in that interaction with Lana, Brandon "receives love" for the first time as a human being.[3] Peirce claims that Lana herself told her about this encounter and therefore it was true to life. In the context of the film, however, which has made no such commitment to authenticity, the scene ties Brandon's humanity to a particular form of naked embodiment that in the end requires him to be a woman.

Ultimately in *Boys Don't Cry*, the double vision of the transgender subject gives way to the universal vision of humanism; the transgender man and his lover become lesbians, and the murder seems to be simply the outcome of a vicious homophobic rage. Given the failure of nerve that leads Peirce to conclude her film with a humanist scene of love conquers all, it is no surprise that she also sacrificed the racial complexity of the narrative by erasing the story of the other victim who died alongside Brandon and Lisa Lambert. As discussed earlier, Philip DeVine, a disabled African American man, has in general received only scant treatment in media accounts of the case, despite the connections of at least one of the murderers to a white supremacist group (Jones 1996, 154). Now in the feature film, Philip's death has been rendered completely irrelevant to the narrative that has been privileged. Peirce claimed that this subplot would have complicated her film and made the plot too cumbersome, but race is a narrative trajectory that is absolutely central to the meaning of the Brandon murder. Philip was dating Lana's sister, Leslie, and had a fight with her the night he showed up at Lisa's house in Humboldt County. His death was neither accidental nor an afterthought; his connection to Leslie could be read as a similarly outrageous threat to the supremacy and privilege of white manhood that the murderers Lotter and Nissen rose to defend. By taking Philip out of the narrative and by not even mentioning him in the original dedication of the film ("To Brandon Teena and Lisa Lambert"), the filmmaker sacrifices the hard facts of racial hatred and transphobia to a streamlined romance.[4] Peirce, in other words, reduces the complexity of the murderous act even as she sacrifices the complexity of Brandon's identity.

In the end, the murders are shown to be the result of a kind of homosexual panic, and Brandon is offered up as an "everyman" hero who makes a claim on the audience's sympathies first by pulling off a credible masculinity, but then by seeming to step out of his carefully maintained manhood to appear before judge and jury in the naked flesh as female. [. . .] *Boys Don't Cry* falls far short of the alternative vision that was articulated so powerfully and shared so beautifully by Brandon and Lana in Lana's bedroom. But even so, by articulating momentarily the specific formal dimensions of the transgender gaze, *Boys Don't Cry* takes a quantum leap away from the crying games, which continued in the past to locate transgenderism in between the male and female gazes and alongside unrelenting tragedy. Peirce's film, in fact, opens the door to a nonfetishistic mode of seeing the transgender body—a mode that looks with, rather than at, the transgender body and cultivates the multidimensionality of an indisputably transgender gaze.

What would a transgender film look like that did not punish the transgender subject for his or her inflexibilities and for failing to deliver the fantasy of fluidity that cinematic audiences so desire? *By Hook or by Crook* offers the spectator not one but two transgender characters, and the two together represent transgender identity as less of a function of bodily flexibility and more a result of intimate bonds and queer, interactive modes of recognition.

Lovely and Confusing: *By Hook or by Crook* and the Transgender Look

> We feel like we were thrown almost every curve in the game. And we managed to make this thing by hook or by crook.
>
> —Harry Dodge and Silas Howard, *By Hook or by Crook* directors

By Hook or by Crook marks a real turning point for queer and transgender cinema. This no-budget, low-tech, high-concept feature, shot entirely in mini digital video, tells the story of two gender bandits, Shy and Valentine. Described by its creators as "utterly post-post-modern, a little bit of country and a little bit of rock and roll," the film conjures up the twilight world of two loners living on the edge without trying to explain or rationalize their reality.[5] The refusal to explain either the gender peculiarities of the heroes or the many other contradictions they embody allows directors Howard and Dodge instead to focus on developing eccentric and compelling characters. While most of the action turns on the bond between Shy and Valentine, their world is populated with a stunning array of memorable characters like Valentine's girlfriend, Billie (Stanya Kahn), and Shy's love interest, Isabelle (Carina Gia). [. . . These appearances] establish the world of *By Hook or by Crook* as a specifically queer universe. [. . .]

Both *The Crying Game* and *Boys Don't Cry* relied heavily on the successful solicitation of affect—whet her revulsion, sympathy, or empathy—in order to give mainstream viewers access to a transgender gaze. And in both films, a relatively unknown actor (Jay Davidson and Hilary Swank, respectively) performs alongside a more well-known actor (Stephen Rea and Chloe Sevigny, respectively); the relative obscurity of the transgender actors allow them to pull off the feat of credibly performing a gender at odds with the sexed body even after the body has been brutally exposed. *By Hook or by Crook* resists the seduction of crying games and the lure of sentiment, and works instead to associate butchness and gender innovation with wit, humor, and style. The melancholia that tinges *The Crying Game* and saturates *Boys Don't Cry* is transformed in *By Hook or by Crook* into the wise delirium of Dodge's character, Valentine. Dodge and Howard (Shy) knowingly avoid engaging their viewers at the level of sympathy, pity, or even empathy, and instead they "hook" them with the basic tools of the cinematic apparatus: desire and identification.

Dodge and Howard pioneer some brilliant techniques of queer plotting in order to map the world of the willfully perverse. As they say in interviews, neither director was interested in telling a story about "being gay." Nor did Dodge and Howard want to spend valuable screen time explaining the characters' sexualities and genders to unknowing audiences. In the press kit, Dodge and Howard discuss their strategy in terms of representing sexuality and gender as follows: "This is a movie about a budding friendship between two people. The fact that they happen to be queer is purposefully off the point. If you call them something, other than sad, rambling, spirited, gentle, sharp or funny . . . you might call them '*butches.*'" [. . .]

In the film, Shy and Valentine visit cafes, clubs, shops, and hotels where no one reacts specifically to their butchness. This narrative strategy effectively *universalizes queerness* within this specific cinematic space. Many gay and lesbian films represent their characters and their struggles as "universal" as a way of suggesting that their film speaks to audiences beyond specific gay and lesbian audiences. But few do more than submit to the regulation of narrative that transforms the specific into the universal: they tell stories of love, redemption, family, and struggle that look exactly like every other Hollywood feature angling for a big audience. *By Hook or by Crook* actually manages to tell a queer story that is more than a queer story by refusing to acknowledge the existence of a straight world. Where the straight world is represented only through its institutions such as the law, the mental institution, or commerce, the queer cinematic world comes to represent a truly localized place of opposition—an opposition, moreover, that is to be found in committed performances of perversity, madness, and friendship. [. . .] *By Hook or by Crook* universalizes queerness without allowing its characters to be absorbed back into the baggy and ultimately heterosexist concept of the "human."

Different key scenes from the film build, capture, and sustain this method of universalizing queerness. In one scene soon after they meet, Shy and Valentine go to a club together. The club scene, filmed in San Francisco's notorious Lexington Bar, is a riotous montage of queer excess. The camera lovingly pans a scene of punky, pierced, tattooed, perverted young queers. [. . .] In *The Crying Game*, the bar scenes were used first to establish the credibility of Dil's womanhood and then, after she has "come out" to Fergus as male bodied, the bar scenes are used to cast her womanhood as incredible. [. . .] Dodge and Howard situate the queer bar as central to an alternative vision of community, space, time, and identity. In the bar, Valentine dances wildly and ecstatically while Shy sits apart from the crowd watching. The camera playfully scans the bar and then lines up its patrons for quick cameos. Here, Dodge and Howard are concerned to represent the bar as both a space of queer community and a place of singularity. The singularity of the patrons [. . .] reveals a difference to be a shared and a collaborative relation to normativity rather than an individualist mode of refusal.

After watching Valentine dance, Shy gets up and steals Valentine's wallet before leaving. The theft of Valentine's wallet should create a gulf of distrust and suspicion between the two strangers, but in this looking-glass world, it actually bonds them more securely within their underground existence. Shy uses Valentine's wallet to find out where she lives, and when Shy returns Valentine's wallet the next day, she is greeted like a long-lost brother—this has the effect of inverting the morality of the world represented in this film by the police.

Other scenes deepen this refusal of conventional law and order. The two butches as wannabe thieves try to hold up a drugstore only to be chased off by an aggressive salesclerk; they try to scam a hardware store and, in a citation of Robert De Niro's famous scene from *Taxi Driver*, they pose with guns in front of the mirror in Shy's run-down motel room. All of these scenes show Shy and Valentine as eccentric, but gently outlaws who function as part of an alternative universe with its own ethics, sex/gender system, and public space.

[. . . While] De Niro's character accidentally hits a vein of humor with his mohawked "fuck you," Shy and Valentine deliberately ride butch humor rather than macho vengeance into the sunset. If the vigilante wants to remake the world in his image, the queer outlaws of *By Hook or by Crook* are content to imagine a world of their own making. When asked about the title of the film, Silas Howard responded: "The title refers to what is involved in inventing your own world—when you don't see anything that represents you out there, how can you seize upon that absence as an opportunity to make something out of nothing, by hook or by crook. We take gender ambiguity, for example, and we don't explain it, dilute it or apologize for it—we represent it for what it is—something confusing and lovely!"

The recent explosion of transgender films forces us to consider what the spectacle of the transgender body represents to multiple audiences. For some audiences, the transgender body confirms a fantasy of fluidity so common to notions of transformation within the postmodern. To others, the transgender body confirms the enduring power of the binary gender system. But to still other viewers, the transgender body represents a Utopian vision of a world of subcultural possibilities. Representations of transgenderism in recent queer cinema have moved from a tricky narrative device designed to catch an unsuspecting audience off guard to truly independent productions within which gender ambiguity is not a trap or a device but part of the production of new forms of heroism, vulnerability, visibility, and embodiment. The centrality of the figure of Brandon in this drama of postmodern embodiment suggests [. . .] that we have a hard time thinking of seismic shifts in the history of representations separate from individual stories of transformation. The hopes and fears that have been projected onto the slim and violated body of one transgender loner in small-town Nebraska make clear the flaws of "representative history," and call for the kind of shared vision that we see in *By Hook or by Crook*—a vision of community, possibility, and redemption through collaboration.

Notes

1. For an excellent discussion of the political contradictions of *The Crying Game*, see Shantanu Dutta Ahmed, " 'Thought You Knew!' Performing the Penis, the Phallus, and Otherness in Neil Jordan's *The Crying Game*" (1998).
2. Patricia White has argued in "Girls Still Cry" (2001) that the gaze in *Boys Don't Cry* is Lana's all along.
3. Interview by Terry Gross on *Fresh Air*, PBS Radio, March 15, 2001.
4. In the review copy of the film I saw, *Boys Don't Cry* was dedicated "To Brandon Teena and Lisa Lambert." This dedication seems to have been removed later on, possibly because it so overtly referenced Philip's erasure.
5. Unless otherwise attributed, all quotes from directors Howard and Dodge are taken from the press kit for *By Hook or by Crook*, www.steakhaus.com/bhobc/.

19 Judith Butler

Queer Feminism, Transgender, and the Transubstantiation of Sex

Jay Prosser

In his 1998 book *Second Skins: The Body Narratives of Transsexuality*, literary scholar Jay Prosser offered one of the most theoretically sophisticated and psychoanalytically informed interdisciplinary interpretations of transgender experience to date. He argued that embodiment is a process of storytelling through which one's identity is communicated to others. In the following selection, Prosser discusses the transgender figure's simultaneous centrality to and marginalization within queer studies generally, and in the work of Judith Butler in particular, to argue that "in retrospect, transgender gender appears as the most crucial sign of queer sexuality's aptly skewed point of entry into the academy." Prosser couples his observations on the ubiquity of transgender content within early queer theory with a pointed critique of the way that certain types of transgender phenomena, notably camp and drag, are celebrated, while others, notably transsexuality, are disparaged. The former modes of transness were deployed to support a theory of gender performativity, while the latter was often held up as an example of an intellectually suspect "foundationalism" or "biological essentialism."

There is little time for grief in the *Phenomenology [of Spirit]* because renewal is always close at hand. What seems like tragic blindness turns out to be more like the comic myopia of Mr. Magoo whose automobile careening through the neighbor's chicken coop always seems to land on all four wheels. Like such miraculously resilient characters of the Saturday morning cartoon, Hegel's protagonists always reassemble themselves, prepare a new scene, enter the stage armed with a new set of ontological insights—and fail again. As readers, we have no other narrative option but to join in this bumpy ride.

—Judith Butler, *Subjects of Desire: Hegelian Reflections in Twentieth-Century France*

Transgender and the Queer Moment

Queer is a continuing moment, movement, motive—recurrent, eddying, troublant. The word "queer" itself means across—it comes from the Indo-European root *twerkw*, which also yields the German *quer* (transverse), Latin *torquere* (to twist), English athwart.

—Eve Kosofsky Sedgwick, *Tendencies*

In its earliest formulations, in what are now considered its foundational texts, queer studies can be seen to have been crucially dependent on the figure of transgender. As one of its most visible means of institutionalization, queer theory represented itself as traversing and mobilizing methodologies (feminism, poststructuralism) and identities (women, heterosexuals) already, at least by comparison, in institutionalized place. Seized on as a definitively queer

DOI: 10.4324/9781003206255-24

force that "troubled" the identity categories of gender, sex, and sexuality—or rather revealed them to be always already fictional and precarious—the trope of crossing was most often impacted with if not explicitly illustrated by the transgendered subject's crossing their several boundaries at once: both the boundaries between gender, sex, and sexuality and the boundary that structures each as a binary category.

Even in Eve Kosofsky Sedgwick's work, which has argued most trenchantly for "a certain irreducibility" of sexuality to gender, and thus one might deduce would follow a certain irreducibility of *homo*sexuality to *trans*gender, homophobic constructions are understood to be produced by and productive of culturally normative gender identities and relations. The implications of this include a thorough enmeshing of homosexual desire with transgender identification. In its claim that women in the nineteenth century served to mediate desire between men, Sedgwick's *Between Men: English Literature and Male Homosocial Desire* suggests that the production of normative heterosexuality depended on a degree of male identification—and yet importantly, the disavowal of this identification—with woman as the object of desire. At the beginnings of queer therefore, in what is arguably lesbian and gay studies' first book, heterosexuality is shown to be constructed through the sublimation of a cross-gendered identification; for this reason, making visible this identification—transgendered movement—will become the key queer mechanism for deconstructing heterosexuality and writing out queer.

Sedgwick's next book foregrounds this methodological function of transgender explicitly. *Epistemology of the Closet* presents transgender as one good reason for the development of a theory of (homo)sexuality distinct from feminism. The critical visibility of transgender—"the reclamation and relegitimation of a courageous history of lesbian trans gender role-playing and identification"—poses a challenge to lesbianism's incorporation within feminism: "The irrepressible, relatively class-nonspecific popular culture in which James Dean has been as numinous an icon for lesbians as Garbo or Dietrich has for gay men seems resistant to a purely feminist theorization. It is in these contexts that calls for a theorized axis of sexuality as distinct from gender have developed." Exceeding feminism's purview of gender, transgender demands and contributes to the basis for a new queer theory; paradoxically, transgender demands a new theory of sexuality. It is transgender that makes possible the lesbian and gay overlap, the identification between gay men and lesbians, which forms the grounds for this new theory of homosexuality discrete from feminism. And it is surely this overlap or cross-gendered identification between gay men and lesbians—an identification made critically necessary by the AIDS crisis—that ushers in the queer moment.

Most recently in her autobiographical narratives and performance pieces, Sedgwick has revealed her personal transgendered investment lying at and as the great heart of her queer project. Her confession of her "identification? Dare I, after this half-decade, call it with all a fat *woman's* defiance, my identity?—as a gay man" "comes out" with the transgendered desire that has been present in her work all along. Similarly in its readings, *Tendencies* derives its queer frisson openly and consistently from an identification across genders: a mobility "across gender lines, including the desires of men for women and of women for men," a transgendered traversal that in its queering (skewing and unraveling) of apparently normative heterosexuality is simultaneously a movement across sexualities. To summon the queer moment, the book begins with a figure for transgender—gay men wearing DYKE T-shirts and lesbians wearing FAGGOT T-shirts.

But Sedgwick is just the tip of the iceberg. The transgendered presence lies just below the surface of most of lesbian and gay studies' foundational texts. Early work on the intersections of race, gender, and sexual identities theorized otherness as produced through a racist, homophobic, and sexist transgendering, and thus again transgendering became the means to challenging this othering. Kobena Mercer's work on the fetishizing/feminizing white gaze of Robert Mapplethorpe at the black male body; Cherríe Moraga's description of the hermaphroditic convergence of the chingón and the chingada; Gloria Anzaldúa's memory of the mita' y mita' figure in the sexual, gender, and geographic borderlands: these various cross-gendered figures emerged both as constructions and, in their articulation by these critics, deconstructions of cultural ideologies that insist on absolute difference in all identity. Other early lesbian and gay studies work invested in the transgendered subject's "trans" a transgressive politics. For Teresa de Lauretis, Sue-Ellen Case, Jonathan Dollimore, and Marjorie Garber whether appearing in contemporary lesbian cinematic representations of butch/femme desire, in theatrical cross-dressing in early modern England, or as popular cultural gender-blending icons, the transgendered subject made visible a queerness that, to paraphrase Garber, threatened a crisis in gender and sexual identity categories. Crucial to the idealization of transgender as a queer transgressive force in this work is the consistent decoding of "trans" as incessant destabilizing movement between sexual and gender identities. In short, in retrospect, transgender *gender* appears as the most crucial sign of queer *sexuality's* aptly skewed point of entry into the academy.

Without doubt though, the single text that yoked transgender most fully to queer sexuality is Judith Butler's *Gender Trouble: Feminism and the Subversion of Identity*. [. . .]

Queer Gender and Performativity

> To realize the difference of the sexes is to put an end to play.
> —Jacques Lacan and Wladimir Granoff, "Fetishism:
> The Symbolic, the Imaginary, and the Real"

Even though it is articulated only in the last of four sections in the final chapter ("Bodily Inscriptions, Performative Subversions" [*GT* 128–141]), that is in less than one-twelfth of the book, it is the account of gender performativity that is most often remembered as the thrust of *Gender Trouble*. Sedgwick illustrates: "Probably the centerpiece of Butler's recent work has been a series of demonstrations that gender can best be discussed as a form of performativity." More intriguing than the disproportionate emphasis accorded the final section of *Gender Trouble* in general remembrance, however, is the way in which *gender* performativity has become so coextensive with *queer* performativity as to render them interchangeable. Sedgwick, again, exemplifies the way in which "gender" has slipped rapidly into "queer." "Queer Performativity" (the title of her essay on James) she writes, is "made necessary" by Butler's work in and since *Gender Trouble*; and in *Tendencies* Sedgwick assigns Butler "and her important book" (*Gender Trouble*) a representative function, "stand[ing] in for a lot of the rest of us" working on queer performativity. How does this slippage from gender to queer in the discussion of performativity come about, and how does *Gender Trouble* come to "stand in for" it?

While it argues that *all* gender is performative—that "man" and "woman" are not expressions of prior internal essences but constituted, to paraphrase Butler, through the repetition of culturally intelligible stylized acts—*Gender Trouble* presents the transgendered subject as the concrete example that "brings into relief" this performativity of gender (*GT* 31). In retrospect we can note that, in concretizing gender performativity with transgender, *Gender Trouble* inadvertently made possible two readings that Butler later returns to refute: first, that what was meant by gender performativity was gender theatricality; and second, that all transgender is queer is syllogistically subversive. The first assumption, that gender performativity means acting out one's gender as if gender were a theatrical role that could be chosen, led to the belief that Butler's theory of gender was both radically voluntarist and antimaterialist: that its argument was that gender, like a set of clothes in a drag act, could be donned and doffed at will, that gender *is* drag. In this reading *Gender Trouble* was both embraced and critiqued. (Even before *Gender Trouble*, however, Butler had carefully argued against any conceptualization of gender as something that could be chosen at will). In fact, Butler's notion of performativity is derived not from a Goffman-esque understanding of identity as role but from Austinian speech-act theory, crucially informed by Derrida's deconstruction of speech-act theory. Not cited in *Gender Trouble* but implicit throughout in its insistence on the cruciality of repetition as destabilizing is Derrida's reading of J. L. Austin and John Searle. *Bodies That Matter* wastes little time before citing Derrida's reading (introduction 13), and in order to clarify this speech-act sense of performativity, the new work emphasizes gender's citationality throughout. To some extent in *Bodies That Matter*, the later term, "citationality," comes to displace the former of *Gender Trouble*, "performativity." Like a law that requires citing to be effective, *Bodies That Matter* argues, sex comes into effect through our citing it, and, as with a law, through our compulsion to cite it. Butler's refiguring of sex as citational law in *Bodies That Matter* is designed to derail the understanding of gender as free theatricality that constituted the misreading of *Gender Trouble*, to clarify how gender is compelled through symbolic prohibitions. The shifts in terms in the books' titles, from "Gender Trouble" to the "Discursive Limits of 'Sex'" (both the shift from "gender" to "'sex'" and from "trouble" to "discursive limits") run as parallel attempts to account for gender's materiality, its nonsuperficiality, and at the same time to foreground the "limits" of the "trouble" subjects can effect to its constitutive prohibitions. That "sex" appears typographically inserted in citation marks suggests sex precisely as a citation.

It is the second assumption drawn from *Gender Trouble*'s illustration of gender performativity with transgender that concerns me most: the assumption that transgender is queer is subversive. For it is this syllogism that enables Sedgwick to make that slide from gender performativity to queer performativity and that effectively encodes transgendered subjectivity as archetypically queer and subversive. It should be understood that, although it never makes such an argument, *Gender Trouble* does set up the conditions for this syllogism: transgender = gender performativity = queer = subversive. We can begin to illustrate the first part of this, the equation of transgender with gender performativity, by examining *Gender Trouble*'s reading of Beauvoir's "One is not born a woman, but rather becomes one." In Butler's reformulation of Beauvoir's famed epigram on the construction of gender nearly half a century later, it is through the suggestion of a possible transgendering that gender appears not simply constructed but radically contingent on the body. To cite Butler: "Beauvoir is clear that one 'becomes' a woman, but always under a cultural compulsion to become one. And clearly, the compulsion does not come from 'sex.' *There is nothing in her account that guarantees that the 'one' who becomes a woman is necessarily female*" (*GT* 8; my emphasis). And again: "Beauvoir's theory implied seemingly radical consequences, ones that she herself did not entertain. For instance, if sex and gender are radically distinct, then it does not follow that to be a given sex is to become a given gender; in other words, *'woman' need not be the cultural construction of the female body, and 'man' need not interpret male bodies*" (*GT* 112; my emphasis). In both citations, Butler's suggestion of a possible transgendered becoming (that men may not be males and women may not be females) not only opens up a conceptual space between gender and sex and leaves sex dispensable to the process of gendering; it also conveys that gender is not a teleological narrative of ontology at all, with the sexed body (female) as recognizable beginning and gender identity (woman) as clear-cut ending. In Butler's reading transgender demotes gender from narrative to performative. That is, gender appears not as the end of narrative becoming but as performative moments all along a process: repetitious, recursive, disordered, incessant, above all, unpredictable and necessarily incomplete. "It is, for [Butler's version of] Beauvoir, never possible finally to become a woman, as if there were a *telos* that governs the process of acculturation and construction. Gender is the repeated stylization of the body, a set of repeated acts within a highly rigid regulatory frame that congeal over time to produce the appearance of substance, of a natural sort of being" (*GT* 33).

If transgender now equals gender performativity, how does this formulation come to acquire the additional equivalencies of queer and subversion? In "Critically Queer," in correcting the tendency to misread *Gender Trouble* as about transgender, Butler underscores that there is no essential identity between transgender and homosexuality: "not only are a vast number of drag performers straight, but it would be a mistake to think that homosexuality is best explained through the performativity that is drag." That she must return to make this qualification, however, is again precisely because *Gender Trouble* has already produced an implicit equivalence between transgender and homosexuality, so that transgender appears as the sign of homosexuality, homosexuality's definitive *gender* style. In one claim key to this imbrication of transgender with homosexuality, "parodic and subversive convergences" are said to "*characterize* gay and lesbian cultures" (*GT* 66; my emphasis). This characterization encodes transgender as homosexual gender difference, a kind of archetypal queer gender.

Where "straight" gender occults its own performativity according to a metaphysics of substance, queer transgender reveals ("brings into relief") the performativity of all gender. Transgender "dramatizes" the process of signification by which all gendered embodiment "create[s] the effect of the natural" or real; drag's imitative workings parallel the imitative workings that structure straight genders, for all "gender is a kind of persistent impersonation that passes as the real" (*GT* x). The metaphysics of substance undergirds the naturalization of sex and of heterosexuality. What Butler terms the "heterosexual matrix," building in particular on Monique Wittig's analyses of the straight mind's naturalization of a dimorphic gender system, sustains heterosexuality as natural and naturalizes gender as sex. The naturalizing mechanism works both ways, shoring up the apparent naturalness of both sex/gender and heterosexual desire. The claim to "be" a man or a woman is made possible by the binary and oppositional positioning of these terms within heterosexuality. Sex, gender, and desire are unified through the representation of heterosexuality as primary and foundational. Female, femininity, and woman appear as stable and conjoined terms through their opposition to male, masculinity, and man. Gender, in other words, appears as *identity*. What stabilizes the association and keeps the two sets discrete and antithetical is the apparent naturalness of heterosexual desire.

Queer transgender's function in *Gender Trouble* can be summarized as twofold: to parallel the process by which heterosexuality reproduces (and reproduces itself through) binarized gender identities; and at the same time to contrast with heterosexuality's naturalization of this process. For whereas the constructedness of straight gender is obscured by the veil of naturalization, queer transgender reveals, indeed, explicitly performs, its own constructedness. In other words, queer transgender serves as heterosexual gender's subversive foil. Thus in the scheme of *Gender Trouble*, heterosexual gender is assigned as ground, queer transgender as figure, dramatizing or metaphorizing the workings of heterosexuality's construction. Even in "Critically Queer," in the very same paragraph that apparently seeks to disentangle homosexuality and transgender, Butler writes that drag "exposes or *allegorizes*" the process by which heterosexualized genders form themselves. Queer transgender is allegory to heterosexual gender's (specious, for it only veils its performativity) referentiality or literality.

Biddy Martin has described her anxiety in response to Butler's and Sedgwick's work over this tendency of "antifoundationalist celebrations of queerness" to represent queer sexualities as "figural, performative, playful, and fun." Martin's anxiety specifically concerns the way in which feminism, gender, and, by extension, the female body, are stabilized in this dynamic, projected by queerness as "fixity, constraint, or subjection . . . a fixed ground." While agreeing that the category of woman is often subject to a degree of a priori stabilization in the very writings that call for its destabilization and proliferation, my concerns, for the following reasons, are particularly with the effective appropriation of transgender by queer. In the first instance, transgendered subjectivity is not inevitably queer. That is, by no means are all transgendered subjects homosexual. While "Critically Queer" itself points this out, *Gender Trouble's* queer transgender illustrates a certain collapsing of gender back into sexuality that, in the particular process of *Gender Trouble's* canonization, has become a tendency of queer studies: a tendency that is, as Martin suggests, the queering of gender through sexuality (and I would add of sexuality through gender). And, more crucially in regard to this first distinction, in the context of a discussion of how gender and sexual subjects have been taken up in theoretical paradigms, by no means are transgendered subjects necessarily queer even in the sense that queer has come to signify in queer studies. That is, although "queer" as a camp term has to some extent lost that referent "homosexual" and now signifies not as homosexual *stricto sensu* but as a figure for the performative—subversive signifier displacing referent— by no means are all transgendered subjects queer even in this figurative, nonreferential sense. Butler's reading of Venus Xtravaganza in *Bodies That Matter* will work as an attempt to demonstrate just this: the way in which not every gender-crossing is queerly subversive. Yet it should be pointed out again that the fact that she must later return to disentangle transgender, queer, and subversion in *Bodies That Matter* as she must in the essay "Critically Queer," is due precisely to their prior entanglement in *Gender Trouble*. (Although, given the importance within Butler's theory of the dynamic of citation, the extent to which her own writing is generated through such reiterative returns should be noted as richly appropriate.)

My second reason for concern with queer's arrogation of transgender is that it allocates to nontransgendered subjects (according to this binary schema, straight subjects), the ground that transgender would appear to *only* figure; this "ground" is the apparent naturalness of sex. For if transgender figures gender performativity, nontransgender or straight gender is assigned (to work within Butler's own framework of speech-act theory) the category of the constative. While within this framework, this allocation is a sign of the devaluation of straight gender, and conversely queer's alignment of itself with transgender gender performativity represents queer's sense of its own "higher purpose," in fact there are transgendered trajectories, in particular *transsexual* trajectories, that aspire to that which this scheme devalues. Namely there are transsexuals who seek very pointedly to be nonperformative, to be constative, quite simply, to *be*. What gets dropped from transgender in its queer deployment to signify subversive gender performativity is the value of the matter that often most concerns the transsexual: the *narrative* of becoming a biological man or a biological woman (as opposed to the performative of effecting one)—in brief and simple the materiality of the sexed body. In the context of the transsexual trajectory, in fact, Beauvoir's epigram can be read quite differently as describing not a generic notion of gender's radical performativity but the specific narrative of (in this case) the male-to-female transsexual's struggle toward sexed embodiment. One is not born a woman, but *nevertheless* may become one—given substantial medical intervention, personal tenacity, economic security, social support, and so on: becoming woman, in spite of not being born one, may be seen as a crucial goal. In its representation of sex as a figurative effect of straight gender's constative performance, *Gender Trouble* cannot account for a transsexual desire for sexed embodiment as *telos*. In this regard *Gender Trouble* serves to prompt readings of transsexual subjects whose bodily trajectories might exceed its framework of the theory of gender performativity.

If *Gender Trouble* enables the syllogism transgender = gender performativity = queer = subversive, it stabilizes this syllogism through suggesting as constant its antithesis: nontransgender = gender constativity = straight = naturalizing. The binary opposition between these syllogisms proliferates a number of mutually sustaining binary oppositions between *Gender Trouble's* conceptual categories: queer versus straight; subversive versus naturalizing;

performativity versus constativity; gender versus sex. The first term in each opposition is ascribed a degree of generativity that puts in question the primacy of the second. The value of this intervention lies in our recognition that it is the second term that is customarily awarded primacy and autonomy over the first. But the transsexual, as Butler later realizes in Venus Xtravaganza, ruptures these binaries and their alignment.

Because it constitutes the focal point of the transsexual trajectory (to *be* a woman) among these binaries, it is the matter of sex that is of interest to me next before Venus, not simply in its conceptually associative opposition to transgendered subjects in *Gender Trouble* but as a conceptual category in itself. Transgender certainly allows Butler to displace an expressivist model of gender where gender is the cultural expression or interpretation of sex (consolidated as bedrock) with a performative model where sex can "be shown to have been gender all along" (*GT 8*). But *Gender Trouble's* most thorough accounting for sex as discursive effect appears in the discussion of melancholia in the second chapter, "Prohibition, Psychoanalysis, and the Production of the Heterosexual Matrix" (*GT* 35–78). Here, although the transgendered subject is not explicitly marshaled to exemplify the theory, the figure of transgender haunts the analyses, and the particular conceptualization of sex as "gender all along," as we shall see, certainly has significant implications for any theory of transsexual subjectivity.

[. . .]

Venus Is Burning: The Transubstantiation of the Transsexual

> I don't feel that there's anything mannish about me except what I might have between me down there. I guess that's why I want my sex change, to make myself complete.
>
> —Venus Xtravaganza, *Paris is Burning*

Because it was released in 1990, hot on the heels of the publication of *Gender Trouble*, Jennie Livingston's film *Paris is Burning* often got taken up in discussions of queer identities in conjunction with Butler's book, as if the subjects of the drag ball—again, the lure of the visual example in transgendered contexts—illustrated Butler's theory of gender performativity. Both texts in their transgendered themes captured what seemed definitive of the queer moment. For this reason they were subject to a certain yoking together in feminist/queer studies—in our readings, course syllabi, conferences, and so on. Butler's chapter in *Bodies That Matter* on the ambivalent effects of transgender in *Paris is Burning*, "Gender is Burning: Questions of Appropriation and Subversion" (*BTM* 121–142), serves by association therefore as a return to the subject of transgender in *Gender Trouble* to mark out *its* ambivalent effects. In this sense "Gender is Burning" functions to complicate those binary syllogisms of *Gender Trouble*. The essay's thesis is that crossing identifications in the film both denaturalize and renaturalize identity norms: "*Paris is Burning* documents neither an efficacious insurrection nor a painful resubordination, but an unstable coexistence of both" (*BTM* 137).

While Butler uses *Paris is Burning* in general to document the ambivalent significance of performative crossings, she uses Venus Xtravaganza as the specific lever to articulate this ambivalence: "Venus, and *Paris is Burning* more generally, calls into question whether parodying the dominant norms is enough to displace them; indeed, whether the denaturalization of gender cannot be the very vehicle for a reconsolidation of hegemonic norms" (*BTM* 125). For Butler it is the particular configuration of Venus's body, gender presentation, desires, and fate that best exemplifies how transgressive crossings can simultaneously reinscribe symbolic norms. The film's representation of this Latina transsexual delimits the subversive possibilities of parodic repetitions. Yet although its argument about ambivalence pivots on the specific material ambivalence of the transsexual body, Butler's essay encodes transsexuality as metaphor in a way that sublimates into theoretical allegory the specific materiality of Venus's sex and of her death as a light-skinned Latina transsexual.

The revelation of Venus's murder in the second part of *Paris is Burning* (filmed in 1989, two years after the first encounter with Venus) is indisputably the moment that most cuts through any sense of the performativity, the fictionality of identities the film provides elsewhere, particularly in the ball scenes. That Venus is killed for her transsexuality, for inhabiting a body which, as that of a preoperative male-to-female transsexual, is not coherently female, is strongly supported by the film's narrative. Angie Xtravaganza, the mother of Venus's house, to whom the film turns to provide an account of the occurrence, firmly fixes Venus's death in the context of a transsexual narrative: "That's part of life. That's part of being a transsexual in New York City." The implication is that Venus is murdered in her hotel bedroom on being "read" by her client, killed for having a body in excess of the femaleness he imagined he was paying for; killed, then, as a transsexual. Butler isolates Venus's death as the most prominent instance in the film in which the symbolic precludes its resignification: "This is a killing that is performed by the symbolic that would eradicate those phenomena that require an opening up of the possibilities for the resignification of sex" (*BTM* 131). Yet while Butler's isolation of this moment and this citation suggest that what matters (to the client, to the film, and to Butler the critic) is Venus's transsexuality and the particular configuration of her sexed body as a male-to-female, Butler's reading of Venus's killing situates Venus's body along a binary of queer man/woman of color, in the split between which Venus's Latina, passing-as-white, transsexual body falls.

Butler attributes Venus's death first to "homophobic violence," staking that it is Venus's "failure to pass completely [that renders her] clearly vulnerable" to this violence (*BTM* 129–130). By "failure to pass completely," Butler clearly intends Venus's penis; yet the presence of the penis on Venus's body renders neither her a homosexual man (a literalization of gender surely symptomatic of the heterosexual melancholia *Gender Trouble* critiqued) nor her death an effect of homophobia. Venus presents herself unambivalently as a transsexual woman, not as a gay man or drag queen. Although the only "genetic girl" is behind the camera, it does not follow that all the bodies in *Paris is Burning* are male. Rather, the film presents a spectrum of bodies and desires, heterosexual and homosexual, in-drag, transsexual, and genetic male, with the subjects frequently articulating the distinctions between these categories in a careful self-positioning. Stating that there's nothing "mannish" about her except what she has "down there," Venus describes looking forward to sex reassignment surgery to make her "complete": in other words, a complete woman. Her identification not as a gay man or a drag queen but as an incomplete (preoperative transsexual) woman highlights the impossibility of dividing up all identities along the binary homosexual/heterosexual. If it applies to Venus at all, her desire—to be a complete woman for a man—is heterosexual, and it is more this desire in combination with her transsex that kills her: not as a homosexual man, then, but as a transsexual woman whose desire is heterosexual—or, as *the failure to be* (an ontological failure) a biological woman.

It is therefore equally inadequate to read Venus's death as equivalent to that of a woman of color, as Butler does in the second instance: "If Venus wants to become a woman, and cannot overcome being a Latina, then Venus is treated by the symbolic in precisely the ways in which women of color are treated" (*BTM* 131). Without disputing that women (of color or white) can be treated identically to Venus, and while underlining that it is crucial that Venus's passing be acknowledged as double-leveled—a race and sex crossing—again, it is not for *being* a woman of color but for failing to be one that Venus is murdered; it is the crossing, the trans movement that provokes her erasure. Her death is indexical of an order that cannot contain crossings, a body in transition off the map of three binary axes—sex (male or female), sexuality (heterosexual or homosexual), and race (of color or white): a light-skinned

Latina transsexual body under construction as heterosexual and female. At work in Venus's murder is not fear of the same or the other but fear of bodily crossing, of the movement in between sameness and difference: not homo- but transphobia, where "trans" here signifies the multileveled status of her crossing. This interstitial space is not foregrounded in Butler's reading of Venus's death.

   If for Butler Venus's death represents the triumph of the symbolic, "Gender is Burning" discovers the symbolic asserting its norms through Venus even before this moment—in particular, in her expressed desires to become a "complete woman," to marry and attain financial security. The second two are of course crucially dependent on the first: a Latina transsexual's desires for sexed realness and domestic comfort. It is to set the realization of these desires in motion that Venus is turning tricks to earn enough for her lower surgery, sex work being a not uncommon, indeed often the only means by which poor/working-class male-to-females can afford to change sex. For Butler these desires reveal the extent to which Venus, even before her murder, is subject to "hegemonic constraint":

> Clearly, the denaturalization of sex, in its multiple senses, does not imply a libera-
> tion from hegemonic constraint: when Venus speaks of her desire to become a whole
> woman, to find a man and have a house in the suburbs with a washing machine, we
> may well question whether the denaturalization of gender and sexuality that she per-
> forms, and performs well, culminates in a reworking of the normative framework of
> heterosexuality.
>
> (*BTM* 133)

Venus's fantasy as a Latina transsexual of becoming "real" (both achieving coherent sexed embodiment and middle-class security) and her corporeal progress in realizing this fantasy mark her out from the drag ball performers who "do" realness and who "resist transsexual-ity" (*BTM* 136). Butler's presupposition is twofold here: first, that inherent to *doing* realness is an agency resistant to and transformative of hegemonic constraint that the desire to *be* real lacks; and following this, that the transsexual's crossing signifies a failure to be subversive and transgressive of hegemonic constraint where it *ought* to be. Hegemony constrains Venus through the "normative framework of heterosexuality." If resisting transsexuality produces a denaturalizing agency, it is because in Butler's scheme transsexuality is understood, by definition, to be constrained by heterosexuality. By extension, to fail to resist transsexual-ity fully (as Venus does in hoping for a sex change) is to reliteralize sex (to be rather than perform it) according to the workings of heterosexual melancholia. While Venus's murder symptomizes the triumph of the heterosexual matrix, in her desires Venus is duped by this same heterosexual ideology into believing that a vagina will make her a woman. The het-erosexual matrix is therefore already asserting its hegemony in Venus's transsexuality even before her death.

   From this scheme it might appear that the binary of heterosexual = literalizing/ queer = performative is still in operation in *Bodies That Matter*, with transsexuality stand-ing in for the first term. The transgendered subject, here exemplified in the transsexual, would accordingly appear simply to have been switched from one side of the binary to the other since *Gender Trouble*. Yet Butler's essay works not to reinforce but to demonstrate the ambivalence of this binary, to delimit (not negate) the queer performativity of transgender. It is the literal ambivalence of Venus's transsexual body that allows for this new theoretical ambivalence. Venus's death represents the triumph of hegemonic norms only as it simulta-neously illustrates Venus denaturalizing these norms: it is a "killing performed by the sym-bolic that would eradicate those phenomena that require an opening up of the possibilities for the resignification of sex." Venus's body, with penis intact, is such a phenomenon that would resignify sex. Even in her death, because of her transsexual incoherence between penis and passing-as-a-woman, Venus holds out for Butler the promise of queer subversion, precisely as her transsexual trajectory is incomplete. In her desire to complete this trajectory (to acquire a vagina), however, Venus would cancel out this potential and succumb to the embrace of hegemonic naturalization. In other words, what awards Venus the status of potential resignifier of the symbolic in Butler's scheme is the fact that Venus doesn't get to complete her narrative trajectory and realize her desires, because she still has a penis at her death. What matters for Butler is the oscillation between the literality of Venus's body and the figurative marks of her gender. Conversely, Venus's desire to close down this tension (what I am calling her desire for sexed realness, for embodied sex) curtails her capacity to resignify the symbolic. That Butler figures Venus as subversive for the same reason that Butler claims she is killed, and considers indicative of hegemonic constraint the desires that, if realized might have kept Venus at least from this instance of violence, is not only strikingly ironic, it verges on critical perversity. Butler's essay locates transgressive value in that which makes the subject's real life most unsafe.

Butler's essay itself is structured on an ambivalence toward transsexuality in its relation to the literal, caught (twice over), both between reading transsexuality literally and metaphorically and between reading the transsexual as literalizing and deliteralizing. That Butler assigns Venus the function of ambivalence in her effect on the literal is encapsulated in the essay's reliance on the theme of transubstantiation, a term that is conjoined to transsexuality twice in the essay, that indeed stands in for transsexuality: first, in reference to Venus; and second, in reference to Jennie Livingston's camera. First, then, Butler writes that Venus's transsexual fantasy of realness is one of transubstantiation: "Now Venus, Venus Xtravaganza, she seeks a certain transubstantiation of gender in order to find an imaginary man who will designate a class and race privilege that to-female transsexual as model perfect, the photographic camera metaphorically phallicizes Livingston's body. For in representing the male-to-female transsexual as woman as object of desire, Livingston, Butler writes, "assumes the power of 'having the phallus.'" (*BTM* 135). The camera's feminization/eroticization of the male-to-female transsexual circulates the phallus from transsexual to lesbian, a circulation that amounts to a "transsexualization of lesbian desire": "What would it mean to say that Octavia is Jennie Livingston's kind of girl? Is the category or, indeed, 'the position' of white lesbian disrupted by such a claim? If this is the production of the black transsexual for the exoticizing white gaze, is it not also the transsexualization of lesbian desire?" (*BTM* 135). Livingston's desire for the transsexual is apparently also her identification with the transsexual; or rather the moment enacts an exchange of identities, with the "real girl" acquiring a phallus (becoming transsexualized) as she represents the transsexual as a "real girl." Extending her metaphorization of transsexuality, Butler designates the camera (photographic symbolizing cinematic) the tool of this (s)exchange, the "surgical instrument and operation through which the transubstantiation occurs" that produces Octavia as woman, which "transplants" the phallus from Octavia's body to Livingston's lesbian body.

Transsexuality and transubstantiation are thus brought together for a second time in Butler's essay, now in a metaphorical context. As in Butler's discussion of Venus's fantasy, transsexuality is again implicitly defined as, rendered equivalent to, transubstantiation. How is the double dynamic of literalization and deliteralization played out in this second moment of transsexualization as transubstantiation? I suggest that Butler's reading here again depends on the literal sexed ambivalence of the preoperative male-to-female transsexual body (the woman with a penis). Yet Butler's metaphor of transsexualization, its application to the lesbian body—and the refiguring of surgery into the camera's look—in effect displaces the materiality of transsexuality, and thus the materiality of sex, to the level of figurative. First, in figuring the phallus as circulated from Octavia to Livingston, the metaphor of transsexualization pivots on, and actually originates in, Octavia's penis. We know that Octavia, like Venus, is indeed preoperative for likewise in her narrative Octavia speaks of looking forward to the surgery that will make her a "complete" woman. However, as in its process of circulation in Butler's essay this penis becomes the phallus (Livingston's camera is said to accord her the phallus, not the penis), this penis is clearly subject in its translation to Lacanian sublimation itself. Butler's metaphor of transsexualization depends upon this crucial substitution of fleshly part with symbolic signifier, a confusion between phallus and penis that certainly does not take place in the film. For while Octavia (like Venus) may yet have a penis, in no way can she be said to "have the phallus": that is, in no way is she accorded or does she assume the position of delegate of the symbolic order. Conversely, while (presumably) Livingston has no penis, her capacity to represent Octavia, Venus, and the rest of the cinematic subjects as embodied others via her authority as disembodied overseer, as hooks's essay argues so convincingly, situates her precisely in this position of the symbolic's delegate—the one who appears to have the phallus. In the context of this film by a white lesbian about black and Latino/a gay men, drag queens, and transsexuals, the penis and phallus might be said to remain not only discrete but oppositional. Worlds apart from her subjects in her whiteness, her middle-classness, her educatedness, and her "real" femaleness, Livingston's position behind the camera is that of an authority with absolute powers of representation.

Moreover, Livingston appears to wield this phallic power most heavily in her representation of the transsexuals, Octavia and Venus, in particular in her representation of their fantasies. The section in the film in which Octavia and Venus are cataloguing their desiderata stands as the most explicitly edited and authored moments in the film. Their sentences, most of which begin "I want," are rapidly intercut with each other's and their visual images likewise interwoven. The technique suggests an identity of their fantasies—not only that there is a generic transsexual fantasy but that the transsexual might be conceived according to what she *lacks*; "I want" reveals all that the subject lacks. At the same time, in its location of these scenes, the cinematic apparatus occults its own framing/authoring function. Both Octavia and Venus are filmed reclining on beds in bedrooms (the viewer is led to believe the subjects' own); Octavia is even dressed for bed. The setting allows the audience to assume an intimacy with the subjects, to forget the extent to which these moments are mediated through Livingston's white female gaze—exactly the dynamic of occultation that provides fodder for hooks's critique. Elsewhere in the film it becomes evident how Livingston's camera mediates what of their lives the subjects reveal. Before her death, for instance, Venus informs Livingston that she no longer works the streets, a claim that her death, of course, proves drastically untrue. (The question of whether Venus would have continued to work the streets to save for her surgery, *of whether Venus would have been killed, had Livingston contracted her* along with the film's subjects as actors is ultimately unanswerable, though the fatal ending of Venus's narrative demands its asking.) To summarize, then: in having the power to represent the other and conceal this power, Livingston not only "has the phallus," this having enables her to represent the transsexual other—Octavia and Venus—as crucially lacking: not so much in spite of, as because of their penises. Along with race and class, the crucial structuring difference between Livingston on the one hand and Venus and Octavia on the other is sexed coherence or biological realness: the difference between the nontransgendered and the embodied transgendered subject.

If phallus and penis are antithetical in *Paris is Burning*, Livingston's "phallicization" in no way reveals her embodiment—even allegorically—as Butler claims. The difference between reality and the allegorical, between the fleshly intractability of the penis and the transcendence of the phallus could not be more marked. As her position behind it renders her unrepresented, only a disembodied voice popping questions, the camera is precisely Livingston's means to disembodiment not to her embodiment. Thus hooks's critique of the filmmaker's bodily erasure still holds. Indeed, Butler's allegorization of Livingston's body in the very vehicle for her disembodiment only places further out of reach the filmmaker's literal corporeality, the notion that Livingston has a "body that matters." And although rendering the camera a lesbian phallus might well disrupt Livingston's identity as a lesbian, it does nothing to disrupt its transcendent whiteness: the reason why hooks has problems with its overseeing position in the first place. Indeed, Butler's wish to curtail hooks's critique of Livingston's disembodiment seems queerly motivated (in both senses)—that is, until she reveals an identification with Livingston: both "white Jewish lesbian[s] from Yale" (*BTM* 133). This moment—exceptionally autobiographical for Butler—suggests that perhaps something quite personal is at stake in Butler's discovering an exception to the disembodied gaze of the auteur representing transgendered subjects. For Butler as much as for Livingston the personal investment in this representation of transgendered subjects may well be there; but the point is that in neither is it ever shown and in both this elision of whatever autobiographical stakes there are exacts the cost of objectification and derealization on the represented subjects.

Most significantly, the essay's metaphorical shifting of transsexuality from Venus's body to Livingston's camera displaces transsexuality to a realm that has nothing to do with the materiality of the body. In the context of a discussion of a film during the making of which one of the protagonists is killed for her transsexuality, for the literal configuration of her sexed body, this sublimation of transsexuality appears more prominent and, in my experience anyway, proves the most disturbing moment in Butler's oeuvre. The critic's metaphorization of the transsexual body transcends the literality of transsexuality in precisely a way in which Venus cannot—Venus who is killed for her literal embodiment of sexual difference. Even in the film we might notice that the literality of Venus's transsexual body and the facticity of her death are already subject to a glossing over. As hooks points out, the film glides over the reality of Venus's death, the moment is rapidly overridden by the spectacle of the ball, and, now that she can no longer function in the service of this spectacle, Venus is abandoned. Indeed, it might be said that not only does the filmic narrative fail to mourn Venus, it markedly includes no scenes of others' bereavement over Venus. We simply have Angie Xtravaganza's terse account of what happened to Venus overlaying footage of Venus filmed on the Christopher Street piers while she was still alive, this montage itself threatening to deny the reality, the finality of Venus's death. In metaphorizing transsexuality, Butler inadvertently repeats something of this deliteralization of the subject, her body, and her death. The substance of the transsexual body is sublimated in the move from the literal to the figurative. In the critical failure to "mourn" her death, Venus's body (surely the lost object of *Paris is Burning*), the most prominent representation we have in this film of the pain and anguish of embodying the experience of being differently sexed, is encrypted in Livingston's camera. And what is not kept in view in the film or the theory on it is the intractable materiality of that body in its present state and its peculiar sex.

Queer Feminism and Critical Impropriety: Transgender as Transitional Object?

> The institution of the "proper object" takes place, as usual, through a mundane sort of violence.
> —Judith Butler, "Against Proper Objects"

In her work since *Bodies that Matter* Butler demonstrates how the founding of lesbian and gay studies as a methodology distinct from feminism has involved a privileging of subjects and categories to the exclusion of others. Her essay in the "More Gender Trouble" issue of *differences* edited by her in 1994, "Against Proper Objects," critiques the way in which lesbian and gay studies has arrogated sexuality as its "proper object" of study, defining itself through and against feminism by assigning gender as feminism's object of study. What comes to appear quite critically improper in Butler's essay is this very investment in theoretical property: both the assurance with which that attribution of the object to the other is made (in effect a restriction of the other to the object) and the claims staked in the name of this attribution and restriction—namely, lesbian and gay studies' claims to "include and supersede" feminism.

Butler's essay implies that it might never be possible to claim methodological distinctness without bringing into play a degree of aggression, that every theory that grounds itself by allocating "proper objects" will be prone to this kind of critical impropriety. Undoubtedly, my attempts to wrest the transsexual from the queer inscription of transgender—and here, my criticisms of Butler's writing on Venus—are not free of aggression. From the point of view of this project, what subtends the difference in such readings is quite primal (theoretical, political, and admittedly personal): concerns about territory, belonging, creating homes; indeed, the extent to which identity is formed through our investment in external "objects"—a fundamental tenet of psychoanalysis, that definition depends on defining and "owning" objects. The question is perhaps quite simple: Where (best) does the transsexual belong? In seeking to carve out a space for transgender/transsexual studies distinct from queer studies, inevitably terrain must be mapped out and borders drawn up (a fact that doesn't render them uncrossable). Representations, subjects, and bodies (such as Venus) serve as the all-important flags that mark the territory claimed. It is additionally inevitable that the establishment of methodological grounds involves the attempt early on to circumscribe neighboring methodologies and approaches, the emphasizing of what *they* do *not* as opposed to what *we do*.

Significantly, "Against Proper Objects" conjures transsexuality in order to complicate articulations of methodological difference (although Butler's language of "domestication" suggests not my frontierscale struggles but tiffs in the kitchen). Butler presents transsexuality as a category that, because of its "important dissonance" with homosexuality (tantalizingly, but importantly for my readings which follow, she doesn't say what this is), falls outside the domain of lesbian and gay studies ("APO" 11). Insofar as lesbian and gay studies delimits its proper object to sexuality and "refuses the domain of gender, it disqualifies itself from the analysis of transgendered sexuality altogether" ("APO" 11). Transsexuality and transgender are invoked as illustrations of the exclusions that lesbian and gay studies has performed in fixing its proper object as sexuality. Transsexuality and transgender number among the categories of "sexual minorities" Butler rightly understands Gayle Rubin insisting in 1984 made necessary a "radical theory of the politics of sexuality." These categories, Butler believes, get sidelined, ironically in lesbian and gay studies' appropriation of Rubin's essay as a foundational text. As I outlined at the beginning of this chapter, my sense of the role of transgender in lesbian and gay studies is quite different: that is, the figure of transgender has, rather, proven crucial to the installation of lesbian and gay studies—its installation *as* queer. Even work purporting to focus exclusively on sexuality and not gender—I suggested Sedgwick's in particular—implicitly engages this transgendered figure and, correlatively, the axis of gender. (In her other mention of transgender and transsexuality Butler writes of Sedgwick's antihomophobic critique that "[b]y separating the notion of gender from sexuality, [it] narrows the notion of sexual minorities offered by Rubin, distancing queer studies from the consideration of transgendered persons, transgendered sexualities, transvestism, cross-dressing, and cross-gendered definition" ["APO" 24, n. 8]). Although it strongly suggests that "an analysis of sexual relations apart from an analysis of gender relations is [not] possible," Butler's essay does not address how lesbian and gay studies might *already* be engaged in gender analyses, if largely unconsciously ("APO" 9). Indeed, toward the end of Butler's interview of Gayle Rubin in the same "More Gender Trouble" issue of *differences*, Rubin provocatively hints that Butler's critique of lesbian and gay studies' exclusion of gender might amount to a tilting at windmills:

> As for this great methodological divide you are talking about, between feminism and gay/lesbian studies, I do not think I would accept that distribution of interests, activities, objects and methods. I cannot . . . imagine a gay and lesbian studies that is not interested in gender as well as sexuality. . . . I am not persuaded that there is widespread acceptance of this division of intellectual labor between feminism, on the one hand, and gay and lesbian studies on the other.

That s/he has received considerably less critical attention than the cross-dresser or drag artist(e), that s/he has not been subject to the same deliberate and concentrated queer recuperation, and indeed, as is demonstrated in Butler's own work on Venus, that s/he is more likely to be deployed to signal the *unqueer* possibilities of cross-gender identifications, suggests that, above all transgendered subjects, the transsexual is more of the limit case for queer studies: the object that exceeds its purview. Yet my sense is that the reasons for transsexuality's exceeding queer lie not so much in queer's refusal of the category of gender (and thus transgender), as Butler argues, as in queer's poststructuralist problems with literality and referentiality that the category of transsexuality makes manifest—particular in relation to the sexed body. Butler's metaphorical displacement of the literality of Venus's sex can serve to exemplify just this.

Indeed, according to Butler, it must remain "an open question whether 'queer' can achieve these same goals of inclusiveness" imagined by Rubin's radical theory of sexual politics, whether queer studies can incorporate all of the "sexual minorities" among which transgender and transsexuality might be categorized ("APO" 11). For Butler the concern is queer's *capacity* to include, a question about queer's elasticity, about how far the term "queer" will stretch. What is not a concern is whether queer *should* even attempt to expand; expansion, inclusion, incorporation are automatically invested with value. One wonders to what extent this queer inclusiveness of transgender and transsexuality is an inclusiveness *for* queer rather than for the trans subject: the mechanism by which queer can sustain its very queerness—prolong the queerness of the moment—by periodically adding subjects who appear ever queerer precisely by virtue of their marginality in relation to queer. For does not this strategy of inclusiveness ensure the conferral on queer of the very open-endedness, the mobility, and—in the language of "Against Proper Objects"—the very means by which to "rift" methodological "grounds" that queer has come to symbolize? If, as Butler writes, "normalizing the queer would be, after all, its sad finish," the project of expansion enables queer to resist this normalization (what Butler fears will be "the institutional domestication of queer thinking") that would herald its end ("APO" 21). Yet if we conceive of "finish" and "end" here not as a limitation in time but a limitation in institutional space, this limited reach is inevitable and arguably necessary for the beginnings of other methodologies, for reading other narratives from other perspectives.

What Butler does not consider is to what extent—and on what occasions—transgendered and transsexual subjects and methodologies might not wish for inclusion under the queer banner. "Against Proper Objects" assesses inclusion and the resistance to inclusion solely from the perspective of queer; it does not imagine possible resistance stemming from the putatively excluded "sexual minorities." Our discussions should address not only—or perhaps not primarily—queer's elasticity but also what is gained and lost for nonlesbian and gay subjects and methodologies in joining the queer corporation. In the case of transsexuality there are substantive features that its trajectory often seeks out that queer has made its purpose to renounce: that is, not only reconciliation between sexed materiality and gendered identification but also assimilation, belonging in the body and in the world—precisely the kinds of "home" that Butler's essay holds at bay in its critical trooping of "domestication." There is much about transsexuality that must remain irreconcilable to queer: the specificity of transsexual experience; the importance of the flesh to self; the difference between sex and gender identity; the desire to pass as "really-gendered" in the world without trouble; perhaps above all, as I explore in my next chapter, a particular experience of the body that can't simply transcend (or transubstantiate) the literal.

Since *Gender Trouble*, "domestication" has figured as something of a specter in Butler's work. Domestication appears to represent the assigning of subjects and methodologies to specific categorical homes, the notion that there is an institutional place to which they belong. For the Butler of 1990 what was at stake was the domestication of gender, and concomitantly the domestication of feminism through gender's domestication beyond sexuality. *Gender Trouble* sought "to facilitate a political convergence of feminism, gay and lesbian perspectives on gender, and poststructuralist theory" to produce a "complexity of gender[,] . . . an interdisciplinary and postdisciplinary set of discourses in order to resist the *domestication* of gender studies or women['s] studies within the academy and to radicalize the notion of feminist critique" (*GT* xiii; my emphasis). As a means of resisting gender/women's studies' domestication, *Gender Trouble* marshaled lesbian and gay sexuality and, as I have suggested, lesbian and gay genders, in effect troubling or queering gender. In analyzing the way in which the sex/gender system is constructed through the naturalization of heterosexuality and vice versa, *Gender Trouble* performed its work in an interstitial space between feminism and lesbian and gay studies, producing a new methodological genre—hence my term for this: queer feminism. In this sense *Gender Trouble* constituted an attempt to queer feminism. Yet although Butler's work might be said to have always conceived of domestication—what we might term object-constancy to push further on the psychoanalytic metaphor—as restrictive, it is interesting to note that in 1994 it is no longer *feminist* but *queer* studies that she perceives to be under threat of domestication: the shift indexes the change in values of the currencies of these methodologies, the ways in which queer and gender studies have "circumscribed" feminism. In "Against Proper Objects" it is (trans)gender that returns as the supplement to trouble the domestication of (homo)sexuality, gender that "troubles" queer. This shift in Butler's theoretical "object-cathexis" is a sure a sign of queer's institutionalization (Oedipalization? with feminism as [M]Other?) if ever there was one.

To resist queer's incorporation of trans identities and trans studies is not to refuse the value of institutional alliances and coalitions (in the form of shared conferences, journals, courses, and so on). But an alliance, unlike a corporation, suggests a provisional or strategic union between parties whose different interests ought not to be—indeed, cannot totally be—merged, sublimated for cohering—or queering—the whole. In closing, it needs emphasizing that it is precisely queer's investment in the figure of transgender in its own institutionalization—and above all the methodological and categorical crossings of Butler's queer feminism—that have made it possible to begin articulating the transsexual as a theoretical subject. It can be said that, in its very origins and its early attempts at self-definition, transgender studies is allied with queer.

20 Getting Disciplined

What's Trans★ About Queer Studies Now?

Cáel M. Keegan

In this 2020 essay published in the *Journal of Homosexuality*, Cáel M. Keegan traces how trans★ studies have (and have not) been incorporated into the institutional frameworks of women's studies and queer studies in the North American academy. He argues that trans★ studies is posited by them as "an epistemic blockage, a distraction from proper objects, a hindrance to customary methods" in queer and feminist approaches that therefore "must be disciplined." While women's studies programs now routinely incorporate trans content, Keegan contends, this inclusion is often predicated on the imagined capacity of trans practices to disrupt fixed notions of gender—a disruptiveness that undermines "woman" as the presumed referent of women's studies, which must then be defensively reasserted. Queer studies, itself often institutionally subsumed within departments of "women's, gender, and sexuality studies," similarly conceptualizes transness as merely a disruptive potential. It often reduces "transgender" and "transsexual" to allegories of gender's inherent instability rather than recognizing these as terms through which some people understand and enact their embodied experiences of gender. In making this argument, Keegan draws on a strand of trans scholarship dating back to the 1990s to highlight how trans★ studies has been utilized in partial and often dismissive ways. He updates and revises this line of thought to acknowledge and account for the rapid institutionalization of trans studies in the 2010s.

Conjunction

(1) *used to introduce something contrasting with what has already been mentioned*
(2) *used to indicate the impossibility of anything other than what is being stated*
(3) *used to introduce a response expressing a feeling of surprise or anger*

Preposition

(1) *except; apart from; other than*

Adverb

(1) *no more than; only*

Noun

(1) *an argument against something; an objection.*

(Shraya, "often brown feels like but")

Interdisciplinarity consists in creating a new object that belongs to no one.

(Barthes, 1972, p. 3)

DOI: 10.4324/9781003206255-25

What is the position of trans★ studies in queer studies now?[1] Thirteen years ago, David L. Eng, Jack Halberstam, and José Esteban Muñoz asked "What's Queer About Queer Studies Now?" (2005) in a special double issue of *Social Text* devoted to examining the upstart field's promises and roadblocks. By 2005, queer studies had become well aware of its rigidification around the investigation of sexuality as a "proper object" (Butler, 1994). Responding to this emerging disciplinary trajectory, the three editors requested a queer studies that would move away from an exclusive focus on sexuality as a "privileged site of critical inquiry" (p. 4), calling for a renewed, intersectional queer studies "calibrated to a firm understanding of queer as a political metaphor without a fixed referent" (p. 1). Yet despite the strong rejoinders contemporaneous transgender scholars had made to queer studies' narrowing focus on sexuality and its allegorizations of trans experience (Namaste, 2000; Prosser, 1998; Stryker, 2004), "transgender" and "transsexuality" are suspiciously absent from the piece. To the extent that "What's Queer?" subsumes the earliest strains of trans★ studies under the aegis of something called "queer studies," it is apparently without attention to the difference and specificity of trans—a "conflation sometimes made because of the suspicion that gender *means* sexuality, that gender . . . is merely a cover story for not only sex but sexuality as well" (Salamon, 2010, p. 103). In this early and formative accounting of the field's promise, trans★ studies is thus obscured within the story of what queer studies can and should do by the precise focus on sexuality the editors seek to address.

To those invested in trans★ studies securing a place in the academy, institutional trajectories since "What's Queer?" seem promising: Over the past 10 years, trans★ studies has gained the status of a recognized field, now boasting two critical readers, a Duke University Press journal, an international conference, and a handful of hires and postdocs at prestigious universities. Courses investigating transgender identities and cultures—if not courses in critical trans★ theories—appear in many university curricula, often within queer studies and women's studies programs. Academia appears to have arrived at a "transgender tipping point" (Steinmetz, 2014) beyond which trans★ studies may find a disciplinary home. Yet the pace and practice of this arrival have been wildly uneven: running fully ahead in elite intellectual centers, forced by student activism in others, taken up through discourses of weak inclusion in many, and often shot through with intergenerational and disciplinary hostilities. The increasing pressure to formalize queer studies and women's studies programs within the neoliberal university also presents epistemic and political barriers to trans★ studies, which is not equivalent to and values specific breaks from the frameworks of both queer theory and academic feminism. Trans★ studies scholars and pedagogues working within queer and women's studies contexts often run the risk of "becoming the problem by bringing up the problem" (Nicolazzo, 2017, p. 212) of trans★ studies' incomplete welcome in these spaces. Given the precarity under which trans lives are lived and trans★ studies is often conducted, is this partial and ragged inclusion something that trans★ studies "cannot not want?" (Spivak, 1996, p. 28).

Inspired by trans of color poet Shraya's (2016) piece "often brown feels like *but*," this essay maps the disciplinary scenarios trans★ studies may face as it is increasingly incorporated into queer studies programs, often housed within women's studies departments. These fields have rapidly professionalized over the past two decades, producing new modes of disciplinary power that may seek to include or cite trans★ studies without fully welcoming its specific material or political investments. Under such conditions, trans★ studies may be perceived as an epistemic blockage, a distraction from proper objects, or a hindrance to customary methods that must be disciplined.[2] We might conceptualize trans★ studies' discursive position in such a disciplinary scenario as *but*. This *but* would perform multiple functions: As a conjunction, *but* might alert us to the existence of a barrier or problem through contrast, surprise, or the assertion of impossibility, only to be viewed as constituting a barrier or problem itself. As a preposition or adverb, *but* might insist on trans★ studies' discreteness or specificity, only to be dismissed as too narrow or limited in scope. As a noun, *but* might be imposed on trans★ studies to frame its claims as merely oppositional, rather than for the creation of new conditions or models. In all these instances, *but* may be perceived as intolerance or frustration by a disciplinary arrangement that cannot acknowledge its own force: *but* becomes both what trans★ studies must say and how trans★ studies might be reciprocally dismissed.

To the extent that such disciplinary conditions exist, trans★ studies might therefore prove "too difficult" (Ahmed, 2014, p. 4) for its institutional hosts, being received only as an interruption, an outburst, a disruptive body. One can presume to include *but*, but such inclusions are often predicated on a silence: a tacit agreement that the *but* will be withdrawn in exchange. If it is not, trouble can follow. The bad feeling of this scene can then be ascribed to the *but* as an "annihilation" (Awkward-Rich, 2017, p. 822) of the terms presumed necessary to any conversation. The *but* might then be "heard as a complaint, which is not actually being heard" (Ahmed, 2017, p. 4). If so, trans★ studies might become a *but* beyond which lies nothing meriting investigation: "If you are heard as complaining then what you say is dismissible. . . . When you are heard as complaining you lose the *about*: what you are speaking *about* is not heard" (Ahmed, 2017, p. 4). The result is a sort of epistemic conundrum: To those constructing and enforcing the disciplinary arrangement, the *but* might be perceived as a form of discursive violence—but not articulating the *but* could be, for transgender bodies, violence of another and far more dire kind. "What does it cost to tell the truth" (Wilchins, 2006), trans★ studies might wonder, when "truth" is a shape that cannot come out of one's mouth as something that might be heard? We do not (yet) know what trans★ studies might become outside of these epistemic confrontations.

Trans★ studies has long been concerned with narratology—with the project of locating narrative structures that will adequately allow for the existence of trans★ bodies and becomings. These concerns arise directly from the epistemic and political needs of transgender people, some of whose lives have only recently begun to count in the accounting of which lives matter. The need for a "good story" is the need for a schema in which one can appear as other than a problem: a good story is one in which we can say something other than *but*. [. . .]

In what follows, I trace an implicit double-bind[3] trans★ studies is faced with as it is invited to join either women's studies or queer studies contexts within the academy. Although the patterns I describe may not be descriptive of every institutional scenario, I seek here to map the epistemic and institutional structures through which women's studies and queer studies might interpellate and move to include trans★ studies. Because these fields each solicit trans★ studies incompletely and to incommensurate purposes, their increasing compression within the academy may exert further discipline on trans★ studies, which must take up contradictory performative positions in relation to each of their expectations. To the extent that women's studies seeks the liberation of women and others (gay men, lesbians) who are oppressed by sex "like women," trans★ studies must perform a *but* that insists against the foundational schema of sexual subordination (M > F), saying *but* gender is *not real like that*. However, in response to queer studies' investment in deconstructing the gender binary (M/F) to unravel heteronormativity, trans★ studies must turn inside out, articulating a constative *but* that asserts *but* gender is *real like this*. This double-bind threatens to strand trans★ studies in an epistemic dilemma that repeats the disciplinary language games transgender subjects are often forced to play (Spade, 2006). Trans★ studies can only thrive, I will claim, in a situation that gives it space to break from the epistemic structures of women's studies and queer studies (Halley, 2006, p. 264). Unless such a space is intentionally created, trans★ studies must retort *but* to the frameworks of both disciplinary invitations.

Disciplinary Position One: Suppression

In the academy, trans★ studies is perhaps most powerfully solicited by women's studies—a field that has labored over the past decade to add "gender" and "sexuality" to its proper objects. Although it has expanded its topical purview to include both LGBT studies and queer theory, areas of this revamped field (sometimes called women, gender, and sexuality studies) have simultaneously become theoretically rigidified by incorporation into the neoliberal university,[4] largely under the guises of "diversity" and "equity." Required to make itself legible to the university in order to secure a home, women's studies has sometimes found it difficult to "sustain gender as a critical self-reflexive category rather than a normative or nominal one" (Brown, 2005, pp. 23–24). Because it increasingly wants to talk about gender and is often compelled to tell a good diversity story, women's studies might solicit trans★ studies as uniquely suited to analyzing the fixed taxonomies of gender. But because women's studies is also a field "whose very essence depends upon gender to conform to just such a fixed economy" (Salamon, 2010, p. 98), it may simultaneously make a number of compensatory moves to close trans★ studies off, working to retain a "fantasy of itself as a field with epistemological and methodological coherence" (Noble, 2012, p. 53). Women's studies programs attempting to incorporate trans★ studies might thus position "women" and "trans" as discrete categories (Malatino, 2015, p. 399), moving to include trans while also retaining the primacy of "women." This strategy ensures that trans★ studies cannot raise the question of what the category of "woman" might contain or whether the object ("woman") actually exists as invoked. Rather than being taken up into the heart of the field's analytic, trans★ studies becomes a "special guest" (Malatino, 2015, p. 399), welcomed into the conversation through a "woman plus" model that strands it on the margin of what is cognizable. Where such strategies are in place, they mark "a self-generating, discipline-sustaining, and disciplining epistemological practice" (Wallach Scott, 2008, p. 51) that restricts what trans★ studies can ask and say.

The seeming paradox of "trans★/feminism" is evidence of this precise situation: As trans★ studies has appeared to arrive in the academy, it has also been met with intensifying force from within more disciplinary feminist orientations, which want to speak about and at trans bodies and identities without offering the space to mount a reply. Much trans★ studies work addressing this situation comes as rebuttal, offering either a contrasting account or a flat objection. For example, Stryker and Bettcher (2016) made clear in their introduction to the *Trans/Feminisms* special double issue of *Transgender Studies Quarterly (TSQ)* that the issue was designed as a retort to Jeffreys's (2014) recent cissexist work, *Gender Hurts: A Feminist Analysis of the Politics of Transgenderism*. Jeffreys's title reiterates the suppressive strategy by which something called "feminism" gets to talk about and at trans subjects while protecting itself from incursion by something called "the politics of transgenderism." Because of the university's institutional will to inclusion, women's studies appears to be at least partially caught in a similar bind—pressed to include and speak about trans★ studies while also needing to suppress its more critical energies through a foundational and self-generated exclusion (Noble, 2012, p. 43). As Cameron Awkward-Rich (2017) put it, "The problem is not so much that (some) feminists would like (trans) gone. Rather, the problem is that (trans) is here, and now we all have to figure out how to live with that" (p. 832). It is not just that trans★ studies challenges the traditional referent of women's studies as a field (queer studies does this as well), but that the political stakes of the epistemic scene render it particularly pressed to defend the legitimacy and place of that challenge. For trans★ studies, to find oneself in such a situation might feel impossible—or, rather, it might produce the feeling that one is being made into an impossibility. In such a disciplinary scenario, trans★ studies might turn to women's studies and say, but—you invited me.

The situation of trans★ studies vis-à-vis women's studies is important to queer studies for a number of reasons: Women's studies departments are increasingly absorbing and/or creating queer studies curricula at both the undergraduate and graduate levels. LGBTQ studies, an amalgam of LGBT studies and queer studies, is often added to women's studies programs through an ostensibly shared commitment to sexual subordination models —the asymptotic assumption that ending patriarchy (M > F) will also end heteronormativity. In this interdisciplinary arrangement, queer is often deployed as a filter through which trans★ studies can be rendered amenable to feminisms that presume sexual subordination as a shared epistemological mode.[5] Because queer threatens to displace "women" through an implicit focus on gay men (Awkward-Rich, 2017, p. 832), women's studies might be prompted to use "queer" to tell a story about how all oppressed subjects are oppressed like women are—i.e., as classes that fail to be hegemonically masculine—thus preserving the central position of "woman" as referent. Trans★ studies might then be affixed to the end of women's studies considerations through the addition of "queer" as a secondary and supporting body of subordination theory, coming only after feminism and on the far side of its trailing objects of concern—"LGB."

To the extent that queer studies is disciplined by the university to accept these frameworks, it cannot account for the unique positionalities of trans bodies and politics, and so trans★ studies must respond, insisting but gender is not real like that. Trans oppression cannot be conceptualized using a subordination model in which one gender or sexuality unilaterally oppresses the others, as if bodies simply are certain genders/sexes unquestionably, or as if binary genders/sexes map neatly onto the operations of power. Subordination feminisms and their disciplinary counterparts must fix gender in order to link it to the binary power relations that undergird their foundational critiques of patriarchy (M > F) and heteronormativity. They therefore need to keep presuming that there are such things as "women" and "homosexuals" (Halley, 2006, p. 113), categories that trans threatens to scramble in its undercutting of the ability to tell which gender or sex is where. To fully acknowledge trans★ studies would be to upend the entire subordination model's investment in gender as a way to know that all women are oppressed as a class, or that all gays or lesbians are oppressed as a class. In a women's studies + LGBTQ studies partnership struck through sexual subordination models, W, L, and G will need T to stay quiet to retain their coherence as categories based on the legibility of gender and sex. [. . .]

Disciplinary Position Two: Citation

Given the disciplinary scenario potentially unfolding within women's studies, trans★ studies might look to queer studies programs unaffiliated with women's studies departments as places to find purchase. Queer studies has indeed been more hospitable to trans★ studies, although often only as an "addendum" (Love, 2014, p. 174) to its chief inquiry—sexuality. Because queer studies tends to privilege sexual orientation as "the primary means of differing from heteronormativity" (Stryker, 2004, p. 214), it often struggles to apprehend trans phenomena and trans oppression as uniquely about both gender identity and sex assignment. Instead, queer studies has historically deployed the category of "transgender" to "contain all gender trouble," thereby securing both homosexuality and heterosexuality as "stable and normative categories" (Stryker, 2004, p. 214). Heather Love reflected on queer studies' use of trans phenomena as an evidentiary archive for its theorizations of sex and gender, noting, "Queer studies has not engaged fully with the material conditions of transgender people but has rather used gender nonnormativity as a sign or allegory of queerness" (p. 174). In this specific mode of queer studies, trans gets cited as an example of something else (queer) that supersedes and speaks for it: Rather than moving to suppress trans★ studies through weak forms of inclusion, queer studies may instead invoke and cite trans★ studies to the extent that trans can serve its aims: the dissolution of heteronormativity and thus the undergirding gender binary. [. . .]

Because queer studies tends to understand gender, sexuality, and identity as effects of normative power, it can erode the bases by which trans★ studies might legitimately claim gender as felt or innately experienced, thereby replicating the denial of transgender experience also found in stigmatizing medical and political discourses. In valuing trans phenomena largely when they subvert gender norms, queer studies has historically sorted, cited, and disciplined some portions of trans into itself while rejecting others as retrograde or conformist (crossdressing, genderqueer, and androgyny are welcome; transsexuality is not). Early on, trans★ studies scholars staged strong objections to queer studies' acquisitive treatment of trans as an allegory for the subversion of gender: Hale's (1997) early piece, "Suggested Rules for Non-Transsexuals Writing About Transsexuals, Transsexuality, Transsexualism, or Trans," recommended that researchers and theorists "beware of replicating the following discursive movement: Initial fascination with the exotic; denial of subjectivity, lack of access to dominant discourse; followed by a species of rehabilitation" (p. 1), while Prosser's (1998) *Second Skins: The Body Narratives of Transsexuality* pointed to how queer theory has used transgender to "institutionalize homosexuality as queer" (p. 5), treating trans as "a symptom of the constructedness of the sex/gender system and a figure for the impossibility of this system's achievement of identity" (p. 6). However, it is perhaps Namaste (2000) who best summed up the need to resist queer studies' emerging, citational relationship with trans phenomena in her largely overlooked book *Invisible Lives: The Erasure of Transsexual and Transgendered People*, which opened with the flat thesis that "Queer theory, as it is currently practiced, needs to be rejected for both theoretical and political reasons" (p. 9). While today trans★ studies is increasingly understood as distinct from queer studies and as possessing its own discrete intellectual trajectories and political frameworks, queer theory remains the more privileged and central discourse.

To the extent that queer studies can strike a deal with women's studies to form a feminist queer studies, it may be through an agreement that women's studies abandon subordination models in favor of social construction—a theory that often enjoys near-disciplinary enforcement where "feminism meets queer theory" (Schor & Weed, 1997). In this more recent alignment between "Third Wave" feminist and queer studies epistemologies, it is not sex that subordinates women and those like women to White patriarchal authority, but instead gender norms that occlude everyone from finding new modes of expression and therefore realizing a new society. This scenario posits the dissolution of gender normativity as the very *precondition* for social progress: The thing to be gotten rid of is no longer M > F, but belief in and repetition of M/F as a source of M > F. Some aspects of trans★ studies do indeed fit under and are amenable to a feminist queer studies project: To the extent that it serves a shared aim to move "beyond the binary," trans★ studies can tell a part of the story, although often in a manner that is rendered indistinguishable from queer studies. However, the adoption of social construction as a foundational concept in feminist queer studies might also produce disciplining effects for transgender bodies, which are uniquely "constructed as constructions" (Bettcher, 2013, p. 298) within the theory itself.[6] An alliance between women's studies and queer studies may thus value trans★ studies for its ability to demonstrate gender as performative, but may struggle to hear its specifically gendered or materially embodied claims as *real*.

Any formalization of social construction as the shared episteme by which a feminist queer studies might cohere must be concerning for trans★ studies, which contains strains of theorization and praxis that understand gender to be innately sensed and actual—in other words, constative rather than performative. Within queer studies, especially, social construction and performativity have been historically deployed in a manner that has opened up the constatively articulated aspects of trans embodiment and identity to political dismissal. As Prosser (1998) wrote, "There is much about transsexuality that must remain irreconcilable to queer: (. . .) the importance of flesh to self; the difference between sex and gender identity; the desire to pass as 'real-ly gendered' in the world without trouble; perhaps above all . . . a particular experience of the body that can't simply transcend (or transubstatiate) the literal" (p. 59). In *Split Decisions: How and Why to Take a Break From Feminism*, Halley (2006) produced a structural mapping of this root division, illustrating through citation how and why Prosser's trans★ studies narratology must break from feminist queer studies' Butlerian social construction. While newer formations such as "transgender" and "trans" have attempted to smooth this epistemological gap, the divide between queer studies' emphasis on deconstruction/failure and trans★ studies' focus on reconstruction/recovery (perhaps not of a "natural" sex but an innately sensed one) remains politically active in any tableau enacted between these fields:

Feminist queer theory affirms:	Transsexuality affirms:
The body as effect	The body as material
The body as surface	The body as interior
Seeing; the visible body	Feeling; the sensible body
Sex1 as language	Sex1 as ground
Nature as law (to be subverted)	Nature as object of desire (to be sought)
Homosexual affirmativity	Rehabilitation of heterosexuality
"Social construction"	"Sexed realness . . . embodied sex" (49)
Deconstructions of literality and referentiality	Literality and referentiality (13, 58)
Deconstruction of monolithic signifiers	Reconstruction of bodily integrity as the aim of transition (6)
The unraveling of identity	The consolidation of identity (6)
Iteration, performance	Narrative (beginning, middle, and desired end) (29)
Trouble	Safety
Performance	Passing
Affirmation of the perversions	Affirmation of the normal
Domesticity as law (to be resisted)	Domesticity as object of desire (to be sought) ("territory, belonging creating homes" [56])
Differentiation	Assimilation (pp. 269-270)

It is here, at the site of what we once referred to as "transsexuality," that trans★ studies may most require a break from feminist queer studies to state *but* gender *is real like this*. Without a legitimizing context for the claims trans★ studies makes to the importance of the body as determinative and gender as known, the a priori propositions of feminist queer studies threaten to render transsexuality politically suspect and retrograde. Transsexuality thus "reveals queer theory's own limits: what lies beyond or beneath its favored terrain of gender performativity" (Prosser, 1998, p. 6). If feminist queer studies thinks this exclusion is a problem (which it does not always think), it might move to defuse the situation by drawing lines between sex and gender or between desire and the body—claiming, for example, that queer is about "nonnormative desires and sexual practices," and trans is about "nonnormative gender identifications and embodiments," (Love, 2014, p. 173). However, such a move cannot account for how sexuality and desire both depend on gender and the materiality of the sexed body for their legibility. Moreover, feminist queer studies' emphasis on antinormativity (i.e., "perversion") as a kind of disciplinary political impetus overlooks the problem that many transgender people seek to live their lives as "real" and "normal" men and women. Because it wants to tell a story about there being no materially fixed difference between M and F, feminist queer studies might seek to cite trans★ studies in its narratives of deconstruction and performativity, but it has not been able to imagine an end to that story without throwing the categories of M and/or F away, and, along with them, the realness of trans desires to have both sex and gender *like this*. To such a story, trans★ studies must say *but—you are forgetting me*.

Conclusion: Giving Each Other a Break

It is important, then, to conclude: To do its work, trans★ studies needs to be permitted "radically interdisciplinary, indeed *trans disciplinary*" (Noble, 2012, p. 50) breaks from the established epistemological frameworks of women's studies and queer studies. While such breaks may have been accomplished in a few leading departments and programs, it is unclear whether similar openings will become possible across the many and varied academic spaces seeking to include or now struggling to acknowledge trans★ studies. To open such breaks, these spaces will need to handle the tensions trans★ studies introduces to their epistemic structures "better than feminism has handled its relationship with queer theory" (Halley, 2006, p. 270). As women's studies and queer studies fall under increasing institutional pressure to defend themselves as disciplines with proper objects and defined methods, they may find themselves compelled to tell stories that discipline trans★ studies in turn. If trans★ studies wants to say more than *but*, it is important for it to get a break from these stories. This would require women's studies and queer studies to consider how the university may coerce them into the same disciplinary shapes they decry, thus (re)generating "much of the political tyranny they claim belongs (over there)" (Wiegman & Wilson, 2015, p. 13).

In the meantime, trans★ studies belongs exclusively to no one and nowhere, and perhaps this condition is the hidden advantage of *but*. To be *except; apart from; other than* is a condition of mourning only for those who value and expect arrival. To wait for invitation into someone else's story about you on other terms may be nothing but a "cruel optimism," in which the thing you desire is "actually an obstacle to (y)our flourishing" (Berlant, 2011, p. 10). Perhaps trans★ studies, with its investments in flex and stretch, need not say anything more legible right now than *but* to those framing the story—to be fixed as nothing more than a reminder of what exceeds the implicit disciplinary frame. Trans★ studies, now, is at least partially a practice of marking where these other stories break, even for only a moment, to offer others a break from themselves. As Prosser noted in 1998, to resist the incorporation of trans★ studies into other fields such as queer studies is not to refuse the value of alliance but to practice how an alliance, unlike a corporation, is "a provisional or strategic union between parties whose different interests ought not to be—indeed cannot totally be—merged" (p. 60). If one side of trans★ studies saying *but* marks an exclusion, the other might be a pedagogy: The *but* is how both women's studies and queer studies might still find where they break—where their stories now fail to find alliance.

Who or what really is broken in such a break?

Notes

1. In what follows, I use *trans* to indicate a set of resistantly gendered/sexed identifications that includes both transgender and transsexual, while I use *trans★* to indicate a broader formation including the theories, cultural productions, political imaginaries, bodies, and material praxes historically created by trans populations. My usage of the asterisk here is consistent with the entry for "asterisk" in the inaugural issue of *Transgender Studies Quarterly*, in which Avery Tompkins (2014) described the function of the asterisk as "to open up *transgender* or *trans* to a greater range of meanings" beyond a set of discrete identities (p. 26). The asterisk also indicates that the presumed referent of *trans* is not settled: While the older fields of WGS and LGBTQ/queer studies have developed more entrenched, centralized referents (e.g., something called "women" and something called "gay and lesbian") that each field has struggled to deconstruct/displace, there is no clear field-specific consensus on the referred object of *trans*. *Trans★* thus

indicates an unsettled condition that reflects historically racialized, classed, and gendered intracommunity politics about who counts as a trans subject, while simultaneously pointing at a range of undetermined potentials for interdisciplinary theoretical elaboration.

2. I use *discipline* throughout this piece to indicate a number of interrelated effects: First, I use it in reference to Foucault's theory of discipline in *Discipline and Punish: The Birth of the Prison* as a primary mode of modern power conducted by and within institutions, most notably carceral and educational spaces, to achieve self-regulation of the body's movements and affects. Second, I use it to indicate the many "disciplinary measures" arrayed at trans bodies within the academy. In his recent award-winning study, *Being and Becoming Professionally Other: The Lives, Voices, and Experiences of U.S. Trans* Academics*, Erich N. Pitcher found broadly punitive measures directed at trans academics, who are largely perceived as "in but not of" the university and who are exposed to a wide range of exclusionary and hostile interpersonal, management, and policy practices. Pitcher described the positionality of trans academics as "always already within a series of interstices: possible and impossible, real and imagined, inside and outside, visible and invisible" (2018, p. 1), a "betwixt" state that defies the categorical and methodological imperatives of disciplinarity. Third, I use "disciplinary position" in suggestive reference to the erotic practices of BDSM, which ironically require more consent than the regulatory and punitive schemas carried out within the academy. Lastly and most obviously, I use "discipline" to refer to the expectation that knowledge production be conducted in rigidly determinative ways that allow certain bodies to attain the privilege of professing status, while others are subjugated beneath or moved outside the borders of the resulting discourse.

3. We might describe this double-bind, to use Sara Ahmed's phrase, as an "affinity of hammers" (2016, p. 22): a situation in which the disciplinary aspects of both women's and queer studies can result in a dual "hammering" that chips away at trans lives simultaneously and from several different directions. Ahmed noted that such a hammering can be turned back on its sources as a tool—a goal I seek here.

4. For an unfolding account of this trajectory, see the 2002 collection *Women's Studies on Its Own: A Next Wave Reader in Institutional Change* (R. Weigman [Ed.], Durham, NC: Duke University Press) as well as the 2008 reader *Women's Studies on the Edge* (J. Wallach Scott [Ed.], Durham, NC: Duke University Press).

5. In *Split Decisions: How and Why to Take a Break From Feminism*, Halley (2006) described sexual subordination feminism as the dominant form of feminism in the United States, which is "persistently a subordination theory set by default to seek the social welfare of women, femininity, and/or female/feminine gender by undoing some part or all of their subordination to men, masculinity, and/or male or masculine gender" (p. 4). Halley wrote that this subordination model has three main components: "A distinction between something m and something f; a commitment to be a theory about, and a practice about, the subordination of f to m; and a commitment to work against that subordination on behalf of f" (pp. 4–5). Later, Halley observed how gay identity politics have borrowed aspects of this subordination formula from feminism (p. 28, 109–111), asserting a model in which homosexuality is subordinated to heterosexuality as F is subordinated to M.

6. Bettcher described the situation of the trans subject within the story of social construction like this: "Consider: If all the world's a stage on which we all play a part, trans individuals play actors. For somebody frustrated at being constructed as an actor, the mere claim that everybody is actually an actor would, by itself, erase the distinctive and oppressive way in which one was specifically constructed as an actor; it would provide no help in undermining being specifically constructed as an actor; and it would reinforce the claim that one was indeed an actor while obscuring the fact that such a reinforcement was being made" (p. 398).

Bibliography

Ahmed, S. (2014). *On being included: Racism and diversity in institutional life.* Durham, NC: Duke University Press.

———. (2016). An affinity of hammers. *Transgender Studies Quarterly, 3*(1–2), 22–34. doi:10.1215/23289252-3334151.

———. (2017, August 9). *A complaint biography* [blog post]. Retrieved from https://feministkilljoys.com/2017/08/09/a-complaint-biography/.

Awkward-Rich, C. (2017). Trans, feminism: Or, reading like a depressed transsexual. *Signs, 42*(4), 819–841. doi:10.1086/690914.

Barthes, R. (1972). Jeunes chercheurs. *Communications, 19*, 1–5. doi:10.3406/comm.1972.1276.

Berlant, L. (2011). *Cruel optimism.* Durham, NC: Duke University Press.

Bettcher, T. M. (2013). Trapped in the wrong theory: Rethinking trans oppression and resistance. *Signs, 39*(2), 383–406. doi:10.1086/673088.

Brown, W. (2005). *Edgework: Critical essays on knowledge and politics*. Princeton, NJ: Princeton University Press.

Butler, J. (1994). Against proper objects. *Differences: A Journal of Feminist and Cultural Studies, 6*(2–3), 1–26.

Eng, D. L., Halberstam, H., & Munoz, J. E. (2005). Introduction: What's queer about queer studies now? *Social Text, 23*(3–4), 2–18. doi:10.1215/01642472-23-3-4_84-85-1.

Hale, J. (1997). *Suggested rules for non-transsexuals writing about transsexuals, transsexuality, transsexualism, or trans* [blog post]. Retrieved from www.sandystone.com/hale. rules.html.

Halley, J. (2006). *Split decisions: How and why to take a break from feminism*. Princeton, NJ: Princeton University Press.

Jeffreys, S. (2014). *Gender hurts: A feminist analysis of the politics of transgenderism*. New York: Routledge.

Love, H. (2014). Queer. *Transgender Studies Quarterly, 1*(1–2), 172–176. doi:10.1215/23289252–2399938.

Malatino, H. (2015). Pedagogies of becoming: Trans inclusivity and the crafting of being. *Transgender Studies Quarterly, 2*(3), 395–410. doi:10.1215/23289252-2926387.

Namaste, V. (2000). *Invisible lives: The erasure of transgendered and transsexual people*. Chicago, IL: University of Chicago Press.

Nicolazzo, Z. (2017). Introduction: What's transgressive about trans★ studies in education now? *International Journal of Qualitative Studies in Education, 30*(3), 211–216. doi:10.1080/09518398.2016.1274063.

Noble, B. (2012). Trans. Panic. Some thoughts toward a theory of feminist fundamentalism. In F. Enke (Ed.), *Transfeminist perspectives in and beyond transgender and gender studies* (pp. 45–59). Philadelphia, PA: Temple University Press.

Pitcher, E. N. (2018). *Being and becoming professionally other: Identities, voices, and experiences of U.S. trans★ academics*. New York: Peter Lang, Inc.

Prosser, J. (1998). *Second skins: The body narratives of transsexuality*. New York: Columbia University Press.

Salamon, G. (2010). *Assuming a body: Transgender and rhetorics of materiality*. New York: Columbia University Press.

Schor, N., & Weed, E. (Eds.). (1997). *Feminism meets queer theory*. Bloomington, IN: Indiana University Press.

Shraya, V. (2016). *Even this page is white*. Vancouver, BC: Arsenal Pulp Press.

Spade, D. (2006). Mutilating gender. In S. Stryker & S. Whittle (Eds.), *The transgender studies reader* (Vol. 1, pp. 315–332). New York: Routledge.

Spivak, G. (1996). Bonding in difference: An interview with Alfred Arteaga (1993–94). In D. Landry & G. MacLean (Eds.), *The Spivak reader* (pp. 15–28). New York: Routledge.

Steinbock, E. (2017). Framing stigma in trans★ mediascapes: How does it feel to be a problem? *Spectator, 37*(2), 48–57.

Steinmetz, K. (2014, May 29). The transgender tipping point [web article]. *Time*. Retrieved from http://time.com/135480/transgender-tipping-point/.

Stryker, S. (2004). Transgender studies: Queer theory's evil twin. *GLQ: A Journal of Lesbian and Gay Studies, 10*(2), 211–215. doi:10.1215/10642684-10-2-212.

Stryker, S., & Bettcher, T. M. (2016). Introduction: Trans/feminisms. *Transgender Studies Quarterly, 3*(1–2), 5–14. doi:10.1215/23289252-3334127.

Tompkins, A. (2014). Asterisk. *Transgender Studies Quarterly, 1*(1–2), 26–27. doi:10.1215/23289252–2399497.

Wallach Scott, J. (Ed.). (2008). *Women's studies on the edge*. Durham, NC: Duke University Press.

Weigman, R. (Ed.). (2002). *Women's studies on its own: A next wave reader in institutional change*. Durham, NC: Duke University Press.

Wiegman, R., & Wilson, E. A. (2015). Introduction: Antinormativity's queer conventions. *Differences: A Journal of Feminist Cultural Studies, 26*(1), 1–25. doi:10.1215/10407391-2880582.

Wilchins, R. A. (2006). What does it cost to tell the truth? In S. Stryker & S. Whittle (Eds.), *The transgender studies reader* (Vol. 1, pp. 547–551). New York: Routledge.

Section V

Sexology and Its Critics

21 "Case 131: Gynandry" From *Psychopathia Sexualis*

Richard von Krafft-Ebing

Richard von Krafft-Ebing, a professor of psychiatry in Vienna in the 19th century, was an important early psycho-medical researcher who played a founding role in the scientific field of "sexology." His landmark compilation of case studies, *Psychopathia Sexualis*, has remained in print in various editions since its first publication in 1877. Krafft-Ebing's text undertakes a vast taxonomic and diagnostic project that attempts to classify an exhaustive range of psycho-sexual variations and offer an etiology of how such variations emerge. Underlying Krafft-Ebing's entire project is the assumption that any departure from procreative heterosexual intercourse represents a form of psychological or physical disease that should be addressed and corrected by medical, psychiatric, forensic, and penal authorities. Before the existence of modern terms and concepts likes *homosexual, transgender*, and *intersex*, Krafft-Ebing understood psychopathic sexuality through the concept of *inversion*. He thought there were "normal" people and "inverts." Krafft-Ebing considered people we would now call cisgender gay men or lesbian women to have a mild form of gender inversion, in that their erotic attractions were like those of normal members of the other sex. Male effeminacy and female masculinity represented more extreme forms of inversion. At its most extreme, inversion culminated in *metamorphosis sexualis paranoica*, the psychotic belief that one was actually a member of the so-called other sex. While they are explicitly pathologizing and profoundly homophobic and transphobic, Krafft-Ebing's case studies are important records in the history of sexuality and gender. They document not only the beginnings of a "medical model" for regulating trans lives but the remarkable persistence of specific ways of expressing trans identity that seem quite familiar in the present day. The person described in Case 131, reprinted here, exemplified what Krafft-Ebing called "gynandry" but seems easily legible as a trans man in contemporary terms.

Case 131. *Gynandry.* History: On November 4, 1889, the stepfather of a certain Count Sandor V. complained that the latter had swindled him out of 800f., under the pretense of requiring a bond as secretary of a stock company. It was ascertained that Sandor had entered into matrimonial contracts and escaped from the nuptials in the spring of 1889; and, more than this, that this ostensible Count Sandor was no man at all, but a woman in male attire,— Sarolta (Charlotte), Countess V.

S. was arrested, and, on account of deception and forgery of public documents, brought to examination. At the first hearing S. confessed that she was born on Sept. 6, 1866; that she was a female, Catholic, single, and worked as an authoress under the name of Count Sandor V.

DOI: 10.4324/9781003206255-27

From the autobiography of this man-woman I have gleaned the following remarkable facts that have been independently confirmed:—

S. comes of an ancient, noble, and highly-respected family of Hungary, in which there have been eccentricity and family peculiarities. A sister of the maternal grandmother was hysterical, a somnambulist, and lay seventeen years in bed, on account of fancied paralysis. A second great-aunt spent seven years in bed, on account of a fancied fatal illness, and at the same time gave balls. A third had the whim that a certain table in her *salon* was bewitched. If anything were laid on this table, she would become greatly excited and cry, "Bewitched! bewitched!" and run with the object into a room which she called the "Black Chamber," and the key of which she never let out of her hands. After the death of this lady, there were found in this chamber a number of shawls, ornaments, bank-notes, etc. A fourth great-aunt, during two years, did not leave her room, and neither washed herself nor combed her hair; then she again made her appearance. All these ladies were, nevertheless, intellectual, finely educated, and amiable.

S.'s mother was nervous, and could not bear the light of the moon.

From her father's family it is said she had a trace too much. One line of the family gave itself up almost entirely to spiritualism: Two blood-relations on the father's side shot themselves. The majority of her male relatives are unusually talented; the females are decidedly narrow and domestic. S.'s father had a high position, which, however, on account of his eccentricity and extravagance (he wasted over a million and a half), he lost.

Among many foolish things that her father encouraged in her was the fact that he brought her up as a boy, called her Sandor, allowed her to ride, drive, and hunt, admiring her muscular energy.

On the other hand, this foolish father allowed his second son to go about in female attire, and had him brought up as a girl. This farce ceased in his fifteenth year, when the son was sent to a higher school.

Sarolta-Sandor remained under her father's influence till her twelfth year, and then came under the care of her eccentric maternal grandmother, in Dresden, by whom, when the masculine play became too obvious, she was placed in an Institute, and made to wear female attire.

At thirteen she had a love-relation with an English girl, to whom she represented herself as a boy, and ran away with her.

Sarolta returned to her mother, who, however, could do nothing, and was compelled to allow her daughter to again become Sandor, wear male clothes, and, at least once a year, to fall in love with persons of her own sex.

At the same time, S. received a careful education, and made long journeys with her father,—of course, always as a young gentleman. She early became independent, and visited *cafés*, even those of doubtful character, and, indeed, boasted one day that in a brothel she had had a girl sitting on each knee. S. was often intoxicated, had a passion for masculine sports, and was a very skillful fencer.

She felt herself drawn particularly toward actresses, or others of similar position, and, if possible, toward those who were not very young. She asserts that she never had any inclination for a young man, and that she has felt, from year to year, an increasing dislike for young men.

"I preferred to go into the society of ladies with ugly, ill-favored men, so that none of them could put me in the shade. If I noticed that any of the men awakened the sympathies of the ladies, I felt jealous. I preferred ladies who were bright and pretty; I could not endure them if they were fat or much inclined toward men. It delighted me if the passion of a lady was disclosed under a poetic veil. All immodesty in a woman was disgusting to me. I had an indescribable aversion for female attire—indeed, for everything feminine—but only in as far as it concerned me; for, on the other hand, I was all enthusiasm for the beautiful sex."

During the last ten years S. had lived almost constantly away from her relatives, in the guise of a man. She had had many *liaisons* with ladies, traveled much, spent much, and made debts.

At the same time, she carried on literary work, and was a valued collaborator on two noted journals of the Capital.

Her passion for ladies was very changeable; constancy in love was entirely wanting.

Only once did such a *liaison* last three years. It was years before that S., at Castle G., made the acquaintance of Emma E., who was ten years older than herself. She fell in love with her, made a marriage-contract with her, and they lived together, as man and wife, for three years at the Capital.

A new love, which S. regarded as a fate, caused her to sever her matrimonial relations with E. The latter would not have it so. Only with the greatest sacrifice was S. able to purchase her freedom from E., who, it is reported, still looks upon herself as a divorced wife, and regards herself as the Countess V.! That S. also had the power to excite passion in other women is shown by the fact that when she (before her marriage with E.) had grown tired of a Miss D., after having spent thousands of guldens on her, she was threatened with shooting by D. if she should become untrue.

It was in the summer of 1887, while at a watering-place, that S. made the acquaintance of a distinguished official's family. Immediately she fell in love with the daughter, Marie, and her love was returned.

Her mother and cousin tried in vain to break up this affair. During the winter, the lovers corresponded zealously. In April, 1888, Count S. paid her a visit, and in May, 1889, attained her wish; in that Marie—who, in the meantime, had given up a position as teacher—became her bride in the presence of a friend of her lover, the ceremony being performed in an arbor, by a false priest, in Hungary. S., with her friend, forged the marriage-certificate. The pair lived happily, and, without the interference of the step-father, this false marriage, probably, would have lasted much longer. It is remarkable that, during the comparatively long existence of the relation, S. was able to deceive completely the family of her bride with regard to her true sex.

S. was a passionate smoker, and in all respects her tastes and passions were masculine. Her letters and even legal documents reached her under the address of "Count S." She often spoke of having to drill. From remarks of the father-in-law, it seems that S. (and she afterward confessed it) knew how to imitate a scrotum with handkerchiefs or gloves stuffed in the trousers. The father-in-law also, on one occasion, noticed something like an erected member on his future son-in-law (probably a priapus). She also occasionally remarked that she was obliged to wear a suspensory bandage while riding. The fact is, S. wore a bandage around the body, possibly as a means of retaining a priapus.

Though S. often had herself shaved *pro forma*, the servants in the hotel where she lived were convinced that she was a woman, because the chambermaids found traces of menstrual blood on her linen (which S. explained, however, as hæmorrhoidal); and, on the occasion of a bath which S. was accustomed to take, they claimed to have convinced themselves of her real sex by looking through the key-hole.

The family of Marie make it seem probable that she for a long time was deceived with regard to the true sex of her false bridegroom. The following passage in a letter from Marie to S., August 26, 1889, speaks in favor of the incredible simplicity and innocence of this unfortunate girl: "I don't like children any more, but if I had a little Bezerl or Patscherl by my Sandi,—ah, what happiness, Sandi mine!"

A large number of manuscripts allow conclusions to be drawn concerning S.'s mental individuality. The chirography possesses the character of firmness and certainty. The characters are genuinely masculine. The same peculiarities repeat themselves everywhere in their contents,—wild, unbridled passion; hatred and resistance to all that opposes the heart thirsting for love; poetical love, which is not marred by one ignoble blot; enthusiasm for the beautiful and noble; appreciation of science and the arts.

Her writings betray a wonderfully wide range of reading in classics of all languages, in citations from poets and prose writers of all lands. The evidence of those qualified to judge literary work shows that S.'s poetical and literary ability is by no means small. The letters and writings concerning the relation with Marie are psychologically worthy of notice.

S. speaks of the happiness there was for her when by M.'s side, and expresses boundless longing to see her beloved, if only for a moment. After such a happiness, she could have but one wish,—to exchange her cell for the grave. The bitterest thing was the knowledge that now Marie, too, hated her. Hot tears, enough to drown herself in, she had shed over her lost happiness. Whole quires of paper are given up to the apotheosis of this love, and reminiscences of the time of the first love and acquaintance.

S. complained of her heart, that would allow no reason to direct it; she expressed emotions which were such as only could be felt,—not simulated. Then, again, there were outbreaks of most silly passion, with the declaration that she could not live without Marie. "Thy dear, sweet voice; the voice whose tone perchance would raise me from the dead; that has been for me like the warm breath of Paradise! Thy presence alone were enough to alleviate my mental and moral anguish. It was a magnetic stream; it was a peculiar power your being exercised over mine, which I cannot quite define; and, therefore, I cling to that ever-true definition: I love you because I love you. In the night of sorrow I had but one star,—the star of Marie's love. That star has lost its light; now there remains but its shimmer,—the sweet, sad memory which even lights with its soft ray the deepening night of death,—a ray of hope." This writing ends with the apostrophe: "Gentlemen, you learned in the law, psychologists and pathologists, do me justice! Love led me to take the step I took; all my deeds were conditioned by it.

God put it in my heart.

"If He created me so, and not otherwise, am I then guilty; or is it the eternal, incomprehensible way of fate? I relied on God, that one day my emancipation would come; for my thought was only love itself, which is the foundation, the guiding principle, of His teaching and His kingdom.

"O God, Thou All-pitying, Almighty One! Thou seest my distress; Thou knowest how I suffer. Incline Thyself to me; extend Thy helping hand to me, deserted by all the world. Only God is just. How beautifully does Victor Hugo describe this in his 'Legendes du Siècle'! How sad do Mendelssohn's words sound to me: 'Nightly in dreams I see thee'!"

Though S. knew that none of her writings reached her lover, she did not grow tired writing of her pain and delight in love, in page after page of deification of Marie. And to induce one more pure flood of tears, on one still, clear summer evening, when the lake was aglow with the setting sun like molten gold, and the bells of St. Anna and Maria-Wörth, blending in harmonious melancholy, gave tidings of rest and peace, she wrote: "For that poor soul, for this poor heart that beat for thee till the last breath."

Personal Examination: The first meeting which the experts had with S. was, in a measure, a time of embarrassment to both sides; for them, because perhaps S.'s somewhat dazzling and forced masculine carriage impressed them; for her, because she thought she was to be marked with the stigma of moral insanity. She had a pleasant and intelligent face, which, in spite of a certain delicacy of features and diminutiveness of all its parts, gave a decidedly masculine impression, had it not been for the absence of a moustache. It was even difficult for the experts to realize that they were concerned with a woman, despite the fact of female attire and constant association; while, on the other hand, intercourse with the man Sandor was much more free, natural, and apparently correct. The culprit also felt this. She immediately became more open, more communicative, more free, as soon as she was treated like a man.

In spite of her inclination for the female sex, which had been present from her earliest years, she asserts that in her thirteenth year she first felt a trace of sexual feeling, which expressed itself in kisses, embraces, and caresses, with sensual pleasure, and this on the occasion of her elopement with the red-haired English girl from the Dresden Institute. At that time feminine forms exclusively appeared to her in dream-pictures, and ever since, in sensual dreams, she has felt herself in the situation of a man, and occasionally, also, at such times, experienced ejaculation.

She knows nothing of solitary or mutual onanism. Such a thing seemed very disgusting to her, and not conducive to manliness. She had, also, never allowed herself to be touched *ad genitalia* by others, because it would have revealed her great secret. The menses began at seventeen, but were always scanty, and without pain. It was plain to be seen that S. had a horror of speaking of menstruation; that it was a thing repugnant to her masculine consciousness and feeling. She recognized the abnormality of her sexual inclinations, but had no desire to have them changed, since in this perverse feeling she felt both well and happy. The idea of sexual intercourse with men disgusted her, and she also thought it would be impossible.

Her modesty was so great that she would prefer to sleep among men rather than among women. Thus, when it was necessary for her to answer the calls of nature or to change her linen, it was necessary for her to ask her companion in the cell to turn her face to the window, that she might not see her.

When occasionally S. came in contact with this companion—a woman from the lower walks of life—she experienced a sexual excitement that made her blush. Indeed, without being asked, S. related that she was overcome with actual fear when, in her cell, she was compelled to force herself into the unusual female attire. Her only comfort was, that she was at least allowed to keep a shirt. Remarkable, and what also speaks for the significance of olfactory sensations in her *vita sexualis*, is her statement that, on the occasions of Marie's absence, she had sought those places on which Marie's head was accustomed to repose, and smelled of them, in order to experience the delight of inhaling the odor of her hair. Among women, those who are beautiful, or voluptuous, or quite young do not particularly interest her. The physical charms of women she makes subordinate. As by magnetic attraction, she feels herself drawn to those between twenty-four and thirty. She found her sexual satisfaction exclusively *in corpora feminæ* (never in her own person), in the form of manustupration of the beloved woman, or cunnilingus. Occasionally she availed herself of a stocking stuffed with oakum as a *priapus*. These admissions were made only unwillingly by S., and with apparent shame; just as in her writings, immodesty or cynicism are never found.

She is religious, has a lively interest in all that is noble and beautiful—men excepted—and is very sensitive to the opinion others may entertain of her morality.

She deeply regrets that in her passion she made Marie unhappy, and regards her sexual feelings as perverse, and such a love of one woman for another, among normal individuals, as morally reprehensible. She has great literary talent and an extraordinary memory. Her only weakness is her great frivolity and her incapability to manage money and property reasonably. But she is conscious of this weakness, and does not care to talk about it.

[Several paragraphs then describe S.'s body in great detail.] The opinion given showed that in S. there was a congenitally abnormal inversion of the sexual instinct, which, indeed, expressed itself, anthropologically, in anomalies of development of the body, depending upon great hereditary taint; further, that the criminal acts of S. had their foundation in her abnormal and irresistible sexuality.

S.'s characteristic expressions—"God put love in my heart. If He created me so, and not otherwise, am I, then, guilty; or is it the eternal, incomprehensible way of fate?"—are really justified.

The court granted pardon. The "countess in male attire," as she was called in the newspapers, returned to her home, and again gave herself out as Count Sandor. Her only distress is her lost happiness with her beloved Marie.

From: Richard von Krafft-Ebing, *Psychopathia Sexualis*, 1886.

22 "Case 13" From *The Transvestites*

The Erotic Drive to Cross-Dress

Magnus Hirschfeld

Magnus Hirschfeld was an influential medical doctor and advocate for sexual liberation in the late nineteenth and early twentieth centuries. He thought that most people could be considered "sexual intermediaries" who combined a variety of physical and psychological traits in innumerable potential mixtures that existed somewhere on a spectrum between a hypothetical "pure heterosexual male" and "pure heterosexual female." What we now call homosexuality or transgender identity were just two of the visible constellations in a rainbow of possibilities that encompassed all people. Hirschfeld founded the Scientific Humanitarian Committee in 1897 based on his belief that, as sexual intermediaries, gay and trans people were part of natural biological diversity and that a rational society should not discriminate against them. In 1919, he opened the world's first Institute for Sexual Science in Berlin. The Institute had trans women on its staff, and doctors associated with it performed the first documented male-to-female genital transformation surgeries. In spite of his explicit targeting by fascists and his generally progressive views, Hirschfeld nevertheless shared some of the eugenicist beliefs that informed Nazism as well as mainstream sexological thought. Hirschfeld's 1910 book *The Transvestites* situated cross-gender behavior within his "sexual intermediaries" framework. He used the word *transvestite* in a more general sense than has become common in recent decades, to refer to all sorts of people who crossed gender—everything from episodic fetishistic cross-dressing for sexual pleasure to non-erotic cross-dressing in daily life to desires for medically assisted gender-transition later classified as "transsexualism." In Case 13, reprinted here, Hirschfeld's informant is someone who seems very much like a contemporary trans woman. She describes always having felt like a girl, experiencing childhood and adolescent gender dysphoria, and running away from home to live as a woman. She tells of her friendships with working-class lesbians and female sex workers, recounts her experiences of sexual assault and harassment by men, and expresses an explicitly feminist politics.

[Editors' note: In this case study, Hirschfeld describes how the publishers of a German feminist journal had forwarded to him a letter they had received in 1905 from someone who wrote to suggest that the publication establish a registry where "manly women" and "womanly men" could find one another—something like a T4T dating service. Hirschfeld then began a correspondence with this person, identified only as Johann or Johanna O., which confirmed his suspicion that "here was a case of a typical representative of the group we are concerned with" (that is, transvestites). "I am abstracting here," Hirschfeld explained, "the most noteworthy parts of his very detailed reports."]

DOI: 10.4324/9781003206255-28

Case 13

"I was born," O. writes, "in 1862. My father was a Tyrolean gamekeeper for the empire for 10 or more years . . .

"My father and my mother were both born in H., Voralberg, as we were, too. Father died in 1867 of consumption; he was supposed to have drunk a lot. Mother died one-and-a-half years later; she was supposed to have been infected by my sick father. I am supposed to be the spitting image of my mother. I later found out that I was still wearing girls' clothing when the brother two years younger than I was wearing pants. Mother told me I did not want any trousers and put up such a fuss that I got to keep the dresses; and since my sister was one year older I could wear her clothes, until Mother died in 1868.

"My aunts then forced me to wear boys' clothing. My sister went to live with an aunt who lived several kilometers from us. Before I was born, Mother was supposed to have wanted a girl.

"Grandfather would have allowed me to wear girls' clothing if my aunts had not been so against it. The doctor was supposed to have said I would be a fine young boy. But I clearly remember I always only wanted to be a girl, and my relatives and acquaintances would tease me with words such as 'li'l girl,' 'girl's face,' or 'Johanna.' Also, many people were supposed to have asked why, then, the little girl wore boy's clothing. I always liked Shrovetide because on that day it was allowed to run around in girls' clothing. I was always envious when I saw my aunt put on her clothes, because I was not allowed to put on girls' clothing, too.

"Because Aunt and Uncle were much more pious than my grandfather and Father, I was soon brought to a Catholic orphanage of the Sisters of Mercy. Soon after I became the favorite of Mother Superior Joachima. I often sat on her lap. She kissed me a lot, and I was allowed to do what the other children might not. Also, I was chosen to run all the errands to clergymen in the area; even at night I would be awakened to bring the priest to someone who was dying. The Mother Superior said that I, Hansel, performed best without asking questions; likewise I kept everything to myself or forgot everything afterward.

"Later, when I was already in America, my sister would often include in her letters regards from Mother Superior; she remembers to this day that I had been such an intelligent child and useful to everyone. I, too, have often thought about the Mother Superior, more than anyone else, and often thought that she had been a good mother. However, she would not allow me girls' clothing; on the contrary, she always dissuaded me from having these thoughts and tried to get me to go to Brixen in the Tyrol and into the pontifical boys' seminary, but I wanted to go to Bregenz to the teachers' seminary, because later, I thought, when I finished at the teachers' seminary, I could go around as a governess or a children's teacher.

"Even at that time I had firm plans to come forward as a woman. But when I realized that my guardian would not give me my father's inheritance unless I went to Brixen, I began to think of ways I could thwart this. The Mother Superior always told me how nice I would have it as a priest, how my parents would be released from purgatory as soon as I said my first Mass, and much more. But at the time I was already praying only because the director wished me to do so. Also, the Mother Superior often took me with her when she went into other regions to visit the sisters who lived there. I was always with her among the Sisters of Mercy, who treated me well and introduced me to the other children as a good example. As a rule, it was customary for the best girl to come along, but the Mother Director preferred me.

"Once she even took me into the home for mothers near Feldkirch, and I heard as the resident director, who was her superior, asked her why she had a boy as a companion. She replied, 'Reverend Mother, Hansel is the most polite, most honest, and most silent child in my charge and in many respects takes the place of many girls.'

"Well, when I saw that they were not going to allow me to study to be a teacher, I still had the thought again and again, in spite of all my religious training, of secretly procuring and setting aside some girls' clothing and running away in them. Then, when I became employed as a general hand for a rich landowner who owned a lot of property, cows, and pasture in the Alps, at the first opportunity I stole from a girl who was my size. I put on her things and took her certificate of domicile and burned my boys' things that night. Everything boyish I left behind in Voralberg and went to Switzerland so that my relatives would not know where I was. I was anxious about writing and was afraid, too, that they could force me to go as a boy.

"Well, I first went to work as a nanny and did general housework. At the same time I learned embroidery. I did not like the first mistress, but I later got another one and even more pay. However, she unfortunately found out that I was not a real girl, but she did not make a big fuss about it, because she said she had never had such a good woman worker. Meanwhile, I grew strong and not ugly, so that boys would lie in wait for me. My mistress gave me much good advice, I followed it and went dancing in the evening in the company of boys. At that time I felt fully a young woman, except when the fellows got fresh with me, and it would occur to me that, unfortunately, I was not one. I mostly enjoyed Sundays, when I could go walking with the children, and me in a starched slip, white pinafore, and little hat; that was when I felt I was in heaven. Only when a handsome man looked at me in a friendly way was I annoyed that I did not have better breasts and hips. Sometimes, when I saw a young woman bathing, I wished I had the shape of her body, and gladly would have given her mine. Since I was still religious, I prayed,

'Dear God, please make me into a girl.'

"At 16 1/2 a man tried to rape me. I protected myself, but he gave me a bad name as being a hermaphrodite, so I had to move away and went to France, where I started as an embroiderer in Luneville. I had a friendship with a girl, who, like me, was in opposition to her sex, namely, manly, and when she went to St. Quentin to the embroidery factory there, I followed her. Not long after, an embroiderer coaxed me to come to Paris where I could earn more. There I had the opportunity for the first time to come together with women who with other women lived like married people, which in France is a rather widespread custom.

"Well, since I was a good woman worker with satin, embroiderers tried to get my employer to loan me out for a time, because their women embroiderers were not as skillful as I. So, one time it happened that I was forced to sleep together with a young woman my own age. I always had the custom of putting my shirt between my legs in such a way that no one could see my organ. In the middle of the night, however, my bed-mate woke me up and said to me that I was not made right. At first I was embarrassed and asked how she could say that. She said, 'I always touch the people I sleep with and found out that you are not like them.'

"I asked her not to betray me, otherwise I would have to disappear immediately. She said I need not be ashamed; that there really were other girls like me. She asked me not to tell that she had touched me. However, that morning she would not leave me alone. I was supposed to show her; maybe she could give me some advice; and because I trusted her words I finally allowed her to examine me. This young woman was the first with whom I entered into a sexual relationship, in which I was the succubus. I had the burning wish to become a mother by her. But she married soon after for money; nevertheless, she wanted me to move in with her.

"But I noticed that her husband, too, was attracted to me, and so, I smelled a rat. But I visited her often. One time her husband was home alone. He invited me in to wait until his wife came, gave me a lot to drink, and suddenly he embraced me, wanted to kiss me and abuse me violently, whereby he found out that I was no young woman. He then threatened to call the police if I did not leave the area.

"I then decided to go around again as a man and as such found work in Claparède, St. Denis on the Seine. However, I wore men's attire only during work; at home I immediately put on women's dresses and kept to myself as much as possible.

"I did not like to work with men at all. The clothing pleased me even less. And I was still afraid that the husband of my girl friend would report me. One evening I bumped into her, and she assured me that I really should go and live with her, that she was finished with her husband, he was too passionate; she thought marriage would be something better. Her husband had made her many nice promises he did not keep and, she said, I really should become her friend. She would never go with another man ever again.

"I did not want to, because at the time I, too, had doubts about myself. If at that time I had had the experience and knowledge I now have, I would have taken the place of a wife for her. But at that time I looked at it as wickedness, suffered terribly amid thoughts of suicide, and no longer took any joy in my life as I was leading it.

"So, in 1882 I left France and went to New York. Here, too, I soon found work as an embroiderer but was discovered and then took a position as a maid on a farm in the State of New York, because I thought I would be able to live there inconspicuously. At the time the farmers had a great need for maids. And it did go along well for a while, but one day the farmer's wife was away and he became fresh. I was afraid of discovery and, as I had read, that in Jersey City they were looking for embroiderers, I left the place and got a good job in Jersey C.

"At that time I bought myself the most modern ladies' apparel, so that I looked charming, and spent all my savings, because, I thought, I would be working there for a long time and be earning a lot of money. However, the other young women made my job miserable, so. I gave it up.

"I could still manage well for a few weeks. Meanwhile I became acquainted with an embroiderer who did not let me out of his sight and followed me everywhere. One night we got drunk, and he found out that I was no young woman. I wanted nothing to do with him, but he did not give in, and I became a victim of his intoxication. He threatened to call the police and tell them that I was playing a masquerade, so I gave him what he wanted. He forced me into sodomy and fellatio and treated me totally as a woman, even bought me pretty toilet articles, so that at that time I became a coquette. A few months passed during which I got more miserable each day and felt more unhappy. One morning, I packed everything together and, when he was away, sold everything of worth, sent my women's clothing off, dressed myself as a man, and traveled to Milwaukee.

"Here I worked as a man in a timber yard, then as a cook. But because I much preferred to wear women's clothing, I went to Montana in the spring as a woman cook. There, however, betrayed again, I took myself to S. Francisco and found myself there in February 1885 and still live there today.

"Soon after I arrived, the woman I lived and boarded with had a baby girl. Happy hours began for me now because I was able to take care of and clean the little thing. Who was happier than I when the woman said, 'Jenny' (I liked to be called by my feminine name when we were alone), 'Rich and I want to go out or go on a trip. Look after the child.'

"With what joy and care did I take it out of its little bed, clean it, throw the wet things into the wash, dress it again, cuddle and caress it, and walk back and forth playing with her. I knew exactly how a mother took care of a child and was happy when the woman praised me and said that I had become a good mother. In the four years I had the child and devoted all my free time to it, I had sexual intercourse only one time. I did not think about it at all, because the child was much too dear to me. Lizzie hung on to me and soon wanted to be taken care of only by me. As soon as she woke up she called my name.

"Her father even got mad because she liked me better than him and she said so. The child grew near to my heart as if she were my own, and never again did I love another child as this one. And that was just as well. When Lizzie left with her parents, I was totally despairing because I loved her so much. I was not as kind to the older boy, even though I certainly did everything for him when his mother was away, but kissed him less. Even today I often wonder if I should give up my bookstore and rather become a nanny. Bringing up and caring for children is my greatest joy, to raise them in the sense of Froebel, Pestalozzi, and other great pedagogues of children. I read everything I can get on the education of children and know for certain that if I had been able to devote all my time to raising children, my sexual desires would have been totally extinguished. To be sure, I did notice that strange children were not as delightful as those at home.

"Meanwhile, in S. Francisco I began as an itinerant bookseller. I sought out the dance halls and sold trashy literature. I also had socialist writings and even took part in the workers' movement because I moved about as a man outside of the apartment. Through the dancers I later even got day jobs, such as cleaning their rooms, sometimes cooking for them, and became good friends with them.

"They often gave me clothes they no longer wore so that many visitors even thought that I was a prostitute. At the time I also drank a lot. It was all the same to me. I got used to all the bad things in society, which, to be sure, I avoided when I was sober.

"But I had to make a living, and at the time it seemed the best thing to do. The dancers, many of whom were educated, had seen better times at home, and accepted me just as nature made me. Finally, with the help of some of these young women, I set up a house and became their room mother, cooked when they invited their friends over, and besides that I also had my job selling books. Only as such did I have to play the man.

"At the time, I easily could have become the lover of one of these young women, but I had no desire and preferred to work rather than be taken care of by them. Well, as soon as I saved some money, I bought a small piece of property, had a house built, and totally gave up the work with the dancers.

"At this time I fell very much in love with a young woman of a manly type; however, she did not understand me, and I could not fully accept her. In short, she married another and is supposed to have never become happy.

"In the 1890s I began traveling for German newspapers, traveled through California, Oregon, and Washington, then back and forth again, and I still carried on the business of bookselling and of the bookstore. I hoped I would forget my feminine nature by traveling, but in vain. It came before everything. "Actually, I felt happy only in my dreams. I dreamed I was a young woman, and a young man whom I loved was waiting for me. I thought, if he really did lie down beside me, as a young woman I would behave by hesitating, but I would only be pretending to resist. And then I would dream I was pregnant and was not ashamed to be a mother out of wedlock. The only thought I had was whether the father would help me raise the child. I went into labor and hardly was the child born and cleaned that I was kissing it and letting my lover know about the birth, and when he came to the bedside, the child held out its arms toward him, whereupon he kissed me and, weeping for joy, asked me if we could not both raise the child. "I put the child to my breast and played with it. When I would wake up I would look for the child next to me, because the feeling of being a mother was still with me. Then I would realize, to my dismay, that it was only a dream, and by feeling my body I would notice that I had had a nocturnal emission. But I felt very satisfied and sometimes I did not have intercourse for years because this and similar dreams, which I had often since about 1881, made me happy and satisfied. Today, I still dream I am an older woman who has ten or more children around her.

"Sometimes they are also grandchildren, and we speak about needlework, new fashions, veils, raising children, and much more, so that I am occupied in my dream totally as a woman. "In 1904 I put a few inserts into a marriage magazine that an effeminate man was looking for a manly woman. I could cook, sew, wash, iron, etc. I got many answers, but most of them were studied women who would do it only for money. "In March 1906 a distant relative came to visit me from Dakota. She seduced me, but it was not successful, and she irritated me by saying I was no good. She was very feminine. But in June of the same year an American woman who lived in my neighborhood, who had a strong manly character and was well-educated, became friends with me. We spoke a lot with each other. I loved her very much and would have liked to have become her wife, but she did not propose to me, and I was not ready to make her any offer. "I expected the woman to make the first move and to be charmed by her, but it had to be an energetic, strong woman who would impress me mentally and physically. I even liked them to have a very small mustache. I would also allow them to wear men's apparel. I alone want to play the female's role, which they have to protect, as it were, as a man. As far as my wardrobe goes, I am exactly like a woman. What the others wear, I, too, must wear, except that the women's clothing must not have any manly cut or look anything like a man's suit. My taste is totally feminine.

"I myself believe that I can be of more service as a woman than otherwise. My earliest tendency was to raise children, and as long as I was with them, I never had thoughts of sex. So, how can people say that that is nothing but a passing fancy, when a person really has the tendency all the time, no matter how people, with the best intentions, try to suppress it?

"I am now 47 years old, born in Austria, worked in Switzerland and in France, in America for twenty-five years, in California since 1885, traveled for a large German newspaper in Milwaukee and always a welcome guest everywhere, and can again enter into every house where I once was, have never been arrested, and today it is still my deepest wish to wear a new princess dress, a new flowered hat, and lace petticoats. I also like needlework, have no time for it any longer, and if I were to find an energetic man-woman as a wife, then for her sake I would do all the work that in today's order of things the wife does, without hesitating. To the contrary, I would enjoy the greatest pleasure living as a wife, if only I did not have to wear hateful men's clothing any longer.

"Today, I have now been wearing women's garments on my property for years, am writing this, too, with a little white cap and white skirt on, decorate my bedroom in the manner of women, and a man seldom enters my room, because I am not a friend to men. Conversations with women satisfy me more, and I am always envious of educated women, because I always look up to them.

"For that reason I always have been an activist for equal rights, and I believe that if ever there is total freedom everywhere, many women would be better fighters than effeminate men, who would do their duty in other ways. If effeminate men would show themselves more often, it would be to their advantage. Really, why should we be ashamed of ourselves! . . . I cannot understand why science has had little to do with effeminate men, when it really is something you see every day and is natural; and, unfortunately, we are often falsely considered to be homosexuals."

From: Magnus Hirschfeld, translated by Michael A. Lombardi-Nash, "Case 13" in *The Transvestites: The Erotic Drive to Cross-Dress*, pp. 83–93. Republished by permission of Michael A. Lombardi-Nash.

23 Trans★ Plasticity and the Ontology of Race and Species

Kadji Amin

In "Trans★ Plasticity and the Ontology of Race and Species," first published in the cultural studies journal *Social Text* in 2019, Kadji Amin develops the concept of *trans★ plasticity* to examine how late nineteenth- and early twentieth-century glandular therapies now called xenotransplantation (non-human to human transfers of tissue or organs) functioned as a eugenic tool for white racial rejuvenation and the promotion of idealized forms of gender. The concept of plasticity has previously been used to describe surgery that changes body shape (i.e., plastic surgery) as well as the ability of the brain and nerves to reconfigure themselves (i.e., neuroplasticity), but Amin uses it here in a new way, to describe the process through which transfers of biological matter from one organism to another cross over the seemingly fixed, natural, hierarchical categories of sex, race, and species. In doing so, these biomatter transfers, often involving hormone-producing glandular tissue, demonstrate the porousness and instability of the categories themselves. The transplants Amin considers, however, do not work to flatten hierarchies of species, race, and sex, but rather use their very plasticity to reinforce gender normativity and white privilege as well as the notion of a humanity superior to mere animality. Amin discusses how various early proponents of glandular science such as Charles-Édouard Brown-Séquard, Serge Voronoff, and Eugen Steinach were all invested in creating an idealized gender dimorphism based on white norms. Their work directly informed the sexological theories and practices of early specialists in trans medicine.

During the 1920s, French surgeon Serge Voronoff became an international sensation for his technique of grafting chimpanzee testicular matter into human testicles. Incredible as it may seem today, "monkey glands" were all the rage among elite European men, and Voronoff's operation was a topic of obsessive interest in the press and in popular fiction alike. For example, Félicien Champsaur's 1929 popular speculative fiction novel, *Nora, la guenon devenue femme (Nora, the Ape-Woman)*, imagines the possibilities of human ape ontological and erotic proximity suggested by Voronoff's practice of gland xenotransplantation, or transspecies transplantation. This article puts *Nora* and the early twentieth-century science of ductless glands (ovaries, testicles, thyroid, thalamus, etc.) into conversation with trans★ new materialist science studies around their shared investment in plasticity. While the term *plasticity* emerged from the neurosciences and stem cell research, I use it in this article to refer broadly to the capacity of bodily tissues to develop, regenerate, and otherwise transform themselves in dynamic relation to matter, technology, and the environment. Plasticity thus understood names one of new materialism's key investments; it is the organic version of "vibrant matter" itself.[1] [. . .] Glandular science, which would later be derided by endocrinologists as "snake medicine," was in essence a science of organic plasticity and its therapeutic uses. It held the ductless glands, particularly the ovaries and testicles, to be the vital activators of bodily plasticity, stimulating growth, development, sexual differentiation, and even intelligence. This article takes shape around the "monkey gland" operation's new materialist challenge to species ontologies: the procedure affirmed humans and apes to be composed of vitally compatible organic substances, to such an extent that a bit of ape testicle (or an ape ovary, for that matter) might reactivate the lost plasticity of aged human bodies.[2] The bygone science and speculative fiction of "monkey gland" operations might therefore serve as a laboratory in which the claims of new materialist and posthumanist trans★ theory might be tested.

This turn in trans★ theory is most clearly delineated in Eva Hayward and Jami Weinstein's introduction to a special issue of *TSQ* on "Tranimalities." This introduction positions *trans★*—an assemblage of all words containing the prefix *trans*—as central to contemporary debates in posthumanist and animal studies scholarship. For Hayward and Weinstein, unlike *transgender* or *trans*, *trans★* does not reference a distinct form of gendered or sexed personhood and thus makes no claims on ontology. Instead, *trans★* is the very "moving mattering" that constitutes being.[3] *Trans★* thus understood is another name for what scholars contributing to the ontological turn have called *affect*, *vibrant matter*, and, yes, *plasticity*. It denotes the excitations, intensifications, and movements through, within, and across matter (because *trans* as a prefix is always prepositional, always in transformative relation to something else) invisible to those who would misperceive matter and organisms to be inert, enclosed, self-same, and classifiable. Trans★ thus at once precedes ontology and "troubles ontologized states," such as those that separate male from female, human from animal, and human from technology or environment.[4] *Transing*, the gerund form, names this process of troubling taxonomy, usually by crossing or entangling two or more categories of ontologized being.[5]

As in most ontological scholarship in affect studies and new materialism,[6] vitalism—which here goes by the name *trans★*—generates scholarly hope. "Trans★," Hayward and Weinstein write, "is movement, excitation, and intensification, or a motor of internal instability that drives self-overcoming, unpredictability, and irreducible multiplicity."[7] Trans★, exemplified in the plastic and generative capacities of matter, is at once that quasi-mystical force that generates being and that unpredictable movement that destabilizes taxonomy, selfhood, and ontology. In the latter guise, trans★ offers an antidote to the ills of the imperialist mania for classification whose chief product is, for animal studies, the human itself, in its foundational disavowal of animality, and, for Wynterian scholars of race, the misrepresentation of Man, in his white Western humanist guise, as the sole genre of the human.[8] "In the beginning is trans," writes Clare Colebrook.[9] If trans★ (or, for Colebrook, transitivity) is indeed primary, then race, gender, sexuality, and so on, are but rough, clumsy, post facto attempts to capture and classify a plasticity that will always exceed such categories.[10] By centering the primary plasticity and vibrancy of matter, which fails to respect human-made divisions of gender, race, and species, trans★ new materialism seeks to undo the harms of humanist taxonomies while envisioning more expansive modes of interinfluence and transformation. This offers a potentially huge payoff for a range of scholarly fields.

Nevertheless, I have two concerns, which this article more fully excavates. The first is that, in this affirmation of trans★ as the primary vitality underlying all being and all life, vitality and its theoretical avatars—plasticity, affect, and movement—go unquestioned as scholarly values.[11] This is the case because vitality, as a preontological and therefore prediscursive force, is imagined to exist prior to power. Hence, while transgender may well be a handmaiden to colonial/racial taxonomies of the human,[12] trans★ is imagined to be exempt from such ontologies—of a different order altogether. By contrast, scholars working in a Foucauldian frame would understand *vitality*, *life*, and other allied terms as invested from the start by biopower—a form of power that takes life as its object. I concur with such scholars that vitality/life/plasticity/affect/trans* are foundational rather than prior to humanist racialized divides between human and animal or being and nonbeing. Second, a simple but oft-overlooked point: if trans* is that dynamic "process through which thingness and beingness are constituted,"[13] then this means that trans* generates ontology. As forces that generate ontological differentiation, trans* and transing cannot be unambivalent antidotes to the ills of ontology and taxonomy.

This article turns to "monkey gland" science and science fiction to flesh out these claims. Glandular science literalizes transing: as I will elaborate below, its signature technology was the vitalizing transplantation of biomatter across the ontological divides of sex and species. Conceptually, its affirmation of human-ape transspecies plasticity undoes ontological divisions between humans and apes. However, the speculative fiction I study demonstrates that such human/animal transings were tethered to the ontology of race. Building on Eva Hayward and Che Gossett's claim that "the Human/Animal divide is a racial and colonial divide," this article zeroes in on the process by which race and animality were produced in relation to each other.[14] In doing so, it contributes to the burgeoning inquiry into transsex, tranimal, and transspecies plasticity—which I refer to, jointly, as trans* plasticity—while interrogating the affirmative and even utopian valance of such inquiry.

Trans* plasticity describes the capacity of organic matter to transform itself in ways that transgress ontological divides between sex, race, and species. As a corrective to the new materialist tendency to focus on the conceptual possibilities of plasticity, I attend to the uses of trans* plasticity, asking what trans* plasticity does. As precursors to transgenic organisms, medical gender affirmation procedures, and the new materialist interest in plasticity as an index of transformative organic agency, early twentieth-century gland transplantations have much to tell us about the historical and racial genealogies of technologies and concepts that today seem freighted with political and conceptual potential. My approach combines the history of science with plot analyses of speculative fiction texts. Speculative fiction unlocks the speculative and unfinished dimensions of a juncture of the history of science that was pregnant with futurity in its own time but was soon discredited by the institutionalization of endocrinology as a legitimate science.[15] Fiction also allows for a crucial exploration of the emotions and sensations evoked by the possible and probable futures of new scientific and medical techniques. Voronoff's "monkey gland" operations activated racialized fantasies, anxieties, and ambitions regarding human-simian recombinations that are best studied not in medical textbooks themselves but, rather, in the cultural fictions they inspired. I turn to Champsaur's *Nora* and H. G. Well's *Island of Doctor Moreau* (1896) to envision both the arrested futures and the erotic unconscious of glandular science.[16] Ultimately, I argue that gland xenotransplantation was a use of trans* plasticity that generated rather than troubled the ontobiological concepts of sexual, racial, and species difference.

Glands and the Plasticity of Life

In the late nineteenth century, emerging theories of glandular secretions positioned the glands, especially the ovaries and testicles, as the mysterious source of messages that disseminated sexual difference throughout the body during puberty, governed the timing and the extent of growth and maturation, and eventually switched off, leading to the body's withering and loss of sexual differentiation with old age. Notably, the ovaries and testicles were not just envisioned as the biological source of sexual differentiation. Rather, glandular theories bound polar sex dimorphism to life itself by situating the glands as both the source of sexual differentiation and the motor of the life cycle of growth, maturation, and decay. Clearly dimorphic sexual difference was the key sign of healthy maturity, whereas its absence or fuzziness signaled the immaturity of childhood, the decay of old age, or the disability of gender inversion—incomplete or degenerate forms of human life. At this same time, sexual dimorphism and clear "mental" gender differentiation between men and women were being theorized as the unique evolutionary and civilizational achievement of the white races.[17] Relative sexual difference positioned the races on the linear path of evolutionary fitness, just as it mapped the relative health, fitness, and maturity of white bodies.[18]

What were considered most exciting about glandular theories were their potential medical applications. As the vital principle of plasticity, healthy glands were capable of inducing growth and development, of activating bodies to reach sex dimorphic forms, and of stimulating (in some not yet understood way) the development of intelligence and good character. The nineteenth- and early twentieth-century sciences primarily valued plasticity for the possibilities for eugenic population control and human engineering that it proffered. As the easily localized source of plasticity, the glands offered a quick fix—a means of correcting faulty bodies and minds. Clinicians sought to "cure" such maladies as homosexuality, impotence, overwork, criminality, and old age with the infusion of fresh glandular matter, leading to the pathologization of a host of new conditions. However, in the moment before the chemical structures of estrogen and testosterone were isolated and replicated, the agent of plasticity was not yet fully liquid. While ovarian secretions could be derived from large quantities of the urine of pregnant human or equine females, testicular secretions remained housed within the form of solid organs. Sourcing testicular secretions was therefore a major problem. Unfortunately, fresh human testicles were in short supply, given the reluctance of humans to part with them. In France, laws prohibited use of the cadavers of executed prisoners for medical science, barring French surgeons from what was a major source of glandular raw material in the United States. Gland therapies were therefore "tranimalities" from the very start. Ovarian secretions were extracted from horse urine, and slurries of goat and bull testicle were injected and consumed to enhance and restore youthful cismanhood and ciswomanhood.[19] One of the most sensational applications, however, was the infamous "monkey gland" operation. Popularized by Voronoff in Paris, the operation consisted of grafting a sliver of chimpanzee testicle into a bisected human testicle. Voronoff believed that because, according to Darwin's theory of evolution, anthropoid apes were biologically close to humans, ape xenotransplants would "take," and the healthy, young ape testicle would reawaken the slumbering human testicle, revitalizing it to the high level of function thought to characterize peak maturity.[20]

The predominant use of glandular transplants was to rejuvenate men and women according to cisnormative and dimorphic models of idealized white gender difference. Nevertheless, glandular science was also transsex from the very start.[21] The agency of the glands rather than the nerves in producing sexual maturation was evidenced by Eugen Steinach's cross-sex transplantation of ovaries or testicles in castrated, immature rats or guinea pigs. These transplantations caused the rats and guinea pigs to sexually mature and, in Steinach's interpretation, to exhibit behavioral characteristics associated with the sex of the transplanted glands rather than their birth sex.[22] In 1930, forty-seven-year-old Lili Elbe, who had lived most of her life as the male painter Einar Wegener, received first the ovaries of a younger woman and, later, perhaps a uterus in an effort to allow her to fully inhabit her youthful female self. She is thought to have died of complications from the latter experimental surgery.[23] In a parallel procedure, Magnus Hirschfeld's Institute for Sexual Science used transplanted testicular tissue to help patients transition to male. According to Hayward, however, the first documented human gender transition surgery was actually transspecific, involving the transplantation of nonhuman ovaries into a human trans woman.[24] Nor is this enmeshment of transspecies with transsex becoming a thing of the distant past. Until recently, Premarin, an estrogen made of the urine of pregnant mares, was a standard prescription for transitioning women,[25] leading Hayward to wonder, in an autoethnographic vein, "if my 'conjugated equine estrogens' are reshaping my species—becoming horse—along with my sex. Could mare chemistry be interlacing my own, giving me more of an insight into horse perception than sex perception?"[26]

These medical applications of glandular science offer concrete examples of trans★ plasticity in action. Here we have a series of material traversals of the ontological categories of human and animal as well as male and female. As Mel Chen writes, in the "new natures" of transspecies biology—including both transgenic stem cell research and the use of animal by-products and hormones to alter sexual and reproductive function in humans—"animals are not a third term; instead, humans and nonhuman animals recombine sexually within the same ontological form in which they are sometimes admitted to belong."[27] Material recombinations of human and nonhuman animal—in "new" transgenic as in "old" glandular research—rely on and activate plasticity, the ability of bodies to transform in response to molecules and transplanted tissue from other species.[28] Transspecies and transsex plasticity were foundational to the endocrinological science that would, by the 1950s, undergird transsexuality as a diagnostic category and set of medical protocols. Yet such trans★ plasticity does not necessarily result in an opening of possibilities for new ethics or forms of life beyond the categories of sexually dimorphic Eurohumanism. [. . .] This is to make a simple but, I think, crucial point: sometimes what transing does is shore up and, in some cases, empirically produce the very boundaries that are being crossed. The hallowed origins of biological sexual difference were sought, empirically speaking, through the method of transsex organ transplantation. Trans★ plasticity generates sexed ontology.

But might trans★ plasticity trouble ontology as well? In what follows, I turn to works of speculative fiction to envision both the arrested futures and the erotic unconscious of glandular science and Darwinian evolution. [. . .]

Transspecies Plasticity in *Nora*

According to the *British Medical Journal* (1924), a monkey graft was "a return, as it were, to our ancestry for refreshment."[29] Within such a return to the evolutionary source of vital plasticity was the potential for a dizzying reversal. What if, in the process, we became more ape than human? Was sex powered by an ape testicle interspecies sex? If the vitality of the ape was so desirable, so erotic, then might apes simply be superior to humans? Was the human species, unlike apes, weakened by generations of straying too far from our "nature"? Such disquieting doubts are given full sway in Champsaur's 1929 popular science fiction novel, *Nora, la guenon devenue femme*, translated into English in 2015 as *Nora, the Ape-Woman*.

Nora compares three sets of xenotransplant recipients. Ernest Paris is an aging French litterateur who undergoes a monkey gland transplant to regain his lost virility and waning creative powers. Narcisse and Nora, two orangutan-human hybrids from *Nora's* prequel, *Ouha: Roi des singes* (*Ouha: King of the Apes*), are the other xenotransplant recipients. The two ape-human hybrids are surgically outfitted with human glands in a bid to, as one character says of Nora, "transform the she-ape into a woman, thus accomplishing in a few months, the work into which nature had put thousands of years!"[30] This is, in other words, a eugenic experiment to direct and accelerate the work of evolution through gland xenotransplantation. Narcisse's and Nora's surgeries are not, however, symmetrical. Nora receives a full set of human glands. The more onerous procedure, for her, is a series of literally bone-breaking plastic surgeries, including ape bone inserts, that give her the silhouette of a fashionable 1920s woman. Nora's flesh is then cultured by placing a chimpanzee testicle within a mold of an idealized woman's figure. Ape testicles are here imagined to have the generative properties of pluripotent stem cells, underlining the fact that the glandular moment, in its obsession with finding and controlling the source of bodily plasticity, was a precursor to contemporary efforts to harness stem cell plasticity.[31] For Narcisse, by contrast, the focus is on intellectual development. Two human pineal glands and two thyroids are grafted into his brain with the intention of making him into a "superhuman."[32] Narcisse's transplants are intended less to retrace the path of evolution from ape to human than to activate his organic plasticity in order to hyperaccelerate evolution beyond what is imagined to be its current human peak. With Narcisse, eugenic gland xenotransplantation reaches toward what Julian Huxley (Aldous Huxley's lesser-known brother) would term transhumanism in 1957. *Transhumanism* names, for Huxley, the human species' savant use of eugenic measures to transcend itself, leading to a new stage of evolution beyond the human.[33] Transhuman though he may be, Narcisse's physical appearance as an orangutan is left unaltered.

As with gland transplantation practices in general, gland grafts and plastic surgeries are here orchestrated to reinforce a particular version of sexual difference. Narcisse represents an ideal fusion of cultivated white manhood and virile masculinity. [. . .] Though intelligent, Nora is no match for the male geniuses that stud this novel. Instead, she represents one male fantasy of the ideal woman as "a magnificent animal of pleasure," pornotropically responding to the sexual advances of any and every man, woman, and ape.[34] Implicitly, the novel asks who is superior, the human man enhanced with ape testicular grafts or the orangutan enhanced with human gland transplants. The novel's conclusion seems to fall resoundingly on the side of the enhanced ape. When Narcisse and Nora finally have sex, Nora finds that he is the only male able to fully satisfy her animal appetites. Soon thereafter, Ernest, revitalized after his ape graft surgery, returns to discover Narcisse and Nora in what appears to be a human-simian embrace (since Nora has a human appearance). Aroused by the sight, he throws himself on Nora—whom he had been grooming to be his mistress—like a beastly rapist "with a savage animal sensuality."[35] Narcisse promptly breaks his neck. Revitalized white men, the novel concludes, are just as beastly, if not more so, as enhanced apes. They remain, nonetheless, physically weaker and less sexually virile. Could this strange narrative be read as an illustration of trans★ plasticity that, by placing apes and humans within the same biomaterial fold, effecting a series of exchanges of matter between them, and playing on the erotic attractions that result, destroys ontological boundaries between human and ape? What would happen to this reading if we considered the difference race makes in transing the human/animal divide?

Figures of Blackness permeate the novel's attempts to illustrate species difference. Nora's first appearance reprises Josephine Baker's sensational banana skirt dance in her 1925 performance with the Revue Nègre at the Théâtre des Champs-Elysées. The novel's spectators' lust and awe at Nora's animal sensuality are thus made equivalent to the response of Parisian spectators to Baker's fantasized Black sexuality. Indeed, the tropes of sexual insatiability, and thus unrapability, of svelte animality, of childlike naivete, and of sexual experience unobtainable with white women that characterize Nora are precisely those that compose the French negrophilic pornotrope of Black femininity during the Jazz Age. Nor was Champsaur the first to make such offensive parallels between Baker and an ape. Sexually suggestive animalizing descriptions were among the stock tropes of Baker's French reception. Gushing over Baker, for instance, dance critic André Levinson evoked "an extraordinary creature of simian suppleness—a sinuous idol that enslaves and incites mankind."[36] He described the finale, Baker's pas de deux with Martinican Joe Alex, titled "Danse du sauvage," as emanating "a wild splendor and ferocious animality."[37] Baker critics Mae G. Henderson and Daphne Brooks have argued that Baker's irony, use of comedy, and savvy fusion of the French imaginary of Black primitivity with the transatlantic modernist styles of American jazz and French music hall constitute forms of agency and resistance.[38] As Henderson notes, however, white French critics and impresarios preferred to interpret and market Baker's virtuoso modernist dance performances as artless expressions of her primitive nature.[39] Likewise, Champsaur describes Nora's *danse sauvage* as the irresistible emanation of her animal nature: the dance has "nothing learned, nothing imposed, and seems instead to be the frolicking of a young animal amusing herself, without worrying about anything whatsoever."[40] The character of Nora literalizes the ape and animal metaphors that were frequently used, often in eroticized and putatively positive contexts, to describe Baker.[41]

So dense is the traffic between Nora's animality and French figures of Blackness that more than one critic misreads Nora as Black.[42] This is contrary to repeated descriptions in the novel of Nora as white, or even blue-skinned beneath her makeup; to her nickname, "la bête blanche" or "the white beast"; and to the fact that she was born of a white, though likely Jewish, father.[43] As with a generation of literary critics who conflated *Tarzan's* apes with its African savages, however, Nora's actual skin color may not ultimately matter for these critics. Brett Berliner, for example, reads Champsaur's apes in general as transparent figures for Blackness in order to condemn his novels as racist portrayals of the threat of miscegenation.[44] In this reading, Nora's orangutan origins are evacuated of any animal specificity: simian animality is nothing but a caricature of Blackness. Such readings illustrate how human/simian figural crossings have become instantly recognizable as blatant icons of racism, to the point that all other possible interpretations are blotted out, even in the presence of evidence (Nora's whiteness) to the contrary.[45] I would argue, however, that the novel's keen interest in the potential scientific basis of human/ape xenotransplantation brings human and ape biomateriality, not merely figuration, into play. Nevertheless, as the parallels between the fictionalized character Nora and Baker's actual reception demonstrate, human/simian crossings, whether figural or material, cannot be read apart from the historic Euro-North American association of race with animality. The next section works through what the confused coimplication of race and species in *Nora* can tell us about the uses of trans* plasticity.

Theorizing Animality With Race

What does trans* plasticity do? First and foremost, gland transplantations were wielded as means of activating and directing bodily and species plasticity with a view to eugenic improvements. The science and speculative fiction of gland transplantation thus demand a rethinking of eugenics itself. Eugenics comprises more than efforts to shape racial stock through positive and negative controls over reproduction, and more even than efforts to perform Lamarckian or glandular alterations on plastic bodies and minds that might then be passed down through the generations. Beyond efforts to shape the race and the species by either targeting reproduction or altering the bodies of current generations, eugenics might be more broadly defined as an effort to modulate the temporality of racial and species evolution. In the late nineteenth and early twentieth centuries, Darwinists reordered the globe into one continuous secular order of being, divided and hierarchized into race and species as avatars of progress or regress, movement or temporal lag. In monogenetic interpretations of Darwinism that held all humans to be descended from a common ancestor, there was no absolute difference between the races, just as there was no absolute divide between humans and apes. Rather than absolute differences of kind, race and species were but temporary figures wrought out of the moving arc of evolution.

[. . .]

Nora speculatively envisions a version of eugenics that seeks, through gland transplantation, to radically accelerate evolutionary change, activating the species plasticity of the orangutan body until it achieves human or, in Narcisse's case, transhuman characteristics. In so doing, *Nora* reminds us that, as scholars such as Jayna Brown, Kyla Schuller, and Jules Gill-Peterson have argued, the source of speculative and scientific interest in plasticity was eugenics.[46] New materialist enthusiasm about the dynamism and vitality of organic matter must contend with this eugenic and racist history of plasticity, as well as the potential eugenic and human engineering uses to which contemporary technologies of plasticity—such as genetic modification and stem cell technologies—may still be put.

The bone-crunching surgeries, surgical suturing of organs and parts from different species, and tissue cultures used to change Nora's form from ape to human are reminiscent of H. G. Wells's 1896 classic, *The Island of Doctor Moreau*, with which Champsaur was likely familiar. *Nora's* similarities with and, more to the point, its generic departures from *Doctor Moreau* offer conceptual insights into the relations among animality, sex, and race. *Doctor Moreau's* plot is well known: on a remote Pacific island, the eponymous Moreau pushes the art of vivisection to extremes, performing excruciatingly painful surgeries on nonhuman animals of a range of species until they approximate the human form. His explicit ambition is "to find out the extreme limit of plasticity in a living shape."[47] Colonialism is the enabling condition of this early scientific inquiry into organic plasticity. After being chased out of Britain by humane resistance to the cruelty of his nonhuman animal vivisection experiments, Moreau, in a settler colonial gesture, claims an entire island as his laboratory, where he reigns unsupervised as absolute sovereign. Moreau creates his loyal subjects, which he names the Beast People, fashions his own Law, which he forces the Beast People to recite, and profits from the primitive accumulation of a wealth of nonhuman animal biomatter for his experiments. As in *Nora*, technologically produced humanoid animals are relentlessly racialized. Of his first vivisection "success," a gorilla, Moreau relates, "I thought him a fair specimen of the negroid type when I had done him."[48] Confronted with these frighteningly beastly humanoid creatures, the shipwrecked narrator, Edward Prendick, repeatedly wonders what "race" of human savages they might be. Within European-authored ontologies of species and race, an animalized human or a humanized animal occupies the same position as the native of color; hence, within science fiction, such figures continually reference and counterreference each other.

[. . .]

The fact that surgical recombinations of human and nonhuman animal evoke racial tropes reveals something about the ontology of race: race was conceptually generated through transings of human and animal. Nineteenth and twentieth-century experiments in transspecies plasticity resonated with the older discourses of natural history, which we might recast as preoccupied with the species plasticity of nonwhite natives and apes. If natives of color and apes were the descendants of human-beast matings, then they exemplified species plasticity: two species hybridizing, their biological material fusing to create a new type of being. Thus, species plasticity buttressed emergent racial and species taxonomies, helping classify racialized natives, particularly Africans and "Hottentots," as "lower" forms of humanity. By the twentieth century, such origin stories either were forgotten or lacked credibility. The ontology of race as a transing of human and animal was nevertheless replayed in unrealized Darwin-inspired schemes for hybridization experiments. In the early twentieth century, evolutionary expert Ernst Haeckle and German sexologist Hermann Rodleder each proposed (unrelated) hybridization experiments between humans and apes. Haeckle thought that the sperm of an African man was necessary for the experiment to succeed, and Rodleder recommended the sperm of a mixed-race native of Tenerife.[49] In the seventeenth and eighteen centuries, trans★ plasticity—in the form of reproduction across species difference—generated ontology, furnishing the evidence that buttressed Euro-humanist racial taxonomies of being. By the twentieth century, this forgotten history haunted speculative proposals to test the trans★ plasticity of humans of color—thought to be evolutionarily "closer" to apes than were white humans—by attempting to hybridize them with apes.

In the (racial) sciences of the seventeenth through twentieth centuries, race either was animality itself or was a transing of animality and humanity—"the animal within the human"—or "*tranimality*," if you will.[50] Material transings generated humanist hierarchies of being. Trans★ plasticity produced the ontology of race and species. Hence, *Nora*'s inquiries into species plasticity—its material recombinations of human and nonhuman animal and experiments in accelerating orangutan evolution—are ultimately powerless against this genealogy of race and species. *Nora*'s play with ape-human xenotransplantation ends up evoking, over and over, figures of surplus animal sexual vitality: Nora's hypersexuality, Narcisse's superior penis. In turn, these figures of animal sexuality cannot but replay the ontology of race as a transing of humanity and animality. Transing is an ineffective means of throwing Darwinism's racial and species hierarchies into disarray, much less of dismantling racism along with speciesism, as some animal studies scholarship might hope. This is because race was already constituted through the transing of human and nonhuman animal in the first place. There is a historical lesson in this revelation. To think transing in the present, without the axis of time, allows scholars to imagine it as what transgressively entangles or destabilizes putatively fixed ontological categories, such as race and species. Restoring the axis of time, however, reveals that at one point these ontologies were emergent rather than fixed. During this moment of emergence, material transings, in their activation of organic plasticity, helped produce the ontobiological concepts of sex, race, and species difference.

Attention to material transings—through gland xenotransplantation, transgenic organisms, interspecies sex, and, more prosaically, the human consumption and digestion of animal and plant matter—can help conceptually unravel the fictions of the determinism and fixity of biology, the purity and self-sameness of organisms, and the exceptionality of the human. It is crucial, however, that in envisioning the conceptual potential of trans★ plasticity, scholars not ignore its speculative and actual uses. This is not to oppose radical speculation to hard historical reality. Modern speculative fiction imagined a more perfect eugenics more often than it promoted radical alternatives to modern ontologies of being. Trans★ plasticity has been both speculatively and actually conscripted into the service of eugenics, human engineering, and the use of nonhuman organisms as raw matter for the renewal of the human. The latter is all too clear, for example, in efforts to create, through transgenic gene splicing, a pig that can grow human organs to be harvested and transplanted into humans.

Transing, in and of itself, is not the answer. What trans★ plasticity calls for is a nuanced political analysis of the power relations, conceptual genealogies, and biopolitical economies brought into play when putatively distinct orders of being are materially combined.

Notes

I am grateful to my research assistant, shelley feller, for their help with research and references, and to Greta Lafleur and Jack Halberstam for their comments on the manuscript chapter and lecture versions of this article.

1. Bennett, *Vibrant Matter*. Jane Bennett's *Vibrant Matter* virtually generated the field of new materialist scholarship.
2. Voronoff claimed to have grafted chimpanzee ovaries into several cisgender women, achieving good results regarding revitalization. This procedure, however, was publicized far less than his operations on cisgender men (*How to Restore Youth*, 185–189).
3. Hayward and Weinstein, "Introduction," 206.
4. Hayward and Weinstein, "Introduction," 197.
5. This represents an ontological turn in the use the term *transing* in Stryker, Currah, and Moore, "Introduction." Hayward writes, for example, that in the lyrics to Antony and the Johnson's "Cripple and the

Starfish," "boundaries of sexual and species differences, artificial and authentic orderings, and nature and culture are affectively and literally trans-ed" ("More Lessons from a Starfish," 69).

6. Affect studies is a broad and diverse field. I am referring here only to affect studies scholarship that thinks affect as ontological or preontological, not to scholarship on the social life of feelings that makes no claims with regards to ontology.

7. Hayward and Weinstein, "Introduction," 200.

8. Wynter, "Unsettling the Coloniality of Being/Power/Truth/Freedom."

9. For Colebrook, *transitivity* names the generative preontological condition of all life ("What Is It Like to Be a Human?" 228).

10. By contrast, C. Riley Snorton poses Blackness as appositional to transitivity "inasmuch as blackness is a condition of possibility for the modern world" (*Black on Both Sides*, 5). Hayward turns to anti-Blackness as the ontology of the human in her short, Afro-pessimist-inspired essay "Don't Exist."

11. For important critiques of the ontological turn, see Hemmings, "Invoking Affect"; and Rosenberg, "Molecularization of Sexuality."

12. Hayward and Gossett, "Impossibility of That."

13. Hayward and Weinstein, "Introduction," 197.

14. Hayward and Gossett, "Impossibility of That," 19.

15. On how glandular science had to be disavowed so that endocrinology could establish itself as a legitimate field, see Sengoopta, *Most Secret Quintessence of Life*.

16. I borrow the notion of arrested futures from Stoler, "'Rot Remains,'" 21.

17. Schuller, *Biopolitics of Feeling*.

18. See Steinach, *Sex and Life*, 11; Sengoopta, *Most Secret Quintessence of Life*; McLaren, *Reproduction by Design*; and Pettit, "Becoming Glandular."

19. See Oudshoorn, *Beyond the Natural Body*; Pettit, "Becoming Glandular"; Sengoopta, *Most Secret Quintessence of Life*; and McLaren, *Reproduction by Design*. On the use of executed and live prisoners in the United States for glandular experiments, see Blue, "Strange Career of Leo Stanley."

20. Voronoff, *How to Restore Youth*; Voronoff and Alexandrescu, *Testicular Grafting from Ape to Man*. In the United States, John Brinkley, the "goat gland doctor," performed immensely popular goat testicular grafts on human men. See Pettit, "Becoming Glandular."

21. I follow Bailey Kier in using the term *transsex* rather than *transgender* for several reasons. First, I am referring to the sexed plasticity of bodies, rather than the gender identifications of subjects. Second, as Kier notes, *transgender* is overloaded with human and humanist connotations; *transsex* seeks to move away from the anthropomorphism of *transgender*. Similarly, I do not use *transsexual*, because this term refers to a specific medicalized narrative of pathologized human gender dysphoria leading to medical transition. See Kier, "Interdependent Ecological Transsex."

22. Steinach, *Sex and Life*.

23. Hoyer, *Man into Woman*; Amin, "Glands, Eugenics, and Rejuvenation."

24. Hayward, "Spider City Sex," 228. Voronoff used this same procedure to rejuvenate middle-aged cisgender women, underscoring the links between glandular rejuvenation and early gender-affirmation surgeries.

25. Premarin is no longer recommended for transitioning women due to an increased likelihood of blood clots. The estrogens prescribed today, as well as testosterone cypionate prescribed to transitioning men, are made from extracts of yam and soy.

26. Hayward, "Spider City Sex," 242.

27. Chen, *Animacies*, 103.

28. Today, the effects of early twentieth-century gland xenotransplants are thought to have been due to the placebo effect. Before the advent of immunosuppressants, xenotransplants would have been reabsorbed into the body. Here, I engage with the imaginaries of speculative science and speculative science fiction without distinguishing which theories were "true" and which were not.

29. Quoted in Sengoopta, *Most Secret Quintessence of Life*, 96.

30. Champsaur, *Nora, the Ape-Woman*, 53. "Changer cette guenon en femme! Accomplir, en qulques mois, l'oeuvre où la nature avait mis des milliers d'années!" (*Nora, la guenon devenue femme*, 55).

31. In stem cell research, *stem cell plasticity* refers to the capacity of pluripotent stem cells to transdifferentiate into distinct types of tissue cells, such as skin, muscle, and fat cells.

32. Champsaur, *Nora, the Ape-Woman*, 63. "Un surhomme" (*Nora, la guenon devenue femme*, 66). Voronoff believed the thyroid gland to be the source of the brain's "ignition spark," without which it would remain "inert" (*How to Restore Youth*, 34).

33. Through transhumanist eugenics, Huxley predicts, "the human species will be on the threshold of a new kind of existence, as different from ours as ours is from the Pekin man [a *Homo erectus* fossil

excavated in Beijing in 1923–27]" ("Transhumanism," 76). For a critical reading of Huxley's "Transhumanism" in relation to posthumanism, plasticity, and eugenics, see Brown, "Being Cellular." Similarly, Megan Glick notes that the first English-language use of the term *posthuman* was by the eugenicist sociologist Maurice Parmelee in *Poverty and Social Progress* in 1914. For Parmelee, once eugenics eliminates socially undesirable stock and improves the remaining stock, the result will be a neither human nor even mammalian but, rather, a superior posthuman animal (Glick, *Infrahumanisms*, 125).

34. Champsaur, *Nora, the Ape-Woman*, 247. "Un magnifique animal de plaisir" (*Nora, la guenon devenue femme*, 284).
35. Champsaur, *Nora, the Ape-Woman*, 220. "Avec une sensualite d'animal sauvage" (*Nora, la guenon devenue femme*, 252).
36. Levinson, "Negro Dance," 291.
37. Levinson, "Negro Dance," 291.
38. Henderson, "Josephine Baker and La Revue Nègre"; Brooks, "End of the Line," 4.
39. Henderson, "Josephine Baker and La Revue Nègre."
40. Champsaur, *Nora, the Ape-Woman*, 25–26. "Rien d'appris, rien d'imposé, et semble plutôt les ébats d'un jeune animal qui s'amuse pour lui-même, sans souci de quoi que ce soit" (*Nora, la guenon devenue femme*, 21).
41. In another example, in Edmond Gréville's *Princesse Tam Tam* (1935), De Mirecourt says of Baker's character, Aouina, a Black North African, "This little animal moves me. She is so naive" (quoted in Sharpley-Whiting, *Black Venus*, 114).
42. "Dark-skinned Nora, Champsaur intimated, was nothing but an atavism, just a gland away from the simian world, a sardonic injunction against miscegenation" (Berliner, "Mephistopheles and Monkeys," 324).
43. Champsaur, *Nora, the Ape-Woman*, 109; Champsaur, *Nora, la guenon devenue femme*, 122.
44. Berliner, "Mephistopheles and Monkeys."
45. For a critique of a generation of literary critics who conflate *Tarzan*'s apes with its savages, see Lundblad, *Birth of a Jungle*, 139. For a critique of the conflation of figures of simian animality with race, see Glick, *Infrahumanisms*, 56–79.
46. See Brown, "Being Cellular," 327; Schuller, *Biopolitics of Feeling*; and Gill-Peterson, *Histories of the Transgender Child*.
47. Wells, *Island of Doctor Moreau*, 66.
48. Wells, *Island of Doctor Moreau*, 67.
49. Rossiianov, "Beyond Species."
50. On tranimality, see Hayward and Weinstein, "Introduction"; Kelley and Hayward, "TRANimalS"; King, "SL Tranimal"; and Steinbock, Szczygielska, and Wager, "Tranimacies."

Bibliography

Amin, Kadji. "Glands, Eugenics, and Rejuvenation in *Man into Woman*: A Biopolitical Genealogy of Transsexuality." *TSQ* 5, no. 4 (2018): 589–605.

Bennett, Jane. *Vibrant Matter*. Durham, NC: Duke University Press, 2010.

Berliner, Brett. "Mephistopheles and Monkeys: Rejuvenation, Race, and Sexuality in Popular Culture in Interwar France." *Journal of the History of Sexuality* 13, no. 3 (2004): 306–325.

Blue, Ethan. "The Strange Career of Leo Stanley: Remaking Manhood and Medicine at San Quentin State Penitentiary, 1913–1951." *Pacific Historical Review* 78, no. 2 (2009): 210–241.

Brooks, Daphne. "The End of the Line: Josephine Baker and the Politics of Black Women's Corporeal Comedy." *Scholar and the Feminist Online* 6, nos. 1–2 (2007): 4.

Brown, Jayna. "Being Cellular: Race, the Inhuman, and the Plasticity of Life." *GLQ* 21, nos. 2–3 (2015): 321–341.

Champsaur, Félicien. *Nora, la guenon devenue femme*. Paris: Ferenczi et Fils, 1929.

———. *Nora, the Ape-Woman*. Translated by Brian Stableford. Encino, CA: Black Coat, 2015.

Chen, Mel. *Animacies: Biopolitics, Racial Mattering, and Queer Affect*. Durham, NC: Duke University Press, 2012.

Colebrook, Claire. "What Is It Like to Be a Human?" *TSQ* 2, no. 2 (2015): 227–243.

Ferriera da Silva, Denise. *Toward a Global Idea of Race*. Minneapolis: University of Minnesota Press, 2007.

Gill-Peterson, Jules. *Histories of the Transgender Child*. Minneapolis: University of Minnesota Press, 2018.

Glick, Megan. *Infrahumanisms: Science, Culture, and the Making of Modern Non/Personhood*. Durham, NC: Duke University Press, 2018.

Hayward, Eva. "Don't Exist." *TSQ* 4, no. 2 (2017): 191–94.

———. "More Lessons from a Starfish: Prefixial Flesh and Transspeciated Selves." In "Trans-," edited by Paisley Currah, Lisa Jean Moore, and Susan Stryker. Special issue, *WSQ* 36, nos. 3–4 (2008): 64–85.

———. "Spider City Sex." *Women and Performance* 20, no. 3 (2010): 225–51.

Hayward, Eva, and Che Gossett. "Impossibility of That." *Angelaki* 22, no. 2 (2017): 15–24.

Hayward, Eva, and Jami Weinstein. "Introduction: Tranimalities in the Age of Trans* Life." In "Tranimalities," edited by Eva Hayward and Jami Weinstein. Special issue, *TSQ* 2, no. 2 (2015): 195–208.

Hemmings, Clare. "Invoking Affect: Cultural Theory and the Ontological Turn." *Cultural Studies* 19, no. 5 (2005): 548–567.

Henderson, Mae G. "Josephine Baker and La Revue Nègre: From Ethnography to Performance." *Text and Performance Quarterly* 23, no. 2 (2003): 107–133.

hooks, bell. "Eating the Other: Desire and Resistance." 1992; repr. in *Media and Cultural Studies: KeyWorks*, edited by Meenakshi Gigi Durham and Douglas M. Kellner, 366–380. Malden, MA: Blackwell, 2006.

Hoyer, Niels, ed. *Man into Woman: An Authentic Record of a Change of Sex*. Translated by H. J. Stenning. London: Jarrolds, 1933.

Huxley, Julian. "Transhumanism." 1957; repr., *Journal of Humanistic Psychology* 8, no. 1 (1968): 73–76.

Jackson, Zakiyyah Iman. "Losing Manhood: Animality and Plasticity in the (Neo)Slave Narrative." *Qui Parle* 25, nos. 1–2 (2016): 95–136.

Kelley, Lindsay, and Eva Hayward. "TRANimalS: Theorizing the Transin Zoontology." Panel Held at the meeting of the Society for Science, Literature, and Art, Atlanta, November 5, 2009.

Kier, Bailey. "Interdependent Ecological Transsex: Notes on Re/Production, 'Transgender' Fish, and the Management of Populations, Species, and Resources." *Women and Performance* 20, no. 3 (2010): 299–319.

King, Katie. "SL Tranimal @ Cardiff 2010: My Distributed Animality." sltranimal.blogspot.com (accessed September 29, 2018).

Levinson, André. "The Negro Dance: Under European Eyes." *Theatre Arts Monthly* 11 (April 1927): 282–93.

Lundblad, Michael. *The Birth of a Jungle: Animality in Progressive-Era U.S. Literature and Culture*. Oxford: Oxford University Press, 2013.

McLaren, Angus. *Reproduction by Design: Sex, Robots, Trees, and Test-Tube Babies in Interwar Britain*. Chicago: University of Chicago Press, 2012.

Oudshoorn, Nelly. *Beyond the Natural Body: An Archaeology of Sex Hormones*. London: Routledge, 1994.

Peterson, Christopher. *Bestial Traces: Race, Sexuality, Animality*. New York: Fordham University Press, 2012.

Pettit, Michael. "Becoming Glandular: Endocrinology, Mass Culture, and Experimental Lives in the Interwar Age." *American Historical Review* 118, no. 4 (2013): 1052–1076.

Rosenberg, Jordy. "The Molecularization of Sexuality: On Some Primitivisms of the Present." *Theory and Event* 17, no. 2 (2014).

Rossiianov, Kirill. "Beyond Species: Il'ya Ivanov and His Experiments on Cross-Breeding Humans with Anthropoid Apes." *Science in Context* 15, no. 2 (2002): 277–316.

Schiebinger, Londa. "The Gendered Ape." 1993; repr. In *Nature's Body: Gender in the Making of Modern Science*, 75–114. New Brunswick, NJ: Rutgers University Press, 2004.

Schuller, Kyla. *The Biopolitics of Feeling: Race, Sex, and Science in the Nineteenth Century*. Durham, NC: Duke University Press, 2018.

Sengoopta, Chandak. *The Most Secret Quintessence of Life: Sex, Glands, and Hormones, 1850–1950*. Chicago: University of Chicago Press, 2006.

Sharpley-Whiting, T. Denean. *Black Venus: Sexualized Savages, Primal Fears, and Primitive Narratives in French*. Durham, NC: Duke University Press, 1999.

Snorton, C. Riley. *Black on Both Sides: A Racial History of Trans Identity*. Minneapolis: University of Minnesota Press, 2017.

Squier, Susan. "Incubabies and Rejuvenates: The Traffic Between Technologies of Reproduction and Age-Extension." In *Figuring Age: Women, Bodies, Generations*, edited by Kathleen Woodward, 88–111. Bloomington: Indiana University Press, 1999.

Steinach, Eugen. *Sex and Life: Forty Years of Biological and Medical Experiments*. New York: Viking Press, 1940.

Steinbock, Eliza, Marianna Szczygielska, and Anthony Wager, eds. "Tranimacies: Intimate Links Between Animal and Trans Studies." Special issue, *Angelaki* 22, no. 2 (2017).

Stoler, Ann Laura. "'The Rot Remains': From Ruins to Ruination." In *Imperial Debris: On Ruins and Ruination*, edited by Ann Laura Stoler, 1–36. Durham, NC: Duke University Press, 2013.

Stryker, Susan, Paisley Currah, and Lisa Jean Moore. "Introduction: Trans-, Trans, or Transgender?" In "Trans-," edited by Paisley Currah, Lisa Jean Moore, and Susan Stryker. Special issue, *WSQ* 36, nos. 3–4 (2008): 11–22.

Voronoff, Serge. *How to Restore Youth and Live Longer*. New York: Falstaff, 1928.

Voronoff, Serge, and George Alexandrescu. *Testicular Grafting from Ape to Man*. Translated by Theodore Merrill. London: Brentano's, 1930.

Wells, H. G. *The Island of Doctor Moreau*. 1896; repr., Oxford: Oxford University Press, 2017.

Wolfe, Cary. *Animal Rites: American Culture, the Discourse of Species, and Posthumanist Theory*. Chicago: University of Chicago Press, 2003.

Woodard, Vincent. *The Delectable Negro: Human Consumption and Homoeroticism Within US Slave Culture*. Edited by Dwight McBride and Justin Joyce. New York: New York University Press, 2014.

Wynter, Sylvia. "Unsettling the Coloniality of Being/Power/Truth/Freedom: Towards the Human, After Man, Its Overrepresentation—An Argument." *CR: The New Centennial Review* 3, no. 3 (2003): 257–337.

24 The Matter of Gender

Nikki Sullivan

Nikki Sullivan is a feminist philosopher and cultural studies scholar who has made several landmark contributions to trans studies, including her essay "Transmogrification: (Un)Becoming Others" in the first volume of the *Transgender Studies Reader*. In "The Matter of Gender," she offers a succinct overview of one of the most influential (and controversial) voices in the study of gender: John Money, who is often credited with inventing the concept of gender itself. Along with medical colleagues at Johns Hopkins University in the 1950s, Money coined the gender-concept to explain how intersex people, who have ambiguous sex anatomy, form identities as men and women, that is, how people with atypical genitals develop a sense of self and a social role in society whose personhood categories are based on a male/female dichotomy. He later applied the gender-concept to the study of transsexuals to explain how a person with one anatomical sex could develop an identity as a person who typically had a different anatomical sex. Money is often considered a "social constructionist" who held that "sex" was biological and "gender" social. As Sullivan shows, however, Money is more accurately understood as an "interactionist" whose full concept of gender-identity/role (G-I/R) is "biopsychosocial"—that is, a complex set of interactions between genetics, brain, and hormones, as well as social structure and individual experience. From its medical point of origin, the concept of gender moved into the social sciences and humanities and eventually provided a foundation for feminist, queer, and trans studies. The concept has become such a ubiquitous part of most people's everyday understanding of the world that it's difficult to remember that it has a surprisingly recent history.

> The social history of our era cannot be written without naming gender, gender role, and gender identity as organizing principles.
>
> —John Money, "The Concept of Gender Identity Disorder in Childhood and Adolescence after 39 Years"

In the popular imaginary of the present, John Money is most often cast as the quintessential social constructionist; as someone who claimed that gender is solely an effect of enculturation[1] and, as such, is radically mutable and alterable. For some, Money's purported theory of gender as an effect of nurture (as opposed to nature), made him "one of the gurus of the [second-wave] feminist movement"[2]—a characterization that seems to sit uncomfortably with Money's criticism of what he saw as feminism's "conceptual neutering of gender."[3]

DOI: 10.4324/9781003206255-30

For others, Money's clinical attempts to "prove" his theory have—particularly in light of the David Reimer case—shown his ideas to be both flawed and dangerous, and his practice to be unethical. Interestingly, in one of the most influential popular cultural texts on Money, *As Nature Made Him: The Boy Who was Raised as a Girl*, John Colapinto's characterization of Money as a constructionist is an inferential effect of the author's narrativization of a world of goodies and baddies, truth and lies, fact and fiction, males and females, rather than something that is convincingly argued through a close engagement with Money's writings. But despite this, Colapinto's text, and in particular his view of Money as a constructionist, seems largely to be taken as gospel.

Money himself would dispute this view of his work, arguing instead that his account of gender identity/role (G-I/R)—a concept I will discuss in detail in due course—is interactionist, that is, it acknowledges the generative effects of both biology and culture. Indeed, it is on this basis that Jennifer Germon has recently argued that "Money's gender offers a third wave of productive potential, one that differs from the second (as in second-wave feminism), precisely because his theories presuppose an interactive relation of cells to environment and to experience(s)."[4] Germon's optimism is challenged, however, by Lesley Rogers and Joan Walsh's much earlier claim that "it is not an interactionist approach to swing towards biological determinism most of the time and then occasionally, when it suits, to swing towards the environmental side."[5] As they see it, insofar as the model of gender attribution that Money and his coauthors articulate is underpinned by extremely conventional assumptions about and attitudes toward sexual difference, any attempt to articulate thoroughly the role of the social in the attribution of gender is wholly undermined. They write: "While Money, Ehrhardt, and co-workers consider the social aspects of gender . . . they take for granted that there are two genders, that there are differences between them, and that fundamentally gender is a consequence of a biological blueprint for behavior as well as physique."[6] Similarly, Ruth Doell and Helen Longino[7] have argued that Money's model of gender is more accurately additive than interactionist since it does not explain how biological and social variables work in tandem,[8] but rather, posits the biological as foundational.

There is little doubt that Money's work—in particular his elaboration of "gender"—has been hugely influential, and that rather than being confined to the worlds of scientific research and/or clinical practice, its influence has shaped us all. Consider, for a moment, the extent to which "gender" (however one might conceive it) has become central to everyday life, so much so that it is difficult to imagine how we might function without such a concept. This alone, it seems to me, is reason enough to engage with Money's vast oeuvre. But further incentive comes from the fact that while competing interpretations of Money's work are readily available to those who choose to seek them out, the popular image of Money as a constructionist abounds. This characterization is an oversimplification of Money's work, and one which can only be maintained through a lack of engagement with his writing. If, as feminists have long argued, ongoing analyses of identity and difference—and in particular, so-called sexual difference—are politically imperative, then a close engagement with Money's highly influential texts, the assumptions that informed his claims, and the ongoing and multifarious effects such claims produce, likewise seems called for. In critically interrogating Money's account of G-I/R, my aim in this chapter is not so much to definitively classify his work as either constructionist or determinist, but rather, to trouble the very tendency to see in dimorphic terms since, as Helen Longino has noted, "as long as dimorphism remains at the centre of discourse, other patterns of difference remain hidden both as possibility and as reality."[9]

Money's "Gender"

In popular parlance, gender tends either to be used as interchangeable with "sex" or, alternately, to refer to the social (as opposed to the so-called biological or "sexed") aspects of femaleness and maleness. In both cases, gender is a term that is commonly used to classify others and to refer to our own sense of ourselves as male or female, men or women, neither or both. Despite the fact that such conceptions of gender feel self-evident, they are, in fact, relatively recent It has been claimed by Money and others that the first use of the term "gender" to refer to something other than feminine and masculine forms within language occurred in Money's 1955 publications "Hermaphroditism, Gender and Precocity in Hyperadrenocortism: Psychologic Findings" and, coauthored with Joan and John Hampson, "Hermaphroditism: Recommendations Concerning Assignment of Sex, Change of Sex, and Psychologic Management."[10] Indeed, it was through his early work with intersex patients that Money came to consider the term "sex" inadequate to describe the lived embodiment of those whose anatomies are either "discordant" or do not appear to match the sex roles associated with masculinity or femininity, and/or the sense of self a particular individual has.[11] For Money, intersexuality challenges the "commonsense" idea that sex (as naturally dichotomous) is a biological characteristic that at once determines genital morphology and can be determined with reference to that morphology, and that sex roles naturally follow from genital morphology and are concordant with it. It is possible, writes Money, "to have the genetical sex of a male . . . ; the gonadal sex of a male; the internal morphologic sex of a male; the external genital morphologic sex of a female; the hormonal pubertal sex of a female; the assigned sex of a female; and the gender-role and identity of a female."[12] Hence, Money's coining of the term "gender"—or, more precisely, gender identity/role (G-I/R)—to refer to the multivariate character of the "totality of masculinity/femininity, genital sex included,"[13] that each person attains even when the multiple aspects of the self (as a "man" or a "woman") are (seemingly) discordant. What we see here, then, is that for Money gender is not synonymous with "sex" (as a set of biological variables), but nor are the five aspects of sex that he identifies in the above quote entirely separable from G-I/R.[14]

Money conceives gender identity and gender role as "obverse sides of the same coin. They constitute a unity."[15] Without this unity, he argues, "gender role . . . become[s] a socially transmitted acquisition, divorced from the biology of sex and the brain"; it becomes "desexualized," "cleaned up."[16] As Money understood it, gender identity is the experience one has of oneself as a man or a woman— "the kingpin of your identity"[17] as he and Patricia Tucker describe it—and gender role is the manifestation of this sense of self in one's daily performance of self. In sum, one's performance of gender reaffirms one's gender identity, in particular because it is through gender role, as "everything that [one] says or does to indicate to others . . . the degree that one is either male, or female, or ambivalent,"[18] that others perceive and position one as gendered (in a specific way). There are, of course, situations in which others' perception of the gender of an individual may not fit with that individual's self-perception, but this is the exception rather than the rule. [. . .]

As Money explains it, gender role is performative in two senses: it is an action or set of actions one articulates corporeally in a world of and with others, and, at the same time, it is constitutive of the self. In other words, gender role makes one be(come) male, female, neither or both, in and through what we might call—although Money himself does not use this term—sedimentation: the more we repeat certain actions, the more naturalized or habituated[19] such actions become, and the more they come to appear (both to others and to ourselves) as external expressions of who we "really" are. Clearly, then, while G-I/R may be effected by, for example, gonadal morphology or hormonal activity, it is never wholly determined by what we commonly think of as "biology." But nor, if G-I/R is intercorporeally (re)produced, can it be radically open and/or free, or, at least, that is what one might suppose. For Money, however, the story is a little more confused and confusing as we shall see.

For Money, the ability to acquire a G-I/R is "phylogenetically given, whereas the actuality is ontogenetically given."[20] In other words, while all humans share the ability to acquire a G-I/R, the G-I/Rs we each develop will differ according to context, pre and postnatal history, morphology, and so on. For Money, then, the ability to acquire a G-I/R—which he refers to as a "phylism"[21]—is, like the ability to acquire language, to breathe, to laugh, or to "pairbond,"[22] sex-shared: he writes, "You were wired but not programmed for gender in the same sense that you were wired but not programmed for language."[23] There are, however, phylisms which, according to Money's conceptual schema, are exclusive to either men or women: these are lactation, menstruation, ovulation, and gestation, which are (allegedly) exclusive to women, and impregnation, which is (allegedly) exclusive to men. Money refers to these as "sex irreducible" dimensions of G-I/R[24] and differentiates them, in kind, from what he classifies as the sex derivative,[25] sex adjunctive,[26] and sex arbitrary or sex adventitious[27] dimensions of G-I/R. What begins to emerge here, then, is a categorical distinction between aspects of G-I/R that are universal and somehow determined by sex (as a set of biological variables)[28] and aspects that are context specific and an effect of a particular "society's customary way of doing things."[29] So, for example, while one can acquire the ability to operate a heavy goods vehicle in and through particular cultural processes (e.g., driving lessons), one cannot acquire the ability to ovulate, ontogenetically.[30] A similar ontological move is apparent in Money's claim that phylisms that are sex-shared are sometimes "threshold dimorphic,"[31] such that, for example, adolescent boys are more readily aroused by "sexy pin-up pictures"[32] than are adolescent girls. It is possible, writes Money:

> that divergent threshold levels are preset as early as in prenatal life when steroidal sex hormones organize bipotential brain regions and pathways to differentiate as predominantly either male or female. From animal experiments, there is abundant evidence that such organization does indeed take place."[33]

Throughout Money's work, the lowering of thresholds is vaguely associated with, although never convincingly connected—at least not in a straightforward causal sense—to prenatal exposure to hormones, most particularly androgen.[34] [. . .] I want to suggest that in both the examples discussed we see that for Money G-I/R is never a purely social phenomenon and, while the acquisition of G-I/R necessarily involves what we might ordinarily think of as biological processes, these processes are never wholly determinative. For example, even though the ability to menstruate is associated with women, it does not guarantee a female G-I/R, as the existence of trans men or FTM (female-to-male) transsexuals shows. Conversely, an inability to menstruate does not mean that a person raised as female will not continue to identify and live as a woman once "amenorrhea" becomes apparent. Consequently, Money describes his model of G-I/R acquisition as biosocial[35] or interactionist, and as developmental (and sequential) as opposed to causal.[36]

As I said earlier, Money's proposition that identity does not strictly follow from anatomy, or, even when it appears to, that anatomy is not the cause of G-I/R, is an outcome of his early work with intersexuals, and later, with individuals desiring to undergo "sex reassignment" procedures. The clinical challenge Money faced in both cases was the question of whether or not surgery should be performed, and if so, on what basis its practice might be justified. Central to Money's theory of G-I/R, and to his recommendation that both infants with atypically sexed bodies and adults whose gender identity is (according to normative logic) at odds with their genital morphology should undergo surgical (trans)formation, is his concept of "the critical period of development."[37] Critical periods occur, according to Money, both

anatomically and in the development of G-I/R more broadly, and each is marked, metaphorically speaking, by a gate that, once closed, is at best unlikely and at worst impossible to
reopen.[38] This closing of gates along a developmental pathway "locks in" G-I/R such that
one's sense of self and one's gendered performance becomes increasingly sedimented as one's
subjectivity develops: you acquire, developmentally, a "native gender,"[39] or, to put it somewhat differently, "bipotentiality becomes monopotentiality.[40] Money writes:

> As you approached each gate's sex-differentiation point, you could have gone in either
> direction, but as you passed through, the gate locked, fixing the prior period of develop-
> ment as male or female. Your gonads, for example, could have become either testicles
> or ovaries, but once they became testicles they lose the option of becoming ovaries. . . .
> In behavior . . . at first you drove all over the highway, but as you proceeded you tended
> to stick more and more to the lanes marked out and socially prescribed for your sex.[41]

[. . .]

Gender Identity Differentiation and/or Gendermaps

Sexology, writes Money, "is the science of . . . the differentiation and dimorphism of sex,"[42]
of the biosocial processes that shape us as women, men, and, very occasionally, androgynous.
Sexology's advantage m the mapping of these processes lies in its multi- or transdisciplinary
approach—an approach that, as Money tells it, allows him to avoid the all-too-common
tendency to divorce the biological from the social, nature from nurture, sex from gender,
body from mind. Indeed, from Money's perspective, the splitting of sex and gender and the
establishment and maintenance of disciplinary boundaries and discipline-specific knowledges and practices have, historically, been mutually constitutive,[43] and have resulted in what
he describes as "enormous doctrinal damage."[44] Money asserts that his work bridges the
chasm between social and biological definitions of gender, as well as that between the "hard"
sciences and the social sciences in and through the conception of G-I/R as the effect of
multivariate and sequential differentiation,[45] or gendermapping. Gendermap, writes Money,

> Is the term used to refer to the entity, template, or schema within the mind and brain
> (mindbrain) unity that codes masculinity and femininity and androgyny. . . . The gen-
> dermap is a conceptual entity wider which are assembled all the male/female differences,
> and similarities also, not only those that are procreative and phylogenetically determined,
> but also those that are arbitrary and conventionally determined, such as male/female
> differences in education, vocation, and recreation. The gendermap . . . ha[s] a history
> of growth and development from very simple beginnings to very complex outcomes.
> [It is] multivariately and sequentially determined and, therefore, complicated to study.
> Explanations of [its] genesis are in terms of temporal sequences, not causal sequences.[46]

[. . .]

Underpinning this model are two assumptions that are ripe for critical attention. The
first is that there is a "normal" developmental teleology that, when followed in an orderly
manner, will result in an ideal(ized), unified G-I/R. Consequently, gender-variant corpo
realities (or "gender identity errors" as Money sometimes calls them)[47] are conceived (and
thus constituted) as the result of developmental deviations in the course of this natural(ized)
universal system. Second, and related, is the assumption that G-I/Rs and the processes by
which G-I/R differentiation occurs are naturally dimorphic and therefore naturally heterosexual.[48] In *Gay, Straight, and In-Between*, Money writes, "Gender coding is by definition

dualistic. One half of the code is for female, the other for male. A child must assimilate both halves of the code, identifying with one and complementating the other."[49] Postnatally, "the child becomes conditioned to adhere to the positive model which is the one congruous with his rearing and, in the normal course of events, consistent with his anatomy. The opposite or negative-valence model becomes a constant reminder of how one should not act."[50] This process of coding by which two gender schemas develop in the "mindbrain" means that gendermaps are never exclusively social or biological in origin. Indeed, since learned behavior shapes the "mindbrain" ontogenetically (by building on what is phylogenetically laid down), it is both wrongheaded and impossible, argues Money, to attempt to differentiate the gendermaps in terms of social and biological aspects. "It is there, in the brain," writes Money, "that ontogeny and phylogeny meet; there that the social customs and traditions . . . are assimilated and fused with one's species heritage. In the brain sociopsycho-physiosomatic and/or somatophysio-psychosocial are one."[51] In short, then, gendermaps consist of "features that are phylogenetically shared with other members of the species, and characteristics that are ontogenetically personal,"[52] such that gendered subjectivity is at once unique, situated, and in-process, and shared, and partially (and increasingly) determined.

[. . .]

Money's Gender and the Question of Influence

At the beginning of this chapter, I suggested that Money is commonly regarded in the contemporary context as a social constructionist—a characterization he himself would strongly refute. I also noted that as such, some have claimed him as the darling of second-wave feminism. Money's model of G-I/R outlined here clearly shows that insofar as the former claim is misguided, the latter too is unlikely to carry any real weight. Indeed, Money's criticism of second-wave feminism's alleged divorcing of sex from gender, combined with the accusation of essentialism made by the very small number of feminists who engaged with Money's work in the period associated with feminism's so-called second wave, clearly points to the dubiousness of such claims.[53] Having said this, however, I do not mean to imply that second-wave feminists embraced a model of gender that was simply opposed to Money's: to do so would be to reaffirm the overly simplistic dichotomy of social constructionism versus biological determinism. What I want to suggest instead is that while at the time of its development Money's model of G-I/R had little impact on second-wave feminism(s),[54] it does, ironically—and this is a claim that may well make Money turn in his grave—share with many second-wave feminist accounts of gender an unacknowledged dependence on "the sexed body" as somehow foundational.[55] In short, it is my contention that both Money's work on gender and the work of the vast majority of second-wave feminists exemplifies what Linda Nicholson refers to as "biological foundationalism."[56]

Nicholson explains this term with reference to what she describes as the "coatrack view of self-identity."[57] On this model, the rack is the aspect of the self that is common to everyone (or, in the case of feminist writing, to all women); it is the thing on which the cultural aspects of selfhood—the things that make us different—are hung. Money's coatrack is what he calls "the phylogenetic," and what gets hung on that foundation are the ontogenetic aspects of G-I/R. This model is also apparent in the work of diverse thinkers associated with second-wave feminism. For example, anthropologist Gayle Rubin introduced the phrase "the sex/gender system"[58] in her landmark essay "The Traffic in Women" (1975), to refer to "a set of arrangements by which the biological raw material of human sex and procreation is shaped by human, social intervention."[59] Feminism, Rubin argued, should aim to create a "genderless (though not sexless) society, in which one's sexual anatomy is irrelevant to who one is, what one does, and with whom one makes love."[60]

In a very different feminist project from the same era, Janice Raymond vehemently attacked MTF (male-to-female) transsexuals, in particular those who identified as lesbian, arguing that "male-to-constructed-female" lesbian feminists "can only play the part"[61] of women, lesbians, and feminists. Further, she claimed that

> All [MTF] transsexuals rape women's bodies by reducing the real female form to an artifact, appropriating this body for themselves. However, the transsexually constructed lesbian-feminist violates women's sexuality and spirit as well. . . . Because [MTF] transsexuals have lost their physical "members" does not mean that they have lost their ability to penetrate women-women's minds, women's sexuality, [MTF] transsexuals merely cut off the most obvious means of invading women so that they seem noninvasive. However, as Mary Daly has remarked in the case of the transsexually constructed lesbian-feminists their whole presence becomes a "member" invading women's presence and dividing us once more from each other.[62]

While I do not want to claim that Raymond explicitly posits a distinction between sex and gender, nature and culture in her work, the criticisms she aims at MTFs clearly imply the existence of a sexuality, a spirit, a body, that is particular to (all) women and that is not, by definition, shared by men. And even though Raymond recognizes differences between men—for example, not all men want to be transsexuals—it nevertheless seems that fundamentally all men are the same at the very least insofar as they are not, and cannot ever be, women.

This sense of sex-shared character(istics) is also apparent in Carol Gilligan's (1983) work on what she perceives as a universal proclivity among women for "relatedness."[63] While Gilligan, like Raymond, describes this tendency as an aspect of "women's culture"—that is, as something that occurs in and through social processes and organization rather than solely as a result of biology—there is a sense in which both writers, "claim a strong [universal(izing)] correlation between people with certain biological characteristics [that is, penises or vaginas] and people with certain character traits."[64] As Nicholson notes, claims that women are different from men (or vice versa) in "such and such ways,"[65] ultimately function to constitute certain characteristics as female or male, and in doing so, to naturalize the differences purportedly described. These differences, Nicholson claims, "tend to reflect the perspective of those making the characterizations . . . and to reflect the biases"[66] of particular social groups, most often those in a position of power and/or authority[67]—a claim I will return to in a moment.

In pointing out what I, following Nicholson, identify as the biological foundationalism of these very different projects, it is not my intention to conflate them, and in so doing, to flatten out the important theoretical and political differences between them. Indeed, what I find so useful about this concept is that it enables a move beyond the black-and-white logic of the essentialism versus constructionism debate: it allows, indeed it calls for, an analysis of the nuances of particular positions, and the (similar and different) effects they produce. As Nicholson puts it, "Biological foundationalism is not equivalent to biological determinism; all of its forms, though some more extensively so than others, include some element of social construction."[68] Biological foundationalism "is best understood as representing a continuum of positions. . . . This counters a commonplace contemporary tendency to think of social constructionist positions as all alike in the role that biology plays within them."[69] Given this, the question is not so much whether biological foundationalism is a good thing or a bad thing since clearly it generates heterogeneous effects even within one particular perspective. Nor is it a question of how to best clarify gender, or of whose/which conception is most correct. If, as Nicholson claims, "the clarification of the meaning of . . . any concept . . . is stipulative"[70] (rather than merely describing a given reality), then it is so within the context of a particular regime of truth, within a particular discipline and/or set of disciplinary practices.[71] Our conceptions of gender are, to quote Nicholson again, situated: "they emerge from our own places within history and culture; they are political acts that reflect the contexts we emerge out of and the futures we would like to see."[72] Nowhere is this clearer than in Money's work on transsexualism in which he simultaneously claims to know of "no proven cause of gender identity disorder,"[73] and yet turns to studies on animals to explain how hormonal coding can affect the G-I/R of sheep who have been androgenized and thereafter try to mount other ewes and are not approached by rams;[74] androgenized female monkeys who "played more boisterously than normal female monkeys" and whose "assertiveness and mating behavior . . . fell somewhere in between the normal male and female";[75] and of developmentally "normal" white leghorn roosters whose sexual attraction to and mounting of a headless model of a chicken demonstrates "the fact that [non-cross-coded] men's erotic arousal, including erection of the penis, is eye-sensitive and can be rather easily triggered by a visual stimuli."[76]

To a humanities scholar, these claims, and the experiments that make them possible, may appear extremely spurious, and yet in the context in which Money carried out his research, it seems they were not. Moreover, the fact that experiments on animals continue to be carried out (in huge numbers, and often in ways that are, to many, inhumane) in the hope that they will one day provide the key(s) to the difference(s) between the sexes is both mind-boggling and profoundly telling in terms of the investment contemporary cultures clearly have in the difference they seem so desperately to desire. If, as Nelson Goodman has stated, "scientific development always starts from worlds already on hand,"[77] then one wonders what worlds shaped Money's ideas and his practice. While a definitive answer to this question is, no doubt, impossible, I want to suggest that one such world is the field of sex endocrinology (including, and perhaps particularly, its uptake by biologists and zoologists), and, more particularly, what has come to be known as brain organization theory.[78] As a consequence, Money's work has tended to find its biggest influence not, as some have suggested, in feminism, or even in politicized accounts of gendered selfhood more generally, but rather, in brain organization research, and in the (largely clinical) discourses and practices surrounding intersexuality and transsexualism. [. . .]

Notes

1. See, for example, John M. Sloop, *Disciplining Gender: Rhetorics of Sex Identity in Contemporary U.S. Culture* (Amherst: University of Massachusetts Press, 2004); Lynn Conway, "Basic TG/TS/IS Information," available at http://ai.eecs.umich.edufpeople/conway/TS/TS.html, accessed November 14, 2011; Maggie McNeill, "Social Construction of Eunuchs" (2011), available at http://maggierncneil.wordpress.com/2011/07/18/social-construction-of-eunuchs, accessed November 10, 2011. In a brief discussion of Harry Benjamin's *The Transsexual Phenomenon*, in an article on *TS Si*—a website "dedicated to the acceptance, medical treatment and legal protection of individuals correcting the misalignment of their brains and their anatomical sex, while supporting their transition into society as hormonally reconstituted and surgically corrected citizens"—the unnamed author claims that Benjamin's approach "ran directly counter to the nurture-oriented claims of John Money"; available at http://ts-si.org/horions/1407-background-on-dr-john-money, accessed November 10, 2011. See also Eliserh, "Some Reflections on the State of Gender: Nature vs. Nurture" (2005), available at http://ts-si.org/horizons/1407-background-on-dr-john-money, accessed November 29, 2011; Sophia Siedlberg, "I'm

Not Dissing You" (2008), available at www.intersexualite.org/Dissing.html. accessed November 20, 2011; Anna Dela Cruz, "Gender Self-Identity among Males: A Case for Biology" (2009), available at http://serendip.brynmawr.edu/exchange/node/4362, accessed November 12, 2011; William Reville, "Gender Can't Be Freely Chosen," *Irish Times* (2011), available at www.irishtimes.com/newspaper/sci-encetoday/2011/0616/1224298993467.html, accessed June 20, 2011; Myria, "From the Forum: Constructed Gender?" (2003), available at www.ifeminists.net/introduction/editorials/2003/0520myria. html, accessed July 20, 2010; Hanna Rosin, "A Boy's Life," *Atlantic* (2008), available at www.theat-lantic.com/magazine/archive/2008/11/a-boy-apos-s-life/7059/5/, accessed August 10, 2011; Wendy Cealey Harrison, "The Shadow and the Substance: The Sex/Gender Debate," in *Handbook of Gender and Women's Studies*, ed. K. Davis, M. Evans and J. Lorber (London: Sage, 2006), 35–52; James H. Liu, "Sexual Assignment and Management of the Transsexual individual," *Journal of Family Practice* 7 (2009), available at www.jfponline.com/Pages.asp?AID=7352, accessed March 5, 2011.

2. Babette Francis, "Is Gender a Social Construct or a Biological Imperative?" 2000, available at www. endeavourforum.org.au/articlesfbabette_social.html, accessed November 14, 2011. See also Schala's post on the blog *Gender Liberation beyond Feminism*, available at www.pellebilling.com/2009/0S/gen der-and-biology, accessed November 10, 2011.

3. See John Money, "The Conceptual Neutering of Gender and the Criminalization of Sex," *Archive of Sexual Behavior* 1.4 (1985): 279–290; John Money, *Gendermaps: Social Construction, Feminism, and Sexosophical History* (New York: Continuum, 1995), 72–73; John Money, *Venuses Penuses: Sexology, Sexosophy and Exigency Theory* (New York: Prometheus, 1986), 591–600.

4. Jennifer E. Germon, *Gender: A Genealogy of an Idea* (New York: Palgrave Macmillan, 2009), 3.

5. Lesley Rogers and Joan Walsh, "Shortcomings of the Psychomedical Research of John Money and Co-Workers into Sex Differences in Behavior: Social and Political Implications," *Sex Roles* 8 (1982): 269–281, 278.

6. Rogers and Walsh, "Shortcomings," 272.

7. Ruth G. Doell and Helen E. Longino, "Sex Hormones and Human Behavior: A Critique of the Linear Model," *Journal of Homosexuality* 15 (1988): 55–78.

8. Rebecca M. Jordan-Young, *Brain Storm: The Flaws in the Science of Sex Differences* (Cambridge, MA: Harvard University Press, 2010), 8.

9. Helen E. Longino, *Science as Social Knowledge: Values and Objectivity in Scientific Objectivity in Scientific Inquiry* (Princeton: Princeton University Press, 1990), 171.

10. See, for example, John Money, "Gender: History, Theory and Usage of the Term in Sexology and Its Relationship to Nature/Nurture," *Journal of Sex and Marital Therapy* 11 (1985): 71–79, 71–72; Money, "Conceptual Neutering," 280; Money, *Gendermaps*, 18; John Money, "The Concept of Gender Identity Disorder in Childhood and Adolescence After 39 Years," *Journal of Sex and Marital Therapy* 20 (1994): 163–177, 163; Germon, *Gender*, 22.

11. In *Gay, Straight, and In-Between: The Sexology of Erotic Orientation* (Oxford: Oxford University Press, 1988), Money writes, "used strictly and correctly, gender is more inclusive than sex. It is an umbrella under which are sheltered all the different components of sex difference, including the sex-genital, sex-erotic, and sex-procreative components" (52–53).

12. Money, "Gender: History, Theory and Usage," 73.

13. Money, "Gender: History, Theory and Usage," 71.

14. Money, *Gendermaps*, 18–20.

15. Money, "Conceptual Neutering," 285. See also Money, "Gender: History, Theory and Usage," 71.

16. Money, "Conceptual Neutering," 275.

17. John Money and Patricia Tucker, *Sexual Signatures: On Being a Man or a Woman* (Boston: Little, Brown, 1975), 5.

18. Money, "Conceptual Neutering," 285. Interestingly, this formulation overlooks the possibility that one might feel certain that one is neither male or female.

19. In *Sexual Signatures*, Money and Tucker talk about how difficult it would be to simply assume a gender at will and/or to perform it "successfully" (i.e., so that one passes), 121–22. This is reminiscent of But-ler's critique in *Bodies that Matter*, of the "wardrobe of gender" theory as a misreading of the notion of gender as performativity. See Judith Butler, *Bodies that Matter: On the Discursive Limits of "Sex"* (New York: Routledge, 1999).

20. Money, *Gendermaps*, 36.

21. Money uses the term "phylism" to refer to what he describes as "a unit or building block of our existence that belongs to us as individuals through our heritage as members of a species." See *Gendermaps*, 36.

22. For an account of Money's theory of "pairbonding" as a basic phenomenon of human existence, see John Money, "Sex, Love, and Commitment," *Journal of Sex and Marital Therapy* (1976): 273–76.

23. Money and Tucker, *Sexual Signatures*, 89.

24. In "Destereotyping Sex Roles," *Society* 14.5 (19n): 25–28, Money refers to the sex irreducible dimensions of G-I/R "sex roles," and differentiates them from "sex-coded roles"—a term he seems to use as an umbrella for the other dimensions of G-I/R listed above. In *Gendermaps* he speaks of impregnation, menstruation, gestation, and lactation as "biological imperatives that are laid down for all men and women" (38).

25. Urinary position is an example Money gives of sex-derivative behavior.

26. Money gives the example of the extension of (what he sees as) men's territorial roaming to truck driving. For a more detailed account of these dimensions of G-I/R see John Money, "Gender: History, Theory and Usage," 74. See also Money "Destereotyping Sex Roles," 26; Money, *Gay, Straight, and In-Between*, 54–70.

27. This includes things such as hairstyles, forms of adornment, etc.

28. Money does accede that what he names as "sex irreducible" differences between women and men can be affected by what we might think of as cultural influences during fetal development. For example, drugs given to pregnant women to lessen the risk of miscarriage have, in some cases, androgenized fetuses otherwise marked as a "female" such that they are born intersexed. In some such cases, those raised as (androgenized) women are not able to ovulate, menstruate, or gestate. See, for example, John Money and Jean Dalery, "Iatrogenic Homosexuality: Gender Identity in Seven 46,XX Chromosomal Females with Hyperadrenal Cortical Hermaphroditism Born with a Penis, Three Reared as Boys, Four Reared as Girls," *Journal of Homosexuality* 1 (1976): 357–371. In "The Future of Sex and Gender," *Journal of Clinical Child Psychology* 9 (1980): 132–133, Money imagines a future in which "male-to-female transsexuals who yearn for a pregnancy may be able to rely on a . . . procedure of induced ectopic pregnancy." This would involve the transplantation of a fertilized egg into the peritoneal cavity such that it would implant itself on the wall of the bowel. He also adds that "whatever can be envisaged for transsexuals can be envisaged for nontranssexuals as well," thus implying the possibility that gestation may not always be the sole domain of women (132).

29. Money, *Gendermaps*, 51.

30. This sort of "commonsense" logic is debatable given that men have been known to lactate, and, more recently, trans men have become pregnant and given birth.

31. Money, *Gendermaps*, 37. See also Money, "Destereotyping Sex Roles," 27–28. In Gendermaps, Money identifies nine parameters of sex-shared, threshold-dimorphic behavior patterns on which educational and vocational male/female differences are developmentally superimposed. These are general kinesis, competitive rivalry, roaming and territorial boundary mapping or marking, territorial defense, guarding of young, nesting and homemaking, parental care of young, sexual positioning, and erotic arousal. (See *Gendermaps*, 39–47.)

32. Money, *Gendermaps*, 37.

33. Money, *Gendermaps*, 38.

34. See, for example *Sexual Signatures*, 67–78. See also John Money, "Gender-Transposition Theory and Homosexual Genesis," *Journal of Sex and Marital Therapy* 10 (1984): 75–82; John Money, "The Influence of Hormones on Sexual Behavior," *Annual Review of Medicine* 16 (1965): 67–82.

35. Money, "Gender: History, Theory and Usage," 77.

36. John Money and Clay Primrose, "Sexual Dimorphism and Dissociation in the Psychology of Male Transsexuals," in *Transsexualism and Sex Reassignment*, ed. Richard Green and Money [1969] (Baltimore: Johns Hopkins University Press, 1975), 115–131, 127; Money and Tucker, *Sexual Signatures*, 6.

37. Money, "Gender: History, Theory and Usage," 74; Money, *Gendermaps*, 23 and 95; John Money, "Ablatio Penis: Normal Male Infant Sex-Reassignment as a Girl," *Archives of Sexual Behavior* 4 (1975): 65–71, 66–67. Early in his career Money used the concept of imprinting to refer to what he later calls the critical period.

38. Money, *Gendermaps*, 75–76. See also Money, "Future of Sex and Gender," 132, in which the author argues that "nature's plan is to resolve the original state of hermaphroditism or indeterminism once and for all, early in development, and from then on the sexual anatomy remains fixed." However, he goes on to envisage a future in which "humankind may unravel the secret of how nature goes about programming spontaneous sex reversal in some species and apply that secret to human beings." Indead, he claims that "nature has already prepared the way" for "reverse embryology" in the figure of the transsexual.

39. Money and Tucker, *Sexual Signatures*, 89.

40. Money, *Gendermaps*, 111.

41. Money and Tucker, *Sexual Signatures*, 73.

42. John Money, "Sexology: Behavioral, Cultural, Hormonal, Neurological, Genetic, Etc.," *Journal of Sex Research* 9 (1973): 1–10, 10. See also John Money, "The Development of Sexology as a Discipline," *Journal of Sex Research* 12 (1976): 83–87, 86.

43. See Money, *Gendermaps*, 23–35, 72–76; Money, "Sexology: Behavioral, Cultural, Hormonal," 3–5; Money, "Gender: History, Theory and Usage," 77; Money, "Conceptual Neutering," 282–285.

44. Money, "Concept of Gender Identity Disorder," 168.

45. See Money, "Conceptual Neutering," 282–285.

46. Money, *Gendermaps*, 96–97. According to Money, the gendermap overlaps with the lovemap but neither is reducible to the other.

47. John Money, "Sex Reassignment as Related to Hermaphroditism and Transsexualism," in *Transsexualism and Sex Reassignment*, ed. Richard Green and John Money (Baltimore: Johns Hopkins University Press, 1969), 91–113. Here Money discusses "errors" that result in intersexuality and transsexualism, but elsewhere configures homosexuality, bisexuality, and transvestism as examples of "gender transposition" effected by developmental errors in gendermapping. See John Money and Michael De Priest, "Three Cases of Genital Self-Surgery and Their Relationship to Transsexualism," *Journal of Sex Research* 12 (1976): 283–294, 292. See also "Sexual Dimorphism and Dissociation," 127, in which Money and Primrose use terms such as "maldevelopment" and "defect" to describe deviations from the developmental norm he posits in the diagram shown in figure 1.

48. In "The Concept of Gender Identity Disorder," Money writes, "The coding of language in the brain is bipolar . . . The developmental coding of C-I/R in the brain is also bipolar" (173).

49. Money, *Gay, Straight, and In-Between*, 72. In order to avoid the kinds of criticisms posed by feminists and others of the association of masculinity with activeness and femininity with passivity in a dimorphic model of gender and heterosexuality, and to gesture toward some sort of "coital parity," Money adds the terms "quim" and "swive" to the analytic vocabulary of sexology to refer respectively to the "tak[ing of] the penis into the vagina and perform[ing], grasping, sliding, and rotating movements on it of varying rhythm, speed and intensity," and the "put[ting of] the penis into the vagina and perform[ing] sliding movements of varying depth, direction, rhythm, speed, and intensity." See John Money, "To Quim and to Swive: Linguistic and Coital Parity, Male and Female," *Journal of Sex Research* 18 (1982): 173–176, 175.

50. Money and Primrose, "Sexual Dimorphism and Dissociation," 129.

51. John Money, "Sexosophy: A New Concept," *Journal of Sex Research* 18 (1982): 364–366, 366.

52. Money, *Gendermaps*, 104.

53. An exception to the generally held view among the few feminists who actually engaged with Money's work that it was mired in biological determinism can be found in Ann Oakley's *Sex, Gender and Society* in which the author recognizes what Money describes as the interactionist character of his work. However, for Oakley, Money's analysis fails to articulate the political nature of gender, and the political import of such an insight. Consequently, she finds little reason to deploy his analysis. See *Sex, Gender and Society* (London: Temple Smith, 1972), 170.

54. One might claim that Money's work had an indirect influence inasmuch as it informed Robert Stoller's work on sex and gender, and this was taken up directly by some second-wave feminists. However, Stoller, unlike Money, makes a distinction between sex and gender. [. . .]

55. My proposition is supported by Celia Roberts's claim that Money and Ehrhardt "positioned biological sex as a structuring materiality that interacts with culture to make gender." See *Messengers of Sex: Hormones, Biomedicine and Feminism* (Cambridge: Cambridge University Press, 2007), 5.

56. Linda Nicholson, "Interpreting Gender," *Signs* 20 (1994): 79–105, 80.

57. Nicholson, "Interpreting Gender," 81.

58. Gayle Rubin, "The Traffic in Women: Notes on the Political Economy of Sex," in *Toward an Anthropology of Women*, ed. Rayna R. Reita (New York: Monthly Review, 1975), 157–210.

59. Rubin, "Traffic in Women," 165.

60. Rubin, "Traffic in Women," 204.

61. Janice Raymond, *The Transsexual Empire: The Making of the She-Male* (London: Women's Press, 1980), 103.

62. Raymond, *Transsexual Empire*, 104.

63. Carol Gilligan, *In a Different Voice: Psychological Theory and Women's Development* (Cambridge, MA: Harvard University Press, 1983). For critiques of the universalizing tendency in Gilligan's work, see John Broughton, "Women's Rationality and Men's Virtues," *Social Research* 50 (1983): 597–642; Linda Nicholson, "Women, Morality and History," *Social Research* 50 (1983): 514–536; Judy Auerbach, Linda Blum, Vicki Smith, and Christine Williams, "Commentary: On Gilligan's *In a Different Voice*," *Feminist Studies* (1985): 149–161.

64. Nicholson, "Interpreting Gender," 94.

65. Nicholson, "Interpreting Gender," 94.

66. Nicholson, "Interpreting Gender," 94.

67. Raymond's work on MTF transsexuals—as fundamentally male, and fundamentally different from the women they allegedly wish to become—has been subject to severe criticism on this basis.

68. Nicholson, "Interpreting Gender," 92.
69. Nicholson, "Interpreting Gender," 88.
70. Nicholson, "Interpreting Gender," 102.
71. Foucault uses the term "regime of truth" to refer to "the types of discourse [a discipline] accepts and makes function as true; the mechanisms and instances which enable one to distinguish true and false statements, the means by which each is sanctioned; the techniques and procedures accorded value in the acquisition of truth; the status of those who are charged with saying what counts as true." See Michel Foucault, "Truth and Power," in *Power/Knowledge: Selective Interviews and Writings, 1972–1971*, ed. Colin Cordon and trans. C. Gordon, L. Marshall, J. Mepham, and K. Soper (New York: Pantheon Books, 1980), 131.
72. Nicholson, "Interpreting Gender," 103.
73. Money, "Concept of Gender Identity Disorder," 170.
74. Money, "Concept of Gender Identity Disorder," 170–172.
75. Money and Tucker, *Sexual Signatures*, 67–68.
76. John Money and John G. Brennan, "Heterosexual vs. Homosexual Attitudes: Male Partners' Perception of Feminine Image of Male Transexuals," *Journal of Sex Research* 6 (1970): 193–209, 205.
77. Nelson Goodman, *Ways of Worldmaking* (Indianapolis: Hackett, 1978), 6.
78. For a detailed account of the emergence of organization theory in the 1950s, Money's contribution to it, and the historico-cultural reasons for its acceptance (in scientific circles), see Marianne Van Den Wijngaard, *Reinventing the Sexes: The Biomedical Construction of Femininity and Masculinity* [1991] (Bloomington: Indiana University Press, 1997), 27–46.

25 Trans of Color Critique Before Transsexuality

Jules Gill-Peterson

Historian Jules Gill-Peterson is the author of the 2018 book *Histories of the Transgender Child*. In this article, based on archival research in the Medical Records Office of the Johns Hopkins University Hospital in Baltimore, Gill-Peterson criticizes the conventional historical narrative of when "transsexuality" first emerged as a discourse of surgical-hormonal-legal transformation that results in a culturally legible "change of sex." The article first appeared in the 2017 "Trans*Historicities" issue of *TSQ: Transgender Studies Quarterly*. Gill-Peterson challenges the conventional wisdom that a transsexual discourse first appeared in the post-WWII period and is best exemplified by hypervisible white transfeminine celebrities like Christine Jorgensen. She shows how this narrative obscures the relationship between gender and race in ways that contribute to the erasure of black trans lives and over-represent transness as white. Gill-Peterson focuses on the patient file of a black transmasculine person in the 1930s named "Billie" who does not desire a vaginectomy, or closure of their vagina, due to the negative consequences this could have on their marriage and the financial stability it provided. While this refusal of genital surgery might mark Billie as "non-transsexual," Gill-Peterson develops a trans-of-color critique that reframes Billie's life choices. In Gill-Peterson's telling, Billie is not just an example of the instrumentalization of Black people's bodies as research subjects for the development of what became trans medicine, nor is Billie simply erased from the history of transsexuality due to the unintelligibility of black trans life in the archives of modern medicine. Rather, Billie is a fugitive who escapes toward a freedom beyond the boundaries of transsexuality as it has been conventionally understood, in ways that showcase that discourse's racial specificity.

The appearance of the patient in street dress . . . was that of a "snappy" young negro woman.
— Hugh Hampton Young, *Genital Abnormalities, Hermaphroditism, and Related Adrenal Diseases*

The Medical Records Office of the Johns Hopkins Hospital in Baltimore is responsible for providing current and recent medical records to patients, but it also stores some of the historical files of the hospital. When I first visited the office, I was there to look at early twentieth-century records from the Harriet Lane Home, the first pediatric clinic in the United States attached to a medical school. With its sizeable Endocrine Clinic, and in concert with the neighboring Brady Urological Institute, the home's records contained several hundred cases falling under the ambiguous catch-all "Hermaphrodism [*sic*]" from the 1910s to 1950s, a complex discursive field that touched on trans life in a period before the terms *transvestism* and *transsexuality* came into widespread usage in the United States.

DOI: 10.4324/9781003206255-31

Because the office's digital microfilm machine was not working the day I arrived, I set up shop on an analog machine in the middle of a room where staff were fielding phone calls and subpoenas for medical records. As the day went on, we got to talking. I asked about the apparent scarcity of resources for such an important office and in return was asked about what I was looking for in such old records. I explained that I was researching medical sex reassignment in the era before transsexuality. I added that I was looking at the racial divide in medicalization to grasp how persistent racial logics inform the later emergence of transsexuality and medicine's claim to know trans life. While we were chatting, a woman next to whom I was working asked if there were any experiments performed on black patients among the cases I was looking at. That prompted a conversation about the long history at Hopkins of nontherapeutic and coercive medical violence perpetrated on black people, from more famous cases like Henrietta Lacks to less well-known but systemic violations of personhood and care (see Washington 2006; Skloot 2010). In an office administrated overwhelmingly by black women there was no shortage of stories about warnings from family and friends that African Americans—whether patients or staff—needed to remain vigilant at Hopkins. My cubicle neighbor mentioned that an older relative of hers used to avoid walking alone at night in East Baltimore, having heard enough rumors about "night doctors" (see Skloot 2010: 158–169) to know that she might be abducted off the street for medical experimentation.

As I read through the archive of "hermaphroditic" patient files from the 1910s–1950s, including those marked "Colored," the weight of my conversation with the staff prompted a question whose epistemological limits this essay pursues. How has the overexposure of medicine as an available archive of transgender history produced an incalculable deflation of trans of color life's intelligibility, especially black trans life? If many black residents of Baltimore have, since the opening of Hopkins, been wary of being medicalized out of legitimate fear of the nontherapeutic violence underwriting "modern" medicine, what effects have practices of self-protection, strategic invisibility, and escape had on the hospital's archive? In other words, how does the use of the medical archive distort the very historicity of black trans and trans of color life through the recording of differing types of absence, silence, or opacity? And, as C. Riley Snorton puts it in *Black on Both Sides* (2017: 57), under such conditions how might we see the "fugitive moments in the hollow of fungibility's embrace"?

If historical practices of illegibility and invisibility inform the limitations of the medical archive from one side, on the other stands not only the racialized logics of medical discourse but also newer limits imposed by the governance of the archive. Contemporary federal health privacy regulations epistemically repeat the historical erasure of black trans and trans of color life at Hopkins.[1]

While doctors carefully compose published medical discourse, the heterogeneous unpublished accounts found in medical records that would undermine that discourse cannot always be made public, for reasons that will be explored later in this essay. Having spent time with these records, I am convinced that the account of black trans life in the archive of Hopkins, despite its dehumanizing and profoundly racist context, is much richer than published medical discourse from the era would lead us to believe. Yet the collision of historical, medical, and privacy ethics prohibits me from describing much of that richness. Ensnared in the position of an enforced ignorance that conspires with and extends the objectifying logic of medical discourse in favor of the privacy of doctors, not patients, this essay works to transform the resulting impossibility of recuperating a clear black trans or trans of color subject into a positive condition for trans of color historiography. Confronting the limits of a "case study" caught at the crossroads of what can be known through the medical archive, I ask what trans of color studies can (and cannot) do to address the continued underappreciation of trans of color knowledge and practice as the disavowed source of the "modernity" of transsexuality and gender.

As a contribution to trans of color historiography, this essay's trans of color critique before transsexuality explores one alternate history of the intersectionality of race and transness by investigating the disavowed reliance of discourses of gender and transsexuality on the embodied knowledge of black trans and trans of color people, asking us to understand more sharply what it means to say that gender and transgender have "always" been racial categories.

The Archiving of Early Twentieth-Century Black Trans Life

Hugh Hampton Young helmed the Brady Urological Institute, which along with the Harriet Lane Home saw patients diagnosed with "hermaphroditism" at Hopkins in the early twentieth century. Young established many of the foundational diagnostic and therapeutic procedures that made American urology modern. In invoking the word *modern*, I mean to resignify it as a result of dehumanizing, violent processes through which the human body was abstracted into distinct parts and systems out of experimental research on living and dead people who were then largely excluded from its supposed universalism. Like gynecology, as Snorton shows in the case of J. Marion Sims's violent experiments on enslaved black women (2017: 18–20), urology constituted itself through the availability of dehumanized bodies for experimental research that was frequently non-therapeutic, dangerous, and ineffective. Black bodies, disabled bodies, women's bodies, and children's bodies, particularly in their overlap with queer, intersex, and trans forms, were frequently those that urology made available to itself at the Brady Institute. The resulting "objectivity" produced by doctors like Young covered over and disavowed its own conditions of production, promising modernizing access to parts of the body long considered unreachable precisely by obscuring the material ways that knowledge was produced through painfully destructive techniques.

During the 1920s and 1930s Young developed a specific expertise for assigning sex to nonbinary infants, children, and adolescents, as well as adults medicalized for various intersex conditions. In 1937 he published a landmark textbook, *Genital Abnormalities, Hermaphroditism, and Related Adrenal Diseases*. Laying out a general nosology and etiological theory with detailed guidelines for clinical and surgical procedures, Young based the book on what Hopkins prided itself on as a "modern" research hospital: extensive case histories. Young pulled the case files of patients he had treated in the 1920s and 1930s to illustrate his methodology for determining sex and making medical reassignments through plastic operations he developed. Although this was the "Age of the Gonads," as Alice Dreger (1998) puts it, during which the presence of ovaries or testes were given by far the greatest weight in producing a "true" sex, the technical means for assessing sex were as disorganized as they were invasive. In these decades before synthetic hormones became standardized and commonly available, Young prioritized visual anatomical evidence. Extensive physical examination preceded diagnoses of hermaphroditism. Cystoscopy and x-ray procedures to picture the inside of the body were, like the physical exam, preludes to exploratory laparotomy, an invasive surgical procedure whose logic was to cut open the body and look inside for gonads or other ostensibly sexed organs. Disqualified from scientificity under this paradigm were a patient's self-identity and embodied self-knowledge.[2]

As trans and intersex studies scholars have noted (Preves 2001; Rubin 2012; Repo 2013), the surgical episteme that grew up around the medical management of nonbinary and intersex patients diagnosed as "hermaphrodites" or "pseudo-hermaphrodites"—which were expansive categories covering dozens, if not more, genetic, hormonal, anatomical, and other forms of embodiment—directly preface the emergence of American transsexual medicine.

The basic protocols of medical transition were first standardized to transform the bodies of infants, young children, and teenagers into a binary sex, while any lingering evidence of an "intermediate" or "mixed" sex was considered pathological, a form of arrested development or atavistic evolutionary regression.

While this field of medical practice was not designed with trans people in mind, it nonetheless began to attract their attention long before the first trans medicine clinics opened in the United States. Doctors like Young exercised an aggressive gatekeeping role around the new protocol of transition and sex reassignment, refusing requests from trans people who began to seek out the services of the Brady Institute in the 1930s. Many of these trans people strategically adopted intersex rhetoric to describe themselves, hoping that would legitimate their requests (5014.10, 5014.11, BUI Records). In this, they reflected a much broader trend: from Lili Elbe ([1933] 2004) in the 1930s to Christine Jorgensen (1968) in the 1960s, many public trans figures claimed to be vaguely intersex so that their transitions could be described as a kind of correction of a mistake made by nature.

Intersex medicine prefaces transsexuality chronologically and conceptually because intersex bodies were framed by medicine as the fullest expression of a concept of sexed plasticity that was central to the medical alterability of the human body in the twentieth century. The broader theory in the biomedical sciences that all human life was to a degree "naturally" mixed in sex in its embryonic and infantile forms was at its height at the time Young was most involved in this work. In its intersex form, this plasticity represented a supposedly arrested or atavistic capacity of the sexed body to take on multiple forms that had not properly waned in early infancy, and it was also racialized in the eugenic and evolutionist paradigms of the era. Sex became in places like Hopkins a phenotype that could be surgically manipulated through its plasticity, leveraged precisely in order to push it into a binary form. The surgical (and, later, hormonal) project of normalizing the intersex body carried a great deal of racial meaning informing the "modernity" of human sex as alterable but binary.[3]

While the medical transformation of intersex plasticity into binary form resulted in the racialization of sex as a pliable phenotype, making it signify through whiteness, this brought other hypervisible forms of race and antiblackness into play. The standard patient forms at Hopkins contained a field not just for sex but also race and "national stock." As a result it is easy to see in the archive that the overwhelming majority of people diagnosed with hermaphroditism at the Brady Institute in this era were white. That is not surprising, for several reasons. First, the institute was not in the habit of providing free treatment nearly as often as the "charitable" mission of Hopkins suggested. Patients were expected to pay for many services and procedures, even if their data were being used as part of research. Unless a local charity or social-work organization was able to sponsor medical treatment, costs for the many procedures and hospital stays were prohibitive for working-class black residents of Baltimore (see 1005.1 BUI Records and 2001.6 Edwards Park Collection).

What's more, the racial discourse of plasticity was synonymous with the calculation of which bodies were worthy of what forms of medicalization. Precisely because of the longer history in American medicine "in which captive flesh functions as malleable matter for mediating and remaking sex and gender as matters of human categorization" (Snorton 2017: 20), black and brown bodies were consistently read as less plastic, as less evolved sexually, and thereby less worthy of medical care now that a universalizing modernity was attached to plasticity as the capacity to remake the white body into a binary form.[4] Moreover, the many ways in which African Americans, in particular, practiced wariness and distance in relation to Hopkins made some people less likely to willingly visit the Brady Institute. For Young, blackness signified both as a devalued fungibility and a kind of super-humanity of the flesh, a combination he saw as desirable for research despite the relative rarity of black patients at the Brady Institute (see Jackson 2016; Harvey 2016). Young was interested in a presumed exceptional pathology he imagined residing somewhere in black bodies, including in those patients who visited the institute in the 1930s who may have been trans rather than intersex. Contrary to his objectifying motivations, however, black trans life could just as much confound as enable the production of racial knowledge about sex.

One of Young's cases in *Genital Abnormalities* in which no medical sex was assigned ignites the paradoxical space occupied by black trans life in this early twentieth-century framework of racial plasticity. Indeed, none of Young's "modern" medical procedures were undertaken. Instead of a rehearsal of surgical laparotomy or plastic surgeries, Young published a short biography of this person's life, including an abridged interview. While the dialogue is paraphrased and highly edited from notes, the archiving of this person's ostensible voice raises a number of interesting challenges to the medical discourse of sex and the intelligibility of black and trans of color life in the era before transsexuality.

The patient, whom I will refer to by the pseudonym "Billie,"[5] was in their[6] mid-twenties when they entered Young's ward. Now in Baltimore, they had previously lived in various places throughout the South and Midwest. In taking Billie's history, Young (1937: 139) emphasized that although they had been raised a girl, they had always been "stronger than the girls" at school, excelling at sports. As a teenager, Billie's mother had taken them to the doctor because they had yet to menstruate. Apparently the doctor, after making an examination, prescribed "medicine to take by mouth" but said "nothing about her condition" (139). As a teenager Billie also began to date girls. Young fixated on their "taking an active male part during sex," something from which, according to him, "the patient derived great pleasure, as did her partner" (139). Still, as a young adult Billie also married a man. The marriage was far from amiable, and Billie continued to see women as well. After less than a year Billie decided to leave their husband and return home to their parents. After trying and failing to reconcile some months later, Billie moved to St. Louis, worked in a factory, and pursued a relationship with a woman, eventually securing a divorce. A second attempt at marriage with another man led to similar conflicts, spurring the move to Baltimore to live with relatives (140).

Young performed a physical exam at admission. As was common with many of his patients, he arranged for nude photographs of Billie's body and genitals to be published in *Genital Abnormalities*, with only a minute censoring of the eyes serving as the slightest gesture at privacy. He also published a photograph of Billie in their clothes, which was more unusual. "The appearance of the patient in street dress," he commented, "was that of a 'snappy' young negro woman with a good figure" (141). A very brief description of a cystoscopy procedure follows, before the case study ends not with the usual laparotomy and sex assignment but with Young's interview. I quote this in its entirety because its public, published status, compared to the unpublished documents from Billie's records in the archive, will become important:

> The patient was asked if she were satisfied with her present life.
> "No," she said, "I feel, sometimes, as if I should like to be a man. I have wondered why my passions always have been directed towards women. I have derived great pleasure from many sexual affairs with women, and never with my two husbands."
> "Would you like to be made into a man?"
> "Could you do that?"
> When assured that this would be quite easy, that it would only be necessary to remove the vagina, and do a few plastics to carry the urethra to the end of the penis the patient said, "Would you have to remove the vagina? I don't know about that because that's my meal ticket. If you did that I would have to quit my husband and go to work, so I think

I'll keep it and stay as I am. My husband supports me well, and even though I don't have any sexual pleasure with him, I do have lots with my girl friends."

(142)

The case history abruptly ends here without any comment from Young.

Billie's apparent reaction to Young's proposal for sex assignment as a man raises a set of interesting questions. Why did Young publish a summary of a case that involved neither a surgical procedure nor a complete diagnosis? And what does the abrupt ending suggest about Billie's embodied knowledge? Valuable in Young's eyes as a case of presumed exceptional pathology, the photograph of Billie in their clothing and the extensive quoted dialogue suggest Young's desire for racialized knowledge to add to his body of research on hermaphroditism. The impression that Young is also sanitizing his account by omitting the reason for which no laparotomy or sex reassignment was carried out is also glaring. Billie does not seem to reject a masculine identity or the possibility of sex reassignment but instead interrogates the surgical premise of the epistemology of sex to which Young is attached. Billie seems to reject the proposal to remove their vagina on the grounds of knowledge gained through lived experience. For someone sometimes hailed as a black woman in the 1930s, marriage to a man seems to represent to Billie a financial and social situation that was in some way worth the emotional and sexual dissatisfaction it entailed. Billie seems to have been willing to live as a masculine person with a penis and a vagina, knowing that their livelihood was secure in an important way. Billie's ease in imagining a life married to a man for practical reasons, while pursuing meaningful relationships with women, is a pointed indictment of the medical model in which Young worked, in which the production and enforcement of heterosexuality was as important as visibly binary sex (Redick 2004: 28–38). Billie assents to no contradiction, no need for a binary sex or heterosexuality in order to live.

Whether Billie's feeling that "sometimes" they "should like to be a man" articulates as clearly trans is, similarly, unknowable. While it would be hasty to claim Billie as trans in the contemporary sense of that term, their lack of conformity to the intersex medical model and the absence of any archival evidence of a lesbian identity makes the entanglement of trans and intersex categories here worth pursuing. Indeed, what interests me in this published case history is precisely the opacity of Billie's self-knowledge. The dominant categories of 1930s urology lose their traction in the partiality and unintelligibility of this account. Billie is fairly invisible throughout, but that position is quite powerful in undermining Young's medical authority. What is at hand in reading this text is not the recovery of a clearly black trans person from the past but a situation more like that described by Snorton (2017: 2) in which "trans . . . finds expression and continuous circulation within blackness, and blackness is transected by embodied procedures that fall under the sign of gender."

I say with great care, then, that Billie "seems to reject" Young's medical discourse because there isn't much reason to take the published account in *Genital Abnormalities* at face value. Indeed, that is precisely why I went to Hopkins to locate Billie's and other medical records of people discussed in *Genital Abnormalities*. I suspected that Billie probably wielded much greater leverage in their encounter with medicine than Young wanted readers to think. I also suspected that Billie's refusal to be given a binary sex and undergo medical reassignment might testify to the ways in which the social heterogeneity of black trans life in this era sought escape or strategic unintelligibility from the reach of medical science. Billie's refusal of categorization also frustrates any impulse to recuperate a legibly black trans subject in this era. Instead, in this short text transgender history is confronted by the limits of its investment in Western forms of knowledge about gender that are archived as meaningfully historical because they emanate from "modern" discourses like urology that squander the intelligibility of trans of color life they nonetheless rely on to produce knowledge.

I suspected that Billie's unpublished records would yield an account in which, despite the epistemic and material violence of medicine, we might read an irruptive heterogeneity of black trans life that could serve as a source for building an alternate account of their experience at Hopkins. And what I read in the archive more than confirmed that hunch. However, here federal privacy regulations collude with Young after the fact, and I cannot disclose what I read. The Health Insurance Portability and Accountability Act (HIPAA) includes regulations that are ostensibly meant to protect the privacy of patients in medical research. Unless a person's death is confirmed or individual permission is secured (the latter being almost always impossible in researching trans history), a presumption of privacy is applied to records containing personal health information (PHI) (see Lawrence 2016). To access these materials, researchers are required to undergo review by their home institutional review board (IRB), as well as the Johns Hopkins Hospital's Privacy Board. In the case of Billie's files, however, an additional ethical problem comes into play. In *Genital Abnormalities* Young published the patient file numbers used by the Brady Institute for the cases he discusses. The consequence of Young's casual approach is that patients like Billie have already had their privacy and confidentiality breached since 1937 under the retrospective criteria of HIPAA. To mitigate that damage, no information in the archive can be disclosed that exceeds what is already public.

HIPAA regulations are supposed to "protect" patients by preserving their privacy. In this case they work much more effectively to protect the privacy of Hugh Hampton Young. Billie's records, which contain unredacted and unabridged sources of information, are disqualified from public circulation, and their possible contradictions of Young's published work are kept unsaid. HIPAA prohibits any further examination of why Billie refused Young's medical model, or evaluation of the honesty of his account in *Genital Abnormalities*. For instance, the full notes from which Billie's quoted speech and interview are derived are archived in these records. An explanation of how Billie was referred to the Brady Institute is also contained there, whereas Young chooses not to disclose that. And while Billie's voice is presented as written by Young in *Genital Abnormalities*, in their medical records there is a handwritten letter from Billie to Young in which they speak through their own voice. Although I can reference the mere existence of these types of documents, that is as far as I can go. The ways that published discourse rely on the deletion or suppression of knowledge generated by patients are left intact. Given how freighted the relation to Hopkins has been for black residents of Baltimore, this continuing silence bears a real magnitude. The use of the medical archive to examine black trans and trans of color life from the early twentieth century may in and of itself reinforce illegibility, but the governance of the archive also constricts and actively antagonizes attempts to pursue a trans of color critique of medicine.

Billie's life is archived in such a way that they are restrained, even after the fact, from challenging the whiteness of the history of transsexuality and the underestimation of the ways in which medicine made sex and gender modern through the simultaneous objectification and devaluation of black life. If Billie is not a visible black trans subject, if Billie's life is besieged by limitations on and limitations of knowledge, then what does the fragmentary evidence of their life in the archive contribute to a trans of color critique of medicine?

Opacity in Trans of Color Critique

Part of why Billie's life matters so much is that their interruption of ordered medical knowledge places blackness in an opaque position to transness at a moment prior to the erasures engendered by transsexuality in the mid-century, proliferating the historical meanings that attach to the sign "trans." Once "the newly-spectacularized medico-juridical discourse of transsexuality" had established itself in the mid-century, as Susan Stryker (2009: 79) puts it, it also got away with making its constitutive racialization scandalously invisible. This is the specifically abstract effect of transsexuality's whiteness that Stryker describes in the case of Christine Jorgensen's global circulation as a marker of modernity in the 1960s. "It is not Jorgensen's pale skin or Scandinavian-American cultural heritage that made her white," argues Stryker, "but rather the processes through which her presence racializes others while rendering opaque her own racialization" (81–82). Transsexuality became exportable as a technology of modernization in the mid-century by activating its whiteness to racialize its others as less than human, making itself innocent of race and transforming itself into a universal category. For that reason, trans of color historicity from the early twentieth century plays a particularly important role in destabilizing the racial innocence of transsexuality and exploring, as Snorton (2017), Elias Vitulli (2016), Kadji Amin (2017), and Emma Heaney (2017) have, the many disavowed racial histories of transness that precede it. The unique task of early twentieth-century trans of color historiography is both to center black trans and trans of color life in contexts that differ from the established narratives of trans history in that moment, while simultaneously pulling the mid-century advent of transsexuality out of joint with itself, showing how its whiteness is built on the forgetting of the black trans and trans of color historicity that directly precedes and exceeds it.

In calling on "trans of color studies," less a fait accompli than a growing horizon of thought and practice, I also draw especially on work by Snorton and Jin Haritaworn (2013), micha cárdenas (2016a, 2016b), Trish Salah (2014), and Kale Fajardo (2016). Trans of color studies exposes how the whiteness of transsexuality actively interferes with the intelligibility and material viability of black, brown, indigenous, and other trans of color and nonbinary lives, making them more invisible, marginal, or exceptional than they otherwise would be in the field of transgender studies. Transgender studies has to an important extent magnified the whiteness of transsexuality by its reliance on its medical archive, for that archive is an artifact of the science of transsexuality, which is to say that it pretends to speak for and grant total access to trans life while obscuring the racial conditions of subjection under which it produces that knowledge as universal.

What is at stake in a trans of color critique of medicine is not only the dehumanization of trans of color life through which medicine emerged but also the undermining of the rationality of medicine and its racialization of knowledge about gender. I argue that before there is a "transsexuality" to hoard attention away from trans of color life it might be easier to see what has for too long remained its penumbra: the fungibility of blackness to the modernity of sex, on one hand, and what Robert F. Reid-Pharr (2017) calls the "announcement of black life," on the other. Following Reid-Pharr's (2016: 9) call for a "post-humanist archival practice" that does not frame Western humanism in rigid terms as a domineering metaphysical force, but seeks out the heterogeneity of sociality in the "archive of flesh" of historically lived blackness, the limits of intelligibility in this archive can serve as grounds for the production of alternate forms of knowledge that affirm opacity and heterogeneity. Billie's life was both postwar trans medicine's disavowed predicate and the limit point of its own diminished epistemology. Billie gives lie to the way that medicine's antiblackness is not only a vehicle of material domination but also simultaneously a profound restraint on what it can know. Billie's blackness and transness take irruptive form as a puncture of medical modernity, coming decades before the discourse of transsexuality. The racialized impasse over their sex in the archive might be read as productive, bringing forth not a subject of the black trans or trans of color past but an invitation to read into the opaque interiority of trans of color life without judging it by the severely partial perspective of the medical science of human sex.

This move toward opacity, interiority, and illegibility, largely driven by broader work in black studies (Ellison et al. 2017), critically responds to the recent turn to biopolitical analysis in transgender studies (see Stryker and Currah 2014: 303). While immensely productive in diagramming how gender and, now, transgender, have become vital domains of administrative regulation and partial normalization for the state, the law, and medicine, trans of color and black trans studies offer conceptual tools for avoiding the pitfalls in Michel Foucault's biopolitical rendering of race and racism, in which colonialism and transatlantic slavery are displaced from modernity, emptying race of its historicity (Weheliye 2014). While the very alterability of sex and gender condensed into the concept of racial plasticity is exemplary of a biopolitical grammar, Billie's blackness and transness also gesture to a more opaque relation to biopolitics, in which the interiority of their embodied knowledge escapes capture by Young and, much later, transgender studies. While it makes sense, then, to insist on seeing the twentieth-century development of trans medicine as part of a broader biopolitical regulation of the sexed and gendered body (see, for example, Preciado 2013), Billie's life places black trans historicity and the question of their opacity in relation to biopolitics at the heart of that historical endeavor.

Trans of color critique can push transgender studies to take up its relationship to the limits of knowledge archived in historical sources like Billie's medical records, not in the hopes of finding a salvageable trans of color subject but to author desubjectivating accounts of the trans of color past.[7] Billie appears in the archive forcibly desubjectified, in the sense of having been deprived of personhood by Young's diagnostic model and its safeguarding by HIPAA. Instead of taking that desubjectification as proof of the unintelligibility of black trans life, however, it can be read as a partial escape from the biopolitical form of subjectivity into which transness was being increasingly confined over the twentieth century. Hardly a triumph or scene of clear-cut resistance, given the partiality of our perspective within a compromised archive, Billie's life registers more akin to what Kevin Quashie (2012: 24–26) calls "the sovereignty of quiet," an expressive form of human interiority that lacks the publicness associated with resistance or subversion. There is a certain risk to this move, as it relies, precisely, on the very opacity of the relation of trans of color life to institutions of capture like medicine, but the potential reward is a kind of counterhistory of privacy that evaded the normative history of concepts of gender, a situation in which, as Snorton puts it, "silence becomes countermythological" (2017: 151).[8]

The call is not to abandon medicine as an archive because of its epistemic bankruptcy (although we need nonmedical archives to supplant its rationality, too). The call, instead, is for forms of archival reading attuned to the unanticipated significance of historical desubjectification. Billie's life may have been highly distorted by medical discourse and further diminished by HIPAA regulations, legally proscribing access to unpublished archived sources of their personhood. Yet the dynamic interplay between the horrific publication of photographs of Billie's naked body and the photo of them in their everyday clothing also announces this black trans person's life as socially meaningful outside the parameters of medicine. From his partial and limited perspective, Young reads Billie as "a snappy young negro woman" in "street dress." The challenge for trans of color critique is to produce out of the surplus of his ignorance saturating that description a different form of knowledge, to take the weakness of medicine in this moment to affirm the rich but opaque interiority of blackness and transness preserved in the archive. That, I would argue, constitutes one distinction between early twentieth-century trans historicity in general and black trans, or trans of color historicity.

This essay has worked to identify and open up this problem for further study. It has not, nor could it, pretend to provide a single model for how to do so. Still, imagine what it might mean for the silence produced through Billie's medicalization to generate insight into black trans historicity not only in a negative sense but also in a move toward the undoing of the genealogy of transsexuality by privileging practices of black trans fugitivity as the reference point for the era "before" transsexuality. If medicine's modernity buries its reliance on racialized knowledge, then we should place black trans and trans of color knowledge in the center of the frame to produce counterhistories of life and embodiment without deference to medicine. Billie's mostly private and opaque embodied knowledge, lavishly lacking scientificity, points the way to another form of trans historiography, just as it points toward another way of life.

Acknowledgment

I am grateful to Kadji Amin, Emma Heaney, and Jennifer Nash for their feedback on this project.

From: Julian Gill-Peterson, "Trans of Color Critique Before Transsexuality," in *TSQ: Transgender Studies Quarterly*, Volume 5, no. 4, pp. 606–620. Copyright 2018, Duke University Press. All rights reserved. Republished by permission of the copyright holder, Duke University Press. www.dukeupress.edu.

Notes

1. I use this phrase because flattening blackness and other forms of racialization into a single "trans of color" denotation would be a reduction of the complexity at hand in this essay, which is about a black trans person in particular.
2. See 5009.7, 5009.8, and 5009.11, BUI Records, Alan Chesney Mason Medical Archives, Baltimore. Due to privacy restrictions on materials at the Alan Mason Chesney Medical Archives and Medical Records Office of the Johns Hopkins Hospital, these numeric codes stand in place of bibliographic citation for certain unpublished documents. A copy of the code's key is stored at the archives, available for access to anyone who applies to the Johns Hopkins Privacy Board. I say "mostly," because in some cases with intersex children Young would wait to see how the sexed body grew into puberty before making a declaration of sex, not out of deference to patient autonomy per se but because he had no predictive model or effective way to override the body's plasticity without synthetic hormones. I look at this issue in detail in my book *Histories of the Transgender Child* (Gill-Peterson 2018).
3. I outline the racialization of modern sex through plasticity in much greater detail in Gill-Peterson 2017.
4. For example, see Edwards A. Park to Hugh Hampton Young, June 19, 1935. Edwards Park Collection, Alan Mason Chesney Medical Archives, Baltimore. In this letter, Parks, who was head of the Harriet Lane Home, analogizes a young black infant diagnosed with an intersex condition to what he construes as less evolved "mammals."
5. This pseudonym is meant to anonymize this person and minimize any implication that I know their actual gender identity (I do not). In *Genital Abnormalities* Young published the ostensible first names and initials for many patients, although these do not necessarily correspond to their actual legal or preferred names. I choose not to use the name that Young ascribes to this person to emphasize my refusal of his ethics.
6. To avoid implying that I know this person's preferred gender marker, I am deliberately using the singular *they/them/their*.
7. In calling for attention to processes of desubjectification I am drawing on Foucault's rendering of that concept in his work on ethics, particularly as developed by Lynne Huffer (2009); but, following Alexander Weheliye (2014), I am also calling for a reckoning with the concept through black feminist work on the desubjectification wrought by the Middle Passage and slavery, most famously in the production of "flesh" (Spillers 1987).
8. I am grateful to Jennifer Nash for raising this point.

Bibliography

Amin, Kadji. 2017. "Transing Intersectionality: Race, Species, and the Emergence of Transsexuality, 1890–1960." Paper presented at National Women's Studies Association Annual Meeting, Baltimore, MD.

cárdenas, micha. 2016a. "Pregnancy: Reproductive Futures in Trans of Color Feminism." *TSQ* 3, nos. 1–2: 48–57.

————. 2016b. "Trans of Color Poetics: Stitching Bodies, Concepts, and Algorithms." *Scholar and Feminist Online* 13, no. 3–14, no. 1. sfonline.barnard.edu/traversing-technologies/micha-cardenas-trans-of-color-poetics-stitching-bodies-concepts-and-algorithms.

Dreger, Alice. 1998. "A History of Intersexuality, from the Age of Gonads to the Age of Consent." *Journal of Clinical Ethics* 9, no. 4: 345–355.

Elbe, Lili. (1933) 2004. *Man into Woman: The First Sex Change*. Edited by Niels Hoyer. London: Blue Boat Books.

Ellison, Treva, et al. 2017. "We Got Issues: Toward a Black Trans★/Studies." *TSQ* 4, no. 2: 162–169.

Fajardo, Kale. 2016. "Queer/Asian Filipinos in Oregon: A Trans★Colonial Approach." Lecture, University of Pittsburgh, February 29.

Gill-Peterson, Julian. 2017. "Implanting Plasticity into Sex and Trans/Gender: Animal and Child Metaphors in the History of Endocrinology." *Angelaki: Journal of the Theoretical Humanities* 22, no. 2: 47–60.

————. 2018. *Histories of the Transgender Child*. Minneapolis: University of Minnesota Press.

Harvey, Sandra. 2016. "The HeLa Bomb and the Science of Unveiling." *Catalyst: Feminism, Theory, Technoscience* 2, no. 2: 1–30.

Heaney, Emma. 2017. *The New Woman: Literary Modernism, Queer Theory, and the Trans Feminine Allegory*. Chicago: Northwestern University Press.

Huffer, Lynne. 2009. *Mad for Foucault: Rethinking the Foundations of Queer Theory*. New York: Columbia University Press.

Jackson, Zakiyyah Iman. 2016. "Losing Manhood: Animality and Plasticity in the (Neo)Slave Narrative." *Qui Parle* 25, nos. 1–2: 95–136.

Jorgensen, Christine. 1968. *Christine Jorgensen: A Personal Autobiography*. New York: Bantam.

Lawrence, Susan. 2016. *Privacy and the Past: Research, Law, Archives, Ethics*. New Brunswick, NJ: Rutgers University Press.

Preciado, Paul B. 2013. *Testo Junkie: Sex, Drugs, and Biopolitics in the Pharmacopornographic Era*. Translated by Bruce Benderson. New York: Feminist Press.

Preves, Sharon E. 2001. "Sexing the Intersexed: An Analysis of Sociocultural Responses to Intersexuality." *Signs* 27, no. 2: 523–556.

Quashie, Kevin. 2012. *The Sovereignty of Quiet: Beyond Resistance in Black Culture*. New Brunswick, NJ: Rutgers University Press.

Redick, Alison. 2004. "American History XY: The Medical Treatment of Intersex, 1916–1955." PhD diss., New York University.

Reid-Pharr, Robert F. 2016. *Archives of Flesh: African America, Spain, and Post-humanist Critique*. New York: New York University Press.

————. 2017. "Effective/Defective James Baldwin." Lecture, University of Pittsburgh, February 2.

Repo, Jemima. 2013. "The Biopolitical Birth of Gender: Social Control, Hermaphroditism, and the New Sexual Apparatus." *Alternatives: Global, Local, Political* 38, no. 3: 228–44.

Rubin, David A. 2012. "'An Unnamed Blank That Craved a Name': A Genealogy of Intersex as Gender." *Signs* 37, no. 4: 883–908.

Salah, Trish. 2014. *Lyric Sexology*. Vol. 1. Berkeley, CA: Roof.

Skloot, Rebecca. 2010. *The Immortal Life of Henrietta Lacks*. New York: Broadway.

Snorton, C. Riley. 2017. *Black on Both Sides: A Racial History of Trans Identity*. Minneapolis: University of Minnesota Press.

Snorton, C. Riley, and Jin Haritaworn. 2013. "Trans Necropolitics: A Transnational Reflection on Violence, Death, and the Trans of Color Afterlife." In *Transgender Studies Reader 2*, edited by Susan Stryker and Aren Z. Aizura, 66–76. New York: Routledge.

Spillers, Hortense. 1987. "Mama's Baby, Papa's Maybe: An American Grammar Book." *Diacritics* 17, no. 2: 64–81.

Stryker, Susan. 2009. "We Who Are Sexy: Christine Jorgensen's Transsexual Whiteness in the Postcolonial Philippines." *Social Semiotics* 19, no. 1: 79–91.

Stryker, Susan, and Paisley Currah. 2014. "General Editors' Introduction." *TSQ* 1, no. 3: 303–307.

Vitulli, Elias. 2016. "Trans★Disability Scholarship Roundtable." Paper presented at "Trans★ Studies: An International Transdisciplinary Conference on Gender, Embodiment, and Sexuality," September 9, University of Arizona.

Washington, Harriet. 2006. *Medical Apartheid: The Dark History of Medical Experimentation on Black Americans from Colonial Times to the Present*. New York: Doubleday.

Weheliye, Alexander. 2014. *Habeas Viscus: Racializing Assemblages, Biopolitics, and Black Feminist Theories of the Human*. Durham, NC: Duke University Press.

Young, Hugh Hampton. 1937. *Genital Abnormalities, Hermaphroditism, and Related Adrenal Diseases*. Baltimore, MD: Williams and Wilkins.

Section VI
Regulating Embodiment

26 Trans Necropolitics

A Transnational Reflection on Violence, Death, and the Trans of Color Afterlife

C. Riley Snorton and Jin Haritaworn

In this jointly authored article, first published in *The Transgender Studies Reader 2*, C. Riley Snorton and Jin Haritaworn bring a transnational perspective to bear on systemic forms of often deadly violence experienced by trans people of color. They suggest that post-colonial theorist Achille Mbembe's concept of "necropolitics," which describes a form of power that marks some fraction of a population for death even while it deems other fractions suitable for life-enhancing social investment, names the conditions of trans of color existence. They assert that value extracted from the deaths of trans people of color vitalizes projects as diverse as inner-city gentrification, anti-immigrant and anti-Muslim moral panics, homonationalism, and white transnormative community formation. Snorton, author of the field-shifting 2018 book *Black on Both Sides: A Racial History of Trans Identities*, offers an account of the 1995 death of Tyra Hunter, an African-American trans woman in Washington, D.C. Jin Haritaworn, who has written widely on trans-of-color necropolitics, then traces how stories of trans-of-color death such as Hunter's circulated in Berlin in the early 2010s. In general, Haritaworn claims, the lives of trans people of color in the global North and West are acknowledged primarily through the memorialization of their deaths, in ways that serve the white citizenry and mask necropolitical violence waged against gender-variant people from the global South and racial minorities in the West.

The concept of an afterlife has a particular resonance for transgender studies. It provides a framework for thinking about how trans death opens up political and social life-worlds across various times and places. Whether through the commemorative, community-reinforcing rituals of Transgender Day of Remembrance (TDOR) or as an *ex post facto* justification for hate crime and anti-discrimination policies, trans death—and most frequently the deaths of trans women or trans-feminine people of color—act as a resource for the development and dissemination of many different agendas. Through the concept of the afterlife, this essay addresses the complex interrelationships between biopower and necropolitics, to consider the discursive and representational politics of trans death and trans vitality. Our formulation of trans necropolitics draws on Achille Mbembe's (2003) necropolitics—a concept he develops for making sense of the centrality of death in contemporary social life. This enables us to understand how biopower—the carving out of subjects and populations (Foucault 1978)—can profess itself at the service of life and yet generate death, in both quotidian and spectacular forms. We also draw on current queer theorizing that attempts to make sense of the expansion of liberal LGBT politics and its complicity with racism, Empire, border

DOI: 10.4324/9781003206255-33

fortification, gentrification, incarceration, and the "war on terror" (Haritaworn, Kuntsman and Posocco forthcoming; Puar 2007).

Working transnationally and intersectionally, we ground our analysis in trans of color critique, whose most urgent present task is explaining the simultaneous devaluation of trans of color lives and the nominal circulation in death of trans people of color; this circulation vitalizes trans theory and politics, we claim, through the value extracted from trans of color death. We bring into one frame the everyday lives of trans and gender non-conforming people of color and the symbiotic (and sometimes parasitic) relationships that develop after their deaths with globalized homonormative and transnormative political projects.

One illustration of the need to think transgender both transnationally and intersectionally is the current globalization of hate crime activism. How is this political method mobilized and assimilated in various locations; what constituencies are interpellated there? What are its seductions for a trans activism for whom traumatized citizenship is more than merely an identitarian pitfall (Berlant 2000; Brown 1993), and is rather a key condition of its own emergence (Agathangelou, Bassichis and Spira 2008)? We ask: how do the biopolitics and necropolitics of trans death and trans vitality play out on the privileged stages of North America and Europe? What are the conditions and effects of their travels? We observe that as a result of U.S. hegemony, the unequal and exploitative stakes in violence and anti-violence are replicated elsewhere, and this forces us to interrogate trans organizing transnationally.

We need to ask how subjectivities and political methodologies travel in predictable directions, from North to South, and West to East (Grewal and Kaplan 2001). Earlier critiques of global feminism and homo-neo-colonialism bear helpful lessons, yet we must be wary of analogizing categories like women, gay and trans, or even "queer of color" and "trans." Rather, the social movements organized under these umbrellas intersect, compete with, and condition each other in complex ways that demand our attention. While important work has examined the uneven ways in which "women's liberation" and "gay liberation" became respectable and assimilable through the abjection of gender non-conformity (see e.g., Namaste 1996; Rivera 2002; Spade 2003), we must question a conception of transgender as first and foremost victimized. Rather, it is necessary to interrogate how the uneven institutionalization of women's, gay and trans politics produces a transnormative subject, whose universalized trajectory of coming out/transition, visibility, recognition, protection and self-actualization largely remains uninterrogated in its complicities and convergences with biomedical, neoliberal, racist and imperialist projects. Thus, while global feminist and homonormative anti-violence politics have been subject to critique, the same is not true for a comparable trans politics. Trans of color positions in particular are as yet so barely conceivable that trying to articulate them (or even marking their absence) almost automatically becomes the "p.c. that goes too far" (Haritaworn 2005).

In Europe, the subject of transgender has gained visibility and viability by joining an older archive of violence and anti-violence discourse, which after years of racist homonationalist mobilizing is already heavily raced and classed. There, the hate crime paradigm arrived in highly racialized and spatialized ways: following a decade-long moral panic over "homophobic Muslims," the figure of "the violent subject" was instantly recognizable as Muslim. The current juncture in Europe between welfare and neoliberal regimes, and the ambivalent desires for diversity and disposal that it produces, invite novel performances of transness as innocent, colorfully diverse, and entitled to survival and protection. Nevertheless, these biopolitical and necropolitical conversions do not accrue value equally to all trans people. While those whose multiple vulnerabilities lend the moral panic its spectacularly violated bodies are continually reinscribed as degenerate and killable, the same process secures a newly professionalizing class of experts in the realm of life. This forces us to examine the rise of trans movements transnationally against the globalization and intersection of various industrial complexes: the prison, non-profit, and increasingly also the academic industrial complex.[1] How do the deaths, both social and actual, of trans people of color provide the fuel and the raw material for this process?

This essay offers two sets of observations on issues of particular relevance to the experiences of trans women of color. The first, on the afterlife of Tyra Hunter, is grounded in Riley Snorton's work; the second, on trans vitality and anti-violence activism in Berlin, is based on Jin Haritaworn's work. We offer meditations on the ways that visibility, legibility, and intelligibility structure a grid of imposed value on the lives and deaths of black and brown trans women. This value grid speaks to some of the intricacies we briefly discussed above—it demonstrates how biopolitics and necropolitics in addition to being modes of governance, are also technologies of value extraction. We demonstrate how these technologies shape the lives and afterlives of particular persons, as well as broader social, cultural, and political projects at this particular historical juncture.

The Afterlife of Tyra Hunter

On October 28, 2009 United States President Barack Obama signed into law the Matthew Shepard and James Byrd, Jr. Hate Crimes Prevention Act, which expanded on previous, similar legislation to include gender identity among other "protected categories." The Act is the first federal law to extend legal "protections" to transgender people. In addition to giving federal authorities greater ability to pursue hate crime enhancements for bias-motivated violent crime, the law also requires the Federal Bureau of Investigation (FBI) to collect data on hate crimes perpetrated against transgender people. As Dean Spade has written, support for such legislation is shored up by advocates' desires for a symbolic declaration of societal/governmental inclusion, which also increases the positive visibility of transgender people (Spade 2009: 356). Hate crimes laws thus legally articulate the value of transgender people's lives, even as this articulation of inclusion is produced by and through their deaths. Simultaneously, hate crimes legislation contributes to a broader biopolitical imperative to manage poor people and people of color by channeling them into a massive carceral project, a "prison industrial complex," through which capital gains through the privatization of prisons.

At one level, centering the experiences of transgender people of color means tuning our critical attention to the biopolitics of everyday life; on another, it requires a raising of the dead, as it were, and an understanding of what Sharon Holland describes as the knowledge of our death, that "determines not only the shape of our lives but also the culture we live in" (Holland 2000: 15). Consequently, I structure this section around the story of a twenty-four-year-old black transgender hairdresser, Tyra Hunter, to illustrate how we might pursue the vexed relationships between neoliberalism and violent forms of governmentality that are materially hostile to trans of color survival.

Drawing on Alexis Pauline Gumbs' work (2010) on the queer survival of black feminism, I suggest that transgender of color survival—and its queer persistence in life and death—provides a vantage point through which to explore the ruptural theoretical and political possibilities precipitated by centering our analysis on transgender people of color. As scholars have noted, biopower found an early and violent instantiation during the Atlantic Slave Trade (Mbembe 2003; Abdur-Rahman 2006; Mirzoeff 2009). This history framed blackness not simply in terms of racial aberrance, but of sexual and gender deviance as well. Thus the un-gendering (or perhaps trans-gendering) of blackness under slavery serves as generative ground for understanding black trans subjectifications and their relationships to contemporary biopolitics. For as Nicholas Mirzoeff explains, "any deployment of 'life' also exists in relation to the 'natural'" (Mirzoeff 2009: 290). The discursive construction of the transgender body—and particularly the transgender body of color—as unnatural creates the precise moment where we as scholars, critics, and activists might apprehend a biopolitics of everyday life, where the transgender body of color is the unruly body, which only in death can be transformed or translated into the service of state power.

Tyra Hunter was headed for work in the passenger side of a vehicle in Washington D.C. on August 7, 1995, when her car was broadsided at an intersection. When fire department personnel arrived on the scene, onlookers already had pulled Tyra and the driver from the car. As a crowd gathered, firefighter Adrian Williams and others began treating the injured— that is, until Williams cut open Tyra's pant leg and noticed she had male genitalia. At that point, according to eyewitnesses, Williams stood up and backed away from Tyra, who was semiconscious, complaining about her pain, and gasping for breath. Williams was quoted by one witness as saying, "This bitch ain't no girl. . . . It's a nigger, he got a dick" (Juang 2006: 712). Another witness heard another firefighter say, "Look, it's got a cock and balls" (Levi n.d.: 1). While the firefighters stood around making derisive remarks, Tyra's treatment was interrupted.

As the "jokes" continued, bystanders began to plead with the emergency responders to resume working to save Tyra's life. One bystander was quoted as saying, "It don't make any difference, he's [sic] a person . . . a human being." After some time, other firefighters attended to Tyra's injuries, and she was transported to D.C. General Hospital, where she was placed under the care of Dr. Joseph A. Bastien, failed to provide a necessary blood transfusion or insert a chest tube necessary for Tyra's medical care. She was pronounced dead later that day.

Of course, the "treatment" Tyra received is not an isolated incident. Popular transgender lore would interpret the events precipitating Tyra's death as medicalized transphobia, which of course they are. But a broader politico-theoretical framework allows us to understand Tyra's body (before and after the accident) as a site where the medical establishment enacted what Henry Giroux calls a "biopolitics of disposability," a "new kind of politics . . . in which entire populations are now considered disposable, an unnecessary burden on state coffers, and consigned to fend for themselves" (Giroux 2006: 174). Thus neoliberal ideologies provide biopower with new ammunition in the creation of life-enhancing and death-making worlds, and offer an insidious addendum to rationales for population control. The consequence of this logic effaces the way power and life are maintained and reproduced through the deaths of certain others.

To return to Tyra's story is to think of her life after death, and to make sense of the excess that constitute her afterlife. In death, Tyra was almost exclusively referred to as Tyrone Michael Hunter. In the series of *Washington Post* articles that chronicled her death, Tyra was described as a man in women's clothes, as a gay man, as a transgender man, and sometimes as a man who lived his life as a woman. Some of this disturbing misattribution of gender is attributable to transphobia in journalistic reporting. But it also underscores why it is necessary to think specifically about transgender of color experiences as distinct from queer subjectivities. A D.C.-based anti-violence coalition, GLOV (Gays and Lesbians Opposing Violence) responded immediately to Tyra's death by calling for the fire department to investigate the incident. Their work turned up eight witnesses willing to testify that the behavior of Williams and others was unacceptable. However, both the media and local government officials framed the death of Tyra—referred to as Tyrone—as a "gay issue." Jessica Xavier, at the time a spokesperson for GLOV and herself a transwoman, was quoted as saying that such transphobic events occur because transgender people "are walking, talking, living, breathing stereotypes of what it means to be gay. They're just trying to lead ordinary lives free from discrimination and violence."

Jin Haritaworn's (2008) analysis of the appropriation of trans of color lives by white queer theorists provides an incisive theoretical framework for understanding Tyra's after-death transformation by layering race onto trans theorist Jay Prosser's supposition about the degree to which transgender and transsexual inclusiveness might really stand in for queer inclusivity. Prosser asks, "to what extent this queer inclusiveness of transgender and transsexuality is . . . the mechanism by which queer can sustain its very queerness . . . by periodically adding subjects who appear even queerer precisely by virtue of their marginality in relation to queer" (1998: 40); we wonder to what degree queer and trans anti-discrimination and anti-violence movements are produced and sustained by the violent and frequently murderous impulses specifically directed toward trans feminine people of color.

Xavier's comments are a key example of a larger project of reincorporating transgender bodies of color under a more legible sign; in this case, the representation of Tyra as a spectacularized gay male body. Whenever the work of legibility is enacted upon transgender bodies, it is always a process of translation—with risks (of appropriation) and payoffs. One "payoff" in this instance was $2.8 million lawsuit Tyra's mother, Margie Hunter, won against the city and hospital on 11 December 1998, when a jury found them guilty of negligence and malpractice. While $500,000 was awarded for damages attributable to the withdrawal of medical care at the accident scene, a further $1.5 million was awarded for conscious pain and suffering endured by Tyra in the emergency room as the result of medical malpractice. The sanitizing of Tyra's transgender body undoubtedly allowed her to be understood more sympathetically as a son. Indeed, Margie Hunter told Washington Post reporters, "Tyrone always was so sure he would be famous, that he'd be on the television," she said. "I don't think he meant this way. I know I didn't. But maybe this is God's will and something good will come of it."

It is important to look beyond statist and mainstream media discourses to see what "good" came from Tyra's life and death. Over 2000 people attended her funeral. A candlelight vigil/protest at the D.C. fire department headquarters drew more than 200 demonstrators. The *Washington Times* quoted Cathy Renna, then co-chairman of the Gay and Lesbian Alliance Against Defamation, as saying, "I have never seen a cause that crossed so many boundaries: gay and straight, black and white . . . All of our work should be this cooperative." The intersections of sexism, transphobia, and racism became the context for an insurgence of political activity, and Tyra's name lives on in the acronym, T.Y.R.A. (or Transgender Youth Resources and Advocacy), a Chicago-based program that continues to support transgender youth of color.

But Tyra Hunter's story is not unique. Her name, frequently invoked at TDOR events, is simply one appellation among many that gestures toward trans of color death. In doing so, it indexes a transnational complicity with racist, transphobic, classist, misogynist and homophobic violence. This violence has continued even after the signing of the Matthew Shepard Act. As a recent report of the National Gay and Lesbian Task Force (NGLTF) suggests:

> It is part of social and legal convention in the United States to discriminate against, ridicule, and abuse transgender and gender non-conforming people within foundational institutions such as the family, schools, the workplace and health care settings, every day. Instead of recognizing that the moral failure lies in society's unwillingness to embrace different gender identities and expressions, society blames transgender and gender non-conforming people for bringing the discrimination and violence on themselves.[2]

Tyra's life and the lives of other transgender people of color gesture in less moral terms toward an understanding of various forms of transgender repudiation. They require a rigorous reconsideration of lives structured alternately by illegibility and spectacle. Those lives also carry a productive force—particularly in death—that sheds light on the borders where biopower and necropower brush against each another in everyday life. These lives stand at the limit of what is livable, and transgender of color survival—in its ghastly presence, which occur before and after life subsides—becomes a unique vantage point for understanding how one might persist in the space of hetero/homonormative unincorporability. As Haritiworn recounts in the subsequent section, Tyra Hunter's story is not confined to a North American context. In fact, her death sutures together a number of transnational political projects that hinge on anti-violence legal protections and transgender-inclusive legislation. In recounting details of her life and death, the aim is not simply to rehearse transmisogynistic violence, but rather to provide an example of how trans women of color act as resources—both literally and metaphorically—for the articulation and visibility of a more privileged transgender subject. The extraction of value from trans of color lives through biopolitical and necropolitics technologies not only serves the Sovereign, but all indexes much more subtle and complex shifts in power. Trans rights activists' participation in and complicity with this process is what compels us to make this intervention.

Transgressive Citizenship in Germany

Hate crime discourse made its entry onto the German scene in 2008. It found its first bodies on the genderqueer scene: in the summer of that year, a group of visitors and performers at Berlin's Drag Festival were involved in a violent incident that was quickly attributed to men of Turkish origin, and which gave rise to media and policy responses that first introduced the term *Hasskriminalität* (hate crime) to a wider German public. The privileged place assumed by the gender non-conforming body in the institutionalization of the hate crime framework may at first surprise. Racialized violence discourses were certainly not alien to white-dominated queer and trans scenes, yet the actors who had invested in them most systematically followed a homonormative politics. The figure of the victim of transphobia nevertheless became instantly legible as the offspring of an already-existing migrant *homophobia* script. Unlike in the U.S., where the death of a homonormative subject-the white middle-class college student Matthew Shepard-was instrumental in forging consent for the inclusion of homophobia and transphobia, German hate crime discourse found its first victims in radical queer and gender non-conforming people, some of whom were migrants. The key "event" that launched the odd neologism *Hasskriminalität* into the German vocabulary was the Drag Festival, an internationally publicized gender/queer performance event, which culminated in an altercation during which several festival visitors and performers were beaten up. Dovetailing with a decade-long moral panic over "homophobic Muslims," and set in the gentrifying "Turkish" area of Kreuzberg—a crime scene par excellence—the incident instantly became an "event" that circulated rapidly through a ready-made queer and trans audience.[3] The representations that followed in its wake, partly as a result of the white festival organizers' own press releases, were highly ambivalent about transgender. In fact, there was an abundance of transphobic images of ridiculous, repulsive and excessive bodies, and it was the homonormative, homoracist trope of "Turks beating up lesbians" that ultimately came to define the incident. (Haritaworn 2011). Nevertheless, and maybe for the first time, the gender non-conforming subject emerged as a body worthy of both protection and celebration. It became an important symbol of the diverse neighborhood that can be colorful even while its older poor and racialized inhabitants are ghosted from it through gentrification and policing. The very excess of the gender non-conforming subject here served to demonstrate how far the tolerant society will go—both in the kind of bodies it is willing to protect, and in the punishments it is willing to mete out to Others who, in a post-fordist and neoliberal context, had been reduced to diversity's constitutive outside.

Spectacularized through the injured bodies of gender non-conforming subjects, the perpetrator of hate crime is nevertheless instantly recognized as the *homo*phobic migrant. This figure emerges in public discourse in the late 1990s, when the big gay organizations turn to "migrants," hitherto marginal to mainstream gay politics, in search of new constituencies, new *raisons d'être*, and an expanded public audience for the recognition of sexual politics as part of a broader, national agenda. Rather than incidental to or a natural result of migrant particularity, the racialization of gender and sexuality that constitutes the ground on which hate crimes discourse arrives is the result of a performative labor which, as Sarah Ahmed puts it, conceals itself through repetition and affective proximities (see Ahmed 2004: 91–92). The homophobic migrant fits this family well—he is instantly adopted as a newcomer whose resemblance makes him seem to have been here forever. The ease with which the homophobic migrant becomes common sense in 2000s Germany belies the decade-long efforts that go into crafting this figure. Its landmarks include, first, the simultaneous integration debates and the Europe-wide "crisis in multiculturalism," blown up into a panic big enough to include even gay expertise (an assimilation which occurs by performing an Other as unassimilable). Second, a domestic violence paradigm increasingly Orientalized as a function of "Muslim" cultures and gender relations, which thus creates space for new metonymies between Muslim sexism and Muslim homophobia, and between women of color and white gay men, who are imagined to suffer from identical forces. Third, the so-called "Muslim Test" of German nationality, which attempts to shore up a belatedly reformed law of blood, or *ius sanguinis*, by inventing new traditions, or "core values," of women-and-gay friendliness. Fourth, the Simon study, a quantitative psychosocial study of homophobic attitudes in "migrant" v. "German" pupils in Berlin, commissioned by the biggest gay organization, funded by the state, and disseminated by the mainstream media, which renders scientific and respectable what by then everybody knows: that "migrants" are *more homophobic* than "Germans," and that the twain, as the unhyphenable categoric opposition under comparison already suggests, shall never meet (see Haritaworn and Petzen forthcoming for an in-depth historiography).

The Drag Festival is thus but the latest episode of a well-rehearsed drama, which nevertheless launches a new victim-subject onto the stage (see Kapur 2005). As so often with moral panics, one incident leads to another, cramming the archive of violence and anti-violence as far as it will stretch (Sudbury 2006; Gilmore 1999). In addition to producing more victim subjects, the moral panic about "homophobic Muslims" has served to proliferate hate crime scenes and cases, perpetrator profiles, experts, numbers, actions, action plans, projects, media, policy and academic texts, along with government funds for more of the same.[4] While homonormative activists have been the main beneficiaries, trans (and radical queer) activists too have joined the stage, with little complication or mutual protest, to co-star in a drama that is characterized by symbiosis and mimesis as much as competition. In summer 2009 the Berlin district of Schöneberg became known as a similarly dangerously "homophobic" and "transphobic" place as neighboring Kreuzberg. Significantly, Schöneberg is home to both the gayborhood and to Frobenstrasse, one of the poorest streets in Berlin, which that summer proved to become a highly productive hate crime scene. Recent migrants from Bulgaria and Romania, many of whom are Roma and/or from the Turkish-speaking minority, live, work and socialize in the street amidst other people of color with longer histories in the area. The area has long been a site of trans street sex work, and many of the new migrants, both trans women, trans-feminine people, non-trans women, and queer- and straight-identified men, use it to sell sex. Of course migrant sex workers of all gender and sexual identities have experienced all kinds of violence for a long time: from residents who blame them for littered condoms and other signs of chronic disinvestment, from police and other authorities who variously target and exclude them as underdocumented migrants and sex workers, and from the utterly unremarkable and uneventful neglect and exploitation to which poor, racialized people and sex workers are regularly subjected. Nevertheless, their lives were long completely uninteresting to queer and trans activists in Berlin. It is arguable that beyond their capacitation as injured victims of hate crime they have largely remained so. Archived as trans sex workers being beaten up by migrant youth gangs, this "event" of violence both fed the moral panic over criminal and violent Muslim youth and accrued value and visibility to more powerful queer and trans positions. In September 2009, a coalition of mainly white trans, mainly non-trans queer of color, and mainly white and non-trans sex work organizations organized a "Smash Transphobia" demo at Frobenstrasse (Siegessäule TV 2009). The demo was visited by mainly white queer and trans activists, most of whom had probably never been to the street before, and would never return thereafter. The speeches, slogans and posters interpellated a transnormative, protectionist victim-subject of "violence against trans people" or "trans women" and called for policy attention to this hitherto neglected group. While sex work occasionally made it into the speeches, the local context was barely mentioned, and where it was, this again occurred in highly racialized and classed ways:

> "You may be unemployed but this is no excuse" (call through the loudspeaker into the open windows of random residents)
> "Transphobic people go to hell" (poster held by a white and presumably secular/Christian organizer)
> "This is our street, too!" (slogan at the demo)

Although the event was ostensibly organized for the benefit of migrant trans sex workers, as happens so often, those injured in the event of violence benefited the least from the remedies offered by a traumatized citizenship model. The two biggest gay organizations were not directly involved in either the Drag Festival or the Frobenstrasse organizing and indeed continue to show no interest in trans people, let alone migrant trans sex workers. However, their long-standing investment in the adjacent gayborhood and ample expertise in racializing homophobia enabled them to swiftly capitalize on the panic. In many ways, the policy attention that resulted from these two spectacles of transphobia fulfilled a long-standing attempt by these organizations, who had authored the first press releases about "homophobic migrants" in the area years earlier, to describe Schöneberg as a dangerous area where (white) gay men live in constant fear of Muslim youth (Haritaworn and Petzen forthcoming). While the bodies that were injured, first in Kreuzberg and then in Frobenstrasse, less than a kilometer away from the office of the Lesbian and Gay Association Germany (LSVD), radically exceeded this binary, the events nevertheless served to consolidate a homonormative constituency and to insert it firmly within urban policies of gentrification, touristification and securitization. Projects that became possible in their wake include the "Rainbow Protection Circle," an association of local businesses and NGOs led by the Berlin branch of the LSVD. [. . .]

The anti-transphobia organizing around violence in Berlin thus points to multiple genealogies and complicities in gay, queer and trans organizing around space, violence and visibility that deserve careful unpacking. We would like to resist the easy ascription of these complicities to neoliberalism. Rather, the homonormative narrative of the creative-class member, who ventures into hitherto ungentrifiable territory and performs himself as a productive citizen and consumer *in contrast to those whose unproductiveness and excessive reproductiveness mark their intimacies as disposable in the current diversity regime*, is sprouting transgressive offshoots that equally need addressing.[5] Thus, as argued by Haritaworn (2011), the degenerate, regenerating ghetto enables a trans subject to emerge whose colorful difference, in a context which increasingly lets go of its people of color, for the first time becomes a pleasant sight. This is also brought home by the fact that white trans activists in Berlin did manage to institutionalize the new space won in the anti/violence archive. In November 2009, a few months after the demo at Frobenstrasse, Transgender Day of Remembrance, a fairly new and until then more DIY event in Berlin, likewise took place in the town hall of Schöneberg.[6] Co-organized by the same predominantly non-trans queer of color group that had collaborated with white trans activists on the Smash Transphobia demo, it nevertheless remained an over-whelmingly white event, and it closely followed the U.S. formula of remembrance (Lamble 2008; Bhanji forthcoming). Most of these dead people were trans people of color from both the Global North and the Global South, whose exotic presence in this overwhelmingly white German trans and ally space was brought home by the chuckles that some of their badly pronounced names evoked. "Their" deaths were not in vain, one of the speakers is said to have stated: "they" made it possible for "us" to come together today. Among "them" was Tyra Hunter.[7] Like so many of its globalizing predecessors, the Berlin TDOR thus incited a trans community into life whose vitality depends upon the ghosting of poor trans people, trans people of color, and trans people in the Global South.

Who benefits from these dominant methodologies of violence and anti-violence? Instead of those most in need of survival, the circulation of trans people of color in their afterlife accrues value to a newly professionalizing and institutionalizing class of experts whose lives could not be further removed from those they are professing to help. Immobilized in life, and barred from spaces designated as white (the good life, the Global North, the gentrifying inner city, the university, the trans community), it is in their death that poor and sex working trans people of color are invited back in; it is in death that they suddenly come to matter.

Conclusion

How do Tyra Hunter and other dead trans women of color circulate, and what are the cor-poreal excesses that constitute their afterlives as raw material for the generation of respect-able trans subjects? We have examined this circulation, which adds value through nominal and numeric repetition, as paradoxically giving birth to both the conditions that allow more recognizable trans subjects to mobilize and ascend into life, and to the forces that immobilize subaltern trans lives. The resulting trans vitalities and socialities must be examined transna-tionally, as bringing trans people into community (both with each other and with a newly sympathetic public) through intensified violence. Thus, we have examined how the ascend-ant politics are symbiotic with the death-making capacities of the market and the state, and cannibalistic upon the lives of other sexually and gender non-conforming people. What would a trans politics and theory look like that refuses such "murderous inclusion" (see Hari-taworn, Kuntsman and Posocco forthcoming)? While radical formulations of violence and anti-violence have tended to focus on colonial feminist and homonormative subjects, domi-nant trans subjects are rarely held accountable and remain awkwardly frozen in positions of analogy and equivalency with other "diversely diverse" locations. Maybe it is time to push our accounts of violence and anti-violence beyond limited formulas such as "race, gender and class," in both their intersectional and post-identitarian formulations. We certainly have examples of such politics to build on (Gossett 2013).

Notes

1. These activations are, of course, terrains of struggle and open to contestation and reappropriation. Par-ticularly in contexts where decolonial struggles have been won, events like TDOR can reflect broader critical agendas, as was the case with the memorial for Sanesha Stewart by Queers for Economic Justice,

Audre Lorde Project, and others in 2008, and for Nizah Morris in Philadelphia in 2002 (Che Gossett, personal communication with Jin on 17 November 2011.)
2. Jaime M. Grant, Lisa A. Mottet, Justin Tanis, Jack Harrison, Jody L. Herman, and Mara Keisling. 2011. *Injustice at Every Turn: A Report of the National Transgender Discrimination Survey, Executive Summary.* Washington: National Center for Transgender Equality and National Gay and Lesbian Task Force.
3. The "event" was heavily contested. Thus, one of the "beaten up" trans people described it as a mutually escalating drunken traffic altercation whose adversaries were conspicuously blond.
4. For example, see the racialized homophobia study by psychologist Simon (2009); the special issue on the Drag Festival aftermath in the left-wing weekly Jungle World (2008); and the homophobia and sexual diversity action plans by the red-red government (SPD/Linke 2009); and the Green opposition (Bündnis 90/Die Grünen 2009). See Haritaworn and Petzen (forthcoming) for a careful mapping of this proliferation.
5. For critiques of queer gentrification, see Manalansan (2005); Fierce (2008); Hanhardt (2008); and Decolonize Queer (2011).
6. Jin would like to credit another trans of color activist in Berlin, who would prefer not to be named, for sharing his brilliant analyses of homo- and trans-whiteness in Berlin.
7. For example, Tyra Hunter appears twice on the list and images of "remembered" trans people on Berlin TDOR's myspace page: (http://www.myspace.com/TDoR#{%22ImageId%22%3A18354015}, http://www.myspace.com/TDoR#!/tdor/photos/4495414).

Works Cited

Agathangelou, Anna, Morgan Bassichis, and Tamara Spira (2008). "Intimate Investments: Homonormativity, Global Lockdown and the Seductions of Empire." *Radical History Review* 100, 120–143.

Abdur-Rahman, Aliyyah (2006). "'The Strangest Freaks of Despotism': Queer Sexuality in Antebellum African American Slave Narratives." *Africall Americau,* 223–237.

Ahmed, Sara (2004). *The Cultural Politics of Emotion.* Edinburgh: Edinburgh University Press.

Berlant, Lauren (2000). "The Subject of True Feeling: Pain, Privacy and Politics." In S. Ahmed, J. Kilby, C. Lury, M. McNeil, and B. Skeggs (eds.), *Transformations: Thinking Through Feminism,* 33–47. London: Routledge.

Bhanji, Nael (forthcoming). *Trans Necropolitics* (working title). PhD thesis, Women's, Gender and Sexuality Studies Department, York University.

Brown, Wendy (1993). "Wounded Attachments." *Political Theory* 21: 3, 390–410.

Bündnis 90/Die Grünen (2008). *Berliner Aktionsplan gegen die Homophobie,* Berlin Senate, Print matter 16/1966, 1/12/2008, 16th election period.

Davis, Angela (2003). *Are Prisons Obsolete?* New York: Seven Stories Press.

Decolonize Queer (2011). "From Gay Pride to White Pride? Why Marching on East London Is Racist." *Decolonize Queer,* www.decolonizequeer.org/?p=1 (accessed 1 January 2012).

Fierce (2008). "LGBTQ Youth Fight for a S.P.O.T. on Pier 40," *Fierce,* 15 September 2008, http://fiercenyc.org/media/docs/3202_PublicHearingPressRelease.pdf (accessed 19 February 2009).

Foucault, Michel [1978] (2004). *The Birth of Biopolitics: Lectures at the Collège de France 1978–1979.* London: Palgrave.

Gilmore, Ruth Wilson (1999). "Globalisation and US Prison Growth: From Military Keynesianism to Post-Keynesian Militarism." *Race and Class* 40: 2–3, 171–188.

Giroux, Henry (2006). "Reading Hurricane Katrina: Race, Class, and the Biopolitics of Disposability." *College Literature* 33: 3, 171–196.

Gossett, Che (2013). "Silhouettes of Defiance: The Memorialization of Historical Sites of Queer and Transgender Resistance in an Age of Neoliberal Inclusivity." In Susan Stryker and Aren Z. Aizura (eds.), *The Transgender Studies Reader,* 2. New York: Routledge.

Grewal, Inderpal and Kaplan, Caren (2001). "Global Identities: Theorizing Transnational Studies of Sexuality." *GLQ: A Journal of Lesbian and Gay Studies* 7: 4, 663–679.

Gumbs, Alexis Pauline (2010). *We Can Learn to Mother Ourselves: The Queer Survival of Black Feminism.* Dissertation retrieved on 1 June 2011 at dukespace.lib.duke.edu.

Hanhardt, Christina B. (2008). "Butterflies, Whistles, and Fists: Gay Safe Streets Patrols and the New Gay Ghetto, 1976–1981." *Radical History Review* 100, 61–85.

Haritaworn, Jin (2005). "Queerer als wir? Rassismus, Transphobie, Queer-Theory" (Queerer than us? Racism, Transphobia, Queer Theory). In E. Yekani Haschemi and B. Michaelis (eds.), *Queering the Humanities*, 216–238. Berlin: Querverlag.

Haritaworn, Jiin. (2008). Shifting Positionalities: Empirical Reflections on a Queer/Trans of Colour Methodology." *Sociological Research Online*, 13: 1, 162–173.

Haritaworn, Jin (2011). "Colorful Bodies in the *Multiklti* Metropolis: Trans Vitality, Victimology and the Berlin Hate Crime Debate." In Trystan Cotton (ed.), *Transgender Migrations: Bodies, Borders, and the (Geo) politics of Gender Transing*, 11–31. New York: Routledge.

Haritaworn, Jin and Petzen, Jennifer (forthcoming). "Invented Traditions" (working title). In C. Flood and S. Hutchings et al. (eds.), *Islam in Its International Context: Comparative Perspectives*. Cambridge: Cambridge Scholars Press.

Haritaworn, Jin, Adi Kuntsman, and Silvia Posocco (eds.) (forthcoming). *Queer Necropolitics*, book project (in review).

Holland, Sharon (2000). *Raising the Dead: Readings of Death and (Black) Subjectivity*. Durham, NC: Duke University Press.

Juang, Richard (2006). "Transgendering the Politics of Recognition." In Susan Stryker and Stephen Whittle (eds.), *The Transgender Studies Reader*. New York: Routledge.

Jungle World (2008). "Bissu schwül oder was?" (You gay or wha'?). Special issue, 26 June 2008.

Kapur, Ratna (2005). "The Tragedy of Victimisation Rhetoric: Resurrecting the 'Native' Subject in International/Postcolonial Feminist Legal Rhetorics." In *Erotic Justice: Postcolonialism, Subjects and Rights*, 95–136. London: Glass House Press.

Lamble, Sarah (2008). "Retelling Racialized Violence, Remaking White Innocence: The Politics of Interlocking Oppressions in Transgender Day of Remembrance." *Sexuality Research and Social Policy: Journal of NSRC* 5: 1, 24–42.

Levi, Jennifer (n.d.) Steatement before the Joint Committee on Judiciary in Support of Raised Bill No. 5723, An Act Concerning Discrimination. Gay and Lesbian Alliance Against Defamation (GLAAD). http://www.glaad.org/uploads/docs/advocacy/Testimony_CT_Transgender_2008_03_18.pdf.

Manalansan, Martin F. (2005). "Race, Violence, and Neoliberal Spatial Politics in the Global City." *Social Text* 23: 3–4, 141–155.

Maneo (2011). "The International Maneo Conference 2011." Posted at www.maneo.de/en/maneo-konferenz.html (accessed 6 January 2012).

Mbembe, Achille (2003). "Necropolitics." *Public Culture* 15: 1, 11–40.

Mirzoeff, Nicholas (2009). "The Sea and the Land: Biopower and Visuality from Slavery to Katrina." *Culture, Theory and Critique* 50: 2, 289–305.

Nair, Yasmin (2009). "Why Hate Crimes Legislation Is a Terrible Idea: A Reminder." *The Bilerico Project*, 17 July 2009, www.bilerico.com/2009/07/why_hate_crimes_legislation_is_a_terrible_ideal_a_r.php (accessed 5 January 2010).

Namaste, Ki (1996). "Tragic Misreadings: Queer Theory's Erasure of Transgender Subjectivity." In B. Beemyn and M. Eliason (eds.), *Queer Studies: A Lesbian, Gay, Bisexual, and Transgender Anthology*, 183–203. New York: New York University Press.

Povinelli, Elizabeth (2008). "The Child in the Broom Closet: States of Killing and Letting Die." *South Atlantic Quarterly* 107: 3, 509–530.

Prosser, Jay. (1998). *Second Skins: The Body Narratives of Transsexuality*. New York: Columbia University Press.

Puar, Jasbir (2007). *Terrorist Assemblages: Homonationalism in Queer Times*. Durham: Duke University Press.

Rivera, Sylvia (2002). "Queens in Exile: The Forgotten Ones." In J. Nestle, C. Howell and R. Wilchins (eds.), *Genderqueer*, 67–85. Los Angeles: Allyson Books.

Schüller, Malini Johar (2005). "Analogy and (White) Feminist Theory: Thinking Race and the Color of the Cyborg Body." *Signs: Journal of Women in Culture and Society* 31: 1, 63–92.

Siegessäule TV (2009). "Transphobe Gewalt im Berliner Frobenkiez—Solidarität mit den Sexarbeiterinnen." www.youtube.com/watch?v=YT_krTlkBzQ&feature=related (accessed 23 December 2011).

Simon, Bernd (2008). "Einstellungen zur Homosexualität: Ausprägungen und psychologische Korrelate bei Jugendlichen mit und ohne Migrationshintergrund (ehemalige UdSSR und Türkei)." *Zeitschrift für Entwicklungspsychologie und Pädagogische Psychologie* 40, 87–99.

Spade, Dean (2003). "Remarks at Transecting the Academy Conference, Race and Ethnic Studies Panel; lltlt· Zinc." http:/fwww.makezine.org/transecling.html (accessed 13 September 2012).

Spade, Dean (2009). "Keynote Address: Trans Law and Politics on a Neoliberal Landscape." *Temple Political and Civil Rights Law Review* 18: 2, 353–373.

SPD/Die Linke (2009), *Initiative Berlin tritt ein für Selbstbestimmung und Akzeptanz sexueller Vielfalt,* www.spdfraktionberlin.de/var/files/pdfzumthema/antrag_sexuelle_vielfalt.pdf (accessed 15 February 2009).

Stanley, Eric and Nat Smith (eds.) (2011). *Captive Genders: Trans Embodiments and the Prison Industrial Complex.* Baltimore: AK Press.

Sudbury, Julia (2006). "Rethinking Antiviolence Strategies: Lessons from the Black Women's Movement in Britain." In Incite! (eds.), *Color of Violence: The Incite! Anthology,* 13–24. Cambridge, MA: South End Press.

Sylvia Rivera Law Project, FIERCE, Audre Lorde Project, The Peter Cicchino Youth Project, and Queers for Economic Justice (2009). "SRLP Announces Non-support of the Gender Employment Non-Discrimination Act." *Sylvia Rivera Law Project,* http://srlp.org/genda (accessed 5 January 2010).

Windy City Times (2011). "International MANEO-Conference Looked at LGBT Neighborhoods Worldwide, Chicago Viewed as Model for Developing, Sustaining LGBT Neighborhoods." Posted at www.windycitymediagroup.com/gay/lesbian/news/ARTICLE.php?AID=35180 (accessed 6 January 2012).

27 Trans Law and Politics on a Neoliberal Landscape

Dean Spade

"Trans Law and Politics on a Neoliberal Landscape" is excerpted from law professor and activist legal theorist Dean Spade's 2015 book *Normal Life: Administrative Violence, Critical Trans Politics, and the Limits of Law*. Spade discusses how, since the 1980s, the lesbian and gay rights movement has become increasingly focused on a narrow set of priorities that serve only to further uplift lesbian and gay people who already enjoy a privileged relation to the state. In contrast to the radical social movements of the 1960s and 1970s that focused on redistribution of resources and expansive ideals of social transformation, Spade argues that the narrow rights-based focus of LGBT activism in recent decades reflects the consolidation of neoliberal values. This activism takes place on a landscape characterized by diminished social safety nets, a vastly expanded prison system, stagnant wages, and lessened capacity for collective labor organizing—all made possible through an array of legal, legislative, and imperialist policies such as the War on Drugs and the War on Terror. Spade then turns his attention to the increased role of non-profit organizations, inclusion-based policies for lesbian and gay people, and, most notably, legal fights for marriage equality to argue that they have served only to increase the precariousness that people of color and Indigenous people, immigrants, disabled folks, poor people, and trans people face in relation to the state.

In order to effectively conceptualize political and economic marginalization, shortened life spans, and an emergent notion of organized resistance among the set of gender rule-breakers currently being loosely gathered under a "trans" umbrella, and to raise questions about the usefulness of law reform strategies in this resistance, it is important to consider the context in which these conditions are embedded. The concept of neoliberalism is a useful tool for describing the context in which emergent forms of trans resistance are appearing. Scholars and activists have used the term "neoliberalism" in recent years to describe a range of interlocking trends in domestic and international politics that constitute the current political landscape. The term is slippery and imperfect. Neoliberalism is used to mean lots of different things by lots of different people, and it is sometimes used to refer to conditions that we could understand as not new at all, like state violence toward people of color, US military imperialism, and attacks on poor people. However, I find the term useful because it allows space for critical insight into the range of practices producing effects at the register of law, policy, economy, identity, organization, and affect. It helps us look at a set of things together and understand their interlocking relationships rather than analyzing them in ways that make us miss key connections.

DOI: 10.4324/9781003206255-34

Neoliberalism has not only shaped the larger social, economic, and political conditions that trans people find themselves in, but has also produced a specific lesbian and gay rights formation that trans politics operates in relation to. The concept of neoliberalism is useful both for raising concerns about the effects of the lesbian and gay rights formation on trans people, and for calling into question the usefulness of the lesbian and gay rights model for trans law reform efforts.

Neoliberalism has been used to conceptually draw together several key trends shaping contemporary policies and practices that have redistributed life chances over the last forty years. These trends include a significant shift in the relationships of workers to owners, producing a decrease in real wages,[1] an increase in contingent labor, and the decline of labor unions; the dismantling of welfare programs; trade liberalization (sometimes called "globalization"); and increasing criminalization and immigration enforcement. Neoliberalism is also associated with the rollback of the gains of the civil rights movement and other social movements of the 1960s and '70s, combined with the mobilization of racist, sexist, and xenophobic images and ideas to bolster these changes. Further, the emotional or affective registers of neoliberalism are attuned to notions of "freedom" and "choice" that obscure systemic inequalities and turn social movements toward goals of inclusion and incorporation and away from demands for redistribution and structural transformation.

At a broad level, the advent of neoliberal politics has resulted in an upward distribution of wealth.[2] Simply put, the rich have gotten richer and the poor have gotten poorer.[3] The real wages of Americans have not increased since the 1970s, and the bargaining power of workers trying to improve the conditions under which they labor has declined significantly. [. . .]

During the same period state programs to support poor people, people with disabilities, and old people have also been dismantled. As a result, more and more people have been left without the basic safety nets necessary to ensure their very survival. The real worth of already inadequate benefits has continuously decreased since the 1970s while the laws and policies governing these programs have simultaneously changed to exclude more and more people from eligibility. Lifetime limits, new provisions excluding immigrants, family caps limiting benefits for new children entering a family, and new regimes of work requirements imposed on those in need of benefits were introduced in the 1990s to "end welfare as we know it."[4] These drastic policy changes have left millions of poor people with less access to basic necessities: these changes have destroyed public housing projects, greatly reduced vital health and social services, and produced a significant increase in the number of people living without shelter.

Globally, the upward distribution of wealth has been aided by trends of trade liberalization combined with coercive rules imposed upon poor/indebted countries by rich/grantor countries. Both of these elements create rules that reduce the ability of countries to protect their workers and natural environments from exploitation and build programs like education and health care systems that increase the well-being and security of their own people. Trade agreements like the North American Free Trade Agreement (NAFTA) and the proposed Trans-Pacific Partnership (TPP) are used by corporations to attack rules that protect workers or the environment, arguing that such rules are barriers to "free trade." At the same time, organizations such as the International Monetary Fund (IMF) and the World Bank place limitations on what indebted countries can do, forcing them to focus on producing cash crops in order to make payments on debts instead of investing money in basic necessities and infrastructure within the country, or growing sustenance crops to feed their people. The structures of trade liberalization and coercive debt allow wealthy countries and corporations to perpetuate resource extraction against poor countries and their populations, leaving their people in peril. These conditions drastically impact the life spans of people in poor countries: deaths from preventable and treatable disease, hunger, and environmental damage are the direct result of economic arrangements that divest exploited nations of control over local human and natural resources.[5] [. . .]

These changes in global economic arrangements, such as the emergence of "free trade agreements" and debt schemes that replaced prior forms of colonialism with new ways of controlling countries, have also had significant impacts within the United States. Domestic job loss has resulted as corporations move their operations to places with more exploitable and unprotected workforces. As more and more working class people feel the effects of economic restructuring that reduces their earnings and employment security, politicians and the media offer racist and xenophobic scapegoating to exploit this dissatisfaction, preventing the discontent from producing interventions on these economic agendas. As workers in the United States experience the impacts of their declining power, the media and government have shaped messages that channel frustration at these changes into policies of racialized control rather than economic reforms that might benefit those workers.

Sexist, racist, and xenophobic images and ideas have been mobilized in the media and by politicians to transform growing economic loss and dissatisfaction into calls for "law and order."[6] Increasingly, social problems rooted in poverty and the racial wealth divide have been portrayed as issues of "crime," and increased policing and imprisonment have been framed as the solution.[7] The last thirty years have seen a massive growth in structures of law enforcement, both in the criminal punishment and immigration contexts, fueled by the rhetorical devices of the War on Drugs and the War on Terror. Numerous law changes have criminalized behaviors that were previously not criminalized and drastically enhanced sentences for existing crimes. Mandatory minimum sentences for drug violations have severely increased the significance of drug convictions, despite an overall reduction of drug use in the United States during this period.[8] "Three strikes" laws, which create a mandatory extended prison sentence for people convicted of three crimes listed as "serious," have been adopted by almost half the states in the United States, contributing to the drastic growth in imprisonment. Behaviors associated with being poor, such as panhandling, sleeping outdoors, entering public transit without paying the fare, and writing graffiti have also been increasingly criminalized, resulting in many poor and homeless people ending up more entangled in the criminal system.[9] Many cities have taken up "quality of life" policing strategies that target for arrest people in the sex trade, homeless people, youth, people with disabilities, and people of color as part of efforts to make cities comfortable for white gentrifiers.[10] The result of these trends has been a rapid growth of imprisonment such that the United States now imprisons one in 100 people.[11] With only 5 percent of the world's population, the United States now has 25 percent of the world's prisoners. Over 60 percent of US prisoners are people of color; and one in three Black men now experience imprisonment during their lifetimes.[12] Native populations also experience particularly high rates of imprisonment; at a rate of 709 per 100,000, the imprisonment rate for Native populations is second only to the rate of imprisonment for Black people, estimated at 1,815 per 100,000.[13] Women are the fastest growing segment of the imprisoned population. The rate of imprisonment for women has increased at nearly double the rate of men since 1985 and there are now more than eight times as many women locked up in state and federal prisons and local jails as there were in 1980. "War on Drugs" policy changes account for much of this shift—40 percent of criminal convictions leading to incarceration of women in 2000 were for drug crimes.[14] Two-thirds of women imprisoned in the United States are women of color.[15]

Such trends have prompted many commentators to observe that imprisonment of communities of color is an extension of systems of chattel slavery and genocide of indigenous people.[16] Angela Davis has described the historical trajectory that formed the criminal punishment system as a response to the formal abolition of slavery. As she and others have pointed out, the Thirteenth Amendment's abolition of involuntary servitude includes a very important caveat: "except as punishment for crime, whereof the party shall have been duly convicted." As Davis traces, in the years following the abolition of slavery, southern prisons drastically expanded and went from being almost entirely white to primarily imprisoning Black people. New laws were passed—the Black Codes—that made an enormous range of behaviors (e.g., drunkenness and vagrancy) criminal solely if the accused was Black. These legal schemes permitted the newly freed slaves to be recaptured into a new system of forced labor, control, and racial violence. The nature of imprisonment changed during this time, taking on the methods of punishment common to slavery, such as whipping, and implementing the convict leasing system that allowed former slave owners to lease the labor of prisoners who were forced to work under conditions many observers have suggested were even more violent than those of slavery.[17] The contemporary criminal punishment system finds its origins in this racially targeted control and exploitation of Black people, and its continuation of those tactics can be seen in its contemporary operations. [. . .]

The specific origins of the criminal punishment system in relation to chattel slavery has not limited the targets of that system to Black people. While Black people continue to be the primary targets, other people of color and poor white people are also profoundly impacted by caging and policing, both through the criminal punishment system and the immigration enforcement system. In the last decade, the War on Terror has prompted a massive growth in immigration enforcement, including imprisonment, significant law changes reducing the rights of people imprisoned in immigration facilities,[18] and an overhaul of the administrative systems that govern identification in ways that lock immigrants out of basic services and make them more vulnerable to exploitation. In the last decade law changes at both the state and federal level have made it more difficult to get id and government benefits. Some of these changes have been fueled by well-publicized campaigns such as the 1994 campaign to pass Proposition 187 in California, a law that aimed to ensure that undocumented immigrants could not use public services such as health care, education, and other social services. The 2005 Real ID Act, passed by Congress, focused on changing how states issue driver's licenses in order to prevent undocumented immigrants from obtaining id. Many other law and policy changes that garnered less attention similarly reduced access to key services and id for undocumented people. During the same period, the federal government has increased its enforcement of immigration laws, imprisoning and deporting more people and creating new programs, like the controversial "Secure Communities" program,[19] that increase the use of state and local criminal enforcement resources for targeting immigrants.

[. . .]

The changes in conditions and the ideas undergirding the neoliberal project have also significantly impacted what social movement politics look like in the United States.[20] The conservative turn has been reflected in social movement politics, where the radical projects of the 1960s and 1970s that were targeted for dismantling by the FBI were replaced by a growing nonprofit sector.[21] Emerging nonprofit organizations both filled the gaps left as the government abandoned key social and legal services designed to assist poor populations, and created a new elite sector of law and policy reform funded by wealthy philanthropists. This new sector differs significantly from the more grassroots and mass-based social movements of earlier eras. Its reform projects reflect the neoliberal shift toward the politics of inclusion and incorporation rather than redistribution and deep transformation. The newly expanded non-profit sector is most concerned with services and policy change. Traditional strategies of mass-based organizing have been underfunded and systematically dismantled, as funders prefer to channel resources toward project-oriented programs with short timelines for quantifiable outcomes. In this context, social justice has become a career track populated by individuals with specialized professional training who rely on business management models to run nonprofits "efficiently." The leadership and decision-making come

from these disproportionately white, upper-class paid leaders and donors, which has significantly shifted priorities toward work that stabilizes structural inequality by legitimizing and
advancing dominant systems of meaning and control rather than making demands for deeper
transformation.

The legal reform work that currently operates under the rubric of lesbian and gay rights
(or sometimes LGBT rights) is an example of this shift from a more transformative social
movement agenda to an inclusion and incorporation-focused professionalized nonprofit legal
reform project. Countless scholars and activists have critiqued the direction that lesbian and
gay rights activism has taken since the incendiary moments of the late 1960s when criminalized gender and sexual outsiders fought back against police harassment and brutality at New
York City's Stonewall Inn and San Francisco's Compton's Cafeteria.[22] The activism that arose
during that period started as street resistance and unfunded ad hoc organizations, initially
taking the form of protests and marches, utilizing strategies that were mirrored across a range
of movements, resisting police brutality and militarism, and opposing patriarchal and racist
norms and violences. This emerging sexuality/gender-focused resistance was institutionalized in the 1980s into nonprofit structures led by white lawyers and other people with class
and education privilege. Critics of these developments have used a variety of terms and
concepts to describe the shift, including charges that the focus became assimilation;[23] that
the work increasingly marginalized low-income people,[24] people of color,[25] and transgender
people;[26] and that the resistance became co-opted by neoliberalism[27] and conservative egali-
tarianism. Critics have argued that as the gay movement of the 1970s institutionalized into
the lesbian and gay rights movement in the 1980s—forming such institutions as Gay and
Lesbian Advocates and Defenders (GLAD), the Gay and Lesbian Alliance Against Defamation (GLAAD), the Human Rights Campaign (HRC), Lambda Legal Defense and Education Fund, and the National Gay and Lesbian Task Force (NGLTF)—the focus of the most
well-funded, well-publicized work on behalf of queers shifted drastically.[28]

[. . .]

Participatory forms of organizing, such as nonprofessional membership-based grassroots
organizations, were replaced by hierarchical, staff-run organizations operated by people with
graduate degrees. Broad concerns with policing and punishment, militarism, and wealth distribution taken up by some earlier manifestations of lesbian and gay activism were replaced
with a focus on formal legal equality that could produce gains only for people already
served by existing social and economic arrangements.[29] For example, choosing to frame
equal access to health care through a demand for same-sex marriage rights means fighting
for health care access that would only affect people with jobs that include health benefits
they can share with a partner, which is an increasingly uncommon privilege.[30] Similarly,
addressing the economic marginalization of queer people solely through the lens of anti-
discrimination laws that bar discrimination in employment on the basis of sexual orientation—
despite the facts that these laws have been ineffective at eradicating discrimination on the
basis of race, sex, disability, and national origin, and that most people do not have access to
the legal resources needed to enforce these kinds of rights—has been criticized as marking
an investment in formal legal equality while ignoring the plight of the most economically
marginalized queers. Framing issues related to child custody through a lens of marital recognition, similarly, means ignoring the racist, sexist, and classist operation of the child welfare
system and passing up opportunities to form coalitions across populations targeted for family
dissolution by that system. Black people, indigenous people, people with disabilities, queer
and trans people, prisoners, and poor people are targeted in child welfare systems. Seeking
"family recognition" rights through marriage, therefore, means seeking such rights only for
queer and trans people who can actually expect to be protected by family law and child welfare systems. Since the availability of marriage does not protect straight people of color, poor

people, indigenous people, prisoners, or people with disabilities from having their families torn apart by child welfare systems, it is unlikely to do so for queer poor people, queer people of color, queer indigenous people, queer prisoners, and queer people with disabilities. The quest for marriage seems to have far fewer benefits, then, for queers whose families are targets of state violence and who have no spousal access to health care or immigration status, and seems to primarily benefit those whose race, class, immigration, and ability privilege would allow them to increase their well-being by incorporation into the government's privileged relationship status. [. . .]

The following chart provides some examples of the framings and demands developed by the most visible and well-resourced lesbian and gay organizations for addressing key problems facing queer and trans communities and compares them to alternative framings offered by queer and trans activists and organizations who center racial and economic justice.[31] Each of these examples makes visible the centering of formal legal equality demands, and the limited potential of those demands to transform the conditions facing highly vulnerable queer and trans people. This chart does not aim to be exhaustive, only to illustrate some of the concerns raised and alternative approaches proposed to the "official" gay and lesbian law reform agenda.

These questions of issue framing and prioritization came to the forefront during the welfare reform debates and subsequent policy changes of the mid-1990s; social justice activists criticized lesbian and gay rights organizations for not resisting the elimination of social welfare programs despite the fact that these policy changes had devastating effects for low-income queers.[32] Similar critiques have been made of the efforts to pass hate crime laws, arguing that the aim of enhancing penalties for assaults perpetrated because of anti-gay animus directs resources to criminal punishment agencies, a move that is deeply misguided and dangerous.[33] Queer activists focused on opposing policing and mass incarceration of low-income people and people of color in the United States have argued that hate crime laws do nothing to prevent violence against queer and trans people, much of which happens at the hands of employees of the criminal punishment system, a system to which hate crime laws lend more resources.[34] The shift in focus from police accountability to partnering with the criminal punishment system and aiming for increased penalties represents a significant betrayal of the concerns of low-income queer and trans people and queer and trans people of color, who are frequent targets of police and prisons. This move centers the perspective and experience of white, economically privileged queers who may feel protected by the police and criminal punishment systems. Those who feel protected and are not directly impacted by the violence of imprisonment and policing are less likely to see the urgent need for a fundamental shift away from relying on that system.

[. . .]

The gay rights agenda, then, has come to reflect the needs and experiences of those leaders more than the experiences of queer and trans people not present in these elite spaces. The mostly white, educationally privileged paid leaders can imagine themselves fired from a job for being gay or lesbian, harassed on the street (often by an imagined assailant of color),[35] excluded from Boy Scouts, or kept out of military service. They do not imagine themselves as potentially imprisoned, on welfare, homeless, in the juvenile punishment and foster care systems, in danger of deportation, or the target of continuous police harassment. Because such figures shaped and continue to shape the "gay agenda," those issues do not receive the resources they warrant and require. Furthermore, these paid nonprofit leaders come out of graduate schools more than from transformative, grassroots social movements of people facing centuries of state violence. Because of this, they do not possess the critiques of notions such as formal legal equality, assimilation, professionalism, and equal rights that are developed through grassroots mobilization work. Even relatively popular feminist critiques of the

The Big Problems	The Official Lesbian & Gay Solutions	Critical Queer and Trans Political Approaches
Queer and trans people, poor people, people of color, and immigrants have minimal access to quality health care	Legalize same-sex marriage to allow people with health benefits from their jobs to share with same-sex partners	Medicaid/Medicare activism; fight for universal health care; fight for transgender health care; protest deadly medical neglect of people in state custody
Violence against queer and trans people	Pass hate crime legislation to increase prison sentences and strengthen local and federal law enforcement; collect statistics on rates of violence; collaborate with local and federal law enforcement to prosecute hate violence and domestic violence	Develop community-based responses to violence that support collective healing and accountability; join with movements addressing root causes of queer and trans premature death: police violence, imprisonment, poverty, lack of health care and housing
Queer and trans people experience violence and discrimination in the military	Eliminate bans on participation of gays and lesbians in US military	Join with movements to oppose racist, sexist, imperialist military actions abroad and at home; demand reduction/elimination of defense budget
Unfair and punitive immigration system	Legalize same-sex marriage to allow people with citizenship to apply for legal residency for a same-sex spouse	Support campaigns to abolish immigration imprisonment and deportation; oppose immigration rules that make legal immigration status dependent on marital relationships
Queer and trans families are vulnerable to legal intervention and separation by the state and/or nonqueer and nontrans people	Legalize same-sex marriage to provide a route to "legalize" families with two parents of the same sex; pass laws banning adoption discrimination on the basis of sexual orientation	Join with other people targeted by family law and the child welfare system (poor families, imprisoned parents, native families, families of color, people with disabilities) to fight for community and family self-determination and the rights of people to keep their kids in their families and communities
Institutions fail to recognize family connections outside of heterosexual marriage in contexts like hospital visitation and inheritance	Legalize same-sex marriage to formally recognize same-sex partners in the eyes of the law	Change policies like hospital visitation to recognize a variety of family structures, not just opposite-sex and same-sex couples; abolish inheritance and demand radical redistribution of wealth and an end to poverty

institution of marriage could not trump the new call for "marriage equality"—meaning access for same-sex couples to the fundamentally unequal institution designed to privilege certain family formations for the purpose of state control.[36]

Where the money for this lesbian and gay rights nonprofit formation comes from, and how it is distributed, is also an area of significant concern. The largest white-founded and white-led organizations doing lesbian and gay rights work have generated much revenue through both foundation grants[37] and sponsorship by corporations such as American Airlines, Budweiser, IBM, and Coors. These partnerships, which include advertising for the corporations, have been criticized by queers concerned about the narrow framework of organizations willing to promote corporations whose labor and environmental practices have been widely critiqued. These partnerships have furthered the ongoing criticism that lesbian and gay rights work has become a "single-issue politics" that ignores vital social justice issues, promoting a political agenda that concerns gays and lesbians experiencing marginalization through a single vector of identity only—sexual orientation. Such a politics excludes queer and trans people who experience homophobia simultaneously with transphobia, poverty, ableism, xenophobia, racism, sexism, criminalization, economic exploitation, and/or other forms of subjection.

[. . .]

Overall, the most well-funded lesbian and gay rights organizations provide stark examples of the critiques made by activists from across a wide range of social justice movements regarding the shift from the transformative demands of the 1960s and '70s to the narrow focus of the grant-funded "social justice entrepreneurs" of today. Lack of community accountability, elitism, concentration of wealth and resources in the hands of white elites, and exploitative labor practices have become norms within these organizations, creating and maintaining disappointing and dangerous political agendas that fail to support meaningful, widespread resistance to violent institutions in the United States—and sometimes even bolstering them. Through the rise of the nonprofit form, certain logics that support criminalization, militarism, and wealth disparity have penetrated and transformed spaces that were once locations of fomenting resistance to state violence.[38] Increasingly, neoliberalism means that social issues taken up by nonprofits are separated from a broader commitment to social justice; nonprofits take part in producing and maintaining a racialized-gendered maldistribution of life chances while pursuing their "good work."

As trans activism emerges and institutionalizes, there is often an assumption that following the strategies of lesbian and gay rights organizations, with their strong focus on law reforms including hate crime and anti-discrimination laws, is our surest path to success. Yet, the picture of economic marginalization, vulnerability to imprisonment, and other forms of state violence that trans communities are describing suggests that the "successes" of the lesbian and gay rights organizations do not have enough to offer in terms of redistribution of life chances—and that their strategies will in fact further endanger the most marginalized trans populations. If formal legal equality at best opens doors to dominant institutions for those who are already closest to inclusion (i.e., they would be included if it wasn't for this one characteristic), very few stand to benefit. Given the context of neoliberal politics, in which fewer and fewer people have the kind of racial and economic access necessary to obtain what has been cast as "equal opportunity" in the United States, and where populations deemed disposable are abandoned to poverty and imprisoned only to be released to poverty and recaptured again, we face serious questions about how to formulate meaningful transformative demands and tactics. Specifically, because changing laws is too often the assumed method of changing the lives of marginalized people, we have to take into account the ways in which law reform has been both ineffective and co-optive in the context of neoliberalism and the nonprofitization of resistance. We have to carefully consider the limitations of strategies that aim for inclusion into existing economic and political arrangements rather than challenging the terms of those arrangements. We must endeavor to create and practice a critical trans politics that contributes to building a political context for massive redistribution. A critical trans politics imagines and demands an end to prisons, homelessness, landlords, bosses, immigration enforcement, poverty, and wealth. It imagines a world in which people have what they need and govern themselves in ways that value collectivity, interdependence, and difference. Winning those demands and building the world in which they can be realized requires an unyielding commitment to center racial, economic, ability, and gender justice. It also requires thoughtful, reflective strategizing about how to build leadership and mobilization in ways that reflect those commitments. Our demands for redistribution, access, and participation must be reflected in our resistance work every day—they can't be something we come back for later.

From: Dean Spade, "Trans Law and Politics on a Neoliberal Landscape," in *Normal Life: Administrative Violence, Critical Trans Politics, and the Limits of Law*, pp. 21–37. Copyright 2015, Dean Spade. All rights reserved. Republished by permission of the copyright holder, and the Publisher. www.dukeupress.edu.

Notes

1. "The decline in real wages over the past two generations also has made unpaid leave impractical for a large majority of American families. Average hourly earnings were $8.03 in 1970 but fell to $7.39 by 1993, while average weekly earnings fell from $298 to $255 over the same time period. The median income for American families was $300 less in 1986 than in 1975. The purchasing power of the dollar (measured by consumer prices) was $4.15 in 1950 but only $0.69 in 1993. By 1985, it took two incomes to maintain the same standard of living that was possible with one income in the 1950s." Arielle Horman Grill, "The Myth of Unpaid Family Leave: Can the United States Implement a Paid Leave Policy Based on the Swedish Model?" *Comparative Labor Law Journal* 17 (1996): 373, 383–390; citing Patricia Schroeder, "Parental Leave: The Need for a Federal Policy," in *The Parental Leave Crisis: Toward a National Policy*, eds. Edward F. Zigler and Meryl Frank (New Haven, CT: Yale University Press, 1988), 326, 331; Bureau of the Census, *US Department of Commerce, Statistical Abstract of the United States*, 114th ed. (Washington, DC: US Department of Commerce, Bureau of the Census, 1994), 396. See also Pew's Economic Mobility Project, "Economic Mobility: Is the American Dream Alive and Well?" 2009, www.economicmobility.org/assets/pdfs/EMP_American_Dream_Key_Findings.pdf; US Bureau of the Census, *Measuring 50 Years of Economic Change Using the March Current Population Survey* (Washington, DC: US Government Printing Office, 1998), www.census.gov/prod/3/98pubs/p60-203.pdf.
2. Lisa Duggan, *The Twilight of Equality? Neoliberalism, Cultural Politics, and the Attack on Democracy* (Boston: Beacon Press, 2004).
3. In 2009, inequality was at the highest level since the US Census began tracking household income in 1967. The top 1 percentile of households took home 23.5 percent of income in 2007, the largest share since 1928. Emily Kaiser, "How American Income Inequality Hit Levels Not Seen Since the Depression." *Huffington Post*, October 22, 2010, www.huffingtonpost.com/2010/10/22/income-inequality-America_n_772687.html.
4. This phrase was one of President Bill Clinton's 1992 campaign promises. The law changes he supported have indeed proven to have severely weakened public benefits systems, throwing many people off benefits and into more severe poverty. "Research show[s] that one in five former recipients ultimately became totally disconnected from any means of support: They no longer had welfare, but they didn't have jobs. They hadn't married or moved in with a partner or family, and they weren't getting disability benefits. And so, after a decline in the late 1990s, the number of people living in extreme poverty (with an income less than half the poverty line, or below about $8,500 for a family of three) shot up by more than a third, from 12.6 million in 2000 to 17.1 million in 2008." Peter Edelman and Barbara Ehrenreich, "Why Welfare Reform Fails Its Recession Test," *The Washington Post* (Washington, DC), December 8, 2009, www.washingtonpost.com/wp-dyn/content/article/2009/12/04/AR2009120402604.html; "According to the think tank Center on Budget and Policy Priorities, federal aid to poor families supported 84 percent of eligible households in 1995, but 10 years later, Temporary Assistance for Needy Families [TANF] reached just 40 percent. Serving a shrinking percentage of needy people means the program has 'become less effective over time' at countering extreme poverty, or those living below half the poverty level." Michelle Chen, "It's Time to Restore the Social Safety Net," *Centre Daily Times* (State College, PA), June 23, 2010; "By 2008, the number of children receiving TANF had fallen to only 22 percent of the number of poor children, down from 62 percent under Aid to Families with Dependent Children [AFDC] in 1995. Eligibility criteria in some states is set at subpoverty levels, making many poor children ineligible, and barriers to access have blocked many poor children who are eligible from actually getting assistance. The percentage of eligible families receiving benefits has declined precipitously under TANF, falling from 84 percent in AFDC's last full year in 1995 to 40 percent in 2005, the most recent year for which the federal government has provided estimates of

the number of families eligible for but not receiving TANF. TANF benefit levels are grossly inadequate for the families the program does reach, and have been eroded by inflation or only minimally increased in most states since 1996. In July 2008, TANF benefit amounts were far below the official poverty guideline in every state." Deepak Bhargava et al., *Battered by the Storm: How the Safety Net Is Failing Americans and How to Fix It* (Washington, DC: Institute for Policy Studies, the Center for Community Change, Jobs with Justice, and Legal Momentum, 2009), www.ips-dc.org/reports/battered-by-the-storm; "Nearly 16 million Americans are living in severe poverty, the McClatchy Washington Bureau reported recently. These are individuals making less than $5,080 a year and families of four bringing in less than $9,903 a year, hardly imaginable in this day and age. That number has been growing rapidly since 2000. And, as a percentage, those living in severe poverty has reached a 32-year high. Even more troubling, the report noted that in any given month only 10 percent of the severe poor received Temporary Assistance for Needy Families and only 36 percent received food stamps." "Tracking Poverty: Continue Survey of Program Effectiveness," *The Sacramento Bee*, March 12, 2007.

5. Ha-Joon Chang, *Bad Samaritans: The Myth of Free Trade and the Secret History of Capitalism* (London: Bloomsbury Press, 2007); Nirmala Erevelles, "Disability in the New World Order," in *Color of Violence: The INCITE! Anthology*, ed. INCITE! Women of Color Against Violence (Cambridge, MA: South End Press, 2006), 25–31; Silvia Federici, "War, Globalization, and Reproduction," in *There Is an Alternative: Subsistence and Worldwide Resistance to Corporate Globalization*, eds. Veronika Bennholdt-Thomsen, Nicholas Faraclas, and Claudia von Werlhof (London: Zed Books, 2001), 133–145; Vijay Prashad, "Debt," in *Keeping Up with the Dow Joneses: Debt, Prison, Workfare* (Cambridge, MA: South End Press, 2003), 1–68; Naomi Klein, *The Shock Doctrine: The Rise of Disaster Capitalism* (New York: Picador, 2007).

6. Duggan, *The Twilight of Equality?*

7. Loïc Wacquant, *Punishing the Poor: The Neoliberal Government of Social Insecurity* (Durham, NC: Duke University Press, 2009).

8. Ruth Wilson Gilmore, "Globalisation and US Prison Growth: From Military Keynesianism to Post Keynesian Militarism," *Race & Class* 40, no. 2–3 (March 1999): 171–188, 173; Angela Y. Davis, *Are Prisons Obsolete?* (New York: Seven Stories Press, 2003).

9. Alex Vitale, *City of Disorder: How the Quality of Life Campaign Transformed New York Politics* (New York: NYU Press, 2008).

10. Vitale, *City of Disorder.*

11. The PEW Center on the States, *One in 100: Behind Bars in America 2008* (2008), www.pewcenter-onthestates.org/uploadedFiles/8015PCTS_Prison08_FINAL_2-1-1_FORWEB.pdf.

12. Thomas P. Bonczar, *Prevalence of Imprisonment in the US Population, 1974–2001, NCJ197976* (Washington, DC: US Department of Justice, Bureau of Justice Statistics, 2003); William J. Sabol and Heather Couture, *Prisoners at Midyear 2007, NCJ221944* (Washington, DC: US Department of Justice, Bureau of Justice Statistics, 2008).

13. Greg Guma, "Native Incarceration Rates are Increasing," *Toward Freedom*, May 27, 2005, www.toward-freedom.com/home/americas/140-native-incarceration-rates-are-increasing-0302.

14. American Civil Liberties Union, "Facts about the Over-Incarceration of Women in the United States" (2007), www.aclu.org/womens-rights/facts-about-over-incarceration-women-united-states.

15. Correctional Association of New York, Women in Prison Project, "Women in Prison Fact Sheet" (March 2002), www.prisonpolicy.org/scans/Fact_Sheets_2002.pdf.

16. Davis, *Are Prisons Obsolete?*; Andrea Smith, "Heteropatriarchy and the Three Pillars of White Supremacy: Rethinking Women of Color Organizing," in *Color of Violence: The INCITE! Anthology*, ed. INCITE! Women of Color Against Violence (Cambridge, MA: South End Press, 2006), 66–73.

17. Davis, *Are Prisons Obsolete?* 29.

18. I intentionally use the term "imprisonment" rather than "detention" and "incarceration" when possible for two reasons. First, I fear that those two terms euphemize the practice of caging people and contribute to how that practice becomes ordinary or a matter of course in American culture. Second, I believe we should analyze the rise in both criminal punishment and immigration enforcement uses of imprisonment as connected concerns and avoid terms that make immigration imprisonment seem more temporary or less violent than it is. While "immigration detention" is often portrayed by immigration enforcement officials as short-term and somehow less concerning because it is officially a part of civil rather than criminal law enforcement, in reality it is marked by the same features as criminal punishment imprisonment: racially targeted; characterized by sexual assault and medical neglect; arbitrary and often indefinite in its duration; and distributed at the population level hidden behind a rationalization of individual culpability and individual rights.

19. Secure Communities was a program where participating jurisdictions submitted the fingerprints of everyone they arrest to federal databases for an immigration check. It was piloted beginning in 2008 with an initial 14 jurisdictions and expanded by the Obama administration, with the goal of including all jurisdictions in the United States by 2013. Immigration Policy Center, *Secure Communities: A Fact Sheet* (Washington, DC: Immigration Policy Center, November 29, 2011), www.immigrationpolicy.org/just-facts/secure-communities-fact-sheet. Activists across the country led campaigns urging their jurisdictions not to participate, and eventually 300 cities and counties plus three states refused to participate. In November 2014, Obama announced that he was ending the unpopular program and replacing it with a Priority Enforcement Program, which critics argue is functionally the same program under a new name. See Center for Constitutional Rights, *Tell Governor Cuomo: Stop Secure Communities in New York* (New York: Center for Constitutional Rights), www.ccrjustice.org/nyscomm; American Friends Service Committee, *Stop "Secure Communities" in Massachusetts* (Philadelphia: American Friends Service Committee, February, 2011), afsc.org/event/stop-secure-communities-massachusetts; Lornert Turnbull, "State Won't Agree to National Immigration Program." *Seattle Times*, November 28, 2010, seattletimes.nwsource.com/html/localnews/2013545041_secute29m.html?prmid=obinsite; Tim Henderson, "More Jurisdictions Defying Feds on Deporting Immigrants," *The Pew Charitable Trust*, October 33, 2014, www.pewtrusts.org/en/research-and-analysis/blogs/stateline/2014/10/31/more-jurisdictions-defying-feds-on deporting-immigrants.

20. Portions of the rest of the text in this chapter are adapted from Dean Spade and Rickke Manzanala, "The Non-Profit Industrial Complex and Trans Resistance," *Sexuality Research and Social Policy: Journal of NSRC* 5, no. 1 (March 2008): 53–71.

21. Dylan Rodríguez, "The Political Logic of the Non-Profit Industrial Complex," in *The Revolution Will Not Be Funded: Beyond the Non-Profit Industrial Complex*, ed. INCITE! Women of Color Against Violence (Cambridge, MA: South End Press, 2007).

22. The Stonewall Rebellion is often understood to be a key incendiary moment for contemporary resistance to sexual and gender norms. The Compton's Cafeteria Riot was far less discussed until Susan Stryker's 2005 documentary, *Screaming Queens: The Riot at Compton's Cafeteria* introduced scholars and activists to the important events that unfolded in 1966 when gender and sexual rule-breakers responded to the constant onslaught of police harassment and violence in San Francisco's Tenderloin neighborhood.

23. Ian Barnard, "Fuck Community, or Why I Support Gay-Bashing," in *States of Rage: Emotional Eruption, Violence, and Social Change*, eds. Renée R. Curry and Terry L. Allison (New York: New York University Press, 1996), 74–88; Cathy J. Cohen, "Punks, Bulldaggers, and Welfare Queens: The Radical Potential of Queer Politics?" *GLQ: A Journal of Lesbian and Gay Studies* 3, no. 4 (1997): 437–465; Mattilda Bernstein Sycamore, ed., *That's Revolting! Queer Strategies for Resisting Assimilation* (Brooklyn, NY: Soft Skull Press, 2004); Ruthann Robson, "Assimilation, Marriage, and Lesbian Liberation," *Temple Law Review* 75 (2002): 709.

24. Richard E. Blum, Barbara Ann Perina, and Joseph Nicholas DeFilippis, "Why Welfare Is a Queer Issue," *NYU Review of Law and Social Change* 26 (2001): 207.

25. Kenyon Farrow, "Is Gay Marriage Anti-Black?" (2004), http://kenyonfarrow.com/2005/06/14/is-gay-marriage-anti-black/; Sycamore, *That's Revolting!*; Darren Lenard Hutchinson, " 'Gay Rights' for 'Gay Whites'? Race, Sexual Identity, and Equal Protection Discourse," *Cornell Law Review* 85 (2000): 1358.

26. Shannon P. Minter, "Do Transsexuals Dream of Gay Rights? Getting Real About Transgender Inclusion," in *Transgender Rights*, ed. Paisley Currah, Richard M. Juang, and Shannon P. Minter (Minneapolis: University of Minnesota Press, 2006), 141–170; Sylvia Rivera, "Queens in Exile, the Forgotten Ones," in *Genderqueer: Voices from Beyond the Sexual Binary*, eds. Joan Nestle, Riki Wilchins, and Clare Howell (Los Angeles: Alyson Books, 2002), 67–85; Dean Spade, "Fighting to Win," in *That's Revolting! Queer Strategies for Resisting Assimilation*, ed. Mattilda Bernstein Sycamore (Brooklyn, NY: Soft Skull Press, 2004), 31–38.

27. Harris, *From Stonewall to the Suburbs?*; Duggan, *The Twilight of Equality?*

28. Harris, *From Stonewall to the Suburbs?*; Urvashi Vaid, *Virtual Equality: The Mainstreaming of Gay and Lesbian Liberation* (New York: Random House, 1996).

29. Dean Spade and Craig Willse, "Freedom in a Regulatory State? Lawrence, Marriage and Biopolitics," *Widener Law Review* 11 (2005): 309.

30. Paula Ettlebrick, "Since When Is Marriage a Path to Liberation?" *Out/Look: National Lesbian & Gay Quarterly* 6 (Fall 1989): 14–16; Spade and Willse, "Freedom in a Regulatory State?"

31. This chart is excerpted from Morgan Bassichis, Alex Lee, and Dean Spade, "Building an Abolitionist Trans Movement with Everything We've Got," in *Captive Genders: Trans Embodiment and the Prison Industrial Complex*, eds. Nat Smith and Eric A. Stanley (Oakland, CA: AK Press, 2011).

32. Blum, Perina, and DeFilippis, "Why Welfare Is a Queer Issue."

33. Laura Magnani, Harmon L. Wray, and the American Friends Service Committee Criminal Justice Task Force, *Beyond Prisons: A New Interfaith Paradigm for Our Failed Prison System* (Minneapolis: Fortress Press, 2006); Dean Spade, "Methodologies of Trans Resistance," in *Blackwell Companion to Lesbian Studies*, eds. George Haggerty and Molly McGarry (London: Blackwell Publishing, 2007), 237–261; Joey L. Mogul, Andrea J. Ritchie, and Kay Whitlock, *Queer (In)Justice* (Boston: Beacon Press, 2011); Katherine Whitlock, *In a Time of Broken Bones: A Call to Dialogue on Hate Violence and the Limitations of Hate Crime Laws* (Philadelphia: American Friends Service Committee, 2001).

34. Dean Spade and Craig Willse, "Confronting the Limits of Gay Hate Crimes Activism: A Radical Critique," *Chicano-Latino Law Review* 21 (2000): 38.

35. Christina Hanhardt describes how early gay vigilante groups aimed at preventing homophobic bashing often took up such work with racist perceptions of bashers in mind, partnering with police to target men of color, often in gentrifying neighborhoods where white gays and lesbians were displacing people of color. Christina Hanhardt, "Butterflies, Whistles, and Fists: Gay Safe Streets Patrols and the 'New Gay Ghetto' 1976–1981," *Radical History Review* 100 (Winter 2008): 61–85.

36. Ruth Colker, "Marriage Mimicry: The Law of Domestic Violence," *William and Mary Law Review* 47 (2006): 1841; Katherine M. Franke, "The Politics of Same-Sex Marriage Politics," *Columbia Journal of Gender and Law* 15 (2006): 236.

37. According to a 2000 study, 66 percent of foundation board members are men and 90 percent are white. Christine Ahn, "Democratizing American Philanthropy," in *The Revolution Will Not Be Funded: Beyond the Non-Profit Industrial Complex*, ed. INCITE! Women of Color Against Violence (Cambridge, MA: South End Press, 2007), 63–76.

38. Rodríguez, "The Political Logic of the Non-Profit Industrial Complex."

28 Artful Concealment and Strategic Visibility

Transgender Bodies and U.S. State Surveillance After 9/11

Toby Beauchamp

The U.S. government put many new surveillance and security measures in place in the aftermath of the 9/11 terrorist attack. Most had little to do directly with trans concerns, although one advisory from the U.S. Department of Homeland Security noted that male terrorists might try to disguise themselves as women—particularly Islamic jihadists donning burkas that disguised their body contours. And yet, as surveillance studies scholar Toby Beauchamp makes clear, all such policies are implicated in the production and regulation of normatively gendered bodies and behaviors. They disproportionately affect people whose bodies differ from societal norms for whatever reason, whether or not those people identify as trans. Beauchamp argues that gender-variant individuals detected by security and surveillance apparatuses are often suspected or accused of practicing some sort of deception for a criminal intent. He is critical not just of the gender-regulating aspects of surveillance but of policy positions that promote "transgender rights" in ways that increase the policing of suspect bodies, ground patriotism in practices of social conventionality, promote exclusionary attitudes regarding who properly belongs to the "body politic," and disadvantage racially minoritized and economically marginalized trans people.

On September 4, 2003, shortly before the two-year anniversary of the attacks on the World Trade Center and Pentagon, the U.S. Department of Homeland Security released an official Advisory to security personnel. Citing ongoing concerns about potential attacks by Al-Qaeda operatives, the advisory's final paragraph emphasizes that terrorism is everywhere in disguise: "Terrorists will employ novel methods to artfully conceal suicide devices. Male bombers may dress as females in order to discourage scrutiny" (Department of Homeland Security 2003). Two years later, the Real ID Act was signed into law, proposing a major restructuring of identification documents and travel within and across U.S. borders. Central components of this process include a new national database linked through federally standardized driver's licenses, and stricter standards of proof for asylum applications. In response to both the Advisory and the Real ID Act, transgender activist and advocacy organizations in the U.S. quickly pointed to the ways trans populations would be targeted as suspicious and subjected to new levels of scrutiny.

Criticizing what they read as instances of transphobia or anti-trans discrimination, many of these organizations offer both transgender individuals and government agencies strategies for reducing or eliminating that discrimination. While attending to the very real dangers and damages experienced by many trans people in relation to government policies, in many

DOI: 10.4324/9781003206255-35

cases the organizations' approaches leave intact the broader regulation of gender, particularly as it is mediated and enforced by the state. Moreover, they tend to address concerns about anti-trans discrimination in ways that are disconnected from questions of citizenship, racialization or nationalism. Nevertheless, by illuminating the ways that new security measures interact with and affect transgender-identified people and gender-nonconforming bodies, transgender activist practices and the field of transgender studies are poised to make a significant contribution to the ways state surveillance tactics are understood and interpreted. The monitoring of transgender and gender-nonconforming populations is inextricable from questions of national security and regulatory practices of the state, and state surveillance policies that may first appear unrelated to transgender people are in fact deeply rooted in the maintenance and enforcement of normatively gendered bodies, behaviors and identities. I argue here that transgender and gender-nonconforming bodies are bound up in surveillance practices that are intimately tied to state security, nationalism and the "us/them," "either/or" rhetoric that underpins U.S. military and government constructions of safety. At the same time, the primary strategies and responses offered by transgender advocacy organizations tend to reconsolidate U.S. nationalism and support the increased policing of deviant bodies.

Normalizing Gender: Medico-Legal Surveillance

In many ways, transgender studies provides an ideal point of entry for thinking through state surveillance of gendered bodies. The field has frequently and primarily dealt with the topic of surveillance in terms of medical and psychiatric monitoring of trans people. The production of the category of "the transsexual" through western medical discourse can be clearly traced through sexologist Harry Benjamin's Standards of Care for Gender Identity Disorders, the first version of which was published in 1979. The Standards, now in their sixth version, define the criteria by which healthcare professionals might measure their clients, in order to determine whether they are so-called "true transsexuals." Clients fitting the profile can then be formally diagnosed with Gender Identity Disorder and allowed to proceed with medical transition in the form of hormones and/or surgeries. Central to this standardized definition of trans identity, however, is the expectation that trans people will, through the process of transition, eliminate all references to their birth gender and essentially disappear into a normatively gendered world, as if they had never been transgender to begin with.

Thus two major forms of surveillance operate relative to trans people in the medical and psychiatric institutions. The first is the monitoring of individuals in terms of their ability to conform to a particular medicalized understanding of transgender identity and performance.[1] But more salient to my argument is the second component, which is the notion that the primary purpose of medical transition is to rid oneself of any vestiges of non-normative gender: to withstand and evade any surveillance (whether visual, auditory, social, or legal) that would reveal one's trans status. To blend. To pass. Medical science relies on a standardized, normative gender presentation, monitoring trans individuals' ability to pass seamlessly as non-trans. Medical surveillance focuses first on individuals' legibility *as* transgender, and then, following medical interventions, on their ability to *conceal* any trans status or gender deviance.

Yet medical science itself determines normative gender through a particular form of raced, classed and sexualized body. As Siobhan Somerville argues in *Queering the Color Line*, western medicine has consistently linked race, gender and sexuality such that the norm of white heterosexuality becomes a marker against which deviance is constructed. Scientific studies from the early 19th century on, Somerville demonstrates, helped to designate particular bodies—typically those that were racially or sexually mixed—as degenerative threats to western norms and security. To be classified as normatively gendered is also to adhere to norms of racial and economic privilege. Under this logic, marginalized gender identities can approximate the norm in part through clinging to ideals of whiteness and class status. Concealing gender deviance is about much more than simply erasing transgender status. It also necessitates altering one's gender presentation to conform to white, middle class, able-bodied, heterosexual understandings of normative gendering.

The notion of "concealment" via medical intervention remains tied to legal gender as well, a link made clear by the fact that most states deny changes of gender on identity documents without proof of irreversible "sex reassignment surgery." Attorney Dean Spade notes that U.S. law depends on medical evidence as proof of gender identity in almost every case involving trans people. Medical science is considered, in his words, "the cornerstone of the determination of [. . .] rights" (Spade 2003: 18).

Moreover, Spade argues that medical science continues to rely on an ideal of "success" when diagnosing and "treating" trans people, where success is typically defined as "the ability to be perceived by non-trans people as a non-trans person" (26). Spade's work points to the ways that medicine and the law work together primarily to "correct" individuals whose bodies or gender presentations fall outside of the expected norm, promoting the concealment of trans status in order to reestablish that norm.

The discourse of concealment haunts transgender populations across a number of cultural sites. The impossibility of fully erasing one's sexed history is evident in the fact that many states still refuse to change gender markers on birth certificates, or allow only a partial change in which the original gender marker is merely crossed out and replaced. Legal gender in these cases cannot be altered, but only cloaked. Similarly, cultural representations of gender variant people depend on the popular notion that with enough scrutiny, one's "true" gender can be revealed at the level of the body. Consider for example the abundance of talk shows and reality television programs that run on the presumably simple premise of uncovering—often literally—the "real" gender of trans-identified individuals. These shows often work to link gender concealment with harmful or dangerous deception in the cultural imagination, revealing the trans person's birth-assigned sex not only to the audience, but also to a shocked and horrified lover. The constant repetition of this narrative structure locates violence not in the institutional practices of media, medicine or law, or in the gender-normative behaviors and relationships they enforce, but instead in individual trans people's apparently fraudulent personal lives. Echoing this perspective, legal cases dealing with violence against gender variant individuals often revolve around the victim's responsibility to disclose their trans status or birth-assigned sex. Such cases imply or outright claim that the individual's dishonest concealment of their "true" sex was the root cause of the violent actions taken against them. This approach is clearly demonstrated in the narratives constructed around transgender teenager Gwen Araujo's murder (and sexual relationships) in 2002. Legal arguments, news articles and made-for-television movies converged to situate Araujo's murder in the context of a "trans panic" defense, centralizing the shock of discovery and frequently faulting Araujo for not revealing her assigned sex. In this and many other instances, the interplay of medical, legal and cultural representations of transgender populations works to associate the notion of transgender identity with that of secrecy, precisely because it is always understood that the secret can and will eventually be discovered.

The Threat of Ambiguity: New State Security Measures

With such a pervasive cultural emphasis on concealment, it may come as no surprise that the slang used by many trans people to describe non-disclosure of trans status is "going stealth." Trans people who are living "stealth" are unknown as transgender to almost everyone in their lives—co-workers, employers, teachers, friends—and instead living only as their preferred genders. The term itself invokes a sense of going undercover, of willful secrecy and concealment, perhaps even of conscious deception. Use of this undeniably militarized language also implies a connection to the state, and going stealth does involve a great deal of complicity with state regulation of gender, for example in the changing of legal identity documents such as passports, drivers licenses and immigration paperwork. These are changes that themselves require documentation of particular medical interventions to "irreversibly" change one's physical sex characteristics. The state requires compliance with specific legal and medical procedures, and ostensibly offers in return official documentation that enables stealth status.

But such complete secrecy is never fully possible in relation to the state. The very idea of "going stealth" depends on the constancy of "going"—of continuing to conceal one's trans status, though that concealment can never be airtight. Granting medical and legal changes of gender enables the state to simultaneously keep ongoing records of these very changes: a paper trail of past identity markers. Moreover, the state's own policies and procedures for gender changes are internally inconsistent. Legal measures to document trans people's gender status frequently conflict with one another, even as they all work towards stricter regulation and surveillance of legal gender. Some states refuse to change the gender marker on birth certificates, while others do so only with documentation of surgery. Other states first require amended birth certificates in order to change the gender marker on driver's licenses, and in some cases state and city regulations contradict each other in their surgical requirements for documentation changes.[2] Such administrative conflicts now emerge in even greater relief as governmental agencies increase their policing of immigrant populations: since 1994, the Social Security Administration has sent "no-match" letters to employers in cases where their employee's hiring paperwork contradicts employee information on file with SSA. Ostensibly used to alert otherwise law-abiding employers to the possibility that they are unwittingly hiring undocumented immigrants, the no-match policy intensified after 9/11, with 2002 seeing more than eight times the typical number of letters mailed than in 2001 (Bergeron 2007: 6). The letters and related data are now also accessed by the Department of Homeland Security, which sends employers guidelines about how to correct the problem and avoid legal sanctions.

The no-match policy aims to locate undocumented immigrants (and potential terrorists) employed under false identities, yet casts a much broader net. Because conflicting legal regulations often prevent trans people from obtaining consistent gender markers across all of their identity documents, gender-nonconforming individuals are disproportionately affected by the policy, whether they are undocumented immigrants or not. The National Center for Transgender Equality (NCTE) website notes that the organization "receives calls regularly from transgender people across the country who have been 'outed' to their employers by the Social Security Administration's (SSA's) unfair gender 'no-match' employment letter policy" (National Center for Transgender Equality 2007). Documents always contain traces of the past, and we might argue that this has never been as true as it is in our contemporary moment. Dean Spade's work and other activist projects have pushed for changes in particular states' approaches to gendered identity documents and moved away from the pathologizing of trans identities and bodies. But such changes emerge within a broader context of U.S. nationalism and the War on Terror that serves to justify ever-closer scrutiny of travel, identity documents and bodies.

It is in this cultural landscape of intensified medical, legal and social surveillance that the DHS Advisory appears. By warning security personnel of the gendered disguises that terrorists may appear in, the Advisory neatly fuses the threat of terrorism-in-disguise with perceived gender transgression, marking particular bodies as deceptive and treacherous. Three days after the Advisory was released, a *New York Times* article described the Pentagon's recent screening of the classic 1965 film *The Battle of Algiers*. The *Times* article suggests that the Pentagon screening was in part to gain tactical insight into the current U.S. war in Iraq. *Algiers* is a film filled with depictions of guerrilla warfare tactics, including those that rely on the links between gender and national identities: Algerian women pass as French to deliver bombs into French civilian settings, while Algerian men attempt to pass as women in hijabs, their disguises broken when French soldiers spy their combat boots. Though neither the DHS Advisory nor the Pentagon's study of the film explicitly reference transgender populations, both nevertheless invoke the ties between gender presentation, national identity and bodies marked as dangerously deceptive.

That the Advisory does not specifically name transgender populations in its text does not make it any less relevant to those populations. The focus on non-normative gender does raise questions about how this framing of state security affects transgender-identified people. But it also raises questions about how state institutions might view non-normative gender presentation as an act not limited to—perhaps not even primarily associated with—transgender identities. In the context of current security rhetoric related to the War on Terror, transgender individuals may not be the primary target of such advisories, particularly if those individuals are conforming to normative racial, class and national presentations. Medical science purports to normalize unruly transgender bodies through surgery and hormones. These interventions are intended to eliminate any signs of deviant gendering, creating a non threatening body that is undetectable as trans in any way. Transgender bodies that conform to a dominant standard of dress and behavior may be legible to the state not as transgender at all, but instead as properly gendered and "safe."

But not all gendered bodies are so easily normalized. Dominant notions of what constitutes proper feminine or masculine behavior are grounded in ideals of whiteness, class privilege and compulsory heterosexuality, and individuals might be read as non-conforming depending on particular racial, cultural, economic or religious expressions of gender, without ever being classified as transgender. For example, Siobhan Somerville historicizes the ways that black people have been medically and culturally understood to have racialized physical characteristics that directly connect to their perceived abnormality in terms of gender and sexuality. She traces this history back to the public displays in the mid-1800s of Saartje Baartman, an African woman popularly known as the Hottentot Venus, whose womanhood was deemed abnormal precisely through racialized readings of her genitalia (Somerville 2000: 26). [. . .] Thus individuals need not be transgender-identified to be classified as gender-nonconforming. Bodies may be perceived as abnormal or deviant because of gender presentations read through systems of racism, classism, heterosexism, and particularly in the case of the Advisory's focus on Al-Qaeda, Islamophobia.

The impetus for state classification and surveillance of deviant bodies has increased dramatically in the context of amplified monitoring of immigration and heightened nationalist security measures justified by the rhetoric of the War on Terror. This environment spurred the passage of the Real ID Act in 2005; legislation endorsed by the 9/11 Commission, which noted that "for terrorists, travel documents are as important as weapons" (Department of Homeland Security 2008). The Real ID Act establishes minimum standards for U.S. driver's licenses and non-driver IDs, with the intention that by 2013 any ID card that is non-compliant with these standards will be invalid for activities such as air travel, access to government buildings, or access to federal funding such as Social Security. Stricter standards are to be used to verify identities, citizenship, names and birthdates. Draft regulations also specify that Real ID cards and all supporting documents used to create them (birth certificates, Social Security cards, court-ordered name changes, etc.) be linked through a federal database and stored there for 7–10 years.

It is noteworthy that the Act was passed through Congress with little debate (and with unanimous final approval from the Senate), four years after 9/11 and as the U.S. waged war in at least two countries. The ease with which the Act passed may be attributed to the fact that it was tacked onto an emergency spending bill to fund the wars in Afghanistan and Iraq. In his historical account of Britain's attempts to institute a national ID card, Jon Agar argues that only during wartime could such universal identification processes be justified and implemented. He notes that increased concern over fraudulent identities proved to be a major argument in favor of continuing the compulsory national identity documents instituted during World War II. Efforts to maintain individual identity converged with efforts to regulate sexual practices and gendered relationship structures, as post-war attempts to shore up the nuclear family took the form of public outcry against bigamy, viewed by the British state and general public as a "foreign" practice that enabled both sexual deviance and multiple identities. Agar writes that "bigamy starkly highlighted the extent to which social institutions depended on individuals living under one, and only one, identity," fuelling desires not just to continue the cards, but to *expand* the amount of information they contained (Agar 2001: 116). For many, compulsory ID cards recalled totalitarian governing associated with Nazi Germany, and conflicted with British ideals of privacy and individualism. Yet the possibility that such cards could eradicate bigamist practices—securing individual accountability alongside normative sexuality and family structure—provided its own form of national differentiation. Moreover, because ID cards were touted as preventative measures against stolen identities, state regulation of identity was encouraged as a personal right and civil liberty, a method of increasing lawful citizens' security. The state thus implied that those who had nothing to hide had nothing to fear from the implementation of national identification.

The Real ID Act and the discourses surrounding it echo much of this rhetoric. In the context of U.S. nationalism that seeks to eradicate the foreign, the Act is most overtly directed at the figures of the immigrant and the terrorist, certainly not imagined as mutually exclusive categories. To eliminate these figures, the Act increases state surveillance of identity by requiring and storing a single identity for each individual. But maintaining a singular, consistent, and legally documented identity is deeply complicated for many gender-nonconforming people: for example, common law name changes mean there is no court order to be filed with a Real ID card. Similarly, different state agencies define "change of sex" differently (with some requiring one surgical procedure, some another, and others no surgery at all), making a single gender marker on the Real ID card difficult if not impossible. Ironically, the state's own contradictory methods of determining and designating legal gender and sex render Real ID cards ineffectual. Even as these cards would work to create and enforce singular and static identities for individuals, they simultaneously work to expose the fluidity and confusion characterizing state policies on identity documents. As Jane Caplan and John Torpey argue, "[t]he very multiplicity of these documents may [. . .] disrupt the state's ostensibly monolithic front" (Caplan 2001: 7). Thus state regulation of gender and gendered bodies can actually function to reveal ambiguities in the state itself.

Moreover, such policies point to the ways that concealing and revealing trans identity actually depend on one another, demonstrating the impossibility of thinking these actions as binary opposites. To conceal one's trans status under the law requires full disclosure to the medico–legal system, which keeps on public record all steps taken toward transition. That same system is later invoked when individuals seek to prove their trans status through medical and legal documents that ostensibly serve to obscure or even disappear such status. Thus concealment necessarily entails disclosure, and vice versa.

That the Real ID Act, created as part of a war funding bill and approved in a climate of fear and militarization, seeks to maintain individual identities and make them more accessible to state agencies speaks to the ways that multiple, ambiguous or shifting identities are viewed as menacing and risky on a national scale. Alongside more overt statements like the DHS Advisory, the Real ID Act and SSA no-match letters function as significant state practices and policies that link gender ambiguity with national security threats. Like other new security measures, the Real ID Act is promoted as benign—even beneficial—for those citizens with nothing to hide. Yet concealment is strongly associated with the category of transgender, a perception fueled by cultural depictions of trans deception and by the medico-legal system that aims to normalize trans bodies while simultaneously meticulously tracking and documenting gender changes. Reacting to these cultural and legislative constraints, transgender activist and advocacy organizations increasingly engage with new state security measures in efforts to maintain safety both of the nation and of individual transgender-identified people.

Nothing to Hide: Organizational Responses

In their responses to the DHS Advisory, the Real ID Act and the SSA no-match letters, transgender advocacy organizations have opposed these measures' effects on transgender individuals. But they have not typically considered the implications for state regulation of gender presentation more broadly, particularly as it might resonate for individuals marked as gender deviant who are not transgender-identified or linked in any obvious way to trans communities or histories. Nor have they addressed the ways in which particular groups of trans-identified people may be targeted differently by such policing. For example, in a 2006 statement to DHS regarding the no-match letter policy, NCTE recommends that gender no longer be one of the pieces of data used to verify employees, arguing that employers are not legally required to submit gender classification to SSA, and therefore any exchange of information about employees' gender is "an invasion of private and privileged medical information" (Keisling 2006: 2). In an effort to protect transgender employees, the NCTE statement aims to limit the information shared between SSA and DHS. Yet it also works to support no-match letters as a form of regulatory state surveillance, by stating clearly the importance of "avoiding fraud" through Social Security number confirmation. The statement does not oppose state surveillance measures more broadly, but instead seeks to improve them, offering recommendations on behalf of trans employees "in order for the employee verification system to be efficient and equitable" (1).

While arguing for privacy rights may benefit some gender-nonconforming employees, this strategy assumes equal access to privacy and legal recourse for all transgender people and fails to consider how privacy rights are compromised or nonexistent for undocumented immigrants, prisoners, and individuals suspected of terrorism, who may or may not be transgender-identified or perceived as gender-nonconforming. Diminished rights to privacy are particularly evident in the wake of the 2001 USA PATRIOT Act, legislation that provides much of the ideological and legal foundation for more recent state surveillance measures. Building on earlier policies such as the 1996 Anti-Terrorism and Death Penalty Act and the FBI's COINTELPRO activities, the USA PATRIOT Act further limits individual privacy rights by expanding the federal government's ability to secretly search private homes; collect medical, financial and educational records without probable cause; and monitor internet activity and messages. Passed in the flurry of anti-immigrant nationalism and increased racial profiling that followed 9/11, the Act bolsters particular understandings of the relationships between citizenship, race, privacy and danger that underpin surveillance measures like the Real ID Act and SSA no-match policy. Though absent from the NCTE statement, this context demonstrates the frailty of any claim to privacy rights, particularly for trans and gender-nonconforming immigrants and people of color. The statement seeks to protect transgender employees, but remains within—and is limited by—the constraints of the current medico-legal system.

That medico-legal system itself works to track and document gender-nonconforming bodies and transgender identities, such that at some level, trans people's medical and legal information was never private or privileged. With this in mind, it is perhaps not surprising that the primary strategy of transgender advocacy and activist groups has been to advise trans individuals to make themselves *visible* as transgender to authorities that question or screen them at places like airports and border checkpoints. In response to the DHS Advisory, The National Transgender Advocacy Coalition (NTAC) released its own security alert to transgender communities, warning that given the recent Advisory, security personnel may be "more likely to commit unwitting abuses" (National Transgender Advocacy Coalition 2003). NTAC suggests that trans travelers bring their court-ordered name and gender change paperwork with them, noting, "while terrorists may make fake identifications, they won't carry name change documents signed and notarized by a court." The organization recommends strategic visibility as a safety precaution, urging those who might otherwise be "going stealth" to openly disclose their trans status to state officials and to comply with any requested searches or questionings. Calling the potential violence and violations against travelers "unwitting abuses" suggests that authorities enacting these measures cannot be blamed for carrying out policy intended to protect the general public from the threat of hidden terrorism. Such a framework neatly sidesteps any broader criticism of the routine abuses of immigrant, Arab and Arab-appearing individuals that have been justified in the name of national security, and implicitly supports the state's increased policing of "deviant" or apparently dangerous individuals. The demand for trans people to make themselves visible as such is couched in terms of distinguishing between the good, safe transgender traveler and the dangerous, deviant terrorist in gendered disguise. This distinction rests on an implicit understanding of trans travelers as compliant and non-threatening, yet such status is only made possible through the linking of deviance to bodies outside of the white middle-class norm, as Somerville and others have demonstrated. In other words, it is only by effacing the particular scrutiny leveled at trans people of color and trans immigrants that the figure of the non-threatening trans traveler emerges. This figure is imagined to be scrutinized on the basis of gender alone, such that medical and legal documentation are assumed to be a readily available and comprehensive solution. Such a move simultaneously entails displacing the racialized elements of state surveillance onto the figure of the terrorist, implicitly marked as both racialized and non-trans in the logic of NTAC's statement. Moreover, by avoiding any larger critique of state surveillance or policing, NTAC also positions *itself* as a non-threatening, safe, even patriotic organization.

Interestingly, the call for strategic visibility does, to a certain degree, resonate with Sandy Stone's call in the late 1980s for trans people to resist the medical impetus to erase or hide their trans status. Urging trans people to remain visible *as transgender* regardless of their medical transition status, Stone writes "in the transsexual's erased history we can find a story disruptive to the accepted discourses of gender" (Stone 1991: 295). Arguing for the transformation of dominant understandings of transsexuality and gender identity, Stone asserts "it is difficult to generate a counterdiscourse if one is programmed to disappear" (295). Written in a historical moment characterized by the suppression of transgender identities within the mainstream gay, lesbian and feminist movements, Stone's argument was viewed both as controversial and as crucial to the galvanization of transgender scholars, activists and communities in the U.S. Stone's initial argument may not be the starting point for a linear progression leading to the current tactic of visibility taken up by transgender advocacy organizations in the fight against perceived terrorist threats, but it does indicate the ways that visibility has long been a key point of contention in relation to gender-nonconforming bodies.

In both Stone's work and NTAC's press release, the recourse to strategic visibility remains grounded in assumptions that *in*visibility was ever possible. Which bodies can choose visibility, and which bodies are always already visible—perhaps even hyper-visible—to state institutions? For whom is visibility an available political strategy, and at what cost? While (some) trans people gain (a particular kind of) visibility through attention from popular media and medical research, such gains must always be evaluated in relation to their dependence on regulatory norms of race, class and sexuality. Not all trans people can occupy the role of the good, safe transgender traveler that NTAC recommends. Moreover, this recommendation does not consider how increased visibility simultaneously places one under greater scrutiny and surveillance by state institutions. Bodies made visible as abnormal or unruly and in need of constraint or correction may likely experience increased vulnerability and scrutiny. For a number of gender-nonconforming individuals, then, visibility may wield more damage than protection. Which bodies would be read under the DHS Advisory's warning as gender deviant, dangerous or deceptive even if they *did* produce paperwork documenting their transgender status? Such documentation may work to decrease suspicion for some bodies, while compounding scrutiny for others.

[. . .]

The Sylvia Rivera Law Project, an organization in New York providing legal services to low-income gender-nonconforming people, argues that the current political climate of "us vs. them" leads to the polarization of communities that could otherwise work in coalition, as individuals attempt to divert surveillance onto other marginalized groups. The Law Project suggests that assimilation—"going stealth," or claiming status as a good transgender citizen—has become a primary tactic for escaping state surveillance, targeting or persecution. But assimilation strategies are often used in conjunction with the scapegoating of other communities. Jasbir Puar and Amit Rai (2002) convincingly address such polarization in their article "Monster, Terrorist, Fag: The War on Terror and the Production of Docile Patriots," arguing that the demand for patriotism in response to past and future terrorist attacks produces "docile patriots," who normalize themselves precisely through distinguishing themselves from other marginalized groups. For example, regarding the profiling of Arab and Arab-appearing people after 9/11, Puar and Rai examine the response of many Sikh communities in the U.S., who emphasized the difference between their respectable turbans and those worn by terrorists. With some even donning red, white, and blue turbans, Puar and Rai note, the actions of these Sikh communities served to mark off Sikhs as a legitimate, patriotic and "safe" group of American citizens, in direct contrast to differently-turbaned terrorists—indeed, the ability of these Sikhs to become good citizens is directly dependent on their ability to clearly distinguish themselves from the figure of the terrorist. Leti Volpp cites similar rhetoric in her article "The Terrorist and the Citizen," writing that "post-September 11, a national identity has consolidated that is both strongly patriotic and multiracial" (Volpp 2002: 1584). Noting that the Bush administration appears inclusive while systematically excluding those racially marked as potential terrorists, Volpp argues that "American" identity and citizenship are in fact constructed against the figure of the terrorist. The terrorist thus *makes possible* the construction of a national identity, providing a contrast that the citizen is formed in opposition to.

This reliance on the notion of legitimacy—as good citizens, as safe travelers, as willing patriots—is similarly evident in the statements made by many transgender advocacy organizations about new security measures that target perceived gender deviance. Suggesting that trans people bring their court documents with them, cooperate with authorities and prove their legitimacy, the advocacy groups no longer rely on the strategy of concealing one's trans status, or what I named earlier as "going stealth." Instead, their primary advice is to *reveal* one's trans status, to prove that trans travelers are good citizens who have nothing to hide. Particularly in the context of the War on Terror, we might reread the notion of "going stealth" to mean not simply erasing the signs of one's trans status, but instead, maintaining legibility as a good citizen, a patriotic American—erasing any signs of similarity with the deviant, deceptive terrorist. The concept of safety thus shifts: rather than protecting trans people from state violence, the organizations now focus on protecting the nation from the threatening figure of the terrorist, a figure that transgender travelers must distinguish themselves from by demonstrating their complicity in personal disclosure. Creating the figure of the safe transgender traveler necessarily entails creating and maintaining the figure of the potential terrorist, and vice versa. Because some bodies are already marked as national threats, the ability to embody the safe trans traveler is not only limited to particular bodies, but in fact requires the scapegoating of other bodies.

While surveillance measures like the DHS Advisory may appear to primarily target transgender individuals as suspicious, the bodies being policed for gender deviance are not necessarily trans-identified, but rather demonstrate non-compliance with gender norms that may have as much to do with race, religion, class and sexuality as with transgender identity. Surveillance of these bodies centers less on their identification as transgender *per se* than it does on the perceived deception underlying transgressive gender presentation. Because normative, non-threatening gender is always read through ideals of whiteness, economic privilege and heterosexuality, "going stealth" is an option available only to those segments of the transgender population able to achieve or approximate those ideals. And in the context of national security and the U.S. War on Terror, going stealth may be less grounded in passing as non-transgender than in maintaining the appearance of a good, compliant citizen, an appearance solidified by the fact that these bodies need not conceal anything from state institutions or authorities, because they have nothing to hide. Approaching the relationship between gender-nonconformity and state surveillance in this way means resisting the urge to think about surveillance of gendered bodies as limited only to medical and legal monitoring of specifically transgender-identified individuals. In fact it points to the importance of thinking more broadly about the interactions between regulatory gender norms, racialization processes and ideals of citizenship. Moreover, it refuses a view of state surveillance as something disconnected from or unconcerned with gender, and instead foregrounds the ways that gendered and racialized bodies are central both to perceptions of safety and security and to the structuring of state surveillance practices. As these bodies attempt to evade surveillance either through careful invisibility or through strategic disclosure—each of which entails engaging the other to some degree—they do so not in isolation, but in the context of war, nationalism and militarization, and power relations that are themselves ever more starkly revealed in the act of going stealth.

Acknowledgements

An early draft of this work benefited from comments at a presentation sponsored by the Consortium for Women and Research at the University of California, Davis, in late 2007. For their careful readings and generous criticism, I am grateful to Cynthia Degnan, Benjamin D'Harlingue, Caren Kaplan and Liz Montegary, as well as two anonymous reviewers.

Notes

1. In "The *Empire* Strikes Back," gender and technology studies scholar Sandy Stone argues that as medical science made available more information about the standards for determining the category of transsexual,

individuals were more able to deliberately perform to these standards, to convince doctors of transsexual identities and personal histories in order to gain access to medical transition. In *Sex Changes*, Patrick Califia discusses similar tactics taken up by trans-identified people in post-operative interviews and medical surveys.

2. For more in-depth analysis of gender reclassification policies and the standardization of U.S. identity documents, see Dean Spade's "Documenting Gender."

Bibliography

Agar, Jon. 2001. Modern horrors: British identity and identity cards. In *Documenting Individual Identity: The Development of State Practices in the Modern World*, ed. Jane Caplan and John Torpey, 101–120. Princeton, NJ: Princeton University Press.

Bergeron, Claire, Aaron Matteo Terrazas, and Doris Meissner. 2007. Social security "no match" letters: A primer. *MPI Backgrounder* 5: 1–11 (October), www.migrationpolicy.org/pubs/BR5_SocialSecurityNoMatch_101007.pdf (accessed July 22, 2008).

Califia, Pat. 2003. *Sex Changes: Transgender Politics*. San Francisco: Cleis Press.

Caplan, Jane and John Torpey. 2001. Introduction. In *Documenting Individual Identity: The Development of State Practices in the Modern World*, ed. Jane Caplan and John Torpey, 1–12. Princeton, NJ: Princeton University Press.

Department of Homeland Security. 2003. DHS advisory to security personnel: No change in threat level. *Department of Homeland Security*, www.dhs.gov/xnews/releases/press_release_0238.shtm (accessed July 28, 2007).

———. 2008. Real ID. *Department of Homeland Security*, www.dhs.gov/xprevprot/programs/gc_1200062053842.shtm (accessed July 28, 2008).

James, Joy. 1996. *Resisting State Violence: Radicalism, Gender, and Race in U.S. Culture*. Minneapolis: University of Minnesota Press.

Kaufman, Michael T. 2003. What does the pentagon see in 'Battle of Algiers'? *New York Times*, September 7, Sec. 4, p. 3.

Keisling, Mara. 2006. NCTE no-match comment. *National Center for Transgender Equality*, http://nctequality.org/Issues/I-9-nomatch-comment.pdf (accessed July 22, 2008).

National Center for Transgender Equality. 2007. Social security gender no-match letters and transgender employees. *National Center for Transgender Equality*, http://nctequality.org/issues/nomatch.html (accessed July 21, 2008).

National Transgender Advocacy Coalition. 2003. Security alert: "Males dressed as females" to be scrutinized when traveling. *Transgender Crossroads*, www.tgcrossroads.org/news/archive.asp?aid=767 (accessed July 30, 2008).

Puar, Jasbir and Amit S. Rai. 2002. Monster, terrorist, fag: The war on terror and the production of docile patriots. *Social Text* 20 (3): 117–148.

Somerville, Siobhan. 2000. *Queering the Color Line: Race and the Invention of Homosexuality in American Culture*. Durham: Duke University Press.

Spade, Dean. 2003. Resisting medicine, re/modeling gender. *Berkeley Women's Law Journal* 18: 15–37.

———. 2008. Documenting gender. *Hastings Law Journal* 59: 731–842.

Stone, Sandy. 1991. The *empire* strikes back: A posttranssexual manifesto. In *Body Guards: The Cultural Politics of Gender Ambiguity*, ed. Julia Epstein and Kristina Straub, 280–304. New York: Routledge.

Sylvia Rivera Law Project. The impact of the war on terror on LGBTSTQ communities. *Sylvia Rivera Law Project*, www.srlp.org/index.php?sec=03M&page=wotnotes (accessed July 15, 2008).

Transgender Law Center and National Center for Transgender Equality. 2005. The real ID act: bad law for our community. *Transgender Law Center*, http://transgenderlawcenter.org/pdf/Joint%20statement%20on%20the%20Real%20ID%20Act%20-%20final.pdf (accessed July 22, 2008).

Volpp, Leti. 2002. The citizen and the terrorist. *UCLA Law Review* 49: 1575–1599.

29 Electric Brilliancy

Cross-Dressing Law and Freak Show Displays in Nineteenth-Century San Francisco

Clare Sears

In this article, historical sociologist Clare Sears explores the production of public space in nineteenth-century San Francisco. She juxtaposes the criminalization of cross-dressing in the streets with the spectacularization of gender-crossing on stage in commercial freak shows. Sears points out that San Francisco's 1863 anti-cross-dressing ordinance was just one of many in a wave of similar statues that swept the United States in the mid-nineteenth century. She argues that these laws were part of a broader regulatory apparatus that targeted gender-variant, Chinese, and disabled people for having "problem bodies" that did not comply with social norms based on whiteness, able-bodiedness, and binary gender. Such bodies, she shows, were spatially segregated through ghettoization, institutionalization, and incarceration, which resulted in a public sphere in which citizens unmarked by those practices of segregation could consider themselves both normal and free. Sears then discusses the flip side of this process to show how problem bodies excluded from the public sphere were hyper-visible in other places, such as the racial enclave of Chinatown, the Tenderloin red-light district, and dime museums and freak shows. All such places offered slumming tourists and urban thrill seekers opportunities to see "exotic" sorts of people excluded from the "normal" public sphere.

In 1863, midway through the Civil War, the San Francisco Board of Supervisors passed a local law against cross-dressing that prohibited public appearance "in a dress not belonging to his or her sex" (*Revised Orders* 1863). That city was not alone in this action: between 1848 and 1900, thirty-four cities in twenty-one states passed laws against cross-dressing, as did eleven additional cities before World War I (Eskridge 1999). Far from being a nineteenth-century anachronism, cross-dressing laws had remarkable longevity and became a key tool for policing transgender and queer communities in the 1950s and 1960s. However, although studies have documented the frequent enforcement of these laws in the mid-twentieth century, far less is known about their operations in the nineteenth century, when they were initially passed. In this essay, I examine the legal and cultural history of cross-dressing law in one city—San Francisco—from the 1860s to 1900s. In particular, I explore cross-dressing law's relationship with another nineteenth-century institution that was centrally concerned with cross-gender practices—the dime museum freak show.

Focusing on the complex, contradictory, and sometimes unpredictable relationships between legal regulation, cultural fascination, and gender transgressions, I develop three main arguments. First, I examine the legal work of cross-dressing law, documenting the

DOI: 10.4324/9781003206255-36

range of practices criminalized, people arrested, and punishments faced. Observing that the law exclusively targeted public cross-dressing practices, I argue that it did much more than police the types of clothing that "belonged" to each sex; it also used the visible marker of clothing to police the types of people who "belonged" in public space. Second, I explore the relationship between cross-dressing law and a host of other local laws that targeted human bodies as public nuisances. In doing so, I argue that cross-dressing law was not an isolated act of government, exclusively concerned with gender, but one part of a broader regulatory project that was also concerned with sex, race, citizenship, and city space. Finally, I analyze the case of Milton Matson, a female-bodied man who was recruited from a jail cell to appear in a dime museum freak show in 1890s San Francisco. Based on this analysis, I argue that cross-dressing law and the freak show had similar disciplinary effects, producing and policing the boundaries of normative gender, albeit in incomplete ways.

A Dress Not Belonging

San Francisco's Board of Supervisors did not initially criminalize cross-dressing as a distinct offense, but as one manifestation of the broader offense of indecency. The full legal text stated:

> If any person shall appear in a public place in a state of nudity, or in a dress not belonging to his or her sex, or in an indecent or lewd dress, or shall make any indecent exposure of his or her person, or be guilty of any lewd or indecent act or behavior, or shall exhibit or perform any indecent, immoral or lewd play, or other representation, he should be guilty of a misdemeanor, and on conviction, shall pay a fine not exceeding five hundred dollars.
>
> (*Revised Orders* 1863)

In turn, this wide-reaching indecency law was not a stand-alone prohibition, but one part of a new chapter of the municipal codebook, titled *Offenses Against Good Morals And Decency*, which also criminalized public intoxication, profane language, and bathing in San Francisco Bay without appropriate clothing. Alongside these newly designated crimes, cross-dressing was one of the very first "offenses against good morals" to be outlawed in the city. In 1866, the original five-hundred-dollar penalty was revised to a five-hundred-dollar fine or six months in jail; in 1875, it increased to a one-thousand-dollar fine, six months in jail, or both (*General Orders* 1866, 1875).

Despite its roots in indecency law, San Francisco's cross-dressing law soon became a flexible tool for policing multiple gender transgressions. Before the end of the nineteenth century, San Francisco police made more than one hundred arrests for the crime of cross-dressing (*Municipal Reports* 1863–64 to 1899–1900).[1] A wide variety of people fell afoul of this law, including feminist dress reformers, female impersonators, "fast" young women who dressed as men for a night on the town, and people whose gender identifications did not match their anatomical sex in legally acceptable ways (people who today would probably—although not definitely—identify as transgender). Those arrested faced police harassment, public exposure, and six months in jail; by the early twentieth century, they also risked psychiatric institutionalization or deportation if they were not U.S. citizens. For example, in 1917, a female-bodied man named Jack Garland was involuntarily institutionalized in a psychiatric ward for refusing to wear women's clothing (Stryker and Van Buskirk 1996), while a male-bodied woman named Geraldine Portica was arrested for violating San Francisco's cross-dressing law and subsequently deported to Mexico (Jesse Brown Cook Scrapbooks n.d.).

San Francisco's cross-dressing law marked the start of a new regulatory approach toward gender transgressions, and it attempted to draw and fix the boundaries of normative gender during a period of rapid social change. However, cross-dressing law signaled not only a new object of regulation, but also a new mechanism of regulation—exclusion from public space. From its inception, cross-dressing law was specifically concerned with public gender displays, and it targeted cross-dressing in public places. Notably, the law made it a crime for someone to "appear *in a public place* . . . in a dress not belonging to his or her sex," and any clothing practices that occurred in private were beyond its scope (*Revised Orders* 1863; italics mine). As a result, some people confined their cross-dressing practices to private spaces and modified their appearance when in public for fear of arrest.

For example, in the 1890s, a male-bodied San Franciscan who identified as a woman named Jenny reported that although she preferred to wear women's clothing, she only dared do so in private, for fear of arrest on the city streets. In a letter to German sexologist Magnus Hirschfeld, Jenny wrote: "Only because of the arbitrary actions of the police do I wear men's clothing outside of the house. Skirts are a sanctuary to me, and I would rather keep on women's clothing forever if it were allowed on the street" (Hirschfeld 1991, 84). Her fears were not unfounded. In 1895, the police arrested a middle-aged carpenter named Ferdinand Haisch for "masquerading in female attire," after Hayes Valley residents called the cops on the "strange appearing woman" who walked through their neighborhood every evening ("Masqueraded as a Woman," *San Francisco Examiner*, April 16, 1895, 4).[2] The police staked out the neighborhood for several weeks before arresting Haisch, who was wearing the latest women's fashions—a three-quarter-length melton coat, green silk skirt, red stockings, silverbuckled garters, high-heeled shoes, and stylish hat. Following a brief stint in the city prison, Haisch was released by the police court judge on the condition that Haisch ceased wearing these clothes in public. Haisch apparently complied, but her ever-vigilant neighbors were still not satisfied, and they demanded her rearrest for wearing women's clothing at home. However, while predictably sympathetic to the neighbors' complaints, the police admitted that they were powerless to intervene, because the law permitted cross-dressing in private ("Crazy on Female Attire," *The Call*, July 3, 1895, 8).

The exclusion of cross-dressing practices from public space—and their concurrent confinement to private spaces—was a form of legal segregation that had significant political consequences, both for individuals whose public appearance constituted a crime and for the "general" public. First, for people excluded from public space, participation in day-to-day city life was curtailed. Everyday activities, such as going to the shops, enjoying a night on the town, or even walking through one's own neighborhood brought surveillance and arrest. As such, cross-dressing was marked as a deviant and secretive practice, rather than a public activity and identification. Second, by excluding cross-dressing practices from public space, the law also severely restricted people's access to the public sphere, which twentieth-century critical theorist Jürgen Habermas (1991) identified as a fundamental precondition of democracy. In Habermas's influential formulation, the public sphere consisted of multiple public venues where individuals came together to discuss common public and political affairs, these spaces including coffee houses, saloons, bars, and meeting halls, as well as the mediated venues of newspapers and journals. By restricting access to these public venues, cross-dressing law effectively excluded multiple people with non-normative gender from civic participation and the democratic life of the city. Finally, cross-dressing law was not only consequential for those excluded from everyday public and political life, but also for the "general" gendernormative public, who faced an artificially narrow range of gender identities in city space. After all, when in public, there were only two ways that people with non-normative gender presentation could avoid arrest—either changing their clothing to comply with the law or evading police detection by fully "passing." Clearly involving different risks and benefits, these strategies nonetheless had a similar effect on city space, removing different-gender appearances and identities from public view. Indeed, by policing gender hierarchies through public exclusion, cross-dressing law reinforced the very notion of "difference" as anomalous by exaggerating the prevalence of the "norm."

Problem Bodies, Public Space

Although cross-dressing law marked a particularly literal attempt to produce and police normative gender, it was not an isolated or idiosyncratic act of government. Instead, it was one part of a broader legal matrix that targeted the public visibility of multiple "problem bodies," including those of Chinese immigrants, prostitutes, and individuals deemed maimed or diseased.[3] These local orders constituted a body of law that targeted the atypical human body as a potential public nuisance, and they appeared in the municipal codebook alongside laws that regulated sewage, slaughterhouses, and the keeping of hogs. However, while these nineteenth-century laws differed significantly from each other in their object of concern, their mechanisms of control were very similar, seeking to manage public nuisances—animal, object, or human body—through regulating city space.

Mirroring the regulatory logic of cross-dressing law, some of these laws sought to directly *exclude* problem bodies from public space. For example, in 1867, the Board of Supervisors passed a law that prohibited anyone who was "diseased, maimed, mutilated," or an otherwise "unsightly or disgusting object" from appearing in public (*General Orders* 1869). One part of a broader law, with the name "To Prohibit Street Begging, and to Restrain Certain Persons from Appearing in Streets and Public Places," this law focused on the intersection of disability and poverty, seeking to exclude the potentially sympathetic figure of the disabled beggar from San Francisco streets (Schweik 2007). Two years later, in 1869, the supervisors passed another law that prohibited persons from carrying baskets or bags on poles on the city streets—this way of moving through public space being common among some Chinese immigrant workers (*General Orders* 1872). Similar to cross-dressing law, these laws focused on public appearances and movements and simultaneously policed problem bodies while producing governable city space.

A second set of laws operated through *confinement*, rather than exclusion, seeking to ban problem bodies from particular neighborhoods, rather than from generic public space. A series of laws in the 1880s and 1890s, for example, targeted houses of prostitution on middle-class, residential streets, in an effort to reduce the visibility of commercial sex work for "respectable," middle-class, Anglo-American women and children, through its confinement in carefully designated, racialized vice districts (*General Orders* 1890, 1892, 1898). Subsequent laws and policies went even further in endeavors to confine vice to specific areas. For example, when the owner of a Barbary Coast "den" attempted to buy property in the upscale Pacific Heights neighborhood, following the 1906 earthquake and fire, the police captain promised to block the sale: "This section of the city must be kept free of such places. They have no business outside of the burned district and I propose to drive them back to where they belong" ("Barbary Coast Harpies Seek to Settle Among Homes of Pacific Heights," *The Call*, September 15, 1906, 3). Two years later, even more dramatically, the chief of police drew territorial boundaries around the Barbary Coast, ordering the district's female residents to remain east of Powell Street and north of Bush Street or face arrest and jailing under vagrancy laws ("Biggy Marks Deadline for Tenderloin Women," *The Call*, January 12, 1908, 32).

A third type of legal intervention required the *concealment*, rather than exclusion or confinement, of problem bodies from the "respectable" public's view. Specifically, in 1863, as the Board of Supervisors enacted its wide-ranging indecency law, the local chief of police,

Martin Burke, attempted to reduce the visibility of prostitution in Chinatown by requiring the owners of "cribs" (small, street-level rooms from which women solicited sex) to buy and erect large screens at the entrance of the streets that housed them (Burke 1887). This specified not only the geographic spaces of concern (namely, Chinatown), but also the characteristics of "the public" that needed to be shielded from these sights. Burke made this explicit in a subsequent annual report, stating that his purpose was to "hide the degradation and vice . . . from the view of women and children who ride the streetcar" through the newly developing downtown area (*Municipal Reports* 1865–66).

Finally, there were several legal attempts to bypass intracity boundaries and *remove* problem bodies from the city entirely, aimed exclusively at Chinese immigrants. In 1865, for example, the Board of Supervisors passed an "Order to Remove Chinese Women of Ill-Fame from Certain Limits of the City" (*General Orders* 1866). This was the first local law to explicitly target a single nationality, and under the advice of the city attorney, the supervisors removed the word "Chinese" from the legal text, prior to publication. The intent of the law, however, remained unchanged, and the following year, 137 women—virtually all Chinese—were arrested as "common prostitutes," an enormous increase over the previous year, when there had been one arrest. These women were subsequently removed from the city, and the chief of police boasted that he had used the law to expel three hundred Chinese women, with fewer than two hundred remaining (*Municipal Reports* 1865–66). Additionally, the Board of Supervisors made numerous attempts to harness the power granted by nuisance law to remove all Chinese residents from San Francisco. This possibility had circulated in anti-Chinese political discourse since at least the mid-1850s and reached its peak in 1880, when an investigative committee of the San Francisco Board of Health published a report declaring Chinatown a nuisance and calling for all Chinese residents to be removed from the city (*Chinatown Declared a Nuisance!* 1880, 6). Judicial restraints ultimately rendered this effort ineffective, but not before the Board of Health unanimously accepted the committee's recommendations, signaling local government's investments in using nuisance law for racialized removal.

Undoubtedly, there were important differences between these laws, as well as between the processes through which cross-dressed, indecent, unsightly, and racialized immigrant bodies were defined as problems and targeted for legal intervention. Nonetheless, I bring these particular laws together here—as they were brought together in nineteenth-century municipal codebooks—for two specific reasons.

First, when these laws are considered together, it becomes clear that cross-dressing law was not alone in its attempt to minimize the public visibility of problem bodies. Instead, it was one part of a broader legal matrix that was concerned not only with gender transgressions, but also with race, citizenship, and disease. Moreover, these were not independent concerns. As numerous scholars have argued, accusations of gender and sexual deviance have frequently been deployed in processes of racialization, while racialized anxieties have informed the policing of gender and sex. In turn, race, gender, and sex have all been linked to disease, and in nineteenth-century San Francisco, the management of public health was key to policing Chinese immigrants and prostitutes. In short, there were numerous intersecting cultural anxieties during this period that become more apparent when cross-dressing law is situated in its broader legal context.

Analyzing cross-dressing law within this context also makes clearer the ways that the law sought to manage not only gender but also city space. As legal historian Lawrence Friedman has stated about nineteenth-century morality laws in general: "What was illegal, then, was not sin itself—and certainly not secret sin—but sin that offended public morality. This was what we might call the Victorian compromise: a certain toleration for vice, or at least a resigned acceptance, so long as it remained in an underground state" (1985, 585). However, before vice in San Francisco could "remain in an underground state," such spaces had to be created. Indecency and nuisance laws were instrumental to this process, creating urban zones where problem bodies could be contained—primarily the racialized vice districts of Chinatown and the Barbary Coast. Consequently, these laws affected not only the public visibility of problem bodies, but also the sociospatial order of the city, drawing a series of territorial boundaries between public and private, visible and concealed, and respectable and vice districts.

Fascination and Freakery

Laws that sought to reduce the visibility of problem bodies—including cross-dressing law— constituted a dense legal matrix that dictated the types of bodies that could move freely through city space and the types of bodies that could not. However, such laws could also incite cultural fascination and the desire to see, which entrepreneurs could exploit. One manifestation of this was the popular commercial "slumming tour," in which tourists were guided through the Barbary Coast and Chinatown, to glimpse the bodies that the law sought to conceal. These tours took in brothels, opium dens, dive bars, and sick rooms housing Chinese patients who were banned from the city's hospital (Evans 1873). Another manifestation was the newspaper scandal, which splashed cross-dressing practices across the front page, as local editors ran sensational stories and interviews with those who broke the law. These scandals publicized normative gender boundaries and ridiculed transgressors, representing gender difference as a titillating private eccentricity or individual moral flaw (Duggan 2000; Sears 2005). However, the starkest manifestation of this cultural fascination was the dime museum freak show, which displayed non-normative bodies and cross-gender performances in seeming conflict with the law.

Dime museum freak shows emerged as a popular form of entertainment in most major U.S. cities after the Civil War, peaking in popularity during the 1880s and 1890s. As one component of the era's new mass entertainment industry, dime museums had their socioeconomic roots in technological, demographic, and economic changes that led to an unprecedented rise in leisure time among working-class and middle-class city residents (Adams 2001).[4] Similar to municipal law, the dime museum freak show was preoccupied with the public appearance of non-normative bodies and offered a variety of attractions for the low price of a dime, including human anatomy exhibits, lectures on morality, sideshow circus artists, and freak show performers. Most studies of dime museums and freak shows have focused on East Coast institutions, with particular emphasis on P. T. Barnum's American Museum in New York (Bogdan 1988; Dennet 1997; McNamara 1974). San Francisco, however, boasted numerous freak shows of its own, ranging from the short-lived Museum of Living Wonders, which operated out of a "leaky tent on Kearny Street" in the early 1870s ("A Shocking Exhibition," *The Call*, December 17, 1873), to the grand exhibitions held at Woodward's Gardens, an expansive family amusement resort that occupied two city blocks in the Mission district from 1866 to 1891 ("Where the 'Old Town' Frolicked," *San Francisco Chronicle*, November 9, 1913, 25). Most of the city's freak shows, however, were clustered on Market Street, operating out of small, seedy, rented storefronts (Asbury 1933; Cowan 1938). Market Street was also home to the Pacific Museum of Anatomy and Science, the city's longest-running dime museum, which claimed to be the "largest anatomical museum in the world" ("Visit Dr. Jordan's Great Museum of Anatomy," *The Call*, September 11, 1902, 2).

In San Francisco, as elsewhere, dime museum entertainment centered upon performances of bodily difference and paid particularly close attention to bodies that challenged gender, racial, and national boundaries or that ostensibly revealed the somatic penalties of immorality through spectacles of disease or deformity. For example, freak shows typically featured a

Bearded Lady or Half-Man/Half-Woman character, while anatomy exhibits included her-maphrodite bodies, such as that of the Pacific Museum's display of "a beautiful dissection" of a hermaphrodite cadaver, featuring "the internal arrangements and dissections of this wonderful freak of nature" (Jordan 1868, 19). Another staple attraction was the popular "Missing Link" or "What-Is-It?" exhibit, which usually featured an African American or a white man in blackface who was presented as the "missing link" between man and animal (Cook 1996). Many dime museums also featured pathology rooms that contained displays of diseased sexual organs and other body parts, damaged by syphilis, gonorrhea, and "the filthy habit of self-abuse" (Jordan 1868, 36). Finally, dime museums regularly staged performances of racialized national dominance that corresponded to contemporary wars. One of the first crowd-drawing exhibits at the Pacific Museum of Anatomy and Science, for example, was the preserved head of Joaquin Murietta, the notorious Mexican "bandit" who fought against Anglo dominance and violence in the southern California gold mines, before being killed by state-sponsored rangers in 1853 (Asbury 1933). Murietta was a popular symbol of Mexi-can resistance, and the display of his severed head graphically dramatized a narrative of Anglo dominance and Mexican defeat, against the backdrop of the Mexican War. Occasion-ally, dime museum exhibits explicitly linked gender and national boundary transgressions, as when Barnum's American Museum displayed a waxwork figure of Jefferson Davis, the defeated leader of the Southern Confederacy, wearing women's clothing, at the close of the Civil War. This exhibit dramatized rumors that Davis had disguised himself in hoopskirts when trying to escape his northern captors, deploying cultural anxieties about cross-gender practices to emasculate the defeated South, fortify territorial boundaries, and reconsolidate the postwar nation (Silber 1989).[5]

As this brief review suggests, the freak show and the law shared a set of cultural anxieties concerning the shifting boundaries of gender, race, health, and the nation, and the disparate bodies gathered on the freak show stage eerily mirrored the bodies targeted by municipal law—the sexually ambiguous, the indecent, the racialized, and the diseased. However, the relationship between the two institutions was complex, not least because the law prohibited the public visibility of problem bodies while the freak show required their public display. These complexities are illustrated by the case of one man who navigated both legal proscrip-tions and freak show visibility in 1890s San Francisco—Milton Matson.

In early January 1895, Matson was arrested in San Francisco, in the room of his fiancée, Ellen Fairweather, and charged with obtaining money under false pretenses. Matson was taken to San Jose County Jail and locked up in a cell with several other men, where he remained for two weeks, until the jailer received a bank telegraph, addressed to Miss Luisa Matson, and realized that Matson was female.[6] After complicated legal wrangling, charges against Matson were dropped, and he walked free from the jail in men's clothing, returning to San Francisco the following month.

The exposure of Matson's "true sex" generated a mass of newspaper coverage and the San Francisco dailies ran numerous stories on this "male impersonator" or "pretender," as Matson was described ("Louisa Has Her Say," *The Call*, January 28, 1895, 1; "Will Again Don Woman's Garb," *San Francisco Examiner*, January 30, 1895, 3). In these stories, the press excitedly debated the possibility of Matson's arrest under cross-dressing law and reported that he publicly dared the police to arrest him. Before this could happen, Matson was approached by a local dime museum manager, Frank Clifton, and offered work, sitting upon a museum platform, wearing men's clothing, for the public to view. In need of employ-ment and money, particularly since the press had undermined his ability to live as a man, Matson accepted Clifton's offer. The strangeness of this transition—"from a cell in the San Jose prison to the electric brilliancy of an amusement resort"—was not lost on Matson, who commented: "Funniest thing . . . I'm getting letters from all sorts of showmen offering good salaries if I will exhibit myself. It amuses me very much. . . . I'm beginning to think it pays to be notorious. It certainly does not seem to be a detriment to people in America" ("Has No Love for Petticoats," *San Francisco Examiner*, February 7, 1895, 16). The appeal of Matson's notoriety proved so popular that several other local freak shows began featuring cross-dressed performers, deceptively advertised as "the only genuine Miss Martson [*sic*] in male attire" ("Louisa Matson's Double Sued," *The Call*, February 15, 1895, 12).

Given the punitive forces impinging on cross-dressing practices in nineteenth-century San Francisco, and the law's insistence on removing them from public view, the concurrent display of cross-dressing performers in city freak shows is initially perplexing. On the one hand, these institutions operated according to very different logics. The law imprisoned, the freak show displayed; the law deprived its subject, the freak show offered a salary; the law disapproved and sought to reduce its subjects "deviance," the freak show was fascinated and sought to exaggerate and increase it.

On the other hand, the operations of cross-dressing law and the freak show overlapped. After all, Matson was recruited into freak show entertainment directly from a jail cell, following a path that other San Francisco performers had walked before him.[7] Moreover, Matson's participation in a freak show exhibition regulated his offstage behavior in a very direct way; his contract forbade him to wear men's clothing on San Francisco's streets, to preserve the mystique—and profitability—of his show ("She Has Been a Man of the World for Over Twenty-six Years," *San Francisco Examiner*, February 10, 1895, 26). Consequently, although the law and the freak show operated through distinct logics of concealment and display, they could have similar regulatory effects on freak show performers.

The freak show also paralleled cross-dressing law as a normalizing discourse that communicated to audiences, in starkly visual terms, the parameters of acceptable behavior and the penalties for violating these norms. While there are few historical records that speak to the disciplinary impact of cross-dressing performers on freak show audiences, a popular 1890s dime novel is highly suggestive of possible effects. In Archibald Gunter and Fergus Redmond's *A Florida Enchantment*, of 1891, a wealthy white woman, Lillian Travers, purchases a box of African sex change seeds from a dime museum in Florida.[8] Following an argument with her fiancé, she swallows a seed and transitions into a man named Lawrence Talbot. Realizing that a wealthy man needs a male valet, rather than a female housekeeper, Lawrence forces his "mulatto maid," Jane, to also swallow a seed and become a man named Jack. Lawrence later realizes with "fearful horror" that dime museums would love to exhibit him as a freak and he has a nightmare in which the city is covered in gigantic dime museum posters, advertising him as "The Freak of All Ages" and "The Woman Man," appearing alongside "The Living Skeleton" and "The Missing Link." Although doubly fictional (first as appearing in a novel, second as appearing as a dream), this scene illuminates the operations of the freak show in two specific ways.

First, by illustrating Lawrence's horror at the prospect of being displayed as a freak, the nightmare suggests that freak show visibility could have disciplinary effects, operating as a threat against gender transgression and an inducement to conform. Second, the context of Lawrence's nightmare, within the novel, suggests that the disciplinary effects of freak show visibility were informed by racialized anxieties, rather than by a universal fear of being labeled "freak." Specifically, Lawrence's nightmare occurs after he has already entered a dime museum to purchase sex change seeds from Africa and after he has learned that his former maid, now Jack, has begun working at a dime museum as "the greatest freak on earth." Additionally, the poster from his nightmare suggests that part of the horror of being displayed as "The Woman Man" is appearing alongside and in association with the racialized "Missing Link" character and the deformed "Living Skeleton." Indeed, throughout the novel, the dime museum appears as a racialized site that serves as both the source of gender transgression (sex change seeds from Africa) and the space of its containment. This suggests that the potential disciplinary effects of freak show visibility were intricately connected to its association with imperial exoticism and racialized difference.

Finally, freak shows worked in tandem with cross-dressing law by producing not only disciplined audiences schooled in gender normativity, but also vigilant audiences trained in the pleasures of suspicion. The possibility of being duped was central to dime museum entertainment, and show managers encouraged audiences to gain pleasure from suspecting, confronting, and unmasking frauds. Performances of sexual and gender ambiguity were particularly susceptible to this suspicion. For example, the Bearded Lady's combination of feminine dress and masculine facial hair confronted audiences with a fascinating gender dilemma—was this a woman who pushed the female body beyond recognizable femininity or was this a man in drag? Visitors sought to resolve this dilemma by prodding at flesh, tugging at beards, and demanding to know the Bearded Lady's marital and maternal status (Wood 1885). Freak show managers encouraged this questioning and occasionally brought in experts to heighten the drama. At New York's American Museum, for example, P.T. Barnum instigated a confrontation, one that ended in court, in which a freak show visitor accused a Bearded Lady of being male, only to be rebuffed by the latter's husband, father, and numerous doctors who testified that she was, indeed, female. Back in San Francisco, Matson's manager also went to court, to sue rivals of his who allegedly featured "fake" Matsons in their shows. Far from resolving the gender confusion at hand, such events reminded audiences of their susceptibility to being duped. As such, freak shows not only reproduced the boundary between permissible and criminal gender displays that cross-dressing law policed—they also popularized and democratized this boundary, turning audiences into aware and vigilant judges of possible gender "fraud."

Despite their different modes of operation, cross-dressing law and the freak show performed similar cultural work in nineteenth-century San Francisco, as techniques of normalization that strove to produce clear, recognizable boundaries between normative and non-normative gender. Additionally, their mutual preoccupation with cross-dressing bodies did not occur in a vacuum, but was one part of a broader set of cultural concerns about the public visibility of problem bodies, particularly those marked by sexual immorality, race, and disease/deformity.

At the same time, however, freak show displays may have had unintended or ironic effects, particularly when the carefully managed distance between viewer and viewed broke down. As cultural scholar Rachel Adams (2001) has argued, freak shows were not only sites of disidentification and disavowal, where audiences secured a sense of normality through their spatial and existential distance from the freaks on stage, but were also sites of identification, where audiences recognized themselves in the freaks and the freaks in themselves. In part, this occurred because the meaning of the freak show performance (like the meaning of any text) was never completely fixed, but was open to multiple interpretations by different audiences. Moreover, as Adams points out, the interactive format of the freak show amplified the possibility of unintended interpretations, as it facilitated unscripted exchanges between disruptive audience members and the freaks who talked back. Such exchanges encouraged alternative readings of the freak show not only among those who participated in them, but also among the wider audience who collectively observed an unintended show.

Adams makes this argument in the context of discussing African American audiences who identified and unmasked racialized freak show performers as local people of color. Such identification, she claims, undermined the fantasy of complete otherness on which the freak show depended and dissolved the boundary between audience and performer, "relocating [the freak] within the community of onlookers" (2001, 170). However, in the context of gender freaks, particularly Matson, the politics of identification could take a slightly different turn, through identifications and desires that did not relocate the freak within the audience but attracted the onlooker to the cross-gender performer on stage. This attraction could be fueled by a shared sense of female masculinity—after all, Matson was not the only female-bodied person to live as a man in 1890s San Francisco.[9] It could also be fueled by an erotic desire for the cross-gender performer, particularly one such as Matson who had described the pleasures of courting women in the pages of the city press.

There is, unfortunately, scant evidence of such identifications and desires in relation to Matson or other cross-dressed freak show performers, as the voices of those who may have appropriated freak discourse in this manner have not made their way into the archive. However, neglecting this possibility because of insufficient evidence may be more problematic than raising it unsupported by positive proof, as it replicates the structure of the archive, amplifying some voices and silencing others. Within the archive, the voice of the newspaper reporter is prominent; a *San Francisco Examiner* reporter described Matson's dime museum exhibit as follows: "Her part will not be a difficult one. She will be faultlessly attired in patent leathers, a handsome dress suit, embroidered linen and a white tie. She will recline in an easy-chair on a little platform and chat with the socially inclined, but whether she will divulge any of the interesting secrets connected with her numerous love episodes is not definitely known" ("Has No Love for Petticoats," *San Francisco Examiner*, February 7, 1895, 16). Consequently, we can imagine the different ways that different audiences may have interacted with Matson—with fascination and titillation, perhaps; with discomfort and disdain; but also perhaps with identification, attraction, and desire.

Conclusion

Through its focus on cross-dressing law, this essay has demonstrated the centrality of gender regulation to nineteenth-century city life and unearthed the hidden history of a law that has appeared in the footnotes of twentieth-century studies, but has not yet been brought to the fore. The essay has also brought together subjects that rarely share the pages of academic inquiry, despite sharing San Francisco streets: male-bodied women and "unsightly" beggars; female-bodied men and sex workers; freak show managers and city police. In doing so I have argued that the policing of gender transgressions needs to be analyzed in relation to the policing of multiple forms of bodily difference and that legal regulations need to be studied alongside cultural fascination. These analytic insights are crucial not only for a study of nineteenth-century cross-dressing law, but also for future studies of the production and regulation of normative gender.

Notes

1. Arrest records were not broken down by gender, but in 1867–68, arrests were reported separately for "wearing female attire" and "wearing male attire." During this year, four people (presumably male bodied) were arrested for "wearing female attire" and two people (presumably female bodied) were arrested "wearing male attire" (*Municipal Reports* 1867–68).
2. Newspapers did not report on Haisch's own gender identification, but they did describe her going to considerable lengths to publicly present as a woman. Consequently, I use female pronouns when discussing Haisch.

3. I use the term "problem bodies" to collectively refer to the multiple sets of bodies that local government officials defined as social problems and targeted for legal intervention in nineteenth-century San Francisco. In particular, I use "problem bodies" as a term that conceptually precedes the related, but narrower, term "deviant bodies" (Terry and Urla 1995), because I identify the construction of deviance, through processes of normalization, as only one of several different strategies used to manage social, political, and economic conflicts. The concept of problem bodies thus allows a wider range of bodies—and a wider range of conflicts—to be brought into view.

4. Vaudeville theater and minstrel shows were also central components of the new entertainment industry and they shared the freak show's emphasis on cross-gender and cross-racial performances (Lott 1993; Toll 1976).

5. Thanks to Susan Stryker for pointing me to the Jefferson Davis reference.

6. Matson was accused of committing this crime in Los Gatos, fifty miles south of San Francisco, and was consequently jailed in San Jose.

7. In 1888, freak show managers recruited another San Francisco performer, "Big Bertha the Queen of Confidence Women," directly from jail, literally paying her bail so as to secure her performance in their Market Street show ("Madame Stanley," *Morning Call*, June 11, 1888, 4).

8. In my discussion of this novel, I draw upon and extend Siobhan Somerville's (2000) earlier analysis.

9. For example, Lou Sullivan (1990) documented the life of Jack Garland (aka Babe Bean), a female-bodied man who lived in or near San Francisco in the late 1890s and 1900s.

Works Cited

Adams, Rachel. 2001. *Sideshow USA: Freaks and the American Cultural Imagination.* Chicago: University of Chicago Press.

Asbury, Herbert. 1933. *The Barbary Coast: An Informal History of the San Francisco Underworld.* New York: A. A. Knopf.

Bogdan, Robert. 1988. *Freak Show: Presenting Human Oddities for Amusement and Profit.* Chicago: University of Chicago Press.

Burke, Martin J. 1887. "The San Francisco Police." Bancroft Library, University of California, Berkeley.

Chinatown Declared a Nuisance! 1880. San Francisco: Workingmen's Party of California.

Cook, James W. 1996. "Of Men, Missing Links, and Nondescripts: The Strange Career of P. T. Barnum's 'What Is It?' Exhibition." In *Freakery: Cultural Spectacles of the Extraordinary Body*, ed. R. G. Thomson. New York: New York University Press.

Cowan, Robert Ernest. 1938. *Forgotten Characters of Old San Francisco, 1850–1870.* Los Angeles: Ward Ritchie Press.

Dennett, Andrea Stulman. 1997. *Weird and Wonderful: The Dime Museum in America.* New York: New York University Press.

Duggan, Lisa. 2000. *Sapphic Slashers: Sex, Violence, and American Modernity.* Durham: Duke University Press.

Eskridge, William N. 1999. *Gaylaw: Challenging the Apartheid of the Closet.* Cambridge: Harvard University Press.

Evans, Albert S. 1873. *A la California: Sketch of Life in the Golden State.* San Francisco: A. L. Bancroft.

Friedman, Lawrence Meir. 1985. *A History of American Law.* 2nd ed. New York: Simon and Schuster. (1st ed. pub. 1973.)

General Orders of the Board of Supervisors. 1866–98. San Francisco: San Francisco Board of Supervisors.

Habermas, Jürgen. 1991. *The Structural Transformation of the Public Sphere: An Inquiry into a Category of Bourgeois Society.* Cambridge: MIT Press (Orig. pub. 1962.)

Hirschfeld, Magnus. 1991. *Transvestites: The Erotic Drive to Cross-Dress.* Buffalo: Prometheus Books (Orig. pub. 1910).

Jesse Brown Cook Scrapbooks Documenting San Francisco History and Law Enforcement. n.d. Vol. 4. The Bancroft Library. University of California, Berkeley. Unit ID: 184.

Jordan, Louis J. 1868. *Handbook of the Pacific Museum of Anatomy and Science.* San Francisco: Francis and Valentine.

Lott, Eric. 1993. *Love and Theft: Blackface Minstrelsy and the American Working Class.* New York: Oxford University Press.

McNamara, Brooks. 1974. "'A Congress of Wonders': The Rise and Fall of the Dime Museum." *ESQ* 20(3):216–231.

Municipal Reports. 1863–64 to 1899–1900. San Francisco: San Francisco Board of Supervisors.

Revised Orders of the City and County of San Francisco. 1863. San Francisco: San Francisco Board of Supervisors.

Schweik, Susan. 2007. "Begging the Question: Disability, Mendicancy, Speech and the Law." *Narrative* 15(1):58–70.

Sears, Clare. 2005. "A Tremendous Sensation: Cross-Dressing in the Nineteenth Century San Francisco Press." In *News and Sexuality: Media Portraits of Diversity,* ed. L. Casteñada and S. Campbell. Thousand Oaks, CA: Sage Press.

Silber, Nina. 1989. "Intemperate Men, Spiteful Women, and Jefferson Davis: Northern Views of the Defeated South." *American Quarterly* 41(4):614–635.

Somerville, Siobhan. 2000. *Queering the Color Line: Race and the Invention of Homosexuality in American Culture.* Durham: Duke University Press.

Stryker, Susan, and Jim Van Buskirk. 1996. *Gay by the Bay: A History of Queer Culture in the San Francisco Bay Area.* San Francisco: Chronicle Books.

Sullivan, Lou. 1990. *From Female to Male: The Life of Jack Bee Garland.* Boston: Alyson.

Terry, Jennifer, and Jacqueline Urla. 1995. *Deviant Bodies.* Bloomington: Indiana University Press.

Toll, Robert. 1976. *On with the Show! The First Century of Show Business in America.* New York: Oxford University Press.

Wood, J. G. 1885. "Dime Museums." *Atlantic Monthly* 55 (January–June):759–765.

30 Incarceration, Identity Politics, and the Trans-Cis Divide

Paisley Currah

Political scientist and trans legal scholar Paisley Currah has, among other accomplishments in a long and influential academic career, co-founded *TSQ: Transgender Studies Quarterly* and co-edited the award-winning book *Transgender Rights*. In this excerpt from a chapter in *Sex Is as Sex Does: Governing Transgender Identity* (2022), Currah offers a new framework for understanding how trans people are affected by the carceral complex. He focuses specifically on policies that "freeze" transition-related healthcare for incarcerated trans people undergoing medical transition or deny access to it altogether for those who seek it but have not yet gotten started. Currah argues that this is not merely an extension of socially pervasive transphobia into the space of the prison but rather reflects "the more general relationship between prisons and civil society." Rather than focusing, as most policy advocacy does, on comparing the proportionally greater rate of incarceration of trans people versus cis people to demonstrate the existence of transphobia, Currah suggests comparing socio-economic disparities between incarcerated and non-incarcerated trans people. Doing so, Currah argues, would shift the analysis from one that revolves around transgender identities and merely documents transphobia to one in which we would could better see how incarceration itself is "central to the constructions of liberal freedom and the principal of state noninterference in free markets." Transphobia is real, but it functions as part of a broader set of racist and anti-poor practices that criminalize people of color, trans people, and poor people to keep the wheels of the capitalist marketplace turning.

In January 2006, the Inmate Sex Change Prevention Act became law in Wisconsin. According to a press release trumpeting the bill's passage, taxpayers would no longer pay for what the two legislators who introduced the legislation described as "extreme prison makeovers." The legislation prohibited the use of federal or state funds to "facilitate the provision of" hormone therapy or gender-affirming surgery for any prisoner in Wisconsin. The law was passed after a Wisconsin prisoner had filed a lawsuit arguing that her inability to undergo gender-affirming surgery in prison violated the US Constitution. It was a violation of the Eighth Amendment, prisoner Donna Konitzer's counsel had argued, to be denied treatment for her serious medical condition, gender identity disorder. "It's the most absurd thing I've ever heard of," said one of the bill's sponsors.[1] Referring to the Eighth Amendment, Representative Mark Gundrum elaborated, "I think the founders of our country—when they wrote that clause—they were envisioning preventing people from being burned in oil or burned at the stake, not simply refusing to use taxpayer dollars to allow inmates to get a sex change or breast implants or whatever else."[2]

DOI: 10.4324/9781003206255-37

The figure of the convict who demands a "sex change" might not have been anticipated in the popular imaginary, but once it was conjured by the press, public outrage erupted. Commenting on a news story about a doctor's recommendation that Ophelia De'Lonta, a transgender women serving a seventy-year sentence in Virginia for robbery, weapons offenses, and drug offenses, be provided with gender-affirming surgery, one individual wrote, "If he/she wants to cut off his/her dick and balls that's his/her choice [but] the state should not pay for the sex change operation." Another chimed in, "Why do ALL trans people want to be victims and claim that they need surgery, want the government and everyone else to pay for it, and use the 'But I'll kill myself if I don't get it!' mantra?" A third wrote, "Ugh, trannies are the worst. Now they actually expect me to pay for their dick-chopping surgery with *my* tax dollars? Just tuck that thing like any other drag queen."[3] And those comments appeared on a website that aggregates news for the *gay* community, a group that generally tends to be more receptive to appeals for equal treatment from transgender people. In a case involving Michelle Kosilek, sentenced in Massachusetts in 1993 and serving a life sentence, a federal judge ruled that she be provided with appropriate counseling, possibly hormone therapy, and potentially even gender-affirming surgery. In response, CBS's Crime Insider headline read, "Tax Dollars at Work: Will State Pay for Wife-Killer's Sex Change?"[4] When Wisconsin's Inmate Sex Change Prevention Act became law in 2006, advocates for trans prisoners knew of no incarcerated people in the United States who had had gender-affirming surgery. Yet the very idea that a prisoner had filed suit for a "taxpayer-funded sex change" generated such social hysteria that similar legislation was introduced in a handful of other state legislatures between 2006 and 2020. Some bills would allow for the provision of hormone therapy to prisoners diagnosed with gender dysphoria, but would explicitly prohibit gender-affirming surgeries. Others would make prisoners pay all the costs of transition-related care.[5]

One could say that trans prisoners find themselves on the wrong side of two sets of exclusions. First, as prisoners, they have fallen into the maw of the criminal justice system in a nation that has the world's highest incarceration rate.[6] Second, as people whose gender identity confounds social expectations, trans prisoners are punished by the gender policies that govern incarcerated populations.[7] In prison, transgender people of all genders suffer the consequences of their gender non-normativity through three mechanisms: the rules of sex classification in a system in which placement is governed by the gender binary, the violence perpetrated by guards and other prisoners, and the lack of access to transition-related medical care. On the question of sex classification, most municipal jails and state and federal prisons assign prisoners to men's and women's prisons based on their genital sex. The Obama-era rules for the Prison Rape Elimination Act, which sets standards for federal and state prisons, had insisted that individuals be evaluated on a case-by-case basis when making decisions about gender placement.[8] The Trump administration reversed even that weak gesture in 2018 with rules specifying that "biological sex" would be the "initial" metric for determining whether a prisoner will go to a men's or women's prison—indeed, the rules advised that "the designation to a facility of the inmate's identified gender would be appropriate only in rare cases."[9] Three years later, the Biden administration reversed course once again, arguing that "categorically refusing" to place transgender prisoners in a facility that corresponds to their gender identity violates the Constitution.[10] Regardless of the political football that trans people seem to have become in regulatory apparatuses driven by partisanship, even under Democratic administrations these rules had little effect. While many trans prisoners prefer to be housed according to the sex they were assigned at birth, many do not. Yet almost all trans inmates remain housed according to the sex they were assigned at birth.[11] Many are denied the personal items—including binders, bras, prostheses—they request.

On the issue of violence, transgender and gender non-conforming prisoners experience high levels of harassment, violence, and humiliation at the hands of fellow prisoners and corrections officials. Transgender women incarcerated in men's institutions are much more likely to be sexually assaulted: one highly regarded study found "59% of transgender women reported having been sexually assaulted in contrast to 4.4%" of a random sample of inmates.[12] In another study, trans prisoners reported being sexually victimized at ten times the rate of other prisoners.[13] In some cases, transgender prisoners—once described as "victim-prone" by a New York State corrections official[14]—are placed in administrative segregation, putatively for their own protection.[15] While that may make transgender and gender non-conforming prisoners less vulnerable to violence at the hands of fellow prisoners, some advocates report that administrative segregation increases the violence and humiliation inflicted by corrections officers. Additionally, prisoners in administrative segregation are isolated, cut off from recreational, social, and educational opportunities.[16] It is a punishment, not a perk.

Between the disciplinary violence of rules for sex classification and the brute violence of physical and sexual assault lie corrections policies on the provision of medical treatment related to gender transition, which is the subject of this chapter. The very title of the Inmate Sex Change Prevention Act, along with the copycat bills from other states, suggests that transgender prisoners across all these United States are receiving all the counseling, hormones, and surgeries they need. That is far from the case. In fact, the first known gender-affirming surgery for an incarcerated person anywhere in the United States did not happen until 2017.[17] One 2017 review of state policies on transition-related health care found that only thirteen states would allow a prisoner to begin hormone therapy while incarcerated; twenty-seven would not, and ten more states had no public policies on that question and would not respond to the investigators' queries. On the question of gender-affirming surgery, thirty-two states had, at the time the study was conducted, policies explicitly banning these procedures.[18]

[. . .]

It's easy to pin the blame for these bad policies and practices on transphobia—or, more broadly, on systems bent on maintaining a rigid, pretty much uncrossable gender binary. Similarly, one can identify the lessening of transphobia and the growing recognition that gender is a spectrum rather than a binary as the impetus driving policy in the right direction. Those explanations are obviously useful to some degree. But here I set aside, at least provisionally, the typical strategy for understanding the injustice. Instead of locating the problem of transgender prisoners as a specifically *transgender* problem, this chapter takes a lateral cut and looks at connections to the larger social logics of incarceration. Certainly, radical and progressive trans advocacy groups and some academics have done exactly that—they have situated the plight of incarcerated trans people firmly within an analysis of capitalism and racism's role in maintaining the world's largest prison population.[19] They have argued, rightly, that the solution to the problems they face is not to reform prison policies seemingly specific to trans people but to abolish prisons.[20] While in alignment with this goal, here I want to stay focused on the present and recent past to figure out how a policy that seems limited to the question of gender transition in prison and that seems to be a result of transphobia might reflect the more general relationship between prisons and civil society; even a policy seemingly particular to trans people might spring from the same ways of thinking that govern incarceration in general. This approach challenges the presumption in mainstream advocacy that transphobic policies in prisons are merely a more severe extension of transphobic policies on the outside. It calls into question the distinction between transgender and cisgender that governs most policy analysis and that has been imported, without question, into research on and advocacy for prisoners who need transition-related medical care. That this argument will be counterintuitive to many (including myself in earlier times) reveals the seductive draw of trans identity politics, which elevates one relatively abstract characteristic (incongruence with the sex assigned at birth) over more historically grounded forms of difference (such as socioeconomic status, race).

[. . .]

In the rest of the chapter, I describe how mainstream advocates frame the problem of incarcerated transgender people and contrast that approach with scholarship that understands incarceration as central to constructions of citizenship and that challenges axiomatic truths about the "free" market's relation to incarceration. Then I read an early and formative policy—the "freeze-frame" policy that dictated that the transition of "transsexual inmates" be "frozen" at the moment of incarceration and that still governs much thinking about transition in prison—with Solzhenitsyn's and Foucault's notions of the "carceral archipelago." The chapter ends with observations on the growing divide between free and incarcerated trans people on the issue of transition-related medical care and the work of trans identity politics in obscuring those divisions.

Arguing That Transphobia Is the Cause of Overincarceration

While the absolute number of prisoners who are transgender is very small, since trans people in general make up a tiny slice of the general population,[21] their rate of incarceration appears to be significantly higher than that of non-trans people. Indeed, according to Lambda Legal, a GLBTQ litigation nonprofit, "nearly one in six transgender Americans—and one in two black transgender people—has been to prison."[22] ("Americans" seems to be a rhetorical gesture here; it's unlikely their survey asked about citizenship status.) Another survey, conducted in 2015, of 27,715 (not randomly selected) self-identified trans people in the United States found that 2 percent of its respondents had spent time in jail or prison or juvenile detention *in the last year*.[23] By way of contrast, a report from the Bureau of Justice Statistics found that 2.7 percent of all people living in the United States *had ever* served time in a state or federal prison.[24] Because the latter percentage doesn't include people who spent time in jail but did not go to prison—jails are run by municipalities and hold people awaiting trial or sentencing as well as those with sentences of less than a year, and prisons are state and federal facilities—these numbers don't allow for a perfectly neat comparison. But the notable difference has led many to conclude that it is very likely that transgender people are incarcerated at much higher rates than cisgender people. The analysis of the same seventy-question survey identified many correlations between experiences of gender-based discrimination and violence and being incarcerated. For example, respondents who had experienced family rejection, domestic violence, or physical or sexual assault in school were more likely to have been incarcerated at some point in their lives than respondents who had not. Those who were currently homeless or unemployed or who had lost a job because of bias against transgender or gender non-conforming people were 85 percent more likely to have been incarcerated than those who had not. Of the survey respondents, 48 percent of those who had engaged in sex work had been incarcerated compared to the overall incarceration rate of 16 percent among all survey respondents.[25] These correlations suggest that disparate rates of incarceration are among the cascading effects of transphobia. Because violating social rules of gender can cause trans people to be cut off from access to family support, education, stable housing, and legal employment and thus to engage more frequently in survival strategies that are criminalized, the chance of a trans person finding themselves on the wrong side of the law is magnified.

The transphobia explanation doesn't capture the whole story, however. Black respondents in the 2009 and 2015 trans surveys were about four times more likely to have been incarcerated than white respondents; in the US population as a whole, the rate of incarceration for Black people has been about five times that of white people (based on the 2010 US census), although the racial gap has narrowed since 2010.[26] Michelle Alexander, Jackie Wang, and others have argued that mass incarceration is an essential element of the apparatus of the nation's ongoing project of white supremacy.[27] Moreover, the rate of incarceration of sex workers in general is also extremely high. For example, one study found that 70 percent of "female" sex workers in Baltimore had been incarcerated at least once—and the mean amount of times was fifteen.[28] As for class, the correlation between unemployment and incarceration is strong. Writing about California, Ruth Wilson Gilmore connects the growing disparity between the number of jobs available and the number of people seeking work to increases in the state's prison population. The "surplus population"—useful to capital by depressing wages—is controlled by shifting large segments of it to prison.[29] [. . .]

These advocacy reports do not fail to underscore discrepancies around race, class, and gender that the research has found. Yet even as they draw attention to what one report calls the "compounding effects of other forms of discrimination" found in their own and others' studies,[30] activists, allies, and sympathetic media stick to a narrative centered on transphobia and the category of transgender.[31] Elías Cosenza Krell aptly ventriloquizes it thus: " 'We need to care about trans lives, especially trans women's lives, especially trans women of color's lives.' "[32] As Nira Yuval-Davis has pointed out in another context, such an "additive" approach to intersectionality conflates different levels of analysis (experiential, structural, representational) and reduces ontologically distinct social divisions to "identities," which are then "often required to 'perform' analytical tasks beyond their abilities."[33] That certainly may be the case here. For example, it's not just that Black trans feminine individuals are much more likely to spend time in jail or prison than white trans feminine individuals. It's that in the United States there is a close relationship between white supremacy and mass incarceration, and, more recently, between the economic dislocations of recent decades and prison. Given the historical circumstances surrounding the construction of the categories of transsexual and transgender, as C. Riley Snorton, Julian Gill-Peterson, and others have suggested, the terms themselves may be constitutively white—or, at the very least, largely fabricated through the elision of anything other than the autonomous liberal employable subject and normative whiteness.[34] Trans, then, might occupy a different position vis-à-vis incarceration than what is suggested by its inclusion in a "triply oppressed" analytic. It's possible that one of the identity categories held out as an axis of oppression may be complicit in the problem it has been charged with dismantling.

Still. For many trans advocates, it is axiomatic that the disproportionate presence of trans people in prison and the mistreatment they face once incarcerated reflect the effects of transphobia on the outside. With regard to this view, the solution requires changing the social and legal landscape in civil society to lessen the possibility that one will enter the downward spiral leading to incarceration. That means working to increase the likelihood that trans children and teens will be accepted at home and at school, and passing laws that prohibit discrimination in housing, employment, and public accommodations. Indeed, the transgender rights apparatus in the United States has largely consolidated around this agenda, which was also reflected in the policy priorities identified by NGLTF's survey respondents in 2011: passing employment nondiscrimination laws, getting insurers to pay for transition-related health care, and improving policies for sex reclassification on identity documents and government records.[35] It's telling that passing hate crime laws was ranked third in the survey's list of priorities while working on transgender and gender non-conforming prisoners' rights was ranked ninth, even though supporting enhanced penalties for particular crimes feeds the carceral leviathan that disproportionately imprisons people of color and trans and gender non-conforming people, especially those who are Black. [. . .]

There's no doubt that, with the exception of passing hate crime laws (which give prosecutors even more power to force plea bargains on members of groups already singled out by the criminal justice system), achieving these policy priorities would certainly go some way toward improving the lives of individuals on the outside who are disadvantaged because they violate social gender norms and reducing the likelihood that they might be imprisoned as a result. But there are other ways of thinking about the question of incarceration. The above account is produced by a conceptual apparatus dependent on a particular set of assumptions, some general to individualism and some specific to the dominant analytics of mainstream movements for transgender justice: that incarceration is an effect of an *individual's* lack of employability; that the declared function of punishment is largely coextensive with its effects; that criminal laws target individuals; that the social and legal regulation of gender and sex on the inside, while more intense than what occurs on the outside, is not qualitatively different from it; and that comparing the treatment of trans prisoners to that of cisgender prisoners will generate the clearest picture of the injustice. But the approach taken in this chapter (the last row in the table below) is to imagine trans *prisoners* as the constitutive other of trans *non-prisoners*, rather than of cisgender prisoners. That framework makes visible the growing differences between trans people who are incarcerated and those who have never been. Instead of focusing on differential rates of discrimination between trans and cisgender people in civil society, or comparing the treatment of trans prisoners to that of cisgender prisoners, incarceration itself becomes the starting point.

Incarceration is central to constructions of liberal freedom and the principal of state non-interference in free markets. As Dylan Rodriguez puts it, the intelligibility of "civil freedom relies on carceral and punitive unfreedom," which requires rendering the prison as "an alien cultural and geographic figuring, a place that is somewhere else altogether, territorially distant and experientially incomprehensible to the ideal-typical 'free' person."[36] In addition to serving as the ideological antipode of the negative freedom that the nonincarcerated are meant to enjoy, Bernard Harcourt argues that prisons function as the "other" in neoliberal notions of limited government—the only arena where state intervention, increasingly draconian and costly, has been not only sanctioned but welcomed.[37] Imprisonment in the United States—from the rate of incarceration to the severity of solitary confinement to felon

Table 1 Perspectives and Comparisons

Perspective	Domain of the comparison	What is compared	What this comparison makes visible
Transgender rights approach in general	Civil society	Trans non-prisoners to cisgender non-prisoners	Higher rates of discrimination leading to higher rates of incarceration Discrimination as the root cause of incarceration
Advocates for trans prisoners	Prisons	Trans prisoners to cisgender prisoners	Gender rules in prisons: sex classification, treatment of gender dysphoria Institutional and informal punishment for violating gender norms Differential vulnerability to sexual assault
Approach taken here	Prisons and civil society (market)	Trans prisoners to trans nonincarcerated	Constitutive role of white supremacy Prisons as part of the economy, not separate from it Widening policy gap (availability of transition-related health care, identity documents, and sex classification) between incarcerated and nonincarcerated

disenfranchisement—is not just an empirical problem of excess, of too much punishment. It's also not just an afterthought to what gets cast as the normal activities of civil life— earning and studying, reproducing and consuming, traveling and nest-making. Incarceration is a load-bearing pillar in the architecture of society, economy, and politics: the racial and structural inequalities not visible in liberal and neoliberal abstractions of the market and the contract, the citizen and their doppelgänger, the earner, are laid bare in the concrete injustices of the criminal justice system.[38]

The Carceral Archipelago and the Freeze-Frame Policy

The first and still formative corrections policy regarding gender transition in prison was the "freeze-frame" policy. The concept of "freeze-framing," in both its formal and informal implementation, rests on two criteria. First, was the prisoner on hormones *before* incarceration, or was hormone therapy sought only *after* they were incarcerated? Second, if the prisoner was receiving hormones prior to incarceration, was the medical treatment provided by medical practitioners, or was it secured through other means—on the streets? In most cases, prisoners who meet the first criterion must have been treated for gender identity disorder (or gender dysphoria) under the supervision of a physician. Maintenance policies expressly preclude the possibility of surgery. The rationale for maintaining prisoners at precisely the level of gender transition they had attained at the moment of incarceration was outlined in guidelines written in 1990 by Robert Dickey, who was on the faculty of the Clarke Institute of Psychiatry in Toronto. (From the 1970s to the aughts, the faculty at the Clarke Institute played an outsized role in policy matters regarding trans people in the Canada, the United States, and internationally. At one time, the Clarke was the only institution in Canada with the power to authorize gender-affirming surgery. They were notorious for treating trans people "with contempt" and for their extreme gatekeeping practices.[39] As Andrea James explains, it was "nicknamed 'Jurassic Clarke' in the trans community for its regressive policies."[40] Indeed, googling "Clarke Institute," "transsexual," and "notorious" generated 1,730 results.) If there is an architect of the freeze-frame policy, it's Dickey. While some prisons already had formal or informal maintenance policies in place, Dickey's interventions cloaked them with the mantle of medical authority. In a 1990 article, "Gender Dysphoria and Antisocial Behavior," he wrote that a "reasonable general policy is to 'freeze' incarcerated gender dysphorics at whatever stage of hormonal or surgical feminization or masculinization they have attained by the time they enter the correctional system."[41] There should be no further surgery while incarcerated, and hormones should be provided in prison, Dickey argued, only if they had been prescribed by a "recognized expert in treating gender disorders" before the individual was incarcerated.[42] He also recommended housing transsexuals—most of his analysis concerns people assigned male at birth, whom Dickey referred to as "transsexual males" or, if they had had genital surgery, as "castrated" males—according to the sex assigned at birth if they had not had genital surgery.[43] As an expert in gender dysphoria among incarcerated populations, Dickey served as a consultant to correctional systems across the United States and Canada.

A few years later, Maxine Peterson, Dickey, and other colleagues from the Clarke Institute conducted a survey of correctional systems in a number of jurisdictions in Australia, Europe, and North America. According to the sixty-three surveys returned (about a 60 percent response rate), just under half the corrections systems indicated they would continue hormone therapy for incarcerated individuals "provided this had been prescribed prior to admission to prison." The rest of the institutions simply discontinued hormone therapy. In some senses, then, Dickey's freeze-frame policy was a progressive one for the time. The policy of "freeze-framing" became the rubric that for many years organized not only transition-related medical care but also sex classification in prison. Since in the majority of corrections systems placement in sex-segregated institutions is based on genitals, the freeze-frame policy meant that one's genitals would not change once one was incarcerated—there would be no surgery. For Dickey, the rationale for maintaining the status quo was based on three factors: "the artificial nature of the prison environment, the inability to assess the intensity of gender dysphoria in such an environment, and the lack of a genuine real-life test in such a controlled setting."[44] As Dickey explains, "The prison environment is not representative of society at large."[45] It's the first and third rationales—the artificiality of the prison environment, and prisoners' inability to engage in the "real-life" test required by the American Psychiatric Association's then-operative treatment protocols—that matter for the purposes of the analysis in this chapter.

The rationale for the policy of preventing prisoners from moving "further along the continuum of transgender changes," then, rests on the distinction between prisons and "real life," a distinction that in turn has been mapped onto the very different registers of space and time between the two. The figure of the archipelago was famously invoked by Aleksandr Solzhenitsyn as a way of imagining the spatial landscapes of incarceration. According to Brady Thomas Heiner, Solzhenitsyn deployed the term both geographically and theoretically. In the first sense, "the archipelago designates a series of . . . scattered carceral 'islands'—sites in which captive bodies were tortured, interrogated, and confined incommunicado." In the latter sense, writes Heiner, "Solzhenitsyn speaks of the archipelago as a grid of 'dead zones,' a 'prison sewage system,' around which the 'seas' of civil society unremittingly flow, and about which civil society remains unaware or inattentive."[46] Foucault, nodding to Solzhenitsyn, speaks of a "carceral archipelago" as "the way in which a form of punitive system is physically dispersed yet at the same time covers the entirety of society."[47] In contrast to real life, prisons, as Solzhenitsyn observed, are islands around which time and civil society flow, but which they do not penetrate. In real life, outside the prison walls, people are apparently at large, free to move; to make decisions; to work; to buy; to sell; to change; to author, edit, and revise their life's story from moment to moment; to reproduce the narratives that fashion the kinship structures of family, community, and race; and to participate in national projects organized around distribution. Opposed to this notion of real life are the carceral islands, the closed spaces where movement is radically constrained or, in the case of super-max institutions, precluded almost completely, and where contingency is managed and aleatory events are prevented. Foucault's musings on the devaluation of space in favor of temporal epistemes speaks to this opposition: "Space was treated as the dead, the fixed, the undialectical, the immobile. Time, on the contrary, was richness, fecundity, life, dialectic."[48] As Regina Kunzel puts it, "the essence of incarceration was forced spatial confinement, of course, but many prisoners experienced it as temporal rupturing as well."[49] Incarceration, "doing time," means immobilizing bodies in place, while "real life" is imagined as structured around flows and temporalities: nation, family, reproductive time, monumental time, even eschatological time.

Of course, imprisoned bodies are not static. Living, becoming ill, suffering, and dying take place in those spaces. [. . .]

[. . .] The situation the freeze-frame policy creates is both critical and chronic. It's both eventful, a crisis, *and* uneventful, "ordinary, chronic and cruddy."[50] Sara Lamble explains, "prison is a site that produces the conditions of living death; it is a place where bodies are subject to regimes of slow death and dying. Not only are deprivation, abuse, and neglect regular features of incarceration but the monotonous regime of caged life—the experience of "doing time"—involves the slow wearing away of human vitality and the reduction of human experience to a bleak existence."[51] Incarceration is not only spatial confinement for a period of time, then, it also has to be understood as a sort of "living death"—an extended dying, a prolonged period of decay, of "bodily and subjective disintegration," that might not end in death.[52]

Instead of seeing the hysteria and hatred directed at the figure of "the convict who demands a sex change" as merely a particularly noxious condensation of a generalized transphobic animus, that reaction might be also understood as a manifestation of the commonsense distinction between being in prison and being free. Prisons are to punish, not reward, criminal behavior. One should not be treated in prison to medical treatments that are not available to most free individuals. In a 1997 decision denying hormone therapy to a transsexual prisoner, Judge Richard Posner, a Chicago School neoliberal and law and economics thinker, explained his logic: "Withholding from a prisoner an esoteric treatment that only the wealthy can afford does not strike us as a form of cruel and unusual punishment. It is not unusual; and we cannot see what is cruel about refusing to benefit a person who could not have obtained the benefit if he had refrained from committing crimes. We do not want transsexuals committing crimes because it is the only route to obtaining a cure."[53] Indeed, the point of incarceration, according to Posner, Gary Becker, and other neoliberal thinkers, is to punish those who have attempted to bypass, in Posner's words, "the system of voluntary, compensated exchange—the 'market.'"[54] As one of the sponsors of Wisconsin's Inmate Sex Change Prevention Act explained, "When most health plans do not cover these types of procedures the state should not have to foot the bill for convicted felons to get it either."[55] The freeze-frame policy—not to mention the complete denial of transition-related care in some correctional systems—ensures that those on the inside do not get services unavailable to those on the outside.[56]

Denaturalizing Gender but Not Markets

The terrain has shifted radically since the Wisconsin Sex Change Prevention Act became law in 2006. Trans people who aren't incarcerated are much more likely to get transition-related medical care now should they want it. In Wisconsin, for example, state policy now bans private insurance companies from discriminating based on gender identity, which means insurance companies can no longer refuse to cover transition-related health care. Moreover, the state's Medicaid plan now also explicitly includes such care. These policy shifts have been widespread in the United States: one advocacy organization suggests that, based on jurisdictions and demographic data, the majority of the LGBTQ population are protected by policies that prohibit trans exclusions in health care coverage.[57] Amid the welter of state and federal policies on private insurance and Medicaid, and state and federal employee health plans, there has been, since at least 2012, an emerging trend line of increasing coverage.[58] The passage of the Affordable Care Act, which went into effect in 2010, has also made a significant difference because it bans sex discrimination in the provision of health care. In 2016, the Obama administration promulgated regulations interpreting sex to include gender identity. As a result, exclusions for transition-related care would run afoul of the law. In 2019 a conservative federal judge in Texas vacated the rule, known as Section 1557 of the Affordable Care Act; that same year the Trump administration, for good measure, also took steps to rescind it. This regulation's prospective future as a political football, changing from one administration to the next, was cut short in 2020 when the Supreme Court ruled, in a 6–3 decision, that "it is impossible to discriminate against a person for being homosexual or transgender without discriminating against that individual based on sex."[59] While the case before it concerned employment discrimination, it's already become clear that the Supreme Court's construction of sex to include transgender individuals will likely apply to nondiscrimination laws in other areas, including health care. Indeed, in 2020 a federal judge in New York granted an injunction against the Trump administration's attempt to change the rules, finding that "the proposed rules are, indeed, contrary to Bostock."[60] Categorical bans on transition-related care will be viewed as a form of sex discrimination—as long as the Affordable Care Act remains undisturbed.[61] [. . .]

Even without the "lure" of free transition-related health care in prison, however, transgender people are still more likely to be incarcerated than cisgender people. According to the downward spiral explanation proffered by mainstream trans rights advocates, it all boils down to discrimination. As the National Center for Transgender Equality explains in a pamphlet promoting federal legislation that would ban employment discrimination based on gender identity, "homelessness, poverty, violence, and working in the street economy are consequences of workplace discrimination. These issues can only be addressed by working to eliminate the root cause. Allowing people to have and keep jobs to support themselves and their families is vital."[62] [. . .] Eliminating transphobia from the workplace would allow for the full participation of responsible, self-governing, and employable transgender individuals. It would then no longer be necessary for trans people to engage in criminalized survival strategies that bypass the market and land them in jail.

The employability narrative, however, leaves out one inconvenient fact—the market cannot provide a job with a living wage to everyone who wants one. From this perspective, prisons do not punish those who bypass the market but instead warehouse some of the populations that the market cannot provide for because, in fact, it depends on their exclusion. [. . .]

If purveyors of the transphobia explanation spent as much time denaturalizing the market as they do denaturalizing gender, the mechanisms that distribute vulnerabilities so unevenly would be more apparent. It might also help us see that the transgender-cisgender binary, the grid of intelligibility that dominates so much of trans studies and advocacy, possibly obscures more than it reveals. Indeed, transgender has become a category of increasing cultural currency in the rhetoric of diversity, stitching together people whose only commonality is that, one way or another, their gender didn't turn out as expected, given the sex they were assigned at birth. For example, the chances of a trans person going to jail or prison differ greatly depending on race, class, and gender, among other things. Earlier, I suggested that rather than comparing transgender prisoners to cisgender prisoners, a more useful juxtaposition might be to compare incarcerated and never-incarcerated transgender people. The increasing policy divergence affecting prisoners and the "free" with regard to rules for sex classification and the provision of transgender-related health care is made very visible by that comparison. This approach doesn't set up transgender as a unifying category of sameness, but rather becomes a method for identifying difference. That trans purports to describe people who are so very differently situated in relation to their vulnerability to violence, incarceration, illness, homelessness, and slow death might be one of the more miraculous feats of identity politics. The fact that removing barriers to the employability of trans people gets cast as the solution to the severe situation now facing trans prisoners is an example of neoliberal rationality in action. Indeed, the three policy changes that would make the *most* difference to the *most* trans people are prison abolition, the adoption of universal public-payer health care, and a large-scale assault on income inequality. None of the specific policies purveyed by mainstream trans rights groups—such as adding gender identity to a federal nondiscrimination law, which Justice Gorsuch effectively accomplished in the June 2020 Supreme Court decision in *Bostock v. Clayton County*[63]—would have anywhere near the effect on the lives of trans people that those three policies would.

To complicate matters a little more—in looking at prisons, it's important not to fall into the trap of reproducing the too-neat distinction between the imprisoned and the free. It might be more apt to rethink the geography of the carceral archipelago, to rearrange the map into zones of safety and precariousness. When the assumptions of the freeze-frame policy are unpacked, it becomes clear that of course time penetrates the realm of the living dead inhabiting those carceral islands. But the converse is also true. Civil society—in the form of the market—contains its own dead zones, warehouses for disposable populations. While Dickey tells us that "the prison environment is not representative of society at large," many parts of "society" are also not representative of what in the social imaginary is thought to constitute living. For example, not all unincarcerated people have access to transition-related care. Prisons aren't "real life," but for many, neither is the realm of putative freedom. For many, it's slow death.[64]

Notes

1. Gina Barton, "Prisoner Sues State over Gender Rights," *Milwaukee-Wisconsin Journal Sentinel*, January 23, 2005, www.jsonline.com.
2. Associated Press, "Transgendered Inmates Push for State-Funded Sex-Change Surgery," *USA Today*, August 19, 2006, http://usatoday30.usatoday.com.
3. "VA Doc Recommends State Pay for Inmate's Gender-Reassignment Surgery," *Queerty*, July 6, 2012, www.queerty.com.
4. Ryan Smith, "Tax Dollars at Work: Will State Pay for Wife-Killer's Sex Change?" *CBS News*, December 1, 2009, www.cbsnews.com.
5. For example: Massachusetts Senate Bill S.1812, "An Act relative to the appropriate use of public funds," 2009–2010 session (prohibiting public funds for "sex reassignment surgery," hormones, or laser hair removal), https://malegislature.gov; California Senate Bill 1079, 2011–2012 session (defining gender-affirming surgery as medically unnecessary), www.leginfo.ca.gov; South Carolina General Assembly Bill 108, 2015–2016 session (prohibiting "sexual reassignment surgery" but allowing hormone therapy if the individual was on hormones before they were incarcerated), www.scstatehouse.gov; Arizona House Bill 2293, 2017–2018 session ("medical and health services do not include gender reassignment surgery"), www.azleg.gov; Michigan House bill 6524, 2017–2018 session ("a prisoner who receives gender reassignment surgery at his or her request is responsible for the entire cost of the treatment"), www.legislature.mi.gov; Alaska House Bill 5, "An Act prohibiting the expenditure of state money on gender reassignment medical procedures," 2019–2020 session www.akleg.gov.
6. John Gramlich, "America's Incarceration Rate Is at a Two-Decade Low," *Pew Research Center*, May 2, 2018, www.pewresearch.org. While the incarceration rate was at a twenty-year low, in 2016 there were still 6.7 million people in the US under some kind of criminal justice supervision. Sentencing Project, "Fact Sheet; Prisons and People in Prisons," August 2017, www.sentencingproject.org.
7. Darren Rosenblum, "'Trapped' in Sing-Sing: Transgendered Prisoners Caught in the Gender Binarism," *Michigan Journal of Gender and Law* 6 (2000): 499–571; Sydney Tarzwell, "The Gender Lines Are Marked with Razor Wire: Addressing State Prison Policies and Practices for the Management of Transgender Prisoners," *Columbia Human Rights Law Review* 38 (2006): 167–220; Dean Spade, *Normal Life: Administrative Violence, Critical Trans Politics, and the Limits of Law* (Durham, NC: Duke University Press, 2015); Elias Vitulli, "Racialized Criminality and the Imprisoned Trans Body: Adjudicating Access to Gender-Related Medical Treatment in Prisons," *Social Justice* 37, no. 1 (2010–11): 53–68; J. Sumner and L. Sexton, "Same Difference: The 'Dilemma of Difference' and the Incarceration of Transgender Prisoners," *Law & Social Inquiry* 41, no. 3 (2016): 616–642.
8. Department of Justice, "Prisons and Jails Standards, United States Department of Justice Final Rules," May 17, 2012, https://bja.ojp.gov.
9. Bureau of Prisons, US Department of Justice, "Transgender Offender Manual," May 11, 2018, www.bop.gov.
10. Statement of Interest of the United States at 2, Diamond v. Ward, No. 5:20-cv-00453-MTT (M.D. Ga, April 21, 2021).
11. According to an investigative report by NBC News, of the 4,890 incarcerated trans prisoners in state prisons that they were able to identify—not every correctional system cooperated with their requests—only 15 were segregated according to their lived gender. Kate Sosin, "Trans, Imprisoned—and Trapped," *NBC News*, February 26, 2020, www.nbcnews.com.

12. Lori Sexton, Valerie Jenness, and Jennifer Macy Sumner, "Where the Margins Meet: A Demographic Assessment of Transgender Inmates in Men's Prisons," *Justice Quarterly* 27, no. 6 (2009): 835–866, https://doi.org/10.1080/07418820903419010; J. Lydon et al., *Coming Out of Concrete Closets: A Report on Black and Pink's LGBTQ Prisoner Survey* (Boston: Black and Pink, 2015), www.issuelab.org.

13. Allen J. Beck, "Sexual Victimization in Prisons and Jails Reported by Inmates, 2011–2012" (Office of Justice Programs, US Department of Justice, December 2014), www.bjs.gov.

14. Dareh Gregorian, "Dozens of Cons Eye Sex Swap," *New York Post*, July 18, 2003, 4.

15. In Black and Pink's 2015 survey of 1,100 LGBTQ prisoners incarcerated at the time of the survey, 85 percent had been placed in solitary confinement during their time in prison or jail. Lydon et al., *Coming Out of Concrete Closets*. See also '*It's War in Here': A Report on the Treatment of Transgender and Intersex People in New York State Men's Prisons* (New York: Sylvia Rivera Law Project, 2007), 18, https://srlp.org.

16. Lisa Guenther, *Solitary Confinement: Social Death and Its Afterlives* (Minneapolis: Minnesota University Press, 2013); Rosenblum, "'Trapped' in Sing-Sing," 530.

17. Associated Press, "California Is First to Pay for Prisoner's Sex-Reassignment Surgery," *New York Times*, January 7, 2017, www.nytimes.com. Indeed, in at least three cases in which courts ordered correctional systems to provide gender affirming surgery, prisoners who had been denied parole were summarily granted it. Beth Schwartzapfel, "Were These Transgender Prisoners Paroled—or Just Kicked Out?" *Marshall Project*, October 8, 2015, www.themarshallproject.org.

18. Douglas Routh et al., "Transgender Inmates in Prisons: A Review of Applicable Statutes and Policies," *International Journal of Offender Therapy and Comparative Criminology* 61, no. 6 (2017): 645–666. Since that article went to press, some state correction departments listed in it as having exclusions on transition-related health care have changed their policies, including Connecticut, Florida, Maine, Rhode Island, and Vermont. See also Elliot Oberholtzer, "The Dismal State of Transgender Incarceration Politics" (Prison Policy Initiative, November 8, 2017), www.prisonpolicy.org.

19. See for example, the TGI Justice Project (www.tgijp.org), Sylvia Rivera Law Project (www.srlp.org), and the now defunct Queers for Economic Justice.

20. Morgan Bassichis, Alexander Lee, and Dean Spade, "Building an Abolitionist Trans & Queer Movement with Everything We've Got," in *Captive Genders: Trans Embodiment and the Prison Industrial Complex*, ed. Eric A. Stanley and Nat Smith (Oakland: AK Press, 2011), 15–40; Lydon et al., "Coming out of Concrete Closets"; Spade, *Normal Life*.

21. The Williams Institute estimates that about 0.6 percent of the adult population in the United States identify as transgender. Flores et al., "How Many Adults Identify as Transgender?" A meta-analysis of large population-based samples came up with a slightly smaller number: 0.39 percent of the adult US population, or 390 per 100,000 people, identified as transgender or answered a question indicating that their gender identity was not congruent with the sex assigned at birth. Esther L. Meerwijk and Jae M. Sevelius, "Transgender Population Size in the United States: A Meta-regression of Population-Based Probability Samples," *American Journal of Public Health* 107, no. 2 (February 2017): E1–8.

22. "Transgender Incarcerated People in Crisis," *Lambda Legal*, accessed August 20, 2020, www.lambdalegal.org.

23. James et al., "Report of the 2015 U.S. Transgender Survey," 190.

24. Thomas P. Bonczar, "Prevalence of Imprisonment in the U.S. Population, 1974–2001," *Bureau of Justice Statistics*, Special Report, August 2003, www.bjs.gov. This report predates the US Transgender Survey by fifteen years, but its analysis centers on the jump in incarceration rates since 1974. By 2001, the US incarceration rate was nearing its peak.

25. Jaime M. Grant, Lisa A. Mottet, and Justin Tanis, *Injustice at Every Turn: A Report of the National Transgender Discrimination Survey* (Washington, DC: National Center for Transgender Equality and the National Gay and Lesbian Task Force, 2011), 65, www.transequality.org.

26. James et al., "Report of the 2015 U.S. Transgender Survey," 190. Another study, of prisoners in the California prison system, found that transgender prisoners are disproportionately Black compared to the general prison population. Sexton, Jenness, and Sumner, "Where the Margins Meet," 12. See also S. L. Reisner, Zinzi Bailey, and Jae Sevelius, "Racial/Ethnic Disparities in History of Incarceration, Experiences of Victimization, and Associated Health Indicators among Transgender Women in the U.S.," *Women Health* 54, no. 8 (2014): 657–767. The rate of incarceration for all Black people in the United States, based on US census data, was five times that of whites. Leah Sakala, *Breaking Down Mass Incarceration in the 2010 Census: State-by-State Incarceration Rates by Race/Ethnicity* (Northampton, MA: Prison Policy Initiative, May 28, 2014), www.prisonpolicy.org. On the declining difference in the racial incarceration gap, see John Gramlich, *The Gap Between the Number of Blacks and Whites in Prison Is Shrinking* (Washington, DC: Pew Research Center, April 30, 2019), www.pewresearch.org. Overall, women's incarceration rates are not falling nearly as quickly as men's; in some jurisdictions,

they are rising. On the difference in incarceration rates between men and women, see Wendy Sawyer, *The Gender Divide: Tracking Women's State Prison Growth* (Northampton, MA: Prison Policy Initiative, January 9, 2018), www.prisonpolicy.org.

27. Alexander, *The New Jim Crow*; Jackie Wang, *Carceral Capitalism* (Cambridge, MA: Semiotext(e), 2018).

28. Anne E. Fehrenbacher et al., "Exposure to Police and Client Violence Among Incarcerated Female Sex Workers in Baltimore City, Maryland," *American Journal of Public Health* 110, no. S1 (2020): S152. On the connections—or possible lack thereof—between transphobia and the heightened vulnerability—from crime, from the police—that trans sex workers face, Mirha-Soleil Ross puts it bluntly. Looking at cases of trans sex workers who were killed by clients who didn't realize they were trans, Ross points out that transphobia can't be the only explanation for the murders of trans sex workers. "My main request is for transgender activists to stop their sinister appropriation of the abuse and violence that transsexual and transvestite prostitutes endure on every continent." Viviane Namaste, "'Activists Can't Go on Forever Acting in the Abstract.' An Interview with Mirha-Soleil Ross," in *Sex Change, Social Change*, 2nd ed. (Toronto: Women's Press, 2011), 122.

29. Ruth Wilson Gilmore, *Golden Gulag: Prisons, Surplus, Crisis, and Opposition in Globalizing California* (Los Angeles: University of California Press, 2007), 70–78.

30. James et al., "Report of the 2015 U.S. Transgender Survey," 6.

31. Certainly, as Joey L. Mogul, Andrea J. Ritchie, and Kay Whitlock point out, emphasizing the policing of queer communities is often a necessary rejoinder to "theories and scholarship that have focused almost exclusively on the disproportionate and selective policing of racial 'minority' communities, presumed on a belief that these communities are monolithic when it comes to class, gender, and sexuality." Joey L. Mogul, Andrea J. Ritchie, and Kay Whitlock, *Queer (In)Justice: The Criminalization of LGBT People in the United States* (Boston: Beacon Press, 2011), 51.

32. Elías Cosenza Krell, "Is Transmisogyny Killing Trans Women of Color? Black Trans Feminisms and the Exigencies of White Femininity," *TSQ: Transgender Studies Quarterly* 4, no. 2 (2017): 226.

33. Nira Yuval-Davis, "Intersectionality and Feminist Politics," *European Journal of Women's Studies* 13, no. 3 (2006): 197.

34. C. Riley Snorton, *Black on Both Sides: A Racial History of Trans Identity* (Minneapolis: University of Minnesota Press, 2017); Julian Gill-Peterson, *Histories of the Transgender Child* (Minneapolis: University of Minnesota Press, 2018); Emily Skidmore, "Constructing the 'Good Transsexual': Christine Jorgensen, Whiteness, and Heteronormativity in the Mid-Twentieth-Century Press," *Feminist Studies* 37, no. 2 (2011): 270–300; Che Gossett, "Blackness and the Trouble of Trans Visibility," in *Trap Door: Trans Cultural Production and the Politics of Visibility*, ed. Reina Gossett, Eric A. Stanley, and Johanna Burton (Cambridge, MA: MIT Press, 2017), 183–90; Snorton, *Black on Both Sides*; Treva Ellison et al., "We Got Issues: Toward a Black Trans★/Studies," *TSQ: Transgender Studies Quarterly* 4, no. 2 (2017): 162–169.

35. Grant, Mottet, and Tanis, *Injustice at Every Turn*, 178.

36. Dylan Rodriguez, *Forced Passages: Imprisoned Radical Intellectuals and the US Prison Regime* (Minneapolis: University of Minnesota Press, 2005), 170.

37. Bernard E. Harcourt, *The Illusion of Free Markets* (Cambridge, MA: Harvard University Press, 2011), 41.

38. Wang, *Carceral Capitalism*; Elizabeth Hinton, *From the War on Poverty to the War on Drugs: The Making of Mass Incarceration in America* (Cambridge, MA: Harvard University Press, 2016); Naomi Murakawa, *The First Civil Right: How Liberals Built Prison America* (New York: Oxford University Press, 2014); Andrew Dilts, *Punishment and Inclusion: Race, Membership, and the Limits of American Liberalism* (New York: Fordham University Press, 2014); Angela Y. Davis, *Are Prisons Obsolete?* (New York: Seven Stories Press, 2011); Mary Fainsod Katzenstein, Leila Mohsen Ibrahim, and Katherine D. Rubin, "The Dark Side of American Liberalism and Felony Disenfranchisement," *Perspectives on Politics* 8, no. 4 (December 2010): 1035–1054; Wacquant, *Punishing the Poor*; Gilmore, *Golden Gulag*; Rodriguez, *Forced Passages*.

39. Denny Dallas, "The Clarke Institute of Psychiatry: Canada's Shame," *Transgender Forum*, April 13, 1998.

40. Andrea James, "Toronto's Clarke Institute (Now CAMH) and Eugenics," accessed 25 September 2020, www.transgendermap.com.

41. Robert Dickey, "Gender Dysphoria and Antisocial Behavior," in *Clinical Management of Gender Identity Disorders in Children and Adults*, ed. R. Blanchard and B. W. Steiner (Washington, DC: American Psychiatric Press, 1990), 196.

42. Maxine Peterson et al., "Transsexuals Within the Prison System: An International Survey of Correctional Services Policies," *Behavioral Sciences and the Law* 14 (1996): 221.

43. Dickey, "Gender Dysphoria and Antisocial Behavior," 195, 197.

44. Peterson et al., "Transsexuals within the Prison System," 221.

45. Peterson et al., "Transsexuals within the Prison System," 226.

46. Brady Thomas Heiner, "The American Archipelago: The Global Circuit of Carcerality and Torture," in *Colonial and Global Interfacings: Imperial Hegemonies and Democratizing Resistances*, ed. Gary Backhaus and John Murungi (Newcastle upon Tyne: Cambridge Scholars Publishing, 2007), 85.

47. Michel Foucault, "Questions on Geography," in *Power/Knowledge: Selected Interviews and Other Writings, 1972–1977*, trans. Colin Gordon (New York: Pantheon, 1980), 68.

48. Foucault, "Questions on Geography," 177.

49. Regina Kunzel, *Criminal Intimacy: Prison and the Uneven History of Modern American Society* (Chicago: University of Chicago Press, 2008), 1.

50. Elizabeth A. Povinelli, *Economies of Abandonment: Social Belonging and Endurance in Late Liberalism* (Durham, NC: Duke University Press, 2011), 3.

51. Sarah Lamble, "Queer Necropolitics and the Expanding Carceral State: Interrogating Sexual Investments in Punishment," *Law Critique* 24, no. 3 (2013): 244. See also Stephen Dillon, "The Only Freedom I Can See: Imprisoned Queer Writing and the Politics of the Unimaginable," in *Captive Genders: Trans Embodiment and the Prison Industrial Complex*, ed. Eric A. Stanley and Nat Smith (Oakland, CA: AK Press, 2011), 169–187.

52. Rodriguez, *Forced Passages*, 185.

53. *Maggert v. Hanks*, 131 F.3d 670, 672 (1997).

54. Richard Posner, "An Economic Theory of the Criminal Law," *Columbia Law Review* 85, no. 6 (1985): 1195. See also Gary S. Becker, "Crime and Punishment: An Economic Approach," in *Essays in the Economics of Crime and Punishment*, ed. Gary S. Becker and William M. Landes (Cambridge, MA: National Bureau of Economic Research, 1974), 1–54.

55. Wisconsin Legislature Representatives Scott Suder and Ted Kanavas, " 'Inmate Sex Change Prevention Act' Becomes Law," *Press Release*, January 6, 2006.

56. Attorney Jennifer Levi, who has been litigating on behalf of transgender prisoners for some time as an attorney with GLBTQ Legal Advocates & Defenders, points out that media and popular criticism of proposals to provide such care to prisoners has centered, in part, on the very idea that trans prisoners should "not receive medical care that those outside prison walls may not be able to afford." Jennifer Levi, "Transgender Exceptionalism Should Not Cloud Legal Analysis," *Jurist*, October 16, 2012, www.jurist.org.

57. Movement Advancement Project, "Equality Maps: Healthcare Laws and Policies," accessed 25 September 2020, www.lgbtmap.org.

58. Kellan E. Baker, "The Future of Transgender Coverage," *New England Journal of Medicine* 376, no. 19 (May 11, 2017): 1801–1814.

59. *Bostock v. Clayton County*, 140 S. Ct. 1731, 1741 (2020).

60. *Asapansa-Johnson Walker v. Azar, Memorandum and Order*, No. 20-CV-2834 (E.D.N.Y. August 20, 2020), 2.

61. It's also possible that this conservative Supreme Court will allow a religious exemption for health care providers, granting them wide latitude to refuse to provide care to transgender people.

62. National Center for Transgender Equality, "ENDA by the Numbers," accessed August 16, 2014, www.transequality.org.

63. *Bostock v. Clayton County*, 140 S. Ct. 1731 (2020).

64. Berlant, "Slow Death."

Section VII

Historicizing Trans

31 Trans, Time, and History

Leah DeVun and Zeb Tortorici

Leah DeVun and Zeb Tortorici's "Trans, Time, and History" was originally published as the introduction to a special issue of *TSQ*, "Trans★historicities" in 2018. Trans studies raises an important metahistorical question: how should one think about the demonstrable variability of sex/gender/body/identity configurations before the current concept of "transgender" existed? The first documented appearance in print of a *trans+gender* word (i.e., *transgenderism*) dates to 1965, in a medical textbook. Between the later 1960s and early 1990s, *trans+gender* words were used in two mutually exclusive ways—first, as a supposedly more accurate way of describing what was then called *transsexualism*; second, as a name for trans people who didn't seek medically assisted transition that distinguished them from those who did. By the later 1980s, some trans people in the United States were beginning to use *transgender* to name the entire spectrum of gender diversity; this is the sense that Leslie Feinberg had in mind when writing *Transgender Liberation: A Movement Whose Time Has Come* in 1992, which catapulted the term into common usage. But as DeVun and Tortorici make clear, *transgender* is a difficult word to use without anachronism. Consequently, questions of change, temporality, chronology, periodization, and nomenclature are quite central to critical trans scholarship. What is ultimately at stake, they argue, in grappling with "transgender history," is not just the recovery of a useable past but how we understand our own position within time as we read, think, write, and act.

Questions of time and chronology have risen to the forefront of scholarship in queer and trans studies in recent years.[1] Carolyn Dinshaw has advocated for anachronistic "touches" across time, Roderick Ferguson has envisioned queer "palimpsests with residues of earlier discourses and histories," and C. Riley Snorton has highlighted intersections of blackness and trans as a condition of temporal possibility—as "movement with no clear origin and no point of arrival" (Dinshaw 1999; Dinshaw et al. 2007: 180; Snorton 2017: 2). Beyond this, a wave of new conferences and publications has explored "trans temporalities," further demonstrating how methods of accounting for and thinking through time have become increasingly relevant to scholarship on trans subjects (e.g., Lau 2016; Fisher, Phillips, and Katri 2017).[2] In an influential essay, Kadji Amin has welcomed this "critical focus on the temporal underpinnings of transgender as a historical category [which] . . . may open the way toward a more transformative politics of justice" (2014: 219). It is to this crux of temporality and temporal crossing—always linked to overlapping modes of history, historiography, and historicity—that our issue of *TSQ* speaks. "Trans★historicities" joins surging interest in gender and sexuality as they relate to both patterns of time and the writing of history, advancing

DOI: 10.4324/9781003206255-39

critical trans politics while simultaneously articulating and confounding our investments in reading, engaging, and cocreating historical pasts.

The notion of a historical past is intricately interwoven with considerations of chronology (time as succession), periodization (time as segmented into units), and the specific cultural experiences of movement and change that undergird how we view our position within time. Efforts to move ostensibly backward in time—to the historical underpinnings of trans—have long been attractive to scholars and activists. Pioneering works such as Kate Bornstein's 1994 *Gender Outlaw* and Leslie Feinberg's 1996 *Transgender Warriors* laid unabashed ancestral claim to gender-nonconforming lives in the past, and they did so to legitimate trans identities in the present. Bornstein, in ways that remain problematic yet illustrative for us, invoked the history of indigenous cultures, writing, "My ancestors were performers. In life. The earliest shamanic rituals involved women and men exchanging genders. Old, old rituals. Top-notch performances. Life and death stuff. We're talking cross-cultural here. We're talking rising way way way above being a man or a woman. That's how my ancestors would fly. That's how my ancestors would talk with the goddesses and the gods. Old rituals" (143). Here, Bornstein draws (necessarily ahistorical) points of comparison between twentieth-century trans experience and that of a utopic, precolonial past, with which she expresses a deep affective bond. Bornstein's claim also naturalizes gender variance in the present by appealing to a shared transgender history, bracketing the "shamanic" as a romanticized, primordial system that exists outside civilizational time and place. As Evan B. Towle and Lynn Marie Morgan have noted, "The danger of portraying the transgender native in this way is that it can perpetuate stereotypes about non-Western societies, with their 'shamanic rituals' and panoply of gods" (2002: 478). It also risks consigning Native peoples to a past that is seemingly irreconcilable with the present or the conditions of modernity.

[. . .]

In some ways this trajectory of trans history resembles that of gay and lesbian history, which once saw social historians and cultural critics looking to the distant past to historicize same-sex desire and locate the origins of LGB identity. These early "ancestral" histories gave way to queer theories that—to use the phrase of Eve Kosofsky Sedgwick—drew on Michel Foucault's "Great Paradigm Shift" to suggest that homosexuality emerged as a discrete identity only toward the end of the nineteenth century (the debate between the two approaches became known, famously, as "essentialism" versus "constructionism"). Queer critiques emphasized the alterity of the past, respect for the contingency of historical phenomena, and the perils inherent in reading contemporary identities backward in time (Doan 2013). Indeed, such projects—inspired by Foucault's *History of Sexuality* [. . .] have tended to foreclose the possibility of any continuous, transhistorical narrative of LGB experience that precedes the formation of modern concepts of sex and selfhood (Halperin 2002; Herring 2007). If we extend this logic, as some scholars have suggested, one cannot write a parallel history of "transgender" or "transsexual" before the advent of the very vocabulary that generated its subject; to do so would risk divesting past gender practice of what made it meaningful in its own time and place. It might also erase what scholar-activist Reina Gossett has called the "different and beautifully expansive" language of gender diversity in history (Boag 2005: 479–480; Beemyn 2013: 113; Walker 2015).

Unsatisfied by this stark choice between ancestral essentialism, on the one hand, and radical altericism, on the other, some scholars have preferred theories of queer or trans temporality—that is, visions of time as asynchronous and nonnormative, and thus enabling of community formation, often through "touches" or "binds" that connect marginalized peoples across time (Dinshaw 1999; Dinshaw et al. 2007; Freeman 2010).[3] Imagination often functions in such works as a means to rethink the past and our relationship to it: speculation about what might have happened, strategic anachronisms, and even defiance against the "tyranny of historicism" (Freccero 2006; Nardizzi, Guy-Bray, and Stockton 2009: 1) have all become hallmarks of queerly temporal projects. [. . .]

History often lends legitimacy to a community's claim that it belongs in the here and now. Given the frequent citation of history by policy makers, there is no doubt that—at least in certain contexts—we imagine a political value in rendering communities visible within history (Currah 2017: 449–450). Take, for instance, the deeply historical statement on the occasion of the North Carolina "bathroom law" of 2016 by US Attorney General Loretta Lynch (2016): "This is not the first time that we have seen discriminatory responses to historic moments of progress for our nation. We saw it in the Jim Crow laws that followed the Emancipation Proclamation. We saw it in fierce and widespread resistance to *Brown v. Board of Education*. And we saw it in the proliferation of state bans on same-sex unions intended to stifle any hope that gay and lesbian Americans might one day be afforded the right to marry." In making such a statement, Lynch embedded the issue of trans access to bathrooms within a long genealogy of political struggles for rights—visualizing an overarching narrative of national progress—amid our inherited legacies of racism and homophobia.

Yet, as Reina Gossett, Eric A. Stanley, and Johanna Burton (2017) have noted, increasing trans visibility creates a double bind: while it promises legitimacy for certain individuals, it erases others, especially those who are economically precarious, who are of color, or whose means of self-representation are limited by systemic racism and sexism. Similar erasures result from what Johannes Fabian has termed the "denial of coevalness," that is, when academics write about racialized others in the present as if they lived in the past, or as if certain people's presents represent other people's futures (Fabian [1983] 2014: 35; Rifkin 2017). As Fabian shows, "such use of Time almost invariably is made for the purpose of distancing those who are observed from the Time of the observer," for they are negated a place in "our" here and now ([1983] 2014: 25). With this in mind, scholars have urged trans studies as a field to reject any interpretive stance that views racialized or "non-European gender-variant cultural practices as timeless 'traditions' bound to a particular location to which they are indigenous and authentic, and which are perpetually at risk of being polluted or diluted by the introduction of exogenous modern forms" (Stryker and Aizura 2013: 9).

How might we deal with these multiple and interconnected binds—of sameness and difference, presence and absence, "tradition" and "modernity"—while also acknowledging our own cravings for (queer and trans) histories? What is it about the gesture of comparison to the past—be it ancestral, asynchronous, or properly contextualized—that provokes such urgency now? How are scholars, artists, curators, and others negotiating these tensions through transhistorical work? We envision this issue as a moment of pause to reflect on new and diverse projects that explore these questions, and that offer a productive set of approaches to trans, time, and history that we call here "trans*historicities."

History and Its Others

Authors Susan Stryker and Aren Z. Aizura devote a section of their anthology *Transgender Studies Reader 2* to "Timely Matters: Temporality and Trans-Historicity." It is to this latter term, *trans-historicity*, that we turn our attention, and that serves as an inspiration for our framing of this issue. "Timely Matters" showcases the methodologically, conceptually, and geopolitically diverse work of five scholars— Mary Weismantel, Deborah A. Miranda, Karma Lochrie, Robert Hill, and Afsaneh Najmabadi—as they engage in cross-temporal analyses that resist ahistorical equivalencies. Through their essays, in the words of Stryker and Aizura, such scholars "envision different methods for excavating pasts that certainly contained gender-variant cultural practices, without necessarily imposing the name 'transgender' on those historical moments" (2013: 11). In doing so, they offer trans as a methodology for thinking about the potential of texts, bodies, artifacts, and narratives from different times and places to reshape our present. They are also attuned to questions of historical context and change over time (whether or not they explicitly use the term *historicity*).

While these scholars differ in their specific topics and approaches, what they share is an interest in making cross-temporal and interdisciplinary comparisons of "gender-variant cultural practices," yet without essentializing those practices or yoking them to progressive teleologies or to timeless traditions. This speaks to the possibility of writing trans history that precedes the relatively recent coinage of the terms *transsexual* and *transgender*—a project that scholars have already begun in earnest (e.g., Stryker 2008; Chiang 2012; Strassfeld 2013; Cleves 2014, 2018; Sears 2015; Karras and Linkinen 2016; Skidmore 2017; Campanile, Carlà-Uhink, and Facella 2017). Indeed, we do not abbreviate all histories of gender simply because past categories accord imprecisely with present ones; we write about women in the distant past even as we acknowledge that premodern subjects dovetail imperfectly with the modern term *woman* (which, of course, few gender studies scholars would characterize as a coherent and intelligible category even now). As Stryker and Aizura write, the field of trans studies wonders "why we think 'man' and 'woman' are any more transhistorical, or less contingent, than any other category of identity, and why we persist in the presentist fallacy of ontologizing a current framework and imposing it on the strangeness of the past" (2013: 6). Allowing the "strangeness of the past" to resonate across a chronologically expansive, historicized framework, as scholars have already suggested, can prompt us to view with new skepticism the seemingly unambiguous categories of "man" and "woman" (Block 2014). Such studies can also enrich our understanding of past gender variance, while preventing us from drawing facile conclusions about what is new or unique about our own era.[4]

[Our goal] is to theorize *historicity* in relation to *trans*, taking Stryker and Aizura's formulation of "transhistoricity" as an invitation to think more carefully about their suturing. As we suggest below, both of these concepts are complex, paradoxical, and mutually illuminating: trans helps us think about time, historical analysis helps us think about trans, and historicity helps us interrogate the nature of evidence and its attendant notions of facticity and historical authenticity. We focus attention here on the prefix *trans* as a method for understanding crossings of time—as in the "trans-temporal" or "transhistorical"—and in ways that encompass the multiple and paradoxical meanings that have accrued to the term *historicity*. In doing so, we seek to put new scholarship—bridging trans studies, historicist inquiry, and queer temporality—into productive conversation to think specifically about history, its meanings, and its place in identity and community formation.

Our approach necessarily challenges the ways in which some queer theorists have set up the figure of "the historian" as a straw man, as if the discipline of history has a priori investments in empiricism and positivist claims of historical truth (for a summary, see Traub 2013; Doan 2013). In our view, such representations unfairly caricature historicist methods by ignoring how historians, at least since the nineteenth century, have engaged with and deeply theorized discursive constructions of (the discipline of) history, as well as their own conflicted relations with archival sources and other forms of historical evidence. While some historians no doubt still view their profession as a transparent retrieval of historical "reality"—keeping aloft the sentiments of nineteenth-century German historian Leopold von Ranke, who claimed that the goal of history was "to show how it essentially was (*wie es eigentlich gewesen*)" (Ranke 2011: 86)—historians have long grappled with problems of narration, representation, speculation, and imagination, as well as with multiple ways of accounting for time and its progression. But, even Ranke himself deeply questioned the meaning and so-called authenticity of historical sources (Berding 2005: 47).

At the same time, historians must acknowledge that in recent years much inventive rethinking and recasting of terms near and dear to them—*chronology, archives, the past*—have taken place outside the discipline of history (e.g., Cvetkovich 2003; Love 2007; Arondekar 2009; Freeman 2010). With this in mind, we suggest that responses to difficult questions about the methods and meanings of historical practice must be situated in debates across the disciplines and yet on the terrain of history. To advance this project, our present issue of *TSQ* unites perspectives from scholars located inside and outside the historical disciplines to look closely at how we might write histories of "trans before trans" and, beyond that, how the conjoining of *trans* and *historicity* might reconfigure our notions of chronology and periodization more broadly.

Genealogies of Historicity

[. . .] Why *historicity*? What does that term and concept offer us that *history* alone does not? Stryker and Aizura's use of *trans-historicity* (as opposed to *trans-history*) is suggestive, especially because they do not define the term explicitly in their volume. Its open-ended use points to just how much might be filled in, something that an even partial genealogy of the word suggests. *Historicity* is a term fraught with meaning, historically labile, and resistant to easy categorization. Its richness and unfixity resemble nothing so much as the heterogeneity and indeterminacy that we tend to associate with *queer* and *trans*. The linkage of *trans* and *historicity* in *trans*historicity*, moreover, suggests how these two analytics might be mobilized together usefully in ways that are relevant to the time-based relations we explore here.

[. . .] Although never part of a unitary method, *historicity* can be traced back at least to the eighteenth century, when the concept became embedded in debates about the nature of time, as well as in considerations of the relationship between past, present, and future. *Historicity* has its etymological roots in the Latin *historicus*, which conveys a sense of both "history" and "the historical," and, at its most basic level, *historicity* is about making sense of things within their proper socio-temporal contexts. The *Oxford English Dictionary* defines the term today simply as "historical authenticity," and, indeed, *historicity* is often used interchangeably with *historicality* (that is, the historical actuality of persons, objects, and events as opposed to their grounding in myth, legend, or fiction). Yet we follow here scholarship that suggests that historicity's meanings are both more subtle and more capacious. Scholars have begun to identify *historicity* as a useful analytic—along the lines of *spatiality* or *materiality*—that communicates a dynamic, mutually conditioning relationship between subjects and objects (Hirsch and Stewart 2005). According to Eric Hirsch and Charles Stewart—editors of a special issue of *History and Anthropology* dedicated to "Ethnographies of Historicity"—*historicity* "draws attention to the connections between past, present and future without the assumption that events/time are a line between happenings 'adding up' to history. Whereas 'history' isolates the past, historicity focuses on the complex temporal nexus of past-present-future" (262). While we disagree that history (as a discipline, practice, method, or lived experience) necessarily "isolates the past," in what follows here we note that the operations identified by Hirsch and Stewart are hardly a new feature of *historicity*: for at least two centuries, the term has been essential to considerations of just this problem of individual and collective experiences of time.

[. . .]

At its heart, historicity gave voice to impassioned critiques of the absolute—that is, it was invoked to make arguments *against* the existence of divine, natural, universal, or other fundamental laws, including reason itself—that supposedly governed human experience and provided temporal continuity through historical linearity. Embedded in the term was a distrust of any grand theory or absolute narrative of world history or development. [. . .]

Perhaps, most importantly, the concept of historicity [. . .] came to subject everything to processes of historical change. Thus, even the divine was subject to the effects of temporality, a stance that made virtually all phenomena available for philosophical and political critique.

From at least the nineteenth century, historicity was therefore wrapped up in explorations of the nature of time and its progression, and in deeply ontological questions of historical being. Moreover, historicity also stoked debates about history's relation to empirical truth: whereas some cited the concept of historicity to bolster the validity of history as a universal science, others, including Friedrich Nietzsche (1844–1900), pointed to the inherent dangers of ever envisioning history as an empirical field. For Nietzsche, history as "science" led to a fixation on the past and relativized all cultural phenomenon (Wittkau-Horgby 2005: 71–72).

A host of later continental philosophers—including Martin Heidegger (1889–1976), Jean-Paul Sartre (1905–80), Michel Foucault (1926–84), and Jacques Derrida (1930–2004), among others—were equally, if not more, invested in the concept of historicity. For Foucault, historicity's potential lay in its ability to account for processes of change, particularly the ways in which discrete cultures forged systems of power, through which identity could be produced or subverted (Malpas 2006: 60). As Foucault reminds us in *The Order of Things*, "a profound historicity penetrates into the heart of things, isolates and defines them in their own coherence, imposes upon them the forms of order implied by the continuity of time," but it too resists those very temporal taxonomies (2002b: xxv). Building on notions of historicity in existentialism, as well as of sequence and narrative among *Annales* school historians (including Fernand Braudel, Marc Bloch, and Lucien Fèbvre), Foucault, in the preface to volume 2 of *The History of Sexuality*, noted that his own turn to "the very historicity of forms of experience" led him to try to "bring to light the domain where the formation, development, and transformation of forms of experience can situate themselves: that is, a history of thought" (1984: 334). As Foucault explained, history was best understood in this context as discontinuous in sequence and constructed of multiple temporal series that "overlap and intersect, without one being able to reduce them to a linear schema" (2002a: 9). In Foucault's and his contemporaries' works, historicity could thus provide a means to interrogate linear or teleological notions of time, to foreground ruptures and discontinuities, and to evaluate the existence of transcendental ideas and experiences. As the literary theorist Krzysztof Ziarek has indicated, "historicity acts as a force of temporal dislocation. [It] both lets the event emerge into presence and withholds (full) presence from it, keeping the event disjointed and incomplete" (2001: 14). From the nineteenth to the twenty-first century, historicity traveled a long way from its earliest associations with "historical authenticity."

[. . .]

Trans*Historicity's Radical Potential

Lest we think these opinions all the vestiges of a stale debate (tied to white, mostly dead European philosophers and historians), historicity continues to serve as an epistemological and ontological touchstone for scholars today, especially those working in critical race theory, posthumanism, colonial studies, and decolonial historiography. In *Silencing the Past: Power and the Production of History*, for instance, anthropologist Michel-Rolph Trouillot distinguishes what he calls "the two sides of historicity" (2015: 23). For him, "historicity 1" refers to the materiality of the sociohistorical process, pointing to those concrete traces— bodies and artifacts, buildings and monuments—of the past. On the other hand, "historicity 2" signifies future historical narratives, which are only partly based on those material traces (29). He asserts that only a focus on the processes and conditions of the production of historical narratives "can uncover the ways in which the two sides of historicity intertwine in a particular context. Only through that overlap can we discover the differential exercise of power that makes some narratives possible and silences others" (25). Historicity, in these two senses, functions to expose the fundamental power imbalances that go into the creation of any—though especially colonial and national—historical narratives.

Historian Marisa J. Fuentes also accounts for the differential exercise of power and its effects on the narration of history in her book *Dispossessed Lives: Enslaved Women, Violence, and the Archive*. She takes up the long discursive tradition of historicity to suggest a mode of *mutilated historicity*, which refers to "the violent condition in which enslaved women appear in the archive disfigured and violated. Mutilated historicity exemplifies how their bodies and flesh become 'inscribed' with the text/violence of slavery. As a result, the *quality* of their historicization remains degraded in our present attempts to recreate their everyday experiences" (2016: 16). The historical record of slavery in Barbados (as elsewhere), in Fuentes's view, consigns enslaved women to a mode of historicity that is precarious at best. Fuentes, as a result, turns to an imaginative encounter with her subjects—a story of what might have happened—through which she harnesses a sense of the possible and finds "an opening to represent the lives of the nameless and the forgotten, to reckon with loss, and 'to respect the limits of what cannot be known'" (141). Fuentes's approach forces us to consider what it means to narrate from a place of silence, as well as to feel deeply the entanglement of present with past—and its deep wells of terror and violence, which represent a continuing "danger to the researcher who sees her own ancestors in these accounts" (146). In Fuentes's work, historicity operates once more as a vehicle for questions of power, agency, speculation, and representation in relation to the narratives and life experiences of enslaved women in the Caribbean, and beyond.

Posthumanist scholars have also left their conceptual mark on historicity, in part by applying it to colonial and postcolonial subjects who have been denied historical consciousness by certain European travelogues, Western historiographies, and strains of anthropological discourse. Anthropologist Neil L. Whitehead, in *Histories and Historicities in Amazonia*, applies the concept of historicity to a range of Amazonian indigenous groups—the Guajá, Wapishana, Dekuana, and Patamuna—who have often been mistakenly perceived as having no conceptualization of "history" as we know it. Whitehead tells us that, for him, *historicities* refers to "the investigation of the cultural schema and subjective attitudes that make the past meaningful," whether or not those pasts operate along constructions of linear time (2003: xi). Whitehead's method operates partly by upending and inverting the originary Eurocentrism of the term *historicity*, and by challenging the temporal logic and absolute nature of settler colonialism (and settler colonial time). By grafting the concept of "historicities" onto Amazonian peoples and onto their nonlinear notions of history, Whitehead and his contributors show how, in comparison to the linear notions of time espoused by European colonizers and their mixed-race descendants in the nation-states that claim land throughout the Amazon River basin (namely, Bolivia, Brazil, Colombia, Ecuador, Guyana, Peru, Suriname, and Venezuela), many indigenous Amazonian peoples have radically different conceptions of both time and history.

If, as Hirsch and Stewart—along with other anthropologists and historians—argue, certain people's literatures, myths, dreams, songs, dramatic performances, perceptions of landscapes, and rituals of spirit possession can "usefully be classified as 'histories'" (even if neither teleological nor linear), then the very notion that any people could ever operate outside historicity is inherently flawed and colonialist (2005: 266). These scholars show that reconfiguring historicity to "index the fuller qualities of this social and personal *relationship* to the past and future makes it a complex social and performative condition, rather than an objectively determinable aspect of historical descriptions" (262). Trans*historicities, for us, conveys this sense of historicity as an embodied reality, an imaginative process, and a performative condition that resonates across time and place. Far from historicity implying any simple notion of "historical authenticity," as its dictionary definition would have it, it finds its own radical potential in this clash of meanings.

[. . .]

As many before us have pointed out, the "now" is fleeting, ephemeral, and lost to the past. Yet "now" might also be an "expanded now"; "now" might extend seamlessly into the past or future; "not now" might erupt into "now"—and all might become entangled in visions of a more radically transformative future (to paraphrase Dinshaw 1999; Muñoz 2009; Butler 2018). It is in this paradoxical, polyvalent spirit that we embrace "trans*historicities." As a synthetic paradigm, trans*historicities cinches together different ways of thinking about time, the historical record, and relations of power—including careful contextualizations, queer touches, temporal drags, and blatant distortions—each as a possibility among possibilities. Together, these fractious modes expand our knowledge of what history is and how we go about finding, crafting, and responding to it. We offer *trans*★ here with an asterisk to signal the overlapping, sometimes contradictory, modes of embodiment and representation that the term has come to signify. The plural *historicities*, moreover, rejects the imposition of any single narrative of events that would demand coherence or continuity, and—even as we acknowledge the complex emotions that often accompany our work—it refocuses us on the pleasures (of identifying or disidentifying; of avowing or disavowing; of imagining, filling in, or leaving blank) that arise when we—through language, image, and sound—are caught up in history. Trans*historicities, we hope, holds a space for these pleasures.

From: Leah DeVun and Zeb Tortorici, "Trans, Time, and History," in *TSQ: Transgender Studies Quarterly*, Volume 5, no. 4, pp. 518–539. Copyright 2018, Duke University Press. All rights reserved. Republished by permission of the copyright holder, Duke University Press. www.dukeupress.edu.

Notes

1. We would like to thank Susan Stryker, Paisley Currah, Abraham Weil, Leif Weatherby, Marvin J. Taylor, Carolyn Dinshaw, and all those who contributed to or gave feedback on this issue. We write this essay from our perspectives as cisgender, white queer historians (one the partner of a trans person) writing about trans, hermaphroditism, sodomy, and the "sins against nature" in a medieval (European), early modern (Iberian Atlantic), and colonial (Latin American) contexts.
2. See, for instance, papers presented at conferences such as "Trans Temporalities" at University of Toronto in April 2016; "Technicity, Temporality, and Embodiment," at University of Queensland and Southern Cross University in November 2016; and "Priors and Priorities: Conceiving Time and Other Bodies" at Harvard University in April 2018.
3. Despite any assumptions that the "turn" to temporality in queer studies represents the inauguration of a new field, de/postcolonial, critical race, and feminist scholarship has long theorized asynchronicity and the temporal dimensions of power; see, for instance, Bhabha 1997; Chakrabarty 2000; Quijano 2000; Lugones 2007, 2008. For some queer theorists, "queer time" occupies a position opposite "straight time," grounded in normative linear and teleological progress, as well as in diachronic history.
4. On broad chronological frameworks, see also the recent focus on "deep" or "big" history, "reception studies," and other modes of transhistorical comparison within the discipline of history, e.g., Shryock and Smail 2012; Hunt 2013; Holmes 2012; among others.

Bibliography

Aizura, Aren, et al. 2014. "Introduction." *TSQ* 1, no. 3: 308–319.

Amin, Kadji. 2014. "Temporality." *TSQ* 1, nos. 1–2: 219–222.

Arondekar, Anjali. 2009. *For the Record: On Sexuality and the Colonial Archive in India*. Durham, NC: Duke University Press.

Beemyn, Genny. 2013. "A Presence in the Past: A Transgender Historiography." *Journal of Women's History* 25, no. 4: 113–121.

Berding, Helmut. 2005. "Leopold von Ranke." In *The Discovery of Historicity in German Idealism and Historism*, edited by Peter Koslowski, 41–58. Berlin: Springer.

Bhabha, Homi K. 1997. "Race, Time, and the Revision of Modernity." In *Postcolonial Criticism*, edited by Bart Moore-Gilbert, Gareth Stanton, and Willy Maley, 166–190. London: Longman.

Block, Sharon. 2014. "Making Meaningful Bodies: Physical Appearance in Colonial Writings." *Early American Studies* 12, no. 3: 524–547.

Boag, Peter. 2005. "Go West Young Man, Go East Young Woman: Searching for the *Trans* in Western Gender History." *Western Historical Quarterly* 36, no. 4: 477–497.

Bornstein, Kate. 1994. *Gender Outlaw: On Men, Women, and the Rest of Us*. New York: Routledge.

Bunnin, Nicholas, and Jiyuan Yu. 2004. *The Blackwell Dictionary of Western Philosophy*. Oxford: Blackwell.

Butler, Judith. 2018. "Susceptibility and Solidarity." Lecture, New York University, February 12.

Campanile Domitilla, Filippo Carlà-Uhink, and Margherita Facella, eds. 2017. *TransAntiquity: Cross-Dressing and Transgender Dynamics in the Ancient World*. New York: Routledge.

Chakrabarty, Dipesh. 2000. *Provincializing Europe: Postcolonial Thought and Historical Difference*. Princeton, NJ: Princeton University Press.

Chiang, Howard, ed. 2012. *Transgender China*. New York: Palgrave Macmillan.

Cleves, Rachel Hope, ed. 2014. "Beyond the Binaries in Early America." Special issue, *Early American Studies* 12, no. 3.

———. 2018. "Six Ways of Looking at a Trans Man? The Life of Frank Shimer (1826–1901)." *Journal of the History of Sexuality* 27, no. 1: 32–62.

Cohen, G. A., et al. 1986. "Historical Inevitability and Human Agency in Marxism [and Discussion]." In "Predictability in Science and Society." Special issue, *Proceedings of the Royal Society of London. Series A, Mathematical and Physical Sciences* 407, no. 1832: 65–87.

Currah, Paisley. 2017. "Transgender Rights without a Theory of Gender?" *Tulsa Law Review* 52, no. 3: 441–451.

Cvetkovich, Ann. 2003. *An Archive of Feelings: Trauma, Sexuality, and Lesbian Public Cultures*. Durham, NC: Duke University Press.

Dinshaw, Carolyn. 1999. *Getting Medieval: Sexualities and Communities, Pre- and Postmodern*. Durham, NC: Duke University Press.

Dinshaw, Carolyn, et al. 2007. "Theorizing Queer Temporalities: A Roundtable Discussion." *GLQ* 13, nos. 2–3: 177–195.

Doan, Laura. 2013. *Disturbing Practices: History, Sexuality, and Women's Experience of Modern War*. Chicago: University of Chicago Press.

Fabian, Johannes. (1983) 2014. *Time and the Other: How Anthropology Makes Its Object*. New York: Columbia University Press.

Feinberg, Leslie. 1996. *Transgender Warriors: Making History from Joan of Arc to Dennis Rodman*. Boston: Beacon.

Fisher, Simon D. Elin, Rasheedah Phillips, and Ido H. Katri, eds. 2017. "Trans Temporalities." Special issue, *Somatechnics* 7, no. 1.

Foucault, Michel. 1984. "Preface to *The History of Sexuality*, Vol. 2." In *The Foucault Reader*, edited by Paul Rabinow, 333–339. New York: Pantheon.

———. 2002a. *Archaeology of Knowledge*. Translated by A. M. Sheridan Smith. London: Routledge.

———. 2002b. *The Order of Things: An Archaeology of Human Sciences*. New York: Routledge.

Freccero, Carla. 2006. *Queer/Early/Modern*. Durham, NC: Duke University Press.

Freeman, Elizabeth. 2010. *Time Binds: Queer Temporalities, Queer Histories*. Durham, NC: Duke University Press.

Fuentes, Marisa J. 2016. *Dispossessed Lives: Enslaved Women, Violence, and the Archive*. Philadelphia: University of Pennsylvania Press.

Gossett, Reina, Eric A. Stanley, and Johanna Burton, eds. 2017. *Trap Door: Trans Cultural Production and the Politics of Visibility*. Cambridge, MA: MIT Press.

Guignon, Charles B. 1983. *Heidegger and the Problem of Knowledge*. Indianapolis, IN: Hackett.

Halperin, David M. 2002. *How to Do the History of Homosexuality*. Chicago: University of Chicago Press.

Haritaworn, Jin, Tamsila Tauqir, and Esra Erdem. 2008. "Gay Imperialism: Gender and Sexuality Discourse in the 'War on Terror.'" In *Out of Place: Interrogating Silences in Queerness/ Raciality*, edited by Adi Kuntsman and Esperanza Miyake, 71–95. New York: Raw Nerve.

Hegel, Georg Wilhelm Friedrich. 1956. *The Philosophy of History*. Mineola, NY: Dover.

Herring, Scott. 2007. *Queering the Underworld: Slumming, Literature, and the Undoing of Gay and Lesbian History*. Chicago: University of Chicago Press.

Hirsch, Eric, and Charles Stewart. 2005. "Introduction: Ethnographies of Historicity." *History and Anthropology* 16, no. 3: 261–274.

Holmes, Brooke. 2012. *Gender: Antiquity and Its Legacy*. Oxford: Oxford University Press.

Hunt, Lynn. 2013. "Globalization and Time." In *Breaking Up Time: Negotiating the Borders Between Present, Past, and Future*, edited by Chris Lorenz and Berber Bevernage, 199–215. Gottingen: Vandenhoeck and Ruprecht.

Karras, Ruth Mazo, and Thomas Linkinen. 2016. "John/Eleanor Rykener Revisited." In *Founding Feminisms in Medieval Studies: Essays in Honor of E. Jane Burns*, edited by Laine E. Doggett and Daniel E. O'Sullivan, 111–122. Woodbridge, UK: Boydell and Brewer.

Koslowski, Peter. 2005. *The Discovery of Historicity in German Idealism and Historism*. Berlin: Springer.

Lau, Jacob Roberts. 2016. "Between the Times: Trans-Temporality and Historical Representation." PhD diss., University of California, Los Angeles.

Love, Heather. 2007. *Feeling Backward: Loss and the Politics of Queer History*. Cambridge, MA: Harvard University Press.

Lugones, María. 2007. "Heterosexualism and the Colonial/Modern Gender System." *Hypatia* 22, no. 1: 186–209.

———. 2008. "The Coloniality of Gender." *Worlds and Knowledges Otherwise* 2 (Spring): 1–17.

Lynch, Loretta E. 2015. "Attorney General Loretta E. Lynch Delivers Remarks at Press Conference Announcing Complaint Against the State of North Carolina to Stop Discrimination Against Transgender Individuals." Remarks as prepared for delivery. US Department of Justice. www.justice.gov/opa/speech/attorney-general-loretta-e-lynch-delivers-remarks-press-conference-announcing-complaint.

Malpas, Simon. 2006. "Historicism." In *The Routledge Companion to Critical Theory*, edited by Simon Malpas and Paul Wake, 55–65. New York: Routledge.

Mills, Robert. 2015. *Seeing Sodomy in the Middle Ages*. Chicago: University of Chicago Press.

Motta, Carlos, dir. 2015. *Deseos/تابغر*. Written by Maya Mikdashi and Carlos Motta. carlosmotta.com/project/2015-deseos-%D8%B1%D8%BA%D8%A8%D8%A7%D8%AA/.

Muñoz, José Esteban. 2009. *Cruising Utopia: The Then and There of Queer Futurity*. New York: New York University Press.

Nardizzi, Vin, Stephen Guy-Bray, and Will Stockton. 2009. "Queer Renaissance Historiography: Backward Gaze." In *Queer Renaissance Historiography: Backward Gaze*, edited by Vin Nardizzi, Stephen Guy-Bray, and Will Stockton, 1–12. Farnham, UK: Ashgate.

Puar, Jasbir. 2007. *Terrorist Assemblages: Homonationalism in Queer Times*. Durham, NC: Duke University Press.

Quijano, Anibal. 2000. "Colonialidad del poder, eurocentrismo y America latina" ("Coloniality of Power, Eurocentrism and Latin America"). In *Colonialidad del Saber: Eurocentrismo y Ciencias Sociales (Coloniality of Knowledge: Eurocentrism and Social Sciences)*, edited by Edgardo Lander, 201–246. Buenos Aires: CLACSO-UNESCO.

Ranke, Leopold von. 2011. *The Theory and Practice of History*. Edited by Georg G. Iggers. New York: Routledge.

Rifkin, Mark. 2017. *Beyond Settler Time: Temporal Sovereignty and Indigenous Self-Determination*. Durham, NC: Duke University Press.

Scott, Joan Wallach. 1999. *Gender and the Politics of History*. New York: Columbia University Press.

Sears, Clare. 2015. *Arresting Dress: Cross-Dressing, Law, and Fascination in Nineteenth-Century San Francisco*. Durham, NC: Duke University Press.

Shryock, Andrew, and Daniel Lord Smail, eds. 2012. *Deep History: The Architecture of Past and Present*. Berkeley: University of California Press.

Skidmore, Emily. 2017. *True Sex: The Lives of Trans Men at the Turn of the Twentieth Century*. New York: New York University Press.

Snorton, C. Riley. 2017. *Black on Both Sides: A Racial History of Trans Identity*. Minneapolis: University of Minnesota Press.

Strassfeld, Max K. 2013. "Classically Queer: Eunuchs and Androgynes in Rabbinic Literature." PhD diss., Stanford University.

Stryker, Susan. 2008. *Transgender History*. Berkeley, CA: Seal.

Stryker, Susan, and Aren Aizura. 2013. "Introduction: Transgender Studies 2.0." In *Transgender Studies Reader 2*, edited by Susan Stryker and Aren Aizura, 1–12. New York: Routledge.

Towle, Evan B., and Lynn Marie Morgan. 2002. "Romancing the Transgender Native: Rethinking the Use of the 'Third Gender' Concept." *GLQ* 8, no. 4: 469–497.

Traub, Valerie. 2013. "The New Unhistoricism in Queer Studies." *PMLA* 128, no. 1: 21–39.

Trouillot, Michel-Rolph. 2015. *Silencing the Past: Power and the Production of History*. Boston: Beacon.

Valentine, David. 2007. *Imagining Transgender: An Ethnography of a Category*. Durham, NC: Duke University Press.

Walker, John. 2015. "Connecting Stonewall to Baltimore: A Conversation with Some Filmmakers Exploring Trans History." *Splinter*, June 4. splinternews.com/connecting-stonewall-to-baltimore-a-conversation-with-1793848182.

White, Hayden. 2007. "Afterword: Manifesto Time." In *Manifestos for History*, edited by Sue Morgan, Keith Jenkins, and Alun Munslow, 220–231. London: Routledge.

Whitehead, Neil L. 2003. Introduction to *Histories and Historicities in Amazonia*, edited by Neil L. Whitehead, vii–xx. Lincoln: University of Nebraska Press.

Wittkau-Horgby, Annette. 2005. "Droysen and Nietzsche: Two Different Answers to the Discovery of Historicity." In *The Discovery of Historicity in German Idealism and Historism*, edited by Peter Koslowski, 59–76. Berlin: Springer.

Ziarek, Krzysztof. 2001. *The Historicity of Experience: Modernity, the Avant-Garde, and the Event*. Evanston, IL: Northwestern University Press.

32 Towards a Transgender Archaeology

A Queer Rampage Through Prehistory

Mary Weismantel

Cultural anthropologist Mary Weismantel has written widely on the material culture of pre-Columbian South America, with a particular emphasis on sex/gender, race, and the non/human. She is especially interested in the interpretative challenges of recovering information from non-literary material artifacts and how artifacts that provide evidence of strikingly different ways of understanding identity and embodiment in the deep past are presented in contemporary museums. In this thought experiment of an article, which first appeared in *The Transgender Studies Reader 2*, Weismantel provides a brief overview of several intriguing archaeological finds that offer evidence for questions raised within transgender studies. She discusses the recovery of cultural patterns from material traces left in bones, grave goods, burial practices, dwelling structures, and artwork and asks how binary and cisgender frames of reference may contribute to the potential misinterpretation of those material traces. Weismantel writes not just about what archeology can offer transgender studies, however, but what transgender studies can offer archaeology. Taking as her point of departure the figure of the "monster," which has been fruitfully elaborated upon within trans studies as well as in studies of premodern and non-Western history, Weismantel turns a critical "transgender rage" against the biocentric, cisgender, and binary assumptions that dominate the contemporary archeological profession.

The Vix burial has attracted considerable attention because of . . . the much-debated sex assessment of the principal burial. . . . Since its excavation in the 1950s, this individual has been described variously as a . . . "nomad princess" . . . a "lady" . . . a "man who did not mind wearing women's clothing" . . . a "transvestite priest" . . . a "rich woman and possibly a chief or tribal ruler" . . . [or] an "honorary male." (Knüdson 2002: 278)

The "Princess of Vix," an Iron Age tomb in France containing an apparently female skeleton surrounded by gold and bronze artifacts usually associated with males, is only one of many archaeological discoveries that hint at a diversity of sexual histories hidden in the ancient past.[1] Very few people outside of professional archaeology know about this intriguing find, and it is not easy for non-specialists to get accurate information about it. The Wikipedia entry about "the Vix grave," for example, describes the fabulous objects found in the tomb, but does not mention the maelstrom of controversy that has raged over the small body buried with so much pomp and circumstance.[2]

The silence that surrounds this grave suggests that archaeology needs to be brought under transgender studies' broad interdisciplinary umbrella. The time is right: professional

DOI: 10.4324/9781003206255-40

archaeology is finally starting to shake off its long history of "sex negativity" and self-censorship (Voss 2008: 318), and as it does, a profusion of incredibly rich evidence of diverse forms of gender identity and gender expression is spilling out from ancient sites around the globe.[3] This newly available data raises provocative questions. Was the body buried at Vix, for example, a woman who attained a lordly political status usually reserved for men? Or an intersex individual who attained the status of a religious leader or shaman,[4] partly because of her unusual body,[5] which was small, asymmetrical, and mostly but not entirely female?[6]

If transgender scholars ignore these archaeological puzzles, we risk impoverishing our sense of the past, and our understanding of who we are and where we came from—not to mention missing out on a whole lot of (somewhat wonkish) fun. It's fascinating to read about the bronze-studded chariot that rolled the bier into the grave at Vix, and the accompanying *krater* (a bronze vessel imported from Greece), the largest and fanciest ever found in the Celtic world—four feet in diameter and five feet tall, and entirely filled with mead (an alcoholic drink made of honey). Or to pore over photographs of the Princess's jewelry, lavish adornments of a kind worn by both men and women, such as the enormous gold *torc* (a large flat necklace or breastplate) adorned with winged horses, lion's paws, and poppies (Knüdson 2002).

However, in inviting you to enjoy these things, I am also inviting you to share my rage. Why is it that the burial at Vix was originally discovered in 1952, but information about the corpse's anomalous sex was not made public until feminist archaeologist Bettina Arnold published a re-study in 1991? Why do so many twenty-first century archaeologists continue to suppress information about discoveries like these? To enter the archaeological record from a transgender perspective is not just a romp through a queer fairyland. In fact, it can turn into a queer *rampage* driven by an angry determination to overturn this systematic repression of knowledge, which constitutes a form of structural violence perpetrated against people, past *and* present, who do not conform to contemporary norms of gender.

Rage can be a defining aspect of transgender identity, as Susan Stryker reminds us in her powerful essay "My Words to Victor Frankenstein above the Village of Chamounix: Performing Transgender Rage" (1994). That rage has its origins in the many forms of violence—physical and psychological, material and symbolic—inflicted on transgender bodies. Transgender scholars transform that rage into a mandate: to write the history of violence so as to bring it back into public memory—and, when we can, to undo it.

Some violence is ancient. For instance, although we remember Classical Greece as a place where sculptors carved sensuous images of the god Hermaphrodite, whose body is both female and male, documents from the period tell a more complicated story. The same society that produced those statues also put women to death by public drowning or burning alive if their bodies were determined by the authorities to be partly male (Ajootian 1995: 102–103). But my focus here is on a modern form of violence: the systematic erasure of lives and histories that are inconveniently queer. Viewed through transgender eyes, the modern history of archaeology looks a little like the history of medicine: where the body of evidence does not fall neatly into a gender binary, the academic doctors just lopped off what doesn't fit.

The first step in creating a transgender archaeology, then, is a destructive one: tearing off the layers of unsupported assumptions about sex and gender that encrust the archaeological record, and freeing the queerly formed bodies trapped underneath. The first section of this article, "Towards a Transgender Archaeology," summarizes the challenges currently facing archaeologists who study sex and gender. The second part surveys some of the work of archaeologists who have moved beyond the gender binary, and shows what an "ungendering" of the archaeological record can do. Ungendering the past has the potential to release us from even the most harmful beliefs about what it means to be human, such as those that denigrate the bodies of transgender persons as "monstrous," "unnatural," or "abnormal." In studying precapitalist, non-Western societies, archaeologists and art historians encounter ontologies of the body in which the damaging modernist fiction of the "natural", with its abhorrence of bodies assembled rather than birthed, never existed. The third and final section of this essay, "Here Be Monsters," enters the arena of the monstrous body. This is the difficult terrain on which Susan Stryker compared her own body to that of Frankenstein, and on which Gloria Anzaldúa called herself "Coatlicue" after the terrifying Aztec goddess (1987). It is here, where the deepest trauma lies, that transgender studies stakes out its most profound battles; and it is here that archaeology offers its most radical promise.

Towards a Trans Archaeology

The "Princess," who died some time around 450 B.C., is a little too old to be called "transgender"—a newly minted term that came into its own in the 1990s.[7] Nevertheless, this find, and others around the globe, demonstrate that many of the behaviors associated with transgender today—"occasional or more frequent crossdressing, permanent cross-dressing and cross-gender living" (Whittle 2006: xi); "transsexuality . . . some aspects of intersexuality and homosexuality, . . . [and] myriad specific subcultural expressions of 'gender atypicality'"(Stryker 2006)—were also part of ancient life.

Vix is far from an isolated case. The evidence defying binary models of gender and sex is truly global, and stretches across the entirety of human history. Let's start with rock art, that earliest and most ubiquitous form of human self-expression. Carved and painted images on caves and cliffs from Australia to Colorado, some of them tens of thousands of years old, provide a rare glimpse of how early humans (and more recent foraging societies) perceived the human body. Surveying these images, Kelley Hays-Gilpin finds little evidence of two sexes. Instead, "With surprising frequency, one encounters figures with something fancy between the legs that can't readily be assigned to one of two categories, neither penis nor vagina" (2004: 15–16).

Interpreting evidence like this from a transgender perspective doesn't mean artificially forcing ancient phenomena into a new and ill-fitting category. If anything, the opposite seems true. It is as if the premodern past had to wait for transgender scholarship to arrive, and with it, an understanding that "'gender' . . . is more complex and varied than can be accounted for by the currently dominant binary sex/gender ideology of Eurocentric modernity" (Stryker 2006: 3). The gender diversity of the past matters for transgender activism. The dominant vision of human history is an oppressive one: an unbroken legacy of manly men and womanly women compelled by biology to create nuclear families devoted to reproduction. Transgender people need to know that the accumulated weight of archaeological data does not support this vision of human history (Joyce 2008). The study of history and prehistory is an inherently political activity, because it reveals this normativizing narrative as the distorting, selective, constructed artifice that it is.

The goal of a transgender archaeology is not to re-populate the ancient past with modern trans men and trans women—that would be a blatant distortion of the archaeological record and of the goals of transgender studies.[8] What we can do is to replace the narrow, reductive gaze of previous researchers with a more supple, subtler appreciation of cultural variation. According to what feminist philosophers of science call "standpoint theory" (Wylie 2003), this is simply good science: turning to the perspective of people from outside the mainstream in order to arrive at hypotheses that a normative person might never generate. Modern researchers' vision of human possibility is inevitably limited by their own cultural biases and personal experience; incorporating a plurality of perspectives is one way to circumvent this limitation.

However, introducing a transgender eye among the archaeology guys will be no easy task. The dominant archaeological model still assumes that every human group, always and everywhere, has been composed of two distinct sexes, male and female:

> . . . the way gender is experienced today is homogenized, made to seem a natural given, and projected back into a timeless past of men and women living life as demanded by genetic capacities and reproductive imperatives deemed to be universal.
>
> (Joyce 2008: 18; see also Voss 2008: 318)

A small but growing number of archaeologists are arguing for a very different picture of human history—one that does not assume a two-sex model, the universality of the nuclear family or the timelessness of heteronormativity. But the work of changing the dominant paradigm is an uneven, ragged, and conflictual process that is far from complete.

The status of research on gender and sexuality in archaeology these days is contradictory. On the one hand, research on women is a well-established subfield. There has been an outpouring of excellent feminist work since the 1980s,[9] and studies of masculinity followed in the 1990s.[10] Anthropology departments at major universities like U.C. Berkeley and Stanford University now boast senior faculty in archaeology who are outspoken feminists. Nevertheless, these researchers and their students are isolated enclaves in a field still largely dominated by heteronormative men, and by research agendas focused on masculinist topics such as warfare and state-level politics.

The picture for the study of sexuality is far more dismal. Although professional archaeologists laugh at their public image as "Indiana Jones," the dominant culture of the discipline is unapologetically testosterone-driven and heteronormative, creating an atmosphere at large mainstream professional meetings that keeps queers barely visible and non-normative voices silent. A small minority of rebels—many of them students of the feminist professors mentioned above—have produced a few really excellent publications and conferences on the archaeology of sexuality, but to many established archaeologists, the very notion of such a subfield is simply ludicrous. With feminist work on gender and queer work on sexuality still struggling to establish a foothold, a transgender archaeology is hard to imagine—and more necessary than ever.

Ungendered

In *Ancient Bodies, Ancient Lives: Sex, Gender and Archaeology*, Rosemary Joyce advocates an archaeology free from "the normative two-sex/two-gender model" (2008: 18). At the moment, though, that binary sex/gender model remains so thoroughly integrated into most archaeological research paradigms that it is invisible—even to the investigators themselves. Gender binaries appear to originate in the data, not in our heads. Occasionally, though, we can glimpse the gap between the actual evidence, which is usually inconclusive, contradictory, and open to multiple interpretations, and the rigid gender straightjacket imposed by the researchers, who may not even be aware that they have foreclosed on the possibility of seeing gender variation in their data.

In the summer of 2011, for example, I saw a colleague make a presentation, which he intended to illustrate some new insights into social structure and site planning at an ancient Middle Eastern city. Inadvertently, however, he showed us something else instead: an unusually graphic illustration of the way restrictive assumptions about gender get superimposed on the open-ended ambiguities of the past. The ancient city in question is a famous one:

> Çatalhöyük, a Neolithic site in the Anatolian region of Turkey that was occupied between 7500 and 5700 B.C.E.; this colleague and I were both part of a small international group of researchers who had gathered for a small conference at the site.

The last slide in my colleague's presentation showed an artist's re-creation of the ancient city. I liked the drawing, which showed a multi-storied compound of rooms, rooftops, and activity areas, with a few people and dogs for scale. What I didn't like was what the speaker had done to it. In thick red lines, he had superimposed a circle over part of one building, to indicate that it was an individual household, and annotated the circle with the words "FAMILY = M + F + others." In assigning these gender markers, and tucking them into a nuclear family, he had recreated a modern middle-class ideal that was not very common in ancient agricultural societies.

In a way, we should be grateful for egregious examples like this, because they make it easy to peel off the offending words and take a look at what lies underneath. At Çatalhöyük, what shows up once we strip away our modern assumptions is fascinating and unexpected. Years of intensive excavation and analysis have resulted in a wealth of information about life in an urban settlement nine thousand years ago, when most human beings still lived in nomadic bands.

The gender picture that is emerging at this early city bears little resemblance to the simplistic model suggested by the words "M + F."

There are two reasons that a different kind of picture is developing at Çatalhöyük. The most important source is the data itself; but we would not necessarily know about that data were it not for another important factor, which is that some of the archaeologists working at the site share Joyce's innovative perspective. After the talk, one of those archaeologists came up to thank me for objecting to the slide: Lynn Meskell, a researcher known for her boldly original work on gender and sexuality. Meskell had particularly good reason to be irritated by the red scrawl projected on the screen, and must have wondered whether the speaker had been listening earlier, when she had presented her research, or whether he had read any of her publications about the site. He seemed oddly unaware that her conclusions differ quite radically from his own. According to Meskell, "[W]hat seems to have been most salient at Çatalhöyük was . . . not a specifically gendered person with discrete sexual markers, but an [unsexed] . . . human form."

When asked, the speaker freely admitted that the idea that Çatalhöyük was inhabited by "M + F"'s, rather by individuals who may not have been "specifically gendered" was based purely on assumption, unsupported by any data. Meskell's conclusions, in contrast, are the result of a long and intensive investigation based on a carefully constructed research paradigm. That work has focused on the hundreds of small clay and stone figurines that litter the site: archaeologists interested in gender often study anthropomorphic figures as evidence of how people in the past conceptualized their own bodies, or the human body in general.

What sets Meskell's work apart from most figurine studies, including earlier work on figurines at Çatalhöyük, is that she did not begin with a binary model, which assumes that all humans are either males or females, and separates the artifacts accordingly into two piles. According to archaeologist Naomi Hamilton, most "interpretation[s] of prehistoric anthropomorphic figurines from eastern Europe and the Near East" rely upon "a methodology which classifies figures primarily by sex and then translates sex into stereotyped Western gender roles which may have no relevance to prehistory" (2000: 17).

[. . .]

Some of the most sophisticated archaeological research on gender to date comes from Mesoamerica (a region that comprises Mexico and parts of Central America). While standard textbooks about Mesoamerican archaeology still describe an unbroken tradition of "men and women engaged in familiarly gendered tasks," several decades of intensive research have overturned that conventional picture. New data has peopled the Aztec cities and Mayan temples with "men wearing women's clothing . . . gods with male and female aspects . . . androgynous figures . . . [and] women rulers . . ." (Stockett 2005: 568). This is not an ungendered world: instead, it is multiply gendered—and elaborately hierarchicalized. In the delicate, aristocratic art produced for royalty cross-dressing kings and gender-morphing gods abound. Androgyny is also a theme that runs throughout Mesoamerican art, much to the confusion of modern viewers. Even experts have been slow to abandon the binary altogether, and to recognize that sometimes, a ferocious argument about whether a figure is male or female should be answered with a simple "yes."

Consider, for example, the history of the Las Limas statue, a beautiful stone figure found in a cornfield by two Mexican children in 1965. This enigmatic seated figure with a flat chest and a rounded, feminine face holds an inert smaller figure lying in the larger figure's lap. The children and their parents initially worshipped this image as the miraculous "Virgin of Las Limas": a Mother holding her Child. But archaeologists quickly recognized the sculpture as pre-Christian. To an informed eye, the graceful, intricate tattoos incised on the larger figure, and the "were-jaguar" facial features of the smaller figure, immediately identify it as Olmec. The experts re-named the statue the "Lord" of Las Limas: a young man holding a sacrificial victim (or possibly an ancestor). Efforts to affix stable gender identities to this Olmec figure seems somewhat misguided, given that a few centuries later, during the Classic Maya period and after, Mesoamerican deities appeared in both male and female manifestations—and sometimes as both/neither. At the Maya site of Palenque (a jewel-like complex of palaces, temples and plazas in southern Mexico famed for its exquisite bas-relief depictions of rulers and deities), walls and doorways were adorned with the lovely face of the Young Maize God, usually described by modern viewers as a very feminine young man.[11] The god was the epitome of perfect beauty—and a perfect androgyne.

This androgynous god lets us question one of the most unquestioned and most damaging assertions of modern gender/sex ideology, namely, that the idea of two sexes originates in nature itself, and expresses the will of God. Ancient Mesoamericans learned a quite different lesson from the natural and supernatural worlds. The Maize God is the human incarnation of the young maize or corn plant—a plant notorious for its sexual ambiguities. Corn and squash, the staples of Native American societies in Mexico and in the U.S. Southwest, reproduce sexually, producing visibly "male" and "female" parts—each with shapes that unmistakably resemble human genitalia. Glyphic depictions of the maize god as a young lord often feature the glossy, pollen-laden strands of silk that erupt from the plant's male sex organs (Taube 1985: 173). But like human parents, corn and squash plants do not always produce fully "male" or fully "female" blooms: ambiguous organs with characteristics of both are extremely common, and healthy plants may produce an exuberance of sexual variations on a single stalk.

The domestication of corn was a great achievement—and one that made generations of Native peoples intimately familiar with the natural phenomenon of intersex individuals. The gently smiling, enigmatic face of the Young Maize God, which hovers so delicately between masculinity and femininity, incarnates the changeable sexuality of this life-giving plant. For the corn farmers who created the great civilizations and religions of Mexico, nature itself offered proof that male and female are mutable categories. Olmec and Maya artists made this connection implicit when they depicted human bodies as ears of corn (Taube 1985, 1996). For ancient Mesoamericans, this—not the inevitability of a fixed biological 'nature'—is the message that the biological world offers to the cultural one.

[. . .]

Ungendering our analyses, then, does not produce only one way of seeing ancient societies. Looking at Čatalhöyük, we are struck by how insistently its egalitarian residents refused to differentiate by gender, in life or in death. In contrast, the rulers and gods of the Maya world appropriated every form of gendering—masculine, feminine, androgynous, even vegetative—as signs of their own multiplicitous power. These glimpses of the past affect our vision of the present: archaeology does its best ungendering when it undermines the claim that modern gender/sex systems are both universal and natural.

Here Be Monsters[12]

Archaeology can certainly contribute to transgender studies' mission of "crosscultural and historical investigations of human gender diversity" (Stryker 2006: 3). At first glance, though, it seems limited in the insights it might provide into contemporary transgender experience. The ritual cross-dressing of ancient kings is an interesting historical footnote, but modern medical practices like hormone replacement and gender reassignment surgery are phenomena of an entirely different order, about which the ancient past presumably has little to say.

Wrong. A deeper look—not at practices but at ontologies—shows that it is precisely here, in thinking about the twenty-first century transsexual body, that a transgender archaeology may have the most profound contribution to make. By juxtaposing premodern, modernist and posthuman understandings of the body, archaeology can perform transgender studies' most critical task: to "disrupt . . . denaturalize . . . rearticulate . . . and make . . . visible the normative linkages we generally assume to exist between [gender and] the biological specificity of the sexually differentiated human body" (Stryker 2006: 3).

As it turns out, the idea of constructing one's body through appropriating and suturing together disparate body parts from diverse origins is not modern at all; many ancient societies would find this way of thinking about oneself completely familiar. It is a peculiarly *modern* state of affairs to have become so estranged from the idea of the body as a hybrid creation, assembled after birth and multiple in its identities and origins. Modernity may have produced the medical system that invented techniques we use today in transitioning, but it also gave rise to an ontology that abhors the constructed body that results, rejecting it as antithetical to the "truth" of the "natural" body (Stryker 1994).

The modern conception of the sexed body claims to be based in immutable, natural truth. One benefit of a cross-cultural and transhistorical perspective is that it helps us see that this 'nature' is not natural at all: it is a carefully constructed intellectual artifice, the product of contingent histories. Like the androgynous Maize God, the two-sex model rests upon a highly selective engagement with nature, one that ignores as much biology as it recognizes, and that was developed to meet specific cultural and ideological needs.

In the canonical modernist novel *Frankenstein*, the unhappy being who inhabits a surgically created body is a monster. This abject role is taken up by Susan Stryker, who claims—and reinvents—monstrosity for her own transsexual body, "torn apart and sewn together again in a shape other than that in which it was born" (1994). Mary Shelley, *Frankenstein's* author, portrayed the unnatural creature as inherently tragic, a being with no future and no past. Stryker absorbs this message and then, like the monster in the novel, rises up in rage to reject it and claim a different history for herself. The transgender body, she suggests, might not belong to the modernist present or the immediate past at all. It might instead be part of a future only now coming into being, in which the constructed body is not terrifyingly inhuman, but "exhilaratingly posthuman"—perhaps one of Haraway's feminist cyborgs (1994) or Rosi Braidotti's "cyberbodies" (2002).

Stryker claims her surgically assembled body as something powerful and new; we might also call it powerful and old. Throughout ancient Europe, the ubiquitous figurines that archaeologists worked so hard to divide into two little piles, male and female, have constantly confounded them with anomalies: a woman/centaur, a man seated on a birthing stool, bodies with a penis and breasts (Hamilton 2000).

In the ancient Americas, a basic premise of Pre-Columbian art is that living beings gain power and beauty through appropriating the body parts of others. At the great Peruvian oracle of Chavín, for instance, stone carvings depict pilgrims processing into the temple accompanied by jaguars and supernatural beings. Humans and superhumans alike are composites: a man wears metal breastplates that are literally shaped like a pair of breasts; the 'angel' on a stone cup has the wings of a bird, the face of a jaguar and a human hand that grasps a baton. Two utterly fantastic composite beings who stand guard at the entrance of the temple may be a male and female pair—but their fearsome, tooth-lined genitalia far exceed anything found on actual bodies of any sex (Burger 1992). In the Western tradition, too, artists use the contrast between women and men, humans and animals to portray power—but never by contaminating the male body with the taint of the female. Instead, tableaux of conquest show the masculine man dominating lesser beings. In the Pre-Columbian tradition, humans demonstrate superiority quite differently: by rising above the limitations of the birthed body through incorporating the bodily aspects of others. To show femininity in this context makes a man more powerful, not less. Underlying this hybrid imagery is a basic theory of the body as permeable and protean, growing throughout life through physical and metaphysical intercourse with others. Because Westerners fear losing control over the boundaries of the body and the self, the art produced in the ancient Americas sometimes creates discomfort and dislike. But for those who do not occupy a privileged body that is masculine and white—or at least respectably feminine and willing to submit—the great corpus of Pre-Columbian art stands as a repository of revolutionary ideas.

In claiming the territory of the monstrous, Stryker walks in the footsteps of Chicana lesbian writer Gloria Anzaldúa, who revolutionized Latino Studies when she embraced the monstrous image of an Aztec goddess, the fearsome Coatlicue, as her own (1987). It was here, in the art of ancient Latin America, that this rebellious writer found a context within which to understand her own nature, which she experienced as both masculine and feminine—and a place where she could embrace her own uncontrollable rage. Coatlicue and her fellow goddesses, Coyalxauqui and Tlaltecuhtli, are ferocious amalgams of human and non-human, masculine and feminine, mother and killer. Standing, like Anzaldúa, in their protective shadows, it becomes easier to follow Stryker in claiming "monstrosity" as a state of redemptive power for gender non-normative people—and for all of us who are stigmatized as deviant in modern Western thought.

The image that Anzaldúa chose is one of the most unforgettable in Pre-Columbian art. At the heart of the Aztec empire, in the center of one of the largest cities in the world, Tenochtitlan (today Mexico City), three enormous female statues were placed in the precincts of the great central temple (Carrasco 1988). For modern Latin Americans, Coyalxauqui is the easiest to understand, and she is the most beloved of Mexicans today. She is a beautiful young woman dressed as a warrior—and killed in combat by her own brother. In the carving, her graceful limbs have been severed from her naked torso, and her eyes are closed in death on her decapitated head. In keeping with modern sensibilities, she is the tragic feminine heroine, young, lovely, and safely dead.

Anzaldúa chose a more difficult figure: not the dead sister, but the vengeful mother. This is Coatlicue, an enormous and terrifying body, human in form but incorporating a fearsome array of non-human creatures. Her head is formed of intertwined serpents; her feet are the curved talons of birds of prey; and, most terrifying of all, her hands are live obsidian blades. The blades are sacrificial knives, and she wears a gruesome necklace of the hearts and hands of her victims. But she herself seems to have been decapitated: the snakes pouring out from her neck and forming her face can also be read as streams of life blood pumping out from a headless corpse. This is no passive victim: erect and powerful, the goddess rises from the dead, her blood forming new and more fearsome dual snakeheads to replace the human head that was taken from her.

Since Anzaldúa wrote her paean to Coatlicue, archaeologists have discovered a third figure, as large and elaborate as the others. This ten-ton stone carving portrays Tlahtecuhtli, a god often portrayed in masculine form, but here a goddess who squats in the birth position, even as sacrificial blood pours from her mouth like tongues.[13] This iconography makes explicit the symbolism of birth and death implicit in the other two; unlike them, she was created as the cover for a coffin, which held the body of a male emperor, Ahuitzotl.

These three goddesses are huge and deadly, and their bodies incorporate more than just elements of masculinity. They are both alive and dead, life-giving and life-taking, and their bodies are composed of bone, blood, flesh, and stone; bird, snake, and woman. They are powerful images, but after all, they are just that: representations of bodies, not real ones.

There is ample evidence, however, that ancient people also saw their actual bodies as things that were assembled over life rather than given at birth—and that this process of accumulating bits and pieces of others was a beneficial process, even though it necessarily involves giving away parts of oneself too. We see this perhaps most strikingly in burial practices: whereas archaeologists originally assumed that the bodies in tombs were intact individuals, new evidence from around the globe shows that premodern people preferred to mix it up. In addition to mass graves, even graves that apparently contain only one person often turn out to contain one whole skeleton—composed of body parts from multiple individuals. In Mexico, Peru, and Turkey, there is evidence that graves were repeatedly re-entered, so that the living could interact with their dead in commemorative rites (see for example Millaire 2004). In the process, they often exchanged, added or subtracted bones, as for example in the grave of a woman at Çatalhöyük who cradles a man's head in her lap, or another young female whose own head has been replaced with that of a man who died long after her.

Theoretically inclined archaeologists are starting to absorb the implications of this data. It suggests that ancient people did not think of themselves and their own bodies in the modern Western sense, as individual bodies with individual identities—a belief that makes interfering with the bodily integrity of a corpse reprehensible. Instead, they conceived of life as a process of constant exchange between bodies, and wished only that such exchange might continue after life. Feminist theorist Marilyn Strathern says that in non-Western societies such as tribal Papua New Guinea, people are not "individuals" but "dividuals" whose bodies and selves—including their gendered sense of themselves as female and male—are multiple and composite in their very essence (1988).

[. . .]

To ungender Çatalhöyük, then, or any society, is not to imagine (or create) a blandly uniform social landscape without appetites or organs. It is to conceptualize bodies and persons as vital assemblages interacting in a field of dynamic material entanglements, where the physical properties of the flesh are not inescapable markers of absolute difference and limitation, but desirable and detachable gifts that can be exchanged in real and imagined interactions between mutable social agents.

[. . .]

Notes

1. I am very grateful to Susan Stryker for the invitation to contribute this article to the second *Transgender Studies Reader*; to my partner, Simon Z. Aronoff, for his careful reading and astute commentaries on various drafts; and to my research assistant, Pilar Escontrias, for her help in assembling the bibliography.

2. The Wikipedia entry is an interesting artifact of the current gender/sex wars in archaeology. On the one hand, it is a triumph for archaeologist Bettina Arnold that the skeleton is described in the entry as female; she fought hard to get Celtic archaeologists to recognize that not all elaborate burials were male. However, neither that debate, nor the further controversy over whether the skeleton might be intersex or occupy an intermediate gender between male and female, is mentioned directly. The fight over gender and sex in archaeology does emerge obliquely in an angry note in the discussion section, which erroneously insists that there is never any doubt about the sex of a skeleton. (On this point, see the recent discussion over osteological identification at the 2011 meetings of the Society for American Archaeology, where a symposium entitled "Exploring Sex and Gender in Bioarchaeology" coined the phrase "the sexism of sexing" to refer to this kind of insistence that identifying biological sex is a simple and unambiguous matter.)

3. Throughout this essay, I use 'ancient' as a broad umbrella term to refer to a wide variety of precapitalist and non-Western societies that have been studied by archaeologists. I am regretfully excluding an entire gamut of excellent archaeological work on sex and gender in historical and Western settings; see for example the essays by historical archaeologists in Schmidt and Voss 2000; Casella and Voss 2011.

4. The word *shaman* has taken on so many meanings in both popular and academic writing that should be used with caution (Klein et al. 2002).

5. I use the female pronoun in accordance with other authors. All researchers agree that this was the individual's primary biological sex, and I do not wish to countervene Bettina Arnold's argument that Celtic individuals buried in this way are not inevitably male.

6. On the Vix debate, see Arnold 1991; Knüdson 2002; and the discussion in Joyce 2008: 75–76 and Voss 2008.

7. Stryker (2006a) and Whittle (2006) describe the 'transgender phenomenon" as a development of the 1990s, the crystallization of cultural effects as diffuse as the rise of the internet, the availability of medical technologies, and the maturation of the feminist and LGBT movements.

8. We no longer naively imagine that other peoples' histories can be treated as a sort of giant thrift shop where we are free to rummage around among discarded and outmoded identities, picking and choosing what pleases us without regard for how our selections were meant to be used, or what might have happened to the original owners. While acknowledging the cultural importance of books like Leslie Feinberg's *Transgender Warriors* for trans people today, or Walter Williams' *The Spirit and the Flesh* for gay men a generation ago, we have seen the ugly racial politics that can ensue. A notable example is the Native American two-spirit tradition, a complex and constantly evolving cultural and religious phenomenon that was reduced by enthusiastic gay outsiders to the simplistic notion of the *berdache* (a term that was itself a homophobic insult, imposed by French colonialists on a cultural phenomenon they neither understood nor respected). For indictments of the cultural whiteness of LGBTQ culture and queer studies, see for example Smith 1977; Moraga and Anzaldúa 1983; Harris 1996; Ferguson 2004; Johnson 2005; McBride 2005; Manalansan 2003.

9. Feminist archaeology has a substantial scholarly history today, beginning with the seminal article by Conkey and Spector (1984). A flurry of gender volumes and articles followed (see, for example, Gero and Conkey 1991; Brumfiel 1992; Jacobs et al. 1997; Nelson and Rosen-Ayalon 2002).

10. See for example Joyce 2000; Buechli 2000; Yates 1993.

11. Looper 2003; see also Klein 2001, Bassie-Sweet 2002. Taube 1985: 171 and passim; although note the discussion of the female-bodied aspects of the Maize God on 1985: 178.

12. Early European cartographers wrote "here be monsters" on the edges of their maps when they reached the limits of the known world.

13. See www.mexicolore.co.uk/index.php?one=azt&two=aaa&id-286&typ=reg, accessed February 7, 2012.

Bibliography

Ajootian, Aileen (1995). "Monstrum or Daimon: Hermaphrodites in Ancient Art and culture." *Greece and Gender*, 93–108. Papers of the Norwegian Institute at Athens. http://digital-ub.uib.no/1956.2/2994, accessed 21 May 2012.

Anzalúa, Gloria (1987). *Borderlands/La Frontera: The New Mestiza*. Aunt Lute Books.

Arnold, Bettina (1991). "The Deposed Princess of Vix: The Need for an Engendered European Prehistory." In Dale Walde and Noreen Willows (eds), *The Archaeology of Gender: Proceedings of the 22nd Annual Chacmool Conference*, 366–374. Calgary: Department of Archaeology, University of Calgary.

Bassie-Sweet, Karen (2002). "Corn Deities and the Male/Female Principle." In Lowell Gustafson and Amy Trevelyan (eds), *Ancient Maya Gender Identity and Relations*, 169–190. Westport, CT: Greenwood Press.

Blackwood, Evelyn (1984). "Sexuality and Gender in Certain Native American Tribes: The Case of Cross-Gender Females." *Signs* 10: 1, 27–42.

Braidotti, Rosi (2002). *Metamorphoses: Towards a Materialist Theory of Becoming.* Cambridge: Polity Press.

Brumfiel, Elizabeth (1992). "Distinguished Lecture in Archaeology: Breaking and Entering the Ecosystem: Gender, Class, and Faction Steal the Show." *American Anthropologist* 94: 3, 551–567.

Buechli, Victor (2000). "Constructing Utopian Sexualities: The Archaeology and Architecture of the Early Soviet State." In Robert Schmidt and Barb Voss (eds). *The Archaeology of Sexuality*, 67–88. London: Routledge Press.

Burger, Richard L. (1992). *Chavín and the Origins of Andean Civilization.* New York: Thames and Hudson.

Casella, Eleanor and Barbara Voss, eds. (2011). *The Archaeology of Colonialism, Gender, and Sexuality.* Cambridge: Cambridge University Press.

Carrasco, David, Eduardo Matos Moctezuma and Joanna Broda (1988). *The Great Temple of Tenochtitlan: Center and Periphery in the Aztec World.* Berkeley: University of California Press.

Conkey, Margaret and Janet D. Spector (1984). "Archaeology and the Study of Gender." *Advances in Archaeological Method and Theory* 7: 1–38.

Feinberg, Leslie (1996). *Transgender Warriors: Making History from Joan of Arc to Dennis Rodman.* Boston: Beacon Press.

Ferguson, Roderick A. (2004). *Toward a Queer of Color Critique: Aberrations in Black.* Minneapolis: University of Minnesota Press.

Gero, Joan M. and Margaret W. Conkey, eds. (1991). *Engendering Archaeology: Women and Prehistory.* Chichester: Wiley.

Hamilton, Naomi (2000). "Concepts of Sex and Gender in Figurine Studies in Prehistory." In Moira Donald and Linda Hurcombe (eds), *Representations of Gedner From Prehistory to the Present*, 17–30. Basingstoke: Palgrave MacMillan.

Haraway, Donna (1994). "A Manifesto for Cyborgs: Science, Technology, and Socialist Feminism in the 1980s." In Steven Seidman (ed), *The Postmodern Turn: New Perspectives on Social Theory*, 82–118. Cambridge: Cambridge University Press.

Haraway, Donna (2006). "A Cyborg Manifesto: Science, Technology and Socialist-Feminism in the Late Twentieth Century." In Susan Stryker and Stephen Whittle (eds), *The Transgedner Studies Reader*, 103–118. New York: Routledge.

Harris, Laura Alexandra (1996). "Queer Black Feminism: The Pleasure Principle." *Feminist Review* 54: 3–30.

Hays-Gilpin, Kelly A. (2004). *Images: Gender and Rock Art.* Rowman Altamira.

Jacobs, Sue-Ellen, Wesley Thomas and Samantha Lang, ed. (1997). *Two-Spirit People: Native American Gender Identity, Sexuality, and Spirituality.* Urbana: University of Illinois Press.

Johnson, E. Patrick (2005). "Introduction: Queer Black Stadius/'Quaring' Queer Studies." In E. Patrick Johnson and Mae G. Henderson (eds), *Black Queer Studies*, 1–20. Durham, NC: Duke University Press.

Joyce, Rosemary A. (2000). "A Precolumbian Gaze: Male Sexuality Among the Ancient Maya." In Robert Schmidt and Barbara Voss (eds), *Archaeologies of Sexuality*, 263–283. New York: Routledge.

——— (2004). "Embodied Subjectivity: Gender, Femininity, Masculinity, Sexuality." In L. Meskell and R. W. Preucel (eds), *A Companion to Social Archaeology*, 82–93. Oxford: Blackwell.

——— (2008). *Ancient Bodies, Ancient Lives: Sex, Gender and Archaeology.* New York: Thames and Hudson.

Klein, Cecelia, ed. (2001). *Gender in Pre-Hispanic America.* Washington, DC: Dumbarton Oaks.

Klein, Cecelia, Eulogio Guzmn, Elisa Mandell, and Maya Stanfield-Mazzi (2002). "The Role of Shamanism in Mesoamerican Art." *Current Anthropology* 43: 3, 383–419.

Knüdson, Christopher (2002). "More Circe than Cassandra: The Princess of Vix in Ritualized Social Context." *European Journal of Archaeology* 5: 275308.

Looper, Matthew George (2003). *Lightning Warrior: Maya Art and Kingship at Quirigua.* Austin: University of Texas Press.

Manalansan, Martin F. (2003). *Global Divas: Filipino Gay Men in the Diaspora.* Durham, NC: Duke University Press.

McBride, Dwight A. (2005). *Why I Hate Abercrombie & Fitch: Essays on Race and Sexuality*. New York: New York University Press.

Millaire, Jean-François (2004). "The Manipulation of Human Remains in Moche Society: Delayed Burials, Grave Reopening, and Secondary Offerings of Human Bones on the Peruvian North Coast." *Latin American Antiquity* 15: 4, 371–388.

Moraga, Cherríe and Gloria Anzaldúa, eds. (1983). *This Bridge Called My Back: Writings by Radical Women of Color*. Kitchen Table: Women of Color Press.

Nelson, Sarah Milledge and Myriam Rosen-Ayalon (2002). *In Pursuit of Gender: Worldwide Archaeological Approaches*. Walnut Creek: AltaMira Press.

Quilter, Jeffrey (2010). *The Moche of Ancient Peru: Media and Messages*. Boston: Peabody Museum Collection Series.

Schmidt, Robert A. (2002). "The Iceman Cometh: Queering the Archaeological Past." In Ellen Lewin and William L. Leap (eds), *Out in Theory: The Emergence of Lesbian and Gay Anthropology*, 155–185. Urbana: University of Illinois Press.

Schmidt, Robert A. and Barbara J. Voss (2000). *Archaeologies of Sexuality*. New York: Routledge.

Smith, Barbara (1977). "Toward a Black Feminist Criticism." In *All the Women are White, All the Blacks are Men, but Some of Us are Brave*, 157–175. New York: Feminist Press.

Stockett, Miranda (2005). "On the Importance of Difference: Re-Envisioning Sex and Gender in Ancient Mesoamerica." *World Archaeology* 37: 4, 566–578.

Strathern, Marilyn (1988). *The Gender of the Gift*. Berkeley: University of California Press.

——— (1990). *The Gender of the Gift: Problems with Women and Problems with Society in Melanesia*. Berkeley: University of California Press.

Stryker, Susan (1994). "My Words to Victor Frankenstein above the Village of Chamounix: Performing Transgender Rage." *A Journal of Lesbian and Gay Studies* 1: 3, 237–254.

——— (2006) "(De)subjugated Knowledges: An Introduction to Transgender Studies." In Susan Stryker and Stephen Whittle (eds), *The Transgender Studies Reader*, 1–18. New York: Routledge.

Taube, Karl (1985). The Classic Maya Maize God: A Reappraisal. In Virginia M. Fields (ed), *Fifth Palenque Round Table, 1983*. Proceedings of the Fifth Palenque Round Table Conference, June 12–18, 1983, Palenque, Chiapas, Mexico. Washington, DC: Dumbarton Oaks.

——— (1996). "The Olmec Maize God: The Face of Corn in Formative Mesoamerica." *RES: Anthropology and Aesthetics* 29/30, 39–81.

Voss, Barbara L. (2000). "Feminisms, Queer Theories, and the Archaeological Study of Past Sexualities." *World Archaeology* 32(2): 180–192.

——— (2008). "Sexuality Studies in Archaeology." *Annual Reviews in Anthropology* 37: 317–336.

Weismantel, Mary (2004). "Moche Sex Pots: Reproduction and Temporality in Ancient South America." *American Anthropologist* 106: 3, 495–505.

——— (2011). "Obstinate Things." In Barbara Voss and Eleanor Casella (eds), *The Archaeology of Colonialism: Intimate Encounters and Sexual Effects*, 303–320. Cambridge: Cambridge University Press.

Whittle, Stephen (2006). "Foreword." In Susan Stryker and Stephen Whittle (eds), *The Transgender Studies Reader*, xi–xvi. New York: Routledge.

Williams, Walter L. (1986). *The Spirit and the Flesh: Sexual Diversity in American Indian Culture*. Boston: Beacon Press.

Wylie, Alison (2003). "Why Standpoint Matters." In Robert Figueroa and Sandra Harding (eds), *Science and Other Cultures: Issues in Philosophies of Science and Technology*, 26–48. New York: Routledge.

Yates, T. (1993). "Frameworks for an Archaeology of the Body." In Christopher Tilley (ed), *Interpretive Archaeology*, 31–72. Oxford: Berg.

33 ONE Inc. and Reed Erickson

The Uneasy Collaboration of Gay and Trans Activism, 1964–2003

Aaron H. Devor and Nicholas Matte

Best known in recent years as the founder of the Transgender Archive at the University of Victoria, Aaron H. Devor first made a name for himself in trans studies with his books *Blending Genders* and *FTM*, his detailed and compassionate sociological studies of masculine women and trans men. Devor has played an important role in preserving the legacy and promoting the significance of Reed "Erick" Erickson, a wealthy mid-twentieth-century trans man and philanthropist who largely underwrote the development and dissemination of the "medical model" of transgender care. In this article, originally published in *GLQ: A Journal of Lesbian and Gay Studies* in 2004, Devor and his former student Dr. Nicholas Matte, who later helped organize an archive at the Mark S. Bonham Centre for the Study of Sexual Minorities at the University of Toronto, recount another dimension of Erickson's generosity: his financial support for the ONE Institute for Homophile Studies in Los Angeles. Devor and Matte focus on the "border wars" between trans and cisgender gay ways of understanding sexuality and gender while highlighting the contributions a trans man made to the gay movement. They also, however, emphasize a trans "respectability politics," foregrounding the important medical and scientific aspects of Erickson's multifaceted philanthropic activism rather than Erickson's eclectic esoteric beliefs, such as psychedelic drugs, Eastern mysticism, and interspecies communication. In recent years, trans studies scholarship has developed a deeper appreciation for the full range of Erickson's interests and activism and how they were all interrelated.

People who are today known as transgendered and transsexual have always been present in homosexual rights movements. Their presence and contributions, however, have not always been fully acknowledged or appreciated. As in many other social reform movements, collective activism in gay and lesbian social movements is based on a shared collective identity. Homosexual collective identity, especially in the days before queer politics, was largely framed as inborn, like an ethnicity, and based primarily on sexual desires for persons of the same sex and gender.[1] However, such definitions make sense only when founded on clearly delineated distinctions between sexes and genders. It becomes considerably harder to delineate who is gay and who is lesbian when it is not clear who is a male or a man and who is a female or a woman. Like bisexual people, transgendered and transsexual people destabilize the otherwise easy division of men and women into the categories of straight and gay because they are both and/or neither. Thus there is a long-standing tension over the political terrain of queer politics between gays and lesbians, on the one hand, and transgendered and transsexual people, on the other.

[. . .]

DOI: 10.4324/9781003206255-41

In this essay, [. . .] we tell the story of how one transsexual man was instrumental in the founding of one of the oldest and longest-running gay and lesbian groups in the United States. In doing so, we attempt to recoup a lost bit of the confluent histories of the transgendered and of the gay and lesbian social movements and to encourage the reexamination of how these two groups might work together more productively.

[. . .]

Early Gay Activism in California

Early efforts to represent and better the social position of sexual and gender minorities in the United States were initiated by people with firsthand knowledge of the pain of trans- and homophobia. They created organizations aimed at undoing the social stigma faced by LGBT people. So when the EEF and ONE began to work together in 1964, their goals and methods were similar in many ways. Nevertheless, the realities of the social stigmas faced by gays and lesbians, on the one hand, and by transgendered and transsexual people, on the other, could be quite different. Thus organizations whose purpose was to eradicate these stigmas also needed to be different in some respects. ONE's main focus was the experience of gay men, whereas the EEF's was that of gender-variant (particularly transsexual) people. Nevertheless, Reed Erickson, the foundation's founder, was keen to have the EEF work with gay and lesbian groups toward common goals. Therefore a brief introduction to the two organizations prior to their partnership is in order.

The early 1950s saw the creation of several groups whose aim was to improve social conditions for sexual minorities. The Knights of the Clock, one of the first homophile groups in the United States, was formed in Los Angeles in 1950 by Merton Bird and W. Dorr Legg. It continued to meet until the mid-1960s, and its function was to provide support for gay people in interracial couples.[2] The better-known, longer-lasting Mattachine Society, originally conceived as a political and civil rights discussion group for homosexual people, was also formed in Los Angeles in 1950, by Harry Hay. Other groups soon emerged in southern California, largely in response to the 1952 arrest of Dale Jennings, a member of the Mattachine Society, for soliciting an undercover police officer.[3] "A veritable flood of social protest" ensued after Jennings, who later accused the arresting officer of entrapment, admitted in court that he was homosexual but denied that this made him guilty of "lewd conduct."[4]

It was in this social climate that ONE, whose founders included Legg, Bird, Jennings, and Martin Block, another former member of the Mattachine Society, was incorporated in Los Angeles in October 1952. Taking its name from a famous quote by Thomas Carlyle, "A mystic bond of brotherhood makes all men one," the organization set about "to aid in the social integration and rehabilitation of the sexual variant."[5] To achieve its goals, which were primarily educational, ONE would produce publications, provide programs, and stimulate and support research.[6] The progress it made toward accomplishing these goals was impressive and swift.

For example, by January 1953 ONE had started to disseminate information about homosexuality by publishing *ONE Magazine*, the first publicly available pro-homosexuality periodical in the United States. The magazine sold for twenty-five cents and was bravely hawked on the streets of Los Angeles, as well as distributed through the U.S. postal system.[7] By October 1954 the magazine had thousands of subscribers, but in that month the U.S. Post Office declared it obscene and unmailable and confiscated the issue. ONE promptly sued the U.S. Post Office for infringement of the constitutional right to freedom of the press. The case was not decided until 1958, when the U.S. Supreme Court ruled that gay and lesbian publications were not a priori obscene and could therefore be mailed legally through the postal system.[8] *ONE Magazine* continued to be published until 1967.[9] In 1958 ONE

Institute also began to publish the first scholarly journal devoted to homophile studies, *ONE Institute Quarterly*, which today continues as the *Journal of Homo sexuality* and as the online *International Gay and Lesbian Review*.[10] *ONE Institute Quarterly* was intended to stimulate further educational publications and research in "homophile studies," a field that ONE itself was pioneering.

[. . .]

ONE Institute sought to provide still other formal educational opportunities. In October 1956 the ONE Institute of Homophile Studies was launched and held its first classes. The word *homophile* was chosen over the word *homosexual* because the founders of ONE Institute felt that *homosexual* implied medicalization and pathologization, whereas the more etymologically correct *homophile* was less encumbered by such negative connotations. The institute's goal was to become a degree-granting research institution in homophile studies.[11] The first course, in which fourteen students met for two hours per week for nine weeks to study homosexuality in biology and medicine, history, psychology, sociology and anthropology, law, religion, literature and the arts, and philosophy was simply called "An Introduction to Homophile Studies." By the 1957–58 term the institute had expanded its schedule to two nine-week semesters, and over the next thirty years it developed a plethora of more specific courses, including "Homosexuality in History," "Sociology of Homosexuality," "The Gay Novel," "The Theory and Practice of Homophile Education," "Homophile Ethics," "Psychological Theories of Homosexuality," "Counseling the Homosexual," "Law and Law Reform," and "Near Eastern Foundations of Biblical Morality" (31–47).

These early courses represent the beginnings of the multitude of college and university courses and programs now devoted to the study of lesbian, gay, bisexual, transgendered, and queer people. When ONE Institute began its pioneering work, however, the support network at colleges and universities for this area of study simply did not exist. The financial support for this work had to come entirely from private sources, and the social stigma associated with offering such support made trying to entice donors extremely difficult. Although ONE had clear goals and methods for accomplishing them, the organization was greatly hindered by its severe shortage of resources. In 1964, badly in need of an injection of funding, ONE Inc. met Reed Erickson.

Reed Erickson and the EEF

Erickson had launched the EEF in June 1964 as a nonprofit philanthropic organization funded and controlled, despite having a board of directors, almost entirely by himself. The foundation's goals were "to provide assistance and support in areas where human potential was limited by adverse physical, mental or social conditions, or where the scope of research was too new, controversial or imaginative to receive traditionally oriented support."[12] A substantial part of the foundation's work, therefore, was funding what Erickson considered to be progressive projects. During the twenty years of its existence, the EEF made available millions of dollars from Erickson's personal wealth for the advancement of causes in which he believed. These fell into three main types, all of them related to social movements that remain important and relevant today. The three main social movements in which Erickson invested were those advocating on behalf of homosexuals, those advocating on behalf of transgendered (specifically, transsexual) people, and those developing what might now be called the "New Age" movement. He also funded a wide range of philanthropic projects outside of these major categories, such as the Interplast (International Plastic Surgery) project, which provided corrective plastic surgeries at no charge to impoverished children in Latin America and Africa.[13] Because the EEF was run almost exclusively by Erickson, his personality was decisive both in the projects that the EEF supported and in the relationship between the EEF and ONE. Considering that his personal wealth sustained so many progressive projects, it is surprising that his vast contributions have not been more widely recognized. His fascinating life story bears on his interaction with ONE Inc. in important ways. Thus a biographical sketch is in order.

Reed Erickson was born as Rita Mae Erickson in El Paso, Texas, on October 13, 1917. Erickson's early years were spent in Philadelphia with his mother, father, and younger sister. After graduating from the Philadelphia High School for Girls, Erickson enrolled in a secretarial course at Temple University. Soon after, the family moved to Baton Rouge, Louisiana, where Erickson's father, Robert B. Erickson, had transferred his lead smelting business. In Baton Rouge, Erickson attended Louisiana State University and became the first woman graduate from its School of Mechanical Engineering. Erickson then returned briefly to Philadelphia to work as an engineer and lived as a lesbian in an intimate relationship for several years. There Erickson and a romantic partner took part in Henry Agar Wallace's 1948 campaign for presidency on behalf of the Progressive Party and were part of a liberal social group that included many gays and lesbians, as well as civil rights activists and theater people. Their political involvement led to harassment by the FBI, and Erickson is rumored to have been blacklisted from several jobs as a result. By the early 1950s Erickson had returned once again to Baton Rouge to work in the family companies. At that time Erickson also started an independent company, Southern Seating, which produced and distributed stadium bleachers.

After Erickson's father's death in 1962, Erickson inherited the family businesses, Schuylkill Products Company Inc. and Schuylkill Lead Corporation, and ran them successfully for several years before selling them to Arrow Electronics in 1969 for around five million dollars. Erickson eventually amassed a personal fortune of over forty million dollars.

In 1963, as a patient of Harry Benjamin, Erickson began the process of masculinizing his body and living as Reed Erickson. That year he also married for the first time. Over the next thirty years he would marry three more times and become father to two children. In 1972 he moved with his wife and children and his pet leopard, Henry, to Mazatlán, Mexico, where he had built an opulent home, which he dubbed the "Love Joy Palace." Later he moved to southern California. By the time of his death in 1992 at the age of seventy-four, he had returned to Mexico, addicted to illegal drugs and a fugitive from U.S. drug indictments.

Before his tragic death Erickson had funded countless researchers and organizations in the fields of homosexuality, transsexualism, and "New Age" spirituality. While this article's focus is his contribution to the field of homosexuality, the EEF was also responsible for many projects in other fields. For example, it funded Harry Benjamin, John Money, Richard Green, and other pioneers of treatment and research connected with transsexualism. The EEF also provided its own services, acting as a referral agency, publicizing news about transgender issues, and giving support to isolated individuals throughout the United States and around the world. The EEF worked with local and national news agencies to make information about transgenderism available to the public. In addition, it provided information for college classes and sent speakers to lecture about their personal experiences of gender. As a clearinghouse for transgendered and transsexual information, the EEF was an essential community resource for transgendered people and their supporters, all of whom lived and worked in isolation during those years. The EEF's work was so valuable to those it benefited that many people have kept copies of the informational pamphlets produced by the EEF for decades after its demise. Working in still other fields, Erickson sponsored workshops and research in spirituality and funded the first printing of *A Course in Miracles*, a three-volume set of channeled spiritual guidance that has been translated into nine languages and has sold over one and a half million copies worldwide.[14] He also encouraged and funded John Lily's work in dolphin communication.

One of Erickson's initial interests was to have the EEF work with those in the field of homosexuality, presumably because of his experience as a lesbian and because in those early days of trans activism, Erickson would no doubt have seen the fights for gay and trans rights as naturally allied. The partnership with ONE was the first one undertaken by the EEF. Eventually, Erickson's long-standing support of ONE enabled it to embark on much more elaborate projects than it otherwise would have been able to do. Further, the patterns of his philanthropy evidence an uncanny ability to pinpoint individuals and organizations who, although still near the beginnings of their long careers, would later become highly successful at their endeavors. His relationship with ONE was no exception.

ONE and the EEF: Building a Relationship

By the time ONE Inc. and the EEF came together in 1964, the former had already established itself as an educational center, whereas Erickson was just starting his own organization and looking for substantial projects to fund. ONE could help Erickson do both, and Erickson could help ONE with much-needed financial resources. Further, both Reed Erickson, the man behind the EEF, and Dorr Legg, the driving force of ONE, had strong personalities that challenged and stimulated each other. As such, their partnership had the potential to be highly productive.

ONE Inc. had taken the unprecedented step of opening a business office in downtown Los Angeles in 1953, and the place had soon become a de facto gay community center and hotline. The staff answered thousands of calls from people all over the United States asking for help with problems ranging from housing to arrests to psychological distress. Such requests came from gay men; lesbian women; bisexual, transgendered, and transsexual people; parents; and teachers. Thus ONE, moving toward the fulfillment of its stated goals, had taken steps to obtain property and to promote the integration of homosexuals into society, but when its landlord put the building that housed the organization's offices up for sale shortly after ONE had moved in, all that ONE had achieved seemed at risk.[15]

It was through the financial appeal that went out to ONE's mailing list that Erickson saw his first potential major funding project. Having spent a frantic year finding the space at 2256 Venice Boulevard after an earthquake had rendered the organization's original offices on Hill Street in downtown Los Angeles unsafe, the staff at ONE had panicked. Not wanting to be out on the street again so soon, they decided that they needed to buy the building themselves and sent a request for donations to their entire mailing list. Few responded, partly because ONE, having s old *ONE Magazine*, had lost its nonprofit status and could no longer offer charitable tax receipts to donors, and partly because many potential donors feared being identified with ONE's high-profile homosexuality.[16] Erickson was one of those few, and his offer of assistance with ONE's larger mission stood out as both generous and eccentric.[17]

According to Legg, "[The] first response was from someone named Reed Erickson. He made numerous phone calls for extended conversation with me. This was in 1963 but went no further at the time."[18] Then in July 1964, only days after the EEF had been incorporated, Erickson asked Legg to see him in Baton Rouge. Legg remembered that "the people here had said, in regard to going down there, 'this is just a Southern queen who wants a date for the weekend and was willing to send an airplane ticket.'"[19] Nevertheless, Legg bought a new suit to wear in the stifling heat and humidity of Baton Rouge in July and boarded an airplane headed east. Legg recalled:

> I was to change in New Orleans and I got on this ancient flapping plane which just barely cleared the tree tops, flapping on to Baton Rouge from New Orleans. I got to the airport which was no kind of an airport at all, it was just a little shanty really with

a wire fence. Eight or ten people got off. Here on the other side of the wire fence was what looked to me like a blonde high school kid. I said, "Are you Reed Erickson?" and he said, "Yes." I just said, "I was expecting somebody older." And I thought, "Uh-oh, maybe they were right." And so we went out and got into this very large car with a built-in telephone. Well, those weren't all that common in 1964. So I thought, "Well there's money here."[20]

[. . .]

During the drive into town I learned I would be put up at a motel. The room turned out to be a veritable presidential suite. Once seated there he said, "Tell me about ONE." After hours of talk with only an occasional question from him he said we would now go over to his house to meet his lover. Entering an old fashioned frame house by the kitchen we went through rooms with bare floors, Southern summer style. Here was what might be a Brancusi, there what might be a Matisse. Now we would meet Henry, his lover. Turning on the lights of a large glassed in porch revealed what looked to me like a ten foot leopard. My host went in and the two proceeded to tumble and roll around with great gusto. I was invited to pat the leopard's head which I most gingerly did. Back to the motel for a few more questions, then a laconic, "I'm very glad you have come." He would return in the morning for more talk. Still no inkling as to why I was there.

Around noon the next day he said, "We have a small foundation and have been observing your *ONE Institute Quarterly* with interest. Do you have any projects you would like funded?" Did we have projects? However, I knew that "consulting engineer" on the letterhead meant that he was not interested in projects as a category but *a project* capable of being presented in detail right then. Fortunately the best talked over [project] had been our long desired bibliography of homosexuality. If this was to be funded by him, I was told, I must go back to my board and set up a foundation for which he would pay. When I reported back to ONE's board their skepticism may well be imagined. A blonde high school student who wrestled with leopards? Clearly the heat in the South had got the best of me. After some weeks of their amused dismissal of my wild story reluctant approval was given to go ahead with the foundation. I flew to New York to complete the details in his beautiful apartment hard by the United Nations building. Thus the "Bibliography Project" was then put in motion, and eventually completed as a two-volume opus of more than 12,700 entries, by far the largest of its kind even yet [in 1993].[21] For the next twenty years other projects were funded. One day without any special reason the scales fell from my eyes and I realized that our benefactor, the small blonde boy, was a female to male transsexual, ONE's first large contributor.[22]

A savvy businessperson, Erickson suggested a solution to ONE Inc.'s tax problem. Under his direction and at his expense, the Institute for the Study of Human Resources (ISHR), a nonprofit corporation, was founded in August 1964, a short six weeks after his first meeting with Legg, for the purpose of accepting charitable donations. It could then donate the money to ONE Inc. or the ONE Institute as it saw fit. Legg chose ISHR's name in recognition of the human resources lost when repressive social attitudes toward homosexuality stifled the human spirit.[23] The title also reflected what the EEF described in an early brochure as the EEF's aim: "to assist where human potential [was] limited by physical, mental, or social conditions, or where the scope of research [was] too new, controversial, or imaginative to receive traditionally oriented support."[24] ISHR's mission greatly resembled the EEF's, reading in part: "to promote, assist, encourage and foster scientific research, study and investigation of male and female homosexuality and various other types of human behavior; to advance education."[25] ONE Inc.'s research, social service, and educational work now shifted to ISHR, which allowed ONE Inc. the freedom to work unabashedly for homosexual law reforms.[26] ISHR's acting directors were Legg (who was also the secretary), Tony Reyes, and Don Slater, all of whom had been among ONE Inc's founders. Erickson was named president, and his soon-to-be wife, Aileen Ashton, was made a founding director, a position she held until 1975.

While Erickson was interested in promoting homosexual law reform and ONE's specific goals, he had his own ideas about the programs that should be offered and the ways that EEF projects and ONE projects could function together. Since he controlled the lion's share of the funding, he greatly influenced ONE's direction during these crucial developmental years. [. . .]

Both ONE and the EEF were interested in providing educational materials for social change. For ONE, this interest had led to a sharp focus on formal educational opportunities in homophile studies, which the EEF eagerly and generously supported. Perhaps ONE's proudest accomplishment came in August 1981, when it received authorization from the state of California to be the first U.S. institution of higher learning to offer master's and doctoral degrees in homophile studies. Courses began in October, and the first degrees were awarded on January 30, 1982, at the thirtieth-anniversary celebration of the founding of ONE Inc. On this auspicious occasion, over six hundred people gathered in the Wilshire Room of the Los Angeles Hilton Hotel saw Erickson and Isherwood awarded honorary doctorates.[27] Remarkably, although Erickson was already a degree holder, this was the first and only college degree that Isherwood had at that time yet received.

Soon after the creation of the ONE Institute graduate school, Erickson suggested that a campus should be found to house the school, its libraries, ONE's business and "community center" offices, and the EEF's offices. The foundation's offices in Baton Rouge and New York City, like ONE's business offices, played a key role as a place to which transgendered and transsexual people could go for education and support. The EEF also had mailing addresses in El Paso, Texas; Los Angeles and Ojai, California; Phoenix, Arizona; and Panama City. Thus the idea of having one centralized location from which to run all these operations (including ONE and its projects) seemed timely. The idea was attractive to ONE because, among other reasons, the owner of 2256 Venice Boulevard had neglected the building, and its maintenance problems were becoming desperate.[28] Late in 1982 Legg met with real estate agent James Dunham, who then helped Erickson negotiate the purchase of an impressive property called "the Milbank Estate," which Erickson had seen only in photographs.[29] Dunham recalled Erickson telling him, "I am buying this property for ONE; we will show the straight world what we can do."[30] Elizabeth Clare Prophet's Church Universal and Triumphant, which occupied the estate at that time, was planning to move its headquarters to Montana. After some wrangling, a sale price of $1.9 million was agreed upon. However, as the completion of the deal neared, there was some concern that the church would not go through with the sale if it knew that the property would be used by a homosexual organization. For this reason, and also because of tax considerations, the ownership of the property was made out to the EEF.[31] A down payment of $95,000 was made, with $1.4 million due at the closing on February 17, 1983, and another $400,000 to be paid out by Erickson over the next four years.[32]

[. . .] Eight months later, on January 29, 1984, ONE Institute held an open house and convocation ceremony at the Milbank mansion during which they awarded one master's and two doctoral degrees in homophile studies, the world's first in that discipline.[33]

ONE and Erickson: The Unraveling of a Relation

Unfortunately, it seemed that no sooner had the ink dried on the contract for the Milbank purchase than the first signs of trouble in the relationship between Erickson and ONE began to surface. The deed to the property was supposed to have been turned over to ONE at a gala event on May 1, 1983, but the transfer was postponed until June 1, and then Erickson apparently abandoned the idea altogether.[34] The problems between ONE and Erickson resulted partly from the intrusion of Erickson's personal problems into the business partnership, partly from longstanding concerns about the relationship between trans and gay politics in the collaborative efforts of ONE and the EEF, and partly from Erickson's desire to use ONE to support projects unrelated to homosexuality.

Like many others, Erickson had experimented with illegal drugs during the previous decade. In the beginning, his use was purely recreational and did not interfere with his ability to conduct his business interests effectively. However, by the early 1980s he had developed a serious drug dependency. Erickson became a regular user of ketamine, a veterinary anesthetic that produced hallucinations in humans, and of cocaine.[35] In addition, he used other recreational drugs, although less extensively. By the time of the Milbank Estate purchase, the cumulative effects of Erickson's drug use were profound. He was frequently difficult to deal with and was often highly distrustful and suspicious of others, particularly those closest to him. He had become uncharacteristically inattentive to his business interests, forgetful, and increasingly unreliable.[36] This trend culminated in a series of arrests for drug offenses during the 1980s. Erickson's subsequent failures to appear in court eventually resulted in the forfeiture of several pieces of real estate and of large sums of money.[37] He was also suffering from bladder cancer, which left him unable to walk and semiconscious for days at a time.[38]

At the same time, tensions were increasing among ONE's leadership concerning the direction in which Erickson's funding was taking them. Jim Kepner later placed more of the blame for the break between Erickson and ONE on Legg than on Erickson. He recalled that Legg "went a little ways off of his rocker" when Erickson refused to turn over the deed to the Milbank estate. But the trouble had started even earlier:

> When ONE got the degree-granting privileges . . . Reed immediately wanted several of his metaphysical and other of his acquaintances, and probably some people involved with dope, to be given degrees. And Dorr flatly refused. Well, under the circumstances, since Reed was paying the bill, I would say Dorr made a serious blunder. Or he should have at least tried to keep negotiations open in some way . . . It [also] reached the point where I began to get kind of nervous: is ONE primarily a homophile organization, or is it a transsexual organization? I felt it got kind of out of balance. I felt that we support these people on our borders. If transsexuals define themselves as gay, well then, they're part of our community; if they define themselves as straight, well, we'll counsel them or help them or so on, but they're not really part of our community, by their own definition.[39]

Clearly, Erickson's ideas about who was "on the borders" were markedly different from Legg's and Kepner's. Additionally, Erickson's drug use and increasingly controlling support of ONE led to a growing confusion among ONE's leaders about ONE's role in relation to other EEF projects.

[. . .]

Late in 1988, Erickson's daughter Monica, then twenty years old, was appointed conservator of his affairs due to Erickson's ill health. In conjunction with her mother, Erickson's ex-wife Aileen, she continued the fight for possession and ownership of the Milbank estate. But on April 4, 1990, the title to Milbank was conveyed by court order to ONE and ISHR. That order was overturned by an appellate court and a new trial was ordered.[40] Appeals launched on behalf of the EEF and Erickson, who died early in 1992, continued until October of that year, when Monica Erickson, now his executor, agreed to a settlement. The property was to be divided between Erickson's heirs and ISHR. Monica Erickson took possession of the Milbank house, the tennis courts, and the surrounding lands, whereas ISHR received the McFie house, also known as the Arlington house; the chauffeur's quarters; a meditation sanctuary; and a few smaller service buildings. ISHR agreed to but never mounted a plaque on the Arlington house that was to acknowledge it as a gift from Reed Erickson and rename it Erickson House.[41] In 1992 the assessed value of the property received by ONE was over one million dollars.[42] By August 1, 1993, ONE had vacated the portion of the estate awarded to Monica Erickson and had turned the keys over to her.[43]

ONE Inc. After Erickson

As the relationship between Erickson and ONE deteriorated, so too had the ability of ONE to function at full capacity. For a decade most of ONE's human and financial resources had been engaged in the fight for the Milbank property. Moreover, the organization's primary source of income, the EEF's grants to ISHR, had ceased. For the first few years, Dorr Legg, Professor Walter L. Williams of the University of Southern California, and a few others had continued to provide courses to a handful of graduate students, but by the late 1980s only Legg still taught at the ONE Institute graduate school. Although he continued to do so until his death in 1994,[44] the institute granted no more degrees.

[. . .]

In January 1995 ONE regained prominence by merging with the International Gay and Lesbian Archives (IGLA) under the name ONE Institute.[45] ISHR, which still functions as a separate entity, supported the move with a donation of thirty-five thousand dollars and has continued to provide grants to ONE Institute.[46] The process of amalgamation was initiated and shepherded to completion by Walter L. Williams, who worked with ONE, IGLA, ISHR, and the University of Southern California to broker a deal that would strengthen all parties concerned. The newly reconstituted ONE Institute dedicated itself to several projects: the lecture series, educational outreach, ONE Institute Press, the new Center for Advanced Studies, and the maintenance of the combined ONE library and the IGLA collection.[47]

[. . .]

Thus, although ONE had encountered both great support and great difficulty in its uneasy collaboration with Reed Erickson and the Erickson Educational Foundation, it has regrouped and joined forces with other organizations that share its vision. Further, it has found a new benefactor in the University of Southern California. However, while ONE Institute continues to accrue public recognition, the work of Erickson and the EEF has gone virtually unnoticed. The proceeds from Erickson's philanthropy quietly continue to fund gay and lesbian research almost forty years after he saw the need for this support and offered his wealth and his expertise to provide it. The custodians of his donations, ISHR's board of directors, have conservatively invested the profits from the sale of the Milbank property and use the income to make small grants in support of gay and lesbian research connected to ONE Institute.[48] In this way Erickson's contributions continue to provide support quietly behind the scenes. ONE Institute thrives once again because of the hard work of dedicated individuals and the financial contributions of many. Yet without the generosity of one crucial benefactor, ONE's success would most likely now be only a chapter in the history of gay and lesbian activism.

Looking Back, Moving On

The relationship between ONE and Reed Erickson and the EEF ultimately ended in dissolution. A combination of factors was responsible, but several important points should be remembered. Both ONE and the EEF had common goals. They both sought to create social change through education, publicity, and the support of marginalized people. Both fostered research that contributed to the social acceptability of marginalized people and that was grounded in fact rather than in prejudice. Both recognized the need for substantial financial support of organizations working on such issues. Leaders of both organizations, mindful of their own experiences, strove to make the world a better place for others. Perhaps most significantly, both organizations recognized the need to work together as communities of marginalized people to effect significant and lasting change.

The story of the organizations' relationship is thus an important one not only for historians but also for activists and community members. The partnership, its problems, and its lessons provide us with valuable insights into the factors that can contribute to effective (or dysfunctional) relationships between transgender and homosexual groups. Since ONE has continued as an institution after the collapse of the EEF, the evidence we are left with and the versions of the story that remain in circulation are mainly from the perspective of ONE and its members. Erickson's personal and professional papers are much more difficult to trace than those of ONE, and many of his closest friends either are guarded in their comments or have died. It is thus unfortunate, both for Erickson and for gay, lesbian, bisexual, and transgender history, that a significant portion of the story remains as yet untold, and it is imperative that the contributions of transgendered and transsexual activists of the past do not go unnoticed.

Although ONE was a relatively unusual organization in the 1950s and 1960s, by the 1970s gay and lesbian social activism had proliferated rapidly. Other individuals and organizations had taken up the work of education and research about homosexuality; courses and programs of gay and lesbian studies had sprung up at many colleges and universities in Europe and North America. As of this writing, however, there are still no other U.S. institutions that offer graduate degrees in an area comparable to ONE's homophile studies.[49]

Much of the recent growth of gay and lesbian pride was built on an ethniclike gay identity that necessarily defined inclusion by the exclusion of others. Gay and lesbian pride has been created at least partly to counteract a society that taught gays and lesbians to be ashamed of who they are.[50] As gays and lesbians have found their pride, many have retreated in shame from the transgendered and transsexual people who had always been among them. This shunning of transgendered and transsexual people remains a dark corner in the struggle for gay and lesbian rights. Transgendered and transsexual people have understood the need for alliances and have made many important contributions to the fight for lesbian, gay, bisexual, and transgendered rights.[51] Reed Erickson was only one of the untold numbers of unsung transgendered and transsexual people who have given generously to a movement that has not always appreciated their gifts. By making more people aware of this one transsexual man's tremendous contributions to the growth and development of a vital arm of the gay and lesbian movement, we hope to have contributed to a reappraisal of the value of a united lesbian, gay, bisexual, and transgender movement. The story of the relationship between ONE and the EEF reminds us of the challenges of creating and maintaining a unified movement. It is important that we recognize the need to work together toward common goals and that as we do so we remember that, as Erickson (and Carlyle) so rightly recognized, we are all one.

From: Aaron H. Devor and Nicholas Matte, "ONE inc. and Reed Erickson: The Uneasy Collaboration of Gay and Trans Activism, 1964–2003," in *GLQ: A Journal of Lesbian and Gay Studies*, Volume 10, no. 2, pp. 179–209. Copyright 2004, Duke University Press. All rights reserved. Republished by permission of the copyright holder, Duke University Press. www. dukeupress.edu.

Notes

1. Joshua Gamson, "Must Identity Movements Self-Destruct? A Queer Dilemma," in *Queer Theory/ Sociology*, ed. Steven Seidman (Cambridge, MA: Blackwell, 1996), 395–420; Steven Seidman, "Introduction," in Seidman *Queer Theory/Sociology*, 1–29.

2. W. Dorr Legg, introduction to *Homophile Studies in Theory and Practice*, ed. W. Dorr Legg et al. (Los Angeles: ONE Institute Press; San Francisco: GLB, 1994), 1–6.

3. C. Todd White, "Dale Jennings (1917–2000): ONE's Outspoken Advocate," in *Before Stonewall: Activists for Gay and Lesbian Rights in Historical Context*, ed. Vern L. Bullough (New York: Harrington Park, 2002), 85.

4. Legg, introduction to *Homophile*, 2.

5. Ibid., 3; ONE Inc., "Articles of Incorporation and By-Laws, 1953," in Legg, *Homophile*, 339.

6. The articles of incorporation state that ONE's purposes were "1. To publish and disseminate magazines, brochures, leaflets, books and papers concerned with medical, social, pathological, psychological and therapeutic research of every kind and description pertaining to sociosexual behavior. 2. To sponsor, supervise and conduct educational programs, lectures and concerts for the aid and benefit of all social and emotional variants and to promote among the general public an interest, knowledge and understanding of the problems of such persons. 3. To stimulate, sponsor, aid, supervise and conduct research of every kind and description pertaining to sociosexual behavior. 4. To promote the integration into society of such persons whose behavior varies from current moral and social standards and to aid the development of social and moral responsibility in all such persons. 5. To lease, purchase, hold, have, use and take possession of and enjoy any personal or real property necessary for the uses and purposes of the corporation."

7. The first out-of-state subscription check came from Alfred C. Kinsey (W. Dorr Legg, "Exploring Frontiers: An American Tradition," *New York Folklore* 19 (1993): 228).

8. "40-Year Dedicated Activist Dorr Legg Dies at 89," *ONE-IGLA Bulletin*, Spring 1995, www.usc.edu/ isd/archives/oneigla/bulletin/articles/LeggBio.html; Legg, *Homophile*, 17.

9. David G. Cameron, "ONE Institute" and "Architecture Notes" (flyer prepared for the Da Camera Society of Mount St. Mary's College on the occasion of the Chamber of Music in Historic Sites concert, March 25, 1984), International Gay and Lesbian Archives (IGLA) collection. At its height *ONE Magazine* had a circulation of eleven thousand (ONE, "ONE 1952–1982: Thirty Year Celebration; Program of Events," 1982, collection of Aaron H. Devor).

10. Legg, *Homophile*, 52–53; Walter L. Williams, interview by Aaron H. Devor, tape recorded via telephone to Palm Springs, CA, May 12, 2000.

11. Legg, *Homophile*, 21–22.

12. Erickson Educational Foundation, brochure, collection of Aaron H. Devor.

13. *Erickson Educational Foundation Newsletter*, Spring 1983, 5.

14. "Introduction to a Course in Miracles," www.acim.org/about_acim_section/into_to_ acim.html (accessed November 7, 2003).

15. Legg, *Homophile*, 16.

16. W. Dorr Legg to Evelyn Hooker, February 8, 1968, IGLA collection.

17. W. Dorr Legg, interview by Vern L. Bullough, Los Angeles, December 15, 20, and 29, 1993.

18. W. Dorr Legg to Thomas Hunter Russell, January 24, 1989, IGLA collection.

19. Legg interview.

20. Ibid.

21. Vern L. Bullough et al., eds., *An Annotated Bibliography of Homosexuality*, 2 vols. (New York: Garland, 1976).

22. Legg, "Frontiers," 233.45. Ibid., 232.

23. Ibid., 232.

24. *Erickson Educational Foundation Newsletter*, Spring 1972, 1.

25. ISHR, "Articles of Incorporation and By-Laws," n.d., IGLA collection.

26. W. Dorr Legg to "Mort," February 14, 1968, IGLA collection.

27. Legg, *Homophile*, 74–77; Legg interview. According to the ONE "Program," presentations at the banquet were also made by Lisa Ben, Del Martin, and Phyllis Lyon. Ben was publisher of *Vice Versa*, "the earliest known American periodical especially for Lesbians. Nine typewritten issues were privately distributed, June 1947—Feb 1948." Martin and Lyon in 1955 had founded the Daughters of Bilitis, "the earliest lesbian emancipation organization in the U.S dedicated to understanding of, and by, the lesbian" (Legg, "Frontiers," 235).

28. Legg interview.

29. The 3.5-acre property known as the Milbank Estate was named after Isaac Milbank, who had commissioned its creation in 1913. In that year Milbank, who had been a vice president and the general manager of the company that later became Borden Milk, was president of the corporation that developed the Country Club Estates area of Los Angeles, so named for its previous use as the Los Angeles Country Club. The Mediterranean-style twenty-seven-room mansion, designed by G. Lawrence Stimson, cost the then huge sum of thirty-five thousand dollars. It was joined by a smaller, but still grand, Georgian-style residence for Milbank's daughter Phila and his son-in-law Lyman McFie and by several lesser buildings used for recreation and service purposes. The Milbanks and the McFies lived in these homes until their deaths in 1976.

30. *Erickson v. Legg*, C 499 120 (c/w C 520 792, C 541 097, C 693 216) U.S. p. 4 (n.d.). Trial brief and related cross-actions and consolidated actions, IGLA collection.

31. Legg wrote to Erickson that "the idea of putting the Milbank property temporarily in the name of Erickson Educational Foundation seems to make good sense." W. Dorr Legg to Reed Erickson, January 14, 1983, IGLA collection; *Erickson v. Legg*, C 499 120 (c/w C 520 792, C 541 097, C 693 216) U.S. p. 5 (n.d.). Trial brief and related cross-actions and consolidated actions, IGLA collection; Walter Williams recalled that Legg objected to this arrangement but that Erickson insisted that it was the best way to proceed (Williams interview, May 12, 2000). Monica Erickson recalled that it was never her father's intention to give title to ONE (e-mail message to Aaron H. Devor, October 21, 2003).

32. James Dunham, interview by Aaron H. Devor, tape recording, Los Angeles, June 12, 1996.

33. Legg, *Homophile*, 413.

34. Zelda Suplee to W. Dorr Legg, August 17, 1987, IGLA collection; Zelda Suplee to Antony Grey, June 1984, quoted in Grey interview.

35. Ketamine has more recently become a popular street and "club" drug also known as K, Ket, Special K, Vitamin K, and Kit Kat. For more information see the National Clearinghouse for Alcohol and Drug Information, www.health.org/pubs/qdocs/ketamine/index.htm.

36. Monica Erickson, interview by Aaron H. Devor, tape recording, Los Angeles, June 3, 1996; Suplee to Grey, June 1984, quoted in Grey interview.

37. Zelda Suplee to Antony Grey, September 26, 1985, quoted in Grey interview.

38. Monica Erickson, handwritten declaration, April 25, 1984, IGLA collection; *California v. Erickson*, FY15759 U.S. 1 (1984). Declaration of Michael S. Pratter, IGLA collection.

39. Kepner interview.

40. *Erickson v. Legg*, B0 51473, CA LASC No. C 499 120, consolidated with C 502 792, C 541 207, C 693 216, CA2/7 4 (1991). Respondents' brief, IGLA collection. That the court order was overturned and a new trial ordered was confirmed by Monica Erickson, e-mail message to Devor.

41. Thomas Hunter Russell to Michael S. Pratter and Alfred R. Keep, October 21, 1992, IGLA collection; Monica Erickson, e-mail message to Devor.

42. County Assessor's Records, "Data Concerning the Milbank Estate," IGLA collection.

43. W. Dorr Legg to Monica Erickson, August 1, 1993, IGLA collection.

44. Williams interview, April 23, 2000.

45. "ONE and IGLA Merge," *ONE-IGLA Bulletin*, Spring 1995, www.usc.edu/isd/archives/oneigla/bulletin/articles/ONE_IGLA_Merge.html.

46. "ISHR Awards $35,000 to General Fund," *ONE-IGLA Bulletin*, Winter 1998, www.usc.edu/isd/archives/oneigla/bulletin/articles/ISHR.html; Rasmussen interview; Walter L. Williams to Aaron H. Devor, May 12, 2000.

47. "ONE and IGLA Merge"; Ernie Potvin, "ONE Institute Organization and Activities," January 25, 1998, www.usc.edu/isd/archives/oneigla/organization_and_activities.htm.

48. Williams interview, April 23, 2000.

49. John G. Younger, "University LGBT Programs, Lesbian, Gay, Bisexual, Transgender, and Queer Studies in the USA and Canada plus Sibling Societies and Study-Abroad Programs," March 28, 2000, www.duke.edu/web/jyounger/lgbprogs.html.

50. Sally R. Munt, "Introduction," in *Butch/Femme: Inside Lesbian Gender*, ed. Sally R. Munt (London: Cassell, 1998), 1–12.

51. Leslie Feinberg, *Transgender Warriors: Making History from Joan of Arc to RuPaul* (Boston: Beacon, 1996), 90–99.

34 Pharmaco-Pornographic Regime

Sex, Gender, and Subjectivity in the Age of Punk Capitalism

Paul B. Preciado

Spanish architectural theorist and transdisciplinary sexuality scholar Paul B. Preciado coins a new term—*farmacopornigráfico* (pharmaco-pornographic)—to describe the post-World War II confluence of drugs, surgery, biotechnology, mass media, social media, cybernetics, and hypersexuality that now governs our lives. He extends and transforms Michel Foucault's influential arguments about power, discipline, and the formation of subjectivity to argue that disciplinary power is no longer "ortho-architectural," applied to the body by apparatuses beyond it. It operates, rather, through new pharmacological technologies that are physically incorporated into the body at the molecular level and regulate everything from birth control and erectile dysfunction to our mood, attention, and sleep. The figure of the transsexual—hormonally altered and surgically modified, rendered hypersexual and deemed obscene—functions a an master symbol of the pharmaco-pornographic era. As such, transness becomes a site of struggle, and DIY practices of "bio-hacking" the drug-based transformation of bodies and minds become a tactic of resistance, for surviving within the pharmaco-pornographic regime. This English version of Preciado's text, a chapter in his book *Testo Junkie*, first appeared in "Installing the Body," a 2009 special issue of the cultural theory journal *Parallax*.

During an era, recent and already irretrievable, Fordism and the automobile industry synthesized and defined a specific mode of production and of consumption. It instituted a Taylorist protraction of life: a smooth and polychrome aesthetic of the unanimated object, a way of thinking about interior space and of living in the city, a conflicting promise of the body and of the machine, a discontinued manner of desiring and of resisting. In the years following the energy crisis and the collapse of the assembly line, new sectors were said to explain the transformations of the global economy. Thus economic "experts" begin to speak of the biochemical industry, electronics, informatics or communication as the new industrial supports of capitalism.[1] But these discourses are not sufficient to explain the production of value and of life in contemporary society.

It seems possible and politically crucial to draw a new cartography of the transformations occurring in industrial production over the last century. With certain radical changes in view, the political management of body technologies that produce sex and sexuality can be seen to progressively become *the* business of the new millennium. It is today philosophically pertinent, following Foucault, to carry out a somatic-political analysis of the "world economy."[2] Economists usually situate the transition to a third type of capitalism around the seventies, after industrial and slavery regimes. These have traditionally been said to set

DOI: 10.4324/9781003206255-42

in motion a new type of "governmentality of the living," emerging from the corporal, physical and ecological urban ruins of the Second World War.[3] The mutation of capitalism that we witness in our time can be characterized by the conversion of "sex," "sexuality," "sexual identity" and "pleasure" into objects used for the political management of life, and also by the fact that this "management" itself takes place through the innovative dynamics of advanced techno-capitalism, global media, and biotechnologies. But first let us review some of the somatic-political events in recent history.

During the period of the Cold War, the United States invested more dollars in scientific research related to sex and sexuality than any other country had done before throughout history. Let us remember that the period between the beginning of the Second World War and the first years of the Cold War constitutes a moment without precedence for women's visibility in public space as well as the emergence of visible and politicized forms of homosexuality in such unexpected places as, for example, the American army.[4] Alongside this social development, American McCarthyism—rampant throughout the 1950s—added to the patriotic fight against communism the persecution of homosexuality as a form of antinationalism while exalting at the same time the family values of masculine labour and domestic maternity.[5] Meanwhile, architects Ray and Charles Eames collaborated with the American army to manufacture small boards of moulded-plywood to use as splints for mutilated appendages. A few years later, the same material was used to build furniture that came to exemplify the light design of modern disposable American architecture.[6] In 1941, George Henry carried out the first demographic study of "sexual deviation," a quantitative study of masses known as *Sex Variants*.[7] The Kinsey Reports on human sexual behaviour (1948 and 1953) and Robert Stoller's protocols for "femininity" and "masculinity" (1968) followed in sexological suit. During the early fifties and into the sixties, Harry Benjamin systemized the clinical use of hormonal molecules in the treatment of "transsexualism," a term first introduced in 1954. In 1941 the first natural molecules of progesterone and estrogens were obtained from the urine of pregnant mares (Premarin) and soon after synthetic hormones (Norethindrone) were commercialized. In 1957, Enovid, the first contraceptive pill was invented using synthetic estrogens, a hormone that would soon become the most used pharmaceutical molecule in the whole of human history.[8] In 1947, the laboratories Eli Lilly commercialized the molecule called Methadone (the most simple opiate) as an analgesic, which became in the seventies the basic substitution treatment for heroin addiction.[9]

Between 1946 and 1949 Harold Gillies was performing the first phalloplastic surgeries in the UK, including work on Michael Dillon, the first female-to-male transsexual to have taken testosterone as part of the masculinization protocol.[10] In 1952, U.S. soldier George W. Jorgensen was transformed into Christine, the first transsexual person discussed widely in the popular press. In 1953, Hugh Hefner founded *Playboy*, the first North American "porno" magazine to be sold in newsstands, with a photograph of Marilyn Monroe naked on the front page of the first publication. In 1957, the North American pedo-psychiatrist John Money coined the term "gender," differentiating it from the traditional term "sex", to define an individual's inclusion in a culturally recognized group of "masculine" or "feminine" behaviour and physical expression. Money famously affirmed that it is possible to "change the gender of any baby up to 18 months."[11] In 1960, the laboratories Eli Lilly commercialized Secobarbital, a barbiturate with anaesthetic, sedative and hypnotic properties conceived for the treatment of epilepsy, insomnia and as an anaesthetic for short surgery. Secobarbital, better known as "the red pill" or "doll," becomes one of the drugs of the rock underground culture of the '60s. At the start of the '60s, Manfred E. Clynes and Nathan S. Kline used the term "cyborg" for the first time to refer to an organism technologically supplemented to live in an extraterrestrial environment where it could operate as an "integrated homeostatic system."[12] They experimented with a laboratory rat, which received an osmotic prosthesis implant that it dragged along—a cyber tail. The first antidepressant that intervenes directly in the synthesis of a neurotransmitter called serotonin was invented in 1966. This would lead to the conception in 1987 of the molecule called Fluoxetine that would be commercialized under various names, the most renowned being Prozac®. In 1969, as part of a military investigation programme, Arpanet was created; it was the predecessor of the global Internet, the first "net of nets" of interconnected computers capable of transmitting information. [. . .] In 1972, Gerard Damiano produced the film *Deep Throat*. The film, starring Linda Lovelace, screened widely in the United States and became the most watched movie of all times, grossing more than $600 million. From this time on, porn film production boomed: from thirty clandestine films in 1950 to 2500 films in 1970. Homosexuality was withdrawn from the *Diagnostic and Statistical Manual of Mental Disorders* (DSM) in 1973. The soviet Victor Konstantinovich Kalnberz patented, in 1974, the first penis implant using polyethylene plastic rods as a treatment for impotency, resulting in a permanently erect penis. These implants were abandoned for chemical variants because they were found to be "physically uncomfortable and emotionally disconcerting." In 1977, the state of Oklahoma introduced the first lethal injection composed of barbiturates similar to the "red pill" to be used for the death penalty. The same method had already been applied in a Nazi German program called Action T4 for "racial hygiene" that euthanatized between 75,000 and 100,000 people with physical or psychic disabilities. The program was abandoned because of the high pharmacological cost; instead they substituted it for the methods of gas chambers or simply death caused by inanition. In 1983, Gender Identity Disorder (clinical form of transsexuality) was included in the DSM with diagnostic criteria for this new pathology. In 1984 Tom F. Lue, Emil A. Tanaghoy and Richard A. Schmidt implanted a "sexual pacemaker" in the penis of a patient. The contraption was a system of electrodes inserted close to the prostate that permits an erection by remote control.

During the '80s, new hormones were discovered and commercialized such as DHEA or the growth hormone, as well as numerous anabolic steroids that would be used legally and illegally in sports. In 1988, the pharmacological use of Sildenafil (commercialized as Viagra® by Pfizer laboratories) was approved for the treatment of penile "erectile dysfunction." It is a vasodilator without aphrodisiac effects that induces muscular relaxation and the production of nitric oxide in the cavernous body of the penis. From 1996 on, American laboratories produced synthetic oxyntomodulin, a hormone found to suppress human appetite by affecting the psycho-physiological mechanisms that regulate addiction; it was quickly commercialized to induce weight loss. At the beginning of the new millennium, four million children are being treated with Ritalin for hyperactivity and for the so-called "Attention Deficit Disorder" and more than two million children consume psycho-tropics destined to control depression.

During the Second World War, we see the exponential multiplication of the production of transuranic elements (the chemical elements with atomic numbers greater than 92—the atomic number of uranium) for use in the civil sector. This included plutonium, which had previously been used as nuclear fuel in military operations. The level of toxicity of transuranic elements exceeds that of any other element on Earth, creating a new form of vulnerability for life. At the same time, a viscous, semi-rigid material that is waterproof, thermally and electrically resistant, produced by artificial propagation of carbon atoms in long chains of molecules of organic compounds derived from petroleum, and whose burning is highly polluting, became generalized in manufacturing the objects of daily life. The mass consumption of plastic defined the material conditions of a large-scale ecological transformation resulting in the destruction of other (mostly lower) energy resources in the world, rapid consumption and high pollution. The *Trash Vortex*, a floating mass of the size of Texas in the north Pacific Ocean made of plastic garbage, was to become the most significant architecture of the twenty-first century.[13]

We are facing a new kind of capitalism that is hot, psychotropic and punk. These recent transformations indicate new micro-prosthetic mechanisms of control emergent from advanced bio-molecular techniques and media networks. The new world economy does not function without the simultaneous and interconnected production and deployment of hundreds of tons of synthetic steroids, without global dissemination of pornographic images, without the manufacturing of new varieties of legal and illegal synthetic psycho-tropics (e.g. enaltestovis, Special K, Viagra®, speed, crystal, Prozac®, ecstasy, poppers, heroin, omeoprazole) without the global dispersal of mega-cities of misery knotted into high concentrations of capital,[14] or without an informatic treatment of signs and numeric transmission of communication.

These are just some snapshots of a post-industrial, global and mediatic regime that I will call from here onwards *pharmaco-pornographic*. This term refers to the processes of a bio-molecular (pharmaco) and semiotic-technical (pornographic) government of sexual subjectivity—of which "the Pill" and *Playboy* are two paradigmatic offspring. During the second half of the twentieth century, the mechanisms of the pharmaco-pornographic regime are materialized in the fields of psychology, sexology and endocrinology. If science has reached the hegemonic place that it occupies as a discourse and as a practice in our culture it is precisely thanks to what Ian Hacking, Steve Woolgar and Bruno Latour call science's "material authority," that is to say, its capacity to invent and produce techno-living artifacts.[15] Techno-science has established its "material authority" by transforming the concepts of the psyche, libido, consciousness, femininity and masculinity, heterosexuality and homosexuality, intersexuality and transsexuality into tangible realities. They are manifest in commercial chemical substances and molecules, biotype bodies, and fungible technological goods managed by multinationals. The success of contemporary techno-science consists in transforming our depression into Prozac®, our masculinity into testosterone, our erection into Viagra®, our fertility/sterility into the Pill, our AIDS into Tritherapy without knowing which comes first: if depression or Prozac®; if Viagra® or an erection; if testosterone or masculinity; if the Pill or maternity; if Tritherapy or AIDS. This performative feedback is one of the mechanisms of the pharmaco-pornographic regime.

Contemporary society is inhabited by toxic-pornographic subjectivities: subjectivities defined by the substance (or substances) that supply their metabolism, by the cybernetic prostheses and various types of pharmaco-pornographic desires that feed the subject's actions and through which they turn into agents. So we will speak of Prozac® subjects, cannabis subjects, cocaine subjects, alcohol subjects, Ritalin subjects, cortisone subjects, silicone subjects, hetero-vaginal subjects, double-penetration subjects, Viagra® subjects, $ subjects . . . There is nothing to discover in nature, there is no hidden secret. We live in a punk hypermodernity: it is no longer about discovering the hidden truth in nature; it is about the necessity of specifying the cultural, political and technological processes through which the body as artefact acquires natural status. The Oncomouse, the laboratory mouse biotechnologically designed to carry a carcinogenic gene, eats Heidegger.[16] Buffy, the mutant vampire on television, eats Simone de Beauvoir. The dildo, a synthetic extension of sex to produce pleasure and identity, eats Rocco Siffredi's cock. There is nothing to discover in sex nor in sexual identity, there is no *inside*. The truth about sex is not a disclosure; it is *sexdesign*. Pharmaco-pornographic bio-capitalism does not produce *things*. It produces mobile ideas, living organs, symbols, desires, chemical reactions and conditions of the soul. In biotechnology and in porno-communication there is no object to be produced. The pharmaco-pornographic business is the *invention of a subject* and then its global reproduction.

In this period of the body's techno-management, the pharmaco-pornographic industry synthesizes and defines a specific mode of production and of consumption, a masturbatory temporization of life, a virtual and hallucinogenic aesthetic of the body, a particular way of transforming the inner in outer space and the city in a private junkspace[17] by means of selfsurveillance devices and ultra fast information distribution, resulting in continuous and uninterrupted loops of desire and resistance, of consumption and destruction, of evolution and self-extinction.

The History of Techno-Sexuality

In thinking about the transformations of European society at the end of the eighteenth century, Foucault describes the transition from what he calls a sovereign society towards a disciplinary society. A new form of power that calculates life technologically in terms of population, health and national interest, he notes, displaces a prior form of power that decided and ritualized death. Foucault calls this new diffuse set of *dispositifs* to regulate life *biopower*. This power overflows the legal and punitive spheres, to become a force that penetrates and constitutes the body of the modern individual. This power no longer behaves as a coercive law or as a negative mandate, but becomes versatile and responsive. Biopower is a *friendly-power* that takes the form of an art for governing life. As a general political technology, biopower morphs into disciplinary architectures (prison, barracks, schools, hospitals, etc.), scientific texts, tables of statistics, demographic calculus, employment options and public hygiene. Foucault underlined the centrality of sex and of sexuality in the modern art of governing life. The biopower processes of the feminine body's hysterization, children's sexual pedagogy, regulation of procreative conduct and the psychiatrization of the pervert's pleasures will be to Foucault the axes of this project that he distinguishes, not without irony, as a process of sexuality's modernization.[18]

The sex-political devices that develop with these new aesthetics of sexual difference and sexual identities are mechanical, semiotic and architectonical techniques to naturalize sex. These devices include *The Atlas of Human Sex Anatomy*, treatises on maximizing the natural recourses available from population growth, judiciary texts about the penalization of transvestism or of sodomy, handcuffs that restrain the hands of masturbating girls to their beds, iron ankle spreaders that separate the legs of hysterics, silver films that engrave photographic images of the dilated anuses of passive homosexuals, straitjackets that hold the indomitable bodies of masculine women. . . .[19] These devices for the production of sexual subjectivity take the form of a political architecture *external* to the body. These systems have a firm command of orthopaedic politics and disciplinary exoskeletons. The model for these techniques of subjectivization, according to Foucault, could be Bentham's architecture for the prison-factory (and in particular, panopticism), the asylum or military barracks. If we think about devices of sex-political subjectivization then we must also speak about the net-like expansion of "domestic architecture." These extensive, intensive and, moreover, intimate architectural forms include a redefinition of private and public spaces, the management of sexual commerce, but also gynecological devices and sexual orthopedic inventions (the corset, the speculum, the medical vibrator), as well as new media techniques of control and representation (photography, film, incipient pornography) and the massive development of psychological techniques for introspection and confession.

It is true that up till here Foucault's analytical overview, though not always historically and chronologically exact, is critically sharp. However, it is also true that the valuable insights he offers begin to blur the closer the analysis comes to contemporary societies. It seems that Foucault does not consider the profound changes, beginning during the Second World War, that occur with a new set of technologies for producing sexual subjectivity. As I see it, these somatic-political technologies require us to conceptualize a third regime of power-knowledge, neither sovereign nor disciplinary, neither pre-modern or modern, in order to take into consideration the deep and lasting impact of these new body technologies on contemporary constructions of subjectivity. In the Postscript of *A Thousand Plateaus*, Deleuze and Guattari are inspired by Williams S. Burroughs to name this "new monster" of social organization derived from biopolitical control a "society of control."[20] I prefer to call it, reading Burroughs along with Bukowski, *pharmaco-porn-power*: a politically programmed ejaculation is the currency of this new sexual-micro-informatic control.

The somatic-political context after the Second World War seems to be dominated by a set of new technologies of the body (e.g. biotechnologies, surgery, endocrinology) and of representation (e.g. photography, film, television and cybernetics) that infiltrates and penetrates everyday life as never before. We live in an era of proliferating bio-molecular, digital and high-speed technologies; of the soft, light, slimy and jelly technologies; of the injectable, inhalable, and incorporable technologies. Testosterone gel, the Pill and psychotropics all belong to this set of *soft technologies*. We are heavily involved in something that can be called—recalling the work of Zygmunt Bauman—a sophisticated form of "liquid" control.[21]

Whereas in the disciplinary society, technologies of subjectivation control the body from the outside as an ortho-architectonic exterior device, in the pharmaco-pornographic society of control, technologies enter the body to form part of it: they dissolve in the body; they become the body. Here somatic-politics become tautological: techno-politics take the form of the body; techno-politics becomes (in)corporate. In the middle of the twentieth century, the first signs of the new somatic-political regime's transmutation were the electrification, digitalization and molecularization of devices of control that specifically produce sexual difference and sexual identities. Little by little, the orthopaedic sexual mechanisms and disciplinary architectonics are being absorbed by pharmacological microinformatics and instant audiovisual transmission techniques. If in the disciplinary society, architecture and orthopaedics served as models to understand the relation of body-power, in the pharmaco-pornographic society, the models for body control are micro-prosthetics: pharmaco-porn-power acts through molecules that become part of our immune system; from the silicon that takes the form of breasts, to a neurotransmitter that modifies our way of perceiving and acting, to a hormone and its systematic affect on hunger, sleep, sexual excitation, aggression and the social codification of our femininity and masculinity. The devices of surveillance and control that are common to a disciplinary sex-political regime will thus progressively assist the pharmaco-pornographic subject's miniaturization, internalization and reflexive introversion (a twist towards the inside, towards the space that is considered to be intimate, private). A common trait of the new soft technologies of microcontrol is that they take the form of the body; they control by transforming into "body", until they become inseparable and indistinguishable from it. Soft technologies become the stuff of subjectivity. Here the body no longer inhabits disciplinary spaces, but is inhabited by them.

The bio-molecular and organic structure of the body is a last resort for these control systems. This moment contains all the horror and exaltation of the body's political potential. Unlike the disciplinary society, pharmaco-pornographic society no longer works over a modern *corpus*. The new pharmaco-pornographic body does not have its limits at the skeletal wrapping that the skin delineates. This new body cannot be understood as a biological substratum outside the framework of production and cultivation, typical features of technoscience. As Donna J. Haraway teaches us, the contemporary body is a techno-living being, "a networking techno-organic-textual-mythic system."[22] Organism and machine, nature and culture are obsolete disciplinary fictions. This new condition of the body blurs the traditional modern distinction between art, performance, media, design, and architecture. The new pharmacological and surgical techniques set in motion tectonic construction processes that combine figurative representations derived from cinema and from architecture (editing, 3D modelling or personality design, etc.), according to which the organs, the vessels, the fluids (techno-blood, techno-sperm, etc.) and the molecules are converted into the prime material from which our pharmaco-pornographic corporality is manufactured. Techno-bodies are either not-yet-alive or already-dead: we are half foetuses, half zombies. Thus, every politics of resistance is a monster politics.

Techno-Gender

The invention of the category *gender* announces the arrival of the new pharmacoporno-graphic regime of sexuality. Far from being the creation of 60s feminism, the category of gender belongs to the bio-technological discourse from the 1950s. "Gender", "masculinity" and "femininity" are inventions of the Second World War that would see their full commer-cial expansion during the Cold War, along with objects such as canned food, the computer, plastic chairs, nuclear energy, television, the credit card, the disposable pen, the bar code, the air bed and the artificial satellite.

Arguing against the rigidity of the nineteenth century concept of "sex", John Money, who conducted the first methodological treatment of intersex babies, advanced the tech-nological plasticity of "gender." In 1957, Money used the notion of "gender" for the first time in speaking about the possibility of technologically modifying, through the use of hormones and surgery, the bodily presentation of babies born with "unclassifi-able" (according to medicine's visual and discursive criteria) feminine or masculine genital organs and/or chromosomes. With Anke Ehrhardt and Joan and John Hampson, Money would later develop his claim into a strict clinical procedure for tinkering with young intersexual bodies.[23] When Money uses the term "gender" to refer to "psychological sex," he basically thinks about the exciting possibility of using technology to modify the deviant body, in order to bring it into accordance with pre-existing prescriptive ideals for feminine and masculine human bodies. If in the nineteenth century disciplinary system sex was natural, definitive, untransferable and transcendental, then *gender* now appears to be synthetic, malleable, variable, and susceptible of being transferred, imitated, produced and technically reproduced. Far from the rigidity of exterior techniques to normalize the body practiced by the disciplinary system at the end of the nineteenth and begin-ning of the twentieth century, the new gender techniques of the bio-capitalist pharmaco-pornographic regime are flexible, internal and assimilable. Twenty-first century gender functions as an abstract device of technical subjectivation: it is glued, it is cut, it is dis-placeable, it is named, it is imitated, it is swallowed, it is injected, it is grafted, it is digital-ized, it is copied, it is designed, it is bought, it is sold, it is modified, it is mortgaged, it is transferred, it is downloaded, it is applied, it is transcribed, it is falsified, it is executed, it is certified, it is exchanged, it is dosed, it is provided, it is extracted, it shrinks, it is sub-tracted, it is denied, it is renounced, it is betrayed, it mutates.

Gender (femininity/masculinity) is not a concept, it is not an ideology, and it is not sim-ply a performance: *it is a techno-political ecology.* The certainty of being a man or a woman is a somatic-political fiction that functions as an operational program of subjectivity through which sensorial perceptions are produced that take the form of affections, desires, actions, beliefs, identities. One of the defining results of this technology of gender is the production of an interior knowledge about oneself, of a sense of the sexual "I" that appears to one's con-sciousness as emotional evidence of reality. "I am man," "I am woman," "I am heterosexual," "I am homosexual" are some of the formulations that condense specific knowledges about oneself, acting as hard biopolitical and symbolic nuclei around which it is possible to attach a set of practices and discourses.

The pharmaco-pornographic regime of sexuality cannot function without the circulation of an enormous quantity of semiotic-technical flows: hormonal flows, silicon flows, digital flows, textual and of representation. *Definitively, this third regime cannot function without the constant trafficking of gender bio-codes.* In this political economy of sex, the normalization of difference depends on the control, re-appropriation and use of these flows of gender.

[. . .]

Forty years after the invention of the endocrine gender control techniques (like the Pill) all sexual bodies are subject to a *common* pharmaco-pornographical platform. Today a bio-man will take a hormonal testosterone supplement to increase his performance in sports; a subcutaneous compound of estrogens and progesterone, active over three years, will be implanted in an adolescent as a contraconceptive; a bio-woman who defines herself as a man could sign a protocol of sex change and access an endocrinology therapy based on testosterone that will make him grow a beard and moustache, increase musculature and pass socially as a man in less than eight months; a sixty year old bio-woman who ingested a high dose of estrogens and progesterone in her contraceptive pills for over twenty years will have kidney failure or breast cancer and receive chemotherapy similar to the kind administered to the victims of Chernobyl; a heterosexual couple will turn to in vitro insemination after discovering that the male of the couple cannot produce sufficient mobile spermatozoids to fertilize the ovule of his partner, due to a high intake of tobacco and alcohol . . .

All this indicates that the diverse sexual identities, the various models of having sex and producing pleasure, the plural ways of expressing gender coexist with a *"becoming-common"*[24] of the technologies that produce gender, sex and sexuality.[25]

Resistances, Mutations . . .

But a process of deconstructing and constructing gender that Judith Butler has called "undoing gender" is always already taking place.[26] Dismantling these gender programmes requires a set of denaturalizing and disidentification operations. These take place, for example, in drag king and criss-cross practices, hormonal self-experiments, crip and postporn practices which in political terms function as techniques for de-installing gender.

In the year 2000, establishing in a certain way our corporal future in the new millennium, the Scottish surgeon Robert Smith became the subject of an international bioethics controversy for accepting the petition of Gregg Furth, a patient who applied for the amputation of his healthy legs. He was suffering from what is known today under the nomenclature of Body Integrity Identity Disorder (BIID), an illness of misidentifying one's real and imagined corporal integration. Furth perceived his own biped body to be contrary to what he thought was *his* ideal body image. Even though the bioethics committee prevented the operation from taking place, Smith confirmed that he had amputated several patients with similar pathologies of "corporal dysmorphism" between 1993 and 1997. To some, nostalgic for the modern body, these operations are considered to be appallingly aberrant. But who would dare to cast the first stone at Furth: candidates for lifting and liposuction, people fitted with pacemakers, consumers of "the Pill," addicts to Prozac, to Tranquimazin or to cocaine, slaves of the hypo-calorie regime, consumers of Viagra, or those who spend an average of eight hours per day connected to an informatic-mediatic prosthesis, i.e. computers, television, games on the net?

Furth is not an isolated madman who wants to submit himself, under medically controlled conditions, to a chirurgical bacchanal worthy of *Texas Chainsaw Massacre*. On the contrary, he is one of the known creators of a set of micro-political movements that demand the right to redefine the living body outside of a hegemonic society's normative restrictions for legitimate able bodies. The political defenders of elective mutilation adopt the slogan of Mies Van der Rohe "less is more" as the new economy for their project's ideal corporal architecture. The BIID project resists corporal normalization imperatives and brutally brings to light the cultural and political law constructed out of the binary disability/normality. In parallel, activists of the self-styled "crip" movement are putting the medical industry on the rack by refusing to receive cochlear electronic prostheses implants that would enable them to hear. Crip activists, inspired by the political tradition of the feminist, black and queer movements, defend their right to stay in the "culture of deafness." They argue that access to sound through prosthesis is a normative imposition that forces them to be part of the dominant auditory culture. Similarly, at the end of the 80s, the transgender movement commenced by criticizing the enforced use of technologies for sex changes, which sought to normalize the transsexual's body. Bio-men and the bio-women (indistinctly heterosexuals and homosexuals), but also those transsexuals who have access to chirurgical, endocrinological or legal techniques to produce their identity, are not simple economical classes in the Marxist sense of the term, but authentic *pharmaco-pornopolitical factories*. These subjects are at the same time prime pharmaco-pornopolitical *material* and the *producers* (rarely the proprietors), as well as consumers of gender's bio codes. Activists like Kate Bornstein, Pat Califia, Del LaGrace Volcano, Dean Spade, Jacob Hale, Sandy Stone and Moisés Martínez reject the psychiatrization of transsexuality (until now defined, in a similar way as BIID, as gender dysphoria) and defend their right to define their own sex, reappropriating hormonal and chirurgical techniques to construct themselves, in loud disagreement with normative codes of masculinity and femininity. They produce self-designed sexes.

Hackers use the Internet and copyleft programs for the free and horizontal distribution of information tools. They affirm that the social movement that they lead is within everyone's reach, via the Internet. The copyleft pharmaco-pornographic movement has a techno-living platform far more accessible than the Internet: the body. But not the naked body, or the body as immutable nature, but the techno-life body as biopolitical archive and cultural prosthesis. Your memory, your desire, your sensibility, your skin, your dick, your dildo, your blood, your sperm, your vulva, your gonads, etc. are the tools of a possible *gender-copyleft* revolution. Gender-copyleft tactics should be subtle but determinant: the future of sex and the open gender of the species is at stake. There should not be one single name that can be patented. It will be our responsibility to remove the code, to open political practices, to multiply possibilities. This movement—that has already begun—could be called Postporno, Free Fuckware, Bodypunk, Opengender, Fuckyourfather, PenetratedState, TotalDrugs, PornTerror, Analinflaction, TechnoPriapismoUniversalUnited . . .

By voluntarily declining politically marginal identities or by electing their own sexpolitical status, these corporal self-determination movements show that the desired "normal body" is the effect of violent devices of representation, control and cultural production. What the BIID, crip or transgender movements teach us is that it is no longer a question of making a choice between a *natural body* and a *techno body*. No, now the question is whether we want to be docile consumers of biopolitical techniques and complicit producers of our own bodies, or, alternatively, if we want to become conscious of the technological processes of which we are made. Either way, we must collectively risk inventing new ways of installing and reinstalling subjectivity.

Notes

Thank you to Yvette Vinke and Eliza Steinbock for helping me with the translation and to Susan Stryker for her sharp reading and editing of the text.

1. Some of the most influential analyses of the current transformations of industrial society and capitalism relevant to my own work are: Mauricio Lazzarato, "Le concept de travail immaterial: la grande enterprise," *Futur Antérieur*, n.10 (1992); Antonella Corsani, "*Vers un renouveau de l'économie politique, anciens concepts et innovation théorique*," *Multitudes*, n.2 (2000); Antonio Negri and Michael Hardt, *Multitudes* (Paris: Editions La Decouverte, 2004); Yann Moulier Boutang, *Le capitalismo cognitif. La grande transformation* (Paris: Ámsterdam, 2007).

2. I refer here to Foucault's notion "*somato-pouvoir*" and "*technologie politique du corps.*" See Michel Foucault, *Surveiller et punir* (Paris: Gallimard, 1975), pp. 33–36; Michel Foucault, "Les rapports de pouvoir passent à l'intérieur du corps," *La Quinzaine Littéraire*, 247 (January 1977), pp. 4–6. Also, here I draw on the well-known expression used by Immanuel Wallerstein, *World-Systems Analysis: An Introduction* (Durham, NC: Duke University Press, 2004).

3. Michel Foucault, *Du gouvernement des vivants* (Collège de France, 1980) (unpublished).

4. Alan Berube, *Coming Out Under Fire: The History of Gay Men and Women in World War Two* (New York: The Free Press, 1990).

5. John D'Emilio, *Sexual Politics, Sexual Communities: The Making of a Homosexual Minority in the United States, 1940–1970* (Chicago: Chicago University Press, 1983).

6. See Beatriz Colomina, *Domesticity at War* (Cambridge, MA: MIT Press, 2007), p. 29.

7. Jennifer Terry, *An American Obsession: Science, Medicine, and Homosexuality in Modern Society* (Chicago: The University of Chicago Press, 1999), pp. 178–218.

8. Andrea Tone, *Devices and Desires. A History of Contraceptives in America* (New York: Hill and Wang, 2001), pp. 203–231; Lara V. Marks, *Sexual Chemistry: A History of the Contraceptive Pill* (New Haven: Yale University Press, 2001).

9. Tom Carnwath and Ian Smith, *Heroin Century* (New York: Routledge, 2002), pp. 40–42.

10. Harold Gillies and Ralph Millard Jr., *The Principles and Art of Plastic Surgery Volume II* (Boston: Little, Brown, 1957), pp. 385–88; Michael Dillon, *Self: A Study in Ethics and Endocrinology* (London: Heinemann, 1946). See also Bernice L. Hausman, *Changing Sex, Transsexualism, Technology, and the Idea of Gender* (Durham, London: Duke University Press, 1995), p. 67.

11. John Money, Joan Hampson, and John Hampson, "Imprinting and the Establishment of Gender Role," *Archives of Neurology and Psychiatry*, 77 (1957), pp. 333–336.

12. M. E. Clynes and N. S. Kline, "Cyborgs and Space," *Astronautics* (September 1960).

13. See Mike Davis, "Planet of Slums," *New Left Review*, 26 (April–March 2004).

14. Ian Hacking, *Representing and Intervening: Introductory Topics in the Philosophy of Natural Science* (Cambridge: Cambridge University Press, 1986); Bruno Latour and Steve Woolgar, *La vie de laboratoire. La construction des faits scientifiques* (Paris: La Découverte, 1979).

15. See: Donna J. Haraway, *Modest_Witness@Second_Millennium. FemaleMan©Meets_OncoMouse™: Feminism and Technoscience* (New York: Routledge, 1997), p. 54; Susan Freinkel, *Plastic: A Toxic Love Story* (Boston: Houghton Mifflin Harcourt, 2011).

16. See Donna J. Haraway, "When Man™ is on the Menu," in *Incorporations*, ed. Jonathan Crary and Sanford K. Winter (New York: Zone Books, 1992).

17. See Rem Koolhaas's notion of "junkspace" in "Junkspace," *October* 100 (June 2002), pp. 175–190.

18. Michel Foucault, *Histoire de la sexualité* (Paris: Gallimard, 1976), pp. 136–139; Michel Foucault, *Naissance de la biopolitique: Cours au Collège de France, 1978–1979* (Paris: Gallimard/Seuil, 2004).

19. For a visual history of hysteria see Georges Didi-Huberman, *Invention of Hysteria: Charcot and the Photographic Iconography of the Salpetriere* (Cambridge, MA: MIT Press, 2004).

20. Gilles Deleuze, "Post-scriptum sur les sociétés de contrôle," in *Pourparlers* (Paris: Minuit, 1990), p. 241.

21. Zygmunt Bauman, *Liquid Modernity* (Cambridge: Polity Press, 2000).

22. Donna J. Haraway, *Simians, Cyborgs, and Women. The Reinvention of Nature* (New York: Routledge, 1991), p. 219.

23. John Money, Joan Hampson, and John Hampson, "Imprinting and the Establishment of Gender Role," *Archives of Neurology and Psychiatry*, 77 (1957), pp. 333–336.

24. I am using here the notion of "becoming-common," "*devenir-commun*" invoked by Michael Hardt and Toni Negri to explain the new common condition of biopolitical work. See: Michael Hardt and Toni Negri, *Multitude: War and Democracy in the Age of Empire* (New York: Penguin Press, 2005), p. 142.

25. See Antonio Negri and Michael Hardt, *Multitudes*.

26. Judith Butler, *Undoing Gender* (New York: Routledge, 2004).

35 Reading *Transsexuality* in "Gay" Tehran (Around 1979)

Afsaneh Najmabadi

In this account of "sex-change" in Tehran before and after the 1979 revolution that established the Islamic Republic of Iran (IRI), feminist historian Afsaneh Najmabadi shows how ordinary citizens can play a role in defining state power. Her meticulous historical and ethnographic research reframes two common Western misconceptions about gayness and transness in Iran in the 1970s— Teheran was neither a "gay mecca" during the Palavi regime before the revolution, nor did the IRI force homosexuals to undergo sex reassignment after the revolution. Drawing on mass media representation, medical and religious literature, and first-person interviews, Najmabadi shows how gender-variant and same-sex-loving people navigated shifting categories of gender and sexual identity across a momentous political transformation. She documents how the line between transness and gayness has always been a site of contestation and struggle. One of the most significant contributions this article makes to trans studies scholarship is the extent to which it shows that what counts as trans is largely determined by state and nation and varies widely across time and in various locales. This version of Najmabadi's research, first published in *The Transgender Studies Reader 2* in 2013, is drawn from her longer book project, *Professing Selves: Transsexuality and Same-Sex Desire in Contemporary Iran* (2014).

Tehran in the early 1970s offered a spectrum of overlapping conceptions of maleness and masculinities. This spectrum structured everyday practices of life with regard to non-heteronormative male gender/sexual desires, and it construed non-heteronormative male-ness as being at once criminal, immoral, and theatrical. This article offers a preliminary mapping of that scene. It is not, and cannot be, a social history of "gay Tehran." Although the available scholarly writing on this topic agrees on the existence of an "active gay subculture"[1] in 1970s Tehran, this literature is anecdotal, and the critical archival research necessary to produce a proper history remains yet to be done. But I also want to argue that to name the 1970s as the decade of a *gay* Tehran obscures important (in)distinctions between what is now named gay (always considered male in this context by all writers on the topic) and what is now considered MtF trans. My purpose is thus to offer an initial survey of the complex overlaps and connections between these sorts of non-heteronormative lives. I want to trace continuities across the "before" and "after" of the 1979 revolution, as well as note the ruptures introduced by regime change into the scene of male non-heteronormativities. Simply casting the advent of the Islamic Republic as the brutal end of Gay Tehran does not do justice to the complexity of the tale.

DOI: 10.4324/9781003206255-43

The story of "Gay Tehran" in the 1970s has been articulated in at least two domains. At the time, there were a number of articles about Tehran's "gay scene" in the American gay press, which reported its extermination by the policies of the Islamic Republic in the 1980s.[2] There is an implicit progressivist dynamic to these stories: the emerging gay subculture of Tehran would have evolved naturally into a livelier, more open, gay Tehran, except that its life was cut short through the 1979 revolution and subsequent Islamization of society. As Jerry Zarit's end-of-the-decade article put it succinctly, "Iran was for me, and for others like me, a sexual paradise. In terms of both quantity and quality it was the most exciting experience of my life."[3] The quests of Western gays for a sexual paradise in Iran specifically, while unselfconsciously reenacting broader cultural tendencies to sexualize an exotic "Orient," were most likely influenced by the publication and enormous popularity of Mary Renault's *The Persian Boy* in 1972, which was widely reviewed and reported on in the American gay press in the 1970s.[4]

A second domain for the formation of the "Gay Tehran" story has been within Iranian diasporic gay communities—some members of which personally experienced the 1970s there.[5] But their recollections are narrated through later *gay* identification developed in their new homes, which, in the 1980s and 1990s when much of this immigration took place, were dominated by a particular style of sexual identity politics. The Iranian gay diasporic progressivist narrative was informed by this sensibility—and through the lens of later identities, earlier sexual and gender subjectivities and practices came to be seen as problematic and backward.

From its earliest manifestation in the diasporic press, Iranian gay identity marked its emergence through a disidentification with that past. This included a very clear demarcation between *hamjinsgara'i* (same-sex inclination/orientation) and *hamjinsbazi* (same-sex playing).[6] The former has been embraced as a modern form of identification that outwardly expresses a true inner self; *hamjinsbazi*, on the other hand, has been disavowed, perhaps because of its pejorative use by government officials, in condemnatory religious texts, in pathologizing contexts by medical professionals, or in hostile general usage within Iranian society and culture at large. The disavowal of *hamjinsbazi* by diasporic gays has been articulated through turning societal and cultural abjection back onto the concept itself: they disavow same-sex-playing due to its presumed abusive character, and its being marked by disparities of age and economics. This is in contrast to same-sex-oriented relations (characterized as *hamjinsgara'i*) that allow for genuinely egalitarian romantic relationships among same-sex partners.[7] The differentiating move between *hamjinsgara'i* and *hamjinsbazi* thus articulates a homonormative response to an anti-heteronormative project.[8]

The imaginary of "Gay Tehran" works differently in these two domains. For the growing gay liberation movement of the 1970s in the United States, traveling to "Gay Tehran," in fiction or in person, was a search for one's "own kind" beyond national borders. In that sense, it fit well with liberationist dreams of the internationalization of activism, and with solidarity work based on "finding the same everywhere" (as in, "Sisterhood is Global").[9] Within diasporic Iranian gay activist politics, imagining the "Gay Tehran" of the 1970s offered a critical intervention into the Iranian cultural politics of denial that insisted on the foreignness of non-normative gender/sexual desires and practices. My point here is not to question the sociological existence of such non-normative desires and practices, but to suggest, rather, that imagining them and the period of 1970s as *gay* may prevent other, equally pertinent ways of thinking about the scene of male non-normative gender/sexuality during that decade. Actively un-familiarizing ourselves with what already has been read through the prism of "Gay Tehran" would, I hope, open up the possibility of seeing differently, and asking different questions about, non-heteronormative practices of life at that time.

The Spectacle of Unmanly Males

The "Gay Tehran" I wish to reread was part of a complex, rapidly growing urban society, in certain domains of which particular styles of non-heteronormative male lives were becoming somewhat visible. This was particularly the case in the growing entertainment industry, which ran the gamut from high-quality modern film and television shows to nightclubs that catered to a range of class-inflected tastes. "Lower class" clubs were performance venues that sustained older and more traditional forms of male dance and entertainment, while the performance of such dances in newer, more cosmopolitan nightclubs, and in film, made them more visible to a layer of the urban middle-class population that may not have been exposed to them in earlier decades; indeed, the urban middle class may well have developed its sense of modern-ness in part from the disavowal of such cultural enactments.

Stories of females living unusual masculine lives fascinated the public during this period; such stories were common features in history books, neighborhood gossip, newspapers, and magazines from 1950s through the 1970s.[10] In many of these cases, especially in the women's press of the 1960s, the stories of females living masculine lives would be rescued from the suspicion of "improper sexuality" through the affirmation of a modern marriage ideal, the failure of which had pushed women into these unusual paths, through cruel arranged marriages or good-for-nothing husbands. Alternatively, economic hardship and the social inhospitality of many professions to women were said to have forced the choice of masculine living. This acceptable configuration of public female non-normative gender self-styling did not have an equivalent for males: males who did not or could not marry and perform their "marital duties" could not get away from their social obligations through a surfeit of feminine performance.

In earlier eras, a male dressing as a woman and opting for a womanly career constituted "housewifery," that is, becoming a male kept by a man.[11] By the mid-twentieth century, such a practice of life was no longer possible; it would have added scandalous shame to the insult and injury of refusing adult manhood. Males then who wanted to *live* womanly lives tended to keep it a secret, fearing censure and punishment. [. . .]

Because male dancers and *zan-push* [woman-attired] actors continued to work in the café entertainment scene as well as in some of the "grittier" nightclubs, these more traditional male dancers and entertainers increasingly may have been marked, for the emerging urban middle classes, as a lower-class taste tainted by the immorality of a suspected sexual availability. But the figure of the female-attired male actor/dancer attained a new, somewhat more respectable, life in the cinema and in "legitimate" theatrical productions.[12] [. . .] It was a style of performance already prevalent in the 1940s and 1950s, and there was a significant traffic, even then, between the worlds of stage and screen and the ongoing public conversations about sex change, which circulated around such figures.

[. . .]

The world of non-heteronormative males was visible in the 1970s not only in the world of "gritty" entertainment. The upper echelons of an expansive art world—painters, photographers, television producers and performers—were also rumored to harbor non-masculine males. Indeed, the two poles of the culture industry were not sealed off from each other. At elite parties catering to males who dressed as women, members of high society mingled with *khanums* who worked in menial day jobs.[13] One difference was that the very rich could dress at home and be safely driven to such parties by their chauffeurs, whereas the less affluent had to change clothes on arrival. These get-togethers were the nonheteronormative male equivalent of daureh parties (women's-night-out parties that rotated on a circuit between different women's homes). The more well-to-do males would throw lavish parties and invite the rest of their circles—sometimes numbering in the hundreds.

[. . .]

The Shame of Unmanly Males and the Hope of Gender Ambiguity

The emergence in the 1970s of more visible scenes of non-heteronormative maleness, along with increased knowledge of such scenes circulating in speech and print, was widely perceived as a moral corruption of Iranian culture through Westernization. The perception had class connotations: only elite society in Tehran was assumed capable of fostering such calamities. The extensive circulation of extravagant rumors about high-society circles of non-heteronormative males became part of the criticism of Pahlavi Court culture, which was seen as corrupt and as encouraging further corruption. While subsequent to the establishment of the Islamic Republic and the world-wide growth of Islamist movements, one tends to associate such criticism with an "Islamist backlash," in the 1970s, attacks against an "excess of cultural liberties" were a much more broadly voiced concern.[14] What sustained the power of non-heteronormative maleness as a sign of excessive liberty (or, as it was by then commonly called "Westoxication"),[15] was the overwhelming feeling of shame and disgust associated with any public spectacle of non-masculine maleness and non-heteronormative sexuality.

What made "it"—this preferably un-named horror—a cultural assault and moral insult was above all *not* its putative Western origin, but the shame of being *kuni*. The most derogatory word in realm of sexuality, *kuni* literally means anal, but in Persian it exclusively means to be receptive of anal penetration. Young male adolescents often first become familiar with the word as that which signals the edge of abjection; for instance, when parents warn their young son to stay away from certain activities (such as dance) and from certain (ill-reputed) persons, lest they become *kuni*. The equivalent word for women, *baruni*, does similar disciplinary work, but its moral load is much lighter.[16]

The gut-shame associated with *kuni* seems to have made it resistant to any measure of self-appropriation and re-signification. When the word *gay* began to arrive in Tehran from the West, some did not take to it. Behzad said he initially "disliked *gay* because in my mind I would translate it into *kuni* and I stayed away from it."[17] Ironically, the more recent acceptance and circulation of *gay* in Persian signifies the same thing: the need for a word that is not-*kuni*.[18] What does that "gut" feeling of revulsion speak to? Why does the spectral threat of be(com)ing kuni seem to be so shattering to a modern (male) Iranian's sense of self? It is impossible—or, at any rate, it is not my project—to give a convincing etiology of disgust. But it is critical to ask what cultural work disgust performs. What does it do to "the disgusting"? What does it achieve for "the disgusted"? Miller asks, "Why is it that disgust figures so prominently in routine moral discourses, even more so perhaps than the idioms of other moral emotions such as guilt and indignation?"[19] And how does this sense of profound aversion to *kuni* relate to the rise in visibility and the increasing prevalence of MtF trans inflections of woman-presenting maleness?

Another source of anxiety directed at males in the 1970s was that of "gender confusion," or ambiguity. Numerous social commentators wrote essays about the current state of youth lamenting the disappearance of manly valor, and of young men with long hair whose demeanor was that of a flirtatious girl, especially when they danced to rock music—all in "blind imitations of the West."[20] For a modern Iranian masculinity that had crafted itself through heterogendering previously androgynous concepts of beauty, and by the adoption of more disciplined and uniform sartorial practices during the first half of the twentieth century, the new fashions and tastes of the young seemed nothing short of a threat to national honor.

Part of this gender anxiety resided in fear of the failure of sex/gender recognition and of what that misrecognition would cause. One woman wrote:

> Once upon a time when we looked at men, we had no doubt that they were men. But now with these Beatle-style hair-dos and [tight] pants that show the body and high-heel shoes and manicured nails, we are forced to look again and again to remove our doubt. In the old days, if you called a man woman, that was an insult, but now they try to make themselves look like women. Several days ago, in Nasir Khusrau Street in Tehran, I ran into a man who had braided hair, was displaying a lot of jewelry and exactly like women had plucked his eyebrows and wore heavy make-up. It is astonishing that these men who always considered women beneath them and thought of themselves as the superior sex are putting themselves in women's place when it comes to dressing and make-up.[21]

Connecting such gender/sex ambiguity to sexual deviation was an easy imaginative leap. Under the bold headline, "The danger of women and men looking alike," another newspaper article cautioned against the clothing, lifestyles, and work of women and men becoming too similar. This kind of confusion

> threatens today's civilization, in the same manner that two thousand years ago civilized nations such as Greece and Rome . . . were overthrown. In ancient Athens, before they were defeated by the Spartans, men had begun to make themselves up like women. . . . In ancient Rome too, similar things happened. . . . Moreover sexual deviancy, as it is today, became so prevalent that it caused their overthrow and destruction.[22]

The spaces opened up by a more visible non-heteronormative maleness and by gender/sex ambiguity nevertheless offered some hopeful possibilities for women-presenting males. As I have already argued, "Gay Tehran" was inclusive of a broad spectrum of male non-heteronormativity. Press reports of genital surgeries beginning to be performed in Iran at this time were particularly important in informing woman-presenting males of more affordable possibilities for changing their bodies, which until then had seemed to be available only at great cost in Europe. On 17 February 1973, the daily *Kayhan* (p. 19), under the headline "In Shiraz, a man voluntarily became a woman!" reported:

> A thirty-one-year-old man was operated in Namazi Hospital in Shiraz and became a woman. This man, who does not wish to reveal his/her [non-gender marked pronoun *u* in original] identity, was a perfectly healthy man, but had an intense desire to become a woman and for a long time s/he was wearing women's clothes and injected female hormones. The patient is a resident of Tehran, had consulted several psychologists before surgery, and the Legal Medical Board in Tehran and Shiraz considered the surgery permissible. The former man has said that soon s/he will be marrying a man who knows her/his condition completely. Doctors say s/he is capable of marriage.

Unlike previous reports of "sex-change" in Iran, which typically involved disambiguation surgery performed on intersex persons, this report specifically emphasized that the person had been "a perfectly healthy man." Inadvertently, it also advertised to any interested reader what the process of sex-change would entail: psychological consultation and acquiring permission from the Legal Medical Board. Most hopefully, it ended in a "happy marriage."

[. . .]

By the mid-1970s, however, the medical establishment, possibly alarmed at the growing rate of sex-change surgeries performed outside any norms of institutional medical supervision, transferred the moral judgment against homosexuality onto trans persons. It took the professional and disciplinary power of the Medical Council of Iran (MCI) to bring the full weight of opprobrium associated with homosexuality to bear on the life-options of woman-presenting males, and thereby to delineate and enforce a kinship relationship between male homosexuality and MtF trans.

Science Rules on Unmanly Males

Formed only in 1969, the Medical Council of Iran established a whole series of regulations for medical practice during the first years of its operation. It also acted as the authority where complaints about medical practice could be filed and reviewed.[23] In the early 1970s, it began to produce guidelines on new medical practices, such as acupuncture. Indeed, its rulings on sex-change surgery and acupuncture were decided in the same session of the Board of Directors on 28 September 1976. Alarmed by the apparent increase in genital surgeries among woman-presenting males, and by the growing public knowledge of these practices, the MCI decided to ban sex-change surgeries, except in the case of the intersex. A huge front-page headline in the daily *Kayhan* informed the public of this decision on 10 October 1976. The newspaper explained that the decision "meant that sex-change through surgical operations and the like which are aimed to solely change someone's apparent condition is no longer permitted." It quoted "an informed source" as saying that "this operation can cause psychological and physical harm and that is why MCI has banned it. . . . From now on any doctor who performs such operations will be legally prosecuted." The paper added that, "up to now some 30 sex-change operations have been performed in Iran."

The full text of the decision was first published some three years later in the *Newsletter of the Medical Council of Iran*. [. . .]

Officially, no sex-change surgeries took place in reputable hospitals after 1976. Dr. Yahya Behjatnia was a prominent gynecologist who for many years headed the Family and Infertility Clinic of Jahanshah Salih Hospital in Tehran, the primary teaching hospital for gynecological training, and the hospital known for having a team of surgeons who operated on the intersex; he recalled that many woman-presenting males would visit him and beg him to change their sex. Often, he explained, by the time such persons would come to him for removal of male sexual organs and vaginal construction, they were already dressing as women and looking like women, and had already obtained hormonal treatment and already had breasts. But he would tell them that genital sex-change was not a permitted practice. If they insisted, he would advise them to go abroad for the surgery.[24]

Some surgeons in the late 1970s, however, still carried out sex-change operations. They either did it surreptitiously in smaller private clinics, or they manipulated the medical system simply by listing their clients as intersex on hospital records.

Another prominent gynecologist, Dr. Mehdi Amir-Movahedi, was a highly regarded specialist in uterine surgeries, intersex surgeries, and vaginal construction for women who were born without vaginas, or with vaginas with very restricted openings.[25] He served on the Board of Directors of MCI for several years, and he echoed the observations of his colleague Dr. Behjatnia. He compared the situation to that of women seeking abortion. At the time, this was illegal except under strict exemptions, such as a pregnancy that threatened the mother's life. Yet with the right connections and money, many doctors would perform abortions.[26] At Jahanshah Salih Hospital, Dr. Movahedi explained, "we were very strict, we would not do anything that was against regulations, nor would we train medical students for illegal surgeries. I worked there for some 20–30 years and I do not recall a single case of sex-change surgery. If any of our trainees performed this in their own clinic, the MCI would prosecute them." Why, then, did the MCI issue an official statement on sex change, I asked?

"If there were any related complaints, it was not when I served there. But many in the old days would do things for money and perhaps that is what happened."[27]

Peculiarities in the timing of the publication of the MCI decision on surgical sex-change, coupled with later interviews with prominent gynecologists who worked at the time in Jahanshah Salih Hospital but insist that no sex-change surgeries were performed by reputable surgeons in this period, lead one to speculate that despite persistent disavowals, reputable surgeons were indeed carrying out a whole range of surgeries that began to endanger the reputability of other surgeons. The division was not a matter of differing professional opinions about the advisability of genital surgery for woman-presenting males; rather, it involved matters of moral reputation. By this time, in the dominant scientific discourse, intersex and trans persons had come to belong to distinctly different categories. The latter had become affiliated with sexual deviancy, rather than birth defect. It was the morality of sex change—or rather, the moral status of the persons requesting or performing sex change—that was at issue. This was indeed at the heart of public conversations at the moment of the MCI decision against surgical sex change in 1976.

The 1976 MCI decision had paradoxical effects. It must have made some surgeons more cautious about sex-change operations; but the practice of surgical sex-change continued, along with media interest in it. The medical community as well, even in the publications of the MCI itself, continued to produce articles that covered the subject of sex-change in supportive terms.[28] Indeed, the MCI's insistence on the impossibility of sex-change, along with the simultaneous banning of surgeries deemed impossible, combined with the prominent coverage of the decision in the national dailies, created a productive public conversation that circulated knowledge of surgical sex-change on an unprecedented scale. Against the MCI's intentions, perhaps, the very possibility of such operations came to broader attention.

[. . .]

Aside from going abroad or using "back-street" surgeons, the other option remained living as a woman-presenting male without surgical transformation (obtaining hormones seems to have continued to be as possible as before). Many took this latter route. One such woman-presenting male, now internationally known, was Maryam Khatun Mulk-ara.[29] Born male in 1950, Mulk-ara, according to her many accounts of her earlier life, was already going out to parties dressed as a woman by her late teens.[30] At age eighteen, walking home from such a party, a car stopped and she noticed the occupants were "three *transsexual* males just like me." The moment she joined them in the car marked for Mulk-ara the beginning of a new life; she referred to this accidental meeting "as the true moment of my entry into a collectivity, a group of people like myself. . . . In those days, there was no distinction between *gay*, two-sexed people, or *transsexuals*. Everyone knew these individuals existed, but no one knew exactly what the problem was. People referred to all these individuals as 'iva-khvahar' [o'sister]" (p. 7). Mulk-ara described the gatherings and parties she attended with her friends as "a place where everyone was a woman, that is, even though they were known as males in social norms of recognition, but they were women. The ambience was just like the ambience of womanly gatherings. We talked about fashion and other women's issues."[31] In the early 1970s, Mulk-ara started working at the Iranian National Radio and Television, and she went to work dressed as a woman. It was there that she was first encouraged to go abroad for a sex-change operation. She spent some time in London in 1975 to learn more about herself and to look into various possibilities, and it was there, she claimed, that she "learned about *transsexuality* and realized I was not a passive *homosexual*."[32] Upon returning from London, Mulk-ara began to lobby various authorities to see what could be done in Iran, but everyone told her that because of the prevailing social atmosphere, the government could not do anything. By this time, of course, the MCI had closed the emerging medical possibilities for sex-reassignment surgery in Iran.

During this same period, Mulk-ara became concerned about the implications of her practices from a religious point of view. "I was in a religious conundrum [az lihaz-i shar'i sardargan]." She visited Ayatollah Bihbihani, who consulted the Qur'an; it opened on the Maryam chapter. Mulk-ara considered this a very auspicious sign, for Maryam is the only chapter bearing a woman's name; this occasion provided her with her eventual post-op name, Maryam). Ayatollah Bihbihani suggested that Mulk-ara should contact Ayatollah Khomeini on this issue, who at the time was in Najaf. Ayatollah Khomeini confirmed that "sex change was permitted and that after surgery, she must live her life as a woman."[33] At this point, she began to plan to go to Thailand, but by then the years of revolutionary upheavals had erupted.

Mulk-ara eventually did go to Thailand for her surgery, in 2002. But in the early months of 1979, once the general strikes came to an end, she, like most people, simply went back to work—and here her troubles began. "They asked me who are you? Why do you look like this? When I insisted that I had a condition, they set up a meeting for me with a doctor at Day Clinic [a top private clinic]. But the doctors' treatment of me was unbelievable; it was gross. This was just the beginning of a series of arrests, questioning me over and over again. . . . Dr. Bahr al-'Ulum and the director of Sida va Sima's [the Islamic Republic of Iran Broadcasting (IRIB), which was previously National Iranian Radio and Television (NIRT)] health clinic threatened me, saying they would set me on fire. Eventually they forced me to take male hormones and go into male clothes. . . . This kind of treatment continued till early 1980s, these were bad years for *gays* and dau-jinsi [double-sex] people. I heard several were arrested and spent time at Evin prison."

[. . .]

In the early 1980s, as the Islamic Republic was taking shape, Maryam Mulk-ara began her persistent lobbying of various authorities to change the situation for woman-presenting males who did not wish to dress and live as men. Under the new regime, the moral purification of society became a systemic priority. Moral purification measures included closing down sites that were considered spaces of corruption, such as the red-light district businesses, bars, night-clubs, and many cafés and cinemas. It meant a series of horrifying public executions of women and men on charges of prostitution and sodomy. It meant intense scrutiny of all institutions, especially those such as the mass media and the universities, which were considered critical for production of a new revolutionary Islamic culture and society, but were thought to be populated by corrupt persons who had to be purged. As Mulk-ara put it in her interview, these were indeed "bad years for *gays* and dau-jinsi people."

The spectrum of non-heteronormative male-bodied persons in the 1970s had included woman-presenting males as well as males who did not dress as or look like women. The latter's non-heteronormativity was focused on their desire for men, while they continued to live lives largely indistinguishable—to the uninitiated—from normative males. These males, some of whom now name themselves as *gay* or are so named by others, had shared in the increased visibility of non-heteronormative males of the 1970s. That visibility became dangerous in the years following the 1979 change of regime. These men had to adopt a more circumspect style of life, something that indeed had been a way of life for many of them already. But while the sexual politics of the new government could be warded off by some non-heteronormative males simply by living more circumspect lives, woman-presenting males faced a peculiar challenge in the new republic, when public gender-separation emerged as an important ethical project. A totally homosocial gendering of public spaces was seen as the ideal, although it was considered largely unachievable in practice. Nevertheless, strict codes of dress and gender presentation in public were put in place by a series of measures over the period 1979–81.[34] The self-perceptions and preferred styles of living for some non-heteronormative males included, and at times critically depended on, their ability to present themselves as women and to be visibly feminine in public—but the gender norms set in place in the early days of the IRI made that nearly impossible. As Mulk-ara and others explained, many people like her felt forced to grow mustaches and beards and live, at least in daytime, as men. Living a double life by presenting as a woman at night, which was practiced by many woman-presenting males even in the 1970s, suddenly became much more hazardous, to the extent that it remained possible at all.

As we have seen, in the 1970s, woman-presenting males had carved for themselves spaces of relative acceptance in particular places and professions. The more public spaces of such "acceptability," for instance in the entertainment industry, were at once spaces of "disrepute" but also spaces in which nonnormative living could be safely cordoned off and marginalized. They provided not only a measure of safety for woman-presenting males, but also for their containment and confinement from the larger society. Woman-presenting males performed the vulgar and the deviant, and the deployment of these semi-licit styles in the popular entertainment of the 1970s provided for partial tolerance of those deemed deviant.[35] The 1979 revolution, particularly the cultural purification campaigns of the first few years of the new republic, ruptured this dynamic. The vulgar, taken in the Islamist discourse (and indeed on the political Left as well) to represent the extreme embodiment of late-Pahlavi corruption, became yet another ground for massive repression of social deviance.

The enforcement of public gender codes in the post-1979 years disrupted the old continuum of male non-heteronormativity. While it was possible to be a closeted *gay* man, living openly as a woman-presenting male became increasingly impossible. Woman-presenting males not only carried the stigma of male same sex practices, they also transgressed the newly imposed regulations of gendered dressing and presentation in public. They were always assumed to be "passive homosexuals," facing the same severe interrogations, sometimes anal rape, imprisonment, or death. Transdressed males walking in the streets would be arrested on charges of prostitution. Some, like Mulk-ara, were forced to take male hormones and change into male clothing, and could no longer go to work looking "like that." One key effect of the policies of the early 1980s was thus the categorical bifurcation of *gay* and *transsexual*. The practices of everyday life within both categories depended on the public disavowal of homosexuality, and both were likewise predicated on the public expression of gender normativity. Given the religious sanction to sex-change offered by Ayatollah Khomeini, the categorical bifurcation of non-heteronormative maleness played out quite differently in the IRI, in the years ahead, than it did in Europe and the United States. Being *transsexual*, rather than gay, emerged as the more socially acceptable way of being a non-heteronormative male.

Acknowledgments

This paper is based on Chapter Five of my manuscript, *Sex-in-Change: Configurations of Gender and Sexuality in Contemporary Iran* (forthcoming, Duke University Press) and was made possible by the superb editorial work of Susan Stryker. I am deeply grateful.

Notes

1. See, for instance, Janet Afary, *Sexual Politics in Modern Iran* (Cambridge: Cambridge University Press, 2009). Afary states, "By the 1970s, a small gay male subculture was gradually taking root in elite circles of Tehran, mostly as a result of interaction with American and European advisors who lived in the country" (243). Similarly, Firoozeh Papan-Matin has suggested, "By the 1970s, Iran had a small and

active gay subculture." "The Case of Mohammad Khordadian, an Iranian Male Dancer," *Iranian Studies*, 42: 1 (February 2009): 127–138; quote from 128.

2. For reports of persecutions and executions in the early months and years of the establishment of the Islamic Republic, see *The Advocate*, 266, May 3 1979, 7; 267, May 17, 1979, 7, and 12–13; 276, September 20, 1979, 17; 281, November 29, 1979, 12; 283, December 27, 1979, 8; 293, May 29, 1980, 12. See also *Homan*, No, 16 (Spring 2000), 16–17, for Iranian newspaper clips of executions from this period on the charge of lavat (sodomy). See also Afary, *Sexual Politics*, 265. In much of such coverage, it is routinely said that Islamic law prohibits homosexuality—even though there is no notion of homosexuality in Islamic law—or that the Islamic Republic made homosexuality a capital offense and that gay men are executed in Iran for expressions of open homosexuality or on charges of homosexuality. On this issue as far as recent executions and the international campaigns are concerned, see Scott Long, "Unbearable Witness: How Western Activists (Mis)recognize Sexuality in Iran," *Contemporary Politics* 15: 1 (March 2009), 119–136. The slippage is important for contemporary politics of sexuality in Iran.

3. Jerry Zarit, "The Iranian Male—an Intimate Look," *GPU* [Gay Peoples Union] *News*, October 1979, 19.

4. See Mary Renault, *The Persian Boy* (New York: Pantheon, 1972), and, for instance, Jim Kepner's review in *The Advocate*, January 31, 1973, 26.

5. The two domains are highly interactive: Jerry Zarit's article in *GPU News* was translated and published in one of the earliest diasporic Iranian gay journals, *Homan*, published first in Sweden [first issue dated May–June 1991] and later in the U.S. See *Homan* 5, April–May 1992, 2–5.

6. In these distinctions, what often is lost is the very modernity of *hamjinsbazi* itself. The nineteenth-century vocabulary of what is at times conceived as the pre-history of modern same-sex relations—such as *amradbazi* (playing with a male adolescent), " *'ubnah'i*' ("afflicted" with a desire for anal penetration), *bachchah'bazi* (playing with a young person)—did not place the two sides in one category (*jins*) of person whether in a pejorative sense (same-sex player) or in its more recent recuperation as same-sex orientation. Even today, some in "same-sex" relationships do not recognize themselves of the same kind.

7. See for instance, Avaz, "Tafavut-i 'hamjins-gara' ba hamjins-baz va bachchehbaz dar chist?" [What is the difference between 'the same-sex-inclined' with the same-sex-player and child-player,"] in *Homan* 9 (October–November 1994), 27–33.

8. See Sima Shakhsari, "From *Hamjensbaaz* to *Hamjensgaraa*: Diasporic Queer Reterritorializations and Limits of Transgression." Unpublished paper.

9. For a feminist critique, see Janet Jakobsen, *Working Alliances and the Politics of Difference: Diversity and Feminist Ethics* (Bloomington: Indiana University Press, 1998).

10. *Khvandaniha*, June 30, 1956, 29, reprinted from *Payam*. For other reports of women opting to live and work as men, see *Ittila'at-i banuvan*, June 17, 1963, 12 and 75; *Zan-i ruz*, special new-year issue, March 1965, 12–14.

11. See Chapter Two in Afsaneh Najmabadi, *Women with Mustaches and Men without Beards: Gender and Sexual Anxieties of Iranian Modernity* (Berkeley: University of California Press, 2005) for some examples of "keeping a young man" (amrad-dari, adam-dari), as it was then called.

12. *Zan-push*, literally meaning dressed in women's clothes, refers to male actors who played women's roles in traditional theatrical performances, whether in passion plays (ta'zieh) or in ruhauzi plays (literally over the pond, because the stage was provided with covering a garden pond with planks of wood) at celebratory occasions. For an important analysis of different styles of enacting female personas in these plays, see William O. Beeman, "Mimesis and Travesty in Iranian Traditional Theatre," in *Gender in Performance: The Presentation of Difference in the Performing Arts*, ed. Laurence Senelick (Medford, MA: Tufts University Press, 2002), 14–25. The expression zan-push has now become part of trans-vocabulary for MtFs who change to female clothes.

13. *Khanum* is a generic form of address for an adult female. I, for instance, am often addressed as Khanum Najmabadi in Iran. In this period, it was also used as an "insider" designation for males living-as-women. Information presented here about this sub-culture of Tehran life in the 1970s is based on conversations with several men in their fifties who now identify as gay, and several male-born adults who now identify as MtF.

14. See, for instance, anonymous report, "Yadi az jashn-i hunar-i Shiraz va barrisi-i iftizahat-i'an. . . ." [Notes on the Shiraz Art Festival and its scandalous embarrassments] in which one of the criticisms is explicit talk of homosexuality in one of the plays. *Khvandaniha*, November 21, 1972, 13 and 54–55.

15. Gharbzadigi, a concept that gained popularity through Jalal Al Ahmad's essay. For an English translation, see *Gharbzadegi—Weststruckness*, trans. John Green and Ahmad Alizadeh (Lexington, KY: Mazda

Publishers, 1982). For a critical discussion, see Mehrzad Boroujerdi, *Iranian Intellectuals and the West: The Tormented Triumph of Nativism* (Syracuse: Syracuse University Press, 1996).

16. *Baruni* literally means raincoat—I have not been able to trace where this word comes from. Another difference between the two words is that kuni is used to designate an individual man; baruni is used within the context of a relationship between at least two women—as in so-and-so is so-and-so's *baruni*.

17. Behzad, interviewed summer 2007.

18. The need for a word that is not derogatory but also not an in-word signifies the emergence of a broader semi-open circulation of these conversations. For that reason, the circulation of *gay* also marks the space of this semi-openness. For a similar dynamic between *gay* and *bantut* in the Philippines, see Johnson, *Beauty and Power*, 89; and for Thailand, between *gay* and *kathoey*, see Megan Sinnott, *Toms and Dees: Transgender Identity and Female Same-Sex Relationships in Thailand* (Honolulu: University of Hawai'i Press, 2004), 6.

19. William Ian Miller, *The Anatomy of Disgust* (Cambridge: Harvard University Press, 1997), xi.

20. No author, "Javanan-i ma chizi mian dukhtar va pisar hastand!" [Our youth are something between girls and boys!], *Khvandaniha*, March 6, 1971, p. 18, reprinted from *Khurasan*.

21. Nadereh Shahram, "Men of the Twentieth Century?" *Zan-i ruz*, August 3, 1974, pp. 7 and 86. For another similar essay, see Mahmud 'Inayat, "Jaff alqalam, jall al-khaliq," *Kayhan*, December 6, 1972, p. 5.

22. *Khvandaniha*, "Khatar-i hamrikhti-i zanan va mardan" [The danger of women and men looking alike], tr. Dr. Kuhsar (no author or source of translation is specified), April 6, 1973, pp. 36–38. Reprinted from *Danishmand*, a general science journal.

23. Attempts to form an association of health professionals had a much longer history. See Cyrus Schayegh, *"Who Is Knowledgeable Is Strong": Science, Class, and the Formation of Modern Iranian Society, 1900–1950* (Berkeley: University of California Press, 2009), 54–60.

24. Interview, December 2007. When I asked about the operation reported in the press in February 1973 that took place in Namazi Hospital of Shiraz, he thought that was a possibility since that hospital had American and American-trained doctors. Doctors trained by Dr. Salih were trained to refuse sex-surgeries except for the intersex. Information about Dr. Behjatnia in the following section is based on interview and on his biographical entry in Muhammad Mahdi Muvahhidi, *Zindigi-nameh-i pizishkan-i nam-avar-i mu'asir-i Iran [Biographies of famous contemporary Iranian physicians]* 2 (Tehran: Abrun, 2000), 61–64.

25. Information about Dr. Amir-Movahedi is based on interview and on his biographical entry in Muvahhidi, *Zindigi-nameh-i pizishkan* 2, 53–59.

26. Interview, December 2007. On abortion regulations, see the text of revision of Article 42, Point 3 of the Penal Code, May/June 1973, in Gholam Reza Afkhami (ed.), *Women, State, and Society in Iran 1963–78: An Interview with Mahnaz Afkhami* (Bethesda, MD: Foundation for Iranian Studies, 2003), 268–269.

27. Interview, December 2007.

28. See, for example, "Akhlaq-i pizishki dar barabar-i pizishki-i nauvin: masa'ili ikhtisasi-i akhlaq-i pizishki" [Medical ethics confronting new medicine: special problems of medical ethics], *Journal of Medical Council of Iran* 6: 5 (1978), 445–447.

29. Mulk-ara has been the subject of numerous interviews and reports, in Iran and internationally, both in print and in film, about Iranian transsexuals. In the book project from which the article is drawn, I will discuss more fully her critical role in creating (and controlling) spaces for trans-activism in Iran over the past decade.

30. I have depended on the following sources for this sketch of Mulk-ara's life. By far, the most extensive interview with her (and the only one in which she talked at length about her life in the 1970s) appeared as part of a four-page social reportage in the daily *I'timad* (May 8, 2005, 7–10). Mulk-ara, including a picture of her at the center of page 7, was featured on 7 and 10 (interviewed by Hamid Riza Khalidi, the total page coverage was over fourth of the full dossier. Unless noted otherwise, the quotes in this section are all from this interview). This dossier remains the most substantive and serious press coverage of transsexuality in Iranian press, though many other newspapers and magazines have covered various aspects of the issues. Other sources on Mulk-ara are a short interview with her as part of a dossier on transsexuals in a popular weekly, *Chilchiraq* (May 26, 2007, 7–13, interview on 11) and several phone conversations with her during summer and fall 2006.

31. In my conversations with her, Mulk-ara spoke about two circles in which she socialized in this period; one she called "darbariha," the Court circle, which according to her included the Shah's cousin, his chief of staff, and several others she named. The other circle, she referred to as lower middle class "zir-i mutivassit." The two circles overlapped in that many of the women most desired in the courtly circles were from the lower middle-class circles and would be brought to parties.

32. Interview, summer 2006. The account of how and when she first identified herself, or was identified by a doctor, as a *transsexual* differed in this conversation from those reported in the *I'timad* and *Chilchiraq* interviews in which she said she was sent to a specialist by the National Iranian Radio and Television who diagnosed her as *transsexual* and suggested she should go for surgery. Nowadays, this moment of "learning about *transsexuality*" has become a central narrative feature in the self-presentation of woman-presenting males. In particular, learning to distinguish oneself from "a passive homosexual" has become a key moment for feminine male-bodied persons. My interviews with Mulk-ara were carried out in 2005–2007 and to some extent reflect the retroactive naming of the consolidation of this distinction in contemporary discourses and practices of transsexuality.

33. "Taghyir-i jinsiyat bilamani'ast va ba'd az 'amal taklif-i yik zan bar shuma vajib ast." Noushin and two other *MtFs* I interviewed each claimed that it was them who had obtained the first fatwa from Ayatollah Khomeini on permissibility of changing sex. Interviews, summer 2006 and 2007. I discuss the significance of these multiple "firsts" in the book from which this article is drawn.

34. There is a huge literature on this period's state policies and resistance by large sections of women against it. Though successfully implemented by the early 1980s, women's dress public code has remained a perennial site of contestation between sections of the government, dissenting women, and at times, young male youth. See Parvin Paidar, *Women and the Political Process in Twentieth-century Iran* (Cambridge: Cambridge University Press, 1995); Minoo Moallem, *Between Warrior Bother and Veiled Sister: Islamic Fundamentalism and the Politics of Patriarchy in Iran* (Berkeley: University of California Press, 2005); Hamideh Sedghi, *Women and Politics in Iran: Veiling, Unveiling, and Reveiling* (Cambridge: Cambridge University Press, 2007).

35. Johnson also discusses, in a different context, the paradox of the *gay/bantut* being "both celebrated as masters of beauty and style and circumscribed as deviant and vulgar," and notes "the historical significance of the beauty parlors as both the site and means for gays' successful occupational reinvention of themselves." One could argue that in the 1970s Iran, the entertainment industry had become such a site for performers such as Farrukhzad and others, who found a place such as NIRT a site of relative acceptance and flourishing of their performative skills. See *Beauty and Power*, 146–147.

Section VIII
Transing the Non/Human

36 A Cyborg Manifesto

An Ironic Dream of a Common Language for Women in the Integrated Circuit

Donna J. Haraway

Feminist science studies scholar Donna J. Haraway's 1983 "Cyborg Manifesto" contributed to innovative thinking across a wide range of humanities and social-scientific disciplines. Its conceptual vocabulary and theoretical framework directly informed one of the founding works of transgender studies, "The 'Empire' Strikes Back: A Possttranssexual Manifesto," by Haraway's doctoral student Sandy Stone. "Cyborg," a word coined in science fiction literature to describe a human-machine hybrid, or "cybernetic organism," was transformed by Haraway into a potent figuration for analyzing three distinct "boundary ruptures" in the late twentieth century that broadly characterize the contemporary situation of embodiment, identity, and desire: the boundaries between humans and nonhuman animals, between organisms and machines, and between the physical world and immaterial things. The cyborg, in Haraway's usage, is a way to grapple with what it means to be a conscious, embodied subject in an environment structured by techno-scientific practices that challenge basic and widely shared notions of what it means to be human. Although Haraway calls her cyborg "a creature in a post-gender world," she does not specifically analyze transgender issues. Rather, she addresses in a more general way several issues of central importance to transgender studies. She helps explain how "gender" is, in part, a story we tell ourselves to naturalize a particular social organization of biological reproduction, family roles, and state powers. Her commitment to troubling the desire for purity in our culture's personhood categories aligns her not just with trans practices of crossing and contesting gender but with postcolonial and women-of-color feminisms that contest biologically essentialist binaries and celebrate mixing.

This essay is an effort to build an ironic political myth faithful to feminism, socialism, and materialism. Perhaps more faithful as blasphemy is faithful, than as reverent worship and identification. Blasphemy has always seemed to require taking things very seriously. I know no better stance to adopt from within the secular-religious, evangelical traditions of United States politics, including the politics of socialist-feminism. Blasphemy protects one from the moral majority within, while still insisting on the need for community. Blasphemy is not apostasy. Irony is about contradictions that do not resolve into larger wholes, even dialectically, about the tension of holding incompatible things together because both or all are necessary and true. Irony is about humor and serious play. It is also a rhetorical strategy and a political method, one I would like to see more honored within socialist-feminism. At the center of my ironic faith, my blasphemy, is the image of the cyborg.

A cyborg is a cybernetic organism, a hybrid of machine and organism, a creature of social reality as well as a creature of fiction. Social reality is lived social relations, our most

DOI: 10.4324/9781003206255-45

important political construction, a world-changing fiction. [. . .] Contemporary science fiction is full of cyborgs—creatures simultaneously animal and machine, who populate worlds ambiguously natural and crafted. Modern medicine is also full of cyborgs, of couplings between organism and machine, each conceived as coded devices, in an intimacy and with a power that were not generated in the history of sexuality. Cyborg "sex" restores some of the lovely replicative baroque of ferns and invertebrates (such nice organic prophylactics against heterosexism). Cyborg replication is uncoupled from organic reproduction. Modem production seems like a dream of cyborg colonization work, a dream that makes the nightmare of Taylorism seem idyllic. And modern war is a cyborg orgy, coded by C^3I, command-control-communication-intelligence, an $84 billion item in 1984's U.S. defense budget. I am making an argument for the cyborg as a fiction mapping our social and bodily reality and as an imaginative resource suggesting some very fruitful couplings. Michel Foucault's biopolitics is a flaccid premonition of cyborg politics, a very open field.

By the late twentieth century, our time, a mythic time, we are all chimeras, theorized and fabricated hybrids of machine and organism—in short, cyborgs. [. . .] The cyborg is a creature in a postgender world. [. . .] It is oppositional, utopian, and completely without innocence. [. . .] Nature and culture are reworked; the one can no longer be the resource for appropriation or incorporation by the other. The relationships for forming wholes from parts, including those of polarity and hierarchical domination, are at issue in the cyborg world. Unlike the hopes of Frankenstein's monster, the cyborg does not expect its father to save it through a restoration of the garden—that is, through the fabrication of a heterosexual mate, through its completion in a finished whole, a city and cosmos. The cyborg does not dream of community on the model of the organic family, this time without the oedipal project. The cyborg would not recognize the Garden of Eden; it is not made of mud and cannot dream of returning to dust [. . .]. Cyborgs are not reverent; they do not remember the cosmos. They are wary of holism, but needy for connection—they seem to have a natural feel for united-front politics, but without the vanguard party. The main trouble with cyborgs, of course, is that they are the illegitimate offspring of militarism and patriarchal capitalism, not to mention state socialism. But illegitimate offspring are often exceedingly unfaithful to their origins. Their fathers, after all, are inessential.

[. . .]

I want to signal three crucial boundary breakdowns that make the following political-fictional (political scientific) analysis possible. By the late twentieth century in U.S. scientific culture, the boundary between human and animal is thoroughly breached. The last beachheads of uniqueness have been polluted if not turned into amusement parks: language, tool use, social behavior, mental events—nothing really convincingly settles the separation of human and animal. And many people no longer feel the need for such a separation; indeed, many branches of feminist culture affirm the pleasure of connection of human and other living creatures. Movements for animal rights are not irrational denials of human uniqueness; they are a clear-sighted recognition of connection across the discredited breach of nature and culture. Biology and evolutionary theory over the past two centuries have simultaneously produced modern organisms as objects of knowledge and reduced the line between humans and animals to a faint trace re-etched in ideological struggle or professional disputes between life and social science. Within this framework, teaching modern Christian creationism should be fought as a form of child abuse.

Biological-determinist ideology is only one position opened up in scientific culture for arguing the meanings of human animality. There is much room for radical political people to contest the meanings of the breached boundary.[1] The cyborg appears in myth precisely where the boundary between human and animal is transgressed. Far from signaling a walling off of people from other living beings, cyborgs signal disturbingly and pleasurably tight coupling. Bestiality has a new status in this cycle of marriage exchange.

The second leaky distinction is between animal—human (organism) and machine. Pre-cybernetic machines could be haunted; there was always the specter of the ghost in the machine. This dualism structured the dialogue between materialism and idealism that was settled by a dialectical progeny, called spirit or history, according to taste. But basically machines were not self-moving, self-designing, autonomous. They could not achieve man's dream, only mock it. They were not man, an author to himself, but only a caricature of that masculinist reproductive dream. To think they were otherwise was paranoid. Now we are not so sure. Late twentieth-century machines have made thoroughly ambiguous the difference between natural and artificial, mind and body, self-developing and externally designed, and many other distinctions that used to apply to organisms and machines. Our machines are disturbingly lively, and we ourselves frighteningly inert.

Technological determination is only one ideological space opened up by the reconceptions of machine and organism as coded texts through which we engage in the play of writing and reading the world.[2] "Textualization" of everything in poststructuralist, postmodernist theory has been damned by Marxists and socialist-feminists for its utopian disregard for the lived relations of domination that ground the "play" of arbitrary reading.[3] It is certainly true that postmodernist strategies, like my cyborg myth, subvert myriad organic wholes (for example, the poem, the primitive culture, the biological organism). In short, the certainty of what counts as nature—a source of insight and promise of innocence—is undermined, probably fatally. The transcendent authorization of interpretation is lost, and with it the ontology grounding "Western" epistemology. But the alternative is not cynicism or faithlessness, that is, some version of abstract existence, like the accounts of technological determinism destroying "man" by the "machine" or "meaningful political action" by the "text." Who cyborgs will be is a radical question; the answers are a matter of survival. Both chimpanzees and artifacts have politics (de Waal 1982; Winner 1980), so why shouldn't we?

The third distinction is a subset of the second: the boundary between physical and non-physical is very imprecise for us. Pop physics books on the consequences of quantum theory and the indeterminacy principle are a kind of popular scientific equivalent to Harlequin romances[4] as a marker of radical change in American white heterosexuality: they get it wrong, but they are on the right subject. Modern machines are quintessentially microelectronic devices: they are everywhere and they are invisible. Modern machinery is an irreverent upstart god, mocking the Father's ubiquity and spirituality. The silicon chip is a surface for writing; it is etched in molecular scales disturbed only by atomic noise, the ultimate interference for nuclear scores.

Writing, power, and technology are old partners in Western stories of the origin of civilization, but miniaturization has changed our experience of mechanism. Miniaturization has turned out to be about power; small is not so much beautiful as preeminently dangerous, as in cruise missiles. Contrast the TV sets of the 1950s or the news cameras of the 1970s with the TV wristbands or hand-sized video cameras now advertised. Our best machines are made of sunshine; they are all light and clean because they are nothing but signals, electromagnetic waves, a section of a spectrum, and these machines are eminently portable, mobile—a matter of immense human pain in Detroit and Singapore. People are nowhere near so fluid, being both material and opaque. Cyborgs are ether, quintessence.

[. . .]

Fractured Identities

It has become difficult to name one's feminism by a single adjective—or even to insist in every circumstance on the noun. Consciousness of exclusion through naming is acute. Identities seem contradictory, partial, and strategic. With the hard-won recognition of their social and historical constitution, gender, race, and class cannot provide the basis for belief in "essential" unity. There is nothing about being "female" that naturally binds women. There is not even such a state as "being" female, itself a highly complex category constructed in contested sexual scientific discourses and other social practices. Gender, race, or class consciousness is an achievement forced on us by the terrible historical experience of the contradictory social realities of patriarchy, colonialism, and capitalism. And who counts as "us" in my own rhetoric? Which identities are available to ground such a potent political myth called "us," and what could motivate enlistment in this collectivity? Painful fragmentation among feminists (not to mention among women) along every possible fault line has made the concept of *woman* elusive, an excuse for the matrix of women's dominations of each other. For me—and for many who share a similar historical location in white, professional middle-class, female, radical, North American, mid-adult bodies—the sources of a crisis in political identity are legion. The recent history for much of the U.S. left and U.S. feminism has been a response to this kind of crisis by endless splitting and searches for a new essential unity. But there has also been a growing recognition of another response through coalition—affinity, not identity.[5]

Chela Sandoval (n.d., 1984), from a consideration of specific historical moments in the formation of the new political voice called women of color, has theorized a hopeful model of political identity called "oppositional consciousness," born of the skills for reading webs of power by those refused stable membership in the social categories of race, sex, or class. *Women of color*, a name contested at its origins by those whom it would incorporate, as well as a historical consciousness marking systematic breakdown of all the signs of Man in "Western" traditions, constructs a kind of postmodernist identity out of otherness, difference, and specificity. This postmodernist identity is fully political, whatever might be said about other possible postmodernisms. Sandoval's oppositional consciousness is about contradictory locations and heterochronic calendars, not about relativisms and pluralisms.

Sandoval emphasizes the lack of any essential criterion for identifying who is a woman of color. She notes that the definition of the group has been by conscious appropriation of negation. For example, a Chicana or U.S. black woman has not been able to speak as a woman or as a black person or as a Chicano. Thus, she was at the bottom of a cascade of negative identities, left out of even the privileged oppressed authorial categories called "women and blacks," who claimed to make the important revolutions. The category "woman" negated all nonwhite women; "black" negated all nonblack people, as well as all black women. But there was also no "she," no singularity, but a sea of differences among U.S. women who have affirmed their historical identity as U.S. women of color. This identity marks out a self-consciously constructed space that cannot affirm the capacity to act on the basis of natural identification, but only on the basis of conscious coalition, of affinity, of political kinship.[6] Unlike the "woman" of some streams of the white women's movement in the United States, there is no naturalization of the matrix, or at least this is what Sandoval argues is uniquely available through the power of oppositional consciousness.

Sandoval's argument has to be seen as one potent formulation for feminists out of the worldwide development of anticolonialist discourse; that is to say, discourse dissolving the "West" and its highest product—the one who is not animal, barbarian, or woman; man, that is, the author of a cosmos called history. As orientalism is deconstructed politically and semiotically, the identities of the occident destabilize, including those of feminists.[7] Sandoval argues that "women of color" have a chance to build an effective unity that does not replicate the imperializing, totalizing revolutionary subjects of previous Marxisms and feminisms, which had not faced the consequences of the disorderly polyphony emerging from decolonization.

[. . .]

It is important to note that the effort to construct revolutionary standpoints, epistemologies as achievements of people committed to changing the world, has been part of the process showing the limits of identification. The acid tools of postmodernist theory and the constructive tools of ontological discourse about revolutionary subjects might be seen as ironic allies in dissolving Western selves in the interests of survival. We are excruciatingly conscious of what it means to have a historically constituted body. But with the loss of innocence in our origin, there is no expulsion from the Garden either. Our politics lose the indulgence of guilt with the *naïveté* of innocence. But what would another political myth for socialist-feminism look like? What kind of politics could embrace partial, contradictory, permanently unclosed constructions of personal and collective selves and still be faithful, effective—and, ironically, socialist feminist?

I do not know of any other time in history when there was greater need for political unity to confront effectively the dominations of "race," "gender," "sexuality," and "class." I also do not know of any other time when the kind of unity we might help build could have been possible. None of "us" has any longer the symbolic or material capability of dictating the shape of reality to any of "them." Or at least "we" cannot claim innocence from practicing such dominations. White women, including socialist-feminists, discovered (that is, were forced kicking and screaming to notice) the noninnocence of the category "woman." That consciousness changes the geography of all previous categories; it denatures them as heat denatures a fragile protein. Cyborg feminists have to argue that "we" do not want any more natural matrix of unity and that no construction is whole. Innocence, and the corollary insistence on victimhood as the only ground for insight, has done enough damage. But the constructed revolutionary subject must give late-twentieth century people pause as well. In the fraying of identities and in the reflexive strategies for constructing them, the possibility opens up for weaving something other than a shroud for the day after the apocalypse that so prophetically ends salvation history.

Both Marxist/socialist-feminisms and radical feminisms have simultaneously naturalized and denatured the category "woman" and consciousness of the social lives of "women." Perhaps a schematic caricature can highlight both kinds of moves. Marxian socialism is rooted in an analysis of wage labor that reveals class structure. The consequence of the wage relationship is systematic alienation, as the worker is dissociated from his (*sic*) product. Abstraction and illusion rule in knowledge, domination rules in practice. Labor is the preeminently privileged category enabling the Marxist to overcome illusion and find that point of view that is necessary for changing the world. Labor is the humanizing activity that makes man; labor is an ontological category permitting the knowledge of a subject, and so the knowledge of subjugation and alienation.

In faithful filiation, socialist-feminism advanced by allying itself with the basic analytic strategies of Marxism. The main achievement of both Marxist feminists and socialist feminists was to expand the category of labor to accommodate what (some) women did, even when the wage relation was subordinated to a more comprehensive view of labor under capitalist patriarchy. In particular, women's labor in the household and women's activity as mothers generally (that is, reproduction in the socialist-feminist sense) entered theory on the authority of analogy to the Marxian concept of labor. The unity of women here rests on an epistemology based on the ontological structure of "labor." Marxist/socialist-feminism does not "naturalize" unity; it is a possible achievement based on a possible standpoint rooted in social relations. The essentializing move is in the ontological structure of labor or of its analogue, women's activity.[8] The inheritance of Marxian humanism, with its preeminently Western self, is the difficulty for me. The contribution from these formulations has been the emphasis on the daily responsibility of real women to build unities, rather than to naturalize them.

Cyborgs: A Myth of Political Identity

I want to conclude with a myth about identity and boundaries that might inform late-twentieth-century political imaginations. I am indebted in this story to writers like Joanna Russ, Samuel R. Delany, John Varley, James Tiptree Jr., Octavia Butler, Monique Wittig, and Vonda McIntyre.[9] These are our storytellers exploring what it means to be embodied in high-tech worlds. They are theorists for cyborgs. Exploring conceptions of bodily boundaries and social order, the anthropologist Mary Douglas (1966, 1970) should be credited with helping us to consciousness about how fundamental body imagery is to worldview, and so to political language.

[. . .]

The cyborgs populating feminist science fiction make very problematic the statuses of man or woman, human, artifact, member of a race, individual entity, or body. Katie King clarifies how pleasure in reading these fictions is not largely based on identification. Students facing Joanna Russ for the first time, students who have learned to take modernist writers like James Joyce or Virginia Woolf without flinching, do not know what to make of *The Adventures of Alyx* or *The Female Man*, where characters refuse the reader's search for innocent wholeness while granting the wish for heroic quests, exuberant eroticism, and serious politics. *The Female Man* is the story of four versions of one genotype, all of whom meet, but even taken together do not make a whole, resolve the dilemmas of violent moral action, or remove the growing scandal of gender. The feminist science fiction of Samuel R. Delany, especially *Tales of Nevèrÿon*, mocks stories of origin by redoing the neolithic revolution, replaying the founding moves of Western civilization to subvert their plausibility. James Tiptree Jr., an author whose fiction was regarded as particularly manly until her "true" gender was revealed, tells tales of reproduction based on nonmammalian technologies like alternation of generations of male brood pouches and male nurturing. John Varley constructs a supreme cyborg in his arch-feminist exploration of Gaea, a mad goddess-planet-trickster-old woman-technological-device on whose surface an extraordinary array of post-cyborg symbioses are spawned. Octavia Butler writes of an African sorceress pitting her powers of transformation against the genetic manipulations of her rival (*Wild Seed*), of time warps that bring a modern U.S. black woman into slavery where her actions in relation to her white master—ancestor determine the possibility of her own birth (*Kindred*), and of the illegitimate insights into identity and community of an adopted cross-species child who came to know the enemy as self (*Survivor*). In *Dawn* (1987), the first installment of a series called *Xenogenesis*, Butler tells the story of Lilith Iyapo, whose personal name recalls Adam's first and repudiated wife and whose family name marks her status as the widow of the son of Nigerian immigrants to the United States. A black woman and a mother whose child is dead, Lilith mediates the transformation of humanity through genetic exchange with extra-terrestrial lovers/rescuers/destroyers/genetic engineers, who re-form Earth's habitats after the nuclear holocaust and coerce surviving humans into intimate fusion with them. It is a novel that interrogates reproductive, linguistic, and nuclear politics in a mythic field structured by late-twentieth-century race and gender.

Because it is particularly rich in boundary transgressions, Vonda McIntyre's *Superluminal* can close this truncated catalogue of promising and dangerous monsters who help redefine the pleasures and politics of embodiment and feminist writing. In a fiction where no character is "simply" human, human status is highly problematic. Orca, a genetically altered diver, can speak with killer whales and survive deep ocean conditions, but she longs to explore space as a pilot, necessitating bionic implants jeopardizing her kinship with the divers and cetaceans. Transformations are effected by virus vectors carrying a new developmental code, by transplant surgery, by implants of microelectronic devices, by analogue doubles, and other means.

Laenea becomes a pilot by accepting a heart implant and a host of other alterations allowing survival in transit at speeds exceeding that of light. Radu Dracul survives a virus-caused plague in his outerworld planet to find himself with a time sense that changes the boundaries of spatial perception for the whole species. All the characters explore the limits of language; the dream of communicating experience; and the necessity of limitation, partiality, and intimacy even in this world of protean transformation and connection. *Superluminal* stands also for the defining contradictions of a cyborg world in another sense; it embodies textually the intersection of feminist theory and colonial discourse in the science fiction I have alluded to in this essay. This is a conjunction with a long history that many "First World" feminists have tried to repress, including myself in my readings of *Superluminal* before being called to account by Zoë Sofoulis (n.d.), whose different location in the world system's informatics of domination made her acutely alert to the imperialist moment of all science fiction cultures, including women's science fiction. From an Australian feminist sensitivity, Sofoulis remembered more readily McIntyre's role as writer of the adventures of Captain Kirk and Spock in TV's *Star Trek* series than her rewriting the romance in *Superluminal*.

Monsters have always defined the limits of community in Western imaginations. The Centaurs and Amazons of ancient Greece established the limits of the centered polis of the Greek male human by their disruption of marriage and boundary pollutions of the warrior with animality and woman. Unseparated twins and hermaphrodites were the confused human material in early modern France who grounded discourse on the natural and supernatural, medical and legal, portents and diseases—all crucial to establishing modern identity.[10] In the evolutionary and behavioral sciences, monkeys and apes have marked the multiple boundaries of late-twentieth-century industrial identities. Cyborg monsters in feminist science fiction define quite different political possibilities and limits from those proposed by the mundane fiction of Man and Woman.

There are several consequences to taking seriously the imagery of cyborgs as other than our enemies. Our bodies, ourselves; bodies are maps of power and identity. Cyborgs are no exception. A cyborg body is not innocent; it was not born in a garden; it does not seek unitary identity and so generate antagonistic dualisms without end (or until the world ends); it takes irony for granted. One is too few, and two is only one possibility. Intense pleasure in skill, machine skill, ceases to be a sin, but an aspect of embodiment. The machine is not an *it* to be animated, worshipped, and dominated. The machine is us, our processes, an aspect of our embodiment. We can be responsible for machines; *they* do not dominate or threaten us. We are responsible for boundaries; we are they. Up till now (once upon a time), female embodiment seemed to be given, organic, necessary; and female embodiment seemed to mean skill in mothering and its metaphoric extensions. Only by being out of place could we take intense pleasure in machines, and then with excuses that this was organic activity after all, appropriate to females. Cyborgs might consider more seriously the partial, fluid, sometimes aspect of sex and sexual embodiment. Gender might not be global identity after all, even if it has profound historical breadth and depth.

The ideologically charged question of what counts as daily activity, as experience, can be approached by exploiting the cyborg image. Feminists have recently claimed that women are given to dailiness, that women more than men somehow sustain daily life and so have a privileged epistemological position potentially. There is a compelling aspect to this claim, one that makes visible unvalued female activity and names it as the ground of life.

But *the* ground of life? What about all the ignorance of women, all the exclusions and failures of knowledge and skill? What about men's access to daily competence, to knowing how to build things, to take them apart, to play? What about other embodiments? Cyborg gender is a local possibility taking a global vengeance. Race, gender, and capital require a cyborg theory of wholes and parts. There is no drive in cyborgs to produce total theory, but there is an intimate experience of boundaries, their construction and deconstruction. There is a myth system waiting to become a political language to ground one way of looking at science and technology and challenging the informatics of domination—in order to act potently.

One last image: organisms and organismic, holistic politics depend on metaphors of rebirth and invariably call on the resources of reproductive sex. I would suggest that cyborgs have more to do with regeneration and are suspicious of the reproductive matrix and of most birthing. For salamanders, regeneration after injury, such as the loss of a limb, involves regrowth of structure and restoration of function with the constant possibility of twinning or other odd topographical productions at the site of former injury. The regrown limb can be monstrous, duplicated, potent. We have all been injured, profoundly. We require regeneration, not rebirth, and the possibilities for our reconstitution include the utopian dream of the hope for a monstrous world without gender.

Cyborg imagery can help express two crucial arguments in this essay: first, the production of universal, totalizing theory is a major mistake that misses most of reality, probably always, but certainly now; and second, taking responsibility for the social relations of science and technology means refusing an antiscience metaphysics, a demonology of technology, and so means embracing the skillful task of reconstructing the boundaries of daily life, in partial connection with others, in communication with all of our parts. It is not just that science and technology are possible means of great human satisfaction, as well as a matrix of complex dominations. Cyborg imagery can suggest a way out of the maze of dualisms in which we have explained our bodies and our tools to ourselves. This is a dream not of a common language, but of a powerful infidel heteroglossia. It is an imagination of a feminist speaking in tongues to strike fear into the circuits of the super savers of the new right. It means both building and destroying machines, identities, categories, relationships, space stories. Though both are bound in the spiral dance, I would rather be a cyborg than a goddess.

Notes

1. Useful references to left and/or feminist radical science movements and theory and to biological/bio-technical issues include Bleier 1984, 1986; Harding 1986; Fausto-Sterling 1985; Gould 1981; Hubbard et al. 1979; Keller 1985; Lewontin et al. 1984. See also *Radical Science Journal* (which became *Science as Culture* in 1987): 26 Freegrove Road, London N7 9RQ; and *Science for the People*, 897 Main Street, Cambridge, Massachusetts 02139.

2. Starting points for left and/or feminist approaches to technology and politics include Cowan 1983, 1986; Rothschild 1983; Traweek 1988; Young and Levidow 1981, 1985; Weisenbaum 1976; Winner 1977, 1986; Zimmerman 1983; Athanasiou 1987; Cohn 1987a, 1987b; Winograd and Flores 1986; Edwards 1985. *Global Electronics Newsletter*, 867 West Dana Street, #204, Mountain View, California 94041; *Processed World*, 55 Sutter Street, San Francisco, California 94104; ISIS, Women's International Information and Communication Service, P.O. Box 50 (Cornavin), 1211 Geneva 2, Switzerland; and Via Santa Maria Dell'Anima 30, 00186 Rome, Italy. Fundamental approaches to modern social studies of science that do not continue the liberal mystification that all started with Thomas Kuhn include Knorr-Cetina 1981; Knorr-Cetina and Mulkay 1983; Latour and Woolgar 1979; Young 1979. The 1984 Directory of the Network for the Ethnographic Study of Science, Technology, and Organization lists a wide range of people and projects crucial to better radical analysis, available from NESSTO, P.O. Box 11442, Stanford, California 94305.

3. A provocative, comprehensive argument about the politics and theories of "postmodernism" is made by Fredric Jameson (1984), who argues that postmodernism is not an option, a style among others, but a cultural dominant requiring radical reinvention of left politics from within; there is no longer any place from without that gives meaning to the comforting fiction of critical distance. Jameson also makes clear why one cannot be for or against postmodernism, an essentially moralist move. My position is that feminists (and others) need continuous cultural reinvention, most modernist critique, and historical materialism; only a cyborg would have a chance. The old dominations of white capitalist patriarchy

seem nostalgically innocent now: they normalized heterogeneity, into man and woman, white and black, for example. "Advanced Capitalism" and postmodernism release heterogeneity without a norm, and we are flattened, without subjectivity, which requires depth, even unfriendly and drowning depths. It is time to write *The Death of the Clinic*. The clinic's methods required bodies and works; we have texts and surfaces. Our dominations don't work by medicalization and normalization anymore; they work by networking, communications redesign, stress management. Normalization gives way to automation, utter redundancy. Michel Foucault's *Birth of the Clinic* (1963), *History of Sexuality* (1976), and *Discipline and Punish* (1975) name a form of power at its moment of implosion. [. . .]

4. The U.S. equivalent of Mills and Boon.

5. Powerful developments of coalition politics emerge from "Third-World" speakers, speaking from nowhere, the displaced center of the universe, earth: "We live on the third planet from the sun"— *Sun Poem* by Jamaican writer Edward Kamau Braithwaite, review by Mackey 1984. Contributors to Smith 1983 ironically subvert naturalized identities precisely while constructing a place from which to speak called home. See especially Reagon (in Smith 1983, 356–368); Trinh T. Minh-ha 1986–87a, 1986–87b.

6. See hooks 1981, 1984; Hull et al. 1982. Toni Cade Bambara (1981) wrote an extraordinary novel in which the women of color theater group the Seven Sisters explores a form of unity. See analysis by Butler-Evans 1987.

7. On orientalism in feminist works and elsewhere, see Lowe 1986; Said 1978; Mohanty 1984; *Many Voices, One Chant: Black Feminist Perspectives* (1984).

8. The central role of object relations versions of psychoanalysis and related strong universalizing moves in discussing reproduction, caring work, and mothering in many approaches to epistemology underline their authors' resistance to what I am calling postmodernism. For me, both the universalizing moves and these versions of psychoanalysis make analysis of "women's place in the integrated circuit" difficult and lead to systematic difficulties in accounting for or even seeing major aspects of the construction of gender and gendered social life. The feminist standpoint argument has been developed by Flax 1983; Harding 1986; Harding and Hintikka 1983; Hartsock 1983a, 1983b; O'Brien 1981; H. Rose 1983; Smith 1974, 1979. For rethinking theories of feminist materialism and feminist standpoints in response to criticism, see Harding 1986, 163–96; Hartsock 1987; and S. Rose 1986.

9. See King 1984. An abbreviated list of feminist science fiction underlying themes of this essay: Octavia Butler, Wild Seed, Mind of My Mind, Kindred, Survivor; Suzy McKee Charnas, Motherlines; Samuel R. Delany, the Nevèrÿon series; Anne McCaffery, The Ship Who Sang, Dinosaur Planet; Vonda McIntyre, Superluminal, Dreamsnake; Joanna Russ.

10. See DuBois 1982; Daston and Mark n.d.; Park and Daston 1981. The noun monster shares its root with the verb to demonstrate.

Bibliography

Athanasiou, Tom. 1987. "High-Tech Politics: The Case of Artifical Intelligence." *Socialist Review* 92: 7–35.

Bambara, Toni Cade. 1981. *The Salt Eaters*. New York: Vintage/Random House.

Baudrillard, Jean. 1983. *Simulations*. Trans. P. Foss, P. Patton, and P. Beitch man. New York: Semiotext[e].

Bird, Elizabeth. 1984. "Green Revolution Imperialism, I and II." Papers delivered to the History of Consciousness Board, University of California, Santa Cruz.

Bleier, Ruth. 1984. *Science and Gender: A Critique of Biology and Its Themes on Women*. New York: Pergamon.

Blumberg, Rae Lessor. 1981. *Stratification: Socioeconomic and Sexual Inequality*. Boston: Little, Brown.

———. 1983. "A General Theory of Sex Stratification and Its Application to Positions of Women in Today's World Economy." Paper delivered to the Sociology Board of the University of California, Santa Cruz.

Burke, Carolyn. 1981. "Irigaray through the Looking Glass." *Feminist Studies* 7 (2): 288–306.

Burr, Sara G. 1982. "Women and Work." In *The Women's Annual, 1981*, ed. Barbara K. Haber. Boston: G. K. Hall.

Busch, Lawrence and William Lacy. 1983. *Science, Agriculture, and the Politics of Research*. Boulder, CO: Westview Press.

Butler-Evans, Elliott. 1987. "Race, Gender and Desire: Narrative Strategies and the Production of Ideology in the Fiction of Toni Cade Bambara, Toni Morrison and Alice Walker." PhD diss., University of California, Santa Cruz.

Butler, Octavia. 1979. *Survivor*. New York: Signet.

———. 1987. *Dawn*. New York: Grand Central Publishing.

———. 1984. *Mind of My Mind*. New York: Grand Central Publishing.

———. 2001. *Wild Seed*. New York: Grand Central Publishing.

———. 2003. *Kindred*. Boston: Beacon Press.

Carby, Hazel. 1987. *Reconstructing Womanhood: The Emergence of the Afro-American Woman Novelist*. New York: Oxford University Press.

Charnas, Suzy McKee. 1955. *Motherlines*. New York: Berkeley.

Christian, Barbara. 1985. *Black Feminist Criticism: Perspectives on Black Women Writers*. New York: Pergamon Press.

Clifford, James. 1985. "On Ethnographic Allegory." In *The Poetics and Politics of Ethnography*, eds. James Clifford and George Marcus. Berkeley: University of California Press.

———. 1988. *The Predicament of Culture: Twentieth-century Ethnography, Literature, and Art*. Cambridge, MA: Harvard University Press.

Cohn, Carol. 1987a. "Nuclear Language and How We Learned to Pat the Bomb." *Bulletin of Atomic Scientists* 43 (5): 17–24.

———. 1987b. "Sex and Death in the Rational World of Defense Intellectuals." *Signs* 12 (4): 687–718.

Collins, Patricia Hill. 1982. "Third World Women in America." In *The Women's Annual, 1981*, ed. Barbara K. Haber. Boston: G. K. Hall.

Cowan, Ruth Schwartz. 1983. *More Work for Mother: The Ironies of Household Technology from the Open Hearth to the Microwave*. New York: Basic Books.

———, ed. 1986. *Feminist Approaches to Science*. New York: Pergamon Press.

Daston, Lorraine and Katherin Park. N.d. "Hermaphrodites in Renaissance France." Unpublished manuscript.

Delany, Samuel R. 1979. *Tales of Nevèrÿon*. New York: Bantam Books.

de Lauretis, Teresa. 1985. "The Violence of Rhetoric: Considerations on Representation and Gender." *Semiotica* 54: 11–31.

———. 1986. "Feminist Studies/Critical Studies: Issues, Terms, and Contexts." In *Feminist Studies/Critical Studies*, ed. T. de Lauretis, 1–19. Bloomington: Indiana University Press.

Derrida, Jacques. 1976. *Of Grammatology*. Trans. G. C. Spivak. Baltimore: Johns Hopkins University Press.

de Waal, Frans. 1982. *Chimpanzee Politics: Power and Sex Among Apes*. New York: Harper and Row.

D'Onofrio-Flores, Pamela, and Sheila M. Pfafflin, eds. 1982. *Scientific-Technological Change and the Role of Women in Development*. Boulder, CO: Westview Press.

Douglas, Mary. 1966. *Purity and Danger*. London: Routledge and Kegan Paul.

———. 1970. *Natural Symbols*. London: Cresset Press.

DuBois, Page. 1982. *Centaurs and Amazons*. Ann Arbor: University of Michigan Press.

Duchen, Claire. 1986. *Feminism in France from May '68 to Mitterand*. London: Routledge and Kegan Paul.

Edwards, Paul. 1985. "Border Wars: The Science and Politics of Artificial Intelligence." *Radical America* (19) 6: 39–52.

Enloe, Cynthia. 1983a. *Women Textile Workers in the Militarization of Southeast Asia*. In Nash and Fernandez-Kelly 1983, 407–25. Albany: State University of New York Press.

———. 1983b. *Does Khaki Become You? The Militarisation of Women's Lives*. Boston: South End Press.

Epstein, Barbara. 1993. *Political Protest and Cultural Revolution: Nonviolent Direct Action in the Seventies and Eighties*. Berkeley: University of California Press.

Evans, Mari, ed. 1984. *Black Women Writers: A Critical Evaluation*. Garden City, NY: Doubleday/Anchor.

Fausto-Sterling, Anne. 1985. *Myths of Gender: Biological Theories About Women and Men*. New York: Basic Books.

Feminist Issues: A Journal of Feminist Social and Political Theory. 1980. 1(1): special issue on Francophone feminisms.

Fernandez-Kelly, Maria Patricia. 1983. *For We Are Sold, I and My People*. Albany: State University of New York Press.

Fisher, Dexter, ed. 1980. *The Third Woman: Minority Women Writers of the United States*. Boston: Houghton Mifflin.

Flax, Jane. 1983. *Political Philosophy and the Patriarchal Unconscious: A Psychoanalytic Perspective on Epistemology and Metaphysics.* In Harding and Hintikka 1983, 245–82. Dordrecht, Netherlands: D. Riedel Publishing Company.

Foucault, Michel. 1963. *The Birth of the Clinic: An Archaeology of Medical Perception.* Trans. A. M. Smith. New York: Vintage.

———. 1975. *Discipline and Punish: The Birth of the Prison.* Trans. Alan Sheridan. New York: Vintage.

———. 1976. *The History of Sexuality, Vol. 1: An Introduction.* Trans. Robert Hurley. New York: Pantheon, 1978.

Fraser, Kathleen. 1984. *Something. Even Human Voices. In the Foreground, a Lake.* Berkeley, Calif.: Kelsey St. Press.

Frontiers: A Journal of Women's Studies. 1980. Volume 1.

———. 1983. Volume 3.

Fuentes, Annette and Barbara Ehrenreich. 1983. *Women in the Global Factory.* Boston: South End Press.

Gates, Henry Louis Jr. 1985. "'Writing 'Race' and the Difference It Makes.' In 'Race,' Writing and *Difference* (special issue)." *Critical Inquiry* 12 (1): 1–20.

Giddings, Paula. 1985. *When and Where I Enter: The Impact of Black Women on Race and Sex in America.* Toronto: Bantam Books.

Gilbert, Sandra M. and Susan Gubar. 1979. *The Madwoman in the Attic: The Woman Writer and the Nineteenth-Century Literary Imagination.* New Haven, CT: Yale University Press.

Gordon, Linda. 1988. *Heroes of Their Own Lives: The Politics and History of Family Violence, Boston 1880–1960.* New York: Viking Penguin.

Gordon, Richard. 1983. "The Computerization of Daily Life, the Sexual Division of Labor, and the Homework Economy." Presented at the Silicon Valley Workshop Conference, University of California, Santa Cruz.

——— and Linda Kimball. 1985. "High-Technology, Employment and the Challenges of Education." Silicon Valley Research Project, Working Paper, no. 1.

Gould, Stephen Jay. 1981. *The Mismeasure of Man.* New York: W. W. Norton.

Gregory, Judith, and Karen Nussbaum. 1982. "Race against Time: Automation of the Office." *Office: Technology and People* 1: 197–236.

Griffin, Susan. 1978. *Women and Nature: The Roaring Inside Her.* New York: Harper and Row.

Grossman, Rachel. 1980. "Women's Place in the Integrated Circuit." *Radical America* 14 (1): 29–50.

Haas, Violet, and Carolyn Perucci, eds. 1984. *Women in Scientific and Engineering Professions.* Ann Arbor: University of Michigan Press.

Hacker, Sally. 1981. "The Culture of Engineering: Women, Workplace, and Machine." *Women's Studies International Quarterly* 4 (3): 341–53.

———. 1984. "Doing It the Hard Way: Ethnographic Studies in the Agribusiness and Engineering Classroom." Presented at the California American Studies Association, Pomona.

———, and Liza Bovit. 1981. "Agriculture to Agribusiness: Technical Imperatives and Changing Roles." Presented at the Society for the History of Technology, Milwaukee.

Haraway, Donna J. 1979. "The Biological Enterprise: Sex, Mind, and Profit from Human Engineering to Sociobiology." *Radical History Review* 20: 206–37.

———. 1983. "Signs of Dominance: From a Physiology to a Cybernetics of Primate Society." *Studies in History of Biology* 6: 129–219.

———. 1984. *Class, Race, Sex, Scientific Objects of Knowledge: A Socialist-Feminist Perspective on the Social Construction of Productive Knowledge and Some Political Consequences.* In Haas and Perucci 1984, 212–29. Ann Arbor: University of Michigan Press.

———. 1984–85. "Teddy Bear Patriarchy: Taxidermy in the Garden of Eden, New York City, 1908–36." *Social Text* 11: 20–64.

———. 1989. *Primate Visions: Gender, Race, and Nature in the World of Modern Science.* New York: Routledge.

Harding, Sandra. 1978. "What Causes Gender Privilege and Class Privilege?" Presented at the American Philosophical Association.

———. 1983. *Why Has the Sex/Gender System Become Visible Only Now?* In Harding and Hintikka 1983, 311–24. Dordrecht, Netherlands: D. Riedel Publishing Company.

———. 1986. *The Science Question in Feminism.* Ithaca, NY: Cornell University Press.

————, and Merrill Hintikka, eds. 1983. *Discovering Reality: Feminist Perspectives on Epistemology, Metaphysics, Methodology, and Philosophy of Science*. Dordrecht, the Netherlands: D. Reidel.

Hartsock, Nancy. 1983a. *The Feminist Standpoint: Developing the Ground for a Specifically Feminist Historical Materialism*. In Harding and Hintikka 1983, 283–310. Dordrecht, Netherlands: D. Riedel Publishing Company.

————. 1983b. *Money, Sex, and Power*. New York: Longman.

————. 1987. "Rethinking Modernism: Minority and Majority Theories." *Cultural Critique* 7: 187–206.

Hogness, Erik Rusten. 1983. "Why Stress? A Look at the Making of Stress, 1936-56." Unpublished manuscript.

hooks, bell. 1981. *Ain't I a Woman*. Boston: South End Press.

————. 1984. *Feminist Theory: From Margin to Center*. Boston: South End Press.

Hrdy, Sarah Blaffer. 1981. *The Woman That Never Evolved*. Cambridge, MA: Harvard University Press.

Hubbard, Ruth and Marian Lowe, eds. 1979. *Genes and Gender*. Vol. 2, Pitfalls in Research on Sex and Gender. Staten Island, NY: Gordian Press.

Hubbard, Ruth, Mary Sue Henifin and Barbara Fried, eds. 1979. *Women Look at Biology Looking at Women: A Collection of Feminist Critiques*. Cambridge, MA: Schenkman Publishing.

Hull, Gloria, Patricia Bell Scott, and Barbara Smith, eds. 1982. *All the Women Are White, All the Men Are Black, But Some of Us Are Brave*. Old Westbury, NY: Feminist Press.

International Fund for Agricultural Development. 1985. *IFAD Experience Relating to Rural Women, 1977–84*. Rome: IFAD, 37.

Irigaray, Luce. 1977. *Ce sexe qui n'en est pas un*. Paris: Les Éditions de Minuit.

————. 1979. *Et l'une ne bouge pas sans l'autre*. Paris: Les Éditions de Minuit.

Jaggar, Alison. 1983. *Feminist Politics and Human Nature*. Totowa, NJ: Rowman and Allenheld.

Jameson, Frederic. 1984. "Post-Modernism, or the Cultural Logic of Late Capitalism." *New Left Review* 146: 53–92.

Kahn, Douglas, and Diane Neumaier, eds. 1985. *Cultures in Contention*. Seattle: Real Comet Press.

Keller, Evelyn Fox. 1983. *A Feeling for the Organism*. San Francisco: W. H. Freeman.

————. 1985. *Reflections on Gender and Science*. New Haven, CT: Yale University Press.

King, Katie. 1984. "The Pleasure of Repetition and the Limits of Identification in Feminist Science Fiction: Reimaginations of the Body after the Cyborg." Presented at the California American Studies Association, Pomona.

————. 1986. "The Situation of Lesbianism as Feminism's Magical Sign: Contests for Meaning and the U.S. Women's Movement, 1968–72." *Communication* 1: 65–92.

————. 1987a. "Canons without Innocence." PhD diss., University of California, Santa Cruz.

————. 1987b. "The Passing Dreams of Choice: Audre Lorde and the Apparatus of Literary Production." Unpublished manuscript (book prospectus).

Kingston, Maxine Hong. 1976. *The Woman Warrior*. New York: Alfred A. Knopf.

Klein, Hilary. 1989. "Marxism, Psychoanalysis, and Mother Nature." *Feminist Studies* 15 (2): 255–78.

Knorr-Cetina, Karin. 1981. *The Manufacture of Knowledge*. Oxford: Pergamon Press.

————, and Michael Mulkay, eds. 1983. *Science Observed: Perspectives on the Social Study of Science*. Beverly Hills, Calif.: Sage Publications.

Kramarae, Cheris, and Paula Treichler. 1985. *A Feminist Dictionary*. Boston: Pandora Press.

Kristeva, Julia. 1984. *Revolution in Poetic Language*. New York: Columbia University Press.

Latour, Bruno. 1984. *Les Microbes: guerre et paix, suivi des irréductions*. Paris: A.M. Métailié.

———— and Steve Woolgar. 1979. *Laboratory Life: The Social Construction of Scientific Facts*. Beverly Hills, CA: Sage Publications.

Lerner, Gerda, ed. 1973. *Black Women in White America: A Documentary History*. New York: Vintage.

Levi-Strauss, Claude. 1973. *Tristes Tropiques*. Trans. John and Doreen Weightman. New York: Atheneum.

Lewontin, R. C., Steven Rose and Leon J. Kamin. 1984. *Not in Our Genes: Biology, Ideology, and Human Nature*. New York: Pantheon Books.

Lorde, Audrey. 1982. *Zami: A New Spelling of My Name*. Watertown, MA: Persephone Press.

————. 1984. *Sister Outsider*. Trumansburg, NY: Crossing Press.

Lowe, Lisa. 1986. "French Literary Orientalism: The Representation of "Others" in the Texts of Montesquieu, Flaubert, and Kristeva." PhD diss., University of California, Santa Cruz.

Mackey, Nathaniel. 1984. "Review." *Sulfur* 2: 200–5.

MacKinnon, Catharine. 1982. "Feminism, Marxism, Method, and the State: An Agenda for Theory." *Signs* 7 (3): 515–44.

———. 1987. *Feminism Unmodified: Discourses on Life and Law.* Cambridge, MA: Harvard University Press.

Many Voices, One Chant: Black Feminist Perspectives. 1984. Feminist Review 17: special issue.

Marcuse, Herbert. 1964. *One-Dimensional Man.* Boston: Beacon Press.

Markoff, John and Lenny Siegel. 1983. "Military Micros." Presented at Silicon Valley Research Project Conference, University of California, Santa Cruz.

Marks, Elaine, and Isabelle de Courtivron, eds. 1980. *New French Feminisms.* Amherst: University of Massachusetts Press.

McCaffery, Anne. 1969. *The Ship Who Sang.* New York: Ballantine.

———. 1978. *Dinosaur Planet.* New York: Ballantine Books.

McIntyre, Vonda. 1983. *Superluminal.* Boston: Houghton Mifflin.

———. 1978. *Dreamsnake.* New York: Dell Books.

Merchant, Carolyn. 1980. *Death of Nature: Women, Ecology, and the Scientific Revolution.* New York: Harper and Row.

Microelectronics Group. 1980. *Microelectronics: Capitalist Technology and the Working Class.* London: CSE Books.

Mohanty, Chandra Talpade. 1984. "Under Western Eyes: Feminist Scholarship and Colonial Discourse." *Boundary* 2, 3 (12/13): 333–58.

Moraga, Cherríe. 1983. *Loving in the War Years: lo que nunca paso por sus labios.* Boston: South End Press.

Moraga, Cherríe, and Gloria Anzaldúa, eds. 1981. *This Bridge Called My Back: Writings by Radical Women of Color.* Watertown, MA: Persephone Press.

Morgan, Robin, ed. 1984. *Sisterhood Is Global.* Garden City, NY: Anchor/Doubleday.

Nash, June, and Maria Patricia Fernandez-Kelly, eds. 1983. *Women and Men and the International Division of Labor.* Albany: State University of New York Press.

Nash, Roderick. 1979. "The Exporting and Importing of Nature: Nature-Appreciation as a Commodity, 1850–1980." *Perspectives in American History* 3: 517–60.

National Science Foundation. 1988. *Women and Minorities in Science and Engineering.* Washington, DC: NSF.

New York Times. 1984. "Focus of U.N. Food Day Tomorrow: Women." October 14.

O'Brien, Mary. 1981. *The Politics of Reproduction.* New York: Routledge and Kegan Paul.

Ong, Aihwa. 1987. *Spirits of Resistance and Capitalist Discipline: Factory Workers in Malaysia.* Albany: State University of New York Press.

Ong, Walter. 1982. *Orality and Literacy: The Technologizing of the Word.* New York: Methuen.

Park, Katherine, and Lorraine J. Daston. 1981. "Unnatural Conceptions: The Study of Monsters in Sixteenth- and Seventeenth-Century France and England." *Past and Present* 92: 20–54.

Perloff, Marjorie. 1984. "Dirty Language and Scramble Systems." *Sulfur* 11: 178–83.

Petschesky, Rosalind. 1981. "Abortion, Anti-feminism, and the Rise of the New Right." *Feminist Studies* 7 (2): 206–46.

Piven, Frances Fox, and Richard Coward. 1982. *The New Class War: Reagan's Attack on the Welfare State and Its Consequences.* New York: Pantheon Books.

Preston, Douglas. 1984. "Shooting in Paradise." *Natural History* 93 (12): 14–19.

Reagon, Bernice Johnson. 1983. *Coalition Politics: Turning the Century.* In Smith 1983, 356–68. New York: Kitchen Table Press.

Reskin, Barbara F. and Heidi Hartmann, eds. 1986. *Women's Work, Men's Work.* Washington, DC: National Academy of Sciences.

Rich, Adrienne. 1978. *The Dream of a Common Language.* New York: W.W. Norton.

Rose, Hilary. 1983. "Hand, Brain, and Heart: A Feminist Epistemology for the Natural Sciences." *Signs* 9 (1): 73–90.

Rose, Stephen. 1986. *The American Profile Poster: Who Owns What, Who Makes How Much, Who Works, Where, and Who Lives with Whom?* New York: Pantheon Books.

Rossiter, Margaret. 1982. *Women Scientists in America.* Baltimore: Johns Hopkins University Press.

Rothschild, Joan, ed. 1983. *Machina ex Dea: Feminist Perspectives on Technology.* New York: Pergamon Press.

Russ, Joanna. 1975. *The Female Man.* New York: Bantam Books.

———. 1983a. *Adventures of Alix.* New York: Timescape.

———. 1983b. *How to Suppress Women's Writing.* Austin: University of Texas Press.

Sachs, Carolyn. 1983. *The Invisible Farmers: Women in Agricultural Production.* Totowa, NJ: Rowman and Allenheld.

Said, Edward. 1978. *Orientalism.* New York: Pantheon Books.

Sandoval, Chela. n.d. *Yours in Struggle: Women Respond to Racism, a Report to the National Women's Studies Association.* Oakland: Center for Third World Organizing.

———. 1984. "Dis-illusionment and the Poetry of the Future: the Making of Oppositional Consciousness." PhD qualifying essay, University of California at Santa Cruz.

Schiebinger, Londa. 1987. "The History and Philosophy of Women in Science: A Review Essay." *Signs* 12 (2): 305–32.

Science Policy Research Unit. 1982. *Microelectronics and Women's Employment in Britain.* Sussex: University of Sussex.

Smith, Barbara, ed. 1983. *Home Girls: A Black Feminist Anthology.* New York: Kitchen Table, Women of Color Press.

Smith, Dorothy. 1974. "Women's Perspective as a Radical Critique of Sociology." *Sociological Inquiry* 44.

———. 1979. "A Sociology of Women." In *The Prism of Sex,* eds. J. Sherman and E. T. Beck. Madison: University of Wisconsin Press.

Sofia [Sofoulis], Zoë. 1984. "Exterminating Fetuses: Abortion, Disarmament, and the Sexo-Semiotics of Extraterrestrialism." *Diacritics* 14 (2): 47–59.

Sofoulis, Zoë. n.d. "Lacklein." Unpublished manuscript.

Sontag, Susan. 1977. *On Photography.* New York: Dell.

Stacey, Judith. 1987. "Sexism by a Subtler Name? Postindustrial Conditions and the Postfeminist Consciousness." *Socialist Review* 96: 7–28.

Stallard, Karin, Barbara Ehrenreich and Holly Sklar. 1983. *Poverty in the American Dream.* Boston: South End Press.

Sturgeon, Noel. 1986. "Feminism, Anarchism, and Non-Violent Direct Action Politics." PhD qualifying essay, University of California, Santa Cruz.

Sussman, Vic. 1986. "Personal Tech: Technology Lends a Hand." *Washington Post Magazine,* 9 Novembe: 45–56.

Tiptree, James Jr. 1978a. *Star Songs of an Old Primate.* New York: Del Rey.

———. 1978b. *Up the Walls of the World.* New York: Berkeley.

Traweek, Sharon. 1988. *Beamtimes and Lifetimes: The World of High Energy Physics.* Cambridge, MA: Harvard University Press.

Treichler, Paula. 1987. "AIDS, Homophobia, and Biomedical Discourse: An Epidemic of Signification." *October* 43: 31–70.

Trinh T. Minh-ha. 1986–87a. "Introduction" and "Difference: 'A Special Third World Women Issue.'" *Discourse: Journal for Theoretical Studies in Media and Culture* 8: 3–38.

———, ed. 1986–87b. "She, the Inappropriate/d Other." *Discourse* 8 (Winter).

Varley, John. 1979. *Titan.* New York: Berkeley.

———. 1981. *Wizard.* New York: Berkeley.

———. 1984. *Demon.* New York: Berkeley.

Weisenbaum, Joseph. 1976. *Computer Power and Human Reason.* San Francisco: W. H. Freeman.

Wilford, John Noble. 1986. "Pilot's Helmet Helps Interpret High-Speed World." *New York Times,* July 1: 21, 24.

Wilfred, Denis. 1982. "Capital and Agriculture, a Review of Marxian Problematics." *Studies in Political Economy* 7: 127–54.

Winner, Langdon. 1977. *Autonomous Technology: Technics Out of Control as a Theme in Political Thought.* Cambridge, MA: MIT Press.

———. 1980. "Do Artifacts Have Politics?" *Daedalus* 109 (1): 121–36.

———. 1986. *The Whale and the Reactor.* Chicago: University of Chicago Press.

Winograd, Terry and Fernando Flores. 1986. *Understanding Computers and Cognition: A New Foundation for Design.* Norwood, NJ: Ablex Publishing.

Wittig, Monique. 1973 [1975]. *The Lesbian Body*. Trans. David LeVay. New York: Avon.

Women and Poverty special issue. 1984. Signs 10 (2).

Wright, Susan. 1982. "Recombinant DNA: The Status of Hazards and Controls." *Environment* 24 (6): 12–20, 51–3.

———. 1986. "Recombinant DNA Technology and Its Social Transformation, 1972–82." *Osiris* (2nd series) 2: 303–60.

Young, Robert M. 1979. "Interpreting the Production of Science." *New Scientist* 29 (March): 1026–28.

———, and Les Levidow, eds. 1981, 1985. *Science, Technology and the Labour Process*. 2 vols. London: CSE and Free Association Books.

Yoxen, Edward. 1983. *The Gene Business*. New York: Harper & Row.

Zimmerman, Jan, ed. 1983. *The Technology Woman: Interfacing with Tomorrow*. New York: Praeger.

37 Biohacking Gender

Cyborgs, Coloniality, and the Pharmacopornographic Era

Hil Malatino

In "Biohacking Gender," Hil Malatino discusses how the concept of "biohacking," a "do-it-yourself" approach to experimental body modification rooted in punk and anarchist sensibilities, nevertheless remains embedded in colonial and neocolonial projects. For trans people, biohacking can be a way to build medical and social networks of care that reroute and rewrite the cisgender-centric ideas of biological and social determinism that would otherwise constrain the possibilities of trans life. This definition aligns with how many marginalized people have taken up Haraway's cyborg as a posthuman figure of connection and kinship. Yet, as Malatino shows, this view conveniently skirts Haraway's own articulation of the cyborg as a figure embedded in Western configurations of sex, gender, race, and capital. It remains entrenched in a transhumanist eugenic fantasy of cheating death and transcending the limitations of the human—itself a category of personhood to which people of color, trans and queer people, and people with disabilities have been denied full access. Malatino engages Paul B. Preciado's *Testo Junkie* as a prime example of the DIY ethos of medically unsupervised hormone use as part of a biohacking practice to acknowledge both the posthuman potentials of hormone-enabled bodily transitions and the colonial roots of hormone research. In doing so, Malatino points us back to the complex relationships between posthumanism and transhumanism, cyborgs and coloniality. Trans people cannot ignore these legacies, Maltino argues; rather, they must acknowledge and work to transform them.

Because I am an athlete—a climber, specifically—I troll the Internet regularly for advice on eating and training. Around early 2014, in the midst of these forages, I started noticing the word "biohacking" appearing on all sorts of articles: articles about green smoothies, about minimizing gluten intake, about the benefits of a paleo diet, about the benefits of a vegan diet, about putting grassfed butter in your coffee. "Hack your health!" (Vennare); "Nutritional biohacking for peak experience!" (Strong); "Biohack yourself: transcend your limits!" (Strong); "Podcasts to take your biohacking to the next level!" (Nightingale).

In this essay, I'm concerned with mapping a tension between very different iterations of biohacking, which is the practice of manipulating biology through engaging biomolecular, medical, and technological innovations. There is, on the one hand, a form of biohacking that engages in corporeal manipulation in a manner that understands the body as an assemblage, as intimately interwoven with other (human and non-human) actants, and cognizes embodiment in terms of a becoming that is not fully predictable nor entirely controlled by a sovereign human agent. On the other hand, there is a form of biohacking that is fully invested in Western technoprogressivist fantasies of transcending the limitations of the human body, in

DOI: 10.4324/9781003206255-46

overcoming (through medical, technological, and nutritional means) disease, frailty, weakness, and—ultimately—human finitude itself. Both of these iterations of biohacking have their roots in cyborg theory, but manifest as radically divergent understandings of cyborg embodiment. The former is deeply invested in a posthumanist ethics; the latter underwritten by a transhumanist mission. Here, I follow Cary Wolfe's distinction between posthumanism and transhumanism. For Wolfe, as for me, posthumanism names both "the embodiment and embeddedness of the human being in not just its biological but also its technical world" as well as a "historical moment in which the decentering of the human by its imbrication in technical, medical, informatic, and economic networks is increasingly impossible to ignore" (xv). By contrast, transhumanism is an "extension of the fundamental anthropological dogma associated with humanism" insofar as "the human" is "achieved by escaping or repressing not just its animal origins in nature, the biological, and the evolutionary, but more generally by transcending the bonds of materiality and embodiment altogether" (xiv, xv). This investment in the power of the human to transcend the body should be understood as an "intensification of humanism" (xv); it is not, in the least, informed by opposition to anthropocentrism or interested in troubling fantasies of human sovereignty (over the body, the "natural" world, or non-human others).

I revisit Donna J. Haraway's "A Cyborg Manifesto: Science, Technology, and Socialist-Feminism in the Late Twentieth Century" in order to emphasize her theorization of these conflicting understandings (and manifestations) of cyborg embodiment. She writes:

> From one perspective, a cyborg world is about the final imposition of a grid of control on the planet, about the final abstraction embodied in a Star Wars apocalypse waged in the name of defense, about the final appropriation of women's bodies in a masculinist orgy of war. From another perspective, a cyborg world might be about lived social and bodily realities in which people are not afraid of their joint kinship with animals and machines, not afraid of permanently partial identities and contradictory standpoints.
>
> (295)

Here, Haraway neatly parses the tensions that Wolfe is also keen to theorize: between transhumanism and posthumanism, between fantasies of immortality, bodily transcendence, and superhumanity and the affirmation of relationality, co-constitution, and collectivity with human and non-human others. Examining the way Haraway's work on cyborgs has been read, received, and redeployed, I discuss the collective intellectual tendency to sidestep her theorization of the violence implicit in cyborg embodiment, and argue that to understand the political and ethical dimensions of contemporary posthuman forms of embodiment we must grapple with this violence, much of which is rooted in ongoing histories of colonization.

Beatriz Preciado's recent *Testo-Junkie* is a text that theorizes posthuman embodiment in a manner that is attentive to the colonial roots of contemporary pharmacopower—a term that Preciado coins to name the biomolecular control of sexual and gendered subjectivity. This attention to these colonial roots reveals the Janus-faced nature of cyborg theory: the simultaneously resistant and oppressive circuits through which posthumanity is routed. S/he explores the political terrain that produces certain subjects that are able to self-determine gender and avail themselves of the biomolecular prostheses on the market, while others experience forced determination, utilized as human test subjects for the profit of big Pharma. I ask after what it means to remind ourselves of the modern-colonial violence in which contemporary understandings of the posthuman are rooted. If we bear this in mind, how does that shift or reorient efforts to demedicalize gender transition, as well as efforts to democratize access to technologies of self-making more broadly? How do we do this without committing ourselves to the kind of troubling cyborg fantasies we see at work in the mainstreaming of biohacking?

Hearkening back to those Internet-based sources I mentioned at the outset: it was strange to encounter the rhetoric of biohacking in such mainstream, heavily commoditized sites. I was familiar with the term, having been interested in cyborg theory, interspecies connections, the blurring of boundaries between nature and artifice, human and machine, just like any good genderqueer science-fiction-loving feminist. I was preoccupied with the subversive potential of posthumanist forms of embodied becoming—that is, forms of embodiment that resist anthropocentrism and individualist understandings of selfmaking, and instead understand the body as an assemblage produced by and through interactions with other agents, both human and non-human. I had encountered biohacking because I was interested in thinking about how understandings of gendered embodiment shift in milieu wherein the technologies of gender transition are at least somewhat accessible.

In other words, I understood biohacking as one method for altering biological composition in the gendered directions one desires, and considered taking hormones or altering muscularity through the use of anabolic steroids as forms of biohacking with gendered consequences. Illegality, or acting through networks that aren't official or institutionalized, is central to the ethos of biohacking. As a form of hacking, it entails the illicit acquisition of material. This acquisition is democratizing because it bypasses systems of bureaucratic gatekeeping and institutional regulation and thus expands accessibility. Accessing testosterone or estrogen through networks beyond the medical industrial complex in order to avoid the red tape and financial cost of appointments with specialists to determine one's fitness for gender transition is an example of biohacking, and one I will return to later in this essay in my discussion of Preciado's *Testo-Junkie*.

Before, I'd been the only person in my family interested in the phenomenon of body modification through biohacking. Now, my mother was calling me up extolling the existential virtues of coconut oil. My brother was telling me about the importance of balancing alkalinity in the body (he's a climber, too). They were obsessed with avoiding xenoestrogens, talking about hitting the "reset button" on their bodies, carefully monitoring their sleep cycles with iPhone apps. All of a sudden, they were *into biohacking*, but they seemed to understand it differently: it was, for them, a means of enhancing health, cheating death, or (minimally) prolonging one's lease on life. Moreover, there was nothing illicit, illegal, or radically democratizing on the face of it. What is being hacked, bypassed, transcended—or at least what is imagined as hacked, bypassed, or transcended—is the finitude and fragility of the body itself.

The futural promises made in the literature on nutritional biohacking are grandiose, more extreme than any dieting article in *Cosmo*. It's the "Biggest Loser" gone cyberpunk. "Faster, Stronger, Smarter, Sexier, Better" reads a digital byline at the popular biohacking website Bulletproof Exec, which also uses this gem of an overwrought catchphrase: "Supercharge your body. Upgrade your brain. Be bulletproof." I can think of no better example of late capitalist superhero fantasies of immortality and hyperperformance. The site rhetorically interrogates you, as you down-scroll: "Can you really lose 100 pounds without using exercise, upgrade your IQ by more than 12 points, and stay healthy by sleeping less than 5 hours?"

The primary target for this adventure in do-it-yourself superhumanity is found in niche demographics dominated by bourgeois men. There are write-ups on biohacking in *Men's Health* and *Fast Company*, and a string of ex-pro-athletes testifying to better living through corporatized biohacking. These websites remind me an awful lot of Viagra commercials, or ads for testosterone supplements (targeted exclusively at cis-men, of course). It's nothing at all like the queer biohacking I'm familiar with: the sexual prostheses, the biomolecular negotiations we go through as we create alternative ways of being gendered, the communities of emotional and financial support we form to aid each other through transition and the often insurmountable-seeming tasks of navigating our everyday lives. The ethos, with this form of biohacking, is collaborative, deindividuated, about troubling ontological boundaries and developing a collective ethics, a kind of being with that doesn't prioritize the liberal, individualist self. It's grounded in a posthuman ethics premised on the idea that our bodies and beings are porous, shared, co-constituted by and through the entities involved in the situations we inhabit, or that inhabit us. Of posthuman ethics, Patricia MacCormack writes:

> Bodies in inextricable proximity [that is, posthuman bodies] involve a threefold ethical consideration—the critique of the detrimental effect a claim to knowledge of another body perpetrates; address as creative expressivity opening the capacity for the other to express; and acknowledgement and celebration of the difficult new a-system of bio-relations as an ongoing, irresolvable (but ethical for being so), interactive, mediative project of desire.
>
> (3)

If bodies are co-constituted, ontologically interwoven, not inviolable or neatly individuated, then there seems to be an ethical injunction to, minimally, dignify the notion that we are beings-in-process, continually affected and mutually transformed through contact and intimacy with the other entities in our milieu. This ethics begins with admitting, as Butler writes in *Undoing Gender*, that "we are undone by each other," and that the fact of this undoneness necessitates thinking the subject, the "I," as something other than sovereign, and consequently relinquishing the fantasy of molding inviolate, indestructible, idealized bodies (19).

Mainstream nutritional biohacking, by contrast, is governed by a marked disdain for corporeal connectivity and the limitations placed on living bodies by their milieu. It is shaped by an investment in the perfectibility of the body unto the point of deathlessness, and underwritten by the idea that economically privileged individuals can become the sovereign authors of their own superhumanity. It is cyborg theory gone venture capitalist; cyborg theory transformed into multi-day self-help conferences and a spate of commodities with outrageous price tags and even more outrageous claims. For example, Bulletproof sells a product called Brain Octane Oil that promises to increase brainpower and reduce brain fog "for maximum cognitive function!" ($45.95, subscriptions available); another called "Unfair Advantage" that claims to deliver "a brand new, activated form of a cellular nutrient called pyrroloquinoline quinine" that "supercharges mitochondria" in a manner that promises to have a "profound effect on your mental and physical energy" ($59.95). There are numerous other supplements, technological devices, coffees, teas, and other food products for sale, each of them issued replete with similarly superhuman promissory notes. My personal favorite is what is colloquially called "the Bulletproof Vibe," which sounds like a sex toy, but sadly is just a vibrating plate mounted on a 30 Hz motor. You stand on it and it shakes you. This supposedly stretches you, works your core, improves brain function and bone density, detoxifies, and improves your immune system ($1,495). You could also probably just do some jumping jacks.

The price tags on these products speak to the very class-specific nature of the niche market they're aimed at: a tired, time-strapped elite desperately seeking a new prime of life with enough expendable income to purchase a vibrating plate and balance on it while guzzling Brain Octane Oil. There is a tension between the strain of biohacking that works as a form of democratized embodied becoming, and the strain of biohacking illustrated by Bulletproof Exec that is a merger of hyper-individualized self-help discourses and the privatized commoditization of technologies of self-making, rhetorically garbed in the promises of folks who seem like the snake-oil salesmen of late liberalism.

To some extent, Haraway warned us about this troubling commoditization of biohack-ing. Her initial articulation of cyborg theory was one of a general ontology, not a rarefied ontology of queer, genderqueer resistance. She was explicit about this, writing early on in the manifesto, "the cyborg is our ontology; it gives us our politics" (292). By "our," she meant those of us operating in milieu predominately shaped by Western science and politics, living in a present molded by multiple destructive traditions—"the tradition of racist, male-dominant capitalism; the tradition of progress; the tradition of the appropriation of nature as resource for the productions of culture; the tradition of reproduction of the self from the reflections of the other" (ibid.). Haraway was very careful to make clear the unavoidability of complicity of all Euro and Westo-centric subjects—no matter how subversive or radical we fancied ourselves—in these destructive, interwoven traditions.

I didn't remember this point about general ontology until I was rereading the manifesto while beginning work on this article. I had preferred an exceptionalist reading of cyborg ontology, one that framed it as an alternative, resistant mode of being-in-the-world, beyond liberal individualism, beyond the vagaries of capitalist exploitation, beyond gender, never realizing that this fantasy of beyond-ness was a way of directly sidestepping that initial point of Haraway's regarding unavoidable complicity in structures of domination, expropriation, and exploitation. When I first encountered the work, I found the following phrases more promising, more exciting, and they became the rabbit holes I burrowed in for a good hand-ful of years.

> The cyborg is a creature in a post-gender world.
>
> (292)

> The cyborg is resolutely committed to partiality, irony, intimacy, and perversity.
>
> (Ibid.)

> The cyborg is "oppositional, utopian, and completely without innocence."
>
> (Ibid.)

> Cyborgs are "monstrous and illegitimate; in our present political circumstances, we could hardly hope for more potent myths for resistance and recoupling."
>
> (293)

I took those conceptual elements—postgender, perverse, oppositional and utopian, mon-strous and illegitimate—and they gradually came to weave the fabric of my understanding of the posthuman as an entity that affirms relationality as primary as it troubles the boundaries of nature/culture, self/other, male/female, and human/non-human. This kind of selective reading was, in part, a form of wish-fulfillment, as I was trying—as an intersex person with some serious scars, physical and otherwise, left from a series of bad dates with the medical industry—to develop an account of queer embodiment that played up collective resistance, that was interested in demedicalizing gender while retaining and democratizing access to technologies of gendered becoming.

[. . .]

But I'm worried I got carried away with the resistant potential of cyborg theory and, given the lineage of the deployment of Haraway's conceptual vocabulary in queer and femi-nist theory, I wasn't the only one. Haraway's position as one of the integral figures in the formation of feminist new materialisms, and the centrality of her concepts—naturecultures, diffractive perception, and situated knowledges, among others—to that field has contributed richly to contemporary understandings of posthuman subjectivity, ontological entanglement and embeddedness, and the deprioritization of anthropocentrism in the formation of feminist political agendas and critiques. Her work has been enormously influential in trans studies; the editors of *The Transgender Studies Reader*, vol. 1, include "A Cyborg Manifesto" and write that

> while she does not specifically address transgender issues [. . .] she addresses several issues of central importance to transgender studies, such as the way that "gender" is, in part, a story we tell ourselves to naturalize a particular social organization of biological reproduction, family roles, and state power.
>
> (103)

The most well-known redeployment of Haraway's work in trans studies is perhaps Sandy Stone's "The Empire Strikes Back," wherein she positions the "post-transsexual"—that is, transsexual persons who are vocal about their embodied histories and refuse the politicosocial imperative to pass-as-cis as a means of resisting the erasure of trans experience—as a form of cyborg embodiment. She writes that the disruptions of the old patterns of desire that the multiple dissonances of the transsexual body imply produce not an irreducible alterity but a myriad of alterities, whose unanticipated juxtapositions hold what Haraway has called the promises of monsters—physicalities of constantly shifting figure and ground that exceed the frame of any possible representation (232).

The posttranssexual cyborg, for Stone, is the harbinger of a promise to scramble, desirably, the codes of gender binarism and thus open up myriad possibilities for queering desire, embodiment, sexuality, and community. Feminist theorist Rita Felski has argued that the cyborg is implicitly transgendered (*sic*), and that Haraway "seeks to recuperate political agency and the redemptive promise of the future" through coding the transgender subject as a "liberating icon" representing "new and unimagined possibilities in hybrid gender identities and complex fusions of previously distinct realities" (568). A promising monster, indeed. In a slightly divergent trajectory, Jasbir Puar has taken the final sentence of "A Cyborg Manifesto" as the title of her 2012 article "'I'd Rather be a Cyborg than a Goddess': Becoming-Intersectional in Assemblage Theory" and positioned Haraway's work as a central component within a feminist genealogy that enables Puar to understand intersectionality as a form of assemblage that moves beyond too-simple conceptions of identity and subjectivity—a move that positions the cyborg as germinal for contemporary women and queer of color scholarship.

We couple up with Haraway's work in order to develop increasingly complex accounts of naturecultures as a means toward building coalitions, alliances, and affinities—with human and non-human actants—capable of resisting destructive traditions, capable of envisioning and enacting life-worlds not entirely constrained by the informatics of domination. It is understandable that, motivated by these desires, some of us (myself, most certainly) have cherry-picked Haraway's most politically sexy assertions; they resonate with a kind of hopefulness, a belief in utopia, in the productivity of radical futural visions, and are informed by a faith in prefigurative politics: the idea that a new world can be built in the shell of the old. Her scholarship is revivifying, even in its skepticism.

It becomes imperative, given this tendency toward a reparative reading of Haraway's work, a style of reading emphasizing the production of pleasurable or joyful affect in the encounter between text and reader, to focus on what of her analysis is left out or minimized on account of this interpretive legacy. One of the conveniently downplayed elements of Haraway's work is her commentary on the violence of cyborg inheritance, on its rootedness in neocolonial technoprogressivism. I have found that returning to the text and finding these admonitions is troubling for readers—like me—who have spent years embracing and emphasizing the more hopeful aspects of her scholarship. I'd like to return, for a moment, to the Haraway citation at the beginning of this essay, in order to think through this phenomenon of selective writing. She asserts:

> from one perspective, a cyborg world is about the final imposition of a grid of control on the planet, about the final abstraction embodied in a Star Wars apocalypse waged in the name of defence, about the final appropriation of women's bodies in a masculinist orgy of war.
>
> (295)

Haraway reiterates this point in her introduction to *The Haraway Reader*, attesting "many of the entities that command my attention [. . .] were birthed through the apparatuses of war" (3). She goes on to critique the legacy of "A Cyborg Manifesto," claiming that "too many people [. . .] have read [it] as the ramblings of a blissed-out, technobunny, fembot" (ibid.). While I hadn't quite construed Haraway as a blissed-out fembot, I had definitely lost touch with the aspects of cyborg theory that emphasized destructive manifestations of cyborg embodiment that are intensely complicit with cultures of dominance. I had begun to habitually overlook the implications of the fact that, as Haraway writes, "the main trouble with cyborgs [. . .] is that they are the illegitimate offspring of militarism and patriarchal capitalism" (293). She goes on to argue, palliatively, that cyborgs are able to be "exceedingly unfaithful to their origins" (ibid.)—but origins are origins, nonetheless. You can take the cyborg out of militarism and patriarchal capitalism, but it may prove significantly more difficult to take the militarism and patriarchal capitalism out of the cyborg.[1] And we know quite a bit about the fundamental colonial and neo-colonial violence—in the form of expropriation, exploitation, and epistemological imperialism—that undergirds contemporary militarism and patriarchal capitalism. The question for me has since become this: *to what extent are contemporary cyborg subjectivities implicated in the coloniality of being?*

By coloniality of being I refer to work by Nelson Maldonado-Torres wherein he describes the Eurocentric taxonomy at work in modern colonial understandings of being. In this colonial taxonomy of being, Western-style scientific rationality is posited as integral to human being, and colonized subjects are constructed as lacking this form of rationality, and thus construed as "what lies below Being" (122). Maldonado-Torres refers to this rendering of beings less-than-being as the construction of "sub-ontological difference" (ibid.). This difference is produced by a coloniality that empowers certain subjects to be future-oriented, to develop an existential comportment that can invest in self-realization, flourishing, attainment of goals, the realization of some kind of ontological authenticity or fullness—a YOLO ontology of maximizing the potential of the present moment which, not coincidentally, seems an awful lot like the hyper-capitalist biohacking I opened this paper describing. This orientation to being contrasts sharply with what Maldonado-Torres, citing Fanon, refers to as the existential reality of the damné (a term Fanon uses to refer to colonized subjects that translates to "damned" or "wretched," as in "the wretched of the earth"). Of this existential reality, Maldonado-Torres writes that the "hellish existence [of the damné] carries with it both the racial and the gendered aspects of the naturalization of the non-ethics of war. *Indeed, the coloniality of being primarily refers to the normalization of the extraordinary events that take place in war*" (255; emphasis in original). For Maldonado-Torres, the coloniality of being refers to existences shaped by the routinization of violence and expropriation. One of the dominating characteristics of existence-in-wartime is nihilism, the futility of action, the desiccation of the future. Thus, he sketches two very different orientations to being, produced by two very distinct structural locations in a world shaped by the coloniality of power. To think the coloniality of being is, to a significant extent, to think about conditions wherein subjects are forced to navigate life in terrains shaped by the non-ethics of war. There is a way in which the valorization of the cyborg works only for those beings with the ability to exercise some degree of autonomy in their utilization of technologies of becoming. For others, features of cyborg ontology are experienced not as *posthumanizing* but as *dehumanizing*.

One can think, for instance, of the histories of forced sterilization that have affected indigenous women, poor women, women of color, and disabled women in the United States and its territories. Andrea Smith, in *Conquest: Sexual Violence and American Indian Genocide*, details the history of sterilization abuse and lab-rat treatment by medico-scientific practitioners—particularly those who worked for Indian Health Services—that has shaped the lives of American Indian women, ranging from coercive hysterectomy to the systematic failure to notify them of the side-effects of DepoProvera and Norplant. Then there are the Rio Piedras trials of the pill, well documented by Iris Lopez in *Matters of Choice: Puerto Rican Women's Struggle for Reproductive Freedom*, wherein poor Puerto Rican women were utilized as test subjects for the garnering of FDA approval: because they would prove the effectiveness of the pill in areas wherein population control was posited as desirable, and because they could be instrumentally utilized to demonstrate the success of the method of daily oral contraceptive ingestion to critics who believed it would be too complicated for these women to self-administer. These instances are significant chapters in the interwoven history of contraceptive technology being utilized in the service of racist eugenics. Much of our contemporary understanding of the biomolecular operations of hormone-based pharmaceuticals stems from research of this sort, meaning that gendered self-determination through biomolecular procedures is intimately tied to forms of knowledge production built on and through neo-colonial violence.

If we're going to embrace the queer potentiality of cyborg ontology we must be simultaneously attentive to these necropolitical instances of cyborg embodiment. These examples allow us to think Haraway and Maldonado-Torres together: if cyborg ontology has become generalized in what we refer to, variously, as late capitalism, late liberalism, or Western hyper-modernity, then the origins of cyborg ontology lie deep in the coloniality of being.

Beatriz Preciado's recent *Testo-Junkie* makes clearer the terrain that has shaped contemporary technologies of gendered becoming. Johanna Fateman, in a review of the volume in *Bookforum*, describes it as an "arresting hybrid work: a philosophical treatise and a literary homage embedded in a sexually explicit drug diary addressed to a ghost" (n. pag.). The volume is structured around Preciado's ritualized practice of administering testosterone, and h/er exhaustive accounts of its effects on h/er body are interwoven with significant research on the transformations in gendered and sexual subjectivity wrought by the development of pharmaceutical extraction and mass production of hormones. The act of self-administering testosterone elicits a book-length meditation on an epochal shift in the logic of gendered being. H/er central argument, like Haraway's, has to do with a shift in general ontology. Preciado explores gender as a posthuman phenomenon, arguing that

> gender in the twenty-first century functions as an abstract mechanism for technical subjectification; it is spliced, cut, moved, cited, imitated, swallowed, injected, bought, sold, modified, mortgaged, transferred, downloaded, enforced, translated, falsified, fabricated, swapped, dosed, administered, extracted, contracted, concealed, negated, renounced, betrayed [. . .] it transmutes.
>
> (129)

One of the most compelling moments in the work comes near the beginning, with h/er account of the ritual of testosterone (T) administration. A couple of days after the dose, s/he writes:

> An extraordinary lucidity settles in, gradually, accompanied by an explosion of the desire to fuck, walk, go out everywhere in the city. This is the climax in which the spiritual force of the testosterone mixing with my blood takes to the fore. Absolutely all the unpleasant sensations disappear. Unlike speed, the movement going on inside has nothing to do with agitation, noise. It's simply the feeling of being in perfect harmony with the rhythm of the city. Unlike with coke there is no distortion in the perception of self, no logorrhea or any feeling of superiority. Nothing but the feeling of strength reflecting the increased capacity of my muscles, my brain. My body is present to itself.
>
> (21)

S/he wraps up this affective account of h/er experience on T with a question and a declaration:

> What kind of feminist am I today: a feminist hooked on testosterone, or a transgender body hooked on feminism? I have no other alternative but to revise my classics, to subject those theories to the shock that was provoked in me by the practice of taking testosterone.
>
> (21–22)

What does it mean to be a feminist hooked on testosterone, one who craves its transformative effects? What does that mean in light of our long history of rejecting biological essentialisms and downplaying the dominant technoscientific narrative that has rendered them the factic determinants of sex difference? What lived knowledge comes from the material transformations called forth by the biomolecular intimacy of blood and T? How do we grapple with these questions, how do we make sense of this transformed terrain of what it is to be and have a gender, with how the mere fact of being gendered places one directly in contact with the transnational circuits that shape research on and the production and consumption of biomolecular agents of corporeal transformation?

[. . .]

The pharmacopornographic era is marked by the literal conversion of concept to product, a commoditization of multivalent, opaque, perhaps even ineffable phenomena. Gender becomes literally encapsulated, as does arousal, sadness, content. The effects of this commoditization are diverse: at the same time as gender floats ever further away from the ostensible constraints of birth sex, access to technologies of gendered becoming are increasingly regulated. Only certain subjects are able to actualize technologies of transition in fully legal, monitored ways: those of us who are moneyed, insured, urban-dwelling, and have access to trans-supportive persons, agencies, and institutions. We are being forced to grapple with gender not as some spiritualized essence, a strictly *social* construction, or an internally felt sense of self to be either closeted or disclosed, but as a product of "*sexdesign*," a curated or imposed (usually, a bit of both) amalgam of circulating, mobile commoditized production that becomes *dissolved into* the body, inseparable from it, productive of it—not simply *used* by the body, which would presuppose a firm division between corporeality and the products at work in the fabrication of gender (35).

Which prompts the question: how did we get to this moment? Historiographically, Preciado submits that pharmacopornography has "lines of force rooted in the scientific and colonial society of the nineteenth century," although "their economic vectors become visible only at the end of WWII" (33–34). S/he documents, drawing heavily on the archaeology of sex hormones written by Nelly Oudshoorn, how hormones came to be theorized in the early 1900s, in a context of increasing transnational information and product exchange whose flows were determined by colonial vectors of exploitative trade in resources (human and otherwise), "according to an early form of information theory" (158). London-based physician Ernest Starling and his brother-in-law, William Bayliss, coined the term "hormone" in 1905 and conceptualized it as a kind of chemical messenger, independent of the nervous system that functioned as a carrier pigeon in the bloodstream, flitting between organs, delivering bits of information that work to elicit corporeal transformation and influencing pre-cognitive affect. Their research, while centered on human subjects, was significantly indebted to slightly earlier work performed by Charles-Edouard Brown-Séquard, a citizen of the French colony of Mauritius and founder of "organatherapy." This mode of therapy involved intense interspecies connectivity (not unlike contemporary hormone therapies such as Premarin, a conjugated estrogen made from the urine of mares) insofar as extracts from the testicles of guinea pigs were posited as the key to "eternal youthfulness and vigor for men" and "potions containing extracts of guinea pigs ovaries were used to treat various forms of uterine disease, as well as cases of hysteria" (155). Proto-hormone therapies based in animal research were also key in the careers of Starling and Bayliss; their discovery of hormones was based on research involving the vivisection of dogs—a practice ill-received by antivivisection activists, but one which was found to be fully legal in the United Kingdom on account of Starling and Bayliss having cleared the proper licensing mechanisms that enabled them to perform such procedures. Bayliss even sued the National Anti-Vivisection League for libel (and won).

Preciado and Oudshoorn both argue—rightly, I think—that the discovery of hormones heralded a massive epistemological transformation in how embodiment is understood, as well as a massive ontological transformation regarding both what bodies *can do* as well as what *can be done with* bodies. The ensemble of practices that led to the isolation, extraction, and production of hormones established "the first regular trafficking networks of biological materials among gynecologists, laboratory researchers, pharmaceutical industries, prisons, and slaughterhouses" (Preciado 163). What this means, for Preciado, is that the act of taking testosterone implicates h/er in a series of posthuman becomings situated in an often-violent web of exchange. S/he writes:

> Each time I give myself a dose of testosterone, I agree to this pact. I kill the blue whale; I cut the throat of the bull at the slaughterhouse; I take the testicles of the prisoner condemned to death. I become the blue whale, the bull, the prisoner. I draft a contract whereby my desire is fed by—and retroactively feeds—global channels that transform living cells into capital.
>
> (Ibid.)

The history of hormone research is a rich example of what Mel Chen has called *trans-substantiation*, a term they use to index exchanges across the bounds of the human/non-human that "extend beyond intimate coexistence" in that they involve "not only substantive exchange, but exchange of substance" (129). To ingest hormones is, in one form or another, to be implicated in processes of trans-substantiation, engaged in exchange of substance with non-human animals. This is, of course, an uneven exchange, as the human and non-human animals utilized in the research and production of hormones are positioned much lower within what Chen has called the "animacy hierarchy," aligned more closely to the necropolitical, with more intensely circumscribed agency, much less able to exercise a degree of autonomy in terms of their becoming (2).[2] It is important to heed Chen's articulation of the function of racialization within animacy hierarchies, which draws on the very long Eurocentric legacy of entwining non-white racialization with beastialization, manifest most vividly in those "pseudo-Darwinian evolutionary discourses tied to colonialist strategy and pedagogy that superimposed phylogenetic maps onto synchronic human racial typologies, yielding simplistic promulgating equations of 'primitive' peoples with prehuman stages of evolution" (102). The construction of colonized and neo-colonized subjects as sub-ontological always tarries with animality, is always implicated in hierarchies of animacy or liveness that work to justify the instrumentalization of the bodies of said subjects through placing their capacity for rational, agentic action under skepticism. Inquiring after how these hierarchies of animacy shape the protocols of medico-scientific research and pharmaceutical production is necessary if we are to have a full picture of the colonial roots of contemporary pharmacopornography.

Examining the colonial roots of the pharmacopornographic era is a way of historicizing the contemporary disjunct between transhumanism and posthumanism. It vividly calls our attention to the racialized and gendered geopolitical bifurcations that produce a small handful of entitled, enfranchised subjects who engage biological modification to overcome human finitude and frailty, to easily mold and mutate corporeality in the direction of their idealized visions of the self-surpassing human, while others find themselves systematically prevented from accessing the technological, medical, and scientific procedures that would enable them to lead more livable lives, whether those come in the form of gender-confirming medical treatment, antiretroviral treatment, or forms of birth control with minimal deleterious side-effects. As we develop and refine accounts of posthumanity that attune us to the intimate imbrications of biology with multiplicitous human and non-human actants, and develop anti-anthropocentric ethics that are companionate with this reconsideration of ontology, it behooves us to remain focused on minoritized subjects who become utilized as research material and labor power for medico-scientific and technological innovations while simultaneously robbed of the means to engage these innovations with a relative degree of agency.

From: Hil Malatino, "Biohacking Gender: Cyborgs, Coloniality, and the Pharmacopornographic Era" in *Angelaki: Journal of the Theoretical Humanities*, 22 (2), pp. 179–190. Copyright 2017, Taylor & Francis. All rights reserved. Republished by permission of the copyright holder, Taylor & Francis (Taylor & Francis Ltd, www.tandfonline.com).

Notes

1. Dillon's work on the centrality of cyborg embodiment to contemporary Western militarism is an excellent rejoinder to valorizations of cyborg ontology that ignore its embeddedness in and indebtedness to military technologies.
2. For an excellent discussion of how this consignment to the necropolitical works for non-human animals, particularly those forced to reside in factory farms, see Stanescu's "Beyond Biopolitics."

Bibliography

Bulletproof Exec. N.d. Web. 8 Dec. 2014.
Butler, Judith. *Undoing Gender.* New York: Routledge, 2004. Print.
Chen, Mel Y. *Animacies: Biopolitics, Racial Mattering, and Queer Affect.* Durham, NC: Duke UP, 2013. Print.
Dillon, Michael. "Intelligence Incarnate: Martial Corporeality in the Digital Age." *Body and Society* 9.4 (2003): 123–147. Web. 8 Dec. 2014.
Fateman, Johanna. "Bodies of Work." *Bookforum.* Sept./Oct./Nov. 2013. Web. 8 Dec. 2014.
Felski, Rita. "Fin de Siècle, Fin du Sexe: Transsexuality, Postmodernism, and the Death of History." *The Transgender Studies Reader.* Ed. Susan Stryker and Stephen Whittle. New York: Routledge, 2006.565–573. Print.

Haraway, Donna. "A Cyborg Manifesto: Science, Technology, and Socialist-Feminism in the Late Twentieth Century." *The Transgender Studies Reader*. Ed. David Bell and Barbara M. Kennedy. New York: Routledge, 2000.103–118. Print.

Lopez, Iris. *Matters of Choice: Puerto Rican Women's Struggle for Reproductive Freedom*. New Brunswick, NJ: Rutgers UP, 2008. Print.

MacCormack, Patricia. *Posthuman Ethics*. Farnham: Ashgate, 2012. Print.

Maldonado-Torres, Nelson. *Against War: Views from the Underside of Modernity*. Durham, NC: Duke UP, 2008. Print.

Nightingale, Rob. "Top Podcasts to Take Your Biohacking to the Next Level." *Make Use of*. 9 June 2014. Web. 8 Dec. 2014.

———. "Nutritional Biohacking for Peak Experience." *Petra8Paleo*. 31 May 2014. Web. 8 Dec. 2014.

Oudshoorn, Nelly. *Beyond the Natural Body: An Archaeology of Sex Hormones*. New York: Routledge, 1994. Print.

Preciado, Beatriz. *Testo-Junkie*. New York: Feminist, 2013. Print.

Puar, Jasbir. "I'd Rather Be a Cyborg Than a Goddess: Becoming-Intersectional in Assemblage Theory." *philoSOPHIA* 2.1 (2012): 49–66. Print.

Sedgwick, Eve Kosofsky. *Touching Feeling: Affect, Pedagogy, Performativity*. Durham, NC: Duke UP, 2003. Print.

Smith, Andrea. *Conquest: Sexual Violence and American Indian Genocide*. Cambridge, MA: South End, 2005. Print.

Stanescu, James K. "Beyond Biopolitics: Animal Studies, Factory Farms, and the Advent of Deading Life." *PhaenEx* 8.2 (2013): 135–160. Web. 8 Dec. 2014.

Stone, Sandy. "The Empire Strikes Back: A Posttransexual Manifesto." *The Transgender Studies Reader*. Ed. Susan Stryker and Stephen Whittle. New York: Routledge, 2006.221–235. Print.

Strong, Winslow. *Biohack Yourself*. N.d. Web. 8 Dec. 2014.

Stryker, Susan, and Stephen Whittle, eds. *The Transgender Studies Reader*. New York: Routledge, 2006. Print.

Vennare, Joe. "Hack Your Health: 6 Biohacks That Might Surprise You." *Daily Burn*. 7 Oct. 2013. Web. 8 Dec. 2014.

Wolfe, Cary. *What Is Posthumanism?* Minneapolis: U of Minnesota P, 2010. Print.

38 Animals Without Genitals

Race and Transsubstantiation

Mel Y. Chen

If the concept of "the human" as it has been developed in the modern West is predicated on marking a fundamental distinction from "the animal" as well as between genders, it follows that concepts of transness and animality are in deep conversation with one another about the domain of the human from their respective positions outside of it. This article by Mel Chen is an early version of work subsequently incorporated into *Animacies: Biopolitics, Racial Mattering, and Queer Affect.* Chen analyzes three eclectic cultural texts, all of which stage encounters between humans and nonhuman animals in which genitals are present and/or absent in various permutations. These include filmmaker Nagisa Oshima's interspecies love story involving a chimpanzee, *Max, mon amour;* philosopher of language J. L. Austin's curious use of a monkey to illustrate varieties of linguistic performativity in his famous series of essays, *How to Do Things With Words;* and artist Xu Bing's conceptual work, *Cultural Animal,* in which a live male pig mounts and penetrates a man-like mannequin. Chen teases out the associative links between genitals, castration, gender transposition, animality, blackness, racialization, and (post)colonialism that operate in and across these texts. What emerges is a conceptual map of the porous and refigurable boundaries that join and separate sexes and species along racialized lines.

How might one think about modes of trans-ness in conjunction with animality? Invoking the theoretical lens of a Deleuzian "body without organs," I bring into suggestive conversation several disparate instances of cultural production from the last few decades of the twentieth century, each of which ostensibly opposes non-human animals to humans in ways that crucially implicate gender. This is a trans-generic thought piece, intentionally speculative in tone as well as consciously promiscuous as it crosses various borders of cultural analysis to examine performatively and rhetorically independent examples that are drawn from film, contemporary art, and language philosophy. I argue that each plumbs animals' symbolic force as a third term, and hence bears its own particular imprint of racialization, sexualization, and globalization in a shared era of geopolitical contestation and postcoloniality. In doing so, I consider the epistemological lessons made possible by thinking about trans-animality in terms of sex.

If mattering turns irrevocably on gender—if, as Judith Butler writes, questions of gender are irretrievably interwoven with questions of materiality, and if human substantiation enduringly depends on the expulsion of animals—then it is imperative that we ask questions about how animals matter sexually.[1] To examine the transness of animal figures in cultural productions or philosophical discourses (beyond their biology, queerness or pure animality,

DOI: 10.4324/9781003206255-47

for instance) is to also interrogate how humans' analogic mapping to and from animals (within imagined, lived or taxonomic intimacies) paradoxically survives the cancellation wrought by the operations of abjection, casting a trans light back on the human. By considering the simultaneous relevance of race, gender, sexuality, and geopolitics in the examples below, each chosen for their potent ambivalences, as well as for their diverse consideration of how trans-animality looks and functions, this piece builds on recent work that treats animal spaces intersectionally.[2] It makes use of the simultaneous mobility, stasis, and border-violation shared among transgender spaces and other forms of trans-being: transnationality, transraciality, translation, transspecies. This is not to conflate these various, importantly distinct terms, but to instead try to think them together in new constellations.

Making the science studies observation that "biology has always meant the thing itself and knowledge of what it is, and equally notoriously, these two biologies have not always been identical," Sarah Franklin (thinking through Haraway) dubs "transbiology" an intensified making of "new biologicals" via "the redesign of the biological in the context of contemporary bioscience, biomedicine and biotechnology,"[3] identifying what might be thought of as a significant shift in the specific depth of imaginative technologies in crafting matter—a shift in the participants in what Charis Thompson has called "ontological choreography."[4] Reframing the transbiological question, Judith Halberstam considers the queer possibilities for human/animal mixings found in the world of animated and other film.[5] Here, thinking less in terms of biotechnologies than attending to the role of visual representation and morphology in mattering, I turn directly to the "trans" in "transbiology." With "trans," I focus on how animal–human boundaries are articulated *in terms of* sex and gender by examining perhaps the most consistent missing morphology in cultural representations of animals: the genitalia.[6]

Animal Spaces: *Max, mon amour*

In the 1988 bilingual French film *Max, mon amour*, directed by Nagisa Oshima, Margaret (played by Charlotte Rampling), the wife of a British diplomat named Peter (played by Anthony Higgins), recounts to her husband that she has fallen in love with a chimpanzee named Max, purchased Max and taken Max home. The film, saturated in bourgeois settings with the blatant exception of Max, proceeds with the ambivalent games of the husband to cope with Max's entrance into the family, Max's moving into the family home, Max's resistances to Peter's mistreatments and violences, Margaret's insistence upon keeping her relationship with Max during a climactic scene during which a rifle changes hands from Peter to Max, and the ultimate, happy reconstitution of the family, Max included.

Max's *linguistic* gender is, throughout, consistently male. Yet the embodied creature is not terribly convincing as a chimpanzee. The non-integrity of the creature is made evident by the fact that the eyes shift around inside the sockets of the chimpanzee hood as Max moves. To a queer (and perhaps forgiving?) skeptic, the middling chimp costume begs further questions, such 1980s special effects notwithstanding: it lacks any form of visible genitalia or easily legible "secondary sex characteristics." While such a visual absence, all else equal, might provoke a tentative reading of "female," it is also true that the default movie sex for costumed monkeys and apes can remain unspecified, genderless, in almost a literalization of the genericity of the animal type. In addition, individual animal specificities like sex cannot survive in a costume unless it is intended as "anatomically accurate," bucking the neutering costume traditions for genitalia. Such a confounding and ultimate undeterminability of possible linguistic and visual sexes and genders points, no less so in the relatively ludicrous case of Max, to the porosity underlying gender/sex systems that structure Western cultural spaces.

[. . .]

Watching the film, my colleagues and I took pleasure in the "failure" of the costume and the awkward monkey-moves of the actor inside. There were gender-queering possibilities: on top of the expected bestial kinkiness offered by a human–animal coupling, why not add a Rampling/chimpanzee lesbian coupling, rather than—as the film seems only to intend—a neatly contained heterosexual narrative?[7] And perhaps, given that the chimp actor was self-evidently a person in a costume, was Margaret's sexual preference in fact for Furries, to borrow a current term for human sexuality imbued with animal signifiers, often while humans wear animal costumes?

For all the amusement of such questions, what cannot be ignored in *Max, mon amour* is the virtual stampede of Africanized racial invocations, overdetermined by Margaret's British husband's diplomatic status and the Parisian locus of the film as both a colonial metropolis, and a host to unwelcome racialized colonial subjects. Such racialized staging was evident from moment to moment in the chimp's expressive limitations, marked "impoliteness" and unfamiliarity with its "civilized" surroundings, its surfeit of embodiment, aggression, and emotional lability in the face of white upper-class cultural sophistication, formal "goodwill," and expressive minimalism. All of these are conditioned by seasoned colonial narrative and visual tropes.[8] The recognizable "fakeness" of the costume's face further invites comparisons to blackface minstrelsy, in which there lingers the possibility that a mask conceals a differently racialized human, undermining the film's pointedly surrealist overtones with a historical legacy of European racism and colonialism.[9]

Austin's Marriage

In 1955, the British language philosopher J. L. Austin put forward a theory of language and action called *How to do things with words*, consisting of a series of transcribed and edited lectures. As the lectures progressed, Austin developed the concept of the performative from a simple class of utterances characterized by special main verbs in finite form, to a more complex tripartite typology of *acts* that not merely the special verbs, but all utterances, would involve: locutionary (speech) content, illocutionary (conventional) content, and perlocutionary (effective) content. In an early lecture, Austin was working off the simple definition of the performative, such as in the example "I thee wed" in a marriage ceremony.

Stating that a performative could not succeed without supporting conditions, Austin wrote: "Suppose we try first to state schematically . . . some at least of the things which are necessary for the *smooth or 'happy' functioning* of a performative (or at least of a *highly developed* explicit performative . . .)" (my emphasis). He went on to list a number of ordered features, among them "a1. There must exist an accepted conventional procedure having a certain conventional effect, that procedure to include the uttering of certain words by certain persons in certain circumstances, and further, a2. the particular persons and circumstances in a given case must be appropriate for the invocation of the particular procedure invoked." Austin's model was also premised on the assumption that communication is "normally" good-willed, and relies on the proper positioning of that person delivering the performative. He wrote: "One might . . . say that, where there is not even a pretence of *capacity* or a *colourable* claim to it, then there is no accepted conventional procedure; it is a *mockery, like a marriage with a monkey*" (my emphasis).[10]

Proper capacity and goodwill were critical to the success of Austin's performative, and these conditions remained through complex developments of the theory. In the moment of defining a critical aspect of the successful performative, Austin turned to marriage, perhaps revealing his own attachments; at other key moments in the text, marriage again emerged as a central exemplar. Finally, how interesting that if a claim to capacity must exist, that it have a kind of substance, that it be, in Austin's words, *colourable*. I read this as an understanding of a role legitimacy that bears an affective weight, a claim to command.

What does Austin's marriage with a monkey suggest, and on what does it rely to make this kind of sense? While Austin's articulation "mockery, like a marriage with a monkey" seems mundane in the sense that monkey-invocations often function as normative dismissals, we can look more closely at the significance of its collocations. More specifically, we can consider what a queer reading might offer. "A mockery, like a marriage with a monkey" equates a particular kind of animal with the performative's excess (and, perhaps, an affective excess inappropriate to the encounter)—that which must be sloughed off for the performative to work efficiently and effectively.[11] Austin's backhanded dismissal of the animal monkey, and his matter-of-fact exclusion of the monkey from the institution of marriage, together consign the marrying monkey to queer life. In citing a particular kind of marriage just as he asserts its invalidity, Austin is responding to a sensed threat. Someone's heteronormative and righteous marriage must be protected against the mockeries of marriage; and we might imagine that someone's righteous and heteronormative speech must be protected against the mockery of performative improprieties, which for all practical purposes are open to convenient definition.

But it is worth asking what might have most registered as a threat. Austin delivered these lectures informed by the social and political context of mid-1950s Britain. The 1950s was a period of intensive societal and legal flux, in which immigrants from formally decolonized sites were arriving in greater numbers as Britain went through the intensified strains of postcolonial revision. 1948 saw the first group of West Indian immigrants enter Britain from sites in the Commonwealth, having been granted citizenship through the *British Nationality Act*. Violence and discrimination against the immigrants grew in the 50s, resulting in 1962's restrictive *Commonwealth Immigrants Act* (also the year of publication of *How to Do Things with Words*). Of course, Austin's monkey was not necessarily innocent of a more generalized history. There was already a long history of British and European associations of apes and monkeys with African subjects, fed and conditioned by the imperialist culture of colonial relations; these were underlain by an abiding pseudo-Darwinian mapping which temporally projected non-European peoples and non-white racialized groups onto earlier stages of human evolution.

The powerfully racialized undertones of "mockery" have been theorized by thinkers such as Homi Bhabha, who opens his essay "Of mimicry and man: On the ambivalence of colonial discourse" with a citation from Sir Edward Cust (1839) that reads: "To give the colony the forms of independence is a mockery."[12] Thus we might say that a racial—*and* freakishly gendered—body haunts Austin's monkey, just as British whiteness may haunt Austin's authorized speaker. Once again, a colonial past might lurk inside a presumably "innocent" cultural form which seems to deploy a presentist animal figure. Austin was working in a specific social and political context, and to tease out the undertones of his language is also to explore contemporary hauntings or habits of epistemological projection with regard to animality, sex, and race. We might also use this example to understand some linguistic animal figures as before-the-fact racialized and sexualized, especially if used in contexts where race has a history of social or cultural presence.

Castrated Animal

A queer analysis of either Max or Austin's monkey, however, does not suffice; for both of these figures are simultaneously engaged with transgender meaning. This dance between *queer* and *trans* evokes debates that have been taken up in recent scholarship, particularly about what degree one might excavate the *trans-* in what has been taken and subsumed under the rubric of *queer*. Ultimately, the opposition of *trans* and *queer* suggests a false dichotomy: just as gender and sex are unavoidably linked, so too are trans and queer. They can be considered as independent factors which participate in intersectional spaces.[13] A *trans critique* is thus invited in the instance of what David Eng calls racialized castration, a kind of transing which is not always considered under a trans rubric, except in the case of male to female transsexuality.[14]

Myra Hird invokes feminist biologist Sharon Kinsman to argue for the idea that human understandings of sex respond not merely to humanity's own intraspecies evidences, but also to those of non-human animals as well, such as fish whose gonads shift from male to female. Concomitantly Hird thinks in terms of "trans" not as an exclusively human construct, challenging readers to fairly consider the implications of evidence of trans in non-human animals. Such analysis perhaps suggests a sense of trans that extends beyond sex alone; as Hird writes, "I want to extend feminist interest in trans as a specifically sexed enterprise (as in transitioning from one sex to another), but also in a broader sense of movement across, through and perhaps beyond traditional classifications."[15]

Of what might be labeled an "organ," the genitals bear tremendous weight, particularly, arguably, in the West/Global North. They are a tremendously loaded "organ," for they simultaneously impute both gender and sexuality and, as so many race and sexuality theorists have demonstrated, race and class.[16] Therefore the "genitals" are directly tied to geopolitical and social orders which are vastly more complex and intersectional than to systems of gender alone. Genitality can be prosthetized through other accouterments in a society which is still wrapped up in styles of modesty. While much has been written of histories in which non-white racialized men are often, due to racism, subject to symbolic castration and representation as non-human animals, less has been suggested of the possibility that the castrated animal is not only a substitute for, but coextensive with, and forming meanings equally with, castrated racialized men.[17]

Frantz Fanon in *Black Skin, White Masks*, in analyzing the postcolonial psychic state of a racialized subject, theorizes relations among animality, castration, and black sexual threat, and in so doing offers us a condensed image of the social possibility of simultaneous *castration* and phallic *presence*.[18] Thinking in particular about transness, Cynthia Fuchs writes about the ways that race, gender identity and sexuality all intervene to produce a sporadically present phallus in Michael Jackson. Fuchs writes: "the problem of his penis remains . . . continually cited by his own choreographed crotch-grabbing. A sign of auto-erotic sexuality (read: perverse, unreproductive, and homosexual), his unseen penis resists visibility, that prevailing emblem of Western cultural Truth."[19] Given the sacrosanct importance of the penis or phallus, we might extend the concurrence of castration and phallic presence to the possibility that non-genitality could impute genitality, or the threat thereof—the threat of genitality's eventual presence.

The introduction of species difference yields a yawning gap around the unresolved question of gender and sexuality, precisely around questions of genericity and gender. If Max, for instance, is a blend between actual (if materialized through costume only) and figural chimpanzee, should there not be another layer of gender confusion between human/animal and actual/figure? Carla Freccero includes an extended discussion of the creative play between the biological and grammatical genders of a female cat (which is grammatically gendered masculine) and shifts in terms of vulnerability and gendered relating in Derrida's engagement with it in his well-known essay "L'Animal que donc je suis." In a critical scene, he considers his domestic female cat, who observes him naked, arousing his anxious concerns about gender, masculinity and sexuality. Freccero notes that Derrida meanders in address between the masculine, generic "le chat" and the feminine, specific "la chatte." Derrida thus genders the cat in multiple, potentially contradictory ways, while presuming that the cat's and his own gender as in some way affected by the relationality between them.[20]

Conveniently perhaps for the design of the film *Max, mon amour*, no linguistic contradictions need be enacted: the French grammatical gender for chimpanzee (*le chimpanzee, lui, il*) is the same as the purported gender/sex of the chimpanzee Max, who is supposed to be a masculine, male chimp. Yet for all the profusion of linguistic gender, in *Max, mon amour*, the incursion of species difference also introduces the presumably threatening possibility of a *genderless* relation, produced by the genericity of the type but literalized in the costume itself. Rampling and the chimp's affections thus yielded something that was *trans* in the sense of the undecidability, elusiveness, or reluctance toward fixity of the chimp's sex, which in spite of its linguistic reinforcements surpasses its otherwise presumptive maleness; that is, to what extent can one trust that a male chimp is sexed *or* gendered "like" a human male?

Returning to the example of Austin's "marriage with a monkey," the genericity of "a monkey" implicates that the monkey threatens being genderless: first, in a general sense, a creature without a gender identity somehow threatens the smooth running of heteronormative society which itself relies on a robust organization of its gender systems; second, a creature without a gender identity must also lack a sex, and thus threaten the possibility of bringing an abject, queer sexuality into (the institution of) marriage. By including "the institution of marriage," I suggest that though Austin insisted in some sense that the performative verbs themselves (like *wed* in "I thee wed") were fixed in purpose and meaning and thus robust, his use of mockery here and the invocation of a kind of animality linked to discourses of colonial and species threat reveals, perhaps, a fear that the institution of marriage (or conventions of language, or rigidities of gender and sex, or divisions of race and nation) itself might be maligned and indeed transformed by a performative's misuse.[21]

Thus, while considering Max's "bad" costume may seem an indulgence, it nevertheless points to the fact that any decision about including or excluding genitals on an imagined non-human animal cannot help but be loaded, since species difference itself cannot help but be fraught with anxieties about reproduction (e.g. miscegenation and animality in discourses of eugenics). Once again the queer/trans relationship is made explicit in the case of Max.

Thus, "trans-animality" can simultaneously refer to gender and species, while sexuality, geopolitics and race remain in full scope. In other words, an analysis of trans-animality must simultaneously identify the quiet imputations of race that are shuttled in along with the animal. Definitions of both "trans-" and "animal" vary both disciplinarily and politically. I consider *animality* not a matter of non-humanity or of creatures considered non-human (for instance the accepted logics of pets or agricultural livestock and our stewardship of them), so much as a quality of animalness, one equally attributable to humans as well as non-human animals. Likewise, *trans* is not as a linear space of mediation between two monolithic, autonomous poles, as for example "female" and "male," not least because the norms by which these poles are often defined too easily conceal, or forget, their interests and contingencies. Rather, *trans* is conceived of as more emergent than determinate, intervening with other categories in a richly intersectional space. Much in the way that the idealized meaning of *queer* signifies an adjectival modification or modulation, rather than a substantive core such as a noun, I wish to highlight a *prefixal* "trans-" not preliminarily limited to gender.

By mobilizing a different form of trans-, I do not mean by any means to evacuate trans entirely of its gendered possibilities. To the contrary, I reassert the complex, multi-factored cultural contingency of transgendered actualizations and affirm that gender is omnipresent, though I am suggesting that it is rarely monolithically masculine or feminine. As Susan Stryker, Paisley Currah, and Lisa Jean Moore write, "The hyphen . . . marks the difference between the implied nominalism of 'trans' and the explicit relationality of 'trans-,' which remains open-ended and resists premature foreclosure by attachment to any single suffix [including gender]."[22] Such a prefixal "trans-" is a way to explore that complexity of gender definition that lies between human gender systems and the gendering of animals.

Animals Without Genitals/Body Without Organs

In two successive coauthored works, *Anti-Oedipus: Capitalism and Schizophrenia*, and *A Thousand Plateaus*, Gilles Deleuze and Félix Guattari describe what they call a "body without organs."[23] The body without organs is that body which actively refuses its own subjectivity, by engaging the dis-ordering of its "organs." In the body without organs, no given organ has merely one functionality, and the organism itself cannot be represented as an ordered system. Instead, the body without organs makes impossible such a systematicity by affirming an infinite functionality and interrelation of the "parts" within, "parts" which can only be individuated by one of an infinite number of permutations of the body into "parts." We might say that in biological research, it does seem that the actual human body is being found to approach the body without organs and to move away from a regularized, systemic representation, both in terms of the multifunctionality of a given organ (the appendix's function has just been discovered, for example), and the increasing numbers of communicative relationships among "organs" that converge to produce behavioral or emotional appearances or effects (e.g. neurophysiological constructs are understood to interact with bodily hormone systems in new ways that influence the measurable emotionality of a body).

Quite unlike Deleuze's "body without organs," the "animal without genitals" would seem to be a body-with-organs-without-genitals, that is, a body with organs from which the genitals have been extracted or pointedly neglected. Nevertheless, the "animal without genitals'" *affective* valence bears closer attention, for I suggest that the animal-without-genitals, just as the directionality of biological research on organism systematicity towards more multiplicity, marks or symbolizes a kind of affective impulse towards a human hope OR repulsion from a marginless being, even as it reiterates the porosity of the very human-animal border. Thus, the animal-without-genitals AFFIRMS the body without organs, while carrying dramatically variant affective valences. The ghostly logic of the racialized, castrated human male/present phallus explored by Fanon and Fuchs is perhaps why, alternatively, the racialized figurative animal that is deployed for purposes of human signification is a body *with* organs *without* genitals, since the body with organs *needs* genitals. Furthermore, affectivities, while they may help leverage narratives to a satisfying conclusion, also yield a result which is ambivalent about the abjection of animality vis-à-vis the weakly solidified human, because the analogies are so vibrant—indeed vital.

Cultural Animal

[. . .]

In the conceptions offered by this paper, several senses of "trans-"have been mobilized and put into conversation: transgender (living outside normative gender definition, or undergoing shift in gender identity), transmogrification (changing of shape or form to something fantastical), translation (across languages), and of course, transspecies (across species). Each of these terms suggests a movement or dynamism, from one site to another, as in the sense of "across." I attempted to make the case for a trans-theorizing that recognizes the distinctness of queer, but at the same time embraces the collaborative possibilities of thinking trans alongside and across queerness. In analyzing a number of theoretical and cultural productions and their (often hostile) articulations or imputations of transness, this paper worked very far away from lived transgender and transsexual lives and identities and does not intend to be in direct conversation with them. Rather, it attended to the coercive conceptual workings of these productions and their way of crafting forms of cultural exile premised on already marginal loci in gender, race, species, and sexuality matrices. Simultaneously, it located zones of possibility that work around and against such coercions, such as the analogic survival of transness that can always be purported back to the human.

Deleuze and Guattari's "body without organs" is both honored and merely suggested in the three examples elaborated in this essay. Their simultaneous limitation and promise is precisely that the genitals (or non-genitals) within them *matter*, but are not necessarily constrained by normative gender and sexuality, and these "animals with/out genitals" possess a trans-materiality which is characterized by a radical uncertainty and a generative affectivity. And so this essay might be thought of as an invitation to consider queer-trans animality, even in its politically most closed of circumstances, not as a tired and fatal venue for human self-making but as a site of unpredictable investment for untraceable animal futurities.

Acknowledgements

I wish to thank Kyla Schuller for bringing the film to my attention, and the members of the Fall 2009 Species Spectacles, University of California Humanities Research Institute Residential Research Group, and two anonymous reviewers for their critical insights. Special thanks go to Julia Bryan-Wilson for being my most lively interlocutor.

Notes

1. Butler 1993.
2. Animal studies is still being formed, and its borders are still in contention. It is a multidisciplinary field, reaching across environmental studies, science and technology studies, psychoanalysis, ecocriticism, and literary and cultural studies. In addition to Donna J. Haraway's corpus, some representative texts include work by Thompson 2002; Anderson 2000; Lutz and Collins 1993; Shukin 2009; Franklin 2007.
3. Franklin 2006.
4. Thompson 2005.
5. Halberstam 2008. Additionally, Akira Lippit (2000) considers the discourse of the animal as a "third term."
6. For two other studies on the intersection of transness and animality, see Hansen 2008; Hayward 2008.
7. Of course, this is a playful reading well outside of standard film criticism, bringing contemporary economies of animal and sexual representation to bear on earlier film practices that did not employ them. For a critically positive psychoanalytic reading of *Max, mon amour*, see Barbara Creed (2006). Creed frames *Max, mon amour* as one example of new "zoocentric" cinema that reflects its interest in resolving questions that remain of a Darwinian blurring of the boundary between human and non-human animal. Creed notes that Margaret's desire for Max foregrounds an even more mysterious female "jouissance" that lies threateningly outside of the male symbolic order (and thus beyond Peter's ken).
8. Shohat and Stam 1994.
9. For work on blackface minstrelsy in the US context, see Lott 1993.
10. Austin 1962, 24.
11. Does this animal expulsive strain still exist in performativity theory itself? To the degree that performative authority is conferred onto to those in strict categories of human role membership (such as a minister), that expulsive strain must live. If performativity theory (thinking here of Judith Butler's *Excitable speech*) delinks performance from the notion of the individual and casts it into realms of iterable citation, I suggest that unless it is extinguished that strain—the human-animal divide and the expulsion inherent inside it—replicates along with scenes of iteration, in ways that might be similar to the ways that traumas might be ushered forth in the reiterations of injurious speech. See Butler 1997.
12. Bhabha 1994, 85.

13. For work that considers the queer-trans relationship, see for example work by Susan Stryker, Jay Prosser, J. Halberstam, and Judith Butler.
14. See Eng 2001.
15. Hird 2006, 37.
16. See, for example, work by Siobhan Somerville, Sander Gilman, Gail Dines, and Patricia Hill Collins.
17. Eng's *Racial castration* offers a brilliant cogent psychoanalytic study of the vexed sexualization of the Asian American male.
18. Fanon [1952] 1994.
19. Fuchs, 1995, 17.
20. Freccero forthcoming.
21. The insecurity I attribute to Austin here is equivalent to a recognition of the importance of iterative renewal for the performative itself to retain its normativity.
22. Stryker, Currah, and Moore 2008.
23. Deleuze and Guattari 1977, 9.

Bibliography

Anderson, Kay. 2000. "The beast within": Race, humanity, and animality. *Environment and Planning D: Society and Space* 18, no. 3: 301–320.

Austin, J.L. 1962. *How to do things with words*. William James Lectures, Harvard University, 1955. Oxford: Clarendon.

Bhabha, Homi. 1994. *The location of culture*. London: Routledge.

Butler, Judith. 1993. *Bodies that matter: On the discursive limits of sex*. London and New York: Routledge.

Butler, Judith. 1997. *Excitable speech: A politics of the performative*. New York and London: Routledge.

Creed, Barbara. 2006. A Darwinian love story: *Max Mon Amour* and the zoocentric perspective in film. *Continuum* 20, no. 1: 45–60.

Cust, Edward. 1839. *Reflections on West African affairs . . . addressed to the Colonial Office*. London: Hatchard.

Deleuze, Gilles, and Félix Guattari. 1977. *Anti-Oedipus: Capitalism and schizophrenia*. New York: Penguin Classics.

Eng, David. 2001. *Racial castration: Managing masculinity in Asian America*. Durham, NC: Duke University Press.

Fanon, Franz. [1952] 1994. *Black skin, White masks*. Trans. Constance Farrington. New York: Grove Press.

Franklin, Sarah. 2006. The cyborg embryo: Our path to transbiology. *Theory, Culture and Society* 23, nos. 7–8: 167–187.

Franklin, Sarah. 2007. *Dolly mixtures: The remaking of genealogy*. Durham, NC: Duke University Press.

Freccero, Carla. Forthcoming. Les chats de Derrida. In *Derrida and Queer Theory*, ed. Michael O'Rourke. Basingstoke: Palgrave.

Fuchs, Cynthia. 1995. Michael Jackson's Penis. In *Cruising the performative*, ed. Sue-Ellen Case, Philip Brett, and Susan Leigh Foster, 13–33. Bloomington: Indiana University Press.

Halberstam, Judith. 2008. Animating revolt/revolting animation: Penguin love, doll sex and the spectacle of the queer nonhuman. In *Queering the Non-Human*, ed. Noreen Giffney and Myra Hird, 265–281. Hampshire: Ashgate.

Hansen, Natalie Corinne. 2008. Humans, horses, and hormones: (Trans) gendering cross-species relationships. *WSQ: Women's Studies Quarterly* 36, nos. 3–4: 87–105.

Hayward, Eva. 2008. Lessons from a Starfish. In *Queering the Non-Human*, ed. Noreen Giffney and Myra Hird, 249–263. Hampshire: Ashgate.

Hird, Myra. 2006. Animal transex. *Australian Feminist Studies* 21, no. 49: 35–50.

Lippit, Akira. 2000. *Electric animal: Toward a rhetoric of wildlife*. Minneapolis: University of Minnesota Press.

Lott, Eric. 1993. *Love and theft: Blackface minstrelsy and the American working class*. New York: Oxford University Press.

Lutz, Catherine A., and Jane L. Collins. 1993. *Reading national geographic*. Chicago and London: University of Chicago Press.

Philo, Chris, and Chris Wilbert. 2000. Introduction to *Animal spaces, beastly places*, ed. Chris Philo and Chris Wilbert. London: Routledge.

Shohat, Ella, and Robert Stam. 1994. *Unthinking Eurocentrism: Multiculturalism and the media.* New York and London: Routledge.

Shukin, Nicole. 2009. *Animal capital: Rendering life in biopolitical times.* Minneapolis and London: University of Minnesota Press.

Stryker, Susan, Paisley Currah, and Lisa Jean Moore. 2008. Introduction, "Trans-." *Women's Studies Quarterly* 36, nos. 3–4: 11–22.

Thompson, Charis. 2005. *Making parents: The ontological choreography of reproductive technologies.* Cambridge, MA: MIT Press.

Thompson, Charis. 2002. When elephants stand in for competing philosophies of nature. In *Complexities: Social Studies of Knowledge Practices*, ed. Jon Law and Annemarie Mol. Durham, NC: Duke University Press.

Xu Bing. 2009. Interview, by Residential Research Group members, "Species Spectacles: Transnational Coordinations of Animality, Race, and Sexuality" at the University of California Humanities Research Institute, Irvine, CA. Beijing, December 2009, with Tonglin Lu translating.

39 Lessons From a Starfish

Eva Hayward

One of several essays in this volume that refuse an identity-based theory of transgender embodiment, Eva Hayward's "Lessons From a Starfish" weaves together music criticism, biology, philosophy, and poetics. It begins by quoting the lyrics from "Cripple and the Starfish," a song recorded by Antony and the Johnsons that deliberately uses a discredited, pejorative term for a disabled person to evoke the difficult or negative feelings associated with being stigmatized. Written before the band's lead singer came out as trans and began using the name ANOHNI, Hayward presciently asks whether the song's refrain—in which the singer proclaims, after being emotionally wounded, that "I'll grow back like a starfish"—might teach us something about transsexual embodiment. From there, the essay explodes into a poetic meditation on cutting and gender-reassignment surgeries. If we resist the idea of cutting as mutilation (as some hostile interpretations of transsexuality would have it), how are we freed to understand cutting as regenerative? The "growing back" capacities of the starfish become an opportunity for thinking through the difference between notions of the "transformative" and the "regenerative" in transsexual discourse. For Hayward, regeneration feels like a more capacious category than transformation. While transformation implies something that changes the body itself, regeneration suggests "re-shaping and re-working bodily boundaries" initiated by a given body.

Cripple and the Starfish

Mr Muscle forcing bursting
Stingy thingy into little me, me, me
But just 'ripple' said the cripple
As my jaw dropped to the ground
Smile smile

It's true I always wanted love to be
Hurtful
And it's true I always wanted love to be Filled with pain
And bruises

Yes, so Cripple-Pig was happy
Screamed 'I just completely love you!'
And there's no rhyme or reason
I'm changing like the seasons

DOI: 10.4324/9781003206255-48

Watch! I'll even cut off my finger
It will grow back like a Starfish!
It will grow back like a Starfish!
It will grow back like a Starfish!'
Mr Muscle, gazing boredly
And he checking time did punch me
And I sighed and bleeded like a windfall
Happy bleedy, happy bruisy

I am very happy
So please hit me
I am very happy
So please hurt me

I am very happy
So please hit me
I am very very happy
So come on hurt me

I'll grow back like a Starfish
I'll grow back like a Starfish
I'll grow back like a Starfish
I'll grow back like a Starfish

I'll grow back like a Starfish
I'll grow back like a Starfish
I'll grow back like a Starfish
I'll grow back like a Starfish
Like a Starfish . . .
(Antony and the Johnsons 2000)

I call this piece a critical poetics rather than a cultural account, so as to foreground the process of writing in it. For I want this to be a doing and a knowing that I get woven into—a kind of phenomenological telling. I am not only describing and articulating, not merely charting the geography, but am pulled into the gerunds of what I write out. That is to say, I am not creating a new narrative; rather I'm simply pulling at the stitches of ongoing processes. I am here not to confess, but to confect; I bear witness through relating.

Of Species and Sexes

I have been in an e-mail exchange with Susan Stryker.[1] During this correspondence, Stryker brought to my attention a particular song, 'Cripple and the Starfish',[2] by Antony and the Johnsons. Stryker thinks that Antony is probably 'trans or at least gender-queer', and that the song seems to point toward 'a yearning for transformation'. Although it is difficult to say anything definitive about someone else's 'transition' or gender identity, I agree with Stryker.[3]

I listen to the song; I find the layered tones in Antony's voice haunting, and the lyrics startling: 'I'll even cut off my finger'; 'I'll grow back like a Starfish'; 'Happy bleedy, happy bruisy'. My iTunes player calls the song 'alternative', that ambiguous over-populated term. The music 'ripples' through styles and textures. Antony's voice vibrates (vibrato), fluctuating and undulating with emotional expressiveness: sometimes soft and tender and ripe with satiety and fulfilment ('I am very happy/So please hit me') then shifting in cadence to declarative and triumphant ('I'll grow back like a Starfish'). Following the rise and fall of the song, Antony's voice shifts between low and high, deep and bright. Antony's voice creates a waving space, a singing sea—the pace and rhythm of his/her phrasing expresses frenetic and calm movements, the periodicity or the punctuated changes of things and events. Could it be that Antony sings the tones of whales calling, the syncopation of herds, the transfiguring surf? This is to ask: how do the tone and the wording of 'Cripple and the Starfish' put us in touch with things that it mentions or hints at?

I wonder, thinking about the transsexual *trans*-formations and the starfish *re*-generations that are suggested in the song, 'What is the transformative and relational power of prefixes like *trans*- or *re*-?' I mentioned this wonderment to Stryker. She wrote in response, 'What this calls my attention to is the need to become more specific in how we think about the *re*-/*trans*- distinction in trans discourse.' My question grew insistent; I wanted to understand how *re*- (as is re-turn or re-new) and *trans*- (as in elsewhere) were differently embodied. Beyond my own identity as a transsexual woman, or the political formation of transgender/transsexual,[4] I wasn't certain about the ontological processes of bodily transformation (my own or others'). How does *re*-assignment define transitioning for some trans-subjects? Moreover, I wondered if starfish—'I'll grow back like a Starfish'—or more properly 'sea stars', might provide some prefixial lessons or guides through language, metaphor and other tropological terrains. Do some starfish not re-generate themselves from injury? Is the 'cripple' not re-pairing him/herself through the act of cutting? Is transsexual transformation also re-generative? Am I not in part a transsexual through the re-working and re-folding of my own body, my tissue and my skin? In being transsexual, am I also becoming 'like a starfish' as the song suggests? When does metaphor transform into metonymy? Is the metaphorical device of 'like-ness' ('like a starfish' or like a woman) too clumsy a rhetorical device for the kind of poetic and material enactments of trans-sexing/speciating?

In addition to stirring my interest, Stryker also provided me with several interviews with Antony and other promotional materials. I have excerpted two key quotations from Antony that evocatively link the group (and Antony him/her-self) both to trans histories and human-animal relationships. During an interview with *Velle Magazine*, Antony, the founder of 'Antony and the Johnsons', discusses the emergence of the band:

> The Johnsons's name is a reference to a hero of mine named Marsha P. Johnson, who was a street activist from the mid 60's [*sic*] all the way through to her death in the early 90's [*sic*]. Marsha P. Johnson was a street prostitute and a very visible figure on Christopher Street through the 70's [*sic*] and 80's [*sic*], very renowned for her kindness. You know, her nickname was Saint Marsha. She was a very gregarious sort of outsider street presence and she was rumored to have thrown the first bottle in the Stonewall Riot—I mean whether that was true or not was a bone of contention among several different queens.[5]

Marsha Johnson,[6] or Saint Marsha, and Sylvia Rivera,[7] an important figure in the nascent 'transgender' civil rights movement, started a group in 1970 called STAR, Street Transvestite Action Revolutionaries.[8] In Antony's own words, a transgender legacy is written into the music group; 'she', an 'outsider', a queen of colour, who threw 'the first bottle', who was murdered in 1992, structures the creative and political intent of the band. Johnson is Antony's 'hero', perhaps, and I say this only speculatively, an ego ideal.

Antony is clear to emphasise the 'collage' quality of her/his music and sound in relation to her/his creative process:

> I think my creative process has always been what I've described as accumulative. I collect a lot of different shards and pieces, and I create something that feels meaningful to me

by finding relationships between them and putting them into a kind of a collage. . . . You know, for me, I'm really drawn to singers that are full of feeling and are seeking transformation. I like transformative singing, you know, singing that starts one place and ends in another place.[9]

Classification is evaded for something more 'transformative', something 'that starts one place and ends in another place'. *Trans-*, a prefix weighted with across, beyond, through (into another state or place), does the now-familiar work of suggesting the unclassifiable. To be trans is to be transcending or surpassing particular impositions whether empirical, rhetorical, or aesthetic. Antony speaks of the affective force of his/her transformation in songs and in singing. Transformations—not unlike transgenders—are produced through emotive forces. 'Shards' and 'pieces' (again, of something broken) are reworked into meaningful integrities, but not wholes.

In another interview with *The Guardian*,[10] Antony discusses her/his album, *I Am a Bird Now*, which was included in the 2004 Whitney Biennial.[11] The record has been described by Antony as 'A record of transformations and survival. Its characters move between states— life and death, male and female, human and animal—searching for sanctuary and fulfil- ment.' Antony proposes transformation as a trope for reworking the relationality of male and female, human and animal. Perhaps I am the only one hearing it, but in the texture of Antony's voice, the instrumental variations and in the lyrics themselves, boundaries of sexual and species differences, artificial and authentic orderings, and nature and culture are affec- tively and literally *trans*-ed in their music.

'Trans' is meant to disturb purification practices; the well defined is confounded at mul- tiple material and semiotic levels. Psychical and corporeal experiences are blended. For example, gender and the embodiment of gender are contingencies that may hold for a moment then fall away into another set of relationships. Species exist in taxonomic differ- ences (*Homo sapiens sapiens* are not the same as *Octopus vulgaris*), but species are also *always already* constitutive of each other through the spaces and places we cohabit—his of course includes language and other semiotic registers. Indeed, species are relationships between species—relationality is world-hood. Matter is not immutable, Antony and the Johnsons suggest, it is discursive, allowing sexes and species to practice trans-materialisation. The meat and meaning for humans and starfish have no structuring lack, no primordial division, but are sensuously intertwined.

Trans-Form

In 'Cripple and the Starfish', transformation is indeed a fusing of organisms, energies and sexes. I am intrigued by the phrase 'cut off my finger, it'll grow back like a starfish.' Let us start with the cut—the 'cripple' wants 'Mr Muscle' to 'please hurt me' and 'cripple' will 'even cut off my finger'. From what has been suggested by the song and Antony him/herself, I presume that 'cripple' wants to transform through cutting (amputation or castration); the 'cripple' can be heard as a transsexual/transgender M2F seeking transformation.[12] At first, the cut finger leads me, and perhaps other listeners/readers, to think that the cut is an act of castration—the finger works as a substitute for the penis. 'Cripple' wants to become a 'woman' through the cutting-off of her penis. Certainly, some transsexual women 'cut off' their penises in order to have solidarity with females[13] or to become female themselves.

I am not interested in how the cut is an absence (as in castration) but how it is a genera- tive enactment of 'grow[ing] back' or healing. The cut enacts trans-embodiment—to cut is not necessarily about castration, but an attempt to re-cast the self through the cut body. The whole (body) and the part (cut) are metonymically bound in an attempt to trans-form *in toto*. However successful or not, however uncomfortable for listeners/readers, however seemingly masochistic, 'cut off my finger' and 'please hit me' can be understood as wished-for metamorphosis by the 'cripple'. To cut off the penis/finger is not to be an amputee, but to produce the conditions of physical and psychical re-growth. *The cut is possibility*. For some transsexual women, the cut is not so much an opening of the body, but a generative effort to *pull the body back through itself* in order to feel mending, to feel the growth of new margins. The cut is not just an action; the cut is part of the ongoing materialisation by which a trans-sexual tentatively and mutably becomes. The cut cuts the meat (not primarily a visual opera-tion for the embodied subject, but rather a proprioceptive one), and a space of psychical possibility is thereby created. From the first, a transsexual embodiment does not foreground a wish to 'look like' or 'look more like a woman' (that is, passing). The point of view of the looker (those who might 'read' her) is not the most important feature of trans-subjectivity—the trans-woman wishes to be *of* her body, to 'speak' from her body.

When I pay my surgeon to cut my penis into a neo-vagina, I am moving *toward myself through myself*. As the surgeon inserts the scalpel and cuts through the thickness of my tis-sue, my flesh immediately empurples. For weeks afterward, my groin remains discoloured and swollen. Between the surgeon's efforts and my body's biomechanics, my cut spills blood and affect. My cut enacts a regeneration of my bodily boundaries—boundaries redrawn. Through my cut, I brush up against invocations and revelations; my cut is not passive—its very substance (materially and affectively) is generative and plays a significant role in my ongoing materialisation. My cut is *of* my body, not the absence of parts of my body. The regenerative effort of my cut is discursive; my transfiguring cut is a material-discursive prac-tice through which I am *of* my body and *of* my trans-self. My cut penis entails being and doing, materiality and affect, substance and form. My cut is generative within material limits but not with affective fixity, my tissues are mutable in so far as they are made of me and propel me to imagine an embodied elsewhere.

Not surprisingly, scholars, activists, students and artists have questioned the meaning and significance of transsexual/transgender embodiment. Some have suggested that the expe-rience of transsexuals is determined, both negatively and positively, by the forms of our bodies. Rather simplistically, it has been suggested that the pre-operative transsexual feels constrained by the 'wrong body' and longs to acquire the whole or healed body, which is represented by the male or female form. According to this account, transsexual selfhood is entangled with images of bodily wholeness—what's more, there is an idea of 'inside' and 'outside' of the body that are at odds. The body is a container—a body-bag of nouns to keep the proper ones in order. The transsexual aspires to make the so-called 'defective body' intact, entire, complete, in order that it may be owned as mine, as me. It is undeniable that such agonising experiences of bodily disownment are true and important for some transsex-uals, nor is it difficult to believe that transsexual alterations are not simply chosen or kinds of mutilation, but the transformation of an unliveable, fragmented body into a 'liveable whole'.

What I find disconcerting about this description of the transsexual is not the trouble of containment; it is the limiting of the body to containment alone. To be comfortable in one's own body is not *only* to be restricted, limited, contained, or constrained, or not this alone. It is to be able to live out the body's vicissitudes—its (our) ongoing process of materialisation. The body (trans or not) is not a clear, coherent and positive integrity. The important dis-tinction is not the hierarchical, binary one between wrong body and right body, or between fragmentation and wholeness. It is rather a question of discerning multiple and continually varying interactions among what can be defined indifferently as coherent transformation, de-centred certainty, or limited possibility. Transsexuals do not transcend gender and sex. We create embodiment by not jumping *out* of our bodies, but by taking up a fold in our bodies, by folding (or cutting) ourselves, and creating a transformative scar of ourselves. For example, neo-vaginas are made from originary penises or skin grafts, and the beards of F2Ms emerge from their own testosterone-invigorated hair follicles. There is no absolute division, but continuity between the physiological and affective responses of my different historical bodies. Again, I am of my body in order that I might experience a subjective, energetic transformation.

A transsexual (myself, for example) is never discontinuous from different states of embodiment, or at least I am only generally distinguished from different historical states of my own beingness. By nature, the body has something tautological about it: skin here is always intractably skin. It is as if a M2F transsexual always carries her various embodiments with herself. Let me be clear here, I am not suggesting anything as banal as that 'male privilege' is carried into female embodiment—I am not making a socio-cultural argument about authenticity (such arguments should be put to rest by now!). If my subjective embodiment has always been 'transgender', then my material transformation is meant to congeal my differently trans-embodied experiences of body and mind. What I am suggesting when I say that embodiment is coherence, is that I am always *of* my tissue even in its ongoing transformation. Whatever the transsexual grants to vision, the subjective embodiment is always only partially visible. We see the physical efforts, but the psychical energies only express themselves within the limits of the body.

Changeability is intrinsic to the transsexual body, at once its subject, its substance and its limit. Our bodies are scarred, marked and reworked into a liveable 'gender trouble', sex trouble, or uneven epidermis. Transsexuals survive not because we become whole, but because we embody the reach and possibility of our layered experience—we have no choice. This is all to say, the transsexual body, my body, is a body created out of necessity, ingenuity and survival—to carry the heft of social identity. I, like many transsexuals, may desire some mythic wholeness, but what is truly intact for me, what I live, what I must be part of, is a body pliant to a point, flexible within limits, constrained by language, articulation, flesh, history and bone.

Re-Form

'I'll grow back like a starfish.' From the start, I notice two things: first, my finger has been substituted for 'I'; secondly, we have moved from the metonymy of the cut to the metaphor of trans-speciation. The starfish seemingly appears as a stand-in for transsexual transformation—the animal appears only as a tool for thinking about beingness. Let us not forget, the metaphor is a displacement: a nominative term is displaced from its everyday context and placed elsewhere so as to illuminate some other context through its reconfiguration. Thus, the relationship is based on the relationship of ideas rather than objects—metaphor does not owe any allegiance to the literal object. The 'cut', in contrast, is structured by a metonymy of embodied correspondences and correlations. Metonymy is a tropological operation quite different from metaphor. Metonymy brings together two objects, each of which constitutes a separate whole. Metonymy refers to conditions of correspondence: cause to effect, instrument to purpose, container to content, 'cut' to trans-body.

I wonder if the starfish is more than metaphor (not that metaphor isn't enough). Playing on the side of zoomorphism, I wonder if being starfish shares in the ontological imaginary of becoming trans-sexed. I don't want to propose that transsexualism is the *same as* trans-speciation, but rather that both share in the materialisation of the transfigure described in 'Cripple and the Starfish'. Both the starfish and the transsexual 'grow back', differently but with similar phenomenological goals of bodily integrity and healing. Is it possible, and here I take a leap, that while the 'cut' has a metonymic force in trans-embodiment, could not 'like a starfish' also suggest a metonymy of trans-speciation. For example, literal animals are always part of figural animals; animals cannot be displaced by words, rather words carry the nervous circuitries, the rhythms, the tempos of the literal. Animals are always constitutively formed in language—human and not, animal and not. Animals (though not necessarily animals alone—but that is for another collection of essays) are bound in language such that language cuts into flesh but does not completely devour the body. The literal 'cut' bleeds around the word 'cut', which is where the conditions of subjective transformation emerge. Likewise, the starfish, an echinoderm, a regenerating body, an invertebrate that can in some species reproduce new individuals through bodily divisions, exceeds the metaphoricity of 'likeness' because the starfish is only ever partially digested, defined, explained, used by language.

Some species of starfish also reproduce asexually by fission, often with part of an arm becoming detached and eventually developing into an independent individual sea star. Some sea stars have the ability to regenerate lost arms. Most species must have the central part of the body intact to be able to regenerate, but a few can grow an entire starfish from a single ray. This bit of morphological knowledge leads me to wonder about *transformative* versus *regenerative*. *Trans-* prefix has more to do with the sense of across, through, over, to or on the other side of, beyond, outside of, from one place, person, thing or state to another. If we think about *re-*prefix however, the original sense of *re-* in Latin is that of 'back' or 'backwards', but in the numerous words formed by its usage, the prefix acquires various shades of meaning. For example, *re-*generate: to form, construct, or create anew, especially in an improved state; to give new life or energy to; revitalise; and in biology, to replace (a lost or damaged organ or part) by the formation of new tissue.

How might the 'Cripple' yearn for *regeneration* in order to transform? 'I'll even cut off my finger. It will grow back like a Starfish.' To me, this is a literal instantiation of sea star biodynamics—s/he will *re-*grow her/his finger, but not necessarily *trans-*form her/his finger. In broader terms, s/he is also *re-*sexed body just as she/he also becomes subjectively transsexed. Although subtle, the work might be in how prefixes shape and re-shape the prepositions of the discourse; *re-* is *of* the body, not *in* the body (as trans embodiment is often articulated—for example, 'trapped in the wrong body'). *Re-* makes all enactments constitutive of the 'form-er' (even if that 'form-er' is an ongoing process of materialisation). *Re-* might offer a more 'crippling' approach to the limit and containment of the flesh. Re-generativity is a process that is enacted through and by containment (the body). In this way, regeneration is a re/iterative enactment of not only growing *new* boundaries (re-bodying), but of imperilling static boundaries (subjective transformation). Re-generation can attend to desire, pathos, trauma, but also to modes of corporeal intimacy, fleshy possibility and, most importantly, re-embodiment.

Re-generation is something that both transsexuals and starfish do. Transsexuals and starfish do other kinds of prefixial relationships between inside/outside, subject/object, or predator/prey, but in re- they share a phenomenological experience of re-shaping and re-working bodily boundaries. How might prefixes help us to understand the ways that we (starfish, transsexuals and others) autonomise and generate embodiment? Re-grow, re-differentiate, re-pattern, re-member, re-nucleate: our bodily structures, our biodynamics, are materiality enacted through ongoing relationships with the world, as part of that world. Transsexuals and starfish challenge disembodied metaphors (such as 'like,' resemblance, or simile), and propose ways in which we are metonymically stitched to carnal substrates. In other words, I'm not like a starfish; I am of a starfish. I am not trapped in my body; I am of my body.

[. . .]

Ripple

'Ripple' (Oxford English Dictionary):

1. A slight cut, scratch, or mark. Verb: to scratch slightly; to graze or ruffle.
2. A piece of shallow water in a river where rocks or sand-bars cause an obstruction; a shoal.
3. A light ruffling of the surface of water, such as is caused by a slight breeze; a wavelet.
4. A wave on the surface of a fluid the restoring force for which is provided by surface tension rather than by gravity, and which consequently has a wavelength shorter than that corresponding to the minimum speed of propagation.
5. A sound as of rippling water.
6. To mark with or as with ripples; to cause to undulate slightly.

'Ripple' creates the ruffling within the subject that allows 'Happy bleedy, happy bruisy' to become the conditions for bodily regeneration, psychical transformation and trans-speciation. 'Ripple' tears and fiddles with the idea that language/representation is a cut between the phenomenal world and the knowing subject. 'Ripple' with the 'Cripple and the Starfish' creates the carnal foundations for prefixial enactments that take meat and meaning seriously. The 'cripple' and 'like a starfish' provide an extreme collapse between the figural and the real. In other words, prefixes (*trans-* and *re-*) are kinds of relationships that ripple and rupture the field of representation. The starfish and the transsexual point beyond the limits of language, allowing both figures to exceed any kind of palliative function ('like a woman' or 'like a starfish').

The transsexual—again I speak of this experience not to the side of my body, but because of my body—energetically ripples the body, marks the meat, with *re*-form, *re*-grow, re-shape so that subjective transformation may occur: transition, transsex, *trans*-be; this is prefixial rippling. The prefix *re*- must take up the body in order that *trans*- might become. The starfish, depending on species, can *re*-grow a damaged ray. The lost ray, again in some species, may become another individual, rippling into another state of being. This is to say, the starfish changes its bio-geometry in relationship to its environment—it is entangled and reshaped and transfigured through encounters. Moreover, the metonymic qualities of embodiment always links semiotics to matter. 'Starfish' is a representation with tube feet; transsexual is an identity that bleeds and is cut.

'Ripple' reminds me of starfish locomotion. Starfish have hydraulic water vascular systems that facilitate movement. Ocean water comes into the system via the madreporite (a small opening in the aboral surfaces of starfish). Saltwater is then circulated from the stone canal to the ring canal and into the radial canals. The radial canals carry water to the ampullae and provide suction to the tube feet. The tube feet latch on to surfaces and move in a wave, with one body section attaching to the surfaces as another releases. 'Ripple' defines the bio-mechanics of tube feet.

'Ripple', on a somatic level, reminds me of my own physical vulnerability—my animate transsex flesh. Might I share this same somatic sensitivity with the starfish in the most basic sense of redressing harm: regeneration as an act of healing. Transsexing is an act of healing. This is some kind of mutuality—some kinds of shared ontology. Trans-morphic as zoomorphic—if we can understand the cut as an act of love, then can we not imagine that 'like a starfish' is an enactment of trans-speciating? We, transsexuals and starfish, are animate bodies; our bodies are experienced and come to be known through encounters with other animate bodies. These epistemological moves describe a shared phenomenological ontology. This is sensate intertwining—inter-corporeal zones between these bodies in language and in experience.

Starfish and transsexuals share world-hood both semiotic (as metonymic kinds) and phenomenological enactments—is this not some form of inter-somaticity?

'It's true I always wanted love to be hurtful', sings Antony in 'Cripple and the Starfish'. If, as I hope I've illustrated here, the literal and the figural—the *matter that means* and the *meaning that means*—emerge as interlocking and dynamic. 'Hurt' is not a masochistic enactment (or, at least, not this alone), but signals a breach in language and a tear in the traditional subject/object formation. The material, the literal matter of being, surfaces and resurfaces as a constitutive force that cannot be digested in the acid fluids of anthropic concerns. 'Animetaphor' and metonymy applies a figurative sense as a literal one, while yet retaining the look or feel of figurality. A phenomenology of the rippling subject having and making sense of the song reveals to us the inter-corporeal function of lived bodies—as both carnal and conscious, sensible and sentient—and how it is we can apprehend the sense of the song both figurally and literally.

Correlatively, a phenomenology of the experience of this lived inter-somaticity and differentiation in the song reveals to us—in the metonymic articulations of language—the reversible and oscillating structure of the lived body's experience of language. To put it simply (if densely): in the act of 'making sense' of the song, metonymy is to language as rippling is to lived bodies. Ambivalently subtending fusion and difference, ambivalent in its structure and seemingly ambiguous in meaning, metonymy not only points to the 'gap' between the figures of language and literal lived-bodies experiences but also inter-corporeally, rippling, 'bridges' and intertwines a sensate ontology. Thus, 'Cripple and the Starfish' mobilises, differentiates and yet entangles lived bodies and language, and foregrounds the inter-somaticity of sensible matter and sensual meaning. As zoomorphic, *re*-morphic and *trans*-morphic subjects, then, we possess an embodied knowledge that both opens us beyond our discrete capacity for listening to a song, opens the song far beyond its containment in iTunes's 'alternative' and opens language to a metonymic and biodynamic knowledge of specific carnal origins and limits. This is what my being transsexual knows about being a starfish.

From: Eva Hayward, "Lessons From a Starfish" in *Queering the Non/Human*, pp. 249–265. Copyright 2016, Taylor & Francis. All rights reserved. Republished by permission of the copyright holder, Taylor & Francis.

Notes

1. Susan Stryker has enormously influenced this essay. She was the first to suggest to me that the song was about transgender transformation, and that the song demonstrated how transformation is a means of 'addressing a hurt, and of moving through that hurt'. Thank you, Susan.
2. Claire Carré has made a 'spec' video of Antony and the Johnsons' 'Cripple and the Starfish'. To watch the video, visit <www.clairesquare.com/starfish.html>. To read Carré's comments about the video and its reception by Rebis Music, visit <www.justonestar.com/forum/viewtopic. php?p=8613&sid=7b35b23c57 02726c6b283b69dd468106>.
3. In a Björk Podcast (#6), Antony explicitly defines as 'transgender'. However, I think the content of the song illustrates a kind of transgender/transsexual embodiment regardless of Antony's own identity— after all musicians do not need to be faithful to their identities.
4. I use transgender and transsexual interchangeably in this essay. I do so not to elide the significant differences between these identities, but to foreground the shared concerns and desires for embodiment. This is to say, being transgender does not exclude bodily change, nor does being transsexual mean one will have sex-reassignment surgery.
5. Antony interviewed by Rebecca K. Uchill <www.vellemagazine.com/contenta/music/antony/ antony.shtml>, 18 January 2007.
6. Several links that offer biographical material on the late Marsha P. Johnson: <http://en.wikipedia. org/wiki/Marsha_P._Johnson>; an obituary <http://gender. org/remember/people/marshajohnson. html>; a poem by Qwo-Li Driskill, <http://www.lodestarquarterly.com/work/248/>.

7. For a bio on Sylvia Rivera, which sadly is also an obituary, see <www. workers.org/ww/2002/syl via0307.php>.
8. My suggestion that STAR was a 'transgender' political organization is a bit ahistorical, considering that 'transgender' as a social identity was still only emerging during these years. All too often, gender variant communities and their contributions to social change, however, get lost in more traditional gay/lesbian historiographies. So, I risk playing the part of a 'bad historian' in the hopes of encouraging more inclusive historical projects.
9. Antony interviewed by Rebecca K. Uchill <www.vellemagazine.com/contenta/music/antony/antony.shtml>, 18 January 2007.
10. Antony interviewed by David Peschek <http://arts.guardian.co.uk/features/story/0,,1438695,00.html>, 18 January 2007.
11. Antony and the Johnsons collaborated with filmmaker Charles Atlas and thirteen trans-women from New York City on a concert/live video installation staged in London, Rome and Paris in autumn 2007. During 'TURNING', Antony and the Johnsons present a concert while Charles Atlas creates live video portraits of each model. 'TURNING' was first presented as a part of the 2004 Whitney Biennial in New York City.
12. Again, I risk reading the 'Cripple' as a trans-subject not to iterate the pathologisation of trans-folks, but to explore the imaginings of the song. For the transsexual/transgender subject, gender assignments can feel 'disabling', even wounding. I'm speaking about this traumatic experience, not about transgressive exceptionalism in which gender/sex changes prompt 'revolutionary potential'. I am simply returning to my own bodily knowledge—carnal logics—of pain and possibility.
13. I use solidarity to suggest something other than identification. I'm not suggesting that transsexual women do not become female (some certainly do), but I want to hold out the possibility that the transsexual woman can also become a kind of woman *made of* her various ontologies. I want to value the experience of becoming transsexual as something particular to transsexuals, even as that experience is constitutive of other sexes and their constitutiveness—together all the way down. This line of reasoning is explored in Stone (1993).

Bibliography

Abraham, N. and Torok, M. (1994), 'Mourning or Melancholia: Introjection Versus Incorporation', in N. Rand (ed. and trans.), *The Shell and the Kernel* (Chicago, IL: University of Chicago Press).

Antony and the Johnsons (2000), 'Cripple and the Starfish', on *Antony and the Johnsons* (song title on music album).

Derrida, J. and Dufourmantelle, A. (2000), *Of Hospitality*, Cultural Memory in the Present (Stanford, CA: Stanford University Press).

Derrida, J., Dufourmantelle, A. and Kamuf, P. (eds) (1991), *A Derrida Reader: Between the Blinds* (New York: Columbia University Press).

Lippit, A. M. (1998), 'Magnetic Animal: Derrida, Wildlife, and Animetaphor', *MLN* 113(5): 1111–1125.

Stone, S. (1993), 'The Empire Strikes Back: A Posttranssexual Manifesto', <www.actlab.utexas.edu/~sandy/empire-strikes-back>, accessed 21 August 2007.

40 Trans Animisms

Abram J. Lewis

In "Trans Animisms," first published in 2017 in *Angelaki: Journal of the Theoretical Humanities*, American studies scholar Abram J. Lewis expands the scope of trans activism by attending to connections with a non-human realm that animated the work of two historically prominent trans activists: Reed Erickson (the philanthropist discussed in the article by Devor and Matte in this volume) and Angela Douglas (who founded the Transsexual Activist Organization in 1970). Rather than sidelining the esoteric, otherworldly, supernatural, or mad elements evident in their lives and careers as irrelevant to their "serious" advocacy work, Lewis argues that attention to the "animistic" was central to their projects of trans survival and worldmaking. He supports this argument through a discussion of two works of art. The first, Chris Vargas's 2012 short video *ONE for All*, playfully engages Erickson's transspecies relationship with a leopard companion named Henry. The second, Craig Calderwood's 2015 drawing *This World Will Soon Be Ours*, is a portrait of Douglas and Randy Towers, the extraterrestrial transsexual lizard person who, she claimed, visited her repeatedly. As Lewis demonstrates, these two influential activists both drew from an animist framework that took nonhuman life and life forces into account to envision and feel enlivened by new modes of existence beyond mere survival.

A thin folder, the "Police" subject file housed in the New York Public Library's LGBT collections, contains a visually unremarkable but peculiar piece of activist ephemera: a flyer from 1970 advertising the LA Gay Liberation Front's (GLF) intent to respond to a spate of police violence by collectively levitating the local precinct building. Describing the action as a "tin-can demonstration," the flyer directs attendees to "Bring a small, empty tin-can [*sic*] and a pencil to beat it with," which, the organizers hope, will produce an "ominous and interesting sound." The flyer presents the action as a kind of memorial: framed by a thick black border, the top of the page bears the names of three gay and trans community members recently dead at the hands of the LAPD. Underneath is a capitalized gloss: "STOP POLICE MURDER, BRUTALITY AND ENTRAPMENT OF HOMOSEXUALS!" The text's presentation of the names, deliberate and unadorned, evokes the meticulous repetition of ritual:

Larry Turner
Black Street Transvestite Killed by Los Angeles Police March 8, 1970

Howard Efland Gay Brother
Killed by Los Angeles Police March 7, 1969

DOI: 10.4324/9781003206255-49

Ginny Gallegos Gay Sister
Killed by Los Angeles Police Spring, 1970

At the demonstration, the flyer explains, activists planned to "raise (by Magick) the Rampart Police Station and hopefully cause it to disappear for two hours." The text at the bottom continues, "if the GLF is successful in this effort we will alleviate a major source of homosexual oppression for at least those two hours [. . .] Support this action with your presence."

Today, the flyer's unselfconscious invocation of "magick" as a technique for ameliorating state violence may incur varied responses: amusement, perhaps, or nostalgia for the era's political optimism, or even distaste for the ineffectual indulgences of the 1970s counterculture, particularly when deployed in response to such an obvious tragedy as queer life lost to police brutality. In fact, within the context of social movement histories, the demo might be most legible as part of a larger decline into demobilized "lifestyle" and "culture," which supposedly helped supplant and undermine the mass movements of the 1960s.[1] Additionally, the flyer's asymmetrical presentation of the deceased evokes the white left's ongoing difficulties in accounting for social difference: excluded from the designations of fraternity afforded to Efland and Gallegos—whose class and race are left unmarked—Turner appears simply as a "Black Street Transvestite." The flyer also hails Turner by her birth name rather than her chosen one, Laverne (Douglas, "Los Angeles" 9). Inasmuch as it recalls the race, class, and gender-based privileges associated with the "hippie" lifestyle, as well as the dubious credibility of the better known 1967 Pentagon levitation, the GLF's levitation flyer may inexorably bear the mark of the counterculture's exclusions and foreclosures.[2]

And yet, today, this archival imprint also retains the capacity to effect a sense of possibility. Writing on the flyer in 2011, New York-based trans activist and filmmaker Reina Gossett reflects:

> I am so inspired by how Laverne, Howard and Ginny are honored as ancestors and are present in the action through a levitated & disappeared police station, ominous and interesting sounds and large turnouts of mourners [. . .] I love how haunting this demonstration is, responding to the killings and ongoing threats of homophobic and transphobic violence from the state by organizing an action filled with accountability to the living, dead and unknown forces that are all fully involved in our struggle for liberation. So outside the normalized organizing tactics preferred by the Non Profit Industrial Complex, forty years later this action feels incredibly accountable to the unborn, the dead and the living present at the Rampart Police Station in 1970.
>
> (N. pag.)

Gossett's remarks position the demo not as a site of the counterculture's divestments from political participation but, rather, as a praxis that is deauthorized under contemporary, state-proctored reform structures (Rodriguez). Her reading urges us to attend more closely to the action's many challenges to orthodoxies of liberal and radical organizing alike. As part of the affective labor of mourning, and as an exercise in the ineluctable sociality of grief, the event partakes in a political labor that cannot be quantified empirically (see Crimp; Butler). An alternative temporality of activism also emerges here: the event was staged not during the work week, when media publicity and the possibility of an LAPD response might have been maximized, but on a Sunday, recognized by many as a Sabbath and a time of reflective nonproductivity. And familiar organizing ideals of "sustainability" are foregone by the demonstration's very inception, which sought to remedy police repression only for a few hours.

But perhaps most intriguing about Gossett's writing is her affirmation of the central mechanism of change to which the activists appealed: what the flyer names simply as "magick," and Gossett aptly characterizes as "unknown forces." The spelling on the flyer harkens to Aleister Crowley's Thelema, which distinguished the "magick" of the occult arts from mere sleight-of-hand or stage magic—the flyer thus suggests the organizers' interest in leveraging supernatural faculties, rather than simply conducting a public performance as form of political theater. Furthermore, to put it bluntly, these activists did not seek to alter conditions of oppression by *signifying* at the police; rather, they declared their intent to *physically* raise the station through the assistance of an unspecified and apparently inhuman force.[3] In both the flyer and in Gossett's remarks, the "magick" that raised the station presents less like a discourse and more like an actant, that is, a mediator with a causal power that is not primarily symbolic and does not reduce to its discursive or phenomenological effects (Latour 237). Arguably, then, Gossett's reading asks after the human-independent efficacy of the magical entity. In so doing, she calls us to consider how—in the past, and to this day—queer and trans movements for social change implicate agencies that are disallowed by anthropocentric as well as secular ontological regimes. Her insights throw into relief techniques of social relating and acting that are not only inadmissible to a statist, neoliberal nonprofit system, they also elude much scholarly thinking on how queer and trans communities work to engage and alter their worlds.

In this article, I situate Gossett's writing alongside two other recent trans artistic productions about the past: Chris Vargas's 2012 short video about transsexual philanthropist Reed Erickson, *ONE for All . . .* and Craig Calderwood's 2015 portrait of trans activists Angela Douglas and Randy Towers, *This world will soon be ours*. Like Gossett's reflections, these two works exhibit remarkable sensitivity to the irreducible presences of enchanted and otherworldly forces. They elicit a reluctance to subsume these forces to human belief or experience, for instance, to treat enchantment as phenomenology, or to distill accounts of the extraordinary as symbolic or "subjective" truths. In other words, these works all resist reading strategies that would systematically bracket the ontological status of enchantment, thereby domesticating it as something that occurs only within the human subject rather than out in the world. In contrast, Gossett, Vargas, and Calderwood all turn their attention to the affectivities that obtain *between* trans humans and other-than-human entities. In rendering enchanted, inhuman presences integral to trans politics, I will suggest that these works proffer "trans" as a form of being with distinct capacities for reciprocity with agencies that dominant historiographies struggle to ratify. Put differently, Gossett, Vargas, and Calderwood evoke trans history as a history forged through relations with "subaltern" agentive entities—entities not recognized within modernist paradigms as actually possessing social agency, or as viable objects of human sociality. Inasmuch as all of these works specifically vex the ontological hierarchies of secular humanism, I think we can read them as animistic. Accordingly, in what follows, I draw not only from recent "post-linguistic" work in US gender and sexuality studies but also from the growing body of anthropological literature known as the "new animism." I hope that by bringing theories of animism in the wake of the ontological turn into conversation with more familiar queer and feminist buzzwords like "animacy" we may further illuminate the impetus of anthro-decentrizing critique as a critique of the politics of secularism. As Gossett's remarks suggest, attending to enchantment as resource for expanding capacities for action on the social plane may be particularly invaluable in the context of a nonprofitized, post-neoliberal world that has seen the foreclosure of many secular and human forms of agency. However, before turning to the trans alter-ontologies of Vargas and Calderwood, a brief comment on the "new animism" in relation to US-based post-humanisms is warranted.

Postsecularizing the Posthuman

Despite the prodigious ink spilled on "nonhuman agency" in recent years, within the US context, much posthuman thought retains an ambiguous relationship to inhuman agencies that are magical or religious in character. On the one hand, as Dana Luciano notes, there is a distinct "quasi-mystical buzz" to speculative philosophy's recurrent appeals to "magic, divinity, wonder, and the miraculous" (717). Additionally, reading practices associated with the "descriptive turn" have sought, in part, to banish the secularizing hermeneutics of demystification privileged by symptomatic criticism (Love; Best and Marcus).[4] At the same time, however, some critics have anxiously distanced discussions of affect and animacy from the apparently damning specter of religion. Notwithstanding the materialist "Nicene Creed" that closes *Vibrant Matter*, for instance, Jane Bennett carefully disaggregates her new vitalist program from the putatively anthropocentric soul vitalism of Christianity (82–87); Teresa Brennan, similarly, has marked the need to develop an expressly "non-occultish" theory of affective transmission (68). With important exceptions, such as Lisa Blackman's work, the posthuman turn of gender and sexuality studies often annexes both affect and the nonhuman to "materiality" (cf. Harman). Finally, many writings render the "nonhuman" synonymous with the "subhuman," without asking how nonhuman reality might also involve entities traditionally located either horizontally or further *up* the great chain of being, such as gods, spirits, demons, or magical creatures (Bennett; Chen).

Outside of the Western context, however, anthro-decentrizing scholarship has been much more decisively involved with the magical and supernatural. Indeed, in its critiques of secular humanism, subaltern studies arguably constitutes one of "correlationism's" early detractors.[5] In *Provincializing Europe* Dipesh Chakrabarty famously asserted the need to reckon with the human-independent agency of gods and spirits. Sounding a lot like Bruno Latour, Chakrabarty indicted the social sciences for reading divinities only as "social facts," as though "the social somehow exists prior to them" (16). In such readings, gods are negated in their capacity as social actors and overwritten as passive objects of human belief. More recently, in her work on South Asian emigrant relations with the dead, anthropologist Jean Langford identifies a similar interpretive problem, wherein human encounters with ghosts are routinely reconfigured by scholars as symbolic (rather than literal) interactions, thereby rendering those relationships commensurate with a secular modern civil order (229). As Rayne Willerslev explains, the problem is that "rather than undermining Western epistemology," this reading instead offers a "culture-transcending interpretation of *all* cultures" in which the Enlightenment reign of the human is ratified and re-enshrined (Willerslev, *Soul Hunters* 184).[6] In admitting nonsecular cosmologies only by reading them through the secularizing humanist rubrics of cultural "symbols" and "metaphors," the scholar affirms her hermeneutic mastery and confirms her subjects as unable to make unqualified claims about reality (Willserslev, "Taking Animism Seriously" 46). Collectively, these anthropological critiques provide an important clarification to the Western new ontologies in underscoring that the ontological singularity of the human is achieved only through disenchantment, and that anthropocentrism is always a project of secularism, always an imperialist and Enlightenment project. These works further remind us that symptomatic or "suspicious" reading styles have uniquely shaped studies of the nonsecular, systematically overwriting the nonsecular as an effect of human culture. In this, symptomatic criticism has colluded with the epistemic hierarchies of liberal modernity by providing a convenient scholarly mechanism for disqualifying the cosmologies of the colonized.

In effort to counter these sublations, works associated with the "new animism" have refused to interpret enchantment only in terms of those relations that obtain within a human community. If prior scholarship anthropocentrically construed spirits and gods as facets of belief, or as mere sublations of an underlying human culture, anthropologists now posit animism as a "relational ontology"—one that recognizes, as Graham Harvey writes, that "the world is full of persons, only some of whom are human" (xi). As Tim Ingold elaborates, animists are united "not in their beliefs but in a way of *being* that is alive and open" (11). Animism

> is not a property of [humans] imaginatively projected onto things with which they per-
> ceive themselves to be surrounded [. . .] it is the dynamic, transformative potential of
> the entire field of relations within which beings of all kinds, more or less person-like or
> thing-like, continually and reciprocally bring one another into existence.
>
> (10)

While the new animism has focused on locations usually considered exterior to Western modernity, these writings can also enable new assessments of episodes in transgender history that have been subjected to similar anthropocentric and secularizing hermeneutics.[7] "Personhood," understood by Harvey and others to include a range of "volitional, relational, cultural and social beings" (xvii), allows us to perceive efforts at collaboration and contact across diverse entities where secular historiographies have recognized only social withdrawal and the attenuation of political participation. In what remains, I turn to two pieces about transgender pasts, which, following the new animism, center practices of trans reciprocity with inhuman, enchanted, and otherworldly presences: Chris Vargas's 2012 short film, *ONE for All . . .* , about transsexual philanthropist Reed Erickson, and Craig Calderwood's portrait of Randy Towers and Angela Douglas, *This world will soon be ours.*

Trans Animisms in the Shadow of the Shadow State

The human subjects featured in Vargas and Calderwood's works have been complicated figures for transgender history in part because of their prominent ties to extraordinary phenomena.[8] Along with his work on trans issues, Erickson funded New Age initiatives and research on parapsychology, hallucinogens, and animal communication. Douglas, who founded the Transexual Action Organization in 1970, was a longtime occultist and UFOlogist. Within historical accounts, Douglas and Erickson have been hailed variously as eccentric, paranoid, psychotic, and delusional (Meyerowitz; Stryker, *Transgender History*; Peña; Devor and Matte). Even in the most sympathetic scholarship, they are subjects who are implicitly understood to have had compromised access to reality, to have imaginatively projected things that were not there. In particular, the fact that Douglas and Erickson recurrently appealed to entities that are not supported by secular scholarship has meant that their own accounts of their lives have been disproportionally represented by historians as subjective—rather than literal or objective—truths.

Vargas's short film *ONE for All . . .* revisits Erickson's failing partnership with the homophile group the ONE Institute, which he backed financially for many years. According to historians Aaron H. Devor and Nicholas Matte, in 1983 Erickson inexplicably reneged on an agreement to turn over a historic LA mansion for use as shared headquarters with ONE. Devor and Matte attribute Erickson's equivocation partly to the intrusion of "personal problems," specifically, his drug dependency, paranoia, and increasingly erratic and unreliable behavior (Devor and Matte 188; Meyerowitz 258). Vargas's video opens on the planned ribbon cutting ceremony for the mansion. Approaching a podium, Erickson, played by Vargas, quietly intones to ONE leader Dorr Legg that he's not sure he still shares ONE's vision for the mansion. Legg (played by Vargas's collaborator Greg Youmans) snaps back, "well, just as long as you don't turn it into some New Age tranny drug compound." The tense exchange marks not only the incommensurability of Erickson's mystically-inflected politics with ONE's secular reformism; it also highlights the interchangeability of gender transgression, psychotropics, and nonnormative religiosity in the liberal imagination. Erickson then steps up to a podium, expected to announce the mansion's official transfer, but instead, looking nervous, he reveals that he will not be turning over the estate, and cannot explain why. A shot of a burning ribbon apprises viewers of Erickson and ONE's doomed partnership, and then the camera cuts to Erickson sitting at a dining room table, poring intently over a copy of the early New Age handbook, *A Course in Miracles*. Chimes play softly in the background, signaling the transition to an ambient space beyond the corporatized non-profit site of the ribbon cutting. Erickson recites aloud: "a miracle inverts perception which was upside down before and thus it ends the strange distortions that were manifest. Now is the perception open to the truth." As he closes the book, the camera cuts back to reveal his companions, seated at the table with him. On one side is Henry, a leopard with whom Erickson lived and enjoyed a close relationship for many years; on the other, an unnamed dolphin—likely Vargas's allusion to Erickson's work with physician John C. Lilly, known for his research on dolphin communication. The passage from *A Course in Miracles* thus announces the video's challenges to the ontological hierarchies that have prefigured accounts of Erickson's life. While scholars have recurrently linked Erickson's interest in relating to animals to his unwieldy "eccentricity" and deteriorating mental health—in other words, to his diminishing viability as a social actor—the video intends to pursue these relationships as integral to Erickson's unique political vision.

Erickson apprises his friends that he'd value their advice about what to do with the Milbank Estate. He explains his doubts about ONE to Henry and the dolphin: "They seem really stuck on supporting the homosexual agenda, with no real care to address other important causes, or integrate other kinds of life." Henry punctuates this remark with a grumble. Erickson turns to Henry, "Henry, I just think that the potential is huge once all these movements are integrated: homosexual people, transsexual people, and animals. We all need to come together: socially, spiritually, and politically." Here, the video reworks the politically demobilized New Age discourse of "human potential" to consider the social possibilities activated by trans relations with untold other-than-human beings. In the spirit of the new animism, Erickson's address might be read not so much as an anthropomorphizing of leopard and dolphin but an anthro-decentrizing of personhood, and a provocation to consider the capacitations offered by queer and trans solidarity with manifold persons. As Erickson talks, the camera alternates between framing him on screen with his companions, and cutting to Henry and the dolphin alone, as they interject into Erickson's remarks with whistles, nods, and sighs. In so doing, the video emphasizes both the relationality and the autonomy of leopard, dolphin and human alike—the three are mutually imbricated, and yet irreducible one to the other. The video's minimalist, low-budget production yields a certain camp effect: the scene was clearly shot against a green screen, and Henry and the dolphin appear to be superimposed images, oddly synchronized with the equally low-resolution dining room table and light fixtures in the background. When Erickson smugly reflects on how he drove down the estate's cost by purchasing it in South African krugerrands—and the camera cuts to a superfluous, clunky shot of plastic coins trickling through his fingers onto a CGI table—the levity and self-awareness of the video are particularly apparent. Nonetheless, the video's glimmers of irony do not finally undermine Erickson's somber deliberations with his companions. To the contrary, these moments seem, if anything, to rehearse a kind of perfunctory avowal of Erickson's unorthodoxies in order to clear the path for a more serious engagement. Moreover, in visually rendering the scene's more unexpected entities (dolphin and leopard), in the same style as their banal household surroundings, the video collapses the animistic into the disenchanted space of Western domesticity, producing them at once as aesthetically and ontologically indistinct.

Erickson's reflections on his life's work become progressively more impassioned, and he finally declares to Henry and the dolphin, "just imagine the human potential in all of us animals . . . we will all truly be ONE!" The camera then cuts to a psychedelic interlude of overlaid, kaleidoscopic images while Erickson's voiceover enumerates the allegiances of this ecological, multi-issue vision: "gender identity and dreams, dolphin communication research, hypnosis, hallucinogenic mushrooms, the full moon and ESP." Cutting back to the table, Erickson reaffirms that ONE cannot conceive these phenomena as interrelated, and resolves: "there are other divided communities that this mansion is destined to bring together." Vargas's video thus attests not to the unraveling of a coalition between humans but to the elaboration of Erickson's politics from liberal reformism into what Eduardo Viveiros de Castro might call a "cosmopolitical theory," one attuned to the solidarity and support of a far more heterogeneous array of persons, fungi, celestial bodies, and other assorted things (56). This animistic vision of a fully integrated trans politics is evoked just as strongly in Craig Calderwood's recent portrait of activists Angela Douglas and Randy Towers, *This world will soon be ours*. Much like Erickson, Douglas has been a recurrent and yet distinctly intractable figure in historical accounts. Douglas's Transexual Action Organization (TAO), which she founded in 1970, has garnered recognition by a number of historians for being one of the first trans activist groups to take up the militancy of the post-Stonewall gay liberation movement. After relocating to Miami Beach in 1972, TAO grew into a multiracial, feminist collective that prioritized the needs of low-income trans immigrants and sex workers (Stryker, *Transgender History*). Over the course of the 1970s, Douglas became an outspoken advocate for trans politics nationally, especially emphasizing issues of police brutality and incarceration (Douglas, *Triple Jeopardy*).

Douglas's more traditional activist work, however, is but one element of a more fraught biography. Throughout her life, Douglas cleaved to the countercultural and iconoclastic, and she had a lifelong fascination with the occult. With the support of TAO president Collette Goudie, a trans woman and self-identified *bruja* of French-Cuban descent, the group drew from occult rites to protect its members from police abuse and hostile feminists. In TAO's newsletter, Goudie remarked that Satanism and black magic were especially invaluable for transsexuals "who need really strong protection in this world from their many, many enemies" (qtd. in Douglas, "Tisha Interview" 10). TAO garnered national media attention when its members hexed feminist Robin Morgan following a spate of transphobic comments at the West Coast Lesbian Feminist Conference in 1973 ("Transsexuals Hex Robin Morgan" 21). Douglas herself was particularly drawn to extraterrestrial beings, and references to UFOs permeate her writings. In her self-published autobiography, she indicates that she was deeply affected to learn that her friend and fellow activist, Randy Towers, was apparently a "reptilian, transsexual ET" that had come to earth to "aid human transsexuals" (Douglas, *Triple Jeopardy* 55). Much like with Erickson, historical accounts report that Douglas's health and material conditions worsened as she aged, and that she gradually alienated her allies with accusations and aspersions (she linked Erickson, in fact, to a CIA plot) (Meyerowitz 240). When Douglas died in 2007, she was apparently homeless and mostly alone. Nonetheless, Douglas remained committed to the idea that otherworldly forces offered important resources for building trans self-defense and self-determination. She speculated on the resonances between transsexual and extraterrestrial existence on multiple occasions, and TAO issued at least one public invitation to extraterrestrials to invade earth (Douglas, "UFOs" 66). While historians have tended to cast Douglas's relations with extraterrestrials as peripheral, if not detrimental, to her proper activist work, Calderwood's portrait instead makes them integral. Calderwood's black and white drawing shows Douglas late in her life, seated, with the reptilian Towers standing over her (see Fig. 3). Towers makes for an impressive figure—her lizard-like face is inscrutable as she gazes intently out at the viewer. Her hand rests on Douglas's shoulder, their fingers interlaced, and Douglas bears a satisfied, toothy smile. Like Calderwood's other works, the piece is intricately detailed in pen—the obsessive attention to specificities of pattern, in their clothes and the texturing of Towers' scaly epidermis, recalls the superfluous, nonfunctional details that produce, for Roland Barthes, a "reality effect" (146). And indeed, the piece is striking as an exercise in rendering reality. Rather than qualifying Douglas's extraordinary friend as a projection of her mind, or a merely "subjective" truth, the portrait manifests Douglas and Towers as equally present, materialized, and real. Calderwood's refusal to subordinate alien to human being is evocative of what Levi Bryant and others might call a "flat ontology" (Bryant 32; Bogost 273). Much like in Vargas's work, the bodies in the drawing are visually indeterminate, and the dense, elaborate patterning of skin and clothing makes it difficult to tell where exactly Douglas's body terminates and Towers' begins. Paired with the aura of impenetrability evoked by Towers' forbidding visage, Calderwood, mirroring Vargas's animals, manages to elicit Towers as co-emergent with Douglas, and yet not finally exhausted by her human relations. But more arrestingly, in Towers' clasping of Douglas's hand, in the intersomatic intimacy of human and alien transsexual, Calderwood's portrait affirms the cross-species solidarity that Douglas long envisioned. In the unearthly alliance summoned forth by this clasping, viewers of the piece are presented not only with an alternative to a historiography in which Douglas died unsupported and alone, they are called to a transgender cosmology that is as expansive as it is chimerical and strange, affixing us sternly—but also, perhaps, protectively—with Towers' coal-black eyes.

What I think is remarkable about Vargas's and Calderwood's pieces—and about Gossett's reading of the GLF tin-can demo—is that all refashion scenes that have been historiographically cast as sites of the erosion of viable sociality and, by extension, the attenuation of social capacity. Gossett responds to the putative decline of "serious" political organizing into inefficacious hippie counterculturalism; similarly, Vargas and Calderwood break from narratives that chart the intrusion of madness into human sociality. These texts, instead, reincarnate these putative withdrawals from relationality as a flourishing of relations with other-than-human presences. In soldering trans political struggles to the powers of the inhuman, I think we can read these texts as activist challenges to the intensifications of debility left in the wake of neoliberal advancement, and equally, as indictments of the hermeneutic foreclosures of secular and correlationist historiographies.

As responses to both statist and scholarly sublations, then, these animisms are neither fortuitous nor merely idiosyncratic. To the contrary, they direct attention anew to how the animistic has long been integral to trans activism and scholarship alike. In this, these works amplify growing recent attention to trans studies' early calls to affinity with inhuman, supernatural forces: like Susan Stryker's reading of the Frankenstein monster, Gossett, Vargas, and Calderwood testify to the creatively agentic as a condition of transgender worldmaking and resistance (Stryker, "My Words"; Barad). But these affinities are not simply "subjugated knowledges," and we would be remiss to disenchant or deconstruct them as such. They are, rather, spaces of emergence, sites where the trans and the inhuman mutually, reciprocally, and continually bring each other into being, and in so doing strive to effect another, more livable reality. They are legacies of capacitation, and especially of survival. These works and others incite us to further explore how an animistic trans politics might mine the occulted forces of the other-than-human to proliferate opportunities for imagination, contact, and action on the social plane—particularly when allegiances with other humans have been foreclosed. Collectively, these works challenge us all to consider what lifeways and worlds might become legible once we begin to listen for the unobtrusive but mysterious sounds of dolphin whistles or pencils tapping on tin cans—once we attend to visions of change that summon together the human, animal, and otherworldly into the empty space of possibility left by a disappeared police station.

Notes

I would like to thank Chris Vargas, Craig Calderwood, and Reina Gossett for their interlocution; *Angelaki*'s special issue editors and peer reviewers; the students of my undergraduate affect studies seminar at Grinnell College; Merlin Matthews for their research assistance; and Steve Dillon for his engaged and thoughtful feedback. I also thank Bryn Kelly, whose animistic ethos was an inspiration to me among many, and whose absence from this article is in letter only—never in spirit.

1. The view of the 1970s as a period of activist decline is prominent in New Left, antiracist, feminist, and LGBT histories alike. Initial social movement histories by Todd Gitlin and James Miller, for instance, mark 1968–69 as a turning point, after which the mass movements deteriorated into irrational sectarianism and depoliticized lifestyle pursuits (Breines 102). In feminist organizing, as Alice Echols put it, women's liberation progressively "succumbed to counterculturalism" as the 1970s progressed (7). LGBT historians such as John D'Emilio and Elizabeth Armstrong offer resonant accounts in which the initial years of radical gay liberation were gradually overtaken by a more reformist, "single-issue" gay rights movement (D'Emilio 247; Armstrong 81). For a recent version of this declension narrative in scholarship on the counterculture, see Binkley.
2. It should be noted that in the following discussion I bracket a number of historical specificities that differentiate the activist trajectories featured in this piece. My intent is not to disavow the historical and cultural discontinuities between the GLF levitation and the Kupferberg—Hoffman Pentagon levitation; or between the various trans experiments with animism in this article's second half. My aim, rather, is to underscore elided resonances between all of these mobilizations of enchantment, in particular how they all occupy a shared trans animistic ethos today. In part, the resonances between these sites of enchantment have been elided precisely because of scholarship's traditional insistence on the primacy of human culture in understanding the nonsecular, a priority that this article resists.
3. And indeed, LA GLF founder Morris Kight would later enthuse that the police station rose "about six feet" (Cleninden 60).
4. As Stephen Best and Sharon Marcus propose, a "surface reading" or "just reading" approach works to encounter "ghosts as presences, not absences, and [to let] ghosts be ghosts, instead of saying what they are ghosts *of*" (13).
5. "Correlationism" is the term given by speculative realists to paradigms of thought that refuse the possibility of making claims about either the subject or the world apart from each other—in the view of speculative realists, this includes all major Western philosophical tradition since Kant. Under correlationism, the horizon of inquiry is constrained to problems concerning the human knower's encounters with the world, making correlationism both thoroughly anthropocentric and epistemological in scope. In this view, "reality appears in philosophy only as the correlate of human thought" (Bryant, Srnicek, and Harman 3).
6. In this context, as Alan Klima further notes, "culture" becomes "a favored form for readmitting alterity into liberal discourse on that discourse's own terms" (20).
7. To be clear, in using a body of indigenous studies work to analyze mostly non-indigenous trans activists, I do not suggest that "indigenous" and "trans" are interchangeable subject positions. Instead, work on animism can be usefully employed here because trans historical subjects raise some of the same basic problems of secularism—as a structure of power—that have been negotiated by scholars of indigenous religion. My use of the new animism in this context, then, might be likened to the use of "queer" to analyze many nonheteronormative subjects that are not strictly LGBT.
8. For a more exhaustive account than I provide here of how and why figures such as Douglas and Erickson have been historiographically challenging, particularly vis-à-vis the politics of archivization, see Lewis 2014.

Bibliography

Armstrong, Elizabeth. *Forging Gay Identities: Organizing Sexuality in San Francisco, 1950–1994*. Chicago: U of Chicago P, 2002. Print.

Barad, Karen. "Transmaterialities: Trans*/Matter/Realities and Queer Political Imaginings." *GLQ: A Journal of Lesbian and Gay Studies* 21.2–3 (2015): 387–422. Print.

Barthes, Roland. *The Rustle of Language*. Trans. Richard Howard. New York: Macmillan, 1987. Print.

Bennett, Jane. *Vibrant Matter: A Political Ecology of Things*. Durham, NC: Duke UP, 2009. Print.

Best, Stephen, and Sharon Marcus. "Surface Reading: An Introduction." *Representations* 108.1 (2009): 1–21. Print.

Binkley, Sam. *Getting Loose: Lifestyle Consumption in the 1970s*. Durham, NC: Duke UP, 2007. Print.

Blackman, Lisa. *Immaterial Bodies: Affect, Embodiment, Mediation*. New York: Sage, 2012. Print.

Bogost, Ian. *Alien Phenomenology, or, What It's Like to Be a Thing*. Minneapolis: U of Minnesota P, 2012. Print.

Breines, Winni. "Sixties Stories' Silences: White Feminism, Black Feminism, Black Power." *NWSA Journal* 8.3 (1996): 101–121. Print.

Brennan, Teresa. *The Transmission of Affect*. Ithaca, NY: Cornell UP, 2014. Print.

Bryant, Levi R. *The Democracy of Objects*. Ann Arbor: Open Humanities, 2001. Print.

Bryant, Levi R., Nick Srnicek, and Graham Harman, eds. *The Speculative Turn: Continental Materialism and Realism*. Melbourne: re.press, 2011. Print.

Butler, Judith. *Precarious Life: The Powers of Mourning and Violence*. New York: Verso, 2006. Print.

Chakrabarty, Dipesh. *Provincializing Europe: Postcolonial Thought and Historical Difference*. Princeton: Princeton UP, 2000. Print.

Chen, Mel Y. *Animacies: Biopolitics, Racial Mattering, and Queer Affect*. Durham, NC: Duke UP, 2012. Print.

Clendinen, Dudley. *Out for Good: The Struggle to Build a Gay Rights Movement in America*. New York: Simon, 2001. Print.

Crimp, Douglas. "Mourning and Militancy." *October* 51 (1989): 3–18. Print.

Crowley, Aleister, et al. *Magick: Liber ABA*. Vol. 4. York Beach: Weiser, 1997. Print.

D'Emilio, John. *Making Trouble: Essays on Gay History, Politics, and the University*. New York: Routledge, 1992. Print.

Devor, Aaron H., and Nicholas Matte. "ONE Inc. and Reed Erickson: The Uneasy Collaboration of Gay and Trans Activism, 1964–2003." *GLQ: A Journal of Lesbian and Gay Studies* 10.2 (2004): 179–209. Print.

Douglas, Angela. "Los Angeles." *Come Out!* 1.5 (Sept.–Oct. 1970): 9. Print.

———. "Tisha Interview." *Mirage* 13 Feb. 1975: 9–12. Print.

———. *Triple Jeopardy: The Autobiography of Angela Lynn Douglas*. N.p.: Angela Douglas, 1983. Print.

———. "UFOs, TSs, and Extra-Ts." Transsexual Action Organization Publications, 1972–1975. Angela Douglas File, Ephemera Collection, GLBT Historical Society, San Francisco.

Echols, Alice. *Daring to be Bad: Radical Feminism in America, 1967–1975*. Minneapolis: U of Minnesota P, 1989. Print.

Gilmore, Ruth Wilson. "In the Shadow of the Shadow State." *The Revolution Will Not Be Funded: Beyond the Non-profit Industrial Complex*. Ed. INCITE! Women of Color Against Violence. New York: South End, 2009. 41–52. Print.

Gossett, Reina. "Occupy Humor & Grief as Transformative Practices." *The Spirit Was . . .* 15 Mar. 2012. Web. 1 May 2015. <http://thespiritwas.tumblr.com/post/19349288742/occupy-humor-grief-as-transformative-practices>.

Harman, Graham. *Immaterialism: Objects and Social Theory*. Malden, MA: Polity, 2016. Print.

Harvey, Graham. *Animism: Respecting the Living World*. New York: Columbia UP, 2005. Print.

Ingold, Tim. "Rethinking the Animate, Re-animating Thought." *Ethnos* 71.1 (2006): 9–20. Print.

Klima, Alan. *The Funeral Casino: Meditation, Massacre, and Exchange with the Dead in Thailand*. Princeton: Princeton UP, 2009. Print.

Langford, Jean. *Consoling Ghosts: Stories of Medicine and Mourning from Southeast Asians in Exile*. Kindle ed. Minneapolis: U of Minnesota P, 2013. Print.

Latour, Bruno. *Politcs of Nature: How to Bring the Sciences into Democracy*. Cambridge, MA: Harvard UP, 2004. Print.

Lewis, Abram J. "'I Am 64 and Paul McCartney Doesn't Care': The Haunting of the Transgender Archive and the Challenges of Queer History." *Radical History Review* 2014.120 (2014): 13–34. Print.

Love, Heather. "Close but not Deep: Literary Ethics and the Descriptive Turn." *New Literary History* 41.2 (2010): 371–391. Print.

Luciano, Dana. "Sacred Theories of Earth: Matters of Spirit in *The Soul of Things*." *American Literature* 86.4 (2014): 713–736. Print.

Meyerowitz, Joanne J. *How Sex Changed: A History of Transsexuality in the United States*. Cambridge, MA: Harvard UP, 2009. Print.

ONE for All . . . Dir. Chris Vargas. Perf. Chris Vargas and Greg Youmans. Chris Vargas, 2012. Video.

Peña, Susana. "Gender and Sexuality in Latina/o Miami: Documenting Latina Transsexual Activists." *Gender and History* 22.3 (2010): 755–772. Print.

Rodríguez, Dylan. "The Political Logic of the Nonprofit Industrial Complex." *The Revolution Will Not Be Funded: Beyond the Non-profit Industrial Complex*. Ed. INCITE! Women of Color Against Violence. New York: South End, 2009.21–40. Print.

———. "Stop Police Murder, Brutality, and Entrapment of Homosexuals." "Police" folder, Ephemera—Subjects. International Gay Information Center. New York Public Library, New York. Flyer.

Stryker, Susan. "My Words to Victor Frankenstein above the Village of Chamounix: Performing Transgender Rage." *GLQ: A Journal of Lesbian and Gay Studies* 1.3 (1994): 237–254. Print.

———. *Transgender History*. Berkeley: Seal, 2008. Print.

"Transsexuals Hex Robin Morgan." *The Advocate* 18 July 1973: 21. Print.

Viveiros de Castro, Eduardo. *Cannibal Metaphysics*. Trans. Peter Skafish. Minneapolis: U of Minnesota P, 2014. Print.

Willerslev, Rane. *Soul Hunters: Hunting, Animism, and Personhood Among the Siberian Yukaghirs*. Berkeley: U of California P, 2007. Print.

———. "Taking Animism Seriously, but Perhaps not Too Seriously?" *Religion and Society* 4.1 (2013): 41–57. Print.

Section IX

Trans Cultural Production

41 Embracing Transition, or Dancing in the Folds of Time

Julian Carter

In this meditation on transgender time and movement, Julian Carter performs a close reading of contemporary choreographer Sean Dorsey's dance work *Lou* (2009), about Lou Sullivan, author of the essay "A Transvestite Answers a Feminist" in this reader, who was a prominent transsexual activist in the 1970s and 80s. Carter begins his essay by reflecting on the paradigmatic expression of transness as physical immobility, "the soul of a woman trapped in the body of a man." He points out that the word typically translated from the original Latin phrase as "trapped," *inclusa*, can also be interpreted as meaning embraced, or enfolded. What happens to the "wrong body" transsexuals are often thought to be trapped in, Carter asks, if we begin to rearticulate *inclusa* as a condition of possibility for being enfolded or moved toward something else, much like the voluptuous sense of folding and regeneration that Hayward writes about in "Lessons From a Starfish"? Carter notes that "transition," in addition to being transgender argot for changing genders, is a choreographic term for how movements are linked. He then offers dance criticism of the transitional gestures and movements that Dorsey uses to stage Lou's transition from social womanhood into gay male community. In a final section, Carter offers a way to understand differently the time and space of gender transition (what he names "transitional time"). Rather than imagining transition as a linear progression, what would happen if we imagine transitions between genders, like choreographic transitions, as places in time in which numerous movements—forward, backward, sideways, tangential—are equally possible and can coexist?

Anima mulieris in corpore virilis inclusa: the soul of a woman imprisoned in a man's body. Karl Ulrichs' 1862 account of trans- experience echoes into our own time in variants of the phrase "trapped in the wrong body." Culturally powerful and politically controversial, claimed and resisted in many ways, such descriptions can feel like a potent form of truth-telling about gender even while they mobilize a troubling vision of embodiment as a form of constraint. To imagine the body as a prison for the soul is to participate, however reluctantly, in a conceptual universe where our flesh is inconvenient matter which limits the free expression of our inner and nobler being. Such a vision seems to cement us into a position of permanent helpless struggle. In this depressive figuration, simply to be embodied is already to be trapped by a wrongness inseparable from the condition of materiality. The historico–cultural slippage from ascription to evaluation—from Ulrich's sexed body to the more contemporary wrong body—deepens the sense of hopeless entrapment: physical sex easily becomes a condition of existential inadequacy. No way out.

DOI: 10.4324/9781003206255-51

But this impasse is not inevitable. *Inclusa* is the feminine perfect passive participle of the Latin verb *includere*, which means to enclose or include. You can use the same word to describe arms extending in embrace, pulling you in. Fem(me)inist explorations of sexual receptivity demonstrate that such gestures of welcome and desire are neither static nor passive but involve active bodily participation in social relationships.[1] It follows that to be *in corpore inclusa*, enfleshed, is not necessarily a trap, but rather the condition of possibility for movement toward one another. Do away with the (assumption of) the trap, and questions arise about what kinds of gestures toward sociality our "wrong" embodiment enables. Do away with the trap, and we can begin to explore the range of motion inherent in the dynamic prefix *trans-*.[2]

I wonder how the wrong body trope can be addressed differently if I put the emphasis on how trans- embodiment mobilizes us. I'm not the first to draw attention to the spatial dynamism of sex/gender change: a powerful tradition in trans- studies theorizes transition as movement, especially movement into the territory of the transformed, the unnatural and monstrous, the cyborg and the transspecies.[3] My focus here is more quotidian. I want to consider transition in terms of physical gestures, movements from place to place (*trans/situ*) that simultaneously shift our relations with our own bodies and the bodies of others. But gesture is not only physical.[4] The English word derives from the Latin *gesturus*, a future active participle of the verb *gerere*, to carry or bear; *gesturus* means "I am about to carry." Gesture is an anticipatory performance of our physical bearing. If we listen to the futural temporality embedded in the word's root, we can hear not only intentionality in relation to actions as we undertake them, but also a triple meaning of the word "to bear," which means to comport one's body in a particular way, to carry something, and to endure. To gesture, then, is to embody one's intention, and may entail assuming a certain open-ended responsibility for what one carries. Taking gender transition literally, as a matter of gesture, can facilitate thinking about its impact on relationality in ways that attend to the physicality of embodiment without bracketing the body's social, psychic and affective dimensions.

Considering gender transition as embodied gesture also raises questions about related issues of continuity, retroflexion, and anticipation.[5] In trans- contexts the term "transition" is most often used to refer to the period of time during which one shifts the sex/gender of one's anatomical body and/or presentation of self in the world. As I'll show, such shifting in space can open time so that developmental sequences, backward turns, and futural impulses coexist and intertwine. Dance has a highly developed technical vocabulary for talking about just such movements in spacetime. In dance worlds, transitions are shifts from one kind of movement to another. They are physical strategies—which may include gestures, motion pathways, adjustments of weight or tension or tempo—that redirect embodied energies so that (for instance) a forward movement becomes a sideways step, or a slowly moving body accelerates. Transitional gestures are the small, often unobtrusive movements that connect and contextualize poses, positions, sequences, or ways of moving that might otherwise seem disjunctive; or conversely they can be ways of interrupting a predictable flow, heightening contrast or calling attention to the moment where one sequence of movements changes into another. Or transitional awareness can index the energetic exchange between bodies, their capacity to sense the presence and proximity of other beings. Transition, as it's realized in dance, joins references to time and references to space in ways that allow us to consider the dimension of embodied relationality that involves movement. As such, dance provides an appropriate analytic framework for trans- work: it is the technical language *par excellence* of bodies in motion. This essay, then, brings dance's precision about physical movement to bear on embodied trans- subjects.

Lou

All dance proceeds via transitions, but very little dance represents transition in terms of gender. Trans- choreographer Sean Dorsey's critically acclaimed work *Lou* (2009) is therefore an especially useful source for this discussion. *Lou* is Dorsey's homage to FTM (female-to-male) activist Lou Sullivan (1951–1991). In 1976 Sullivan began seeking sex reassignment but was routinely rejected from gender clinics because then-current medical protocols defined eligibility for sex change according to medico-psychiatric gatekeepers' assessment of whether the person seeking to transition would be able to function socially as a "normal" man or woman.[6] As a woman whose erotic gestures were directed toward men, Sullivan's social movements already appeared to conform to normative expectations for his embodiment; therefore his desire for transition seemed simply perverse to his doctors. His insistence on the legitimacy of his intention to move in the world as a gay man, and his persistent post-transition engagement with psychiatrists positioned to parlay their convictions into recommendations for practice, were instrumental in changing standards of care to accommodate queer outcomes: Sullivan's trailblazing activities expanded opportunities for medically-assisted transition toward embodiments legible as gay for later generations of trans men.[7] He also helped to found an international FTM community, initially through a support group in San Francisco and later through editing a newsletter that circulated nationally and internationally, linking its readers through community announcements, political and medical news, and historical anecdotes. And almost every day for thirty years, Lou Sullivan kept a diary in which he detailed his relationship to himself as well as his many and varied encounters with thousands of people.[8]

This is the figure at the center of Dorsey's *Lou*. The dance is performed by four men moving to an original score featuring spoken excerpts from Sullivan's diaries, supplemented with Dorsey's reflections on those texts and on his own affective and creative responses to the issues they raise. At the core of this piece is a certain productive refusal to maintain clear subjective and temporal boundaries between the choreographer and the object of his homage. Not only does Dorsey mix his words with Sullivan's, he physically embodies his sense of Sullivan's experience by dancing the title character's role.[9] But while Dorsey's physical re-creation and inhabitation of Sullivan's social gestures work to extend Sullivan's presence into the moment of performance, Dorsey's written text insists that the past is gone and can't be regained. The first and last movements of *Lou* are meditations on the permanence of loss, the transience of memory, and the unreliability of history. "History," Dorsey declares, "is a trick the living play on the dead," not least because it so often forgets or conceals the poverty of its representation of their lives.

Lou thus stages the tension between the material reality of historical loss—the past as dead and gone—and the equally material reality of physical rememory—the past as embodied in the living present.[10] The four dancers' gestures are not literal enactments of the voice-over text. Instead they develop a bodily representation of loss that can't be separated from their simultaneous fleshly recreation of and relationship to the lost subject. For instance, one of the dance's core motifs is a sequence in which one dancer embraces another's chest and shoulders, then stands while the one being held dips his knees to slide out of the embrace and step away. The result is an empty circle of arms with the palms turned inward toward the face.

Dorsey's voice-over tells us that people die and we are left with the space they once filled, until over time we come to imagine that space as an adequate reflection of who they were in life. Yet while the words are about absence and grief, the changing experience of loss is made tangible on stage through the continued living presence of the "dead" subject, theatrically embodied by the very survivor who mourns its loss.

When we experience the dead as present in living flesh that nonetheless invokes, remembers, and mourns their absence, we are sensing time's ability to fold in on itself. This isn't another way of indicting our untrustworthy memories or faulty accounts of the past. The *when* of the dance in performance and the *when* it depicts in its movements lie over one another like transparencies in an anatomical textbook, in which the layers of the body are necessarily perceived simultaneously and as a whole, while they are also palpably, if not always exactly visibly, distinct and separable. Watching, we see that the body's past both is and is not present in the present. Further, the present is not the past's future so much as its re-embodiment. The present does not merely cite the past (acknowledging, tacitly or overtly, that it is pointing to something outside of and other than itself in order to claim a particular relation of identity or alterity in relation to it), but is instead a rematerialization of it.

This approach to the past is a sensuous operation as well as an analytic one. The body is always in its present, which does not prevent it from both rubbing up against and remaking its past in a way that utterly defies historical logic. Embodiment provides a compelling model for developmental, sequential history in its progressive physical maturation through years of growth and aging, and yet at the same time the body's capacity not only to index but also to embody a past it never experienced presents a major challenge to any such notion of linearity. This complexly invaginated, profoundly relational experience of temporality is especially significant in the sections of Dorsey's dance that stage Sullivan's transition from female to male. The first of these sections, titled "I Want to Look Like What I Am," presents gender transition as entry into relationship, an entry that sends time swirling around itself and around people who are set in motion by the decision to change sex. The second section, "Desire," stages the physicality and consequentiality of trans- interventions into the social.

Joy

"I Want to Look Like What I Am" opens with the cast reading excerpts from Sullivan's diaries that highlight both Sullivan's pre-transition identification with gay men and his uncertainty about making that identification real through transitioning. As the other dancers file off the stage and leave Dorsey alone, the soundtrack continues with Dorsey's voice reading the words "*I want to look like what I am, but I don't know what someone like me looks like.*" Wandering passages of movement, frequently executed with Dorsey's back to the audience or with his focus curled into his torso, provide visual counterpoint to the soundtrack's evocation of solitary self-questioning. We hear how Sullivan's library research yields no evidence that anyone like him has ever existed, and learn the consequences for him of this lack of human recognition: "*Hidden from view I'm losing touch.*" Sullivan's choice of words is telling: the split subjectivity of the unrealized transsexual produces both the sensation and the performance of a physical disconnection indistinguishable from lack of social engagement.

Dorsey interrupts his performance of isolation by staging the classic transgender experience of wrong embodiment. Walking downstage center, face to face with the audience, Dorsey introduces gender transition as a move toward relationality via folds in time, recognition, and embodiment. As he faces us, his recorded voice says: "*I look in the mirror and say to myself, that's you? That girl over there is you.*" The proscenium stands in for the frame of the mirror such that the audience is positioned as looking through it at him while he looks at himself. What we see there is importantly different from what he tells us he sees in that the person on the stage does not occupy a social space marked "girl." The resulting stumble of perception marks Dorsey's queer inscription of his viewing audience into the wrong-body narrative. We are called to occupy the position of the outsider whose visual perception of sexed embodiment doesn't align with the transsexual sense of self. Yet at the same moment and through the same summons to relationship we are positioned as transsexuals, at risk of seeming deluded because we perceive Dorsey's masculinity even though the "objective reality" that pertains within the dramatic situation—what we are told the mirror reflects—says "girl." And we in the audience are summoned as affirmative witnesses to the temporal transitivity of the transgender embodiment on the stage in front of us.

Through the looking glass we see the trans man's body standing in for its own potential before it was brought into being.

On one level, "I Want to Look Like What I Am" follows a conventional narrative arc that maps neatly onto a triumphalist model of time as progress: in this section, we see Lou Sullivan moving from isolation and confusion toward self-realization and, eventually, sociosexual affirmation. But the arc of that story is the narrative equivalent of the proscenium arch in that, while it lends authority to a particular view of the action on the stage, it does not fully contain the potential of the movement that unfolds there. Dorsey's depiction of transition as progress toward sociality provides a stabilizing frame for his depiction of transition as an elaborately transtemporal relational formation. Such an arrangement may appear like an aesthetic compromise, a pulling-back from his own exploration of transitional time in the interests of accessibility; audiences are comfortable with that narrative arc, and telling tales of becoming-transsexual transpiring within its frame may serve a normalizing, universalizing function. One could come away from this piece with dreams of social progress confirmed, the hope for a more perfect body renewed. But it's also true that Dorsey shows triumphalist and invaginated time as co-existing, a convergence which challenges the assumption that they are opposed and mutually exclusive modes of temporality. In doing so he pushes us to consider through what gestures, and through what physical relationships, the time of transition unfolds.

Transition pleats time, and in so doing transforms our relational capacities. Dorsey enacts that folding as inseparable from Sullivan's frustrated need for embodied social contact: "*My voice and my body betray me. I mean, no one looks deeper than the flesh, do they. So practice being invisible. Learn to look in the mirror and see only the mirror.*" At this point dancer Brian Fisher walks up behind Dorsey and stands at his back, mirroring his moves while Dorsey's recorded voice, speaking Sullivan's words, announces an intention to "*See only the person there that I imagine myself to be. And make this change.*"

With this utterance Dorsey shifts from Sullivan's remembrance of the "years of this wondering, not validated by anybody" to his own enactment of Sullivan's transition. This is simultaneously a narrative transition from female to male and a choreographic transition in which Dorsey turns away from his imaginary mirror and toward physical relationship with another dancing body on the stage.

These transitions are explicitly romantic in gesture and in utterance. The core movement motif of this section is an embrace, and Sullivan's words record his experience of transition as a romance that is none the less social because it is with the self: "I think of myself as two people, finally coming together in peace with each other, but of my other half I sing, 'Nobody loves me, but me adores you.' I am positive I want to do this, this change. My own body. This limitless joy. Imagine. I am finally going *to be able to look in the mirror and see the person there I imagine myself to be.*" Holding hands, the dancers twine. They step around one another's legs and through one another's arms, resting their heads against one another, lifting one another off the floor and circling one another with their weight until Dorsey pulls Fisher face-to-face and suddenly Fisher is leading this same-sex couple in a few measures that quote a tango. We are being shown that they are passionate partners in a movement pattern that is formally structured by gender, but which does not duplicate the conventional heterogendered relations of social dance. Then just as suddenly, Dorsey turns out of Fisher's arms, pulls him against his back, closes Fisher's arms around his chest and dips his knees to slide out of the embrace he has made.

With this movement Dorsey repeats the core motif of the opening section of *Lou*, the sequence that enacts the transition from loss to grief to memory to history. This slipping-through is a repetition of the previous gesture but it is enacted now to the words *"I am positive I want to do this."* This is a repetition with a difference, a gesture that fills the space of loss with the realization of connection.[11] Dorsey, who has slipped out of Fisher's grasp, turns his back to his partner and faces us with the words *"My own body,"* just as Fisher's hands land softly on Dorsey's hips and Dorsey opens his arms soft and wide as his weight wavers in Fisher's hands. In its earlier iteration this gesture signified memory, the last personal trace of the dead before they are abstracted into history. Repeated now, it combines the lightness and uncertainty of flight toward the future, and it is grounded in the present by his partner's touch. Dorsey is staging "this change" as the transtemporal enactment of self-love, a relation of mutual trust and reliance between the gay man who is coming into being and the person who has been a girl and a woman before this point in his life. As the narrator anticipates *"I am finally going to be able to look in the mirror,"* the dancers, facing one another, take turns creating openings with their arms for the other to slip through. The gestural sequence that once performed loss and memory's fading into historical misrepresentation now communicates not only transformation but also the delights of looking forward to a scene of secure recognition.

Yet the transformations and recognitions the dancers anticipate have in fact already taken place. Dorsey offers a vision of transsexual self-fashioning in which the gay man who will be the end product of transition guides and supports the trans man-in-the-making as he begins to realize himself. The trans man dancing the role of a female-bodied person just embarking on transition could be seen as a turn toward the past that Dorsey and Sullivan, as trans men, can be said to share insofar as both were once girls: but it is also a kind of folding forward of her life into his, a suggestion that her body held its breastless future just as his holds its breasted past. The supple cisgendered gay man dancing the role of the trans fag who has not yet come into being is also folding time forward, toward the erotic masculinity that transition enabled Sullivan to access, and back toward a past in which the trans man was a man all along. Time's pleating here is inseparable from affective and intercorporeal connection.

This magical temporality, where many layers of anticipation, experience, loss, and memory fold into one another, takes physical shape as an extraordinarily delicate intimacy between the dancers. Fisher, in black, melts visually into the dark stage so that his movement can be perceived primarily as his body shadows the cream-clad Dorsey. Like a shadow, his body is not quite the same as Dorsey's, but instead of rendering Dorsey's embodiment uncanny or inauthentic in its similitude without sameness, Fisher's shadow-role serves to provide Dorsey's embodiment with a visual depth of field that is emotionally analogous to intersubjective context. One embodied aspect of the self dances with another. We witness transsexual self-fashioning as inherently, physically relational, and as deeply tender.

The narration underscores this relational quality by introducing an interlocutor; the voice-over tells us *"He asked if I was scared and I said 'Just the opposite.' Afraid for so long, I now know I can do anything, be anything, exactly who I am."* On this phrase, Dorsey walks forward with Fisher at his back, holding Fisher's hands gently on his hips and stopping downstage center in a spotlight. We are looking through the mirror again. Head turned to the side, remaining in touch with his partner, Dorsey's hands follow Fisher's briefly as Fisher circles Dorsey's chest, but this time Dorsey doesn't slip through. Instead Fisher lifts Dorsey's shirt from the bottom hem. For a moment Dorsey's hands hover, suspended, and then together they slide the shirt off over his head. As Dorsey stands and looks at himself in his imaginary mirror, his mouth slightly open and his hand on his solar plexus, the narration folds time in on itself again with the whisper *"I always knew it would turn out to be like this."*

The movement of taking off a shirt is simple both as gesture and as concept, but in this context it has disproportionate performative force. It is not a moment of coming out; we already know that Lou Sullivan and Sean Dorsey are transsexual men. When Dorsey bares his chest, he occupies Sullivan's bodily remaking for us to witness and celebrate. The gesture's evident communicative content, in this performance context, is something like "look at Sullivan's success by looking at my success! We are no longer wrongly embodied." But the physical presence in the spotlight exceeds its overt reference to the prior achievement of gendered rightness. Both dancers are sweating and breathing hard, and in their, and our, larger stillness, it's impossible not to feel the labor of their ribcages' pulsing, their collarbones rising with the air they suck. The gestures of respiration Dorsey presents at this moment reveal and solicit the sheer physical work of making connection. Knowledge here precedes both the existence of its object—the realized trans- body—and the existence of the subject who will know that body in and through its movement of disrobing. It's the attempt to make connection that sets these bodies in motion, that makes time fold and pleat. Watching these men breathe together while their larger travels from place to place are temporarily suspended, we see transition as a physical practice that exceeds alterations in individual embodiment. It's not only about the contours of Dorsey's chest, but also about the way his rematerialization of Sullivan's relation to himself performs and transforms the spatial and temporal transitivity of bodies. The fold in time produces a fold toward relationship: Dorsey turns his head ask though to ask his shadow "*Did you know? I always knew it.*" Still holding his hip with one hand, the other caressing an arm, Fisher rests his head on the back of Dorsey's shoulder and the two of them sway with their shared breath as the narrator whispers "*Limitless joy. Just, joy.*"

Desire

To push at what thinking transition as embodied movement can accomplish, I want to consider transitional gestures. Recall that transitions, in dancer-talk, are movements that accomplish change; they redirect moving bodies' relation to tempo, energetic focus, spatial orientation or intercorporeal connection. The transitional sequence of *Lou* to which I now turn is about forty seconds long and connects the duet that ends "I Want to Look Like What I Am" to the next movement of Lou, a full-company segment titled "Desire." I want to linger on a very brief—three-second—passage within this transitional sequence. Such lingering is not only for the pleasure it yields, though pleasure turns out to be a lot of what's at stake here. It also allows me to demonstrate transition's effectiveness as a conceptual tool for unpacking movement that is not explicitly or intentionally "about" changing sex.

After Dorsey takes off his shirt the stage goes dark and in that darkness Dorsey's recorded voice reads passages from Sullivan's diary about his emergence as a gay man. Three dancers enter wearing white boxer briefs and tanktops. Spread out in a line near the back of the stage, they pose while we hear Sullivan exulting in his discovery that he is "a social being." "*I am desired, and I desire other men. I've got lost time to make up for,*" he tells us. "*I've got to make up for lost time.*" Again a temporal fold enables Sullivan's turn toward embodied relationship; the fantasy of re-occupying the past, using it better, animates his determination to occupy his masculinity through sexual contact. As the narrator invokes time, the dancers reach toward one another. Wrists crossed and holding hands, they sketch the first steps of *Swan Lake*'s Dance of the Cygnets before unraveling their tidy full-frontal pattern into a loose chain. While the three men—still holding hands—turn and twist through one another's arms, the narrator reads from Sullivan's diary about the sexual acceptance and pleasure he experienced among gay men.

The three seconds Dorsey borrows from *Swan Lake* serve as a transition from a sequence in which the men preen as individuals, connected only by the precise timing of their movements, to a sequence in which their gestures become socially intertwined so that they respond to and flow out of one another's bodies. In between—during the cygnets' steps—they hold hands and step in unison, physically and temporally connected but not yet motivating or responding to one another's gestures. It's a moment of proximity that has not yet become sociality.

On the level of narrative, it connects the longing to embody masculinity depicted in "I Want to Look Like What I Am" to the longing to touch other men. It takes us from the desire for gender to sexual desire, from the desire to be a man to the desire to have men.[12] And it accomplishes that transition into the social through a gestural image that returns us to the "wrong body" trope, this time heavily laden with normative expectations for the gendered temporality through which we enter into relationships.

Swan Lake's Dance of the Cygnets is a famous *pas de quatre* for four young women who demonstrate the purity and precision of their ballet technique by executing increasingly bravura steps side by side while holding hands across one another's waists. It stages mutual support among adolescent girls as a charming phase to be superseded by heterosexual pairing: in the ballet world, a cygnet transitions into a swan when she is offered a romantic *pas de deux* with a male lead, a framing expectation that sentimentalizes the ephemerality of same-sex companionship. The cygnets' shoulder-to-shoulder configuration embodies the cultural demand that girls identify with other girls. Simultaneously, it displays them for an implied masculine viewer, anticipating the dissolution of their identificatory intimacy through sexual competition.

When Dorsey gives these girlish steps to three adult men, the choreography's references to conventional gender and sexual development fracture into a representation of a particularly gay temporality. Three men are not four girls, and as such they are clearly the wrong bodies for the Dance of the Cygnets. Or one could say that the Dance of the Cygnets is culturally wrong movement for adult male bodies: whether you place the emphasis on the form or the gesture, morphologies and movements don't line up in conventional ways. Much of that queer disjunction has to do with time. Because these men dance steps that "belong" to adolescents, they can be imagined as performing their own developmental failure.[13] For a grown man to embody a cygnet suggests a perverse refusal to grow out of same-sex intimacies: men acting like teenagers materialize their homosexuality as an arrest of development. Further, because the men's gestures invoke a past in which they were girls, these gestures suggest that the putative effeminacy of proto-gay boys overlaps the youthful femininity of the trans man-to-be.[14] The temporal disjunctions launched by the cygnets' steps serve to connect the three dancing men to one another along an axis of shared physical and dynamic wrongness, which, in turn, launches their creation of a mutually supportive intimacy. When adult men's arms and ankles cross to compose the cygnets' network of intersecting lines, *Swan Lake*'s sentimental homophobia is replaced with a web of connection. These cygnets transition us into gay community. And by staging this transition with three dancers instead of *Swan Lake*'s four, Dorsey opens a space on the stage where the fourth dancer belongs even before he appears.

His entry will matter all the more because his absence carries such a powerful charge. Dorsey is offstage during this transitional sequence, which means that the figure of the gay trans man literally stands to one side of the Dance of the Cygnets. His spatial marginalization during this sequence suggests that the intersection of gay tropes of arrested development with trans- tropes of wrong embodiment works differently for trans- subjects than for gay ones. The narrator has already hinted that Sullivan's transition will enable his entry into gay men's public sexual culture, where he'll "make up for lost time," but he can't do that by turning toward the adolescent femininity the cygnets' steps evoke. Retroflexion and delay would seem particularly complex for trans- subjects. Because Sullivan once embodied the category "teenage girl," arresting his development at that stage would foreclose his access to gay masculinity, not confirm it.[15] For Dorsey to dance toward girlhood, however gay the irony, does not constitute a queer arrest of development as much as a return to a non-consensually feminized past. In its movement away from trans- self-realization, such a return rejects futurity and in doing so forecloses Sullivan's desire to make up for the sexual time he lost by being embodied as a girl on his first tour through adolescence. When the future is refused, the past loses its dynamic potential and the subject finds itself stuck on the margins of time and social relationship. Making up for lost time requires a return with a difference, rather than an arrest.

Hence Dorsey/Sullivan does not—in some senses, cannot—do the cygnets' dance. This matters because that dance provides the choreographic transition that brings spatially separate, though visually connected, individuals into physical contact and communication. If the trans man cannot physically take the place of the fourth cygnet, how can he enter into gay sexual community? Dorsey answers with a return to the embrace. Still holding hands, the trio melts out of the little swans' lateral formation to collaborate on a low traveling lift, two of the men containing the third with their linked hands circling his waist, one pair of hands clasping in front and the other behind. The gesture sustains and intensifies the cygnets' interwoven arms. Held between his partners' hands and propelled by their forward motion, the third dancer arches back and extends his neck. The gesture feels intensely sexual in its exaggerated openness and sense of being carried along, as though the boundaries of the self were dissolving in sensation—but if the self dissolves, it's safely contained by the intimate touch of surrounding bodies.

We've just seen another form of intimate, containing touch in the embrace at the end of "I Want To Look Like What I Am," in which Fisher's hands provide physical and symbolic stabilization for Dorsey/Sullivan as he commits himself to realizing his masculinity in his flesh. What's different about this embrace is the affect generated by its traveling execution with four arms, two dancers' hands clasped around a third body. Intimacy looks and feels different when it involves three people. *Pas de deux*—movement passages for two dancers who sustain physical contact with one another—are conventionally used to develop and express romance. Dorsey staged Sullivan's gender transition as a *pas de deux* in a way that emphasizes his vision of transition as expressing love for and reconciliation between halves of the self (one masculine, one feminine). In the transitional movement borrowed from the Dance of the Cygnets, Dorsey expands the embrace in a way that expands the relational connections among the bodies on stage. Through this visual reference to a *ménage a trois* we're offered a vision of eroticism as social contact, an expansion beyond privatized dyadic romantic love toward the sex clubs Sullivan frequented. Then the embrace expands again: the three cygnets land the traveling embrace face to face with Dorsey/Sullivan, who has entered quietly and stands watching their approach. They look at one another for a heartbeat, then two, before the cygnets extend their hands and Dorsey joins their chain, weaving through their arms. His passage through their hands concludes with his chest arched back and neck extended, ecstasy running through his spine.

Folding

Dorsey offers us a vision of the embrace as a gesture that transitions bodies to new sociotemporal contexts. At the beginning of *Lou*, circling arms indicate the progressive stages of response to death—from loss, to grief, to memory, to history. In "I Want To Look Like What I Am," variations on the same motif move the Sullivan character along a developmental path from isolation and confusion to self-recognition and, eventually, love. But other uses of this gesture interrupt conventional expectations of linear temporal and affective development.

For instance, when Dorsey draws on the embrace used in partnered social dancing to depict the psychic and physical process of gender transition, he stages that transition as inherently relational in a way that makes time fold around the subject. In "Desire," increasing expansions of the cygnets' embrace generate a sexual community wide enough to include Sullivan despite his temporal difference from other gay men. The expanded embrace produces a ripple effect out from the individual body of the transsexual man into the social body: the *ménage a trois* becomes a quartet, suggesting the possibility that we could keep adding more and more partners in an almost infinite expansion of possible intimacies. Further, the trans man's disruptive effect on the cygnets' signifying chain stages the historical expansion of the category "gay" to include transsexuals, and the category "transsexual" to include "gay," at the end of the 1980s. Such transformations demonstrate that bodies can change the social contexts in which they move. Dorsey shows us that Sullivan's transition did more than make him a gay man: it helped widen the social worlds in which bodies natally assigned to femininity could embrace, and be included in, erotic manhood. Because we watch Dorsey's work in a moment subsequent to the historical change he depicts, our current engagement with Sullivan's past must involve our own willingness to allow time to fold around our bodies as well. Thus the remaking of the body that is becoming-transsexual changes both the content and the form of social relationships, with profound temporal implications.

This essay can't finish with a conventional conclusion because the medium it engages works against tidy endings. Movement doesn't conclude when the dancers bow. There's always another transition ahead, another step, another opportunity to change direction and approach other bodies; not to attend to that embodied and relational reality would be to betray this project's deepest investments. Besides, there's something compelling about the circular, recursive temporality that emerges from the gesture of the embrace. And so we circle back to the question with which I began: how the wrong-body trope works differently when being *in corpore inclusa* is considered not as a flesh trap but as the condition of possibility for our movement toward other bodies. The wrong-body trope most often drives an understanding of gender transition as a reparative process through which one alters a bad form so that its structure aligns with and reflects a particular content more precisely. That understanding presumes that content exists prior to and separate from its expression; further, it tends to impose a linear temporality on transition so that it serves as a hinge between two distinct conditions linked and separated by a point of redirection in an otherwise intact timeline (e.g., not this future, in a woman's body, but that future, in a man's body).[16] The problem with such accounts of transition is that they can consider time only as an inert substance linking physical moments or embodied states that are static in themselves. In contrast, Dorsey offers us a vision of transitional time, and transitioning bodies, as dynamic and relational negotiations of wrongness. He shows us how transition enfolds the body in its own material substance, yet allows for that substance's alteration. Anticipation, retroflexion, and continuity coexist in the same body, at the same moving moment of space and time.

Transitioning subjects anticipate a gender content they generate recursively out of their physical medium's formal potential in relation to the context of its emergence. One might say transition wraps the body in the folds of social time.

Transitional time's folds may drag on the body in a way that produces the sense of arrest, deferral, and delay so richly explored by queer theorists of temporality.[17] Queer time is widely theorized in opposition to temporal straightness, the normative and limiting "logic of development" that subtends and legitimizes many objectionable discursive constructions and sociopolitical formations, from individual maturation through reproduction to eugenic imperialism.[18] From this analytic perspective, when Dorsey opens a representation of gay sexual community by having adult men execute steps choreographed for adolescent girls, he is staging the social and libidinal joys of arrested development—joys worth celebrating not only for their physical pleasure but also for their interruption of normative expectations for how, and through which forms of relationality, individual lives should progress. This works fine as a description of the way that Dorsey's choreography communicates the gay sexuality of the three men dancing together, but as I suggested above, queer valorizations of temporal lag are not quite adequate to theorizing the fourth dancer's absence, or the way his entry shifts the social field. As the temporal lag of arrested development opens the space for same-sex bonding and polymorphous perversity, it simultaneously shuts down the space for becoming-trans. For a trans- subject like Lou Sullivan, developmental arrest can lead to imprisonment in a wrong body: remaining a teenage girl forecloses rather than instantiates his adult male homosexuality.

Fortunately, transitional time's folding can have other effects beyond drag. It may heighten the body's sensitivity, invaginating so that it touches itself in several different moments at once; thus, after transition materializes Sullivan's adult gay masculinity, he might return to his girlhood as a site of youthful effeminacy. He might embody the boy, the girl, and the adult man all at the same time. Or transitional time's pleats may propel the body forward: Sullivan left girlhood behind to become a man. Sex change does involve purposive movement toward an embodied future, even as that future is summoned into being in and through a body that does not yet exist, and while the body that does exist in the present is the medium for the future body's becoming-form. Transitional time's incorporation of both straight and queer temporalities exemplifies a certain heuristic spaciousness in the concept of trans-, a spaciousness wide enough to enclose the notion of queer time in a trans- embrace.

From: Julian Carter, "Embracing Transition, or Dancing in the Folds of Time" in *Transgender Studies Reader, Volume 2*, pp. 130–144. Copyright 2013, Routledge. All rights reserved. Republished by permission of the publisher.

Notes

1. In addition to Joan Nestle's classic works, especially *A Restricted Country* (Firebrand Books, 1987), see descriptions of femme sexual agency in Heidi Levitt and Katherine Heistand, "Gender Within Lesbian Sexuality: Butch and Femme Perspectives," *Journal of Constructivist Psychology* 18 (2005): 39–51; Juana María Rodríguez, "Gesture and Utterance: Fragments from a Butch/Femme Archive," in *A Companion to LGBT Studies*, ed. George Haggerty and Molly McGarry (Malden, MA: Blackwell Publishing, 2007), 282–291.

2. On the trans- prefix see Susan Stryker, Paisley Currah, and Lisa Jean Moore, "Trans-, Trans, or Transgender?" *WSQ* 36: 3–4 (2008), 11–22.

3. Several essays in *The Transgender Studies Reader*, ed. Susan Stryker and Stephen Whittle (New York: Routledge, 2006) provide an introduction to these themes. See especially Susan Stryker, "My Words to Victor Frankenstein Above the Village of Chamounix: Performing Transgender Rage" (244–256); Donna J. Haraway, "A Cyborg Manifesto: Science, Technology, and Socialist-Feminism in the Late Twentieth Century" (103–120). For a critical exploration of the social and legal consequences of phobic figuration of transsexuality as monstrous, see Abigail Lloyd, "Defining the Human: Are Transgender People Strangers to the Law?" *Berkeley Journal of Gender, Law and Justice* 20 (2005), 150–195. See also Myra Hird, "Animal Transsex" in *Queering the Non/Human*, ed. Noreen Giffney and Myra Hird (Ashgate 2008), 227–248; Eva Hayward, "More Lessons from a Starfish: Prefixial Flesh and Transspeciated Selves," *WSQ* 36: 3–4 (2008), 64–85.

4. Adam Kendon, *Gesture: Visible Action as Utterance* (Cambridge University Press, 2004); David McNeill, *Gesture and Thought* (University of Chicago Press, 2007); Carrie Noland, *Agency and Embodiment: Performing Gestures/Producing Culture* (Harvard University Press, 2009).

5. Current queer theoretical examinations of temporality emphasize the extent to which non-normativity can scramble time, undoing the linear sequentiality characteristic of straight temporality; but despite Halberstam's work on trans- subjects in *In a Queer Time and Place: Transgender Bodies, Subcultural Lives* (New York: New York University Press, 2005), this critical literature rarely treats gender in terms sensitive to or informed about trans- scholarship and experience. See, for instance, "Theorizing Queer

Temporalities: A Roundtable Discussion," *GLQ: A Journal of Lesbian and Gay Studies* 13: 2–3 (2007), 177–195; Elizabeth Freeman, *Time Binds: Queer Temporalities, Queer Histories* (Durham: Duke University Press, 2010).

6. "Medical Correspondence Regarding Sex-Reassignment, 1976–1990," especially correspondence with the Stanford Gender Dysphoria Clinic, Louis G. Sullivan Papers, 97–1, San Francisco GLBT Historical Society.

7. Susan Stryker, "Portrait of a Transfag Drag Hag as a Young Man: The Activist Career of Louis G. Sullivan," in *Reclaiming Gender: Transsexual Grammars at the Fin de Siècle*, ed. Kate More and Stephen Whittle (London: Cassells, 1999), 62–82.

8. "Guide to the Louis Graydon Sullivan Papers," 97–91, San Francisco GLBT Historical Society.

9. This subjective overlapping extends offstage, where Dorsey is a trailblazing transgender presence in dance and the founder of an important arts organization, Fresh Meat, which stages a festival of trans-arts each June. As a writer of texts and of dances, and as a trans- community organizer, Dorsey extends Sullivan's social roles into a historical and cultural moment Sullivan didn't live to see.

10. "Rememory" is the term Toni Morrison uses in her novel *Beloved* (New York: Alfred A Knopf, 1987) to capture the complexity of memories that exceed individual experience and consciousness. See Caroline Rody, "Toni Morrison's *Beloved*: History, 'Rememory' and a 'Clamor for a Kiss'," *American Literary History* 7: 1 (1995), 92–119.

11. See Judith Butler, *Undoing Gender* (New York: Routledge, 2004), especially Chapter One, "Beside Oneself: On the Limits of Sexual Autonomy."

12. The phrase "the desire for gender" has been floated by at least two previous theorists, Sheila Jeffreys and Robyn Weigman. For Jeffreys, the desire for gender is a symptom of collusion with the existing sexist binary system; she assumes that "gender" is a reflection of heteronormativity, such that without its asymmetrical polarizations "gender" would have no meaning. See "Heterosexuality and the Desire for Gender," in *Theorizing Heterosexuality*, ed. Diane Richardson (Buckingham, UK: Open University Press, 1996), 75–90. For Weigman, the desire for gender describes a feminist analytic: it "serves as a way to name how, as gender has been pursued as an object of study, it has proliferated, instead of settled, meaning, becoming one thing and then another as it has traveled across different domains where it has been wielded, differently, as both explanation and solution to the problems it has named." "The Desire for Gender," in *A Companion to LGBT Studies*, 231. My usage is (oddly enough) more aligned with Jeffreys' political argument than with Weigman's analytic, in that Jeffreys does think of the desire for gender in terms of the longing to take up a particular embodied place in the social order and thus making oneself available for particular kinds of relationships; further, she recognizes that gender has an erotic dimension and that much eroticism mobilizes gender. Susan Stryker would seem to concur, describing "gender categories (like man and woman)" as enabling "desire to take shape and find its aim." "Transgender Studies: Queer Theory's Evil Twin," *GLQ: A Journal of Lesbian and Gay Studies* 10:2 (2004), 212. In my usage, the desire for gender is not an alternative to sexual desire—so much of eroticism is bound up with gender, and vice versa, that any firm theoretical distinction (let alone opposition) between them will inevitably falter on the evidence of experience. But the desire for gender does not always overlap sexual desire in the sense that desire may prioritize gender itself as its aim. For instance, when Dorsey stages Sullivan's romance with his own futural dream of gay manhood, the relationship unfolding on stage is a materialization of Sullivan's longing to occupy masculinity, a longing that contains a fantasy of the social but that is nonetheless distinct from the social act of moving toward another person.

13. Juana María Rodríguez, writing about erotic gesture, has argued that no movement can be said to "belong" to a particular group ("Gesture and Utterance," 284). The point holds for ballet. Yet gestures also embody cultural traditions of which bodies will perform them and how—traditions that necessarily inflect their performance by other bodies.

14. Boyish effeminacy can also lead to a transfeminine future, of course. My formulation here is not meant to occlude this point but instead reflects the fact that in the context of Dorsey's dance, what's at stake is the way that femininity in youth can be a precursor to adult gay masculinity.

15. I am arguing here against Judith Halberstam's stance that "For queers, the separation between youth and adulthood quite simply does not hold . . . I want to return here to the notion of queer time, a different mode of temporality that might arise out of an immersion in . . . queer sex cultures." Judith Halberstam, "What's That Smell," *In a Queer Time and Place*, 174. Such a valorization of delay and arrest works to marginalize a trans subject like Sullivan, for whom access to queer sex cultures depended on leaving adolescence.

16. The linear temporality of this construction has a spatial counterpart that appears in the travel narrative of trans-becoming, which figures sex change as a journey. Aren Aizura offers an able and elegant

critique in "The Persistence of Transgender Travel Narratives," in *Transgender Migrations: The Bodies, Borders, and Politics of Transition*, ed. Trystan T. Cotten (New York: Routledge, 2011), 139–156.

17. See especially J. Jack Halberstam, *In A Queer Time and Place*; Heather Love, *Feeling Backward: Loss and the Politics of Queer History* (Cambridge, MA: Harvard University Press, 2005); Kathryn Bond Stockton, *The Queer Child: Growing Sideways in the Twentieth Century* (Durham: Duke University Press, 2009).

18. (2005), 57–58; 59. Also see Julian Carter, *The Heart of Whiteness: Normal Sexuality and Race in America* (Durham: Duke University Press, 2007) for a discussion of evolution's developmental narrative. Against developmental timelines and their political consequences, queer theorists have argued for the critical importance of putting on the brakes, turning backward or stepping sideways: evasive movements undertaken in part out of the conviction that resisting neoliberalism's claims for privatization as progress necessarily involves rejecting all developmental accounts or, for some, rejecting futurity as inherently complicit with reproductive investments that work to recreate a corrupt social order in its own image. See Lee Edelman, *No Future: Queer Theory and the Death Drive* (Durham, NC: Duke University Press, 2004); against Edelman, see José Esteban Muñoz, *Cruising Utopia: The Then and There of Queer Futurity* (New York University Press, 2009); Juana María Rodríguez, "Queer Sociality and Other Sexual Fantasies," *GLQ: A Journal of Lesbian and Gay Studies* 17. 2–3 (2011), 331–348.

42 Performance as Intravention

Ballroom Culture and the Politics of HIV/AIDS in Detroit

Marlon M. Bailey

Marlon M. Bailey has conducted research on HIV/AIDS prevention practices in queer African-American and Latino/a communities in Detroit, Michigan, using a methodology known as "performance ethnography." Bailey, who trained as an actor before entering academe, works to understand the communities he researches by participating in them. He has participated in the stylized, semi-public performance scene known as the "ballroom" or "house" sub-culture, made known more broadly by television shows like *Pose* and documentary films like *Paris Is Burning*. Houses are chosen-family kinship groups that compete against one another for fame and money. The ballroom culture Bailey describes has a six-part gender system: butch queens (people assigned male at birth who have sex with men), femme queens (trans women), butch queens up in drags (people assigned male at birth who live as men and sometimes cross-dress or do drag), butches (masculinity in a person assigned female at birth, whether identifying as a lesbian or trans man), women (people assigned female at birth who are feminine, regardless of sexual orientation), and men (heterosexual males who live as men). Participants in the ballroom subculture are either children (those who are less established in the scene) or parents (more seasoned members of the scene who act as house mothers and fathers.) In documenting how ballroom culture promotes HIV/AIDS prevention, Bailey demonstrates how communities often deemed "at risk" are also "communities of care" whose members look after one another in life-affirming ways. In this article, he argues that ballroom culture accomplishes a public health "intravention" rather than "intervention," enabling better health practices to emerge from within communities in empowering ways rather than as campaigns imposed on them or imported from the outside.

I see Ballroom as an artistic community that can connect with youth on issues of HIV/AIDS prevention, and the relationship between drugs and unsafe sex.
—Wolfgang Busch, Filmmaker, *How Do I Look*[1]

Despite the feelings of some in black communities that we have been shamed by the immoral behavior of a small subset of community members, those some would label the underclass, scholars must take up the charge to highlight and detail the agency of those on the outside, those who through their acts of nonconformity choose outside status, at least temporarily.
—Cathy J. Cohen, "Deviance as Resistance"[2]

The house structure is geared specifically toward the ball scene (particularly in Detroit). As far as its purpose, houses provide a source of family nurturing that often times a lot of kids don't get at home.
—Prada Escada from the House of Escada in Detroit

DOI: 10.4324/9781003206255-52

"What's going on in the USA? George Bush got us in a disarray. We got soldiers in Baghdad; we should be fighting AIDS instead," chanted Chicago Ballroom commentator Neiman Marcus Escada.[3] Usually spoken in front of a captive crowd of Black queer members of the Ballroom community during a ball, Escada's words serve as both an astute critique of U.S. imperialism in the name of "national security" and its unwillingness to take appropriately aggressive measures to curtail the spread of HIV/AIDS infection among Black gender and sexual marginals locally and abroad. Consisting of Black and Latina/o LGBTQ people, Ballroom culture is a minoritarian social sphere where performance, queer genders and sexualities, and kinship coalesce to create an alternative world. Thus, within and through performance at balls, Neiman Marcus Escada contributes to the creation of a counterdiscourse of HIV/AIDS. This is but one example of the important role that performance plays within Ballroom culture and how it is a part of a critical practice of survival in which many of the members of this community are engaged.

Ballroom culture, sometimes called "house ball culture," is a relatively clandestine community consisting of African American and (in locations such as New York, Miami, and Los Angeles) Latino/a GLBTQ people. Although Jenny Livingston's popular documentary film *Paris Is Burning* (1991) provides only a glimpse into the world of Ballroom culture, it was the first exposé to bring mainstream exposure to Ballroom practices in the late 1980s in New York City. Since its beginnings in Harlem more than fifty years ago, Ballroom culture has expanded rapidly to every major city in the United States, including Chicago, Atlanta, Baltimore, Charlotte, Cleveland, and Philadelphia. Notwithstanding the popular media coverage of Ballroom culture in recent years from its members appearing in Madonna's music video "Vogue" (1990) to the deaths of two of the community's most prominent icons, Pepper LaBejia (2003) and Willie Ninja (2006), to date this unique and generative culture has received scant scholarly attention.

Perhaps more importantly, out of the limited scholarship on Ballroom culture, the disproportionate impact of the HIV/AIDS epidemic on its members has barely been mentioned let alone examined. An increasing number of community-based organizations (CBOs) have received federal and/or state/local funding for their prevention programs that target Ballroom communities.[4] Yet the funding support for these prevention programs has yet to garner comprehensive studies that can help determine their overall effectiveness in reducing HIV/AIDS infection among Ballroom communities. As a result, little is known about the sociocultural challenges that members of this community face, and how social practices that are organic to Ballroom culture assist its members in withstanding the scourge of the disease and challenging the stigmatization associated with it.

In this performance ethnography[5] of Ballroom culture and HIV/AIDS in Detroit, Michigan, I delineate three aspects of Ballroom culture that are potential strategies for HIV/AIDS prevention that already exist within the community. First, I highlight three core dimensions of the Ballroom community: the gender and sexual identity system, the kinship structure, and the performances at the ball. Second, I argue that, generally, HIV/AIDS prevention programs that target Black communities have relied on research and intervention models that are based on individual sexual behavior and are devoid of cultural analyses. As a result, the organic practices and strategies of prevention that emerge from within so-called at-risk communities have been woefully neglected. For instance, even though HIV/AIDS infection is disproportionately high among Black men who have sex with men (MSM), a substantial portion of Black MSM remains HIV-negative. More research needs to be conducted to identify and support strategies deployed by Black MSM that protect them from infection. I argue that these strategies are forms of *intravention*. *Intravention* describes HIV/AIDS *prevention* activities that are conducted and sustained through practices and processes within at-risk communities themselves.[6]

Finally, I delineate three forms of *intravention* that are rooted in Black performance traditions and are integral to Ballroom culture: the creation of a social epistemology, social support, and prevention balls. These three aspects demonstrate that the Black queer members of the Ballroom scene are communities of support rather than simply communities of risk.[7] Looking to performance and other cultural work, in theory and in practice, will not only yield more socioculturally nuanced theories, methods, and models for HIV/AIDS prevention, but it can also help guide CBOs to forge more effective and sustained programs aimed at reducing HIV infection in Black communities in general and Black queer communities in particular.

Black Queer Performance and HIV/AIDS

I approach this examination of Ballroom culture using the methodology of performance, emphasizing research and community activism in HIV/AIDS prevention. My nine years of performance ethnographic research on Ballroom culture and HIV/AIDS consist of my participation in the very performances and cultural practices that I analyze.[8] Hence, as I describe later in this essay, I competed in balls as a member of both the Detroit and Los Angeles Chapters of the House of Prestige. Accordingly, my performance approach involved me being a member of the Ballroom community and working for two CBOs that collaborated with the Ballroom community.[9] I have also been engaged in extensive HIV/AIDS prevention research and activism among Black gay men and transgender women. Given my particular vantage point, this essay seeks to build a conceptual framework and a language between public health and (Black) cultural studies that can illuminate the central role that performance plays in the lives of Ballroom members as it relates to the epidemic.

By and large, the research on HIV/AIDS and culture has been produced in disparate domains of scholarship. Research on the disproportionate impact of HIV/AIDS on Black communities has been beset by a failure to employ truly interdisciplinary approaches to HIV/AIDS prevention studies to explicate the multifaceted nature of this epidemic, and to identify innovative strategies to combat it. More or less, HIV/AIDS research has been dominated by biomedicine, epidemiology, and social science.[10] Calls for radical interdisciplinarity and cultural criticism have been only marginally addressed at best and outright rejected at worst.[11] As a result, the topic of HIV/AIDS among Black queer communities falls through the cracks, so to speak, of several disparate intellectual conversations that fail to account for the multifarious social context in which Black queer people live.

As a site of cultural inquiry, African American studies has been markedly absent from discourses and sites of inquiry and advocacy in HIV/AIDS prevention studies. With the exception of Cathy J. Cohen's groundbreaking work, *The Boundaries of Blackness: AIDS and the Breakdown of Black Politics*,[12] African American studies has failed to theorize sufficiently or even address the social and cultural dimensions and implications of AIDS among Black communities, particularly since its epidemiological profile has become primarily Black and queer. Founded on the principle of creating theoretical and practical knowledges that can effect social change in the lives of everyday people, remarkably, African American studies has not translated its fundamental intellectual and political principles into a praxis to confront the AIDS crisis on the ground. Of note, in "Deviance as Resistance: a New Research Agenda for the Study of Black Politics," Cathy J. Cohen calls for a "paradigmatic shift" in African American studies that builds on Black queer studies and that attempts to reduce, if not eliminate, the superficial distance between researchers in the academy and the communities from which many of us hail and purport to study.[13] Indeed, any sociocultural site of inquiry or "studies" should both emerge from and be applicable to the experiences of everyday people.[14]

Recent trends in performance studies, however, have opened a space to examine not only the theatrical and quotidian dimensions of performance, but also the relationship between performance and social change as well. According to D. Soyini Madison and Judith Hamera, performance studies has been concerned with analyzing how, through performance and performativity, human beings fundamentally make culture, affect power, and reinvent their ways of being in the world, especially those who have limited or no access to state power.[15] Perhaps most germane to this study of the Ballroom community and HIV/AIDS is Dwight Conquergood's argument that performance is at once a radically multidisciplinary and embodied approach to examining an object of inquiry, and an active participation in performance as "tactics of *intervention*" in spaces of alterity and struggle.[16]

Theorizing HIV/AIDS through performance, or what Robin D. G. Kelley refers to as cultural labor,[17] necessarily shifts the emphasis in HIV/AIDS research away from individual sexual behavior that supposedly leads to infection to a focus on culture, as an arsenal of resiliency strategies upon which marginalized communities rely to survive the social crisis. For instance, in his analysis of the forms of cultural expression among Black urban youth on the street, Kelley suggests that Black urban youth undertake cultural labor within an increasingly politically powerless and economically deprived urban sphere.[18] Likewise, in my larger project on Ballroom culture, I frame its members' reconstitution of gender and sexual subjectivities, family/kinship, and community as a form of cultural labor as one way to withstand and creatively respond to the sociocultural and economic forms of exclusion that they experience. And, as I will elaborate, in the Ballroom community, these forms of cultural labor are inextricably linked to performance.

Performance-studies scholars such as José Muñoz, David Román, and Barbara Browning have made invaluable contributions to the study of HIV/AIDS, queer communities of color, and performance.[19] Since there is scant research on the Ballroom community and the epidemic, in general, and almost no literature on this topic within public health, this ethnographic study of Ballroom culture in Detroit is an appropriate basis from which to forge cross-disciplinary dialogues and research. For instance, one of the core concepts in HIV/AIDS prevention theory and practice is *intervention*. Within public health, intervention models are designed programmatically to facilitate behavioral change in order to reduce incidents and prevalence of HIV infection among targeted communities that have been identified as "high risk" or as "risk communities." In "AIDS: Keywords," Jan Zita Grover defines "risk groups" as an epidemiological concept that serves to isolate identifiable characteristics among certain communities that are predictive of where infection is most likely to occur so as to contain and prevent it.[20] In other words, within public health, the aim is to identify, isolate, and contain infection within a particular risk community so that the general population remains safe from infection.[21]

[. . .]

Conceptually, I call for a move from *intervention* to *intravention* in HIV/AIDS prevention studies to capture what so-called communities of risk do, based on their own knowledge and ingenuity, to contest, to reduce, and to withstand HIV in their communities. In my critique of the concept of intervention that is so prevalent in public-health and prevention studies, I draw from the work of performance theorist David Román, who suggests that cultural performance is, indeed, an act of intervention into the cultural politics of race, sexuality, and AIDS.[22] Such cultural politics pathologize Black sexuality and represent Black queer men as vectors of HIV infection. Thus, I join performance (as it is an arena in which minoritarian communities engage in social struggle) with Friedman and colleagues' notion of "communities of *intravention*."[23] In their study of HIV/AIDS prevalence among communities of injection drug users (IDU), they further argue, "Cognitive-behavioral theories that focus on the individual may not provide sufficient understanding for such efforts because they lack the concepts and methodologies needed to identify, understand or intervene in structures and processes that are at the cultural system, community network levels."[24]

My analysis here attends to the ways in which such communities of risk deploy strategies to address the correlative social factors that make people more vulnerable to the epidemic such as, but not limited to, social isolation, low self-worth, violence, and poverty. Thus, the concept of *intravention* is a key point of entry for performance into the analysis and development of targeted HIV/AIDS prevention programs within a Black queer cultural context.

In what follows I delineate the aspects of performance that are central to the Ballroom community that intravene in the HIV/AIDS epidemic. Instead of referring to the Ballroom community as a community of risk, I suggest that Ballroom is a community of support. In the Ballroom community, performance is the means through which members create a counterdiscourse (through a social epistemology), provide social support (kin labor) for its members, and produce prevention balls in order to reduce Black queer people's vulnerability to HIV/AIDS infection through competitive performance. Thus, Ballroom cultural practices are a form of intravention, deploying protective and prevention efforts that emerge from within the culture itself, efforts that the larger Black community and society as a whole fail to do. This community constitutes a site of refuge where its members have the opportunity to be nurtured, to experience pleasure, and to access a better quality of life in the face of the AIDS epidemic, particularly for those that are located at the very bottom of society. Clearly, enhancing the quality of life is a precondition to reducing the spread of HIV in the community.

Ballroom Culture: A Community of Social Support

Although Ballroom culture had existed for decades prior to Jennie Livingston's documentary *Paris Is Burning*, the film has become the primary prism through which this rich and long-standing cultural practice is recognized and understood. Even in some of the more recent glances of Ballroom to which the American public has been exposed, very little has been revealed about the day-to-day lives of the people involved and the multiple purposes that the social structures within the community serve.[25]

Two inextricable features sustain the community: flamboyant competitive ball rituals and houses, and the anchoring family-like structures that produce these rituals of performance. Ballroom subjectivities and familial roles are based on an egalitarian gender/sexual identity system that offers more gender and sexual identities from which to choose than available to members in the "outside" world (see Table 1).[26]

Because gender performance is central to self-identification and can imply a whole range of sexual identities in Ballroom culture, the system reflects how the members define themselves largely based on the categories that they walk/perform. All members of the Ballroom community identify as either one of the six categories in the gender/sexual identity system. If/when one "walks a ball," that participant competes in the competitive categories that coincide with their gender/sexual identity within the Ballroom community. For instance, a femme queen can only "walk/perform" in categories that are listed under that heading on the ball flyer. The intensely competitive performances at the ball events create a space of celebration, affirmation, critique, and reconstitution as well as in the everyday lives of its Black queer members.

It is worth noting that there are no balls without houses and there are no houses without balls. And in the kinship system of Ballroom culture, houses are led by "mothers" (butch queens, femme queens, and women) and "fathers" (butch queens and butches), who, regardless of age, sexual orientation, and social status, provide a labor of care and love with/for numerous Black queer people who have been rejected by their blood families, religious institutions, and society at large. Houses, for instance, are one of the core features of the Ballroom community, and houses serve as social, and sometimes literal, homes for its members.[27]

Table 1 Gender/Sexual Identity System

Ballroom Culture: Three Sexes
1. Woman (one born with female sex characteristics)
2. Man (one born with male sex characteristics)
3. Intersex (one born with both male and female sex characteristics or with sex characteristics that are indeterminate)

Six-Part Gender/Sexual Identity System
1. Butch queens (biologically born male who identify as gay or bisexual and are and can be masculine, hypermasculine, or effeminate)
2. Femme queens (male to female transgender people or at various stages of gender reassignment—that is, hormonal and/or surgical processes)
3. Butch queens up in drags (gay males that perform drag but do not take hormones and who do not live as women)
4. Butches (female to male transgender people or at various stages of gender reassignment or masculine lesbian or a female appearing as male regardless of sexual orientation)
5. Women (biologically born females who are gay or straight identified or queer)
6. Men (biologically born males who live as men and are straight identified)

House Parents
1. Mothers: Butch queens, femme queens, and women
2. Fathers: Butch queens, butches, and men

Thus the ball, combined with the social relations within the houses outside of it are mutually constitutive and, taken together, make up the world of Ballroom culture.

[. . .]

Ballroom Culture and HIV/AIDS

I begin this portion of my examination by situating Ballroom culture and HIV/AIDS within the context of Detroit, Michigan.[28] Given the disproportionate impact of HIV/AIDS on Black communities across the country, and its particular devastation of Black people in Detroit, and given that the Ballroom community is embedded in Black communities in the city, HIV/AIDS and its impact on Ballroom is an instructive case study. Invariably, the interlocking oppressions of race, class, gender, and sexuality shape Black queer people's experiences as they exacerbate the suffering of marginalized groups at the hands of the virus.[29]

In Michigan, although African Americans comprise of only 14 percent of the total population, according to HIV epidemiological data for 2008, new infection rates for African Americans were 59 percent; this was compared to a 35-percent infection rate for whites. By race and gender, HIV infection rates were 41 percent compared to 29 percent for white men. And it is worth noting that African American women make up 73 percent of all HIV cases among women in Michigan.[30] HIV infection rates among MSM were 45 percent compared to 13 percent for heterosexual transmission.[31] Based on this epidemiological data in Michigan, we can infer that Black MSM have increasing disproportionate rates of new HIV infections (that is, there are higher HIV infection rates among Blacks, among Black men, and among Black MSM, and among men, the primary route of HIV transmission is male-to-male sexual intercourse).[32]

Detroit carries the majority of HIV prevalence in Michigan.[33] Known as both the "chocolate city" and the "motor city," Detroit has the most distinct racial and class demographics of any large U.S. city. According to the 2000 U.S. Census, Detroit is the largest city with a Black majority population in the United States. Out of approximately 951,270 residents, 83 percent identified themselves as Black or African American. In socioeconomic terms,

Detroit has one of the poorest populations in the country; between 26.8 and 33.4 percent of the city's residents live in poverty.[34] Like many other cities with large Black populations, Detroit is one of the places hardest hit by the disease.[35]

HIV/AIDS workers in Detroit, some of whom are HIV-positive, have a unique vantage point when considering the intersections of gender, sexuality, and HIV/AIDS. The prevention workers that I interviewed suggested that the dominant discourse on HIV/AIDS, one that pathologizes and sutures the disease to homosexuality and that disallows a candid dialogue about sexuality and HIV risk reduction, hampers their ability to reduce infections rates in the city. Compounded by the disturbing socioeconomic conditions, most HIV/AIDS cases among men in Detroit are Black MSM. Black people infected with HIV/AIDS in large cities like Detroit do not have access to AIDS prevention and treatment resources that are equal to their white counterparts.[36] Thus, Black MSM who are infected with or at high risk for HIV/AIDS infection experience a simultaneity of oppression, structured not only by and through race, class, gender, and sexuality, but also through HIV/AIDS.

For example, when I asked Tino Prestige, a butch queen and caseworker at the Horizons Project, an HIV/AIDS prevention and services agency in Detroit, why he thinks the HIV/AIDS epidemic is so severe among African American men in Detroit, he said, "There's a lack of information in the school system, *no* discussion of sexuality, and no discussion of how to be sexually responsible even if you are heterosexual. People have a whole lot of ignorance about LGBTQ issues, and people still think that it's wrong because of their religious views."

Similarly, Noir Prestige, also a butch queen, described how once, while he worked for the Men of Color Motivational Group (MOC), a now-defunct HIV/AIDS prevention agency in Detroit, he delivered a presentation on HIV/AIDS, a school administrator insisted that he not encourage homosexuality, as if HIV/AIDS were "naturally" linked to homosexuality and as if talking about homosexuality would lead to young people adopting it. That is why Noir reiterated the need to "de-gay" or "de-homosexualize" HIV/AIDS so that all people will take the problem seriously. A public discussion of HIV/AIDS, especially among young people, requires this delinking of HIV/AIDS from homosexuality in order to ease homophobic fears held in society. At the same time, prevention workers are faced with a conundrum of sorts because when homosexuality is not discussed Black MSM and/or gay men are rendered invisible, while still viewed as the primary vectors of HIV/AIDS infection.

Both Tino and Noir attest to the fact that explicit and implicit homophobia resulting from familial and cultural expectations to adhere to hegemonic gender and sexual norms directly influence the information that Black queer people receive about HIV/AIDS. As Lester K. Spence argues, in general, the larger Black community's knowledge about HIV/AIDS; Black people's perception of their own risk of contracting the virus; and their preferences concerning HIV/AIDS policy are all intrinsically linked to their views on homosexuality.[37] Ultimately, the treatment and policing of sexuality that Black queer people endure from the outside create deep-seated internal struggles that influence the way they self-identify and interact with others, both gays and heterosexual.

[. . .]

Therefore, Ballroom culture is compelled to be proactive and multifaceted in its struggle against the disease and the Othering discourses that accompany it. As David Román aptly points out, AIDS cannot be separated from the discourses that construct and in fact "sustain it."[38] Discourse regarding AIDS informs the specific priorities (defining those whose lives are worth saving) that public-health institutions devise regarding prevention. Recalcitrant racism, sexism, homophobia/heterosexism, poverty, and other forms of disenfranchisement are inextricably linked to scurrilous representations of AIDS as a Black gay disease.

In Michigan, the scant HIV/AIDS reduction strategies consist of the distribution of brochures, condoms, and other safe-sex materials, discussion groups, and safe-sex training,[39] but they ignore the crucial role that cultural values play in shaping the stigmatization associated with race, class, gender, sexuality, and AIDS. Directly related to this issue, few CBOs create programs that move beyond simply reducing individual "risk behaviors," by addressing the social conditions that contribute to them.

[. . .]

Ballroom Community Practices as HIV/AIDS Intravention

What do Black queer members *do* about such conditions? How does the cultural work of creating an alternative minoritarian sphere help to refract feelings of worthlessness caused by stigmatization and oppression? How does Ballroom provide a space to forge alternatives realities for its members? Part of what is at stake in the Ballroom community here is a struggle for alternative community representation and community preservation in midst of a health and social crisis.[40] In what follows, I delineate three forms of intravention that are organic aspects of Ballroom culture or what Friedman and colleagues refer to as collective risk-reduction reinforcement.[41] Members of the Ballroom community create a counterdiscourse of HIV/AIDS that recasts its members as people with lives worth saving, not merely risk groups; the structure of the community provides social support; and the community produces prevention balls that are based on Ballroom community values and practices in an attempt to destigmatize HIV/AIDS so that its members can be more receptive to messages of risk reduction.

Social Epistemology of Ballroom Culture

First, I highlight the ways in which Ballroom members construct a social epistemology as a critical aspect of the overall work of creating an alternative social sphere. This alternative social sphere is a crucial source of value for Ballroom members. I emphasize key characteristics of Ballroom culture/spaces that are strategies for addressing HIV/AIDS that reflect its members' desire for recuperative forms of self and collective representations.[42] I contend that Ballroom practices and their potentialities unveil the difference between *prevention* approaches and the on-the-ground practices of cultural *intravention*.

[. . .]

All of my informants agree that doing HIV/AIDS prevention work within the Ballroom scene is difficult; however, some believe that it is a cultural space of hope. One such possibility is the notion of self-renewal, a way of reconstituting the self within Ballroom to contend with the negative representations in the outside world. For instance, Ballroom is what Diva D from the House of Bvlgari calls a "fictitious existence." When I asked him whether "low self-worth" was a motivating factor for Black queer people to join the Ballroom scene, he responded, "Yes, it gives them a brand-new identity; it gives them a brand-new slate. If your family don't care about you because you are gay and what not or if you can't get a job, the Ballroom scene helps you start anew. It creates a brand-new identity that you can feel comfortable with."

The social knowledge of Ballroom links the balls to the community-fashioned kinship system that both sustains the community and facilitates HIV/AIDS prevention. Therefore, Ballroom social knowledge enables effective HIV/AIDS prevention that is based on the values and norms established by its community members as opposed to those imposed on it from the outside.

Kinship and Social Support

As the house mother of the Detroit chapter of the House of Prestige and former HIV/AIDS prevention worker at the time of the interview, Duchess suggests that Ballroom is built on social relations that redefine prevention work. He stated further, "The structure of the [Ballroom] community already allows for familial prevention work, you know, just in the fact that someone can say to you, 'Now you know you need to wear a condom' and it be from someone that you have built that trust factor with. People in the community do prevention work all of the time."

Within these houses, members consult with their house parents and their siblings on issues that, either by choice or necessity, they do not discuss with their biological kin. House mothers and fathers, in particular, provide daily parental guidance for Ballroom kids on issues such as intimate/romantic relationships, sex, gender and sexual identities, health, hormonal therapy, and body presentation, just to name a few matters.

[. . .]

Black Queer Performance and HIV/AIDS Prevention Balls

Despite the inability of some public-health departments to devise and sustain effective HIV/AIDS prevention strategies for so-called high-risk communities, some Ballroom houses have joined forces with a few CBOs to create "prevention houses" and "prevention balls." As I have noted, Ballroom houses, in general, are spaces of social support that often reinforce messages of HIV/AIDS prevention either directly or indirectly. But, prevention houses usually have formal funding from and/or programmatic ties with CBOs, and they engage in HIV/AIDS prevention activities and coordinate balls based on HIV/AIDS prevention themes.

Again, since there are no houses without balls and there are no balls without houses, part of the important discursive work of prevention houses occurs at prevention balls. On one hand, the importance placed on image and status in Ballroom makes HIV/AIDS prevention work difficult because members distance themselves from the topic of HIV/AIDS for fear that it will tarnish them. But on the other hand, competitive performance, image, and status are used to disseminate and promote messages about HIV risk reduction among Ballroom members. Out of the numerous balls that I attended and/or participated in, most of them were packed with hundreds of Black queer people from all over the country. As Francisco Roque from Gay Men's Health Crisis said, "The Ballroom community is a captive 'at-risk' population, and modeling behavior is built in the community." Albeit imperfect, it is a necessary strategy to use competition and image within a Ballroom cultural context to disseminate information and simultaneously reduce stigma.

As a hallmark of Ballroom culture, competition is another means through which image and status are formed and repaired. Since individual members and houses can gain recognition and status only by "snatching trophies,"[43] competition is an integral aspect of the social world of Ballroom that offers possibilities for effective HIV/AIDS prevention. Former Father of the House of Infiniti and the Executive Director of Empowerment Detroit, an HIV prevention agency targeting Black gay youth, Jonathon Davis confirmed this when he said, "In terms of the Ballroom community in Detroit, if it ain't got nothing to do with a trophy, these girls don't care." And when I asked Pootaman, a twenty-year-old member of the House of Ninja and an HIV/AIDS prevention worker at MOC at the time of the interview, why he became interested in walking balls, he said, "I enjoy the competition, the feeling of sitting someone down to prove a point, that I could take home a trophy." Father Infiniti and Pootaman speak to the centrality of the trophy, the accoutrements that come along with it and how both represent the attainment of value and affirmation that Ballroom members are usually otherwise denied in the outside world.

Last, in order to illustrate more vividly how prevention balls work, I describe my experience as a performance participant and witness. In March 2005, I competed in the annual

Love is the Message Ball in Los Angeles.[44] As a member of the Los Angeles chapter of the House of Prestige at the time, I walked, along with Pokka, the father, in the "schoolboy realness versus executive realness" category for the mini grand prize. The description of the category on the flyer read:

> School Boy Realness—Let's see if U were paying attention in Sex Ed. Bring us School Boy realness w/ a safe sex production. Props a must and you will be graded on your project and knowledge.
>
> VS.
>
> Executive—U have been promoted to CEO of a condom company of your choice. U must have a prop and be prepared to sell your product to the board.

Pokka planned our performance and was determined to win the trophy and the $100.00 cash prize. Since Pokka and I walk executive realness, I dressed the part and played the role of a CEO, and Pokka was the president of the board of directors of the Lifetime Condoms Corporation. He had spent time and money to prepare everything we needed to mount this miniproduction.

When Kodak Kandinsky, the commentator for the evening, announced our category, members from various houses came out as schoolboy realness wearing clothes with several condoms attached to them. Because I was in the waiting area of the hall, I could not see them perform their mini production. When it was our turn, Pokka walked out ahead of me, dressed in an all-black suit and carrying his laptop computer case. As he approached the judges' table, he read a statement about the crisis of HIV/AIDS in the Black community, stressing that condom use is an effective strategy in the fight against the spread of the disease. "Now, I bring to you Professah Prestige, our new CEO, to make a brief statement," said Pokka. I came strutting down the runway in a navy blue suit carrying my laptop computer in a black leather computer bag in one hand and a large black portfolio case full of billboards in the other. When I got to the judges table, I took the microphone and said, "My name is Professah Prestige, the new CEO of Lifetime Condoms. We have new durable condoms that do not reduce sensation. I hope that you all will give them a try. Be safe and use condoms." After my statement, the commentator asked the judges to score me. "Are they real? Do you see it? Judges score him (all of the judges flashed their cards with "10" written on them). Ok, tens across the board. Prestiges step to the side. Next contestants please," said Kodak. "Thank God, I did not get chopped," I thought.

After other competitors were eliminated, "chopped," there were only five competitors left, Pokka and I from the House of Prestige and three members from another house who walked schoolboy realness. Then, someone from the Minority AIDS Project posed the following question to all of us: "What is a dental dam?" Each of us was told to whisper the answer in Kodak's ear. When he came to me, I explained that a dental dam is used for oral sex, and it provides a barrier of protection between the mouth and the anus or the vagina. Then, Kodak announced that only two of us said the correct answer, a schoolboy realness kid from the other house and me. Apparently, Pokka gave him the wrong answer. I felt kind of bad because Pokka had done most of the preparation for our production.

Finally, the judges had to choose who looked more real between the realness kid and me. "Who is realer?" said Kodak. When Kodak got to the final two out of the seven judges, one of them pointed at me and said, "He look like a real executive." At the end, I won the category. I was shocked and thrilled at the same time. They gave me a trophy and the $100.00 prize. I kept the trophy and gave the money to the house mother to put in our house fund. I had won the category for the House of Prestige. Most importantly, within the competitive spirit at the balls, members of the Ballroom community were exposed to knowledge about safe sex without individuals being singled out and stigmatized. Clearly, performance, kinship, and social knowledge function as cultural practices that allow Ballroom community members to intravene radically in the AIDS crisis, since the practices are derived from within the community itself.

Conclusion

Ballroom members perform the labor of caring for and the valuing of lives that are integral to building and sustaining a community in the midst of crisis. Ballroom practices are important alternatives that attend to the multifarious challenges that HIV/AIDS poses, especially the attendant public and scientific discourses that render Black queer people dysfunctional and dangerous, and further stigmatized them as vectors of disease. These values sustain the community and constitute a critical component to any form of intervention not just aimed at reducing the spread of HIV/AIDS, but also attempting to cultivate the necessary systems and structures (within Ballroom) that redress the violence done to Black queers. This is violence not only at the hands of the HIV/AIDS epidemic, but also the Othering discourses that coproduce it.

The focus here is the Ballroom community's creation of "communities" and of new and counter modes of self-representation and self-identification that offer possibilities for members of the minoritarian communities to alter the conditions for themselves. And those of us who are ensconced in notions of "at-risk" communities know that HIV/AIDS—the disease itself—does not discriminate. It has no boundaries. On the contrary, it is the public-health and sociopolitical responses to it, on a local, national, and global scale, that do. This fact marks the difference between *prevention* (from the outside) from *intravention* and the dialectic between the two that are necessary to ameliorate the epidemic.

I do not romanticize performance by suggesting that it can totally overhaul or transform the social and material conditions in which Ballroom members live. Some members fall through the cracks, and many die. But some survive, and they do so with the assistance of fellow Ballroom members. Ballroom culture demonstrates how performance can add value and meaning to the lives of those rendered valueless and meaningless. But, as cultural critic and homo-hip hop artist Tim'm West aptly argues, since there are few safe spaces for Black queers, especially those suffering from HIV, many of us must claim all spaces as salvageable in whichever ways they support our breathing.[45]

From: Marlon M. Bailey, "Performance as Intravention: Ballroom Culture and the Politics of HIV/AIDS in Detroit" in *A Critical Journal of Black Politics, Culture, and Society* 11: 3, pp. 253–274. Copyright 2009, Taylor & Francis. All rights reserved. Republished by permission of the copyright holder, Taylor & Francis (Taylor & Francis Ltd, www.tandfonline. com).

Notes

1. I interviewed Wolfgang Busch on November 30, 2003 in New York City. His film, *How Do I Look* (2006), is the most recent documentary on Ballroom culture in NYC. During the interview, Wolfgang said that he wants the proceeds from the film to be dedicated to HIV/AIDS prevention. For more information and updates on his work go to www.howdoilooknyc.org
2. Cathy Cohen, "Deviance as Resistance: A New Research Agenda for the Study of Black Politics," *Du Bois Review* 1, no. (2004): 27–45, 27.
3. This chant by Neiman Marcus Escada is taken from a CD of house music mixes called *Bamabounce*.

4. Currently, the Gay Men's Health Crisis (GMHC) has the longest standing HIV/AIDS prevention program that focuses on the Ballroom community. The House of Latex of the GMHC has held its annual Latex Ball (an HIV/AIDS prevention ball) for eighteen years. The Latex Ball is by far the most popular ball in the country, usually drawing between 2,500 and 3,000 audience members/participants. Ironically, the CDC does not recognize this program as an intervention, and it is not federally funded.

5. Performance or performative ethnography is a method of data collection that requires the researcher to actively participate in the very performances and cultural practices that he or she is analyzing. Simply put, for the performance ethnographer, performance is the object and the method of study, as well as the theoretical framework through which the data are analyzed. More discussion on performance ethnography can be found in D. Soyini Madison, *Critical Ethnography: Method, Ethics, and Performance* (Thousand Oaks, CA: Sage Publications, 2005); Norman K. Denzin, *Performance Ethnography: Critical Pedagogy and the Politics of Culture* (Thousand Oaks, CA: Sage Publications, 2003); E. Patrick Johnson, *Appropriating Blackness: Performance and the Politics of Authenticity* (Durham, NC: Duke University Press, 2003).

6. Samuel Friedman, Melissa Bolyard, Carey Maslow, Pedro Mateu-Gelabert, Alan Neaigus, and Milagros Sandoval, "Urging Others to Be Healthy: 'Intravention' by Injection Drug Users as a Community Prevention Goal," *AIDS Education and Prevention* 16, no. 3 (2004): 250–263, at 251.

7. Ibid.

8. E. Patrick Johnson, *Sweet Tea: Black Gay Men of the South* (Chapel Hill: University of North Carolina Press, 2008), 8.

9. In 2003, I worked for Men of Color Motivational Group Inc. (MOC) in Detroit, Michigan. MOC had a CDC-funded program that emphasized HIV/AIDS prevention among the Ballroom community. The program lost its funding, and the organization eventually closed in the midst of controversy. For more information, see Brent Dorian Carpenter, "Sexual Harassment Allegations Rock Men of Color: Funding Could Be at Risk," *Between the Line* (June 2003), 12–18.

10. It is worth noting that most qualitative studies that are conducted on HIV/AIDS within public health are not ethnographic. In my experience working with and among other HIV/AIDS researchers, I am usually the only ethnographer involved in any given research project.

11. Carlos Ulises Decena, "Surviving AIDS in an Uneven World: Latina/o Studies for a Brown Epidemic," in *A Companion to Latina/o Studies*, ed. Juan Flores and Renato Rosaldo, 276–296 (Malden, MA: Blackwell, 2007), 278.

12. Cathy Cohen, *The Boundaries of Blackness: AIDS and the Breakdown of Black Politics* (Chicago: University of Chicago Press, 1999).

13. Cathy J. Cohen, "Deviance as Resistance: A New Research Agenda for the Study of Black Politics," *Du Bois Review* 1, no. 1 (2004): 27–45, 28.

14. Ki Namaste, "The Everyday Bisexual as Problematic: Research Methods Beyond Monosexism," in *Inside the Academy and Out: Lesbian/Gay/Queer Studies and Social Action*, ed. Janice L. Ristock and Catherine G. Taylor, 110–135 (Toronto: University of Toronto Press, 1998), 113.

15. D. Soyini Madison and Judith Hamera, "Performance Studies at the Intersections," in *The Sage Handbook of Performance Studies*, ed. D. Soyini Madison and Judith Hamera (Thousand Oaks, CA: Sage Publications, 2006), xii. For more elaboration on theories of performance and cultural formations and/or deployments of performance as resistance, see José Muñoz, *Disidentifications: Queers of Color and the Performance of Politics* (Minneapolis: University of Minnesota Press, 1999).

16. Dwight Conquergood, "Performance Studies: Interventions and Radical Research," *The Drama Review* 46, no. 2 (Summer 2002): 145–156, at 145.

17. Robin D. G. Kelley, *Yo' Mama's Disfunktional! Fighting the Culture Wars in Urban America* (Boston: Beacon Press, 1997), 45.

18. Robin D. G. Kelley, *Yo' Mama's Disfunktional! Fighting the Culture Wars in Urban America* (Boston: Beacon Press, 1997), 45.

19. David Román, *Acts of Intervention: Performance, Gay Culture, and AIDS* (Bloomington: Indiana University Press, 1998); Barbara Browning, *Infectious Rhythm: Metaphors of Contagion and the Spread of African Culture* (New York: Routledge, 1998).

20. Jan Zita Grover, "AIDS: Keywords," in *AIDS: Cultural Analysis, Cultural Activism*, ed. Douglas Crimp, 17–30 (Cambridge, MA: MIT Press, 1998), 27.

21. Cindy Patton, *Fatal Advice: How Safe-Sex Education Went Wrong* (Durham, NC: Duke University Press, 1996), 23.

22. David Román, *Acts of Intervention: Performance, Gay Culture, and AIDS* (Bloomington: Indiana University Press, 1998), 155.

23. Friedman et al., "Urging Others to Be Healthy," 250.

24. Ibid., 260.

25. Karen McCarthy Brown, "Mimesis in the Face of Fear: Femme Queens, Butch Queens, and Gender Play in the Houses of Greater Newark," in *Passing: Identity and Interpretation in Sexuality, Race, and Religion*, ed. María Carla Sánchez and Linda Schlossberg (New York: New York University Press, 2001), 208–227, at 208.

26. What I call the "gender/sexual identity system" is typically called the "gender system" within Ballroom culture. My outline of the six subjectivities within the system is drawn from my ethnographic data that include my attendance/participation in balls, my analysis of numerous ball flyers, and interviews that I conducted with members from all over the country over a nine-year period. Despite a few discrepancies among different sectors of the community, the general components of the system are standard throughout the Ballroom scene. The gender/sexual identity system is separate but inextricably linked to the competitive categories that appear on ball flyers. At balls, competitive performance categories abound, but the gender and sexual identity system serves as the basis upon which the competitive categories are created. For an example and an analysis of a ball flyer/program, see David Valentine's *Imagining Transgender: An Ethnography of a Category* (Durham, NC: Duke University Press, 2007), 78–84.

27. Emily Arnold and Marlon M. Bailey, "Constructing Home and Family: How the Ballroom Community Supports African American GLBTQ Youth in the Face of HIV/AIDS," *Journal of Gay and Lesbian Social Services: Issues in Practice, Policy, & Research* (Summer 2009): 1–34, at 6.

28. While I acknowledge the participation of Latina/o queer people in Ballroom culture in some locations, most Ballroom members are Black queer people. Since my primary site of examination is Detroit, where the Ballroom scene is almost exclusively Black, all of my interlocutors and the communities to whom I refer are Black queer people.

29. Brett C. Stockdill, *Activism Against AIDS: At the Intersections of Sexuality, Race, Gender, and Class* (Boulder, Colo.: Lynne Rienner, 2003), 4.

30. All statistics cited here are from the Michigan Department of Community Health (2008), www.michigan.gov/mdch.

31. In a five-city study of HIV infection among Black MSM conducted by the CDC in 2005, it was estimated that 46 percent of Black MSM are infected with HIV/AIDS, and 64 percent of those who tested positive were unaware of their status. "HIV Prevalence, Unrecognized Infection, and HIV Testing Among Men Who Have Sex with Men—Five U.S. Cities, June 2004—April 2005," *Morbidity and Mortality Weekly Report* 54: 597–601.

32. One of the critical problems with the reporting of HIV epidemiological data by local health departments is that the data is not often disaggregated by race, gender, and "sexual risk categories." As a result, most of the data collected on the local level do not provide specific numbers on Black MSM.

33. Michigan Department of Community Health (2008), https://www.michigan.gov/documents/mdch/2008_Forward_10.01.08_251297_7.pdf.

34. U.S. Census (2000), www.census.gov/main/www/cen2000.html.

35. Cathy J. Cohen, "Contested Membership: Black Gay Identities and the Politics of AIDS," in *Queer Theory/Sociology*, ed. Steven Seidman (Cambridge, MA: Blackwell, 1996), 372.

36. Roy Cain, "Gay Identity Politics in Community-Based AIDS Organizations," in *Inside the Academy and Out: Lesbian/Gay/Queer Studies and Social Action*, ed. Janice L. Ristock and Catherine G. Taylor, 110–135 (Toronto: University of Toronto Press, 1998), 200. More elaboration on this can be found in Cathy Cohen, *The Boundaries of Blackness: AIDS and the Breakdown of Black Politics* (Chicago: University of Chicago Press, 1999); Steven Seidman, *Queer Theory/Sociology*, ed. Steven Seidman (Cambridge, MA: Blackwell, 1996); Brett C. Stockdill, *Activism Against AIDS: At the Intersections of Sexuality, Race, Gender, and Class* (Boulder, CO: Lynne Rienner, 2003).

37. Lester K. Spence, "Uncovering Black Attitudes About Homosexuality and HIV/AIDS," paper presented at the 2005 National Conference of Black Political Scientists, Alexandria, Va., 1.

38. David Román, *Acts of Intervention: Performance, Gay Culture, and AIDS* (Bloomington: Indiana University Press, 1998), xxiii.

39. Nancy E. Stoller, *Lessons from the Damned: Queers, Whores, and Junkies Respond to AIDS* (New York: Routledge, 1998), 2.

40. Stuart Hall, "What Is This 'Black' in Black Popular Culture?" in *Black Popular Culture*, ed. Gina Dent, 1–21 (Seattle: Bay Press, 1992), at 24.

41. Samuel Friedman, Melissa Bolyard, Carey Maslow, Pedro Mateu-Gelabert, Alan Neaigus, and Milagros Sandoval, "Urging Others to Be Healthy: 'Intravention' by Injection Drug Users as a Community Prevention Goal," *AIDS Education and Prevention* 16, no. 3 (2004): 251.

42. Kim D. Butler, "Defining Diaspora, Refining a Discourse," *Diaspora* 10, no. 2 (2001): 189–218, at 192.

43. In Ballroom lingo, "snatching a trophy" means winning the category and being awarded a trophy and/or a cash prize. This is also called "slay and snatch: slaying the competitors and snatching the trophy."
44. This annual ball is cosponsored by the House of Rodeo and the Minority AIDS Project in Los Angeles.
45. Tim'm West, "Keepin' It Real: Disidentification and Its Discontents," in *Black Cultural Traffic: Crossroads in Global Performance and Popular Culture*, ed. Harry J. Elam Jr. and Kennell Jackson, 162–184 (Ann Arbor: University of Michigan Press, 2005), 163.

43 The Labor of Werqing It

The Performance and Protest Strategies of Sir Lady Java

Treva Ellison

Treva Ellison offers a framework for understanding the complexities of Black femme performance under racial capitalism in their essay, "The Labor of Werqing It: The Performance and Protest Strategies of Sir Lady Java," first published in the 2017 anthology *Trap Door: Trans Cultural Production and the Politics of Visibility*. Ellison redeploys the term "werq," drawn from the slang of ballroom culture, to name and celebrate the excessive performance of Black femininity by iconic transfeminine nightclub entertainer Sir Lady Java. Ellison understands Java's *werq* as an exercise of power, rooted in resistance and survival within racial capitalism. When Java relocated from New Orleans to Los Angeles, she found success and celebrity on stage there in the 1960s, only to be targeted by the LAPD for violating its nebulous and unevenly enforced "Rule No. 9," which forbade cross-dressing in entertainment venues. Java protested and garnered favorable attention in the gay community press; she and her supporters picketed the clubs that would no longer hire her, and, with the ACLU's backing, she took her employment discrimination suit all the way to the California State Supreme Court (where the case was dismissed on a technicality). But rather than concentrating on questions of laws, rights, and recognition, Ellison highlights the ways in which the praxis of Java's embodied performance of femme Blackness itself reworked—and *werqed!*—the conditions of labor under racial capitalism. The labor of Java's werqing it, Ellison suggests, helped forge new worlds for Black trans women and gender-nonconforming people in a culture that consigned them to social death.

"Werq Queen!" "Yaaaas!" "Slay!" These terms, which have become mainstream in US popular culture, circulate through Black queer and trans culture and social life to affirm and express excitement over a performance and praxis of existence that exceed the commonsense of normative categories of social being like gender, race, class, and sexuality. In the house and ball scene, the declarative "Werq!" asserts the sartorial, the expressive, the performed, and the embodied over the biologic, the state record, the birth certificate, the checkbox; it affirms the potential and creativity in being surplus and the potential of reworking and repurposing the signs, symbols, and accoutrements of Western modernity. Werqing it is a relational gesture of world-making at the spatial scale of both the body and the community that aligns sender and receiver in a momentary network of fleshly recognition. That is to say, werqing it and having that werq seen, felt, or heard is a power-generating praxis, a force displacement in and over time, that arises from Black queer and Black trans culture, performance, and politics and through the re/production of Black trans social life. It reminds us that under racial capitalism, all Black life is trans, transient, transductive, and transformative.

DOI: 10.4324/9781003206255-53

To werq is to exercise power through the position of being rendered excessive to the project of the human and its dis/organizing social categories: race, gender, sexuality, and class. Werqing it deforms, denatures, and reforms the very categories in which werqers can find no stable home.

As an act of making power, werqing it has become attractive; it's trending.[1] We are in a moment in which everyone wants to "werq werq werq werq werq," from Young Thug to Jaden Smith to Beyonce, each of whom has adopted either sartorial strategies, terminology, or other performative elements arising from Black queer and trans culture and presented them to more mainstream audiences. A 2014 issue of *Time* magazine that features Laverne Cox on the cover termed this current moment a "transgender tipping point,"[2] a historically significant time of representational saturation of transgender people, identity, and struggles in popular culture, media, and public discourse and debate. The visual economy of the so-called transgender tipping point is driven by Blackness and Black femme embodiment. Black women have become emblematic of and instrumental to the tipping point narrative: they are the representational figures of transgender issues and politics and the martyrs of political struggles for civil rights for trans people—a hyper-present absence. The facts that trans is trending and that Black trans performance, embodiment, and politics are desirable are tempered by the images of spectacular violence against transgender people, particularly Black trans women. Black trans women like Cox, CeCe McDonald, and Janet Mock have named and resisted the exceptionalism/death binary that pervades popular culture narratives of transgender rights and transgender vulnerability, insisting on visibility and representation as limited and partial strategies for transgender people of color that do not challenge structures and systems of violence and oppression.

This essay thinks through the labor of werqing it—the practices, performances, and protests that constitute Blackness, queerness, and transness as relational and para-identitarian approaches to existence, knowledge, and power. To do this, I focus on the protest and performance strategies of Sir Lady Java, a Los Angeles-based Black femme performer who rose to national and international acclaim in the 1960s. As Java ascended to local and national prominence, the Los Angeles Police Department (LAPD) began to track and monitor her performances: they sent plainclothes officers to observe her performances; they attempted to strip search her to confirm her "real" gender; they sent a police battalion to intimidate her and other Black femme performers; and, in October 1967, they even attempted to get her off the stage by filing an injunction against one of the bars that regularly employed her. Using archival documents and excerpts from an April 2015 conversation I had with Sir Lady Java and C. Jerome Woods, founder and director of the Black LGBT Project,[3] this essay outlines Java's strategies in the context of her struggle against LAPD harassment, the burgeoning gay liberation movement, and the rise of Black middle-class power.

Java's struggle against the LAPD elucidates the labor of werqing it: both the labor politics of being a Black gender nonconforming woman and entertainment industry worker in postwar Los Angeles and the liminal labor of insisting on and inventing an undercommons for Black and queer social life through and under the oppressive forces of racial capitalism. Her protest and performance strategies evince a nuanced, nimble analysis of the position of Black femme embodiment in the postwar Los Angeles political economy. Java's fight as a Black femme performer and her fight against the LAPD emphasize that under racial capitalism, visibility is a flexible capacity whose motive potential is derived from the conjoining of subjection and subjectification.[4] Gender studies scholar Grace Kyungwon Hong argues that the political and intellectual formations of women of color mark the violent transition between US capital's national phase and its global phase after World War II. Hong argues that before World War II attempts to resolve contradictions between the abstract labor needs of racial capital and the coherence of the nation-state hinged on abstraction. The universal citizen–subject of US democracy is defined by a capacity for ownership of self and of objects, but racial capital operates precisely by dispossessing racialized subjects of land, property, and the capacity of self-actualization and self-possession.[5] After World War II, Hong explains, attempts to resolve contradictions between global racial capital and an increasingly delocalized nation–state started to hinge not on the abstraction of difference but on the fetishization of difference, which she calls "flexibility."[6] This formulation of flexibility riffs on the concept of flexible accumulation, which marks a transition from a Fordist model of production characterized by the incorporation of labor into highly formalized production processes, to a post-Fordist model characterized by the integration of informal production processes alongside formal processes. [. . .] As a logic that underwrites the articulation of subjectivity, flexibility is, in part, a response to the long arc of anti-imperialist and Black freedom struggles in the US that threw the abstract citizen–subject of the US racial state into crisis. Flexibility is itself an abstracting logic because it repositions the racial state as the purveyor and guarantor of racial, class, gender, and sexual citizenship and demands a constant forgetting of the exclusions and erasures that imbue race, class, gender, and sexuality with the appearance of stability and coherence.

[. . .]

Flexibility, as a logic of the post-Keynesian racial state, overwrites oppositional social formations with propriety and attempts to position self-possession and self-actualization as the end goals of social movements. It is a mechanism of subjectification via strategic disavowal. Under the logic of flexibility, sex workers, people who are regular drug users, people with mental illnesses, people with disabilities, and people who in general cannot perform a hegemonic ideal of professionalism or rationality become re-thingified. As an expression and accretion of racial progress or class power, they become the objects of recovery, renewal, and remediation, often by people who claim an identitarian commonality with them. To follow Hong's argument, in racial capitalism's flexible phase, political and cultural visibility and representation, which were never not commodifiable to begin with, find new and multiple pathways for commodification and instrumentalization. Java's struggle calls our attention to those rendered surplus even to oppositional social movements, and reminds us that Black women's political and intellectual formations are capacious terrains that facilitate the coherence of race, gender, class, and sexuality as social and political categories. This, then, is what is encapsulated in the phrase "the labor of werqing it": Black femme embodiment and labor act as the fulcrums of racial capital's flexible capacity in the articulation of politics and culture. That is to say, Black femme embodiment is one point of passage through which subjection and subjectification reach a dynamic (and often deadly) equilibrium via mechanisms of power and social sedimentation, including visibility, recognition, legibility, and representation.

In the hegemonic visual and political culture of the United States, Black femme embodiment appears as that which flits in and out of sight and sound, that which can be simultaneously erased and affirmed, enlivened with vitality and agency or rendered void in order to tell someone else's story. Understanding Java's struggle in relation to the burgeoning gay liberation movement in Los Angeles and the context of the rise of the Black middle class throughout the 1960s underscores the limits of visibility as a tool of political power, as both of these groups instrumentalized Black femme embodiment and labor to build political power but failed to disrupt the relationships and logics that undergird Black femme precarity.

I am using the terms "Black femme" and "Black femme embodiment" to describe Java because, while she never labeled herself or identified her gender during the course of our interview, she lived her life as a woman. I am also using "Black femme" in a similar vein to critical studies theorist Kara Keeling to think about how Black trans and gender nonconforming femme labor, politics, and cultural production pose challenges to social and identity categories that were themselves constructed as a response to racism, sexism, and homophobia.[7] Keeling writes that the Black femme as a figure "exists on the edge line . . . between the visible and the invisible, the thought and the unthought. . . . [I]t could be said that the Black femme haunts current attempts to make critical sense of the world along lines delineated according to race, gender, and/or sexuality. Because she often is invisible (but nonetheless present), when she becomes visible, her appearance stops us, offers us time in which we can work to perceive something different, or differently."[8] Sir Lady Java's protest and performance strategies ask us to think different and differently by putting pressure on the normative categories and epistemologies of progress that both scholars and activists use to build power-terms and ideas such as transgender, the transgender tipping point, transgender history, and the Black community. It is my humble hope that the telling of this story offers time and space to think different and differently about the terms and narratives through which we envision and articulate political struggle, LGBT history, transgender studies, and Black studies.

Sir Lady Java and Rule No. 9

Sir Lady Java was born in New Orleans, Louisiana, in 1940, the eldest of six children. Java climbed through the ranks of the entertainment industry working as a go-go dancer at a club in Hemet, California, doing stand-up comedy and female impersonation (the term used at the time). Java has described her stage act as combining the humor of Pearl Bailey, the facial beauty of Lena Horne, and the sartorial style and presence of Josephine Baker.[9] The fact that Java lived her everyday life as a Black woman but earned her living as a female impersona-tor and performer made "passing" an incoherent framework for her. She instead leveraged passing as a source of livelihood while using her performances to poke fun at and question the coherence of gender. During her performances, Java would often come on stage dressed in a full suit, portraying a debonair gentleman, and take the audience through her gender transition over the course of her stage act, metamorphosing first into a femme in the style of Horne or Baker and ending her shows in a sequined bikini. Java's stage act challenged view-ers' trust in gender as a visually verifiable trait. While many drag performers of the era wore elaborate gowns, suits, and costumes, Sir Lady Java performed primarily in bikinis, which allowed her not only to stand out, but also to invoke the spectacle of her body as a challenge to the audience's faith in the rigidity of gender: "I came in a bikini. That's what made me famous. [Knocks on the table.] Even at the drag shows, when they had a ball, the girls wore such outlandish gowns that I couldn't compete with. So I'd come in chiffon and floral prints and a bikini on where they could see it. You know, and that would win the ball. All the time."[10] Reviews of Java's performances made continual reference to how spectacular and unbelievable her appearance was,[11] and Java has recounted that employers and co-performers (notably Richard Pryor) voiced disbelief and overzealous interest upon learning that she was not a cisgender woman. Java's ability to earn a living as an openly gender nonconforming performer troubles today's tipping point narrative and asks us to think about public interest in and discourse around gender and sexuality as iterative and connected to conflicts or crises of economic, social, and political capital. For example, at the turn of the twentieth century, gender impersonation was considered family entertainment, and the conservative capitalist elite of Los Angeles—the Merchants and Manufacturers Association—used to sponsor a huge gender-bending party in Los Angeles called All Fools' Night, which was celebrated as a successful tourist event until the growing Protestant merchant class decried its immorality and had the party outlawed in 1898.[12]

As a Creole woman, Java also troubled racial boundaries and emphasized throughout our interview that she "chose" to be Black, as she could have passed as Latina in the racial visual economy of Los Angeles at the time.[13] Java's ability to slip between identities was always tempered by the possibility of harassment and violence from employers or obsessed audience members.[14] Although she emphasized that she did not "walk in fear," Java recounted experiencing and witnessing multiple incidents of anti-Black racial profiling and anti-Black gendered violence throughout her young adult years.[15] Java actively built community with Black trans and gender nonconforming femmes, whom she refers to as her sisters, and hosted an annual Halloween ball that flexed her personal notoriety and connections to create a performative and labor undercommons for other Black femme performers to hone their craft.[16]

As Java gained local and national prominence, the LAPD began to target her by sending plainclothes and uniformed officers to monitor her performances and to warn bars against employing her. This harassment reached a fever pitch in October 1967, when the Los Angeles Police Commission (LAPC) filed an injunction against the Redd Foxx, a Black-owned bar that employed Java, demanding that the bar cancel all of her upcoming performances or risk losing its business license. Before filing the injunction, an LAPC investigator went to the Redd Foxx and attempted to strip search Java to confirm her "true" gender, but Java refused to comply. The LAPC claimed that by employing Java, the Redd Foxx was in violation of one of the commission's rules governing public entertainment venues, Rule No. 9, which read: "No entertainment shall be conducted in which any performer impersonates by means of costume or dress a person of the opposite sex, except by special permit issued by the Board of Police Commissioners."[17] Java responded by staging a picket outside of the Redd Foxx on October 21, 1967, and later, with the help of the American Civil Liberties Union (ACLU), filed a lawsuit against the LAPD.[18] The LAPD's harassment of Java and other femme of color queens and werqers occurred in a climate in which gender nonconforming people could be arrested for "masquerading," or dressing as the "opposite" gender. Java's struggle against the LAPD and the LAPC is a powerful story in the unkempt and unruly archive of the labor of werqing it.

LGBT studies scholars have been quick to fold Java's struggle against Rule No. 9 into genealogies of male-to-female transgender activism, gay history, and struggles over queer spaces without acknowledging that her protest was, at its core, a response to anti-Black racism.[19] In news articles and interviews at the time, Java framed her struggle against the LAPD and Rule No. 9 as a workplace discrimination issue: "It's discrimination, allowing some people this privilege and not others. . . . It's got to stop somewhere, and it won't unless somebody comes forward and takes a stand. I guess that's me."[20] But, reflecting on the incident in 2015, Java framed her fight with the LAPD as a struggle against anti-Black and gendered racial profiling:

> We didn't know of any establishment that was white that they [the LAPD] were stopping [from employing impersonators], but they were definitely targeting me, because I was queen of the Black ones and they feel that they had more trouble out of the Black ones. You see, we didn't have places to go to, places to eat, and they would not allow us in the places and it was against the law to wear women's clothing, you know that? They could arrest you if you walk down the street in women's clothing [if you were being read as biologically male], in male clothing [if you were being read as a biologically female].[21]

Java felt that the LAPD chose to suspend the Redd Foxx's business license rather than the licenses of the numerous other venues where she performed across the city because the bar's owner, Redd Foxx, stood out in the area as one of the few Black club owners on the

Westside. LAPC records corroborate this: the investigator's report about Java's scheduled performances at the Redd Foxx notes that other venues had been "warned about employing this individual"; warned, but not threatened with the loss of livelihood.[22] Also, Java was granted a permit from the Police Commissioner to perform for a charity benefit at the Coconut Grove, a club with a mostly white patronage, weeks after the incident at the Redd Foxx.[23] Java recalled that the performance at the Coconut Grove was the first time she had performed in front of a majority white audience.[24] She links the LAPD's effort to make female impersonators unemployable to larger issues of employment for gender nonconforming people and the criminalization of sex work, noting:

> You have to understand that we didn't have jobs, because they wouldn't hire us and those that would dress, the pioneers . . . it hurts to talk about it. . . . We could not. . . . But they wouldn't let us work, so we had to turn tricks to work. And, baby, that was so-called "our job" and we'd get ready to work at night, and baby, we was come out! Police or no police, we was coming out, snapping our wrists, flirting, walking down the street I told them [the American Civil Liberties Union] that we have no place to work and the only place we can work is at night in the club. We had no right to work. [When] we come to work, we had to come as men [because it was illegal to dress as the "opposite" gender on the street] and then transform ourselves into women when we get on stage. Well, that was hard to do both. I won the fight for us to appear on stage, but I didn't win the fight for us to walk the streets.[25]

When Java asked the ACLU of Los Angeles to sue the LAPC after the commission tried to pull Redd Foxx's business license, she ran into difficulty. While Rule No. 9 targeted drag performers, it made the bar owner the *subject* of the law. Thus, Java's civil suit required a bar owner willing to be the named plaintiff. Her case could not be heard in a court of law with Java as the sole plaintiff and was eventually rejected by the courts on these grounds. So, while the LAPD could track Java from venue to venue under the guise of Rule No. 9, she had little recourse to challenge the LAPD. Unable to legally challenge Rule No. 9, Java effectively subverted it by finding a way to adhere technically to its requirements: she tested the threshold of its stipulation that performers must wear at least three items of "properly gendered attire" by incorporating a wristwatch, a bowtie, and men's socks into her act. This became a strategy, according to Java, that other performers mimicked: "They [other female impersonators] say: We're able to work, and we're all going [to] work the next day, and we're going to put on the three male articles [of clothing], and they did the same thing I did: socks and the wristwatch and the bowtie if they wore bikinis; if they wore gowns, they wore little bowties, some of them were jeweled."[26]

The transgender tipping point narrative suggests that public interest in transgender people, transgender representation, and transgender power is progressive and has reached an apotheosis in our current time. Even critical counter-narratives of the tipping point stage their arguments by remarking that despite advances in visibility and representation, violence against trans people has reached a climax today.[27] Besides being hard to verify, both of these narratives also miss the way that the visibility and containment of gender and sexual nonconformity are cyclical and related to crises in capital. By framing her challenge to Rule No. 9 and LAPD harassment as a labor issue informed by anti-Black racism, and by connecting unemployment for gender nonconforming people to the criminalization of sex work, Sir Lady Java calls our attention to the linked histories of containing gender nonconformity and criminalizing sex work in Los Angeles and how these histories intersect with the racialization of space and ruptures in capital.

The Labor of Werqing It: Criminalizing Black Femme Embodiment in Los Angeles

Public interest in and discourse around gender and sexual nonconformity in Los Angeles have been iterative and related to dramatic, qualitative changes in the organization of economic, political, and social life. For example, in 1942, when faced with the threat of the disintegration of the nuclear family and traditional gender roles because World War II production needs had shuffled the gendered division of labor, then-mayor Fletcher Bowron petitioned the city council to make it illegal for women employees to wear pants in city hall.[28] And slightly earlier than that, in the late 1930s, policing gender and sexual deviance became a way to resolve a political fissure between middle-class reformers and organized labor on one side and the mayor and the LAPD on the other. Middle-class reformers and organized labor pointed to the unchecked spread of sex work, gambling, and the immorality of night life as evidence that the LAPD and mayor were under the control of commercial vice organizations. However, the racialization of space served as a primary organizing trope for the criminalization of gender and sexual deviance, as Bowron's predecessor, Mayor Frank Shaw, and the LAPD responded to reformers' critiques by punishing the most vulnerable people in the social hierarchy, reinforcing race- and class-based spatial containment strategies such as redlining, racially restrictive covenants, and vigilante violence. The LAPD responded by increasing the number of arrests of Black and Mexican women for sex work and by establishing a Sex Crimes Bureau in 1937 to fingerprint, study, and contain so-called sexual criminals.[29] Earlier, between 1932 and 1933, the LAPD had responded to the increasing popularity of impersonation by raiding the pansy clubs where impersonators performed.[30] Raiding drag venues and criminalizing women of color were convenient ways to temporarily resolve a political crisis without actually disrupting the more powerful commercialized vice conglomerates that had already paid off the LAPD and city hall. Sir Lady Java's insistence on her struggle as an issue of gendered racial discrimination is an insistence that we not forget that the racialization of urban space is a structuring phenomenon for queer and trans criminality. It's not surprising, then, that after winning office on an anti-vice platform, Bowron would try to ban women from wearing pants in an effort to stave off gender inversion, which he saw as a consequence of wartime labor needs.

Throughout the late 1960s, LGBT activists in Los Angeles increasingly used visibility as a strategy to build political power. Activists held touch-ins and kiss-ins at public parks and bars, led public consciousness-raising circles in the new Gay Community Services Center (now the Los Angeles Gay and Lesbian Center), held political forums for local politicians to meet with the "gay electorate," and organized marches and protests against LAPD harassment. However, as a political strategy, LGBT visibility became increasingly anchored to the neighborhoods of West Hollywood and Hollywood. Even when the acts of police harassment and deadly police violence that cohered LGBT as an oppressed cluster targeted racialized LGBT people outside these two neighborhoods, gay liberation groups in Los Angeles still mostly failed to understand how the racialization of space and the criminalization of cross-dressing and sex work underpinned the criminalization of sexual deviance. Gay Liberation Front Los Angeles, for example, had internal fissures develop both around including trans people in the group-especially trans women-and around taking up issues that impacted people who were not cisgender men.[31] At the same time, Gay Liberation Front and other groups struggled to welcome and retain trans and gender nonconforming femmes, lesbians, and people of color.

While gay liberation organizations in Los Angeles failed to see the criminalization of sex work and trans and gender nonconforming people as structuring components of queer criminality, Black middle-class activists fought to curb sex work in certain sections of Los

Angeles throughout the 1960s and '70s. In October 1960, a group of Black businessmen led by Cecil B. Murrell formed the Council of Organizations Against Vice (COAV), which sought to eradicate prostitution in the West Adams neighborhood of Los Angeles.[32] Murrell, one of the cofounders of the famed Golden State Mutual Life Insurance Company, the first Black-owned insurance company established west of the Mississippi, led an effort to increase punitive fines for sex workers, not to penalize those soliciting sex work. Murrell worked with the LAPD and city council to increase the fine for sex workers from $50 to $100, and he lobbied municipal judges to sentence sex workers for the maximum possible 180 days instead of the average ten-day sentence in 1960.[33] Even the *Los Angeles Sentinel* criticized Murrell's and COAV's approach as shortsighted, arguing that police resources should not be used to entrap Black women and should instead be directed toward arresting white male motorists, who residents complained would come through the neighborhood and proposition and harass any Black woman walking down the street.[34] Although COAV noted that sex work was pervasive throughout Los Angeles and that the Central and Newton districts had the "worst" prostitution, they focused their energy on Westside, whose Black communities have historically been more middle class. COAV saw eradicating sex work as a part of a larger self-help politics of racial equality and progress. A review of LAPC records throughout the 1960s shows similar instances of Black residents petitioning the police commission for LAPD intervention to curb prostitution, burglaries, and other proclaimed nuisances in South Central and West Adams.[35]

Leveraging Black middle-class political power as a way to curb prostitution was based on the idea that Black people have the same right to safety, protection, and a say in policing priorities as middle-class whites. COAV's anti-sex worker activism rerouted a real communal concern about racist sexual harassment in West Adams into a script of gender and sexual conformity as a method of building class power. This framing of equality and identity-based class power rendered Black femme sex workers outside of the terrain of Black middle-class neighborhood politics and disregarded the extent to which gender and sexual deviance function as the staging grounds for Black fungibility. Gay and lesbian activists, on the other hand, disavowed the centrality of race and racism in the production of sexuality-based criminalization. Understanding Java's struggle as both surplus to the gay liberation movement and excessive to Black middle-class activism and Black middle-class visions of Black neighborhoods and communities, we can see how flexibility—as a cultural logic underwriting subjectivity in racial capital's global phase—manifests itself in social and political formations organized around race, class, gender, and sexuality. For Los Angeles-based gay and lesbian institutions like Gay Liberation Front and the Gay Community Services Center, the local expansion of voluntary sector governance initiatives under the Bradley mayoral administration and the Nixon presidency created opportunities for activists to fund survival programs, which they modeled on those of the Black Panther Party. The professional requirements of these funding initiatives, however, privileged the skills and expertise of middle class and educated gays and lesbians; thus, activists increasingly positioned sex workers, drug users, raucous partiers, people with mental illnesses, gays and lesbians of color, and working-class trans people as excessive to the project of gay Los Angeles. For the Black middle-class activists in COAV, civil rights-era gains created an opportunity for Black middle-class activists to cohere Blackness around middle-class performances of gender and sexual conformity, property ownership, and racial uplift.

Java's praxis of producing social life-creating an undercommons for Black queer labor, performance, and desire and her hesitance around transgender as an identity offer us so much to consider. First, Java's story issues a warning against investing in transgender as the penultimate horizon or new frontier of social difference. Her struggle has been rendered through the language of trans activism, MTF activism, and LGBT history. What does it mean to recover this story as an episode in the production of transgender history, when, from Java's perspective, so much of her understanding of herself as a woman-the kinds of labor she performed as a lover, a daughter, and a friend-and her framing of her struggle with the LAPD are both anchored in a strident critique of anti-Black racism? Considering Java's life story on her own terms delivers a word of caution to the burgeoning field of transgender studies: transgender studies becomes a scene of the subjection and instrumentalization of Blackness when scholars and proponents of the field use the lives and stories of Black people to make transgender cohere as a category of analysis and a field of inquiry without a full acknowledgment of how the racialization of space dis/organizes the articulation and production of queer and trans culture and politics.

[. . .]

Java's life and praxis also offer an alternative approach to thinking about Blackness and theories of Blackness and of Black ontology that posit social death as an axiom or universal law of Black existence-namely, Blackness as a relation of ontological death. Such theorizations dismiss the ways that Black femmes, in particular, and Black people, in general, create and exercise power through the production of social life and social underworlds that are always already denaturing and deforming the "world as we know it." The over-representation of social death as an axiom of Blackness also relies on a dismissal of gender and sexuality as one of the staging grounds of Black fungibility. The idea that Blackness is related to death relies on the reality of natal alienation for enslaved Black women as a defining characteristic of "Blackness as social death," but then twists that fact to render anti-Blackness as the primary structuring mode of the human project, relative to gender and sexuality, which, under this framework, become strategic modes of oppression. This logic de-particularizes and abstracts gendered anti-Black violence to do the work of rendering anti-Blackness as a universal or axiomatic theory of Blackness. For example, Black communal violence against gender and sexually nonconforming Black people, as outlined by Black feminist scholars like Beth Richie and Cathy Cohen, becomes reduced to a case of "borrowed institutionality," or white man mimesis,[36] instead of opening a space and a time to critically reflect on how racial capitalist logics reproduce themselves within oppositional political-intellectual formations precisely through the frameworks of gender and sexual conformity.[37] What does it mean to relegate Blackness to the position of social death, when, as Java's life and times suggest, Blackness itself is uncertain, as it is both a medium and relation of social death and social life? Black is; Black ain't; Black is in flux between is and ain't. This tension is what is summoned in naming the labor of werqing it: the power and potential in creating underworlds and undercommons for Black social life and its collision with logics and strategies of subjectification that rely on Black femme subjection, abuse, and premature death. Naming the labor of werqing it incites and stokes tension and uncertainty because flexibility, as a cultural and epistemological logic of racial capitalism, does try to position Blackness as fungible. At the same time, flexibility is also a Black femme method of cultivating the undercommons, the unkempt, and the unrulable—the very potentialities that drive social and political transformation and threaten the coherence of civil society and the world as we know it.

From: Tourmaline, Eric A. Stanley, and Johanna Burton, eds., *Trap Door*, pp. 1–22, © 2017 Massachusetts Institute of Technology, by permission of The MIT Press. Treva Ellison, "The Labor of Werqing It: The Performance and Protest Strategies of Sir Lady Java".

Notes

1. See Manuel Arturo Abreu, "Transtrender: A Meditation on Gender as a Racial Construct," *Newhive*, April 18, 2016, https://newhive.com/b/transtrender-a-meditation-on-gender-as-a-racial-construct/. Abreu raises similar questions about the instrumentalization of transness, writing: "Trans is trending,

which may or may not help, but most likely hurts, actually existing trans people. A concrete institutional definition of trans is still 'under construction,' itself having undergone various 'queerings.' But both above and under the carnival of signifiers and the circulation of theoretical concepts, trans people, especially of color, still inordinately suffer and die. Our voices are still unheard and ignored, even as aspects of the condition become generalized and hypervisible. The world cheers on as we agonize. Statistics about trans people of color get subsumed into the general trans struggle to intensify empathy. What, precisely, is this necropolitics of conceptualization whereby trans pain, particularly the pain of Black trans people, continues to transmute into metaphors, generalities, theoretical developments, queerings, coping mechanisms for people who think they were 'born into the wrong race,' and much more, but basic human rights and even expectancy of life itself still elude many in the global trans community? When did queerness become a post-critical theory clickbait machine?"

2. Katy Steinmetz, "The Transgender Tipping Point: America's Next Civil Rights Frontier," *Time*, May 29, 2014, http://time.com/135480/transgender-tipping-point.

3. The Black LGBT Project, founded and directed by C. Jerome Woods, is the largest and, perhaps, only archive in existence dedicated to preserving the history of the Black LGBT people of Los Angeles and their partners. Woods, a retired Los Angeles Unified School District teacher, started the archive from materials he had collected over the years and creates local exhibitions of archival materials. The Black LGBT Project consists of over one thousand photos, over one hundred books, thousands of paper documents, and several hundred pieces of ephemera relating to Black LGBT life in the United States, with the bulk of the materials focused on Black LGBT life in Los Angeles.

4. Several recent books in ethnic studies and gender and sexuality studies theorize how processes of material and ideological subjection animate and capacitate processes of producing and rendering subjects in the context of US racial capitalism. Jodi Melamed terms this contradiction "represent-and-destroy," or the incorporation of the management of difference into the aegis of the post-civil rights US state, alongside the creative destruction of racial capitalism evinced in the buildup of the prison industrial complex at state, federal, and global scales beginning in the late 1960s; see Jodi Melamed, *Represent and Destroy: Rationalizing Violence in the New Racial Capitalism* (Minneapolis: University of Minnesota Press, 2011). Chandan Reddy names this contradiction "freedom-with-violence" to underscore the productive tension between the expansion of sexual citizenship alongside the expansion of racialized carceral violence; see Chandan Reddy, *Freedom with Violence: Race, Sexuality, and the US State* (Durham, NC: Duke University Press, 2011). Lisa Marie Cacho uses the term "unprotectability" to identify the gap between the socio-spatial multiplicity that criminality indexes and the particular embodiments that become reified through the production of identity-based political subjects. Cacho argues that when one is rendered unprotectable, the interpretive violence of the law attempts to make one politically, economically, and socially illegible. Additionally, she argues that these modes of representation and subjectification (the law, law enforcement, and political representation) *work* and are reconstituted precisely through the very endurance of unprotectability as a mode of existence, the disciplinary double to political subjecthood; see Lisa Marie Cacho, *Social Death: Racialized Rightlessness and the Criminalization of the Unprotected* (New York: New York University Press, 2012), 5. These scholars illustrate, in different ways, how the fungibility of criminality marks both the potential and limits of identity-based political formations.

5. Grace Kyungwon Hong, *The Ruptures of American Capital: Women of Color Feminism and the Culture of Immigrant Labor* (Minneapolis: University of Minnesota Press, 2006), 2, 9.

6. Ibid., 110. Other scholars of race and racial capitalism might disagree with Hong's periodization of capital into two major phases in the twentieth century: nation-state and global. Certainly, we can find many examples of global racial capital before World War II. Katherine McKittrick, Denise Ferreira da Silva, and Sylvia Wynter, for example, all chronicle the formulation of the onto-epistemological creation of "Man" (white, cisgender, able-bodied, propertied) as the corollary project to the world-organizing strategies and projects of racial capitalism: enclosure, extraction, colonialism, and transatlantic slavery. What is helpful to me about Hong's formulation is that she identifies flexibility as a logic that organizes culture, politics, and subjectivity and manifests alongside the shift in modes of capital accumulation from more formal, production-oriented modes to more multi-varied ones. Today, even work once thought of as informal, like domestic work, cleaning, personal assistance, sex work, food delivery, and even gifting, can be integrated into formal, corporate modes of accumulation.

Companies such as Google, Airbnb, Facebook, Instacart, Tumblr, and PayPal fold all kinds informal labor into a formal corporate chain of production. Hong asks us to consider how flexibility as a mode of accumulation for racial capital manifests in our cultural, social, and political formations.

7. Kara Keeling, *The Witch's Flight: The Cinematic, the Black Femme, and the Image of Common Sense* (Durham, NC: Duke University Press, 2007), 2.

8. Ibid.

9. Sir Lady Java, interview by C. Jerome Woods and Treva Ellison (unpublished transcript), April 19, 2015, 1.

10. Sir Lady Java, interview by C. Jerome Woods and Treva Ellison (unpublished transcript), April 19, 2015, 12.

11. See, for example, Gertrude Gibson, "Lady Java Unbelievable," Candid Comments, *Los Angeles Sentinel*, January 13, 1966, B6; Gertrude Gibson, "World's Greatest: Farewell L.A. Appearance of 'Lady Java' Monday," Candid Comments, *Los Angeles Sentinel*, May 11, 1967, B7; Gertrude Gibson, "Lady Java Gets a Double," Candid Comments, *Los Angeles Sentinel*, December 29, 1966, BS; Gertrude Gibson, "Lady Java Fantastic," Candid Comments, *Los Angeles Sentinel*, February 13, 1975, B7, which reads: "Sir Lady Java . . . did it again, packing them in at Larry Hearns' Memory Lane displaying the 'topless' look. One spectator got so carried away she spilled a whole table of drinks on the floor. The unbelievable 'Female Impersonator' has them standing on their feet to watch the great show. First show at 9 p.m."

12. Lillian Faderman and Stuart Timmons, *Gay L.A.: A History of Sexual Outlaws, Power Politics, and Lipstick Lesbians* (New York: Basic Books, 2006), 15–17.

13. Sir Lady Java, interview by Woods and Ellison, 2.

14. Sir Lady Java, interview by Woods and Ellison, 17.

15. Sir Lady Java, interview by Woods and Ellison, 2–5, 17.

16. Archival data suggests the annual ball happened at least several times. A 1974 promotion for the ball in the *Los Angeles Sentinel* reads: "Unbelievable . . . but it's true. THE LADIES ARE MEN and represent some of the prettiest 'female impersonators' in the business. Monday night at Memory Lane Club, you will see a bevy of other performers on hand for the Pre-Halloween Ball with Sir Lady Java crowning the beautiful queen." The promo article shows pictures of Java and two Black femme performers: Tawny Tann and Sahji. See "Pre-Halloween Ball Monday Night," *Los Angeles Sentinel*, October 24, 1974, BS.

17. "Board Rules Governing Cafe Entertainment," Minutes of the Board of Police Commissioners, City of Los Angeles, June 24, 1964, 452, available at the Los Angeles City Archives, Erwin C. Piper Technical Center.

18. James Gilliam, "Pride: Sir Lady Java and the ACLU/SC," *ACLU of Southern California*, December 17, 2010, www.aclusocal.org/pride-sir-lady-java-and-the-aclusc/.

19. The GLQ Archive: Members of the Gay and Lesbian Historical Society of Northern California, "MTF Activism in the Tenderloin and Beyond, 1966–1975," *GLQ: A Journal of Lesbian and Gay Studies* 4, no. 2 (1998): 365, doi:10.1215/10642684-4-2-349; Monica Roberts, "Sir Lady Java: Trans Civil Rights Warrior," blog post, *TransGriot*, December 9, 2010, http://transgriot.blogspot.com/2010/12/sir-lady-java-trans-civil-rights.html.

20. "Sir Lady Java Fights Fuzz-Y Rule Nine," *Advocate* 1, no. 3 (November 1967): 2.

21. Sir Lady Java, interview by Woods and Ellison, 4.

22. "Los Angeles Police Commission Investigative Report: Redd Foxx Enterprises," Meeting Minutes of the Los Angeles Police Commission, October 3, 1967, 3, available at the Los Angeles City Archives, Erwin C. Piper Technical Center.

23. "Sir Lady Java Fights Fuzz-Y Rule Nine," 2.

24. Sir Lady Java, interview by Woods and Ellison, 1.

25. Sir Lady Java, interview by Woods and Ellison, 10.

26. Sir Lady Java, interview by Woods and Ellison, 3.

27. In the past year, several articles have suggested that violence against transgender people is at its highest point in US history. See, for example, Cleis Abeni, "Two Black Trans Women Killed in 48 Hours," *Advocate*, February 23, 2016, www.advocate.com/transgender/2016/2/23/two-black-trans-women-killed-48-hours; Zach Stafford, "Transgender Homicide Rate Hits Historic High in US, Says New Report," *Guardian*, November 13, 2015, www.theguardian.com/us-news/2015/nov/13/transgender-homicide—victims-us-has-hit-historic-high.

28. Lillian Faderman and Stuart Timmons, *Gay L.A.: A History of Sexual Outlaws, Power Politics, and Lipstick Lesbians* (New York: Basic Books, 2006), 93–94. This is doubly interesting knowing that Fletcher Bowron was elected mayor in a recall election aimed at ousting mayor Frank Shaw, who was accused of corruption and of having mob ties. The coalition of organized labor and progressive middle-class reformers who pushed for Bowron pointed directly at vice as a sign of the decaying morality in Los Angeles.

29. Treva Ellison, "Towards a Politics of Perfect Disorder: Carceral Geographies, Queer Criminality, and Other Ways to Be" (PhD dissertation, University of Southern California, 2015), 73; Kaitlin Therese

Boyd, "The Criminalization of Black Angeleno Women: Institutionalized Racism and Sexism in Los Angeles" (PhD dissertation, University of California, Los Angeles, 2012).

30. Daniel Hurewitz, *Bohemian Los Angeles and the Making of Modern Politics* (Berkeley: University of California Press, 2007), 120–121.

31. The GLQ Archive, "MTF Activism in the Tenderloin and Beyond" summarizes the struggles that Angela Douglas, a trans woman who is an active member of Gay Liberation Front Los Angeles, has had with the patriarchy within the organization. Gay Community Alliance, another Los Angeles-based gay group that organized against homophobic policing in the early 1970s, defined its work as explicitly for gay men only and made a specific point to exclude transgender and transsexual women in its printed materials inviting people to join the organization; see "An Invitation to Participate in Activities of the Gay Community Alliance," May 10, 1971, Gay Community Alliance Collection, Coll. 2011–045, ONE National Gay and Lesbian Archives at the USC Libraries, Los Angeles.

32. See "Westside Businessmen Organize Fight Against Dope, Prostitution: Vice Council Formed," *Los Angeles Sentinel*, November 3, 1960, Al; "Prostitution Resurgence Noted in Southwest L.A.: Vice Crusader Calls for Help, Gives Partial Blame to Municipal Court Judges," *Los Angeles Sentinel*, November 19, 1961, ClO; "Vice Meeting Tonight at Golden State Los Angeles Sentinel," *Los Angeles Sentinel*, December 1, 1960, Al; Cecil B. Murrell, "Anti-Vice Organization Lauds Los Angeles Police Department," *Los Angeles Times*, August 2, 1962, AS.

33. "Prostitution Resurgence Noted in Southwest L.A."

34. "Policemanship," *Los Angeles Sentinel*, November 17, 1960, A6; Paul Coates, "Vice Casts Its Shadow on West Adams District: White Men on Prowl for Negro Streetwalkers," *Los Angeles Times*, April 11, 1965, B.

35. "Western-Adams Residents Seek Public Vice Action," *Los Angeles Times*, January 30, 1961, 2; Walter Ames, "Problem of Prostitution Never Ending for Police: Arrests, Difficult . . .," *Los Angeles Times*, April 12, 1965, 3.

36. For a detailed and excellent deconstruction of the articulation of anti-Black racism as a paradigm of emasculation, see LaKeyma King, "Inversion and Invisibility: Black Women, Black Masculinity, and Anti-Blackness," *Lies: A Journal of Materialist Feminism* (August 2015): 31–48. King demonstrates how Black women and Black femme embodiment are instrumentalized to do the work of rendering narratives of anti-Blackness that hinge on racial castration or the idea of anti-Blackness as a flattening ontology in relation to gender (anti-Blackness negates gendered difference among Black people and Black women get treated "like men"). King argues that "theories of racial castration are fused to a narrative about racial authenticity that leaves Black women politically isolated from the overarching Black community, their efforts to survive attacked as forms of race-betrayal, their struggles within and without their homes elided" (32).

37. See Beth E. Richie, *Arrested Justice: Black Women, Violence, and America's Prison Nation* (New York: New York University Press, 2012); Cathy J. Cohen, *The Boundaries of Blackness: AIDS and the Breakdown of Black Politics* (Chicago: University of Chicago Press, 1999).

44 Transgender Chican@ Poetics

Contesting, Interrogating, and Transforming Chicana/o Studies

Francisco J. Galarte

Francisco J. Galarte, a long-serving editor of *TSQ: Transgender Studies Quarterly*, is the author of *Brown Trans Figurations: Rethinking Race, Gender, and Sexuality in Chicanx/Latinx Studies*. In "Transgender Chican@ Poetics," first published in the journal *Chicana/Latina Studies* in 2014, Galarte posits "transgender" as a category ripe with potential to expand the longstanding critical projects of Chicana feminism and to counter the exclusionary dismissal of trans people present in some of that work. He discusses how, on the one hand, Chicana lesbian feminists Gloria Anzaldúa and Cherríe Moraga expanded the concept of "queer" in the early 1990s beyond the predominantly white, Anglocentric academic spaces in which "queer theory" had taken root; they called instead for a Chicano/a studies and a queer Aztlán inclusive of all Chicano/a peoples, "including its *joteria* (queer folks)." On the other hand, Moraga did not imagine *joteria* to include trans people. In a 2011 essay on gay marriage and respectability politics, Moraga, as Galarte notes, criticizes *transgender* "as an identity category invested in recognition, visibility, and legibility in a normative framework." In her desire to "keep queer queer," by which she means radically disruptive of heteronormative privilege, she resurrects arguments advanced by transphobic second-wave feminists such as Janice Raymond to argue that transsexuals reassert patriarchal constructs of femininity and masculinity. In directly addressing transphobic elements in Moraga's version of Chicana feminism, Galarte works to expand Chicanx politics beyond a needlessly narrow, limiting, and exclusionary understanding of transness that reduces it to reactionary complicity with homonormativity and heteropatriarchy. He advocates instead for a Chicanx studies and a Chicana feminist politics that embrace an even more expansive concept of *joterίa* that includes a broader range of queer and trans perspectives.

Please don't. I have a family.

—Gwen Amber Rose Araujo[1]

I begin this essay by conjuring a scene of literal, corporeal violence, the epigraph above is reportedly the last words uttered by Gwen Amber Rose Araujo, a transgender, Mexican American teen brutally murdered in 2002 by a group of young men.[2] Araujo's story has accompanied me along my trajectory in academia, in my aim to point to the necessity in addressing transgender phenomena within Chicana/o Studies.[3] Araujo and Angie Zapata, and the countless number of Mexican and Mexican American transgender women who have been killed, are indeed the specters and ghosts who haunt Chicana/o Studies at its current juncture. Avery Gordon reminds us that, specters and ghosts appear "when the trouble they represent and symptomize is no longer being contained or repressed or blocked from view" (Gordon 2008, xvi).

DOI: 10.4324/9781003206255-54

In order to write an essay that addresses institutional violence against trans/queer folks in Chicana/o Studies, it is imperative to begin with the staggering realities of violence faced by transgender and gender non-conforming jotería.[4] The lives of transgender and gender non-conforming Chican@s are structured by regulating regimes maintained by institutional, epistemic, and quotidian violence. These three types of violence are sustained by an unwillingness to engage, understand, and see transgender Chican@s. There is an assumption that through the use of *queer* or LGBT that there is a place at the table for transgender issues, politics, and subjects; however, this is not always the case. Such affinities are presumed but not necessarily honored in practice, especially in the realm of mainstream LGBT politics.[5] The question remains: are transgender Chican@s part of the imagined community of jotería? As a transgender Chicano and scholar committed to the pedagogical aims of Chicana/o Studies, I want to help define *jotería* as a familia to which transgender Chican@s belong.

It is important to note that the term *Chican@s*, and Chican@ Studies should be understood to be different from Chicana/o and Chicana/o Studies. It is imperative that Chican@ is recognized as more than shorthand for *Chicana/o* or *Chicana and Chicano*. Simply regarding Chican@ as a shorthand alternative to get around post-1980s gender-inclusive formulations is quite possibly the resurgence of heteronormative patriarchal disciplining. According to Sandra K. Soto, Chican@ as a queer performative "at first sight looks perhaps like a typo and seems unpronounceable," and "disrupts our desire for intelligibility . . . and certain visual register of a gendered body" (2010, 2). Chican@ then has the possibility to function as a visual citational code for racialized gender outside the regularized categories of male and female as well as a direct resistance to heteronormative patriarchal disciplining.

Just as Chicana feminists demanded and fought for paradigmatic shifts in Chicano Studies that were attentive to gender and sexuality, the time has arrived to interrogate the field once more in terms of transgender inclusion. In this essay, I argue that "trans-" has the potential to provoke the kind of paradigmatic shift necessary to critically engage gender and sexuality in such a way that disrupts the heteronormative patriarchal authority and conformity with which Chicana/o Studies is currently entangled. At the end of her book, *Reading Chican@ Like a Queer: The De-Mastery of Desire*, Soto asks, "What responsibilities does the younger Chican@ scholar have to the ethnonationalist ethos of Chicano Studies as elaborated in 'El Plan de Santa Barbara' and to the feminist platforms launched in response to those foundations" (Soto 2010, 126)? As a young transgender Chican@ scholar, this question deeply resonates and identifies a core issue that must be faced when considering the place of transgender phenomena in Chicana/o Studies: how can we expand existing Chicana feminist lexicons currently attending to gender and sexuality to include gender non-conformity and transgender people? When Chicana lesbians initially responded to Chicana feminisms' elision of queer issues, they created what Emma M. Pérez describes as a "sitio y lengua" for attending to the intimate dimensions of racialized, gendered sexuality.[6] The challenge that 'transgender' presents is that it cuts across sexuality; therefore, transgender Chican@s further complicate and destabilize approaches to theorizing gender and sexuality in the current Chicana/o context. Do the varied sexual and gender practices and narratives of transgender Chican@s have a place in the theoretical space envisioned in Cherríe Moraga's "Queer Aztlán?"

[. . .]

This essay does not presume that transgender throws categories into crisis, but rather argues that transgender transforms our reading practices. To trans- our approach to Chicana/o Studies is to invite change and transformation and perhaps spark a moment of reflexivity in the field that is attentive to the "sensuous intersectionalities that mark our experience" (Muñoz 2009, 96). [. . .] There already exists a vocabulary within Chicana lesbian feminist thought to attend to such material, discursive, and institutional violence: much of this work was done in the early 1990s, around the same time as the emergence of queer studies and the increased use of 'transgender' as an term with utopian possibility.

Chican@ Studies should have as a central concern, a methodology for theorizing the "related yet distinct" systematic operations we know as ableism, racism, homophobia, misogyny, and transphobia (Keeling 2009, 566). Centering trans- and exposing the faltering present, as noted by the ghosts whose presence remind us that, "what's been concealed is very much alive and present, interfering with those always incomplete forms of containment and repression directed toward us" (Gordon 2008, xvi), is a reminder that Chicanas/os have not heeded Gloria E. Anzaldúa's call to "listen to what your jotería is saying" (1987, 85). Araujo's last words not only remind us of the asymmetries of violence that affect transgender women of color, but provoke us to assert through our methodologies and pedagogies in Chicana/o Studies that indeed, she does have a familia.

[. . .]

The normalization of violence against transgender women of color is an example of the contingent nature of queer familia. In an important essay by Linda Heidenreich—notably one of the few essays on the death of Gwen Araujo—she argues that there are "shades of queer," or a queer spectrum, noting that there are definitely embodiments of queerness that are much more valuable than others in terms of societal recognition. [. . .] When discussing the lives and experiences of transgender women of color, especially when the topic is violence, "'transgender' increasingly functions as the site in which to contain all gender trouble, thereby helping secure both homosexuality and heterosexuality as stable and normative categories of personhood (Stryker 2004, 214). Heidenreich's "Queer Chicana methodology" resists this stabilization, and what is most important is how she mobilizes Chicana and Latina feminist writings as the starting place for writing about gendered and sexual violence directed at transgender Chicanas and Latinas. In doing so, Heidenreich theoretically locates Chicana feminism as a starting point carved out by "this first generation of overtly queer Chicana and Latina writers; Anzaldúa, [Cherríe] Moraga, [Ana] Castillo, [Carla] Trujillo, [Juanita] Ramos, and [Norma] Alarcón," whose writings created a space "where we could imagine ourselves, in the flesh, and then move on to critique those other spaces in the dominant society and our own communities that would make us invisible" (Heidenreich 2006, 54–55). Heidenreich's methodology and attentiveness to understanding transphobic racial violence effectively demonstrates how we can mobilize Chicana feminist paradigms to attend to gendered and sexual violence as enacted against transgender folks. Araujo's story and the stories of many other transgender women of color who have been brutally murdered elucidate the critical observations made in the work of early Chicana feminists that, "contemporary gender systems cannot be separated from race and economic status but rather must be understood as mutually intersecting to produce the poor woman's circumstance and experience" (Taylor-Garcia 2012, 112).

A Trans Chicana Interlude

As pointed out by Pérez in her monograph *The Decolonial Imaginary: Writing Chicanas Into History*, in Chicano history there is a desire to correlate Chicano history in relationship to grand events, and a desire to narrate history in relationship to heroes (who are always men). In my desire to illuminate how the contributions of transgender Chican@s have been elided in the narration of Chicana/o history, as well as queer Chicana/o recuperative projects, I will offer a preliminary reading of the short film *Felicia*, directed by Mark O'Hara, that features Felicia Flames Elizondo, one of the women featured in Susan Stryker's documentary *Screaming Queens*. *Felicia* features the story behind the 1966 riot and protest against police repression by transgender women in the Tenderloin district in San Francisco.[7] Felicia Flames Elizondo, is a figure to be remembered and acknowledged as part of Chicana/o history.[8] In analyzing this film, I demonstrate the complimentary affinities of queer, trans- and Chicana feminist approaches to contesting institutional violence through our reading practices.

O'Hara's short film features Felicia discussing the realities of aging alone, and the first few minutes of the film captures her narrating her day-to-day routine. She notes, "We never think of getting old until we get there." Felicia also comments that she refuses to conform to what she describes as dominant notions around aging: "In my time, when you get old you were useless and nobody cared about you, so I made it a point that I have a group of friends . . . it is important to have friends." Felicia is letting us know, and quite possibly reminding herself, that she indeed does have people who care about her and witness (as we are witnessing) the rhythms of her everyday life: her routine of walking her dogs, keeping up with world events via television, and checking in with her friends. The director then transitions the film into a montage of old photos of Felicia; the last photo is Felicia in her Navy uniform, marking the "reveal" that Felicia is not the person the viewer presumed her to be. The director's surprise to the viewer both informs them that they are not just watching a film about aging alone, but a film about a transgender woman aging alone, and violently exploits Felicia's vulnerability and loneliness. We see this, too, at the end of the film, but not before the trope of transgender women as "deceiver" is reiterated through the reveal that Felicia is a Vietnam War veteran. At the end of the film, the camera frames Felicia's hands showing her jewelry and then pans across what are presumably Felicia's performance costumes, but all the viewer can make out are sequins and glitter. Finally, as Rocio Dúrcal's recording of "El Dia Que Me Acaricies Llorare" plays in the background, we see Felicia lying on her bed, pensive and as melancholy as the refrains of the ranchera in the background.[9] Felicia's gaze is fixed upon something above and soon the camera position moves so that our gaze becomes Felicia's: We see that she is looking up at a mirrored disco ball hanging from the ceiling in her bedroom. As the song continues to play, the frame of the disco ball fades and is replaced by a much more modern club light fixture with spinning neon lights. We first hear, and then see, Felicia center stage, dressed in a glittering dress, with sorrow and dolor consuming her face as she is singing along with Rocio Dúrcal:

> Estoy acostumbrada a tus desprecios/
> Que el día que me acaricies llorare/
> Te quiero tanto y tanto que aunque quiera/
> Dejarte y olvidarte no podré.

The film ends with the sound of scattered applause from a crowd; however, we are not able to see who, besides the film viewers, is Felicia's audience. The film's final scenes are much more remarkable than the transgender reveal; the end of the film leaves effective traces of queer temporalities that are disjointed, out of sync with the time-anchored, ethnonationalist ethos that underpins Chicana/o Studies. This moment is a temporal interruption, a moment that calls into question the ways "people are bound to one another, engrouped, made to feel coherently collective, through particular orchestrations of time" (Freeman 2010, 3). The pedagogical intervention from this temporal interruption challenges institutional violence by showing viewers that it is imperative to acknowledge the presence of a transgender Chicanas in proximity to and/or alongside historical moments and spaces that align with Chicano ethnonationalist narratives of community, resistance, and liberation. For example, as a survivor of a place and time that sparked the first well-documented mass trans resistance to police surveillance, repression, and discrimination, Elizondo bears witness to Chicana participation in this important act of resistance and liberation, yet we continue to invest in the forgetting and erasure of such struggles because they do not neatly align with the masculinist ethos of Chicano cultural nationalism. Perhaps this disjointing or disrupting of normative time can help us rethink and or reconceptualize what constitutes Chicana resistance and liberation.

Testifying Dolor en Aztlán, Trans Chican@ Poetics

In many ways I developed my transgender identity via exposure to Chicana lesbian feminist writings. I am a transgender-identified Chican@, and I am not a threat, nor am I a deceiver. Chicana feminist politics has guided my identity development through the recognition that my freedom is intrinsically connected to the freedom of my hermanas. My survival has depended on the ways in which I saw my experience reflected in the words of Chicana lesbian feminist writings, and now, to my chagrin I feel as though I am no longer a part of that community. At the moments in which I decided to transition, I never thought such a decision was at odds with the Chicana lesbian lineage I so powerfully felt a part of. I envisioned myself part of a queer familia because of my Chicana butch identification at the time. The debates regarding trans- inclusion in Mujeres Activas en Letras y Cambio Social (MALCS), in email conversations I was not a part of and chisme about who of my longtime feminist heroes stood on what side, and in recent writings by Cherríe L. Moraga, have increasingly alienated me from the community and familia I assumed would always be there for me.[10] I saw myself as one of the "butch daughters" lost to a transgender identity Moraga mourns in her 2011 essay "Still Loving in the (Still) War Years." In some ways the loss I'm experiencing feels violent and in others it foments a strong desire to theorize from that place of loss. My training in Chicana feminist paradigms that emphasized "productive contradictions," the "salience of sexuality" and encouraged the critique of Chicana feminist discourses that elided queer issues, led me to believe that changing my body did not change my ability to enact, transform, and participate in Chicana feminisms (Yabro-Bejarano 2007, 402–403). At the time, I was naive to believe that the so-called "Ftm/Butch Border Wars"[11] were over; however, now I realize that such debates are necessary and that there is just not enough written about the Transgender Chican@ experience.

I return to one of the questions guiding this personal and academic scholarship: when scholars committed to theorizing gender and sexuality in Chicana/o Studies say "Chicana/o queers," are we/they including those who are transgender? Given the ways in which 'queer' is mobilized within Chicana/o Studies, could we even include 'transgender' under that framework? Just as the first edition of Carla Trujillo's edited volume, *Chicana Lesbians: The Girls Our Mothers Warned Us About*, was published in 1991, as Chicana lesbian feminists were waging the war against Chicano nationalists and homophobia among Chicanas at the then National Association of Chicano Studies (NACS) and MALCS, that 'transgender,' as well as 'queer,' were being taken up in academic and activist circles as terms with significant political promise. As a result, transgender and transsexual and queer became entangled (Stryker 1998, 148). Chicana lesbian feminists such as Anzaldúa and Moraga, for example, mobilized 'queer' in very different way. Anzaldúa describes her queerness in a 1993 interview with Jamie Lee Evans as "not just White, but Indian, Mexican, Chicano, a regional queerness, a working-class queerness of my growing up in South Texas" (Anzaldúa 2000, 203–204).[12] Moraga's essay, "Queer Aztlán: The Re-formation of Chicano Tribe," also published in 1993, envisions a queer Aztlán that addressed the limitations of the "anglocentricity" of "Queer Nation" and the elisions of gays and lesbians in Chicano Nationalism (Moraga 1993, 147). Moraga's "Queer Aztlán" would be a "Chicano homeland that could embrace *all* its people, including its *jotería* (queer folk)" (Moraga 1993, 147). Moraga's vision in this essay is a capacious one:

> Chicana lesbians and gay men do not merely seek inclusion in the Chicano nation; we seek a nation strong enough to embrace a full range of racial diversities, human sexualities, and expressions of gender. We seek a culture that can allow for the natural expression of our femaleness and maleness and our love without prejudice or punishment.
>
> (Moraga 1993, 164)

While not explicitly naming transgender folks, perhaps we can claim that they are included within the vision under the subtle nuance "expressions of gender." Transgender Chican@s are the absent presence and the audible silence. As noted by Karen Mary Davalos, "Chicana feminism looks differently at silence, examining what is said, what is not said, and what is said by the silences (2008, 154).

In her recent and controversial 2011 essay, "Still Loving in the (Still) War Years," Cherríe Moraga breaks the silence of discussing transgender issues among queer communities of color. The first half of the essay is a critique of gay marriage, and points to the inequities inherent in the institution of state-sanctioned marriages, while the second half of the essay takes up the silences around transgender issues. It is important to note that the impetus of this essay is Moraga's desire to remind us that we must "keep queer queer," and in doing so questions what constitutes queer resistance in the time of mainstream LGBT political agendas that are centered around recognition in heteronormative, neoliberal institutions such as "marriage, military and the market" (Duggan 2012). Pairing a critique of gay-marriage with fears and anxieties around the fashioning of transgender identities by youth of color to reinvigorate discussions about what constitutes queer resistance implicates transgender as an identity category invested in recognition, visibility, and legibility in a normative framework. Moraga notes that the "political agenda of the transgender movement . . . may preempt young people from simply residing in that queer, gender-ambivalent site for as long as and deeply necessary" (184). In this statement, Moraga is insinuating that transgender politics are not queer politics—or resistant—conjuring second wave feminist arguments that transsexuality reasserts patriarchal standards of femininity and masculinity.[13] As Moraga fleshes out her concerns, staking her connection and approximating her role as queer elder to this younger generation of queer and trans- folks of color, she explicitly laments, "I do not want to keep losing my macha daughters to manhood through any cultural mandates that are not derived of our own making" (186). In the essay, it would be too easy point and identify Moraga's anxieties, and name them as wrong, hurtful, and transphobic. This type of approach does not aptly attend to what is the seemingly more important issue at hand in this essay.[14] The reaction of many transgender folks (myself included) was one of hurt feelings, defensiveness, a desire to be heard, and most importantly, the desire to be invited to a dialogue. I appreciate Moraga's effort to break the silence caused by "in-house censorship wherein questioning any aspect of the identity one risks being labeled transphobic" (184), and I admire her commitment to a Chicana feminist and U.S. third world feminist politic that she as a key figure has championed, and subsequently bequeathed, to generations of Chicanas and Chicanos. Her essay, in its aim to incite consciousness and invigorate discussions around what constitutes queer resistance in the time of neoliberal LGBT political organizing that further marginalizes queers of color, implicates transgender folks of color within such politics of conformity. She does this by explicitly pairing the discussion of transgender folks of color with a critique of the politics of respectability, recognition, and visibility that underpin the homonormative aims of gay marriage. Moraga's anxieties clearly concern folks who are assigned female at birth and chose to transition and live as male and will further the work of heteropatriarchy and heterosexism, should they construct their masculinity through a rejection of femaleness. This is most evident as she reminds her "daughters and granddaughters of color" that:

> Should you choose to transition to a man's body, you must still hold on desperately to your womanhood in the shaping of that masculinity. You must know that there is something in being born female from a female in a female-hating world that still matters.

> (Moraga 2011, 189)

This section, when read in relationship to the context of the larger aim of the essay, reiterates Yarbro-Bejarano's assertion that Moraga has created a "public voice for Chicana lesbian identity politics, making demands for entitlement as 'citizens' in multiple arenas of historical exclusion and marginalization" (128). In her 2011 essay, Moraga seeks to protect and re-center the Chicana lesbian feminist politic she and others struggled and fought vehemently to articulate in theory and in practice (Yabro-Bejarano 2001). Moraga is not eschewing the presence and contributions of transgender folks of color to queer politics and struggles; rather, she is one of the few (in the Chicana/o and Chicana/o queer context I have been writing about) that actually *sees* transgender Chican@s. As Sandra K. Soto has noted, Moraga's style of writing places a "high premium on the public elaboration of private feelings of anxiety, guilt and fear" and thus the fear she expresses in this essay is potentially a conduit for "both individual and political transformation" (33). While at the conclusion of the essay Moraga concedes to the invitation of a young transman to be seen and she accepts him as a member of her queer nation, Moraga's text forces transgender folks to bear the burden of proving loyalty to a nation as well as being the figure that is the exemplar of race, sex, and gender abjection and liberation. In the aim to take up the question of queer resistance in the time of homonormativity, the essay renders transgender folks of color as a nodal point for discussions of inclusion, exclusion, and marginality. My reading of Moraga's essay echoes La Fountain-Stokes's question: "What does it mean for this subject position to be raised to the status of an absolute embodiment of difference" (2011, 64)?

On Chican@ Futurity

The thing that remains certain for me is that I still wholeheartedly believe that Chicana/o Studies is a collective project, through which our pedagogy and criticism "impart knowledges that students take with them as they graduate to become professionals, artists, and activists, helping to develop a new social imaginary that extends beyond the university" (Yabro-Bejarano 2007, 404). I have met transgender Chican@ students at undergraduate institutions who long to see themselves represented in the texts they read or even remotely represented in a pedagogy that does not naturalize heteronormativity and binary gender systems. It is our responsibility to teach our classes so as not to advance the violence of heteropatriarchy through transphobic and homophobic pedagogies. Changing our pedagogical practices can only lead to transformation and the necessary interrogation of the categories of male and female, which is not something new for Chicana and other U.S. third world feminists. As noted by Chela Sandoval (2000):

> US third world feminists argued that feminists of color represent a third term, another gender outside the regularized categories of male and female, as represented in the very titles of publications such as *All the Women Are White, All the Blacks Are Men, but Some*

of Us Are Brave, Ain't I a Woman?, This Bridge Called My Back, and *Sister Outsider.* These books proposed that the social space represented by these "third-term" identities is that place out of which a politicized differential consciousness arises.

(70)

We must be committed to creating such social spaces for our students so that they are much more generous in how they understand varying categories of gender. It is through our students that we can combat the type of violence enacted in face-to-face relations at the intersections of racism, transphobia, homophobia, and sexism. We must teach our students to engage in what Daphne Taylor-Garcia (2012) has identified as a "dialogical ethics," integral to enacting decolonial politics. She describes this as "being willing and committed to take seriously many different perspectives and, in particular pay special attention to those perspectives that are seen as dispensable, irrelevant, and/or insignificant" (110). Contesting contemporary gender systems in relation to race, sexuality, class, and ability furthers the decolonial project set forth in the work of Pérez, who notes that "the decolonial is a dynamic space in which subjects are actively decolonizing their lives. Unlike the colonial imaginary, which is a narrow, binary, 'us' versus 'them' standpoint, the decolonial imaginary instead is a liberatory, mobile frame of mind. The decolonial is a deconstructive tool" (Pérez 2012, 195). If we take Maria Lugones' proposition that gender is a colonial construct defined by patriarchy and heteronormativity seriously, then we must assume that gender is a decolonial feminist project and commit ourselves to dismantling systems of heteropatriarchy and heterosexism (Lugones 2007, 186). Peréz's "decolonial imaginary" remains relevant to a queer and feminist politic that is inclusive of transfolks. The decolonial imaginary is the interstitial, in-between space; the transgender body is not. In the decolonial imaginary, transgender Chican@s are also actors and part of the project of re-writing and disputing what is written in history. The decolonial imaginary allows for the unraveling of binary gender categories and relations we have inherited from historical circumstances that have rendered the transgender Chican@ impossible, unseen, or adrift in a sea of discourse.

[. . .]

Our definition of jotería must be capacious, but must also remain committed to the disruption of heteropatriarchy and conformity; it must be guided by the mandate that "the here and the now is simply not enough" (96). Queer and transgender need not be mutually antagonistic terms under the rubric of jotería; we must do the work to prove that this is so and actively assert and define jotería as a family to which transgender Chican@s belong. To return to Soto's question: "What responsibilities does the younger Chican@ scholar have to the ethnonationalist ethos of Chicano Studies as elaborated in 'El Plan de Santa Barbara' and to the feminist platforms launched in response to those foundations?"

The responsibilities are twofold: to continue to resist the heteropatriarchal and heterosexist disciplining of the ethnonationalist ethos of Chicano Studies and to cultivate a politicized Chican@ Studies that bridges epistemological feminist platforms with renewed commitment to a heterogeneity of voices and embodiments we can recognize as queer, trans-, or some other iteration not yet known. Invigorating the field with such a commitment to transformation galvanizes our intellectual and political aims to impart upon our students new paradigms for conceptualizing community, identity, and subjectivity.

From: Francisco J. Galarte, "Transgender Chican@ Poetics: Contesting, Interrogating, and Transforming Chicana/o Studies" in *Chicana/Latina Studies*, 13 (2), pp. 118–139. Republished by permission of the publisher.

Notes

1. Araujo's last words are dramatized in the Lifetime television movie, *A Girl Like Me: The Gwen Araujo Story*. This film was based on testimony from the two trials of Michael Magidson, Jose Antonio Mérel, and Jason Cazares.
2. I use Chican@ with the arroba to symbolically gesture a rejection of the imposition and implied male/female binaries of "Chicana/o". The essay takes up the use of Chican@ in Chicana/o Studies in further detail.
3. For more on the death of Gwen Araujo and the politics of remembrance see the essay, "Siempre en Mi Mente: On Trans★ Violence."
4. A note on terminology: "transgender phenomena" is a term commonly used in Transgender Studies. Transgender in this essay can be understood as, "not to refer to one particular identity or way of being embodied but rather as an umbrella term for a wide variety of bodily effects that disrupt or denaturalize heteronormative linkages constructed between an individual's anatomy at birth, a non-consensually assigned gender category, psychical identifications with sexed body images and/or gendered subject positions, and the performance of specifically gendered social, sexual, or kinship functions (Stryker 1998, 148). I also use "Chicana/o Studies" as well as "Chican@ Studies," which are not meant to be synonymous.
5. "Gender non-conforming" refers to persons who may or may not identify as transgender but do not embody, identify or present as either male or female.
6. There is a sustained elision of transgender issues in mainstream LGBT political platforms and advocacy, an example being the Human Rights Coalition's refusal to support a trans-inclusive version of ENDA (Employee Non-Discrimination Act).
7. For an invigorating critique of hate crimes legislations and the workings of the neoliberal state's deployment of (institutional) violence against peoples perceived as non-normative, see Chandan Reddy, *Freedom with Violence: Race, Sexuality and the US State* (Durham, NC: Duke University Press, 2011).
8. In addition to the Chicana lesbian writings in *This Bridge*, see Alarcón, Castillo, and Moraga, eds., *The Sexuality of Latinas* (Berkeley, CA: Third Woman Press, 1983); Juanita Ramos, ed., *Compañeras: Latina Lesbians* (New York: Latina Lesbian History Project, 1987); Carla Trujillo, ed., *Chicana Lesbians: Girls Our Mothers Warned Us About* (Berkeley, CA: Third Women Press, 1991), which contains writings by Castillo, Moraga, Anzaldúa, Emma Pérez, and others.
9. The work of Horacio N. Roque Ramírez is central to this recuperative project, specifically his works that center the oral histories of transgender Latinas in San Francisco. See Horacio N. Roque Ramírez, "A Living Archive of Desire: Teresita la Campesina and the Embodiment of Queer Latino Community Histories," in *Archive Stories: Facts, Fictions, and the Writing of History*, edited by Antoinette M. Burton (Durham, NC: Duke University Press, 2005); "Sharing Queer Authorities: Collaborating for Transgender Latina and Gay Latino Historical Meanings," in *Bodies of Evidence: The Practice of Queer Oral History*, edited by Nan Alamilla Boyd and Horacio N. Roque Ramírez (New York: Oxford University Press, 2012).
10. For more information on Felicia Flames Elizondo see: www.screamingqueens1.com/. The Association for Jotería Arts, Activism, and Scholarship (AJAAS) recently awarded Felicia Flames Elizondo the "Jotería Lifetime Achievement Award" at their inaugural Conference on October 19, 2012.
11. "El Dia Que Me Acaricies Llorare" was written by Juan Gabriel, which is important to note given Gabriel's inimitable and notorious queer performances of the canción ranchera.
12. For more about debates held within MALCS regarding "women only" spaces, see Francisco J. Galarte (2011) "Notes from a Trans★ Chican@ Survivor," http://mujerestalk.malcs.org/2011/10/ notes-from-trans-chican-survivor.html. Also see Marie 'Keta' Miranda (2012) "TransGenderInter," http://mujer estalk.malcs.org/2012/10/transgenderinter.html.
13. FTM/butch border wars refers specifically to an exchange between Judith Halberstam and Jacob C. Hale in their respective essays, "Transgender Butch: Butch/FTM Border Wars and the Masculine Continuum" and "Consuming the Living, Dis(re)membering the Dead in the Butch/ FTM Borderlands." For a discussion of Ftm/butch border wars that is relevant to a Chican@/ Latin@ context, see the film *Mind If I Call You Sir?*, directed by Mary Guzmán.
14. Gloria E. Anzaldúa is critiquing what becomes known as "Queer Studies" after the publication of Michael Warner's *Fear of a Queer Planet: Queer Politics and Social Theory* (1993), which discusses queer politics and ideology in social theory. Yvonne Yarbro-Bejarano has also made similar critiques of queer studies for its elision of race in her 2007 essay, "Reflections on Thirty Years of Critical Practice in Chicana/o Cultural Studies."

Works Cited

Alarcón, Norma, Ana Castillo, and Cherríe Moraga. 1993. *The Sexuality of Latinas.* Berkeley, CA: Third Woman Press.

Anzaldúa, Gloria E. 1987. *Borderlands/La Frontera: The New Mestiza.* San Francisco: aunt lute.

———. 2000. *Interviews/Entrevistas/Gloria Anzaldúa.* Edited by Ana Louise Keating. New York: Routledge.

Calvo, Luz and Catriona Rueda Esquíbel. 2011. "Our Queer Kin." In *Gay Latino Studies: A Critical Reader,* edited by Michael Hames-Garcia and Ernesto Javier Martinez, 105–112. Durham, NC: Duke University Press.

Davalos, Karen Mary. 2008. "Sin Verguenza: Chicana Feminist Theorizing." *Feminist Studies* 34, no. 1 and 2 (Spring and Summer): 151–171.

Duggan, Lisa. 2012. "After Neoliberalism? From Crisis to Organizing for Queer Economic Justice." *Scholar and Feminist Online* 10, no. 1 and 2 (Fall 2011 and Spring 2012): n.p.

Felicia. 2007. Dir. Tim O'Hara gdfilms.com and frameline.

Freeman, Elizabeth. 2010. *Time Binds: Queer Temporalities, Queer Histories.* Durham, NC: Duke University Press.

Galarte, Francisco J. 2011a. "Notes from a Trans★ Chican@ Survivor." *Mujeres Talk: A MALCS Discussion Site.* http://mujerestalk.malcs.org.

———. 2011b. "El Sabor del Amor y del Dolor: Affect, Violence and the (Trans)Body in the Chican@ Historical Imaginary." PhD diss., University of Illinois Champaign-Urbana.

———. 2012. "Siempre En Mi Mente: On Trans★ Violence." *The Feminist Wire* (October 10). http://thefeministwire.com/2012/10/siempre-en-mi-mente-on-trans-violence/.

Gordon, Avery. 2008. *Ghostly Matters: Haunting and the Sociological Imagination.* Minneapolis: University of Minnesota Press.

Halberstam, Judith. 1998. "Transgender Butch: Butch/FTM Border Wars and the Masculine Continuum." *GLQ: Gay and Lesbian Studies* 4, no. 2: 287–310.

Hale, Jacob C. 1998. "Consuming the Living, Dis(re)membering the Dead in the Butch/FTM Borderlands." *GLQ: Gay and Lesbian Studies* 4, no. 2: 311–348.

Hames-Garcia, Michael. 2011. "Queer Theory Revisited." In *Gay Latino Studies: A Critical Reader,* edited by Michael Hames-Garcia and Ernesto Javier Martinez, 19–45. Durham, NC: Duke University Press.

Heidenreich, Linda. 2006. "Learning From the Death of Gwen Araujo?—Transphobic Racial Subordination and Queer Latina Survival in the Twenty-First Century." *Chicana/Latina Studies* 6, no. 1: 50–86.

Keeling, Kara. 2009. "Looking for M—. Queer Temporality, Black Political Possibility and Poetry from the Future." *GLQ: Journal of Gay and Lesbian Studies* 15, no. 4: 565–582.

La Fountain-Stokes, Lawrence. 2008a. "Trans/Bolero/Drag/Migration: Music, Cultural Translation, and Diasporic Puerto Rican Theatricalities." *WSQ: Women's Studies Quarterly* 36, no. 3 and 4: 190–209.

———. 2008b. "Gay Shame Latina- and Latino-Style: A Critique of White Queer Performativity." In *Gay Latino Studies: A Critical Reader,* edited by Michael Hames-Garcia and Ernesto Javier Martinez, 55–80. Durham, NC: Duke University Press.

Lugones, Maria. 2007. "Heterosexualism and the Colonial/Modern Gender System." *Hypatia* 22, no. 1 (Winter): 186–219.

Mind If I Call You Sir? A Discussion Between Latina Butches and Female-to-Male Transgendered Latinos. 2004. Dir. Mary Guzmán. Lantham, MD: National Film Network. DVD.

Miranda, Marie. 2012. "TransGenderInter." *Mujeres Talk: A MALCS Discussion Site.* http://mujerestalk.malcs.org/2012/10/transgenderinter.html.

Moraga, Cherríe. 1993. *The Last Generation: Prose and Poetry.* Cambridge, MA: South End Press.

———. 2011. *A Xicana Codex of Changing Consciousness: Writings, 2000–2010.* Durham, NC: Duke University Press.

Moraga, Cherríe and Gloria E. Anzaldúa, eds. 1983. *This Bridge Called My Back: Writings by Radical Women of Color.* New York: Kitchen Table, Women of Color Press.

Muñoz, José Esteban. 2009. *Cruising Utopia: The Then and There of Queer Futurity.* New York: New York University Press.

Namaste, Viviane. 2000. *Invisible Lives: The Erasure of Transsexual and Transgendered People.* Chicago: University of Chicago Press.

Pérez, Emma. 1991. "Sexuality and Discourse: Notes from a Chicana Survivor." In *Chicana Lesbians: Girls Our Mothers Warned Us About,* edited by Carla Trujillo, 159–184. Berkeley, CA: Third Women Press.

———. 1999. *The Decolonial Imaginary: Writing Chicanas into History.* Bloomington: Indiana University Press.

———. 2012. "Decolonial Border Queers: Case Studies of Chicana/o Lesbians, Gay Men, and Transgender Folks in El Paso/Juárez." In *Performing the US Latina and Latino Borderlands,* edited by Arturo Aldama, Chela Sandoval, and Peter J. Garcia, 192–209. Bloomington: Indiana University Press.

Ramos, Juanita, ed. 1987. *Compañeras: Latina Lesbians.* New York: Latina Lesbian History Project.

Raymond, Janice. 1994. *The Transsexual Empire: The Making of the She-Male.* New York: Teachers College Press.

Reddy, Chandan. 2011. *Freedom with Violence: Race, Sexuality and the US State.* Durham, NC: Duke University Press.

Rodriguez, Richard T. 2009. *Next of Kin: The Family in Chicano/a Cultural Politics.* Durham, NC: Duke University Press.

———. 2010. "The Locations of Chicano/a and Latino/a Studies." In *A Concise Companion to American Studies,* edited by John Carlos Rowe, 190–209. Oxford: Blackwell Publishers.

Roque Ramirez, Horacio N. 2005. "A Living Archive of Desire: Teresita la Campesina and the Embodiment of Queer Latino Community Histories." In *Archive Stories: Facts, Fictions, and the Writing of History,* edited by Antoinette M. Burton, 111–135. Durham, NC: Duke University Press.

———. 2012. "Sharing Queer Authorities: Collaborating for Transgender Latina and Gay Latino Historical Meanings." In *Bodies of Evidence: The Practice of Queer Oral History,* edited by Nan Alamilla Boyd and Horacio N. Roque Ramirez, 184–201. New York: Oxford University Press.

Sandoval, Chela. 2000. *Methodology of the Oppressed.* Minneapolis: University of Minnesota Press.

Screaming Queens: The Riot at Compton's Cafeteria. 2005. Dir. Tim O'Hara. San Francisco, CA: Frameline. DVD.

Soto, Sandra K. 2010. *Reading Chican@ Like a Queer: The Demastery of Desire.* Austin: University of Texas Press.

Stryker, Susan. 1998. "The Transgender Issue: An Introduction." *GLQ: A Journal of Lesbian and Gay Studies* 4, no. 2: 145–158.

———. 2004. "Transgender Studies: Queer Theory's Evil Twin." *GLQ: A Journal of Lesbian and Gay Studies* 10, no. 2: 212–215.

Taylor-Garcia, Daphne. 2012. "Decolonizing Gender Performativity: A Thesis for Emancipation in Early Chicana Feminist Thought (1969–1979)." In *Performing the US Latina and Latino Borderlands,* edited by Arturo Aldama, Chela Sandoval, and Peter J. Garcia, 107–126. Bloomington: Indiana University Press.

Trujillo, Carla. 1991. *Chicana Lesbians: The Girls Our Mothers Warned Us About.* Berkeley: Third Women Press.

Valentine, David. 2007. *Imagining Transgender: An Ethnography of a Category.* Durham, NC: Duke University Press.

Warner, Michael, ed. 1993. *Fear of a Queer Planet: Queer Politics and Social Theory.* Minneapolis: University of Minnesota Press.

Yabro-Bejarano, Yvonne. 2001. *The Wounded Heart: Writing on Cherríe Moraga.* Austin: University of Texas Press.

———. 2007. "Reflections on Thirty Years of Critical Practice in Chicana/o Cultural Studies." In *A Companion to Latina/o Studies,* edited by Juan Flores and Renato Rosaldo, 397–405. Malden, MA: Blackwell Publishing.

45 Shimmering Phantasmagoria

Trans/Cinema/Aesthetics in an Age of Technological Reproducibility

Eliza Steinbock

Trans and film studies scholar Eliza Steinbock has written widely on trans aesthetics and art and has served on the editorial teams for *TSQ: Transgender Studies Quarterly* and Duke University Press's books series *ASTERISK: Gender, Trans-, and All That Comes After*. In this selection, drawn from the first chapter of their book *Shimmering Images*, Steinbock analyzes the relationship between trans embodiments and film. As the author notes, some of pioneering filmmaker George Méliès's first works involved cinematic "trick shots" based on stop-motion, cutting, and splicing techniques that created the illusion of instantaneous on-screen gender transformations. Part of what early cinema-watchers saw when they looked at such images, Steinbock argues, was not just a representation of gender-change as a bit of trickery: they saw as well, with a sense of marvel, how the new technology of motion pictures rearranged time and space, light and (later) sound, allowing viewers to imagine themselves, and the world, in new ways. Contemporary trans artists have continued to explore this cinematic capacity, often in ways that subvert the assumption that the camera records some obvious truth of the body captured by its gaze and then reveals that body to its audience.

Opening a phantasmagoria show in Paris in 1793, Philip Philidor proclaimed to the crowd, "I do not wish to deceive you; but I will astonish you."[1] The Enlightenment's investment in rational, clear thinking achieved by shining a light on the natural world takes a perverse twist in this popular form of entertainment that projects phantoms during an aural and visual dialogue between the living and the dead. The double view of trans bodies as both engineered by medical science and as fundamentally illusory holds the same tension, and protracted appeal, as proto-cinematic phantasmagoria shows. In our twenty-first-century cultural moment when trans characters and talent are inundating televisual series, reality shows, and films, yet still with their transition forming a main attraction and plot device, it seems pertinent to ask, Are trans people the heirs of phantasmagoric visual culture?[2] Taking a historical view, Rita Felski argues that the perceived undecidability of gender leads the figure of the transsexual to become a metaphor for cultural crisis. Citing the epigram *fin de siècle, fin de sexe*, Felski notes how the anxieties of suspended sex from the late nineteenth century return before the millennium during the postmodern moment in which "gender emerges as a privileged symbolic field for the articulation of diverse fashionings of history and time," be they apocalyptic or redemptive.[3]

What is missing in trans origin myths and interpretations of their existence—a bellwether—is an appreciation for how trans subjects narrate and represent their lives and thereby mold

DOI: 10.4324/9781003206255-55

the available conceptual models of gendered embodiment. This chapter submits that diverse conceptualizations for trans embodiments and identities emerge together with phantasmagorical visual practices that offer them a horizon of intelligibility by interlacing science with entertainment. I foremost explore the continuity of a stuttering, flickering type of transformation as a type of shimmering found in the early cinematographic "fantastic views" of filmmaker George Méliès (1896–1912). [. . .] At the close I consider how shimmering phantasmagoria return in the contemporary trans artworks of Zackary Drucker and A. L. Steiner, who collaborate on a photography series entitled "Before/After" (2009–present), and the flipbook and life-size zoetrope project "Becoming" by Yishay Garbasz (2010), documenting the year before and after her gender clarification surgery. Forgoing the foundational terms of either *trans* or *film* is imperative to tracing the phantasmagoria's lingering hold on how a transformative embodiment is conceptualized within visual culture. Following Elizabeth Freeman's queer historical concept of "temporal drag" to register the pull of the deep past on the present, I focus on how some trans bodies carry forward "the genuine *past*-ness of the past—its opacity and illegibility," that seems intransient and anachronistic, that is, unless viewed from the perspective of the phantasmagoria.[4] To grasp the parallel and overlapping tracks of trans and phantasmagoria's temporal drag, I map the genealogy of an expansive trans concept interacting with invert, hermaphrodite, and deviant sex theories relying on the dichotomy of illusion/real, and I conduct media archaeology to trace phantasmagoric aesthetics of deception/reproduction across divergent cultural series. A veritable mountain of literature discusses phantasmagoria as the name for the ancient or modern exhibition of optical illusions, or the literary creation of a shifting series of imagined phantasms, or the key term of intellectual and aesthetic discussions during the nineteenth and twentieth centuries. Straddling the era of incipient and full-blown technological reproducibility, Tom Gunning explains, "Phantasmagoria takes on the weight of modern dialectics of truth and illusion, subjectivity and objectivity, deception and liberation, and even life and death."[5] Or, as Terry Castle has shown, in the history of the phantasmagoria we can find the latent irrationalism haunting the rationalist conception of the mind, what she calls the "spectralization" of the world of thought.[6] Its persistence today in the syntax of trans lives and representation points toward the strong undertow of these larger categorical anxieties deflected onto gender then as now, and thus complicates the notions of transsexual and transgender as formatively modern or postmodern.

My argumentation goes against the grain of scholars such as Bernice Hausman or R. Nick Gorton who attribute the emergence of trans identities foremost to the development of surgical technologies by modern science and to the taxonomy of mental and sexual pathologies in sexology.[7] The evolving system of medico-scientific discourses certainly determines the so-called truth about a subject's status vis-à-vis differentiating between pathological and healthy definitions of sexual and gender practices. Trans subjects who articulate the feeling of being in the "wrong body" become a sign of pathology, and therefore a subject to reform back to health. But this view of trans embodiment is limited to explaining discourses of clinical experiences that arose during the modern era, however much of a hold they retain today in spite of competition from juridical definitions of self-determination.[8] In addition, I also contest the conclusion of trans scholars such as Jack Halberstam who claim this modern formation of trans has been superseded by postmodern theories that question any form of universal truth and challenges the fixity of all meaning, including the designations sex and gender.[9] [. . .] However, the modern and the postmodern claims for conceptualizing trans are primarily about epistemological correction, or uncertainty. Running through both claims, and both eras, is the perpetuation of the trans stereotype of *being* illusory or unreal, which places a heavy stigma on those who assert a trans identity. That is, the trans "onto-epistemological" condition, in which being and knowing are always already entangled, appears symbolically as either an aberration or a deconstructive supplement to constructed normal, natural, or healthy binary gender identities that match the sex assigned at birth, often referred to as cisgender.[10] The visual legacies of inscribing gender truths onto the visual body-as-text can be heard in trans vocabularies, such as being read (for trans), passing (for cisgender), female impersonator, or masculine presenting. Trans subjectivity is pulled taut between gestures of concealing and revealing with its literal translation into the violence of the genital reveal I discussed in the introduction. First I address the perilous investment in an one/none visual truth of sex and gender before coming to see how trans subjects engage the phantasmagoria *dispositif* to effectively shift the visual and discursive order toward a model of sensorial reckoning best described as shimmering.

Cultural Series

Machines for Perceiving "Self-Evidences"

The experience of transitioning is often conceptualized as a visual effect of a personal disclosure, a "coming out" of the hidden epistemological closet into the revealing light of truth. Jay Prosser, for example, considers the transsexual to exist only during a medically assisted physical transition to become the desired perceptible gender. "The immediate purpose of transsexuality," he writes, "is to make real the subject's true gender on the body," and in this pursuit he names "the visual media" as being highly valuable for the "promise (like transition itself) to make visible that which begins as imperceptible—there but underexposed."[11] People who "cross over (*trans-*) the boundaries constructed by their culture to define and contain gender" thereby lose access to conventional evidence for making truth claims for their gender identity.[12] This places a tremendous amount of onto-epistemological weight on the indexical, referential, and highly visual dimension of their truth statements. The visual media of photographic images especially "realize the image of the 'true' self that is originally only apparitional" to others and potentially to oneself.[13] The photographic portrait accompanying written testimony functions, for Prosser, as an incarnation of gendered realness, bringing to the apparitional yet truer version of self as described in language a sense of heft paradoxically through its paper or digital materiality. In Prosser's brilliant analysis of how written trans autobiographies often integrate personal and artistic photographs, he is aware of the dangers of awarding visual media with less (perceived) mediation between signifier and soma than writing's rhetorical strategies. Borrowing language from Roland Barthes, the photograph, he notes, appears "co-natural" or fully in alignment with the bodily referent and even confused with it as it begins to function as more referential to the anchored gendered self (I am there, I am that) than the actual body that remains stubbornly in flux. In fact, the photographic portrait that realizes a true gender by index risks over time not offering the indexed subject a sustained form of gendered realness, but rather its illusion. The "now you see it, now you don't" quality of visual trans self-representation can function like a phantasmagoric technique. Like Philidor's disclaimer for his phantasmagoria, the production of visual gendered realness oscillates between deception and astonishment.

The optical device and conceptual vehicle of the phantasmagoria stresses the spectacular and spectral quality of bodies. Not only did the phantasmagoria incorporate the necessary, underlying lens technologies, perspectival physics, and techniques for capturing light for photographic arts, it also readied an audience eager to be astonished by cinematographic views. For a methodological frame to study the continuities between previous popular trick technologies and early film, André Gaudreault suggests the inclusive term of a "cultural series" for moments of transition through "intermedial meshing" between media rather than looking to pinpoint a historical rupture.[14] The process of institutionalization through the normalization of codes later set the animated views of cinema apart from other cultural forms such as magic shows and vaudeville theatre, consolidating it into a relatively autonomous media institution during Hollywood's Golden Age (1917–1960s). Even from a twenty-first-century point of view though, the series element of spectacular and specular bodies continues to play across differing cultural and media forms, linking together phantasmagoric aesthetic impulses with new technical advances. The cultural series approach that tracks intermedial meshing might also be applied to the scientific series of sexual intermediacy in which earlier notions of trans concepts were strongly related to homosexuality and intersexuality as well. Dating from the late nineteenth century, this kaleidoscopic blending and turning of trans-inter-queer inflections has a distinctly visual and psychosexual lineage. Take for example Magnus Hirschfeld's "Yearbooks for Sexual Intermediaries" (1899–1923), which consist of 20,000 pages of images showing the variance of psychic and physical hermaphroditism, transvestism, and homosexuality between the poles of what he called the "full woman" and the "full man."[15] These meshings of sexual intermediacy shifted again when judicial rulings compared intersex and transsexual claims to change gender status (1950s) and when homosexuality was largely replaced by transsexuality in a key reference psychology book on diagnosing mental disorders (1973).[16] My framing of phantasmagoria as a cultural series has the benefit of bringing together, and thinking together, two historical transitional moments: when technological reproducibility first affected visual culture by heightening the volatility of an audiovisual image, and when surgical and sexological science also first acknowledged the mutability of gender.

[. . .]

In the case of the phantasmagoria, I see that it patterns the supposedly self-evident or knowable visibilities of both cinema images and trans bodies as astonishing illusions or more generally as a shimmer. Deleuze defines visibilities to be "forms of luminosity which are created by the light [of the era] itself and allow a thing or object to exist only as a flash, sparkle or *shimmer*."[17] The "first light" of an era acts as a virtual visibility producing all perceptible experiences; it "brings forth visibilities as flashes and shimmerings, which are the 'second light.'"[18] Thus, the pervasive lights of an era can be analyzed as a potentate form that is capable of creating other forms and movements.[19]

[. . .]

I look methodologically at how the cultural series of the phantasmagoria developed in order to understand how the sense of trans right about now is oddly not that anachronistic with trans from back then. Although trans identification and means to attain a gender transition then and now are clearly not the same, the lingering phantasmagoric aesthetic achieves a continued problematic sense of a sex change as self-evidently illusory by wavering on the tip of deception/astonishment. My archaeological method involves "breaking open" the self-evidence of an audiovisual cultural form that is suspended in the "strata" of an age, leading to the question, How did the era of technological reproducibility become filled with this particular cultural series of phantasmagoric shimmerings?[20] Principally, according to a media archeology perspective, as the means of image reproduction became more sophisticated so did the concealment of its production, contributing further to the sense of self-evident realness and the ever-greater popular success of phantasmagoric devices. The original phantasmagoria that used rear projection from behind the screen to keep the audience unaware of the lanterns became improved with new optical technologies of film that further hid the source of production by projecting images from behind the audiences' backs. Jonathan Crary's historical study of visual devices and techniques determines that of the many competing optical experiences of the 1830s most disappeared by the 1850s because they were insufficiently "phantasmorgoric" in the sense of creating an illusion of the image's standalone realness.[21] [. . .] The occultation of production through its concealment makes a commodity a "very queer thing," Marx noted, because it seems to take on an animated life of its own.[22] Hiding the production of gender, sometimes in plain sight with gender-marked clothing, gesture, and so on, enables one's outer appearance to do the work of "claiming the status of being." The very queer shimmer of a thing in the era of technological reproducibility shows up under the aegis of competing phantasmagorical optical novelties that create a world of images so real that they threaten to replace the actual experiences they represent.

The genre of fantastical stories of transformation also trades in the troubling division of illusion from realness. One of the first self-authored memoirs of someone who was relentlessly investigated for their "true" sex and gender identity was written by Herculine (Adélaîde/ Abel) Barbin (1838–68), who also referred to herself as Alexina or Camille and was living in France during the phantasmagoria craze. Foucault came across Barbin's story through an entry in a sexological encyclopedia published by Auguste Tardieu that details Barbin's youth spent in an all-girl's convent school and later a women's teaching college. Foucault extracts from the personal narrative and surrounding medical documents an emerging social perception of monstrous and foolish embodiments that deviate from the ideal form of a singular sex—a new shimmer in the audiovisual archive. Changes of sex or claims of multiple sexes increasingly became considered as "insulting to 'the truth,'" or "not adequate to reality," and "seen as belonging more or less to the realm of chimeras."[23] Even if not an outright crime, sexual irregularity is suspected to be fictitious, a mere disguise that should be stripped off through the declaration of one's true sex.

[. . .]

The fantastic view that gender is transformable, and sex changeable, acknowledges an interest in the waning sense of incommensurable difference between the sexes.[24] The cinematographic shimmer of trans, however flickering in and out of focus with hermaphrodites and sexual deviants, indicates that long before Christine Jorgenson attained her international celebrity for having a "sex change" in the early 1950s, the visual field was peppered with sex change—type narratives and morphing imagery. In the scientific series of trans sex transformation, a significant shift occurred when Western scientific traditions of surveillance, measurement, and physical transformation utilized cinema to perform a "fantastic construction of 'human life' as a dynamic entity to be tracked, studied, and transformed in the social 'theatre' of the laboratory."[25] The ontology of cinema, in its special relation to animating life and suspending death in a cinematic theatre, strongly resembles the ontology of the trans body that undergoes surgery, which takes place in an operating theatre. In the phantasmagoria cultural series, cinema, with its system of editing cuts and suturing images, parallels the incisions and sutures that take place in a surgical theatre. Attention to the construction of human life with respect to the ways in which surgical and cinematic cuts refigure bodies may offer insight into the cultural and technical conditions that enabled trans identity to emerge differentiated from an otherwise perplexing limbo identity.

[. . .]

Trickality Aesthetics

Georges Méliès and the Quick Change

The model of cinema-as-surgical theatre bears out surprisingly literally in the practice of early filmmaking, flipping Susan Stryker's insight into the "cinematic logic of transsexual embodiment" into a confirmation of the transsexual logic of cinema at work since its inception. In 1888 Georges Méliès bought the famous Théâtre Robert-Houdin in Paris and worked as a conjuring magician some eight years before he started experimenting with new cinematographic devices. Playing the impresario in most all of his films, Méliès swapped a magic wand for scissors. "Méliès was one of the first to think of the cinema in terms of cuts!" exclaims Gaudreault, who points to the often overlooked stigmata of the numerous cuts found through all of Méliès's films, hidden in the upper corner of the celluloid film strip where the glue sutures together two distinct successive moments that comprise the trick effect.[26] The presence of scissors and glue indicate the slice-and-splice creative thinking that surgeons also apply. Even closer to the surgical cutting edge though was how along with developing his achievements in editing Méliès developed a penchant for demonstrating an instant sex change on film. Both the match-on-action trick edit and gender transformation are birthed in the origin story of his discovery of the stop-camera technique. It occurred one day through a happy accident when he was filming at the Place de l'Opéra around October or November 1896, less than a half year after he began filmmaking. He claims that "[. . . .] the camera I used in the early days (a primitive thing in which the film tore or frequently caught and refused to advance) jammed and produced an unexpected result; a minute was needed to disengage the film and to make the camera work again. During this minute, the passers-by, a horse trolley and other vehicles had, of course, changed positions. In projecting the strip, rejoined [*ressoudée*: glued back together] at the point of the break, I suddenly saw a Madeleine-Bastille horse trolley change into a hearse and men become women."[27] Gaudreault analyzes this quote to show that Méliès rightly belongs to the history of editing, as he is clearly aware from this moment of the possibility to glue together mismatching frames (that link different content by shared action) to achieve an astonishing effect.[28] This is the animated effect of the before-and-after photograph, speeding up the minute during which the scene became rearranged to an instant.

However, the quick change of men becoming women was perhaps more than just a lucky metamorphosis; it precipitated in cinematic aesthetics the avant-garde of the surgical and hormonal science of sex transformation by at least a decade.[29] Charles Darwin wrote in 1868, "in many, probably in all cases, the secondary characters of each sex lie dormant or latent in the opposite sex ready to be evolved under peculiar circumstances."[30] Méliès's filmic trick effect discovered a quarter of a century later seems to offer up this "peculiar circumstance" of sexual morphing as imaginable in the blink of an eye. This first substitution or stop-camera trick, Méliès says, sent him into a frenzy of experimentation: "Two days later, I produced the first metamorphoses of men into women and the first sudden disappearances [. . .]. One trick led to another."[31] Although Méliès used narrative, all his films are "trick-motivated" in that the story is accessory and theatricality is a pretext to the centering of what Gaudrealt coins cinema's inherent capacity for "trickality."[32] In the cinema's trickality one can grasp the transformative possibility of reproductive technology for human identity.

[. . .]

Principally, the stop-motion effect is technically simple in that the camera operator is required to stop the motion of filming and then resume it, but in the laboratory the montage was also always recut on the negative to ensure that the desired continuity of action between frames match perfectly, which hides the splice in an unbroken rhythm. The splice proves that the perceived filmic instant is not just the instant of stopping, like that captured by a photography camera, but also a jump forward in real time. The on-match cut must be practically invisible to ensure the viewer experiences the continuity of time when introduced to any factors of discontinuity (man into woman, trolley into hearse). Different from the continuity system of editing that ensures smoothness in the narrative by suturing together cause and effect or diegetic relationships, Méliès used match-on-action cutting for magical ends rather than dramatic purposes.[33] Frank Kessler clarifies how trick films go against the presumption of a "cinematic specificity" that lies in the camera's capability for "reproducing visible reality"; instead the trick intervenes to manipulate "the exact rendition of the visual impression that an actual scene would provide to an eye-witness."[34] The illusion lies in the presumption of the perceived instant, that is, in the illusion of temporal continuity. This false sense of temporal continuity is "enhanced by the unchanging spatial arrangement" of the frontal shot with its fixed framing.[35] Although performed on the same stage, a gulf of difference lies between Méliès's real-time theatrical magic and the collapsed temporal instant of his filmic tricks: the location is not changed, the body is. The stop-camera edit provides a view of gender that is based on montage and assembly, departing from the naturalization of a body's gender that exists without a noticeable, conspicuous cut.

[. . .]

Reparative Practices of Cut and Suture

Resequencing Trans Hirstories

Aesthetically, this era of reproducibility and instant change is today still seeded by the chrononormativity of trans before-and-after photography, which derives from the same tricks Méliès used to "effectuate instantaneous transformations" in the flick from one image to another, approximating the editing done with a scalpel.[36] Of course the reality of any surgically wrought change is far less speedy, not to mention the long time lapse between various surgeries or stages of a surgical change, and as presented in *Man into Woman*, a transition can follow nonchronological sequencing. The phantasmagoria's "techno-necro" roots of bringing the dead to life—by way of confusing categories dead/alive, truth/falsity, past/present—throws up an opportunity for contemporary trans artists.[37] In returning to the novelty of phantasmagoric aesthetics they purchase a discourse bent on disorienting juxtapositions. Retro-phantasmagoric images offer a cover for the awkward, impossible split framing forced on to the transsexual body "in transition" to both pass and be revealed, that is, to have a true and a false identity, to be dead or relegated to the past but still alive in the present. With a phantasmagoric vision artists can foreground presenting the trick to the viewer, to tickle their desire for optical mastery while withholding a full reveal. Knowledge of the technological mechanism that presents the vision does not necessarily undermine the reality of that vision. As Gunning puts it, the phantasmagoric effect is "I know very well, and yet I see . . ."[38] Trans artists who invoke early modern optical toys and tricks not only practice temporal drag via a return to a so-called outdated medium, but also show acute awareness of the hangover of the true sex conceptual apparatus, for it drags on in contemporary sociocultural and certainly psycho-sexological discourses. Their harkening of these "throwback" concepts, aesthetics, and technologies facilitates time travel to resequence trans histories as well as their own transition histories.

Deriving from beauty, fashion, and surgical advertisements, before-and-after photographs obey the imperative to portray the self, improved. Thus the pairing of images might not necessarily cite a gender transition but is always gendered. The photography project "Before/After" (2009–) of Zackary Drucker in collaboration with A. L. Steiner occurs in the context of Drucker's performance, photographic, and video work that draws on her trans experience, particularly during the period 2008–10, when she first started physically transitioning.[39] The images currently circulating use some of the same trick techniques that Méliès pioneered in his films, for example, double exposure and duplex photography, which achieve cinematic aesthetics through capturing the moment of transformation in a single image. Other images use an opaque sheet recalling the vanishing lady trick, and more include diptychs of switched bodies back-to-front as well as switched bodies side-by-side. The project's cheeky joke is before and after what exactly? What event or temporal jump has taken place, on which body? Two bodies are presented, rotund and thin, large-breasted and budding, straight blond hair and dark curls, older and younger. Each masquerades as the other transformed, if we follow the invited trans logic of before and after. This series performs a preposterous split temporality distributed across dual, dueling bodies. The series has been installed wrapped around both sides of a corner and is also available in a printed postcard bundle one might thumb through. The multiples of "Before/After" made available simultaneously to the viewer trouble the search for the time of past perfect in which one event is supposed to have happened *before* another one in the past. Without anchoring in a before/body, which is the moment of the after/body?

Ducking the portrait's investment in realist resemblance, these split images suggest the viewer recall the magic simplicity used in theatrical and then cinematic magic acts of disappearance/reappearance, for instance by citing a sheet over a body. The blanket functions as a screen for our projections of which body might be more desirable: Steiner's curves or Drucker's leanness? It is unclear in which direction or into which body we place the unsatisfactory before and the desired after. The wonky double exposure of their bodies, seated and smiling, overlaid imperfectly, also invokes the ghostly apparitions of the phantasmagoria; but who is channeling whom here? It's attention to layering implicates a generosity of sharing a body, an act of gifting in which body areas and parts could be gained/lost through an optical game of addition, subtraction, multiplication, and division. Engaging Roland Barthes's theory of the photographic referent, Prosser writes that visual media promise to "realize the image of the 'true' self that is originally only apparitional," thereby incarnating the trans subject.[40] And yet these before-and-after portraits depict bodies cloaked in the transitioning narrative without any clear resolution of which would be this true self, or even which body should be taken as realized after the transformative event. The pairing of Steiner and Drucker seem to contribute in different, even contradictory ways to the notion of incarnating the trans subject via a radical split. Instead of a real woman emerging, transfemininity here incarnates through mutual longing.

"Before/After" takes a formalist approach to trans portraiture by ignoring who might be in transition, which is usually signaled by a named person in transition, even one in backslash like Einar/Lili. Instead its continued interrogation is of the aesthetic named in all the titles that comprise the series. Yishay Garbasz's two-year project of weekly self-documentation of her transition marked by a vaginoplasty, which resulted in a flipbook and large-scale zoetrope both called "Becoming" (2010), also uses seriality to foreground the forms her body takes over an expanded before/after time. The title's gerund *becoming* with its ever-expanding present futurity echoes with how the series presents a transition as progressively accretive instants. The 911 photographs of her nude body against a white backdrop show her one year before and one year after her gender clarification surgery on November 18, 2008, detailing the slight changes under way in hairstyle, nail color, facial expression, posture, and so on. Through appearing as "a straightforward look" at a physical transformation, as she writes,[41] the basic animation technology of a flipbook allows the viewer to control the movement of her becoming. Holding the book's edge with your thumb, you can flip forward, back, or stop to play "spot the difference" on the full-frontal body lying small scale in your palm.[42]

By contrast the zoetrope project installed at the 2010 Busan Biennale in South Korea insists on the unique physics of Garbasz's movement.[43] Here a select number of self-portraits were printed life-size, then were lit from within the enormous wheel and cast spinning along in a rhythmic movement that follows the transition's physical changes. Crucial to Garbasz's decision for this format of the early modern optical device is that it injects movement into the images without requiring projection or animation from elsewhere.[44] Not only is the documentation self-made, but also the display retains authority over the pace of Garbasz's bodily transformation. The flipbook and zoetrope animations insert a stuttering movement into her transition; the breaks in uniformity create small jerks that recall the shimmers resulting from the minute, overall "effort for difference," as Barthes phrases it (see the introduction).

Despite her full-frontal nudity, the optical devices point foremost to the things unseen, to the nuance of where difference arrives. Sobchack makes the point that the pages "visibly stutter a bit as we flick them, reminding us of the temporal gaps in between, pointing to things unseen—cut out but nonetheless re-membered (pun intended)."[45]

These works meditate on the expansions and disorientations possible in the format of before/after, calling for a formalist approach to their analysis, "an impulse to dilate the aesthetic encounter as such, to *prolong* it by means of analysis and reading," as Richmond describes it.[46] The overt references to the format of optical toys, visual illusions, and the thrill of seeing human movement conjured out of still images shake off the hold before/after has on defining trans embodiment. In the dilated aesthetic encounter—walking around the edge to see where the series goes, flipping through the changing bodies and watching them whirl by—a formalist approach "reveals instead something hidden, yet nevertheless also given, in our perception and our feeling" about trans shimmers.[47] The formalism applied to the trans experience by these artists refuses to disclose a hidden meaning of who they really are; the highly self-reflexive choice of formats shifts into view the operations of the hidden structure of feelings that coalesce around their phantasmagoric bodies.

In anticipating the imperative for a trans reveal, these artworks seek to link the surprise associated with glimpsing the difference of a trans body to other affective responses than negatively tinted ones. Writing on the queer paranoiac's tenet that the violence of gender reification must be anticipated, Sedgwick explains that surprise is the one thing that the paranoid tries to eliminate through mastery of knowledge.[48] The necessity of forestalling painful surprises produces an anticipatory response she describes as proposing, "*Anything you can do (to me) I can do worse,* and *Anything you can do (to me) I can do first*—to myself."[49] While aware of how a reveal usually results in violence, these artworks—by taking a phantasmagoric form for their reveals—challenge the paranoid's unshakable faith in demystifying exposure. Following from Melanie Klein, Sedgwick explains that to a reparatively positioned reader (or viewer) it can seem realistic and necessary to experience surprise: "Because there can be terrible surprises, however, there can also be good ones."[50] The artworks pivot on the goodwill of the artist revealing something of themselves, but also on the viewer's goodwill to demonstrate openness to the new in the anticipation of the "after" shot, or what emerges in the becoming. The reparative assemblage of a new object—transition—with associated positive affects takes place through an anachronistic identification with sexual intermediacy—not coincidentally, I might add. Entering the reparative mode via the temporal drag of the phantasmagoria enables a resequencing of trans histories; it gives pause to reflect that if the past could have been different than it actually was, maybe the future will be too.

Reaching through a tear in the skin of time, these works extract life-giving substance from a culture that avows not to sustain them. The age of reproducibility in which the phantasmagoria rose in popularity also gave rise to the technological ability for projecting one's self: the trans/cinema agency to cut and splice together audiovisual images into a new sequence. The phantoms recalled from the dead also herald a posttranssexual moment à la Stone in which the binary personae do not have to be forever split, but shown in a lengthy progression (Garbasz) or out of synch (Drucker/Steiner). Through the delinking and relinking of images the phantasmagoric gender transitions reshuffle the sensorium of the artist and viewer alike. In discussing intercultural cinema, Laura Marks makes an addendum to Foucault's categorical orders of the sayable and seeable, which Deleuze tracks in film's audio and visual levels, that an order of the *sensible* is "the sum of what is accessible to sense perception at a given historical and cultural moment."[51] The temporal drag of the phantasmagoria in trans artworks might thus be a means of accessing across a wrinkle in time another organization of the senses in order to open up our cultural moment to a new sensorium that is in fact renewed. "Aesthetics concerns the struggle for control over the human sensorium," insists Sean Cubitt in *The Practice of Light*, which is why control over light and its mediations in the age of reproducibility is so charged—for Benjamin writing on the brink of fascism but also for trans representation created in an era of great violence against gender nonconformity.[52] The incorporation of the phantasmagoria haunting trans bodies into art-making practices reflects how "the machine is always social before it is technical. There is always a social machine that selects or assigns the technical elements used," in Deleuze and Claire Parnet's words.[53] Rather than seeing the phantasmagoria exclusively as either an ideological machine sustaining illusions or a process of demystification, Gunning persuades that its great capacity for producing startling effects could provide "an aesthetic model for the manipulation of the senses."[54] The showmanship, audience pleasure, and scrambling of what is perceptible by the senses all lend the phantasmagoria an air of highly politicized aesthetics. Rather than fostering credulity or incredulity, then, the phantasmagoria becomes a training ground for a sensorial reckoning of those psychic and affective currents of being that fall away from rational belief. The sensorial experience of trans shimmers may not be easily grasped or cast as real, but in the framing of a phantasmagoria, in which misty forms float into view and men incrementally or suddenly change into women, the so-called illusion is experienced as a real entity.

Finally, the reparative work being carried out on trans visual hirstories indicates that some trans bodies, more than others, appear phantasmagoric from a contemporary perspective.[55] The inheritance of trans phantasmagoric imagery with the specter of a horrific or hilarious surprise seems to be passed down mainly, if not specifically, to trans women who seem to carry the burden of "the genuine *past*-ness of the past—its opacity and illegibility."[56] [. . . R]ecent trans cultural productions also participate in the historical revival with films that reimagine the Stonewall riots by foregrounding the role of trans women of color and street queens such as Marsha P. Johnson and Silvia Rivera, who are honored in *Happy Birthday, Marsha!* (dir. Reina Gossett and Sasha Wortzel, 2016).[57] As the Silent Generation and Baby Boomer trans godmothers taper off, younger artists have started to grapple with making sense of the ensuing generational shift by investigating the query, What is our inheritance? To the question of how their life stories will be told, one can already find substantiation of a highly willing temporal drag, or identification across generations, in recent feature-length documentaries about the influential lives of the prison abolition and trans woman of color activist Miss Major Griffin-Gracy and the theorist and theatre-maker Kate Bornstein, and in the archiving of Flawless Sabrina's organization of a national drag beauty pageant and performance career.[58] The reparative impulse within these younger trans-led projects seems linked to an intransient and anachronistic identification that mixes up the temporal order of progressive narratives. These deeply historical projects enter their subjects into the phantasmagoric pantheon of visual culture as trans women who refuse both to fade into the population and to acquiesce to the logic of a full reveal. The next chapter continues an investigation of how trans subjects have negotiated the reveal but in the pornographic register, where genital optics are closely tied to the documented authenticity of the sexual performance and the performer's gender identity.

Notes

1. Quoted in Laurent Mannoni, *The Great Art of Light and Shadow* (Exeter: University of Exeter Press, 2000), 144.

Shimmering Phantasmagoria 549

2. Here I refer to Laverne Cox playing Sophia Burset on *Orange Is the New Black*, Jamie Clayton playing Nomi on *Sense8*, numerous characters on *Trans-parent*, Scott Turner Schofield on *The Bold and the Beautiful*, *I Am Cait* about Caitlyn Jenner, *I Am Jazz* on the life of a young trans woman, RuPaul's *Drag Race*, and so on. I mention specific films in the introduction and in this chapter refer to Tom Hooper's 2015 dramatization of *The Danish Girl*.

3. Rita Felski, "*Fin de siècle, Fin de sexe*: Transsexuality, Postmodernism, and the Death of History," *New Literary History* 27 (1996): 338.

4. Elizabeth Freeman, *Time Binds: Queer Temporalities, Queer Histories* (Durham, NC: Duke University Press, 2010), 62–64.

5. He further writes, "I know of no word more complex than 'Phantasmagoria,'" in Tom Gunning, "Illusions Past and Future: The Phantasmagoria and Its Specters" (paper presented at the Refresh! First International Conference on the Histories of Art, Science and Technology, 2004). Consulted via Media Art History accessed March 24, 2016, http://pl02.donau-uni.ac.at/jspui/handle/10002/296/.

6. Terry Castle, "Phantasmagoria: Spectral Technology and the Metaphorics of Modern Reverie," *Critical Inquiry* 15, no. 1 (1988): 29.

7. On surgeries see Dwight Billings and Thomas Urban, "The Socio-Medical Construction of Trans-sexualism: An Interpretation and Critique," *Social Problems* 29, no. 3 (1982): 266–282; Bernice Hausman, *Changing Sex: Transsexualism, Technology, and the Idea of Gender* (Durham, NC: Duke University Press, 1995).

   On diagnostic categories see Jay Prosser, *Second Skins: The Body Narratives of Transsexuality* (New York: Columbia University Press, 1998); and the provocative R. Nick Gorton, "Transgender as Mental Illness: Nosology, Social Justice, and the Tarnished Golden Mean," in *The Transgender Studies Reader 2*, ed. Susan Stryker and Aren Aizura (New York: Routledge, [2007] 2013), 644–52.

8. Legal and administrative hurdles to gender self-determination in the U.S. context are elaborately discussed in Dean Spade, *Normal Life: Administrative Violence, Critical Trans Politics, and the Limits of Law* (Durham, NC: Duke University Press, 2015).

9. Early examples include Jack (formerly Judith) Halberstam, "F2M: The Making of Female Masculinity," in *The Lesbian Postmodern*, ed. Laura Doan (New York: Columbia University Press, 1994), 210–228; Susan Stryker, "My Words to Victor Frankenstein Above the Village of Chamounix: Performing Transgender Rage" [1994], in *The Transgender Studies Reader*, ed. Susan Stryker and Stephen Whittle (New York: Routledge, 2006), 244–256.[. . .]

10. Karen Barad, *Meeting the Universe Halfway: Quantum Physics and the Entanglement of Matter and Meaning* (Durham, NC: Duke University Press, 2007).

11. Prosser, *Second Skins*, 211.

12. Susan Stryker, *Transgender History* (Berkeley: Seal Press, 2008), 1.

13. Prosser, *Second Skins*, 211.

14. André Gaudreault, *Film and Attraction: From Kinematography to Cinema*, trans. Timothy Barnard (Chicago: University of Illinois Press, [2008] 2011), 68. Gaudreault acknowledges that Eric de Kuyper articulates ideas similar to his "intermedial meshing" to describe the hodgepodge of technologies among kinematographic phenomena.

15. Vern L. Bullough, "Magnus Hirschfeld, An Often Over-Looked Pioneer," *Sexuality and Culture* 7, no. 1 (2003): 62–72. See commentary on the role of Hirschfeld in Merl Storr and Jay Prosser, "Introduction to Part III Transsexuality and Bisexuality," in *Sexology Uncensored: The Documents of Sexual Science*, ed. Lucy Bland and Laura Doan (Chicago: Chicago University Press, 1998), 75–77. Sexology today differentiates cross-gender identification from intersex conditions. Conceptualization of trans identification evolved into a psychic cross-gender desire aligned with requested bodily modifications, whereas intersex was kept from becoming an identity by framing bodies as atypical through diagnosis and (nonconsensual) treatment. Hence, both involve hormonal and surgical practices but deployed in one case to treat the psyche and in the other case, the physical irregularity. Today intersex social movements and trans rights organizations both use the language of self-determination and informed consent models to enable people access to voluntary treatment that is seen from a more holistic perspective.

16. See Stryker, *Transgender History*, 95–98; Ulrike Klöppel, "Who Has the Right to Change Gender Status? Drawing Boundaries Between Inter- and Trans- Sexuality," in *Critical Intersex*, ed. M. Morgan Holmes (Farnham, U.K.: Ashgate, 2009), 171.

17. Deleuze, *Foucault*, 52, emphasis mine.

18. Deleuze, *Foucault*, 57–58. In Deleuze's reading of Foucault, the method of tracing secret statements and the light that makes a thing shimmer underline all of Foucault's historical works. From *The Archaeology of Knowledge* onward, discourse precedes the visible field he designates as "non-discursive." For

Foucault, however, this suggests irreducibility, not a reduction. The nonrelation of words and images implies for Foucault an important cultural process of mutual grappling and capture.

19. Foucault tried to locate visibilities in his study of Roussel and isolate them in Manet, tracing an aesthetics of an era in a manner close to that of the French artist Robert Delaunay (1885–1941), argues Deleuze (*Foucault*, 52).

20. Deleuze, *Foucault*, 53.

21. Jonathan Crary, *Techniques of the Observer: On Vision and Modernity in the Nineteenth Century* (Cambridge, MA: MIT Press, 1990), 132–36.

22. Karl Marx, "Section 4 The Fetishism of Commodities and the Secret Thereof," in *A Critique of Political Economy: Vol I Part I—The Process of Capitalist Production*, ed. Friedrich Engels (New York: Cosimo Classics, [1867] 2007), 81.

23. Michel Foucault, "Introduction," in *Being the Recently Discovered Memoirs of a Nineteenth-Century French Hermaprodite (1838) by Herculine Barbin*, trans. Richard McDougall (New York: Pantheon, 1980), x. Foucault's study of Barbin's conjectured hermaphroditism recalls and to an extent reproduces the early entanglements of inversion theory relying on the notion of physical and psychic hermaphroditism that enfolds sexological histories of both transsexuality and homosexuality.

24. The shifting notion of sexual difference(s) is documented by Joanne Meyerowitz, *How Sex Changed: A History of Transsexuality in the United States* (Cam-bridge, MA: Harvard University Press, 2002). From the early twentieth century, she writes, "the concepts of sex change and sex-change surgery existed well before the word transsexual entered the medical parlance" (15).

25. Lisa Cartwright, *Screening the Body: Tracing Medicine's Visual Culture* (Minneapolis: University of Minnesota Press, 1995), 9.

26. André Gaudreault, "Theatricality, Narrativity, and Trickality: Reevaluating the Cinema of Georges Méliès," *Journal of Popular Film and Television* 15, no. 3 (1987): 118.

27. Georges Méliès, "Cinematographic Views," *October* 29 (1984): 30, with additional translation borrowed from André Gaudreault, "Méliès the Magician," trans. Timothy Barnard, *Early Popular Visual Culture* 5, no. 2 (2009): 171.

28. Gaudreault, "Méliès the Magician," 171–173.

29. See Meyerowitz, *How Sex Changed*, 15–20. Beginning with the Austrian physiologist Eugen Steinach in the 1910s, so-called sex transformation experiments were first tried on animals. The successful results were put into practice for humans in the 1920s and 1930s by doctors associated with Hirschfeld's Institute for Sexual Science in Berlin, who reported on their human sex-change surgeries to much acclaim. Meyerowitz notes that Dorchen Richter was the first male-to-female to undergo complete genital transformation, arranged through Hirschfeld's institute. In 1931 Felix Abraham published an article on two such surgeries (one of which was on Richter); in addition, Ludwig Levy Lenz was reputed to have performed several surgeries at this time, the total of which are unknown.

30. Darwin, quoted in Meyerowitz, *How Sex Changed*, 22–23.

31. Méliès, "Cinematographic Views," 30. Méliès calls his produced views "fantastic" because they include transformation scenes of appearance and disappearance like the phantasmagoria, but also effects using theatrical machines, optical illusions, and editing of metamorphosis trick shots.

32. Gaudreault, "Theatricality, Narrativity, and Trickality," 115.

33. Gaudreault, "Méliès the Magician," 171–173.

34. Frank Kessler, "Trick Films," in *Encyclopedia of Early Cinema*, ed. Richard Abel (London: Routledge, 2005), 643.

35. Kessler, "Trick Films," 643.

36. Katherine Singer Kovács, "Georges Méliès and the 'Féerie'," *Cinema Journal* 16, no. 1 (1976): 11.

37. Gunning, "Illusions Past and Future," 16.

38. "The purveyors of magical illusions learned that attributing their tricks to explainable scientific process did not make them any less astounding, because the visual illusion still loomed before the viewer, however demystified by rational knowledge that illusion might be," writes Tom Gunning, "Animated Pictures: Tales of Cinema's Forgotten Future After 100 Years of Film," in *The Nineteenth-Century Visual Culture Reader*, ed. Vanessa R. Schwartz and Jeannene M. Przyblyski (New York: Routledge, 2004), 104.

39. Zackary Drucker has eight images from the series on her website, accessed March 24, 2016, http://zackarydrucker.com/photography/b4-after/. A. L. Steiner has nine images from the series on her website, accessed March 24, 2016, http://www.hellomynameissteiner.com/filter/collaborations/BEFORE-AFTER-1. More images can be found in the digital essay version of the installation that includes some eighty statements, to which one can answer either true or false, ironically typical of an intake form given

to people who try to access medical treatment for gender "dysphoria." A. L. Steiner and Z. Drucker, "IMG MGMT: Before/After 2009–Present," *Art F City* website, May 16, 2011, accessed March 24, 2016, http://artfcity. com/2011/05/16/img-mgmt-z-drucker-a-l-steiner-beforeafter-2009-present/.

40. Prosser, *Second Skins*, 211.
41. Yishay Garbasz, *Becoming: A Gender Flipbook* (New York: Mark Batty, 2010), 180.
42. Vivian Sobchack remarks on the potential for playfulness in her essay in the book, "On *Becoming*," in Garbasz, *Becoming*, 183–184.
43. A video documentation of the "Becoming" zoetrope installation can be viewed on YouTube, published September 25, 2010, accessed February 20, 2016, www.youtube.com/watch?v=F5diBtcul_4.
44. Yishay Garbasz, personal communication with author, April 18, 2015.
45. Sobchack, "On *Becoming*," 185.
46. Richmond, "The Persistence of Formalism."
47. Richmond, "The Persistence of Formalism."
48. Eve Kosofsky Sedgwick, "Paranoid Reading and Reparative Reading, Or, You're So Paranoid, You Probably Think This Essay Is About You," in *Touching Feeling: Affect, Pedagogy, Performativity* (Durham, NC: Duke University Press, 2003), 132–133.
49. Sedgwick, "Paranoid Reading and Reparative Reading," 131, emphasis in original.
50. Sedgwick, "Paranoid Reading and Reparative Reading," 146.
51. Laura Marks, *The Skin of the Film: Intercultural Cinema, Embodiment, and the Senses* (Durham, NC: Duke University Press, 2000), 30–31.
52. Sean Cubitt, *The Practice of Light: A Genealogy of Visual Technologies from Prints to Pixels* (Cambridge, MA: MIT Press, 2014), 10–11.
53. Gilles Deleuze and Claire Parnet, *Dialogues II*, trans. Hugh Tomlinson and Barbara Habberjam (London: Continuum, 1997), 126–127.
54. Gunning, "Illusions Past and Future," 14.
55. I expand on how to theorize trans art historical and visual culture hirstories in "Collecting Creative Transcestors: Trans★ Portraiture Hirstory, from Snapshots to Sculpture," in *Companion to Feminist Art Practice and Theory*, ed. Maria Buszek and Hilary Robinson (Hoboken, NJ: Wiley-Blackwell Publishing, forthcoming).
56. Freeman, *Time Binds*, 63.
57. Link to official website for *Happy Birthday, Marsha!*, posted February 19, 2015, accessed March 24, 2016, www.happybirthdaymarsha.com/. This factual element of the historical narrative of the Stonewall riots has been erased in the Hollywood version, *Stonewall* (dir. Roland Emmerich, 2015), which was released to poor reviews.
58. Annalise Ophelian, dir., *Major!*, Floating Ophelia Productions, USA, 2016, accessed March 16, 2016, www.missmajorfilm.com/; Sam Feder, dir., *Kate Bornstein Is a Queer and Pleasant Danger*, produced by Sam Feder and Karin Winslow, USA, 2014, accessed March 16, 2016, http://katebornsteinthemovie. com/. The Flawless Sabrina Archive, a nonprofit organization founded by Flawless Sabrina, Zackary Drucker, and Diana Tourjee in 2014 (accessed March 16, 2016, www.flawless-sabrina.com/flawless-sabrina-archive/). Mother Flawless Sabrina/Jack Doroshow passed away November 18, 2017.

Section X

Intersectionality and Embodiment

46 Pauli Murray's Peter Panic

Perspectives From the Margins of Gender and Race in Jim Crow America

Simon D. Elin Fisher

Pauli Murray has gained a reputation, since the publication of Rosalind Rosenberg's 2017 biography *Jane Crow: The Life of Pauli Murray* and the Netflix debut of Julie Cohen and Betsy West's 2021 documentary *I Am Pauli Murray*, as the most important person in twentieth-century U.S. history that most people have never heard of. Murray's legal analyses of the intersecting forms of discrimination and oppression faced by Black women in the South directly informed Thurgood Marshall's argument in the *Brown v. Board of Education Supreme Court* case that overturned racial segregation in schools, Ruth Bader Ginsburg's defense of women's reproductive rights, and Kimberlé Crenshaw's concept of intersectionality. In this article, originally published in *TSQ: Transgender Studies Quarterly*, historian Simon D. Elin Fisher discusses one of the lesser-known dimensions of Murray's life: though Murray was assigned female at birth and answered to she/her pronouns, they also quite openly expressed transmasculine identifications and desires and thought of their gender in non-binary terms. Murray repeatedly sought, and was repeatedly denied, access to masculinizing hormones for a medically assisted gender transition before ultimately reconciling to life as a gender-nonconforming woman (exemplifying the white-centered and anti-black dimensions of the mid-twentieth-century discourse of transsexuality discussed in this volume by Jules Gill-Peterson). The title of the article is taken from one of Murray's pseudonyms, "Peter Panic," used when writing for African-American newspapers in California in the 1940s. As Fisher demonstrates, Murray made a foundational contribution to contemporary understandings of intersectionality in non-academic writing and did so from a specifically trans of color perspective. Fisher helps reposition trans critique not as a recent development that makes use of a pre-existing notion of intersectionality but rather as a constitutive component of that concept's original articulation.

Intersectionality argues that racism and sexism cannot be treated separately as single oppressions, especially when considering the lives of black women (Crenshaw 1989). The history of intersectional feminism demonstrates that the theory is grounded in a trans-of-color analysis of the racial caste system known as "Jim Crow." In 1944, Pauli Murray, an African American activist, journalist, and lawyer, began exploring the simultaneous structural and affective impacts of "white supremacy as well as male supremacy" (Murray 1947: 5). Murray argued that Jim Crow, a system of binary racial categorization, social segregation, violence, and political and economic repression, had a companion: "Jane Crow" similarly classified humans into two binary gender categories, segregated the groups and violently policed their intimate interactions, and restricted the economic and political possibilities of those labeled "woman" (Panic 1944; Murray 1947, 1950; Murray and Eastwood 1965). For three decades,

DOI: 10.4324/9781003206255-57

Murray wrote prominent legal briefs and policy recommendations about Jane Crow and the negative effects it had on women of color, and when Murray moved from law to the priesthood in the 1970s, Jane Crow's perilous affects became the focus of a number of spiritual tracts and sermons.

This article explores Murray's writing on Jane Crow, but instead of charting the progression of Murray's thesis forward through the Civil Rights and feminist movements, I look backward. I build upon the historiography of Civil Rights activists that connects an individual's early encounters with racist oppression and their radical thoughts and actions, and I examine Murray's experiences as a person whose racial appearance and gender expression fell outside black/white and female/male binaries. Jane Crow was developed out of Murray's early navigations of Jim Crow gender and racial categories. At times, Murray purposefully played with the norms that shifted as s/he[1] moved across geographies and institutional settings, but s/he was acutely aware that the power to name her/his race and gender was rarely in her/his hands. Following Kenneth Mack (2012), I ask, how does a life of navigating these hegemonic binaries shape one's analysis of their operation and effects? Through exploring this question, I highlight the trans-of-color analysis of and resistance to Jim Crow central to the historical and theoretical development of intersectional feminism.

Pauli Murray was born in 1910 in Baltimore, a child of what s/he calls "my dual family heritage" (Murray 1987: xiv). Descended from a free woman and freeman, an enslaved woman and her owner, Murray was light-skinned but did not pass as white in the strict racial binaries constituted by Jim Crow. Especially salient to Murray was her/his childhood experiences of segregation that split her/his own family. Out of six siblings, only Murray and one other did not pass as white, separating the siblings in both the public spaces they could inhabit and the social statuses they were afforded. Even with light skin, Murray was designated as black and was "very, very conscious" that her/his movements were regulated and restricted throughout her/his childhood in the South (Murray 1976: 6).

Therefore, from a young age, Murray was a keen observer of the processes of racial categorization, in which, in any (and every) given situation, a more powerful white individual could observe and determine her/his race and admit or refuse her/him entrance into these local, privileged spaces. Murray was simultaneously also restricted by contemporary binary gender norms that insisted each individual be demarcated as either female or male. S/he expressed a pronounced masculine sense of self throughout childhood, and during her/his twenties and thirties, Murray (1937a) wrote that s/he "desired experimentation on the male side." In 1939, s/he clipped an article from the African American *Amsterdam News* reporting that experiments with testosterone "transform[ed] effeminate males into normal men, strong and virile" (*New York Amsterdam News* 1939). S/he immediately visited the hospital where the experiments were conducted, inquiring whether "the clinic would experiment" on her/him "with the male hormone" (Murray 1940).

Recently, and finally, historians (Azaransky 2011, 2013; Gilmore 2009; Mack 2012) have begun to read Murray's archive using a trans-analytical lens, refuting the conflation of her/his identification as a heterosexual male with internalized homophobia in an era before the modern gay liberation movement. From this perspective, Murray was attempting to align her/his physical body with her/his sense of normative male gender (described as her/his sexual attraction to feminine women, drive to compete in "men's" occupations, a desire to partner with a woman in a monogamous marriage, and "wearing pants" [Murray 1937a]). Even though Murray implored endocrinologists for treatment, stating that her/his "desire to be male was so strong," s/he was rejected—it was recommended s/he "accept treatment using female hormone[s]" instead (Murray 1940). Murray pursued testosterone therapy until at least 1944; there is no record that her/his numerous appeals were ever fulfilled.

During this period, Murray was hospitalized three times, each for "emotional break-downs" from a combination of intense overwork, heartbreak, and the struggle to normalize her/his gender and sexuality through testosterone therapy (Azaransky 2011: 23). Murray's personal notes (1937a, 1937b, 1938, 1940) from these episodes are centered on these "conflicts," and her/his race, and others' perception of it, is always in play. In one document (1937a), s/he wonders if part of this inner turmoil is not also racial—that being "hemmed in" by Jim Crow "restrictions" adds additional strain on her/his precarious gendered life. S/he wonders why, since s/he is so eager to become more masculine to ease this "conflict," s/he does not desire to pass as white, or make efforts to do so: "Why is [it] I am proud of my Negro blood?" While considering these critical questions, hospital staff "palmed [her/him] off as Cuban" so that s/he might receive a higher level of treatment.[2] Murray (1937b) simply left "the race question in the open" and let others decide what racial category to place her/him into.

Murray spent a great deal of time and energy observing the operations of racialization and gendering at work as those surrounding her/him tried to categorize her/him for their own purposes. In her/his 1938 poem "Mulatto's Dilemma," Murray writes:

Oh God! My face has slipped them . . .
Can I endure the killing weight of time it takes them To be sure? (Murray 1938)

Although the poem centers on the "killing" wait while others attempt to identify Murray as either black or white, her/his gender was simultaneously appraised. Racial and gender nonnormativity explicitly crossed paths on Murray's body, and as s/he walked through the world, others were always taking measure of this dual nonbelonging.

I argue that it is this trans perspective, not only Murray's experience "as a black woman" as others have concluded (Hartmann 2002: 75; Lewis 1977), that led to her/his first formulation of *Jane Crow*. Murray first introduced the term in a short 1944 *Los Angeles Sentinel* article, "Little Man from Mars: He's All Mixed Up," penned under the name Peter Panic (Panic 1944). The nom de plume is a nod to the character Peter Pan, traditionally played onstage by a woman. But Murray isn't Pan—s/he is Panic, perhaps referencing her/his failed quest for masculinization therapy and gender alignment. The article itself centers not on this gender tension but rather on the panic over the arbitrary violences of Jim Crow. Published in the largest African American newspaper on the West Coast, it is told from the perspective of a "little man from Mars" who observes the processes of racial and gender categorization from above. The martian literalizes Jim Crow as a bird that bites "culud" people, giving them "something like an itch" that "nearly drives them crazy." Keeping the words "culud folks" and "white folks" in quotation marks demonstrates that it is actually the bite of the bird and its harmful effects that demarcates who is "culud" and who is "white," not a physiological "truth" that stands outside processes of subjectification.

The martian rarely sees the bird, but humans erect "certain signs" that delineate not only space but also the people within it. Describing the infamous "white only" signs that littered the public spaces of the South, including the cemeteries, Murray/Panic writes, "If you get buried with the wrong sign on you, they dig up your bones, put the proper label on you, and bury you in the designated graveyard." To the martian, this represents the extreme in racial categorization, in that even without skin, proper racial binaries must be retained. While these strictures might hold in the daylight, at night, "sometimes they're careless and forget to put up their signs . . . then everybody gets mixed up." Alluding to the interracial intimacies, consensual and not, that occur throughout segregated communities, Murray/Panic is also connecting these hidden relationships within her/his own ancestry. Intimacies that cross racial lines leave people "all mixed up," just like the man from Mars is. Murray writes, "Being changeable color—green-and-blue— I don't know which sign to choose" (Panic 1944).

In the last paragraphs, the martian introduces Jim Crow's mate, Jane Crow. Although Murray/Panic does not expound upon Jane Crow's "bite," it is clear that Murray sees similarities between their operations and effects. Articulating an early form of social constructionism, s/he argues that both racialization and gendering are violent binary systems imposed from without—"the bite"—rather than from truths that emerge from the body. Those that are "bit" by these birds, those labeled black and/or woman, suffer both the internalized sense of inferiority—the "itch" that "drives them crazy"—and the material effects of systemic racism and sexism. However, as exemplified by the little man from Mars, Peter Panic, and Pauli Murray herself/himself, there are those who do not easily fit into these binarized categories and are themselves "all mixed up."

During this period, Murray took several interstate trips, sometimes in the company of a lover. S/he carefully recorded others' perceptions of her/his race and gender, which changed as s/he traveled through different parts of the country. In 1940, Murray, dressed in men's clothes, and her/his partner Adelene MacBean were arrested in Virginia during the first recorded utilization of Gandhian nonviolence in the struggle against Jim Crow. While some reports of the incident describe Murray and MacBean as two women, another describes one of the arrestees as "a young colored girl" and the other as a "young man . . . lighter than she, of slight build" (Gilmore 2009: 322). In the South, Murray was read as black regardless of gender.[3] But upon leaving the region, the perception of Murray's racial identity was more fluid, as was the case during Murray's hospitalization in 1937. For example, on a 1935 hitch-hiking trip through Illinois, one woman thought Murray "was a Boy Scout," while another "thought [s/he] was Indian" (Murray 1935).

Contemporary trans and critical race scholarship (Omi and Winant 1994; Serano 2009; Snorton 2009) invites us to see Murray as passed rather than passing. Instead of the responsibility for identification falling solely on the individual, it rests on the racial and gender norms that shape the way they are assessed. One's visible and audible embodiments are read through governing hegemonic categories, and the identification of the individual as a particular race and gender is created through that process. In this way, the experiences of people who are passed as more than one race and/or gender can teach us about the structural norms of that historical moment. Each time the individual is read and then categorized as one singular race and gender, the local racial and gender norms are exposed. Witnessing this quotidian yet fundamental process can build comprehension of complex hegemonic discourses.

Murray was labeled in ways that changed day to day and place to place. This, then, is a set of experiences that sets Pauli Murray apart from most of her/his movement activist counterparts—other "race women" who made black women's experiences a central focus of their racial justice work. While race women spent the majority of their time in the public sphere, most kept the details of their intimate lives well hidden. Darlene Clark Hine (1989: 914–915) argues that many black women who "desire[d] to achieve personal autonomy" developed a "culture of dissemblance" wherein they denied whites and black men access to their interior psychic and sexual selves. This was crucial for black women in leadership positions, toward whom stereotypes about black female sexual excess was explicitly and implicitly directed. Race women crafted personas of "openness" while "actually remaining an enigma," allowing them to inhabit culturally held white heteronormative ideals of virtuous womanhood, industriousness, emotional regulation, and gender respectability.

A long historiographical conversation regards the negative impact of the culture of dissemblance on black women, lesbians, and gender-nonnormative people. Hine highlights black middle-class women's attempted management of poor women, nonmonogamous women, and sex workers. Evelynn Hammonds (1999: 101) argues that lesbian and queer black women have been and are among those labeled as "traitors," in that not only do they invite additional scrutiny, but their expression of queerness enunciates their nonnormative sexual desires. Fearing that revelation might displace them from their racial community, black queer women police themselves, furthering the silences surrounding black women's intimacies.

Matt Richardson (2003) uses Hine's analytic to understand the absence of transgender people from black history. He cites her research on Cathy Williams, who lived under the name William Cathy, was read consistently as a black man, and served as a buffalo soldier in the late nineteenth century. Richardson argues that what is missing from Hine's analysis is the connection between Cathy's race and gender expression and the racial and gender norms in which Cathy was read and categorized. Separating William Cathy from the historical governing hegemonies results in the relegation of her/his gender and sexual nonnormativity to a biographical aside, rather than a lens through which to view the historical effects of changing cultural discourses.

Hammonds and Richardson argue that scholars perpetuate the culture of dissemblance in two ways. First, dissemblance maintains a closet for historical figures, denying queer and trans African Americans a place in the historiography. Second, it refuses the likelihood that one's sexuality or desire for gender self-definition is woven into one's race work, even if it is not spoken outright. Murray's crucial role in the histories of Civil Rights activism and intersectional feminism has been marginalized because both disciplines have yet to fully include transgender as a category of analysis that offers a distinct perspective on systemic operations of subjectification. Only a handful of scholars have recognized Murray's transgender history, and only Mack (2012) has begun to unpack how those experiences shaped Murray's theoretical analysis of Jane Crow.

Making her/his way through Jim Crow's strict racial and gender norms, Pauli Murray had plenty to Peter Panic about. Before studying law at Howard University, Murray was rejected from the University of North Carolina on account of her/his race; after graduating from Howard as valedictorian, s/he was rejected from Harvard Law School on account of her/his sex. In response to this latest exclusion, Murray famously wrote, "Gentlemen, I would gladly change my sex to meet your requirements, but since the way to such change has not been revealed to me, I have no recourse but to appeal to you to change your minds. Are you to tell me that one is as difficult as the other?" (Mayeri 2013: 87).

Just one month later, Murray introduced Jane Crow to an African American readership rapidly coalescing into a national civil rights movement. S/he articulated what would be intimately resonant to many: white supremacy and male supremacy operated in tandem, and their combined effects fell squarely across the bodies and psyches of African American women. As the analysis gained popularity among Murray's colleagues and friends, s/he used her/his full name when writing about Jane Crow, and by the mid-1960s, Murray was regarded as the legal expert on the civil rights of black women. But the bird's first sighting was by Peter Panic—the spirited boy played by a woman, and a little man from Mars—a color-changing observer from another planet. These caricatures represent Murray's sense of nonbelonging in a social world built on racial and gender binaries, and these outsider observations became the theoretical foundation of intersectional feminism. Murray's transgender is more than a biographical aside in feminist and Civil Rights historiography; these experiences informed Murray's racial justice work and shaped her/his analysis of hegemonic racism and sexism.

Acknowledgments

An earlier version of this article was presented at the Sixteenth Annual Graduate Student Conference in African American History at the University of Memphis, February 13, 2015. I wish to thank Jessi Lee Jackson for her careful reading and astute comments in preparation for publication.

From: Simon D. Elin Fisher, "Pauli Murray's Peter Panic: Perspectives from the Margins of Gender and Race in Jim Crow America," in *TSQ: Transgender Studies Quarterly*, Volume 3, no. 1–2, pp. 95–103. Copyright 2016, Duke University Press. All rights reserved. Republished by permission of the copyright holder, Duke University Press. www.dukeupress.edu.

Notes

1. I use *s/he* pronouns for Murray to both accentuate Murray's internal sense of male/masculine gender during the 1930s–1950s and also Murray's identification with female experience after this period until her death. My desire is to use a third-gender pronoun; yet I feel the contemporary *they* is ahistorical. As scholars continue to consider the lives of gender-nonconforming people living before the availability of a transgender/transsexual identity, a more uniform system of pronoun usage will likely emerge.
2. It is unclear whether the Long Island Rest Home (Amityville, New York) excluded African American patients at this time, but regardless of the admittance policy, a light-skinned Cuban client would likely receive better treatment than an African American.
3. This has much to do with the discursive expansiveness of the racial category "colored," constituted as such to maintain white racial purity and enfold the greatest number of individuals into a politically and economically subordinate position.

Bibliography

Azaransky, Sarah. 2011. *The Dream Is Freedom: Pauli Murray and American Democratic Faith*. Oxford: Oxford University Press.

———. 2013. "Jane Crow: Pauli Murray's Intersections and Antidiscrimination Law." *Journal of Feminist Studies in Religion* 29, no. 1: 155–160.

Crenshaw, Kimberle′. 1989. "Demarginalizing the Intersection of Race and Sex: A Black Feminist Critique of Antidiscrimination Doctrine, Feminist Theory, and Antiracist Politics." *University of Chicago Legal Forum* 140: 139–167.

Gilmore, Glenda Elizabeth. 2009. *Defying Dixie: The Radical Roots of Civil Rights, 1919–1950*. New York: W. W. Norton.

Hammonds, Evelynn M. 1999. "Toward a Genealogy of Black Female Sexuality: The Problematic of Silence." In *Feminist Theory and the Body: A Reader*, edited by Janet Price and Margrit Shildreck, 93–104. New York: Taylor and Francis.

Hartmann, Susan M. 2002. "Pauli Murray and the 'Juncture of Women's Liberation and Black Liberation'." *Journal of Women's History* 14, no. 2: 74–77.

Hine, Darlene Clark. 1989. "Rape and the Inner Lives of Black Women in the Middle West." *Signs* 14, no. 4: 912–920.

Lewis, Diane K. 1977. "A Response to Inequality: Black Women, Racism, and Sexism." *Signs* 3, no. 2: 339–361.

Mack, Kenneth W. 2012. *Representing the Race: The Creation of the Civil Rights Lawyer*. Cambridge, MA: Harvard University Press.

Mayeri, Serena. 2013. "Pauli Murray and the Twentieth-Century Quest for Legal and Social Equality." *Indiana Journal of Law and Social Equality* 2, no. 1: 80–90.

Murray, Pauli. 1935. Travel Diary, April 27–May 24. Box 1, Folder 25, Pauli Murray Papers (PMP), Schlesinger Library, Cambridge.

———. ca. 1937a. "Interview with Dr. ." Box 4, Folder 71, PMP.

———. ca. 1937b. "Questions Prepared for Dr. Titley." Box 4, Folder 71, PMP.

————. 1938. "Mulatto's Dilemma (A Poem)." *Opportunity* 16: 180.

————. 1940. "Summary of Symptoms of Upset—Pauli Murray. March 8, 1940." Box 4, Folder 71, PMP.

————. 1947. "Why Negro Girls Stay Single." *Negro Digest*, July: 4–8.

————. 1950. *States' Laws on Race and Color.* Athens: University of Georgia Press.

————. 1976. "A Legal Activist Discusses Her Work in the Civil Rights and Women's Liberation Movements." Oral History Interview with Pauli Murray, February 13, 1976. Interview G-0044. Southern Oral History Program Collection (#4007): Electronic Edition. Docsouth.unc.edu/sohp/G-0044/G-0044. html (accessed January 29, 2015).

————. 1987. *Proud Shoes: The Story of an American Family.* New York: Harper and Row.

Murray, Pauli, and Mary O. Eastwood. 1965. "Jane Crow and the Law: Sex Discrimination and Title VII." *George Washington Law Review* 34, no. 2: 232–256.

New York Amsterdam News. 1939. "Sex Tablets Stir Medics." November 11.

Omi, Michael, and Howard A. Winant. 1994. *Racial Formation in the United States: From the 1960s to the 1990s.* New York: Taylor and Francis.

Panic, Peter [Pauli Murray]. 1944. "Little Man from Mars." *Los Angeles Sentinel*, July 14.

Richardson, Matt [published as Mattie Udora Richardson]. 2003. "No More Secrets, No More Lies: African American History and Compulsory Heterosexuality." *Journal of Women's History* 15, no. 3: 63–76.

Serano, Julia. 2009. *Whipping Girl: A Transsexual Woman on Sexism and the Scapegoating of Femininity.* Berkeley, CA: Seal.

Snorton, C. Riley. 2009. "'A New Hope': The Psychic Life of Passing." *Hypatia* 24, no. 3: 77–92.

47 A Black Feminist Statement

The Combahee River Collective

Part manifesto, part Black feminist history, the Combahee River Collective Statement asks readers to confront the racism of the feminist movement, the sexism and heteronormativity of the Black nationalist movement, and the lack of analysis of race within Marxist thought. It argues against the bio-essentialist assumption that characterizes a great deal of liberal white feminism and, in doing so, articulates a position shared by trans critique. It adamantly rejects the sexism and misogyny of many men but does not embrace "the misguided notion that it is their maleness per se—i.e., their biological maleness—that makes them what they are. As black women, we find any kind of biological determinism a particularly dangerous and reactionary basis on which to build a politic." In this view, what another black feminist scholar, Sylvia Wynter, termed "biocentrism" and post-colonial feminist Maria Lugones called "somato-centriticity" is regarded as a pernicious ideological legacy of the transatlantic slave trade. Biological determinism inhibits the means of Black survival and diminishes the capacity to imagine or manifest different and better futures. Perhaps the most powerful point the Collective makes, however, is the fundamental assertion that "Black women are inherently valuable." This perspective informs the contemporary Black Lives Matter movement and the related slogan that "Black Trans Lives Matter." When the most marginalized and disparaged constituencies are valued and centered in movements for social transformation, they suggest, true liberation for all becomes more possible.

We are a collective of Black feminists who have been meeting together since 1974.[1] During that time we have been involved in the process of defining and clarifying our politics, while at the same time doing political work within our own group and in coalition with other progressive organizations and movements. The most general statement of our politics at the present time would be that we are actively committed to struggling against racial, sexual, heterosexual, and class oppression, and see as our particular task the development of integrated analysis and practice based upon the fact that the major systems of oppression are interlocking. The synthesis of these oppressions creates the conditions of our lives. As Black women we see Black feminism as the logical political movement to combat the manifold and simultaneous oppressions that all women of color face.

We will discuss four major topics in the paper that follows: (1) the genesis of contemporary Black feminism; (2) what we believe, i.e., the specific province of our politics; (3) the problems in organizing Black feminists, including a brief herstory of our collective; and (4) Black feminist issues and practice.

DOI: 10.4324/9781003206255-58

1. The Genesis of Contemporary Black Feminism

Before looking at the recent development of Black feminism we would like to affirm that we find our origins in the historical reality of AfroAmerican women's continuous life-and-death struggle for survival and liberation. Black women's extremely negative relationship to the American political system (a system of white male rule) has always been determined by our membership in two oppressed racial and sexual castes. As Angela Davis points out in "Reflections on the Black Woman's Role in the Community of Slaves," Black women have always embodied, if only in their physical manifestation, an adversary stance to white male rule and have actively resisted its inroads upon them and their communities in both dramatic and subtle ways. There have always been Black women activists—some known, like Sojourner Truth, Harriet Tubman, Frances E. W. Harper, Ida B. Wells Barnett, and Mary Church Terrell, and thousands upon thousands unknown—who have had a shared awareness of how their sexual identity combined with their racial identity to make their whole life situation and the focus of their political struggles unique. Contemporary Black feminism is the outgrowth of countless generations of personal sacrifice, militancy, and work by our mothers and sisters.

A Black feminist presence has evolved most obviously in connection with the second wave of the American women's movement beginning in the late 1960s. Black, other Third World, and working women have been involved in the feminist movement from its start, but both outside reactionary forces and racism and elitism within the movement itself have served to obscure our participation. In 1973, Black feminists, primarily located in New York, felt the necessity of forming a separate Black feminist group. This became the National Black Feminist Organization (NBFO).

Black feminist politics also have an obvious connection to movements for Black liberation, particularly those of the 1960s and 1970s. Many of us were active in those movements (Civil Rights, Black nationalism, the Black Panthers), and all of our lives were greatly affected and changed by their ideologies, their goals, and the tactics used to achieve their goals. It was our experience and disillusionment within these liberation movements, as well as experience on the periphery of the white male left, that led to the need to develop a politics that was anti-racist, unlike those of white women, and anti-sexist, unlike those of Black and white men.

There is also undeniably a personal genesis for Black Feminism, that is, the political realization that comes from the seemingly personal experiences of individual Black women's lives. Black feminists and many more Black women who do not define themselves as feminists have all experienced sexual oppression as a constant factor in our day-to-day existence. As children we realized that we were different from boys and that we were treated differently. For example, we were told in the same breath to be quiet both for the sake of being "lady-like" and to make us less objectionable in the eyes of white people. As we grew older we became aware of the threat of physical and sexual abuse by men. However, we had no way of conceptualizing what was so apparent to us, what we knew was really happening.

Black feminists often talk about their feelings of craziness before becoming conscious of the concepts of sexual politics, patriarchal rule, and most importantly, feminism, the political analysis and practice that we women use to struggle against our oppression. The fact that racial politics and indeed racism are pervasive factors in our lives did not allow us, and still does not allow most Black women, to look more deeply into our own experiences and, from that sharing and growing consciousness, to build a politics that will change our lives and inevitably end our oppression. Our development must also be tied to the contemporary economic and political position of Black people. The post-World War II generation of Black youth was the first to be able to minimally partake of certain educational and employment options, previously closed completely to Black people. Although our economic position is still at the very bottom of the American capitalistic economy, a handful of us have been able to gain certain tools as a result of tokenism in education and employment which potentially enable us to more effectively fight our oppression.

A combined anti-racist and anti-sexist position drew us together initially, and as we developed politically we addressed ourselves to heterosexism and economic oppression under capitalism.

2. What We Believe

Above all else, our politics initially sprang from the shared belief that Black women are inherently valuable, that our liberation is a necessity not as an adjunct to somebody else's but because of our need as human persons for autonomy. This may seem so obvious as to sound simplistic, but it is apparent that no other ostensibly progressive movement has ever considered our specific oppression as a priority or worked seriously for the ending of that oppression. Merely naming the pejorative stereotypes attributed to Black women (e.g. mammy, matriarch, Sapphire, whore, bulldagger), let alone cataloguing the cruel, often murderous, treatment we receive, indicates how little value has been placed upon our lives during four centuries of bondage in the Western hemisphere. We realize that the only people who care enough about us to work consistently for our liberation are us. Our politics evolve from a healthy love for ourselves, our sisters and our community which allows us to continue our struggle and work.

This focusing upon our own oppression is embodied in the concept of identity politics. We believe that the most profound and potentially most radical politics come directly out of our own identity, as opposed to working to end somebody else's oppression. In the case of Black women this is a particularly repugnant, dangerous, threatening, and therefore revolutionary concept because it is obvious from looking at all the political movements that have preceded us that anyone is more worthy of liberation than ourselves. We reject pedestals, queenhood, and walking ten paces behind. To be recognized as human, levelly human, is enough.

We believe that sexual politics under patriarchy is as pervasive in Black women's lives as are the politics of class and race. We also often find it difficult to separate race from class from sex oppression because in our lives they are most often experienced simultaneously. We know that there is such a thing as racial-sexual oppression which is neither solely racial nor solely sexual, e.g., the history of rape of Black women by white men as a weapon of political repression.

Although we are feminists and lesbians, we feel solidarity with progressive Black men and do not advocate the fractionalization that white women who are separatists demand. Our situation as Black people necessitates that we have solidarity around the fact of race, which white women of course do not need to have with white men, unless it is their negative solidarity as racial oppressors. We struggle together with Black men against racism, while we also struggle with Black men about sexism.

We realize that the liberation of all oppressed peoples necessitates the destruction of the political-economic systems of capitalism and imperialism as well as patriarchy. We are socialists because we believe that work must be organized for the collective benefit of those who do the work and create the products, and not for the profit of the bosses. Material resources must be equally distributed among those who create these resources. We are not convinced, however, that a socialist revolution that is not also a feminist and anti-racist revolution will guarantee our liberation. We have arrived at the necessity for developing an understanding of class relationships that takes into account the specific class position of

Black women who are generally marginal in the labor force, while at this particular time some of us are temporarily viewed as doubly desirable tokens at white-collar and professional levels. We need to articulate the real class situation of persons who are not merely raceless, sexless workers, but for whom racial and sexual oppression are significant determinants in their working/economic lives. Although we are in essential agreement with Marx's theory as it applied to the very specific economic relationships he analyzed, we know that his analysis must be extended further in order for us to understand our specific economic situation as Black women.

A political contribution which we feel we have already made is the expansion of the feminist principle that the personal is political. In our consciousness-raising sessions, for example, we have in many ways gone beyond white women's revelations because we are dealing with the implications of race and class as well as sex. Even our Black women's style of talking/testifying in Black language about what we have experienced has a resonance that is both cultural and political. We have spent a great deal of energy delving into the cultural and experiential nature of our oppression out of necessity because none of these matters has ever been looked at before. No one before has ever examined the multilayered texture of Black women's lives. An example of this kind of revelation/conceptualization occurred at a meeting as we discussed the ways in which our early intellectual interests had been attacked by our peers, particularly Black males. We discovered that all of us, because we were "smart," had also been considered "ugly," i.e., "smart-ugly." "Smartugly" crystallized the way in which most of us had been forced to develop our intellects at great cost to our "social" lives. The sanctions in the Black and white communities against Black women thinkers is comparatively much higher than for white women, particularly ones from the educated middle and upper classes.

As we have already stated, we reject the stance of Lesbian separatism because it is not a viable political analysis or strategy for us. It leaves out far too much and far too many people, particularly Black men, women, and children. We have a great deal of criticism and loathing for what men have been socialized to be in this society: what they support, how they act, and how they oppress. But we do not have the misguided notion that it is their maleness, per se—i.e., their biological maleness—that makes them what they are. As Black women we find any type of biological determinism a particularly dangerous and reactionary basis upon which to build a politic. We must also question whether Lesbian separatism is an adequate and progressive political analysis and strategy, even for those who practice it, since it so completely denies any but the sexual sources of women's oppression, negating the facts of class and race.

3. Problems in Organizing Black Feminists

During our years together as a Black feminist collective we have experienced success and defeat, joy and pain, victory and failure. We have found that it is very difficult to organize around Black feminist issues, difficult even to announce in certain contexts that we are Black feminists. We have tried to think about the reasons for our difficulties, particularly since the white women's movement continues to be strong and to grow in many directions. In this section we will discuss some of the general reasons for the organizing problems we face and also talk specifically about the stages in organizing our own collective.

The major source of difficulty in our political work is that we are not just trying to fight oppression on one front or even two, but instead to address a whole range of oppressions. We do not have racial, sexual, heterosexual, or class privilege to rely upon, nor do we have even the minimal access to resources and power that groups who possess anyone of these types of privilege have.

The psychological toll of being a Black woman and the difficulties this presents in reaching political consciousness and doing political work can never be underestimated. There is a very low value placed upon Black women's psyches in this society, which is both racist and sexist. As an early group member once said, "We are all damaged people merely by virtue of being Black women." We are dispossessed psychologically and on every other level, and yet we feel the necessity to struggle to change the condition of all Black women. In "A Black Feminist's Search for Sisterhood," Michele Wallace arrives at this conclusion:

> We exists as women who are Black who are feminists, each stranded for the moment, working independently because there is not yet an environment in this society remotely congenial to our struggle—because, being on the bottom, we would have to do what no one else has done: we would have to fight the world.[2]

Wallace is pessimistic but realistic in her assessment of Black feminists' position, particularly in her allusion to the nearly classic isolation most of us face. We might use our position at the bottom, however, to make a clear leap into revolutionary action. If Black women were free, it would mean that everyone else would have to be free since our freedom would necessitate the destruction of all the systems of oppression.

Feminism is, nevertheless, very threatening to the majority of Black people because it calls into question some of the most basic assumptions about our existence, i.e., that sex should be a determinant of power relationships. Here is the way male and female roles were defined in a Black nationalist pamphlet from the early 1970s:

> We understand that it is and has been traditional that the man is the head of the house. He is the leader of the house/nation because his knowledge of the world is broader, his awareness is greater, his understanding is fuller and his application of this information is wiser. . . . After all, it is only reasonable that the man be the head of the house because he is able to defend and protect the development of his home. . . . Women cannot do the same things as men—they are made by nature to function differently. Equality of men and women is something that cannot happen even in the abstract world. Men are not equal to other men, i.e. ability, experience or even understanding. The value of men and women can be seen as in the value of gold and silver—they are not equal but both have great value. We must realize that men and women are a complement to each other because there is no house/family without a man and his wife. Both are essential to the development of any life.[3]

The material conditions of most Black women would hardly lead them to upset both economic and sexual arrangements that seem to represent some stability in their lives. Many Black women have a good understanding of both sexism and racism, but because of the everyday constrictions of their lives, cannot risk struggling against them both.

The reaction of Black men to feminism has been notoriously negative. They are, of course, even more threatened than Black women by the possibility that Black feminists might organize around our own needs. They realize that they might not only lose valuable and hardworking allies in their struggles but that they might also be forced to change their habitually sexist ways of interacting with and oppressing Black women. Accusations that Black feminism divides the Black struggle are powerful deterrents to the growth of an autonomous Black women's movement.

Still, hundreds of women have been active at different times during the three-year existence of our group. And every Black woman who came, came out of a strongly felt need for some level of possibility that did not previously exist in her life.

When we first started meeting early in 1974 after the NBFO first eastern regional conference, we did not have a strategy for organizing, or even a focus. We just wanted to see what we had. After a period of months of not meeting, we began to meet again late in the year and started doing an intense variety of consciousness-raising. The overwhelming feeling that we had is that after years and years we had finally found each other. Although we were not doing political work as a group, individuals continued their involvement in Lesbian politics, sterilization abuse and abortion rights work, Third World Women's International Women's Day activities, and support activity for the trials of Dr. Kenneth Edelin, Joan Little, and Inéz García. During our first summer when membership had dropped off considerably, those of us remaining devoted serious discussion to the possibility of opening a refuge for battered women in a Black community. (There was no refuge in Boston at that time.) We also decided around that time to become an independent collective since we had serious disagreements with NBFO's bourgeois-feminist stance and their lack of a clear political focus.

We also were contacted at that time by socialist feminists, with whom we had worked on abortion rights activities, who wanted to encourage us to attend the National Socialist Feminist Conference in Yellow Springs. One of our members did attend and despite the narrowness of the ideology that was promoted at that particular conference, we became more aware of the need for us to understand our own economic situation and to make our own economic analysis.

In the fall, when some members returned, we experienced several months of comparative inactivity and internal disagreements which were first conceptualized as a Lesbian-straight split but which were also the result of class and political differences. During the summer those of us who were still meeting had determined the need to do political work and to move beyond consciousness-raising and serving exclusively as an emotional support group. At the beginning of 1976, when some of the women who had not wanted to do political work and who also had voiced disagreements stopped attending of their own accord, we again looked for a focus. We decided at that time, with the addition of new members, to become a study group. We had always shared our reading with each other, and some of us had written papers on Black feminism for group discussion a few months before this decision was made. We began functioning as a study group and also began discussing the possibility of starting a Black feminist publication. We had a retreat in the late spring which provided a time for both political discussion and working out interpersonal issues. Currently we are planning to gather together a collection of Black feminist writing. We feel that it is absolutely essential to demonstrate the reality of our politics to other Black women and believe that we can do this through writing and distributing our work. The fact that individual Black feminists are living in isolation all over the country, that our own numbers are small, and that we have some skills in writing, printing, and publishing makes us want to carry out these kinds of projects as a means of organizing Black feminists as we continue to do political work in coalition with other groups.

4. Black Feminist Issues and Projects

During our time together we have identified and worked on many issues of particular relevance to Black women. The inclusiveness of our politics makes us concerned with any situation that impinges upon the lives of women, Third World and working people. We are of course particularly committed to working on those struggles in which race, sex, and class are simultaneous factors in oppression. We might, for example, become involved in workplace organizing at a factory that employs Third World women or picket a hospital that is cutting back on already inadequate heath care to a Third World community, or set up a rape crisis center in a Black neighborhood. Organizing around welfare and daycare concerns might also be a focus. The work to be done and the countless issues that this work represents merely reflect the pervasiveness of our oppression.

Issues and projects that collective members have actually worked on are sterilization abuse, abortion rights, battered women, rape and health care. We have also done many workshops and educationals on Black feminism on college campuses, at women's conferences, and most recently for high school women.

One issue that is of major concern to us and that we have begun to publicly address is racism in the white women's movement. As Black feminists we are made constantly and painfully aware of how little effort white women have made to understand and combat their racism, which requires among other things that they have a more than superficial comprehension of race, color, and Black history and culture. Eliminating racism in the white women's movement is by definition work for white women to do, but we will continue to speak to and demand accountability on this issue.

In the practice of our politics we do not believe that the end always justifies the means. Many reactionary and destructive acts have been done in the name of achieving "correct" political goals. As feminists we do not want to mess over people in the name of politics. We believe in collective process and a nonhierarchical distribution of power within our own group and in our vision of a revolutionary society. We are committed to a continual examination of our politics as they develop through criticism and self-criticism as an essential aspect of our practice. In her introduction to *Sisterhood is Powerful* Robin Morgan writes:

> I haven't the faintest notion what possible revolutionary role white heterosexual men could fulfill, since they are the very embodiment of reactionary-vested-interest-power.

As Black feminists and Lesbians we know that we have a very definite revolutionary task to perform and we are ready for the lifetime of work and struggle before us.

From: Combahee River Collective, "The Combahee River Collective Statement" in *Capitalist Patriarchy and the Case for the Socialist Feminism*. Copyright 1978, Monthly Review Press. All rights reserved. Republished by permission of the publisher.

Notes

1. This statement is dated April 1977.
2. Wallace, Michele. "A Black Feminist's Search for Sisterhood," *The Village Voice*, 28 July 1975, pp. 6–7.
3. Mumininas of Committee for Unified Newark, Mwanamke Mwananchi (The Nationalist Woman), Newark, N.J., ©1971, pp. 4–5.

48 Selection From *Brilliant Imperfection*

Grappling With Cure

Eli Clare

Eli Clare is a writer and activist who lives and works at the intersection of trans, disability, peace, and anti-racist movements for social justice. In "Gender Transition," a selection from his 2017 book *Brilliant Imperfection*, Clare reframes trans phenomena through a disability studies lens. He examines how concepts of "curability" inform common understandings of medicalized trans embodiment and thus influence some trans people to reproduce ableism by pathologizing trans gender-difference as a "defect" to be corrected. Not only does this way of thinking imagine medical transition as a cure for transness, it imagines transness itself as an unwanted and limiting disability. Clare is compassionate but critical in his opposition to framing transness through the language of defect. He insists that trans people who seek to medicalize their gender transitions should not expect medicalization to confer normalcy or to offer a cure for the social stigma attached to being different. At the same time, medical transition can offer new ways of relating to socially compulsory notions of "the normal" in ways that make trans lives more livable. Clare focuses his discussion on Alexandre Baril, a transsexual disabled scholar whose work carefully distinguishes between rejecting the idea that transness is in itself a mental or physical defect or disability while also acknowledging that being trans can feel emotionally disabling by reducing one's capacity to be at ease in the world. One implication of approaching trans issues through a disability studies framework is whether the "social model" of disability—the view that disability is not inherent in the body but rather is produced by organizing the physical and social environment around able-bodied norms—can usefully contribute to trans studies and intervene in trans movements. Can the perception of "gender normativity" be thought of as conferring access and the perception of transness denying access to normatively gendered space? To what extent is the failure to regard transness as socially disabling an expression of ableism, and to what degree is the exclusion of transness from disability discourse (and from civil rights legislation such as the Americans with Disabilities Act) a consequence of transphobia?

Gender Transition

My slow turn from butch dyke to genderqueer living as a white man in the world was never about curing disorder or fixing brokenness, but rather about desire and comfort—transition a door, a window, a cobalt sky. That said, trans people who want to transition using surgeries, hormone replacement therapy, or both have many different relationships to cure. Some folks name their transness a birth defect, a disability in need of repair. The work *defect* always takes my breath away. It's a punch in my stomach. These folks reason, "I should have easy access to competent respectful heath care just as other disabled people do. I simply need a cure." Their logic makes me incredulous, even as I work to respect people who name their

DOI: 10.4324/9781003206255-59

transness this way. Do they really believe disability ensures decent—much less good—health care? I could tell a thousand stories, cite pages of statistics, confirming the opposite, and rant for hours about ableism in the medical-industrial complex. I hate their unquestioned acceptance of cure.

But I need to pause my rant for a moment. Until the early 1990s, when trans communities began finding strong, collective voices, medical providers' explicit goal for gender transition was to create normal heterosexual men and women who never again identified as trans, gender-nonconforming, gay, lesbian, or bi. In other words, the framing of transness as defect, an abnormality to be corrected, didn't start with trans people but with the medical-industrial complex.

And then there are the real forces of gender dissonance and body-mind dysphoria. Scholar Alexandre Baril reflects, "The problem with framing transness as a defect resides, I believe, not in the concept of transness as disability, but in the individualist, ableist, pathologising views of disabilities."[1] He continues, describing his experience as a transsexual disabled man: "My transness has been and continues to be a debilitating and disabling component of my life. My dysphoria, although much less intense than before my transition, is a constant presence that manifests itself through a variety of concerns that, taken separately, might seem insignificant but that, taken together, reveal a persistent discomfort about my body. This dysphoria is as psychologically disabling as my other mental disabilities."[2] Rather than resorting to some naïve and stereotyped notion of defect, Baril is grappling with a complex tangle. His words ask me to sit with the reality of body-mind dysphoria as a sometimes overwhelming or disabling force.

Still other trans people turn the idea of gender dissonance inside out, refusing to name transness a disease and gender nonconformity a pathology. Their refusal locates dysphoria not in individual trans people but rather in a world that often denies, mocks, and criminalizes our genders.

Transition as an open door, transness as defect to fix, gender dysphoria as disability, transgender identities as nonpathologized body-mind difference—all of these various realities exist at the same time, each with its own relationship to cure and the medical-industrial complex.

Even as my transition was not about fixing disorder, the promise of cure still called out to me, burrowing into my body-mind and channeling what I wanted. The medical-industrial complex taps into our desires, promising us so much. Through cure, it assures us that we can control and reshape our body-minds; restore them to some longed-for, imagined, or former state of being. Assures us that the unhappiness we feel resides within our individual selves. Assures us that on an individual level we can be whole and that on a collective level disability, illness, and body-mind difference can be eradicated. This assurance—that medical technology can align our body-minds with what we desire (whether it be an end to pain or depression, the ability to walk again, the loss of weight, or reshaping of our sexed and gendered selves)—is so seductive.

When I started taking testosterone, I was impatient for facial hair and a deeper voice, slimmer hips and a squarer jaw. But underneath those defined body-mind changes, I hungered for a settledness that *girl* and *woman* had never given me. I caught myself thinking of that pale yellow synthetic hormone as honey and light, the smell of sugar pine, infusing me. Through metaphor, I was trying to wrench my transformation away from the medical-industrial complex.

But in truth, the people who control transition technology—surgeons, therapists, endocrinologists, family doctors—are all embedded in the white Western system of medicine, trained to identify and repair body-mind trouble. Diagnosis in the form of gender dysphoria and the recently discarded gender identity disorder plays a significant role in who receives treatment in the form of hormones and surgery and who doesn't. Multinational pharmaceutical companies develop, produce, distribute, and profit from hormones. In short, the medical-industrial complex shapes gender transition in dozens of ways. I wasn't injecting honey and light into me but rather a chemical compound, contributing to the profits of Sun Pharmaceutical Industries. I was stepping through the door held open by the promise of cure.

Trans people aren't alone in our encounters with the promise of cure. Any time we—trans and cisgender, disabled and nondisabled—access medical technology to change our body-minds in little ways or big ways, we are engaging with that seductive assurance. We go to a fertility clinic wanting to become pregnant, to our primary care doctor wanting meds to stop daily full-blown panic attacks, to the emergency room wanting to mend a broken leg. We enter the medica-industrial complex with many different needs and desires, interacting with cure's promise in many different ways.

But cure doesn't only follow the lead of our body-mind yearnings; it also pushes us toward normality. Transition certainly didn't make me a normal guy. Yet I'm not longer "ma'am" on one street corner and "sir" on the next—my body-mind no longer a pry bar, leveraging space between man and woman. For the first time in my life, I'm read consistently as a single gender. Even as I've remained twisted, bent, rebellious, unrepentantly queer, my relationships to *normal* has definitely changed.

The promise of cure held the door open, and I stepped through. I listened to desire. I found body-mind comfort. I live more easily inside the gender binary. I still feel akin to my nine-year-old self who flew her kite in the hayfields and knew she was neither girl nor boy. I cured nothing because there was nothing to cure. All of these forces jostle through me.

From: Eli Clare, *Brilliant Imperfection: Grappling With Cure*, pp. 177–180. Copyright 2017, Eli Clare. All rights reserved. Republished by permission of the copyright holder, and the Publisher. www.dukeupress.edu.

Notes

1. Alexandre Baril, 2015, "Transness as debility: Rethinking intersections between trans and disabled embodiments," *Feminist Review* 111 (59–74), 66.
2. Alexandre Baril, 2015, "Transness as debility: Rethinking intersections between trans and disabled embodiments," *Feminist Review* 111 (59–74), 71.

49 Hermaphrodites With Attitude

Mapping the Emergence of Intersex Political Activism

Cheryl Chase

This article by the pseudonymous Cheryl Chase, founder of the Intersex Society of North America (ISNA), explores the intersections of trans and intersex activism. It was first published in the 1998 "Transgender Issue" of *GLQ: A Journal of Lesbian and Gay Studies*. Chase played a pivotal role in the formation of a political intersex movement in the 1990s. She generated considerable controversy among politically engaged intersex people in 2006 by signing off on the "Consensus Statement on the Management of Intersex Disorders," which she and a handful of other activists had hammered out with the pediatricians who treated neonatal intersex conditions, and then disbanding ISNA. The consensus involved, on the one hand, medical service providers agreeing to no longer consider non-consensual neonatal corrective genital surgeries "best practices" for the management of intersex conditions and to include intersex people and advocates on expert panels deciding on the best course of action with regard to each individual intersex case. On the other hand, it involved intersex activists framing intersex conditions more narrowly as a medical rather than social problem and, as a rationale for appropriate medical treatment, acknowledging intersex conditions to be "disorders" rather than "differences." Some intersex activists found this a pragmatic way to reduce the harm of invasive, irreversible, and ethically questionable surgeries performed on children unable to consent to the permanent modification of their genitals; others considered the "Consensus Statement" a betrayal of the political intersex movement's broader agenda and a sacrifice of its intersectional relationships to other social movements that addressed bodily autonomy and self-determination. Nearly a quarter-century after its original publication, "Hermaphrodites With Attitude" now exemplifies a visionary moment in the early history of a movement that has since fractured. The article remains useful for Chase's paradigmatic first-person account of coming to political consciousness as an intersex person, its narrative account of her formative role in an intersex movement, and the close association of that movement with transgender activism in the 1990s. It offers a devastating critique of the silence then surrounding medicalized genital cutting practiced on intersex individuals in the West relative to the feminist outrage in the global North over traditional "African" genital cutting as a "harmful cultural practice," thereby exposing the racial and colonial roots of those differing responses.

The insistence on two clearly distinguished sexes has calamitous personal consequences for the many individuals who arrive in the world with sexual anatomy that fails to be easily distinguished as male or female. Such individuals are labeled "intersexuals" or "hermaphrodites" by modern medical discourse.[1] About one in a hundred births exhibits some anomaly in sex differentiation,[2] and about one in two thousand is different enough to render

DOI: 10.4324/9781003206255-60

problematic the question "Is it a boy or a girl?"[3] Since the early 1960s, nearly every major city in the United States has had a hospital with a standing team of medical experts who intervene in these cases to assign—through drastic surgical means—a male or female status to intersex infants. The fact that this system for preserving the boundaries of the categories male and female has existed for so long without drawing criticism or scrutiny from any quarter indicates the extreme discomfort that sexual ambiguity excites in our culture. Pediatric genital surgeries literalize what might otherwise be considered a theoretical operation: the attempted production of normatively sexed bodies and gendered subjects through constitutive acts of violence. Over the last few years, however, intersex people have begun to politicize intersex identities, thus transforming intensely personal experiences of violation into collective opposition to the medical regulation of bodies that queer the foundations of heteronormative identifications and desires.

Hermaphrodites: Medical Authority and Cultural Invisibility

Many people familiar with the ideas that gender is a phenomenon not adequately described by male/female dimorphism and that the interpretation of physical sex differences is culturally constructed remain surprised to learn just how variable sexual anatomy is.[4] Though the male/female binary is constructed as natural and presumed to be immutable, the phenomenon of intersexuality offers clear evidence to the contrary and furnishes an opportunity to deploy "nature" strategically to disrupt heteronormative systems of sex, gender, and sexuality. The concept of bodily sex, in popular usage, refers to multiple components including karyotype (organization of sex chromosomes), gonadal differentiation (e.g., ovarian or testicular), genital morphology, configuration of internal reproductive organs, and pubertal sex characteristics such as breasts and facial hair. Because these characteristics are expected to be concordant in each individual—either all male or all female—an observer, once having attributed male or female sex to a particular individual, assumes the values of other unobserved characteristics.[5]

Because medicine intervenes quickly in intersex births to change the infant's body, the phenomenon of intersexuality is today largely unknown outside specialized medical practices. General public awareness of intersex bodies slowly vanished in modern Western European societies as medicine gradually appropriated to itself the authority to interpret—and eventually manage—the category which had previously been widely known as "hermaphroditism." Victorian medical taxonomy began to efface hermaphroditism as a legitimated status by establishing mixed gonadal histology as a necessary criterion for "true" hermaphroditism. By this criterion, both ovarian and testicular tissue types had to be present. Given the limitations of Victorian surgery and anesthesia, such confirmation was impossible in a living patient. All other anomalies were reclassified as "pseudohermaphroditisms" masking a "true sex" determined by the gonads.[6]

With advances in anesthesia, surgery, embryology, and endocrinology, however, twentieth-century medicine moved from merely labeling intersexed bodies to the far more invasive practice of "fixing" them to conform with a diagnosed true sex. The techniques and protocols for physically transforming intersexed bodies were developed primarily at Johns Hopkins University in Baltimore during the 1920s and 1930s under the guidance of urologist Hugh Hampton Young. "Only during the last few years," Young enthused in the preface to his pioneering textbook, *Genital Abnormalities*, "have we begun to get somewhere near the explanation of the marvels of anatomic abnormality that may be portrayed by these amazing individuals. But the surgery of the hermaphrodite has remained a terra incognita." The "sad state of these unfortunates" prompted Young to devise "a great variety of surgical procedures" by which he attempted to normalize their bodily appearances to the greatest extents possible.[7]

Quite a few of Young's patients resisted his efforts. One, a " 'snappy' young negro woman with a good figure" and a large clitoris, had married a man but found her passion only with women. She refused "to be made into a man" because removal of her vagina would mean the loss of her 'meal ticket," namely, her husband.[8] By the 1950s, the principle of rapid post-natal detection and intervention for intersex infants had been developed at John Hopkins with the stated goal of completing surgery early enough so that the child would have no memory of it.[9] One wonders whether the insistence on early intervention was not at least partly motivated by the resistance offered by adult intersexuals to normalization through surgery. Frightened parents of ambiguously sexed infants were much more open to sugges-tions of normalizing surgery, while the infants themselves could of course offer no resistance whatever. Most of the theoretical foundations justifying these interventions are attributable to psychologist John Money, a sex researcher invited to Johns Hopkins by Lawson Wilkins, the founder of pediatric endocrinology.[10] Wilkins's numerous students subsequently car-ried these protocols to hospitals throughout the United States and abroad.[11] Suzanne Kes-sler notes that today Wilkins and Money's protocols enjoy a "consensus of approval rarely encountered in science."[12]

In keeping with the Johns Hopkins model, the birth of an intersex infant today is deemed a "psychosocial emergency" that propels a multidisciplinary team of intersex specialists into action. Significantly, they are surgeons and endocrinologists rather than psychologists, bioethicists, representatives from intersex peer support organizations, or parents of inter-sex children. The team examines the infant and chooses either male or female as a "sex of assignment," then informs the parents that this is the child's "true sex." Medical technology, including surgery and hormones, is then used to make the child's body conform as closely as possible to that sex.

The sort of deviation from sex norms exhibited by intersexuals is so highly stigmatized that the likely prospect of emotional harm due to social rejection of the intersexual provides physicians with their most compelling argument to justify medically unnecessary surgical interventions. Intersex status is considered to be so incompatible with emotional health that misrepresentation, concealment of facts, and outright lying (both to parents and later to the intersex person) are unabashedly advocated in professional medical literature.[13] Rather, the systematic hushing up of the fact of intersex births and the use of violent techniques to normalize intersex bodies have caused profound emotional and physical harm to intersexu-als and their families. The harm begins when the birth is treated as a medical crisis, and the consequences of that initial treatment ripple out ever afterward. The impact of this treat-ment is so devastating that until just a few years ago, people whose lives have been touched by intersexuality maintained silence about their ordeal. As recently as 1993, no one publicly disputed surgeon Milton Edgerton when he wrote that in forty years of clitoral surgery on intersexuals, "not one has complained of loss of sensation, *even when the entire clitoris was removed.*"[14]

The tragic irony is that, while intersexual anatomy occasionally indicates an underlying medical problem such as adrenal malfunction, ambiguous genitals are in and of themselves neither painful nor harmful to health. Surgery is essentially a destructive process. It can remove and to a limited extent relocate tissue, but it cannot create new structures. This technical limitation, taken together with the framing of the feminine as a condition of lack, leads physicians to assign 90 percent of anatomically ambiguous infants as female by excising genital tissue. Members of the Johns Hopkins intersex team have justified female assignment by saying, "You can make a hole, but you can't build a pole."[15] Positively heroic efforts shore up a tenuous masculine status for the remaining 10 percent assigned male, who are subjected to multiple operations—twenty-two in one case[16]—with the goal of straightening the penis and constructing a urethra to enable standing urinary posture. For some, the surgeries end only when the child grows old enough to resist.[17]

Children assigned to the female sex are subjected to surgery that removes the troubling hypertrophic clitoris (the same tissue that would have been a troubling micropenis if the child had been assigned male). Through the 1960s, feminizing pediatric genital surgery was openly labeled "clitorectomy" and was compared favorably to the African practices that have been the recent focus of such intense scrutiny. As three Harvard surgeons noted, "Evidence that the clitoris is not essential for normal coitus may be gained from certain sociological data. For instance, it is the custom of a number of African tribes to excise the clitoris and other parts of the external genitals. Yet normal sexual function is observed in these females."[18] A modified operation that removes most of the clitoris and relocates a bit of the tip is variously (and euphemistically) called clitoroplasty, clitoral reduction, or clitoral recession and is described as a "simple cosmetic procedure" to differentiate it from the now infamous clitorectomy. However, the operation is far from benign. Here is a slightly simplified summary (in my own words) of the surgical technique—recommended by Johns Hopkins Surgeons Oesterling, Gearhart, and Jeffs—that is representative of the operation:

> They make an incision around the phallus, at the corona, then dissect the skin away from its underside. Next they dissect the skin away from the dorsal side and remove as much of the corpora, or erectile bodies, as necessary to create an "appropriate size clitoris." Next, stitches are placed from the pubic area along both sides of the entire length of what remains of the phallus; when these stitches are tightened, it folds up like pleats in a skirt, and recesses into a concealed position behind the mons pubis. If the result is still "too large," the glans is further reduced by cutting away a pie-shaped wedge.[19]

For most intersexuals, this sort of arcane, dehumanized medical description, illustrated with close-ups of genital surgery and naked children with blacked-out eyes, is the only available version of *Our Bodies, Ourselves*. We as a culture have relinquished to medicine the authority to police the boundaries of male and female, leaving intersexuals to recover as best they can, alone and silent, from violent normalization.

My Career as a Hermaphrodite: Renegotiating Cultural Meanings

I was born with ambiguous genitals. A doctor specializing in intersexuality deliberated for three days—sedating my mother each time she asked what was wrong with her baby—before concluding that I was male, with a micropenis, complete hypospadias, undescended testes, and a strange extra opening behind the urethra. A male birth certificate was completed for me, and my parents began raising me as a boy. When I was a year and a half old my parents consulted a different set of experts, who admitted me to a hospital for "sex determination." "Determine" is a remarkably apt word in this context, meaning both "to ascertain by investigation" and "to cause to come to a resolution." It perfectly describes the two-stage process whereby science produces through a series of masked operations what it claims merely to observe. Doctors told my parents that a thorough medical investigation would be necessary to determine (in the first sense of that word) what my "true sex" was. They judged my genital appendage to be inadequate as a penis, too short to mark masculine status effectively or to penetrate females. As a female, however, I would be penetrable and potentially fertile. My anatomy having been relabeled as vagina, urethra, labia, and outsized clitoris, my sex was determined (in the second sense) by amputating my genital appendage. Following doctors' orders, my parents then changed my name, combed their house to eliminate all traces of my existence as a boy (photographs, birthday cards, etc.), changed my birth certificate, moved to a different town, instructed extended family members no longer to refer to me as a boy, and never told anyone else—including me—just what had happened. My intersexuality and change of sex were the family's dirty little secrets.

At age eight, I was returned to the hospital for abdominal surgery that trimmed away the testicular portion of my gonads, each of which was partly ovarian and partly testicular in character. No explanation was given to me then for the long hospital stay or the abdominal surgery, nor for the regular hospital visits afterward, in which doctors photographed my genitals and inserted fingers and instruments into my vagina and anus. These visits ceased as soon as I began to menstruate. At the time of the sex change, doctors had assured my parents that their once son/now daughter would grow into a woman who could have a normal sex life and babies. With the confirmation of menstruation, my parents apparently concluded that that prediction had been borne out and their ordeal was behind them. For me, the worst part of the nightmare was just beginning.

As an adolescent, I became aware that I had no clitoris or inner labia and was unable to orgasm. By the end of my teens, I began to do research in medical libraries, trying to discover what might have happened to me. When I finally determined to obtain my medical records, it took me three years to overcome the obstruction of the doctors whom I asked for help. When I did obtain them, a scant three pages, I first learned that I was a "true hermaphrodite" who had been my parents' son for a year and a half and who bore a name unfamiliar to me. The records also documented my clitorectomy. This was the middle 1970s, when I was in my early twenties. I had come to identify myself as lesbian, at a time when lesbianism and a biologically based gender essentialism were virtually synonymous: men were rapists who caused war and environmental destruction; women were good and would heal the earth; lesbians were a superior form of being uncontaminated by "men's energy." In such a world, how could I tell anyone that I had actually possessed the dreaded "phallus"? I was no longer a woman in my own eyes but rather a monstrous and mythical creature. Because my hermaphroditism and long-buried boyhood were the history behind the clitorectomy, I could never speak openly about that or my consequent inability to orgasm. I was so traumatized by discovering the circumstances that produced my embodiment that I could not speak of these matters with anyone.

Nearly fifteen years later, I suffered an emotional meltdown. In the eyes of the world, I was a highly successful businesswoman, a principal in an international high tech company. To myself, I was a freak, incapable of loving or being loved, filled with shame about my status as a hermaphrodite and about my sexual dysfunction. Unable to make peace with myself, I finally sought help from a psychotherapist, who reacted to each revelation about my history and predicament with some version of "no, it's not" or "so what?" I would say, "I'm not really a woman," and she would say, "Of course you are. You look female." I would say, "My complete withdrawal from sexuality has destroyed every relationship I've ever entered." She would say "Everybody has their ups and downs." I tried another therapist and met with a similar response. Increasingly desperate, I confided my story to several friends, who shrank away in embarrassed silence. I was in emotional agony, feeling utterly alone, seeing no possible way out. I decided to kill myself.

Confronting suicide as a real possibility proved to be my personal epiphany. I fantasized killing myself quite messily and dramatically in the office of the surgeon who had cut off my clitoris, forcibly confronting him with the horror he had imposed on my life. But in acknowledging the desire to put my pain to some use, not to utterly waste my life, I turned a crucial corner, finding a way to direct my rage productively out into the world rather than destructively at myself. I had no conceptual framework for developing a more positive self-consciousness. I knew only that I felt mutilated, not fully human, but that I was determined to heal. I struggled for weeks in emotional chaos, unable to eat or sleep or work. I could not accept my image of a hermaphroditic body any more than I could accept the butchered one the surgeons left me with. Thoughts of myself as a Frankenstein's monster patchwork alternated with longings for escape by death, only to be followed by outrage, anger, and a determination to survive. I could not accept that it was just or right or good to treat any person as I had been treated—my sex changed, my genitals cut up, my experience silenced and rendered invisible. I bore a private hell within me, wretchedly alone in my condition without even my tormentors for company. Finally, I began to envision myself standing in a driving storm but with clear skies and a rainbow visible in the distance. I was still in agony, but I was beginning to see the painful process in which I was caught up in terms of revitalization and rebirth, a means of investing my life with a new sense of authenticity that possessed vast potentials for further transformation. Since then, I have seen this experience of movement through pain to personal empowerment described by other intersex and transsexual activists.[20]

I slowly developed a newly politicized and critically aware form of self-understanding. I had been the kind of lesbian who at times had a girlfriend but who had never really participated in the life of a lesbian community. I felt almost completely isolated from gay politics, feminism, and queer and gender theory. I did possess the rudimentary knowledge that the gay rights movement had gathered momentum only when it could effectively deny that homosexuality was sick or inferior and assert to the contrary that "gay is good." As impossible as it then seemed, I pledged similarly to affirm that "intersex is good," that the body I was born with was not diseased, only different. I vowed to embrace the sense of being "not a woman" that I initially had been so terrified to discover.

I began searching for community and consequently moved to San Francisco in the fall of 1992, based entirely on my vague notion that people living in the "queer mecca" would have the most conceptually sophisticated, socially tolerant, and politically astute analysis of sexed and gendered embodiment. I found what I was looking for in part because my arrival in the Bay Area corresponded with the rather sudden emergence of an energetic transgender political movement. Transgender Nation (TN) had developed out of Queer Nation, a post-gay/lesbian group that sought to transcend identity politics. TN's actions garnered media attention—especially when members were arrested during a "zap" of the American Psychiatric Association's annual convention when they protested the psychiatric labeling of transsexuality as mental illness. Transsexual performance artist Kate Bornstein was introducing transgender issues in an entertaining way to the San Francisco gay/lesbian community and beyond. Female-to-male issues had achieved a new level of visibility due in large part to efforts made by Lou Sullivan, a gay FTM activist who had died an untimely death from HIV-related illnesses in 1991. And in the wake of her underground best-selling novel, *Stone Butch Blues*, Leslie Feinberg's manifesto *Transgender Liberation: A Movement Whose Time Has Come* was finding a substantial audience, linking transgender social justice to a broader progressive political agenda for the first time.[21] At the same time, a vigorous new wave of gender scholarship had emerged in the academy.[22] In this context, intersex activist and theoretician Morgan Holmes could analyze her own clitorectomy for her master's thesis and have it taken seriously as academic work.[23] Openly transsexual scholars, including Susan Stryker and Sandy Stone, were visible in responsible academic positions at major universities. Stone's "*Empire* Strikes Back: A Posttranssexual Manifesto" refigured open, visible transsexuals not as gender conformists propping up a system of rigid, binary sex but as "a set of embodied texts whose potential for productive disruption of structured sexualities and spectra of desire has yet to be explored."[24]

Into this heady atmosphere, I brought my own experience. Introduced by Bornstein to other gender activists, I explored with them the cultural politics of intersexuality, which to me represented yet another new configuration of bodies, identities, desires, and sexualities from which to confront the violently normativizing aspects of the dominant sex/gender system. In the fall of 1993, TN pioneer Anne Ogborn invited me to participate in a weekend retreat called the New Woman Conference, where postoperative transsexual women shared their stories, their griefs and joys, and enjoyed the freedom to swim or sunbathe in the nude with others who had surgically changed genitals. I saw that participants returned home in a state of euphoria, and I determined to bring that same sort of healing experience to intersex people.

Birth of an Intersex Movement: Opposition and Allies

Upon moving to San Francisco, I started telling my story indiscriminately to everyone I met. Over the course of a year, simply by speaking openly within my own social circles, I learned of six other intersexuals—including two who had been fortunate enough to escape medical attention. I realized that intersexuality, rather than being extremely rare, must be relatively common. I decided to create a support network. In the summer of 1993, I produced some pamphlets, obtained a post office box, and began to publicize the Intersex Society of North America (ISNA) through small notices in the media. Before long, I was receiving several letters per week from intersexuals throughout the United States and Canada and occasionally some from Europe. While the details varied, the letters gave a remarkably coherent picture of the emotional consequences of medical intervention. Morgan Holmes: "All the things my body might have grown to do, all the possibilities, went down the hall with my amputated clitoris to the pathology department. The rest of me went to the recovery room—I'm still recovering." Angela Moreno: "I am horrified by what has been done to me and by the conspiracy of silence and lies. I am filled with grief and rage, but also relief finally to believe that maybe I am not the only one." Thomas: "I pray that I will have the means to repay, in some measure, the American Urological Association for all that it has done for my benefit. I am having some trouble, though, in connecting the timing mechanism to the fuse."

ISNA's most immediate goal has been to create a community of intersex people who could provide peer support to deal with shame, stigma, grief, and rage as well as with practical issues such as how to obtain old medical records or locate a sympathetic psychotherapist or endocrinologist. To that end, I cooperated with journalists whom I judged capable of reporting widely and responsibly on our efforts, listed ISNA with self-help and referral clearinghouses, and established a presence on the Internet (www.isna.org). ISNA now connects hundreds of intersexuals across North America, Europe, Australia, and New Zealand. It has also begun sponsoring an annual intersex retreat, the first of which took place in 1996 and which moved participants every bit as profoundly as the New Woman Conference had moved me in 1993.

ISNA's longer-term and more fundamental goal, however, is to change the way intersex infants are treated. We advocate that surgery not be performed on ambiguous genitals unless there is a medical reason (such as blocked or painful urination), and that parents be given the conceptual tools and emotional support to accept their children's physical differences. While it is fascinating to think about the potential development of new genders or subject positions grounded in forms of embodiment that fall outside the familiar male/female dichotomy, we recognize that the two-sex/gender model is currently hegemonic and therefore advocate that children be raised either as boys or girls, according to which designation seems most likely to offer the child the greatest future sense of comfort. Advocating gender assignment without resorting to normalizing surgery is a radical position given that it requires the willful disruption of the assumed concordance between body shape and gender category. However, this is the only position that prevents irreversible physical damage to the intersex person's body, that respects the intersex person's agency regarding his/her own flesh, and that recognizes genital sensation and erotic functioning to be at least as important as reproductive capacity. If an intersex child or adult decides to change gender or to undergo surgical or hormonal alteration of his/her body, that decision should also be fully respected and facilitated. The key point is that intersex subjects should not be violated for the comfort and convenience of others.

One part of reaching ISNA's long-term goal has been to document the emotional and physical carnage resulting from medical interventions. As a rapidly growing literature makes abundantly clear (see the bibliography on our website, www.isna.org/bigbib.html), the medical management of intersexuality has changed little in the forty years since my first surgery. Kessler expresses surprise that "in spite of the thousands of genital operations performed every year, there are no meta-analyses from within the medical community on levels of success."[25] They do not know whether postsurgical intersexuals are "silent and happy or silent and unhappy."[26] There is no research effort to improve erotic functioning for adult intersexuals whose genitals have been altered, nor are there psychotherapists specializing in working with adult intersex clients trying to heal from the trauma of medical intervention. To provide a counterpoint to the mountains of medical literature that neglect intersex experience and to begin compiling an ethnographic account of that experience, ISNA's *Hermaphrodites with Attitude* newsletter has developed into a forum for intersexuals to tell their own stories. We have sent complimentary copies of the newsletter filled with searing personal narratives to academics, writers, journalists, minority rights organizations, and medical practitioners— to anybody we thought might make a difference in our campaign to change the way intersex bodies are managed.

ISNA's presence has begun to generate effects. It has helped politicize the growing number of intersex organizations, as well as intersex identities themselves. When I first began organizing ISNA, I met leaders of the Turner's Syndrome Society, the oldest known support group focusing on atypical sexual differentiation, founded in 1987. Turner's Syndrome is defined by an XO genetic karyotype that results in a female body morphology with nonfunctioning ovaries, extremely short stature, and a variety of other physical differences described in the medical literature with such stigmatizing labels as "webnecked" and "fishmouthed." Each of these women told me what a profound, life-changing experience it had been simply to meet another person like herself. I was inspired by their accomplishments (they are a national organization serving thousands of members), but I wanted ISNA to have a different focus. I was less willing to think of intersexuality as a pathology or disability, more interested in challenging its medicalization entirely, and more interested still in politicizing a pan-intersexual identity across the divisions of particular etiologies in order to destabilize more effectively the heteronormative assumptions underlying the violence directed at our bodies.

When I established ISNA in 1993, no such politicized groups existed. In the United Kingdom in 1988, the mother of a girl with androgen-insensitivity syndrome (AIS, which produces genetic males with female genital morphologies) formed the AIS Support Group. The group, which initially lobbied for increased medical attention (better surgical techniques for producing greater vaginal depth, more research into the osteoporosis that often attends AIS), now has chapters in five countries. Another group, K. S. and Associates, was formed in 1989 by the mother of a boy with Klinefelter's Syndrome and today serves over one thousand families. Klinefelter's is characterized by the presence of one or more additional X chromosomes, which produce bodies with fairly masculine external genitals, above-average height, and somewhat gangly limbs. At puberty, people with K. S. often experience pelvic broadening and the development of breasts. K. S. and Associates continues to be dominated by parents, is highly medical in orientation, and has resisted attempts by adult Klinefelter's

Syndrome men to discuss gender identity or sexual orientation issues related to their intersex condition.

Since ISNA has been on the scene, other groups with a more resistant stance vis-à-vis the medical establishment have begun to appear. In 1995, a mother who refused medical pressure for female assignment for her intersex child formed the Ambiguous Genitalia Support Network, which introduces parents of intersexuals to each other and encourages the development of pen-pal support relationships. In 1996, another mother who had rejected medical pressure to assign her intersex infant as a female by removing his penis formed the Hermaphrodite Education and Listening Post (HELP) to provide peer support and medical information. Neither of these parent-oriented groups, however, frames its work in overtly political terms. Still, political analysis and action of the sort advocated by ISNA has not been without effect on the more narrowly defined service-oriented or parent-dominated groups. The AIS Support Group, now more representative of both adults and parents, noted in a recent newsletter,

> Our first impression of ISNA was that they were perhaps a bit too angry and militant to gain the support of the medical profession. However, we have to say that, having read [political analyses of intersexuality by ISNA, Kessler, Fausto-Sterling, and Holmes], we feel that the feminist concepts relating to the patriarchal treatment of intersexuality are extremely interesting and do make a lot of sense. After all, the lives of intersexed people are stigmatized by the cultural disapproval of their genital appearance, [which need not] affect their experience as sexual human beings.[27]

Other more militant groups have now begun to pop up. In 1994, German intersexuals formed both the Workgroup on Violence in Pediatrics and Gynecology and the Genital Mutilation Survivors' Support Network, and Hijra Nippon now represents activist intersexuals in Japan.

Outside the rather small community of intersex organizations, ISNA's work has generated a complex patchwork of alliances and oppositions. Queer activists, especially transgender activists, have provided encouragement, advice, and logistical support to the intersex movement. The direct action group Transsexual Menace helped an ad hoc group of militant intersexuals calling themselves Hermaphrodites with Attitude plan and carry out a picket of the 1996 annual meeting of the American Academy of Pediatrics in Boston—the first recorded instance of intersex public protest in modern history.[28] ISNA was also invited to join GenderPAC, a recently formed national consortium of transgender organizations that lobbies against discrimination based on atypical expressions of gender or embodiment. More mainstream gay and lesbian political organizations such as the National Gay and Lesbian Task Force have also been willing to include intersex concerns as part of their political agendas. Transgender and lesbian/gay groups have been supportive of intersex political activism largely because they see similarities in the medicalization of these various identities as a form of social control and (especially for transsexuals) empathize with our struggle to assert agency within a medical discourse that works to efface the ability to exercise informed consent about what happens to one's own body.

Gay/lesbian caucuses and special interest groups within professional medical associations have been especially receptive to ISNA's agenda. One physician on the Internet discussion group glbmedical wrote:

> The effect of Cheryl Chase's postings—admittedly, after the shock wore off—was to make me realize that THOSE WHO HAVE BEEN TREATED might very well think [they had not been well served by medical intervention]. This matters a lot. As a gay

man, and simply as a person, I have struggled for much of my adult life to find my own natural self, to disentangle the confusions caused by others' presumptions about how I am/should be. But, thankfully, their decisions were not surgically imposed on me!

Queer psychiatrists, starting with Bill Byne at New York's Mount Sinai Hospital, have been quick to support ISNA, in part because the psychological principles underlying the current intersex treatment protocols are manifestly unsound. They seem almost willfully designed to exacerbate rather than ameliorate already difficult emotional issues arising from sexual difference. Some of these psychiatrists see the surgical and endocrinological domination of a problem that even surgeons and endocrinologists acknowledge to be psychosocial rather than biomedical as an unjustified invasion of their area of professional competence.

ISNA has deliberately cultivated a network of nonintersexed advocates who command a measure of social legitimacy and can speak in contexts where uninterpreted intersex voices will not be heard. Because there is a strong impulse to discount what intersexuals have to say about intersexuality, sympathetic representation has been welcome—especially in helping intersexuals reframe intersexuality in nonmedical terms. Some gender theory scholars, feminist critics of science, medical historians, and anthropologists have been quick to understand and support intersex activism. Years before ISNA came into existence, feminist biologist and science studies scholar Anne Fausto-Sterling had written about intersexuality in relation to intellectually suspect scientific practices that perpetuate masculinist constructs of gender, and she became an early ISNA ally.[29] Likewise, social psychologist Suzanne Kessler had written a brilliant ethnography of surgeons who specialize in treating intersexuals. After speaking with several "products" of their practice, she, too, became a strong supporter of intersex activism.[30] Historian of science Alice Dreger, whose work focuses not only on hermaphroditism but on other forms of potentially benign atypical embodiment that become subject to destructively normalizing medical interventions (conjoined twins, for example), has been especially supportive. Fausto-Sterling, Kessler, and Dreger will each shortly publish works that analyze the medical treatment of intersexuality as being culturally motivated and criticize it as harmful to its ostensible patients.[31]

Allies who help contest the medicalization of intersexuality are especially important because ISNA has found it almost entirely fruitless to attempt direct, nonconfrontational interactions with the medical specialists who themselves determine policy on the treatment of intersex infants and who actually carry out the surgeries. Joycelyn Elders, the Clinton administration's first surgeon general, is a pediatric endocrinologist with many years of experience managing intersex infants but, in spite of a generally feminist approach to health care and frequent overtures from ISNA, she has been dismissive of the concerns of intersexuals themselves.[32] Another pediatrician remarked in an Internet discussion on intersexuality: "I think this whole issue is preposterous. . . . To suggest that [medical decisions about the treatment of intersex conditions] are somehow cruel or arbitrary is insulting, ignorant and misguided. . . . To spread the claims that [ISNA] is making is just plain wrong, and I hope that this [on-line group of doctors and scientists] will not blindly accept them." Yet another participant in that same chat asked what was for him obviously a rhetorical question: "Who is the enemy? I really don't think it's the medical establishment. Since when did we establish the male/female hegemony?" While a surgeon quoted in a *New York Times* article on ISNA summarily dismissed us as "zealots,"[33] there is considerable anecdotal information supplied by ISNA sympathizers that professional meetings in the fields of pediatrics, urology, genital plastic surgery, and endocrinology are buzzing with anxious and defensive discussions of intersex activism. In response to the Hermaphrodites with Attitude protests at the American Academy of Pediatrics meeting, that organization felt compelled to issue the following statement to the press: "The Academy is deeply concerned about the emotional, cognitive, and body image development of intersexuals, and believes that successful early genital surgery minimizes these issues." Further protests were planned for 1997.

The roots of resistance to the truth claims of intersexuals run deep in the medical establishment. Not only does ISNA critique the normativist biases couched within most scientific practice, it advocates a treatment protocol for intersex infants that disrupts conventional understandings of the relationship between bodies and genders. But on a level more personally threatening to medical practitioners, ISNA's position implies that they have—unwittingly at best, through willful denial at worst—spent their careers inflicting a profound harm from which their patients will never fully recover. ISNA's position threatens to destroy the assumptions motivating an entire medical subspecialty, thus jeopardizing the ability to perform what many surgeons find to be technically difficult and fascinating work. Melissa Hendricks notes that Dr. Gearhart is known to colleagues as a surgical "artist" who can "carve a large phallus down into a clitoris" with consummate skill.[34] More than one ISNA member has discovered that surgeons actually operated on their genitals at no charge. The medical establishment's fascination with its own power to change sex and its drive to rescue parents from their intersex children are so strong that heroic interventions are delivered without regard to the capitalist model that ordinarily governs medical services.

Given such deep and mutually reinforcing reasons for opposing ISNA's position, it is hardly surprising that medical intersex specialists have, for the most part, turned a deaf ear toward us. The lone exception as of April 1997 is urologist Justine Schober. After watching a videotape of the 1996 ISNA retreat and receiving other input from HELP and the AIS Support Group, she suggests in a new textbook on pediatric surgery that while technology has advanced to the point that "our needs [as surgeons] and the needs of parents to have a presentable child can be satisfied," it is time to acknowledge that problems exist that "we as surgeons . . . cannot address. Success in psychosocial adjustment is the true goal of sexual assignment and genitoplasty. . . . Surgery makes parents and doctors comfortable, but counseling makes people comfortable too, and is not irreversible."[35]

While ISNA will continue to approach the medical establishment for dialogue (and continue supporting protests outside the closed doors when doctors refuse to talk), perhaps the most important aspect of our current activities is the struggle to change public perceptions. By using the mass media, the Internet, and our growing network of allies and sympathizers to make the general public aware of the frequency of intersexuality and of the intense suffering that medical treatment has caused, we seek to create an environment in which many parents of intersex children will have already heard about the intersex movement when their child is born. Such informed parents we hope will be better able to resist medical pressure for unnecessary genital surgery and secrecy and to find their way to a peer-support group and counseling rather than to a surgical theater.

First-World Feminism, African Clitorectomy, and Intersex Genital Mutilation

> We must first locate and challenge our own position as rigorously as we challenge that of others.
> —Salem Mekuria, "Female Genital Mutilation in Africa"

Traditional African practices that remove the clitoris and other parts of female genitals have lately been a target of intense media coverage and feminist activism in the United States and other industrialized Western societies. The euphemism *female circumcision* largely has been supplanted by the politicized term *female genital mutilation* (FGM). Analogous operations performed on intersexuals in the United States have not been the focus of similar attention—indeed, attempts to link the two forms of genital cutting have met with multiform resistance. Examining how first-world feminists and mainstream media treat traditional African practices and comparing that treatment with their responses to intersex genital mutilation (IGM) in North America exposes some of the complex interactions between ideologies of race, gender, colonialism, and science that effectively silence and render invisible intersex experience in first-world contexts. Cutting intersex genitals becomes yet another hidden mechanism for imposing normalcy upon unruly flesh, a means of containing the potential anarchy of desires and identifications within oppressive heteronormative structures.

In 1994, the *New England Journal of Medicine* paired an article on the physical harm resulting from African genital surgery with an editorial denouncing clitorectomy as a violation of human rights but declined to run a reply drafted by University of California at Berkeley medical anthropologist Lawrence Cohen and two ISNA members detailing the harm caused by medicalized American clitorectomies.[36] In response to growing media attention, Congress passed the Federal Prohibition of Female Genital Mutilation Act in October 1996, but the act specifically exempted from prohibition medicalized clitorectomies of the sort performed to "correct" intersex bodies. The bill's principal author, former Congresswoman Patricia Schroeder, received and ignored many letters from ISNA members and Brown University professor of medical science Anne Fausto-Sterling asking her to recast the bill's language. The *Boston Globe*'s syndicated columnist Ellen Goodman is one of the few journalists covering African FGM to respond to ISNA. "I must admit I was not aware of this situation," she wrote to me in 1994. "I admire your courage." She continued, however, regularly to discuss African FGM in her column without mentioning similar American practices. One of her October 1995 columns on FGM was promisingly titled, "We Don't Want to Believe It Happens Here," but it discussed only immigrants to the United States from third-world countries who performed clitorectomies on their daughters in keeping with the practices of their native cultures.

While clitorectomized African immigrant women doing anti-FGM activism in the United States have been receptive to the claims made by intersex opponents to medicalized clitorectomies and are in dialogue with us, first-world feminists and organizations working on African FGM have totally ignored us. To my knowledge, only two of the many anti-FGM groups contacted have responded to repeated overtures from intersex activists. Fran Hosken, who since 1982 has regularly published a catalogue of statistics on female genital mutilation worldwide, wrote me a terse note saying that "we are not concerned with biological exceptions."[37] Forward International, another anti-FGM organization, replied to an inquiry from German intersexual Heike Spreitzer that her letter was "most interesting" but that they could not help because their work focuses only on "female genital mutilation that is performed as a harmful cultural or traditional practice on young girls." As Forward International's reply to Spreitzer demonstrates, many first-world anti-FGM activists seemingly consider Africans to have "harmful cultural or traditional practices," while we in the modern industrialized West presumably have something better. We have science, which is linked to the metanarratives of enlightenment, progress, and truth. Genital cutting is condoned to the extent that it supports these cultural self-conceptions.

Robin Morgan and Gloria Steinem set the tone for subsequent first-world feminist analyses of FGM with their pathbreaking article in the March 1980 issue of *Ms.* magazine, "The International Crime of Genital Mutilation."[38] A disclaimer warns, "These words are painful to read. They describe facts of life as far away as our most fearful imagination—and as close as any denial of women's sexual freedom." For *Ms.* readers, whom the editors imagine are more likely to experience the pain of genital mutilation between the covers of their magazine than between their thighs, clitorectomy is presented as a fact of foreign life whose principal relevance to their readership is that it exemplifies a loss of "freedom," that most cherished possession of the liberal Western subject. The article features a photograph of an African girl with her legs held open by the arm of an unseen woman to her right. To her left is the disembodied hand of the midwife, holding the razor blade with which she has just performed a ritual clitorectomy. The girl's face—mouth open, eyes bulging—is a mask of pain. In more than fifteen years of coverage, Western images of African practices have changed little. "Americans made a horrifying discovery this year," *Life* soberly informed its readers in January 1997 while showing a two-page photo spread of a Kenyan girl held from behind as unseen hands cut her genitals.[39] The 1996 Pulitzer Prize for feature photography went to yet another portrayal of a Kenyan clitorectomy.[40] And in the wake of Fauziya Kassindja's successful bid for asylum in the United States after fleeing clitorectomy in Togo, the number of FGM images available from her country has skyrocketed.[41]

These representations all manifest a profound othering of African clitorectomy that contributes to the silence surrounding similar medicalized practices in the industrialized West. "Their" genital cutting is barbaric ritual; "ours" is scientific. Theirs disfigures; ours normalizes the deviant. The colonialist implications of these representations of genital cutting are even more glaringly obvious when images of intersex surgeries are juxtaposed with images of African FGM. Medical books describing how to perform clitoral surgery on white North American intersex children are almost always illustrated with extreme genital close-ups, disconnecting the genitals not only from the individual intersexed person but from the body itself. Full-body shots always have the eyes blacked out. Why is it considered necessary to black out the eyes of clitorectomized American girls—thus preserving a shred of their privacy and helping ward off the viewer's identification with the abject image—but not the eyes of the clitorectomized African girls in the pages of American magazines?[42]

First-world feminist discourse locates clitorectomy not only "elsewhere," in Africa, but also "elsewhen" in time. A recent *Atlantic Monthly* article on African clitorectomy asserted that the "American medical profession stopped performing clitoridectomies decades ago," and the magazine has since declined to publish a contradictory letter to the editor from ISNA.[43] Academic publications are as prone to this attitude as the popular press. In the recent *Deviant Bodies* anthology, visual artist Susan Jahoda's "Theatres of Madness" juxtaposes nineteenth- and twentieth-century material depicting "the conceptual interdependence of sexuality, reproduction, family life, and 'female disorders.'"[44] To represent twentieth-century medical clitorectomy practices, Jahoda quotes a July 1980 letter written to *Ms.* magazine in response to Morgan and Steinem. The letter writer, a nurse's aide in a geriatric home, said she had been puzzled by the strange scars she saw on the genitals of five of the forty women in her care: "Then I read your article My God! Why? Who decided to deny them orgasm? Who made them go through such a procedure? I want to know. Was it fashionable? Or was it to correct 'a condition'? I'd like to know what this so-called civilized country used as its criteria for such a procedure. And how widespread is it here in the United States?"[45] While Jahoda's selection of this letter does raise the issue of medicalized American clitorectomies, it safely locates the genital cutting in the past, as something experienced a long time ago by women now in their later stages of life.

Significantly, Jahoda literally passed over an excellent opportunity to comment on the continuing practice of clitorectomy in the contemporary United States. Two months earlier, in the April 1980 issue of *Ms.*, feminist biologists Ruth Hubbard and Patricia Farnes also replied to Morgan and Steinem:

> We want to draw the attention of your readers to the practice of clitoridectomy not only in the Third World but right here in the United States, where it is used as part of a procedure to "repair" by "plastic surgery" so-called genital ambiguities. Few people realize

that this procedure has routinely involved removal of the entire clitoris and its nerve supply—in other words, total clitoridectomy. . . . In a lengthy article, [Johns Hopkins intersex expert John] Money and two colleagues write that "a three-year old girl about to be clitoridectomized should be well informed that *the doctors will make her look like all other girls and women*' (our emphasis), which is not unlike what North African girls are often told about their clitoridectomies. But to date, neither Money nor his critics have investigated the effect of clitoridectomies on the girls' development. Yet one would surely expect this to affect their psychosexual development and their feelings of identity as young women.[46]

While Farnes and Hubbard's prescient feminist exposé of medicalized clitorectomies in the contemporary United States sank without a trace, there has been an explosion of work that keeps "domestic" clitorectomy at a safe distance. Such conceptualizations of clitorectomy's geographical and temporal cultural remoteness allow first-world feminist outrage to be diverted into potentially colonialist meddling in the social affairs of others while hampering work for social justice at home.[47]

Feminism represents itself as being interested in unmasking the silence that surrounds violence against women. Most medical intersex management is another form of violence based on a sexist devaluing of female pain and female sexuality. Doctors consider the prospect of growing up as a boy with a small penis to be a worse alternative than growing up as a girl *sans* clitoris and ovaries; they gender intersex bodies accordingly and cut them up to make the assigned genders support cultural norms of embodiment. These medical interventions transform many transgressive bodies into ones that can be labeled safely as women and subjected to the many forms of social control with which women must contend. Why then have most first-world feminists met intersexuals with a blank stare?

Intersexuals have had such difficulty generating mainstream feminist support not only because of the racist and colonialist frameworks that situate clitorectomy as a practice foreign to proper subjects within the first world but also because intersexuality undermines the stability of the category "woman" that undergirds much of first-world feminist discourse. We call into question the assumed relation between genders and bodies and demonstrate how some bodies do not fit easily into male/female dichotomies. We embody viscerally the truth of Judith Butler's dictum that "sex," the concept that accomplishes the materialization and naturalization of power-laden, culturally constructed differences, has really been "gender all along."[48] By refusing to remain silenced, we queer the foundations upon which depend not only the medical management of bodies but also widely shared feminist assumptions of properly embodied feminine subjectivity. To the extent that we are not normatively female or normatively women, we are not considered the proper subjects of feminist concern.

As unwilling subjects of science and improper subjects of feminism, politicized intersex activists have deep stakes in allying with and participating in the sorts of poststructuralist cultural work that exposes the foundational assumptions about personhood shared by the dominant society, conventional feminism, and many other identity-based oppositional social movements. We have a stake, too, in the efforts of gender queers to carve out livable social spaces for reconfigured forms of embodiment, identity, and desire. In 1990, Suzanne Kessler noted that "the possibilities for real societal transformations would be unlimited" if physicians and scientists specializing in the management of gender could recognize that "finally, and always, people construct gender as well as the social systems that are grounded in gender-based concepts. Accepting genital ambiguity as a natural option would require that physicians also acknowledge that genital ambiguity is 'corrected' not because it is threatening to the infant's life but because it is threatening to the infant's culture."[49] At that time, intersexuals had not yet been heard from, and there was little reason to think that physicians or other members of their culture would ever reflect on the meaning or effect of what they were doing. The advent of an activist intersex opposition changes everything.

From: Cheryl Chase, "Hermaphrodites with Attitude: Mapping the Emergence of Intersex Political Activism," in *GLQ: A Journal of Lesbian and Gay Studies*, Volume 4, no. 2, pp. 189–211. Copyright 1998, Duke University Press. All rights reserved. Republished by permission of the copyright holder, Duke University Press. www.dukeupress.edu.

Notes

My appreciation goes to Susan Stryker for her extensive contributions to the structure and substance of this essay.

1. Claude J. Migeon, Gary D. Berkovitz, and Terry R. Brown, "Sexual Differentiation and Ambiguity," in *Wilkins: The Diagnosis and Treatment of Endocrine Disorders in Childhood and Adolescence*, ed. Michael S. Kappy, Robert M. Blizzard, and Claude J. Migeon (Springfield, IL: Charles C. Thomas, 1994), 573–715.

2. Lalitha Raman-Wilms et al., "Fetal Genital Effects of First-Trimester Sex Hormone Exposure: A Meta-Analysis," *Obstetrics and Gynecology* 85 (1995): 141–148.

3. Anne Fausto-Sterling, *Body Building: How Biologists Construct Sexuality* (New York: Basic Books, forthcoming).

4. Judith Butler, *Gender Trouble: Feminism and the Subversion of Identity* (New York: Routledge, 1990); Thomas Laqueur, *Making Sex: Body and Gender from the Greeks to Freud* (Cambridge, MA: Harvard University Press, 1990).

5. Suzanne Kessler and Wendy McKenna, *Gender: An Ethnomethodological Approach* (New York: John Wiley and Sons, 1978).

6. Alice Domurat Dreger, "Doubtful Sex: Cases and Concepts of Hermaphroditism in France and Britain, 1868–1915" (Ph. D. diss., Indiana University, 1995); Alice Domurat Dreger, "Doubtful Sex: The Fate of the Hermaphrodite in Victorian Medicine," *Victorian Studies* (Spring 1995): 336–370; Alice Domurat Dreger, "Hermaphrodites in Love: The Truth of the Gonads," *Science and Homosexualities*, ed. Vernon Rosario (New York: Routledge, 1997), 46–66; Alice Domurat Dreger, "Doctors Containing Hermaphrodites: The Victorian Legacy," *Chrysalis: The Journal of Transgressive Gender Identities* (Fall 1997): 15–22.

7. Hugh Hampton Young, *Genital Abnormalities, Hermaphroditism, and Related Adrenal Diseases* (Baltimore: Williams and Wilkins, 1937), xxxix–xl.

8. Young, *Genital Abnormalities*, 139–142.

9. Howard W. Jones Jr. and William Wallace Scott, *Hermaphroditism, Genital Anomalies, and Related Endocrine Disorders* (Baltimore: Williams and Wilkins, 1958), 269.

10. John Money, Joan G. Hampson, and John L. Hampson, "An Examination of Some Basic Sexual Concepts: The Evidence of Human Hermaphroditism," *Bulletin of the Johns Hopkins Hospital* 97 (1955): 301–319; John Money, Joan G. Hampson, and John L. Hampson, "Hermaphroditism: Recommendations Concerning Assignment of Sex, Change of Sex, and Psychologic Management," *Bulletin of Johns Hopkins Hospital* 97 (1955): 284–300; John Money, *Venuses Penuses* (Buffalo: Prometheus, 1986).

11. Robert M. Blizzard, "Lawson Wilkins," in Kappy et al., *Wilkins*, xi–xiv.

12. Suzanne Kessler, "The Medical Construction of Gender: Case Management of Intersexual Infants," *Signs: Journal of Women in Culture and Society* 16 (1990): 3–26.

13. J. Dewhurst and D. B. Grant, "Intersex Problems," *Archives of Disease in Childhood* 59 (1984): 1191–1194; Anita Natarajan, "Medical Ethics and Truth-Telling in the Case of Androgen Insensitivity Syndrome," *Canadian Medical Association Journal* 154 (1996): 568–570; Tom Mazur, "Ambiguous Genitalia: Detection and Counseling," *Pediatric Nursing* (1983): 417–422; F. M. E. Slijper et al., "Neonates with Abnormal Genital Development Assigned the Female Sex: Parent Counseling," *Journal of Sex Education and Therapy* 20 (1994): 9–17.

14. Milton T. Edgerton, "Discussion: Clitoroplasty for Clitoromegaly due to Adrenogenital Syndrome without Loss of Sensitivity (by Nobuyuki Sagehashi)," *Plastic and Reconstructive Surgery* 91 (1993): 956.

15. Melissa Hendricks, "Is It a Boy or a Girl?" *Johns Hopkins Magazine*, November 1993, 10–16.

16. John F. Stecker et al., "Hypospadias Cripples," *Urologic Clinics of North America: Symposium on Hypospadias* 8 (1981): 539–544.

17. Jeff McClintock, "Growing Up in the Surgical Maelstrom," *Chrysalis: The Journal of Transgressive Gender Identities* (Fall 1997): 53–54.

18. Robert E. Gross, Judson Randolph, and John F. Crigler, "Clitorectomy for Sexual Abnormalities: Indications and Technique," *Surgery* 59 (1966): 300–308.

19. Joseph E. Oesterling, John P. Gearhart, and Robert D. Jeffs, "A Unified Approach to Early Reconstructive Surgery of the Child with Ambiguous Genitalia," *Journal of Urology* 138 (1987): 1079–1084.

20. Kira Triea, "The Awakening," *Hermaphrodites with Attitude* (Winter 1994): 1; Susan Stryker, "My Words to Victor Frankenstein above the Village of Chamounix: Performing Transgender Rage," *GLQ* 1 (1994): 237–254.

21. Leslie Feinberg, *Stone Butch Blues* (Ithaca, NY: Firebrand, 1993); Leslie Feinberg, *Transgender Liberation: A Movement Whose Time Has Come* (New York: World View Forum, 1992).

22. See, for example, Judith Butler, *Bodies That Matter: On the Discursive Limits of "Sex"* (New York: Routledge, 1993); Butler, *Gender Trouble*; Laqueur, *Making Sex*; Julia Epstein and Kristina Straub, eds., *Body Guards: The Cultural Politics of Gender Ambiguity* (New York: Routledge, 1991).

23. Morgan Holmes, "Medical Politics and Cultural Imperatives: Intersexuality Beyond Pathology and Erasure" (Master's Thesis, York University, Toronto, 1994).

24. Sandy Stone, "The *Empire* Strikes Back: A Posttranssexual Manifesto," in Epstein and Straub, *Body Guards*, 280–304, quotation on 296.

25. Suzanne Kessler, *Lessons from the Intersexed* (New Brunswick, NJ: Rutgers University Press, forthcoming).

26. Robert Jeffs, quoted in Ellen Barry, "United States of Ambiguity," Boston *Phoenix*, 22 November 1996, 6–8, quotation on 6.

27. AIS Support Group, "Letter to America," *ALIAS* (Spring 1996): 3–4.

28. Barry, "United States of Ambiguity," 7.

29. Anne Fausto-Sterling, "The Five Sexes: Why Male and Female Are Not Enough," *The Sciences* 33, no. 2 (March–April 1993): 20–25; Anne Fausto-Sterling, *Myths of Gender: Biological Theories about Women and Men*, 2nd ed. (New York: Basic Books, 1985), 134–141.

30. Kessler, "The Medical Construction of Gender"; Suzanne Kessler, "Meanings of Genital Variability," *Chrysalis: The Journal of Transgressive Gender Identities* (Fall 1997): 33–38.

31. Anne Fausto-Sterling, *Building Bodies: Biology and the Social Construction of Sexuality* (New York: Basic Books, forthcoming); Kessler, "Meanings of Genital Variability"; Alice Domurat Dreger, *Hermaphrodites and the Medical Invention of Sex* (Cambridge, MA: Harvard University Press, forthcoming).

32. "Dr. Elders' Medical History," *New Yorker*, 26 September 1994, 45–46; Joycelyn Elders and David Chanoff, *From Sharecropper's Daughter to Surgeon General of the United States of America* (New York: William Morrow, 1996).

33. Natalie Angier, "Intersexual Healing: An Anomaly Finds a Group," *New York Times*, 4 February 1996, E14.

34. Hendricks, "Is It a Boy or a Girl?" 10.

35. Justine M. Schober, "Long Term Outcomes of Feminizing Genitoplasty for Intersex," in *Pediatric Surgery and Urology: Long Term Outcomes*, ed. Pierre Mouriquant (Philadelphia: W. B. Saunders, forthcoming).

36. Patricia Schroeder, "Female Genital Mutilation," *New England Journal of Medicine* 331 (1994): 739–740; Nahid Toubia, "Female Circumcision as a Public Health Issue," *New England Journal of Medicine* 331 (1994): 712–716.

37. Fran P. Hosken, *The Hosken Report: Genital/Sexual Mutilation of Females*, 4th ed. (Lexington, MA: WIN News, 1994).

38. Robin Morgan and Gloria Steinem, "The International Crime of Genital Mutilation," *Ms.*, March 1980, 65–67ff.

39. Mariella Furrer, "Ritual Agony," *Life*, January 1997, 38–39.

40. Pulitzer Prize Board, "Feature Photography: Stephanie Welsh," 1996. Available online at ners/1996/winners/works/feature-photography/.

41. Celia Dugger, "U.S. Grants Asylum to Woman Fleeing Genital Mutilation Rite," *New York Times*, 14 June 1996, A1; Celia Dugger, "New Law Bans Genital Cutting in the United States," *New York Times*, 12 October 1996, 1; Furrer, "Ritual Agony."

42. Dugger, "U.S. Grants Asylum"; Salem Mekuria, "Female Genital Mutilation in Africa: Some African Views," *Association of Concerned African Scholars Bulletin* (Winter–Spring 1995): 2–6.

43. Linda Burstyn, "Female Circumcision Comes to America," *Atlantic Monthly*, October 1995, 28–35.

44. Susan Jahoda, "Theatres of Madness," in *Deviant Bodies*, ed. Jennifer Terry and Jacqueline Urla (Bloomington: Indiana University Press, 1995), 251–276.
45. Letter to the editor, *Ms.*, July 1980, 12.
46. Ruth Hubbard and Patricia Farnes, letter to the editor, *Ms.*, April 1980, 9–10.
47. Seble Dawit and Salem Mekuria, "The West Just Doesn't Get It," *New York Times*, 7 December 1993, A27.
48. Butler, *Gender Trouble*, 8.
49. Kessler, "Medical Construction of Gender," 25.

50 Undetectability in a Time of Trans Visibility

Christopher Joseph Lee

In "Undetectability in a Time of Trans Visibility," first published in *TSQ: Transgender Studies Quarterly* in 2020, Christopher Joseph Lee repurposes the term *undetectability*, used to describe an HIV viral load below the threshold of noticeability, to explore questions of trans representation in mass media. He pays particular attention to questions of responsibility for "detection" and "undetectability" and whether that responsibility is assigned to the individual or the systems and structures the individual lives within. Lee explores these ideas of detection and responsibility in critiquing David France's film *The Death and Life of Marsha P. Johnson* for its narrative strategy, which seeks to identify an individual perpetrator responsible for the death of that legendary foremother of contemporary transfeminine people. To personalize anti-trans violence in this way, Lee argues, effaces the structural and institutional forms of racist and anti-trans violence that Johnson confronted throughout her life and which arguably contributed to her death. The film argues, in essence, that the life of a Black HIV+ trans person would have been saved, and could still receive justice, by better policing. Drawing from Toby Beauchamp's work on how gender-nonconforming bodies are subjected to heightened surveillance and criminalization by the state, Lee suggests that the concept of "opacity" might offer a trans people a better survival strategy than the concept of "undetectability." Trans opacity, in Lee's words, "short-circuit[s] the seeming promise of recognition." To be opaque is to refuse the logic of visibility that infuses the neoliberal state's discourse of inclusion and diversity, which glosses over what Dean Spade calls the "administrative violence" that the state routinely enacts against trans people. Lee finds this strategy of "trans opacity" at work in another film about Marsha Johnson's life, Tourmaline and Sasha Wortzel's *Happy Birthday, Marsha!* Lee suggests that this film offers a rich yet deliberately incomplete portrait of Johnson's life by intercutting archival footage of her with scripted reenactments of the day leading up to the Stonewall Riots. In so doing, Lee claims, the filmmakers move their audience beyond the individualizing forensic concerns of France's film and depict instead a more radical political imaginary that better honors Johnson as a revolutionary anti-carceral activist.

In 1996, the advent of highly active antiretroviral therapy (HAART) as an effective treatment for HIV marked a watershed moment in which a commonly fatal infection could be seen as a manageable chronic condition. In the wake of this medical breakthrough, researchers investigating the effectiveness of antiretroviral medication found that early and prolonged use of HAART could also serve as a deterrent to spread of HIV, suggesting that treating the virus contributed to its prevention. Put simply, by suppressing viral load to a level undetectable by conventional testing, HAART also suppressed transmission of the virus. More recently, this

DOI: 10.4324/9781003206255-61

concept of treatment as prevention (TasP) has gained traction in public health campaigns, designating "undetectability" as an essential tool and term in the fight against HIV.[1]

While undetectability guides the promise of a once unimaginable normal life, critics, curators, and activists have also pointed to the limits of undetectability discourses, asking how overemphasizing treatment as prevention might leave out broader discussions of access, class, education, race, and community care. In his essay exploring HIV, incarceration, and art, Ted Kerr (2019) suggests that public health campaigns' embrace of undetectability simultaneously promotes the effectiveness of HIV treatment as prevention and the "individual work of ending the crisis by choosing to become undetectable." Jan Huebenthal (2017: 2) argues, likewise, that undetectability signals fitness for good citizenship, promising "a post-AIDS world inhabited by gay men who, having suffered though the horrors of AIDS, have returned to their healthy, authentic selves." In reflecting on the relative privilege necessary to access treatment, Nathan Lee (2013) posits that undetectability might "displace the positive/negative binary with the more urgent categories of the insured/uninsured." Registered collectively, these critics suggest that, far from acting as a guarantee of HIV destigmatization, undetectability might overdetermine questions of individual responsibility and health at the cost of forgoing discussions of the structures barring access to widespread testing and treatment.

Beyond its medical and public health definitions, the term *undetectable* carries different resonances in a time of heightened trans visibility predicated on a theory that more or better trans representation might better protect trans people.[2] This discourse of trans visibility has crept into public HIV/AIDS campaigns that name trans people of color as an underrecognized risk group, and, according to the *US News and World Report*, warn of a growing trans population of the "infected and invisible" (Marcus 2018). But while nonprofit organizations like the Human Rights Campaign continually call for greater trans "visibility and inclusiveness" within HIV/AIDS campaigns, scholars like Eric Stanley and Toby Beauchamp have highlighted the imbrication of trans visibility with targeted surveillance practices (Human Rights Campaign n.d.). In *Going Stealth* (2019), Beauchamp examines how overemphasizing trans recognition can expand the reach of surveillance programs like identification documents and airport body screening that monitor gender conformity. Beauchamp's interrogation of visibility dovetails with Stanley's (2017: 617) movement from trans "optics" to "opacity," putting forward a call to interrogate a "visual regime hostile to black trans life." In short-circuiting the seeming promise of trans recognition, Stanley asks: "How can we be seen without being known and how can we be known without being hunted?" (618).

Such critiques of trans visibility offer another inroad to unpacking undetectability, not just as a shorthand for the management of viral risk but also as a space for navigating the violence of surveillance and exposure in a "discourse of concealment" germane to trans life (Beauchamp 2019: 32). To invoke undetectability in a time of trans visibility might mean exploring how demands for trans recognition parallel an enduring and equally fraught demand to recognize those living with and lost to HIV/AIDS, in a time before undetectability could even be imagined. Bound up with the problem of trans representation and visibility, moreover, is the struggle to represent HIV/AIDS altogether, given what Paula A. Treichler (1987: 31) has called, in her early analysis of the AIDS crisis, an "epidemic of signification." Treichler's call to reckon with the multitude of interpretations seeking to signify the virus is a reminder that the battle against HIV/AIDS has always comprised medical and scientific breakthroughs as well as a crisis of meaning. When confronted with undetectability, as with the social construction of the virus itself, we are wrestling with the many contradictions this term might hold for those living with HIV/AIDS and for those living in an intensified moment of trans visibility and precarity. Can undetectability serve as an adjacent term to trans opacity or trans invisibility? And what lessons might follow from thinking about undetectability alongside metaphors of vocalization from silence, visibility from opacity, and clarity in the absence of clear or certain narratives?

Undetectability and the Detective Story

In the midst of these discussions, I want to turn to David France's *Death and Life of Marsha P. Johnson* (2017) as an attempt to constellate questions of undetectability, trans visibility, exposure, and remembrance. In recent years, a resurgent attention has been devoted to the revolutionary figure, Marsha "Pay It No Mind" Johnson, owing largely to the work of community historians in shining a light on her roles as freedom fighter, activist, and cofounder, alongside Sylvia Rivera, of the Street Transvestite Action Revolutionaries (STAR). Simultaneously, such an attention has also revived intrigue around the mysterious circumstances of Johnson's death, which, to this day, remains unsolved. In 2017, France, director of the Oscar-nominated film *How to Survive a Plague*, released *The Death and Life of Marsha P. Johnson*, which centers Johnson's unexplained death as well as the efforts of Victoria Cruz, a close friend of Johnson's, to find answers. That France's latest film features the death of Marsha P. Johnson—a black, trans woman noted for her revolutionary movement work—appears to serve as a corrective to critiques that *How to Survive* privileged the perspectives of white men over queer people of color, life over death, and medical advancements over direct action and activism.[3] The narrative emphasis that *Death and Life* places in Johnson's mysterious demise poses another frame of detection and undetectability connected to trans life and antitrans violence: the detective story. France's film folds in archival footage, Cruz's investigation, and the present-day trial of Islan Nettles, a trans woman beaten to death in 2013, as a means to explore how detection can potentially mediate and deter, or potentially fail to resolve antiqueer violence.

By weighing *Death and Life*'s emphasis on detective work—namely, the film's tracking of Cruz's investigation as a means of closing a chapter on transphobic violence— I reflect on both detection and undetectability as tools for confronting acts of transphobic violence, as well as the multiple causes, spectacular and otherwise, of trans precarity. While the film's privileging of forensic detection, investigation, and state-sponsored resolution strikes an odd contrast to Johnson's movement work on behalf of people living the HIV/AIDS, prisoners, sex workers, and other survivors of state violence, I argue that the film points both to the affective thrill of pursuing detection *and* its inevitable disappointments. Revisiting undetectability within these efforts to memorialize Johnson—who herself had been living with HIV prior to her mysterious death—reminds us how practices of looking, investigation, and the fantasy of "knowing" operate in the interlocking discourses of trans and HIV/AIDS visibility, both of which demand forms of secrecy and disclosure.

In one of the first scenes of *Death and Life*, we are introduced to Victoria Cruz, a counselor at the Anti-Violence Project who serves as the narrator of much of France's film. Cruz remarks that Johnson's case, in particular, has been "cold" for twenty-five years, and that she seeks justice for slain trans women of color, beginning with Johnson. As Cruz asks, "If we can't bring justice to Marsha, how can we bring justice for all these other unsolved cases?" Cruz's nondiegetic narration plays out in this early scene, where she assembles a rough time line in the days leading up to Johnson's death (fig. 1). Writing on various Post-it notes, Cruz pins one note after another to a largely bare wall of corkboard. A close-up of one note reads, "July 6 1992, found at 5:23 PM," the time at which Johnson's body was first discovered. This scene launches the long investigatory arc of France's film, in which Cruz's attempt to bring justice to Johnson's unsolved death dovetails with a broader effort to confront and resolve the violence facing trans women of color. As Cruz conducts interviews and chases leads, the once empty space of the corkboard fills up with printed articles, interviews, and diagrams relating to Johnson's death, all annotated with Cruz's hand-written comments. This wall becomes a recurring visual motif for the investigatory motor of France's film, in which Cruz assembles clues and details that will point to answers in Johnson's cold case.

This quest for justice is at the heart of France's film as well as Cruz's investigation, but the question of justice—whose justice, what type of justice is served, and whom it serves—is far murkier. Cruz's method of detection, whereby she pores over eyewitness accounts and forensic reports, places her firmly in the frame of the hard-boiled crime story, which, according to Bill Pronzini and Jack Adrian (1997: 3), generally centers "a social misfit" in the role of the amateur or professional sleuth and deals principally with "disorder, disaffection, and dissatisfaction" with the prevailing social order. The detective story, especially of the hard-boiled variety, serves as a well-worn genre through which to channel frustration with the failures of the police to adequately address Johnson's mysterious death. By beginning with death, the film suggests that detection, foremost, can clear the fog of mystery hanging over Johnson. In Jeffry J. Iovannone's (2017) account, France's film deemphasizes Johnson's remarkable contributions to queer liberation in favor of "focusing disproportionately on the more spectacular and suspenseful details of her death." *Death and Life*'s meditation on Johnson's mysterious demise follows a broader trend to draw political and symbolic meaning from trans death. Though memorials might serve as a crucial outlet to publicly mourn the loss of trans lives, scholars like Jin Haritaworn and C. Riley Snorton have also critiqued the ritualized remembrance of transphobic attacks and murders. As they discuss, public memorials for trans women of color increasingly feed the institutionalization of a trans politics that converges with rather than against state power. Haritaworn and Snorton (2013: 74) describe how trans-of-color death is invoked to "accrue value to a newly professionalizing . . . class of experts whose lives could not be further removed from those they are professing to help." In this way, it is only through death that "poor and sex working trans people of color are invited back in" to policy, legal, and nonprofit discussions of trans protections and rights.

As Victoria Cruz and many of those in Johnson's close community seek answers for the loss of a friend and sister, their quest for personal justice is frustrated by the ineffectiveness of state-sponsored inquiries. Their anger at do-nothing cops is channeled at an effort to carry out their own investigation. But even this provisional opposition to the state is another feature of the hard-boiled crime story, as the detective will often have "a jaundiced view of government, power, and the law" (Pronzini and Adrian 1997: 3). And despite capturing a palpable anger at the police, France's film remains enmeshed in a model of detection that privileges forensic investigation and state-sponsored inquiries into transphobic violence. In a secondary arc of the film, Cruz and other activists seek justice for Islan Nettles, a trans woman of color beaten to death in an act of brutal transphobia. One of the last sequences of France's film takes place in a New York courtroom, where Nettles's killer is sentenced to ten and a half years in prison. Xena Grandichelli, a volunteer with the Anti-Violence Project and an attendee of the court proceedings, is shown to be outraged at the judge's decision, indicating that the relatively light sentencing amounts to a failure of the system in deterring and accounting for transphobic violence.

Nettles's death in 2013 marks a significant but contested moment in which trans-of-color death drove public and media narratives around antiqueer violence, including efforts to propose and advance carceral expansion.[4] As Lena Carla Palacios (2016: 43) writes, Nettles's case "has been used as a poster child by journalists, legislators, and even members of their own kin to expand police surveillance in racially marginalized communities and to bolster the passage of criminal punishment—enhancing laws that purportedly address transphobic violence." In her broader study, Palacios suggests that reductive accounts of Nettles's death discount the circumstances contributing to transphobic harm, like gentrification and increased police surveillance of Harlem. *Death and Life* plays a part in this flattening of context, and its narrative centering of a courtroom sentencing scene suggests that carceral resolutions of transphobic violence mark, in its framing, a horizon of trans justice. To be clear, though, the trans activists depicted in France's film are not merely mouthpieces for the documentary's carceral model of justice. Any critique of *Death and Life*'s framing of justice must also weigh the extent to which trans women themselves— Cruz, Grandichelli, and others—push for longer sentencings and punitive responses to transphobic violence. Palacios's analysis of the media outcry following Nettles's death cautions that trans women of color's responses vary in their responses to the institutionalization of trans remembrance, and they can both "reproduce and challenge dominant logics of social value" (45). While capturing a passionate outcry for state intervention into trans violence, the film overlooks what Palacios calls an "outlaw vernacular" that works against a straightforward politics of recognition and visibility (39).

How might we rethink detecting the origins of transphobic harm and, in doing so, reconceptualize its supposed resolution? And what relationship might the fantasy of criminal guilt have to a term like *undetectability*? *Death and Life* investigates the untimely deaths of Johnson and Nettles in search of an individual perpetrator to account for the enormity of transphobic violence. Likewise, discourses of undetectability that emphasize personal management follow what Trevor Hoppe (2017: 118) has called a "responsibility politics" that emerged in the late 1990s and early 2000s, just as the advancement of antiretroviral treatments "transform[ed] HIV-positive people from passive victims into active managers." In analyzing the Centers for Disease Control and Prevention's (CDC) shift from promotion of condom use and "safer sex" to campaigns like "HIV Stops With Me," Hoppe describes how efforts to endow HIV-positive people with a sense of individual responsibility "resonate[d] with efforts to assign blame, punish, and, ultimately, criminalize individuals viewed as failing to live up [to] those [expectations]" (119). These notions of individual responsibility, well-meaning or otherwise, drive, in Hoppe's terms, an "epidemic of criminalization" that expands HIV-specific laws to punish the spread of disease (294).[5] As with carceral solutions to transphobic harm, it is within this punitive framework of detection, exposure, shame, and guilt that an individual wrongdoer must surface.[6]

The quest to find a missing perpetrator to account for Johnson's death defines the investigatory arc of France's documentary. By the end of the film, though, Cruz appears to hit a limit in her own investigation. Methodically removing her notes and clues, she files her evidence into a hefty dossier, stripping the corkboard wall as bare as it had begun. She hand addresses the file folder, and the camera follows her as she delivers the binder to the Federal Bureau of Investigation's (FBI) New York office. France's film thus ends with the transfer of Johnson's case to a bureau that notoriously utilized state power throughout 1960s to infiltrate, surveil, and quell the activities of the Black Panthers, suspected communist organizations, and civil rights groups.[7] Framed as a search for Johnson's presumable killer(s), *Death and Life* ends in this melancholic space, with Cruz looking off mournfully into the New York skyline. Cruz's search for justice is forestalled, perhaps indefinitely. My argument suggests that *Death and Life*'s framing as a hard-boiled detective story, complete with forensic detail and intrigue, offers a poor juxtaposition to Johnson's lifelong struggle with the police and state power (by her own count, having been arrested over a hundred times). However, I also argue that in offering up an ultimately failed detective story, the film lays bare the limits of forensic investigation.

In searching for a criminal account to clear the mystery around Johnson's death, *Death and Life* takes on the impossible task of mediating transphobic harm writ large, which, as Eric Stanley (2011: 7) reminds us, is more a foundational and "epistemic force" than a state of exception. Without an individual perpetrator to account for Johnson's death, the film suggests that something—a narrative thread or piece of evidence—is missing. In his account of

HIV criminalization, Kane Race (2017: 117, 120) argues that "criminal law aims to isolate the human subject in its framing of responsibility for HIV events," and he asks, alternatively, "What capacities exist within juridical discourse to conceive the participation of a wider range of actors . . . in undesirable events such as HIV infection?" The same question might be asked of the death of Marsha P. Johnson: that is, how can the juridical frame account for a death absent an explicit cause or human actor? I am not suggesting that viral exposure, death, and potentially murder are at all commensurate in scale, but rather, that the logic of criminalization demands that a perpetrator emerge in each instance.[8] Without a culpable subject to anchor such a loss, what sense of justice remains?

Undetectability in Trans Remembrance

Shortly after the release of *The Death and Life of Marsha P. Johnson*, a controversy erupted around France's film, ignited by claims that his ideas were heavily borrowed, if not outright lifted, from the historical and archival research of filmmaker Tourmaline, who herself had been working on a documentary about Johnson.[9] The revelation that France's well-funded *Netflix* film might derive from the intellectual labor of an underfunded trans woman raises serious questions about the institutionalized remembrance of trans life (and death), particularly in its reproduction of violent power asymmetries that Johnson herself negotiated. Tourmaline, alongside codirector Sasha Wortzel, released her own short film about Johnson entitled *Happy Birthday, Marsha!* in 2018. Though there is much evidence and significance to weigh in this controversy, I want to, instead, close by taking note of the striking formal contrast between France's handling of Johnson's legacy and her depiction in *Happy Birthday, Marsha!*

If *Death and Life* is premised on exposure and detection—a documentary-cum-detective story that drives toward state-sponsored and forensic resolution of Johnson's mysterious demise—*Happy Birthday, Marsha!* is premised on exploring Johnson's legacy through a lens of opacity. With Mya Taylor cast in the role of Marsha P. Johnson, Tourmaline and Wortzel's film combines elements of archival research and fantastic reimagining, depicting the hours in Johnson's life leading up to the famous Stonewall Uprising of 1969, the police riot widely considered to be the modern birthplace of the gay liberation movement. As Jeannine Tang (2017: 382) remarks, *Happy Birthday, Marsha!* is steeped in a soft-focused aesthetics of glamour that works against a visual logic that features "trans bodies as . . . mangled and murdered." Rather than linger on Johnson's mysterious death, Tourmaline and Wortzel craft a small, intimate portrait of Johnson that culminates in a stand off with the police at the Stonewall Inn. Notably, the film stops meaningfully short of the uprising itself, though Johnson (as played by Taylor) is shown to throw the shot glass that, legend has it, launched the multiday demonstrations (fig. 2). The historical and temporal space that Tourmaline and Wortzel work in is relatively contained but rich with affection, style, and intrigue. Cutting between recorded footage and a fictional reimagining of Johnson, the film intermingles what is apprehensible in the archive with what remains (or must remain) unseen. Thinking alongside *Happy Birthday, Marsha!* and France's documentary is one space in which to reflect on undetectability, trans visibility, and the promise of opacity.[10]

What would it mean to sit with the historical and archival registers and gaps in Marsha P. Johnson's legacy and leave what is unexposed, unruly, and undetectable? What would it mean to refuse criminal investigation—beginning first with the FBI and forensic investigation altogether—and decline declaring any singular cause of transphobic harm?

There is little doubt that the state-sponsored justice system failed Johnson in overlooking the circumstances of her death. There is little doubt, however, that this system was built on that failure, punishing and criminalizing people like Johnson: poor people of color, sex workers, houseless people, and those living with HIV/AIDS. In her time, Johnson saw many of her own community, "transvestites," as she called them, locked up "for no reason at all" (Jay 1992: 113). She observed how the justice system trapped her trans sisters by demanding bail and legal fees from those who had no money to give. She marched on Wall Street with ACT UP to decry the overpricing of AIDS medications and called on people to "stand as close to [people living with AIDS] as much you can . . . help them out as much as you can."[11] Honoring Johnson's legacy asks us to reflect on crafting a sense of justice commensurate with those who have lived under and resisted, in oftentimes revolutionary ways, the reach of the carceral state. What is left unknown, I argue, moves beyond the mysterious causes of her death, extending into the remarkable political imaginary that she crafted, a portrait of mutual aid that we have yet to fully realize. This model of collective liberation necessitates rethinking the privatization of viral management and the joint orientation of criminal investigation toward individual choice, responsibility, and guilt.

Notes

1. The Undetectable=Untransmittable movement (U=U) launched in 2016 with a consensus statement affirming that "people living with HIV on HAART with an undetectable viral load in their blood have a negligible risk of sexual transmission of HIV." U=U has played an especially significant role in promoting undetectability to normalize and destigmatize HIV as a manageable condition. See Prevention Access Campaign 2016.

2. The edited collection, *Trap Door*, offers a number of reflections on the paradox of trans visibility, questioning, in the editors' words, whether it is "a goal to be worked toward or an outcome to be avoided at all costs" (Burton, Stanley, and Tourmaline 2017: xx).

3. France's earlier work, *How to Survive a Plague*, has been the subject of both mainstream acclaim and intense scrutiny. Despite the film's offering an oftentimes moving account of the early years of the AIDS crisis, scholars like Jih-Fei Cheng (2016: 73) point to the gaps in *How to Survive's* framing, depicted through a "lens of white male heroes" that largely overlooks queer-of-color contributions to early AIDS activism. Cheng describes how the film trains its attention to the search for a medical breakthrough (like undetectability). White men are positioned as central to the eventual development of HAART, and the survival of some of these men "become[s] the film's evidence that biomedical interventions can and should work for everyone" (74). See also Shahani 2016.

4. Dean Spade's (2015) work on critical trans politics has been particularly instructive in illuminating the failure of hate crime legislation to effectively deter transphobic harm.

5. As of today, according to the CDC, twenty-six states in the United States have laws criminalizing HIV exposure. See CDC n.d.

6. Perhaps the most infamous example of HIV/AIDS discourses' intersecting with individual responsibility resides in the case of Canadian flight attendant Gaëtan Dugal, the man popularly dubbed "Patient Zero." Through a work of investigative journalism by Randy Shilts, *And the Band Played On*, Dugal was sensationally scapegoated as the man who brought the AIDS virus to the Western world. Philip James Tiemeyer (2013: 258) describes the speed with which the "patient zero" mythos ignited a new narrative in which "AIDS was a disease born of gay immorality, a threat to the nation that came from the post-Stonewall gay credo of unchecked sexual excess." Tiemeyer suggests that the popularization of the term *patient zero*, though only tenuously based in truth, served as an effective bogeyman for conservative lawmakers to rapidly advance the criminalization of people with HIV. In the case of Dugal, detecting "patient zero" helped propagate even more emphasis on medical exposure of and criminalization of potentially "dangerous" individuals.

7. In David Cunningham's (2004: xi–xii) analysis of the FBI's counterintelligence programs, he remarks that COINTELPRO and other actions taken up by the bureau should not be seen as "purely historical artifacts" but rather as "key to comprehending the FBI's fragile orientation to civil liberties generally."

8. In a time before undetectability was understood and accepted, such comparisons between viral exposure and murder were commonplace. Gay journalist Charles Kaiser was infamously quoted as saying, "A person who is HIV-Positive has no more right to unprotected discourse than he has the right to put a bullet through another person's head" (quoted in Jacobs 2005).

9. Two articles in *Teen Vogue* (Weiss 2017; Tourmaline 2017) offer a clear portrait of this controversy. For more on the question of narrative authority and *Death and Life*, see Calafell 2019.

10. As with visibility, there are limits to the promise of opacity. To be marked illegible, or to mark oneself in such a way, is also to be uncounted, unheard, and potentially discarded; indeed, the tactics of early AIDS organizing demanded visibility and vocalization amidst a deafening silence. In a time of trans exposure and HIV criminalization, though, we must also weigh, in Ted Kerr's (2019) words, how "visibility has become a state-enforced demand."

11. From an interview in an earlier documentary, *Pay It No Mind: Marsha P. Johnson* (Kasino 2012).

Bibliography

Beauchamp, Toby. 2019. *Going Stealth: Transgender Politics and U.S. Surveillance Practices*. Durham, NC: Duke University Press.

Burton, Johanna, Eric Stanley, and Tourmaline. 2017. "Known Unknowns: An Introduction to Trap Door." In *Trap Door: Trans Cultural Production and the Politics of Visibility*, edited by Johanna Burton, Eric Stanley, and Tourmaline, xv–xxvi. Cambridge, MA: MIT Press.

Calafell, Bernadette Marie. 2019. "Narrative Authority, Theory in the Flesh, and the Fight Over *the Death and Life of Marsha P. Johnson*." *QED* 6, no. 2: 26–39.

CDC (Centers for Disease Control and Prevention). n.d. "HIV-Specific Criminal Laws." www.cdc.gov/hiv/policies/law/states/exposure.html (accessed June 15, 2020).

Cheng, Jih-Fei. 2016. "How to Survive: AIDS and Its Afterlives in Popular Media." *WSQ* 44, no. 1: 73–92.

Cunningham, David. 2004. *There's Something Happening Here: The New Left, the Klan, and FBI Counterintelligence*. Berkeley: University of California Press.

France, David, dir. 2017. *The Death and Life of Marsha P. Johnson*. Netflix.

Haritaworn, Jin, and C. Riley Snorton. 2013. "Trans Necropolitics: A Transnational Reflection on Violence, Death, and the Trans of Color Afterlife." In *The Transgender Studies Reader 2*, edited by Susan Stryker and Aren Z. Aizura, 66–76. New York: Routledge.

Hoppe, Trevor. 2017. *Punishing Disease: HIV and the Criminalization of Sickness*. Oakland: University of California Press.

Huebenthal, Jan. 2017. "Un/Detectability in Times of 'Equality': HIV, Queer Health, and Homonormativity." *European Journal of American Studies* 11, no. 3. journals.openedition.org/ejas/11729.

Human Rights Campaign. n.d. "Transgender People and HIV: What We Know." www.hrc.org/resources/transgender-people-and-hiv-what-we-know/.

Iovannone, Jeffry J. 2017. "Should Netflix Viewers Boycott *the Death and Life of Marsha P. Johnson*?" *Medium*, October 8. medium.com/queer-history-for-the-people/should-netflix—viewers-boycott-the-death-and-life-of-marsha-p-johnson-cdf0a4057217.

Jacobs, Andrew. 2005. "Gays Debate Radical Steps to Curb Unsafe Sex." *New York Times*, February 15. www.nytimes.com/2005/02/15/health/gays-debate-radical-steps-to-curb-unsafe-sex.html.

Jay, Karla. 1992. *Out of the Closets: Voices of Gay Liberation*. New York: New York University Press.

Kasino, Michael, dir. 2012. *Pay It No Mind: Marsha P. Johnson*. Redux Pictures.

Kerr, Ted. 2019. "From Tactic to Demand: HIV Visibility Within a Culture of Criminalization." *ONCURATING*, no. 42. www.on-curating.org/issue-42-reader/from-tactic-to-demand—hiv-visibility-within-a-culture-of-criminalization.html.

Lee, Nathan. 2013. "Becoming-Undetectable." *E-flux*, no. 44. www.e-flux.com/journal/44/60170/becoming-undetectable/.

Marcus, Noreen. 2018. "Infected and Invisible: Fla. Housing Troubles Hit Transgender Residents." *US News and World Report*, April 11. www.usnews.com/news/healthiest-communities/articles/2018–04–11/hiv-transgender-residents-hit-by-south-florida-housing-crunch.

Palacios, Lena Carla. 2016. "Killing Abstractions: Indigenous Women and Black Trans Girls Challenging Media Necropower in White Settler States." *Critical Ethnic Studies* 2, no. 2: 35–60.

Prevention Access Campaign. 2016. "Consensus Statement." July 21. www.preventionaccess.org/consensus.

Pronzini, Bill, and Jack Adrian, eds. 1997. *Hardboiled: An Anthology of American Crime Stories.* Oxford: Oxford University Press.

Race, Kane. 2017. *The Gay Science: Intimate Experiments with the Problem of HIV.* New York: Taylor and Francis.

Shahani, Nishant. 2016. "How to Survive the Whitewashing of AIDS: Global Pasts, Transnational Futures." *QED* 3, no. 1: 1–33.

Spade, Dean. 2015. *Normal Life: Administrative Violence, Critical Trans Politics, and the Limits of Law.* Durham, NC: Duke University Press.

Stanley, Eric. 2011. "Near Life, Queer Death: Overkill and Ontological Capture." *Social Text*, no. 107: 1–19.

———. 2017. "Anti-trans Optics: Recognition, Opacity, and the Image of Force." *South Atlantic Quarterly* 116, no. 3: 612–620.

Tang, Jeaninne. 2017. "Contemporary Art and Critical Transgender Infrastructures." In *Trap Door: Trans Cultural Production and the Politics of Visibility*, edited by Johanna Burton, Eric Stanley, and Tourmaline, 363–392. Cambridge, MA: MIT Press.

Tiemeyer, Philip James. 2013. *Plane Queer: Labor, Sexuality, and AIDS in the History of Male Flight Attendants.* Berkeley: University of California Press.

Tourmaline. 2017. "Why Transgender People Should Be the Ones Telling Transgender Stories." *Teen Vogue*, October 11. www.teenvogue.com/story/reina-gossett-marsha-p-johnson-op-ed.

Tourmaline, and Sasha Wortzel, dirs. 2018. *Happy Birthday, Marsha!* San Francisco: Frameline, DVD.

Treichler, Paula A. 1987. "AIDS, Homophobia, and Biomedical Discourse: An Epidemic of Signification." *October*, no. 43: 31–70.

Weiss, Suzannah. 2017. "'The Death and Life of Marsha P. Johnson' Creator Accused of Stealing Work from Filmmaker Tourmaline." *Teen Vogue*, October 8. www.teenvogue.com/story/marsha-p-johnson-documentary-david-france-reina-gossett-stealing-accusations.

Index